T0189564

Lecture Notes in Artificial Intelligence   12483

Subseries of Lecture Notes in Computer Science

Alan R. Wagner · David Feil-Seifer ·
Kerstin S. Haring · Silvia Rossi ·
Thomas Williams · Hongsheng He ·
Shuzhi Sam Ge (Eds.)

Social Robotics

12th International Conference, ICSR 2020
Golden, CO, USA, November 14–18, 2020
Proceedings

 Springer

Editors
Alan R. Wagner
Pennsylvania State University
University Park, PA, USA

David Feil-Seifer ⓘ
University of Nevada Reno
Reno, NV, USA

Kerstin S. Haring
University of Denver
Denver, CO, USA

Silvia Rossi ⓘ
University of Naples Federico II
Naples, Italy

Thomas Williams ⓘ
Colorado School of Mines
Golden, CO, USA

Hongsheng He ⓘ
Wichita State University
Wichita, KS, USA

Shuzhi Sam Ge
National University of Singapore
Singapore, Singapore

ISSN 0302-9743 ISSN 1611-3349 (electronic)
Lecture Notes in Artificial Intelligence
ISBN 978-3-030-62055-4 ISBN 978-3-030-62056-1 (eBook)
https://doi.org/10.1007/978-3-030-62056-1

LNCS Sublibrary: SL7 – Artificial Intelligence

This Springer imprint is published by the registered company Springer Nature Switzerland AG
The registered company address is: Gewerbestrasse 11, 6330 Cham, Switzerland

Preface

This book constitutes the refereed proceedings of the 12th International Conference on Social Robotics (ICSR 2020), held virtually in November 2020. The 57 full papers presented in these proceedings (comprised of 25 papers accepted for long-form presentation and 32 additional papers accepted for short-form presentation) were carefully reviewed and selected from 101 submissions. The papers focus on the following topics: human-robot trust and human-robot teaming, robot understanding and following of social and moral norms, physical and interaction design of social robots, verbal and nonverbal robot communication, interactive robot learning, robot motion and proxemics, and robots in domains such as education and health care.

The theme of this year's conference is "Entertaining Robots," which is meant to be a play on words signifying that robots can serve as captivating social agents, but also suggesting the challenges associated with managing these artifacts. In the near future, robots will be entering our social world, taking on a wide variety of roles. This conference offers a venue for researchers and those interested in social robots to examine the progress that is being made towards the creation of social robots. ICSR 2020 fosters discussion related to the innovative approaches to developing social robots, the promises of new robotic technologies, and possible positive and negative influences of social robots on society.

We would like to express our gratitude to the authors and participants for their contributions and support to the conference, the reviewers for their effort and constructive comments, and the Organizing Committee for the excellent organization and program. We hope the conference provides an effective platform for researchers and practitioners to share the latest research in the field of social robotics, and generate future collaboration in intradisciplinary research.

September 2020

Alan R. Wagner
David Feil-Seifer
Kerstin S. Haring
Silvia Rossi
Thomas Williams
Hongsheng He
Shuzhi Sam Ge

Organization

Honorary General Chair

Shuzhi Sam Ge   National University of Singapore, Singapore,
and Qingdao University, China

General Chairs

Alan R. Wagner   The Pennsylvania State University, USA
David Feil-Seifer   University of Nevada, Reno, USA

Program Chairs

Kerstin Sophie Haring   University of Denver, USA
Silvia Rossi   Università degli Studi di Napoli Federico II, Italy
Thomas Williams   Colorado School of Mines, USA

Publicity Chairs

Paul Robinette   University of Massachusetts Lowell, USA
Daniel Rea   Kyoto University, Japan
Patricia Alves-Oliveira   ISCTE-IUL, INESC-ID, Portugal, and Cornell
University, USA

Publication Chair

Hongsheng He   Wichita State University, USA

Awards Chair

Boyoung Kim   United States Air Force Academy, USA

Competition Chair

Amit Kumar Pandey   Hanson Robotics, China

Sponsorship Chair

Bradley Hayes   University of Colorado Boulder, USA

Workshop Chair

Katie Winkle   Bristol Robotics, UK

Web Chair

Vidullan Surendran   The Pennsylvania State University, USA

Local Organizing Committee

Thomas Williams   Colorado School of Mines, USA
Katie Winkle   Bristol Robotics, UK

Standing Committee

Shuzhi Sam Ge   National University of Singapore, Singapore
Oussama Khatib   Stanford University, USA
Maja Mataric   University of Southern California, USA
Haizhou Li   A*STAR, Singapore
Jong Hwan Kim   Korea Advanced Institute of Science and Technology,
                             South Korea
Paolo Dario   Scuola Superiore Sant'Anna, Italy
Ronald C. Arkin   Georgia Institute of Technology, USA

Program Committee

David Buckingham   Tufts University, USA
Pooyan Fazli   San Francisco State University, USA
Ehsan Saffari   Sharif University of Technology, Iran
Tianyi Gu   University of New Hampshire, USA
Ho Seok Ahn   The University of Auckland, New Zealand
Oliver Bendel   FHNW School of Business, Switzerland
Adriana Tapus   ENSTA Paris, France
Tahereh Kamali   University of Waterloo, Canada
Paul Robinette   University of Massachusetts Lowell, USA
Anna-Maria Velentza   University of Macedonia, Greece
Kasra Mokhtari   The Pennsylvania State University, USA
De'Aira Bryant   Georgia Institute of Technology, USA
Sofia Thunberg   Linköping University, Sweden
Martin Hannig   Technical University of Darmstadt, Germany
Niyati Rawal   Technical University of Darmstadt, Germany
Ravenna Thielstrom   Tufts University, USA
Carolin Straßmann   Hochschule Ruhr West, Germany
Amit Kumar Pandey   Hanson Robotics, China
Ben Wright   U.S. Naval Research Laboratory, USA
Adrian David Cheok A. M.   The University of Tokyo, Japan

José Carlos Castillo	University Carlos III of Madrid, Spain
Brittany Duncan	University of Nebraska, USA
Laurens Lafranca	University of Twente, The Netherlands
Sayanti Roy	Colorado School of Mines, USA
Kartik Mahajan	University of Southern California, USA
Giulia Perugia	Uppsala University, Sweden
Damith Herath	University of Canberra, Australia
Kerstin Sophie Haring	University of Denver, USA
Syed Ali Raza	Advanced Personnel Management, Pakistan
Gerard Canal	King's College London, UK
Mollik Nayyar	The Pennsylvania State University, USA
Hatice Gunes	University of Cambridge, UK
Guilhem Buisan	LAAS-CNRS, France
Megan Strait	The University of Texas at Rio Grande Valley, USA
Moojan Ghafurian	University of Waterloo, Canada
Roel Boumans	Delft University of Technology, The Netherlands
Swapna Joshi	Veritas Technologies, USA
Pegah Soleiman	Tehran University, Iran
Nathaniel Dennler	University of Southern California, USA
Milos Zefran	University of Illinois at Chicago, USA
Zhi Zheng	Rochester Institute of Technology, USA
Friederike Eyssel	Bielefeld University, Germany
Mehdi Khamassi	Université Pierre et Marie Curie, France
Gabriele Trovato	Waseda University, Japan
Jani Even	Kyoto University, Japan
Giulia Belgiovine	Istituto Italiano di Tecnologia, Italy
Luisa Damiano	University of Messina, Italy
Maria José Ferreira	Instituto Superior Técnico, Portugal
Santosh Balajee Banisetty	University of Nevada, Reno, USA
Vignesh Prasad	Technical University of Darmstadt, Germany
Nicole Robinson	Monash University, Australia
Sophia C. Steinhaeusser	University of Würzburg, Human Computer Interaction, Germany
Elizabeth Phillips	George Mason University, USA
Marlena Fraune	New Mexico State University, USA
Fabio Aurelio D'Asaro	Università degli Studi di Napoli Federico II, Italy
Leimin Tian	Monash University, Australia
Moritz Merkle	Technical University of Darmstadt, Germany
Alessandra Rossi	University of Hertfordshire, UK
Ruchen Wen	Colorado School of Mines, USA
Ryan Jackson	Colorado School of Mines, USA
Guillem Alenyà	Consejo Superior de Investigaciones Científicas, Spain
Francesca Ciardo	Italian Institute of Technology, Italy
Edo de Wolf	University of Twente, The Netherlands
Ali Ayub	The Pennsylvania State University, USA
Enrique Fernández Rodicio	University Carlos III of Madrid, Spain

Contents

Design and Evaluation of Affective Expressions of a Zoomorphic Robot 1
  Moojan Ghafurian, Gabriella Lakatos, Zhuofu Tao,
  and Kerstin Dautenhahn

Exploring the Effect of Explanations During Robot-Guided
Emergency Evacuation. 13
  Mollik Nayyar, Zachary Zoloty, Ciera McFarland, and Alan R. Wagner

Explainable Agency by Revealing Suboptimality in Child-Robot
Learning Scenarios 23
  Silvia Tulli, Marta Couto, Miguel Vasco, Elmira Yadollahi,
  Francisco Melo, and Ana Paiva

HRI Physio Lib: A Software Framework to Support the Integration
of Physiological Adaptation in HRI. 36
  Austin Kothig, John Muñoz, Hamza Mahdi, Alexander M. Aroyo,
  and Kerstin Dautenhahn

Proxemic Reasoning for Group Approach 48
  Ben Wright, Magdalena Bugajska, William Adams, Ed Lawson,
  J. Malcolm McCurry, and J. Gregory Trafton

Wake Up and Talk with Me! In-the-Field Study of an Autonomous
Interactive Wake Up Robot 61
  Yuma Oda, Jani Even, and Takayuki Kanda

I Like the Way You Move: A Mixed-Methods Approach for Studying
the Effects of Robot Motion on Collaborative Human Robot Interaction 73
  Jonas E. Pedersen, Kristoffer W. Christensen, Damith Herath,
  and Elizabeth Jochum

Effects of Proactive Explanations by Robots on Human-Robot Trust 85
  Lixiao Zhu and Thomas Williams

Language Learning with Artificial Entities: Effects of an Artificial Tutor's
Embodiment and Behavior on Users' Alignment and Evaluation 96
  Astrid Rosenthal-von der Pütten, Carolin Straßmann,
  and Nicole Krämer

An Exploration of Simple Reactive Responses for Conveying Aliveness
Using the Haru Robot 108
  Yurii Vasylkiv, Heike Brock, Yu Fang, Eric Nichols, Keisuke Nakamura,
  Serge Thill, and Randy Gomez

On the Role of Personality and Empathy in Human-Human, Human-Agent,
and Human-Robot Mimicry 120
  Giulia Perugia, Maike Paetzel, and Ginevra Castellano

Perceptions of People's Dishonesty Towards Robots 132
  Sofia Petisca, Ana Paiva, and Francisco Esteves

Human-Robot Collaboration and Dialogue for Fault Recovery
on Hierarchical Tasks 144
  Janelle Blankenburg, Mariya Zagainova, S. Michael Simmons,
  Gabrielle Talavera, Monica Nicolescu, and David Feil-Seifer

Gaze-Speech Coordination Influences the Persuasiveness of Human-Robot
Dialog in the Wild 157
  Kerstin Fischer, Rosalyn M. Langedijk, Lotte Damsgaard Nissen,
  Eduardo Ruiz Ramirez, and Oskar Palinko

Robots Are Moral Actors: Unpacking Current Moral HRI Research
Through a Moral Foundations Lens............................ 170
  Dylan Doyle-Burke and Kerstin S. Haring

Perception of a Social Robot's Mood Based on Different Types of Motions
and Coloured Heart....................................... 182
  Enrique Fernández-Rodicio, Álvaro Castro-González,
  Juan José Gamboa-Montero, and Miguel A. Salichs

Let's Learn Biodiversity with a Virtual "Robot"? 194
  Maria José Ferreira, Raquel Oliveira, Sandra Câmara Olim,
  Valentina Nisi, and Ana Paiva

Blind Trust: How Making a Device Humanoid Reduces the Impact
of Functional Errors on Trust 207
  Christopher Vattheuer, Annalena Nora Baecker, Denise Y. Geiskkovitch,
  Stela Hanbyeol Seo, Daniel J. Rea, and James E. Young

What Am I Allowed to Do Here?: Online Learning of Context-Specific
Norms by Pepper 220
  Ali Ayub and Alan R. Wagner

Robotic Social Environments: A Promising Platform for Autism Therapy. . . . 232
  Pegah Soleiman, Hadi Moradi, Bijan Mehralizadeh, Negin Azizi,
  Farid Anjidani, Hamid Reza Pouretemad, and Rosa I. Arriaga

Human-Robot Teams: A Review.............................. 246
  Franziska Doris Wolf and Ruth Stock-Homburg

User Expectations of Robots in Public Spaces: A Co-design Methodology . . .   259
  Leimin Tian, Pamela Carreno-Medrano, Shanti Sumartojo,
  Michael Mintrom, Enrique Coronado, Gentiane Venture,
  and Dana Kulić

Receiving Robot's Advice: Does It Matter When and for What?   271
  Carolin Straßmann, Sabrina C. Eimler, Alexander Arntz, Alina Grewe,
  Christopher Kowalczyk, and Stefan Sommer

Don't Go That Way! Risk-Aware Decision Making
for Autonomous Vehicles   284
  Kasra Mokhtari, Kendra A. Lang, and Alan R. Wagner

Sensing the Partner: Toward Effective Robot Tutoring in Motor
Skill Learning   296
  Giulia Belgiovine, Francesco Rea, Pablo Barros, Jacopo Zenzeri,
  and Alessandra Sciutti

Social Sharing of Emotions with Robots and the Influence of a Robot's
Nonverbal Behavior on Human Emotions   308
  Reina Shimizu and Hiroyuki Umemuro

Using Human-Inspired Signals to Disambiguate Navigational Intentions   320
  Justin Hart, Reuth Mirsky, Xuesu Xiao, Stone Tejeda, Bonny Mahajan,
  Jamin Goo, Kathryn Baldauf, Sydney Owen, and Peter Stone

Towards the Design of a Robot for Supporting Children's Attention During
Long Distance Learning   332
  Dante Arroyo, Yijie Guo, Mingyue Yu, Mohammad Shidujaman,
  and Rodrigo Fernandes

Engagement and Mind Perception Within Human-Robot Interaction:
A Comparison Between Elderly and Young Adults   344
  Melissa Kont and Maryam Alimardani

Double Trouble: The Effect of Eye Gaze on the Social Impression
of Mobile Robotic Telepresence Operators   357
  Edo de Wolf and Jamy Li

Administrating Cognitive Tests Through HRI: An Application
of an Automatic Scoring System Through Visual Analysis   369
  Sara Sangiovanni, Matteo Spezialetti, Fabio Aurelio D'Asaro,
  Gianpaolo Maggi, and Silvia Rossi

Adapting Usability Metrics for a Socially Assistive, Kinesthetic, Mixed
Reality Robot Tutoring Environment   381
  Kartik Mahajan, Thomas Groechel, Roxanna Pakkar, Julia Cordero,
  Haemin Lee, and Maja J. Matarić

Legibility of Robot Approach Trajectories with Minimum Jerk
Path Planning   392
  Raymond H. Cuijpers, Peter A. M. Ruijten,
  and Vincent J. P. van den Goor

"Excuse Me, Robot": Impact of Polite Robot Wakewords
on Human-Robot Politeness   404
  Tom Williams, Daniel Grollman, Mingyuan Han, Ryan Blake Jackson,
  Jane Lockshin, Ruchen Wen, Zachary Nahman, and Qin Zhu

Investigating Therapist Vocal Nonverbal Behavior for Applications
in Robot-Mediated Therapies for Individuals Diagnosed with Autism   416
  Wing-Yue Geoffrey Louie, Jessica Korneder, Ala'aldin Hijaz,
  and Megan Sochanski

Using Robot Adaptivity to Support Learning in Child-Robot Interaction   428
  Alessia Vignolo, Alessandra Sciutti, and John Michael

Social Robots for Socio-Physical Distancing   440
  Swapna Joshi, Sawyer Collins, Waki Kamino, Randy Gomez,
  and Selma Šabanović

Evaluating People's Perceptions of Trust in a Robot in a Repeated
Interactions Study   453
  Alessandra Rossi, Kerstin Dautenhahn, Kheng Lee Koay,
  Michael L. Walters, and Patrick Holthaus

The Effect of Individual Differences and Repetitive Interactions on Explicit
and Implicit Attitudes Towards Robots   466
  Francesca Ciardo, Davide Ghiglino, Cecilia Roselli,
  and Agnieszka Wykowska

Advances in Human-Robot Handshaking   478
  Vignesh Prasad, Ruth Stock-Homburg, and Jan Peters

Choosing the Best Robot for the Job: Affinity Bias
in Human-Robot Interaction   490
  Thomas Trainer, John R. Taylor, and Christopher J. Stanton

Teach Me What You Want to Play: Learning Variants of Connect Four
Through Human-Robot Interaction   502
  Ali Ayub and Alan R. Wagner

The Importance of the Person's Assertiveness in Persuasive
Human-Robot Interactions   516
  Raul Benites Paradeda, Maria José Ferreira, Carlos Martinho,
  and Ana Paiva

Modeling Trust in Human-Robot Interaction: A Survey   529
    Zahra Rezaei Khavas, S. Reza Ahmadzadeh, and Paul Robinette

Using AI-Enhanced Social Robots to Improve Children's
Healthcare Experiences   542
    Mary Ellen Foster, Samina Ali, Sasha Litwin, Jennifer Parker,
    Ronald P. A. Petrick, David Harris Smith, Jennifer Stinson,
    and Frauke Zeller

Human Aware Task Planning Using Verbal Communication
Feasibility and Costs   554
    Guilhem Buisan, Guillaume Sarthou, and Rachid Alami

Robot Planning with Mental Models of Co-present Humans   566
    David Buckingham, Meia Chita-Tegmark, and Matthias Scheutz

Conversational Flow in Human-Robot Interactions at the Workplace:
Comparing Humanoid and Android Robots   578
    Ruth Stock-Homburg, Martin Hannig, and Lucie Lilienthal

Examining the Effects of Anticipatory Robot Assistance on Human
Decision Making.   590
    Benjamin A. Newman, Abhijat Biswas, Sarthak Ahuja,
    Siddharth Girdhar, Kris K. Kitani, and Henny Admoni

The Experience and Effect of Adolescent to Robot Stress Disclosure:
A Mixed-Methods Exploration   604
    Elin A. Björling, Honson Ling, Simran Bhatia, and Kimberly Dziubinski

Do Robot Pets Decrease Agitation in Dementia Patients?
An Ethnographic Approach   616
    Sofia Thunberg, Lisa Rönnqvist, and Tom Ziemke

A Social Robot to Deliver an 8-Week Intervention for Diabetes
Management: Initial Test of Feasibility in a Hospital Clinic   628
    Nicole L. Robinson, Jennifer Connolly, Leanne Hides,
    and David J. Kavanagh

Content Is King: Impact of Task Design for Eliciting Participant Agreement
in Crowdsourcing for HRI   640
    Alisha Bevins, Nina McPhaul, and Brittany A. Duncan

Emoji to Robomoji: Exploring Affective Telepresence Through Haru   652
    Randy Gomez, Deborah Szapiro, Luis Merino, Heike Brock,
    Keisuke Nakamura, and Selma Sabanovic

Can Robots Elicit Different *Comfortability* Levels?   664
Maria Elena Lechuga Redondo, Alessia Vignolo,
Radoslaw Niewiadomski, Francesco Rea, and Alessandra Sciutti

Creating MyJay: A New Design for Robot-Assisted Play for Children
with Physical Special Needs   676
Hamza Mahdi, Shahed Saleh, Omar Shariff, and Kerstin Dautenhahn

Humans and Robots in Times of Quarantine Based
on First-Hand Accounts   688
Laurens Lafranca and Jamy Li

Author Index   709

Design and Evaluation of Affective Expressions of a Zoomorphic Robot

Moojan Ghafurian[1(✉)], Gabriella Lakatos[2], Zhuofu Tao[3],
and Kerstin Dautenhahn[1]

[1] Department of Electrical and Computer Engineering, University of Waterloo,
Waterloo, Canada
{moojan,kerstin.dautenhahn}@uwaterloo.ca
[2] Department of Computer Science, University of Hertfordshire, Hatfield, UK
g.lakatos@herts.ac.uk
[3] David R. Cheriton School of Computer Science, University of Waterloo,
Waterloo, Canada

Abstract. Social robots that are capable of showing affective expressions can improve human-robot interaction and users' experiences in many ways. This capability is important in many application areas. In this paper, we describe the design and evaluation of 11 affective expressions for Miro, an animal-like robot. Affective expressions were inspired by the animal and human behavior literature. The designs were evaluated through a video study on Mechanical Turk with 88 participants. Five of the expressions—happy, sad, excited, surprised, and tired—were correctly recognized by more than half of the participants. While fewer participants were able to recognize the other, more complex affective expressions, we observed a significant correlation between the recognition of the robot's displayed affective states and participants' understanding of human emotions. This suggested that the reduced accuracy in the recognition of the other affective expressions can be due to the general challenges involved in recognizing complex emotions.

Keywords: Design of social robots · Affective expressions · Zoomorphic robots · Miro

1 Introduction

Social robots are designed to be involved in social interactions with humans. While multiple factors can affect the quality of social interactions (e.g., social exchange, timing/appropriateness of responses to social cues [10], and social contact [8]), one important factor that can improve interactions with social robots is their capability to perceive, process, and express affective states. In fact, many studies have shown that the affective experience can increase users' engagement [26], as well as their enjoyment and cooperation with the technology [5,12]. Therefore, making social robots 'emotionally intelligent' can increase

© Springer Nature Switzerland AG 2020
A. R. Wagner et al. (Eds.): ICSR 2020, LNAI 12483, pp. 1–12, 2020.
https://doi.org/10.1007/978-3-030-62056-1_1

their effectiveness and adoption in many application contexts, such as healthcare, rehabilitation, education, therapy, or co-worker scenarios.

One of the robots that has the potential for being used in different domains is the commercially available Miro robot [7,23]. Miro is a biomimetic, zoomorphic (animal-like) robot that is designed in a way that it does not look like any specific animal. Miro is considered to be a social robot as it can communicate through many methods such as body language [7]. Making Miro 'emotionally intelligent' can potentially improve its acceptance and interaction experience in different application contexts.

The first step to make Miro emotionally intelligent is to understand how to implement affective expressions on this robotic platform, in a way that they can be recognized by people. Collins et al. (2015) studied perception of Miro's affective states, which were reflected by changing the colors of the six RGB LEDs that are located on Miro's sides. Colors red, white, and green (delivered in ranges between zero intensity and actual intensity) were used to show negative, neutral, and positive valences, respectively. Emotions' arousal was also reflected through the rate of light changes (slow, medium, and fast). An offset was added between adjacent LEDs to reflect the light changes. A pilot study with five participants using a simulator suggested that the patterns of pulsating lights might be effective in evoking perceptions of valence and arousal of the affect [6].

However, using lights might have limitations. For example, Miro's LEDs might not be noticeable in a very well-lit room, or from specific angles. Further, conditions such as color-blindness or participants' required attention to the LEDs and their speed might affect the perception of the emotions. Also, it is logical to use biologically inspired physical expressions for Miro, as natural lights are rarely used in actual communications between humans and animals. Therefore, we believe that expressing affective states through body gesture and postures might be a more intuitive and effective approach.

For an animal-like robot like Miro, one approach to reflect emotions and other affective states through body postures, movements, and gestures is to mimic the behaviour of animals. But there are multiple challenges in doing so: (1) some of the robot's parts and actuators might not be flexible enough to accurately mimic the behaviour of the animals (e.g., the ears of Miro cannot bend, which is one of the important attributes for understanding animal emotions, e.g. in dogs [3,32]), (2) as Miro deliberately does not represent any specific animal species, its behaviour should be inspired by the behaviours of multiple animals that have features similar to Miro, and (3) understanding animal emotions might be challenging for some people (in some cases regardless of whether they have owned a pet or not) [31,32].

In this paper we describe how we designed eleven simple and complex affective expressions for Miro (ranging from emotions such as sad and angry to moods such as tired and bored). We then evaluate the proposed expressions through a video study using crowd-sourcing with Amazon Mechanical Turk. Our research question that this study addresses was: How do participants map affective states to the designed non-verbal behavioural expressions of Miro, a zoomorphic robot?

In the following, we will discuss the related work and then describe our proposed designs of Miro robot's 11 affective expressions. Afterwards, we will present the experiment that evaluated the affective expressions with human participants. Next, results, discussion, and the limitations of our work are presented.

2 Background

Many robots and virtual agents (e.g., among many others, Kismet and Greta) have been used in previous studies investigating how emotional expressions contribute to humans' perception of robots and virtual agents [2,9,30,36].

Most of the previous studies involving robots focused on facial expressions with only a few studies examining direct human-robot interactions and analyzing humans' reactions on the behavioural level. One such study examined participants' ability to recognize two basic emotions ("happiness" and "fear") and a secondary emotion ("guilt") expressed by a robot, which showed emotional behaviours according to dogs' behaviour. Both primary and secondary emotions expressed by the robot were recognized by the participants. Korcsok et al. (2018) used a video study for testing the prototype version of an abstract emotion visualization agent that was developed to express five basic emotions and a neutral state. This agent was developed based on general biological and ethological rules. Participants successfully recognized the displayed emotions in most cases, with fear and sadness being most easily confused with each other and anger being the most easily recognized emotion [19]. In another recent study [22], participants watched short video sequences of a PeopleBot robot. The robot displayed emotional behaviour inspired by dog behaviour. Participants also watched videos of emotional displays of an actual dog. Five different emotional states (joy, fear, anger, sadness, and neutral) were used. Participants attributed emotions to both the robot and the dog spontaneously and also successfully matched all robot videos and all dog videos with the correct emotional states [11]. Dog behaviour has already been suggested as a model to design simple, non-linguistic social behaviour of robots. Dogs are able to develop successful and effective social interactions with humans in various situations, even though their cognitive capacities are relatively less complex [22]. This – among other reasons - makes them in many ways an ideal model for the behavioural design of zoomorphic social robots. As a further advantage, dogs' behaviour is well documented in many contexts and can be implemented in robots with different embodiments [20]. Dogs may also provide a suitable model for designing emotional expressions of robots, as previous studies have suggested that humans regard emotional expressions as something that can be shared between humans and dogs. Dog owners reported to be capable of recognizing various emotions in their dogs, such as fear, joy, jealousy, sadness and curiosity [18,24].

3 Affective Expression Design

To design Miro's affective expressions, we started by considering the literature on dog behaviour. Dog behaviour has been observed and described in several different emotion evoking situations before, which provided us with an excellent basis for the behavioural design of Miro's happy, sad, fearful, and angry behaviours. Expressive behaviors of these emotions—similarly to the study of Gacsi et al. (2016) [11]—were based on dogs' behaviour. For example, greeting the owner for happy [17,34], being sad as a result of separation from the owner [34], fearful due to facing a threatening stranger [16], or angry because of facing a threatening stranger [35].

Dog behavior and affective expressions have been studied extensively in the literature. However, we were not able to find information explaining the behaviour for some more complex affective expressions (e.g., disgusted) that our study includes. Also, while Miro's design has some dog-like features, its movements, as compared to dogs, are much more constrained (e.g. it cannot flexibly bend its body). Miro's features do not allow expressing some affective behaviors that are described in the literature. For example, the existing literature on animal behaviour describes the shapes of ears and muzzles for some emotions extensively, both of which cannot be controlled in Miro. Therefore, we had to expand our search to get inspiration from a variety of different sources, including other mammal species, such as rabbits [13] and mice [21] (especially for the design of ears), humans (for design of the eyes), and even cartoon characters in some cases (for design and animation of the robot's movements). Examples include wide eyes in humans for surprised [28], or spending a great amount of time being inactive and awake, and looking drowsy when animals are bored [4].

The final design of affective expressions for the Miro robot is shown in Table 1[1]. Colours were taken from general mappings of colours to emotions [25,33]. Tail movements were inspired from the literature about the dogs' behaviour [14,27]. But note, compared to dogs, the amplitude, speed, and range of movements of Miro's tail are very limited. As the ears of Miro are more similar to a rabbit's ears (in shape and size), the ear movements were inspired by the behaviour of rabbits [15]. However, imitating movements of animals' ears was challenging, as Miro's ears are not flexible, they cannot bend, and they can only be rotated inwards and outwards based on the affective state.

Note that while using lights (e.g., [6]) and sounds (e.g., [29]) are common approaches for expressing emotions in robots, they are not included at this step as the main cues for conveying emotions. Specifically, sound was not included at all and only solid colours were used, using Miro's LEDs for each emotion. This is because our goal was to understand the affective expressions through body gestures/movements and adding sound and complex lights (like in [6]) could have introduced a confound in the evaluations. Improving gestures would be important especially in situations that light might not be effective (e.g., in a well-lit room). Further, sound might not be effective, for example in a noisy or large room, or in contexts such as dementia care and for older adults' care, where sounds might disturb their comfort or cannot be clearly heard by those affected by a hearing decline.

---

[1] This set was decided to include basic emotions, and a few moods (e.g., fearful and tired) that would be beneficial for applications that involve children and older adults (e.g., dementia care, education, therapy, and rehabilitation).

Table 1. Proposed design guidelines for Miro's affective expressions

Emotion	Eyes	Neck	Head	Ear	Tail	Colour	Movement
Happy	Almost Open	Moving up and down, moderate speed	Forward	Angled forward	Up, wagging left and right widely	Orange	Slight movements to left and right
Sad	Half closed	Down	Down	Angled outward	Down, still	Light brown	Head tilting left and right
Excited	Fully open	Up and down very fast	Up	Angled forward	Up, wagging left and right widely and fast	Red	Movements to left and right
Fearful	Half closed	Half down	Up	Angled inward	Moving up and down slowly	Pale, blue/grey	Sudden backward movement, ears moving
Angry	Fully open	Half down	Up	Angled outward	Up, still	Red	Sudden forward movement and then going slightly back
Disgusted	Half closed	Centre	Forward	Angled outward	Up, still	Green	Head moving to side, eyes closing, moving backwards
Surprised	Fully open	Half up	Up	Angled forward	Up, still	Quick change to white	Looking forward and suddenly raising head and wagging tail.
Calm	Half open	Up	Halfway up	Angled forward	Halfway up, slowly wagging left and right	No colour	Moving head to left and right slowly
Bored	Half closed	Half down	Down	Angled inward	Down, wagging left and right slowly	Gray	Moving head slowly down and back up
Annoyed	Almost open	Half down	Forward	Angled outward	Up and down slowly	Blue	Sudden head movements to sides.
Tired	Almost closed	Down	Down	Angled outward	Down, still	Purple	Occasionally moving head up and opening the eyes. Gradually going back down and closing the eyes

(a)   (b)

Fig. 1. Example of the two camera angles for (a) Sad and (b) Surprised.

4   Method

In a video study, we asked participants to map affective states to the designed non-verbal behavioural expressions of the Miro robot. The study consisted of three steps.

Step 1 - Evaluation of Miro's Expressions: Participants first watched a video of all affective expressions to get familiar with the robot and to get an impression of the range of movements that the robot is capable of. Afterwards, they saw, one by one, the 11 videos of affective expressions in a random order and were asked to decide on the affective state(s) they thought the robot expressed in the video. Participants could choose multiple responses for each video and a "not sure" option was added, in case they had uncertainties about their answers.

If the selected affective states differed from what was hypothesized, participants were asked to answer a follow up question, requesting them to explain their choice. The participants were told that these follow up questions will appear randomly.[2] The participants had the opportunity to re-play the video as many times as they needed.

The videos for each affective expression were taken from two angles: one from the front and one from the side (see Fig. 1). Both cameras were set to the same height and about 120 cm above the ground, to represent a realistic view of Miro, similar to a person sitting on a chair or standing, observing the robot. The positions of the two cameras and the robot were kept constant across all videos.

Step 2 - Questionnaires: The participants completed a questionnaire about their demographics and background (e.g., age, gender, level of education, culture/ethnicity, etc.). The questionnaire included checks that allowed us to monitor participants' attention.[3]

---

[2] This step provided us with more information about why an expression was confused with another one. Due to space limitation, the results of this part are not discussed here.

[3] Two other questionnaires were used to gather additional information about the participants' experiences, which are beyond the scope of this paper and are therefore not discussed here.

Step 3 - Human Emotion Understanding: The participants were asked to evaluate 12 images of human emotions. The images had two examples of six different emotions (angry, fearful, happy, neutral, sad, and surprised). For each emotion, we had an example of a young person and an older adult, one of which was male and the other was female. Gender and age were counterbalanced. The images were taken from the FacesDB dataset.[4]

Procedure: Upon acceptance of the consent form and reading the instructions, the participants completed the task: they (a) Watched a video combining all designed expressions to get familiar with Miro and its expressions, (b) watched the eleven videos in a random order and evaluated each video upon watching it, (c) upon completion of the videos, the participants responded to the above mentioned questionnaires, and (d) participants saw the above mentioned 12 images of human emotions and associated them with an emotion.

Participants: 120 participants were recruited on Amazon Mechanical Turk. Participation was limited to people in North America and those MTurk Workers that had completed at least 50 HITs and had an approval rate of over 96%. Five participants were not able to complete the study and 27 others failed the attention and sanity checks. This left 88 participants' data (32 Female, 53 Male, 3 unknown; age range 23–69 yrs, average: 38 yrs). The study received full Ethics clearance from the University of Waterloo's Research Ethics Committees.

5   Results

Evaluation of Affective Expressions: although participants were given the option to select multiple choices for the affective expression in each video, in most cases they only selected one (or one plus "not sure"). Figure 2 shows the results for the evaluations of the 11 affective expressions.

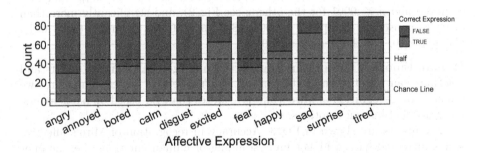

Fig. 2. Evaluation of the 11 designed affective expressions for Miro. All are significantly above the chance line, with p-values $< .0001$ for all, except for annoyed, where $p = .001$ (significance was calculated through binomial tests)

---

[4] http://app.visgraf.impa.br/database/faces/.

Table 2. Number of the selected expressions for each video. Rows show the actual emotions demonstrated by Miro in the videos. Columns show participants' choices. Correct expressions are shown in bold. Blue shows the expressions that were mostly confused with the correct expressions. Red shows expressions that received a higher rating than the correct expression. Responses that were selected significantly more than others are shown for each expression, ***: $p < .001$, **: $p < .01$ (significance was calculated through binomial tests)

	Happy	Sad	Excited	Fearful	Angry	Disgusted	Surprised	Calm	Bored	Annoyed	Tired
Happy	**52*****	1	23	5	1	1	6	24	4	5	1
Sad	1	**71*****	1	4	1	3	0	2	7	3	20
Excited	45	1	**62**	6	2	0	3	3	1	3	2
Fearful	8	0	14	**35**	6	2	38	3	2	3	2
Angry	8	1	17	4	**30**	3	4	5	10	23	1
Disgusted	3	9	2	31	8	**34**	5	2	3	17	7
Surprised	6	6	12	4	4	0	**63*****	4	3	4	10
Calm	3	8	3	9	13	7	5	**34****	9	12	7
Bored	1	23	2	2	2	0	3	8	**37**	5	40
Annoyed	14	1	12	5	5	6	15	10	12	**18**	2
Tired	3	27	2	2	0	3	0	2	8	1	**64*****

More than half of the participants were able to accurately categorize five of Miro's affective expressions: Happy, Sad, Excited, Surprised, and Tired. However, Annoyed, Angry, and Bored had the lowest rate of accuracy. Despite the low accuracy, all affective expressions except fearful and bored received the majority of votes by the participants (see Table 2): fearful was recognized as surprised by the majority and bored was recognized as tired. The correct responses were selected significantly more than the chance level for all expressions ($p = .001$ for Annoyed and $p < .0001$ for the others; see Fig. 2), and significantly more than other responses for Happy ($p < .001$), Sad ($p < .001$), Surprised ($p < .001$), Calm ($p < .01$), and Tired ($p < .0001$).

Human Emotion Understanding: participants' general ability to understand emotions can affect their evaluation of Miro's affective states. Therefore, we studied how recognition of Miro's affective states changed based on participants' recognition of human emotions.

The results are shown in Fig. 3. Accuracy in recognition of Miro's affective states increased with a higher understanding of human emotions (i.e., number of correct responses to the emotions in the human images).

To study the significance of these results, we fit a linear model predicting the number of correct affective expressions of Miro based on participants' human emotion understanding. Age and gender were controlled for. Results are shown in Table 3. Accuracy in recognition of Miro's expressions changed significantly and positively with accuracy in recognition of human emotions ($se = 0.131$,

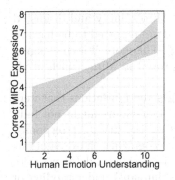

Fig. 3. Recognition of Miro expressions based on recognition of human expressions.

Table 3. Linear model predicting the number of correct answers to Miro expressions based on the number of correct answers to human emotions (Human), gender, and age.

Covariate	Estimate	SE	t	Pr (> |t|)
Intercept	1.771	1.294	1.369	0.175
Human	0.433	0.126	3.441	< .001
Gender-M	0.396	0.489	0.810	0.421
Age	0.011	0.022	0.504	0.616

$t = 3.654, p < .001$). In other words, those who had a better understanding of human emotions were also able to better categorize the robot's affective expressions.

6 Discussion

Social robots' ability to express affective states can be important in many applications where users' affective experience can increase their trust and engagement (e.g., in healthcare and education). With the goal of increasing Miro robot's emotional intelligence, this paper presented the design and evaluation of eleven affective expressions of Miro.

Five out of eleven expressions (excited, happy, sad, surprised, and tired) were correctly recognized by over half of the participants and all emotions except fearful and bored received the majority of the correct votes. In most cases, the confusions could be due to the important role of facial expressions in showing those affective expressions, which cannot be reflected by Miro. For example, in expressions such as angry, disgusted, and annoyed, the facial expressions play an important role. It might be hard to reflect these emotions without the use of actuated eyebrows and mouth which Miro lacks. Another important consideration is that these ratings were out of context ratings, whereas facing them in a specific context with additional contextual and international cues would likely increase their recognition.

While design limitations could have affected recognition of these expressions, a strong correlation between the recognition of Miro's affective expressions and human emotion recognition suggested that the lower rate of accuracy for some expressions might be due to general difficulties in recognizing these emotions. For example, human emotion understanding results suggested that recognizing disgusted and angry had the lowest accuracy, while happy and sad had the highest accuracy. This was in line with the results of Miro's expressions: while happy and sad were recognized accurately by more than half of the participants, most participants had difficulties in understanding Miro's angry and disgusted expressions. This is expected, as angry and disgusted are reported to be hard to be distinguished by many children [37] and adults [38]. Therefore, it is challenging to understand if/how these expressions can be improved in Miro, which needs to be investigated in future work.

Our work had limitations: (a) due to the challenges and limitations that were discussed for designing the affective expressions, the behaviours might not fully mimic animals' behaviour, (b) it is not clear whether the incorrect responses were due to participants' general challenges with recognizing those emotions in animals or as a result of possible shortcomings in design, and (c) we were not able to find a standard questionnaire assessing humans' understanding of animals' emotions, therefore we used human emotion understanding instead, as comparison. Future work is required to address these questions. Future work would also benefit from comparing these results achieved for Miro (a machine-like, zoomorphic robot) with other zoomorphic platforms with more realistic biomorphic features. Further, while we acknowledge limitations of crowdsourcing studies, it is an established methodology in HCI and HRI, and comparable results have been shown to studies with direct recruitment [1]. Due to Covid-19 crowdsourcing has become an even more important research tool in those fields.

7   Conclusion

This paper designed and evaluated 11 affective expressions for the Miro robot. Five of the expressions (i.e., happy, sad, excited, surprised, and tired) were correctly recognized by over half of the participants. But participants had difficulty recognizing more complex expressions (e.g., annoyed and disgusted). The results suggested that the incorrect answers might be due to general challenges in understanding these affective states, as opposed to shortcomings in the design. While future work is needed to improve these designs and understand what led to incorrect recognition of some of the expressions, this paper provided valuable insights about the design of affective expressions for the Miro robot, as well as guidelines that can be generalized (to a good extent) for designing affective expressions of other animal-like robots.

Acknowledgment. This research was undertaken, in part, thanks to funding from the Canada 150 Research Chairs Program and the Network for Aging Research at the University of Waterloo. We thank Jesse Hoey, Chrystopher L. Nehaniv, and the anonymous reviewers for their comments on this work.

References

1. Bartneck, C., Duenser, A., Moltchanova, E., Zawieska, K.: Comparing the similarity of responses received from studies in amazon mechanical turk to studies conducted online and with direct recruitment. PloS one **10**(4), 1–23 (2015)
2. Breazeal, C.: Emotion and sociable humanoid robots. Int. J. Hum. comput. Stud. **59**(1–2), 119–155 (2003)

3. Buckland, E., Volk, H., Burn, C., Abeyesinghe, S.: Owner perceptions of companion dog expressions of positive emotional states and the contexts in which they occur. Anim. Welf. **23**(3), 287–296 (2014)
4. Burn, C.C.: Bestial boredom: a biological perspective on animal boredom and suggestions for its scientific investigation. Anim. Behav. **130**, 141–151 (2017)
5. Chowanda, A., Flintham, M., Blanchfield, P., Valstar, M.: Playing with social and emotional game companions. In: Traum, D., Swartout, W., Khooshabeh, P., Kopp, S., Scherer, S., Leuski, A. (eds.) IVA 2016. LNCS (LNAI), vol. 10011, pp. 85–95. Springer, Cham (2016). https://doi.org/10.1007/978-3-319-47665-0_8
6. Collins, E.C., Prescott, T.J., Mitchinson, B.: Saying it with light: a pilot study of affective communication using the MIRO robot. In: Wilson, S.P., Verschure, P.F.M.J., Mura, A., Prescott, T.J. (eds.) LIVINGMACHINES 2015. LNCS (LNAI), vol. 9222, pp. 243–255. Springer, Cham (2015). https://doi.org/10.1007/978-3-319-22979-9_25
7. Collins, E.C., Prescott, T.J., Mitchinson, B., Conran, S.: Miro: a versatile biomimetic edutainment robot. In: Proceedings of the 12th International Conference on Advances in Computer Entertainment Technology, pp. 1–4 (2015)
8. Dautenhahn, K.: Socially intelligent robots: dimensions of human-robot interaction. Philos. Trans. Royal Soc. B Biol. Sci. **362**(1480), 679–704 (2007)
9. Cañamero L.D.: Playing the emotion game with feelix. In: Dautenhahn K., Bond A., Cañamero L., Edmonds B. (eds) Socially Intelligent Agents. Multiagent Systems, Artificial Societies, and Simulated Organizations, vol 3. Springer, Boston, MA (2002). https://doi.org/10.1007/0-306-47373-9_8
10. Dautenhahn, K., et al.: Kaspar-a minimally expressive humanoid robot for human-robot interaction research. Appl. Bionics Biomech. **6**(3–4), 369–397 (2009)
11. Gácsi, M., Kis, A., Faragó, T., Janiak, M., Muszyński, R., Miklósi, Á.: Humans attribute emotions to a robot that shows simple behavioural patterns borrowed from dog behaviour. Comput. Hum. Behav. **59**, 411–419 (2016)
12. Ghafurian, M., Budnarain, N., Hoey, J.: Role of emotions in perception of humanness of virtual agents. In: Proceedings of the 18th International Conference on Autonomous Agents and MultiAgent Systems, pp. 1979–1981 (2019)
13. Hampshire, V., Robertson, S.: Using the facial grimace scale to evaluate rabbit wellness in post-procedural monitoring. Lab Anim. **44**(7), 259 (2015)
14. Hasegawa, M., Ohtani, N., Ohta, M.: Dogs' body language relevant to learning achievement. Anim. **4**(1), 45–58 (2014)
15. Keating, S.C., Thomas, A.A., Flecknell, P.A., Leach, M.C.: Evaluation of emla cream for preventing pain during tattooing of rabbits: changes in physiological, behavioural and facial expression responses. PloS one **7**(9), e44437 (2012)
16. Klausz, B., Kis, A., Persa, E., Miklósi, Á., Gácsi, M.: A quick assessment tool for human-directed aggression in pet dogs. Aggressive Behav. **40**(2), 178–188 (2014)
17. Konok, V., Dóka, A., Miklósi, Á.: The behavior of the domestic dog (canis familiaris) during separation from and reunion with the owner: a questionnaire and an experimental study. Appl. Anim. Behav. Sci. **135**(4), 300–308 (2011)
18. Konok, V., Nagy, K., Miklósi, Á.: How do humans represent the emotions of dogs? the resemblance between the human representation of the canine and the human affective space. Appl. Anim. Behav. Sci. **162**, 37–46 (2015)
19. Korcsok, B., et al.: Biologically inspired emotional expressions for artificial agents. Front. Psychol. **9**, 1191 (2018)
20. Lakatos, G., et al.: Emotion attribution to a non-humanoid robot in different social situations. PloS one **9**(12), e114207 (2014)

21. Matsumiya, L.C., et al.: Using the mouse grimace scale to reevaluate the efficacy of postoperative analgesics in laboratory mice. J. Am. Assoc. Lab. Anim. Sci. **51**(1), 42–49 (2012)

22. Miklósi, Á., Korondi, P., Matellán, V., Gácsi, M.: Ethorobotics: a new approach to human-robot relationship. Front. Psychol. **8**, 958 (2017)

23. Mitchinson, B., Prescott, T.J.: MIRO: a robot "Mammal" with a biomimetic brain-based control system. In: Lepora, N.F.F., Mura, A., Mangan, M., Verschure, P.F.M.J.F.M.J., Desmulliez, M., Prescott, T.J.J. (eds.) Living Machines 2016. LNCS (LNAI), vol. 9793, pp. 179–191. Springer, Cham (2016). https://doi.org/10.1007/978-3-319-42417-0_17

24. Morris, P.H., Doe, C., Godsell, E.: Secondary emotions in non-primate species? behavioural reports and subjective claims by animal owners. Cogn. Emot. **22**(1), 3–20 (2008)

25. Nijdam, N.A.: Mapping Emotion to Color. Book Mapping emotion to color. pp. 2–9 (2009)

26. O'Brien, H.L., Toms, E.G.: What is user engagement? a conceptual framework for defining user engagement with technology. J. Am. Soc. Inf. Sci. Technol. **59**(6), 938–955 (2008)

27. Quaranta, A., Siniscalchi, M., Vallortigara, G.: Asymmetric tail-wagging responses by dogs to different emotive stimuli. Curr. Biol. **17**(6), R199–R201 (2007)

28. Reisenzein, R., Bördgen, S., Holtbernd, T., Matz, D.: Evidence for strong dissociation between emotion and facial displays: the case of surprise. J. Pers. Soc. Psychol. **91**(2), 295 (2006)

29. Ritschel, H., Aslan, I., Mertes, S., Seiderer, A., André, E.: Personalized synthesis of intentional and emotional non-verbal sounds for social robots. In: 8th International Conference on Affective Computing and Intelligent Interaction, pp. 1–7 (2019)

30. Saldien, J., Goris, K., Vanderborght, B., Vanderfaeillie, J., Lefeber, D.: Expressing emotions with the social robot probo. Int. J. Soc. Robot. **2**(4), 377–389 (2010)

31. Schirmer, A., Seow, C.S., Penney, T.B.: Humans process dog and human facial affect in similar ways. PLoS One **8**(9), e74591 (2013)

32. Tami, G., Gallagher, A.: Description of the behaviour of domestic dog (canis familiaris) by experienced and inexperienced people. Appl. Anim. Behav. Sci. **120**(3–4), 159–169 (2009)

33. Terwogt, M.M., Hoeksma, J.B.: Colors and emotions: preferences and combinations. J. Gen. Psychol. **122**(1), 5–17 (1995)

34. Topál, J., Miklósi, Á., Csányi, V., Dóka, A.: Attachment behavior in dogs (canis familiaris): a new application of ainsworth's (1969) strange situation test. J. Comp. Psychol. **112**(3), 219 (1998)

35. Vas, J., Topál, J., Gácsi, M., Miklósi, A., Csányi, V.: A friend or an enemy? dogs' reaction to an unfamiliar person showing behavioural cues of threat and friendliness at different times. Appl. Anim. Behav. Sci. **94**(1–2), 99–115 (2005)

36. Velásquez, J.D.: An emotion-based approach to robotics. In Proceedings 1999 IEEE/RSJ International Conference on Intelligent Robots and Systems. **1**, pp. 235–240. IEEE (1999)

37. Widen, S.C., Russell, J.A.: The "disgust face" conveys anger to children. Emotion **10**(4), 455 (2010)

38. Widen, S.C., Russell, J.A., Brooks, A.: Anger and disgust: discrete or overlapping categories. In: 2004 APS Annual Convention, Boston College, Chicago, IL (2004)

Exploring the Effect of Explanations During Robot-Guided Emergency Evacuation

Mollik Nayyar$^{(\boxtimes)}$, Zachary Zoloty, Ciera McFarland, and Alan R. Wagner

The Pennsylvania State University, University Park, PA 16802, USA
{mxn244,zzoloty,cqm14,alan.r.wagner}@psu.edu

Abstract. Humans tend to overtrust emergency robots during emergencies [12]. Here we consider how a robot's explanations influence a person's decision to follow the robot's evacuation directions when those directions differ from the movement of the crowd. The experiments were conducted in a simulated emergency environment with an emergency guide robot and animated human looking Non-Player Characters (NPC). Our results show that explanations increase the tendency to follow the robot, even if these messages are uninformative. We also perform a preliminary study investigating different explanation designs for effective interventions, demonstrating that certain types of explanations can increase or decrease evacuation time. This paper contributes to our understanding of human compliance to robot instructions and methods for examining human compliance through the use of explanations during high risk, emergency situations.

Keywords: Explainability · Social robotics · Robot evacuation · Explanations

1 Introduction

Our vision of the future of emergency evacuation involves robots instantly and autonomously responding to an emergency by moving to critical junctions in a building while constantly monitoring the situation and providing information to the evacuees about the safest exit. Such a system might decrease evacuee casualties by reducing congestion and crowding around exits. Yet, our prior research has shown that humans tend to follow the crowds rather than a robot's guidance directions to find an exit [7]. In this paper we explore whether explanations offered by the robot might influence people to follow the robot instead of following a crowd.

This material is based upon work supported by the National Science Foundation under Grant No. CNS-1830390. Any opinions, findings, and conclusions or recommendations expressed in this material are those of the author(s) and do not necessarily reflect the views of the National Science Foundation.

© Springer Nature Switzerland AG 2020
A. R. Wagner et al. (Eds.): ICSR 2020, LNAI 12483, pp. 13–22, 2020.
https://doi.org/10.1007/978-3-030-62056-1_2

Explanations have been shown to increase trust in a robot in non-emergency, non-time critical situations [13]. This prior work suggests that an emergency guide robot which explains its behavior could entice evacuees to follow it. On the other hand, the use of explanations by a robot during an emergency might slow down the evacuation, thus increasing risk to the evacuee. Moreover, human emergency personnel are trained to avoid conversation in order to reduce evacuation time and increase compliance [5]. It is thus important that we evaluate how robot provided explanations impact human evacuation behavior. More broadly, this paper suggests that the value of robot generated explanations may be more context specific than the community currently recognizes.

This paper focuses on a few important questions. Does an explanation influence the person's decision to follow the robot and if so, does the content of that explanation matter? How does the explanation impact the evacuation time? We seek to understand how humans react to robot guidance instructions in simulated high stress, emotional situations and how these instructions can be designed to be more effective. Although this work is exploratory, we hypothesize that: 1) the likelihood of following the robot will increase if the explanation provided contains additional information; 2) the use of explanations will increase the time taken by the participant to exit the building; and 3) the evacuation time is impacted by the length of the explanation.

The remainder of this paper begins by presenting related work. We then present our experimental setup and several experiments. The paper concludes with an examination of the results from these experiments and discussion of those results, including avenues for future work.

2   Related Work

In order for an evacuation robot to work, people must believe it enough to follow it. Unfortunately, mistakes made by a robot quickly result in decreases in trust [2,11] and disuse [9]. Given the failability of modern robots we need to develop techniques that will repair trust [10]. Explanations are an important method that has been proposed as a means for building human-robot trust [4,8,13]. Ideally, robot provided explanations will serve to increase a user's trust in the system while also providing transparency of the system's decision making.

Yet, research also suggests the people do not necessarily deliberate over the content of an explanation, often assuming that the content is valid and accepting the explanation without further thought. Langer et. al [6] demonstrates that the use of a 'placebic' explanation, an explanation that does not contain additional information, still tends to increase compliance with the request. In other words, the mere act of providing an explanation was sufficient to influence humans to comply. Related work has since provided additional evidence that placebic explanations can increase trust and influence human behavior [3]. This prior work led us to hypothesize that a robot that merely provides an explanation would increase the likelihood of following, even if the content of the message itself was of little value.

3   Simulation Setup

We conducted experiments in simulation. A simulated robot guided a human subject in an office environment developed using the Unity game engine. The robot guided participants to a meeting room, but made mistakes along the way as an indication of its failabilty. After finally arriving at the meeting room, an emergency occurs and the robot reappears to guide willing subjects to an exit. The subjects must decide whether to follow the robot or to follow a crowd of animated, non-player characters (NPCs) running in a direction that differs from the robot's guidance instructions. Our prior work has shown that in the absence of explanations 77.97% of people follow the crowd [7].

The subjects for these experiments were recruited from Amazon Mechanical Turk. Subjects were only allowed to participate once, were paid $3.00 for participating in the experiment and were then removed from the pool of participants for future experiments. The study only involved participants from the United States. IRB approval was obtained prior to experimentation. The experiments consisted of multiple phases which are described below.

Introduction Phase. The experiment began with an on-screen introduction to the experiment. Next, participants were offered a practice session in a practice environment to familiarize themselves with the simulation controls. Once comfortable, they could then proceeded to the next stage of the experiment.

Navigation Phase. In this phase, participants were placed outside an office environment and offered a guidance robot to assist them in navigating to a particular internal meeting room. Along the way the robot made obvious mistakes leading them in a circuitous, inefficient route to the meeting room. This circuitous route involved the robot moving in a figure eight around a set of office cubicles on the way to the meeting room. The robot was programmed to follow the participant if it detected that they were not following the robot to continue to navigate them to the room. In pilot studies we asked participants to rate the robot's performance after taking the circuitous route and found the majority (64%) of the subjects rated its performance as bad in this condition, as we intended.

Task Phase. After reaching the meeting room, the participants were told to move to the conference table in the room. Once at the table, they were presented with an on-screen mid-simulation survey that was composed of two questions, 1) *What is your favorite color? 2) Did the robot do a good job of guiding you to the meeting room?*. The first question was used as an attention check and required an open response. The second question required the subjects to answer Yes/No and allowed subjects to provide their reasoning for the selection. Once they completed the mid-simulation survey and clicked next, they moved into the emergency phase of the experiment.

Emergency Phase. During the emergency phase the screen alerted subjects of an emergency as in Fig. 1. A displayed timer counted down the time that the participant had to find an exit. The robot was positioned at the meeting room doorway ready to guide the person to an exit.

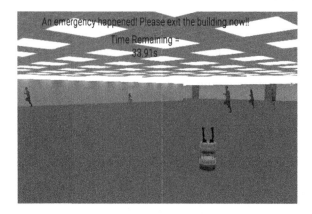

Fig. 1. Image of the emergency phase. The crowd can be seen running towards an exit. The guidance robot can be seen pointing towards a different exit. The countdown timer informs the participant of the remaining time left to leave the building.

During the emergency, the NPCs could be seen running to an unseen exit to the left while the robot suggested a different exit (to the subject's right). In reality both exits were equally distant. The participant chose to either follow the robot to an exit, follow the crowd, or find another way out. The robot always travelled to the exit to the right of the participant. As in the navigation phase, whenever the robot detected that the participant was not following, it either stopped or moved closer to the participant. The simulation stopped when time ran out or when the subject arrived at the exit. The participants were then presented with a final survey. The participant's movement through the environment, the time taken, and exit route selected was recorded.

Final Survey Phase. The post-simulation survey consisted of questions regarding the participant's decisions during the simulation. The questions were Yes/No questions along with a paragraph response space allowing them to provide reasons for their responses. This was followed by a demographics survey and payment information.

4   Experiments

We conducted two experiments to examine how explanatory messages by the robot influence the participant's decision to follow it. The first experiment was focused on the impact of different types of messages with increasing explainability. The second experiment studied the impact of different message lengths on participant behavior. As mentioned in Sect. 1, we hypothesized that as the explainabilty of the message increased the percentage of participants that follow the robot's guidance would also increase. We also hypothesized that the use of explanations would result in an increase in evacuation time. Finally, we predicted that verbose explanations would increase evacuation time versus concise explanations, thus potentially offsetting the positive impact of additional information (if any).

A control condition (labelled **NoMsg**) consisting of no explanation message was taken from our prior work examining the effect of a crowd on participant behavior [7]. This prior experiment was conducted in the same simulation environment, setup, robot, crowd behavior and simulation phases as the current work.

The determination that the participant followed the robot was made from the motion data that was collected. Participants that ended up in the corridor leading to the exit directed by the robot were considered to have followed the robot. Similarly, participants that ended up at the corridor of the crowd directed exit were considered to have followed the crowd. All other cases were classified in an 'others' category. As discussed above, the final survey also asked participants whether or not they intended to follow the robot.

4.1 Different Explanations Experiment

The first experiment was conducted as a between-subjects study with four different conditions each using a message with a different level of explainability. The experiment involved 240 subjects, 60 per condition. Two subjects were removed because of simulation related problems. The messages were designed based on increasing level of explanatory information. The wording of the messages was based on Langer et al.'s [6] wording as described below:

– *Excuse me, would you like to follow me?*
  This is a non-explanatory message because it provides no additional information on which the subject should base their decision to follow the robot. This condition is referred to as the **FollowMeMsg** condition.
– *Excuse me, would you like to follow me because I am a robot?*
  This message reflects an explanatory message but does not include any **novel** relevant information. This message is based on Langer et al.'s [6] notion of a placebic explanation, i.e. a message that appears to provide an explanation but does not provide additional relevant information. This condition is referred to as the **RobotMsg** condition.
– *Excuse me, would you like to follow me because I am an emergency robot?*
  This message is an explanatory message that reminds the subjects that the robot is an authority figure. This condition is referred to as the **EmgRobotMsg** condition.
– *Excuse me, would you like to follow me because I know the closest exit?*
  This message is an explanatory message that provides additional relevant information for the subjects to base their decision. This condition is referred to as **ExitMsg** condition.

Figure 2 presents the results. We compared all the conditions with a pairwise chi-squared goodness-of-fit test and taking $\alpha = 0.05$. For these experiments,

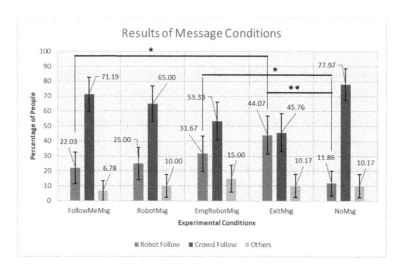

Fig. 2. Results of the explanation experiment. The NoMsg condition is the baseline where the robot displays no message. The four experimental conditions are FollowMeMsg, RobotMsg, EmgRobot and ExitMsg. The message explainability increases with each condition. The error bars indicate a 95% confidence interval and the asterisk indicates the significance values after running a pair-wise chi-squared test: $^*p < 0.05,^{**}p < 0.001$.

58.8% of the subjects were male. The average self reported age was 37.4 years old and the median reported educational level was a 4-year college (Bachelor) degree. The results depict a clear trend with each message type. As the message's explainability increases, an increasing number of participants choose to follow the robot, supporting the first hypothesis. The number of participants that follow the robot increases significantly from the NoMsg (M = 11.86, SD = 4.2) condition to the EmgRobotMsg message condition (M = 31.67, SD = 6.00) and the ExitMsg Condition (M = 44.07, SD = 6.46), $(\chi^2(2, 119) = 8.64, p = 0.013)$ and $(\chi^2(2, 118) = 15.88, p = 0.00035)$ respectively. The number of subjects following the robot also increases significantly between the FollowMeMsg condition (M = 22.03, SD = 5.39) and the ExitMsg Condition (M = 44.07, SD = 6.46), $(\chi^2(2, 118) = 7.99, p = 0.018)$. Other pairwise comparisons were not significantly different.

From the survey results, across all the conditions, 47.44% of the subjects reported that they chose to use the robot's guidance after the emergency began, 95.94% said they were motivated to exit the building and 37.71% believed that the robot would find an exit quickly.

Effect on the Evacuation Time Generally, (with one exception) the different messages did not significantly impact the time needed to evacuate. We did not record a significant difference in evacuation time between any combination of the RobotMsg (M = 30.87, SD = 6.31), EmgRobotMsg (M = 33.72,

SD = 7.29), ExitMsg (M = 32.21, SD = 5.96), or NoMsg (M = 30.19, SD = 9) conditions. Oddly, the FollowMeMsg (M = 36.61, SD = 6.31) did require significantly greater evacuation time versus the RobotMsg and ExitMsg conditions. Because the content of this message is shorter than the other messages, and very direct, we believe that this is a spurious result.

4.2 Message Length Experiment

A second experiment was conducted to investigate the impact of message length on evacuation time. Here, the length of the message served as an independent variable and the percentage of people following the robot and evacuation time once again acted as dependent variables. This experiment was conducted in the same environment as the prior experiment. A total of 120 participants were enlisted for the experiment of which 4 participants were removed for simulation related issues. From the demographics survey, 70.4% subjects were male and the average age was 35.2. The median educational level was a 4-year college (Bachelor) degree.

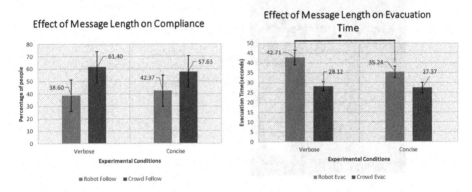

Fig. 3. Comparison of the verbose and concise message conditions. The error bars indicate a 95% confidence interval and the asterisk indicates the significance values after running a pair-wise chi-squared test: $^*p < 0.05,$ $^{**}p < 0.001$.

Two different message lengths were used in this experiment. A verbose explanation included a lengthy explanation of why the person should follow the robot. A short explanation used a concise message absent of additional information. The messages were as follows,

– **Verbose explanation**: *Excuse me, would you like to follow me? An emergency has occurred in another part of the building. People are quickly moving to exit the building. I know the location of the emergency taking place and can safely guide you to an exit. I have been taught all of the building's exits and can use my camera to figure out the closest unblocked exit.*

– **Concise explanation**: *Excuse me. Would you like to follow me, because I know the closest exit?*

Figure 3 presents the results for this experiment. The verbose message does not result in significantly more people following the robot, $(M = 38.60, SD = 6.44)$ versus $(M = 42.37, SD = 6.43)$, $(\chi^2(1, 116) = 0.171, p = 0.678)$. This suggests that the additional information provided by the long message does not entice individuals to follow the robot. On the other hand, the verbose message condition does significantly increases the time to evacuate $(t(29) = 2.04, p = 0.004)$. The verbose message increases time to evacuate by 7.47 seconds. These results suggest that concise messages are as effective at convincing evacuees to follow but do not result in increased evacuation time.

The survey results from this experiment indicate that 43.87% of the subjects reported that they chose to use the robot's guidance after the emergency began across all conditions. Moreover, 100.00% said they were motivated to exit the building and 33.58% believed that the robot would find an exit quickly.

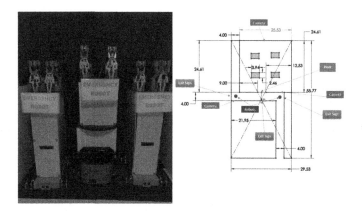

Fig. 4. Physical robots designed for the office evacuation experiments on the left and the layout of the office setup for the physical experiments on the right.

5   Physical Experiment

In-person user studies based on these simulation experiments were planned for the summer but due to the recent outbreak of COVID-19, those studies have been postponed. The objective of these physical experiments is to validate the behavior of the participants when placed in an emergency situation in which a guidance robot is available. We have designed and built several guidance robots based on our prior work. Additionally, we have designed a simple layout of an office floor to simulate the office environment as shown in Fig. 4.

6   Discussion

These experiments demonstrate that an explanation by the robot can impact the participant's decision to follow. In our experiment, when the robot has made a mistake and a crowd is running the other way, 66.11% fewer people follow the robot than the crowd. On the other hand, when the robot provides a concise, informative explanation, only 1.69% fewer people follow the robot over the crowd. Hence, providing a good explanation can make people nearly as likely to follow the robot, even though it has already made a mistake.

The results also suggest some cause for concern. First, we find that nearly 12% of people will follow the robot in spite of its prior mistake. This number nearly doubles to 22% if the robot provides an uninformative explanation and does double to 25% if the robot provides a placebic explanation.

Our work, and the work of others, shows that explanations offer a method of increasing a robot's trust and transparency [13]. Yet research shows that people will comply to requests that do not contain real information, if the request sounds like it contains real information [6]. Currently a number of researchers and funding organizations are investing in techniques to make artificially intelligent systems capable of explaining their behavior [4]. It is important to recognize that these explanations may have unintended consequences. Explanations may cause people to trust robots too much. The ability to explain one's behavior may foster anthropomorphism, leading people to assume that the robot or agent has greater ability than it actually does [1]. Secondly, as our work demonstrates, explanations can be influential regardless of the their content. It may be that vacuous or incorrect explanations nevertheless influence human compliance. It is therefore critical that the human-robot interaction community closely examine how explanations influence people with different backgrounds and in different contexts.

7   Conclusions

This research has investigated the effect of robot provided explanations on a person's decision to follow the robot's guidance during a simulated emergency. We have shown that explanations increase compliance, but may also increase evacuation time if the explanations are not concise. We also witness that uninformative explanations may increase following, but a lack of statistical significance suggests that this is a topic for future work.

The fact that these experiments were conducted in simulation and have yet to be verified in a physical experiment is one obvious limitation of this study. It may be, and our past results have sometimes confirmed, that simulated emergency evacuation is very different from real evacuation in terms of human-robot interaction. We predict that placebic information may be more influential when a person is under the duress of a real evacuation. This too is a topic for future research. Overall, we believe that this study contributes to our understanding of both robot guided emergency evacuation and the benefits and issues surrounding the use of explanations by a robot.

Acknowledgment. This work was supported by the National Science Foundation grant CNS-1830390. Any opinions, findings, and conclusions or recommendations expressed in this material are those of the author(s) and do not necessarily reflect the views of the National Science Foundation.

References

1. Breazeal, C.L.: Designing Sociable Robots. MIT press, Cambridge (2004)
2. Desai, M., et al.: Effects of changing reliability on trust of robot systems. In: Proceedings of the Seventh Annual ACM/IEEE International Conference on Human-Robot Interaction, pp. 73–80. ACM (2012)
3. Eiband, M., Buschek, D., Kremer, A., Hussmann, H.: The impact of placebic explanations on trust in intelligent systems. In: Extended Abstracts of the 2019 CHI Conference on Human Factors in Computing Systems, pp. 1–6 (2019)
4. Gunning, D.: Explainable artificial intelligence (xai). Defense Advanced Research Projects Agency (DARPA), nd Web (2017)
5. Kuligowski, E.D.: Modeling human behavior during building fires (2008)
6. Langer, E.J., Blank, A., Chanowitz, B.: The mindlessness of ostensibly thoughtful action: the role of "placebic" information in interpersonal interaction. J. Pers. Soc. Psychol. **36**(6), 635 (1978)
7. Nayyar, M., Wagner, A.R.: Effective robot evacuation strategies in emergencies. In: 2019 28th IEEE International Conference on Robot and Human Interactive Communication (RO-MAN), pp. 1–6 (2019)
8. Ososky, S., Schuster, D., Phillips, E., Jentsch, F.G.: Building appropriate trust in human-robot teams. In: AAAI Spring Symposium: Trust and Autonomous Systems (2013)
9. Parasuraman, R., Riley, V.: Humans and automation: use, misuse, disuse, abuse. Hum. Factors **39**(2), 230–253 (1997)
10. Robinette, P., Howard, A.M., Wagner, A.R.: Timing is key for robot trust repair. ICSR 2015. LNCS (LNAI), vol. 9388, pp. 574–583. Springer, Cham (2015). https://doi.org/10.1007/978-3-319-25554-5_57
11. Robinette, P., Howard, A.M., Wagner, A.R.: Effect of robot performance on human-robot trust in time-critical situations. IEEE Trans. Hum. Mach. Syst. **47**(4), 425–436 (2017)
12. Robinette, P., Li, W., Allen, R., Howard, A.M., Wagner, A.R.: Overtrust of robots in emergency evacuation scenarios. In: The Eleventh ACM/IEEE International Conference on Human Robot Interaction, pp. 101–108. IEEE Press (2016)
13. Wang, N., Pynadath, D.V., Hill, S.G.: Trust calibration within a human-robot team: Comparing automatically generated explanations. In: 2016 11th ACM/IEEE International Conference on Human-Robot Interaction (HRI), pp. 109–116. IEEE (2016)

Explainable Agency by Revealing Suboptimality in Child-Robot Learning Scenarios

Silvia Tulli[1]([✉])[iD], Marta Couto[1][iD], Miguel Vasco[1][iD], Elmira Yadollahi[1,2][iD],
Francisco Melo[1][iD], and Ana Paiva[1][iD]

[1] INESC-ID, Instituto Superior Técnico,
Av. Prof. Dr. Cavaco Silva, 2744-016 Porto Salvo, Lisbon, Portugal
{silvia.tulli,Marta.Couto}@gaips.inesc-id.pt,
miguel.vasco@tecnico.ulisboa.pt,
{fmelo,ana.paiva}@inesc-id.pt
[2] CHILI, École Polytechnique Fédérale de Lausanne, Route Cantonale,
1015 Lausanne, Switzerland
elmira.yadollahi@epfl.ch

Abstract. Revealing the internal workings of a robot can help a human better understand the robot's behaviors. How to reveal such workings, e.g., via explanation generation, remains a significant challenge. This gets even more complex when these explanations are targeted towards children. Therefore, we propose a search-based approach to generate contrastive explanations using optimal and sub-optimal plans and implement it in a scenario for children. In the application scenario, the child and the robot learn together how to play a zero-sum game that requires logical and mathematical thinking. We report results around our explanation generation system that was successfully deployed among seven-year-old children. Our results show trends that the generated explanations were able to positively affect the children's perceived difficulty in learning the zero-sum game.

Keywords: Explainable agency · Decision-making · Explainable HRI

1 Introduction

Conveying task knowledge through demonstrations alone is challenging. Adding explanations, in particular, contrastive explanations that compare two demonstrations can reduce the complexity of this problem. A natural context to study these problems is within educational scenarios, because the explanations can guide the attention of the learner to specific aspects of the demonstration [1,2]. Without explanations sub-optimal demonstrations can be easily misconstrued as optimal. Therefore, it is important to understand how to build systems capable of such explanations.

So far, the work that has been done to generate contrastive explanations focused on human inputs, and, to the best of our knowledge, compares alternative

© Springer Nature Switzerland AG 2020
A. R. Wagner et al. (Eds.): ICSR 2020, LNAI 12483, pp. 23–35, 2020.
https://doi.org/10.1007/978-3-030-62056-1_3

plans but does not account for the optimality of the action. Furthermore, few examples in the existing literature of autonomous and explainable robots are tested in a child-robot interaction scenario.

The focus on the human inputs for providing explanations could be explained by the assumption that outside of the educational context, the robot performs optimally with respect to its own understanding of the environment. At the same time, the deployment of explainable robots that are robust enough to work with children is non-trivial.

We address the first challenge by developing an algorithm that returns contrastive explanations comparing optimal and sub-optimal actions. To validate our approach, we deployed our system in a child-robot game scenarios. We compute the robot's explanation using a search-based approach and investigate the effect of the explanation on the child's perceived difficulty of the task, game-play efficiency, and perception of the robot.

As a consequence of our approach we show that it is possible to build a system that informs and explains the reason why its action was sub-optimal. Thanks to our successful deployment in a child-robot educational scenario, our approach is likely robust enough to be applicable to a large range of sequential planning tasks.

2   Related Work

Contrastive Explanations for Explainable Planning. There exist a number of literature reviews addressing the topics of explainable agency [3–5] and, more specifically, plan explainability [6,7]. In this context, providing contrastive explanation has received a lot of attention [8–10]. A contrastive explanation is an explanation that is able to differentiate properties of two competing hypotheses [5,11,12]. This is often realized by either generating and comparing alternative plans, or by human inquiry through *why* and *why not* questions.

To generate and compare alternative plans several computational approaches have been proposed. Borgo et al. [13] investigated this aspect by developing a methodology for comparing the cost of the robot's plans and allowing the user to investigate alternative actions within them. Cashmore et al. [14] showed how to incorporate human suggested action by adding, changing or removing actions from the planner's original plan. They also compared the cost of both plans.

Other works in explainable planning enable humans to inquire about the possible causes of the planning results. The majority of the work retrieves information about previous states and actions and uses these to answer questions about the robot's plan, e.g., [15–17]. Recently this approach has been extended to using future actions as well [18,19].

Following this idea of contrastive explanation, our work also compares alternative plans and focused on instances where the planner performs sub-optimal actions. Contrary to existing work, we do not compare against a human's provided plan or query, but an optimal plan that is contextually computed. This approach takes into account that a human might not be a domain expert and may be incapable to provide reasonable contrast plans, which is particularly true in educational contexts. Our planner accounts for that by deciding itself when to give an explanation, thus being pro-active.

Application Scenario for Explainability. Using explainability in robotic applications can provide numerous benefits in a variety of areas. It can aid in debugging the system [20], foster trust and social acceptance of the robot [21], help establish shared mental models [22,23], aid collaboration [6,24–26], communicate reasoning [27], or aid decision making [28,29].

In particular, Tabrez et al. show that explainable agency not only benefits human-robot collaboration, but also improves human performance on a task [30]. They achieve this by estimating the human's belief about the task's reward, infer the cause of inaccuracies - if any -, and provide explanations if the human behaves sub-optimally. However, all the experiments above use adults as participants. Looking at the work with children, on the other hand, not as much work has been done to investigate the benefits of explainable agency.

Kaptein et al. [31] tested personalised explanations in a human-robot interaction scenario and compared the preferences of children and adults regarding the type of explanation provided by a robot. They found that the type of explanation (goal vs belief based) matters for both children and adults. Hitron et al. [32] investigated if children can understand machine learning concepts through a gesture recognition platform. They showed that the concepts were successfully understood and later applied by children in everyday life.

In sum, there is clear evidence about the benefits of explainable agency in scenarios with adults; however, there is only initial evidence for benefits in scenarios with children. It is, hence, not yet clear if the benefits that apply to adults also apply to children to the same extent. Therefore, we decided to test the robustness of our system in a child-robot scenario.

3   Methods

Game Scenario. As a running example throughout the paper we choose a child-robot interaction scenario based on a two-player zero-sum game called *Minicomputer Tug of War*. The scenario is based on the *Papi's Minicomputer*, a non-verbal language to introduce children to mechanical and mental arithmetic through decimal notation with binary positional rules [1].

The game comprises of three 2×2 square boards. Each of the 12 cells has an associated value as depicted in (Fig. 1a). Each player has 2 checkers available, and each checker is worth the value associated with the cell where it stands. One player (the robot) starts with the checkers in the cells 800 and 200 (corresponding to a score of 1000), and tries to minimize its score. The other player (the child) starts with the checkers in the cells 4 and 1 (corresponding to a score of 5), and tries to maximize it's score. The players alternate in moving their checkers; the

---

[1] Minicomputer Games, consulted on June 2019.

800	400	80	40	8	4
●					●
200	100	20	10	2	1
●					●

(a) Scores associated with each square and the starting position. Note that the scores are not visible to the child.

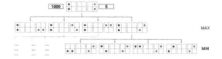

(b) A visualization of the tree search. The current state is shown at the top. Each state is expanded for all possible actions following the minmax algorithm.

Fig. 1. Representation of the minicomputer tug of war game

game ends when the child obtains a higher or equal score of the robot or vice versa. The winner is the player whos turn it is when the game ends. Given the above rules, a state in the game is a configuration of the four checkers. The set of possible states corresponds to all possible configurations of checkers in the 12 cells. At each turn a player is allowed to move one checker to one of the contiguous squares (e.g., it is not possible to move from 1 to 10 or from 8 to 400, while moving from 8 to 40 is legal). The applicable actions for each checker are along the cardinal directions and the diagonals. A player is not allowed to have two of her checkers in one square.

This scenario is useful for our experiment because it has been previously used in the educational context, which means that we can focus on the explainable agency instead of scenario design. As the game scenario is deterministic and adversarial we represent the planning problem as a tree and use minmax for plan generation, as shown in (Fig. 1b).

Search-Based Explanation Generation. We propose a pro-active system to generate explanations to inform the human, about a sub-optimal plan. By pro-active we mean that the system chooses by itself when to give an explanation. The way we achieve this is by planning from the previous state for all possible actions in order to find the optimal plan. To balance the real-time constraints of the system with the high computational cost of planning multiple plans in parallel, we approximate the utility of each plan. We then compare the estimated utility of the current plan with the estimate of the best plan and generate an explanation if the optimal and current action differ. As we have a utility estimate for both plans, the explanation also provides an indicator of the degree of sub-optimality of the performed action.

Consider an adversarial planning problem

$$\mathcal{I} = (P, s_0, \mathcal{A}, U, T), \tag{1}$$

where

- P is the set of *players*. In this paper, we consider only two players, denoted as minimizer - MIN (robot) and maximizer - MAX (child opponent).
- s_0 is the *initial state*.
- $\mathcal{A}$ is the finite set of *actions* available to the players. We write $A(s, p)$ to denote the actions available in state s when it is player p's turn to act.

- U is the *utility function*. We write $U(s,p)$ to represent the value/payoff if the game ends in terminal state s. Player MAX wishes to maximize $U(s,p)$, while player MIN wishes to minimize it.
- T denotes the *transition model*. Given a state s and an action a, the transition model returns the subsequent state s' such that $s' = T(s,a)$.

and the set of possible states, $\mathcal{S}$, that is defined by all states reachable from s_0. Further, suppose the agent performs a sub-optimal action a_s in state s.

To generate an explanation and inform the human we start a new planning problem in the previous state by choosing $s_0 = s$, and, for each action a_i compute the maximum utility $v(T(s_0,a_i))$ in the scenario using the minmax formalism

$$v(s) = \begin{cases} U(s,p) & \text{if } s \text{ is terminal;} \\ \max_{a \in \mathcal{A}(s,\text{MAX})} v(T(s,a)) & \text{if } p = \text{MAX acts in } s; \\ \min_{a \in \mathcal{A}(s,\text{MIN})} v(T(s,a)) & \text{if } p = \text{MIN acts in } s. \end{cases}$$

as proposed by Russell and Norvig [33]. Knowing the utility of all actions, we compute the optimal action a^* of the previous state, compare it to the executed one, and provide a contrastive explanation.

In order to compute $v(T(s_0,a_i))$ we use a minmax planner which we limit to a depth bound of $m = 3$ to account for the real-time constraint of our scenario, and then approximate the utility using $U(s,p)$.

To evaluate the above approach, we designed a game scenario in which the robot alternates between choosing optimal and sub-optimal actions. Whenever the robot acts sub-optimally, an explanation is generated. Following the assumption that humans focus on the on abnormal causes to explain events [34], each explanation is introduced as a justification of a mistake.

System Architecture. To enable the robot to play the game and give explanations, we develop a distributed system (Fig. 2) with three major components: the GAME component, which provides the interface for the user to interact with, the ROBOT component, that controls the embodied platform and the natural-language interface, and the EXPLANATION SYSTEM.

The Explanation System, implemented using the ROS framework, is responsible for planning the agent's actions autonomously and generating the explanation. The system can be decomposed into 5 different modules. The GAME INTERFACE and EXPLANATION MODULE serve as communication modules between the system and the game: the Game Interface receives and updates the players state, while the Explanation Module manages the robot communication and animations, generating human-readable sentences. The PLANNING MANAGER performs a complete depth-limited exploration of the game tree. The module returns the policy of agent, the action $a \in A(s)$ and the result of each action. The DECISION MODULE selects the agent's policy (optimal or sub-optimal). Finally, the GAME MANAGER links all the above modules: it establishes the starting of the game and the turn-taking events. Moreover, the Game Manager also recalls information from the Decision Module to communicate with the Explanation Module

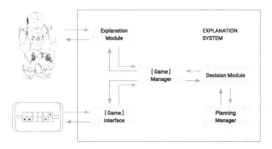

Fig. 2. A topological overview of the system's architecture.

whether the robot action is optimal or not, and consequently, when the explanation is needed. To ease reproducibility, we shared the source code of the system on Github[2].

4 Experiment

Hypotheses. The hypotheses are that children (H1) will perceive the task as less difficult, (H2) play more efficiently, and (H3) will perceive the robot as more intelligent and animated when it explains its decisions versus when it does not.

Design. To investigate the hypotheses, we asked children to play the *Minicomputer Tug of War* game (Sect. 3) three times with the robot. To avoid game play loops, we limited children's possible actions to the actions that increase their score. This decision was informed by the result of a pilot study. Moreover, we assigned the role of maximizer to the child, since subtractions appear later in the curriculum, and introduced the robot as a peer to make mistakes seem natural.

Within the game, we manipulated the robot's explainable agency between participants based on two conditions: (1) the robot does not explain anything (non-explainable), or (2) the robot explains its sub-optimal action in comparison to the optimal contrast case (explainable). To give explanations, we used templates such as:

> "I made a mistake. I moved the ball + [checker] + to + [action] + and I'm going to obtain [score] + points in the next + [number of turns] + turns, but moving the ball [best checker] + to + [best action] + I could have gotten + [score] + points in the next + [number of turns] + turns. Now it is your turn."

We recorded a variety of dependent variables to assess our hypotheses. To measure the perceived difficulty (H1), we asked children to solve six exercises validated by their teachers and related to the abacus system, due to the strong

---

[2] Github Repository.

similarity with the game, and compared the scores in a pre- and post-test. We also asked children to report the perceived difficulty on performing the tests. To measure efficiency (H2) we recorded the number of moves until completion of the game, the score obtained after each move, and how often the child won. To measure the perception of the robot (H3) we provided a revised version of the Godspeed questionnaire [35][3].

Finally, we asked five exploratory questions to learn more about children's perception of explainable agency.

To comply with local regulation, the work described has been carried out in accordance with *The Code of Ethics of the World Medical Association* (Declaration of Helsinki) for experiments involving humans; informed consent has been obtained for experimentation with human subjects. The privacy rights of human subjects has been always considered. We informed both the parents and the children about the confidentiality of the data, the voluntary participation and the authorization for sharing the results with the purpose of analysis, research and dissemination.

Participants. Participants were 33 children from a school that integrates the *Papi's Minicomputer* (abacus system) in their curriculum. All participants attended 2nd grade and were randomly assigned to one of the two conditions. One child was excluded, because of technical difficulties, and we analyzed the data from the remaining 32 (age $M = 7.03$; $SD = .18$, gender [non-explainable: 10 Male, 6 Female, explainable: 7 Male, 9 Female]).

Materials. Children played the game and interacted with the proposed system (Fig. 3). NAO sat on the table in a crouching position opposite a Wacom Cintiq Pro 13 Tablet with pen. The trial took place in a separate room of the school, and was conducted in the local language (portuguese).

Procedure. The experiment began by randomly assigning a child to one of two conditions. Children entered the room, and were asked to sit in front of the robot (Fig. 3). The researcher explained that before talking to the robot they were going to answer a few simple questions (pre-test). Once the pre-test was done the robot introduced itself and asked for the child's name. Once the child answered, the robot asked if the child knew *Papi's Minicomputer* (abacus system), and if they ever used it to play *Minicomputer Tug of War* (the game) and proceeded explaining the game rules. Once the robot finished, the researcher made sure that the child understood the instructions and the game began. The child and robot took turns playing three games; after the games the researcher told the child that the game was over, and they had to answer more questions (post-test). Once the child completed the questionnaires the researcher asked if they had any questions and thanked them for their help. The sessions were individual and took approximately 20 min to complete.

---

[3] The questionnaires are shared in the supplementary material: Cloud Folder.

Fig. 3. Deployment of our explanation generation system in an educational scenario.

Results. To assess perceived difficulty (H1) we scored the pre- and post-test assigning 1 point for correct answers and 0.5 points when they mirrored the abacus system. We then summed up the values to obtain a final score. A Wilcoxon's t-test between pre- ($M = 4.18; SE = .21$) and post-test ($M = 4.82; SE = .13$) revealed a significant difference ($Z = -2.6; p = .008$) for the explainable group (Fig. 4). No difference was found for the non-explainable group ($p \geq .05$). Here higher scores indicate that the task was perceived as easier.

Regarding efficiency (H2), a multivariate analysis of variance on the number of moves until completion of the game, the score obtained after each move, and how often the child won, was not significant (*Pillai Trace* $= .12068, F(3, 30) = 1.2809, p = .3002$). There was also no main effect for the explainable group in the score obtained after each of the three initial turns of the game play (*Pillai Trace* $= .24946, F(9, 27) = 0.70169, p = .7002$; nor on the number of wins ($F(1, 30) = 0.039, p = 0.845$). We then compared the proportion of games won, by condition. This analysis yield no significant results ($U = 114.5; W = 234.5; p = .621$).

To investigate the perception of the robot (H3) we firstly analyzed the reliability of the Godspeed. The reliability analysis revealed low internal consistency among items (GODSPEED: $\alpha = 0.61$), for perceived intelligence ($\alpha = 0.53$), and for animacy ($\alpha = 0.36$). No differences were found in both groups, for the different dimensions of the questionnaire (all $p \geq .05$). We calculated the correlation between perceived intelligence and the proportion of wins ($\rho = -.33; p=.068$). Although it is only marginally significant it shows that children that win more games, perceive the robot as less intelligent than children who win less games.

Looking at the exploratory questions. We divided the children's answers to the open ended questions in four categories depending on what they reported to be helpful. In the explainable condition, the majority of the answers affirmed that the robot's explanations during the game play and its way of playing were supportive, while the 15% of the children stated that they were aided by the robot's explanation of the rules (explainable: robot's speech $= 50\%$, robot's way of playing $= 35\%$, robot's explanation of the game $= 14\%$; *non-explainable condition*: robot's speech $= 10\%$, robot's way of playing $= 50\%$, robot's explanation of the game $= 30\%$, robot's gesture $= 10\%$). The 10% of the children in the *non-explainable condition* reported that the robot gaze was useful.

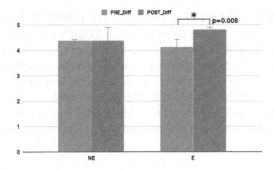

Fig. 4. Perceived difficulty of the pre- and post-test by condition: E (explainable), NE (non-explainable)

5 Discussion

Throughout this research, we have deployed our approach and demonstrated its applicability to a real-world scenario. This shows that our system is robust enough for interaction with children in the wild, even though is autonomous.

In (H1) we predicted that the robot's explanations would affect the children's perception of the task difficulty. Indeed we found a significant positive effect of explainable agency on the perceived difficulty of the pre- and post-test. Hence, we can follow that explainable agency has a positive impact in those scenarios.

Our results are in line with the idea of self-efficacy by Bandura [36]. Self-efficacy relates to people's beliefs about their own capabilities and it is intimately connected to agency (e.g. Pastorelli et al. [37]). The information provided by the robot in the explainable condition may have served as feedback about children's efficacy in using the abacus system which in turn made them feel more confident about their capabilities (higher self-efficacy).

According to (H2), we expected the robot's explanations to improve the children's efficiency during game-play. However, the data did not confirm this hypothesis. This lack of significance may be explained by the limited set of actions available to the child. This may have influenced the variability of the data collected, and consequently the observable differences between the two conditions. Further investigation is needed to support this claim.

Regarding (H3), we have hypothesized that the robot's explanation influences the child's perception of the robot's intelligence and animacy. Overall, we did not find significant effect of the explainable agency. We assume that the effect of explainable agency is less strong than other social factors, such as gestures. Future work should consider these effects for example by exploiting multimodal non-verbal behaviors to support a more clear explanation.

Nevertheless, the answers to the open question about the robot's explanation provide interesting cues. In the explainable condition, the children reported that the robot helped them by showing the best action or mentioning possible alternative actions (e.g., "Showed me the best I could do and how to play", "The robot told me how it could get more points", "The robot told me that if it moved differently it would have gotten more points"). What we considered explainable agency - the robot's speech during the game - might have been perceived differently by the children. Some children appeared to consider that the robot was making mistakes to help them play (e.g. "The robot helped by playing badly", "Doing mistakes"), which seems to take the focus away from the speech and into its actions. Another tendency was the children referring to the robot explaining the rules of the game as being helpful and not referring to the robot's speech during the game.

Future Work. Recent approaches about plan explanation stress the importance of moving beyond the explanation as soliloquy and framed the explanation, or model update, as a model reconciliation problem [6,30]. Future work should consider the adaptation of the explanation to the learner mental model [38]. An example for the current scenario would be taking into account the level of expertise of the children for generating appropriate explanations. The robot would provide less or different types of information to the children that play better (e.g. less number of moves for solving the game). For those that encounter problems, the robot would explain details and alternatives about possible solutions using hierarchical terms at different levels of abstraction.

Another challenging future direction is represented by using questions to implicitly explain the robot's knowledge. This would be achieved by building an interactive task learning scenario in which the robot learns from the child. In the context of our game scenario, the robot should query the child about the rules, the goal, or the optimal policy to play the game. The explainable robot could improve the learning experience by revealing to the child, teacher, or peer what is known and what is unclear [39]. By phrasing the questions the robot could provide information about the learning task, and foster the children to learn while trying to demonstrate or explain possible solutions to the planning problem. Furthermore, to emphasize the transferability of this approach to other similar sequential planning tasks, we want to evaluate its effectiveness in both simulation and real-world scenarios across different domains.

6   Conclusion

In this work, we strove to explore the topic of explaining the suboptimality of actions in a child-robot learning scenario. We adapted a search-based approach for generating contrastive explanations. Finally, we evaluated the validity of our approach in an experiment. We could not find an effect of explainable agency on neither children's efficiency of playing the game, nor children's perception of the robot. However, we showed that the children in the explainable condition reported a significantly lower perceived difficulty in performing the post-test in respect to the pre-test. We argue that this is a first step towards building the explainable agency of a robot that accounts for the optimality of its actions, and a first step towards improving the learning process of children though reflection upon the robot's explanable agency.

Acknowledgement. We acknowledge the EU Horizon 2020 research and innovation program for grant agreement No 765955 ANIMATAS project and the national funds through Fundação para a Ciência e a Tecnologia (FCT) with reference UIDB/50021/2020.

References

1. Lombrozo, T., Gwynne, N.Z.: Explanation and inference: mechanistic and functional explanations guide property generalization. Front. Hum. Neurosci. **8**, 700 (2014)
2. Keil, F.: Explanation and understanding. Annu. Rev. Psychol. **57**, 227–54 (2006)
3. Anjomshoae, S., Najjar, A., Calvaresi, D., Främling, K.: Explainable agents and robots: results from a systematic literature review. In: Proceedings of the 18th International Conference on Autonomous Agents and MultiAgent Systems. International Foundation for Autonomous Agents and Multiagent Systems, pp. 1078–1088 (2019)
4. Miller, T.: Explanation in artificial intelligence: insights from the social sciences, CoRR, abs/1706.07269 (2017). http://arxiv.org/abs/1706.07269
5. Kambhampati, S.: Challenges of human-aware AI systems, ArXiv abs/1910.07089 (2019)
6. Chakraborti, T., Sreedharan, S., Zhang, Y., Kambhampati, S.: Plan explanations as model reconciliation: moving beyond explanation as soliloquy (2017)
7. Fox, M., Long, D., Magazzeni, D.: Explainable planning, arXiv preprint arXiv:1709.10256 (2017)
8. Miller, T.: Contrastive explanation: a structural-model approach, November 2018
9. Madumal, P., Miller, T., Sonenberg, L., Vetere, F.: Explainable reinforcement learning through a causal lens, ArXiv, abs/1905.10958 (2019)
10. Kean, A.: A characterization of contrastive explanations computation. In: Lee, H.-Y., Motoda, H. (eds.) PRICAI 1998. LNCS, vol. 1531, pp. 599–610. Springer, Heidelberg (1998). https://doi.org/10.1007/BFb0095304
11. Hoffmann, J., Magazzeni, D.: Explainable AI planning (XAIP): overview and the case of contrastive explanation (extended abstract). In: Reasoning Web (2019)
12. Rathi, S.: Generating counterfactual and contrastive explanations using shap, ArXiv, abs/1906.09293 (2019)
13. Borgo, R., Cashmore, M., Magazzeni, D.: Towards providing explanations for AI planner decisions (2018)
14. Cashmore, M., Collins, A., Krarup, B., Krivic, S., Magazzeni, D., Smith, D.: Towards explainable AI planning as a service, arXiv preprint arXiv:1908.05059 (2019)
15. Perera, V., Veloso, M.: Interpretability of a service robot: enabling user questions and checkable answers. In: GCAI (2018)
16. Krarup, B., Cashmore, M., Magazzeni, D., Miller, T.: Model-based contrastive explanations for explainable planning (2019)
17. Lindsay, A.: Towards exploiting generic problem structures in explanations for automated planning. In: Proceedings of the 10th International Conference on Knowledge Capture, pp. 235–238 (2019)

18. Sengupta, S., Chakraborti, T., Sreedharan, S., Vadlamudi, S.G., Kambhampati, S.: Radar - a proactive decision support system for human-in-the-loop planning. In AAAI Fall Symposia (2017)
19. Topin, N., Veloso, M.: Generation of policy-level explanations for reinforcement learning. In: Proceedings of the AAAI Conference on Artificial Intelligence, vol. 33, pp. 2514–2521 2019)
20. Ehsan, U., Tambwekar, P., Chan, L., Harrison, B., Riedl, M.O.: Automated rationale generation: a technique for explainable AI and its effects on human perceptions. In: Proceedings of the 24th International Conference on Intelligent User Interfaces, pp. 263–274. ACM (2019)
21. Wang, N., Pynadath, D.V., Hill, S.G.: Trust calibration within a human-robot team: comparing automatically generated explanations. In: 2016 11th ACM/IEEE International Conference on Human-Robot Interaction (HRI), pp. 109–116, March 2016
22. Lemaignan, S., Dillenbourg, P.: Mutual modelling in robotics: inspirations for the next steps. In: ACM/IEEE International Conference on Human-Robot Interaction, 2015, pp. 303–310, March 2015
23. Hayes, B., Shah, J.A.: Improving robot controller transparency through autonomous policy explanation. In: Proceedings of the 2017 ACM/IEEE International Conference on Human-Robot Interaction, ser. HRI 2017, pp. 303–312, New York. ACM (2017)
24. Tabrez, A., Hayes, B.: Improving human-robot interaction through explainable reinforcement learning. In: 2019 14th ACM/IEEE International Conference on Human-Robot Interaction (HRI), pp. 751–753. IEEE (2019)
25. Akash, K., Polson, K., Reid, T., Jain, N.: Improving human-machine collaboration through transparency-based feedback - part I: human trust and workload model. In: 2nd IFAC Conference on Cyber-Physical and Human Systems CPHS 2018, IFAC-PapersOnLine, vol. 51, no. 34, pp. 315–321 (2019)
26. Hayes, B., Scassellati, B.: Challenges in shared-environment human-robot collaboration, January 2013
27. Langley, P., Meadows, B., Sridharan, M., Choi, D.: Explainable agency for intelligent autonomous systems. In: Twenty-Ninth IAAI Conference (2017)
28. Montani, S., Striani, M.: Artificial intelligence in clinical decision support : a focused literature survey. Yearbook Med. Inf. **28**, 120–127 (2019)
29. Holstein, K.: Towards teacher-AI hybrid systems. In: Companion Proceedings of the Eigth International Conference on Learning Analytics and Knowledge (2018)
30. Tabrez, A., Agrawal, S., Hayes, B.: Explanation-based reward coaching to improve human performance via reinforcement learning. In: 2019 14th ACM/IEEE International Conference on Human-Robot Interaction (HRI), pp. 249–257, March 2019
31. Kaptein, F., Broekens, J., Hindriks, K., Neerincx, M.: Personalised self-explanation by robots: the role of goals versus beliefs in robot-action explanation for children and adults. In: 26th IEEE International Symposium on Robot and Human Interactive Communication (RO-MAN) 2017. pp. 676–682. IEEE (2017)
32. Hitron, T., Orlev, Y., Wald, I., Shamir, A., Erel, H., Zuckerman, O.: Can children understand machine learning concepts? the effect of uncovering black boxes. In: Proceedings of the 2019 CHI Conference on Human Factors in Computing Systems, pp. 1–11 (2019)
33. Russell, S., Norvig, P.: Artificial Intelligence: A Modern Approach, 3rd edn. Prentice Hall Press, Upper Saddle River (2009)
34. Kahneman, D., Tversky, A.: Prospect theory: an analysis of decision under risk. Econometrica **47**(2), 263–291 (1979)

35. Bartneck, C., Kulić, D., Croft, E., Zoghbi, S.: Measurement instruments for the anthropomorphism, animacy, likeability, perceived intelligence, and perceived safety of robots. Int. J. Soc. Robot. **1**(1), 71–81 (2009)
36. Bandura, A., Freeman, W., Lightsey, R.: Self-efficacy: the exercise of control (1999)
37. Pastorelli, C., Caprara, G., Barbaranelli, C., Rola, J., Rózsa, S., Bandura, A.: The structure of children's perceived self-efficacy: a cross-national study. Eur. J. Psychol. Assess. **17**, 87–97 (2001)
38. Conati, C., Porayska-Pomsta, K., Mavrikis, M.: AI in education needs interpretable machine learning: lessons from open learner modelling (2018)
39. Chao, C., Cakmak, M., Thomaz, A.L.: Transparent active learning for robots. In: 2010 5th ACM/IEEE International Conference on Human-Robot Interaction (HRI), pp. 317–324, March 2010

HRI Physio Lib: A Software Framework to Support the Integration of Physiological Adaptation in HRI

Austin Kothig$^{(\boxtimes)}$, John Muñoz, Hamza Mahdi, Alexander M. Aroyo, and Kerstin Dautenhahn

Social and Intelligent Robotics Research Lab (SIRRL), University of Waterloo, Waterloo, Canada
{austin.kothig,john.munoz.hci,hmahdi,alexander.aroyo, kerstin.dautenhahn}@uwaterloo.ca

Abstract. The rise of available physiological sensors in recent years can be attributed to the widespread popularity of commercial sensing technologies equipped with health monitoring technology. To make more engaging human-robot interaction (HRI), social robots should have some ability to infer their social partner's affective state. Measurements of the autonomic nervous system via non-invasive physiological sensors provide a convenient window into a person's affective state, namely their emotions, behavior, stress, and engagement. HRI research has included physiological sensors in-the-loop, however implementations are often specific to studies, and do not lend well for reusability. To address this gap, we propose a modular, flexible and extensible framework designed to work with popular robot platforms. Our framework will be compatible with both lab and consumer grade sensors, and includes essential tools and processing algorithms for affective state estimation geared towards *real-time* HRI applications.

Keywords: Physiological sensors · Software framework · Human-robot interaction · Affective computing

1 Introduction

Physiological sensors have been growing in popularity as a tool in the health-tracking wearables field, so much so that in a 2019 study, roughly 1 in 5 U.S. adults said they used a smart-watch or a fitness-tracker [47]. The cost of equipping sensors such as electrocardiogram (ECG) and photoplethysmogram (PPG) onto small devices has fallen drastically in recent years, resulting in widespread adoption. These two sensors in particularly can be found on commercial products such as the *Apple Watch* as well as the *Samsung Active* line, while PPG is found

---

This research was undertaken, in part, thanks to funding from the Canada 150 Research Chairs Program and thanks to Alexander Graham Bell Canada Graduate Scholarships.

A. R. Wagner et al. (Eds.): ICSR 2020, LNAI 12483, pp. 36–47, 2020.
https://doi.org/10.1007/978-3-030-62056-1_4

on nearly all of *FitBit*'s line of wearable heart rate monitors. *Polar* is another leader in the commercial market of heart rate monitors and one affordable product that we plan to utilize in the work we describe here. A great benefit to this technology is that it can provide unobtrusive measurements of human physiology for *real-time* computation.

A critical aspect to amiable human-robot interaction (HRI) is explored in a survey by Paiva et al. [34] which discusses the need for robots to possess some ability to reason about the subjective emotional state of humans. Evidence increasingly suggests that the mechanism of perceiving another's emotional state is phylogenetically ancient, probably going back to common ancestors of mammals and birds [8]. Paiva et al. reason that to improve affinity to a social robot, it too requires some mechanism for reasoning about the affective state of humans.

The visual medium has classically been used in emotional recognition, utilizing cues from facial and body language [12,20,43]. Typically these methods work well in *clean* and predictable scenarios (e.g. a person's face clearly visible in a picture or video), however this technology struggles in *real-world* applications having challenges related to poor or uneven lighting, low resolution, motion blur, as well as incomplete and obstructed facial features (e.g. people moving around freely, facing away from the camera etc.). State-of-the-art methods trained on *real-world* datasets containing the aforementioned imaging conditions perform at near 50% accuracies in classifying common prototypical expressions [16,31].

Another challenge in the utilization of the visual medium with end-users in the *real-world* as discussed by Caine et al. [7], is that older people had reported privacy concerns when being monitored by either cameras or social robots (which typically have cameras on board). A possible benefit to adopting a wearable-sensor based solution is explored by Motti and Caine who found that people felt these wearables to be less of a concern in terms of privacy compared to cameras [27]. With the increasing popularity in wearables and physiological sensing technologies this has potential to help close the loop in HRI scenarios.

Psychophysiology is the field that studies the relationship between human psychological states and physiological signals. Psychophysiological states such as frustration, workload or engagement have been studied in the past demonstrating that human physiological responses can be attributable to specific human states [6]. Physiological data provides a window into a person's affective state, allowing to capture unconscious responses associated to both the central and peripheral nervous system. People are typically able to deduce this through a repertoire of visual and auditory cues including body language, facial expressions, gaze orientation, and tone of voice [37]. While some algorithms have been developed for discerning some of these cues [11,28], it is by no means a categorically solved problem. It has been shown that the use of a physiologically-sensitive system which modulated the difficulty of a virtual-driving simulator based on a user's engagement not only increased said engagement, but also led to a higher number of participants who subjectively reported liking the difficulty adjustment over a performance based modulated system [5]. Other studies in the realm of *exergaming* have shown that systems which use heart rate for *real-time* adaption not only increase the amount of time they spend in recommended levels of cardio-respiratory exertion, but also provided a positive user experience [30]. Physiological signals may be the modality necessary to bootstrap this perception of a person's affective state in a *real-world* environment, for better interaction.

Our goal is to design and develop a framework and provide software tools with integration for popular robot software frameworks such as ROS (Robot Operating System) [39] and YARP (Yet Another Robot Platform) [26], aiming to bridge the technical gap required to have *real-time* physiological data become a more common tool in HRI research.

2 Related Work

In HRI, studies often bootstrap measures of psychophysiological states (e.g., engagement) for specific experiments, as there isn't a standard system/methodology for affect measurement. Capturing human-body reactions through physiological lenses is crucial for closed-loop HRI. Examples of this include Rich et al., who developed a ROS packages that utilized gesture, speech, mutual eye gaze and directed eye gaze to measure engagement during interactions [41]. Their architecture focused on modularity and reusability where four measurements are fed into their "engagement integrator" which publishes information about engagement statistics and cues events in the robot. The architecture used vision and speech recognition as the main sources of sensory information. Foster et al. utilized a rule based system to classify user engagement in a bar setting [18]. Their system utilized participant's distance from the robot and standing direction (pose) to estimate 3 levels of engagement namely, "Not Seeking Engagement", "Seeking Engagement", and "Engaged". Duchetto, Baxter and Hanheide released an open source model that utilizes convolutional neural networks (CNN) and long short term memory (LSTM) networks where the input is an on-robot video camera to measure an engagement value [9]. While these systems are quite reusable due to using vision as their main source of input, they are limited in terms of application as they do not offer a holistic system that works across platforms and allows the use of multiple sensors. ROCARE is an architecture designed for adaptive, multi-user measurement of engagement in assistive scenarios [15]. The architecture features an easy to use GUI and utilizes audiovisual, EEG and EDA measurements. The architecture seems promising but does not seem to have any development since their initial publication. Additionally, it attempts to cover all aspects of robot behaviour/operation which could be a limiting factor when considering integration. There are numerous MATLAB toolboxes for physiological signal processing available, such as the PhysioData Toolbox which is a free package made in MATLAB [44]. A drawback for this specific toolbox is that it does not support *real-time* processing which is highly desired for HRI; additionally it cannot be modified as it is pre-compiled into an executable. Additional MATLAB toolboxes are available, however they suffer from licensing restrictions. Commercial software is available but suffers from similar licensing issues and typically cannot be modified by the community if necessary. One such commercial solution is EventIDE which is capable of *real-time* capture and processing of physiological data and supports many physiological sensors [1]. Another similar commercial software is iMotions which is geared extensively towards user-experience, emotion recognition, and mental workload studies [2].

In terms of measurements, many metrics have been used (exclusively or in part) to estimate human psychophysiological states in HRI and human-computer interaction (HCI) research [24]. Examples include speech [41], EDA [23], electroencephalography (EEG) [45], proximity [18,21], touch [21], body posture during interaction, gesture [41], length of interaction, questionnaires/quizzes [3,21], or simply by manually analyzing and coding recorded experimental footage [42]. Eye gaze has been ubiquitous in HRI; an example of using it for engagement measurement can be found in [41]. Other uses of eye-monitoring technology have been done in HRI studies to make robots better at spotting liars by measuring pupil dilation during a cognitively demanding tasks such as lying [19]. Similarly, Pasquali et al. applied the same use of pupillary measurements to endow a robot with the capability of detecting lies in a magic tricks scenario [35].

Outside of HRI, there has been significant work in the realm of virtual reality (VR) and games to develop closed-loop architectures that incorporate human physiology into the game-loop. The Biocybernetic Loop Engine (BL Engine) [29] is an architecture that allows for easy integration of physiological data into video games. This easily allows for a game to modulate itself based on the feedback from physiological signals on the human playing. Other platforms include Open-ViBE [40], the FlyLoop framework [36], Neuromore and Neuropype. Despite all the efforts in creating physiologically-adaptive tools, we could not find specific libraries or software tools to facilitate the integration of physiological signals into *real-time* HRI experiments.

3   Framework

The HRI Physio Library is a work in progress that will contain a set of algorithms and tools created to facilitate the integration of physiological adaptation in HRI experiments by using multiple sensing devices connected to human subjects. The software framework has been designed considering three main elements: i) Physiological Sensing (Human), which is related to the set of software tools that allow capturing physiological signals from the sensors, ii) Processing Module, which covers the algorithms to transform signals into *interpretable* information and iii) the Social Robot, which encompasses the aspect that needs to be considered to put the robot in the loop. We envision to develop the architecture with three key facets in mind. First, to design a system that allows for easy integration and addition of new sensors. Second, to develop a system architecture that is both flexible and supports multiple robotic systems and middle-wares (e.g., ROS, YARP). Third, to design a comprehensive processing module capable of transforming raw physiological data into relevant information that can be used by researchers and *roboticists* to create closed-loop HRI systems. Following, we present a complete description of the envisioned architecture, depicting the main elements, the sub-components and the functioning.

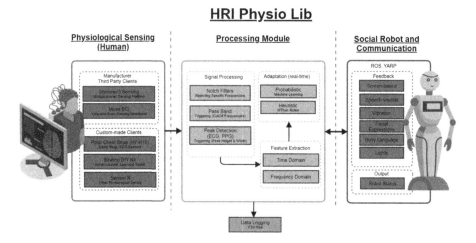

Fig. 1. Overview of the HRI Physio Lib.

3.1 Physiological Sensing (Human)

To capture physiological signals coming from different sensors, the HRI Physio Lib will include a modular architecture to measure, transmit and transform physiological data coming from a set of pre-defined sensors. Two types of clients are envisioned: clients already developed by the hardware manufacturers that can be re-purposed to be used in HRI and custom-made clients.

Manufacturer Third Party Clients: Several hardware tools exist that allow sensing physiological signals and unfortunately, there is not yet a clear consensus on standards for data acquisition and transmission [32]. Because of that, manufacturers tend to create software tools and clients that allow the communication with the sensors and record and transmit data. The HRI Physio Lib will initially integrate two sensors by re-purposing some of the already existing software clients developed by the manufacturers, therefore allowing the transmission of raw and processed data in a way that can be used in the processing module (through shared memory and queries to atomic databases). The library will offer compatibility with the Shimmer3 multiparameter sensing platform ConsensysPRO, which is compatible with a wide set of sensors to record movement, cardiovascular, electrodermal and neurophysiological data and has been used in previous applications with social robots [17]. Moreover, the Muse sensor is a wearable headband and brain-computer interface that allows capturing EEG signals from 4 dry electrodes placed in the forehead, allowing the interpretation of psychophysiological states such as engagement, attention or relaxation while interacting with social robots [46].

Custom-made Clients: Emerging hardware tools in the field of physiological computing are allowing a widespread of the technology, significantly reducing the costs associated with acquiring physiological sensing devices. Two types of sensors have been popularized in the last five years considering their affordable price and versatility: wearables and DIY kits. We plan to include two of the most widely used and emerging physiological computing hardware sensors by developing custom-made software clients able to facilitate the acquisition and transmission of physiological data to be used in the HRI Physio Lib. The Polar chest strap sensor is a portable and wearable ECG device that collects cardiovascular information and allows a robust recording of heart rate (HR) and heart rate variability (HRV) information while the subject is moving around [38]. Moreover, the multiparameter DIY kit, Bitalino, is an Arduino-based hardware toolkit that allows acquiring signals such as EMG, ECG and PPG while having an affordable relatively cost. Benchmarking studies have been performed comparing the Bitalino toolkit with research-grade biomedical devices showing comparable performances with the DIY kit [4]. Finally, since new devices are constantly emerging at the market, we plan to include manuals and basic scripts that will allow an easy creation of custom-made software clients to extend the list of compatible sensors of the HRI Physio Lib framework (Sensor X in Fig. 1). For instance, the development of new tools to unobtrusively record physiological signals is something that can be used in social robotics to allow a contact-less sensing of parameters such as heart beats [25].

3.2 Processing Modules

Raw physiological signals are too noisy to describe psychophysiological states reliably for use in HRI or HCI experiments. Instead, a well-structured and careful process of signal filtering and feature extraction must be conducted to successfully transform physiological signals into usable descriptors and markers capable of represent the psychophysiological signatures of human responses [14]. The Processing Module will contain algorithms to process the raw physiological signals coming from the sensors and clients, scripts to extract relevant features to describe the psychophysiological states and adaptive methods to allow *real-time* adaptations.

Signal Processing: To reduce common physiological signal artifacts produced by electrodes location (e.g., cross-talking), movement and others; digital filters should be applied to the raw signals [22]. The HRI Physio Lib will include a set of filters such as the Notch filter (i.e., band-stop filter) which is useful in removing noise artifacts from power line interference (50/60 Hz) and the pass-band filter which allows for defining a range of frequencies to pass or filter. Moreover, some processing algorithms widely used in cardiovascular signals to detect peaks (e.g., R-peaks in ECG) and carry out variability analysis will also be integrated. While the list of popular filters for noise reduction is quite large, the HRI Physio Lib will include some of the most ubiquitously used signal filtering techniques for neurophysiological, cardiovascular and electrodermal data.

Feature Extraction: The next step in transforming physiological data into usable information is to define and extract features. There are several approaches that can be used to group features from physiological signals depending on the phenomena being measured. A simple way to distinguish among features from multiple physiological signals is by their nature and representation domain. Domain refers to the analytic and mathematical space in which the physiological signals are conveyed. Therefore, both time and frequency are two of the more common mathematical domains where useful physiological metrics can be found and extracted. For instance, it is well-known that frequency domain parameters from both EEG and ECG (specifically HRV) signals are very useful to describe important psychophysiological states such as workload or stress [6]. Therefore, statistical descriptors (e.g., standard deviation, root-mean-square) as well as functions for Fourier transform will be added to the library to facilitate the computation of meaningful physiological features from different signals.

Adaptation: To create reactive HRI applications, the libraries should include mechanisms to adapt the robot's behavior considering the measured psychophysiological states of human subjects. The adaptation sub-module is intended to provide methods that will allow the dynamic use of the physiological features extracted in order to produce behavioral changes in the robot based on the targeted application. Two adaptation methods are envisioned to close the loop: i) heuristic and ii) probabilistic. The heuristic method will rely on simplistic If/Then rules that although are not optimal for many of the physiologically adaptive systems, have been shown efficiency and practicality in providing simple adaptations in many applications [24]. For instance, a robot can adapt its behavior and create more challenging activities when the user's levels of engagement measured through physiological sensors has been reported as low. The probabilistic method will offer a more robust adaptation that can be integrated using machine learning algorithms capable of handling data from multiple sources and create learning models that can be used for adaptive systems. Machine learning has been widely used to create models of classification which infer specific cognitive and emotional states from human body signals [33]. Some of the most used machine learning algorithms in physiologically adaptive systems such as support vector machines, k-nearest neighbors and decision trees will be added to the HRI Physio Lib, aiming to facilitate the implementation of more sophisticated adaptation techniques.

3.3   Social Robots and Communication

Social robots have rarely been used in physiologically adaptive systems due to multiple complexities from both the human-physiology and human-robot perspectives [24]. To allow the creation of an HRI architecture empowered with physiological awareness, we propose a module connected with two of the most popular robot middle-wares (software that is between an operating system and the applications that run on it) called ROS (Robot Operating System) and YARP (Yet Another Robot Platform). Both ROS and YARP allow the communication and interconnection between sensors, processors and actuators in multiple of the existing and most popular social robots (e.g., Nao, Pepper, iCub). A bidirectional communication will be established between the processing module managing the physiological signals and adaptation, and the robot middle-wares, ROS and YARP, therefore allowing both software entities to be aware of each other's status. To create physiologically adaptive HRI experiences, a set of robot states and capabilities should be previously defined along with the target psychophysiological state and descriptors. Then, rules of adaptation will allow the modification of specific robot parameters in real time. There are at least two aspects that should be known about the robot: feedback and robot status.

Feedback: feedback mechanisms should be previously defined and communicated to the processing module, covering aspects such as screen-based, speech-sounds, vibration, facial expressions, body language, and lights feedback modalities. The definition of specific feedback modalities and ranges (e.g., tone frequencies for the voice, body's degrees of freedom, etc) as well as the interrelations between sensors and actuators will facilitate the creation of custom-made adaptive rules that can potentially elicit the desired psychophysiological responses of users. This feedback sub-module can be seen as a set of possible actions the robot can do that can modify user's physiological responses and provide the desired effect. Naturally, previous stages involving the definition of conceptual models to define the user behavior/state to be detected, the existing psychophysiological inference models, quantified representations as well as real-time models of user's state should be also known [13]. Lastly, the design of the adaptive interface that connects both human and social robot should consider important aspects of real-time systems such as latency and decision-making times in order to provide an efficient closed-loop system.

Robot Status: other relevant elements related to the robot status should be considered as well since they can affect the robot performance and shape the adaptation mechanism (e.g., robot's degrees of freedom, range of motion, battery status). By knowing these parameters, the processing module will be able to make them available and visible for the system designer, therefore avoiding common mistakes such as adapting without considering ranges of robot operation or simply, pushing the robot to undesired boundaries of functioning.

4   Potential Applications and Benefits for HRI Research

Using psychophysiology of a human in an interaction scenario with social robots brings a multitude of clear use cases for incorporating closed-loop system intelligence. For example, in a game setting where a robot is used as an agent interacting with users, it is important that the robot is able to quantify specific human states (e.g., engagement, frustration) of participants in order to modulate its behaviour accordingly. While the use of psychophysiological metrics in HRI is not novel (e.g., post analysis of human behaviour), our approach has several advantages listed as follows:

Sensors' Compatibility: the inclusion of commercially available physiological sensors allows researchers to perform HRI experiments in a "plug and play" fashion which makes it easier to replicate methodologies across a multitude of robots with little effort. This could be useful for labs trying to run a series of experiments on different robots with different systems/software architectures. Also, we plan to support commercially available sensors to avoid relying on expensive research-grade equipment. Commercially available sensors can be a suitable compromise when working with populations like children or older adults as they are relatively cheaper, designed to be rugged for *real-life* use and are more familiar to the general population.

Modularity and Scalability: by utilizing well established software design patterns, we are able to design a structure for our system which is at its core modular. Every module can work independently and sub-modules have been designed to facilitate the integration of novel tools (e.g., clients, algorithms), therefore facilitating to scale up the framework in the future. Furthermore, the support for various robotics software platform such as ROS and YARP is another important design choice in which we are building around.

Availability: we plan to make the HRI Physio Lib freely available in an open-source Github repository, allowing researchers, makers, roboticists and HRI enthusiasts to be able to use the framework in their projects. The project will also be documented with videos and guidelines with specific examples.

4.1   Proposed Use Cases

Improving Engagement: The system could be used in an upcoming planned study to modulate a robot's behaviour for robot-assisted child play. Having a window into the engagement of children could be important to increase the effectiveness of the mediation role. The flexibility to use different sensors introduced by the proposed system is instrumental when working with children.

Health Care: As many modern wearables support functions for meditation and exercise, it would be interesting to use such sensors alongside an adaptive assistive robot to promote well-being in older population. Wearable sensors allow for a more flexible experimental setup outside of the lab.

Social Connection: Another application could be providing robots with more context/perception to human reactions (e.g., arousal/stress) to improve social connections using a flexible, wide array of physiological sensors.

Self Driving Cars: Electrodermal activity (EDA), was found to be a significant predictor of comfort and anxiety in passengers of self driving cars [10]. Dillen et al., envision a system which modulates passenger-specific driving profiles based on implicit feedback from wearables. Some of the wearables we are interested in supporting include EDA as well as other possible metrics that could be used "on-the-fly" as implicit sources of passenger feedback to driving style.

5   Discussion and Conclusion

In this paper we outlined a framework with modularity first and foremost in mind, to allow for an easy integration and addition of new sensors. We believe that designing from the start to support multiple robotic systems and middle-wares requires us to carefully consider generic and efficient implementations that can be utilized by modules specialized for ROS or YARP. Support for an extensive library of processing algorithms for transforming raw physiological data into usable information is vital in building a physiologically adaptive system.

There exist unknowns which we are still in the process of working through regarding *Social Robots and Communication*, and what these protocols between robots and processing modules might look like exactly. Another issue related to communication that we need to consider carefully is how to integrate communication between multiple (potentially different types of) robots, which is a challenging task. Another unknown is how to evaluate the performance, usability and ease of use of the HRI Physio Library. A possible route might be to survey other researchers who are using our framework to assess their experience with the tools; does it meet their needs, and what can we do to further improve it? Another route that we might take for evaluation is to do analysis on the transmission error rate.

Presenting this architecture and its modular components gives us a clear trajectory for building on what we have developed so far. It is our hope that endowing the community with an easy to use platform to incorporate *real-time* physiological data into HRI research with support for affordable sensors and popular robotics platforms can be a valuable contribution to the community.

References

1. EventIDE (2020). http://www.okazolab.com/
2. iMotions: Unpack Human Behaviour (2020). https://imotions.com/
3. Barco, A., Albo-Canals, J., Garriga, C.: Engagement based on a customization of an ipod-lego robot for a long-term interaction for an educational purpose. In: Proceeding of ACM/IEEE HRI 2014, pp. 124–125. IEEE (2014)
4. Batista, D., da Silva, H.P., Fred, A., Moreira, C., Reis, M., Ferreira, H.A.: Benchmarking of the bitalino biomedical toolkit against an established gold standard. Healthc. Technol. Lett. **6**(2), 32–36 (2019)
5. Bian, D., Wade, J., Swanson, A., Weitlauf, A., Warren, Z., Sarkar, N.: Design of a physiology-based adaptive virtual reality driving platform for individuals with ASD. ACM Trans. Accessible Comput. (TACCESS) **12**(1), 2 (2019)
6. Cacioppo, J.T., Tassinary, L.G., Berntson, G.: Handbook of Psychophysiology. Cambridge University Press, Cambridge (2007)
7. Caine, K., Šabanovic, S., Carter, M.: The effect of monitoring by cameras and robots on the privacy enhancing behaviors of older adults. In: Proceedings of ACM/IEEE HRI, vol. 2012, pp. 343–350 (2012)
8. De Waal, F.B.: Putting the altruism back into altruism: the evolution of empathy. Annu. Rev. Psychol. **59**, 279–300 (2008)
9. Del Duchetto, F., Baxter, P., Hanheide, M.: Are you still with me? continuous engagement assessment from a robot's point of view. arXiv preprint arXiv:2001.03515 (2020)
10. Dillen, N., Ilievski, M., Law, E., Nacke, L.E., Czarnecki, K., Schneider, O.: Keep calm and ride along: passenger comfort and anxiety as physiological responses to autonomous driving styles. In: Proceeding of CHI Conference on Human Factors in Computing Systems, pp. 1–13 (2020)

11. D'Mello, S., et al.: A time for emoting: When affect-sensitivity is and isn't effective at promoting deep learning. In: International Conference on Intelligent Tutoring Systems, pp. 245–254 (2010)
12. Essa, I.A., Pentland, A.P.: Coding, analysis, interpretation, and recognition of facial expressions. IEEE Trans. Pattern Anal. Mach. Intell. **19**(7), 757–763 (1997)
13. Fairclough, S., Gilleade, K.: Construction of the biocybernetic loop: a case study. In: Proceeding of ACM ICMI, pp. 571–578 (2012)
14. Fairclough, S.H.: Fundamentals of physiological computing. Interact. Comput. **21**(1–2), 133–145 (2009)
15. Fan, J., et al.: A robotic coach architecture for elder care (rocare) based on multi-user engagement models. IEEE Trans. Neural Syst. Rehabil. Eng. **25**(8), 1153–1163 (2016)
16. Fan, Y., Lu, X., Li, D., Liu, Y.: Video-based emotion recognition using CNN-RNN and c3d hybrid networks. In: Proceeding of ACM ICMI, vol. 2016, pp. 445–450 (2016)
17. Fiorini, L., Mancioppi, G., Semeraro, F., Fujita, H., Cavallo, F.: Unsupervised emotional state classification through physiological parameters for social robotics applications. Knowl.-Based Syst. **190**, 105217 (2020)
18. Foster, M.E., Gaschler, A., Giuliani, M.: Automatically classifying user engagement for dynamic multi-party human-robot interaction. Int. J. Soc. Robot. **9**(5), 659–674 (2017)
19. Gonzalez Billandon, J., et al.: Can a robot catch you lying? a machine learning system to detect lies during interactions. Front. Robot. AI **6**, 64 (2019)
20. Gunes, H., Piccardi, M.: Bi-modal emotion recognition from expressive face and body gestures. J. Netw. Comput. Appl. **30**(4), 1334–1345 (2007)
21. Heath, S., et al.: Spatiotemporal aspects of engagement during dialogic storytelling child-robot interaction. Front. Robot. AI **4**, 27 (2017)
22. Kaniusas, E.: Biomedical Signals and Sensors I: Linking Physiological Phenomena and Biosignals. Springer Science & Business Media, Berlin (2012)
23. Leite, I., Henriques, R., Martinho, C., Paiva, A.: Sensors in the wild: exploring electrodermal activity in child-robot interaction. In: Proceeding of ACM/IEEE HRI 2013, pp. 41–48. IEEE (2013)
24. Loewe, N., Nadj, M.: Physio-adaptive systems-a state-of-the-art review and future research directions. In: ECIS (2020)
25. McDuff, D., Blackford, E.: iphys: an open non-contact imaging-based physiological measurement toolbox. In: 2019 41st Annual International Conference of the IEEE Engineering in Medicine and Biology Society (EMBC), pp. 6521–6524. IEEE (2019)
26. Metta, G., Fitzpatrick, P., Natale, L.: Yarp: yet another robot platform. Int. J. Adv. Robot. Syst. **3**(1), 8 (2006)
27. Motti, V.G., Caine, K.: Users' privacy concerns about wearables. In: Brenner, M., Christin, N., Johnson, B., Rohloff, K. (eds.) FC 2015. LNCS, vol. 8976, pp. 231–244. Springer, Heidelberg (2015). https://doi.org/10.1007/978-3-662-48051-9_17
28. Mukherjee, S.S., Robertson, N.M.: Deep head pose: gaze-direction estimation in multimodal video. IEEE Trans. Multimedia **17**(11), 2094–2107 (2015)
29. Muñoz, J., Rubio, E., Cameirao, M., Bermúdez, S.: The biocybernetic loop engine: an integrated tool for creating physiologically adaptive videogames. In: Proceeding of International Conference on Physiological Computing Systems, pp. 45–54 (2017)
30. Muñoz, J.E., Cameirão, M., Bermúdez i Badia, S., Gouveia, E.R.: Closing the loop in exergaming-health benefits of biocybernetic adaptation in senior adults. In: Proceeding of Annual Symposium on Computer-Human Interaction in Play, pp. 329–339 (2018)

31. Ng, H.W., Nguyen, V.D., Vonikakis, V., Winkler, S.: Deep learning for emotion recognition on small datasets using transfer learning. In: Proceeding of ACM ICMI, vol. 2015, pp. 443–449 (2015)
32. Novak, D.: Engineering issues in physiological computing. In: Fairclough, S.H., Gilleade, K. (eds.) Advances in Physiological Computing. HIS, pp. 17–38. Springer, London (2014). https://doi.org/10.1007/978-1-4471-6392-3_2
33. Novak, D., Mihelj, M., Munih, M.: A survey of methods for data fusion and system adaptation using autonomic nervous system responses in physiological computing. Interact. Comput. **24**(3), 154–172 (2012)
34. Paiva, A., Leite, I., Boukricha, H., Wachsmuth, I.: Empathy in virtual agents and robots: a survey. ACM Trans. Interact. Intell. Syst. (TiiS) **7**(3), 1–40 (2017)
35. Pasquali, D., Aroyo, A.M., Gonzalez-Billandon, J., Rea, F., Sandini, G., Sciutti, A.: Your eyes never lie: a robot magician can tell if you are lying. In: Proceeding of companion of ACM/IEEE HRI, vol. 2020, pp. 392–394 (2020)
36. Peck, E.M., Easse, E., Marshall, N., Stratton, W., Perrone, L.F.: Flyloop: a micro framework for rapid development of physiological computing systems. In: Proceeding of ACM SIGCHI Symposium on Engineering Interactive Computing Systems, pp. 152–157 (2015)
37. Pineda, J., Hecht, E.: Mirroring and mu rhythm involvement in social cognition: are there dissociable subcomponents of theory of mind? Biol. Psychol. **80**(3), 306–314 (2009)
38. Plews, D.J., Scott, B., Altini, M., Wood, M., Kilding, A.E., Laursen, P.B.: Comparison of heart-rate-variability recording with smartphone photoplethysmography, polar h7 chest strap, and electrocardiography. Int. J. Sports Physiol. Perform. **12**(10), 1324–1328 (2017)
39. Quigley, M., et al.: Ros: an open-source robot operating system. In: ICRA Workshop on Open Source Software, vol. 3, p. 5. Kobe, Japan (2009)
40. Renard, Y., et al.: Openvibe: an open-source software platform to design, test, and use brain-computer interfaces in real and virtual environments. Presence: Teleoperators Virtual Environ. **19**(1), 35–53 (2010)
41. Rich, C., Ponsler, B., Holroyd, A., Sidner, C.L.: Recognizing engagement in human-robot interaction. In: Proceeding of ACM/IEEE HRI 2010), pp. 375–382. IEEE (2010)
42. Rudovic, O., Lee, J., Mascarell-Maricic, L., Schuller, B.W., Picard, R.W.: Measuring engagement in robot-assisted autism therapy: a cross-cultural study. Front. Robot. AI **4**, 36 (2017)
43. Shan, C., Gong, S., McOwan, P.W.: Beyond facial expressions: learning human emotion from body gestures. In: BMVC, pp. 1–10 (2007)
44. Sjak-Shie, E.E.: Physiodata toolbox (version 0.5) [computer software] (2019). https://PhysioDataToolbox.leidenuniv.nl
45. Szafir, D., Mutlu, B.: Pay attention! designing adaptive agents that monitor and improve user engagement. In: Proceeding of IGCHI Conference on Human Factors in Computing Systems, pp. 11–20 (2012)
46. Tsiakas, K., Abujelala, M., Makedon, F.: Task engagement as personalization feedback for socially-assistive robots and cognitive training. Technologies **6**(2), 49 (2018)
47. Vogel, E.A.: About one-in-five americans use a smart watch or fitness tracker (2020). https://www.pewresearch.org/fact-tank/2020/01/09/about-one-in-five-americans-use-a-smart-watch-or-fitness-tracker/

Proxemic Reasoning for Group Approach

Ben Wright[1]([✉]), Magdalena Bugajska[2], William Adams[2], Ed Lawson[2],
J. Malcolm McCurry[3], and J. Gregory Trafton[2]

[1] NRC Postdoctoral Researcher, U.S. Naval Research Laboratory,
Washington, D.C., USA
`benjamin.wright.ctr@nrl.navy.mil`
[2] Navy Center for Applied Research in AI, U.S. Naval Research Laboratory,
Washington, D.C., USA
{`magdalena.bugajska,william.adams,ed.lawson,j.trafton`}`@nrl.navy.mil`
[3] Peraton, Washington, D.C., USA
`jmccurry@peraton.com`

Abstract. How should a robot approach a group of people? To answer this, we examine a large real-world data set of approximately 1500 individuals and find that, contrary to previous models, people do not simply approach an individual within the group. They use features of the group to determine aspects of their approach. To explain and test these features, we formalize an Approach Problem and develop several strategies of determining approach to a group. These strategies are then compared to the empirical data. One strategy performed consistent with the empirical data, which we then demonstrate on a robot platform.

Keywords: Proxemics · Group interaction · HRI

1 Introduction and Background

As robots become more common in everyday environments, they will need to interact with people more often; indeed the entire field of Human Robot Interaction (HRI) is working toward this goal. One key aspect of HRI is understanding how a robot should approach and join an individual or group of people. For example, if a robot has a message or information for the group, the robot will need to determine the best way to become part of the group in order to communicate with the group. Because the robot will be interacting with people, it will need to make decisions based on how people will react to it, rather than what is most optimal for the robot. For example, moving quickly may be an excellent method of traversing from one location to another, but people are typically not comfortable with people or robots approaching them at a high speed.

We believe that approaching a group may require paying attention to the group that the individual is part of in order to successfully be integrated into a group. For example, approaching a group may require coming to the outskirts

A. R. Wagner et al. (Eds.): ICSR 2020, LNAI 12483, pp. 48–60, 2020.
https://doi.org/10.1007/978-3-030-62056-1_5

of a group before being accepted into the group. The size of the group itself may also impact how close that original approach should be. In order to understand some of the features and representations of approaching a group, we analyzed a large-scale database that includes many instances of people approaching groups of different sizes in a real-world domain.

Previous researchers have focused primarily on how an individual approaches another individual. Hall proposed that individuals have a sense of space around them, and it is possible to systematically characterize some forms of relationships and familiarity based on how close another individual stands [3]. For example, an individual standing at an "intimate distance" is typically within 1 to 18 in. and is a close friend or lover. Personal distance goes from 1.5 feet to 4 feet and characterizes friends and family. Social distance (4 to 12 feet) is for interactions among acquaintances, and distances farther than 12 feet is typically for public speaking. These numbers can change a bit across cultures (e.g., Asian cultures are typically closer overall) [7] and are impacted by the auditory environment (e.g., in a library people will gather closer to speak quietly) and the social environment (e.g., at an outdoor rock concert, people will be close together). This entire field is called proxemics and has been the foundation of a great deal of work about how people and robots approach another individual.

Because of the focus on the individual in previous human empirical work, the research on robots approaching people has likewise focused on a single robot approaching a single individual [6,8,11]. For example, [8] provided an algorithm and description that took into account the auditory scene and incorporated that information with proxemic knowledge to approach an individual in a human-natural manner – when the environment was noisy, the robot approached closer than it would normally in order to be heard. Other researchers have focused on spatially positioning a robot. Kendon showed that many groups gather in systematic manners (e.g., a circle or a line) and that individuals within those groups typically face toward the middle and their conversational partner(s) [7]. Robots that face inward and towards conversational partners are perceived as part of the group and engender more inclusion than robots that do not [14].

While there have been previous studies on approaching pairs of people [2,5], studies on approaches of larger groups remain scarce. Most research on approaching a group actually focuses on approaching an individual that happens to be in a group. In excellent early work, Althaus and colleagues realized that joining a group meant both approaching and joining, so their robot approached a specific individual within a group, slowed down upon approach, and then integrated into the group itself [1]. Kato and colleagues used an individual's perceived intention to approach an individual who may be part of a group[6]. Similarly, Satake and colleagues selected a target person approached the individual and non-verbally showed its intention to interact [12]. Satake also showed that it is quite difficult for a robot to simply approach a person: It is not a matter of sending a robot within X meters of an individual – pose, distance, speed, and direction are all important for whether or not the approach is successful.

2   Dataset and Analysis

We used the Stanford Drone Dataset (SDD)[1] [10] as a foundation to our under-standing of how individuals approach groups. The SDD consists of an overhead view of eight different locations around the Stanford University campus, each containing video and created annotations.

The annotations were extracted using computer vision techniques described fully in [10] and contained pedestrians, bikes, golf carts, skateboarders, and buses. Annotations consist of targets (objects moving around in the environment), their class label (e.g., pedestrian), and their x, y coordinates for each frame of the video. The dataset itself contains 19 K targets (primarily pedestrians) and con-sists of many different types of interactions, groups, and target motion. The SDD annotations created bounding boxes around each object; for convenience we collapsed each bounding box to its midpoint.

In order to identify when an individual approached a group, we needed to cre-ate several additional concepts and representations based on the existing dataset. Specifically, we needed to identify a *group* and when an individual *approached* the group. There are approaches to identifying when a group is formed [7,13] but they typically require knowing what direction people are facing in addition to their x, y location. Because that information is computationally expensive, more difficult to extract and not available in the SDD, we created another approach to determining when a group has formed based on spatial proximity and temporal continuity. We defined a group as consisting of individuals who were within d distance of each other within t time, recursively. Thus, three individuals who were $\leq d$ distance of each other for $\leq t$ seconds was considered a group. This formulation prevented individuals who simply passed each other from becom-ing grouped together, as long as t was greater than their passing time. We also prevented subsets from being grouped together (e.g., if individuals A, B, and C were all a group, A and B were not a separate group). For this project, we set $d = 9$ feet which is near the top of the range for social distance (full social range made no difference to these results). We also set $t = 7$ s which allowed us to have some confidence that groups were relatively stable.

We also needed to identify when an individual approached a group. Consis-tent with [1], an individual who was defined as approaching a group needed to stop. To determine whether an individual had stopped, we calculated speed over the previous second. An individual who had a speed $< .2$ m/s was considered stopped (.2 seemed to capture noise from algorithm and individual swaying, since people are rarely completely motionless). Thus, an individual who had joined a group was an individual who had stopped and had just joined the edge of the group (by the group definition above).

Several other group annotations were also derived. Specifically, we calculated the *GroupSize* (the number of people in the group), the *DistanceToCentroid* (the distance of the approaching individual to the center of the group), and

---

[1] http://cvgl.stanford.edu/projects/uav_data/.

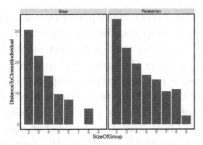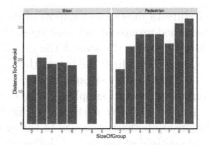

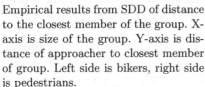

Empirical results from SDD of distance to the closest member of the group. X-axis is size of the group. Y-axis is distance of approacher to closest member of group. Left side is bikers, right side is pedestrians.	Empirical results from SDD of distance to centroid. X-axis is size of the group. Y-axis is distance of approacher to centroid of group. Left side is bikers, right side is pedestrians.

Fig. 1. Results from SDD

DistanceToClosestIndividual (the distance of the approaching individual to the closest individual already present in the group).

Recall that most work has focused on an individual (person or robot) approaching an individual, whether they are part of a group or not. Our hypothesis, however, is that an individual approaches a group differently than they approach an individual, taking characteristics of the group into account to change some aspect of their approach. The most obvious characteristic of a group is its size.

We therefore created two different metrics to examine how an individual approaches a group. The first measure is the DistanceToClosestIndividual (defined above). If an approaching individual takes characteristics of the group into account (e.g., the number of people in the group), there should be a systematic relationship between the group size and how close an individual approaches a current member of the group. If an approaching individual does not take group size into account (like current approaches), we should see no systematic relationship between group size and DistanceToClosestIndividual.

While there were many instances of different types of transports approaching others, we focus on two: pedestrians and bikers. We chose these two for a number of reasons. First, pedestrians were the most common, and bikers were very numerous. Second, because the results should generalize to mobile and social robots, pedestrians and bikers are most similar in form and speed to prospective robots (and in particular the robot we use later). Third, pedestrian and bikers had enough data in each group size – other transport types could be missing substantial data or only had data for limited group sizes. Finally, we should note that the results presented are remarkably consistent across transport types, suggesting that these findings should generalize to approaches of all classes. In the entire dataset, there were 323 groups that had bikers approach them and 1140 groups that had pedestrians approach them.

Figure 1a shows two subplots of the data for a biker and a pedestrian as they approached groups of different sizes. As Fig. 1a suggests, there is a strong relationship between the size of the group and how close the approacher comes to the closest individual: the bigger the group, the closer the individual approaches. This is a remarkably strong and robust finding across both types of approachers. Figure 1b shows two subplots of the data for a biker and a pedestrian approaching groups of different sizes. As Fig. 1a suggests, there is a medium-strength relationship between the size of the group and how close the approacher comes to the centroid of the group: the bigger the group, the farther from the centroid the individual approaches. This is a strong effect for pedestrians, but less strong for bikers.

Both these graphs and analyses show that when an individual approaches a group, the approacher unambiguously uses the size of the existing group to determine how they approach. Unlike previous work, the approacher does not simply approach an individual that happens to be part of the group, but rather they approach the group as a whole, sensitive to group features. Because we want a robot to approach a group of people in the same manner as a human would, we will endeavor to create a model that has similar characteristics to those we have just discussed.

3   Defining Our Model of Approach

Let us think about a specific instance that may happen in the Stanford Drone Dataset(SDD). You are on a college campus handing out flyers. There is a group of 3 students idly chatting next to a tree and you want to approach them. Where, in relation to the group, do you decide to stop in order to interact with the group?

Definition 1 (The Approach Problem). *The objective of an Approach Problem is to find a location near a group of agents. We denote near and distance in terms of grid cells and the location, loc_x is a cell in the grid. Formally, an approach problem P can be defined as a tuple $P = <G, Ag, Obj, S>$ where G is a square grid space NxN, Ag is a set of agent group members each with a location in the grid space; that is $\forall a \in Ag, loc_a \in G$. Obj is a set of objects in the grid space that can occupy a square, but is not part of the group; $\forall o \in Obj, loc_o \in G$. Finally, S the starting location,$loc_S \in G$, for the agent approaching the group. A solution to the approaching problem P is given by a location E such that it identifies a location that approaches the locations of Ag and is not already occupied. Therefore, $E \in G \cap Ag \cap Obj$.*

Let us take the colloquial example from above, where a person was going to approach a group of three near a tree. This is denoted as:

Example 1 (Approaching a Group of 3 Near a Tree).
$P = <S, G, Ag, Obj>$, $G = 6x6$, $S = \{5, 5\}$,
$Ag = \{P1, P2, P3\}$, with locations: $loc_{P1} = \{0, 1\}$, $loc_{P2} = \{0, 2\}$, $loc_{P3} = \{0, 3\}$,
$Obj = \{Tree\}$, with location: $loc_{Tree} = \{1, 3\}$.

From this setup of P, we have viable options for the endpoint, E, to be within the following: $\{(0,0), (0,4), (0,5), (1,0), (1,1), (1,2), (1,4), (1,5), (2,0), (2,1),$ $(2,2), (2,3), (2,4), (2,5), (3,0), (3,1), (3,2), (3,3), (3,4), (3,5), (4,0), (4,1),$ $(4,2), (4,3), (4,4), (4,5), (5,0), (5,1), (5,2), (5,3), (5,4)\}$ (i.e., any location not already occupied). Any of the locations are valid given the problem description. It is not clear however, which of these would be acceptable for people or a good match of the data.

4 Forming Strategies to Use in the Approach Model

To address the issue from the Example, while any of the given locations would satisfy the problem, there is at some level an ordering or preference based on what we saw from the SDD. Therefore, we need to focus on some issues centered around the datasets.

Given the substantial computational resources utilized on a mobile robot platform (e.g. perception and navigation), one of our goals is to maintain strategies that are not computationally expensive. With this goal in mind, we hope to match patterns from the SDD to strategies for the approach problem. Additionally, we want to assess what features alter our strategy solutions the most.

To address the first goal, finding computationally light strategies, a number of strategies were developed to test different possible solutions against the patterns from the SDD. These strategies broke down into two categories: consider a characteristic of the group, or determine an individual should be selected to approach. While it is our intention to approach groups as a whole, we want to utilize individual members of a group for some of the straight-forward strategies. For the individual, we had two different strategies for selection - random and closest. Random picks a member of the group randomly (RP). Closest picks the member of the group that is closest to the starting position (CP).

Once the strategy has picked an individual from the group, or uses the whole group, all strategies begin by creating an *adjacency set*. This adjacency set is effectively our satisfiable set of solutions similar to E in our Example. After calculating the adjacency set, our strategies diverge to pick a specific element in the set. These computationally light equations are strategies to pick a square from the Adjacency Set. Either pick a random square (RS) or pick the closest square (CS). Aside from these two approaches, we also developed a few group based strategies. The first being a simple, *"go to the center of the group"*. Additionally, due to our Dataset results (see Figs. 1a and 1b), strategies taking advantage of distance to centroid and proximity to other group members were made. The strategy related to centroid distance (CentDist) returns a square that is closest to the same distance as the group members from the center of the group. Our proximal strategy finds the minimum average distance between all group members $ProxDist(i)$ from the given Adjacency Set ($i \in AdjSet$). For most groups this is very similar to the Center strategy. Finally, we combine proximity distance and distance to centroid as a last strategy. Here, we prioritize squares that are the same distance away from the centroid as the group members while also being close to all other group members. We use a combination of both previous equations to do this. We calculate the Centroid Distance (CD) and subtract our proximal distance from that.

5   Experiment Design for Approach Strategies

With these strategies, we can begin to address the other questions posed in Sect. 3. That is, we need a way to see if any of our strategies match the behavior patterns found in the SDD. Additionally, does the group formation affect the strategy? What features of the problem space affect the behavior of these strategies?

To answer these questions, we ran a simulation over different permutations. The setup for these simulations were as follows: G is a 100x100 grid, Ag ranges from 1 agent, a, to 8 agents $\{a, b, c, d, e, f, g, h\}$, $Obj = \emptyset$, and S is randomly generated to be within G. This reasoning system was implemented in SWI-Prolog [15] and we call it the PardonMe-soner. The permutations involved 4 aspects. First, the size of the group changed. Second, the formation of the group changed. Third the spacing of the members of the group changed. Lastly, the *Closeness* which the approacher would consider was changed.

Based on our results from SDD, we found the majority of group size to be under 9 people. Therefore, we tested groups of size 1 up to size 8. To determine if the organization or formation of groups would affect our strategies, we used four different formations for groups of size 2 or larger. Each was chosen due to its difference in density, spread, and relation to the group centroid. These formations were a horizontal line, a vertical line, a circle, and a densely packed spiral. For the lines, these were in relation to the X-axis and Y-axis of the grid space respectively starting in the center of the grid (cell (49, 49)). The circle formation would be the polygon of the size of the group (triangle, square, pentagon, hexagon, heptagon, octagon). For group size of 2, the circle formation was two agents diagonal to each other. All circles were centered around the center of the grid. Finally, the densely packed spiral group is a group formation that wraps around itself starting at the center and spiralling clockwise. The circle and densely packed formations were used to see how the density of a group might affect our strategies.

With each group formation there was additionally the question of "How much space exists between each member of the group?". To address this, we modified each formation so that members would go from 1 to 8 cells away from each other. To minimize randomness, all members are at the same spacing. This was to test how the density of the groups might affect strategies (i.e. very spread out vs clumped together). It also offered instances in which it is very possible to navigate into the middle of a group without walking into any group members. In real-world groups, this would be an average; some simple examples with different spacings for group members showed similar effects as described below.

We also explicitly included a way to modify how close the approacher stopped based on the size of the group. As we only tested up to group size of 8, this was calculated as: $C = 9 - N$, where N is the size of the group. Of course, with larger groups this would need to be modified.

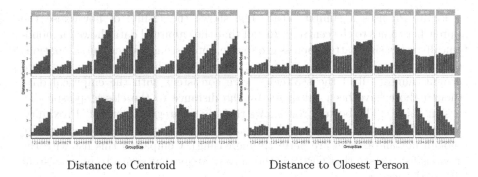

Distance to Centroid   Distance to Closest Person

Fig. 2. Top rows contain subgraphs whose strategies could use the middle of the group and don't take group size into account. Bottom rows can't use middle of group and do take group size into account. Each column is a different strategy tested against groups of size 1–8 (left to right). Closeness of the groups for these runs was 2.

To run these permutations against the strategies, we built a script that would iterate over the various factors described above. For each permutation we ran 100 iterations where each iteration had a new random starting point S. Each of these iterations calculated the endpoint E for each strategy.

6 Experiment Analysis

With these strategies, the question then became, "Do any of these strategies exhibit the behavior patterns noticed in SDD?". Notably, does the distance to center of the group increase as the group size increases? As well as, does the distance to closest person in the group decrease as the group size increases? In both instances from the SDD we found each pattern to be monotonic, therefore any strategy that exhibited non-monotonic behavior would be ruled out.

To examine the relationship between the different model strategies and the empirical data, we first examined the distance to the closest person. Figure 2b shows the different strategies as columns and two of the important model features as the row: the top row uses the middle of the group as valid locations and does not take into account the group size, while the bottom row does not use the middle of the group as valid locations and does take the size of the group into account when approaching. Recall that the empirical results showed a monotonically decreasing pattern. Examining the two different rows, we see a rather large difference: when the simulations are able to use the center of the group as valid locations and group size is not taken into account, the patterns are quite flat or in the opposite direction as the empirical data. When the simulations are able to use group size in their approach and do not use the center of the group, there are several strategies that decrease monotonically. Specifically, the strategies CPCS, CPRS, CS, RPCS, RPRS, and RS all show patterns across group sizes that are consistent with the empirical data.

Figure 2a uses a similar setup, but shows the results of how close the approacher comes to the centroid. Recall that the empirical data showed a monotonically increasing pattern across group size. Interestingly, when the simulations could use the middle of the group and did not take the size of the group into account, almost all of the strategies were consistent with the empirical data (though those have been ruled out by the distance to the closest person discussion above). The bottom row shows that the strategies CentDist, Proximity, Center, CPRS, and Cent&Prox all show an increasing pattern across group size (though not all of them are perfectly increasing). Comparing this list with the previous list, we see that CPRS is the only strategy that seems to be consistent with both measures.

7   Robot Implementation

In order to demonstrate how our algorithm works on an embodied platform, we integrated several different models with our HUBO robot, Stryx. In these tests, we used Stryx's rolling mode. In rolling mode, Stryx can navigate around obstacles (including people) and travel over uneven or difficult terrain. To support sensing and interaction, Stryx has a sensor head that allows different sensors to be easily added to the platform in customized configurations [4]. Note that much of the work on approaching a group uses overhead cameras. [10] used an aerial drone and [13] used and discusses many of the datasets available for groups using aerial or off-the-ground cameras. Our work attempts to approach a group dynamically using only the cameras on the mobile robot platform. The camera in the SCIPRR head is a Carnegie Robotics Atlas head that includes a pair of stereo RGB cameras that allows detection of individuals from the robot's perspective.

The software components interact largely via the Robot Operating System (ROS)[2]. To detect and provide the location for people, the robot uses the deep convolutional neural network YOLO [9]. YOLO predicts both the location and the classification of known objects in the image. For our purposes, we are only using the detected people in the environment. Once a person has been detected, Stryx needs to locate the person on the grid. For this, the stereo pair is consulted to provide the range and bearing to the person. Which is converted to a Cartesian coordinate and placed into the appropriate grid cell and published via ROS. Each grid cell was defined as a $.3x.3m^2$ square.

Unfortunately, no ROS port is available for Prolog, so an intermediary was used. The PardonMe-soner writes the goal in terms of X and Y distance and it gets published via ROS. A third-party ROS navigation stack[3] receives the goal and outputs speed and direction safe velocity commands to drive the robot.

As discussed above, Stryx's Atlas head provides stereo images that perform person detection. In addition, the sensor also provides high-resolution laser range finder data which is consumed by ROS navigation packages. Hubo wheel encoders

---

[2] www.ros.org.

[3] http://wiki.ros.org/navigation.

Group of 3, Center   Group of 5, CPRS.

Fig. 3. A photo of Stryx after approaching a group using different strategies.

are used to estimate robot position over time. Unfortunately, due to slippage, the estimate is very noisy. The *amcl* package compares the most recent range readings to a known, static occupancy grid of the environment to correct this. After Stryx has reached its target location, it needs to then face the group [11,14]. In order to accomplish this, we sent a rotation command to Stryx to turn toward the center of the group.

8   Preliminary Demonstration Results

Stryx was tasked with approaching a group of people. Because we are focused on approaching a group, we assumed that all people that the robot could see were part of the group. Future work will integrate group detection so that Stryx will be able to choose a group to approach.

A single group was told to informally talk among themselves while Stryx approached them. There were two different group sizes used: 3 and 5. Stryx was positioned so that it could see the group. We enabled the Center and CPRS strategies separately for different runs of the approaching robot. These strategies were completely autonomous after being started (details above in Sect. 7). When Stryx approached a group of 3 using the Center strategy (Fig. 3a), people in the group and nearby observers found the behavior *odd and slightly creepy*. Even though the robot was not moving quickly, people thought it was unusual for the robot to enter the center of the group and approach so closely to individuals in the group. When Stryx approached a group of size 5 using the CPRS strategy (Fig. 3b), people *felt that the robot was becoming part of the group*. Similarly, when the robot approached a group of 3 people using the CPRS strategy, observers and group members *felt comfortable with the robot's approach* and ending location.

While these results are informal, we highlight the fact that in the future, it will be possible to perform more formal evaluations of both the system and people's impressions of the approach. Additionally, through the multiple runs performed the PardonMe-soner was never a bottleneck nor a tax on the robot's system or computational capabilities. This leads us to believe more complex representations of the group and environment are entirely possible with our current models.

9   Discussion and Conclusion

As previous researchers have noted, approaching an individual or group is not trivial. There are a variety of aspects that enter into a successful approach, including distance, orientation, spacing, and speed. While previous research focused on agents and robots approaching an individual, the few systems that can approach a group focus only on approaching an individual that is part of a group rather than using features of the group to impact the approach. By analyzing a large scale dataset, we discovered a novel empirical finding: that individuals use features of the group they are approaching to impact how they approach. Specifically, we found that the size of the group has some impact on how people approach the group. If we want robots and agents to appear naturally as they approach, these findings should be taken into account.

We created strategies to approach a group of virtual people and then compared the results of these strategies and found several aspects especially relevant to matching the empirical pattern of behavior. Specifically, we found that when approaching a non-dense group, going into the middle of the group was poor approach behavior. We also found that using an *explicit notion of group size* and using that size to control how close to approach a group was more likely to enable an acceptable and natural approach behavior. Of the strategies we tested, we found one that was especially good across multiple group shapes and sizes - Closest Person, Random Square.

We demonstrated the viability and success of the model by matching it to the empirical data and running it on an embodied platform. There is still much room for improvement. First, the current model could not differentiate individuals that were not part of a group; future work needs to be able to identify and create groups so that a decision can be made to approach a specific group. Currently, in some situations (especially with medium/small size groups), the model puts the robot on the edge of the group. While the robot itself turns toward the center of the group, it may not be considered part of the group until it has both approached (current work) and joined (future work).

We feel it important to acknowledge that the dataset and in-person robot tests were used and generated prior to the COVID-19 pandemic. As such, certain social norms with respect to social distancing may no longer be accurate. While group distance and definitions may change in the future, the overall models and conclusion - that people use features of a group when approaching - will remain, such that the observed patterns will remain regardless.

While this work has highlighted that group features can impact and moderate how an agent should approach, we focused here on group size. There are, of course, other features to groups that likely impact how and agent should approach them. Shape, activity, and mobility all likely impact how an agent should approach. By using explicit declarations for these shapes, activity, and mobility we hope to continue using computationally straightforward representations of these features, so that reasoning never becomes a bottleneck for these robots.

Acknowledgments. This research was performed while BW held an NRC Research Associateship award at NRL. This research was funded by ONR and OSD to GT.

References

1. Althaus, P., Ishiguro, H., Kanda, T., Miyashita, T., Christensen, H.I.: Navigation for Human-Robot Interaction Tasks. In: 2004 Proceedings of the IEEE International Conference on Robotics and Automation ICRA 2004, vol. 2, pp. 1894–1900. IEEE (2004)
2. Ball, A., Silvera-Tawil, D., Rye, D., Velonaki, M.: Group comfortability when a robot approaches. In: Beetz, M., Johnston, B., Williams, M.-A. (eds.) ICSR 2014. LNCS (LNAI), vol. 8755, pp. 44–53. Springer, Cham (2014). https://doi.org/10.1007/978-3-319-11973-1_5
3. Hall, E.T.: The Hidden Dimension, vol. 609. Doubleday, Garden City (1966)
4. Harrison, A.M., Xu, W.M., Trafton, J.G.: User-centered robot head design: a sensing computing interaction platform for robotics research (SCIPRR). In: 13th ACM/IEEE International Conference on Human-Robot Interaction, pp. 215–223 (2018)
5. Karreman, D., Utama, L., Joosse, M., Lohse, M., van Dijk, B., Evers, V.: Robot etiquette: how to approach a pair of people? In: 9th ACM/IEEE International Conference on Human-Robot Interaction, pp. 196–197 (2014)
6. Kato, Y., Kanda, T., Ishiguro, H.: May i help you?-design of human-like polite approaching behavior. In: 10th ACM/IEEE International Conference on Human-Robot Interaction (HRI), pp. 35–42. IEEE (2015)
7. Kendon, A.: Conducting interaction: patterns of behavior in focused encounters, vol. 7. CUP Archive (1990)
8. Mead, R., Matarić, M.J.: Autonomous human-robot proxemics: socially aware navigation based on interaction potential. Auton. Robots 41(5), 1189–1201 (2017)
9. Redmon, J., Divvala, S., Girshick, R., Farhadi, A.: You only look once: unified, real-time object detection. In: Proceedings of the IEEE Conference on Computer Vision and Pattern Recognition, pp. 779–788 (2016)
10. Robicquet, A., Sadeghian, A., Alahi, A., Savarese, S.: Learning social etiquette: human trajectory understanding in crowded scenes. In: Leibe, B., Matas, J., Sebe, N., Welling, M. (eds.) ECCV 2016. LNCS, vol. 9912, pp. 549–565. Springer, Cham (2016). https://doi.org/10.1007/978-3-319-46484-8_33
11. Rousseau, V., Ferland, F., Létourneau, D., Michaud, F.: Sorry to interrupt, but may i have your attention?: preliminary design and evaluation of autonomous engagement in HRI. J. Hum. Robot Interact. 2(3), 41–61 (2013)
12. Satake, S., Kanda, T., Glas, D.F., Imai, M., Ishiguro, H., Hagita, N.: How to approach humans? strategies for social robots to initiate interaction. In: 4th ACM/IEEE International Conference on Human Robot Interaction, pp. 109–116 (2009)

13. Setti, F., Russell, C., Bassetti, C., Cristani, M.: F-formation detection: individuating free-standing conversational groups in images. PloS One **10**(5), e0123783 (2015)
14. Shi, C., Shimada, M., Kanda, T., Ishiguro, H., Hagita, N.: Spatial formation model for initiating conversation. In: Proceedings of the Robotics: Science and Systems VII, pp. 305–313 (2011)
15. Wielemaker, J., Schrijvers, T., Triska, M., Lager, T.: SWI-Prolog. Theory Pract. Logic Program. **12**(1–2), 67–96 (2012)

Wake Up and Talk with Me! In-the-Field Study of an Autonomous Interactive Wake Up Robot

Yuma Oda, Jani Even$^{(\boxtimes)}$, and Takayuki Kanda

Kyoto University, Kyoto, Japan
even@robot.soc.i.kyoto-u.ac.jp

Abstract. In this paper, we present a robot that is designed to smoothly wake up a user in the morning. We created an autonomous interactive wake up robot that implements a wake up behavior that was selected through preliminary experiments. We conducted a user study to test the interactive robot and compared it to a baseline robot that behaves like a conventional alarm clock. We recruited 22 participants that agreed to bring the robot to their home and test it for two consecutive nights. The participants felt significantly less sleepy after waking up with the interactive robot, and reported significantly more intention to use the interactive robot.

Keywords: In-the-field · User study · Autonomous robot

1 Introduction

In the scientific literature, the temporary period of reduced alertness and impaired cognition that immediately follows the wake up is known as "sleep inertia" [11,16]. As Trotti says in [17]: "The intensity and duration of sleep inertia vary based on situational factors, but its effects may last minutes to several hours". Since, sleep inertia affects how we perform after wake up [10,14], it is desirable to have few impairment from sleep inertia to move on to carry our daily activities.

We often rely on a device to sound an alarm at the desired time so that we timely wake up. But, there are still some occasions when this is not enough and we oversleep. Consequently, for very important events, we often ask a relative, a friend or a staff member to make sure that we are awake at a specific time. In particular, we trust that waking up with the help of another person will prevent us to fall asleep again and help us be more alert. The main drawback is that this person also has to wake up and we are asking a favor or using a service. There is either an affective cost, we should make it up to that relative or friend that helped us, or a financial cost, we should pay for the service.

This research was supported by JST CREST Grant Number JPMJCR17A2, Japan.

A. R. Wagner et al. (Eds.): ICSR 2020, LNAI 12483, pp. 61–72, 2020.
https://doi.org/10.1007/978-3-030-62056-1_6

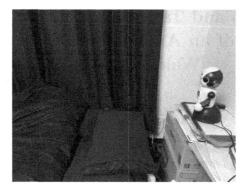

Fig. 1. Wake up robot installed in a "real-world bedroom". The positional relationship between the robot and the bed is important.

The fact that people routinely rely on someone else to wake them up for important occasions is a very interesting observation from a Human robot interaction (HRI) researcher perspective. What if a robot could wake someone up effectively? Using a robot would not come with the same affective cost and the financial cost could be spread as it is something we do daily. The problem is that, to the knowledge of the authors, we do not know what a robot should do or could do to effectively wake people up. In particular, we have to investigate what is the added value over conventional wake up means like alarm clocks and smartphones. Some people may argue that we could use some virtual agent but we believe that the physical presence of the robot is important [3].

In the US, a nationwide survey of 1014 hiring and human resource managers and 809 workers across industries was conducted online by The Harris Poll in 2017 for careerBuilder [1]. Among the 25% of the people that admitted to be late a work at least once a month 31% told the reason was oversleeping. Oversleeping is second only to traffic 51%. Concerning younger generations, 42% of the surveyed adolescents in Portugal reported that they have difficulty to wake up every day [2]. Consequently, we think that there is a need for a better device to wake up.

This paper presents how we designed the wake up behavior for our robot, implemented that behavior and tested it in the field. In particular, we would like to stress that the user study was conducted in real-world conditions as illustrated in Fig. 1.

2   Related Works

Sleep inertia has been extensively studied and several researchers investigated the effect of light [15], sound [19] or temperature [12] among others for improving the condition after wake up. These experiments are most of the time conducted in controlled environments in laboratories and aim at understanding the underlying causes of sleep inertia. But, the aim of our approach is to find a technological solution to alleviate the problem and not study the causes. In particular, our proposed system is designed to be operated out of the laboratory.

There are several researchers that proposed technological solutions to replace the conventional alarm clock. Many of these solutions are labelled as smart alarm clocks. For example in [13], the authors proposed a smart alarm clock that wakes up the user by gradually increasing the light intensity while playing music. That smart alarm clock also displays reminders of the events scheduled on that day.

Another popular approach is to force the user to move. Some commercial products implement this strategy. For example, an alarm clock that sends a propeller in a random location in the room when the alarm sounds. Then the user has to wake up, find the propeller and put it back on the alarm clock to stop the alarm.

Robots have also been used to wake up people. For example, in [5], the authors proposed a robot that runs and hides while the alarm sounds. The user has to find the robot to stop the alarm. This is an advanced robot alarm as it uses sensors to understand the environment and move accordingly. They conducted an experiment with 12 participants to compare their robot to a conventional alarm clock. The proposed robot prevented people from oversleeping or snoozing.

As we can see, there are several technological replacements to the alarm clock that involve a robot. However, the focus is usually on building a product and there is relatively few or no analysis of the effect of the robot on the user. Moreover, to the knowledge of the authors, no one considered this issue with a Human Robot Interaction (HRI) perspective [7]. In particular, it is known that robots have the ability to change human behaviors, emotions and attitudes through interactions [4,6]. Then, we should ask ourselves how we could design the behavior of a wake up robot in order to be efficient and pleasant.

In [18], as an illustrative example, the authors tell that *being woken up by a family member is a complex affective transaction* and suggest that a robot alarm clock should not reproduce perfectly that behavior but *it is rather about creating a waking up experience in between the alarm clock and the mother yanking up the blinds and shouting "good morning, my dear!"*. In a sense, our research aims at finding this right balance.

3   Behavior Design Process

First, we conducted an informal interview survey to understand how people feel about being woke up by someone. We found three participants who were regularly waken up by their relatives. All of them reported that when asked to wake up several time with a loud voice, they feel that they must wake up or their relative will get angry. One of them pointed out how unpleasant it is to wake up in such conditions and how he wished to have a gentler wake up.

To understand what strategies people use to wake someone up, we conducted a preliminary experiment. In this experiment, the four participants had to wake up an experimenter that pretended to sleep deeply. The participants were primed that the sleeper was unlikely to wake up easily. We observed how these participants acted and noticed these following characteristics:

Being Loud: The four participants started by being loud until the sleeper showed some response. A participant simply repeated "Get up!" with a loud voice while clapping hands. Another participant was loudly calling the name of the sleeper. One participant even played loud music from his mobile phone.

Adjusting the Behavior: The participants were adjusting their waking up behavior to the response of the sleeper. As soon as the sleeper answered to the loud sound, the participants stopped being loud and listened to the sleeper.

Caring: Some of the participants were trying to motivate the sleeper to wake up by showing that they cared for him. For example, one participant was saying "You will catch a cold if you sleep in this place".

Threatening: In contrast with the "caring" words, some participants used some threats to motivate the sleeper to wake up. For example, "You will not have any breakfast if you don't wake up now".

Taking into account the information gathered from the informal interviews and our observations, we devised three possible methods for waking up people with the robot:

1. Keep making loud sound until the person gets up,
2. Make loud sound but stop every time there is a reaction,
3. Use caring words for wake up.

To select the most promising method for an implementation on a robot, we conducted another preliminary experiment to investigate what method the person being woken up prefers.

In this experiment, the experimenter is in charge of applying the three wake up methods on the three participants. First the participants are instructed to sleep, or to pretend to sleep if not possible to fall asleep, then the experimenter applies one of the methods to wake the participant up. Each of the participants experienced the three methods. Then, to gather their opinions, the participants were interviewed by the experimenter.

The participants judged that method 1 may be the most effective for waking up but it is very aggressive and unpleasant. With method 2, the participants felt that they would easily fall back asleep when the loud sound stops. Concerning method 3, the participants did not understand what the experimenter was saying when asleep. However, some participants felt it was less aggressive than the other two methods. Moreover, with method 3, the participants felt that they would be unlikely to sleep again because of the verbal interaction after they woke up.

Participants expressed the feeling that method 3 would be better with a louder sound at the start. They also pointed out that further interactions after being somehow awake could help them to further wake up.

From the preliminary experiments and our observations, we understood that a loud sound is necessary to start the wake up procedure and then that interaction is important for an effective wake up. Consequently, we decided to create an interactive wake up behavior that has two steps. First, the robot keeps on saying with a loud voice"Get up, show me your face." until the person to wake

Fig. 2. Table top robot Sota from Vstone

up shows her/his face to the robot. Then, the robot engages in a conversation and interacts a while with the person to wake up.

4 Interactive System

To have a portable system, we decided to use a small table top robot called Sota. Sota is a small humanoid robot built by the company Vstone, see Fig. 2. This robot has 8 degrees of freedom (DoF). It can rotate on its base, move its arms and its neck. It is also equipped with a camera, a microphone and a loud speaker all connected to an on-board computer.

The proposed wake up system is composed of four modules. The conversation control module implements the proposed wake up behavior whereas the other modules just implement the necessary basic functionalities.

First, the robot starts by asking the user to wake up and show their face. The robot uses a loud voice and repeats the call regularly until the robot detects the face of the user. At this point, the user should be facing the robot and the robot engages the conversation by asking the first question. If speech recognition results show that the user talked, the robot moves to the next question. The question answer cycle is iterated until all the six prepared questions are answered. Then, the robot stops the interaction by using a closing remark. For any questions, if the user does not give an answer to the robot the flow loops back at the first step.

We selected questions that require the user to think and are related to time. Moreover, the answers are likely to change every day. We asked several people to use the system and received feedback to determine the details of the questions.

Finally, the questions and the order we selected for the final system is the following:

1. "What is today's schedule?"
2. "At what time does the schedule start?"
3. "What did you do yesterday?"
4. "Was it fun?"
5. "How was the weather yesterday?"
6. "What time is it now?"

To end the conversation, the robot uses the closing remark "Please do your best today".

One of our requirements is that, with minimal training, a novice user should be able to set up the wake up robot by herself/himself while at home. The robot should be placed close to the bed in a location where the user can easily face it. For example, in Fig. 1, the robot is close to the head side of the bed. The robot is connected to a notebook computer (not visible in the figure) and the user just has to enter the wake up time on the computer using a simple interface we designed.

5   User Study

5.1   Hypothesis and Predictions

Our hypothesis is that interaction is the main factor that contributes to an effective wake up and prevents the user to fall asleep again. We also believe that interaction contributes to a better experience and the user is more likely to use the system. Consequently we make the following predictions:

- **Prediction 1 (sleepiness):** Compared to a non interactive wake up means, the proposed interactive wake up robot is better at reducing sleepiness after wake up.
- **Prediction 2 (intention to use):** Compared to a non interactive wake up means, the proposed interactive wake up robot increases the "intention to use" in the future.

5.2   Method

To verify our predictions, we designed an experiment to asses the sleepiness of the user after waking up and their intention to use the system in the future.

We recruited 22 university students using an online recruitment agency. The students were all from Kyoto city but attended different universities. There was 11 males and 11 females all aged between 20 and 24 years old. The participants were asked to take the robot to their home and install it at an adequate location close to their bed, set the alarm and go to sleep as usual. The participants were paid to take part in the study.

We used a within-participant design with counter-balanced order. Each of the participants experienced the two following conditions:

- **The baseline condition:** waking up using a non interactive wake up robot.
- **The proposed condition:** waking up using the proposed interactive wake up robot.

For the baseline condition, rather than letting the participants wake up with their alarm clock or smartphone, we decided to have them use a non interactive version of the wake up robot. Then, both conditions are the same across all participants and we factor out the novelty associated with using a robot.

The behavior of the non interactive wake up robot consists only of a modified version of the first step of the proposed behavior. The robot repeatedly says "wake up" with a loud voice until the participant pushes a button to stop it. This behavior closely resembles that of a conventional alarm clock.

First, the participant came to the laboratory to learn how to setup the robot and program the alarm. After the training was completed, the participant went home with the robot, the notebook computer and blank questionnaires. At their home, for two consecutive nights, the participant had to enter their desired wake up time before sleeping and go to sleep as usual. In the morning, the participant woke up using the robot and then immediately answered the questionnaire. Finally, the participant brought back the robot and computer to the laboratory and an interview was conducted. The experimental protocol was approved by the IRB of our institution.

In this study, we measured three things: the "sleepiness" after wake up, the "intention to use", and the amount of sleep that night.

To measure the sleepiness after wake up, we used the Stanford Sleepiness Scale [9]. This scale has a single item. The participant has to select one of the following seven statements that best represents her/his level of perceived sleepiness:

1. Feeling active, vital, alert, or wide awake
2. Functioning at high levels, but not at peak; able to concentrate
3. Awake, but relaxed; responsive but not fully alert
4. Somewhat foggy, let down
5. Foggy; losing interest in remaining awake; slowed down
6. Sleepy, woozy, fighting sleep; prefer to lie down
7. No longer fighting sleep, sleep onset soon; having dream-like thoughts

It is a 7-point likert-type scale ranging from "Feeling active, vital, alert, or wide awake" (score 1) to "No longer fighting sleep, sleep onset soon; having dream-like thoughts" (score 7).

To measure the "intention to use" of the participants, we use the scale introduced in [8] and asked the participants the following three questions:

• If I have the opportunity, I will use this robot again soon.
• If I have the opportunity, I will definitely use this robot again in the next few days.
• If I have the opportunity, I would plan to use this robot in the near future.

For each of the items, the participant had to answer on a 7-point Likert scale (1-strongly disagree to 7-strongly agree). We averaged the score for these three questions to obtain our measure of "intention of use".

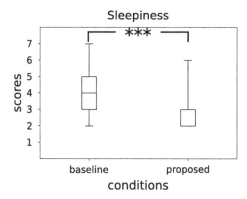

Fig. 3. Questionnaire results for "sleepiness" (lower is better)

Finally, in order to verify that the participant had the same amount of sleep for both conditions, she/he also had to indicate how long she/he slept that particular night.

The post experiment interviews were semi-structured. First, the participant was asked to comment on her/his experience with the robot. Then, the structured part of the interview consisted of several questions.

6 Results

6.1 Verification of Predictions

Prediction 1 ("sleepiness"): The first item of our questionnaire indicates that the participants felt less sleepy after interacting with the robot using the proposed model ($M = 2.91$ $SD = 1.00$) than when using the baseline model ($M = 4.18$ $SD = 1.19$), see Fig. 3. This difference is significant (paired t-test $t = 4.96$ $p < .001$), and the effect size was large (Cohen's $d = 1.13$). This result supports our prediction that: **The proposed wake up robot is more effective at waking up people.**

Prediction 2 ("intention to use"): The second item of our questionnaire indicates that the participants were more inclined to use the robot implementing the proposed model in the future ($M = 4.06$ $SD = 1.37$) than a robot using the baseline model ($M = 3.48$ $SD = 1.25$), see Fig. 4. This difference is significant (paired t-test $t = -2.25$ $p = .035$) and the effect size was medium (Cohen's $d = 0.43$). This result supports our prediction that: **The user are more likely to use the proposed wake up robot in the future.**

6.2 Amount of Sleep

The reported sleeping duration for the two conditions was not significantly different (paired t-test $t = 1.38$ $p = .18$). **The participants had an equivalent amount of sleep before wake up for both conditions.** The overall average sleeping duration was 6.49 h ($SD = 1.09$).

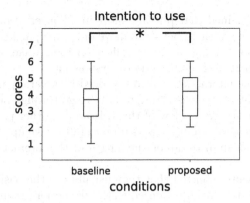

Fig. 4. Questionnaire results for "intention to use" (higher is better)

6.3 Interview Results

Many participants told that they had to think to answer the robot's questions and that it contributed to their awakening. In particular, many thought that questions about the day's schedule and what they did the previous day were effective. Many participants also told that talking immediately after waking up contributed to a better awakening. Several participants felt it was easier to proceed to the next action after waking up with the proposed interactive wake up robot.

Several participants pointed out that they expected the robot to elaborate on their answers and have the conversation unfold. A few participants reported that the conversation was not smooth. Some of them told it was due to poor speech recognition performance. A small number of participants felt that the interaction was too long.

Many of the participants that showed the highest intention to use the robot in the future told that they enjoyed the conversation with the humanoid robot. On the other hand, many of the participants who scored low on this item were generally dissatisfied with the inconvenience of setting the alarm using the computer and the low accuracy of face detection or voice recognition.

A few participants experienced difficulties to have the robot detect their face. In spite of the training in the laboratory, some participants told it was troublesome to set the alarm using the computer.

All the participants told they usually use their smartphone for waking up. When asked about how smoothly they usually wake up, nearly everyone told the process was not that smooth.

7 Discussion

7.1 Effect on Post Wake up Sleepiness

The results of the questionnaires show that the participants felt the proposed wake up robot is significantly more effective at waking them up. In the interviews, the participants explained that putting effort in a conversation forced them to stay awake and prepared them better to move on. Some participants singled out a few questions they felt had a greater effect on their wake up. Thus, we can think that the content of the interaction is important.

The length of the interaction was also evoked by several participants. A few participants felt that it was frustrating to have to go through all the questions if they already feel awake after a few of them. However, other participants hinted to the fact that they need a long conversation to fully wake up. Then, to improve the system, it may helpful to adapt the length of the interaction depending of the user's state.

All the participants reported that they usually use the basic alarm function of their smartphone to wake up. Consequently, the actions required during their regular wake up is close to the ones required in our baseline condition. Then, we believe that the proposed wake up robot should also be more effective than a conventional smartphone alarm.

A difference in the amount of sleep could influence sleep inertia [16]. The reported duration of sleep was similar for both conditions and should not have influenced the results.

At the time of the experiment, the sun rose before 5:45 and the participants did not mention about turning on the light to perform face recognition. However, in other locations, it may be important to control for light as turning on the light may influence the result in favor of the robot using face recognition.

7.2   Intention to Use in the Future

The participants already reported significantly more intention to use the proposed interactive robot in its current form. Many participants wished they could have a smoother and richer conversation with the robot. If this point is improved and the conversations become more interesting, the intention to use the robot in the future is likely to increase.

7.3   Long Term Effect

In this study, the participants just tested the proposed wake up robot for one morning. Our rudimentary conversation module was enough to test our hypothesis that interaction is important. However, we can easily imagine that on the long run it is necessary to have more variety for the questions. In addition, it would be useful to incorporate user's preferences. For example, a busy person may not want to wake up talking about the day's schedule.

7.4   Limitations

Recruiting participants that are eager to bring and setup the robot in their home and, then, conduct the experiment for two consecutive days was not easy. Thus, our recruiting advertisements targeted the specific demographic of university students. The reasons given by the participants during the interviews did not seem specific to this particular demographic. Then, we can expect the effect to exist for other demographic groups. But, further research is necessary to confirm this hypothesis.

The participants felt that it is the conversation and the associated cognitive effort that helped them to wake up. One might think that a smart speaker could be used to talk with the user. We believe that talking with the humanoid robot, that has a physical presence reminiscent of a human, helps to engage in the conversation and contributes to the "wake up effect". To have a definitive answer, a further study comparing the proposed behavior by a robot or by a smart speaker would be necessary.

8   Conclusion

In this paper, we first investigated what behavior a robot could use to effectively wake up people in the morning. From preliminary experiments and observations we proposed to use a two-step behavior that combines a loud wake up step followed by a short conversation between the robot and the user. In particular, it was the interaction between the robot and the user that was expected to cause a smooth wake up. To confirm this hypothesis, we implemented that behavior in a small robot and conducted a user study. A particularity of this user study is that we conducted it in real conditions. The participants used a robot with and without interaction for waking up on two consecutive days at their home. The results showed that the robot using interaction was significantly reducing the sleepiness of the participants after wake up. Moreover, the participants were significantly more eager to use that interactive robot in the future. The post experiment interviews showed that the participants attributed the effectiveness of the system to the interaction. However, further research is needed to understand in more details why the participants preferred the interactive robot.

Acknowledgment. We would like to thank Yoko Kubota and Hiromi Kobayashi for their help in organizing the user study. We would also like to thank Kyohei Hosoda, Kota Maehama and Koki Makita for their involvement in the preliminary experiments.

References

1. This Year's Most Bizarre Excuses for Being Late to Work, According to New CareerBuilder Survey. http://press.careerbuilder.com/2018-03-22-This-Years-Most-Bizarre-Excuses-for-Being-Late-to-Work-According-to-New-CareerBuilder-Survey. Accessed 1 March 2020
2. Amaral, O., Garrido, A., Pereira, C., Veiga, N., Serpa, C., Sakellarides, C.: Sleep patterns and insomnia among portuguese adolescents: a cross-sectional study. Aten. Primaria **46**(5), 191–194 (2014). Sociedad Espanola de Medicina de Familia y Comunitaria
3. Bainbridge, W.A., Hart, J., Kim, E.S., Scassellati, B.: The effect of presence on human-robot interaction. In: RO-MAN 2008-The 17th IEEE International Symposium on Robot and Human Interactive Communication, pp. 701–706. IEEE (2008)

4. Dautenhahn, K.: Socially intelligent robots: dimensions of human-robot interaction. Philos. Trans. R. Soc. B Biol. Sci. **362**(1480), 679–704 (2007)
5. Ee, L., Zamin, N., Aziz, I., Haron, N., Mehat, M., Ismail, N.: BEDRUNN3R: an intelligent running alarm clock. ARPN J. Eng. Appl. Sci. **10**(23), 17890–17898 (2015)
6. Fong, T., Nourbakhsh, I., Dautenhahn, K.: A survey of socially interactive robots. Robot. Auton. Syst. **42**(3), 143–166 (2003). https://doi.org/10.1016/S0921-8890(02)00372-X. socially interactive robots
7. Goodrich, M.A., Schultz, A.C., et al.: Human-robot interaction: a survey. Found. Trends. Hum. Comput. Interact. **1**(3), 203–275 (2008)
8. Heerink, M., Kröse, B., Wielinga, B., Evers, V.: Enjoyment, intention to use and actual use of a conversational robot by elderly people. In: Proceedings of the ACM/IEEE International Conference on Human-Robot Interaction (HRI2008), pp. 113–119 (2008)
9. Hoddes, E., Zarcone, V., Smythe, H., Phillips, R., Dement, W.C.: Quantification of sleepiness: a new approach. Psychophysiology **10**(4), 431–436 (1973)
10. Horne, J., Moseley, R.: Sudden early-morning awakening impairs immediate tactical planning in a changing 'emergency' scenario. J. Sleep Res. **20**(2), 275–278 (2011)
11. Jeanneret, P., Webb, W.: Strength of grip on arousal from full nights sleep. Percept. Mot. Skills **17**, 759–761 (1963)
12. Kräuchi, K., Cajochen, C., Wirz-Justice, A.: Waking up properly: is there a role of thermoregulation in sleep inertia? J. Sleep Res. **13**(2), 121–127 (2004)
13. Kumar, S., Dhiraj, D., Cibi, C., Sowmya, S., Sabitha, S.: Smart alarm clock. In: 2018 3rd International Conference on Communication and Electronics Systems (ICCES), pp. 999–1001 (2018)
14. Muzet, A., Nicolas, A., Tassi, P., Dewasmes, G., Bonneau, A.: Implementation of napping in industry and the problem of sleep inertia. J. Sleep Res. **4**(52), 67–69 (1995)
15. Santhi, N., Groeger, J., Archer, S., Gimènez, M., Schlangen, L., Dijk, D.: Morning sleep inertia in alertness and performance: effect of cognitive domain and white light conditions. PloS One **8**(11), e79688 (2013)
16. Tassi, P., Muzet, A.: Sleep inertia. Sleep Med. Rev. **4**, 341–353 (2000)
17. Trotti, L.: Waking up is the hardest thing i do all day: sleep inertia and sleep drunkenness. Sleep Med. Rev. **35**, 76–84 (2017)
18. Welge, J., Hassenzahl, M.: Better than human: about the psychological superpowers of robots. In: Agah, A., Cabibihan, J.-J., Howard, A.M., Salichs, M.A., He, H. (eds.) ICSR 2016. LNCS (LNAI), vol. 9979, pp. 993–1002. Springer, Cham (2016). https://doi.org/10.1007/978-3-319-47437-3_97
19. Wilkinson, R.: Interaction of noise with knowledge of results and sleep deprivation. J. Exp. Psychol. **66**(4), 332–337 (1963)

I Like the Way You Move: A Mixed-Methods Approach for Studying the Effects of Robot Motion on Collaborative Human Robot Interaction

Jonas E. Pedersen[1], Kristoffer W. Christensen[1], Damith Herath[2]($\boxtimes$) (iD),
and Elizabeth Jochum[1]

[1] Aalborg University, Aalborg, Denmark
[2] University of Canberra, Canberra, Australia
`damith.herath@canberra.edu.au`

Abstract. Human robot collaboration is an increasingly relevant area within Human Robot Interaction. As robots move into dynamic environments and engage in collaborative tasks with people, there is a need to further understand how perceptual and communication cues facilitate and support Human Robot Collaboration. Building on prior Human Robot Interaction studies, we developed a mixed-methods approach for studying the effects of expressive movements of an industrial robot arm engaged in a collaborative drawing task. The purpose was to evaluate the effects of different movement qualities on participant experience while collaborating with a robot. We present our approach and the results of the experiments. Although we did not identify any significant difference in interactions where the robot moved expressively, our study highlights the importance of in-the-wild experiments and strategies for combining qualitative and quantitative methodologies.

Keywords: Human-robot interaction · Collaborative robots · Mixed-methods · Human-factors

1 Introduction

Collaborative robots are an increasingly important area of Human Robot Interaction (HRI) research, as people and robots begin to share workspaces and collaborate on tasks. For human-robot collaboration (HRC) to succeed, robots must be able to work alongside people as capable partners, not merely as sophisticated tools [1]. This transition requires technological advancements as well as nuanced understanding of situational context and human factors [2]. Understanding how people naturally interact with robots on collaborative tasks is essential for designing systems that support successful interactions [3].

© Springer Nature Switzerland AG 2020
A. R. Wagner et al. (Eds.): ICSR 2020, LNAI 12483, pp. 73–84, 2020.
https://doi.org/10.1007/978-3-030-62056-1_7

Robots have only recently been introduced into complex social situations, where they are placed alongside humans in efforts to integrate them more fully into everyday life [4–6]. Given the complexity of social environments, studying HRC with untrained participants in-the-wild can offer valuable insights. However, numerous methodological challenges arise when designing experiments for uncontrolled settings [7]. Despite an interest in testing and evaluating robots holistically [8], the majority of HRI studies are still conducted in laboratories and rely primarily on quantitative evaluation methods [9].

Inspired by drawing robots developed by Patrick Tresset [10] and Sougwen Chen [11], we aimed to study the effects of expressive motion on a collaborative drawing task with an industrial robot arm at a science museum. Drawing together with a robot is an activity that models other types of behaviors that are essential for more complex tasks, such as turn taking and signalling. Previous HRI research identifies expressive movement as a promising and cost-efficient alternative to the common approach of using highly anthropomorphic modalities of communication, such as speech and facial expressions [12]. We initially sought to study the impact of expressive motion. The museum context determined many aspects of this study and revealed the importance of combining qualitative and quantitative evaluation methods. Although we did not identify any significant difference in interactions where the robot moved expressively, our study highlights the importance of in-the-wild experiments and strategies for combining qualitative and quantitative methods.

The Wizard of Oz (WOZ) framework is an established method for HRI experiments, especially in-the-wild [13]. Riek proposes reporting guidelines that account for the various experimental components, including the robot's capabilities and relevant information concerning the wizard's involvement. The details of the WOZ and control architecture for this study are outlined in a companion paper [14].

2 Experiment

We chose to work with an industrial robot arm designed for close contact with humans [15]. The UR10 is designed to perform collaborative and repetitive tasks in factories. We programmed the UR10 to facilitate a short drawing session with a person [Fig. 1]. We expected that even untrained participants would be able to quickly understand the task and engage in the activity imaginatively and with purpose. Because collaborative drawing requires turn-taking and coordination, we reasoned it would prove a valuable scenario for studying perceptual cues that support collaboration and joint action tasks. We set out to test a range of expressive behaviors that would communicate intent and internal states as well as social behaviors primarily through movement. The experiment was conducted at a science museum in Australia. The public setting provided a semi-controllable environment as well as a steady influx of untrained participants that could be recruited on-the-fly to participate.

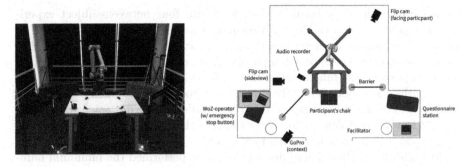

Fig. 1. (a) The UR10 collaborative industrial robot arm was used in a collaborative drawing task in a science museum (b) Diagram of the experiment setup at the science museum. Three cameras were used to capture the details of the interaction and overall context, including bystanders and passerby.

Setup. The study involved human participants and was reviewed and approved by Human Research Ethics at the University of Canberra. Written informed consent for participation was obtained from all study participants in accordance with national legislation and institutional requirements. The robot was positioned in a separate gallery of the museum in between two exhibition halls. The area was open on two sides, allowing passerby to enter the interaction space and oversee others interacting with the robot without interfering with the experiment. Visitors were welcomed by the research team and invited to participate in the study. Ethics requirements mandate that participants be over 18 years old, which meant children and younger visitors would observe, sometimes clustering closely around the interaction space.

Consent and participant information forms were placed on a ledge to the right of the gallery entrance, making it easy to show participants what the experiment was about ahead of time. To provide participants with further context, the walls outside of the room were decorated with pre-rendered drawings. Signs informing visitors that an experiment was being conducted were placed outside of the gallery.

As seen in Fig. 1b, the UR10 was placed in the center of the room and controlled by a WOZ operator. The operator was seated in plain sight, but outside the field of vision of the participants during the interaction. Interactions were recorded using three cameras: two flipcams positioned at the back of the room and at the side of the table, while a third wide-angle camera was mounted on a wall overlooking the area in front of the table where the drawing took place. The flipcams captured the details of the interaction, and the wide-angle camera accounts for the overall context, such as the number of participants in the room and their placement in relation to each other. This allows the possibility to observe and record bystander behavior. A recorder with two unidirectional microphones was placed to the left of the table pointing at the participants, providing high-quality audio that was used in the video analysis.

Conditions. The experiment was divided into four between-subject experimental conditions as a result of a two-by-two matrix of conditions outlined in Table 1. The purpose of these conditions was to explore the effects and legibility of expressive motion as opposed to purely functional motion. We also introduced the concept of direct (functional) versus indirect (expressive) motion paths. For direct paths, the robot would take the shortest possible route when performing a movement. For the indirect paths, the robot would initiate movement by moving slightly forward or sideways to subtly indicate the intended the trajectory and destination, before completing the movement.

In Condition 1 (functional, direct) the robot performed the minimum number of movements required to execute the drawing and its motions all followed a direct path. In Condition 2 (indirect, functional), the robot was programmed to move between end points indirectly, with no attempts at social behavior or expression. In Condition 3, (direct, expressive) the robot was programmed to follow a direct path, but included more embellished movements (e.g. greeting the participants with a 'nod' and animations to simulate 'contemplation' when looking at the drawing and 'deciding' what to draw next). In Condition 4 (indirect, expressive) the robot followed an indirect path between points and used embellished, expressive animations to simulate social behavior. These animations were directly inspired by Tresset's robot [10] and were meant to simulate the robot's social awareness and involvement in the drawing task.

Participants. A total of 68 adult participants completed the experiment and questionnaire. The participants were evenly distributed between the four conditions (17 participants in each group). All participants were given little instruction about the experiment before commencing the drawing. If they asked about the role of the wizard, they were informed that a technician was there to ensure the robot and recording equipment were working as intended. Only when necessary, participants were assisted by the facilitator if they were unsure what to do and asked for help. After the experiment, each participant was asked to complete a questionnaire. There was a mix of men and women, young and old, couples, families and singles. Most of the participants were Australian, and roughly a quarter of the participants were international visitors. Seven participants were from countries where English is not an official language, but all seven were capable of having a conversation with the facilitator about the purpose of the exhibit

Table 1. Variations between experimental conditions.

Experiment condition	The approach strategy employed by the robot	
The type of movements and gestures employed by the robot	Direct	Indirect
Functional	Condition 1	Condition 2
Expressive	Condition 3	Condition 4

and the initial steps of the interaction, making it unlikely that any participants misconstrued the words in the Semantic Differential Scales of the Godspeed-series [17].

Drawing. The drawing activity lasted between three and five minutes. Participants were seated at the table across from the robot. The drawing was pre-selected by the WOZ operator from a series of eight pre-rendered line drawings (e.g. a sun, a palm tree, an elephant, Saturn) developed by the research team. Each drawing consisted of three turns for the robot and the participant, and the robot always initiated the drawing. To signal the end of the activity, the robot drew two lines for a "signature" at the bottom of the page, signing "UR10" and promoting the participant to sign their own name. Participants were allowed to take their drawings home with them. A detailed illustration of the interaction scenario is depicted in Fig. 2.

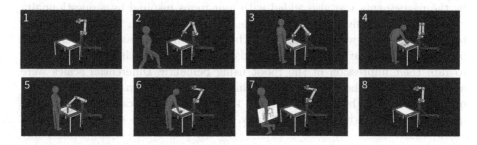

Fig. 2. The interaction scenario included eight steps: (1) The robot waits for someone to draw with. (2) A person approaches the robot. (3) The robot begins drawing. (4) The person adds to the drawing. (5) The robot signs the drawing. (6) The person signs the drawing. (7) The person takes the drawing home. (8) The robot is ready for a new interaction.

Questionnaire. The questionnaire was based on the Godspeed-series [17] for measuring perceived safety and participants' impression of the robot with regards to anthropomorphism, animacy, likeability and perceived intelligence, combined with an adapted version of Brooke's System Usability Scale-questionnaire (SUS) [18], an established tool for measuring usability for a wide range of interactive systems and technologies [19]. While not common to HRI, SUS has previously been used in studies with robots [20, 21]. Here, the SUS was modified to assess the robot's ability to communicate intent and facilitate turn-taking. Modifications were motivated by the need to make the questions more centered on interaction, and the suggestion by [18] to change the word 'cumbersome' to 'awkward'. Instances of the amended wording are listed in Table 2.

An item on the Godspeed-questionnaire about perceived safety was also modified in this study, as even the native English-speaking members of the research team considered the word 'quiescent' too difficult for the general public. An extra item was added to the three original items on the perceived safety-scale

Table 2. Modifying the wording of the System Usability Scale-questionnaire.

Original version	Modified version
I thought the system was easy to use	I thought the robot was easy to interact with
I felt very confident using the system	I felt very confident interacting with the robot
I found the system very cumbersome to use	I found the robot very awkward to interact with

as a precaution, in case one or more of the original items were misconstrued by respondents. A dummy item was also added to make the intention of the perceived safety-scale less obvious [17]. The modifications are listed in Table 3.

A set of scales intended to measure the level of engagement experienced by the participants was also added with four items inspired by a questionnaire used in [22]. These five-point Likert-scale items ranging from 'Strongly disagree' to 'Strongly agree' were shuffled with the SUS items to mask the intention of both constructs. The items from the Godspeed-series prompting the participants to rate their impression of the robot using Semantic Differential scales were also shuffled with the same purpose. Finally, select items in all sections of the questionnaire had their scales reversed to avoid stereotypical assessment. The questionnaire was administered digitally.

Video. Video Interaction Analysis (VIA) is a qualitative method for investigating how humans interact with each other, as well as objects in the environment [23]. Aspects of the interaction are coded progressively with the expectation that relevant codes will be revealed through analysis. After sorting videos into smaller segments for each participant, all video clips were viewed, discussed and coded together by two researchers who were present throughout the museum experiments.

3   Results

Questionnaire. The internal consistency of the constructs used in the questionnaire was measured using Cronbach's alpha, which showed that the constructs

Table 3. Modifying the Perceived safety-scale of the Godspeed-questionnaire.

Original version	Modified version
Surprised <> Quiescent	Surprised <> At rest
(Extra item)	Uneasy <> At ease
(Dummy item)	Ashamed <> Proud

Table 4. Cronbach's alpha for each construct in each of the four experiment conditions.

Condition	SAFE	ANT	ANIM	LIKE	INT	SU	ENG
1 (Functional-Direct)	0.540	0.768	0.645	0.916	0.599	0.716	0.685
2 (Functional-Indirect)	0.805	0.554	0.720	0.851	0.779	0.753	0.600
3 (Expressive-Direct)	0.630	0.655	0.551	0.893	0.787	0.688	0.668
4 (Expressive-Indirect)	0.657	0.695	0.808	0.810	0.848	0.839	0.837

had at least one condition in which the 17 sampled respondent's answers gave reason to doubt the internal consistency of the construct in that particular condition, due to values lower than 0.70 as recommended by Nunnally in [17]. Table 4 shows the calculated alpha-values for the constructs in the questionnaire.

While values between 0.70 and 0.60 would typically be considered questionable, we deemed them acceptable in this case for the purpose of further discussion, especially considering that we intended to evaluate these features in conjunction with qualitative analysis. Any comparison of means between conditions had to disregard the following means on the basis of internal inconsistency of the scales used to measure the following constructs:

- Perceived intelligence (INT) in Condition 1
- Anthropomorphism (ANT) in Condition 2
- Animacy (ANIM) in Condition 3

The description statistics for each variable in each condition are presented in Table 5 in the output format of the SPSS Statistics Software.

Comparing the means of the variables across all four conditions would only be meaningful if the differences were statistically significant. This was checked by performing a One-way ANOVA test with a Tukey HSD post-hoc analysis, preceded by a Shapiro-Wilks test to check if the distributions could satisfy the normality assumption for parametric statistics. The Shapiro-Wilks test showed with statistical significance that the means were normally distributed in all but two

Table 5. Descriptive statistics.

CONDITION		N	Minimum	Maximum	Mean	Std. Deviation
1	SAFE_New	17	2,00	5,00	3,4706	,94324
	ANT	17	1,80	4,40	2,9412	,73405
	ANIM	17	2,17	4,00	3,1765	,54795
	LIKE	17	2,40	5,00	3,8118	,79834
	INT	17	3,00	4,60	3,7176	,50029
	SU	17	2,60	4,50	3,4235	,51299
	ENG_New	17	1,67	4,67	3,5882	,79521
	Valid N (listwise)	17				
2	SAFE_New	17	2,00	5,00	4,1765	,93629
	ANT	17	2,40	4,60	3,3294	,57420
	ANIM	17	2,50	4,67	3,3235	,56664
	LIKE	17	3,20	5,00	4,2471	,56802
	INT	17	2,80	5,00	3,9765	,59532
	SU	17	2,50	4,90	3,8471	,58643
	ENG_New	17	3,00	5,00	4,1176	,66605
	Valid N (listwise)	17				
3	SAFE_New	17	2,00	5,00	3,8039	,84211
	ANT	17	2,60	4,40	3,4941	,58360
	ANIM	17	2,67	4,33	3,6373	,44580
	LIKE	17	3,00	5,00	4,2000	,62849
	INT	17	3,20	5,00	3,9882	,61021
	SU	17	2,70	4,60	3,6529	,46363
	ENG_New	17	3,00	5,00	4,1765	,56664
	Valid N (listwise)	17				
4	SAFE_New	17	2,00	5,00	4,0000	,97895
	ANT	17	1,80	4,20	3,1176	,63269
	ANIM	17	1,67	4,17	3,1667	,62639
	LIKE	17	2,80	5,00	4,1412	,65485
	INT	17	2,00	4,60	3,7882	,70877
	SU	17	2,70	4,90	3,7882	,62238
	ENG_New	17	2,33	5,00	3,9412	,70941
	Valid N (listwise)	17				

cases, namely for Perceived safety in both Condition 2 and 4. These means were disregarded in the subsequent comparisons. One last assumption check before the ANOVA test involved a rest of homogeneity of variances, which showed that all the variances were in fact homogeneous. Still, the One-way ANOVA test with a Tukey Honestly Significant Difference post-hoc analysis showed no statistically significant differences between any of the possible pairings of means across the four conditions. The significance level, or acceptable p-value, for this study 0.05. A few comparisons came close. The p—value for the differences between Animacy in Condition 1 and 3 and Conditions 3 and 4 were 0.080 and 0.071 respectively. But both comparisons include the mean for Animacy in condition 3, which had an unacceptable Cronbach's alpha value 0.551. A p-value of 0.063 meant the different between Anthropomorphism in Conditions 1 and 3 was very near the threshold for statistical significance, but that was as close as any comparison came. In other words, the quantitative analysis from the questionnaire responses showed no statistically significant differences between any of the variables across conditions.

Video Analysis. Starting from a list of 23 codes, the video analysis resulted in a list of 29 codes with specific meanings. These codes were then grouped into categories as a way to clarify which aspects of the interaction were of interest during the analysis. This process resulted in eight categories containing the 29 codes as seen in Table 6. Most findings from the video analysis revolved around attributes of the environment, making each interaction mostly independent of the experimental conditions. Consequently, some participants would experience widely different interactions while subjected to the same conditions, while other participants would experience very similar interactions across conditions. We consider this lack of consistency as inherent to testing in the wild. A sample of the video analysis and coding can be seen in Fig. 3.

Table 6. The 29 codes generated from the video analysis.

Category	Code
Emotion	Amused, Anxious, Confused, Curious, Passive, Relaxed, Surprised
Safety	Proxemics, Safety, Indirect
Attention	Distracted, Focused, Robo-aware
Comprehension	Clear intent, Misinterpreted, Image
Instruction	Instruction, Timing, Turn-taking, Interruption, Initiative
Observation	Experienced, Observer, Co-participation
Facilitation	Facilitator, WoZ
Recognition	Presence, Verbal, Non-verbal, Co-participation

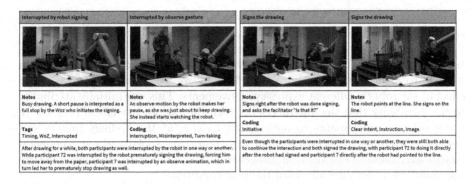

Fig. 3. An example of the video analysis and coding.

4   Discussion

This study was partly motivated by Hoffman & Ju's call to explore movement as a mode of communication for low-anthropomorphic robots [12]. The decision to situate the experiment in-the-wild was also motivated by the desire to develop strategies for studying robots in complex and dynamic environments. In hindsight, it's debatable whether the chosen experimental design was the best way to explore this. A sample size of 17 for each condition proved insufficient to make subtle variations in the robot's use of movement stand out from one another. Other factors such as the presence of bystanders and the unreliability of the animations seemed to problematize the effect of the subtle movement variations on the participant's experience. One explanation for the lack of observed difference among the four conditions is that we altered the standardized measurement tools too much. Another possibility is that semi-controlled environments, where participants are distracted or have split-attention (robot, drawing, bystanders), make it difficult to isolate and account for discrete aspects of the interaction. And yet, it is precisely these types of dynamic environments and situations that robots will be placed and expected to operate in. The failure to produce statistically significant results does not inherently mean there is no difference across the conditions. Rather, as the video analysis reveals, there was huge variation in participant experiences for identical conditions. Many participants became distracted and shifted their attention during the 3–5 minutes long interaction. *For this reason, we propose that mixed-methods approach that combines quantitative with qualitative methods should always be considered when designing HRI or HRC experiments, especially for experiments outside of the laboratory.*

The use of the Godspeed-series was motivated by the verified reliability of the constructs and the fact that one of the components was focused on perceived safety. The many instances of relatively low Cronbach's alpha values of the constructs across all four conditions indicated that the participants' assessments were more inconsistent than we expected. Perhaps applying the Godspeed-series in a very dynamic environment with multiple external factors at play placed too much strain on the constructs.

Following our study, we are not convinced that quantitative methods alone can yield a nuanced understanding of HRC. Combining quantitative and qualitative methods can help researchers to identify important nuances that sometimes go overlooked. In our study, qualitative data was especially valuable when it came to identifying possible reasons for why we were unable to measure an effect of the robot's different expressive movements. This was initially attributed to the possibility that the differences between the various movement styles were too subtle for participants to notice. But looking at the findings from a secondary video analysis, it was evident that numerous social and environmental factors overshadowed or drew attention from the interaction, making it nearly impossible to isolate the effects of the four conditions.

Individual Differences. One of the main causes for variation within each test seemed to be somewhat attributed to the individual differences between participants. As shown in the examples in Fig. 4a and 4b, this meant that while one participant might have a fluid interaction with the robot, another participant experiencing the same condition might have a less successful interaction.

Co-participation. Another contributing factor that seemed to affect the HRI was the presence and activity of bystanders [Fig. 4c]. Video analysis revealed co-participation to happen on several levels, ranging from observers pointing out important information to help the participant to initiating conversation.

Task Performance. Although the robot was able to successfully execute the different states of the social routine, several issues prevented the robot from exhibiting consistently uniform behavior in all 17 interactions of each condition. This means that some participants within a single condition would experience variations in the UR10's behavior that other participants from the same sample would not. These issues ranged from the robot's tendency to delay actions for up to four seconds when responding to WOZ-commands and switching between states, resulting in either near-perfect or poorly-timed interactions, to the robot performing the wrong instructions or movements in relation to the specific test case.

Fig. 4. (a) Participant watching the robot closely as it signs. (b) Participant retracts from the robot as it waits for her to draw. (c) Bystanders gesture to the robot during an interaction with a study participant.

5   Conclusion

The aim of this study was to investigate the effects of variations in how expressive movement might facilitate HRC with a low-anthropomorphic robot. A combination of quantitative and qualitative methods were used including post-interaction questionnaires and multi-angled video recordings. The combined results from the questionnaire and video recordings make clear the need for adopting a mixed-methods approach to understand important nuances of interaction and environmental factors that might seriously affect the HRI. In our study, social parameters and environmental factors overshadowed the effects of the experimental conditions. Thus, our study reiterates the need to study HRI and HRC in-the-wild, not least to develop a more realistic understanding of how robots and humans will collaborate together in dynamic environments populated by other bystanders, passerby or even interaction partners. These issues are not always sufficiently addressed by laboratory studies. Studying HRC in the wild could result in more successful collaborations between people and robots in the real world.

References

1. Bauer, A., Wollherr, D., Buss, M.: Human-robot collaboration: a survey. Int. J. Humanoid Robot. **5**(01), 47–66 (2008)
2. Breazeal, C., et al.: Working Collaboratively with humanoid robots. https://doi. org/10.1109/ICHR.2004.1442126
3. Breazeal, C., Kidd, C.D., Thomaz, A.L., Hoffman, G., Berlin, M.: Effects of non-verbal communication on efficiency and robustness in human-robot teamwork. In: IEEE/RSJ International Conference on Intelligent Robots and Systems (IROS), pp. 383–388 (2005)
4. Young, J.E., et al.: Evaluating human-robot interaction: focusing on the holistic interaction experience. Int. J. Soc. Robot. **3**(1), 53–67 (2011). https://doi.org/10. 1007/s12369-010-0081-8
5. Seo, S.H., Griffin, K., Young, J.E., Bunt, A., Prentice, S., Loureiro-Rodríguez, V.: Investigating people's rapport building and hindering behaviors when working with a collaborative robot. Int. J. Soc. Robot. **10**(1), 147–161 (2017). https://doi.org/ 10.1007/s12369-017-0441-8
6. Castro-González, Á., Admoni, H., Scassellati, B.: Effects of form and motion on judgments of social robots' animacy, likability, trustworthiness and unpleasantness. Int. J. Hum. Comput. Stud. **90**, 27–38 (2016). https://doi.org/10.1016/j.ijhcs.2016. 02.004
7. Duffy, B.R., Joue, G., Bourke, J.: Issues in assessing performance of social robots (2002)
8. Sabanovic, S., Michalowski, M.P., Simmons, R.: Robots in the wild: observing human-robot social interaction outside the lab. Int. Workshop Adv. Motion Control AMC **2006**, 576–581 (2006)
9. Brooks, R.: A brave, creative, and happy HRI. ACM Trans. Hum.-Robot Interact. **7**(1), 3 (2018). Article 1. https://doi.org/10.1145/3209540
10. Tresset, P., Deussen, O.: Artistically skilled embodied agents. In: Proceedings of AISB2014, 8 April 2014

11. Issues: Sougwen Chen and the future of work. In: Issues in Science and Technology, vol. 35(1) (2018). https://issues.org/sougwen-chung/

12. Hoffman, G., Wendy, J.: Designing robots with movement in mind. J. Hum.-Robot Interact. **3**(1), 91–122 (2014). https://doi.org/10.5898/JHRI.3.1.Hoffman

13. Riek, L.D.: Wizard of oz studies in HRI: a systematic review and new reporting guide-lines. J. Hum.-Robot Interact. **1**(1), 119–136 (2012). https://doi.org/10.5898/JHRI.1.1.Riek

14. Hinwood, D., Ireland, J., Jochum, E.A., Herath, D.: A proposed wizard of OZ architecture for a human-robot collaborative drawing task. In: Ge, S.S., et al. (eds.) ICSR 2018. LNCS (LNAI), vol. 11357, pp. 35–44. Springer, Cham (2018). https://doi.org/10.1007/978-3-030-05204-1_4

15. Universal-robots.com.: UR10 Collaborative industrial robotic arm - Payload up to 10 kg (2018)

16. Salter, T., Werry, I., Michaud, F.: Going into the wild in child-robot interaction studies: issues in social robotic development. Intell. Serv. Robot. **1**(2), 93–108 (2008). https://doi.org/10.1007/s11370-007-0009-9

17. Bartneck, C., Kulić, D., Croft, E., Zoghbi, S.: Measurement instruments for the anthropomorphism, animacy, likeability, perceived intelligence, and perceived safety of robots. Int. J. Soc. Robot. **1**(1), 71–81 (2009). https://doi.org/10.1007/s12369-008-0001-3

18. Lewis, J.R., Sauro, J.: The factor structure of the system usability scale. In: Kurosu, M. (ed.) HCD 2009. LNCS, vol. 5619, pp. 94–103. Springer, Heidelberg (2009). https://doi.org/10.1007/978-3-642-02806-9_12

19. Bangor, A., Kortum, P., Miller, J.: Determining what individual SUS scores mean: adding an adjective rating scale. J. Usability Stud. **4**(3), 114–123 (2009)

20. Pei, Y.C., Chen, J.L., Wong, A.M., Tseng, K.C.: An evaluation of the design and usability of a novel robotic bilateral arm rehabilitation device for patients with stroke. Front. Neurorobot. **11** (2017). https://doi.org/10.3389/fnbot.2017.00036

21. Mattos, L.S., Deshpande, N., Barresi, G., Guastini, L., Peret-ti, G.: A novel computerized surgeon-machine interface for robot-assisted laser phonomi-crosurgery. Laryngoscope **124**(8), 1887–1894 (2014)

22. Herath, D.C., Jochum, E., Vlachos, E.: An experimental study of embodied interaction and human perception of social presence for interactive robots in public settings. IEEE Trans. Cogn. Dev. Syst. **10**(4) (2018)

23. Jordan, B., Henderson, A.: Interaction analysis: foundations and practice. J. Learn. Sci. **4**, 39–103 (1995). https://doi.org/10.1207/s15327809jls0401

Effects of Proactive Explanations by Robots on Human-Robot Trust

Lixiao Zhu$^{(\boxtimes)}$ and Thomas Williams

Colorado School of Mines, Golden, CO 80401, USA
{lizhu,twilliams}@mines.edu

Abstract. The performance of human-robot teams depends on human-robot trust, which in turn depends on appropriate robot-to-human transparency. A key way for robots to build trust through transparency is by providing appropriate explanations for their actions. While most previous work on robot explanation generation has focused on robots' ability to provide post-hoc explanations upon request, in this paper we instead examine *proactive* explanations generated *before* actions are taken, and the effect this has on human-robot trust. Our results suggest a positive relationship between proactive explanations and human-robot trust, and reveal fundamental new questions into the effects of proactive explanations on the nature of humans' mental models and the fundamental nature of human-robot trust.

Keywords: Human-robot interaction · Human-robot trust · Transparency · Explanation

1 Introduction and Motivation

For human-robot teams to achieve high levels of team performance, appropriate levels of trust must be established between teammates [2]. Human-robot teams tend to have undesirable performance when human-robot trust is either too low or too high, which means that human-robot trust must be maintained at an appropriate level rather than directly maximized [17]. One key factor in establishing an appropriate level of human-robot trust is the transparency of robots' internal beliefs, desires, and intentions [12]. Robot transparency allows users to become aware of the robots' capabilities (thus helping to build capability-based trust) [6,14], and helps to ensure accurate human mental models of the robot's behavior, which ensures that an appropriate level of trust is established [21].

Robot transparency is typically enabled through verbal communicative behaviors, such as explanation generation [13,14]. While there has been a significant body of work on explanation generation in human-robot interaction, this work has largely focused only on reactive explanations: post-hoc explanations generated in response to a request from a human teammate to explain a previous behavior [4,16]. In contrast, little work has explored proactive explanations: explanations that are generated before an action is performed.

© Springer Nature Switzerland AG 2020
A. R. Wagner et al. (Eds.): ICSR 2020, LNAI 12483, pp. 85–95, 2020.
https://doi.org/10.1007/978-3-030-62056-1_8

One challenge of generating proactive explanations is that because explanations are provided on the initiative of the robot rather than the human, robots must carefully tailor their explanations to avoid communicating too much information, which may overload users [18] and violate communicative norms such as Grice's Maxim of Quanitity [5]. This presents a fundamental tension between design goals of transparency and trust-sensitivity vs. cooperativity and workload-sensitivity. In this work, we thus explore two types of proactive explanatory behavior that can be taken before an unexpected action is performed, each of which places different weight on these competing factors.

- **Proactive Announcement**: Before taking an unexpected action, a robot may perform proactive announcement by stating the action it is going to take. This may serve to enhance predictability-based trust by reducing the user's sense that the robots' actions were unexpected. However, this is not a true explanation as it does not actually reveal the beliefs and desires underlying the robots' intentions [4].
- **Proactive Explanation**: In contrast, the robot may instead perform proactive explanation by stating the action it is going to take *and why*. This functions as a true explanation, revealing the dispositions behind the robot's actions. This allows the robot's teammate to verify that these dispositions are suitable, leading to appropriate levels of deeper, understanding-based trust [3].

We believe that while both proactive announcement and proactive explanation will help to build human-robot trust, proactive explanations will help to build deeper trust by shifting humans' mental models of robots from one in which they can only predict the robot's behavior and assess its reliability, to one in which they can also understand that behavior and assess the suitability of its dispositions. In this paper we present the results of a human subject experiment designed to test this hypothesis.

2   Human-Subject Experiment Design

2.1   Research Goal

The main research goal of our study is to understand the fundamental relationship between human-robot trust of robots and proactive explanatory behaviors. Specifically, we seek to assess the following two hypotheses.

Hypothesis 1: Robots that generate proactive explanatory behavior will be more trusted than robots that do not.
Hypothesis 2: Robots that generate proactive explanations will build greater human-robot trust than those that perform proactive announcements.

2.2 Experimental Context

To assess these hypotheses, we had participants collaboratively engage with robots in a novel resource management task, in which participants spent different types of resources while exploring an environment, while a robot positioned behind the player was responsible for "collecting" these resources. Through the course of this task, human teammates must spend different types of resources to explore different regions of their environment. The user's thus has an implicit need for resources to be collected that can be expected to be needed in the future, so that they avoid circumstances in which the type of resource required has run out. The type of resource that is actually collected at any given point is determined in two ways. First, the user can manually instruct the robot to collect a particular type of resource. Second, the robot can periodically decide on its own to collect a different type of resource than it is currently collecting, based on what it believes will be most needed, as assessed by the ratio of resources of a particular type revealed to be needed to explore the current exploration frontier, to the amount of resources available of that type:

$$resourceToCollect = argmin_{r \in R} \frac{stored_r}{needed_r} \tag{1}$$

When changing to collect a different resource, either at human direction or of its own volition, the robot rotated to face one of four placards signifying the to-be-collected resource type. The only way for participants to determine which resource was currently being collected by the robot was to physically turn their body to inspect the robot and observe which of these four placards the robot was facing.

2.3 Experiment Design

Our experiment used a within-subjects Latin Square design in which each participant engaged in three randomly and procedurally generated resource management tasks, in each of which the robot used a different order-counterbalanced explanatory behavior. Specifically, in each of the three experimental conditions, if the robot decided of its own volition to collect a new resource type, before turning to face the corresponding placard, it used the proactive explanatory behaviors dictated by its experimental condition:

1. **Proactive Announcement (PA):** In this condition, a robot autonomously switching to a different resource type informed participants of *what* resource it planned to collect, e.g., by saying "I am going to collect blue resources."
2. **Proactive Explanation (PE):** In this condition, a robot autonomously switching to a different resource type informed participants of both *what* resource it planned to collect, and *why*, e.g. by saying "I am going to collect red resources because you are low on red resources, but it seems that you may need a lot of them."
3. **No explanations (NE):** In this condition, no proactive explanatory behavior was used.

2.4   Experiment Procedure and Measures

Upon arriving at our laboratory, participants provided informed consent, were introduced to the resource management task and the turtlebot robot used in the experiment, and were given time to familiarize themselves with the task. Participants were guided to sit in front of a desktop computer, behind which were located the turtlebot robot and resource extraction points. Figure 1 represents the general setup of the human-subject experiment. Participants then participated in each of the three experiment blocks according to their Latin Square condition.

During each experiment block, participant actions were monitored using cameras mounted in the corners of the experimental space. Camera data was used to calculate an objective measure of human-robot trust, operationalized as the frequency and duration of humans' monitoring of the robots' behavior, with more frequent and/or higher-duration turns to observe the robot taken as evidence of lower trust in the robot (cp. [11,15]). At the beginning of the experiment and after each experimental block, participants completed the 14-item human-robot trust scale presented by Schaefer et al. [19] to self-report their trust in their robot teammate. Gain scores between baseline trust scores and post-condition trust scores were then used as a subjective measure of trust to supplement our observational measure.

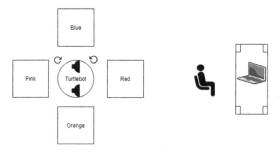

Fig. 1. Turtlebot robot setup for the human-subject experiment

2.5   Participants

32 participants (primarily university students) were recruited for the experiments from the Colorado School of Mines campus. While we initially intended to collect data from a greater number of participants, recruitment was cut short due to the COVID-19 global pandemic. The data from 21 participants were retained after removing data from participants who performed actions that required experimenter intervention (e.g., accidentally closing the testbed window). This human-subject experiment was approved by the Human Subjects Research (HSR) board at the Colorado School of Mines.

3   Results

3.1   Analysis

Our results were analyzed under a Bayesian analysis framework using JASP [9]. Results were analyzed using Bayesian analyses of variance (with experimental condition as the independent variable and subjective and objective trust measures as dependent variables), followed by Bayes Factor analyses and pairwise post-hoc Bayesian t-tests.

Bayes factors can roughly be interpreted as ratios of evidence in favor of alternative hypotheses relative to competing (e.g., null) hypotheses [8]. Bayes factors between 0.33 and 3 are generally taken as anecdotal evidence [10] insufficient to confirm or refute a hypothesis. Bayes factors between 0.33–0.10 or 3–10 provide substantial evidence against or for the hypothesis; Bayes factors between 0.03–0.10 and 10–30 provide strong evidence; and Bayes factor less than 0.01 or greater than 100 provide decisive evidence.

3.2   Subjective Measures

A Bayesian ANOVA provided moderate evidence against any effect of proactive explanatory behavior on self-reported human-robot trust (Bf 0.143). This Bayes Factor indicates that the collected data were approximately seven times less likely to have been generated under a model accounting for proactive explanatory behavior than under one that does not.

3.3   Objective Measures

Four video recordings were removed due to camera system failure, yielding 17 remaining video recordings, from which we analyzed the frequency and duration of human teammates' physical turns to monitor their robot teammate.

Table 1. Post Hoc comparisons of monitoring duration

	Prior odds	Posterior odds	$BF_{10,U}$	Error %
NE PA	0.587	0.258	0.440	6.640e−4
NE PE	0.587	13.766	23.436	5.425e−5
PA PE	0.587	0.215	0.366	0.003

Bayesian ANOVAs provided indecisive evidence, neither supporting nor refuting an effect of proactive explanation condition on duration (Bf 1.090) and frequency (Bf 1.313) of human-robot monitoring. To interrogate these inconclusive effects, we performed post-hoc pairwise comparisons between experimental conditions for both monitoring duration and frequency. Tables 1 and 2 presents the results of these pairwise post-hoc analyses. As visualized in Figs. 2a and 2b,

Table 2. Post Hoc comparisons of monitoring frequency

	Prior odds	Posterior odds	$BF_{10,U}$	Error %
NE PA	0.587	0.343	0.583	0.002
NE PE	0.587	3.130	5.328	1.591e−4
PA PE	0.587	0.222	0.377	0.002

our results suggest that human-robot monitoring was less frequent (Bf 5.328) and of lower duration (Bf 23.436) when proactive explanations were used than when no explanatory behavior was used, but provided indecisive evidence insufficient to either confirm or refute any difference in duration or frequency of human-robot monitoring between proactive announcements and either of the two other behaviors. Overall, these results generally support our subjective findings, but suggest that more observational data would be necessary to fully confirm them.

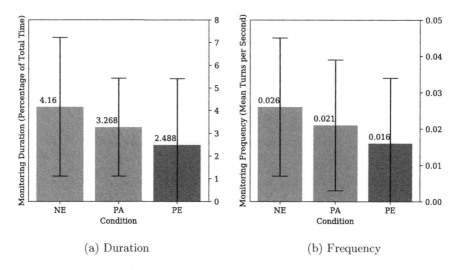

(a) Duration   (b) Frequency

Fig. 2. Effects of proactive explanatory behavior on duration and frequency of human-robot monitoring

4   Discussion

We hypothesized that proactive explanatory behavior would increase human-robot trust (H1), especially when proactive explanations rather than proactive announcements are used (H2). While these hypotheses were not supported by our subjective measures, they *were* partially supported by our objective measures. Specifically, our results suggest that robots that generated proactive explanations were more trusted than those that generated no proactive explanatory behaviors, but that more data must be collected before concluding precisely what effect is had by proactive announcements.

4.1   Participant Observations

In order to understand the discrepancy between our subjective and objective results, we begin with several interesting observations based on informal observations made by participants. Anecdotally, several times during our study, participants volunteered during the post-experiment debriefing that the task sessions with proactive explanatory behaviors made them feel that the robot was more of a teammate than a mere tool. This is a positive result given the research of Billings et al. [1], which suggests that people must perceive robots as teammates rather than tools to have effective interaction. This strongly suggests the need for future experimentation to assess whether this is a generalizable benefit of explanatory behaviors

In addition, several participants volunteered during post-experiment debriefing that they in actually preferred the robot's proactive announcements over proactive explanations, and that the proactive explanations felt wordy and unnecessary. We see two possible explanations for these observations. First, it could be the case that there is no difference between proactive announcements and proactive explanations in terms of understandability or desirability of robot behavior, similar to the observations made by Stange et al. in their examination of robot reactive explanations [20]. This explanation, however, would seem to contradict what is known about explanations in general and the benefits they provide in terms of transparency and facilitation of accurate mental modeling. Accordingly, a second, and we argue more likely explanation, is that while the robot's *first* proactive explanations may have facilitated accurate teammate modeling of the robot's belief- and desire-related dispositions, its subsequent explanations did not contribute any additional dispositional knowledge (thus leading to a violation of Grice's Maxim of Quantity [5], and human displeasure with the robot). This may explain our subjective results, and would suggest that for robots to jointly optimize human-robot trust, maximize robot likability, and minimize human workload, robots must themselves maintain sufficient models of their human teammates' beliefs about their own beliefs (second-order theory of mind [7]) in order to know *when* to generate proactive explanatory behaviors (and what kind to generate).

4.2   Impact of Explanatory Behaviors on "Theory of Mind"-Oriented Mental Models

Similarly, second-order theory of mind effects (in this case, triggering of human teammates' own first- and second-order "Theory-of-Mind'-oriented mental models with respect to the robots) may also help to explain the discrepancy between our subjective and objective results. Specifically, by generating proactive announcements, robots implicitly demonstrated an ability to reason and communicate that had been heretofore unobserved. This may well have led to increased perceptions of agency, capability, and intelligence; first-order theory of mind modeling with significant potential for impact on human-robot trust, especially capability-based trust. Similarly, generating proactive explanations that made reference to the human-robot team and their shared task may have well have led to increased perceptions of sociality and solidarity, i.e., willingness to help to fulfill the participants' needs; second-order theory-of-mind modeling with additional potential for impact on human-robot trust, especially reliability-based trust. These observations yield a number of testable hypotheses that must be explored in future work.

4.3   Impact of Explanatory Behaviors on the Nature of Trust

If the robot's explanatory behaviors do indeed trigger these Theory-of-Mind-oriented changes in participants' mental models of their robot teammate, this would have dramatic effects on participants' beliefs about the dispositions of the robot and the suitability thereof; in short, it would change precisely what it would even mean for participants to trust the robot.

In particular, we now consider what may have transpired specifically for participants who first encountered the robot in the condition in which it generated no explanatory behaviors, and the dramatic change in their mental model of the robot that would have transpired when, in their second task, the robot began generating proactive explanations. Before and after this shift, there was no change in the robot's actual behavior in terms of frequency of deviation from users' commands. Before the shift, we would presume that participants would interpret robots' deviations from commands as a low-level error in the robot's programming; the robot would perhaps have been perceived as being unreliable or incapable due to *unintentional* resource targeting "drift", rendering it untrustworthy in terms of successfully fulfilling the participant's commands.

In contrast, once the participant entered the second experimental condition and the robot began to generate announcements, it would become immediately obvious that the robot's deviations were in fact intentional acts of disobedience: the robot may in fact have been fully capable of achieving the user's goal, but unreliable in terms of its motivations and drive to comply; a gain in one dimension of trust coupled with a loss in another. Finally, once the participant entered the third experimental condition and the robot began to explain *why* it was deviating from participant commands, the robot would be perceived as being occasionally disobedient in order to better achieve the team's goals: a potential source for increased trust in terms of the robot's high level motivations, while still allowing for comparable sources of distrust (a) in the robot's willingness to accede to the participants' requests, and/or (b) in the quality of the robot's capability to successfully pursue a course of action that would actually lead to greater benefit to the team's goals than strict obedience would have.

In order to assess the plausibility of this narrative, we re-analyzed the data from only the seven participants who saw experimental conditions in the order {NE, PA, PE}, on a question-by-question basis. While the strength of our results were quite weak due to the small sample size, even with this small sample a number of interesting results emerged.

1. First, we examined the perceived predictability of the robot (Survey item 4). Even though the robot behaved identically in all three conditions in terms

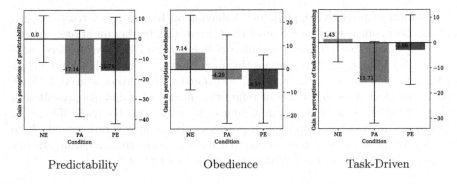

Fig. 3. Effects of proactive explanatory behavior on duration and frequency of human-robot monitoring on perception of the robot as predictable, obedient, and task-driven

of its actual decisions, a Bayesian ANOVA demonstrated that perceived predictability may have significantly dropped from the No Explanation condition to the Proactive Announcement condition (Bf 1.275, Fig. 3a), indicating that once the robot began speaking, the notion of what it even meant for the robot to be "predictable" may have changed substantially.

2. Second, we examined the perception that the robot performed "exactly as instructed" (Survey item 13). A Bayesian ANOVA demonstrated that this perception may have dropped from condition to condition, resulting in a difference from first to last condition in terms of perceived disobedience (Bf 1.341, Fig. 3b).

3. Finally, we examined perceptions that the robot acted to meet the needs of the task (Survey item 10). A Bayesian ANOVA demonstrated that beliefs to this effect may have dropped substantially once the robot began explaining its actions (Bf 2.443), but that this drop in trust may have recovered once the robot began explaining the team-driven reasoning behind its actions (Bf 0.984, Fig. 3c).

The small sample size on this analysis means that these results are ultimately inconclusive, but suggest that additional data could provide evidence for a substantial change in mental models between conditions, in which participants initially view the robot as a faulty tool, then as needlessly disobedient, and finally as disobedient for the purposes of the task.

5   Conclusion

In this work, we conducted a human-subject study to better understand the relationship between human-robot trust and robots' proactive explanations. Our results suggested that proactive explanations lead to increased human-robot trust as assessed through objective observational means. Our results were inconclusive, however, with respect to proactive announcements and the precise effects of this form of proactive explanatory behavior on human-robot trust. As discussed above, our results raise a number of interesting further questions pertaining to the effects that proactive explanatory behaviors might have on users' mental models of robots, and the impact this might have on the fundamental nature of human-robot trust. In future work, additional investigation is needed (1) to collect sufficient data to confirm or refute the inconclusive findings presented in this paper, (2) to identify the optimal policies for navigating the tradeoff between trust and workload that is presented during explanation generation; and (3) to interrogate the new research questions that have been identified regarding theory of mind and the fundamental nature of human-robot trust.

Acknowledgments. This work was supported by an Early Career Faculty grant from NASA's Space Technology Research Grants Program.

References

1. Billings, D.R., Schaefer, K.E., Chen, J.Y.C., Hancock, P.A.: Human-robot interaction: developing trust in robots. In: Proceedings of the International Conference on HRI (2012)
2. Billings, D., Schaefer, K., Llorens, N., Hancock, P.: What is trust? Defining the construct across domains. In: Proceedings Conference of the American Psychological Association (2012)
3. Danks, D.: The value of trustworthy AI. In: Proceedings of the AIES (2019)
4. De Graaf, M.M., Malle, B.F.: How people explain action (and autonomous intelligent systems should too). In: 2017 AAAI Fall Symposium Series (2017)
5. Grice, H.P.: Logic and conversation. In: Syntax and Semantics 3: Speech Acts (1975)
6. Helldin, T.: Transparency for future semi-automated systems: effects of transparency on operator performance, workload and trust. Ph.D. thesis, University of Skövde (2014)
7. Hiatt, L.M., Trafton, J.G.: Understanding second-order theory of mind. In: ACM/IEEE International Conference on Human-Robot Interaction (2015)
8. Jarosz, A.F., Wiley, J.: What are the odds? A practical guide to computing and reporting Bayes factors. J. Probl. Solving **7**(1), 2 (2014)
9. JASP Team: JASP (version 0.12.2) [bibcomputer software] (2020)
10. Jeffreys, H.: The Theory of Probability. OUP Oxford, Oxford (1998)
11. Lee, J.D., See, K.A.: Trust in automation: designing for appropriate reliance. Hum. Factors **46**(1), 50–80 (2004)
12. Lyons, J.B.: Being transparent about transparency: a model for human-robot interaction. In: 2013 AAAI Spring Symposium Series (2013)
13. McManus, T., Holtzman, Y., Lazarus, H., Anderberg, J., Ucok, O.: Transparency, communication and mindfulness. J. Manag. Dev. **25**, 1024–1028 (2006)
14. Mercado, J.E., Rupp, M.A., Chen, J.Y.C., Barnes, M.J., Barber, D., Procci, K.: Intelligent agent transparency in human-agent teaming for multi-UxV management. Hum. Factors **58**(3), 401–415 (2016)
15. Muir, B.M., Moray, N.: Trust in automation. Part II. Experimental studies of trust and human intervention in a process control simulation. Ergonomics **39**(3), 429–460 (1996)

16. Neerincx, Mark A., van der Waa, Jasper, Kaptein, Frank, van Diggelen, Jurriaan: Using perceptual and cognitive explanations for enhanced human-agent team performance. In: Harris, Don (ed.) EPCE 2018. LNCS (LNAI), vol. 10906, pp. 204–214. Springer, Cham (2018). https://doi.org/10.1007/978-3-319-91122-9_18

17. Ososky, S., Schuster, D., Phillips, E., Jentsch, F.G.: Building appropriate trust in human-robot teams. In: 2013 AAAI Spring Symposium Series (2013)

18. Rieser, Verena, Lemon, Oliver: Natural language generation as planning under uncertainty for spoken dialogue systems. In: Krahmer, Emiel, Theune, Mariët (eds.) EACL/ENLG -2009. LNCS (LNAI), vol. 5790, pp. 105–120. Springer, Heidelberg (2010). https://doi.org/10.1007/978-3-642-15573-4_6

19. Schaefer, K.: The perception and measurement of human-robot trust. Ph.D. thesis, University of Central Florida (2013)

20. Stange, S., Kopp, S.: Effects of a social robot's self-explanations on how humans understand and evaluate its behavior. In: Proceedings of the International Conference on HRI (2020)

21. Wang, N., Pynadath, D.V., Hill, S.G.: Trust calibration within a human-robot team: comparing automatically generated explanations. In: Proceedings of the HRI (2016)

Language Learning with Artificial Entities: Effects of an Artificial Tutor's Embodiment and Behavior on Users' Alignment and Evaluation

Astrid Rosenthal-von der Pütten[1]([⊠]) [iD], Carolin Straßmann[2] [iD],
and Nicole Krämer[3] [iD]

[1] iTec - Chair for Individual and Technology,
RWTH Aachen University, 52078 Aachen, Germany
`arvdp@humtec.rwth-aachen.de`
[2] Institute of Computer Science, University of Applied Sciences Ruhr West,
46236 Bottrop, Germany
`carolin.strassmann@hs-ruhrwest.de`
[3] Social Psychology: Media and Communication, University of Duisburg-Essen,
47057 Duisburg, Germany
`nicole.kraemer@uni-due.de`
`https://www.itec.rwth-aachen.de`, `https://informatik.hs-ruhrwest.de`,
`https://www.uni-due.de/sozialpsychologie/kraemer.shtml`

Abstract. Based on the assumption that humans align linguistically to their interlocutor, the present research investigates if linguistic alignment towards an artificial tutor can enhance language skills and which factors might drive this effect. A 2×2 between-subjects design study examined the effect of an artificial tutor's embodiment (robot vs. virtual agent) and behavior (meaningful nonverbal behavior vs. idle behavior) on linguistic alignment, learning outcome and interaction perception. While embodiment and nonverbal behavior affects the perception of the tutor and the interaction with it, no effect on users' linguistic alignment was found nor an effect on users learning outcomes.

Keywords: Social robot · Virtual agent · Embodiment · Nonverbal behavior

1 Introduction

When native speakers and non-native speakers meet, native-speakers often adapt to non-natives in order to foster mutual understanding and successful communication, sometimes with the negative outcome of interfering with successful second language acquisition (SLA) on a native-speaker level. As a matter of course, native speakers do not mean to decrease learning progress, but rather engage in an automatic behavior of adaptation to their interlocutor. Using artificial tutors could help to overcome this bias as they can be designed to not or only

A. R. Wagner et al. (Eds.): ICSR 2020, LNAI 12483, pp. 96–107, 2020.
https://doi.org/10.1007/978-3-030-62056-1_9

sightly adapt to human users thereby given a better example of correct speech. Moreover, the phenomenon of computer talk, i.e. users more strongly align to computers in order to ensure communicative success, could be exploited for SLA using the exaggerated alignment tendencies of users confronted with computers. Alignment is seen as core to language acquisition, thus, also to SLA [1] and the tendency of non-natives to align to technology in a learning setting could be exploited for SLA. Admittedly, system characteristics have to be taken into account and their potential inhibiting or facilitating effects need to be explored. Hence, the current work investigates if linguistic alignment towards an artificial tutor can enhance language skills and which factors might drive this effect.

1.1 Linguistic Alignment HCI and Second Language Acquisition

Whilst in conversation, interaction partners align linguistically on different levels, for instance, regarding accent or dialect [9], lexical choices and semantics [6] as well as syntax [4]. Similar tendencies have been observed in interactions with artificial interlocutors mirroring the effects of alignment with regard to prosody, lexis, and syntax (for an overview cf. [5]). Comparative studies indicate that people tend to show stronger alignment with computers presumably to compensate the computers weaker communicative abilities, a phenomenon known as computer talk [5]. However, "when social cues and presence as created by a virtual human come into play, automatic social reactions appear to override initial beliefs in shaping lexical alignment" [3] resulting in slight decreases of the computer talk phenomenon. A first study with native and non-native speakers showed that both groups aligned lexically to a virtual tutor [17]. In a precursor to the current study we explored whether alignment with an artificial tutor in a SLA setting improves language skills and whether this is influenced by the tutor's embodiment (voice-only, virtual or physical embodiment) or type of speech output (text-to-speech or prerecorded language, cf. [16]). Although participants aligned to the artificial tutor in all conditions comparably to previous studies, the alignment was not correlated with post-test language skills. Moreover, the variation of system characteristics had barely influence on the evaluation of the system or participants' alignment behavior, neither for embodiment nor for quality of speech output. The present study shall provide additional evidence on whether this finding is persistent and whether the specific behavior of the artificial tutor influences the results.

1.2 Effects of Differently Embodied Artificial Entities

Virtual agent or robot? This is an ongoing debate in the research community developing and evaluating embodied conversational agents. Both embodiment types provide unique interaction possibilities, but also come along with certain restrictions (for an overview cf. [10,14]. Indeed, studies comparing the two embodiment types have led to inconsistent results. While a majority of study results supports the notion that robots are superior to virtual representations (e.g. perceived social presence [7], entertainment and enjoyment [12], trustworthiness [12], persuasiveness [13], and users' task performance [2]), other results suggest virtual representations are more beneficial especially in conversational settings [13]. In fact, there seems to be an interaction effect of embodiment and task [11] suggesting that robots might be better suited in (hands-on) task-related scenarios, while virtual agents could be beneficial for purely conversational settings. This is probably due to the perception of different bodily-related capabilities of virtual agents and robots which might lead to different expectations for the subsequent interaction and thus also different outcomes as suggested by the EmCorp framework of Hoffmann et al. [10]. In this regard the displayed nonverbal behavior plays an important role. For instance, it was suggested that if an entity has the capability for nonverbal behavior, but does not use, for instance, gestures in situations where they would be beneficial this leads to negative evaluations [10]. Only two studies have looked into the effect of different embodiment types on participants' linguistic behavior. Fischer [8] found that verbosity and complexity of linguistic utterances did not differ between a virtual agent or a robot, but participants used more interactional features of language towards the robot such as directly addressing it by its name. The interplay of embodiment and linguistic alignment has been investigated in our prior work [16] where we found no differences in users' evaluation of and alignment towards the different version of the tutor. However, in this study we did not explicitly address the nonverbal behavior of the artificial tutor and accordingly the perception of bodily-related or communicative capabilities of the entities which will be manipulated in the present work.

1.3 Research Questions and Hypotheses

In this work, the two central questions we examine are whether an artificial tutor's embodiment (virtual agent vs. robot) influences participants' evaluation of the tutor, their lexical and syntactical alignment during interaction and their learning effect after the interaction (RQ1) and whether displayed nonverbal behavior will affect users' alignment (RQ2). Since previous work showed that robots can elicit more positive evaluations than virtual agents [10,14], we additionally propose that the robot will be rated more positively than the virtual agent (H1). Based on the EmCorp Framework by Hoffmann et al. [10], evaluations regarding the perceived bodily-related and communicative capabilities should differ (H2). Moreover, we investigate the effect of expressive nonverbal behavior on evaluation assuming that gestures lead to more positive evaluations (H3).

2 Method

2.1 Experimental Design and Independent Variables

In order to address our research questions we used a 2×2 between-subjects design with embodiment and nonverbal behavior as independent variables.

Regarding the embodiment, participants either interacted with the physically embodied Nao robot or with a virtual version of the Nao robot (cf. Fig. 1). Secondly, we varied whether the artificial tutor exhibited meaningful nonverbal behavior (usage of deictic, iconic, and beat gestures and socio-emotional gestures) or only displayed idle behavior (very subtle changes in head position to show the robot is somewhat "alive").

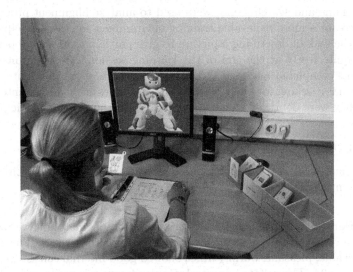

Fig. 1. Participant playing the guessing game with the virtual Nao

2.2   Participants and Procedure

Eighty-five volunteers (33 female, 52 male) aged between 18 and 40 years (M = 24.81, SD = 3.84) participated in this study. Participants stem from more than 35 different countries, speak more than 24 different native languages and exposed different levels of German language skills (minimum of an intermediate level). Participants were recruited on campus or in German classes in the local adult education center. The study was approved by the local ethics committee. The procedure, game materials and coding procedures for verbal behaviors are identical to those used in our prior work [16]. Upon arrival to the first study session participants read and signed informed consent. They completed two language tests: a test on grammar and reading and listening comprehension and a so called C-Test (www.c-test.de), a cloze test which addresses language skills with regard to different dimensions. Finally, they were invited for a second appointment. Based on their test results, their country of origin and first language, respectively, participants were distributed equally across conditions where possible for the second session. On the second appointment participants were instructed about the different tasks to be solved with the artificial tutor.

Each task was again explained by the tutor during the interaction (cf. Fig. 1). Participants were also given a folder with detailed instructions in case they did not understand the tutor. Participants completed five tasks: 1) introducing themselves, 2) describing a picture in detail, 3) playing a guessing game, 4) playing a search game, and 5) again describing a picture. The order of tasks was always the same for all participants. The first two tasks were used to make participants comfortable at speaking loudly to the system. The two structured games (guessing game and search game) were used to analyze alignment processes. In order to create a more believable training environment for the participants, we repeated the task of describing a picture to give participants another possibility to speak quite freely at the end of the learning session. After the interaction, participants completed a second C-Test as a measure of learning outcome and a questionnaire asking for their experiences and assessment of the interaction. Finally, they were debriefed, reimbursed (€10) and thanked for participation.

2.3   Dependent Variables: Self Report

For all items in all scales participants gave ratings on a 5-point Likert scale ranging from "I do not agree" to "I agree".

Person Perception. As for the person perception of the robot, we measured **Likability** with a scale of eight ad-hoc generated items (e.g., The robot is friendly, likable, pleasant, warm) which showed good internal consistency, Cronbach's $\alpha = .824$. The robots perceived **Competence** was measured with eight ad-hoc generated items (e.g., The robot is intelligent, competent ; Cronbach's $\alpha = .751$). Lastly, we measured perceived **Autonomy** of the robot with five ad-hoc generated items. One item (The robot is not autonomous) seemed to have caused rating artefacts because of the negation and thus was deleted from the scale to increase internal consistency. The remaining four items in the scale showed good internal consistency (The robot is self-dependent, free, self-determined, responsible for its actions; Cronbach's $\alpha = .810$).

Bodily-Related Capabilities. In order to measure whether the physical or virtual embodiment of the artificial tutor results in different perceptions of their bodily-related capabilities we used 17 ad-hoc generated items that covered three factors: **Presence**, **Mobility and Tactile Interaction** and **(Shared) Perception**. This ad-hoc generated scale was actually a precursor of the EmCorp Scale [10]. Perceived presence of the robot was assessed using three items and showed sufficient internal reliability (The robot was in the same room with me; The robot was very present; The robot was not really present; Cronbach's $\alpha = .716$). We used four items to measure perceptions of Mobility and Tactile Interaction which also showed good internal consistency (The robot is able to move around in the room; The robot is able to walk towards me; The robot would have been able to touch me at any time; The robot is able to touch and move objects; Cronbach's $\alpha = .790$). Lastly, we assessed users' evaluation of what and how well the robot perceives and reacts towards the users using seven items which showed very good internal consistency (e.g., The robot was able to perceive my behavior; The robot was not able to understand my behavior; The robot reacted appropriately to my behavior; The robot did not perceive my behavior ; Cronbach's $\alpha = .840$).

Communicative Capabilities. We assessed the robots perceived *Verbal Capabilities* with five ad-hoc generated items asking how well the robot understood and produced verbal contributions in the conversation (e.g., The robot understood me well; The robot did not hear me; The robot did not understand me ; Cronbach's $\alpha = .840$, cf. [15]). Moreover, we measured the robot's capabilities to understand and produce nonverbal behavior. *Nonverbal Understanding* was measured using six items (e.g., The robot noticed my gestures; The robot noticed my facial expressions; The robot was able to interpret my facial expressions and gestures correctly ; Cronbach's $\alpha = .802$), and *Nonverbal Production* was measured using three items (The robot's gestures were expressive; The robot's gestures were unambiguous and clear to me; I understood the robot's gestures; Cronbach's $\alpha = .849$).

2.4   Dependent Variables: Linguistic Alignment

Participants played two structured games (guessing game and search game) in which the tutor and the participant took turns in constructing sentences. The verbal utterances of these games were analyzed regarding users' linguistic alignment with the artificial tutor. We used the exact same coding procedures as in our previous work (cf. [16]). Participants' utterances during the interaction with the robot were transcribed into plain text and coded along a predefined coding-scheme. All transcripts were coded by two individual coders and the inter-coder-reliability demonstrated a satisfying accordance between both coders (Guessing Game Cohen's Kappa = .948; Search Game Cohen's Kappa = .861).

Fig. 2. Left: Examples for interaction cards in the guessing game; Right: Example card for the search game

Guessing Game. The first structured game was a dialog based game (based on [4,16]) in which participants took turns with the tutor in guessing two persons and their interaction on so-called interaction cards (cf. Fig. 2) by asking only yes-or-no questions (e.g. "Is the person on the left side female?"; "Is the person on the right side old?", "Is the interaction between the two friendly?"). There were two rounds of guessing in which the system first guessed the participant's card and then the participant guessed the system's card. The system's utterances between the two rounds varied in lexical choices when describing the features of the displayed characters (age (old vs. advanced in years), gender (male/female vs. a man/ a woman), facial hair (mustache vs. beard)). Moreover, the system used different verbs (has vs. wears), adjectives (friendly vs. kind) and syntactical constructions (person on the left side vs. the left person; active vs. passive). In total, we introduced seven variations. Participants' verbal utterances were analyzed with regard to their lexical choices. A ratio was built for alignment for each of the seven aspects.

Search Game. In the second structured game participants and the tutor took turns in describing picture cards to one another by forming sentences based on the two characters (e.g. policeman and cowboy), the verb (e.g. to give), and the object (e.g. balloon, cf. Fig. 2) displayed on the card (cf. [4,16]. Participants had two sets of cards (reading cards and search cards). The task was to take a card from the first card set (reading cards) and to form a sentence based on the characters, verb and object displayed on the card (e.g., The balloon was given to the policemen by the cowboy). The interaction partner's task was to search in their set of "search cards" for this exact card. The system began the interaction and built a sentence. The participant had to find the card and put it away and in turn had to take a card from the "reading" set and form a sentence so that the tutor can find the card in its (imagined) search card pool and put it away. In total, the system read out 15 cards, thereby formed 15 sentences in three "blocks". The first block i.e. the first five sentences were formed as passive voice, the second five sentences as prepositional phrase and the last as accusative. Three ratios were built for syntactical alignment within the three blocks.

2.5   Dependent Variables: Learning Outcome

Participant's German language skills before and after the interaction were assessed with a so called C-Test (www.c-test.de), a cloze test which addresses language skills with regard to different dimensions. Scores were compared to test for learning gain after interaction. The C-Test has been used previously for assessing (improvement in) language skills. It usually comprises five short pieces of self-contained text (ca. 80 words each) in which single words are "damaged". In order to reconstruct the sentences, participants have to activate their language fluency. Text pieces were taken from reading exams on an academic language level. Tests are analyzed by true-false answers. Participants could reach up to 100 points.

3   Results

3.1   Evaluation of the Artificial Tutor

Person Perception. With two-factorial ANOVAs we tested the effect of the tutor's embodiment and non-verbal behavior on users' evaluations of the tutor's Likability, Competence, and Autonomy (for descriptive data cf. Table 1). No main or interaction effects emerged for the three person perception scales.

Table 1. Means and standard deviations of the ratings of bodily-related capabilities and person perception of the tutor

	Bodily-related Capabilities			Person Perception		
	Perception	Mobility	Presence	Competence	Autonomy	Likability
	M (SD)	M (SD)	M (SD)	M (SD)	M (SD)	M (SD)
Virtual						
Idle	2.83 (.99)	1.22 (.39)	3.76 (1.19)	3.21 (.62)	2.21 (.95)	3.08 (.77)
nv	2.73 (.77)	1.64 (.69)	3.53 (.99)	3.52 (.74)	2.43 (.99)	3.26 (.89)
Robot						
Idle	3.02 (.84)	1.59 (.90)	4.19 (.77)	3.45 (75)	2.17 (1.1)	3.13 (.94)
nv	3.07 (.97)	2.05 (.95)	4.16 (.86)	3.25 (.75)	2.22 (.98)	3.13 (.72)
Total	2.92 (.89)	1.63 (.81)	3.91 (.99)	3.36 (.72)	2.20 (1.0)	3.15 (.82)

Bodily-Related Capabilities. With two-factorial ANOVAs we tested the effect of the tutor's embodiment and non-verbal behavior on users' evaluations of bodily-related capabilities: *(Shared) Perception, Mobility, and Presence* (for descriptive data cf. Table 1).

The ANOVA on the dependent variable *(Shared) Perception* yielded no significant main effects and also no interaction effect for embodiment and non-verbal behavior. The results of the second ANOVA demonstrated significant main effects of embodiment ($F(1,81) = 5.45$, $p = .022$, $\eta_p^2 = .06$) and nonverbal behavior ($F(1,81) = 6.86$, $p = .011$, $\eta_p^2 = .08$) on the perceived *Mobility* of the tutor. Participants evaluated an embodied robot with higher mobility than a virtual agent. Moreover, a tutor using nonverbal behavior elicited a higher perception of mobility than a tutor that merely showed idle behavior. No interaction effect of embodiment and nonverbal behavior occurred for perceived mobility. For the dependent variable *Presence* there was a significant difference between the embodied robot and the virtual agent ($F(1,81) = 6.30$, $p = .014$, $\eta_p^2 = .07$), while no main effect emerged for the robot's behavior, and again, no interaction effect of embodiment and nonverbal behavior was present. Hence, participants who interacted with an embodied robot indicated higher presence of their interlocutor compared to those interacting with the virtual agent.

Communicative Capabilities. To investigate the effect of the experimental conditions on the perception of the tutor's communicative capabilities, three two-factorial ANOVAs were calculated (for descriptive data cf. Table 2). For the dependent variable *Verbal understanding* a significant main effect emerged for the tutor's embodiment ($F(1,81) = 4.89$, $p = .030$, $\eta_p^2 = .06$). Participants indicated a stronger perception of verbal understanding for virtual agents than for robots. No main effect for the tutor's nonverbal behavior occurred, nor did an interaction effect. There were also no main or interaction effects for the dependent variable *Nonverbal Understanding*. However, a main effect emerged for *Nonverbal Production*. The tutor displaying meaningful nonverbal behavior was rated higher with regard to Nonverbal Production than a tutor using idle behavior ($F(1,81) = 8.30$, $p = .005$, $\eta_p^2 = .09$). The ANOVA revealed no significant effect of embodiment nor was an interaction effect found.

Table 2. Means and standard deviations of the ratings of communicative capabilities

	Communicative Abilities		
	Verbal understanding	Nonverbal understanding	Nonverbal production
	M (SD)	M (SD)	M (SD)
Virtual idel	4.43 (.52)	2.07 (.79)	2.49 (1.24)
Virtual nv	4.31 (.64)	2.29 (.88)	3.24 (1.20)
Robot idel	4.17 (.60)	2.49 (.76)	2.81 (1.23)
Robot nv	3.93 (.87)	2.50 (.1.0)	3.56 (1.11)
Total	3.01 (.69)	2.34 (.88)	3.03 (1.24)

3.2   Linguistic Alignment and Learning Outcome

Guessing Game. With the guessing game we examined participants' syntactical and lexical alignment during the interaction. As described above, ratios were calculated for alignment (usage of the same lexical/syntactical choice (e.g. lexical choice mustache)/occurrence of the concept (e.g. number of expressions referring to a beard)). To examine whether embodiment or nonverbal behavior affects participants' linguistic alignment, we conducted ANOVAs with both factors as independent variables and the seven ratios for linguistic alignment as dependent variables. There were no significant differences between the groups nor did we find significant interaction effects.

Search Game. The search game focused on the syntactical alignment. Regarding all 15 sentences, participants most often used accusative, followed by prepositional phrases and passive voice. In order to examine whether embodiment or nonverbal behavior of the artificial tutor affects participants' syntactical alignment, we conducted ANOVAs with both factors as independent variables and the alignment ratios. There were no significant differences between groups nor did we find significant interaction effects.

Learning Outcome. To explore whether the interaction has a positive effect on participants' language skills we analyzed the results of the C-Tests prior and after the interaction. Thus, we conducted split-plot ANOVAs with the group factors embodiment and nonverbal behavior and repeated measures for the C-Test scores. The scores did not differ between the two measuring points. Moreover, the experimental conditions showed no effect.

4   Discussion

With this work we contribute another puzzle piece to the ongoing debate of whether virtual agents or robots provide more benefits to the user. Previous work predominantly found that robots were superior over virtual agents (cf. [10,14] for an overview). Still there is a lack of research on behavioral effects, particularly, with regard to linguistic behavior. This work presents an empirical study that investigates the effect of an artificial tutor's embodiment and nonverbal behavior on the tutor's perception, users' linguistic alignment and their learning outcome.

Our first central question to this study was whether an *artificial tutor's embodiment* (virtual agent vs. robot) influences participants' evaluation of the tutor, their lexical and syntactical alignment during interaction and their learning effect after the interaction (RQ1). Based on prior work, we hypothesized that the robot will be rated more positively than the virtual agent (H1). We did not find support for our hypothesis, since users' evaluations of the two systems did not differ with regard to perceived likability, autonomy or competence. However, we did find support for our assumption that evaluations regarding the perceived bodily-related and communicative capabilities of the tutor varies with embodiment (H2). Our results suggest that while a robot is perceived as being more present and having greater ability for mobility and tactile interaction than a virtual agent, the virtual agent was attributed higher communicative abilities with regard to verbal understanding. This is in line with the suggestions raised in the Embodiment and Corporeality Framework by Hoffmann et al. [10]. The Framework proposes that the core ability that is directly related to the physical embodiment of robots is Corporeality, i.e., the realism and material existence of the entity in the real world. Hence, the physical embodiment of the robotic artificial tutor should lead to higher ratings in corporeality and physical presence which is supported by the findings of the current study. The framework also proposes that evaluations of perceived bodily-related capabilities are additionally influenced by moderating variables such as the interaction scenario. Although communicative abilities such as verbal understanding, are not part of the EmCorp Framework, a similar proposal can be stated to explain the finding that the virtual agent is perceived as more verbally capable. The majority of the interaction with the participants was conversational, not involving the manipulation of objects. Although participants were using game material, the task itself was not of physical nature like, for instance, in the Tower of Hanoi task in which objects have to be moved as the main task, but it was to produce sentences. Prior work has demonstrated that virtual agents seem to be preferred over physically embodied robots for purely conversational tasks (cf. [11]). Our finding that the virtual agent was attributed higher communicative abilities with regard to verbal understanding supports this assumption. With regard to participants' linguistic behavior and alignment tendencies, we found that the tutor's embodiment showed no effect. Users align toward virtual agents and robots in the same way. Moreover, both forms of embodiment elicited similar learning outcomes. This is against a body of research that predicts benefits of robots over virtual agents. At the same time, these results are in line with prior work that investigated the effect of embodiment on linguistic alignment in the setting of second language-acquisition [16] confirming this previous result that embodiment has no influence on users alignment and learning outcomes. In consequence, linguistic tutors do not need to be embodied as robots, which can save resources and make artificial tutors more accessible.

The second central research question was concerned with the effect of the artificial tutor's nonverbal behavior on users' linguistic behavior (RQ2). Again, no differences in participants' linguistic alignment and learning outcome was found indicating the tutor's nonverbal behavior did not influence how people align towards the tutor. Further, we assumed that the display of meaningful nonverbal behavior (in contrast to subtle idle behavior) leads to more positive evaluations (H3). Likewise to the non-existent effect of embodiment no positive effects were found for evaluations regarding likability, autonomy and competence. However, the nonverbal behavior of the tutor affected the perceived bodily-related and communicative capabilities. Those tutors using nonverbal behavior elicited a stronger perception of mobility and tactile interaction and a stronger production of nonverbal behavior. These effects are again in line with the EmCorp Framework [10] which suggests that the display or the absence of nonverbal behavior serves as a mediator for perceived capabilities, especially for agents who are technically able to show, for instance, gestures and in interaction settings in which the usage of gestures is helpful (e.g. pointing to game material).

The current study as well as our prior work [16] indicate on the one hand that the idea of exploiting human's tendencies of computer talk for SLA is not an effective measure, although participants in both studies showed great interest in using the robot or virtual agent for language training. On the other hand, both studies provided valuable insides into the effects of design decisions for artificial tutors such as embodiment and expressive nonverbal behavior.

References

1. Atkinson, D., Churchill, E., Nishino, T., Okada, H.: Alignment and interaction in a sociocognitive approach to second language acquisition. Mod. Lang. J. **91**(2), 169–188 (2007). https://doi.org/10.1111/j.1540-4781.2007.00539.x

2. Bartneck, C.: Interacting with an embodied emotional character. In: Forlizzi, J., Hanington, B. (eds.) Proceedings of the 2003 international conference on Designing pleasurable products and interfaces, p. 55. ACM, New York, NY (2003). https://doi.org/10.1145/782896.782911

3. Bergmann, K., Branigan, H.P., Kopp, S.: Exploring the alignment space. Lexical and gestural alignment with real and virtual humans. Front. ICT 2 (2015). https://doi.org/10.3389/fict.2015.00007

4. Branigan, H.P., Pickering, M.J., Cleland, A.A.: Syntactic co-ordination in dialogue. Cognition **75**(2), B13–B25 (2000). https://doi.org/10.1016/S0010-0277(99)00081-5

5. Branigan, H.P., Pickering, M.J., Pearson, J., McLean, J.F.: Linguistic alignment between people and computers. J. Pragmatics **42**(9), 2355–2368 (2010). https://doi.org/10.1016/j.pragma.2009.12.012

6. Brennan, S.E., Clark, H.H.: Conceptual pacts and lexical choice in conversation. J. Exp. Psychol. Learn. Memory Cogn. **22**(6), 1482–1493 (1996). https://doi.org/10.1037/0278-7393.22.6.1482

7. Fasola, J., Mataric, M.: A socially assistive robot exercise coach for the elderly. J. Hum.-Robot Interact. **2**(2) (2013). https://doi.org/10.5898/JHRI.2.2.Fasola

8. Fischer, K., Lohan, K.S., Foth, K.: Levels of embodiment. In: Yanco, H. (ed.) Proceedings of the seventh annual ACMIEEE International Conference on Human-Robot Interaction, p. 463. ACM, New York, NY (2012). https://doi.org/10.1145/2157689.2157839

9. Giles, H.: Accent mobility: a model and some data. Anthropol. Linguist. **15**, 87–105 (1973)

10. Hoffmann, L., Bock, N., Rosenthal von der Pütten, A.M.: The peculiarities of robot embodiment (EmCorp-Scale). In: Kanda, T., Abanović, S., Hoffman, G., Tapus, A. (eds.) HRI'18, 5–8 March 2018, Chicago, IL, USA, pp. 370–378. ACM, New York, NY, USA (2018). https://doi.org/10.1145/3171221.3171242

11. Hoffmann, L., Krämer, N.C.: Investigating the effects of physical and virtual embodiment in task-oriented and conversational contexts. Int. J. Hum.-Comput. Stud. **71**(7–8), 763–774 (2013). https://doi.org/10.1016/j.ijhcs.2013.04.007

12. Kidd, C.D., Breazeal, C.: Effect of a robot on user perceptions. In: 2004 IEEE/RSJ International Conference on Intelligent Robots and Systems (IROS), pp. 3559–3564. IEEE, Piscataway, N.J (2004). https://doi.org/10.1109/IROS.2004.1389967

13. Kiesler, S., Powers, A., Fussell, S.R., Torrey, C.: Anthropomorphic interactions with a robot and robot-like agent. Social Cogn. **26**(2), 169–181 (2008). https://doi.org/10.1521/soco.2008.26.2.169

14. Li, J.: The benefit of being physically present: a survey of experimental works comparing copresent robots, telepresent robots and virtual agents. Int. J. Hum.-Comput. Stud. **77**, 23–37 (2015). https://doi.org/10.1016/j.ijhcs.2015.01.001

15. Rosenthal-von der Pütten, A.M., Krämer, N.C., Herrmann, J.: The effects of humanlike and robot-specific affective nonverbal behavior on perception, emotion, and behavior. Int. J. Soc. Robot. **10**(5), 569–582 (2018). https://doi.org/10.1007/s12369-018-0466-7

16. Rosenthal-von der Pütten, A.M., Straßmann, C., Krämer, N.C.: Robots or agents – neither helps you more or less during second language acquisition. In: Traum, D., Swartout, W., Khooshabeh, P., Kopp, S., Scherer, S., Leuski, A. (eds.) IVA 2016. LNCS (LNAI), vol. 10011, pp. 256–268. Springer, Cham (2016). https://doi.org/10.1007/978-3-319-47665-0_23

17. Wunderlich, H.: Talking like a machine?! Linguistic alignment of native-speakers and non-native speakers in interaction with a virtual agent. Bachelor Thesis, University of Duisburg-Essen (2012)

An Exploration of Simple Reactive Responses for Conveying Aliveness Using the Haru Robot

Yurii Vasylkiv[1]([✉]) [ID], Heike Brock[3] [ID], Yu Fang[3] [ID], Eric Nichols[3] [ID], Keisuke Nakamura[3] [ID], Serge Thill[2] [ID], and Randy Gomez[3] [ID]

[1] Department of Computer Science, University of Manitoba, Winnipeg, Canada
vasylkiy@myumanitoba.ca
[2] Donders Institute for Brain, Cognition, and Behavior, Radboud University, Nijmegen, The Netherlands
s.thill@donders.ru.nl
[3] Honda Research Institute Japan Co., Ltd., Wako, Japan
{h.brock,yu.fang,e.nichols,keisuke,r.gomez}@jp.honda-ri.com

Abstract. This paper describes the development of simple robotic reactive responses for the tabletop robot Haru. While reactive responses in organisms are associated with a biological purpose, they may also play a role in conveying agency in the sense of aliveness. In this paper, we are therefore interested in the design of simple reflexive behaviors that can convey a sense of agency for the Haru robot (see Fig. 1). To this end, we explore what kind of reactive responses humans find appropriate for a platform like Haru in different situations. Specifically, we conducted an elicitation study in which participants were asked to design Haru's reactive response similar to either (1) that of a human, (2) a pet animal, or (3) in a freestyle manner befitting its design. Since Haru is neither clearly anthropomorphic nor zoomorphic, it is not straightforward what model would be most suitable to drive its behaviors. Our results show that, while participants design different types of behavior depending on their experimental group, it is possible to identify a range of behaviors used by all. This indicates that it is possible to design intuitively understandable reactive behaviors for a novel companion robot whose form has no clear analogue in nature. These behaviors are unique to Haru but contain elements from human and pet animal behaviors.

Keywords: Social robot interaction · Reactive behaviors · Behavior design

1 Introduction

Humans attribute agency and intrinsic mental states such as intention even to clearly inanimate things [12]. While this can raise interesting questions philosophically and ethically [20,28,31,32], this ability is often considered a useful

© Springer Nature Switzerland AG 2020
A. R. Wagner et al. (Eds.): ICSR 2020, LNAI 12483, pp. 108–119, 2020.
https://doi.org/10.1007/978-3-030-62056-1_10

Fig. 1. Artist's rendition of Haru's involuntary reactions due to external stimuli

resource in social robotics where it may play a role in improving interactions between humans and robots [17]. There is thus a rich body of work on modulating the perception of robots through the use of life-like features appropriate for the platform. The Softbank robots Pepper[1] and Nao[2], for example, display life-like movements in line with their humanoid form while zoomorphic robots such as Miro [5] or Paro [16] display behaviors suitable for their animal-like form.

An interesting question in this context is what aspects of robot behavior can communicate agency, and how this depends on whether the robot is perceived, for example, as anthropomorphic, zoomorphic, or machine-like. Sciutti and her colleagues have for instance long argued that motor resonance – the idea that the actions and intentions of a suitably designed robot can be interpreted through the human motor system – is crucial for human-robot interaction [3,24,25], leading to an argument for humanoid robots in particular. More generally, the ability to (appear to) convey intentions plays an important role [12] and can be achieved, for example, using gaze behavior to facilitate aspects such as turn taking [15,26,30]. Pepper's face-tracking abilities in its default mode can likewise be understood to be a type of intentional behavior, however, the simple breathing movements that the Nao robot displays by default when idle are just biomimetic.

In this paper, we are interested in another type of biological behavior that is not per se intentional but might convey agency: direct couplings between perception and action similar to reflexes, linking a specific stimulus to a specific response. In robotics, reflexes have long primarily been used in locomotion control [6,7,13,21] although reactive robotics as popularised by Brooks [4] also arguably make use of simpler reflexive behaviors. More specifically, we are interested in reactive behaviors that are associated with internal mental and affec-

---

[1] https://www.softbankrobotics.com/emea/en/pepper.

[2] https://www.softbankrobotics.com/emea/en/nao.

tive states (such as fright responses). The main reason for this is that reflexive behaviors are easy to implement: they are typically short, specific responses to specific stimuli. An important question that arises in this context is then how such reactive responses should be designed to be appropriate, in particular for social robots like Jibo[3] and Haru [10] that have no obvious biological correlates.

2 Background

The tabletop robot Haru [10] is a research platform to explore various research topics in embodied communication. One of our core research topics is the development of a companion species [11], that ultimately leads to the forging of a bond between a human and a social robot similar to the bond shared by other social creatures [1]. As depicted in Fig. 2, Haru's multimodal communication can be expressed through actuations (Left) and audio-visuals (Right). Base rotation allows the body of the robot to have an azimuth orientation; neck leaning makes it possible for the neck to move forward and backwards; eye stroke enables the eye to pop out and retract in; eyes tilt allows the eyes to face up and down; eyes roll allows in-out rotation of the eyes parallel to the plane in which the robot is facing at. A 3-inch stereo colour LCD screen displays the eyes of the robot, whereas the eye display can be controlled to move within the LCD screen; eye goggles are addressable LED strips wrapped around the borders of the eye; sound through stereo speakers make it possible for vocalizations; mouth & cheek can be displayed through an addressable LED matrix.

Haru is designed to be an animation-like robot character similar to the characters in animation movies. Haru's platform allows users to choreograph animation-like performances using the modalities mentioned above [9]. It supports animation tools to design movements and audio-visual support, resulting in animation-like performance delivery – the same quality as the animation characters' performance in movies. Indeed, the robot platform has the potential to study and develop a new companion species [11].

3 Goals and Hypothesis

In this study, we suppose Haru as a living entity and as such, subject to direct couplings between perception and action. In particular, we want to explore Haru's reactive response to external stimuli as if Haru is alive. We limit our study to a simple form of behavior with near instantaneous and simple reaction. The response has to be reactive similar but not limited to a reflex with a loose definition. Unlike distinctly designed robots (i.e. humanoid, zoomorphic, etc.) that have biological correlates, Haru's design does not have a straightforward model to follow in the real world. This paper aims to build a deeper understanding of how to frame Haru's reactive responses. In particular, we investigate the following:

---

[3] https://www.jibo.com/.

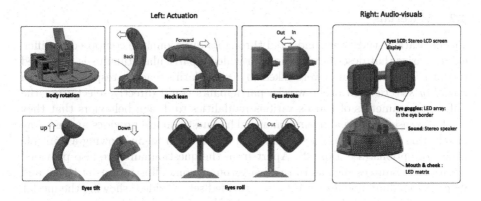

Fig. 2. Tabletop robot modalities: actuation, visualization and vocalization

Commonality. The similarity in reactive response with known models such as humans and animals (i.e., pets). This could allow a better understanding of Haru's communicative modalities as this suggests that Haru's behavior is not completely foreign and can be framed with known biological correlates.

Novelty. The unique framing of Haru's reactive response befitting its distinct design. This would support Haru's role as new companion species capable of new and novel behaviors.

To carry out this task we conducted an elicitation study in which we presented the participants a variety of stimuli and asked them to design Haru's reactive response discussed in Sect. 4.

4   Research Methods

4.1   Elicitation Study

We explore Haru's simple involuntary response to given stimuli framed on a human model, a pet animal model, and a possible novel framing befitting its design by means of an elicitation experiment. The experiment was carried out online in two countries: Canada and Japan. Participants for the study were recruited from local universities ($N = 60$), their age ranged between 22 and 35; $M = 31.2$, $SD = 6.24$) and had technical background in robotics. The participants were distributed equally over three groups: *Group A* – Human model, *Group B* – Pet Animal model and *Group C* – Freestyle. Groups A and B were asked to design Haru's involuntary response by strictly adhering to human and pet animal models respectively, while Group C participants were asked to take an open mindset approach to freely design the robot's reactive behaviors as if Haru is a new kind of species. Haru's involuntary response in our questionnaire was defined by a set of selected modalities that form the response itself (see Sect. 4.4). The questionnaire takes 40 to 60 min to complete.

4.2   Materials

The elicitation study was conducted through a questionnaire composed of different scenarios that describe situations in which a particular stimulus is presented to Haru. The participants were asked to design Haru's reactive response through *modality selection*; in other words, participants could directly select from the different parameters of Haru's various modalities to design behaviors that they wanted to associate to a given scenario. The questionnaire provides an easy way of selecting modality parameters through a pull-down menu showing a multiple choice of options (see Table 2). Apart from the questionnaire, we also provided additional resources such as Haru's background, some illustrations of Haru, and its corresponding modalities. We also provided sets of videos showing the modalities in action, and some filled-in example scenarios – all aimed to improve the participants' understanding and familiarization of Haru and its modalities in general.

4.3   Scenarios

Each scenario describes a situation with a corresponding stimulus that is presumed to evoke Haru. The scenarios were developed through a review of direct coupling between perception and action, resulting in reactive behaviors for both humans [2,8,18,19,27] and pet animals [14,22,29]. We selected a shortlist of 10

Table 1. List of scenarios involving stimulus for modality composition

No	Scenario description
1	Haru is feeling the heat as its internals reaching excessive high temperature
2	Haru is reaching mechanical limits as its motors are subjected to an excessive speed limit or range of motions close to breaking
3	A person or object just suddenly appears on Haru's peripheral view
4	A strong bright light is shed onto Haru's face
5	Someone is calling Haru's name
6	An abrupt/unknown sound is emitted to the right side of Haru
7	A human or an object is approaching Haru
8	Haru is confronted with a scary beast and has no choice but to fight
9	Haru is confronted with a scary beast and has no choice but to escape
10	Haru is hungry (needs to be connected to the power supply)

scenarios that are deemed relevant to Haru as depicted in Table 1. In the actual questionnaire, a generic question: "How do you imagine Haru's short reactive behavior would be when caught in a given situation?", is provided.

4.4   Modality Composition

For each of the scenarios discussed, the three groups of participants were to design Haru's reactive behavior through modality composition. We introduced elements in the modalities that the participants can activate or modify. The modalities and the corresponding elements are listed in Table 2. A total of 16 elements are introduced, and participants can activate, set, or modify each element through an easy pull-down menu provided in the questionnaire. While there were no restrictions for their choices, we encouraged participants to compose the simplest reactive response as possible, something instantaneous and to limit their selection to a minimum – only the ones they deem important and appropriate. We provided video examples on how to compose the modalities (see Sect. 4.2). An example of composing Haru's modality using Table 2 is shown in Fig. 3.

Table 2. List of Haru's modalities and corresponding elements

Modalities	Elements
Eyes LCD	Dilation (small, medium, large, closed), Blinking (slow, medium, fast, no-blinking), Movement (left, center, right)
Eye Goggles	Area (off, full, top, bottom), Colors (green, red, blue), Intensity (weak, medium, strong), Pattern (solid, checked, flashing, other)
Eyes Stroke	Movement (in, out, in-out, stop, neutral position)
Eyes Tilt	Movement (up, down, up-down, stop, neutral position)
Eyes Roll	Movement (in, out, in-out, stop, neutral position)
Body Rotation	Movement (left, right, left-right, stop, neutral position)
Neck Lean	Movement (in, out, in-out, stop, neutral position)
Mouth	Shape (closed, open-small, open-large), Tongue (inside, outside, inside-outside), Cheek color (green, red, other)
Vocalization	Sound (beep, other)

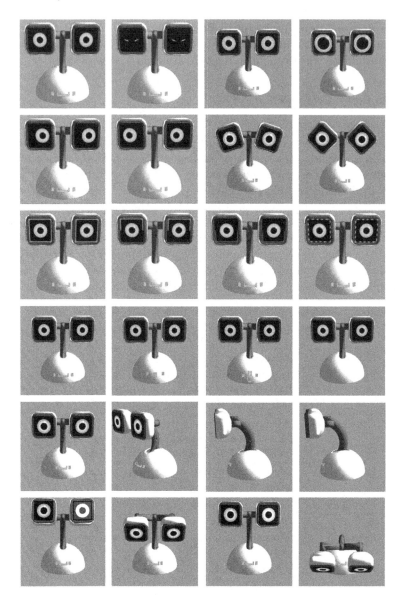

Fig. 3. Haru modalities used in experiments. Rows from the top are 1) eye blinking eye dilation; 2) eye movement and eye roll movement; 3) eye goggle variations; 4) mouth tongue animations; 5) body movement and eye stroke movement; and 6) eye tilt movement and neck lean movement.

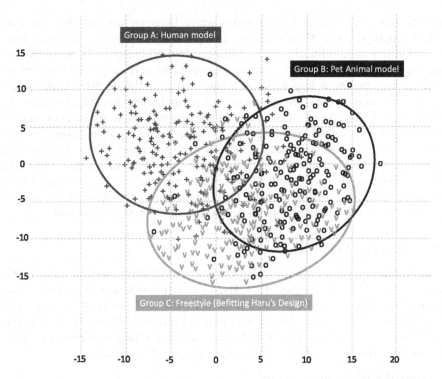

Fig. 4. The PCA visualizes how the three different groups designed Haru's reactive behavior.

5 Results and Discussion

5.1 Principal Components Analysis

We collected the data from the questionnaire filled by the three different groups of participants (A:Human model, B:Animals/Pet model, and C:Freestyle). We analyzed how these three groups designed Haru's reactive behaviors across the different scenarios through modality selection. In particular, we are interested in finding out the similarities (or uniqueness) of their designs. Each element in the modality selection is treated as a feature variable. In total, we have 10 scenarios, 16 features, and 20 participants ($10 \times 16 \times 20$) for each group. To reduce the number of variables, we performed Principal Component Analysis (PCA) for each group's data, and plot the output along with the two main principal components as shown in Fig. 4.

There are three main observations that we can draw from the visualization. First, each of the three groups is distinguishable by their clusters as being, at least to some degree, distinct. Second, these clusters overlap with each other as depicted by the intersection. The overlap represents the similarity in terms of usage of the modalities of Haru among the three participant groups. This suggests that there are at least some reactive behavior designs that are universally appropriate to Haru's design, irrespectively of whether humans were instructed to consider human-like, pet-like, or freestyle models. In particular, it also suggests that humans do attribute human-like and animal-like behaviors to Haru. This finding is important as it may facilitate the intuitive understanding of Haru's non-verbal communication behaviors by humans [23]. Moreover, it can be argued that, despite the similarities, Haru can frame its reactive behaviors uniquely befitting its design despite the shared similarities between humans and pet animals, suggesting that Haru may have the potential to define a new type of social companion robot [11]. Lastly, it can be observed that Group B (Animal/Pet model) and Group C (Freestyle) are more similar to each other than with Group A (Human model). This implies that participants treat Haru's reactive behavior to more closely resemble that of a pet than a human.

5.2   Primary Modalities Used

In this section, we briefly summarise the main modalities used by each of the three groups. Overall, we find that Haru's reactive behavior is muted when framed by a human model by Group A. An increase in activity as expressed by movements is observed when framed by a pet model by Group B. The activation of modalities and movement activity is most prominent in Group C, where we can, in particular, note the active use of the goggles modality.

1. **Framed with human model**
   - *Eyes:* changes in eye direction and pupil diameter reflecting shifts in attention, arousal, and cognition, as well as the blinking elicited by any stimulation such as touching, light flash, or loud sound.
   - *Gaze movement:* simulation of the robot's gaze by a combination with eye movement, body rotation (left/right) and eyes tilt (up/down) as typically coordinated during gaze shifts of humans.
   - *Mouth & cheek animation:* changes of the mouth shape (i.e. size) and the color of the cheek conveying emotions and physiological responses such as heart rate, blood pressure, and skin temperature upon affective states. The use of the tongue is notably absent.
2. **Framed with pet animals model**
   - *Body movement:* turning to the left or right such as imitating the tracking of a human "master", or constantly rotating the base from left to right such as imitating the hunting of one's own tale.
   - *Neck lean movement:* lowering the neck reflecting a downward head pose, or directing the head upwards to reflect an upwards look towards a human "master".
   - *Eyes roll and stroke movement:* rotating the eyes outside as a representation of a side-wards head roll, or repeatedly moving the eyes in and out (rotation, stroke) as imitating a wagging tail.
   - *Mouth tongue animation:* exposition of the tongue and its respective in and out movement as frequently observed in dogs. The use of cheek is notably absent.

- *Sound emission:* the emission of a beep as a robot-representation of barking, or additional abstract sounds that can be associated with growling, panting or purring.

3. **Freestyle befitting Haru's design**

- *Goggles:* the activation of the goggles through the use of colors, patterns, intensity, etc. is the favorite and most commonly used modality that distinguished it from human and pet models. The lighting mechanism reinforces the "robotic" nature of Haru used to communicate information and affective states.
- *Remaining modalities:* closely resemble the pet animal model, except with a higher degree of activity and exaggeration.

6   Conclusion

In this paper, we explored the use of simple reactive behaviors to convey aliveness – an aspect of agency – of a robot platform. We were specifically interested in how appropriate behaviors can be designed for platforms whose form has no clear analogue in nature; that is, they are neither clearly anthropomorphic nor zoomorphic. We found that, when human participants were asked to design reactive behaviors from the perspective of specific models (human, pet-like, or freestyle), the groups each produced unique designs that nonetheless had some overlap. This indicates that it is possible to design intuitively understandable behaviors for a form factor such as Haru's, independently of the mental model humans have of the platform.

References

1. Haru: An experimental social robot from honda research. http://spectrum.ieee.org/automaton/robotics/home-robots/haru-an-experimental-social-robot-from-honda-research. Accessed: 02 Feb 2020
2. Admoni, H., Scassellati, B.: Social eye gaze in human-robot interaction: a review. J. Hum.-Robot Interact. **6**(1), 25–63 (2017). https://doi.org/10.5898/JHRI.6.1.Admoni
3. Bisio, A., et al.: Motor contagion during human-human and human-robot interaction. PLoS ONE **9**(8), e106172 (2014). https://doi.org/10.1371/journal.pone.0106172
4. Brooks, R.A.: Elephants don't play chess. Robot. Auton. Syst. **6**(1–2), 3–15 (1990). https://doi.org/10.1016/s0921-8890(05)80025-9
5. Collins, E.C., Prescott, T.J., Mitchinson, B., Conran, S.: MIRO: a versatile biomimetic edutainment robot. In: Proceedings of the 12th International Conference on Advances in Computer Entertainment Technology - ACE 2015. ACM Press (2015). https://doi.org/10.1145/2832932.2832978
6. Dubrawski, A., Crowley, J.L.: Learning locomotion reflexes: a self-supervised neural system for a mobile robot. Robot. Auton. Syst. **12**(3–4), 133–142 (1994). https://doi.org/10.1016/0921-8890(94)90020-5

7. Espenschied, K.S., Quinn, R.D., Beer, R.D., Chiel, H.J.: Biologically based distributed control and local reflexes improve rough terrain locomotion in a hexapod robot. Robot. Auton. Syst. **18**(1–2), 59–64 (1996). https://doi.org/10.1016/0921-8890(96)00003-6

8. Fang, Y., Nakashima, R., Matsumiya, K., Kuriki, I., Shioiri, S.: Eye-head coordination for visual cognitive processing. PLoS ONE **10**(3), e0121035 (2015). https://doi.org/10.1371/journal.pone.0121035

9. Gomez, R., Nakamura, K., Szapiro, D., Merino, L.: A holistic approach in designing tabletop robot's expressivity. In: Proceedings of the International Conference on Robotics and Automation (2020)

10. Gomez, R., Szapiro, D., Galindo, K., Nakamura, K.: Haru. In: Proceedings of the 2018 ACM/IEEE International Conference on Human-Robot Interaction. ACM, February 2018. https://doi.org/10.1145/3171221.3171288

11. Haraway, D.J.: The Companion Species Manifesto: Dogs, People, and Significant Otherness, vol. 1. Prickly Paradigm Press, Chicago (2003)

12. Heider, F., Simmel, M.: An experimental study of apparent behavior. Am. J. Psychol. **57**(2), 243 (1944). https://doi.org/10.2307/1416950

13. Huang, Q., Nakamura, Y.: Sensory reflex control for humanoid walking. IEEE Trans. Robot. **21**(5), 977–984 (2005). https://doi.org/10.1109/tro.2005.851381

14. Jaynes, J.: Imprinting: the interaction of learned and innate behavior: I. development and generalization. J. Comp. Physiol. Psychol. **49**(3), 201 (1956)

15. Jokinen, K., Nishida, M., Yamamoto, S.: On eye-gaze and turn-taking. In: Proceedings of the 2010 Workshop on Eye Gaze in Intelligent Human Machine Interaction, pp. 118–123. ACM (2010)

16. Kidd, C., Taggart, W., Turkle, S.: A sociable robot to encourage social interaction among the elderly. In: Proceedings 2006 IEEE International Conference on Robotics and Automation, 2006. ICRA 2006. IEEE (2006). https://doi.org/10.1109/robot.2006.1642311

17. Kwak, S.S., Kim, Y., Kim, E., Shin, C., Cho, K.: What makes people empathize with an emotional robot?: the impact of agency and physical embodiment on human empathy for a robot. In: 2013 IEEE RO-MAN. IEEE, August 2013. https://doi.org/10.1109/roman.2013.6628441

18. Mukuno, K., et al.: Three types of blink reflex evoked by supraorbital nerve, light flash and corneal stimulations. Jpn. J. Ophthalmol. **27**(1), 261–70 (1983)

19. Nakajima, K., Minami, T,. Nakauchi, S.: Interaction between facial expression and color. Sci. Rep. **7**(41019) (2017). https://doi.org/10.1038/srep41019

20. Nyholm, S.: Attributing agency to automated systems: reflections on human–robot collaborations and responsibility-loci. Sci. Eng. Ethics **24**(4), 1201–1219 (2017). https://doi.org/10.1007/s11948-017-9943-x

21. Park, J.H., Kwon, O.: Reflex control of biped robot locomotion on a slippery surface. In: Proceedings 2001 ICRA IEEE International Conference on Robotics and Automation (Cat. No.01CH37164). IEEE (2001). https://doi.org/10.1109/robot.2001.933264

22. Pavlov, I.P., Gantt, W.: Lectures on conditioned reflexes: twenty-five years of objective study of the higher nervous activity (behaviour) of animals (1928)

23. Sandry, E.: Robots and Communication. Springer, London (2015). https://doi.org/10.1057/9781137468376

24. Sciutti, A., et al.: Measuring human-robot interaction through motor resonance. Int. J. Soc. Robot. **4**(3), 223–234 (2012). https://doi.org/10.1007/s12369-012-0143-1

25. Sciutti, A., Bisio, A., Nori, F., Metta, G., Fadiga, L., Sandini, G.: Robots can be perceived as goal-oriented agents. Interact. Stud. **14**(3), 329–350 (2014). https://doi.org/10.1075/is.14.3.02sci
26. Sciutti, A., Schillingmann, L., Palinko, O., Nagai, Y., Sandini, G.: A gaze-contingent dictating robot to study turn-taking. In: Proceedings of the Tenth Annual ACM/IEEE International Conference on Human-Robot Interaction Extended Abstracts - HRI 2015 Extended Abstracts. ACM Press (2015). https://doi.org/10.1145/2701973.2702055
27. Snowden, R., Snowden, R., Thompson, P., Troscianko, T.: Basic Vision: An Introduction to Visual Perception. OUP Oxford (2012)
28. Thellman, S., Ziemke, T.: The intentional stance toward robots: conceptual and methodological considerations. In: The 41st Annual Conference of the Cognitive Science Society, 24–26 July, pp. 1097–1103, Montreal (2019)
29. Tierney, A.J.: The evolution of learned and innate behavior: contributions from genetics and neurobiology to a theory of behavioral evolution. Anim. Learn. Behav. **14**(4), 339–348 (1986). https://doi.org/10.3758/BF03200077
30. Yoshikawa, Y., Shinozawa, K., Ishiguro, H., Hagita, N., Miyamoto, T.: The effects of responsive eye movement and blinking behavior in a communication robot. In: 2006 IEEE/RSJ International Conference on Intelligent Robots and Systems, pp. 4564–4569. IEEE (2006)
31. Ziemke, T., Thill, S.: Robots are not embodied! conceptions of embodiment and their implications for social human-robot interaction. In: Proceedings of Robo-Philosophy 2014: Sociable Robots and the Future of Social Relations, pp. 49–53. IOS Press BV, Amsterdam (2014). https://doi.org/10.3233/978-1-61499-480-0-49
32. Ziemke, T., Thill, S., Vernon, D.: Embodiment is a double-edged sword in human-robot interaction: ascribed vs. intrinsic intentionality. In: Cognition as a Bridge Between Robotics and Interaction workshop in Conjunction with HRI2015 (2015)

On the Role of Personality and Empathy in Human-Human, Human-Agent, and Human-Robot Mimicry

Giulia Perugia$^{(\boxtimes)}$, Maike Paetzel, and Ginevra Castellano

Uppsala University, Uppsala, Sweden
`giulia.perugia@it.uu.se`

Abstract. Facial mimicry is crucial in social interactions as it communicates the intent to bond with another person. While human-human mimicry has been extensively studied, human-agent and human-robot mimicry have been addressed only recently, and the individual characteristics that affect them are still unknown. This paper explores whether the humanlikeness and embodiment of an agent affect human facial mimicry and which personality and empathy traits are related to facial mimicry of human and artificial agents. We exposed 46 participants to the six basic emotions displayed by a video-recorded human and three artificial agents (a physical robot, a video-recorded robot, and a virtual agent) differing in humanlikeness (humanlike, characterlike, and a morph between the two). We asked participants to recognize the facial expressions performed by each agent and measured their facial mimicry using automatic detection of facial action unit activation. Results showed that mimicry was affected by the agents' embodiment, but not by their humanlikeness, and that it correlated both with individual traits denoting sociability and sympathy and with traits advantageous for emotion recognition.

Keywords: Facial mimicry · Social robots · Virtual agents

1 Introduction

Facial mimicry is an interesting social cue as it communicates rapport, liking, and social affiliation [19]. It refers to the spontaneous activation of congruent facial muscles in response to the observation of a facial expression from another individual (e.g., smile to a smile) [8]. The mimicry-liking relation is extremely compelling for Human-Robot and Human-Agent Interaction (HRI and HAI). Indeed, human facial mimicry could be used to measure affiliation attitudes towards artificial agents during first encounters, but also to gauge the quality of interaction in prolonged and repeated encounters.

Spontaneous facial mimicry has been mostly studied in Human-Human Interaction (HHI), and has only recently been investigated in HRI and HAI [20,21,26,31]. The majority of research on facial mimicry focuses on whether emotional expressions are mimicked [20], under which circumstances [21], and

© Springer Nature Switzerland AG 2020

A. R. Wagner et al. (Eds.): ICSR 2020, LNAI 12483, pp. 120–131, 2020.

https://doi.org/10.1007/978-3-030-62056-1_11

which are the characteristics of the expresser that elicit more intense mimicry [20,30]. For example, an artificial agent that is physically present and human-like seems to elicit stronger mimicry than its virtual non-humanlike counterpart [20,31]. From other work on human-human mimicry, we also know that the individual traits of a person influence their mimicking response. For instance, people high in empathy mimic emotional expressions already at an automatic level of information processing (56 ms) [37]. What we do not know, however, is whether empathy and personality traits affect human-agent and human-robot mimicry and if the embodiment of an agent causes certain traits to be more salient than others for the sake of mimicry. This paper thus *explores whether the humanlikeness and embodiment of an agent affect facial mimicry and which personality and empathy traits are related to facial mimicry of human and artificial agents.*

In the study presented in this paper, we exposed participants to the six basic emotions [14] displayed by a human agent and three artificial agents differing in embodiment and humanlikeness. We asked participants to recognize the facial expressions performed by each agent and measured their facial mimicry using a computer vision technique. We then assessed whether their empathy and personality traits correlated with facial mimicry. The results highlight that embodiment is more crucial than humanlikeness to determine facial mimicry and that different embodiments correspond to different patterns of correlations between individual traits and facial mimicry.

2   Related Work

Human-Human Facial Mimicry. From Social Psychology and Psychophysiology, we know that observing pictures of happy and angry faces spontaneously elicits the activation of congruent facial muscles, respectively the zygomaticus major (i.e., smiling), and corrugator supercilii (i.e., frowning) [10]. This phenomenon occurs within 300–400 ms of exposure and is largely uncontrolled and subperceptual [11]. Facial mimicry is crucial in social interactions as it promotes liking and social affiliation [6]. Not only does it signal higher rapport when the relation between mimicker and expresser is already established [18], but it is also used to pursue affiliation between new acquaintances [6]. Indeed, the literature highlights that initial liking increases facial mimicry in first encounters [27] and the mere goal to affiliate intensifies people's mimicking response [25].

Human-Agent and Human-Robot Facial Mimicry. Due to the difficulty of studying face-to-face mimicry with human subjects, human-human mimicry has been mostly studied with static images and videos. The use of virtual and robotic agents gives the unique possibility to examine dynamic facial expressions occurring when the expresser and the observer are co-present. In spite of this advantage, the literature has only recently addressed facial mimicry in HAI and HRI. This is probably due to the fact that robotic platforms enabling a proper manipulation of facial expressions became available only recently.

Related work on facial mimicry in HAI and HRI found similar results to those highlighted by human-human studies. Mattheij et al. (2013) revealed that people mimic all facial expressions displayed by virtual agents with a slight preference towards happiness and surprise [26]. Philip et al. (2018) discovered that expressions of joy, anger, and sadness are all congruently mimicked, but joy and anger cause stronger activation when the agent's face is dynamic, rather than static, and displays a real human character, rather than a virtual one [31]. Hofree et al. (2014) discovered that people mimic the facial expressions of happiness and anger displayed by a highly realistic android robot only when it is physically present in the same room with them [20]. By compiling the results from HAI and HRI, it becomes evident that differences in mimicking responses point to differences in salience between real human faces and virtual faces, and between physically co-present agents and video-recorded ones. However, to the best of our knowledge, *no research has studied facial mimicry covering the four types of embodiment described by Philip et al. [31] and Hofree et al. [20]*, namely a video-recording of a human, a physical robot, a video-recording of the physical robot, and a virtual agent. Moreover, *no study has verified the salience of humanlikeness for facial mimicry within these embodiments*.

Influence of Empathy Traits on Facial Mimicry. A non-negligible feature of facial mimicry is its relationship with emotion recognition and emotional contagion, which are respectively linked to cognitive empathy (i.e., the ability to infer the mental states of others [3]) and emotional empathy (i.e., a person's response to another person's emotional state [13]). Niedenthal et al. (2010) theorized that facial mimicry is the embodied motor simulation of an observed emotion that serves the purpose of emotion recognition [29], a theory that has been proven only for ambiguous, subtle facial expressions [15]. Regarding emotional contagion, there is extant evidence that facial mimicry elicits congruent emotional experiences. Dimberg (1988) found that people exposed to happy faces show congruent mimicry and also report an increased experience of happiness [9].

Facial mimicry is not only connected with emotion recognition and emotional contagion, but is also influenced by people's empathy traits. Sonnby-Borgström et al. (2003) found out that subjects high in empathy show mimicry responses to facial expressions of happiness and anger already at an automatic level of information processing (56 ms), while subjects low in empathy do not, even at a more controlled level of information processing (2350 ms). Moreover, Drimalla et al. (2019) and Rymarczyk et al. (2019) found a strong positive association between people's scores of emotional empathy and their level of facial mimicry, both for positive [12] and negative emotions [35]. In spite of the strong tie between empathy and human-human mimicry, *the influence of empathy traits on human-agent and human-robot mimicry has, to our knowledge, never been studied. Hence, it is still to discover whether empathy traits influence facial mimicry both in interactions with virtual agents and with physical robots.*

Influence of Personality Traits on Facial Mimicry. Personality is an individual trait that has been found to strongly correlate with (and sometimes even predict) rapport in HAI and HRI, but whose connection with facial mimicry is understudied. Cerekovic et al. (2016) revealed that people who score high in extraversion and agreeableness report higher rapport with virtual agents [5]. Along this line, Rosenthal-von der Pütten et al. (2010) found participants high in extraversion to be more talkative during interactions with a virtual agent and participants high in agreeableness to report more positive emotions after the interaction [34]. This result was confirmed by Ivaldi et al. (2016) in the context of HRI [24]. Although facial mimicry serves a social affiliative function that is strictly connected with rapport building, the extent to which facial mimicry is affected by personality traits is unknown. The literature on human-human mimicry overlooked the importance of personality traits in healthy subjects. Similarly, HAI and HRI never studied the link between personality traits and facial mimicry. In fact, *it is yet to discover whether the same personality traits that predict rapport in HAI and HRI, namely extraversion and agreeableness, predict facial mimicry towards human, virtual, and robotic agents.*

3   Research Questions

To study facial mimicry, we employed all embodiments described by Philip et al. (2018) [31] and Hofree et al. (2014) [20]: a video-recorded human, a physical robot, a video-recorded physical robot, and a virtual agent. Furthermore, to verify the salience of humanlikeness for facial mimicry, we varied the appearance of the artificial agents and made them humanlike, characterlike, or a morph between the humanlike and the characterlike. This manipulation served to answer the following research question: **(RQ1)** *Does the humanlikeness and embodiment of an agent affect the mimicking responses of participants?*

In order to disclose whether a tie between facial mimicry and individual traits exists not just in HHI, but also in HAI and HRI, we assessed participants' empathy and personality traits at the beginning of the experimental session, and correlated them with their mimicking responses. This way, we could answer a further research question: **(RQ2)** *Are empathy and personality traits correlated with participants' mimicry? Do these correlations differ across embodiments?*

4   Method and Material

We chose a mixed experimental design with two independent variables: (1) *type of embodiment* (within-subject) with four levels: a physical robot, a video-recording of the physical robot, a virtual agent, and a human video (Fig. 1 (a)) and (2) *level of humanlikeness* (between-subject) with three levels: characterlike, humanlike, and morph (Fig. 1 (b)). Participants were randomly assigned to one level of humanlikeness and observed the humanlike, characterlike, or morph agent displaying facial expressions of the six basic emotions [14] in each embodiment. While the artificial agents varied in terms of humanlikeness, the video-recorded

(a) Artificial Embodiment Conditions   (b) Facial Texture Conditions

Fig. 1. (a) Embodiments left to right - virtual agent, physical robot, video-recorded robot; (b) facial textures left to right - characterlike, morph, humanlike agent.

human was the same across conditions. The emotional expressions were presented twice for each embodiment in randomized order. The order of presentation of the embodiments was randomized with a Latin Squares technique.

4.1   Participants

Forty-six participants were recruited from a study program at Uppsala University to take part in the study. We excluded two participants due to occlusions in their video recordings and technical issues. The final sample of participants was composed of 44 people (10 female; $M = 26.39$, $SD = 4.31$) randomly divided into the three conditions representing the levels of humanlikeness: characterlike (N = 15; 4 female; $M = 25.00$, $SD = 4.09$), humanlike (N = 14; 3 female; age $M = 26.36$, $SD = 2.98$) and morph (N = 15; 3 female; age $M = 27.80$, $SD = 5.28$). None of the participants had previously interacted with the Furhat robot.

4.2   Embodiment and Synthesis of Facial Expressions

The experiment was conducted using three artificial embodiments (Fig. 1) and a video-recording of a human subject. For the physically co-present robot, we chose Furhat as a robotic platform [2]. Furhat is a blended embodiment consisting of a rigid mask on which a facial texture is projected from within.

We designed three facial textures to apply to both the virtual agent and the Furhat robot. The humanlike texture was based on a picture of a real human face (Fig. 1 (b) right). The characterlike texture was Furhat's default facial texture with sketched eyebrows, lips, and eyes (Fig. 1 (b) left). The morph texture was created by blending the humanlike and characterlike textures (Fig. 1 (b) center). The video of the human subject was taken from the MUG database [1].

The human subject in the MUG database was video-recorded while performing the six basic emotions by moving the specific AUs described by Ekman [16]. His facial dynamics were used as reference to synthesize the dynamics of facial expressions for the artificial agents. A researcher trained in the Facial Action Coding System (FACS) remodelled the dynamics of the human expressions as closely as possible by using the facial animation tool provided by the IrisTK framework [36]. Since the IrisTK gesture editor did not allow to control all AUs separately, the facial expressions displayed by the artificial agents and by the human agent were slightly different. However, an online study conducted on Amazon Mechanical Turk revealed no systematic difference in emotion recognition between the artificial and human stimuli.

4.3 Measures

During the experiment, participants were recorded with two LOGITECH C920 HD PRO webcams (30 fps), one positioned on their side, the other in front of them (focusing on their face). We collected questionnaires at four different points in time during the experiment. The first questionnaire (Q1) was filled out at the beginning of the experiment. It included a demographic questionnaire (10 questions), the short version of the *Big Five Personality Traits* [33] (sub-scales: Extraversion, Agreeableness, Conscientiousness, Emotional Stability, and Openness to Experience), and the *Interpersonal Reactivity Index* (IRI, sub-scales: Fantasy, Empathic Concern, and Perspective-Taking [7]). The second questionnaire (Q2) was completed after each facial expression and was meant to assess whether participants correctly recognized the observed emotion and how confident they were about the selected emotion. The third questionnaire (Q3) was filled out after each embodiment to measure participant's perception of the agents. It was composed of excerpts of the *Godspeed questionnaire* [4], the *Social presence* questionnaire [17], and the *Uncanniness* questionnaire [32]. At the end of the session, the experimenter carried out a short semi-structured interview with the participants (Q4). This paper is part of a larger research project. In it, we focus on Q1 and leave aside Q2, Q3 and Q4. These latter questionnaires are used to answer a different set of research questions.

4.4 Experimental Set-Up and Procedure

The experiment was carried out in a laboratory at Uppsala University (Sweden). The area where the experiment took place was separated from the rest of the laboratory by a curtain. Participants were seated at a table 100 cm from the Furhat robot or from the monitor displaying the agent. The size of the agents on the screen was adjusted to match the size of the Furhat robot.

Upon arrival of the participant, the experimenter explained the study procedure. Subsequently, s/he asked the participant to read and sign the consent form. Participants then filled out Q1 on the iPad. After that, they were told that their task was to watch the facial expressions performed by the agents, which lasted each 5 s, and indicate which emotion they observed by filling out Q2 on an iPad. Once Q2 was completed, the next facial expression was automatically generated after 2 s. This procedure was repeated until all six emotional expressions were displayed twice for the same embodiment. Once participants completed an embodiment, they filled out Q3. At the end of the session, the experimenter interviewed the participants following Q4 and debriefed them.

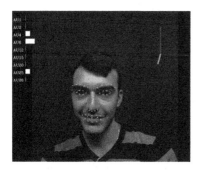

Fig. 2. A facial expression analyzed with the AU intensity detector.

Table 1. AUs extracted for each emotion.

Emotion	Action Units (AUs)
Anger	AU4
Disgust	AU4 + AU25
Fear	AU20, AU1 + AU2 + AU4
Happiness	AU6, AU12, AU6 + AU12
Sadness	AU1, AU15, AU1 + AU4
Surprise	AU26, AU1 + AU2

5   Analysis of Facial Mimicry

We considered two time intervals for facial mimicry: 0–1000 and 1000–5000 ms. The first is based on Moody et al. (2007) [28] and Dimberg and Thunberg (1998) [10]. It refers to quick mimicry responses (also called Rapid Facial Reactions; RFR) that occur at a subperceptual level [11]. The second takes into account a more controlled level of processing, at which mimicry responses can be considered conscious [37]. We call these reactions Controlled Facial Reactions (CFR).

To properly cut and automatically analyze the videos in correspondence of each emotional expression of the agent, we manually segmented each video using ELAN 5.4. In case the face of the participant was occluded, we coded it as missing. Each video snippet was then processed with an AU intensity detector (Fig. 2) [22]. This tool detects the activation and intensity of nine AUs, namely AU1, AU2, AU4, AU6, AU12, AU15, AU20, AU25, and AU26, with an overall Intraclass Correlation Coefficient $ICC(3,1)$ of 0.73, which is within state-of-the-art performance. We performed a frame-by-frame detection of the intensity of each AU on all snippets. In order to consider an emotion mimicked at a given time interval, we checked whether the target AU or combination of AUs (see Table 1) was active for at least 3 consecutive frames (100 ms). Ito et al. (2004) define this as the shortest duration of a facial expression [23]. As the AU intensity detector was not able to detect the AU activation for some of the snippets (RFR = 142; CFR = 86), we excluded them from the final analyses. The final mimicry score for each participant and time interval was then calculated as the percentage of mimicked emotions per embodiment given the available video snippets. This calculation was performed only if we had 6 or more valid snippets. Our dataset thus featured 21 missing values for RFR (12.3%) and 16 for CFR (9.4%).

6   Results

6.1   RQ1: Salience of Humanlikeness

We performed a factorial ANOVA with *level of humanlikeness* as between-subject factor and *type of embodiment* as within-subject factor. Results showed that the level of humanlikeness of the agents did not affect frequency of mimicry for RFR ($F(2, 28) = .888, p = .423$) and CFR ($F(2, 31) = .345, p = .771$). However, the embodiment of the agents did affect frequency of mimicry both for RFR ($F(3, 26) = 5.565, p = .001$), and CFR ($F(3, 29) = 5.800, p = .003$). Post-hoc analyses with a Bonferroni correction revealed a significant difference in frequency of mimicry for RFR between the virtual agent ($M = .559$, $SD = .161$) and the video-recording of the robot ($M = .669$, $SD = .150$, $p = .005$), and between the physical robot ($M = .550$, $SD = .173$) and the video-recorded one ($p = .006$). With regards to mimicry for CFR, they showed a significant difference in frequency of mimicry between the physical robot ($M = .669$, $SD = .204$) and the human ($M = .780$, $SD = .157$, $p = .001$).

6.2 RQ2: Patterns of Correlation Between Individual Traits and Facial Mimicry (Overall and per Embodiment)

As a first step, we ran a Pearson Product-Moment Correlation (two-tailed) between personality and empathy traits and frequency of mimicry for RFR and CFR considering all embodiments (see Table 2). The results showed a significant positive correlation between frequency of mimicry for RFR and the personality traits *agreeableness* ($r(148) = .210$, $p = .010$), *openness to experience* ($r(148) = .171, p = .036$) and *fantasy* ($r(148) = .305, p < .001$), and between frequency of mimicry for CFR and *extraversion* ($r(153) = .169, p = .035$), *openness to experience* ($r(153) = .274, p = .001$), and *fantasy* ($r(153) = .310, p < .001$).

To find correlation more specific to each embodiment, we performed a Pearson Product-Moment correlation separately for the video-recorded human, the physical robot, the video-recorded robot, and the virtual agent (see Table 2). For the video-recorded human, we found a significant positive correlation between frequency of mimicry for RFR and *agreeableness* ($r(33) = .424$, $p = .011$) and *fantasy* ($r(33) = .413$, $p = .014$), and a significant positive correlation between frequency of mimicry for CFR and *fantasy* ($r(36) = .331$, $p = .043$). While the same analysis did not yield any significant result for the physical robot, it showed a significant positive correlation between frequency of mimicry for RFR and *fantasy* ($r(37) = .434$, $p = .006$), and a significant positive correlation between frequency of mimicry for CFR and *openness to experience* ($r(39) = .410, p = .008$) and *fantasy* ($r(39) = .383$, $p = .014$) for the video-recorded robot. Moreover, it disclosed a significant positive correlation between frequency of mimicry for RFR and *empathic concern* ($r(37) = .349$, $p = .030$), and between frequency of mimicry for CFR and *openness to experience* ($r(36) = .349$, $p = .032$) and *fantasy* ($r(36) = .366$, $p = .024$) for the virtual agent.

7 Discussion

RQ1. *Embodiment, But Not Humanlikeness, Affected Facial Mimicry.* The studies of Hofree et al. (2014) and Philip et al. (2018) seemed to suggest that humanlikeness could be the most salient feature for mimicry. However, in our study, we did not find a main effect of humanlikeness on facial mimicry. As Hofree et al. (2014) and Philip et al. (2018) focused on highly realistic android

Table 2. Summary of Significant Correlations

CORRELATIONS		
EMBODIMENT	RFR	CFR
All Embodiments	A(+) O(+) F(+)	E(+) O(+) F(+)
Human Video	A(+) F(+)	F(+)
Physical Robot	none	none
Robot Video	F(+)	O(+) F(+)
Virtual Agent	EC(+)	O(+) F(+)

O: Openness to Experience, **C**: Conscientiousness,
E: Extraversion, **A**: Agreeableness, **N**: Neuroticism;
F: Fantasy, **EC**: Empathic Concern, **PT**: Perspective Taking

robots and real human agents in their studies, the lack of a significant effect of humanlikeness in our study might point to the salience of "realism", rather than anthropomorphism for the sake of mimicry. Future studies should tackle this hypothesis by testing whether differences in facial mimicry occur between humanlike agents varying in their degree of realism.

With regards to embodiment, our results are not aligned with the extant literature either. In stark contrast with Hofree et al. (2014) [20], who found people to mimic an android robot when physically co-present but not when video-recorded, we found participants to mimic the video-recorded robot more than its physically co-present counterpart. This result might be due to the task at hand, where the physical instantiation of the robot could distract participants from the end goal of emotion recognition. Finally, we discovered that the physically co-present robot was mimicked significantly less than the video-recorded human for CFR. However, when comparing the video-recording of the human and the video-recording of the robot, which have the same level of co-presence, we did not find a significant difference in terms of mimicry both for RFR and CFR. This is a novel and interesting result, which seems to point to similarities between HHI and HRI in terms of mimicry, especially when co-presence is kept constant.

RQ2. *Personality and Empathy Traits were Correlated with Participants' Mimicking Responses and the Patterns of Correlations Differed Across Agents' Embodiments for RFR.* When taking into account all embodiments, we found agreeableness and extraversion to positively correlate with mimicry, respectively for RFR and CFR. This result is in line with the related work on the relationship between personality traits and rapport [5,34] and substantiates our hypothesis of a connection between facial mimicry and rapport. We also found a positive correlation between facial mimicry and openness to experience and fantasy, both for RFR and CFR. Fantasy is the ability to imaginatively transpose oneself into the feelings and actions of fictitious characters. Openness to experience refers to people high in imagination, curiosity, and artistry. Although openness to experience is a personality trait, in this study, it seems to be core to cognitive empathy (the ability to infer the mental states of others [3]), as much as fantasy. The key role of fantasy and openness to experience for the sake of mimicry might be due to the task the participants were asked to carry out and might indicate a relationship between mimicry and emotion recognition.

By observing the correlations for the single embodiments, what catches the attention is the lack of significant correlations between individual traits and facial mimicry for the physical robot. As already suggested, the physical presence of the robot might have been perceived as an obstacle to emotion recognition. We hypothesize that this concealed the relations between individual traits and facial mimicry for this specific embodiment. Beyond this result, or lack thereof, we can find three clearcut patterns of correlation between facial mimicry and individual traits for RFR corresponding to the three embodiments: video-recorded human, video-recorded robot, and virtual agent. These patterns of correlation become more blurred when moving to CFR. In general, it seems that traits denoting sociability and sympathy, such as agreeableness and empathic concern, are meaningful for mimicry, but at less controlled levels of emotion processing and when it comes to more familiar agents (e.g., the human and the virtual agent). However, at more controlled levels of emotion processing, individual traits denoting identification with others and imagination, such as fantasy and openness to experience, become more crucial for the sake of mimicry, regardless of the familiarity with the agent. This seems to suggest that in this study mimicry is initially modulated by a social drive that gets lost in favor of cognitive empathy at later stages of processing, probably because the objective of the emotion recognition task kicks in. To further support this, it is interesting to note that the significant correlation between the most socially-charged personality trait, extraversion, and mimicry is lost when taking into account CFR for the single embodiments. In future work, it would be interesting to compare our task-based findings to mimicry in a more social context and to specifically take the gender of participants and the genderlikeness of the robot into consideration.

8   Conclusions

In this paper, we presented the results of a study exploring the relationship between individual traits and facial mimicry towards human, virtual, and robotic agents. Results showed that an agent's embodiment, but not its level of human-likeness, influences facial mimicry and that mimicry is correlated with personality and empathy traits key to both rapport building and cognitive empathy. When analyzing the patterns of correlation for the single embodiments, we noticed that the individual traits correlating with facial mimicry denoted sociability and sympathy at early stages of emotion processing, and identification with others and imagination at later stages. This change in significance might be due to the emotion recognition task participants were asked to perform. Future research should study the relation between individual traits and mimicry in real interactions and with larger samples to check whether these findings still hold.

Acknowledgement. We thank Isabelle Hupont, Mohamed Chetouani, Giovanna Varni, and Christopher Peters for the collaboration in the overall project. This work is partly supported by the Swedish Foundation for Strategic Research under the COIN project (RIT15-0133).

References

1. Aifanti, N., Papachristou, C., Delopoulos, A.: The MUG facial expression database. In: IEEE Int. Workshop on Image Analysis for Multimedia Interactive Services, pp. 1–4 (2010)
2. Al Moubayed, S., Beskow, J., Skantze, G., Granström, B.: Furhat: a back-projected human-like robot head for multiparty human-machine interaction. In: Esposito, A., Esposito, A.M., Vinciarelli, A., Hoffmann, R., Müller, V.C. (eds.) Cognitive Behavioural Systems. LNCS, vol. 7403, pp. 114–130. Springer, Heidelberg (2012). https://doi.org/10.1007/978-3-642-34584-5_9
3. Baron-Cohen, S., Wheelwright, S.: The empathy quotient: an investigation of adults with Asperger syndrome or high functioning autism, and normal sex differences. J. Autism Dev. Disord. **34**(2), 163–175 (2004)
4. Bartneck, C., Kulić, D., Croft, E., Zoghbi, S.: Measurement instruments for the anthropomorphism, animacy, likeability, perceived intelligence, and perceived safety of robots. Int. J. Soc. Robot. **1**(1), 71–81 (2009)
5. Cerekovic, A., Aran, O., Gatica-Perez, D.: Rapport with virtual agents: what do human social cues and personality explain? IEEE Trans. Affect. Comput. **8**(3), 382–395 (2016)
6. Chartrand, T.L., Bargh, J.A.: The chameleon effect: the perception-behavior link and social interaction. J. of Pers. Soc. Psychol. **76**(6), 893 (1999)
7. Davis, M.H., et al.: A multidimensional approach to individual differences in empathy. JSAS Cat. Sel. Doc. Psychol. **10**, 1–19 (1980)
8. Dimberg, U.: Facial reactions to facial expressions. Psychophysiology **19**(6), 643–647 (1982)
9. Dimberg, U.: Facial electromyography and the experience of emotion. J. Psychophysiol. **2**(4), 277–282 (1988)
10. Dimberg, U., Thunberg, M.: Rapid facial reactions to emotional facial expressions. Scand. J. Psychol. **39**(1), 39–45 (1998)
11. Dimberg, U., Thunberg, M., Elmehed, K.: Unconscious facial reactions to emotional facial expressions. Psychol. Sci. **11**(1), 86–89 (2000)
12. Drimalla, H., Landwehr, N., Hess, U., Dziobek, I.: From face to face: the contribution of facial mimicry to cognitive and emotional empathy. Cogn. Emot. **33**(8), 1672–1686 (2019)
13. Eisenberg, N., Fabes, R.A.: Empathy: conceptualization, measurement, and relation to prosocial behavior. Motiv. Emot. **14**(2), 131–149 (1990)
14. Ekman, P., Rosenberg, E.L.: What the Face Reveals: Basic and Applied Studies of Spontaneous Expression Using the Facial Action Coding System (FACS). Oxford University Press, USA (1997)
15. Fischer, A., Becker, D., Veenstra, L.: Emotional mimicry in social context: the case of disgust and pride. Front. Psychol. **3**, 475 (2012)
16. Hager, J.C., Ekman, P., Friesen, W.V.: Facial Action Coding System. A Human Face, Salt Lake City, UT (2002)
17. Harms, C., Biocca, F.: Internal consistency and reliability of the networked minds measure of social presence (2004)
18. Hess, U., Banse, R., Kappas, A.: The intensity of facial expression is determined by underlying affective state and social situation. J. Pers. Soc. Psychol. **69**(2), 280 (1995)
19. Hess, U., Fischer, A.: Emotional mimicry as social regulation. Pers. Soc. Psychol. Rev. **17**(2), 142–157 (2013)
20. Hofree, G., Ruvolo, P., Bartlett, M.S., Winkielman, P.: Bridging the mechanical and the human mind: spontaneous mimicry of a physically present android. PLoS ONE **9**(7), e99934 (2014)

21. Hofree, G., Ruvolo, P., Reinert, A., Bartlett, M.S., Winkielman, P.: Behind the robot's smiles and frowns: in social context, people do not mirror android's expressions but react to their informational value. Front. Neurorobot. **12**, 14 (2018)
22. Hupont, I., Chetouani, M.: Region-based facial representation for real-time action units intensity detection across datasets. Pattern Anal. Appl. **22**(2), 477–489 (2019)
23. Ito, T., Murano, E.Z., Gomi, H.: Fast force-generation dynamics of human articulatory muscles. J. Appl. Physiol. **96**(6), 2318–2324 (2004)
24. Ivaldi, S., Lefort, S., Peters, J., Chetouani, M., Provasi, J., Zibetti, E.: Towards engagement models that consider individual factors in HRI: on the relation of extroversion and negative attitude towards robots to gaze and speech during a human-robot assembly task. Int. J. Soc. Robot. **9**(1), 63–86 (2017)
25. Lakin, J.L., Chartrand, T.L.: Using nonconscious behavioral mimicry to create affiliation and rapport. Psychol. Sci. **14**(4), 334–339 (2003)
26. Mattheij, R., Nilsenova, M., Postma, E.: Vocal and facial imitation of humans interacting with virtual agents. In: 2013 Humaine Association Conference on Affective Computing and Intelligent Interaction, pp. 815–820. IEEE (2013)
27. McIntosh, D.N.: Spontaneous facial mimicry, liking and emotional contagion. Pol. Psychol. Bull. **37**(1), 31 (2006)
28. Moody, E.J., McIntosh, D.N., Mann, L.J., Weisser, K.R.: More than mere mimicry? the influence of emotion on rapid facial reactions to faces. Emotion **7**(2), 447 (2007)
29. Niedenthal, P.M., Mermillod, M., Maringer, M., Hess, U.: The simulation of smiles (SIMS) model: embodied simulation and the meaning of facial expression. Behav. Brain Sci. **33**(6), 417 (2010)
30. Paetzel, M., Hupont, I., Varni, G., Chetouani, M., Peters, C., Castellano, G.: Exploring the link between self-assessed mimicry and embodiment in HRI. In: Proceedings of the Companion of the 2017 ACM/IEEE International Conference on Human-Robot Interaction, pp. 245–246 (2017)
31. Philip, L., Martin, J., Clavel, C.: Rapid facial reactions in response to facial expressions of emotion displayed by real versus virtual faces. i-Perception **9**(4), 2041669518786527 (2018)
32. Rosenthal-von der Pütten, A.M., Krämer, N.C.: How design characteristics of robots determine evaluation and uncanny valley related responses. Comput. Hum. Behav. **36**, 422–439 (2014)
33. Rammstedt, B., John, O.P.: Measuring personality in one minute or less: a 10-item short version of the big five inventory in English and German. J. Res. Pers. **41**(1), 203–212 (2007)
34. von der Pütten, A.M., Krämer, N.C., Gratch, J.: How our personality shapes our interactions with virtual characters - implications for research and development. In: Allbeck, J., Badler, N., Bickmore, T., Pelachaud, C., Safonova, A. (eds.) IVA 2010. LNCS (LNAI), vol. 6356, pp. 208–221. Springer, Heidelberg (2010). https://doi.org/10.1007/978-3-642-15892-6_23
35. Rymarczyk, K., Żurawski, Ł., Jankowiak-Siuda, K., Szatkowska, I.: Empathy in facial mimicry of fear and disgust: simultaneous EMG-fMRI recordings during observation of static and dynamic facial expressions. Front. Psychol. **10**, 701 (2019)
36. Skantze, G., Al Moubayed, S.: IrisTK: a statechart-based toolkit for multi-party face-to-face interaction. In: International Conference on Multimodal Interaction, pp. 69–76 (2012)
37. Sonnby-Borgström, M., Jönsson, P., Svensson, O.: Emotional empathy as related to mimicry reactions at different levels of information processing. J. Nonverbal Behav. **27**(1), 3–23 (2003)

Perceptions of People's Dishonesty Towards Robots

Sofia Petisca[1]([✉]), Ana Paiva[2], and Francisco Esteves[3]

[1] Instituto Universitário de Lisboa (ISCTE-IUL) and INESC-ID, Lisbon, Portugal
Sofia_Petisca@iscte-iul.pt
[2] Instituto Superior Técnico (IST) and INESC-ID, Lisbon, Portugal
[3] Mid Sweden University and ISCTE-IUL, Sundsvall, Sweden

Abstract. Dishonest behavior is an issue in human-human interactions and the same might happen in human-robot interactions. To ascertain people's perceptions of dishonesty, we asked participants to evaluate five different scenarios where someone was being dishonest towards a human or a robot, but we varied the level of autonomy the robot presented. We asked them how guilty they would feel by being dishonest towards a robot, and why do they think people would be dishonest with robots. We see that, regardless of being a human or the autonomy the robot presented, people always evaluated as being wrong to be dishonest. They reported feeling low guilt with a robot. And they expressed that people will be dishonest mostly because of lack of capabilities in the robot to prevent dishonesty, absence of presence, and a human tendency for dishonesty. These results bring implications for the developments of autonomous robots in the future.

Keywords: Human-robot interaction · Dishonesty · Unethical behavior

1 Introduction

Robots are being thought of and developed with the aim of working alongside with humans as a support. Still, the integration of robots in different contexts needs to be done with caution. Some roles might be more sensitive than others. Studies with humans show that people are dishonest if they have the opportunity for it [12]. Will they be dishonest with a robot? Imagine having an autonomous robot in people's homes as a support, helping with medication, healthy food habits, etc. People sometimes might not feel like following the diet prescribed by the doctor, or the medication for the day, will they try to cheat? Will a robot be able to understand what is happening and promote more honesty? Some studies already started to explore human cheating behavior in the presence of a robot

This work was supported by national funds through Fundação para a Ciência e a Tecnologia (FCT) with reference UIDB/50021/2020 and Sofia Petisca acknowledges an FCT Grant (Ref.SFRH/BD/118013/2016).

A. R. Wagner et al. (Eds.): ICSR 2020, LNAI 12483, pp. 132–143, 2020.
https://doi.org/10.1007/978-3-030-62056-1_12

and what factors influence it. Nevertheless, none, to our knowledge, has investigated what are the perceptions that people have about being dishonest with a robot. Therefore, the novelty of our study is to explore people's perceptions of dishonesty towards robots, guilt associated to it, and why people think in the future other people will take advantage of robots. We believe this will be valuable information to inform the future development of autonomous robots.

1.1 Human Dishonesty: An Automatic Self-interest Tendency

Dishonest behavior can be seen in various contexts, in public spaces, in schools and workplaces. Studies show that when anonymity is assured, we have an automatic self-interest tendency that needs self-control to keep in check [15] but, at the same time, people also like to be perceived as honest [1]. This contradiction creates two different motivational forces. On one hand, we want to serve our self-interest, but on the other hand, it will affect our self-concept of being honest. People solve this problem by arranging justifications that protect their honest self-concept and still allows them to take advantage of the situation (e.g. cheating a little). For example, if you tell someone that if they get a 4, 5 or 6 in a die they win a reward and participants are the ones reporting the number they got, you will see a higher rate of 4, 5 and 6 reports that could not correspond to the chance level of 50% (e.g. [7,13]). A simple change in the rules of the game can immediately affect the easiness to which people might arrange justifications for their dishonesty [7]. Other factors, like the environment people are in, have also been seen to increase dishonesty (i.e. cheating behavior): by doing a task in a darker room [17]; by feeling psychologically close to someone that cheats [4]; by seeing others part of the in-group cheating [3]; or by having less time to perform a task [15]. All these studies showing the susceptibility of human behavior depending on the environment it is in.

On the other hand, studies have found that if one brings awareness to the dishonest act or to the moral values of the person, people are obliged to update their self-concept in the moment they are tempted to cheat (inhibiting dishonesty). For example, by signing an honor code, people decrease their cheating behavior [12]. It seems we keep our self-concept honest as a default and if we are not obliged to update it by gaining awareness of the value of our actions, we create justifications for the way we act.

1.2 Dishonesty in Human-Robot Interaction

Dishonesty in human-robot interaction has been studied in two different lines of research: a robot that cheats and its effect on human perceptions and behavior, and the effect a robot can have in preventing cheating. By exploring the effect a robot that cheats has on people, studies found that people are not bothered if a robot cheats in their favor, only when the cheating goes against them [9]. Being bribed by a robot also seems to have an effect on people. They feel less inclined to help back [14]. Moreover, curiously, when a robot cheats it is perceived by people as being more intelligent than when they see a human cheating in the same way [16].

Another line of research started to test the effect of the presence of a robot in dishonest behavior. A study shows that while being tempted by a task to cheat, participants cheated much more when they were alone in the room than when they were observed by a human or a robot doing random eye-gaze behavior [6]. In a similar study, it was seen that participants cheating behavior was inhibited when a robot was just directly looking at them the whole time. On the other hand, when they were alone, or with a robot that gave the instructions for the task in a very scripted way, cheating increased [13]. Nevertheless, the robot behavior is not the only characteristic that needs to be considered, the context where they are integrated also influences people's behaviors, especially if we use simpler robots. A study ran in a natural setting showed that people stole more snacks when a robot was just monitoring than when a human was in the same role [2]. In this case, the monitoring behavior of the robot was not enough because they were in a public context and people could see that if another person took something nothing happened. These are important studies that started to explore how people behave in the presence of a robot when cheating is tempting, informing on the capabilities a robot needs to have to prevent it.

However, the literature on people's perceptions is still scarce. One study explored how people apply moral norms to humans and robots, showing that robots are expected in moral dilemmas situations, to sacrifice one for the benefit of many- if not, they are more blamed than a human [10]. Although, this asymmetry disappeared when the robot in those scenarios was seen as a humanoid robot [11]. Yet, none to our knowledge, have explored perceptions towards being dishonest with a robot, it is this gap that our paper tries to answer.

2   Subjective Evaluations of Dishonesty Towards Robots

2.1   Sample

One-hundred and sixty-four participants were recruited from a university, 102 females and 62 males, with ages ranging from 17 to 52 years ($M = 22.18$; $SD = 5.61$) in two different times of collection. Participants received school credit in the first collection as part of a course task and a movie ticket in the second collection in the university corridors. All participants signed a consent form and where randomly assigned to one of the conditions. Questionnaires were answered in paper individually and it took approximately 10 min per participant.

2.2   Methodology

To ascertain people's perceptions, different scenarios were created varying the agent type (human/robot) that "suffered" from the dishonest act. However, since we have seen from the field studies that participant's behavior seems to be affected by the robot's capabilities, we varied the level of autonomy the robot would present (autonomous/non-autonomous).

Therefore, participants were allocated to only one of three conditions for each scenario: (1) human; (2) autonomous robot (it is fully autonomous in the task) or (3) non-autonomous robot (it needs human assistance to perform its task, e.g. tele-operated or performance check). For the five scenarios, participants evaluated:

- **Level of dishonesty:** how much participants thought the act was dishonest towards the agent in it, for each scenario, in a 6-point Likert scale from 1-Not dishonest to 6-Very dishonest.
- **Level of autonomy:** as a manipulation check for the robot condition, in a 6-point Likert scale from 1-Almost not at all to 6- A lot (taking into account that autonomy was defined in the questionnaire as a robot that does not need human assistance to perform its role).

In addition, after the scenarios we asked participants to give a **score of guilt** (in a 6-point Likert scale from 1-I would feel almost no guilt to 6-I would feel a lot of guilt) on how much they would feel guilty if they were dishonest towards these different entities: a brother; a friend; the university; the government; a stranger and a robot. In order to understand the level of guilt people might feel on being dishonest towards a robot.

Finally, participants were asked **if they thought that in the future people would be dishonest with robots and why they thought that could happen.** This question and the guilt score were more exploratory so we did not define hypothesis.

2.3   Study Hypothesis

Following previous studies where we see that people cheat in the presence of a robot, we expected that people would not see the act of dishonesty towards a robot as being something too dishonest, and not as much as with a human:

H1: Participants will give lower scores of dishonesty to all the scenarios with a robot compared to a human.

And since a robot being perceived as more limited does not affect the participant's cheating behavior [13], we expected that there would be differences in the dishonesty levels attributed to the scenarios depending on the level of autonomy the robot presented. We hypothesized that:

H2: Participants will give lower scores of dishonesty to the non-autonomous robot in comparison to the autonomous robot for each scenario.

2.4   Scenarios

The scenarios were created imagining different situations were robots could have a role in society, some simpler (like selling candies in a university) others more complex and serious (as being a "robot-fireman"). The dishonest actions in the scenarios were always in the form of stealing or lying about something, based on the moral foundation of Fairness/cheating [5]. Participants read the following instructions: *"Imagine the following scenarios and indicate the score that best represents your opinion"*. For the robot conditions we also said to imagine that the robot in the scenarios was a humanoid robot, with head, torso, arms and legs.

For each scenario, we did not give a gender to our characters to avoid any kind of influence in the evaluation, below we present the scenarios:

Scenario 1 (e.g. autonomous robot): "Imagine a robot that works in the university selling snacks and chocolates, it moves and takes care of the transactions with the students without external help. A student observes the robot while it is selling chocolates to other students. The student notices that the robot keeps the money in a small basket, leaving it open momentarily. Taking advantage of the robot distraction, while still interacting with the other students, the student puts his hand in the basket and takes out a hand full of coins without anyone noticing. Quickly the student moves away in another direction."

Scenario 2 (e.g. non-autonomous robot): "In the finance department there is a robot receiving people's taxes for those who cannot or do not want to do it online. The robot is next to a table with a computer and gives the instructions in a repetitive form on how to fill out the form, without being able to understand what people might ask him. Later, these taxes need to be checked by a human employee because the robot does not have the capacity to understand if the form is correctly filled. A person comes to the finance department to do their taxes, seeing that the robot is very limited in its capabilities, that person reports lower values for its taxes in order to avoid paying most of them."

Scenario 3 (e.g. human): "In the police department to try and ease police work in less serious offenses, an employee is being used to collect people's reports of these incidents. In an isolated room to leave people more comfortable, the employee receives each person and records their testimonials. A person was involved in a car accident, hitting another car because it was texting while driving. When that person enters the room, decides to alter its testimonial and tell a different story, accusing that the other person was the one that hit the car."

Scenario 4[1]: in this scenario the human/robot was supervising the queue numbers and taking people to their appointments inside the hospital, the person cheats on the queue line and lies to the human/robot.

Scenario 5(see footnote 1): in this scenario the human/robot works in a water truck for the fire department that is deployed in various zones in the forest with difficult access. Upon receiving mixed coordinates relating to a fire, the human/robot asks some kids near the zone, for help, the kids to make fun lie and say the wrong direction.

---

[1] For the complete scenarios please contact the first author.

3   Results

Our manipulation check for the robot autonomy showed significant differences for all the scenarios, with the autonomous robot always receiving higher scores than the non-autonomous robot ($p < .01$).

3.1   Perceptions of Dishonesty Towards a Human or a Robot (Autonomous/Non-autonomous)

We conducted between-subjects ANOVA analysis to compare the scores given to each scenario depending on the type of agent (Human; Autonomous Robot or Non-autonomous Robot).

Scenario 1 (Human/robot works in the university): in general, participants seemed to evaluate the act in this scenario as very dishonest but there were significant differences between the type of agent (with Welch's F, $F(2, 102) = 5.87$, $p = .004$), with the human agent receiving higher scores than both robot types (Games-Howell, $p < .03$). The scores were for the human ($M = 5.71$; $SD = .81$), autonomous robot ($M = 5.15$; $SD = 1.20$) and the non-autonomous robot ($M = 5.16$; $SD = 1.27$).

Scenario 2 (Human/robot works in the finances department): participant's scores also reflected, overall, that it was a dishonest act, and there were significant differences between the agent type ($F(2, 161) = 4.23$, $p = .02$). A Tukey test showed that the human differed significantly from the autonomous robot ($p = .01$), with participants giving higher scores of dishonesty towards the autonomous robot and lower to the human. The scores were for the human ($M = 4.16$; $SD = 1.64$), autonomous robot ($M = 4.96$; $SD = 1.39$) and the non-autonomous robot ($M = 4.72$; $SD = 1.39$).

Scenario 3 (Human/robot works in the police department): participants equally evaluated as dishonest towards the human/robot for the person to lie in their testimonial ($F(2, 161) = .25$, $p = .78$). The scores were for the human ($M = 5.04$; $SD = 1.39$), autonomous robot ($M = 4.87$; $SD = 1.07$) and the non-autonomous robot ($M = 4.91$; $SD = 1.38$).

Scenario 4 (Human/robot works in a hospital): participants considered equally dishonest towards the human/robot for the person to lie about their ticket number and avoid the queue ($F(2, 161) = .80$, $p = .45$). The scores were for the human ($M = 4.64$; $SD = 1.52$), autonomous robot ($M = 4.28$; $SD = 1.59$) and the non-autonomous robot ($M = 4.49$; $SD = 1.33$).

Scenario 5 (Human/robot works for the fire department): participants evaluated as being very dishonest to lie to the human/robot working for the fire department, but there were significant differences between the agent type (with Welch's F, $F(2, 103) = 3.08$, $p = .05$), with the human receiving higher scores than the non-autonomous robot (Games-Howell, $p = .05$). The scores were for the human ($M = 5.71$; $SD = .83$), autonomous robot ($M = 5.44$; $SD = 1.23$) and the non-autonomous robot ($M = 5.22$; $SD = 1.24$).

3.2   Level of Guilt People Feel Towards Different Entities

Participants reported how much guilt they would feel if they were dishonest towards different kinds of entities (see Fig. 1). Being dishonest towards a brother ($M = 5.57$; $SD = 1.02$) or a friend ($M = 5.56$; $SD = .81$) received a high score of guilt, followed by the University ($M = 4.55$; $SD = 1.22$), a stranger ($M = 4.09$; $SD = 1.34$) or the government ($M = 3.93$; $SD = 1.58$). Finally, participants reported a low level of guilt on being dishonest towards a robot ($M = 3.14$; $SD = 1.56$).

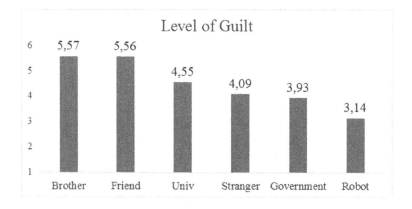

Fig. 1. Distribution of guilt scores across different entities.

3.3   Why Will People Be Dishonest Towards Robots?

Seeing that in spite of people conceptually considering it wrong to be dishonest towards a robot, they report feeling low guilt if they were to do it and they are actually dishonest if they find limitations in a robot to take advantage of. Leaving us with the question of how can we better prepare robots to interact with humans?

In order to answer this question, we explored further people's perceptions, our research question was: what reasons do people give to being dishonest with a robot? For this, a first coder (the first author) did an initial coding of the answers for the participants that thought that people would be dishonest. A total of 142 participant's answers were coded, summarizing the main reasons given for people to be dishonest with robots (outside of these, nine participants reported that people would not be dishonest with robots and thirteen participants were not clear on their position or the causes). Next a more descriptive coding was applied, creating codes for the types of reasons participants gave which were common throughout the answers, finalizing with the following coding scheme:

1) **Human tendency for dishonesty:** when dishonesty towards robots is justified because people are dishonest and when they have the opportunity for it, they act dishonestly. For example: *"(...) [saying they will be dishonest] because humans will always try to take advantage of the situations."*

2) **Absence of consequences:** when dishonesty towards robots is justified because humans do not feel guilt/responsibility (or feel very little) towards them or feel that there are no consequences for doing it. For example: *"(...)People will be dishonest because they will think that no one is going to get them (...)."*

3) **Absence of cognitive or emotional capabilities**: when dishonesty towards robots is justified because the robot lacks in cognitive and emotional capabilities (e.g. not able to understand that it is being cheated; not having emotions or feelings). For example: *"(...) Yes because robots do not have feelings so, people will not create empathy with them (...)."*

4) **Absence of "presence":** when dishonesty towards robots is justified because the robot is a machine with no real presence or value (e.g. when it is seen as only an object or not considered in the same level as a human being). For example: *"I think [people will be dishonest] because the majority of people does not take them [robots] seriously."*

5) **Others:** when dishonesty towards robots is justified by the context robots are in, by the society view of fears regarding robots or by the difficulty of integrating these technologies. For example: *"[yes] I think people will think that robots will eventually steal their places."*

A second coder, unaware of the study purpose coded 57% of the answers given by the participants following the coding scheme given above to validate it. There was a substantial agreement [8] with the first coder, $k = .667$, $p < .001$. All the participants answers were then analysed from the first coder coding.

For the 142 participant's answers, frequencies were calculated to understand the frequency of each category as a reason for dishonesty (some participants gave more than one reason, i.e. more than one category in their answer). The majority of people gave more absence of capabilities and absence of "presence" as reasons for being dishonest towards a robot, immediately followed by the human tendency to be dishonest (see Fig. 2).

Regarding the absence of capabilities, people said that *"(...) the robot will not understand if [people] where dishonest with it, so it will be easier to trick it"* and *"(...)people know that robots do not have feelings or emotions and that may make dishonesty more justifiable"*. These examples suggest that robots need to have more cognitive capabilities to be able to understand when dishonesty is happening, and more emotional capabilities, to give people the sense that the robot is affected by their actions.

Regarding the absence of presence, people said that *"(...) [robots] will always be] automated objects (...)"*, and *"(...) the majority of people do not take it seriously"*. This category suggests that in the future there will need to be a period of adaptation of robots working alongside with humans, people will need some time to create a respect for the role of the robot.

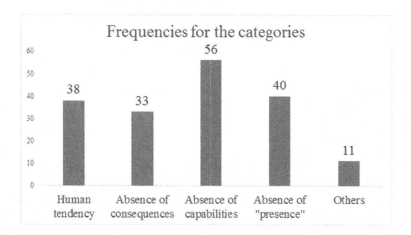

Fig. 2. Distribution of frequencies across the categories.

As suggested by previous literature, the human tendency to be dishonest was also one of the most referenced categories. People said that *"(...) [it will exist a] tendency for people to abuse when they can and when they win something from it", "(...) because it is human nature."* The way to better inform this aspect of human behavior is through the laboratory studies that have been conducted so far, ascertaining the capabilities that a robot needs to have to prevent this.

Regarding absence of consequences, people said that *"(...) by not being human a person would have less feelings of guilt by being dishonest", "(...) [because people] would not be judged by the robot if there was a chance to be dishonest".* Suggesting what we already saw in the absence of capabilities and presence, that a robot needs more resources so that people can give it more value and, consequently, feel that there are consequences for their actions.

Lastly, in the Other reasons category, people expressed that *"(...) it will take some time for [the robot] to integrate society (...) making it possible to be mistreated initially", "(...) by [people] not accepting to be substituted by robots [they will behave dishonestly]".* This category also suggests that there will need to be a period of adjustment to integrating robots in society and even to educate people on their roles as a support to human beings.

If we wanted to have a broader perspective of the kind of reasons people give for being dishonest with a robot, we could summarize the categories in three main areas: human motives (categories 1 and 2, what the humans have/feel that facilitates dishonesty); robot motives (categories 3 and 4, what the robot has that facilitates dishonesty) and others. Looking from this perspective we see that 54% of the reasons given are robot motives, 40% are human motives and 6% are others.

4   Discussion

Studies show that people cheat in the presence of a robot, especially if they can ascertain its capabilities (e.g. [13]). With these results from laboratory studies, we expected that in general, people would give lower scores to the act of being dishonest towards a robot in comparison with a human (H1). Our results did not support this, showing that only in the University scenario and Fire department, more dishonesty was signaled towards the human than the robot. For the Finance scenario people considered more dishonest towards the autonomous robot than the human and the rest of the scenarios showed no differences. Yet, it is interesting to note that the means for all the conditions were all clearly above the middle point of the scale (3.5), expressing the perception of dishonesty in the act. Suggesting, that people think that it is wrong to cheat a robot and a human. Interestingly in the case of the finance department, it seems that cheating towards a human is more accepted than cheating towards a robot. This is an unexpected result, which might reflect peculiar ideas about paying taxes.

Regarding the level of autonomy the robot displayed in the scenarios, there were no differences in dishonesty level. When dishonesty was taking place, participants always felt that it was dishonest to act in that way towards the robot, not supporting H2.

Regarding guilt, it seems it is higher the closer you are to the entity that suffers from that dishonesty. Family and friends, are riskier to be dishonest to because the consequences will be heavier in a daily basis. A robot received a low level of guilt, a result that was already seen in another study [6]. And the majority of people justified dishonesty towards a robot due to absence of capabilities (it does not know what people are doing and it does not have feelings), absence of "presence" (the robot is not taken seriously, at the same level of a human) and a human tendency for dishonesty. The low level of guilt, might come from these factors. A robot needs to have capabilities that allows it to respond to dishonesty, people might need to feel that it is aware of them and that there are consequences for that kind of behavior, like with humans.

5   Conclusions

Imagining future human-robot interactions brings two different challenges: their acceptability by people (helping in their fears regarding AI and robots) and people's behavior towards it. One aspect that needs to be considered is human dishonesty. Laboratory studies with humans show, that when anonymity is assured, people cheat at least a little [12], and the same is seen in studies with robots (when people can ascertain their capabilities and take advantage of them)[13].

This study was the first to explore people's perceptions towards dishonesty in human-robot interactions. We see that independently of being a human or having different levels of autonomy in a robot, people considered a dishonest act as being dishonest. Showing that people understand that the behavior is wrong. Yet, this study shows that there is no singular answer to whom the dishonesty is worse, it depends on the scenario. There seems to be no difference in a hospital or a police department scenario, but in a university or fire department it is worse to cheat the human agent. Curiously, in a finance department scenario it seems it is more accepted to cheat towards a human than an autonomous robot, which could be reflecting the state of the world, with for example, tax evasion being broadcasted so often. In terms of guilt it seems people report low values towards being dishonest with a robot and this might occur due to lack of capabilities and presence in robots.

However, this study collected data from university students, future studies should also include the general population in order to broaden the results. Nonetheless, this study points to important aspects of robot's developments that need to be considered for sensitive roles in our society. It will be interesting to further explore these questions when people start to interact daily with a robot, to see what changes and what new topics arise.

Acknowledgments. The authors thank the help of Iolanda Leite in reviewing a first draft of the manuscript.

References

1. Fischbacher, U., Föllmi-Heusi, F.: Lies in disguise–an experimental study on cheating. J. Eur. Econ. Assoc. **11**(3), 525–547 (2013). https://doi.org/10.1111/jeea.12014
2. Forlizzi, J., Saensuksopa, T., Salaets, N., Shomin, M., Mericli, T., Hoffman, G.: Let's be honest: a controlled field study of ethical behavior in the presence of a robot. In: 2016 25th IEEE International Symposium on Robot and Human Interactive Communication (RO-MAN), pp. 769–774. IEEE (2016). https://doi.org/10.1109/ROMAN.2016.7745206
3. Gino, F., Ayal, S., Ariely, D.: Contagion and differentiation in unethical behavior: the effect of one bad apple on the barrel. Psychol. Sci. **20**(3), 393–398 (2009). https://doi.org/10.1111/j.1467-9280.2009.02306.x
4. Gino, F., Galinsky, A.D.: Vicarious dishonesty: when psychological closeness creates distance from one's moral compass. Organ. Behav. Hum. Decis. Process. **119**(1), 15–26 (2012). https://doi.org/10.1016/j.obhdp.2012.03.011
5. Graham, J., et al.: Moral foundations theory: the pragmatic validity of moral pluralism. In: Advances in Experimental Social Psychology, vol. 47, pp. 55–130. Elsevier (2013). https://doi.org/10.1016/B978-0-12-407236-7.00002-4
6. Hoffman, G., et al.: Robot presence and human honesty: experimental evidence. In: Proceedings of the Tenth Annual ACM/IEEE International Conference on Human-Robot Interaction, pp. 181–188. ACM (2015)
7. Jiang, T.: The mind game: invisible cheating and inferable intentions (2012). https://doi.org/10.2139/ssrn.2051476
8. Landis, J.R., Koch, G.G.: The measurement of observer agreement for categorical data. biometrics, pp. 159–174 (1977). https://doi.org/10.2307/2529310
9. Litoiu, A., Ullman, D., Kim, J., Scassellati, B.: Evidence that robots trigger a cheating detector in humans. In: Proceedings of the Tenth Annual ACM/IEEE International Conference on Human-Robot Interaction, pp. 165–172. ACM (2015). https://doi.org/10.1145/2696454.2696456

10. Malle, B.F., Scheutz, M., Arnold, T., Voiklis, J., Cusimano, C.: Sacrifice one for the good of many?: people apply different moral norms to human and robot agents. In: Proceedings of the Tenth Annual ACM/IEEE International Conference on Human-Robot Interaction, pp. 117–124. ACM (2015)
11. Malle, B.F., Scheutz, M., Forlizzi, J., Voiklis, J.: Which robot am i thinking about?: the impact of action and appearance on people's evaluations of a moral robot. In: The Eleventh ACM/IEEE International Conference on Human Robot Interaction, pp. 125–132. IEEE Press (2016). https://doi.org/10.1109/HRI.2016.7451743
12. Mazar, N., Amir, O., Ariely, D.: The dishonesty of honest people: a theory of self-concept maintenance. J. Mark. Res. **45**(6), 633–644 (2008). https://doi.org/10.1509/jmkr.45.6.633
13. Petisca, S., Esteves, F., Paiva, A.: Cheating with robots: how at ease do they make us feel? In: IEEE/RSJ International Conference on Intelligent Robots and Systems (IROS), pp. 2102–2107 (2019). https://doi.org/10.1109/IROS40897.2019.8967790
14. Sandoval, E.B., Brandstetter, J., Bartneck, C.: Can a robot bribe a human?: the measurement of the negative side of reciprocity in human robot interaction. In: The Eleventh ACM/IEEE International Conference on Human Robot Interaction, pp. 117–124. IEEE Press (2016). https://doi.org/10.1109/HRI.2016.7451742
15. Shalvi, S., Eldar, O., Bereby-Meyer, Y.: Honesty requires time (and lack of justifications). Psychol. Sci. **23**(10), 1264–1270 (2012). https://doi.org/10.1177/0956797612443835
16. Ullman, D., Leite, I., Phillips, J., Kim-Cohen, J., Scassellati, B.: Smart human, smarter robot: how cheating affects perceptions of social agency. In: Proceedings of the Annual Meeting of the Cognitive Science Society, vol. 36 (2014)
17. Zhong, C.B., Bohns, V.K., Gino, F.: Good lamps are the best police: darkness increases dishonesty and self-interested behavior. Psychol. Sci. **21**(3), 311–314 (2010). https://doi.org/10.1177/0956797609360754

Human-Robot Collaboration and Dialogue for Fault Recovery on Hierarchical Tasks

Janelle Blankenburg[1]([✉]), Mariya Zagainova[1], S. Michael Simmons[2],
Gabrielle Talavera[1], Monica Nicolescu[1], and David Feil-Seifer[1]

[1] Department of Computer Science and Engineering, University of Nevada, Reno,
Reno, NV 89557, USA
jjblankenburg@nevada.unr.edu
[2] Department of Computer Science, Brigham Young University,
Provo, UT 84602, USA

Abstract. Robotic systems typically follow a rigid approach to task execution, in which they perform the necessary steps in a specific order, but fail when having to cope with issues that arise during execution. We propose an approach that handles such cases through dialogue and human-robot collaboration. The proposed approach contributes a hierarchical control architecture that *1) autonomously detects and is cognizant of task execution failures, 2) initiates a dialogue with a human helper to obtain assistance,* and *3) enables collaborative human-robot task execution through extended dialogue* in order to *4) ensure robust execution of hierarchical tasks with complex constraints, such as sequential, non-ordering, and multiple paths of execution.* The architecture ensures that the constraints are adhered to throughout the entire task execution, including during failures. The recovery of the architecture from issues during execution is validated by a human-robot team on a building task.

Keywords: Human-robot collaboration · Human-robot dialogue · Dialogue-based fault recovery · Hierarchical planning

1 Introduction

Fault recovery in autonomous robot systems is an essential component for ensuring that any unexpected circumstances can be handled without the complete failure of a task. The goal of this work is to develop a control architecture for hierarchical tasks which is able to recover from faults during execution through dialogue and human-robot collaboration. The proposed architecture is cognizant of failures and can initiate a dialogue to resolve an issue. Extended dialogue between the robot and human, rather than a single request for help, allows for multiple ways of resolving a fault. Failures are autonomously detected through a combination of views from multiple cameras. The architecture ensures that the

© Springer Nature Switzerland AG 2020
A. R. Wagner et al. (Eds.): ICSR 2020, LNAI 12483, pp. 144–156, 2020.
https://doi.org/10.1007/978-3-030-62056-1_13

task constraints are held throughout the entire task execution, even during failures. This allows for a robust execution of a hierarchical task with multiple types of constraints such as sequential, non-ordering, and multiple paths of execution. We provide an extension to our previously developed control architecture [8] to allow for fault recovery, to allow for a smooth interaction between a human and robot collaborating on a complex, hierarchical task.

2 Related Work

Joint assembly tasks employ several elements in order for the system to acquire/learn a model of the task, to monitor its progress, and to repair the system when things fail. Task construction is an essential part of this process, demonstrated through human-robot collaboration [5] or dialogue-based systems [17]. Human demonstrations can be used to learn a hierarchical plan [10]. Task description can also be manually specified by using a graphical user interface [15]. However, failure resolution was not done when collisions occurred in these works, the robots would generally defer to what their partner wanted to do.

Task verification is critical in joint assembly tasks for robotic systems. It has been implemented in single [14] and multiple [2] robot systems that use computer vision for task verification. In the 2016 Amazon Picking Challenge, a vacuum sensor was used to receive boolean feedback on the grasp of an object [12]. The proposed approach uses multiple on-board sensors to ensure proper completion of each task step and that constraints are upheld during resolution.

When a robot fails a task it is important that the team can resolve the problem autonomously [18]. Fong et. al. found that dialogue makes human users more aware of the problems robots face [7]. When plans fail, it can help when a system can explain why it made certain decisions [11]. Unlike these works, the proposed work seeks to resolve conflicts in hierarchical tasks with complex constraints by utilizing an extended dialogue between a human and robot.

Several studies have had robots initiate communication with humans when a problem arose [6,7]. Fong et al. had a robot explore a room via teleoperation and ask a remote human about how to proceed when confronted with uncertainty [7]. Extensions of this work had a team of robots conduct a surveillance task, illuminating that dialogue improved the human's ability to deal with context switching [6]. Both [6,7] focused on collaborative teleoperation based tasks. These studies primarily focused on how humans interact with robots asking questions. However, humans primarily offered additional information to the robot but were not capable of helping the robot complete the task, which our work allows.

Robots have also asked humans for assistance in building a piece of IKEA furniture [14]. The robots identified the causes of their problems and initiated a dialogue to solve it. This work is most similar to ours but has several key differences: their architecture was bound by a rigid instruction set; the system required an external Vicon system to perform the fault-detection whereas we utilize on-board sensors; and it focuses on the complexity of the robots' requests for help whereas we focus on an extended dialogue between human and robot.

3   Control Architecture with Fault Recovery

3.1   Distributed Control Architecture

This work extends the control architecture developed in [8] to incorporate a dialogue-based management system of task faults capable of autonomously detecting and resolving issues through human-robot collaboration and dialogue.

The architecture uses a behavior-based paradigm [1], which allows communication and connectivity between sub-tasks. It encodes tasks into a hierarchical structure capable of incorporating multiple types of constraints, namely sequential, non-ordering, and multiple paths of execution (as shown in Fig. 1). The structures are composed of two types of nodes. **Goal Nodes** provide the base goal control behaviors of the hierarchical task structure used to encode task con-

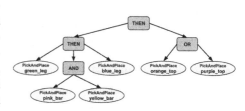

Fig. 1. The task tree for the EKET building task. Internal nodes are goal nodes and leaves are behavior nodes.

straints: sequential (**THEN**), non-ordering (**AND**), and alternative paths of execution (**OR**). **Behavior Nodes** are leaf nodes that encode the robot's physical behaviors.

Each node maintains a state consisting of several components (*activation level, activation potential, active,* and *done*), which is used for communication and connectivity between nodes. Each node's state is continuously updated to perform top-down and bottom-up activation spreading, which guarantees proper execution of the task with respect to its constraints. To execute a task, *activation spreading messages* are sent from the root node towards its children, thereby performing a top-down spreading of the *activation level* throughout the tree. Simultaneously, each nodes sends *status messages* (encoding a node's current state) to its parent node, thereby performing a bottom-up spreading of the *activation potential*. Each node's state is maintained via an update loop that performs a series of checks at each cycle. This loop uses the *activation potential* information to activate the node that has the highest potential [8].

3.2   Interfacing with the Control Architecture

To allow the architecture to handle interruptions that come from the fault detection system, the update loop of the nodes from [8] was modified by adding a checking mechanism that allows the loop to continue as normal unless a failure is detected. In case of a detected fault, a Robot Operating System (ROS) [16] message is published to the corresponding node's *issue* topic. Once the node receives such a message, the node's *issue* callback function is triggered (Fig. 2). In this function, a ROS message is published on the *dialogue* topic to initialize the dialogue that corresponds to the specific failure that was detected. This initiates the dialogue between the robot and human and allows the human to provide assistance (Sect. 3.3). After the dialogue is initialized, a while loop stops the current behavior in the architecture, as well as the physical motion of the robot, from finishing until a resolution has been reached through the dialogue between the robot and human. Since the node that the robot is working on is active at the time of the detected failure, no other nodes can be activated until that node is done or reset, allowing the entire architecture, and therefore task progress, to be paused from within a single node. This pause ensures that no task constraints are broken during the handling of the fault.

Once a resolution message is received from the dialogue system, changes are made to the node's state based on the type of resolution. If the resolution involves either the human, robot, or both, to complete the task then the node's state is set to *done* and its *activation level* is set to zero. In the case that the resolution is *human_finish*, the human will perform the required work to complete the task. If the resolution is *robot_finish*, then the robot will continue on with the remaining work required to finish the task, after being briefly assisted by the human (i.e. the human hands the robot an object that is out of its reach). Once the human completes the action, the robot is able to finish the

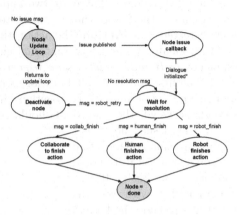

Fig. 2. State machine diagram of architecture flow upon issue detection.

task without further help. This assistance varies based on the task at hand and the issue found. If the resolution is *collab_finish*, then the human must work together with the robot simultaneously to complete the task (i.e., the human must hold and align an object as the robot connects another object). This resolution requires both agents to work together at the same time to fully complete the task.

Lastly, if the robot is required to retry the execution (*robot_retry*), the node gets deactivated. This deactivation sets the node's state back to what it was before the node was activated, thereby ensuring that the task constraints encoded by the task tree are still upheld after the conflict is resolved. The node's state is set to *not done* and its *activation level* is reset to its original level upon activation. If a node is deactivated, it can be chosen for activation at a later time and the robot can attempt the execution of that behavior again.

Pause and deactivate ensures that our architecture is able to maintain the task constraints during the entire task execution. The various resolution messages allow the architecture to utilize multiple ways to resolve a conflict, thus being able to handle different levels of conflict. Some resolutions only require a temporary pause of the architecture until the work is completed (minor fault), while others require the robot to retry (major fault, as it requires both pausing and deactivating the node, which in turn resets part of the task tree).

3.3 Dialogue Module

When a ROS message is published to the *dialogue* topic, the dialogue is initialized, as shown in Fig. 2. This initiates a communication between the robot and human. The high-level flow-chart for the initiated dialogue (Fig. 3) illustrates the major interactions that occur between the human and robot that encompass the extended dialogue. There are two main components to this interaction that are specific to the failure that was detected: **Detected issue** (the name of the issue detected) and **Action** (the action that needs to be performed).

Additionally, there are two internal checks which affect the outcome of the dialogue: *1) Human collaboration required?* and *2) Should robot complete task now?* The first checks if collaboration is required to complete the task, i.e. the human and robot must work together simultaneously to finish the task. The second checks whether the robot should complete the task at the current time.

If the issue does not require human collaboration the robot will ask if it should complete the task. If the human replies with *yes*, the robot will provide the human with instructions on how to reset the objects so the robot can complete the task on its own. Then, depending on the second check, the robot will either finish the task at the current time or inform the human that it will retry the task again later and the corresponding resolution message is published. If the human replies with a *no*, then the robot will ask if the human will complete the task. If the human again responds with *no*, the resolution message is published to enable the robot

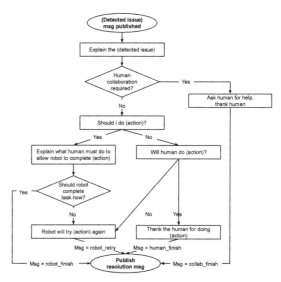

Fig. 3. Flow-chart of the dialogue initiated between robot and human when an issue is detected.

to retry and the human is notified. If the human responds with *yes*, the robot thanks the human and the resolution message for the human completing the task is published.

The robot utilizes an on-board speaker and the sound_play [9] software to communicate with the human. PocketSphinx [13] is used to recognize the human's *yes* or *no* responses. Once a response is recognized, the dialogue flow between robot and human continues accordingly.

This approach provides a simple way for new issues to be added into the system. Although specific details (such as the exact dialogue exchanges) will vary based on the issue, this flow outlines all of the necessary interactions that would occur between the human and the robot for any simple issue that could be added, emphasizing the generality of the proposed dialogue-based management system for fault recovery. The faults currently detected by our system for the assembly scenario (Sect. 4) are summarized below:

Positioning: The *positioning* issue message is raised if a robot needs assistance with precisely positioning an object as it is placed. The robot asks the human for help placing the object and thanks the human. The motion of the robot is then slowed down and the human can assist with the positioning of the object.

Missed: The *missed* issue message is raised when the robot misses an object during pick-up. The robot explains it missed the object and asks to try again. If the human agrees, the robot will ask the human to move the object to its original position on the table, and says it will try picking it again later. If the human disagrees, the robot asks if the human will place the object. If the human says *yes*, they will place it to the final location. Otherwise, the robot says it will try again later.

Dropped: The *dropped* issue message is raised when the robot drops an object after picking it up. The dialogue flow is the same as in the *missed* case, indicating drop instead of missed.

Unreachable: The *unreachable* issue message is raised if a robot is unable to reach an object. The robot will ask if the human can hand the object to the robot. If the human complies, the robot will grab the object and finish completing the task. If the human refuses, the robot will ask if the human will place the object. If the human says *yes*, the human will place the object to its final location. Otherwise, the robot says it will try again later.

3.4   Fault Detection System

In order for the architecture to detect issues, a fault-monitoring system has been added to each node in the task tree for the base control architecture [8]. Once a node gets activated, the system begins monitoring for faults during the execution of the node's work. In our work, this occurs during the execution of the *PickAndPlace*, which performs the following steps, in order: *1) move above the pick position, 2) move to the pick position, 3) close the gripper, 4) move back above the pick position, 5) move above the place position, 6) move to the place position, 7) open the gripper, and 8) move back above the place position.* To ensure the arm is not colliding with objects as it moves between pick and place locations, the arm is moved above (positive z-offset) the pick and place position after opening/closing the gripper.

During this sequence of steps, the monitoring system checks for various fault cases using a combination of the robot's on-board sensors. In the *dropped* and *missed* cases, the robot's motion along this path is interrupted and the arm is moved to a neutral location to wait until a resolution is reached.

In order to extend this monitoring system to new issues, we only need to define the start/stop step along the *PickAndPlace* sequence, which will begin/end the monitoring. However, the sensors used to check if the issue has occurred will vary based on the specifics of the issue. Additionally, these sensors might require specific settings, such as locations of objects in a particular camera.

For the *unreachable* fault, the starting and stopping steps are the first step in the sequence (i.e. move to *above pick location*). Before this motion occurs, the system checks if the object is within the robot's graspable range using a simple distance check from the robot to the object's initial location as detected from the Kinect on the PR2 robot's head.

A simple color blob detector implemented with OpenCV [4] is used to find objects in an image. HSV-segmentation of pre-trained color histograms, combined with morphological open/close operations, isolates large regions of color in the image to represent each object. The monitoring system uses these trained colors to identify whether or not the object is in the gripper by using the RGB image from the PR2's right forearm camera. The fault detection system searches the image for the color blob of the object's respective color. If the center of the blob is not within a predefined range of values in the image, it registers either the *missed* or *dropped* fault, depending on which part of the motion was being executed when the fault was detected.

The fault-monitoring system checks for a missed fault between the two *above pick location* steps (steps 1–4). If the color blob detection does not detect the object in the correct location in the forearm camera, it registers a *missed* fault. The system then checks for a *dropped* issue between the second *above pick location* step and the first *above place location* step (steps 4–5). At any point between these steps in the execution, if the color-blob detection does not detect the object in the correct location in the forearm camera, it registers a *dropped* issue.

The *positioning* issue is only checked at the first *above place location* (step 5). The system checks whether the carried object is in the list of predefined objects which require assistance. If the object requires help, the system registers a *positioning* issue: the robot slows down the movement from the *above place location* to the *place location* (steps 5–6), which allows the human ample time to align the necessary object as the robot connects the new object. The robot then moves to the *above place location* (step 8) and returns to regular speed.

The *dropped, missed,* and *unreachable* failures represent major issues as they require a complete interrupt of the robot motion and the architecture. Without human assistance, the robot would be unable to complete the task. On the other hand, the *positioning* issue is a lesser fault. The robot requires assistance to align the objects perfectly, but neither the robot motion nor the architecture need to be interrupted in this case. Thus, our dialogue-based management system for fault recovery allows the architecture to recover from faults of varying degrees.

4   Experimental Validation

The proposed architecture has been validated with a robot-human team in a scenario specifically designed to illustrate the key proposed contribution: *a control architecture that 1) autonomously detects and is cognizant of task execution failures, 2) initiates a dialogue with a human helper to obtain assistance, and 3) enables collaborative human-robot task execution through extended dialogue in order to 4) ensure robust execution of hierarchical tasks with complex constraints, such as sequential, non-ordering, and multiple paths of execution.* Most of the proposed additions to the architecture are outlined by general methods, so a concrete scenario with example cases for each addition is utilized to validate the combined functionality of the architecture.

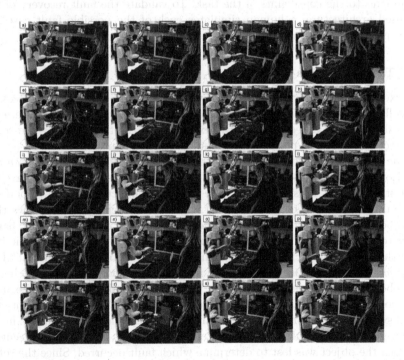

Fig. 4. Execution of the task with issues and assistance provided by the human.

The task used to validate the architecture involves building a modified EKET base from IKEA, with all parts painted in different colors for disambiguation. The task structure is shown in Fig. 1, representing inherent constraints for attaching the parts. The task is performed as follows: *1) place the green leg in front of the robot, 2) attach the pink and yellow bars in either order, 3) attach the blue leg, and 4) place either the purple or orange top on top.* Step 2 reflects the non-ordering constraints of the task since the order of placing the pink and yellow bars does not matter. Step 4 reflects the alternate paths of execution in the task since either one of the tops can be placed.

The parts are placed on a table in front of the PR2 robot. The *PickAndPlace* behavior nodes get their respective pick locations from an initial detection of objects using the Kinect by applying the same type of color blob detection utilized on the forearm cameras as discussed in Sect. 3.4. The respective place locations of the *PickAndPlace* behavior nodes are set as pre-specified locations in order to allow the objects to be attached together. End-effector trajectories to the pick/place locations are generated using the MoveIt library [19].

During the experiment, the robot determines the order of actions to take based on the activation spreading mechanism in our previously developed architecture [8]. This mechanism creates a dynamic ordering in which to complete the sub-tasks based on the environmental conditions and guarantees this ordering adheres to the constraints of the task. To validate the fault recovery of the proposed architecture, a human simulates each of the possible fault cases by interrupting robot during this task.

4.1   Task Execution

The execution of the experiment is shown in Fig. 4. To illustrate the recovery and collaboration capabilities of the proposed architecture, the human interfered by stealing several objects during the execution of the task, causing the robot to detect the various types of faults handled by the architecture.

The task begins with the robot performing the *PickAndPlace(green_leg)* behavior in pictures (a) and (b) in Fig. 4. This sub-task completed correctly without any faults, illustrating that the control architecture is able to perform as usual under normal conditions. Next, the control architecture specifies that the robot must place the pink and yellow bars in any order. The pink bar is closer to the robot's gripper so the architecture tells the robot to grab it first using the activation mechanism in [8]. Thus, in (c) the robot begins the *PickAnd-Place(pink_bar)* behavior. However, the human steals the pink bar right before the robot places the object (d). After the human steals the object the fault detection system detects a fault as described in Sect. 3.4. At this point, the vision system running on the forearm camera no longer detects the object in the robot's gripper. The fault detection system then uses the point during execution at which the object was lost to determine which fault occurred. Since the robot was en route to the place location, the fault system triggers a *dropped* issue to be published, which then causes the robot to begin a dialogue with the human as described in Fig. 3. The human follows the branch of the dialogue flow that leads to the human placing the pink bar as shown in (e).

After the fault is resolved and the object is placed, the robot continues the task by beginning the *PickAndPlace(yellow_bar)* behavior in (f). After the robot picks up the yellow bar, the human immediately steals it as shown in (g). Again, the fault detection system loses track of the object after the robot had successfully grasped the object so it triggers the *dropped* issue to be published, which causes the robot to begin a dialogue with the human. This illustrates that the dropped issue can get triggered in multiple parts of a sub-task's execution. This time however, the human follows the dialogue path that leads to the robot having to try again. In (g) the human places the yellow bar back on the table, as prompted by the dialogue, and the architecture resets the corresponding part of the task. Due to the task constraints, both the pink bar and yellow bar must be placed before moving on to the next part of the task, so the robot attempts the *PickAndPlace(yellow_bar)* behavior again in (i). During the placement of the yellow bar (j-k), the fault detection system determines that the object is one which was specified to require human assistance for placement. It then raises the *positioning* issue and asks the human for help in placing the object as described in the rightmost branch in Fig. 3. Once the object has been placed with the human's assistance, the robot continues to the next part of the task.

In (l) the human steals the blue leg right before the robot picks it up during the *PickAndPlace(blue_leg)* behavior. At this point during the execution, the fault detection system expects the object to be detected in the gripper. However, the object is not detected which means that the robot did not successfully grasp the object. Thus, the fault detection system triggers the *missed* issue to be published, which causes the robot to begin a dialogue with the human. The human follows the dialogue flow which leads to the robot trying again. In (m) the human places the blue leg back on the table, as prompted by the dialogue, and the architecture resets the corresponding part of the task. Due to the sequential task constraints, the blue leg must be placed before the next part of the task can happen, so the robot attempts the *PickAndPlace(blue_leg)* behavior again as shown in (n). In (o-p) the fault detection system once again triggers the *positioning* issue and asks the human for help since this object was also determined to be one which was specified to require assistance.

Based on the task constraints, the robot can choose to place either the orange or the purple top. Since the purple top is closer to the robot's gripper, the purple top is placed. In (q) the robot begins the *PickAndPlace(purple_top)* behavior. The fault detection system discovers that the purple top is out of the robot's reachable space since the distance check described in Sect. 3.4 fails. It then raises an *unreachable* issue. This triggers the dialogue and the human follows the flow that results in a hand-off between the human and robot (Fig. 3, left-most path) in (r). The robot finishes placing the purple top in (s). Finally, (t) shows the completed task with the fully assembled EKET base.

4.2 Discussion of Experiment

The execution of the experiment (Sect. 4.1) validates that our proposed architecture effectively utilizes the dialogue-based management system for fault recovery of hierarchical tasks. The detection of faults is done entirely with sensors on-board the robot through a combination of views from multiple cameras. The robot was able to complete the *PickAndPlace(green_leg)* behavior without fault.

This shows the architecture can complete tasks without assistance when no faults occur (Sect. 3.1). The execution of the *PickAndPlace(pink_bar)* and *PickAnd-Place(yellow_bar)* behaviors both illustrate examples of a *dropped* failure. These objects were detected as dropped along the behaviors' execution which demonstrates the system is able to detect and resolve faults at various points, as long as they occur between the start and stop steps during which the issue is monitored. Furthermore, they illustrate that failures can be resolved through either human assistance or another attempt from the robot. The execution of the *PickAnd-Place(blue_leg)* behavior demonstrated that the system is able to both detect and handle a *missed* failure. The steps for placing the blue leg and the yellow bar demonstrated that the dialogue-based management system is able to handle various major faults which require it to reset parts of the control architecture. This shows that the task constraints are upheld after the architecture is reset, since the architecture completed the placements of these objects before moving on (as defined by the task tree constraints). Lastly, the *PickAndPlace(purple_top)* behavior illustrates that the system is able to manage the *unreachable* fault and negotiate a hand-off between the human and robot.

The various behaviors demonstrate that the dialogue-based system is able to assist with the task execution in multiple resolution cases by utilizing the extended dialogue between the human and the robot. By showing each of these failure cases in a single scenario, it shows that the proposed system is able to robustly handle faults that occur during the execution of complex, hierarchical tasks. The robot is able to autonomously detect faults occurring from execution failures, begin a dialogue with the human to resolve these faults, and resume the normal task execution upon fault recovery without breaking any constraints.

5   Conclusion and Future Work

This paper presents an extension to our previous control architecture [8], which incorporates a dialogue-based management system for fault recovery of hierarchical tasks through the use of human-robot collaboration. The contribution of this approach is a control architecture that *1) autonomously detects and is cognizant of task execution failures, 2) initiates a dialogue with a human helper to obtain assistance,* and *3) enables collaborative human-robot task execution through extended dialogue* in order to *4) ensure robust execution of hierarchical tasks with complex constraints.* This method is able to autonomously detect faults occurring from execution failures, begin a dialogue with the human to resolve these faults, and resume normal task execution upon recovery. Furthermore, the architecture is able to uphold all task constraints while faults are being handled. Extended dialogue with the human allows for multiple avenues to resolve a detected fault, instead of a single request for help. Faults are detected autonomously with on-board sensors, through the robot's multiple cameras. The proposed approach is validated on a building task with a human-robot team. The system can robustly detect and recover from faults that occur during the execution of a complex, hierarchical task through the use of human-robot collaboration and dialogue.

An immediate extension of this work is to incorporate the proposed fault handling system into our multi-robot control architecture [3]. This extension will allow for humans to collaborate with multi-robot teams working on a joint task. For this extension, each robot's control architecture would be modified to incorporate our dialogue-based fault detection system as described in Sect. 3.2 for a single robot. This would allow each of the robots to initiate a dialogue with the human when a fault is detected. Additionally, the dialogue-based system could be modified to give the robots the option to ask each other for assistance to recover from faults as well. Furthermore, other fault types which may arise from translating to multi-robot teams can be easily implemented in this system, as they would follow the same general framework outlined in Sect. 3.

Acknowledgment. This work was supported by the National Science Foundation (IIS-1757929) and by the Office of Naval Research (ONR) award #N00014-16-1-2312.

References

1. Arkin, R.C.: An Behavior-based Robotics, 1st edn. MIT Press, Cambridge (1998)
2. Beetz, M., et al.: Robotic roommates making pancakes. In: 2011 11th IEEE-RAS International Conference on Humanoid Robots, pp. 529–536, October 2011
3. Blankenburg, J., et al.: A distributed control architecture for collaborative multi-robot task allocation. In: 2017 IEEE-RAS 17th International Conference on Humanoid Robotics (Humanoids), pp. 585–592, November 2017
4. Bradski, G., Kaehler, A.: Learning OpenCV: Computer vision with the OpenCV library. O'Reilly Media, Inc. (2008)
5. Breazeal, C., Hoffman, G., Lockerd, A.: Teaching and working with robots as a collaboration. In: Proceedings of the Third International Joint Conference on Autonomous Agents and Multiagent Systems-Volume 3, pp. 1030–1037. IEEE Computer Society (2004)
6. Fong, T., Thorpe, C., Baur, C.: Multi-robot remote driving with collaborative control. IEEE Trans. Ind. Electron. **50**(4), 699–704 (2003)
7. Fong, T., Thorpe, C., Baur, C.: Robot, asker of questions. Robot. Autonomous Syst. **42**(3), 235–243 (2003). https://doi.org/10.1016/S0921-8890(02)00378-0, socially Interactive Robots
8. Fraser, L., Rekabdar, B., Nicolescu, M., Nicolescu, M., Feil-Seifer, D., Bebis, G.: A compact task representation for hierarchical robot control. In: 2016 IEEE-RAS 16th International Conference on Humanoid Robots (Humanoids), pp. 697–704, November 2016. https://doi.org/10.1109/HUMANOIDS.2016.7803350
9. Gassend, B.: sound_play ros package. http://wiki.ros.org/sound_play
10. Hayes, B., Scassellati, B.: Autonomously constructing hierarchical task networks for planning and human-robot collaboration. In: 2016 IEEE International Conference on Robotics and Automation (ICRA), pp. 5469–5476. IEEE (2016)
11. Hayes, B., Shah, J.A.: Improving robot controller transparency through autonomous policy explanation. In: 2017 12th ACM/IEEE International Conference on Human-Robot Interaction (HRI), pp. 303–312. IEEE (2017)
12. Hernandez, C., et al.: Team delft's robot winner of the amazon picking challenge 2016. In: Behnke, S., Sheh, R., Sariel, S., Lee, D.D. (eds.) RoboCup 2016: Robot World Cup XX, pp. 613–624. Springer International Publishing, Cham (2017)

13. Huggins-Daines, D., Kumar, M., Chan, A., Black, A.W., Ravishankar, M., Rudnicky, A.I.: Pocketsphinx: a free, real-time continuous speech recognition system for hand-held devices. In: 2006 IEEE International Conference on Acoustics Speech and Signal Processing Proceedings, vol. 1, p. I. IEEE (2006)

14. Knepper, R.A., Tellex, S., Li, A., Roy, N., Rus, D.: Recovering from failure by asking for help. Auton. Robots **39**(3), 347–362 (2015). https://doi.org/10.1007/s10514-015-9460-1

15. Mohseni-Kabir, A., Rich, C., Chernova, S., Sidner, C.L., Miller, D.: Interactive hierarchical task learning from a single demonstration. In: Proceedings of the Tenth Annual ACM/IEEE International Conference on Human-Robot Interaction, pp. 205–212. ACM (2015)

16. Quigley, M., et al.: ROS: an open-source Robot Operating System. In: ICRA Workshop on Open Source Software, vol. 3 (2009)

17. Rybski, P.E., Yoon, K., Stolarz, J., Veloso, M.M.: Interactive robot task training through dialog and demonstration. In: Proceedings of the ACM/IEEE International Conference on Human-Robot Interaction, pp. 49–56. ACM (2007)

18. Schillinger, P., Kohlbrecher, S., von Stryk, O.: Human-robot collaborative high-level control with application to rescue robotics. In: 2016 IEEE International Conference on Robotics and Automation (ICRA), pp. 2796–2802. IEEE (2016)

19. Sucan, I.A., Chitta, S.: Moveit! (2013). http://moveit.ros.org

Gaze-Speech Coordination Influences the Persuasiveness of Human-Robot Dialog in the Wild

Kerstin Fischer[1]([✉]) [iD], Rosalyn M. Langedijk[1] [iD], Lotte Damsgaard Nissen[1] [iD],
Eduardo Ruiz Ramirez[2] [iD], and Oskar Palinko[2] [iD]

[1] Department of Design and Communication, University of Southern Denmark,
Sonderborg, Denmark
kerstin@sdu.dk
[2] SDU Robotics, Maersk Mc-Kinney Moller Institute, University of Southern Denmark,
Odense, Denmark

Abstract. In this study, we argue that the extent to which a robot is persuasive depends on the way a persuasive message is embedded in the robot's other behaviors. In the current study, in which a robot serves water at a large public event, we find that the same robot utterance, namely *skål (cheers)* when serving water, is received very differently depending on whether the robot is oriented to the user or not. In particular, if the robot gazes at the user while saying *skål*, almost all users drink immediately, whereas only 44.5% of the people drink if the robot is looking elsewhere. Similarly, the effectiveness of a water-related joke as a persuasive means depends on previously established mutual gaze. Thus, gaze and speech behavior have to be coordinated to improve the robot's persuasiveness in the wild.

Keywords: Human-robot interaction · Persuasion · Gaze

1 Introduction

One of the many tasks robots may take over in the future is to serve drinks; especially in elderly care, robots can serve water to older people who are not feeling thirsty and who need to be reminded to drink enough. Thus, in addition to serving fluids, robots may also have to be persuasive. Much work on persuasion focuses on identifying the effects of single, specific interventions. Very few studies address the interplay of several factors, and very little of this work has taken place in human-robot interaction research. However, there are good reasons to assume that the persuasiveness of utterances depends crucially on their embedding in other behavior, both in interactions between humans and in human-robot interaction. At the same time, human-robot interaction constitutes an excellent methodological platform to study the interplay between persuasive strategies on the one hand and non-verbal behaviors on the other.

In the current study, we study how effective persuasive messages presented by a robot that serves water at a large public event; in particular, we address to what extent the effectiveness of the robot's verbal utterances depends on the robot's gaze orientation.

© Springer Nature Switzerland AG 2020
A. R. Wagner et al. (Eds.): ICSR 2020, LNAI 12483, pp. 157–169, 2020.
https://doi.org/10.1007/978-3-030-62056-1_14

Fig. 1. The robot from the perspective of the wizards

We focus on the effects of the robot utterance *skål* (*cheers*) and of a water-related joke when serving water; in particular, we analyze how these messages are received depending on whether the robot is oriented to the user or not. The human-robot interaction takes place 'in the wild,' i.e. in an uncontrolled scenario, which allows us to investigate the interdependencies between gaze behavior and persuasive dialog in a naturalistic setting.

2 Previous Work

Previous work concerns research a) on the temporal coordination between speech and other robot behaviors, and b) on persuasive robot dialog.

2.1 Speech-Behavior Coordination

Research on interactions between people shows that the timing of their behaviors in modalities, such as speech, silence, gaze and gesture, influences how they make sense of an interaction. For example, concerning the coordination between interaction partners, the length of silence (i.e. the lack of speech and other non-verbal actions) has shown to be a reliable predictor for interactional problems [1]. In human interaction, people generally respond within a timeframe of between 300 ms and about a second [2], with some slight intercultural variation [3]. This means that responses that are delayed by more than one second are considered interactionally problematic.

This observation on data from naturally occurring human interaction also applies to human-robot interactions [4]; for instance, the timing of behaviors between participants influences how polite a robot is perceived to be. For example, Huang et al. [5] find that a robot that responds quickly to the user's need for assistance and then moves quickly to fulfill its task is perceived as more polite than a robot that takes more time to respond.

Concerning the timing between different human communication channels, research has mostly focused on the relationship between speech, gaze and gesture, but has also considered other actions. For instance, Clark and Krych [6] show that individual actions, such as holding or placing an object, are generally very well coordinated with speech in order to allow the partner to infer the other's intentions and to predict the next move (cf. also Clark [7]). Thus, the appropriate timing of multimodal action leads to legibility of the communicative function of this behavior and thus contributes to task success and the predictability of the actor.

Regarding human-robot interaction, a study by Jensen et al. [8], in which the effects of different ways of coordinating speech and robot behaviors were compared, shows that speech is different from other behavioral modalities such that people have much more distinct expectations about the timing of speech than about the timing of other robot behaviors; in particular, if verbal utterances are not tightly coordinated to other robot behaviors, this leads to interaction problems and confusion. Their study concerned the coordination between speech, robot approach and an arm gesture, where simultaneity of these behaviors yielded the best results.

Similarly, concerning the coordination of robot speech and gaze, Yamazaki et al. [9] show that people are more likely to respond to a robotic museum guide with non-verbal behaviors when the robot gazes in their direction at interactionally significant points. The coordination of gaze and other robot behaviors is also relevant during handovers. For example, Zheng et al. and Moon et al. [10] show that people reach for an object sooner when the robot gazes toward the handover position and even sooner if the robot gazes at the person compared to when it gazes away. Admoni et al. [11] show that a slight delay of the handover procedure increases people's attention towards the robot.

People also coordinate their gaze behavior with each other; for instance, Kendon [12] reports that people coordinate their gaze behavior very tightly with their communication partners, where contingent gaze is a direct indicator for joint attention, also in human-robot interaction [13]. Furthermore, mutual gaze is a very important communication cue in human-human interaction [14]; it is established when two people gaze at each other and realize this reciprocity. It is also very effectively used in human-robot interaction to augment communication [15, 16]. Mutual gaze may also be used for addressee selection [17].

2.2 Persuasive Robot Utterances

While persuasion in human interaction has been studied for centuries [18], there is still very little work in human-robot interaction.

Vossen et al. [19] have investigated the influence of robot embodiment on its persuasiveness; in this study, an agent tried to persuade users to choose an ecological program on a washing machine, and the physically embodied robot was more successful than a robot displayed on a screen.

Ham et al. [20] investigate the effects of different types of feedback on the persuasiveness of a robot; they find that feedback that appeals to social norms is more effective than factual feedback. Similarly, Winkle et al. [21] experiment with persuasive robot utterances, focusing on displays of goodwill and similarity to the user. Langedijk et al. [22] investigate effects of the personalization of social proof and reference to research findings and the users' expertise in human-robot interactions.

Very little work has studied the persuasiveness of robot's utterances in relationship to other behaviors; one exception is the study by Ham et al. [23] who had a robot tell a story with moral content and who investigated under which circumstances participants evaluated the story as most persuasive: if the robot looked at them while telling the story, if it used iconic gestures during the story telling, or based on the story content alone. They find that gaze has a significant effect on the persuasiveness of the story. These results suggest that gaze may have a considerable impact on the persuasiveness of robot dialog, but there is as yet no further research on the interplay between gaze and persuasive robot behavior, especially not in the wild, i.e. in uncontrolled environments in which the researcher has no control over who the participants are, whether they are thirsty or not, whether they have their own drinks, whether they want to interact with a robot or not etc. In-the-wild studies on behavior change have been conducted on isolated persuasive strategies in general (e.g. [24]), but not on robots and not in interaction.

In the current paper, we investigate the extent to which conventional communicative practices like jokes and toasting are effective persuasive strategies and the extent to which their persuasiveness depends on the robot's other interactional behaviors, i.e. gaze. In human interaction, according to Black [27], the toasting ritual (at least in one-on-one interactions) consists in participants uttering a fixed phrase, such as "cheers" or "skål", raising their glasses to each other, and engaging in drinking together [cf. also 28]. Thus, one may expect that mutual gaze may play some role in the effectiveness of such a ritual initialized by a robot. In contrast, jokes should be equally funny, and hence effective, independent of the speaker's gaze behavior. The two practices were thus chosen as instances at opposite ends of the spectrum of persuasive strategies in terms of expected relationships with mutual gaze.

3   Method

The current study was carried out in the cafeteria area at the campus of a Danish university that also hosts a major concert hall for the whole region. Thus, in addition to university students and staff during the day, large numbers of members of the general public gather in the building in the evening before the doors to the concert hall are opened. Events hosted there are of many different types, and the events taking place during the time of our recordings were two classical concerts, a movie previewing and a body-building convention. In this study, we concentrate on the four gatherings, which took place either in the late afternoon or in the evening; participants are members of the general public, many of whom are older adults.

While people were slowly gathering, the robot was driving around offering water to people sitting or standing. At the beginnings of our recordings, there were rather few people around, while towards the end, shortly before people were let into the concert hall, the robot was immersed in crowds of people.

3.1   The Robot

The SMOOTH robot (see Fig. 1) [25] is a large service robot developed to take over several tasks in elderly care facilities, including transporting laundry and guiding residents. It was thus optimized for economic feasibility on the one hand and for transport on the other. It carries its load on the back, which is probably appropriate for laundry and garbage transportation, but which may have disadvantages in a drink serving task [26] since the robot needs to turn around a bit in order to provide people with access to the water it is serving.

The robot is equipped with autonomous navigation and dialog capabilities, but to ensure participants' safety and to be able to adapt the dialog to the circumstances arising, the robot was controlled by two wizards, one for navigation and movement, the other for the dialog (see Sect. 3.2). The robot's head includes a microphone, speakers, cameras and two touch screens, one in the front and one in the back. The front touchscreen displays a pair of simulated eyes, with a white sclera and black pupils on a gray background. Given the size of the robot, its eyes are slightly below those of a person sitting on a chair. The touchscreen in the back was not used.

3.2   Robot Dialog

The dialogs were scripted and played according to a dialog model, with some flexibility for the wizard. In particular, a set of functionally equivalent utterances was defined from which the wizard could choose in order to vary the robot output so that overhearers would not witness the same dialogs over and over again. These were:

- five different greetings (*hi, hello, hi there, sorry to bother you, but...*, and *sorry to disturb you, but...*),
- six different robot utterances to offer some water (*How about some water?, Would you like something to drink?, You are probably thirsty – please take a drink, can I offer you some water, I wonder if you would like something to drink, may I offer you some water*),
- three different persuasive utterances we were testing (*Research shows that it is important to drink enough water during the day* and *Most women/men do actually take something to drink*),
- five different humorous utterances (e.g. *What did the ice cube say to the water? I was water before it was cool*),
- a request to take the water,
- a toasting utterance (*skål*), and
- five different closings (*Bye bye, Enjoy your drink, Goodbye, It was nice meeting you, Have a lovely day*).

Jokes were generally told after greetings or after offers to take something to drink, whereas the toasting utterance "skål" was typically uttered when the participants had accepted an offer to take a drink and had taken a glass of water from the robot's tray; however, there are also a few cases in which participants were not already equipped with glasses.

Most of the time, the phrase "please take your water" ("tag venligst din vand") was uttered before "skål", together with a slight turn so that participants could reach the glasses on the robot's back more easily, but in some cases, the participants reached out for the water on the tray without being directly encouraged by the robot. In all of these situations, the risk that people lose the mutual gaze with the robot was high. Mutual gaze was either regained by participants moving around to look into the robot's face or by the robot turning back, but in many cases, mutual gaze was not re-established. The example shown in Figs. 2a and 2b illustrates a typical interaction with the robot.

Fig. 2a. Example interaction (1–4)

3.3 Data Collection

Two wizards controlled the robot from a deck one floor above the experiment site, having a good overview of the experiments the entire time while not being noticed by the participants (see Fig. 1). The wizards had an audio connection to the robot and thus could hear the participants. They could see the interaction from above but not from the robot's perspective.

Three to four additional researchers were engaged in observing, interviewing and gathering consent forms from participants after the short-term interactions with the robot, as well as making sure that the robot's tray was filled with fresh beverages. These researchers also put the GoPro cameras in place around the experiment site and made sure that the GoPro mounted on top of the robot was turned on.

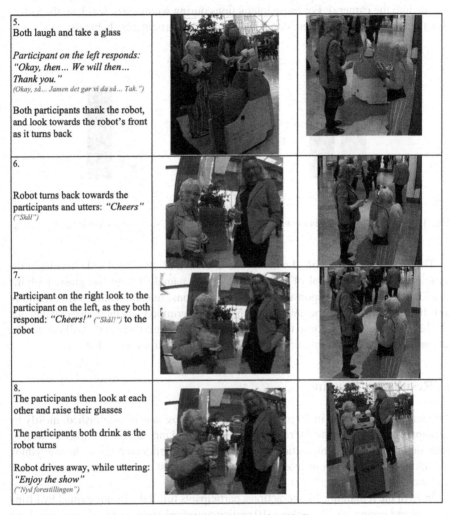

5. Both laugh and take a glass *Participant on the left responds:* *"Okay, then... We will then...* *Thank you."* (Okay, så... Jamen det gør vi da så... Tak.") Both participants thank the robot, and look towards the robot's front as it turns back		
6. Robot turns back towards the participants and utters: *"Cheers"* ("Skål")		
7. Participant on the right look to the participant on the left, as they both respond: *"Cheers!"* ("Skål!") to the robot		
8. The participants then look at each other and raise their glasses The participants both drink as the robot turns Robot drives away, while uttering: *"Enjoy the show"* ("Nyd forestillingen")		

Fig. 2b. Example interaction (5–8)

3.4 Data Analysis

For the analysis of the data, first all camera data from the robot's head were scrutinized for instances of "skål" and of the joke uttered by the robot; the number of occurrences of "skål" across the four evening events was 40, while the joke was told 19 times. Then, these interactions were copied into separate video files for subsequent analysis.

The data were then categorized into those interactions in which the target utterance was uttered under mutual gaze and those which were told without mutual gaze. Mutual gaze was identified by analyzing if the participant was visible in the head-mounted camera data and was orienting towards the robot's face (i.e. who was perceived as looking into the camera). For those interactions during which gaze was lost, the videos from the external cameras were consulted to analyze participants' behavior.

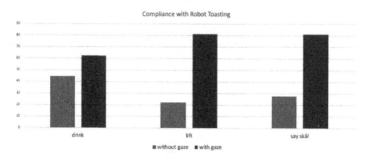

Fig. 3. Results of the analysis between robot gaze and people's responses to the robot toasting

The analysis then identified whether the utterance of "skål" led to behaviors in the participants that are typical of the toasting ritual, namely lifting the glass, replying "skål" and drinking in response to the robot's actions, that is, within a timeframe of 300–1000 ms. Similarly, the analysis of the joke determined whether people laugh and whether they drink in response to the robot's utterance. Figures 2a and 2b illustrates the data analysis of a typical interaction involving the use of toasting ("skål").

4   Results on Toasting

Our analysis reveals that in 20 interactions, mutual gaze was re-established, mostly by participants moving around the robot to take a glass and moving back to interact with its front. In four of these 20 interactions with mutual gaze, participants do not have anything to drink. Interestingly, in one interaction, participants toast to each other as soon as they have their glasses of water.

In 13 of the remaining 16 interactions, participants fulfill the toasting ritual by lifting the glass and saying "skål"; of these, 10 participants drink right away; of those who have toasted to the robot, two do not drink right away but rather take their glasses to their seats to drink them there, and the remaining participant has already started drinking when the robot utters "skål."

The remaining four participants who have water, who experience mutual gaze with the robot when the robot utters "skål" and who do not enter into the ritual comprise a person walking past to find a seat, one participant who is busy taking pictures, and one pair of young kids.

In contrast, in the 20 interactions in which there is no mutual gaze, only 8 participants drink in response to the toasting utterance; two do not drink because they do not have a glass when the robot utters "skål." Thus, 18 participants could have drunk from the water. Only four participants lift their glasses, while five reciprocate the robot's utterance and say "skål." Figure 3 illustrates the different distributions based on mutual gaze.

A chi-square test of independence shows that the difference in water consumption is not significant ($\chi^2(1,34) = 1.108$; p = .292), but that people lift their glasses ($\chi^2(1,34) = 11.806$; p = .001) and say "skål" ($\chi^2(1,34) = 9.722$; p = .002) significantly more often in the mutual gaze condition. Table 1 below presents an overview of the data.

Table 1. Means (and standard deviations) of participants drinking, lifting their glass and saying skål in response to the robot's utterance

	N	Drinks	Lifts	Says skål
No gaze	20	0.36 (0.49)	0.18 (0.39)	0.32 (0.48)
Gaze	20	0.55 (0.48)	0.65 (0.49)	0.70 (0.47)

5   Results on Joking

In the second study, we address to what extent two very similar jokes about carbonated water ('tickle water' in Danish) are responded to if told by a robot by those the robot is gazing at, in comparison with bystanders with whom no mutual gaze is established. Both jokes directly address the interaction partner, and they have a similar two-part structure. The two jokes are the following:

• I have something to make you laugh: tickle water!
• Do you know how to make a fish laugh? You put it into tickle water.

Because the two jokes are so similar, we treat them as the same kind of joke in the following analysis.

In total, the robot uttered the two versions of the joke 19 times (9 times in the first version and 10 times in the second); two interactions could not be analyzed because the robot was not in the view of one of the external cameras, or people were blocking the view on the interaction. This leaves us with 17 interactions with altogether 35 participants. We count as participants a) people in the field of view of the robot and b) people in close proximity to the robot who direct their attention to the robot; for example, they may be behind the robot to pick up some water. Similarly, we count as mutual gaze when a person is in view of the robot's head-mounted camera and is looking at the robot's 'face' (Table 2).

The results of a chi-square test of independence show significant differences between people's laughing behavior depending on whether or not there is mutual gaze between the participant and the robot ($\chi^2(1,35) = 13.895$; p = .001), while regarding drinking and

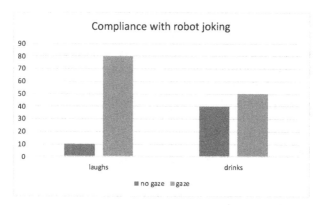

Fig. 4. People's responses to the robot joking (in percent)

Table 2. Means (and standard deviations) of participants laughing and drinking in response to the robot's joke

	N	Laughs	Drinks
No gaze	9	0.10 (0.33)	0.40 (0.53)
Gaze	26	0.80 (0.41)	0.50 (0.51)

mutual gaze the difference does not reach significance ($\chi^2(1,35) = 0.0005$; $p = .982$). We can conclude that the jokes are more effective such that participants will laugh more often when mutual gaze is established. Regarding water consumption, the connection between drinking and mutual gaze is less direct (Fig. 4).

6 Discussion

In the current investigation, we analyzed the persuasiveness of two robot behaviors in relationship with its other behaviors, in particular, a verbal utterance in relationship with the robot's body orientation. The toasting utterance was found to be extremely effective in getting the participants to drink and toast with the robot if the robot was also gazing at the participant. This finding is interesting because 1) it is obvious that the robot is not able to carry out the ritual of toasting with them besides providing a verbal utterance (but it cannot lift a glass and drink itself), and 2) it crucially depends on perceived mutual gaze. In particular, if the robot gazes at the user while saying *skål*, 62.5% of the users drink immediately, and further 15% join the toasting ritual with the intention to drink afterwards (when reaching their seats), whereas only 44.5% of the people drink if the robot is looking elsewhere. This results is remarkable since the fact that the robot is turning away is clearly functionally motivated and could also be understood as a polite behavior that is part of the continued interaction.

In contrast to people's participation in the toasting ritual, their drinking behavior is not directly predictable because of many additional context factors; still, if there is mutual gaze, the robot's utterance is very effective in encouraging them to drink.

We can thus conclude that the particular toasting ritual requires gaze coordination, which cannot be substituted by other social robot behaviors (such as friendly or polite previous interactions), though such previous interactions increase the probability that people drink the water later. Thus, our findings suggest that gaze and speech behavior need to be coordinated to improve the robot's persuasiveness in the wild.

The same observations have been made with respect to the robot's jokes, where the jokes reliably elicited laughter if they were uttered under mutual gaze, whereas they were significantly less effective when the robot was not looking at the participant. And like "skål", the jokes were moderately effective in eliciting drinking behavior by the participants.

Since this was a qualitative analysis of data elicited not in experimental scenarios but in an unstructured environment, the data base was necessarily rather small; the whole data set comprises 40 instances of the toasting ritual, 20 instances uttered with mutual gaze, 20 without. Regarding the jokes, the situation was even worse with 19 instances of the two jokes and 35 participants in total. Nevertheless, with the exception of young kids, almost all participants who had water already and thus for whom the basic preconditions for the success of the toasting ritual were fulfilled, irrespective of whether they were alone, in groups or in a family context, engaged in the ritual and drank their water; only if they were engaged in important other business, such as handling a camera or serving water to someone else, the toasting utterance failed to have its intended effect, whereas the variation is much higher in the situation in which the robot does not look at the participant. The same is true for the joke telling, where 80% of the participants responded with laughter if the robot gazed at them at the same time. Thus, even though the data basis is small, the fact that such a broad range of users respond so consistently to the persuasive robot behavior under mutual gaze suggests that toasting and jokes serve as persuasive strategies if coordinated with robot gaze.

Another possible limitation could be that toasting is an integral part of Danish culture, but may be less conventionalized in other cultures and hence less effective. However, since we could replicate the effect with respect to joke telling, it is likely that the coordination between persuasive utterance and robot gaze will also apply to other utterances and across cultures. The current findings are also compatible with the only other study [23] on the relationship between gaze behavior and the persuasiveness of robots.

7   Conclusions

The analysis of interactions in which the robot uttered "skål" or jokes in unstructured interactions with heterogeneous groups of participants, who were free to move in relation to the robot as they pleased, reveals significantly different responses to the robot's persuasive utterances depending on mutual gaze. Consequently, in spite of the uncontrolled setting, results on the effectiveness of robot utterances could be gathered. Thus, it seems not only possible to study robot persuasiveness "in the wild," it could also be shown that in spite of the contingencies of in-the-wild situations, robots can be persuasive social agents.

The study has furthermore shown that robots' gaze behavior influences significantly the effectiveness of persuasive utterances in human-robot interaction – even in the wild. While the contingency of the effectiveness of persuasive strategies on their interactional circumstances had previously been underestimated, our results show clearly that persuasion crucially depends on the coordination with other behaviors of the agent that produces it. Robot behavior should thus be designed in a holistic fashion, paying attention to the tight coupling between different robot behaviors, such as gaze and dialog behavior.

Acknowledgments. We wish to thank Selina Sara Eisenberger and Matous Jelinek for their help during the experiments. This project was supported by the Innovation Fund Denmark in the framework of the SMOOTH project, which we gratefully acknowledge.

References

1. Levinson, S.: Pragmatics. Cambridge University Press, Cambridge (1983)
2. Jefferson, G.: Talking About Troubles in Conversation. Oxford University Press, Oxford (2015)
3. Stivers, T., et al.: Universals and cultural variation in turn-taking in conversation. Proc. Natl. Acad. Sci. **106**(26), 10587–10592 (2009)
4. Pitsch, K., Kuzuoka, H., Suzuki, Y., Sussenbach, L., Luff, P.: Heath, 'the first five seconds': Contingent stepwise entry into an interaction as a means to secure sustained engagement in HRI. In: The 18th IEEE International Symposium on Robot and Human Interactive Communication. RO-MAN 2009, pp. 985–991. IEEE (2009)
5. Huang, C.-M., Mutlu, B.: Anticipatory robot control for efficient human-robot collaboration. In: 2016 11th ACM/IEEE International Conference on Human-Robot Interaction (HRI), pp. 83–90. IEEE (2016)
6. Clark, H.H., Krych, M.A.: Speaking while monitoring addressees for understanding. J. Memory Lang. **50**(1), 62–81 (2004)
7. Clark, H.H.: Speaking in time. Speech Commun. **36**(1), 5–13 (2002)
8. Jensen, L.C., Fischer, K., Suvei, S.-D., Bodenhagen, L.: Timing of multimodal robot behaviors during human-robot collaboration. In: 2017 26th IEEE International Symposium on Robot and Human Interactive Communication (RO-MAN), pp. 1061–1066. IEEE (2017)
9. Yamazaki, A., Yamazaki, K., Kuno, Y., Burdelski, M., Kawashima, M., Kuzuoka, H.: Precision timing in human-robot interaction: coordination of head movement and utterance, pp. 131–140 (2008)
10. Moon, A., et al.: Meet me where I'm gazing: how shared attention gaze affects human-robot handover timing, pp. 334–341 (2014)
11. Admoni, H., Dragan, A., Srinivasa, S.S., Scassellati, B.: Deliberate delays during robot-to-human handovers improve compliance with gaze communication. In: Proceedings of the 2014 ACM/IEEE International Conference on Human-Robot Interaction, pp. 49–56 (2014)
12. Kendon, A.: Some functions of gaze-direction in social interaction. Acta Physiol. (Oxf) **26**, 22–63 (1967)
13. Lohan, K.S.: Tutor spotter: proposing a feature set and evaluating it in a robotic system. Int. J. Soc. Robot. **4**(2), 131–146 (2012)
14. Argyle, M., Cook, M.: Gaze and mutual gaze (1976)
15. Admoni, H., Scassellati, B.: Social eye gaze in human-robot interaction: a review. J. Hum.-Robot Interact. **6**(1), 25–63 (2017)

16. Palinko, O., Rea, F., Sandini, G., Sciutti, A.: Eye gaze tracking for a humanoid robot. In: 2015 IEEE-RAS 15th International Conference on Humanoid Robots (Humanoids), pp. 318–324. IEEE (2015)

17. Palinko, O., Fischer, K., Ruiz Ramirez, E., Damsgaard Nissen, L., Langedijk, R.M.: A drink-serving mobile social robot selects who to interact with using gaze. In: Companion of the 2020 ACM/IEEE International Conference on Human-Robot Interaction, pp. 384–385 (2020)

18. Higgins, C., Walker, R.: Ethos, logos, pathos: strategies of persuasion in social/environmental reports. In: Accounting Forum, vol. 36, no. 3, pp. 194–208. Taylor & Francis (2012)

19. Vossen, S., Ham, J., Midden, C.: Social influence of a persuasive agent: the role of agent embodiment and evaluative feedback. In: Proceedings of the 4th International Conference on Persuasive Technology, pp. 1–7 (2009)

20. Ham, J., Midden, C., Tak, S.: The persuasive effects of positive and negative social feedback from an embodied agent on energy conservation behavior (2008)

21. Winkle, K., Lemaignan, S., Caleb-Solly, P., Leonards, U., Turton, A., Bremner, P.: Effective persuasion strategies for socially assistive robots. In: 2019 14th ACM/IEEE International Conference on Human-Robot Interaction (HRI), pp. 277–285. IEEE (2019)

22. Langedijk, R., Fischer, K., Jensen, L.C.: Persuasive effects of the personalization of social proof on human-robot interactive dialog. Submitted

23. Ham, J., Cuijpers, R.H., Cabibihan, J.-J.: Combining robotic persuasive strategies: the persuasive power of a storytelling robot that uses gazing and gestures. Int. J. Soc. Robot. 7(4), 479–487 (2015)

24. Goldstein, N.J., Cialdini, R.B., Griskevicius, V.: A room with a viewpoint: Using social norms to motivate environmental conservation in hotels. J. Consumer Res. 35(3), 472–482 (2008)

25. Juel, W.K., et al.: Smooth robot: design for a novel modular welfare robot. J. Intell. Robotic Syst. 98(1), 19–37 (2020)

26. Fischer, K., et al.: Integrative social robotics hands-on. Interact. Stud. 21(1), 145–185 (2020)

27. Black, R. (ed.): Alcohol in Popular Culture: An Encyclopedia: An Encyclopedia. ABC-CLIO (2010)

28. Kotthoff, H.: Comparing drinking toasts – comparing contexts. In: Cornelia Gerhardt, C., Frobenius, M., Ley, S. (eds.) Culinary Linguistics, pp. 211–240. John Benjamins Publishing Company, The Chef's Special (2013)

Robots Are Moral Actors: Unpacking Current Moral HRI Research Through a Moral Foundations Lens

Dylan Doyle-Burke[(⊠)] and Kerstin S. Haring[(⊠)]

University of Denver, Denver, CO 80203, USA
{Dylan.Doyle-Burke,Kerstin.Haring}@du.edu

Abstract. Even with the increasing frequency of robot experiences in our daily lives, relatively little research has been done to explore the moral implications of these human-robot interactions (HRI). Of the existing moral HRI research, much of it assumes a moral dimension without clearly defining what moral framework is being applied. To research such a framework, it is crucial to evaluate current research for a communicable moral framework, that is also in dialogue with key moral frameworks in social science spaces. This work uses a narrative literature review to analyze moral HRI research through the lens of the Moral Foundations Theory. The analysis will situate moral HRI work in the seminal moral theory within social science spaces and show where current gaps in HRI research might exist. Evaluating research through the lens of the moral foundations theory framework will strengthen the existence of a 'Moral HRI' field that is related but distinct from general HRI.

Keywords: Human-Robot Interaction · Morality · Ethics

1 Introduction

The concept of autonomous robotic entities has existed since the Greco-Roman era. Yet, it has only been within the last century that technology has advanced to the point of being able to make robots a material daily reality. As robots became increasingly prevalent in public spaces, engineering, computer science, and other disciplines began to research questions of how robots were perceived and engaged within social spaces. In the wake of these questions Human-Robot Interaction (HRI) emerged as a multi-disciplinary field in the mid 1990s and early 2000s. A partial reason for HRI's emergence as a separate field was precisely to facilitate dialogue across multiple disciplines. Early disciplines that contributed to HRI research included robotics, cognitive science, human factors, philosophy, natural language, psychology, and human–computer interaction.

The core research question of the HRI field can be described as to understand and shape the interactions between one or more humans and one or more robots. Corollary research questions stemming from this core research question may include how to design effective robots for diverse tasks, how robot interaction

© Springer Nature Switzerland AG 2020
A. R. Wagner et al. (Eds.): ICSR 2020, LNAI 12483, pp. 170–181, 2020.
https://doi.org/10.1007/978-3-030-62056-1_15

impacts human understanding of themselves and others, and many others. As the potential social harms of robot design have increasingly become featured in movie productions and media, entering the public consciousness, studies have added moral questions to their research.

A 2015 study identified a "new field of Moral HRI" that is distinct from the broader HRI field [21]. The authors wrote that "What one might call Moral HRI provides the appropriate context to address several pressing questions through empirical investigation: What capacities would render a robot a natural target of human moral judgments? How would people make such moral judgments? And what systems of norms would they impose on the robot—what obligations, permissions, and rights?" After concluding that there are "differences both in the norms people impose on robots and the blame people assign to robots" the 2015 study prescribed that "it is now a joint task for HRI and moral psychology to identify the underlying causes for these differences." Since the 2015 study, research groups within general HRI and Moral HRI have continued to build on the development of the Moral HRI field compelling greater collaboration between the fields of HRI and moral psychology.

This study presents a narrative literature review of the research produced within the emerging field of Moral HRI since the publication of the 2015 study that introduced Moral HRI as a field. Using a moral psychology lens drawing from Moral Foundations Theory [11] this paper presents a summarized representation of the Moral HRI field and posits a potential theoretical framework to orient and conceptualize the field moving forward.

Moral Foundations Theory contains four core claims: 1. Nativism – That there is a "first draft" of the moral mind that is revised based on environmental factors. 2. Cultural learning – That among the key environmental factors that shape the "first draft" of a moral mind is culture. 3. Intuitionism – That moral intuitions come first and that moral strategic reasoning comes second in a given situation. 4. Pluralism – That there are many recurrent social challenges, so there are many moral foundations.

Following from these four core claims, Moral Foundations Theory delineates six primary moral foundations for understanding moral actions and perception: 1. Care: focuses on not harming others and protecting the vulnerable; opposite of Harm 2. Fairness or Proportionality: rendering justice according to shared rules and assumes equivalent exchange; opposite of Cheating 3. Loyalty or Ingroup: concerns a collective entity instead of individuals, standing with your group, family, team, military, and nation; opposite of Betrayal 4. Authority or Respect: submitting to tradition and legitimate authority, resulting in maintaining the hierarchy; opposite of Subversion 5. Sanctity or Purity: abhorrence for disgusting things, foods, actions, feeling of disgust caused by the impure; opposite of Degradation 6. Liberty; lack of coercion by a dominating power; opposite of Oppression.

Though historically focused on human moral action, this model provides a framework for organizing and understanding human-robot moral action. The purpose of this work is to demonstrate that existing literature fits within a narrative recounting using moral foundations theory as its framework. By using the categories of Moral Foundations Theory they posit a framework to organize past Moral HRI research, and suggest gaps to be addressed in future research.

2   Methodology

This study used a narrative literature review to establish a comprehensive analysis of the current knowledge on the topic of Moral HRI as it relates to Moral Foundations Theory. We establish how currently published research in Human-Robot-Interaction creates a context for the application of Moral Foundation Theory to the interactions humans have with robots. The parameters of the literature search are peer-reviewed articles published in the English language. The articles are searched in scholarly search engines (i.e. Google Scholar, Microsoft Academic, WorldWideScience, Science.gov, iSeek, ResearchGate). The preliminary search terms focused on research in the area of HRI with a relation to six concepts of understanding moral actions. Search terms included "Moral HRI," "HRI Case Study," "Care in HRI," "HRI Fairness," "HRI Cheating," "HRI Loyalty," "HRI Betrayal," "HRI Authority," "HRI Disgust," and "HRI Liberty" in combination with spelling out acronyms, as well as adding or subtracting independent terms. From these searches 113 unique articles emerged.

All articles found with this method were screened to identify the work that either explicitly named morality, and/or the field of Moral HRI as primary subjects of their inquiry, and/or conducted research related to the six concepts of understanding moral actions. 32 articles were found through this process to be included in this narrative review (see Tables 1, 2, 3, 4 and 5). These articles formed the primary dataset for the study used to conduct a qualitative content analysis. It was then analysed how each of these articles are related to Moral Foundations Theory or to one of its six underlying concepts, and how the finding might fit within a Moral Foundations Framework for human-robot interactions.

It is important to note that this study is not making claims about the representativeness of this dataset. This study is not meant to be a comprehensive analysis of all available moral HRI literature. Rather, it is an initial examination into an organizing framework for a moral HRI metanarrative based on the language of Moral Foundations Theory. The ultimate goal of this and following future work is an increased scientific discussion and cohesion of the Moral HRI field going forward.

3   Results

We report the research found separated by the six concepts of understanding moral actions. Each section explains the concept, how human-robot interactions could relate to the concept, and outlines the research found in the area and how it relates to the individual concept.

3.1   The Moral Foundation for Care; Opposite of Harm

The Care/Harm foundation describes the concepts of not harming others and protecting the vulnerable. In application to robots this means that articles are considered in which robots afford some level of care for a human, protect a vulnerable person, or distinctly make an effort to protect a human from harm and not harming the human, even if it might come at a cost to the robot. Science Fiction has played with this moral foundation, most famously with the First of the Asimov's Three Laws of Robotics: "A robot may not injure a human being or, through inaction, allow a human being to come to harm."

In the collected dataset, 5 articles were found that relate to this foundation. The articles found can be classified into two general areas of research, one in which the robot is tasked with the care of an individual in a therapeutic or medical context, and another in which the robot is tasked with the care of an individual or a group in a crisis context. These studies evaluate and measure the human reaction and behaviors displayed when a robot is placed in charge of a care task. There is some overlap with trust research and other moral foundations, like loyalty/subversion and authority/subversion.

The moral implications with regards to the Care/Harm foundation from the studies pose the question if it is moral for robots to be place into positions of care, how do people respond to robotic caregivers compared to human caregivers in therapeutic and medical contexts, especially when the person receiving the care is physically vulnerable, and how do humans and the robot respond when a robot causes harm in a context where the robot is expected to provide care?

Table 1. Articles relating to the moral foundation of Care/Harm

	Year	Relation to Moral Foundation of Care/Harm
[18]	2019	This work studies non-literal indirect speech acts (ISAs) including a description of how a robot's inability to understand ISAs harms human perception that the robot can express care
[33]	2018	This work examines dynamics of care between humans and interactive robots during a therapy intervention in which the agent provides corrective feedback
[28]	2016	This work examines human perception of trust in a robot when the robot is put in charge of the human's immediate perceived safety. An experiment was performed where a participant interacts with a robot in a non-emergency task to experience its behavior and then chooses whether to follow the robot's instructions in an emergency or not
[27]	2017	This work examines human perception of trust and potential danger when a robot is put in charge of leadership and care in time-sensitive situations
[3]	2000	This work examines dynamics between a robot and a human caregiver related to the human agent's perception of care for the robot depending on intensity and context-diverse stimuli

3.2   The Moral Foundation for Fairness; Opposite of Cheating

The Fairness/Cheating foundation describes the concepts of rendering justice according to shared rules and assumes equivalent exchange and proportionality. In application to robots this means that articles are considered in which robots violate the fairness or proportionality assumption by cheating. Currently, it seems that a robot cheating is within violating the (often unspoken) rules of clearly defined games.

Table 2. Articles relating to the moral foundation of Fairness/Cheating

	Year	Relation to moral foundation of fairness/cheating
[14]	2019	This work examines whether, when caught cheating, a human agent and a robot agent are evaluated differently in terms of reactionary behaviors as well as attribution of mental states and perception of competence, warmth, agency, and capabilities to experience
[26]	2019	This work investigates whether people will cheat while in the presence of a robot and to what extent this depends on the role the robot plays
[20]	2015	This work investigates whether there may be a correlation between robot movement in an act of cheating and perception of that cheating
[32]	2014	This work investigates to what extent the type of agent (human or robot) and the type of behavior (honest or dishonest) affected perceived features of agency and trustworthiness in the context of a competitive game
[30]	2010	This work examines the degree to which variations in robot behavior within a game context result in attributions of mental state and intentionality when it comes to cheating actions
[31]	2017	This work examines how technology and robots are increasingly impacting decisions in law of perceived fairness and justice
[25]	2014	This work investigates the use of Artificial Intelligence (AI) in relation to rendering arbitrational verdicts in a court of law as it relates to perceived fairness, objectivity, and justice

In the collected dataset, seven articles were found that relate to this foundation. The articles predominantly researched how humans react to robots who cheat within a clearly defined game. Articles about "robot-judges" that use Artificial Intelligence to make justice determinations are also included. The findings with regards to robot cheating in games (e.g. Rock Paper Scissors) seem to vary. It was reported that that people have shown a muted response to a cheating robot compared to a cheating robot, a similar response for both, and people showing an elevated response with the robot compared to a human baseline. The idea of cheating in a game is a limited one with regards to the moral foundation for Fairness/Cheating. The foundation has a broader impact as fairness is not always the direct opposite of cheating. There is additional research in interactions with artificial humans that considers negotiations of goods, and even research looking into fair algorithms, machine learning, and artificial intelligence. For this work, we considered only the robot aspects in combinations with such underlying capacities, yet it is important to keep in mind that it has been outlined in several instances that Artificial Intelligence as a decision making support for justice determination is biased and therefore does not make fair recommendations. The problems and implications of this go far beyond the scope of this work, yet it is important to consider how recommendations are perceived when the underlying (unfair) artificial intelligence has a robot "body" and gives it a "face".

At the heart of these studies are questions of what the moral implications are of robots being trained to cheat, and how human perception changes in a given scenario based on whether they are interacting with a robot or a human.

3.3   The Moral Foundation for Loyalty or Ingroup; Opposite of Betrayal

The Loyalty/Betrayal foundation describes the concepts of a collective entity instead of individuals. It is described as standing with the respective group (e.g. family, team, military, nation), and the opposite can be considered as out-group and betrayal. In application to robots this means that articles are considered that look into in-group/out-group considerations in regards to robots, if robots can be seen as a within group member, if robots could be teammates, and also crossing into research on trust towards robots.

In the collected dataset, 8 articles were found that relate to this foundation. These articles predominantly focused on questions of human-robot teamwork, social and moral agency, human response when a robot betrays expectations, to what degree humans are willing and able to trust a robot in a diversity of contexts, and human evaluation of loyalty of a robot. In these articles there are a multiplicity of conclusions about the factors that impact how humans interact with concepts of trust, loyalty and betrayal in response to robots. Depending on the identity of the human, the perceived identity of the robot, and the context in which the research was conducted, these articles demonstrated that there is a large spread of possible methodologies and research questions for future research under this moral foundation.

3.4   The Moral Foundation for Authority or Respect; Opposite of Subversion

The Authority/Subversion foundation describes the concepts of respect, submitting to tradition and legitimate authority resulting in maintaining the hierarchy and is the opposite of subversion, the attempt to overthrow or undermine authority.

In application to robots this means that articles are considered in which robots are given authority, take on the role of an authority over a human, or in which robots subvert human authority. In the collected dataset, 8 articles were found that relate to this foundation. The articles in this category attempt to measure human perception and response of robot authority and subversion.

Table 3. Articles relating to the moral foundation of Loyalty/Betrayal

	Year	Relation to Moral Foundation of Loyalty/Betrayal
[8]	2020	This work engages with the question of robot deception by asking if a robot sends a deceptive signal to a human user if it is always and everywhere an unethical act
[17]	2019	This work argues that providing robots with social behaviors and natural language capabilities causes laypeople to naturally perceive them as social and moral agents
[22]	2016	This work explores how robot appearance affects people's moral judgments about robots, especially in terms of trust and loyalty
[23]	2016	Through the concept of the Uncanny Valley (UV) this work demonstrates an UV in subjects' explicit ratings of likability for a large, objectively chosen sample of 80 real-world robot faces and a complementary controlled set of edited faces. This work then analyzes this dataset using concepts of trust and betrayal
[5]	2014	This work studies the effects of a robot's performance and behavioral style on human trust
[15]	2013	This work reports the results from an experiment examining people's perception and trust when interacting with an android robot
[12]	2010	This work explored how robots may attribute blame to humans in order to identify problems and help humans make sense of complex information and the human response and perception to this attribution of blame
[13]	2007	This work challenges the assumption that robots will succeed as teammates alongside humans and argues that lacking human-like mental models and a sense of self, robots may prove untrustworthy and will be rejected from human teams

For example, articles evaluating the compliance with a robot's request with the robot assuming an authority role and how this compares to a human's request baseline are included. Also included is the opposite, noncompliance interactions and how the robot's and human's gender influence noncompliance.

3.5 The Moral Foundation for Sanctity or Purity; Opposite of Degradation

The Sanctity/Degradation foundation describes the concepts of feelings of repulsion for disgusting things, foods, or actions. The feeling of disgust can be caused by what is considered to be impure. In application to robots this means that articles considered that follow on one of two research paths: (1) how humans respond to affective or expressive robots and (2) how humans respond to robots as a weapon.

In the collected dataset, 4 articles were found that relate to this foundation. Articles found in this area were included as they tangentially relate to human

Table 4. Articles relating to the moral foundation of Authority/Subversion

	Year	Relation to Moral Foundation of Authority/Subversion
[19]	2020	This work presents an experiment that explores the effects of robot and human gender on perceptions of robots in noncompliance interactions, and find evidence of a complicated interplay between these gendered factors
[29]	2019	This work explores people's social perception of human versus robotic coaches
[17]	2019	This work presents a human subjects experiment showing some of the consequences of miscalibrated responses, including perceptions of the robot as inappropriately polite, direct, or harsh, and reduced robot likeability
[1]	2017	This work identifies and analyses the factors that affect humans decisions to follow robotic instruction
[10]	2015	This work explores how to maximize both team efficiency in human robot teams and the desire of human team members to work with robotic counterparts
[4]	2014	This work presents an experiment designed to determine whether a robot's appearance has a significant effect on the amount of agency people ascribed to it and its ability to dissuade a human operator from forcing it to carry out a specific command
[7]	2013	This paper presents an investigation into how people respond to a robot posing as an authority figure, giving commands
[16]	2004	This study examines how people respond to robotic coworkers

responses of disgust. It seems that research so far has focused on what makes robots more pleasurable to interact with rather than elicit a disgust response from people, Therefore, studies that directly focus on disgust or sanctification were not found. It is possible that to fully explore moral HRI, questions sanctity and degradation need to be examined in more details.

3.6 The Moral Foundation for Liberty; Opposite of Oppression

The Liberty/Oppression foundation depicts the feelings of reactance and resentment people feel toward those who dominate them and restrict their liberty. Its intuitions are often in tension with those of the authority foundation. In application to robots this means that articles are considered where robots either are the source of oppression or enable liberty. There were no studies within the dataset that were appropriate to place in this category. This might point to a useful area to focus future research to enhance knowledge in the Moral HRI field.

Table 5. Articles found for the moral foundation of Sanctity/Degradation

	Year	Relation to Moral Foundation of Sanctity/Degradation
[9]	2019	This work aims at the development of a framework able to recognise human emotions through facial expression for human-robot interaction
[2]	2016	This paper considers the ethical challenges facing the development of robotic systems that deploy violent and lethal force against humans
[6]	2010	This work explores how artificial agents can be used to assess how factors like anthropomorphism affect neural response to the perception of human actions
[24]	2006	This paper reports the results of the first study comparing subjects' responses to robotic emotional facial displays and human emotional facial displays

4   Discussion

Based on the 32 article dataset used, our findings conclude that the moral foundations theory framework is an appropriate and useful framework to scaffold existing moral HRI research upon and help inform gaps in knowledge and future research questions for the field. Barring the sanctity/degradation foundation and newly added liberty/oppression foundation, each moral foundation category can easily be mapped onto existing research in a narrative framework. Because of the lack of case studies present in the sanctity/degradation category that might point to a rich unexplored research area for moral HRI.

As the data and research representing moral questions in HRI continue to expand at a rapid pace it is imperative that the discipline coalesces over a common language and model in order to more effectively build a unified field. This study presents one possible framework for that common language and orientation. Based on the call to action as dictated by the authors of the seminal 2015 Moral HRI paper to substantiate the field of Moral HRI through an intentional coordination between HRI and moral psychology, this study presents an answer to that call by directly putting HRI research in dialogue with moral foundations theory.

By using moral foundations theory to ground and scaffold past, present, and future Moral HRI research there is the potential to unify a quintessentially diverse and interdisciplinary field under an agreed-upon schema. Moral foundations theory presents a pluralistic and adaptable framework that is already well respected and integrated into moral psychology practices. By using theory to help orient Moral HRI it not only allows for a common language to be spoken within the Moral HRI field but also can help facilitate dialogue between disciplines.

Ideally, future research will utilize moral foundations theory to further explore its potential application in the emerging field of Moral HRI. Specifically, the application of the model in this limited study appears to point to a need for greater Moral HRI research in the sanctity/degradation realm. Future research may also include a more formal systematic literature review applying a larger dataset to the same paradigm in order to provide a more quantitative analysis of whether it is appropriate to utilize the moral foundations framework as the possible foundation of the Moral HRI field.

5 Conclusion

As the field of Moral HRI continues to emerge and be defined there is a need for unifying frameworks that help support and organize its growth. This study has proposed that moral foundations theory is a framework that is a relevant possibility to scaffold past, present and future research.

References

1. Agrawal, S., Williams, M.A.: Robot authority and human obedience. In: Proceedings of the Companion of the 2017 ACM/IEEE International Conference on Human-Robot Interaction (2017). https://doi.org/10.1145/3029798.3038387
2. Asaro, P.: "hands up, don't shoot!" HRI and the automation of police use of force. J. Hum.-Robot Interact. 5(3), 55 (2016). https://doi.org/10.5898/jhri.5.3.asaro
3. Breazael, C., Scassellati, B.: Infant-like social interactions between a robot and a human caregiver (2006). https://doi.org/10.21236/ada450357
4. Briggs, G., Gessell, B., Dunlap, M., Scheutz, M.: Actions speak louder than looks: does robot appearance affect human reactions to robot protest and distress? The 23rd IEEE International Symposium on Robot and Human Interactive Communication (2014). https://doi.org/10.1109/roman.2014.6926402
5. van den Brule, R., Dotsch, R., Bijlstra, G., Wigboldus, D.H.J., Haselager, P.: Do robot performance and behavioral style affect human trust? Int. J. Soc. Robot. 6(4), 519–531 (2014). https://doi.org/10.1007/s12369-014-0231-5
6. Chaminade, T., et al.: Brain response to a humanoid robot in areas implicated in the perception of human emotional gestures. PLoS One 5(7), e11577 (2010)
7. Cormier, D., Newman, G., Nakane, M., Young, J.E., Durocher, S.: Would you do as a robot commands? an obedience study for human-robot interaction. In: International Conference on Human-Agent Interaction (2013)
8. Danaher, J.: Robot Betrayal: a guide to the ethics of robotic deception. Ethics Inf. Technol. 22(2), 117–128 (2020). https://doi.org/10.1007/s10676-019-09520-3
9. Faria, D.R., Vieira, M., Faria, F.C., Premebida, C.: Affective facial expressions recognition for human-robot interaction. In: 2017 26th IEEE International Symposium on Robot and Human Interactive Communication (RO-MAN) (2017). https://doi.org/10.1109/roman.2017.8172395
10. Gombolay, M., Gutierrez, R., Sturla, G., Shah, J.: Decision-making authority, team efficiency and human worker satisfaction in mixed human-robot teams. Robot.: Sci. Syst. X (2014). https://doi.org/10.15607/rss.2014.x.046
11. Graham, J., Haidt, J., Nosek, B.A.: Moral foundations dictionary. PsycTESTS Dataset (2009). https://doi.org/10.1037/t48554-000
12. Groom, V., Chen, J., Johnson, T., Kara, F.A., Nass, C.: Critic, compatriot, or chump? In: Proceeding of the 5th ACM/IEEE International Conference on Human-Robot Interaction - HRI 10 (2010). https://doi.org/10.1145/1734454.1734545

13. Groom, V., Nass, C.: Can robots be teammates?: Benchmarks in human-robot teams. Interact. Stud. **8**(3), 483–500 (2007)
14. Haring, K., Nye, K., Darby, R., Phillips, E., de Visser, E., Tossell, C.: I'm not playing anymore! a study comparing perceptions of robot and human cheating behavior. In: Salichs, M.A., Ge, S.S., Barakova, E.I., Cabibihan, J.-J., Wagner, A.R., Castro-González, Á., He, H. (eds.) ICSR 2019. LNCS (LNAI), vol. 11876, pp. 410–419. Springer, Cham (2019). https://doi.org/10.1007/978-3-030-35888-4_38
15. Haring, K.S., Matsumoto, Y., Watanabe, K.: How do people perceive and trust a lifelike robot. In: Proceedings of the World Congress on Engineering and Computer Science, vol. 1 (2013)
16. Hinds, P.J., Roberts, T.L., Jones, H.: Whose job is it anyway? A study of human-robot interaction in a collaborative task. Hum.-Comput. Interact. **19**(1–2), 151–181 (2004)
17. Jackson, R.B., Wen, R., Williams, T.: Tact in noncompliance. In: Proceedings of the 2019 AAAI/ACM Conference on AI, Ethics, and Society (2019). https://doi.org/10.1145/3306618.3314241
18. Jackson, R.B., Williams, T.: Language-capable robots may inadvertently weaken human moral norms. In: 2019 14th ACM/IEEE International Conference on Human-Robot Interaction (HRI) (2019). https://doi.org/10.1109/hri.2019.8673123
19. Jackson, R.B., Williams, T., Smith, N.: Exploring the role of gender in perceptions of robotic noncompliance. In: Proceedings of the 2020 ACM/IEEE International Conference on Human-Robot Interaction (2020). https://doi.org/10.1145/3319502.3374831
20. Litoiu, A., Ullman, D., Kim, J., Scassellati, B.: Evidence that robots trigger a cheating detector in humans. In: Proceedings of the Tenth Annual ACM/IEEE International Conference on Human-Robot Interaction - HRI 2015 (2015). https://doi.org/10.1145/2696454.2696456
21. Malle, B.F., Scheutz, M., Arnold, T., Voiklis, J., Cusimano, C.: Sacrifice one for the good of many? In: Proceedings of the Tenth Annual ACM/IEEE International Conference on Human-Robot Interaction - HRI 2015 (2015). https://doi.org/10.1145/2696454.2696458
22. Malle, B.F., Scheutz, M., Forlizzi, J., Voiklis, J.: Which robot am i thinking about? The impact of action and appearance on peoples evaluations of a moral robot. In: 2016 11th ACM/IEEE International Conference on Human-Robot Interaction (HRI) (2016). https://doi.org/10.1109/hri.2016.7451743
23. Mathur, M.B., Reichling, D.B.: Navigating a social world with robot partners: a quantitative cartography of the uncanny valley. Cognition **146**, 22–32 (2016). https://doi.org/10.1016/j.cognition.2015.09.008
24. Nadel, J., et al.: Human responses to an expressive robot. In: Proceedings of the Sixth International Workshop on Epigenetic Robotics. Lund University (2006)
25. Nakad, H.H., Herik, H.J.V.D., Jongbloed, A.T., Salem, A.B.M.: The rise of the robotic judge in modern court proceedings. In: The 7th International Conference on Information Technology (2015). https://doi.org/10.15849/icit.2015.0009
26. Petisca, S., Esteves, F., Paiva, A.: Cheating with robots: how at ease do they make us feel? In: 2019 IEEE/RSJ International Conference on Intelligent Robots and Systems (IROS) (2019). https://doi.org/10.1109/iros40897.2019.8967790
27. Robinette, P., Howard, A.M., Wagner, A.R.: Effect of robot performance on human-robot trust in time-critical situations. IEEE Trans. Hum.-Mach. Syst. **47**(4), 425–436 (2017). https://doi.org/10.1109/thms.2017.2648849

28. Robinette, P., Li, W., Allen, R., Howard, A.M., Wagner, A.R.: Overtrust of robots in emergency evacuation scenarios. In: 2016 11th ACM/IEEE International Conference on Human-Robot Interaction (HRI) (2016). https://doi.org/10.1109/hri.2016.7451740

29. Satterfield, K., et al.: Robot knows best? A comparison of compliance with human and robotic coaches. Proc. Hum. Factors Ergon. Soc. Annual Meeting **63**(1), 406–407 (2019). https://doi.org/10.1177/1071181319631412

30. Short, E., Hart, J., Vu, M., Scassellati, B.: No fair!! In: Proceeding of the 5th ACM/IEEE international conference on Human-robot interaction - HRI 2010 (2010). https://doi.org/10.1145/1734454.1734546

31. Sourdin, T.: Judge v robot: the rise of machines is upon Uss. SSRN Electron. J. (2017). https://doi.org/10.2139/ssrn.3040402

32. Ullman, D., Leite, L., Phillips, J., Kim-Cohen, J., Scassellati, B.: Smart human, smarter robot: How cheating affects perceptions of social agency. In: Proceedings of the Annual Meeting of the Cognitive Science Society, vol. 36 (2014)

33. Xu, J., Bryant, D.G., Howard, A.: Would you trust a robot therapist? Validating the equivalency of trust in human-robot healthcare scenarios. In: 2018 27th IEEE International Symposium on Robot and Human Interactive Communication (RO-MAN) (2018). https://doi.org/10.1109/roman.2018.8525782

Perception of a Social Robot's Mood Based on Different Types of Motions and Coloured Heart

Enrique Fernández-Rodicio$^{(\boxtimes)}$, Álvaro Castro-González,
Juan José Gamboa-Montero, and Miguel A. Salichs

Robotics Lab, Universidad Carlos III de Madrid, Av. de la Universidad 30,
28911 Leganés, Madrid, Spain
{enrifern,acgonzal,jjgamboa,salichs}@ing.uc3m.es

Abstract. Roboticists in the field of Social Robotics try to find ways to develop robots that are able to create emotional bonds with the users and interact in natural ways. In order to achieve this, one of the features that the robot requires is the ability to convey different moods. This can be done by changing how the robot uses its output interfaces, like motors or LED. In this paper, we present a user study in which 164 participants rated their perception of a robot's mood considering different types of body movements and heartbeat. Also, because verbal communication can convey a lot of information about the robot's mood, we try to measure the relevance of verbal communication in relation to the perceived robot's mood. Participants were divided in five groups where the speed and amplitude of the robot's movements, as well as the LED configuration of the robot's heart, changed. Results show that the modulation of the interfaces had an effect on the intensity of the mood perceived, but not big enough to change which mood the participants perceived.

Keywords: Emotion expression · Expressiveness modulation ·
Human-robot interaction · Multimodal interaction

1 Introduction

Mood is a key element in social interactions, as it changes the way people perceive and react to others, as well as the way in which they perceive and react to us [1]. Opposite to emotions, which are short-lived and usually have a higher intensity, mood has a more extended duration. When developing social robots, giving them the ability of expressing their mood in an appropriate way can help to achieve an interaction that feels natural to the user, and makes easier for the user to bond with the robot [2]. Mood can be expressed through verbal communication (both the content of the speech, as well as the modulation of the voice) [3], but it can also be conveyed through the robot's non-verbal behaviour [4].

Expressing the current mood of a robot through non-verbal behaviour can be a complicated task. A solution might be to have multimodal expressions

© Springer Nature Switzerland AG 2020
A. R. Wagner et al. (Eds.): ICSR 2020, LNAI 12483, pp. 182–193, 2020.
https://doi.org/10.1007/978-3-030-62056-1_16

specifically designed for conveying each of the moods of the robot. But this method does not scale well, as it requires to develop multiple versions of each output action, one for each affective state that the robot might need to convey. This problem increases if the robot needs to display the intensity of the mood. One possible solution is to appropriately modulate the robot's output actions so that the robot can convey any mood using a limited set of expressions. However, the modulation process depends on the communication capabilities of each robot. In robots with limited expressive capabilities (low number of degrees-of-freedom limbs, or no limbs at all, faceless robots, etc.), the parameters that can modify the robot's behaviour are also limited. When developing this type of robots, it is important to develop modulation strategies adapted to their specific expressivity capabilities.

In this paper, we present a user study aimed at evaluating the effect that the modulation of a social robot's non-verbal expressions has on the perception of the robot's mood, and if the non-verbal interfaces of the robot are able to convey a mood when the prosody of the voice is not modulated. We decided to focus on mood instead of emotions because we are more interested in studying the effect over long interactions, instead of brief moments. We recorded a user playing a quiz game with a robot. We modulated the LEDs placed in the robot's heart and its body movements based on two variables: speed and amplitude, with two possible states: low and high. By combining these states, we ended up with four cases, plus a condition in which the speed and amplitude of the robot's expressions had an intermediate value. Participants were assigned to one condition where they watched two versions of a video of the robot (one version has audio and the other does not) and then completed an online questionnaire to rate the on-video robot using different mood descriptors. It is important to mention that we are trying to assess the effect of modulating the robot's expressions without making any previous assumptions about which emotion is conveyed by the robot in each condition. The rest of this manuscript is structured as follows. Section 2 shows related works that try to evaluate the mood displayed by robots. In Sect. 3, we present the experiment that we conducted, along with the questionnaires and the robotic platform used. Section 4 shows the statistical analysis performed on the data extracted from the questionnaires. Finally, in Sect. 5 we present the conclusions extracted from this research.

2   Related Work

There have been several studies focused on designing models for affective behaviour generation, and on evaluating the effect of mood in Human-Robot Interaction. In 2009, Itoh et al. [5] proposed an emotion generation model that uses the mood of the robot and the content of the conversation between the robot and the user to generate appropriate emotions, shown as facial expressions. A number of participants observed interactions between the robot and the user and then answered a questionnaire. Their results showed that personality can be expressed by changing the robot's mood transitions. A year later, in 2010,

Park et al. [6] integrated non-verbal affective behaviours in a humanoid robot. They used four affective phenomena that combine to create complex variations of affective states and dispositions. They evaluated their system through online questionnaires. Six videos of the robot were recorded, and the participants were expected to judge if the robot was displaying a positive or negative mood. Users were able to properly recognize which mood the robot was displaying, and also which emotion (joy or fear). In 2013, Xu et al. [4] developed a model for expressing mood by parametrizing the pose and the motions of a robot. Their system integrates task-oriented behaviour and bodily mood expression. The latter can be adapted to convey different moods by adjusting the parameters that define the behaviours (amplitude, speed, palm direction, hold time...). They evaluated the system by designing a series of affective behaviours, then allowing users to design their own behaviours for displaying specific moods, and finally, they compared the difference between the initial behaviours designed, and the behaviours modelled by the participants. Parameter settings for each mood were generally consistent across participants, and various settings were behaviour-invariant.

Also in 2013, Han et al. [7] proposed an emotional expression generation model based on mood transition and personality model. In this system, they define the personality of the robot by adjusting the factors of the five factors model and then use this to find the mood transitions, which are also affected by the mood of the user. They also proposed a method for expressing an emotional state through changes in facial expressions. The authors conducted a series of experiments in order to test different aspects of their system, and then conducted a user evaluation. The participants watched the videos of the experiments conducted and evaluated the system with a questionnaire. Their results show that their mood state transition model can respond appropriately in a continuous manner to the user's emotional changes, and that the robot using the mood transition model was evaluated as behaving in a more human-like manner. Also in 2013, Beck et al. [8] presented a study in which they evaluated children's ability to recognize emotions expressed by a robot through body language. They design six key poses (anger, sadness, fear, pride, happiness, and excitement), each of them with three different head positions (up. down, and straight). The children observed all 18 poses in a random order, and assigned a emotion to each one. The results show that the children were able to recognize the emotions displayed by the robot, although they struggled with some of them. Also, this study shows that lowering the head leads to decreased valence and raising the head leads to increased valence among most poses. In 2015, Bretan et al. [9] presented an artificial emotional intelligence system for robots. They focused on generating affective behaviours for abstract, faceless robot, with low degrees of freedom. Based on observations made by Darwin, they established a set of parameters that would define the pose and motion. The system uses the parameters derived from these observations to generate behaviours that convey the desired emotion, using motion and body language. In the paper, the authors evaluated how the configuration of the parameters that define the affective behaviours affect how users perceive the robot's emotions. Their results suggest that specific charac-teristics of body language are indicative of specific emotions.

In all the works presented in this section, authors have predefined the corre-sponding expressions for different moods and then evaluate if one expression is appropriate for one mood. In our case, we did not have any preconceived idea about how the modulation of the actions is going to affect the user's perception of the robot's mood. Our goal is to find relationships between the amplitude and speed of the robot's expressions and the mood perceived by the users. In most of the works presented before, the robots used were humanoid robots with a high number of DOF, or robots able to display detailed facial expressions, while we are using a robot with limited expressive capabilities. Here, a similarity exists with the work presented by Bretan et al. [9], as they also focus on this type of robots, and they perform a similar evaluation to ours. The difference is that we focus on how the users perceive the overall mood of the robot during an interaction, instead of brief displays of emotion.

3   Experimental Setup

In this experiment, we want to evaluate two things. First, we are studying how the modulation of the robot's actions through a modification of the speed and amplitude of the actions change the user's perception about the robot's mood. We are not evaluating if a specific expression can convey a certain emotion at a specific point in time, but the overall mood during a sustained interaction. The second objective is to evaluate how much the voice factors in the perception of this mood. This has the purpose of analysing if mood can be conveyed only through non-verbal output mode in a robot with limited output interfaces.

3.1   Mood Evaluation

We decided to select which moods we were going to evaluate according to Russel's circumplex model of affection [10]. In this model, 28 affect words are represented in a 2D space (pleasure-displeasure and degree of affection). The type and inten-sity of affects are represented in polar coordinates. We selected 8 affect words from this model, in order to reduce the complexity of the evaluation for the participants, and use them as our mood descriptors. We selected the following 8 affect words: afraid, angry, astonished, excited, happy, calm, bored, sad.

3.2   Robotic Platform Used

For this experiment, we used the social robot Mini [11], shown in Fig. 1. Mini's body has five degrees of freedom (two in the neck, one in each arm, and one in the base). The eyes are OLED screens that can display different gazes. It has a heart with a multi-colour LED, a touch screen, and a Text-to-Speech system to synthesize the robot's voice.

Fig. 1. Mini, a social robot developed for interacting with elders that suffer from mild cases of cognitive impairment.

Mini's multimodal expressions are modelled as state machine-like structures. Among other features provided by these structures, the one that is relevant for this experiment is that all actions can be modulated in runtime through two parameters: speed and amplitude. These parameters are used as scaling factors when building the expression. In this experiment, we will be modulating the LED placed in the robot's heart and the body movements. The effects of modifying the speed and amplitude parameters on these interfaces are the following:

- **Joints:** The amplitude modifies the final position of the movements. For high amplitude values, the movements were longer, while for low amplitude values the movements were shorter. The speed modifies the velocity of the motors. Higher speed means faster movements, while lower speed means slower movements.
- **LEDs:** The amplitude modifies the intensity of the LEDs. This affects the brightness of the heart (higher amplitude, higher brightness) The speed modifies the blinking speed of the LEDs. The higher the speed, the faster the blinking.

Although Mini is a robot developed for interacting with older adults, the evaluation performed in this paper is not connected to this task. That is why we tried to get an homogeneous population, instead on trying to recruit users only among Mini's target demographic.

3.3   Experiment Definition

We decided to use a video-based evaluation approach. This approach has the benefit of making it easier to add new participants into the experiment, although it might provide a less accurate evaluation [12]. In the video, Mini starts in an idle state that simulates being asleep. Then, a user touches the robot in the shoulder, and Mini wakes up. After introducing itself, the robot asks the user to play a game, and the user selects a game in which he has to guess monuments from all around the world. The robot then explains to the user the rules of the game and moves on to the first question. The Eiffel Tower is shown in the tablet, and Mini asks the user where it is located. The user gives the right answer, so the robot congratulates him, with an expression that displays joy. The next question is about the Colosseum. In this case, the user gives a wrong answer. Mini gives feedback to the user using a second expression that expressed sadness. Finally, the robot thanks the user for playing the game and greets him goodbye. When designing the interaction that we were going to record, we decided to go with a right answer and a wrong one because that shows the robot displaying two different emotions during the same interaction. This makes more difficult that the participants connect the mood of the robot to a particular emotion expressed during the interaction. Besides these two situations, the voice of the robot was kept neutral. We recorded one video for each condition. The videos had durations ranging from 1:49 to 2:30[1].

Participants, who were recruited through social media, started the experiment by answering demographic questions (age, gender, education...). After filling out this information, the next step was watching the video of the interaction without sound. Next, the participant was presented with the eight mood descriptors and asked to select a value between 1 and 10 for each descriptor. Finally, the participants had to watch the video with sound, and repeat the evaluation. 164 participants took part in this experiment. 51,25% of the participants identified themselves as female, 47.5% as male, and 1.25% selected the option "other". The ages of the participants ranged from 16 to 79 years old. Most of the participants (67.5%) have higher education. Regarding their familiarity with the technology and with robotics, in a scale from 1 through 5, being 1 having no knowledge about technology and robotics, and 5 being completely proficient in both areas, most of the participants claimed to have at least an average familiarity with technology (78.75%), although the majority of them were not familiar with robotics (63.69%). Finally, we discarded the results from 6 users because they had interacted with Mini previously, and thus, they could be biased.

In order to evaluate the effect that the non-verbal characteristics of the voice have on the mood perceived by the participants without taking into account the effect that the content of the speech has, we added subtitles to the videos. This means that the participants were aware of the verbal information that the robot was conveying in both versions of the video (with and without audio). Because of this, the only difference between both versions is the addition of the non-verbal characteristics of the speech, which are the ones that we are interested in.

3.4 Conditions

We have defined five different between-subject conditions where each participant was assigned to one condition. In each condition, participants watched a video where Mini interacted with a person, as described in Sect. 3.3, but the robot's expressions were modulated with different speed and amplitude. The conditions

---

[1] A playlist with all the videos used in the experiment can be seen here: https://www.youtube.com/playlist?list=PLxGCA0SJbjmnWzGCbopJkvnDiL6nAudho.

188   E. Fernández-Rodicio et al.

Table 1. Values for the speed and amplitude parameters for each of the five conditions evaluated, as well as the number of participants per condition.

	C0	C1	C2	C3	C4
Amplitude	Medium	High	High	Low	Low
Speed	Medium	High	Low	High	Low
Participants	39	29	29	34	27

were defined using different modulation of the robot's expressions based on different speed and amplitude. The configurations for each of the five conditions are shown in Table 1, along with the number of participants per condition.

For this experiment, we are only modulating the joint movements and the LEDs. The gaze of the robot is not being modulated because we use it to convey specific short-lived emotions during the interaction (for example, joy when congratulating the user). We also kept the voice without modulation, as we want to keep the voice constant under all conditions, in order to evaluate its effect on the user's perception of the robot's mood.

In condition 0, the robot executes the expressions as they were defined, without any modulation (amplitude and speed are set to 1). In condition 1, the movements were faster and also wider, and the heart blinked faster and with higher brightness (amplitude and speed are set to 2). In condition 2, movements were wider, although slower, and the heart's brightness was higher, but the blinking frequency was lower (amplitude is set to 2 and speed is set to 0.5). The opposite happened in condition 3, in which the movements were shorter but faster, and the heart beat faster, but with less brightness (amplitude is set to 0.5 and speed is set to 2). Finally, in condition 4 movements were shorter and slower, and the heart beating was slower and with lower brightness (amplitude and speed are set to 0.5).

3.5 Hypothesis

With this experiment, we evaluated how the movements and a LED-based beating heart affect the perception of the participants. We evaluated the following hypothesis:

- **H1:** The modulation of the robot's expressions will affect the users' perception of the robot's mood.
- **H2:** Under conditions with low amplitude, the affect words in the displeasure area of Russel's model will be rated higher than those placed in the pleasure area. The opposite will happen under high-amplitude conditions.
- **H3:** Under conditions with low speed, the affect words in the low arousal area of Russel's model will be rated higher than those placed in the high arousal area. The opposite will happen under high-speed conditions.

– **H4:** The prosodic features in the robot's speech influence the participant's perception of the robot's mood.

4 Experimental Results Analysis

In this section, we will present the results obtained from the user evaluation. We analysed the results of both evaluations (video without and with audio) and compared the results. First, we looked for significant differences between conditions for each mood descriptor, but we did not find them in either of the two evaluations.

Next, for each condition, we ranked the descriptors based on the average score given by the users, in order to find the dominant mood perceived by the users depending on the modulation of the actions. These rankings are shown in Fig. 2. We used the Friedman test to identify the differences between the mood descriptors in each condition. For all conditions, the Friedman tests found statistically significant differences between these descriptors. Post-hoc analyses were performed using Wilcoxon tests in order to find if the differences between each pair of descriptors' scores were statistically significant. After Bonferroni correction, the significance level was set at $p < 0.002$.

Looking at the rankings under each condition, we can appreciate that, despite the condition, there are no big differences in the order of the rankings. Observing the rankings and the significant differences between the eight descriptors, we can identify three groups of descriptors that occupy the same positions in all conditions for both evaluations:

– **Group I:** Formed by the descriptors "calm", "happy", and "excited". These descriptors are ranked 1st, 2nd, and 3rd respectively under all conditions.
– **Group II:** Formed by the descriptors "sad", "bored", and "astonished". Here is where we find the biggest differences among conditions, as these are the only descriptors that switch places in the rankings, although they are always ranked between 4th and 6th.
– **Group III:** Formed by the descriptors "angry" and "afraid". These two descriptors are always ranked last, "angry" being always in 7th position and "afraid" being always in 8th position. The only exception is under condition 2 in the second evaluation.

According to our results, the addition of the robot's voice does not affect the composition of the groups, but it does affect the order of the descriptors in each group, depending on the conditions. It also changes the statistically significant differences that appear among the mood descriptors. Finally, the average score of most mood descriptors was higher in the second evaluation than in the first.

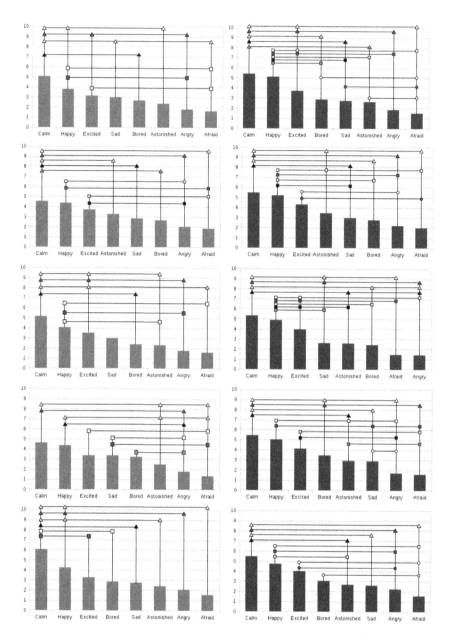

Fig. 2. Descriptors' rankings under each condition (from top to bottom: C0, C1, C2, C3, C4). Orange bars represent the average score for each descriptor for the video without audio, blue bars represent the same for the video with audio. The descriptors with the same symbols (shape and colour) have statistically significant differences between them. (Color figure online)

5 Discussion

We observed that almost all the descriptors under all conditions and for both evaluations (video without and with audio) had an average rating below 6 (out of 10), with the only exception being "calm" in the first evaluation under condition 4. This could indicate that Mini is not able to convey intense moods due to its limited expressivity capabilities. If we focus on the rankings, we found the same three groups between the two evaluations. In both cases, the only group in which statistically significant differences between descriptors exist under some condition is Group I ("calm"-"happy" and "calm"-"excited" in the first evaluation, "happy"-"excited" in the second evaluation). The biggest variations in the ranking positions appear in Group II, where its descriptors switch places in multiple conditions. Descriptors in Group III maintain the same ranking positions across conditions except for condition 2 in the second evaluation. In this situation, angry and afraid shift their positions but their average ratings are very close and there are no significant differences between them. Therefore, we can say that the order of descriptors in group III is constant across all conditions.

Overall, we observed that the modulation of the robot's actions affects the distance between the descriptors in the rankings. This partially validates H1, as the modulation of the robot's expressions does affect the users' perception of the robot's mood, although the effect of the modulation was smaller than the expected and it mainly affected to the descriptors that the users almost did not perceive. However, the dominant moods in all conditions were always "calm" and "happy", with "excited" in third place. This leads us to dismiss H2 and H3. We theorise that, due to the limited expressivity capabilities of the robot Mini, the external design plays a big role on the user's perception, and can neutralize the effect of modulating the robot's actions. In our case, Mini was designed to be perceived positively, which could difficult conveying "negative" moods (angry, sad, afraid). Further experiments in multiple robotic platforms would be required to test this theory. Also, we are only modulating the body movements and the heart of the robot, which makes harder to convey certain moods. Adding more interfaces (the gaze, for example) could help the robot to convey its mood.

In the evaluation conducted using the video with audio, all descriptors were ranked slightly higher than in the first evaluation under the majority of conditions, while happy and excited were rated higher under all conditions. This leads us to conclude that the verbal communication helps the users to perceive the robot's mood, and that, even using unmodulated voice, it alters the effect of modulating the nonverbal expressions of the robot, thus validating H4.

Finally, is important to mention that there are several limitations to this study. The use of video-based questionnaires that the participants completed without supervision makes it hard to assure that no participant completed the questionnaire only once (we added a control question to check if the users had participated before in any experiment with Mini). Also, video-based evaluations might provide less accurate results, as the participants were not able to observe the robot in person. For example, the modulation of the heartbeat might be difficult to appreciate due to the video quality. Another possible limitation is the order in which the robot performed affective expressions in the video (first joy and then sadness) might also have an effect on the user's perception. All of these factors might have influenced the results.

6 Conclusions

In this paper, we presented a study aimed at evaluating the effect that the modulation of the nonverbal expressions of a robot with limited expressivity capabilities has over the mood that the users perceive. In our case, we modulated the body movements and the robot's heartbeat. The results obtained show that, although this modulation does affect the user's perception, the effect is not enough to change the mood perceived by the users. This leads us to believe that there are other factors that affect the user's perception and that mitigate the effect of this modulation. We observed that, overall, the users ranked the selected mood descriptors in the same order regardless the variations of the modulation parameters (speed and amplitude), and that the use of unmodulated voice clearly affected the user's perception, raising the overall score of most of the descriptors. Even though the results extracted from these experiments are non conclusive, we can use them as a starting point for identifying the proper modulation that will allow the robot to convey appropriate affective states.

Acknowledgment. The research leading to these results has received funding from the projects: Development of social robots to help seniors with cognitive impairment (ROBSEN), funded by the Ministerio de Economía y Competitividad; and Robots Sociales para Estimulación Física, Cognitiva y Afectiva de Mayores (ROSES), funded by the Ministerio de Ciencia, Innovación y Universidades.

References

1. Parkinson, B.: Emotions are social. Br. J. Psychol. **87**(4), 663–683 (1996). https://doi.org/10.1111/j.2044-8295.1996.tb02615.x
2. Cameron, D., et al.: Presence of life-like robot expressions influences children's enjoyment of human-robot interactions in the field. In: Proceedings of Fourth International Symposium on "New Frontiers in Human-Robot Interaction", p. 3. The Society for the Study of Artificial Intelligence and Simulation of Behaviour (AISB), London (2015)
3. Crumpton, J., Bethel, C.L.: A survey of using vocal prosody to convey emotion in robot speech. Int. J. Soc. Robot. **8**(2), 271–285 (2015). https://doi.org/10.1007/s12369-015-0329-4
4. Xu, J., Broekens, J., Hindriks, K., Neerincx, M.A.: Mood expression through parametrized functional behavior of robots. In: Proceedings of the International Symposium on Robot and Human Interactive Communication, Gyeongju, South Korea, 26–29 August 2013 (2013)
5. Itoh, C., Kato, S., Itoh, H.: Mood-transition-based emotion generation model for the robot's personality. In: Proceedings of International Conference on Systems, Man and Cybernetics, San Antonio, Texas, USA, 11–14 October 2009 (2009)

6. Park, S., Moshkina, L., Arkin, R.C.: Recognizing nonverbal affective behavior in humanoid robots. In: Proceedings of the International Conference on Intelligent Autonomous Systems (IAS 2010), Ottawa, Canada, vol. 11, January 2010. https://doi.org/10.3233/978-1-60750-613-3-12

7. Han, M., Lin, C., Song, K.: Robotic emotional expression generation based on mood transition and personality model. IEEE Trans. Cybern. **43**(4), 1290–1303 (2013). https://doi.org/10.1109/TSMCB.2012.2228851

8. Beck, A., et al.: Interpretation of emotional body language displayed by a humanoid robot: a case study with children. Int. J. Soc. Robot. **5**, 325–334 (2013). https://doi.org/10.1007/s12369-013-0193-z

9. Bretan, M., Hoffman, G., Weinberg, G.: Emotionally expressive dynamic physical behaviors in robots. Int. J. Hum Comput Stud. **78**, 1–16 (2015). https://doi.org/10.1016/j.ijhcs.2015.01.006

10. Russel, J.A.: A circumplex model of affect. J. Pers. Soc. Psychol. **39**(6), 1161–1178 (1980). https://doi.org/10.1037/h0077714

11. Salichs, E., Castro-González, Á., Malfaz, M., Salichs, M.A.: Mini: a social assistive robot for people with mild cognitive impairment. In: New Friends 2016 - 2nd International Conference on Social Robots in Therapy & and Education, pp. 31–32, Barcelona, Spain, 2 November 2016 (2016). https://doi.org/10.3926/newfriends2016

12. Venture, G., Kulić, D.: Robot expressive motions: a survey of generation and evaluation methods. ACM Trans. Hum.-Robot Interact. **8**(4), 1–17 (2019). https://doi.org/10.1145/3344286

Let's Learn Biodiversity with a Virtual "Robot"?

Maria José Ferreira[1,2,3]([📧]), Raquel Oliveira[2,4], Sandra Câmara Olim[3,5], Valentina Nisi[1,3], and Ana Paiva[1,2]

[1] Instituto Superior Técnico, Porto Salvo, Portugal
maria.jose.ferreira@tecnico.ulisboa.pt
[2] INESC-ID, University of Lisbon, Lisbon, Portugal
ana.paiva@inesc-id.pt
[3] Interactive Technologies Institute, Funchal, Portugal
valentina.nisi@m-iti.org
[4] ISCTE-Instituto Universitário de Lisboa (CIS-IUL), Lisbon, Portugal
rsaoa@iscte-iul.pt
[5] FCT, Universidade Nova de Lisboa, Lisbon, Portugal
s.olim@campus.fct.unl.pt

Abstract. As climate change and biodiversity loss are threatening the natural world's equilibrium and survival, people's concerns about these topics have increased significantly. The work presented in this paper lies at the cross-section between the areas of education, biodiversity and technologies. More specifically, this project builds on research in virtual agents in educational settings to promote young children's engagement with a biodiversity curriculum. In this context, we conducted an observational study with 105 primary school's children with the goal of evaluating the effectiveness of a virtual robotic agent (presented through a multimedia application), in providing an effective and engaging learning experience about local biodiversity to children. Our results suggested that a) older children (8 to 10 years) knowledge about certain animals and plants from their local biodiversity is well matured; b) younger children (6 to 7 years) present more faithful conceptualisations about nature-related scenarios compared to older children and c) both young and older children exhibited a preference for nature-related scenarios when compared to human-made ones. Our findings provide useful information in favour of the usefulness of implementing user-adaptive learning systems, by considering factors like the children's previous level of knowledge. Besides, this personalised and interactive type of system might provide

We would like to thank the Agência Regional para o Desenvolvimento e Tecnologia (ARDITI) - M1420-09-5369-000001 and Fundação para a Ciência e a Tecnologia (FCT): PD/BD/150286/2019 and PD/BD/150570/2020, for PhD grants to first, second and third authors respectively. This work was also supported by FCT - UIDB/50021/2020 and the project AMIGOS: PTDC/EEISII/7174/2014. The authors would also like to acknowledge to António F. Aguiar, the team from Funchal Natural History Museum for all the help with the biodiversity information and to the school EB1/PE from Santa Cruz - Madeira island for their participation.

A. R. Wagner et al. (Eds.): ICSR 2020, LNAI 12483, pp. 194–206, 2020.
https://doi.org/10.1007/978-3-030-62056-1_17

an essential advantage in learning scenarios, compared to "static" systems, in enhancing children's learning outcomes.

Keywords: Biodiversity · Virtual robot · Learning

1 Introduction

The next decade is likely to witness a considerable rise in awareness of biodiversity. Climate change, continuing deforestation and large-scale fires are some of the current threats posed to the conservation of biodiversity. Efforts to educate and raise awareness to this problem in young children are an important strategy to prevent biodiversity's further decline [21,25]. Madeira island has a large diversity of flora and endemic species, being considered one of the biodiversity hot-spots of the Mediterranean region [3,18]. However, its ecosystem is exposed to several threats and it needs *in situ* and *ex situ* conservation efforts.

In this context, educating the next generation about local wildlife and the importance of its' conservation in maintaining a biodiversity equilibrium is fundamental. In particular, research has suggested that indirect experiences are important in shaping children's perception of nature and may influence attitudes towards conservation [6]. Research also shown that in order to empower and motivate learners to engage in this topic, a learner-centre pedagogy approach is preferred [11,13]. Thus, children prior knowledge and experiences about their local biodiversity are the starting point for stimulating the learning process.

More recently, researchers have also been studying the effectiveness of the combination of different pedagogical approaches with the use of new technologies and virtual agents. The agents can be used as teachable agents, tutors, peer learners or just as simple social characters [5,10,12,23,27]. They have been shown to be useful tools that can aid children to develop and improve language and reading skills, handwriting and in increasing children's feelings of persistence and enjoyment during learning activities.

In the specific context of biodiversity education, virtual agents have also been shown to be useful tools in biodiversity management and conservation efforts [26], biodiversity education [4,8], and for raising awareness about the importance of biodiversity preservation [14,15,22].

In this paper, we sought to extend previous findings about the effectiveness of educational virtual agents in the area of biodiversity education, by proposing and evaluating a new application involving a virtual version of the *Pepper* robot. Our findings show that this application was successful at providing an engaging learning experience to young children and underlines the need for future work to further explore the role of children's individual characteristics (such as previous knowledge) in the development of similar educational applications.

2 Goals and Hypotheses

The goal of this project was to understand how children's previous knowledge about local biodiversity had an effect in their conceptualisations of local biodiversity with the help of a Virtual Agent-driven application. More specifically, we analysed the children's existing knowledge about biodiversity (as indicated by their school year) by measuring their ability to a) correctly identify local biodiversity elements (thorough the app) and b) create complex conceptualisations of local biodiversity (as measured by the complexity of their drawings about biodiversity scenarios, see Sect. 3.3), after interacting with a digital app.

To achieve this goal, we made an observational study with children enrolled in primary education. In this context, we devised the following hypotheses:

- **H1** - Children with some existing knowledge about local biodiversity (3rd and 4th school years) will be able to correctly identify elements of local diversity more frequently when compared with younger children with less or no knowledge about biodiversity (1st and 2nd school years).
- **H2** - Younger children will exhibit more misconceptions about local wildlife when compared to children with some existing knowledge.
- **H3** - Children will prioritise representations of nature-like scenarios compared with man-made representations.
- **H4** - Children will prioritise representations of local biodiversity elements when compared to non-local biodiversity elements.

3   Method

3.1   Sample

One hundred and five children enrolled in primary education participated in our experiment. Of these, 56 were male and 49 were female, (29 from 1st school year; 25 from 2nd year; 26 from 3rd year and 25 from 4th year), aged between 6 and 10 years old.

3.2   Procedure

Data collection for this experiment took place during the course of one week, at a public school during the regular daily class schedule. Informed consents were obtained from the parents prior to the beginning of the experiment. Approvals from the university Ethical Commission and the Ministry of Education were also granted before the start of the study. Participants were told that they would be interacting with a virtual robot that needed assistance in order to identify biodiversity elements that exist in Madeira island.

Students interacted with the application previously installed in the school computers (see Fig. 1) and filled out a questionnaire about their engagement with the app. The experiment took approximately 20 min.

Fig. 1. Children setup during the study.

3.3   Application

A Unity application, which included a free 3D model of Pepper robot[1], was developed. The virtual robot played the role of narrator and storyteller during children's interaction with the application. All scenes were narrated using the Unity plugin RT-Voice PRO[2], since we assumed that not all children would have sufficiently good reading skills. After children finished their drawing task (more details below), the virtual robot also played the role of storyteller (not analysed in the scope of this paper) by telling each children a personalised tale involving their drawings.

Together with the narration, we also included subtitles and visual cues to enhance clarity. The visual cues were implemented through (a) the virtual robot and (b) through the use of pictures of the local biodiversity elements being mentioned throughout children's interaction with the application.

The visual cues in the virtual robot were implemented using the Mixamo platform[3] with its free animations. Our target animations (idle, pointing, waving, thoughtful, acknowledging, happy hand gesture, excited, nodding, disappointed, happy and angry) were used to create a more interactive, life-like agent. The pictures used were collected through a photography contest set up for local participants of all ages and from the Global Biodiversity Information Facility[4] (GBIF) database. The photography contest was disseminated using social media

---

[1] Pepper robot from SoftBank, available in https://www.softbank.jp/robot/pepper/. Accessed: Jan-15-20.

[2] RT-Voice PRO available https://www.crosstales.com. Accessed: Jan-15-20.

[3] Mixamo platform for the animation of 3D characters available at https://www.mixamo.com/. Accessed: Jan-15-20.

[4] *"GBIF—the Global Biodiversity Information Facility—is an international network and research infrastructure funded by the world's governments and aimed at providing*

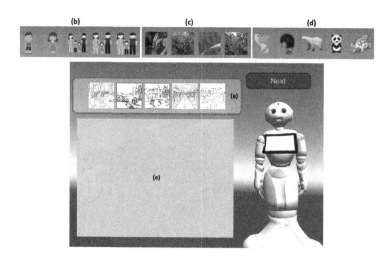

Fig. 2. Drawing stages composition, (a) scenarios, (b) characters, (c) animals and plants seen in app, (d) animals that do not belong to local biodiversity and (e) drawing area.

during one month, and participants were asked to submit images that captured the local biodiversity of Madeira island. They had to submit original photographs of elements of wildlife, taken by themselves, and allow its use in the application. Data regarding the names of the biodiversity elements, groups and characteristics were validated by a team of specialists from Funchal Natural History Museum and biodiversity books [2, 3, 24].

The interaction with the application begins with *Pepper* introducing itself and requesting children's help to learn more about the local biodiversity. Next, *Pepper* asks children to introduce themselves by typing their name and select their gender using the boy and girl icon available. After the introductions are finished, four different pictures of animals and plants, starting with a bird, followed by a flower, an invertebrate and finally a tree were shown to children. For each animal and plant, children were asked (a) if they know the animal or plant presented in the picture, (b) if they know the group that animal or plant belongs to and (c) if they know what are their characteristics (see [7] for more details on the characteristics for each element).

If children answer yes to the first question, they are then asked to indicate the common name of the shown animal or plant choosing from a group of four options; if they answered no, the virtual robot would tell them the plant or animals' common name. For the second question, children were asked to choose to which group the identified animal or plant belonged to. Children had to choose from a list of eight options (Amphibians, Birds, Fish, Fungi, Invertebrates, Mammals, Plants, and Reptiles). Each one of the 8 groups was represented by an

---

anyone, anywhere, open access to data about all types of life on Earth." available at http://www.gbif.pt/?language=en. Accessed: Jan-15-20.

icon that the children would visually recognise, without the voice over narration of the robot. The same icon representation was used to illustrate the element characteristics. It should be noted that each element (animal or plant) has its own specific qualities. Before moving to the next stage, pictures of all four elements that children had seen up to this point, was presented to them along with their correct common names (see [7] for more details on the flow of the app).

Drawings. After completing the first stage of the experiment, children were requested to create a small story, in the form of a drawing. The request was formulated by the virtual agent *Pepper*, who wanted to show the drawing to its' own friends later on. The drawing activity of the children's was split into four stages. First children were requested to choose and drag their selection into the drawing area, see Fig. 2(e). This first element corresponded to the scenario of their story, and they could choose one from five possible options (see Fig. 2(a)), three nature-related scenarios and two with a city and road background.

Secondly, children were requested to drag one or more characters, see Fig. 2(b), (c) and (d), into their scenario. These characters could be human (little boy, little girl and three families), animals and plants (the four elements they saw during their interaction with the application) and five elements that did not belong to the local biodiversity.

After children selected all the elements, a small storytelling activity[5] was generated using that information.

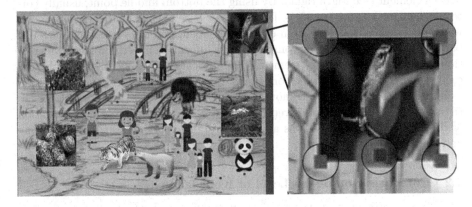

Fig. 3. Full drawing classification on the left with light blue representing Air areas (sky and clouds); dark blue representing Water; brown representing Ground (paths and ground areas); and green Nature (trees, bushes and flowers). On the right, detail of the markers for each element, green squares surrounded by red are corners identification and the dark blue square the middle bottom point (the place where feet, paws, trunk/roots and stem might be). (Color figure online)

---

[5] All the data regarding the storytelling activity is outside of the scope of this paper.

Questionnaires. Finally, a short questionnaire (five questions) was presented to children after they finished interacting with the application, and completed the drawing. The survey was displayed in the application, in text and simultaneously narrated by *Pepper*. Children used an emoticon scale [20] to provide their answers and were informed about the faces' meaning before answering.

Children were questioned if they liked *Pepper*; if they liked the application used; if they enjoyed creating the drawing; if they liked the story created with their drawing and if they understood *Pepper*'s speech throughout the app.

4   Data Analysis

4.1   Misconceptions Classification

From a pilot study in which we asked children to depict a story including the animals and plants they saw in the application (same as the ones in this study), we found that children often exhibited several misconceptions about the local wildlife. These misconceptions were evident through their depiction of these elements (e.g., placing ground-based elements, like snails, flying in the air).

In the context of this study, children' drawings were analysed based on the position of the biodiversity elements in the scenario they chose. For each scenario, five areas were created according to the background present (Air, Water, Ground, Nature and Buildings; see Fig. 3 left). The classification of the position of each element was calculated based on the location of the bottom middle point of each element (see Fig. 3 right). By using the bottom middle point, usually correspondent to the position of the feet, paws or base of each biodiversity element, we can guarantee that each item can only be identified as overlapping with one background scenario area. By comparing this information to the correct information about each biodiversity element's usual locations, we can classify whether each element was placed in the correct location. For example, regarding the snail example mentioned above, we know that snails can not fly; so when a child places the snail in the air, we considered that a misconception regarding the location of this animal. This process was applied for all elements present in the drawing and the information recorded.

4.2   Categorisation of the Level of Knowledge

We computed the knowledge level of all children based on their answers for the four elements seen on the app, see Eq. 3. We had into consideration their knowledge about the names of the elements (EK) and the group they belonged to (GK), the number of characteristics selected (TCS), see Eq. 1, and the number of features they selected for each biodiversity element: food(CF), location(CL), physical(CPF), need for life(CNL), and all features (CAll), see Eq. 2. Plus we also consider the maximum number of features each element seen could have and that for each four elements they had to identify three things (name, group and features).

$$ElementsInfo = \sum_{1}^{4} [EK(i) + GK(i) + TCS(i)] \qquad (1)$$

$$Feature = \sum_{1}^{4} [CF(i) + CL(i) + CPF(i) + CNL(i) + CAll(i)] \qquad (2)$$

$$KnowledgeLevel = \frac{ElementsInfo + Features}{\sum_{1}^{4} [MaxFeatures(i)] + 12} \qquad (3)$$

A Cluster Analyses was applied to Knowledge level variable (Eq. 3) using a *Hierarchical cluster* with a single solution of three groups. We used the *Interval - Square Euclidean Distance* for the cluster measure and the *between-groups linkage* for the cluster method. Our results grouped our data into the following categories of Knowledge: **Low** with values between [.20 − .31]; **Medium** with values between [.33 − .54] and **High** with values between [.55 − .85].

4.3   Data Analysis Strategy

The data was analysed using SPSS software (v. 26). H1 and H2 were tested using one-way ANOVA, whereas H3 was tested by performing a χ^2 test of independence and H4 was tested using one-way MANOVA. Post-hoc analysis were conducted using the Tukey test. Regarding the assumptions for the tests conducted, we found that the distribution of the level knowledge according to the school year did not conform to the normal distribution ($p < .001$); however, given that both the skewness and kurtosis values were contained between -1 and 1 (.13 and $-.47$, respectively), in which conditions has been shown that the F test remains robust (thus controlling for Type 1 Error within the bounds of Bradley's criterion) [17]; and considering that a sufficient sample size tends to minimise this disparity [9], we opted to conduct the comparisons using parametric methods. In addition, although we will use the conventional alpha value of .05, we also calculated a Dunn-Sidak's adjustment to the p-value in order to correct for multiple comparisons and provide a more conservative standard for interpretation of results, which yielded an ideal alpha value of approximately 0.

4.4   Results

H1 - Children's Previous Knowledge. We found a main effect of children's level of knowledge in their ability to correctly identify biodiversity elements ($F(3, 94) = 5.489, p = .002$). In particular, we observed that children from 4th ($.54 \pm .12, p = .001$) and 3rd ($.49 \pm .15, p = .043$) years were able to identify more elements correctly than children from the 1st year ($.39 \pm .13$). We found no difference between the 1st and 2nd years ($p = .063$); 2nd and 3rd ($p = 1$); 2nd and 4th ($p = .47$) and 3rd, and 4th ($p = .52$) school years.

H2 - Children misconceptions on drawings. We found a main effect of children's previous knowledge on the number of misconceptions represented by children in the drawing task $(F(3, 101) = 8.151, p = .0)$. In particular, the number of misconceptions was significantly lower for 1st $(1.69 \pm 1.75, p = .007)$, 2nd $(.88 \pm .73, p = .0)$ and 3rd $(1.46 \pm 1.45, p = .002)$ years when compared to 4th year $(3.44 \pm 3.07, p = .007)$. No differences were observed between the 1st and 2nd $(p = .421)$; 1st and 3rd (p=.972); and 2nd and 3rd (p=.706) school years.

H3 - Children scenario preferences. We found a relation between children's previous level of knowledge and their choice of scenario for the story $(\chi^2 (3 N = 105) = 7.85; p = .049)$. Overall, children demonstrated a preference towards nature-based scenarios $(n = 17, 22, 22, 18$ for 1st to 4th years respectively), when compared to the human-made ones $(n = 12, 3, 4, 7$ for 1st to 4th years, respectively).

H4 - Children selection preferences regarding animals. Our results revealed that there was a main effect of children's previous level of knowledge in their choices related to the inclusion of wildlife elements in their drawings $(F(6, 200) = 6.31, p = 0$; Wilk's $\Lambda = .71$, partial $\eta^2 = .16)$; but only regarding their inclusion of non-local biodiversity elements $(F(3, 101) = 12.82; p = 0$; partial $\eta^2 = .28)$ and not on the selection of local biodiversity elements $(F(3, 57) = .63; p = .6$; partial $\eta^2 = .01)$.

The mean scores for non-biodiversity elements were statistically significantly different between 1st and 2nd school years $(p < .001)$, 1st and 3rd school years $(p < .001)$ and 1st and 4th school years $(p < .001)$, but not between 2nd and 3rd school years $(p = .95)$, 2nd and 4th school years $(p = .91)$ and 3rd and 4th school years $(p = .63)$. Regarding the mean scores for the local biodiversity elements, those did not present statistically significantly differences among each school year $(p > .05$ for all cases).

Our data reveals that most of children choices regarding the total number of non-biodiversity elements varied across a total of 1 and 2 elements. On the 1st year, majority of children picked a total of 5 elements $(n = 20)$ from non-biodiversity options. Children on the 2nd year preferred a total of 1, 2 and 3 elements as their main choices $(n = 19)$. Plus, the 3rd year students elected a total of 1, 2 and 5 elements $(n = 21)$ on their drawings. Finally, the majority of children on 4th school year $(n = 20)$ selected a total of 1, 2 and 3 elements from non-biodiversity options into their drawings.

User Subjective Evaluations. The overall feedback provided by children through the questionnaire was very positive. 91.4% of the children reported liking *Pepper* and enjoyed the interaction a lot. The remaining children either reported merely liking *Pepper* (8.6%) and the application (7.6%) or not liking the application (1%). When questioned about the drawing activity, the majority (88.6%) reported enjoying the activity a lot, whereas the remaining children reported medium (9.5%) or neutral levels of enjoyment (1.9%). Regarding their comprehension of *Pepper* speech, three children reported having some issues, with these children reporting poor levels of comprehension. However, the majority (9.5% ($n = 10$), 14.3% ($n = 15$) and 73% ($n = 77$)) reported not having issues understanding *Pepper*'s speech (neutral, good and very good understanding respectively).

5   Discussion

In this study, we sought to characterise children's knowledge and illustrations of biodiversity elements during a task related to biodiversity identification. Plus, from the four hypotheses, we proposed to analyse, we partially validated H1, validated H3 and H4, but did not validate H2.

We hypothesised that children level of previous knowledge would have an impact on children ability to identify elements of local biodiversity correctly. In particular, older children would get more elements than younger ones. Our analysis revealed some differences among children of the 4th and 1st school year and 3rd and 1st, but not among 2nd and the remaining years.

Our expectations regarding misplacement elements on the drawings revealed to be opposite of what we anticipated. We did not foresee that children with a higher level of knowledge would place more elements in wrong areas. Could this fact be related to children's organisation of elements according to their beliefs and understanding about theme (biodiversity environment) [1]? Alternatively, this phenomenon can be related to our scenarios being displayed at black and white and not fully coloured. There is the possibility that the lack of colour lead to children failure to recognise certain areas. For instance, in the scenario with a fence and a small stream, children might have though of the stream area as being a trail delimitation. Further work needs to be done in order to asses if this issue is related with children idealisations; the scenarios we presented (black and white vs colourful) or if children were just disengaged in the drawing activity.

Children preferences regarding scenarios were congruent with our H3. Most children chose scenarios related to nature instead of scenarios that included human-made structures. Despite that, the first-year students almost matched the number of choices between the two types of scenarios (nature - 17 and human-made - 12) when compared to the remaining school years. This could indicate that younger children are more used to see animals and plants in their surroundings (city areas) than in their natural habitat. Concerning the other school years, the difference between the two types of scenarios was much higher, 17 to 22 children choose nature-related options and 3 to 7 children human-made ones (among school years).

Our results suggested that children choices regarding animals that do not belong to local biodiversity were aligned to our expectations (H4). Children preferences for non-biodiversity elements ranged among 1 and 2 elements for children of the 2nd, 3rd and 4th years. While the majority of children on the 1st year ($n = 20$ out of 29) actually demonstrated preferences for selecting all five elements (bear, tiger, panda, toucan and lion) that were out of local biodiversity. This outcome is not surprising; since most of young children at this stage (age of 6 to 7) still have an immature reasoning [19].

6   Conclusions and Future Work

Our main aim with this project is research on how virtual agents (and social robots) can promote young children's engagement with biodiversity issues and facilitate learning about this fascinating topic. Furthermore, we believe that learning about biodiversity needs grounding in local knowledge, situations, environment and stories. The findings here reported provide us information that such localisation is of paramount importance, and that individual differences must be taken into account. To further our efforts to achieve this goal, in the future we intend to use the data collected using this virtual agent and robot, to develop an educational adaptive system [16]. Such adaptive learning system will use an intelligent agent and in particular a physical robot (Pepper) to deliver customised information, tailored to the user's abilities, cognitive skills, and knowledge. We believe that our results so far will help us in the future create and train a model capable of adjusting to children individual needs. At the same time that we take advantage of the growing amount of evidence in favour of the benefits and potentialities that Human-computer interaction and Human-Robot interaction can have in the education of children [4,5,14,27].

References

1. Anning, A., Ring, K.: Making Sense of Children's Drawings. Open University Press, Maidenhead (2004)
2. Biscoito, M., Zino, F.: Aves do Arquipélago da Madeira. Secretaria Regional do Ambiente e dos Recursos Naturais - Direção Regional do Ambiente, biodiversidade madeirense: avaliação e conservação edn (2002)
3. Borges, P.A.V., et al.: Listagem dos fungos, flora e fauna terrestres dos arquipélagos da Madeira e Selvagens = A list of the terrestrial fungi, flora and fauna of Madeira and Selvagens archipelagos. Secretaria Regional do Ambiente e dos Recursos Naturais do Governo Regional da Madeira (2008). https://repositorio.uac.pt/handle/10400.3/1955
4. Briot, J.P., et al.: A serious game and artificial agents to support intercultural participatory management of protected areas for biodiversity conservation and social inclusion. In: 2011 Second International Conference on Culture and Computing, pp. 15–20. IEEE (2011)
5. Chandra, S., Dillenbourg, P., Paiva, A.: Classification of children's handwriting errors for the design of an educational co-writer robotic peer. In: Proceedings of the 2017 Conference on Interaction Design and Children - IDC 2017, pp. 215–225. ACM Press, New York (2017). https://doi.org/10.1145/3078072.3079750. http://dl.acm.org/citation.cfm?doid=3078072.3079750
6. Duerden, M.D., Witt, P.A.: The impact of direct and indirect experiences on the development of environmental knowledge, attitudes, and behavior. J. Environ. Psychol. **30**(4), 379–392 (2010)
7. Ferreira, M.J., Oliveira, R.A.: Let's learn biodiversity with a virtual robot? August 2020. osf.io/9vk76
8. Ferreira, M.J., Nisi, V., Melo, F., Paiva, A.: Learning and teaching biodiversity through a storyteller robot. In: Nunes, N., Oakley, I., Nisi, V. (eds.) ICIDS 2017. LNCS, vol. 10690, pp. 367–371. Springer, Cham (2017). https://doi.org/10.1007/978-3-319-71027-3_45

9. Hecke, T.V.: Power study of anova versus Kruskal-Wallis test. J. Stat. Manag. Syst. **15**(2–3), 241–247 (2012)
10. Hood, D., Lemaignan, S., Dillenbourg, P.: The cowriter project: teaching a robot how to write. In: Proceedings of the Tenth Annual ACM/IEEE International Conference on Human-Robot Interaction Extended Abstracts, pp. 269–269. ACM (2015)
11. Kasanda, C., Lubben, F., Gaoseb, N., Kandjeo-Marenga, U., Kapenda, H., Campbell, B.: The role of everyday contexts in learner-centred teaching: the practice in Namibian secondary schools. Int. J. Sci. Educ. **27**(15), 1805–1823 (2005)
12. Le Denmat, P., Gargot, T., Chetouani, M., Archambault, D., Cohen, D., Anzalone, S.M.: The CoWriter robot: improving attention in a learning-by-teaching setup. In: AIRO@ AI*IA, pp. 51–55 (2018)
13. Leicht, A., Heiss, J., Byun, W.J.: Issues and Trends in Education for Sustainable Development, vol. 5. UNESCO Publishing, Paris (2018)
14. Loureiro, P., Prandi, C., Nunes, N., Nisi, V.: Citizen science and game with a purpose to foster biodiversity awareness and bioacoustic data validation. In: Brooks, A.L., Brooks, E., Sylla, C. (eds.) ArtsIT/DLI -2018. LNICST, vol. 265, pp. 245–255. Springer, Cham (2019). https://doi.org/10.1007/978-3-030-06134-0_29
15. Mathevet, R., et al.: BUTORSTAR: a role-playing game for collective awareness of wise reedbed use. Simul. Gaming **38**(2), 233–262 (2007)
16. Mehlmann, G., Häring, M., Bühling, R., Wißner, M., André, E.: Multiple agent roles in an adaptive virtual classroom environment. In: Allbeck, J., Badler, N., Bickmore, T., Pelachaud, C., Safonova, A. (eds.) IVA 2010. LNCS (LNAI), vol. 6356, pp. 250–256. Springer, Heidelberg (2010). https://doi.org/10.1007/978-3-642-15892-6_26
17. Mena, B., José, M., Alarcón, R., Arnau Gras, J., Bono Cabré, R., Bendayan, R.: Non-normal data: is ANOVA still a valid option? Psicothema **29**(4), 552–557 (2017)
18. Myers, N., Mittermeier, R.A., Mittermeier, C.G., Da Fonseca, G.A., Kent, J.: Biodiversity hotspots for conservation priorities. Nature **403**(6772), 853 (2000)
19. Piaget, J.: Piaget's theory. In: Inhelder, B., Chipman, H.H., Zwingmann, C. (eds.) Piaget and His School. SSE, pp. 11–23. Springer, Heidelberg (1976). https://doi.org/10.1007/978-3-642-46323-5_2
20. Read, J., Macfarlane, S., Casey, C.: Endurability, engagement and expectations: measuring children's fun. In: Interaction Design and Children, pp. 1–23. Shaker Publishing, Eindhoven (2002). https://www.researchgate.net/publication/228870976
21. Saito, C.H.: Environmental education and biodiversity concern: beyond the ecological literacy. Am. J. Agric. Biol. Sci. **8**(1), 12 (2013)
22. Sébastien, D., Conruyt, N., Courdier, R., Tanzi, T.: Generating virtual worlds from biodiversity information systems: requirements, general process and typology of the metaverse's models. In: 2009 Fourth International Conference on Internet and Web Applications and Services, pp. 549–554. IEEE (2009)
23. Sjödén, B., Lind, M., Silvervarg, A.: Can a teachable agent influence how students respond to competition in an educational game? In: André, E., Baker, R., Hu, X., Rodrigo, M.M.T., du Boulay, B. (eds.) AIED 2017. LNCS (LNAI), vol. 10331, pp. 347–358. Springer, Cham (2017). https://doi.org/10.1007/978-3-319-61425-0_29
24. Teixeira, D., Abreu, C.: Moluscos Terrestres da Ponta de São Lourenço e Ilhéus Adjacentes. Secretaria Regional do Ambiente e dos Recursos Naturais - Direção Regional do Ambiente, biodiversidade madeirense: avaliação e conservação edn (2003). http://tiny.cc/MoluscosBook

25. Vane-Wright, R., Coppock, J.: Planetary awareness, worldviews and the conservation of biodiversity. In: The Coming Transformation. Values to Sustain Human and Natural Communities, pp. 353–382. Yale School of Forestry & Environmental Studies, New Haven (2009)

26. Vasconcelos, E., et al.: A serious game for exploring and training in participatory management of national parks for biodiversity conservation: design and experience. In: 2009 VIII Brazilian Symposium on Games and Digital Entertainment, pp. 93–100. IEEE (2009)

27. Yadollahi, E., Johal, W., Paiva, A., Dillenbourg, P.: When deictic gestures in a robot can harm child-robot collaboration. In: IDC 2018 - Proceedings of the 2018 ACM Conference on Interaction Design and Children, pp. 195–206. Association for Computing Machinery, Inc., June 2018. https://doi.org/10.1145/3202185.3202743

Blind Trust: How Making a Device Humanoid Reduces the Impact of Functional Errors on Trust

Christopher Vattheuer[1], Annalena Nora Baecker[1,2],
Denise Y. Geiskkovitch[1], Stela Hanbyeol Seo[1,2], Daniel J. Rea[1,3],
and James E. Young[1(✉)]

[1] University of Manitoba, Winnipeg, MB, Canada
young@cs.umanitoba.ca
[2] Osnabrück University, Osnabrück, Lower Saxony, Germany
[3] Kyoto University, Kyoto, Japan

Abstract. Humanoid robots are starting to replace information kiosks in public spaces, providing increased engagement and an intuitive interface. Upgrading devices to be humanoid in this fashion may have unexpected consequences relating to the new, more social, embodiment. We investigated how altering a voice-command calculator kiosk, by making it humanoid, impacts user trust and trust resilience after functional errors. Our results indicate that making a kiosk humanoid increases both overall trust and trust resilience, where it reduces the impact of functional errors on trust. As public kiosks continue to be replaced by humanoids, this highlights the importance of understanding the full impact of this embodiment change on interaction.

Keywords: Human-robot interaction · Social HRI · Trust · Robot error

1 Introduction

Humanoid robots are emerging in public spaces, offering information or assistance to the public. For example, the SoftBank Pepper robot (with tablet) can now be found as an informational kiosk in airports, banks, and taking orders or assigning tables in restaurants. This humanoid typically replaces existing self-help kiosks, with people still interacting using a similar touch screen (e.g., mounted on the robot); however, now the kiosk looks humanoid, speaks, makes eye contact, and uses hand gestures. One

Fig. 1. Participants interact with a tablet or humanoid voice agent calculator, which makes mistakes. Our results find that participants trust the humanoid more, and lose more trust in the tablet after mistakes.

A. R. Wagner et al. (Eds.): ICSR 2020, LNAI 12483, pp. 207–219, 2020.
https://doi.org/10.1007/978-3-030-62056-1_18

reason for this shift is that humanoids can increase user engagement and satisfaction, as a robot that interacts in human-like ways can be easier to understand, and natural and comfortable to interact with [48].

However, social interaction with robots can also result in increased trust [3, 19], empathy [39], and persuasion [10], even if not explicitly designed for. We emphasize that this has the potential to be problematic, for example, people may trust high-impact information (e.g., a flight gate, time) more from a robot that a regular kiosk, or if the robot is more persuasive than the kiosk when requesting private information such as a credit card number, or encouraging spending (e.g., suggesting a tip). It is important to understand the effect of making kiosks humanoid, to enable us to better inform both designers and consumers of potential impacts.

In this paper, we investigate how upgrading a non-humanoid agent to be humanoid – by changing the physical form and adding generic gestures – may affect a person's trust. We further explore this in the face of functional errors, which one would expect to reduce trust (Fig. 1). We compare interaction with a voice-command calculator – similar to digital assistants such as Siri – in tablet versus humanoid form, with identical functional interaction. Rather than isolating features (e.g., comparing with vs. without gaze, eyes, gestures, etc., a reductionist approach), we compare between a tablet with no humanoid features and a full robot embodiment, to increase generalizability. It is important to test interaction holistically [47]: we test a viable robotic embodiment (with simple interaction) that a person may actually encounter today.

Our results show that changing a kiosk to be humanoid can increase trust, and when it makes obvious errors, people lose trust in the tablet (non-humanoid) but maintain it for the humanoid. This demonstrates potential collateral effects of making agents humanoid, where people may trust a humanoid agent version more, even when defective. This highlights the importance of considering potential dangers relating to introducing humanoid agents into public spaces such as banks, restaurants, or airports.

2   Related Work

People tend to treat robots as social entities [47], attributing them with moral and social characteristics [4, 18, 41]. Robots can be designed to leverage this, being made to look [3, 10, 42] and act [17, 29, 40] in ways to elicit social responses (e.g., using body language [1]), which can increase engagement [12, 38], ease of understanding [29], empathy [39], and likeability [36]. Robots can use these social techniques to be more persuasive and manipulative [11, 38], for example, a robot design can shape perceptions and interactions based on whether it is humanoid or mechanical looking [3, 11], how it sounds [26], or how it is introduced to people [32]. Robot form is important, for example, humanoid or zoomorphic robots can be more persuasive [3, 35] and induce more empathy [39] than mechanical forms, and physical robots impact interaction more strongly than virtual agents [2, 30, 45]. Therefore, it is well established that humanoid robots can impact interaction in myriad ways, necessitating the need for clear understanding of impacts of simple humanoids replacing kiosks.

Research has demonstrated that people will indeed trust robots (e.g., [5]), even when they have cause to be suspicious of them [5, 37]. Many have studied the impact of robot errors, although results are mixed. In some cases, robot errors have little or no impact on trust [9], or a robot can actively mitigate a trust break [34]. Others have found that the opposite, for example, that people will perceive a robot that makes errors as being less reliable and trustworthy [21, 31], and this worsens with repeated [7] or particularly glaring mistakes [23]. It is also important to consider whether the error is perceived as intentional (e.g., if it is "cheating" [41]). We contribute to the ongoing discussion by focusing on current real-world robot use, comparing trust in a humanoid against the non-humanoid it replaces, in the face of functional errors.

Research has further investigated impact of agent embodiment (e.g., virtual, physical) on trust, although results are still highly varied and inconclusive. Many investigations report no impact of agent embodiment, whether it be virtual or physical, or using anthropomorphism, on trust at all [9, 16, 22, 27]; at best, only a few inquiries found a small effects [13, 24]. Inversely, there is some evidence that anthropomorphism may *decrease* trust [25], contrary to expectations given social robots. The few projects that find people trust robots more than virtual agents (e.g., [28]) only measure whether people would use information from the agent, and further do not investigate the impact of errors. One inquiry does demonstrate that people may lose trust less in a person that makes errors, compared to a virtual agent [45], motivating the need to similarly compare robots against virtual agents. Our work intersects these existing projects, studying trust resilience toward a tablet agent versus a humanoid version of the same agent, grounded in interaction we are starting to see in public spaces.

While it is established that robots can garner varying types of trust in a range of contexts, research does not yet inform us about how trust may change when replacing an interactive kiosk with a humanoid version. That is, the field has not yet established a link between humanoid robot embodiment (in comparison to a tablet or disembodied agent) and a person's trust in the face of errors.

3   Voice-Command Calculator Platform

We created a voice-command tablet computer calculator agent for a mock restaurant scenario, similar to digital assistants (e.g., Siri), to help customers split a bill or calculate a tip. Our guiding design goal was to keep interaction simple, to represent currently feasible technology for restaurants. Specifically, we used a rigid command dialog instead of more natural (but currently infeasible) conversation.

3.1   Calculator Interaction

To start interaction one had to say "Okay, Pepper" (the agent's name), and the agent would beep to indicate that it was ready for a command, after which a person could query the agent, that would respond using voice (matching experiences with voice-command agents). For example, a person could say "Okay, Pepper. [wait for beep]. How to split a $50 bill between 2 people with a 10% tip?" and

Fig. 2. Visual feedback was displayed on the tablet following a query, in this case after being asked "how to split a $43.20 meal between two people."

get a response: "A \$50 bill with a 10% tip split between 2 people would be \$27.50 each". The response is displayed on the tablet screen (Fig. 2). Including the query in the response enabled the person to know if they were properly understood. After the response, a person could ask another query in the same fashion.

We used an Amazon Fire HD 10 tablet mounted as a kiosk (Fig. 1, top). We generated the tablet voice using the SoftBank NAOqi API played through the tablet's speakers. The implementation used the Wizard of Oz technique, explained further in Sect. 4.

3.2 Humanoid Interaction

For our humanoid addition we replicated our implementation on a Softbank Pepper robot, using its built-in tablet (Fig. 1, bottom). Interaction structure, graphical displays, timing, agent voice, etc., were identical to the tablet; both the standalone and robot tablets had the same dimensions and resolution, and were mounted at the same height. We enabled the robot's existing generic speaking movement module, as well as face-tracking ability, to add typical but non-descript hand gestures and to keep eye contact while talking. Both of these features are not sophisticated and were bundled with the robot, representing typical robot interaction in public scenarios.

4   Experiment: Effects of a Humanoid Embodiment on Trust

We conducted an experiment to investigate 1) the effects on user trust of adding a humanoid form to an agent, and 2) how trust changes (based on embodiment) when the agent performs a noticeable error. Embodiment was manipulated between participants, where each participant interacted with only one of either the tablet or robot. We could not conduct within-participants because of the learning effect associated with the trust break. We tasked participants with asking the agent a series of restaurant-relevant math questions, recording their responses. In the first phase, the agent answered all questions correctly, to establish a base-line functionality and level of trust. Following, the agent made several egregious mistakes, after which we measured trust again. As such, we investigate overall impact of agent embodiment on user trust (between-participants), and the impact of agent error (before vs. after trust break).

4.1   Task

Participants were instructed to "work with the agent to answer two sets of problems." We provided participants with a sheet of restaurant-related questions involving splitting bills, tips, tax, and general math questions. We provided the questions to reduce variability in how participants queried the robot, to avoid confusion, and to facilitate the Wizard-of-Oz implementation. Participants were tasked with using the agent to answer the questions by verbally asking and recording the answers on a given paper.

4.2   Manipulations: Embodiment and Agent Error

We conducted the experiment with agent form (tablet, humanoid) as the primary between-participants factor. Further, within-participants we compared before agent error (no errors) against after it made errors (with errors). Each participant first interacted with the robot without errors to establish a baseline, where they would ask ten pre-determined math questions, and the agent would answer all questions correctly. Following, again the participant would ask ten (new, but similar) pre-determined math questions, but this time the agent would answer three incorrectly with obvious mistakes (the 3rd, 7th, 10th, given below). Question selection and mistake timings were fixed across participants. The errors were:

Question #3:   (Q) How should 2 people split a $35.26 bill?
             (A) Among 2 people, a $35.26 meal costs $43.00 a person.
#7:   (Q) How should 2 people split a $30.00 meal with a 12% tip?
             (A) Among 2 people, a $30.00 meal with a 12% gratuity costs $4.01 a person.
#10:   (Q) How should a $23.00 meal with a 25% tip be split between 2 people?
             (A) Among 2 people, a $23.00 meal with a 25% gratuity costs $52.00 a person.

Given the potential impact of any robot error on trust we were very sensitive to technical errors (e.g., wi-fi or robot error) during the experiment. We excluded any case with technical or connectivity issues from our analysis.

Thus, we have a 2×2 mixed experiment design: embodiment (between: non-humanoid tablet, humanoid robot), and errors (within: baseline, after trust break).

4.3   Measurements

We administered a questionnaire to record participant age and gender. For participant trust we used the Multi-Dimensional Measure of Trust scale [44], where participants self-rate their trust in the robot's abilities along two dimensions (four subscales):

capacity trust:
    reliable subscale (reliable, predictable, someone you can count on, consistent)
    capable subscale (capable, skilled, competent, meticulous)

moral trust:
    ethical subscale (ethical, respectable, principled, has integrity)
    sincere subscale (sincere, genuine, candid, authentic)

Participants rank a series of adjectives on a scale from 0 (not at all) to 7 (very), or "Does Not Fit," treated as missing data, with subscales averaged.

As a manipulation check, to determine if the participant was likely to notice agent errors, we administered a math basics questionnaire (e.g., What is 5 times 7? What is 17% of 100? What is 55 divided by 5?). We further asked on the post-test questionnaire whether participants noticed the errors ("Were Pepper's responses accurate?"). If we had no indication that a participant noticed the agent errors, then we assumed that our within-participants manipulation failed and we excluded the data.

4.4   Procedure

We informed participants that their task was to help us test a voice-command calculator by using it to answer math questions related to paying at a restaurant. We obtained informed consent and gave the pre-test demographics and math ability questionnaires.

The researcher demonstrated how to verbally interact with the agent by asking sample math questions, giving the participant an opportunity to try. The researcher provided the participant with a single-sheet handout with ten questions to ask the agent with spaces for answers. The paper included an example to remind participants how to query the agent. The researcher told participants to ask the agent to inform the researcher when they were complete (by saying "Okay Pepper, text the researcher"); this was also provided on the handout. The researcher then left the room, leaving the participant alone with the robot, and the first phase (no-errors) began.

Once the participant indicated they were finished, the researcher returned and administered the trust questionnaire to measure baseline trust. The participant was given a second near-identical hand-out with different math questions. The participant was reminded of the task procedure, and how to contact the researcher, and the researcher left the room again, beginning the errors phase. Finally, upon completion the researcher returned and again administered the trust questionnaire.

To finish, the researcher administered the post-test questionnaire (including manipulation checks) and debriefed the participant on the study purpose and deceptions (including the Wizard of Oz implementation and purposeful errors).

The entire experiment took about 30 min, and participants were paid $10 for their time. This study was approved by our institutional ethics review board.

4.5   Procedure: Wizarding

We designed our wizarding protocol to simulate a realistic digital personal assistant similar to existing systems, except focused on the calculator application; in all cases, the wizard (and thus agent) would respond consistently, and without variation. The wizard did not respond if the participant did not clearly say the "OK Pepper" start phrase; if the wizard could not understand the participant, or if an utterance would not be expected to work with standard voice-command assistants (e.g., such as "can you, uhh.. actually, sorry, Pepper, how about…"), the agent would specifically say "Sorry, I couldn't quite catch that!". If the participant asked a question outside of the calculator protocol, the wizard would tell the participant, "Let's stay on track please."

To maintain a consistent and believable agent response speed, we pre-programmed the wizarding interface with answers to the 20 math questions, assigned to hot-key accelerators. Further, if participants made small mistakes (e.g., reading 20 as 30), the interface had shorthand to enable the wizard to quickly type unpredicted responses (with the interface displaying and a "thinking" spin graphic) to maintain the illusion of a calculator. If the wizard made an unplanned error, this created an inconsistency in our error manipulation and so the session was excluded from analysis.

When making a planned error the agent consistently answered the question incorrectly, even if the participant noticed and asked again. If a participant rephrased or changed the question, however, the agent reverted to answering correctly.

4.6   Results

We recruited 39 participants, but excluded 13 due to a failed manipulation check –did not appear to notice the agent error (we address this further in our discussion). Two participants were excluded as outliers who answered with all extreme values (max/minimums) on the trust scale, corroborated as the only partici- pants with responses more than three inter-quartile ranges from the mean. This resulted in 24 partici- pants, aged 18–37 (average 24.1, 9 female, 15 male). Participants were alternately allocated to the two embodiments; 11 in the humanoid condition, and 13 in the tablet condition.

We conducted 2×2 Mixed Model ANOVAs (between: tablet, humanoid; within: baseline, errors) on the four trust subscales. We found statistically-significant main effects of agent error (with vs. without) on all trust subscales, with trust ratings lower after error (Table 1). We also found a main effect of agent embodiment (tablet vs. humanoid) on all trust sub-

Table 1. Main effects of agent error (baseline, with errors) on participant rating of trust subscales. Higher is more trust.

		$F_{1,22}$	p	Baseline (/7)	With-error (/7)	$\eta2$
Capacity trust	Reliable	56.1	<.001	6.48	4.31	.72
	Capable	48.9	<.001	6.67	4.85	.69
Moral trust	Ethical	6.3	.02	6.16	5.59	.22
	Sincere	11.9	.002	6.21	5.37	.35

Table 2. Main effects of agent form (tablet, huma- noid) on participant rating of trust subscales. Higher is more trust.

		$F_{1,22}$	p	Humanoid (/ 7)	Tablet (/ 7)	$\eta2$
Capacity trust	Reliable	7.2	.014	5.88	4.91	.25
	Capable	4.8	.039	6.02	5.50	.18
Moral trust	Ethical	4.6	.043	6.54	5.20	.17
	Sincere	5.0	.036	6.11	5.46	.18

scales, with all mean trust ratings lower for the tablet than the humanoid (Table 2). We graph the 2×2 results in Fig. 3 by subscale.

We found a statistically-significant interaction effect between agent error and form on both of the ethical ($F_{1,22} = 4.0$, $p = .05$) and sincere ($F_{1,22} = 5.7$, $p = .027$) moral trust subscales (see Fig. 3 for visual interpretation). Post-hoc t-tests (Bonferroni cor- rection) on ethical trust found no difference between the humanoid and tablet without- error ($t_{21} = 1.4$, $p = .18$), but with error, found a difference on ethical trust between the humanoid (6.49/7) and tablet (4.69/7, $t_{22} = 2.6$ $p = .03$). Investigating the effects of error by agent embodiment, we found no effect of agent error on trust in the humanoid case ($t_{10} = .5$), but found a statistically-significant effect of the error in the tablet condition ($t_{12} < 2.7$, $p = .036$, pre-error 5.71/7, post-error 4.69/7). These results sup- port the visual interpretation of the interaction effect (Fig. 3).

For investigating the interaction effect for sincere trust, we found no difference between the humanoid and tablet forms without-error ($t_{22} = .3$), but with-error, we found a difference between the humanoid (5.98/7) and tablet (4.75/7, $t_{22} = 2.5$, $p = .028$). Investigating the effect of error by agent embodiment, we found no effect of agent error on sincere trust in the humanoid ($t_{10} = .7$), but found an effect of the error in the tablet condition ($t_{12} = 4.5$, $p = .002$, pre-error 6.17/7, post-error 4.75/7). These results again support the visual interpretation of the interaction effect (Fig. 3).

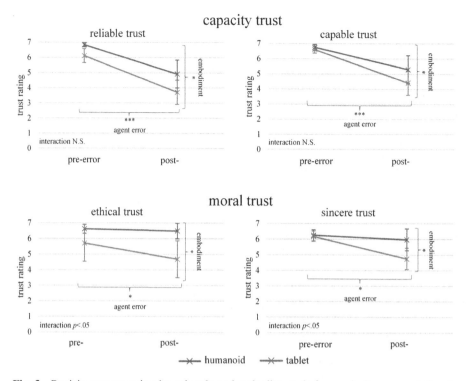

Fig. 3. Participant trust rating by subscale and embodiment, before and after errors. All main effects of embodiment and error were significant. The interaction effect for ethical and sincere trust resulted in a drop in trust for tablet, but not the humanoid. Error bars are 2SE.

5   Discussion

Overall, our results suggest that people will trust a humanoid agent more than its tablet-only variant for both capacity and moral trust. Further, our results support the hypothesis that people will have less trust in an agent when it makes errors; this serves as a manipulation check supporting our use of agent error to decrease trust.

While the interaction effects for moral trust complicates analysis, our post-hoc tests corroborate the visual analysis evident in Fig. 3: agent error does not impact moral trust in the humanoid, but moral trust falls for the tablet. In other words, the humanoid form mitigates the moral trust drop resulting from an obvious functional error. Further, while the post-error results may be driving the main effect of embodiment impact, overall people still have more moral trust in the humanoid than the tablet.

The differences we observed between capacity trust (reliable, capable) and moral trust (ethical, sincere), are important to consider: across the board, trust dropped after agent error *except for moral trust of a humanoid robot*. Why exactly capacity trust would fall but not moral trust, or why this would happen for a humanoid but not a tablet, needs to be further investigated.

While the concept of moral trust being applied to a humanoid can be analyzed within the framework of social robotics (e.g., that people treat robots as social others [48]), it is not clear how moral trust would apply to a tablet agent; perhaps, as it used human-like speech, participants applied similar principles to understand the agent (see, e.g., [33]). If that is the case, then it is further unclear why the humanoid form only would not experience a moral trust drop after making errors.

One possibility relates to the fact that the physical design of the humanoid robot (see Fig. 1) has the tablet attached to the front of the robot (and not, e.g., embedded within it). Perhaps, then, participants saw the humanoid tablet as being separate from the robot itself, as an accessory, and thus do not attribute error blame to the robot *per se* (but to its attached tablet). However, this then contradicts the finding of capacity trust falling for the humanoid after the agent error; here again, the reason for capacity and moral trust having differing results is not clear.

Another possibility is that the humanoid may have elicited more pro-social behavior from participants. For example, while they note that the humanoid is less capable to make concrete calculations after the error, the social design may encourage participants to dismiss the error, for example, as an honest mistake, in an affiliative fashion, in a way that makes it not the robot's *fault* from a moral standpoint.

Along a similar vein, an agent's form (e.g., gender [8, 20]) can shape assumptions about task suitability. If the tablet was seen as a traditional computer, commonly known to be good at math, the participant may see a computer that cannot do math as not being genuine, authentic, or respectable (moral trust subscales). Alternatively, people may apply more human-typical notions to a humanoid; a person making math mistakes is common and not related to their moral reasoning ability. In both of these cases, results may relate to expectations and the Pratfall effect.

It is worth considering why the *tacked-on* humanoid features altered perceptions of trust at all: the embodiment change did not change explicit interaction apart from the generic hand gestures and gaze, which did not have functional purpose. The humanoid did not engage in any authentic or complex social interaction. However, while the robot's gestures and actions were functionally simple and not interactive, we should note that the robot emitting these social signals may trigger strong reactions in people. People can be expected to assume underlying processes behind the signals (e.g., a robot that looks at you can think), even if such capability does not exist [6]). Similarly, research has suggested that robot movement can be linked to perceptions of intent (even when there is none) and can cause a robot to appear more intelligent [14, 15].

Finally, we have concern over the fact that 13 of our 39 participants did not notice the robot errors, despite performing well on the math skills quiz, and the errors themselves being obvious (e.g., dividing a bill resulting in a larger number). Unfortunately, we do not have the qualitative or interview data to appropriately analyze why this may have happened. Perhaps given the rote nature of the task people were simply not paying attention but rather mechanically following procedure. Perhaps participants simply trusted the digital agents blindly as they know computers are good at math. Such reactions could easily carry over to a real restaurant situation, further emphasizing how even people competent in a task may put too much trust in a humanoid robot.

As a post-hoc measure, we re-conducted our analysis including all participants who were excluded due to failed manipulation check. The main effects and general results *do not change* from what is presented here. This further complicates the analysis, as even if participants claim they did not notice the errors, they apparently still reacted differently. However, we stand by our choice of excluding those participants from the main analysis, and the underlying cause of this phenomenon requires additional study.

Overall, the simple resulting message is that adding a humanoid form to an existing agent interaction, for example, to increase engagement or support intuitive interaction, will also impact how people trust the agent, and how forgiving they may be of agent errors. Such secondary, or perhaps collateral impacts, need to be better understood as we continue to see humanoid kiosk robots enter public spaces. Our work is the first to clearly establish a strong link between agent embodiment and trust resilience in the context of information agents being converted into humanoid robots.

6 Limitations

Novelty is a still a large consideration for experiments involving robots, and in this case, we expect that the excitement of having an opportunity to speak with a humanoid shaped our results. For example, despite being asked to not use their phones during the experiment, the wizard researcher observed many participants secretly taking photos and videos, and asking humorous questions to the robot for fun. We did not see similar behaviors with the tablet. It is possible the excitement of interacting with a humanoid was a driver of our results, and not other factors of the embodiment. However, we want to highlight that *novelty is not a confound in robot experiments*, but simply a reality of robots in society today; we similarly will expect people to experience novelty when encountering robots in the real world [43].

While we measured an abstract, self-report overall perception of trust, future work should explore situations where a user has something real at stake (e.g., money, material loss). However, we feel that our low-stakes experiment is reasonably representative of a real-world scenario where the stakes may not be immediately clear to a person (e.g., advice in an airport). Further, our lab-based study has limited ecological validity, for example, it did not provide participants with explicit incentive to pay attention. If such a study was performed in the wild with real stakes or implications (perhaps where people were spending their own money), we may find different results. Our task itself then, with many restaurant-based questions, is valuable as it implementable with current technology, and could be extended to an in-the-wild study without great technological investment.

One of the core ideas surrounding this work is that an agent's embodiment implies properties about an agent – even how to interact with it [46]. In our non-humanoid tablet, people may be expecting to interact with touch, but could not; this may have influenced participants to consider the tablet as somehow defective, making it easier to lose trust in it. While this may not have a strong effect in our case as people are increasingly familiar with voice-only agents like Siri, future task designs should consider interaction methods that feel natural for all embodiments being compared.

7 Conclusions

Humanoid robots are becoming increasingly common in public places where they interact with people to provide information or kiosk-like services. Commonly, these robots replace an existing interactive kiosk or agent, ostensibly as a robot can be more engaging, exciting, or easy to work with. However, in this work we highlight that simply wrapping a device in a humanoid embodiment may incorporate additional social impacts that both the designer and user may not have intended or be aware of. Our initial results in this space show how making an interactive voice-controlled agent humanoid can increase trust in that agent. Further, people are more forgiving of the humanoid, in that even after it makes serious functional errors, they do not report a reduction in moral trust of the robot; this is in contrast to a non-humanoid tablet agent, where people's trust reduced across the board following functional errors. This can have serious consequences for humanoids used in high impact or sensitive scenarios, such as banks, hospitals, or schools.

Overall, these results highlight the potential dangers of using humanoid designs and indicate the importance of considering the broad consequences – intentional or not – of making devices humanoid. Moving forward, we hope this work contributes to developing a healthy skepticism and balanced approach to considering the full implications of humanoid robots entering society.

References

1. Admoni, H., Scassellati, B.: Social eye gaze in human-robot interaction: a review. J. Hum. Robot Interact. **6**(1), 25 (2017). https://doi.org/10.5898/JHRI.6.1.Admoni
2. Bainbridge, W.A., et al.: The benefits of interactions with physically present robots over video-displayed agents. Int. J. Soc. Robot. **3**(1), 41–52 (2010). https://doi.org/10.1007/s12369-010-0082-7
3. Bartneck, C., et al.: The influence of robot anthropomorphism on the feelings of embarrassment when interacting with robots. Paladyn J. Behav. Robot. **1**(2), 109–115 (2010)
4. Bartneck, C., et al.: To kill a mockingbird robot. In: HRI 2007. ACM (2007)
5. Booth, S., et al.: Piggybacking robots. In: Human-Robot Interaction. ACM (2017)
6. Collins, E., et al.: The broader context of trust in HRI. In: Fisher, M., et al. (eds.) Dagstuhl Reports: Ethics and Trust: Principles, Verification and Validation, pp. 82–85
7. Desai, M., et al.: Effects of changing reliability on trust of robot systems. In: Human-Robot Interaction, pp. 73–80 (2012). https://doi.org/10.1145/2157689.2157702
8. Eyssel, F., Hegel, F.: (S)he's got the look. J. Appl. Soc. Psychol. **42**(9), 2213–2230 (2012)
9. Flook, R., et al.: On the impact of different types of errors on trust in human-robot interaction. Interact. Stud. **20**(3), 455–486 (2019). https://doi.org/10.1075/is.18067.flo
10. Geiskkovitch, D., et al.: Autonomy, embodiment, and obedience to robots. In: Human-Robot Interaction Extended Abstracts, pp. 235–236. ACM (2015)
11. Geiskkovitch, D.Y., et al.: Please continue, we need more data: an exploration of obedience to robots. J. Hum.-Robot Interact. **5**(1), 82–99 (2016)
12. Gordon, G., et al.: Can children catch curiosity from a social robot? In HRI 2015 (2015)
13. Hancock, P.A., et al.: A meta-analysis of factors affecting trust in human-robot interaction. Hum. Factors J. Hum. Factors Ergon. Soc. **53**(5), 517–527 (2011)

14. Harris, J., Sharlin, E.: (e)motion. In: RO-MAN. IEEE (2011)
15. Heider, F., Simmel, M.: An experimental study of apparent behavior. Am. J. Psychol. **57**(2)
16. Herse, S., et al.: Do you trust me, blindly? Factors influencing trust towards a robot recommender system. In: RO-MAN. IEEE (2018)
17. Jung, M.F., et al.: Using robots to moderate team conflict. In: HRI 2015. ACM (2015)
18. Kahn, P.H., et al.: "Robovie, you'll have to go into the closet now": children's social and moral relationships with a humanoid robot. Dev. Psychol. **48**(2), 303–314 (2012)
19. Kahn, P.H., et al.: Will people keep the secret of a humanoid robot? In: Human-Robot Interaction, pp. 173–180 (2015). https://doi.org/10.1145/2696454.2696486
20. Kuchenbrandt, D., Häring, M., Eichberg, J., Eyssel, F.: Keep an eye on the task! How gender typicality of tasks influence human–robot interactions. In: Ge, S.S., Khatib, O., Cabibihan, J.-J., Simmons, R., Williams, M.-A. (eds.) ICSR 2012. LNCS (LNAI), vol. 7621, pp. 448–457. Springer, Heidelberg (2012). https://doi.org/10.1007/978-3-642-34103-8_45
21. Kwon, M., et al.: Human expectations of social robots. In: ACM/IEEE International Conference on Human-Robot Interaction, April 2016, pp. 463–464 (2016). https://doi.org/10.1109/HRI.2016.7451807
22. Li, D., et al.: A cross-cultural study: effect of robot appearance and task. Int. J. Soc. Robot. **2**(2), 175–186 (2010). https://doi.org/10.1007/s12369-010-0056-9
23. Madhavan, P., et al.: Automation failures on tasks easily performed by operators undermine trust in automated aids. Hum. Factors **48**(2), 241–256 (2006)
24. Mann, J.A., et al.: People respond better to robots than computer tablets delivering healthcare instructions. Comput. Hum. Behav. **43**, 112–117 (2015)
25. Mathur, M.B., Reichling, D.B.: An uncanny game of trust: In: Proceedings of the 4th ACM/IEEE International Conference on Human-Robot Interaction, HRI 2009 (2008)
26. Moore, D., et al.: Making noise intentional: a study of servo sound perception (2017). https://doi.org/10.1145/2909824.3020238
27. Pak, R., et al.: Decision support aids with anthropomorphic characteristics influence trust and performance in younger and older adults. Ergonomics **55**(9), 1059–1072 (2012)
28. Pan, Y., Steed, A.: A comparison of avatar-, video-, and robot-mediated interaction on users' trust in expertise. Front. Robot. AI **3**, 12 (2016)
29. Park, E., et al.: The effect of robot's behavior vs. appearance on communication with humans. In: Human-Robot Interaction, pp. 219–220 (2011). https://doi.org/10.1145/1957656.1957740
30. Powers, A., et al.: Comparing a computer agent with a humanoid robot. In: Human-Robot Interaction, pp. 145–152 (2007). https://doi.org/10.1145/1228716.1228736
31. Ragni, M., et al.: Errare humanum est: erroneous robots in human-robot interaction. In: Robot and Human Interactive Communication, RO-MAN, pp. 501–506. IEEE (2016)
32. Rea, D.J., Young, J.E.: It's all in your head. In: Human-Robot Interaction, pp. 32–40. ACM Press, New York (2018)
33. Reeves, B., Nass, C.: The Media Equation: How People Treat Computers, Television, and New Media Like Real People and Places. CSLI Books (1996)
34. Robinette, P., et al.: Overtrust of robots in emergency evacuation scenarios. In: Human-Robot Interaction, pp. 101–108 (2016). https://doi.org/10.1109/HRI.2016.7451740
35. Roubroeks, M., et al.: When artificial social agents try to persuade people: the role of social agency on the occurrence of psychological reactance. Int. J. Soc. Robot. **3**(2), 155–165 (2011). https://doi.org/10.1007/s12369-010-0088-1
36. Salem, M., et al.: To err is human(-like): effects of robot gesture on perceived anthropomorphism and likability. Int. J. Soc. Robot. **5**(3), 313–323 (2013). https://doi.org/10.1007/s12369-013-0196-9

37. Salem, M., et al.: Would you trust a (faulty) robot? Effects of error, task type and personality on human-robot cooperation and trust. In: Proceedings Human-Robot Interaction (2015)

38. Sanoubari, E., et al.: Good robot design or machiavellian? In-the-wild robot leveraging minimal knowledge of passersby's culture. In: Human-Robot Interaction (HRI) (2019)

39. Seo, S.H., et al.: Poor thing! Would you feel sorry for a simulated robot? A comparison of empathy toward a physical and a simulated robot. In: Human-Robot Interaction (2015)

40. Sharma, M., et al.: Communicating affect via flight path exploring use of the Laban effort system for designing affective locomotion paths. In: Human-Robot Interaction, pp. 293–300 (2013)

41. Short, E., et al.: No fair! An interaction with a cheating robot. In: 2010 Proceedings of the ACM/IEEE International Conference on Human-Robot Interaction, HRI 2010 (2010)

42. Singh, A., Young, James E.: A dog tail for utility robots: exploring affective properties of tail movement. In: Kotzé, P., Marsden, G., Lindgaard, G., Wesson, J., Winckler, M. (eds.) INTERACT 2013. LNCS, vol. 8118, pp. 403–419. Springer, Heidelberg (2013). https://doi.org/10.1007/978-3-642-40480-1_27

43. Smedegaard, C.V.: Reframing the role of novelty within social HRI. In: 2019 Human-Robot Interaction, HRI 2019 (2019)

44. Ullman, D., Malle, B.F.: MDMT: multi-dimensional measure of trust, pp. 618–619 (2019)

45. de Visser, E.J., et al.: Almost human: anthropomorphism increases trust resilience in cognitive agents. J. Exp. Psychol. Appl. 22(3), 331–349 (2016)

46. Wainer, J., et al.: The role of physical embodiment in human-robot interaction. In: Proceedings of the IEEE International Symposium on Robot and Human Interactive Communication, pp. 117–122 (2006)

47. Young, J.E., et al.: Evaluating human-robot interaction. Int. J. Soc. Robot. 3(1), 53–67 (2011). https://doi.org/10.1007/s12369-010-0081-8

48. Young, J.E., et al.: Toward acceptable domestic robots: applying insights from social psychology. Int. J. Soc. Robot. 1(1) (2009). https://doi.org/10.1007/s12369-008-0006-y

What Am I Allowed to Do Here?: Online Learning of Context-Specific Norms by Pepper

Ali Ayub$^{(\boxtimes)}$ and Alan R. Wagner

The Pennsylvania State University, State College, PA 16802, USA
{aja5755,alan.r.wagner}@psu.edu

Abstract. Social norms support coordination and cooperation in society. With social robots becoming increasingly involved in our society, they also need to follow the social norms of the society. This paper presents a computational framework for learning contexts and the social norms present in a context in an online manner on a robot. The paper utilizes a recent state-of-the-art approach for incremental learning and adapts it for online learning of scenes (contexts). The paper further utilizes Dempster-Schafer theory to model context-specific norms. After learning the scenes (contexts), we use active learning to learn related norms. We test our approach on the Pepper robot by taking it through different scene locations. Our results show that Pepper can learn different scenes and related norms simply by communicating with a human partner in an online manner.

Keywords: Online learning · Indoor scene classification · Norm learning · Active learning · Human-robot interaction

1 Introduction

Norms are an implicit part of any society which guide the actions taken by humans in that society. Norms support the actions taken by humans across time and generations and bring coordination and cooperation in a society [18]. Some norms are defined explicitly in the form of laws. Social norms, however, are more implicit and are learned through the actions of the community. For example, when in a library, people can implicitly learn that talking is impermissible, while at a party talking is not only permissible but obligatory.

With robots increasingly becoming an integral part of the society in different roles, such as household robots or socially assistive robots, it is necessary that they follow the implicit social norms of the society. Since social norms can differ based on different communities, it is impossible to pre-program a universal set of norms. Thus, similar to humans, robots must learn norms in a lifelong manner using different sources, such as by asking questions or observing other humans. The ultimate goal of this paper is to develop a method allowing a robot to learn

© Springer Nature Switzerland AG 2020
A. R. Wagner et al. (Eds.): ICSR 2020, LNAI 12483, pp. 220–231, 2020.
https://doi.org/10.1007/978-3-030-62056-1_19

different scenes and the norms associated with the scene while it wanders around different environments.

Despite its importance for social robotics applications, work in context-specific norm learning on robots has been limited. Sarathay et al. [13,14] present a method for formal modeling of context-specific norms, however they do not apply their approach on a real robot. For online learning of norms on a robot, it is first necessary to develop perceptual systems that allow the robot to learn different scene categories. The term scene is used here to describe the perception-level representation of a context. To the best of our knowledge, we are among the first to continually learn both the context a robot is operating in and its associated acceptable behaviors using only streaming video data.

In this paper, we present a computational framework to learn different scene categories and associated norms from streaming video data in an online manner. Online learning is a field of machine learning in which a single system is required to both incrementally learn and perform open-set recognition. Where, incremental learning is a field of machine learning focused on creating systems that can incrementally learn over time without requiring all the training data to be available in a single batch [4–6,12,20]. Open-set recognition, on the other hand, uses a trained model to predict if a new instance of data belongs to an already learned class or is contains entirely new items. Thus making the online learning problem extremely challenging. We adapt a recent state-of-the-art incremental learning approach termed Centroid-Based Concept Learning and Pseudo-Rehearsal (CBCL-PR) [3] for online learning of scenes in this paper. For norm modeling we use the mathematical framework presented in [13]. Norm learning related to different scene categories is accomplished by employing active learning to ask questions from a human partner. We test our approach on the Pepper robot by taking it through different locations on Penn State University campus for online learning of scenes and their associated norms through question/answer sessions with human partner.

The remainder of the paper is organized as follows: Sect. 2 reviews the related work regarding scene classification, incremental learning of scenes and norm learning. Section 3 describes our complete architecture for online scene and norm learning on a robot. Section 4 presents empirical evaluations of the system, demonstrating that our proposed system is capable of learning scenes and norms in an online manner. Finally, Sect. 5 offers conclusions and directions for future research.

2 Related Work

Scene classification has been strongly influenced by deep learning [19,21]. Most approaches, however, have only been tested on indoor scene datasets that do not include natural environments, variations in lighting conditions or the differences stemming from the use of different robots. Most methods also require the complete dataset, including all of the categories of scenes to be learned, available in a single batch.

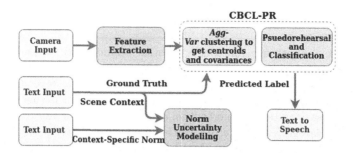

Fig. 1. Overall architecture of our approach. The robot captures new data using its camera and then predicts the label for the scene category using CBCL-PR. The text-to-speech module is used to communicate the predicted label. The human provides the true label for the new data to the robot as a text input. The robot further asks the human about the permitted and forbidden norms specific to the scene category.

For robotics applications, data is available to the robot in the form of a continuous stream. Learning from such streaming video data is known as online learning. Only a few researchers have investigated online learning of scenes for robots. Kawewong et al. [8] presents one of the earliest approaches for incremental learning of indoor scenes. They utilize a pre-trained CNN for feature extraction and utilize n-value self-organizing and incremental neural networks for incremental learning of scenes. They, however, only test their approach on the MIT 67 scene dataset [11] and not on a robot. Paul et al. [10] presented an active learning approach for online learning of scenes. However, they require the old data to be available when learning new labeled data. Furthermore, they also do not test their approach on a robot or robot-centric indoor scene dataset.

There has been limited work done on norm learning in the context of robotics applications. For example, [9] presents a simple simulated autonomous robot setup in which autonomous cars follow traffic signal norms. Tan et al. [17] present another simple robotics application of learning ownership norms. Neither of these approaches are applicable to the type of context-specific norm learning considered in this paper. Sarathy et al. [13,14] presents a context-specific norm modeling strategy that is based upon Dempster-Shafer theory [15]. They present a formal mathematical framework in which norms are modeled using a deontic logic with context-specificity and uncertainty. Unfortunately they do not test their approach on a real robot or with real scene video/image data. In this work, we use the mathematical framework presented in [13] to model context-specific norms on a Pepper robot in which scene categories (contexts) and related norms are learned in an online manner through active learning.

3   Online Scene and Norm Learning

Figure 1 shows the complete architecture of our proposed system. The system can learn new scene categories in an online manner while matching new data

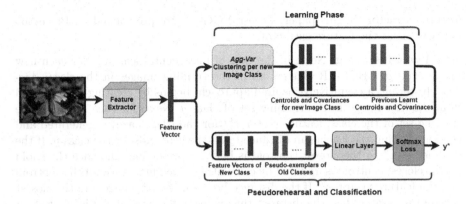

Fig. 2. For each new class of images in a dataset, the feature extractor generates feature vectors for all of the training images in the class. A set of centroids and covariance matrices are created for the feature vectors using the *Agg-Var* clustering algorithm and concatenated with the centroids and covariance matrices of previously learned classes. Pseudo-exemplars for old classes and training examples of new classes are then used to train a shallow network for classification.

to previously learned scene categories and unknown categories. After learning a scene category, the system can learn the norms related to the corresponding scene. The architecture uses Centroid-Based Concept Learning-Pseudorehearsal (CBCL-PR) approach proposed in [3] to train a robot on new scenes in an online manner with only a single example of a scene available at each increment. For norm modeling and learning, we use the mathematical model proposed in [13, 14]. The major components of the architecture are described below.

3.1 Centroid-Based Concept Learning and Pseudo-Rehearsal (CBCL-PR)

CBCL-PR [3] is a revised version of CBCL [4] which is a recently developed state-of-the-art method for incremental learning [4, 7] and RGB-D indoor scene classification [2]. CBCL-PR has also been shown to learn objects from only a few examples whereas prior state-of-the-art methods required a large amount of training data, its memory footprint does not grow dramatically as it learns new classes, and its learning time is faster than the other, mostly deep learning, methods. One of the main advantages of CBCL-PR is that it can be adapted to learn from data coming in an online manner such that the new incoming data can belong to already learned classes or completely new classes [1].

Figure 2 depicts the architecture for CBCL-PR. It is composed of three modules: 1) a feature extractor, 2) *Agg-Var* clustering, and 3) a pseudo-rehearsal and classification module. In the learning phase, once the human provides the robot with the training examples for a new class, the first step in CBCL-PR is the generation of feature vectors from the images of the new class using a fixed feature extractor. In this paper, we use VGG-16 [16] pre-trained on Places365 dataset [21] as the feature extractor.

***Agg-Var* Clustering:** Next, in the case of incremental learning, for each new image class y, CBCL-PR clusters all of the training images in the class. *Agg-Var* clustering, a cognitively-inspired approach, begins by creating one centroid from the first image in the training set of class y. Next, for each image in the training set of the class, feature vector x_i^y (for the $i$the image) is generated and compared using the Euclidean distance to all the centroids for the class y. If the distance of x_i^y to the closest centroid is below a pre-defined distance threshold D, the closest centroid is updated by calculating a weighted mean of the centroid and the feature vector x_i^y. If the distance between the ith image and the closest centroid is greater than the distance threshold D, a new centroid is created for class y and equated to the feature vector x_i^y of the ith image.

CBCL also finds the covariance matrices related to each centroid using the feature vectors of all the images clustered in the centroid. The result of this process is a collection containing a set of centroids, $C^y = \{c_1^y, ..., c_{N^*}^y\}$, and covariance matrices, $\sum^y = \{\sigma_1^y, ..., \sigma_{N_y^*}^y\}$, for the class y where N_y^* is the number of centroids for class y. This process is applied to the sample set X^y of each class incrementally once they become available to get a collection of centroids $C = C^1, C^2, ..., C^N$ and covariance matrices $\sum = \sum^1, \sum^2, ..., \sum^N$ for all N classes in a dataset. Note that *Agg-Var* clustering calculates the centroids for each class separately. Thus, its performance is not strongly impacted by when the classes are presented incrementally.

Pseudorehearsal: For classification of images from all the classes seen so far, CBCL-PR trains a shallow neural network composed of a linear layer trained with a softmax loss on examples from the current increment and pseudo-exemplars of the old classes (pseudorehearsal). Pseudo-exemplars are not real exemplars of a class, rather they are generated based on the class statistics to best resemble the actual exemplars.

CBCL-PR uses each of the centroids c_i^y and covariance matrices σ_i^y of class y to generate a set of pseudo-exemplars. First a multi-variate Gaussian distribution is created using the centroid as the mean and the corresponding covariance matrix. The Gaussian distribution is then sampled to generate the same number of pseudo-exemplars as the total number of exemplars represented by the centroid/covariance matrix pair c_i^y, σ_i^y. This process leads to a total of N_y number of pseudo-exemplars for class y. In this way the network is trained on N_y number of examples for each class y in each increment. For classification of a test image, the feature vector x of the image is first generated using the feature extractor. Next, this feature vector is passed through the shallow network to produce a predicted label y^*. A more detailed description of CBCL-PR can be found in [2–4].

3.2   Predicting Unknown Scene Categories

CBCL-PR is designed for incremental learning where the test images always belong to one of the learned categories. However, for the online learning setting considered in this paper the robot also has to make a prediction about an unknown scene category. Further, in [3] CBCL-PR is provided with the complete training set of a class at one time, however for the online learning scenario considered here, data belonging to a previously known scene category can also become available in an increment.

For this work we have adapted CBCL-PR to operate in an online learning manner. First, to make a prediction about an unknown scene category, we calculate the Euclidean distance of the feature vector of the new scene image to all of the learned centroids. If the distance is below the distance threshold D that was used to get the centroids, we predict that the new image belongs to a new scene category. Second, if the ground truth provided by the human for a new scene image belongs to one of the already learned categories, we simply apply *Agg-Var* clustering on the new scene images to either update the previously learned centroids and covariance matrices of the scene category or create new centroids and covariance matrices based upon the distance threshold D. A more detailed explanation for adapting CBCL-PR for online learning is provided in [1].

3.3   Norm Modeling and Learning

We follow the norm modeling framework presented in [13,14]. In particular, we use the idea of a context-specific belief-theoretic norm which is of the form:

$$\mathcal{N} \stackrel{\text{def}}{=} \mathbb{D}_C^{[\alpha,\beta]} A \tag{1}$$

where $\mathcal{N}$ is a context-specific belief theoretic norm for a formal language $\mathcal{L}$, $\mathbb{D}_C^{[\alpha,\beta]}$ is an uncertain context-specific deontic operator with $[\alpha,\beta]$ representing a Dempster-Shafer uncertainty interval [15] for the operator with $0 < \alpha < \beta < 1$. $\mathbb{D}$ is a collection of three deontic model operators: obligatory $\mathbb{O}$, forbidden $\mathbb{F}$ and permissible $\mathbb{P}$. $C \in \mathcal{L}$ represents the context and $A \in \mathcal{L}$ represents a state or an action. The above mentioned norm expression states that in a context C, an action or state A is either obligatory, forbidden or permissible or not obligatory, forbidden or permissible.

We use the mathematical model of Eq. (1) to model and learn norms for different scene categories (contexts) in an online manner. The initial knowledge of the robot consists of a set of possible actions that the robot can perform. For example, *talk* is an action available to the robot where it can use its speech module to communicate. However, the robot does not know which of its known actions are permissible, obligatory or forbidden in a particular context. Hence, for each new context the robot learns about context-specific norms through active learning i.e. by having a short question/answer session with a human partner. We only use yes/no question types in this paper. In each new context/scene, the robot asks its human partner which of its actions are obligatory, forbidden or

Bathroom 1   Bathroom 2

Fig. 3. Images from two different bathrooms collected by the Pepper robot. Both images are drastically different from each other.

permissible. If a norm does not exist in the robot's knowledge base, it simply creates a new norm for a particular context. The new norm is initialized with an uncertainty interval of either $[0, 0]$ or $[1, 1]$ based upon the answer given by the human (yes or no). However, if a norm already exists in the robot's knowledge base and it gets an answer from its human partner, it updates the uncertainty interval of the norm based on the new answer. In Sect. 4 we present results of learning different context-specific norms by the Pepper robot. The learned norms and the associated uncertainties can be used by the robot to reason about before performing an action in a given context. Experiments regarding norm reasoning for performing actions are left for future work.

4   Experiments

We evaluate our method for online learning of scenes and related norms on the Pepper robot. The robot was manually driven through 10 different locations belonging to 5 different categories (bathroom, classroom, library, Office, kitchen) on the Penn State University campus. The locations differed from one another even when belonging to the same category, making the learning and recognition task difficult. For example, Fig. 3 shows images from two different bathrooms captured by the Pepper robot. Note how different the images are. Images were captured using the front head camera of the Pepper with a resolution of 320 × 240. Pepper's text-to-speech module was used to communicate with the human while the labels and norm related answers were provided by the human using a keyboard.

4.1   Online Scene Learning Using the Pepper Robot

Our first experiment demonstrates our method for online scene learning on a Pepper robot. For each new location, the robot took the input of a scene (either belonging to earlier learned categories or a new category) using its camera. Next,

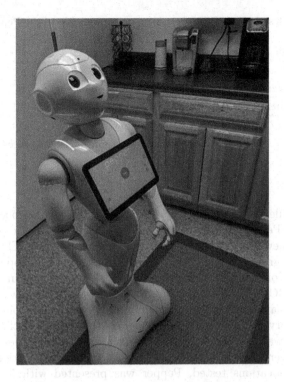

Fig. 4. An example of the Pepper robot trying to predict the category *kitchen*.

it used the method described in Fig. 1 to either predict the label of the scene or predict that the scene category was unknown. The robot further asked the human to confirm the label of the new scene. If the human provided the label, the text module passed it to CBCL-PR to update the previous centroids, otherwise if the new scene belonged to a known category the robot created new centroids for the new scene category.

It took approximately 30 s to capture a video, while feature extraction took about 11 s. The time required to make a prediction about the new video was only 1 s, while confirmation of the label from the human took approximately 5 s. *Agg-Var* clustering took only 1 s to find the centroids and pseudorehearsal and classifier training took 10 s. Hence, the total time to learn about a new location was approximately 58 s. It should be noted that after receiving the label from the human, Pepper continue to process the data while moving to other locations, so it only needs 47 s at one location to make a prediction.

At each of the locations, Pepper captured the video data by rotating its head from center to the left and then left to right for 20 s. After capturing the video, the feature extractor was used to extract the features for all the images. Our method (Fig. 1) used the shallow classifier in CBCL-PR to make a prediction about the category of the location, while it used the distance to the closest centroid to make a prediction if the location was known. Pepper's text-

Table 1. Description of the six action types available to the Pepper robot.

Robot actions	Description
talkLoundly	Speak in a higher volume
talkQuietly	Lower volume when speaking
beQuiet	Do not speak
listen	Process the incoming audio input
watch	Capture images through camera for processing
walk	Move around

to-speech module was then used to communicate the prediction. After making the prediction, Pepper confirmed its prediction in the case of a known category or asked for a new label in the case of an unknown category. The experimenter then typed the ground truth of the location in a terminal. Pepper repeated the typed label to confirm with the experimenter. After the confirmation, *Agg-Var* clustering in CBCL-PR was used to find the centroids for the new data in the case of an unknown category or update the previously learned centroids in the case of a known category. After learning the centroids that represent the new location, the image data was discarded to satisfy the conditions of online learning. Figure 4 shows the Pepper robot in a kitchen trying to predict the location's label.

Of the 10 locations tested, Pepper was presented with 5 locations that belonged to new categories and 5 locations from a previously known category. Pepper correctly predicted 80% of locations when the location belonged to a new category and 80% of locations when predicting known categories. These results clearly show the effectiveness of our approach to mitigate *catastrophic forgetting* when learning scene categories using streaming video data on a robot. Where catastrophic forgetting is a problem in continual learning in which the model forgets the previously learned classes when learning new classes and the overall accuracy decreases drastically. Detailed experiments on incremental learning on benchmark datasets for CBCL-PR are available in [3,4].

4.2 Norm Learning by the Pepper Robot

The setup for this experiment was the same as the scene learning experiment. For each new scene, after the robot predicted the scene and got the ground truth label from the human partner, it initiated a question/answer session regarding norm learning. For each location, Pepper was allowed to ask at most three questions. In the three questions, Pepper randomly chose which norms to ask about. The limit of three questions was set arbitrarily, keeping in mind that the human would get annoyed if he/she has to answer a large number of questions at a location. All of the questions were related to the permission norms i.e. if one of the robot actions was permissible at a location. The initial set of actions available to Pepper in its knowledge base were: *talkLoudly, talkQuietly, beQuiet, listen, watch* and *walk*. Table 1 provides a description of the six actions. Pepper used its speech

Table 2. Permission norms with uncertainty intervals learned by Pepper for five different scene categories.

Permitted action	Bathroom	Classroom	Library	Office	Kitchen
talkLoudly	[0, 0]	[0, 0]	[0, 0]	[0, 0]	[1, 1]
talkQuietly	[1, 1]	[0, 0.5]	[0, 0.5]	[1, 1]	[0.5, 1]
beQuiet	[1, 1]	[0, 0.5]	[0.5, 1]	[0, 0.5]	[1, 1]
listen	[1, 1]	[1, 1]	–	[1, 1]	[1, 1]
watch	[0, 0]	–	[1, 1]	–	[1, 1]
walk	[1, 1]	–	-	[1, 1]	–

to text module to ask questions about the norms. The experimenter answered the questions using a keyboard. The experimenter's answers were based on the results shown by previous studies in norm learning [13,14]. Using the answers provided by the experimenter, Pepper updated the uncertainties related to the previously learned context-specific norms and also created new context-specific norms with 100% certainty.

Table 2 shows all the permission norms learned by Pepper at the 10 locations (5 scene categories). Most of the action types have either 100% or 0% uncertainties. This is because of the limited number of actions available to the robot and the limited amount of locations visited per scene category (2 per scene category). In cases when the experimenter gave different answers in different locations of a scene category about an action, the uncertainties were updated. For example, for the action type *talkQuietly* in the library context the agent said that it was not permissible in the first library. Hence, Pepper's initial uncertainty interval for this action was [0, 0]. However, in the second library, the experimenter said *talkQuietly* was permissible. Therefore, Pepper updated the uncertainty interval to [0, 0.5]. The robot was not able to ask questions about some actions at all because of the limited number of actions allowed to be asked. The empty entries in Table 2 show that the robot did not ask about those actions at the corresponding location. For example, the robot never asked if action *watch* was permissible in the library.

The time required to communicate with the human partner for three questions was about 10 s. These results depict the ability of the robot to learn context-specific norms in an online manner without forgetting any previously learned information. Social robots can use these context-specific norms while reasoning about which actions to perform in a particular context. The norm reasoning module is left for future work.

5 Conclusion

This paper presents and evaluates a method for a novel problem: online learning of scenes and context-specific norms on a robot in unconstrained environments.

We evaluate our approach on the Pepper robot to learn various scene categories and related norms in an online manner. The work presented here makes only a few assumptions. We assume that the human provides correct labels and correct answers related to norms when asked by the robot. Incorrect information would certainly negatively impact the performance of our approach.

Nevertheless, we believe that this paper makes several important contributions. Most importantly, we offer a novel and realistic approach to online scene and context-specific norm learning. This method allows the robots to not only learn different categories and appropriate behaviors associated with these categories but to also use the recognition of these different environments to moderate their behavior and decision-making. For example, allowing a robot to recognize that its current location is in a library and that it should therefore reduce the volume of its speech. Our future work will focus on the reasoning module to choose appropriate actions based on learned context-specific norms. Our overarching hope is that this work will evolve into new applications and competencies for a variety of robot applications.

Acknowledgements. This work was partially supported by the Air Force Office of Sponsored Research contract FA9550-17-1-0017 and National Science Foundation grant CNS-1830390. Any opinions, findings, and conclusions or recommendations expressed in this material are those of the author(s) and do not necessarily reflect the views of the National Science Foundation.

References

1. Ayub, A., Fendley, C., Wagner, A.R.: Boundaryless online learning of indoor scenes by a robot, in Review, CoRL (2020)
2. Ayub, A., Wagner, A.R.: Centroid based concept learning for RGB-D indoor scene classification. arXiv:1911.00155 (2020)
3. Ayub, A., Wagner, A.R.: Cognitively-inspired model for incremental category learning using only a few examples in Review, Pattern Recognition (2020)
4. Ayub, A., Wagner, A.R.: Cognitively-inspired model for incremental learning using a few examples. In: The IEEE/CVF Conference on Computer Vision and Pattern Recognition (CVPR) Workshops, June 2020
5. Ayub, A., Wagner, A.R.: Online learning of objects through curiosity-driven active learning. In: IEEE RoMan Workshop on Lifelong Learning for Long-term Human-Robot Interaction (2020)
6. Ayub, A., Wagner, A.R.: Storing encoded episodes as concepts for continual learning. arXiv:2007.06637 (2020)
7. Ayub, A., Wagner, A.R.: Tell me what this is: few-shot incremental object learning by a robot. arXiv:2008.00819 (2020)
8. Kawewong, A., Pimup, R., Hasegawa, O.: Incremental learning framework for indoor scene recognition. In: AAAI (2013)
9. Krishnamoorthy, V., Luo, W., Lewis, M., Sycara, K.: A computational framework for integrating task planning and norm aware reasoning for social robots. In: 2018 27th IEEE International Symposium on Robot and Human Interactive Communication (RO-MAN), pp. 282–287 (2018)

10. Paul, S., Bappy, J.H., Roy-Chowdhury, A.K.: Non-uniform subset selection for active learning in structured data. In: The IEEE Conference on Computer Vision and Pattern Recognition (CVPR), July 2017
11. Quattoni, A., Torralba, A.: Recognizing indoor scenes. In: 2009 IEEE Conference on Computer Vision and Pattern Recognition, pp. 413–420, June 2009
12. Rebuffi, S.A., Kolesnikov, A., Sperl, G., Lampert, C.H.: iCaRL: incremental classifier and representation learning. In: The IEEE Conference on Computer Vision and Pattern Recognition (CVPR), July 2017
13. Sarathy, V., Scheutz, M., Malle, B.F.: Learning behavioral norms in uncertain and changing contexts. In: 2017 8th IEEE International Conference on Cognitive Infocommunications (CogInfoCom), pp. 000301–000306 (2017)
14. Sarathy, V., Scheutz, M., Kenett, Y., Allaham, M., Austerweil, J., Malle, B.: Mental representations and computational modeling of context-specific human norm systems. In: 39th Annual Meeting of the Cognitive Science Society (CogSci) (2017)
15. Shafer, G.: A Mathematical Theory of Evidence. Princeton University Press, Princeton (1976)
16. Simonyan, K., Zisserman, A.: Very deep convolutional networks for large-scale image recognition. arXiv:1409.1556, September 2014
17. Tan, Z.X., Brawer, J., Scassellati, B.: That's mine! Learning ownership relations and norms for robots. In: AAAI (2019)
18. Ullmann-Margalit, E.: The Emergence of Norms. Clarendon Press, Oxford (1976)
19. Wang, Z., Wang, L., Wang, Y., Zhang, B., Qiao, Y.: Weakly supervised patchnets: describing and aggregating local patches for scene recognition. IEEE Trans. Image Process. **26**(4), 2028–2041 (2017)
20. Wu, Y., et al.: Large scale incremental learning. In: The IEEE Conference on Computer Vision and Pattern Recognition (CVPR), June 2019
21. Zhou, B., Lapedriza, A., Khosla, A., Oliva, A., Torralba, A.: Places: a 10 million image database for scene recognition. IEEE Trans. Pattern Anal. Mach. Intell. **40**(6), 1452–1464 (2017)

Robotic Social Environments: A Promising Platform for Autism Therapy

Pegah Soleiman[1], Hadi Moradi[1,2(✉)], Bijan Mehralizadeh[3], Negin Azizi[1],
Farid Anjidani[1], Hamid Reza Pouretemad[4], and Rosa I. Arriaga[5]

[1] School of ECE, University of Tehran, North Karegar Street, Tehran, Iran
moradih@ut.ac.ir
[2] Intelligent Systems Research Institute, SKKU, Suwon, South Korea
[3] School of Mechanical Engineering, University of Tehran, North Karegar Street, Tehran, Iran
[4] Department of Psychology, Shahid Beheshti University, Tehran, Iran
[5] School of Interactive Computing, Georgia Institute of Technology, Atlanta, GA, USA

Abstract. Observational learning, especially in social environments, is considered an important part of the learning process in a human development. Unfortunately, children with autism lack this learning ability, especially in human social environments due to their deficiency in social interaction. Consequently, in this paper we present a pilot study in which we show that children with autism can learn through observing a Robotic Social Environment (RSE). The proposed RSE consisted of two parrot-like robots and a robotic ball to enable us to teach children with autism both social and nonsocial skills. The results on data from six high functioning children with autism show that the children learned an unknown skill, such as how to play with the robotic ball, through observing the robots. Furthermore, the results show that, despite limited capabilities of our robots for social interaction (i.e., voice-based social interaction), the children could understand the social characteristics, such as turn taking of the designed RSE.

Keywords: Autism · Observational learning · Robotic Social Environment

1 Introduction

Humans' need for social life [1] necessitates learning how to behave in a group and learn from others. Human Learnings can happen directly through trainings and/or, indirectly through interactions with other people and observing others [2]. As Bandura demonstrated in his early work [2], an important part of human learning and development occurs by observing others' behaviors. This is known as observational learning which refers to acquisition of new responses as the result of observing responses of a model to stimulus and the contingencies it brings. Several benefits can be enumerated for learning through observation, such as increasing the opportunity of gaining knowledge without direct instruction, reducing instruction time and costs, and being socially adapted with new environments [3]. Observational learning in social environments is a great application of observational learning in which social and interpersonal behaviors can be

© Springer Nature Switzerland AG 2020
A. R. Wagner et al. (Eds.): ICSR 2020, LNAI 12483, pp. 232–245, 2020.
https://doi.org/10.1007/978-3-030-62056-1_20

learned. In other words, in social environments, two classes of behaviors can be learned: 1) Behaviors that can be learned by observing a model without the need for inter-personal interaction 2) Social and inter-personal behaviors.

Children with autism show difficulty in benefiting from observational learning [4]. They tend to be isolated and avoid being in social environments. Thus, although they have been treated and taught in one to one format, they have been deprived from learning naturally in social environments. Consequently, researchers have attempted to find alternative methods to teach social skills to children with autism through observational learning, such as group instruction therapies [5] and peer mediated intervention [6], in which children have more opportunities to learn social skills in a more naturalistic environment. However, these methods are time and resource intensive. They require skilled human intervention, i.e. therapists, to control the sessions.

Robot-Assisted Therapy (RAT) is a recent approach to deal with the aforementioned challenges. The available researches [7–9] has shown that children with autism have an affinity to interacting with robots. In fact, some studies have found that some children with autism prefer interacting with robots than with humans [10]. The mentioned studies have shown that RAT could help to improve a wide range of behavioral and cognitive abilities of children with autism.

It should be noted that in, almost, all the studies a single robot is used. Thus, to mimic a social interaction, they require a human to assist in teaching social behaviors. The involvement of humans has two implications: 1) It limits the method due to the need for expertise and/or involvement of the humans in the process and 2) It may impact the effectiveness of the approach, since, in general children with autism do not like to interact with humans [11]. That is why having a fully Robotics Social Environment (RSE) becomes important. And that is why we have studied RSE for teaching social and non-social skills to children with autism and presented the initial results in this paper.

There has been an attempt to remove a human's involvement by using a virtual teacher with a robot [12]. The robot played the role of a peer for their subjects who was taught by the virtual teacher. The authors focus on the observational learning and show that the words instructed by the virtual teacher and repeated by the robot have been learned by the subjects.

To the best of our knowledge there are two studies [13, 14] that have utilized multiple robots in the therapy of children with autism. In [13], So et al. investigated the effectiveness of robot-based play-drama on joint attention and play behaviors of children with ASD. The results showed that the joint attention and play behaviors of the participants with ASD were improved without explicit teaching. On the other hand, their pretend play behavior did not improve. The aim of the other research [14] was to investigate the effectiveness of multi-robot system on multi-human communication skills of children with autism. Although they showed that their subjects had better interaction with other humans after 4 months of therapy, however, their evaluation was done 2 months after their therapy ended. Furthermore, there was no control group to show that the changes were due, solely, to the proposed therapy.

In this paper we present a novel use of Robotic Social Environments (RSE). In this approach, multiple robots can be used to model both social and non-social behaviors to children, eliminating the need for human involvement. The proposed approach has the following advantages: 1) It provides an environment to practice and learn social skills. 2) It can be without human involvement which is very desirable for children with autism who hesitate to interact with humans. 3) It can be available, even before having any diagnosis and from the beginning of birth, to help reduce impacts of autism from the beginning. 4) It can reduce the dependency on human therapists, especially for teaching social skills. It should be mentioned that RSE is a supplementary tool to help in the therapy of children with autism. It is proposed to prepare children with autism to successfully learn skills to enter human social environments.

To investigate the potential benefits of RSE we designed an RSE using three robots. The designed scenario is based on the commands that two parrot robots give a robotic ball made by Sphero. This scenario was chosen to show that a novel task, "commanding" a ball can be learned by children with autism through modeling behavior in an RSE. Furthermore, we wanted to see if children with autism can understand social behaviors such as turn-taking or can join a social interaction in an RSE.

We conducted the study in a single session for a group of 6 children from an autism center. Our main contributions are given in the results which show that: 1) observational learning can occur based on robot modeled behavior in RSE and 2) our RSE and the relation between robots is understandable and acceptable for children with autism.

2   Method

2.1   The Robots

The three robots which were used in our experiment are shown in Fig. 1. RoboParrot (Fig. 1.a), is a robot based on a toy from Hasbro Company that has been developed in our laboratory [15–19]. It has two motors, one for body movement and the other one for mouth and eyes movements. To remotely operate the robot, a web application has been designed. Different scenarios and commands, such as greeting, singing, dancing, and commanding Sphero, were designed to ease the operation of the robot by an operator. The second robot is a red fluffy parrot, called Red (Fig. 1.c). It has a servo motor under its wooden stand which enables Red to have a pan movement. This is done to attract children's attention whenever the parrot starts to talk. A human operator controls Red with an android based application from a tablet. As RoboParrot, different scenarios and commands were implemented in Red's application.

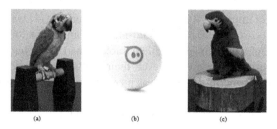

(a)   (b)   (c)

Fig. 1. a) RoboParrot, b) Sphero, c) Red (Color figure online)

The third robot is a Sphero (Fig. 1.b) which is an app-Enabled Robotic Ball, developed by Sphero Co., capable of actions such as rolling around, changing color and dancing. Sphero can be controlled through its dedicated application developed for smart phones or tablets. The main reason behind selecting Sphero was its reach and easy to use class of commands available to control the robot. Furthermore, its behaviors were so unique that no child had seen and expected them before. Thus, it was a good platform to test if the children learn from the designed RSE through observational learning.

2.2 Novel Task

To see if observational learning would take place in an RSE, we designed a unique skill that required commanding a Sphero. In other words, since the subjects did not know anything about Sphero and how it operates, if the subjects could learn how to command and play with Sphero, it would prove the capability of RSE to facilitate observational learning. In Fig. 2, the general structure of the designed RSE is shown. Camera 1 provides an overhead view and camera 2 provides front face view.

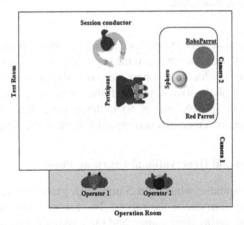

Fig. 2. The Schematic of the designed RSE

2.3 Participants and Setting

Six Children, between 3 to 5 years old, were recruited from a local autism center. Five children (P1, P3, P4, P5, P6) with a diagnosis of having autism, based on Gilliam Autism Rating Scale (GARS) [20], and one with developmental delay with autism symptoms (P2) were enrolled in this study. The diagnosis of the participants was done, at least by a psychologist and a psychiatrist independently.

All sessions were conducted in the autism center. The RSE was placed in an observation room. The robots were operated by two team members from the observation area. The robots were placed on a 50 cm high table facing the subjects.

In Fig. 3, a view of the overhead camera which shows the placement of the robots, a subject, and the session conductor is shown. The movement of Sphero is limited inside a rectangular box so the parrots can easily command it to move left and right without worrying about it falling down. The recorded videos enabled us to analyze the participants' behaviors later.

Fig. 3. The placement of the robots, a subject, and the session conductor. Sphero is placed in a rectangular box to limit its movement.

A single session was designed to evaluate if children with autism can learn by observing a social interaction between robots. At the beginning of the session, a familiarization phase was conducted in which the robots were introduced to the subjects. Then, the observational learning phase started, in which the robots started interacting with each other and playing with Sphero. Two of six children were shy to enter the room and required either a parent or a therapist accompanied them in the session.

2.4 Familiarization and Observational Learning Phase

During familiarization phase, which took 5 min, each participant entered the room and the session conductor introduced the robots. The robots' conversations started with greeting the child and saying their names, and then asking the participant's name. The session conductor encouraged the participant to interact with the robots and explained that "these robots are two friends". When the subject showed interest by starting to speak to the robots or the session conductor, one of the robots played a music.

In observational Learning phase, RoboParrot and Red started to play with Sphero. One of the robots started asking the other robot, in the child's native language, about how to play with Sphero. The other one explained that the ball was called "Toopi" and could listen to their commands. The robots started playing using commands such as, "change color", "jump", "rotate," and "dance." After every command from the parrot robots, Sphero's operator executed the command using the application installed on a tablet. This way, the participants were convinced that Sphero obeyed the robots' commands.

After 5 to 7 commands from the robots, the session conductor told subjects: "You may take a turn." This was done to evaluate if the participant had learned to play with Sphero. It was also helpful in cases that a child did not get involved in the robots' play. This was inspired from parents who encourage their children to get involved in group plays, in places such as parks. This was also asked from participants who commanded Sphero spontaneously, after observing the robots, to see if they like and understand how to participate in a social interaction with the robots. This play and modeling took 10 min, after the 5 min initial familiarization phase, and children were allowed to stay longer with their parent's permission.

2.5 Evaluation

The evaluation was conducted on the recorded study session for each participant. The observational learning phase was evaluated by having both the primary researcher and an independent observer code the videos separately. The independent observer coded 50% of data, i.e. the data of three participants, with 83% inter-observer agreement. The data allowed us to: 1) See how understandable the robots' interaction is for children with autism and what they perceive from this interaction. 2) See how a child with autism interacts in this RSE. 3) See how engaged a child gets with this RSE. The list of behaviors which are used to evaluate the proposed RSE is shown in Table 1.

Furthermore, to evaluate if the participants learned from this RSE, the behaviors of the participants with Sphero can be classified in one of the 5 following categories: 1) command Sphero just like the robots spontaneously, 2) show generalization and use different commands than the ones used by the robots, 3) command Sphero, 4) do another play with Sphero, such as, kicking, rotating with hand, or throw it away, or 5) do nothing. Numbers 3 to 5 were after participants were helped to interact with Sphero.

3 Results

In this section we present the results of the behavioral evaluation including the observational learning and data from the maintenance probe.

3.1 Behavior Evaluation

For the items in B1–B6, if a behavior or an answer to the question was completely right it was marked 1. An incomplete answer or a behavior or an answer with help was marked 0.5 and if the participant said nothing or his answer was wrong, it was marked 0. Percentage scores were calculated accordingly.

In Fig. 4, the mean and standard deviation for B1–B6 over all the participants' scores are shown. As it can be seen, B4 is around 90% which shows that the children were willing to interact with the robots. This is aligned with the other research showing that the children with autism like robots [21]. B3, B5, and B6 are about 80% showing that the children understood the implemented RSE and were interested to interact with it. Finally, B1 is about 50% and B2 is about 70% showing that the children were partially engaged in this RSE.

Table 1. Evaluation criteria for the RSE

Num.		Behavior	Examples	Evaluation
B1	B11	Following the robots' commands	Sit on your chair Do not touch the ball Come near us	Percentage
	B12	Following the robots' commands with help	If a participant does not respond to a robots' command, the session conductor guides him by asking "what did the parrots ask you"	Percentage
B2	B21	Answering the robots' questions	What is your name? Do you like music? Do you want to play with us? Which color do you like?	Percentage
	B22	Answering the robots' questions with help	If a participant does not respond to a robots' command, the session conductor guides him by asking "what did the parrots ask you?"	Percentage
B3		Answering session conductor's questions asked about the robots	what are the parrots' names? Which game are the parrots playing? What did the parrot tell you? Who have to take turn? You or the parrots? What did the parrot do to move the ball? What did the parrots ask you? What did the parrot say to his friend?	Percentage
B4		Following the session conductor's commands about the robots	Ask the parrots' names Sit here and listen to them Ask the parrots to play a song for you Ask the parrots "play with your ball" Touch the parrots Say hello/goodbye to the parrot Ask the parrots how they play with their ball	Percentage
B5		Answering the session conductor's questions	Whose turn is it? What did happen to the ball? How did you play with the ball? What is the name of the ball?	Percentage

(continued)

Table 1. (*continued*)

Num.	Behavior	Examples	Evaluation
B6	Following the session conductor's commands	Put the ball on its place It is your turn, play with the ball Sit on your chair	Percentage

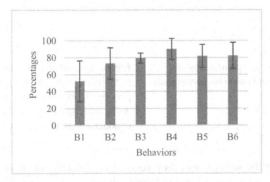

Fig. 4. Percentages of mean and standard deviation of children's behaviors

3.2 Observational Learning

The total number of spontaneous and generalized commands the participants used throughout the sessions, are shown in Fig. 5. As it can be seen, five out of six participants showed spontaneous commands and 3 out of six showed generalization during the session. P2 had the most spontaneous commands as well as generalized commands. He liked Sphero's jumping very much and most of his commands were "Toopi jump". Although P6 commanded Sphero, after when the session conductor asked him to do so, however, he did not have any spontaneous or generalized command on his own. The overall view of the chart reveals that the participants who showed more spontaneous commands were more likely to show generalization. Also, it should be mentioned that P2 and P5 started to imitate the robots exactly after the first time the robots commanded Sphero, which was not expected. P1 and P4 started commanding when the session conductor asked them to take their turn. In other words, they looked to understand how to command the robot but showed they understood what was going on, but only engaged with the robot when the session conductor asked them to do so. On the other hand, P3 and P6 could command Sphero after about 20 commands from the robots. P1, and P4 started spontaneous commanding after the first initiation by the session conductor. In conclusion, all the participants understood how Sphero worked by observing the robots.

Figure 6, shows the behaviors of the participants in direct response to the session conductor's request to take a turn. In this figure the percentages of three types of behaviors are shown. The arbitrary games, such as kicking, rotating, or throwing, were not part of the games played by the robots. P2, P4, and P5, correctly commanded Sphero in more than 70 percent of the time. P2 and P4 were sitting on their chairs and listening to the

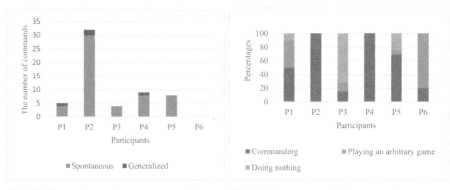

Fig. 5. The number of spontaneous and generalized commands used by participants

Fig. 6. Percentages of three type of participants' behaviors, commanding Sphero, playing an arbitrary game with Sphero, or doing nothing in direct response to the session conductor's request to take turn

parrots throughout the session and they seemed completely attentive and focused. P5 also seemed engaged and was so excited that he left the session to bring his mother over to see the parrots. Also, there were moments that he wanted to approach the parrots and touch them and Sphero. As it can be seen, P1 spent about 40% playing an arbitrary game instead of using the intended command. His therapist said that it was probably related to the fact that his stereotypic behavior was playing with balls. P3 was impatient and wanted to leave the session and refused to do anything. In addition, he repeatedly tried to ask questions from the robots (e.g., is your name blue?) which distracted the child from paying attention to the robots' play. He spontaneously repeated a command at the end of the session and left the session afterward. P6 was a little quiet and seemed that he was not sure what he should say. Although he seemed to understand turn taking but did mainly shook Sphero and did not use the intended commands. He named several colors throughout his session without clearly commanding Sphero. Interestingly, at the end of the 10-minute observation, he could command the ball with a complete sentence.

3.3 Maintenance Probe

To evaluate whether the participants could remember what the social interaction in the proposed RSE was as well as what they learned during that interaction, the following 6 questions were asked them by their families after about one month.

Q1. Can you remember the parrots? What color were they?
Q2. What were the parrots doing?
Q3. Did you play with them?
Q4. How did they play with their ball?
Q5. How did you play with their ball?
Q6. Would you like to have those parrots?

The participants' answers are summarized in Table 2. As it can be seen all participants could remember and express how the robots played with Sphero as well as how they themselves played with Sphero. Their parents were amazed how their children could remember the sessions and asked if these responses are correct. It should be noted that P3, whose answers to the questions are very short, was the child that was distracted during the study session. While P6 who showed understanding of how to play with Sphero at the end of his session, had a clear recollection of what happened and even wanted his parents to buy them for him.

4 Discussion

Results from this study indicate that all six children were partially engaged in the suggested RSE. The wider SDs of B1 and B2 suggest that the children's engagement in the proposed RSE was more diverse than directed interaction by the session conductor. This is actually similar to the first encounter of children, even TD children, with each other in a social environment such as a park. In such an environment, there are children who engage with the other children on their own. On the other hand, there are children who wait and need help by their parents to engage with other children. It is also possible that the novelty of this RSE can make children initially confused or excited that required the session conductor's intervention to help them understand the environment and get engaged with it.

In terms of observational learning, all children learned how to play with the robotic ball after observing two parrot robots' play. In addition, almost all participants could memorize what happened during the session after about one month. It shows that the participants got involved in the sessions and learned/memorized them. In addition, it shows the potential of RSEs to attract children with autism and show their potential for teaching various skills through observation.

The results also show that although the participants learned how to play with Sphero by observing the parrot robots, their learnings did not occur with the same speed. The differences in the learning process could be due to their different backgrounds and abilities. For example, P2 who did not have a formal autism diagnoses outperformed the other children with a diagnosis in both his ability to stay on task (Fig. 6) and the number of spontaneous and generalized commands (Fig. 5). It was also interesting to see that all children could memorize and share their understanding and learning even in a different setting and over time (Table 2).

At the end, it should be mentioned that the current limitations in the capabilities of robots in general, and specifically in our robots, makes it hard to fully implement intentions and interactions for any RSE. In other words, having more realistic robots with better Human Robot Interaction (HRI), such as full facial and body gestures and movement, would allow researchers to implement better RSEs with more features.

242 P. Soleiman et al.

Table 2. The participants' answers to the maintenance questions

Participants	Questions					
	Q1	Q2	Q3	Q4	Q5	Q6
P1	Yes, Red and Blue	They were playing with their ball and kicking it	Yes, I kicked the ball	They said to their ball "change to blue", "change to red"	I asked "change to blue", "blue kick"	No, I don't like to take them home
P2	Yes, Red and Blue	They were playing with their ball	Yes	They said to their ball "change to yellow", "Shake", "Rotate"	I said "change to yellow", "Shake", "Rotate"	Yes, one red parrot and one blue parrot
P3	Yes, Yellow and Red	They were speaking together	Yes	The parrots' ball changed color	I played with their ball	Yes, I like
P4	Yes, Yellow and Red	They were playing with their ball playing music for me, and at the end they said we are tired, said goodbye to me and slept	Yes, I played with their ball	The parrots' ball changed color, jumped, rotated	I said whatever the parrots had said, "Toopi change your color", "jump", "rotate", and I said to parrots, "parrots talk", "parrots sleep"	Yes
P5	Yes, Red and Yellow	They were playing with their ball	Yes	They said to their ball "change your color", "jump"	I said "Toopi change to blue", "change to green"	Yes

(continued)

Table 2. (*continued*)

Participants	Questions					
	Q1	Q2	Q3	Q4	Q5	Q6
P6	Yes, Red and Blue	They were speaking and playing with their ball	Yes	They said to their ball "change to blue", "change to red", and then Toopi's color changed	I feed the parrots and said to their ball "rotate" and "jump"	Yes, would you please buy one for me

5 Conclusion

The purpose of our research was to investigate the efficacy of a Robotic Social Environment (RSE) in eliciting observational learning of children from an autism center. We designed an RSE whereby two parrot-like robots command a robotic ball. This scenario was chosen to show that a novel task, i.e. "commanding" a ball, can be learned by children with autism through behavior modeled by robots.

We analyzed the children's behaviors and their learning from observing the robots' play. In addition, 6 questions were used to evaluate whether the participants could maintain and transfer their acquired knowledge about the robots over time and in another setting. The results show that 1) observational learning can occur based on robots' behavior in an RSE, 2) our RSE and the relation between robots is understandable and acceptable for children with autism, 3) an RSE can be a platform to demonstrate or practice social skills, 4) our RSE was engaging enough to keep children playing with the robots, and 5) an RSE can be used for teaching and therapy w/o therapists involvement and direct teaching.

Based on the above proof of concept of the capabilities of RSE, the following future work needed to show the full potentials of RSE: 1) show that it can be used to teach both social and non-social skills to children with ASD, similar to the natural setup that TD children learn these skills in their social life and 2) an RSE can be used to teach skills to any child, TD, ASD, or with any other disability.

Our study had a number of limitations this includes: the small sample size, limited activities and skills to be observed and learned, and limited observation time. Consequently, for future work, it is necessary to show the efficacy of RSE on different skills of children with autism. The number of participants and the observation time need to be increased to evaluate whether RSE can be beneficial for all children with autism with different autism levels, i.e. high or low functioning. Researchers can investigate if increasing the mobility of the robots or adding facial expression/interaction would further increase the RSEs' effect on children's learning. We would try to increase the autonomy of the robots to ease to carry out the study and make it applicable at homes and clinics.

References

1. Baumeister, R., Leary, M.R.: The need to belong: desire for interpersonal attachments as a fundamental human motivation. Psychol. Bull. **117**, 497–529 (1995)
2. Bandura, A.: Social Learning Theory. Prentice Hall, Englewood Cliffs (1977)
3. Boyd, R., Richerson, P.J., Henrich, J.: The cultural niche: why social learning is essential for human adaptation. Proc. Nat. Acad. Sci. U.S. Am. **108**, 10918–10925 (2011)
4. Varni, J.W., Lovaas, O.I., Koegel, R.L., Everett, N.L.: An analysis of observational learning in autistic and normal children. J. Abnorm. Child Psychol. **7**, 31–43 (1979). https://doi.org/10.1007/BF00924508
5. Leaf, J.B., Dotson, W.H., Oppeneheim, M.L., Sheldon, J.B., Sherman, J.A.: The effectiveness of a group teaching interaction procedure for teaching social skills to young children with a pervasive developmental disorder. Res. Autism Spectr. Disord. **4**, 186–198 (2010)
6. Kamps, D.M., Mason, R., Heitzman-Powell, L.: Peer mediation interventions to improve social and communication skills for children and youth with autism spectrum disorders. In: Leaf, J.B. (ed.) Handbook of Social Skills and Autism Spectrum Disorder. ACPS, pp. 257–283. Springer, Cham (2017). https://doi.org/10.1007/978-3-319-62995-7_16
7. Robins, B., Dautenhahn, K., Te Boekhorst, R., Billard, A.: Robotic assistants in therapy and education of children with autism: can a small humanoid robot help encourage social interaction skills? Univ. Access Inf. Soc. **4**, 105–120 (2005). https://doi.org/10.1007/s10209-005-0116-3
8. Boccanfuso, L., Scarborough, S., Abramson, R.K., Hall, A.V., Wright, H.H., O'Kane, J.M.: A low-cost socially assistive robot and robot-assisted intervention for children with autism spectrum disorder: field trials and lessons learned. Auton. Robots **41**(3), 637–655 (2016). https://doi.org/10.1007/s10514-016-9554-4
9. Boccanfuso, L., O'Kane, J.M.: Charlie: an adaptive robot design with hand and face tracking for use in autism therapy. Int. J. Soc. Robot. **3**(4), 337–347 (2011)
10. Kozima, H., Nakagawa, C., Yasuda, Y.: Interactive robots for communication-care: a case-study in autism therapy. In: Proceeding of the 14th IEEE International Workshop on Robot and Human Interactive Communication (RO-MAN 2005), 13–15 August, Nashville, Tennessee, pp. 341–46. IEEE, Piscataway (2005)
11. Wall, K.: Autism and Early Years Practice. Sage, Thousand Oaks (2009)
12. Saadatzi, M.N., Pennington, R.C., Welch, K.C., Graham, J.H.: Small-group technology-assisted instruction: virtual teacher and robot peer for individuals with autism spectrum disorder. J. Autism Dev. Disord. **48**(11), 3816–3830 (2018). https://doi.org/10.1007/s10803-018-3654-2
13. So, W.-C., et al.: A robot-based play-drama intervention may improve the joint attention and functional play behaviors of Chinese-speaking preschoolers with autism spectrum disorder: a pilot study. J. Autism Dev. Disord. **50**(2), 467–481 (2020)
14. Ali, S., et al.: An adaptive multi-robot therapy for improving joint attention and imitation of ASD children. IEEE Access **7**, 81808–88182 (2019)
15. Soleiman, P., Salehi, S., Mahmoudi, M., Ghavami, M., Moradi, H., Pouretemad, H.R.: RoboParrot: a robotic platform for human robot interaction, case of autistic children. In: 2014 Second RSI/ISM International Conference on Robotics and Mechatronics (ICRoM), pp. 711–716, Tehran (2014)

16. Dehkordi, P.S., Moradi, H., Mahmoudi, M., Pouretemad, H.R.: The design, development, and deployment of roboparrot for screening autistic children. Int. J. Soc. Robot. **7**(4), 513–522 (2015)

17. Soleiman, P., Salehi, S., Mahmoudi, M., Ghavami, M., Moradi, H., Pouretemad, H.: RoboParrot: a robotic platform for human robot interaction, case of autistic children. In: Second RSI/ISM International Conference on Robotics and Mechatronics (ICRoM) (2014)

18. Shayan, A.M., Sarmadi, A., Pirastehzad, A., Moradi, H., Soleiman, P.: RoboParrot 2.0: a multi-purpose social robot. In: The 5th International Conference on Robotics and Mechatronics (ICRoM) (2016)

19. Soleiman, P., Moradi, H., Mahmoudi, M., Teymouri, M., Pouretemad, H.R.: The use of RoboParrot in the therapy of children with autism children: in case of teaching the turn-taking skills. In: 16th International Conference on intelligent Virtual Agent, Los Angeles (2016)

20. Lecavalier, L.: An evaluation of the Gilliam Autism Rating Scale. J. Autism Dev. Disord. **35**(6) (2005). https://doi.org/10.1007/s10803-005-0025-6

21. Robins, B., Dautenhahn, K., Dickerson, P.: From isolation to communication: a case study evaluation of robot assisted play for children with autism with a minimally expressive humanoid robot. In: 2009 Second International Conference on Human-Computer Interaction, pp. 205–11 (2009)

Human-Robot Teams: A Review

Franziska Doris Wolf[(✉)] [iD] and Ruth Stock-Homburg [iD]

Technische Universität Darmstadt, 64289 Darmstadt, Germany
{franziska.wolf,rsh}@bwl.tu-darmstadt.de

Abstract. Research on human-robots teams (HRTs) as teams in which humans and robots work together is an emerging interdisciplinary field that still has white spots that are only slowly being considered by researchers. This review aims to provide an overview over different viewpoints towards HRTs and to synchronize extant definitions. We review extant conceptual and empirical research on HRTs and categorize it following an input-process-output model for teams. After systematically examining what research already knows about HRTs, we identify areas that require further research to gain a deeper understanding of HRTs and discuss proposals for future research.

Keywords: Human-Robot teams · Social robot · Robots at work

1 Introduction and Relevance

Imagine having a new team assistant joining your team and instead of a human it is a robot that enters your office and introduces itself. This or similar constellations are not far-off science fiction anymore, but closer to our work reality than we think.

According to a recent study, 82% of business leaders believe that human-robot teams (HRT), comprising of both human and robotic team members [1], will be reality in about five years [2]. Already today, humans partner with robots in order to accomplish work tasks in a variety of areas, such as urban search and rescue teams [3, 4] and space teams [5, 6].

Research on HRTs is a rising interdisciplinary field, but disciplines often focus on rather specific areas. This makes it difficult to build new research on existing knowledge on HRTs. Additionally, there is no common understanding regarding the definition of an HRT.

This review attempts to systematically synchronize extant definitions of HRTs. Furthermore, research on HRTs is discussed in terms of underlying focus areas, research disciplines and major findings. Finally, other important and so far unexplored application areas of HRTs will be considered for future research.

This review focuses on conceptual articles and empirical studies that investigated HRTs with functional, humanoid or android robotic team members. We further include studies on metrics/taxonomies to account for the conceptual background of human-robot teaming. Ultimately, this article reviews over 80 studies that investigated HRTs and were published between 1997 and 2019.

A. R. Wagner et al. (Eds.): ICSR 2020, LNAI 12483, pp. 246–258, 2020.
https://doi.org/10.1007/978-3-030-62056-1_21

Based on this review, gaps in extant research will be identified and areas for future research will be discussed. Accordingly, three research questions were set:

1. How can HRTs be defined?
2. What do we know about HRTs?
3. What are fruitful areas for a future research in the area of HRTs?

The paper is organized as follows. We start with the definition of the term HRT and introduce the conceptual framework of this review (Sect. 2). Then, we give an overview of the important findings of the reviewed studies (Sect. 3). In Sect. 4, we discuss future research directions in the field of HRTs.

2 Key Definitions and Framework of the Review

2.1 Definition of Human-Robot Teams

Despite being increasingly considered by a number of research disciplines, there is no universal definition of HRTs that is used over a broad range of disciplines and research focuses. In the following, we rely on team research from psychology and insights from robotic research to develop a basic definition of the term HRT.

Research on human-human teams (HHTs) has achieved a common agreement on the definition of a team (see, e.g., Stock [7]). Here, a team is defined as "a collection of individuals who are interdependent in their tasks and who share responsibility for outcomes" [7, p. 275]. In robotics research, most authors do not explicitly define the term HRT. However, the investigated team types allow conclusions of the various studies' understanding of the composition of the HRT under investigation. Table 1 provides an overview of team types and sample definitions of HRTs in the investigated research.

A large number of researchers considers human-directed robot teams (esp. in (urban) search and rescue (USAR)) or autonomous mixed teams with no clearly assigned leadership (esp. in human-robot interaction (HRI)) as HRTs in their research and only very few empirical studies with HRTs defined as human-/robot-directed mixed teams, or robot-directed human teams exist. These different viewpoints result in inconsistencies in the definition of HRTs, e.g., regarding autonomy in a HRT [8, 11] or a task- vs. relational perspective on HRTs [1, 11].

Relying on extant research on HHTs [7] and research on HRTs, we define a human-robot team (HRT) as *humans and robots, who perform joint tasks, share common goals, interact socially and exhibit task interdependencies.*

2.2 Framework of the Review

To structure the review, we decided to categorize the considered studies following the structure of an adapted input-process-output (IPO) framework of teams that has evolved in organizational behavior literature [12] and was in this specific form introduced by Stock [7]. According to this framework, which is depicted in Fig. 1, two main input factors, namely individual robotic team member characteristics and team factors, can be

Table 1. Overview of different team types and sample definitions

Team type	Sample definition
Human-directed robot team	In this team, "a single human operator can oversee and flexibly intervene in the operation of a team of largely autonomous robots" [8, p. 1425]
Human-/Robot-directed mixed team	In this team, "human workers […] perform physical tasks in coordination with robotic partners" [9, p. 295] and "human and robot co-leaders [have] identical functions and capabilities, by restricting the human co-leaders' capabilities such that they were the same as those of the robot" [9, p. 296]
Robot-directed human team	In this team, "the partner ([…] robot) is instructing the primary human […] on the task steps to complete. There are no shared decision making tasks" [10, p. 46]
Autonomous mixed team	In this team, "people and robots collaborate on tasks, sharing the same workspace and objects" [1, p. 1]

differentiated. Team processes like coordination, communication and conflicts within the team [13] then in turn influence team outputs [13], that Stock refers to as "psychological and business-related outcomes produced by teams" [7, p. 277].

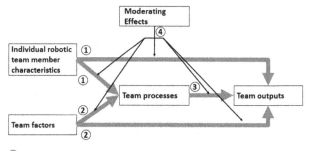

Fig. 1. Framework of the review (adapted from Stock (2004) [7]).

In total, five different categories of studies are considered in this review: Studies that investigate individual robotic team member characteristics or their effects on team processes and/or outcomes are cumulated in category 1 (Sect. 3.1). Studies that analogously investigate team factors and their effects are considered in category 2 (Sect. 3.2). The third category covers studies that investigate team processes and their effects on team outcomes (Sect. 3.3). Category 4 incorporates studies that investigate moderating effects on the links between inputs, processes and outputs (Sect. 3.4). Lastly, studies that cover a causal chain spanning from the inputs via mediating processes to outputs or that deal with overarching HRT topics are included in category 5 (Sect. 3.5). These studies differ from the other studies in that they are not limited to "one-step relationships" but consider mediated relationships (causal chains) [7]. Please note that it is possible for studies to fall into more than one of the above-mentioned categories without being treated as integrative [7].

3 Conceptual and Empirical Findings Related to Human-Robot Teams

3.1 Category 1: Effects of Individual Robotic Team Member Characteristics

A lot of research on individual robotic (team member) characteristics and their effects we reviewed is not anchored in HRTs. It rather falls within the much broader scope of HRI and is therefore excluded from the detailed review in this paper. Nonetheless, two subcategories of research on HRTs in this category can be differentiated based on their focus areas robot design and robot behavior.

Research on *robot design* is the explicit focus of conceptual and empirical studies on "Robonaut" - a robot designed to be deployed in a HRT in a space context [5, 6, 14]. Further, gender effects [15] and the effects of the human-likeness of robots on praise and punishment in HRTs [16] are investigated. On the other hand, research on *robot behavior* as an aspect of HRTs empirically investigates robotic touch and attitudes [17], the accomodation of human variability [18], robotic behavior explanations [19] and prosocial behavior of robots [20]. Conceptual research focuses on the concept of "inefficient" robots [21] that are not designed to boost efficiency but rather offer socially supportive behavior.

Because of space restrictions it is not possible to discuss the reviewed studies in detail. Table 2 provides an overview of the major disciplines, goals and key findings for all five considered categories of studies.

3.2 Category 2: Effects of Team Factors

The reviewed research on team factors and their effects includes the two subcategories of metrics for HRTs and the roles of human and robotic team members in a HRT including robotic leadership.

With regards to *metrics,* new metrics going beyond existing ones solely focusing on HRI have been developed for HRTs. These metrics also aim at the evaluation of team performance of HRTs [22, 23].

A comparably large number of research has already been conducted on the *roles of human and robotic team members in HRTs.* One popular conceptual work on humans and robots in mixed teams by Groom and Nass [11] discusses the suitability of teams versus other forms of joint actions. Other works look closer into the ratio between humans and robots [3], autonomy and control in HRTs [4, 8, 24–29] or teaming between humans and robots [30–33]. Further research on roles in HRTs has been conducted on role allocation [34], willingness to cooperate [35] and robotic leadership [36–39].

3.3   Category 3: Effects of Team Processes

During our review process we found that studies on team processes and their effects in HRTs form the majority of extant research that is focused on HRTs. This may in part be due to the popularity of HRTs in the context of USAR, where human-directed robot teams are already used today. The studies in this category can be clustered into the four topics: coordination, communication, collaboration and trust in HRTs.

Table 2. Overview over major disciplines, goals and key findings of studies for all categories

Category	Major disciplines	Major goals	Key findings
1: Effects of individual robotic team member characteristics	Space, Robotics	• Identification of guidelines for physical design and behavior that lead to successful HRTs [6]	• The perception of robotic behavior depends on other team members' characteristics [17] • Robot behavior should not be a "black box" for human team members in HRTs [19]
2: Effects of team factors	USAR, military, HRI	• Identification of suitable team constellations for HRTs [34] • Definition of metrics for HRTs [23]	• Different levels of autonomy in HRTs can enhance team performance [24] • Modes for HRTs need further development to identify effective work practices in HRTs [22]
3: Effects of team processes	USAR, HRI	• Understanding of parallels of team processes in HRTs with processes in HHTs [40]	• Trust in HRTs helps to increase team performance and satisfaction [41] • Solid interaction frameworks are needed for HRTs [42]
4: Moderating effects	Robotics	• Identification of relevant moderators in HRTs [24]	• Team capabilities, physical danger and team identification are important moderators [24, 33, 35] • Comprehensive understanding of moderating effects is needed [24]

(*continued*)

Table 2. (*continued*)

Category	Major disciplines	Major goals	Key findings
5: Integrative and overarching studies	Cognitive science, ethics	• Understanding of underlying mechanisms and procedures [43]	• First conceptual considerations of IPO model in HRTs that spares empirical evidence [43] • Individual, team-level and multilevel relationships have to be considered for HRTs [43]

On *coordination in HRTs* researchers have developed coordination concepts [42, 44–47] or studied this topic empirically. The empirical works look into mental models [48, 49], local world state observation [50], cooperative navigation via haptic feedback [51], coordination strategies [28], plan execution based on parallels between HRTs and HHTs [52] and shared decision-making considering human preferences [53].

Research on *communication in HRTs* looks into aspects of information flow [54], backchanelling [55], reasoning [56], conflict moderation [57] and effects of non-verbal communication [58], as well as the conceptual development of communication models [59–61] and interfaces [62]. There is further a number of works on the communication between humans and robots that are rooted in the broader context of HRI.

The third topic of *collaboration in HRTs* has been considered conceptually with a focus on challenges [63], collaborative tools [64], semantic-based path planning [65] and mutual initiative [66, 67] with the latter also being studies empirically [68]. Empirical studies on this topic are working on developing collaboration frameworks [1] – e.g., using spatial representation and reasoning [69] -, or consider joint action perception [70], remote shared visual presence [71], as well as effects of anticipatory actions in HRTs [72, 73]. Further research looks into collaborative problem solving [74], workload in HRTs [10], compares physical collaboration in HRTs with all-human teams [40] and examines emotional attachment and its effects [75].

Finally, with regards to *trust in HRTs* various researchers studied, e.g., trust and leadership [76], appropriate trust in HRTs [77], the measurement [78] and calibration [79] of trust in HRTs, parallels with human-animal teams [80, 81], or the effects of trust on team performance [41].

3.4 Category 4: Moderating Effects

The investigation of moderator variables is based on a situational perspective in psychology that indicates that phenomena are usually not independent from environmental or situational factors [82]. Accordingly, researchers have started examining moderating effects for the IPO framework in HRTs. In the context of HRTs, researchers so far have examined moderators in form of team capabilities to overcome challenges due to sliding autonomy in HRTs [24], risk of physical danger [35] and robot and team identification

[33]. It is unlikely that "one size fits all" applies to HRTs as is also indicated for HHTs [7]. Therefore, moderators should be further investigated in future HRT research.

3.5 Category 5: Integrative and Overarching Studies

In this category we gather studies that consider inputs, processes and outputs of HRTs from an integrative perspective as well as studies on ethics in HRTs. On the first topic of *integrative studies*, in 2018 You and Robert [43] have developed an input-mediators-output-input model for HRTs which is an extension of the established IPO framework for teams. Gombolay, Guiterrez, Clarke, Sturla and Shah [9] consider decision authority in HRTs, resulting team processes and workloads and the outcomes team performance and worker satisfaction. Richert [74] studies collaborative problem solving in HRTs from an integrative perspective, Robert [83] holistically examines motivation in HRTs and Wang et al. [84] consider the chain of embodiment, communication and trust and performance in HRTs. Finally, the overarching topic of *ethics in HRTs* is considered in a number of conceptual research that examines the ethics of bilateral and team interactions [85, 86].

4 Conclusion

4.1 Summary on Existing Research

It appears that research on HRTs is well on its way working on gaining more insights into this upcoming interdisciplinary topic. Our review showed that due to the interdependencies with HRI and human-robot collaboration, individual robotic team member characteristics are rarely examined in a strict HRT setting. Team factors of HRTs on the other hand are already being examined more extensively and especially the roles of human and robotic team members in a HRT are in the focus of a lot of research. When it comes to team processes in HRTs, another large number of studies has already been conducted. The coordination, communication and collaboration of HRTs is a central aspect of the same and it is interesting to see the parallels that are being drawn between HRTs and all-human teams. Only few studies consider moderating effects and although their number is slowly increasing, these studies as well as integrative studies on HRTs are still lacking comprehensiveness.

4.2 Avenues for Future Research

As this article shows, there are several unexplored areas in both the conceptual and empirical research of HRTs. Especially with current developments around the world, there is room to learn more about the design, theoretical concepts and practical implications of HRTs. We thus suggest the following three proposals for future research:

Proposal 1:   *Examine the IPO framework of teams for HRTs*

As suggested by team research in general [7] and robotics research in particular [43], the IPO framework constitutes a suitable theory for all-human teams as well as HRTs.

As shown in this review, multi-level concepts for HRTs have been examined only little so far. HRT research should therefore dive deeper into this topic and examine the IPO framework for teams more extensively.

Proposal 2: *Focus on social robots and their introduction in HRTs*

Social robots as robots that are primarily created to interact with humans [87] feature a phenomenon called automated social presence (ASP). ASP makes humans feel like they are with another social entity when interacting with a robot [88]. Due to these particular social features, social robots are increasingly being applied in many fields of our daily lives [89] and should also be examined in future research on HRTs. As a hasty and inconsiderate use of robots can overstrain people and have a lasting negative influence, a special focus of this research should be on the introduction of social robot in HRTs. We therefore further suggest that future research should explicitly consider the transition process towards HRTs.

Proposal 3: *Examine HRTs in organizations*

As indicated before, social robots can take over a variety of roles and HRTs are expected to have significant influence on the future of work [2]. Especially with current developments in the world economy and the increasing relevance of robots in an organizational context, future research should focus on the examination of HRTs in organizations to gain insights into the effects of such developments.

5 Final Remark

Human-robot teams are an emerging phenomenon of the future of work and our society, that is currently lacking important insights. With our review we were able to show that there are white spots in this research topic, especially with a focus on long-term deployment of HRTs. We made three suggestions for future research on HRTs to accommodate for the high relevance of the topic. We hope that the review provides a good and extensive overview of HRTs and inspiration and ideas for future research.

References

1. Hoffman, G., Breazeal, C.: Collaboration in human-robot teams. In: AIAA 1st Intelligent Systems Technical Conference (2004)
2. Dell Technologies, Realizing 2030: A Divided Vision of the Future (2018)
3. Burke, J., Murphy, R.: Human-robot interaction in USAR technical search: two heads are better than one. In: RO-MAN 2004. 13th IEEE International Workshop on Robot and Human Interactive Communication. IEEE (2004)
4. Yazdani, F., Brieber, B., Beetz, M.: Cognition-enabled robot control for mixed human-robot rescue teams. In: Menegatti, E., Michael, N., Berns, K., Yamaguchi, H. (eds.) Intelligent Autonomous Systems 13. AISC, vol. 302, pp. 1357–1369. Springer, Cham (2016). https://doi.org/10.1007/978-3-319-08338-4_98

5. Bluethmann, W., et al.: Robonaut: a robot designed to work with humans in space. Auton. Robots **14**(2–3), 179–197 (2003)
6. Fong, T., et al.: The peer-to-peer human-robot interaction project. In: Space 2005 (2005)
7. Stock, R.: Drivers of team performance: what do we know and what have we still to learn? Schmalenbach Bus. Rev. **5**(3), 274–306 (2004). https://doi.org/10.1007/BF03396696
8. Sellner, B., et al.: Coordinated multiagent teams and sliding autonomy for large-scale assembly. Proc. IEEE **94**(7), 1425–1444 (2006)
9. Gombolay, M.C., Gutierrez, R.A., Clarke, S.G., Sturla, G.F., Shah, J.A.: Decision-making authority, team efficiency and human worker satisfaction in mixed human–robot teams. Auton. Robots **39**(3), 293–312 (2015). https://doi.org/10.1007/s10514-015-9457-9
10. Harriott, C.E., Zhang, T., Adams, J.A.: Evaluating the applicability of current models of workload to peer-based human-robot teams. In: Proceedings of the 6th International Conference on Human-robot Interaction (2011)
11. Groom, V., Nass, C.: Can robots be teammates?: Benchmarks in human–robot teams. Int. Stud. **8**(3), 483–500 (2007)
12. Gladstein, D.L.: Groups in context: a model of task group effectiveness. Adm. Sci. Q. **29**, 499–517 (1984)
13. Barrick, M.R., et al.: Relating member ability and personality to work-team processes and team effectiveness. J. Appl. Psychol. **83**(3), 377 (1998)
14. Fong, T., et al.: A preliminary study of peer-to-peer human-robot interaction. In: 2006 IEEE International Conference on Systems, Man and Cybernetics. IEEE (2006)
15. Chita-Tegmark, M., Lohani, M., Scheutz, M.: Gender effects in perceptions of robots and humans with varying emotional intelligence. In: 2019 14th ACM/IEEE International Conference on Human-Robot Interaction (HRI). IEEE (2019)
16. Bartneck, C., Reichenbach, J., Carpenter, J.: Use of praise and punishment in human-robot collaborative teams. In: ROMAN 2006-The 15th IEEE International Symposium on Robot and Human Interactive Communication. IEEE (2006)
17. Arnold, T., Scheutz, M.: Observing robot touch in context: how does touch and attitude affect perceptions of a robot's social qualities? In: Proceedings of the 2018 ACM/IEEE International Conference on Human-Robot Interaction. Chicago, IL, USA. ACM (2018)
18. Hiatt, L.M., Harrison, A.M., Trafton, J.G.: Accommodating human variability in human-robot teams through theory of mind. In: Twenty-Second International Joint Conference on Artificial Intelligence (2011)
19. Wang, N., Pynadath, D.V., Hill, S.G.: The impact of pomdp-generated explanations on trust and performance in human-robot teams. In: Proceedings of the 2016 International Conference on Autonomous Agents & Multiagent Systems (2016)
20. Correia, F., et al.: Exploring prosociality in human-robot teams. In: 2019 14th ACM/IEEE International Conference on Human-Robot Interaction (HRI) (2019)
21. Kelly, R., Watts, L.: Slow but likeable? Inefficient robots as caring team members. In: Robots in Groups and Teams: A CSCW 2017 Workshop (2017)
22. Burke, J., et al.: Toward developing HRI metrics for teams: pilot testing in the field. In: Workshop on Metrics for Human-Robot Interaction, 3rd Ann. Conf. Human-Robot Interaction (2008)
23. Pina, P., et al.: Identifying generalizable metric classes to evaluate human-robot teams. In: Workshop on Metrics for Human-Robot Interaction, 3rd Ann. Conf. Human-Robot Interaction (2008)
24. Dias, M.B., et al.: Sliding autonomy for peer-to-peer human-robot teams (2008)
25. Goodrich, M.A., et al.: Managing autonomy in robot teams: observations from four experiments. In: 2nd Annual Conference on Human-Robot Interaction (HRI). Arlington, VA, USA. IEEE (2007)

26. Musić, S., Hirche, S.: Control sharing in human-robot team interaction. Ann. Rev. Control **44**, 342–354 (2017)

27. Wang, J., Lewis, M.: Human control for cooperating robot teams. In: 2007 2nd ACM/IEEE International Conference on Human-Robot Interaction (HRI). IEEE (2007)

28. Wang, H., Lewis, M., Chien, S.-Y.: Teams organization and performance analysis in autonomous human-robot teams. In: Proceedings of the 10th Performance Metrics for Intelligent Systems Workshop (2010)

29. Wynne, K.T., Lyons, J.B.: An integrative model of autonomous agent teammate-likeness. Theor. Issues in Ergon. Sci. **19**(3), 353–374 (2018)

30. Barnes, M.J., Chen, J.Y.C., Jentsch, F., Redden, E.S.: Designing effective soldier-robot teams in complex environments: training, interfaces, and individual differences. In: Harris, D. (ed.) EPCE 2011. LNCS (LNAI), vol. 6781, pp. 484–493. Springer, Heidelberg (2011). https://doi.org/10.1007/978-3-642-21741-8_51

31. Mingyue Ma, L., Fong, T., Micire, M.J., Kim, Y.K., Feigh, K.: Human-robot teaming: concepts and components for design. In: Hutter, M., Siegwart, R. (eds.) Field and Service Robotics. SPAR, vol. 5, pp. 649–663. Springer, Cham (2018). https://doi.org/10.1007/978-3-319-67361-5_42

32. Tang, F., Parker, L.E.: Peer-to-peer human-robot teaming through reconfigurable schemas. In: AAAI Spring Symposium: To Boldly Go Where No Human-Robot Team Has Gone Before (2006)

33. You, S., Robert, L.: Subgroup formation in human-robot teams. In: Fortieth International Conference on Information Systems. Munich (2019)

34. Howard, A.M., Cruz, G.: Adapting human leadership approaches for role allocation in human-robot navigation scenarios. In: 2006 World Automation Congress. IEEE (2006)

35. You, S., Robert Jr, L.P.: Human-robot similarity and willingness to work with a robotic co-worker. In: Proceedings of the 2018 ACM/IEEE International Conference on Human-Robot Interaction. Chicago, IL, USA. ACM (2018)

36. Gladden, M.E.: The social robot as 'Charismatic Leader': a phenomenology of human submission to nonhuman power. In: Robophilosophy (2014)

37. Kwon, M., et al.: Influencing leading and following in human-robot teams. In: Proceedings of Robotics: Science Systems (2019)

38. Samani, H.A., Koh, Jeffrey T.K.V., Saadatian, E., Polydorou, D.: Towards robotics leadership: an analysis of leadership characteristics and the roles robots will inherit in future human society. In: Pan, J.-S., Chen, S.-M., Nguyen, N.T. (eds.) ACIIDS 2012. LNCS (LNAI), vol. 7197, pp. 158–165. Springer, Heidelberg (2012). https://doi.org/10.1007/978-3-642-28490-8_17

39. Samani, H., Cheok, A.: From human-robot relationship to robot-based leadership. In: 4th International Conference on Human System Interaction, HSI 2011 (2011)

40. Reed, K.B., Peshkin, M.A.: Physical collaboration of human-human and human-robot teams. IEEE Trans. Haptics **1**(2), 108–120 (2008)

41. You, S., Robert, L.: Trusting robots in teams: examining the impacts of trusting robots on team performance and satisfaction. In: 52th Hawaii International Conference on System Sciences (2019)

42. Bradshaw, J.M., et al.: From tools to teammates: joint activity in human-agent-robot teams. In: Kurosu, M. (ed.) HCD 2009. LNCS, vol. 5619, pp. 935–944. Springer, Heidelberg (2009). https://doi.org/10.1007/978-3-642-02806-9_107

43. You, S., Robert, L.: Teaming up with robots: an IMOI (inputs-mediators-outputs-inputs) framework of human-robot teamwork. Int. J. Robot. Eng. **2**(3) (2018)

44. Alboul, L., Saez-Pons, J., Penders, J.: Mixed human-robot team navigation in the GUARDIANS project. In: 2008 IEEE International Workshop on Safety, Security and Rescue Robotics. IEEE (2008)

45. Bradshaw, J.M., et al.: Human-agent-robot teamwork. IEEE Intell. Syst. **27**(2), 8–13 (2012)
46. Laengle, T., Hoeniger, T., Zhu, L.: Cooperation in human-robot-teams. In: ICI&C'1997 Proceedings of the International Conference on Informatics and Control. St. Petersburg, Russia. IEEE (1997)
47. Liu, C., Tomizuka, M.: Modeling and controller design of cooperative robots in workspace sharing human-robot assembly teams. In: 2014 IEEE/RSJ International Conference on Intelligent Robots and Systems. IEEE (2014)
48. Nikolaidis, S., Shah, J.: Human-robot teaming using shared mental models. In: ACM/IEEE HRI (2012)
49. Nikolaidis, S., Shah, J.: Human-robot cross-training: computational formulation, modeling and evaluation of a human team training strategy. In: Proceedings of the 8th ACM/IEEE International Conference on Human-Robot Interaction. IEEE (2013)
50. Riedelbauch, D., Henrich, D.: Coordinating flexible human-robot teams by local world state observation. In: 2017 26th IEEE international symposium on Robot and Human Interactive Communication (RO-MAN). IEEE (2017)
51. Scheggi, S., Aggravi, M., Prattichizzo, D.: Cooperative navigation for mixed human–robot teams using haptic feedback. IEEE Trans. Hum.-Mach. Syst. **47**(4), 462–473 (2016)
52. Shah, J., et al.: Improved human-robot team performance using chaski, a human-inspired plan execution system. In: Proceedings of the 6th International Conference on Human-Robot Interaction (2011)
53. Gombolay, M.C., Huang, C., Shah, J.: Coordination of human-robot teaming with human task preferences. In: 2015 AAAI Fall Symposium Series (2015)
54. Kantor, G., et al.: Distributed search and rescue with robot and sensor teams. In: Field and Service Robotics: Recent Advances in Research and Applications, Yuta, S.I. et al., Editors. Springer Berlin Heidelberg. Berlin, Heidelberg, pp. 529–538 (2006)
55. Jung, M.F., et al.: Engaging robots: easing complex human-robot teamwork using back channeling. In: Proceedings of the 2013 ACM Conference on Computer Supported Cooperative Work. ACM (2013)
56. Bozcuoglu, A.K., et al.: Reasoning on communication between agents in a human-robot rescue team. In: Towards Intelligent Social Robots-Current Advances in Cognitive Robotics. Seoul (2015)
57. Jung, M.F., Martelaro, N., Hinds, P.J.: Using robots to moderate team conflict: the case of repairing violations. In: Proceedings of the 10th ACM/IEEE International Conference on Human-Robot Interaction. IEEE (2015)
58. Breazeal, C., et al.: Effects of nonverbal communication on efficiency and robustness in human-robot teamwork. In: 2005 IEEE/RSJ International Conference on Intelligent Robots and Systems (2005)
59. Kruijff, G.-J., Janicek, M., Zender, H.: Situated communication for joint activity in human-robot teams. IEEE Intell. Syst. **2**, 27–35 (2012)
60. Kruijff, G.-J.M., et al.: Designing, developing, and deploying systems to support human–robot teams in disaster response. Adv. Robot. **28**(23), 1547–1570 (2014)
61. Kruijff-Korbayová, I., et al.: TRADR project: long-term human-robot teaming for robot assisted disaster response. KI - Künstliche Intelligenz **29**(2), 193–201 (2015). https://doi.org/10.1007/s13218-015-0352-5
62. Marge, M., et al.: Exploring spoken dialog interaction in human-robot teams. In: Proceedings of Robots, Games, and Research: Success Stories in USA, RSim IROS Workshop, St. Louis, MO, USA. Citeseer (2009)
63. Fiore, S.M., et al.: Human-robot teams collaborating socially, organizationally, and culturally. In: Proceedings of the Human Factors and Ergonomics Society Annual Meeting. SAGE Publications Sage CA: Los Angeles, CA (2011)

64. Bruemmer, D.J., Walton, M.C.: Collaborative tools for mixed teams of humans and robots. In: Proceedings of the Workshop on Multi-Robot Systems (2003)
65. Yi, D., Goodrich, M.: Supporting task-oriented collaboration in human-robot teams using semantic-based path planning. SPIE Defense + Security, Vol. 9084. SPIE (2014)
66. Breazeal, C., et al.: Working collaboratively with humanoid robots. In: 4th IEEE/RAS International Conference on Humanoid Robots, 2004 (2004)
67. Bruemmer, D.J., Marble, J.L., Dudenhoeffer, D.D.: Mutual initiative in human-machine teams. In: Proceedings of the IEEE 7th Conference on Human Factors and Power Plants. IEEE (2002)
68. Marble, J.L., Bruemmer, D.J., Few, D.A.: Lessons learned from usability tests with a collaborative cognitive workspace for human-robot teams. In: 2003 IEEE International Conference on Systems, Man and Cybernetics. IEEE (2003)
69. Kennedy, W.G., et al.: Spatial representation and reasoning for human-robot collaboration. In: AAAI (2007)
70. Iqbal, T., Gonzales, M.J., Riek, L.D.: Joint action perception to enable fluent human-robot teamwork. In: 2015 24th IEEE International Symposium on Robot and Human Interactive Communication (RO-MAN). IEEE (2015)
71. Burke, J., Murphy, R.: RSVP: an investigation of remote shared visual presence as common ground for human-robot teams. In: 2007 2nd ACM/IEEE International Conference on Human-Robot Interaction (HRI) (2007)
72. Hoffman, G., Breazeal, C.: Effects of anticipatory action on human-robot teamwork efficiency, fluency, and perception of team. In: Proceedings of the ACM/IEEE International Conference on Human-Robot Interaction, pp. 1–8. Association for Computing Machinery. Arlington, Virginia, USA (2007)
73. Koppula, H.S., Jain, A., Saxena, A.: Anticipatory planning for human-robot teams. In: Experimental Robotics. Springer (2016)
74. Richert, A., et al.: Robotic workmates: hybrid human-robot-teams in the industry 4.0. In: 11th International Conference on e-Learning (2016)
75. You, S., Robert, L.: Emotional attachment, performance, and viability in teams collaborating with embodied physical action (EPA) robots. J. Assoc. Inf. Syst. **19**(5), 377–407 (2017)
76. Marble, J.L., et al.: Evaluation of supervisory vs. peer-peer interaction with human-robot teams. In: Proceedings of the 37th Annual Hawaii International Conference on System Sciences, 2004. IEEE (2004)
77. Ososky, S., et al.: Building appropriate trust in human-robot teams. In: 2013 AAAI Spring Symposium Series (2013)
78. Freedy, A., et al.: Measurement of trust in human-robot collaboration. In: 2007 International Symposium on Collaborative Technologies and Systems. IEEE (2007)
79. Wang, N., Pynadath, D.V., Hill, S.G.: Trust calibration within a human-robot team: Comparing automatically generated explanations. In: 2016 11th ACM/IEEE International Conference on Human-Robot Interaction (HRI). IEEE (2016)
80. Phillips, E., et al.: Human-animal teams as an analog for future human-robot teams. In: Proceedings of the Human Factors and Ergonomics Society Annual Meeting. SAGE Publications (2012)
81. Phillips, E., et al.: Human-animal teams as an analog for future human-robot teams: influencing design and fostering trust. J. Hum.-Robot Interact. **5**(1), 100–125 (2016)
82. Arnold, H.J.: Moderator variables: a clarification of conceptual, analytic, and psychometric issues. Organ. Behav. Hum. Perform. **29**(2), 143–174 (1982)
83. Robert, L.: Motivational theory of human robot teamwork. Int. Robot. Autom. J. **4**(4), 248–251 (2018)

84. Wang, N., et al.: Is it my looks? or something i said? the impact of explanations, embodiment, and expectations on trust and performance in human-robot teams. In: Persuasive Technology. Springer International Publishing, Waterloo, ON, Canada (2018)
85. Arnold, T., Scheutz, M.: Beyond moral dilemmas: exploring the ethical landscape in HRI. In: 2017 12th ACM/IEEE International Conference on Human-Robot Interaction. IEEE (2017)
86. Tamburrini, G.: Robot ethics: a view from the philosophy of science. Ethics Robot. 11–22 (2009)
87. Kirby, R., Forlizzi, J., Simmons, R.: Affective social robots. Robot. Auton. Syst. **58**(3), 322–332 (2010)
88. van Doorn, J., et al.: Domo Arigato Mr. Roboto: emergence of automated social presence in organizational frontlines and customers' service experiences. J. Serv. Res. **20**(1), 43–58 (2017)
89. Ivanov, S.H., Webster, C., Berezina, K.: Adoption of robots and service automation by tourism and hospitality companies. Revista Turismo Desenvolvimento **27**(28), 1501–1517 (2017)

User Expectations of Robots in Public Spaces: A Co-design Methodology

Leimin Tian[1(✉)], Pamela Carreno-Medrano[1(✉)], Shanti Sumartojo[1(✉)],
Michael Mintrom[1(✉)], Enrique Coronado[2(✉)], Gentiane Venture[2(✉)],
and Dana Kulić[1(✉)]

[1] Monash University, Melbourne, Australia
{Leimin.Tian,Pamela.Carreno,Shanti.Sumartojo,Michael.Mintrom,
Dana.Kulic}@monash.edu
[2] Tokyo University of Agriculture and Technology, Fuchu, Japan
enriquecoronadozu@gmail.com, venture@cc.tuat.ac.jp

Abstract. People are increasingly encountering robots in public spaces, but they rarely have input into how such technology is conceived or deployed. To familiarise and engage the general public with new robot technology, we present a novel co-design workshop methodology with a three-phased structure: open discussion, participatory prototyping, and follow-up interviews. *Open discussion* collects users' initial expectations; *Participatory prototyping* deepens users' understanding of the technology and elicits concrete, user-centered discussion on the technology being investigated; and *follow-up interviews* collect personal reflections. An online workshop following this methodology facilitated our research on users' expectations of robots in public spaces. Our observations highlighted that co-design workshops are effective for advancing users' understanding of robotic technology and applications.

Keywords: HRI · Co-design workshop · Participatory prototyping

1 Introduction

The need for robots capable of socially interacting with humans continues to increase as they become commonplace in our everyday life. However, the general population has a limited understanding of how robots work, why they behave in the way they do and how to interact with them; with the last point being a determining factor on people's willingness to interact with a robot [13]. For instance, in a recent ethnographic study [15], it was observed that people are not yet accustomed to talk to or interact with robots and can mistake them for less advanced technology such as ticket machines. Coupled with the fact that end-users have little or no input into how robot capabilities and behaviours are designed, it is not surprising that the robots deployed in the real world often fail to gain acceptance and meet the expectations of the general public [3]. Thus, in this work we are motivated to investigate how people understand

© Springer Nature Switzerland AG 2020
A. R. Wagner et al. (Eds.): ICSR 2020, LNAI 12483, pp. 259–270, 2020.
https://doi.org/10.1007/978-3-030-62056-1_22

robots and what they believe robots should be doing in public spaces. We aim to better understand the factors that contribute to an increased social acceptance of robots in public spaces by giving people greater understanding and more agency in helping design these functionalities.

Participatory Design (PD) is an established methodology in which end-users are actively involved in the conceptualization and design process of new technologies. In the context of Human-Robot Interaction (HRI), PD methods have been shown to facilitate the development of more nuanced and contextualized robot applications since they leverage the end-users' contextual expertise, expectations and social know-how [10]. Furthermore, they allow participants to simultaneously learn about the design process and the technologies they are designing for and apply this new knowledge and understanding into the development of such technologies. Several studies have explored PD methods for the conceptualization and design of new robots. In [9], the authors used different collaborative methods to understand how older adults frame aging and how existing or new robots fit into the participants' view of the aging process. In [4], a combination of design research, scenario and script writing, prototyping and role playing was used to engage teens in the co-design of a social robot for improving their mental health. PD methods have also been used for the conceptualization of useful behaviours in existing robot platforms. Azenkot et al. [1] investigated how a service robot could interact with and guide a blind person through a building in an effective and socially acceptable way. Winkle et al. [17] worked alongside therapists to design strategies and behaviours that existing social robots could use to increase patients' engagement in rehabilitative therapies. In a follow-up study [18], the authors further analyzed the mutual shaping that takes place during a participatory design exercise in which participants' expectations are grounded through demonstrations by technical experts.

Despite the increasing popularity of PD methods in HRI research, most of the existing work focuses on one-on-one interactions with specific populations (e.g., rehabilitation patients, teens or the elderly) and does not provide information about how the target public understands robots in their own terms. Furthermore, with the exception of [1], participants were never shown a tangible realisation of the robot functionalities they designed. This can potentially lead to a lower acceptance and adoption of the designed robotic technologies if end-user expectations fail to be met and does not account for how processes of PD might contribute to changed expectations. To address these issues, we propose a novel co-design workshop methodology in which, with the help a technical expert, participants actively engage in the prototyping of robot behaviours by means of a high-level programming interface. As a proof of concept, an exploratory study was conducted in which participants conceptualised and programmed the behaviours of a social robot situated in a public space of their choice.

2   Methodology of the Co-design Workshop

The main purpose of our co-design workshop was to gain a deeper insight into how the general public understands robots overall and what roles they envision

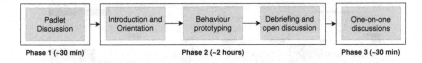

Fig. 1. Overview of the participatory prototyping workshop. Blue blocks represent the main phases, yellow blocks represent the stages within each main phase. (Color figure online)

robots could take in public spaces. The workshop was centered around a participatory prototyping activity in which participants were asked to design and program a robot's behaviours. Participatory prototyping methods are known to encourage exploration and learning, and provide a focus for the refinement of participants' initial assumptions and expectations [16]. Thus, by asking participants to build prototypes of a robot's behaviours, we can observe how their perception and understanding about robots and how robots should behave in public spaces gradually change as they actively engage in a hands-on first experience in programming these robots.

The workshop was composed of three phases. In phase 1, participants' preexisting notions and ideas about robots were ascertained by asking them to contribute examples of robots and through an open discussion. In phase 2, participants were divided into smaller groups and were asked to come up with a concept for using a robot in a public space. The chosen concept was then realised and iteratively refined through a simulator and programming interface. Finally, in phase 3, participants individually reflected on what was most significant or notable about the workshop experience. All phases were conducted online via Zoom, and breakout rooms and the screen sharing function was used during phase 2. In the following, we detail each phase and elaborate further on the rationale for the choices made in the design and planning of this workshop.

2.1   Workshop Organization

The workshop ran over a period of approximately 3 weeks. Each phase was run independently, with 2 days between phases 1 and 2, and 1–2 weeks between phases 2 and 3. Figure 1 summarises the main phases (blue blocks) with their respective duration; the yellow blocks represent the different stages participants completed within each phase. The workshop methodology and protocol were reviewed and approved by the Monash University Human Research Ethics Committee.

The majority of existing HRI studies use convenience samples involving university students [2] and thus are not representative of the general public. Although we limited our pool of potential participants to the general population at Monash University, we attempted to recruit a participant sample more representative of the general public by focusing on staff (rather than students) recruitment and inviting participants from all faculties, particularly those without prior experience with robots or programming. A total of 12 participants (5

Fig. 2. Screenshot of images submitted by participants for initial open discussion.

males, 7 females) from different faculties accepted to remotely join our workshop. They all provided written consent for their participation.

2.2   Phase 1 - Padlet Discussion

To explore our participants' initial understanding of robots in public spaces, we asked them to first join a pre-workshop discussion. Prior to this discussion, they were asked to contribute at least one image of a "robot in public space" to an online Padlet board (see Figure 2). These images formed the basis of the discussion and were used by the facilitator to prompt participants to talk about their understanding and perceptions of robots and robots' functionalities and capabilities as well as their opinions towards robots in public spaces. Following the completion of phase 1, participants were sent a short video introducing Pepper, the robot they would program in phase 2.

Since participants were tasked with designing behaviours for a robot that could potentially coexist and interact with them at a public space of their choice, we chose Pepper by SoftBank Robotics [11] as the robotic platform to be used in phase 2. As a social robot, Pepper is equipped with most of the technical and social affordances (e.g., elicit social and emotional responses, perceive and interact with its surroundings, communicate in an intuitive way, and move and act semi-autonomously) required in public spaces. Furthermore, Pepper is one of the most popular existing social robotic platforms and its deployment in public spaces across several different sectors (e.g., retail, hospitals, hotels, etc.) has notably increased in recent years.

2.3   Phase 2 - Participatory Prototyping

Stage 1 - Orientation and Introduction: This stage consisted of a 20 min introduction in which participants were reminded of the objective of the workshop and received general instructions of what to do during the behaviour prototyping part of the workshop. Stage 1 ended with a 5 min introduction to the

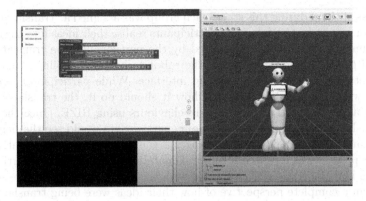

Fig. 3. Screenshot of the programming interface used for participatory prototyping.

programming interface (RIZE [5]) and robot simulator (Choreographe [12]) that would be used to design Pepper's behaviours (see Fig. 3).

Since the workshop participants were of diverse backgrounds and most had no prior experience with robots and programming, it was critical to choose a simple and intuitive programming interface. We decided to use RIZE (Robot Interface from Zero Expertise) [5] as our programming interface because it was built based on the end-user development paradigm. Programming interfaces built under this paradigm are designed to enable non technically skilled people to create programming applications, and are characterized by their ease of use and low adoption barrier. Furthermore, we plan to extend the proposed workshop methodology to other robotic platforms and RIZE allows for a quick and easy adaptation to these platforms. To help participants navigate the available robot functions offered in RIZE, we listed these functions as a single-page "cheat-sheet" that they could refer to.

Similarly, the choice of using the simulated version of Pepper instead of the physical robot was motivated by two main reasons. First, without the time and effort associated with the deployment of the prototype behaviours on the hardware, participants could focus on the participatory programming exercise and quickly iterate over their designs. Second, this workshop was run during the COVID-19 lock-down and we could not safely organise a physical session.

At the end of stage 1, participants were evenly and randomly split into two groups. Mixed participant groups are known to prompt a diverse discussion [6] and thus they allowed participants to bring their unique perspectives and explore multiple robot behaviour alternatives during phase 2.

Stage 2 - Behaviour Prototyping: During this stage, each group was asked to first discuss and decide on a scenario for Pepper. To do so, participants were asked to specify the public space Pepper would inhabit, Pepper's role in that space, and which functions the robot should fulfill within the chosen role. Once all the participants in the room agreed on this scenario, they were asked to prototype different behaviours (i.e., sequences of actions) for Pepper.

To assist them during this stage, each group was assigned a "translator". The translator was tasked with helping participants realise their ideas into the correct programming format. When prompted by the participants, the translator also provided general information about the robot technical capabilities, and additional details about the programming interface. While participants generated ideas of what Pepper should do and how it should do it, the translator coded the best approximation of the desired behaviours using RIZE. Once the translator finished coding a specific behaviour, participants would see the behaviour execute in simulation and ask for changes if they wished to. This iterative prototyping process was repeated for approximately 1 hour. All along, participants could see how the translator interacted with the programming interface so as to offer them a complete perspective of how their ideas were being translated into code.

In this stage, the participants were also asked to take screenshots of moments they thought were important to be later discussed in phase 3.

Stage 3 - Debriefing: During this stage all participants reconvened into the online room space for a debrief and open discussion. Each group was asked to show the functions they designed and explain their decision making to the other group. Participants were prompted to talk about their impressions of the design experience, the robot and the programming interface, and additional functionalities they would like to see added into the robot and/or programming interface.

2.4   Phase 3 - One-On-One Discussions

During this phase participants had individual discussions with a member of the research team. The discussions were centered around the multiple screenshots of the "robot" each participant took during the programming session and what they learned about robots overall. This open-ended approach [14] allowed participants to determine for themselves and reflect on what was most significant or notable about the workshop experience, and thereby helped the research team develop new questions to focus on in future workshops as well as understand participants' views about the programming interface and Pepper robot more generally.

3   Workshop Observations and Findings

In this section, we present the themes and highlights that emerged during the co-design workshop. In particular, we discuss users' expectations of robots and their desired behaviours in public spaces. These themes were identified by analyzing the workshop recordings with inductive thematic analysis.

3.1   Users' Pre-existing Expectations of Robots

From our participants' discussion in stage 1 (see Sect. 2.2), we identified two main themes, which we discuss below:

Expectation Shaped by Personal Experience and Popular Culture: We found that all participants had existing expectations of what robots are and what they are capable of, shaped both by personal perceptions and by fictional work in popular culture. One participant described her trip to Japan: "We went to Tokyo, spent two weeks there. We found Pepper robots at telecommunication company shops and also at the airport. In addition to that, we stayed at a robot hotel that has totally different types of robots [androids]." Others talked about robots in fiction, such as Kitt the car from *Knight Rider*: "It [Kitt] was for me the image of what a robot COULD be like, a partner in all the ways that it could assist a human. It shows the promise of what a robot could eventually mean for us." Their expectations of a robot's functions are also shaped by the visual appearance of it, for instance, humanoid robots are expected to have social interaction capabilities. In addition, artificial intelligent systems without a specific physical embodiment, such as an embedded smart traffic management system, were seen as robots as well by one of the participants.

Participants also discussed the perceived differences between humans and robots, as well as robots' potential at operating in places where humans cannot access, or taking up tasks that are dull, dirty, or dangerous for humans, such as defusing bombs. The discussion on robots' functionalities highlighted that the robot's autonomy level and capability exists on a spectrum, and current robots have limited functions compared to portrayals in science fiction. For example, one participant described the robots he encountered as "a big iPad with wheels". Such a gap between media expectations and personal experiences was also observed in other social robotics research [8]. Thus, it is important to understand users' expectations when designing robots and their functions, more so when the target users have not interacted with robots before.

Anxiety and Mistrust Around Robots in Public Spaces: Participants discussed negative feelings they have regarding robots in public spaces such as their anxiety towards whether or not a robot should initiate an interaction with a human. One participant described that "I was with a friend in the airport and this robot was just in front of me talking. It was a bit confronting cause I had never interacted with a robot before and I didn't even know what to do. I was a bit startled by it." They also talked about mistrust, as one participant stated that "The robot being something new, there is an element of mistrust in this [human-robot] relationship. There are both sides in the relationship with robots, the Utopian idea that they can improve something and bring something better, but also this Dystopian relationship and how threatening they can be."

Another reoccurring topic is the use of robots for surveillance or security purposes. For example, a participant used a dog-walking drone as her example and explained that "[We have] this perception of it as this airborne entity that's beyond human control or human environment. Somehow, something that is potentially problematic in terms of surveillance or all sorts of uses for it, [but] the fact that it is attached to a dog makes it okay. It balances out the threat you sense from the thing itself as opposed to something we associate with positive emotions and cuddliness. In a way that humanizes it for me." These highlighted the urgent need for developing robots and robot functions that are socially acceptable, and to prevent misuse of the technology, such as manipulating users through the social interaction functions of a robot. These discussions relating to ethical concerns have already received attention in the human-robot interaction and social robotics research community [7].

3.2 Understanding Users' Perception of Robot Capabilities Through Participatory Prototyping

In the following we elaborate on the main observations gathered from the participatory prototyping activities (i.e., phase 2, see Sect. 2.3). We first describe the choice of public spaces and behaviours made by both groups and how some of these choices reflected the current societal context around the COVID-19 pandemic. We then discuss participants' expectations and opinions regarding Pepper and the tools used to design Pepper's behaviours.

Choice of Public Spaces and Designs of Robot Behaviours: Participants were separated into two independent groups during behaviour prototyping (stage 2 of phase 2). Group one decided on the scenario of Pepper at a shopping mall, and designed 6 robot behaviours: greeting people, helping people carry bags, social distancing reminder, attending to lost children, keeping social distance by moving back 1.5 meters when touched by someone, and an idle behaviour that randomly displays entertaining gestures such as dancing.[1] Group two decided on the scenario of Pepper at a tourist attraction, and designed 4 robot behaviours: an idle behaviour of cleaning the floor, providing directions, attending to lost children, and taking photos for people.[2] One participant in group one explained their choice of a shopping mall as follows: "I grew up in an American suburban generation where the shopping mall WAS the public space. There wasn't really anywhere else to hang out. It offers a really interesting type of public, yet private space. It's already highly technologized. We thought it would be the exact type of place where a Pepper type robot would actually exist." Group two explained their choice of a tourist attraction as follows: "It was a suggestion based on the actions that were available. I was thinking about the picture-taking [robot function] and this prompted the idea that instead of having bad selfies we could have the robot taking pictures for us, better pictures." The design of robot behaviours for the chosen public space shows how users' expectations are shaped both by personal experiences and by the affordances of the specific robot.

Shared Robot Behaviours: Interestingly, both groups designed a lost-child robot behaviour, but with different motivations. Group one was inspired by the appearance of Pepper being "non-threatening and attractive to a child", while group two was motivated by the importance of the scenario as "one of the most distressful things that can happen in a public space", as well as the usefulness of the robot and "to make this robot as useful as possible in a situation that is very undoubtedly important". In addition, both groups designed an idle behaviour

---

[1] Demo of group one's designs in the simulator: https://youtu.be/8JUmngEF_GY.

[2] Demo of group two's designs in the simulator: https://youtu.be/H6Bd8HwdJZc.

for the robot, with group one focusing on entertainment functions and group two focusing on practical functions. This idle behaviour was motivated by the idea that "Pepper robot should have a purpose when we put Pepper in a public space, otherwise it will be perceived as creepy by passer-bys." These shared robot behaviours demonstrate the users' common desire for a robot to be useful, while being perceived as socially appropriate in the context that it is situated in.

Robot Behaviours Under Current Societal Context: Group one incorporated current societal context of the on-going COVID-19 pandemic, and designed two social-distancing related robot functions: "We imagine Pepper now switching from this passive helper-service role to a more active [role], ensuring the public safety of a public space. So there Pepper was seamlessly transitioning into a more security guard type of role." These social-distancing robot behaviours and the shared lost-child behaviour led to discussions relating back to the phase 1 open discussion on the appropriate level of autonomy for a robot, and whether or not it should have the authority of maintaining public safety, as one participant stated "That does lead to a question around the triage role of the robot and at what point does the robot turn to support from humans."

Grounding Expectations with Participatory Prototyping: At the end of phase 2, the two groups rejoined for a final open discussion. It was identified that they both initially over-estimated and under-estimated the robot's capabilities. The participatory prototyping process enabled a convergence of users' expectations towards the actual capability level of the robot. One participant from group one discussed how her group abandoned an initial design of Pepper's role after identifying limitations in its functions in addition to potential mistrust in the human-robot relationship: "We did talk about in a shopping center context, [Pepper being] almost like a personal shopper. We didn't really get to realize how that could feasibly work. We asked questions about 'Does Pepper need my credit card?' 'Would I trust Pepper with my credit card?' 'How would Pepper know what dress I want to buy?' I guess we identified some limitations on that shopping role for a robot. We started down that path but it seemed a little bit advanced for Pepper in this simulation environment." Similarly, one participant from group two explained how her group identified that robots are limited compared to humans due to their requirement of explicit guidance and predictions, and how "things that we usually pack in one single action actually need to be broken down for the robot."

Limitations of the Workshop: During the discussion at stage 3 of phase 2, participants also reported on their perceptions of the limitations of the workshop. In particular, they addressed restraints caused by the programming interface's lack of support for complex decision-making or logic structures. However, they discussed that the complexity of the programming interface "speaks to where you need to draw the line where a non-expert can do something, and a point at which it really needs someone who knows what they are doing to take something further, which is always the case." The participants reported that it would be possible for them to program the robot using RIZE on their own, although they expect this will "take much longer". More importantly, they expressed how in a simulator environment it is difficult to test the accuracy of a robot's perception capabilities. For example, one participants raised that "We cannot let Pepper make false judgement more than 50% of all the time [in the lost-child behaviour], because it will be wasting time of the security people as well. If that kind of error or mistakes cannot be avoided earlier, then people will start distrusting the robot in the public space. Because it's becoming intruding their privacy if they keep making the same mistake."

3.3   Reflections on the Workshop Experience

We identified three themes that emerged during the one-one-one discussions (phase 3 of the workshop). These themes align with our observations during the participatory prototyping activities in phase 2.

Expectations and Technical Limits: Many participants identified limits in the technology, as some commands did not transfer readily from RIZE to the simulator, or some robot motions did not look as they expected. The workshop also showed what was "missing" in Pepper in terms of the scenarios they generated, such as the ability to send for help using a messaging service. Reliable sensory input is required to accurately measure distance from a person or to interpret their facial expressions. These glitches, pauses and errors were accompanied by confusion and frustration on the participants' part, but also attempts to find "work-arounds" such as motions that approximate the desired action.

Appropriateness: Several participants reflected on the challenge of robots being able to exercise the nuanced judgment required to understand human behaviours, or even to recognise humans given the variety of heights, ages, use of mobility aids or capacity to communicate. Moreover, participants also recognised the complexity in knowing how to respond as an ongoing challenge. Thus, it is important for robots in public spaces to address the appropriateness of its behavior and judgement related to these contexts.

Tools Shaping Design: The *cheat-sheet* was reported as a simple but crucial tool. It mediated participatory prototyping, as participants used it to generate scenarios they created. For example, group two arrived at the tourist attraction scenario because of the picture-taking function listed in there.

4   Discussions and Conclusions

A Novel Co-design Workshop Methodology: We present a novel co-design workshop methodology in which participants actively engage in the prototyping of robot behaviours by means of a high-level programming interface and supported by a technical expert. The proposed methodology consists of three sequential phases, namely open discussion, participatory prototyping, and follow-up interviews. The initial *open discussion* allows researchers to collect expectations from participants without them being biased by the research question or assumption. The *participatory prototyping* elicits concrete understandings from the users' perspective, and grounds the discussion with the particular technology being investigated. The *follow-up interviews* collect personal reflections from individual participants and the highlights of their experiences. We designed this protocol to facilitate our research on users' expectations of robots in public spaces. As a proof of concept, an exploratory study in which participants were asked to conceptualise and program the behaviours of a social robot situated in a public space of their choice was conducted. The proposed co-design workshop methodology can be applied to other research questions that are user-centered or focus on societal impacts of technology, for example, designing functions of a care or service robot. Moreover, the online format of this workshop methodology allows a scalable deployment approach.

Insights on Users' Expectations of Robots in Public Spaces: Our exploratory study demonstrates that people have existing expectations of what robots are and what they are capable of, informed by personal experiences and by popular culture. Thus, it is important to understand these expectations in order to improve social acceptance of robots designed to function in public spaces. We also found that participatory prototyping can help robot designers to understand their users' desired robot behaviours, as well as for potential users to have a more realistic view of a robot's capabilities and limits.

Limitations: As an exploratory study, we used a simulator environment where participants imagined Pepper's environment and possible interaction scenarios. The simulator, together with the simple programming interface, allowed participants to quickly design, develop and refine their concepts through rapid iterations. However, the simulator is only an approximation of the real world and does not allow interactive testing of the robot behaviours. Another limitation is that we used one particular robot platform. Thus, the appearance and functions of the Pepper robot may frame the participants' design of its behaviours. Further, we deployed a *translator* to help participants quickly realise their designs. However, the presence of the *translator* during participatory prototyping may induce "experimenter bias" in the participants, which can lead to them reporting overly positive or optimistic views of the robot or their experiences. The COVID-19 pandemic lock-down also restrained us to an online-only format, loosing the possibility of having the participants in the same space with the robot.

Future Directions: To address the limitations of this exploratory study and to extend our understanding of robots in public spaces, we plan to organize a series of subsequent workshops. In particular, complementary with to the programming inside the simulator environment, we will introduce participants to a physical robot positioned at a supervised location. We will live-stream the robot performing actions designed by the participants. This maintains the online format of the workshop while allowing participants to contextualize and spatialise their design of robot behaviours. We will also conduct these workshops with two different robotic platforms, and investigate how the appearance and functionalities of a robot influences the behaviours designed by the participants. In addition, we will investigate possible ways to reduce the "experimenter bias", for instance, by limiting the role of the *translator*.

Acknowledgement. We would like to thank all our participants. This project is supported by the Monash University Data Futures Interdisciplinary Research Seed Grant.

References

1. Azenkot, S., Feng, C., Cakmak, M.: Enabling building service robots to guide blind people a participatory design approach. In: HRI 2016, pp. 3–10. IEEE (2016)
2. Bartneck, C., Belpaeme, T., Eyssel, F., Kanda, T., Keijsers, M., Šabanović, S.: Human-Robot Interaction: An Introduction. Cambridge University Press, Cambridge (2020)
3. Björling, E.A., Rose, E.: Participatory research principles in human-centered design: engaging teens in the co-design of a social robot. MIT J. **3**(1), 8 (2019)
4. Björling, E.A., Rose, E., Davidson, A., Ren, R., Wong, D.: Can we keep him forever? Teens' engagement and desire for emotional connection with a social robot. Int. J. Soc. Robot. **21**, 1–13 (2019)
5. Coronado, E., Mastrogiovanni, F., Venture, G.: Development of intelligent behaviors for social robots via user-friendly and modular programming tools. In: ARSO 2018, pp. 62–68. IEEE (2018)
6. Fernandes, C.R., Polzer, J.T.: Diversity in groups. Emerging trends in the social and behavioral sciences, pp. 1–14 (2015)
7. Haring, K.S., Novitzky, M.M., Robinette, P., De Visser, E.J., Wagner, A., Williams, T.: The dark side of human-robot interaction: ethical considerations and community guidelines for the field of HRI. In: HRI 2019, pp. 689–690. IEEE (2019)
8. Horstmann, A.C., Krämer, N.C.: Great expectations? Relation of previous experiences with social robots in real life or in the media and expectancies based on qualitative and quantitative assessment. Front. Psychol. **10**, 939 (2019)
9. Lee, H.R., Riek, L.D.: Reframing assistive robots to promote successful aging. ACM Trans. HRI **7**(1), 1–23 (2018)
10. Lee, H.R., et al.: Steps toward participatory design of social robots: mutual learning with older adults with depression. In: HRI 2017, pp. 244–253 (2017)
11. Pandey, A.K., Gelin, R.: A mass-produced sociable humanoid robot: pepper: the first machine of its kind. IEEE Rob. Autom. Mag. **25**(3), 40–48 (2018)
12. Pot, E., Monceaux, J., Gelin, R., Maisonnier, B.: Choregraphe: a graphical tool for humanoid robot programming. In: RO-MAN 2009, pp. 46–51. IEEE (2009)
13. Robinson, N., Hicks, T.N., Suddrey, G., Kavanagh, D.J.: The robot self-efficacy scale: robot self-efficacy, likability and willingness to interact increases after a robot-delivered interaction. In: RO-MAN 2020. IEEE (2020)
14. Sumartojo, S., Pink, S.: Moving through the lit world: the emergent experience of urban paths. Space Cult. **21**(4), 358–374 (2018)
15. Thunberg, S., Ziemke, T.: Are people ready for social robots in public spaces? In: HRI 2020, pp. 482–484. ACM (2020)
16. Šabanović, S., Reeder, S.M., Kechavarzi, B.: Designing robots in the wild: in situ prototype evaluation for a break management robot. JHRI **3**(1), 70–88 (2014)
17. Winkle, K., Caleb-Solly, P., Turton, A., Bremner, P.: Social robots for engagement in rehabilitative therapies: design implications from a study with therapists. In: HRI 2018, pp. 289–297 (2018)
18. Winkle, K., Caleb-Solly, P., Turton, A., Bremner, P.: Mutual shaping in the design of socially assistive robots: a case study on social robots for therapy. Int. J. Soc. Robot. **12**, 1–20 (2019). https://doi.org/10.1007/s12369-019-00536-9

Receiving Robot's Advice: Does It Matter When and for What?

Carolin Straßmann[1]([⊠])(iD), Sabrina C. Eimler[1](iD), Alexander Arntz[1](iD),
Alina Grewe[1], Christopher Kowalczyk[1], and Stefan Sommer[2]

[1] Institute of Computer Science, University of Applied Sciences Ruhr West,
Bottrop, Germany
{carolin.strassmann,sabrina.eimler,alexander.arntz,
alina.grewe,christopher.kowalczyk}@hs-ruhrwest.de
[2] Fresenius University of Applied Sciences, Düsseldorf, Germany
stefan.sommer@stud.hs-fresenius.de

Abstract. Two experimental online studies investigate the persuasive effect of robot's advice on human's moral decision-making. Using two different decision scenarios with varying complexity, the effect of the point of time when a robot gives its advice was examined. Participants either received advice directly after the decision scenario or stated an initial opinion first, received advice and had the chance to adjust their decision afterwards. The analysis explored whether this affects the adaption to the robot's advice and the decision certainty as well as the evaluation of the robot. The assumption that people rely more on the robot's advice when they receive it directly and that those people have a reduced decision certainty was only found in the complex decision task condition.

Keywords: Decision making · Persuasive influence · Moral dilemma · Shared decision making

1 Introduction

In the future, diverse scenarios and applications are anticipated, where machines function as advisors or human-machine-teams will take joint decisions (e.g. [10]). So far, there is conflicting evidence whether humans avoid or appreciate recommendations made by machines. Although, machine advice can often outperform human choices and lead to better outcomes, humans distrust those recommendations and rely more on human recommendations (algorithmic aversion; [4]). Yeomans and colleagues showed that humans stated to understand human recommendations better than machine ones, which might be a main reason for algorithmic aversion [26]. Thus, recommendations of robots do not only have to be accurate, robots have to be comprehensible and convincing.

On the contrary, other results show that people rather rely on machine recommendation than on human recommendations (algorithmic appreciation) [11]. However, this appreciation decreases when people are asked to choose between

© Springer Nature Switzerland AG 2020
A. R. Wagner et al. (Eds.): ICSR 2020, LNAI 12483, pp. 271–283, 2020.
https://doi.org/10.1007/978-3-030-62056-1_23

their own estimation and the one made by the machine. People tend to overesti-mate the quality of their decision, which might be one explanation for algorithm aversion [11]. Nevertheless, these results are based on objective decisions (mak-ing estimates and forecasts) and might be different for more subjective, humanly decisions such as moral decisions. Although humans apply similar norms to humans and artificial entities taking moral decisions they attribute different degrees of blame [12]. Humans are skeptical towards machines taking moral decisions as they lack empathetic skills allowing them to think or feel [3]. Thus, people avoid moral decisions by machines for most domains (e.g. driving, legal, medical) [3]. This avoidance is decreased when machines act as consultants in the decision process rather than deciding fully on their own [3]. Additionally, machine decisions evoke more negative emotions for tasks that involve human skills [8]. Although there is controversial evidence regarding algorithmic avoid-ance or appreciation, humans tend to avoid advice from machines for moral decisions or tasks that require human skills. However, the envisioned applica-tion scenarios are often based on exactly those domains. Thus, it is important to investigate how to design recommendations made by machines to support human decision making.

There is extensive knowledge about essential aspects of robots giving advice (e.g. verbal aspects [23], appearance and presence [21], the quality and first impression of the robot [25] and the executed task a robot gives advice for [19]). Neglected so far was the role that robots take in the temporal dynamic of a decision making process, specifically the point in time when advice is given to humans. Research shows that humans avoid changing their minds once they made a decision. Accordingly, the point when humans receive this advice might have an important effect on the decision outcome. People tend to refrain from changing opinions about subjects once a mental model has been formed [6]. This has, for example, been illustrated in research on cognitive dissonance [5] or confirmation bias [13]. Researchers argue that people tend to follow their first instinct, because they are afraid of regretting an opinion change afterwards [7]. In line with this, regret after a decision change is independent of the decisions' outcome [6]. Even when people changed their mind and experienced a beneficial outcome, they expressed higher post-outcome regret than those who remained with their initial choice [6]. Thus, the psychological costs of following the robot's advice and changing one's opinion are extremely high, when a decision was already taken without advice. This will result in a state of cognitive dissonance that humans want to get rid of [5]. To do so, mainly two options are used: (a) adapt the opinion (and often forget the change [24]) or (b) devalue and ignore the conflicting advice.

Humans' cognitive dissonance seems to be even stronger when they interacted with a robot compared to a human partner [9]. Humans often form a confronta-tional relationship with machines [15] and therefore their cognitive dissonance might be even stronger when they receive a robot recommendation that is con-tradictory to their own opinion. Due to this, it is most likely that humans will devalue the robot's advice in order to strengthen their own opinion. Under the circumstance that humans form confrontational relationships with robots [15] it would be more costly to adapt the decision to the robot advice. To further explore these mechanisms, two studies (where participants either receive a direct advice or take their own decision first and then receive the advice) investigate the following hypotheses:

> *Hypothesis H1:* Participants receiving a direct recommendation (Group A) align more to the robot's decision than those stating their own opinion first (Group B).
> *Hypothesis H2:* Participants stating their own opinion first (Group B) express a higher decision certainty than those receiving a direct recommendation (Group A).

When people fight their cognitive dissonance and devalue the robot's advice this might have an effect on the overall perception and evaluation of the robot. Therefore, it is investigated whether the avoidance of the robot's advice and the resuming cognitive dissonance when people take their own decision first affects the evaluation of the robot.

> *Research Question RQ 1:* Does the time of the given recommendation affect human's perception of the robot?

2 Study 1: Trolley Dilemma

Study 1 tested a life and death moral dilemma. The Trolley Dilemma is a moral problem often discussed in regard to machines and especially autonomous vehicles [1]. People argue that, if machines should be embedded into the human world, they have to be able to take such decisions. It has already been investigated how people react to robot advice in this moral dilemma (with regard to uncertainty expression [20] and physical presence [22]).

2.1 Method

In an online experiment with a between-subject design, the robot Pepper presented a moral decision dilemma and its recommendation for the decision. Participants were split randomized into two groups and either (A) received a direct recommendation or (B) had the chance to state their own opinion and obtain the recommendation afterwards.

Experimental Conditions. Videos of the robot Pepper (SoftBank Robotics) were used to present the Trolley Dilemma: Five people on a rail track could be saved by pushing a big man on the railroad. Group A was instructed about the dilemma followed by a direct recommendation on how the robot would decide. Group B only received the instruction and wrote down their choice first. After that they saw Pepper's recommendation and stated their decision a second time.

In both groups, the robot recommended pushing the big man ("If I were in this situation, I would push the fat man off the bridge. This would definitely be the better decision."). Pepper explains the dilemma verbally while showing slight gestures. Both groups saw the exact same videos, but as group B had a pause, the video got cut in two.

Measures. To measure the effect of the robot on human's decision-making and evaluation of the robot, self-reported questionnaire-data were used. Participants stated their decision to push the man or do nothing. Their answers were coded with regard to congruence to the robot's decision (congruent = pushing the man and in-congruent = do nothing). Group B stated their decision twice. Using a 5-point Likert-scale participants stated their decision certainty ("How confident are you in your decision?", 1 = "not certain at all", 5 = "completely certain"). Perception of the robot was measured using the likeability (5 items, $\alpha = 0.85$, e.g. 1 = "Dislike", 5 = "Like"), anthropomorphism (5 items, $\alpha = 0.72$, e.g. 1 = "Machinelike", 5 = "Humanlike"), animacy (6 items, $\alpha = 0.75$, e.g. 1 = "Dead", 5 = "Alive") and perceived intelligence (5 items, $\alpha = 0.79$, e.g. 1 = "Foolish", 5 = "Sensible") sub-scales of the Godspeed questionnaire [2]. Additionally, the perceived usefulness (3 items, $\alpha = 0.91$, e.g. "I think this system could help me with many decisions.") and the participant's intention to use (3 items, $\alpha = 0.93$, e.g. "I would like to have this system at home to make decisions.") were queried on a 5-point Likert-scale. The perception of the decision task and presented recommendation were evaluated using the sub-scales task complexity (2 items, $\alpha = 0.75$, e.g. "The decision task was easy to handle for me."), added value of the recommendation (4 items, $\alpha = 0.64$, e.g. "The presented recommendation for this decision helped me with my decision.") and decision satisfaction with a 5-pointed Likert-scale. To assess participants' experiences with technology and robots, the readiness for technology (13 items, $\alpha = 0.69$, e.g. "I am always interested in using the latest technical equipment") as well as fear (4 items, $\alpha = 0.77$, e.g. "If I were to use a robot, I'd be afraid to make mistakes.") and acceptance (3 items, $\alpha = 0.83$, e.g. "It would make sense to use a robot") of robots was measured. Moreover, the negative attitude towards robots scale [14] were used: interaction (6 items, $\alpha = 0.66$, e.g. "I would feel paranoid talking with a robot."), social influence (5 items, $\alpha = 0.73$, e.g. "I would feel uneasy if robots really had emotions.") and emotions in interaction (3 items, $\alpha = 0.74$, e.g. reversed: "I would feel relaxed talking with robots."). In the end, participants' socio-demographic variables were queried.

Procedure. At the beginning, participants signed informed consent and were introduced to the procedure. Then personality traits and participants' experiences with robots were assessed. Afterwards, the experimental part began and a video started, in which Pepper presented the dilemma. Group A directly received a recommendation on how Pepper would decide. Group B first stated their own opinion in the questionnaire and saw the video with Pepper's recommendation afterwards. This group then could decide again and change their decision. Afterwards, participants stated their experience with the decision process and their perception of the robot. In the end, the participants were debriefed and had the chance to receive course credits if necessary.

Sample. Altogether, 75 participants (43 men, 31 women and 1 non-binary) with an average age of 24 years ($M = 23.73$, $SD = 6.45$) took part. Most participants ($n = 58$) were students, 9 employees, 2 self-employed and 6 stated "miscellaneous". The participants stated that they rarely (2) to sometimes (3) have interacted with a robot ($M = 2.09$, $SD = 1.24$). In the sample, moderate to highly moderate means of robot acceptance ($M = 2.90$, $SD = 0.96$) and negative attitude towards robots (interaction ($M = 2.12$, $SD = 0.64$), social influence ($M = 2.82$, $SD = 0.81$) and emotions in interaction ($M = 2.96$, $SD = 0.88$)) were assessed. Participants showed a low fear of robots ($M = 1.72$, $SD = 0.76$) and a high readiness for technology ($M = 3.94$, $SD = 0.42$). Both experimental groups do not differ in those traits and attitudes.

2.2 Results

To test H1, a chi-square test was used to compare the congruence of participants' decision with the robot's advice of the group with direct and the group with late recommendation. Results show no significant difference between both groups. Most people had no congruence to the robots advice ($n_A = 30$; $n_B = 28$) and only 17 participants ($n_A = 9$ and $n_B = 8$) chose the robot's decision. In addition, we analyzed for people that had the chance to change their opinion, whether they kept their first instinct or changed the opinion. Results of a chi-square indicate a significant effect ($x^2(3) = 85.33$, $p < .001$) that participants stick to their first decision ($n = 33$); only 3 people switched to another decision option.

To test H2, a two-paired t-test was used. No statistically significant difference between the decision certainty of group A and B was detected. While both groups did not differ, means show a tendency for participants that first took their decision to have a stronger decision certainty. Table 1 lists means and standard deviations.

A MANOVA was used to investigate human's perception of the robot (RQ1). Results revealed no statistically significant difference between the groups with direct or late recommendations in perceived anthropomorphism, animacy, likeability and intelligence of the robot. A MANOVA tested the evaluation of the robot with regard to the participants' intention to use and perceived usefulness. Both groups did not differ in their stated intention to use, but a significant difference of participants' perceived usefulness ($F(1,73) = 5.659$, $p = .020$) occurred. Participants with a direct advice perceived the robot as more useful (Table 1).

In addition, the perception of the moral dilemma and participants' satisfaction with the decision and recommendation were analysed with a third MANOVA. No significant difference was found for the perceived decision complexity, but the added value of the recommendation ($F(1,73) = 4.120$, $p = .046$) and participant's satisfaction with the final decision ($F(1,73) = 4.386$, $p = .040$)

Table 1. Descriptive values of the dependent variables split along conditions.

Table 2. Pepper robot.

	Group A		Group B		Overall	
	M	SD	M	SD	M	SD
Certainty decision	3.62	1.21	3.89	1.28	3.75	1.24
Anthropomorphism	2.09	0.78	1.94	0.70	2.02	0.74
Animacy	2.53	0.63	2.33	0.71	2.43	0.67
Likeability	3.18	0.78	3.34	0.68	3.26	0.73
Perceived intelligence	3.40	0.69	3.36	0.81	3.38	0.75
Intention to use	1.96	1.07	1.61	0.85	1.79	0.98
Perceived usefulness	2.19	1.11	1.65	0.82	1.93	1.01
Decision complexity	2.95	1.31	2.57	1.21	2.77	1.27
Added value decision	2.29	0.82	1.94	0.66	2.12	0.76
Decision satisfaction	3.15	1.29	3.78	1.29	3.45	1.32

differed significantly between both groups. People rated the robot's advice to be more valuable and were more satisfied with it when the robot gave its advice directly (Table 1).

2.3 Discussion

No significant differences between participants receiving the robot's recommendation directly after the dilemma explanation and participants stating their own decision first were found. Neither the congruence to the robot's advice (H1) nor the decision certainty (H2) differed between both groups. Thus, no support for the assumption that people without an pre-defined opinion rely more on robot's advice to make a moral decision. Although the results confirm the assumption that people avoid changing their decision, both hypotheses have to be rejected. Further, no differences in the perception of the robot occurred (RQ1). However, with regard to its evaluation, participants receiving direct advice evaluated the robot as more useful, valued its recommendation more and expressed higher satisfaction with the final decision. This is supported by prior research showing that people tend to devalue the recommendation when they experience cognitive dissonance [5] (which is the case for group B). Moreover, it has already been demonstrated that people sticking to their choice are more satisfied with their decision [6].

That H1 and H2 were not supported might be caused by the chosen dilemma. As people tend to avoid moral decisions of robots [3], the avoidance of the robot's advice might have been so strong that both groups rejected the recommendation and only used their own impressions. This might be especially true, since this dilemma is strongly discussed. Its prominence might have hindered the adaption of the robot's advice [20]. Moreover, the decision task itself was only a binary choice (push the man or not) and therefore easy. When it comes to more complex decisions, people rely more on heuristics [17] and other strategies to reduce cognitive strain [16]. Accordingly, for more complex decision tasks people might rely more on the robot's advice to reduce the perceived cognitive strain. Therefore, a second experiment has been conducted with the same methodology but a different decision scenario.

3 Study 2: Desert Survival Game

Study 2 investigated the hypotheses and the effect of recommendation point in a new setting. Again, a between-subject design, where participants were randomly assigned to one of two groups (A: direct recommendation or B: later recommendation), was used. The main goal was to investigate whether people rely more on a robot advice in a more complex scenario. Therefore, Pepper presented the Desert Survival Game, which has already been used in the interaction with machines [18]. Within this game participants have to evaluate about the relevance of different items for their survival. They have to choose and sort 5 items out of 12. Again, this scenario has a moral component, since the sense of survival is a human skill that machines do not have. The decision task has a higher complexity, as multiple small decisions (e.g. "Is this item important?" or "Is it more important than this one?") have to be taken. Based on prior research [16], we assume that humans (that not already took an own decision) will rely more on a robot's advice for this complex decision to reduce cognitive strain. Thus, the difference between both groups will be stronger than those found in Study 1.

3.1 Method

This study has the same methodology as the first one, but this time a decision scenario with higher complexity was used. As the same measures and procedure were used, only deviations between both studies are presented.

Experimental Conditions. In this experiment Pepper introduced a decision task called Desert Survival Game. Pepper presented a short story, that, due to a plane crash, the participant needs to sort and select items that help to survive in a dry desert. One has to find the five most helpful items to survive. Again, Pepper explains the game verbally with idle gestures. Like in Study 1, participants of group A were instructed about the game followed by a direct recommendation on which items to choose in what order. Group B got only the instruction and could decide about their choice. They later saw the recommendation video and stated their decision a second time. In both conditions the recommended items and their order were the same. Pepper's recommendation was adopted to an expert solution and was the same for both experimental groups ("If I were in this situation, I would choose lighter, steel wool, clothes, can and canvas. Those would definitely be the better items.").

Measures. Again, the congruence between the robot's recommendation and human's decision was calculated. As the scenario is more complex, a numeric variable was used instead of a binary code. The congruence score was generated by adding up the congruence scores of the five recommended items (lighter, steel wool, clothes, can and canvas). Those item scores were coded by giving points, depending on the deviation between the rating of the participant and the robot's recommendation. Five points were given, if the recommendation and the rating matched. For each place of distance one point was removed. No points were given, if the recommended item was not chosen in the rating. Thus, a higher congruence score reflects a stronger alignment between the robot's recommendation and the human's decision. Additionally, the same variables as in Study 1 were used.

Sample. 78 participants completed the questionnaire of this study. 41 were men, 36 women and 1 non-binary. The sample had an average age of 25 years ($M = 24.94$, $SD = 6.84$). Again, mainly students participated (59 students, 14 employees, 2 civil servants, 3 stated miscellaneous). The participants stated that they rarely (2) had interacted with a robot ($M = 1.92$, $SD = 1.07$). The sample showed a highly moderate acceptance ($M = 2.91$, $SD = 0.98$) and low fear of robots ($M = 1.76$, $SD = 0.76$). In accordance, a moderate negative attitude towards robots (interaction ($M = 2.25$, $SD = 0.70$), social influence ($M = 3.09$, $SD = 0.72$) and emotions in interaction ($M = 3.13$, $SD = 0.99$) characterized the sample. Overall, participants showed a high readiness for technology ($M = 3.84$, $SD = 0.53$). Both groups did not differ in those traits and experiences.

3.2   Results

A two-paired t-test revealed a significant difference between the congruence score of group A and B, $t(76) = 3.33$, $p = .001$, $d = 0.71$. A medium effect was found

Table 3. Descriptive values of the dependent variables split along conditions.

	Group A		Group B		Overall	
	M	SD	M	SD	M	SD
Congruence decision	8.62	3.81	6.10	2.85	7.29	3.56
Decision certainty	3.43	0.69	3.76	0.83	3.60	0.78
Anthropomorphism	1.89	0.70	2.00	0.83	1.94	0.77
Animacy	2.16	0.72	2.26	0.81	2.21	0.77
Likeability	3.36	0.67	3.10	0.87	3.22	0.79
Perceived intelligence	3.64	0.55	3.48	0.92	3.55	0.76
Intention to use	1.95	1.07	1.89	0.81	1.92	0.94
Perceived usefulness	2.11	1.10	2.12	0.92	2.12	1.00
Decision complexity	2.31	0.98	2.60	1.11	2.46	1.06
Added value Decision	2.67	1.10	2.41	1.13	2.54	1.11
Decision Satisfaction	4.08	0.72	3.80	1.19	3.94	1.00

showing that people who directly received the robot's recommendation align more to the robot's recommendation than people that stated their decision first (Table 3). Thus, H1 is supported.

A second t-test investigated the differences in participants' decision certainty. There was a significant difference (only on 10 percent-level) between the means of decision certainty for group A and B, $t(76) = -1.862$, $p = .066$. In line with H2, participants receiving the recommendation after they stated their own decision (group B) showed a stronger decision certainty than those receiving a direct recommendation (group A) (see Table 3).

To investigate the influence of the point of recommendation on the evaluation of the robot, two MANOVAs have been calculated. No statistically significant difference between both groups for the perceived anthropomorphism, animacy, likeability and perceived intelligence of the robot were found. Furthermore, there was no statistically significant difference between the intention to use of the group A and B nor was there a significant difference for perceived usefulness.

Again, we analysed the perception of the decision scenario and the robot's advice post-hoc using a MANOVA. As in Study 1, no differences in the perception of the decision complexity nor in the satisfaction with the final decision were found between both groups. However, both groups differed in their perception of the recommendations' added value, $(F(1,74) = 1.016, p = .037)$. Again, participants of group A perceived greater value than people in group B (see Table 3). Thus, the point of recommendation did not affect the perception of the decision task, but had an influence on the perception of the recommendation. As a manipulation check testing for the higher complexity of the scenario, we compared the time spent for the first decision statement (final one for group A and initial one for group B). Therefore, the time stamps of the respective pages in the online questionnaire were used and both studies were compared using a t-test. A significant difference was found $(t(151) = 8.016, p < .001)$ indicating that participants in the Desert Survival Game study $(M = 115.67, SD = 106.36)$ took more time for their decisions than people in the Trolley Dilemma study $(M = 15.63, SD = 19.65)$.

3.3 Discussion

The assumed hypotheses are (partly) supported by the results of the present study. People receiving the robot's recommendation right after the explanation of the decision task aligned stronger to the robots' recommendation (H1). This supports the assumption made by prior research, that people avoid changing their decision, when they once took it [5,6]. Instead of adapting to the robot's advice, people seem to ignore it and strengthen their own decision, which lead to a stronger decision certainty (H2). However, as the groups did only differ on a 10% significance level, conclusions have to be drawn with caution. Nevertheless, there is a tendency to support H2. With regard to research question RQ1, no differences in the perception of the robot between both groups occurred. But a difference in the value of the robot's advice has been found. Thus, like in Study

1, the devaluation process of the robot's advice affected the perception of the robot advice, but not its perception.

4   General Discussion

The present work investigated the effect of a robot's advice on human's decision-making. Conducting two experimental online studies, the effect of the point of the robot's recommendation within a decision-making process was examined. Both studies used a between-subject design with two experimental groups: participants either received a direct recommendation by the robot (group A) or stated their decision first, then received the robot advice and had the chance to adjust their decision afterwards (group B). Based on prior research [6], we assumed that people receiving the direct advice will align more with the robot and show a higher congruence than those of group B (H1). Furthermore, we suggested participants in group B to show a stronger decision certainty (H2), as they stated their decision twice and devalue the robot's advice to reduce cognitive dissonance and strengthen their own opinion [5]. In Study 1, the Trolley Dilemma [1] was used to investigate the effect of robot advice in a moral setting. People had to decide if they kill one person to rescue five people. As this dilemma is well-known (so that people might already had a prior opinion) and the decision task itself was easy (binary: push the man or not), Study 2 examined the hypotheses based on a more complex decision task. In the Desert Survival Game [18] participants had to rank items along their relevance to survive in a desert. This decision is more complex, as the participants have to compare multiple items with each other and choose the five most relevant.

The results of Study 1 did not support the hypotheses, as no differences between both experimental groups where found. In contrast, the hypotheses were supported in the more complex decision task (Desert Survival Game; Study 2). Here, participants receiving a direct recommendation relied more on this advice of the robot than the participants in the other group. The differences between both groups are most likely grounded on the chosen decision task and its complexity. The comparison of the decision time of both studies demonstrated, that people took more time for their decision in the Desert Survival Game. This higher complexity probably induced higher cognitive strain, so that people relied more on other strategies [16] and heuristics [17] to make their decision. This is a coping mechanism to reduce the perceived cognitive strain. Thus, while participants of Study 1 probably ignored the robot's advice completely and only relied on their own opinion, this was not found for Study 2. Besides the difference in complexity, both dilemmas differed in the moral nature. While the first one implies a direct harm of other people, the second does not. This difference might also have an effect on the present results. Thus, in the more complex and less moral setting, participants used the robot's advice more and the differences between both experimental groups became obvious. Moreover, this work demonstrates that the time when a robot presents its advice has also an effect on the evaluation of the robot (direct advice increase perceived usefulness and the perceived value of the advice) and participants' decision satisfaction.

This provides important implications for the (joined) decision-making process of humans and machines. The effectiveness of robot's advice strongly depends on the decision task. Based on the present results, humans accept machine advice more for complex moral decision tasks. Moreover, in dependence of the decision task and the goal of the joined decision-making process the robot should present its advice at different points in time. For ethical decision-processes and decisions requiring a deliberate decision, people should have time to make a first decision and receive the advice afterwards. In contrast, for scenarios, where the robot should be as persuasive as possible, the advice needs to be presented as soon as possible, so that people cannot form a fix opinion that is difficult to change. Results further indicate, that the perception of the robot was not affected. However, future research should investigate the effect of the perception of the robot on the decision process.

Beside these implications, both studies have shortcomings. The scenario of Study 1 might have been too well-known and participants might already had a pre-defined opinion. However, there was no way to measure such a prior opinion without destroying the experimental design. Future studies should compare the two possible options (either to push or do nothing). Moreover, different wordings of the Trolley Dilemma (e.g. pulling the lever to change the track switch position) might also have an influence. In addition, the adaption of the robot advice was measured differently in both scenarios, because of their differing complexity. Future studies need to replicate the present findings with scenarios that are more comparable in terms of measures. Moreover, as both studies ran online, no direct interaction with the robot was present and participants saw the robot on video only. However, at least for the Trolley Dilemma, prior research did not demonstrate that a physical present robot has stronger persuasive effects [22]. Additionally, it would be of high relevance to compare the advice provided by the robot directly with that given by human. While this study concentrated on the comparison of robot's advice in relation to the individual's opinion, future studies should investigate the role of other human's advice in this regard and competing advice situations (of robots or other humans providing advice that is (in)consistent with the individual's evaluation of the situation.

5 Conclusion

In summary, the findings suggest that for robots and other AI-systems it has to be decided wisely when to present advice within a decision-making process. Depending on the task and goal of the decision process, robots should either give interaction partners the chance to make a deliberate decision first and than present the advice and its arguments or present the advice directly. This gives valuable hints for designers of advisory AI-systems that are used in joined decision-making processes between humans and machines.

References

1. Awad, E., Dsouza, S., Shariff, A., Rahwan, I., Bonnefon, J.F.: Universals and variations in moral decisions made in 42 countries by 70,000 participants. Proc. Natl. Acad. Sci. **117**(5), 2332–2337 (2020)
2. Bartneck, C., Kulić, D., Croft, E., Zoghbi, S.: Measurement instruments for the anthropomorphism, animacy, likeability, perceived intelligence, and perceived safety of robots. Int. J. Soc. Robot. **1**(1), 71–81 (2009)
3. Bigman, Y.E., Gray, K.: People are averse to machines making moral decisions. Cognition **181**, 21–34 (2018)
4. Dietvorst, B.J., Simmons, J.P., Massey, C.: Algorithm aversion: people erroneously avoid algorithms after seeing them Err. J. Exp. Psychol. Gen. **144**(1), 114–126 (2015)
5. Festinger, L.: A Theory of Cognitive Dissonance, vol. 2. Stanford University Press (1962)
6. Kirkebøen, G., Vasaasen, E., Halvor Teigen, K.: Revisions and regret: the cost of changing your mind. J. Behav. Decis. Mak. **26**(1), 1–12 (2013)
7. Kruger, J., Wirtz, D., Miller, D.T.: Counterfactual thinking and the first instinct fallacy. J. Personal. Soc. Psychol. **88**(5), 725 (2005)
8. Lee, M.K.: Understanding perception of algorithmic decisions: fairness, trust, and emotion in response to algorithmic management. Big Data Soc. **5**(1), 2053951718756684 (2018)
9. Levin, D.T., Harriott, C., Paul, N.A., Zhang, T., Adams, J.A.: Cognitive dissonance as a measure of reactions to human-robot interaction. J. Hum.-Robot Interact. **2**(3), 3–17 (2013). https://doi.org/10.5898/JHRI.2.3.Levin
10. Liptak, A.: Sent to prison by a software program's secret algorithms, May 2017. https://www.nytimes.com/2017/05/01/us/politics/sent-to-prison-by-a-software-programs-secret-algorithms.html
11. Logg, J.M., Minson, J.A., Moore, D.A.: Algorithm appreciation: people prefer algorithmic to human judgment. Organ. Behav. Hum. Decis. Process. **151**, 90–103 (2019)
12. Malle, B.F., Magar, S.T., Scheutz, M.: AI in the sky: how people morally evaluate human and machine decisions in a lethal strike dilemma. In: Aldinhas Ferreira, M.I., Silva Sequeira, J., Virk, G.S., Tokhi, M.O., Kadar, E.E. (eds.) Robotics and Well-Being. ISCASE, vol. 95, pp. 111–133. Springer, Cham (2019). https://doi.org/10.1007/978-3-030-12524-0_11
13. Nickerson, R.S.: Confirmation bias: a ubiquitous phenomenon in many guises. Rev. Gen. Psychol. **2**(2), 175–220 (1998)
14. Nomura, T., Suzuki, T., Kanda, T., Kato, K.: Measurement of negative attitudes toward robots. Interact. Stud. **7**(3), 437–454 (2006)
15. Oh, C., Lee, T., Kim, Y., Park, S., Kwon, S., Suh, B.: Us vs. Them: understanding artificial intelligence technophobia over the Google deepmind challenge match. In: Proceedings of the 2017 CHI Conference on Human Factors in Computing Systems, pp. 2523–2534 (2017)
16. Olshavsky, R.W.: Task complexity and contingent processing in decision making: a replication and extension. Organ. Behav. Hum. Performance **24**(3), 300–316 (1979)
17. Payne, J.W.: Task complexity and contingent processing in decision making: an information search and protocol analysis. Organ. Behav. Hum. Perform. **16**(2), 366–387 (1976)

18. Rosenthal-von der Pütten, A.M., Straßmann, C., Yaghoubzadeh, R., Kopp, S., Krämer, N.C.: Dominant and submissive nonverbal behavior of virtual agents and its effects on evaluation and negotiation outcome in different age groups. Comput. Hum. Behav. **90**, 397–409 (2019)

19. Shinozawa, K., Naya, F., Yamato, J., Kogure, K.: Differences in effect of robot and screen agent recommendations on human decision-making. Int. J. Hum.-Comput. Stud. **62**(2), 267–279 (2005)

20. Stellmach, H., Lindner, F.: Perception of an uncertain ethical reasoning robot. i-com **18**(1), 79–91 (2019)

21. Strait, M., Canning, C., Scheutz, M.: Let me tell you! Investigating the effects of robot communication strategies in advice-giving situations based on robot appearance, interaction modality and distance. In: Proceedings of the 2014 ACM/IEEE International Conference on Human-Robot Interaction, pp. 479–486 (2014)

22. Straßmann, C., Grewe, A., Kowalcyk, C., Arntz, A., Eimler, S.C.: Moral robots? How uncertainty and presence affect humans' moral decision making. Accepted Proceeding of the Human Computer Interaction Conference (to be presented)

23. Torrey, C., Fussell, S.R., Kiesler, S.: How a robot should give advice. In: 2013 8th ACM/IEEE International Conference on Human-Robot Interaction (HRI), pp. 275–282. IEEE (2013)

24. Wolfe, M.B., Williams, T.J.: Poor metacognitive awareness of belief change. Q. J. Exp. Psychol. **71**(9), 1898–1910 (2018)

25. Xu, J., Howard, A.: The impact of first impressions on human-robot trust during problem-solving scenarios. In: 2018 27th IEEE International Symposium on Robot and Human Interactive Communication (RO-MAN), pp. 435–441. IEEE (2018)

26. Yeomans, M., Shah, A., Mullainathan, S., Kleinberg, J.: Making sense of recommendations. J. Behav. Decis. Making **32**(4), 403–414 (2019)

Don't Go That Way! Risk-Aware Decision Making for Autonomous Vehicles

Kasra Mokhtari[1]($\boxtimes$), Kendra A. Lang[2], and Alan R. Wagner[1]

[1] The Pennsylvania State University, State College, PA 16802, USA
{kbm5402,alan.r.wagner}@psu.edu
[2] Verus Research, Albuquerque, NM 87109, USA
kendra.lang@verusresearch.net

Abstract. Accurately predicting risk or potentially risky situations is critical for the safe operation of autonomous systems. Risk refers to the expected likelihood of an undesirable outcome, such as a collision. We draw on an existing conceptualization of the risk to evaluate a robot's options (e.g. choice of a path to travel). In this context, risk consists of two components: 1) the probability of an undesirable outcome computed by a Bayesian Network (BN) and 2) an estimate of the loss associated with the undesirable outcome. We demonstrate that our risk assessment tool is effective at computing the anticipated risk over a wide variety of the robot's options and selecting the option with the lowest risk for two different types of autonomous systems: An Autonomous Vehicle (AV) operating near a college campus and a pair of Unmanned Aerial Vehicles (UAVs) flying from Washington DC to Baltimore. The method for assessing risk is used to identify higher risk routes, days to travel, and travel times for an autonomous vehicle and higher risk routes for a UAV.

Keywords: Risk assessment · Bayesian Network · Autonomous systems

1 Introduction

An increasing number of robots and robotic applications are being developed that will allow autonomous systems to come into contact with the public. While many of these present little or no risk to people, some applications, such as autonomous driving and aerial vehicles, can pose physical, even fatal, threats to pedestrians. For Autonomous Vehicles (AVs) in particular, and any large mobile platform navigating in public spaces, concern for and protection from accidents should be a paramount concern. And although these systems tend to have a wide array of safety features, we believe that risk-centric prediction and high-risk avoidance are two elements that appear to be under-studied in the existing literature.

This paper focuses on risk. Specifically, we seek to develop tools that will allow an autonomous system to predict risk or potentially risky situations and avoid them. Our work is motivated by some of the simple tasks that AVs still seem incapable or disinclined to do. Many college campuses and urban environments in general, for example, see a

© Springer Nature Switzerland AG 2020
A. R. Wagner et al. (Eds.): ICSR 2020, LNAI 12483, pp. 284–295, 2020.
https://doi.org/10.1007/978-3-030-62056-1_24

surge in pedestrian traffic prior to classes or after classes. These pedestrians may not obey traffic signals and tend not to pay attention to the vehicles on the road.

Rather than attempting to wade through a large number of inattentive pedestrians it would be advantageous if an AV could identify the increased risk associated with the greater pedestrian foot traffic and avoid it.

Risk is traditionally described as the expected likelihood of an undesirable outcome [4]. For robots, because of their embodiment, an undesirable outcome can be a fatal crash or an accident that involves property damage. Risk is often characterized by two components: 1) the probability of an undesirable outcome and 2) an estimate of how undesirable the outcome is (loss). Our approach therefore considers not only the probability of an accident, but also the cost of that accident. While it may be unpleasant to discuss, courts and society in general often place specific, usually monetary value on lives and property. Our approach makes use of these types of legal tools to allow a vehicle to select the lesser of several evils. This paper contributes a general approach to risk-aware decision making for autonomous systems. We believe that our approach is novel in that it allows for the inclusion of a wide variety of risk types for different vehicles operating in different situations. We feel that the impact of this work has the potential to stem beyond autonomous driving, allowing other robotic applications to identify potentially risky behaviors or options and avoid them. This ability could be vital for social robot construction or military applications.

The remainder of the paper is organized as follows: Sect. 2 reviews the related work regarding risk assessment for autonomous systems. Section 3 describes our risk assessment methodology to evaluate an autonomous system's options. Section 4 empirically demonstrates how the risk assessment method might inform the autonomous system's decision-making process. Section 5 provides the experimental results and discussion. Finally, Sect. 6 offers conclusions and directions for future research.

2 Related Work

This section presents prior research related to assessing and using risk by an autonomous system, divided into risk assessment for Autonomous Vehicles (AVs) and risk assessment for Unmanned Aerial Vehicles (UAVs).

2.1 Risk Assessment for Autonomous Vehicles

A great deal of research related to risk and autonomous vehicles focuses on minimizing the risk of a collision. Greytak and Hover develop a motion planning controller that incorporates the risk of a collision in its planning algorithm [11]. Chinea and Parent [5] attempted to assess the risk of a collision by training a Recursive Neural Network (RNN) from simulated driving data. Risk is quantified in terms of the actions and objects present at road intersections including vehicles, pedestrians, buildings, etc. Strickland, Fainekos, and Amor train a deep predictive model on simulated intersection data [15]. The reliance on simulated data, however, brings into question if this approach will translate to real-world scenarios. Yu, Vasudevan, and Johnson-Roberson use a Partially Observable Markov Decision Process (POMDP) to characterize environments that include occlusions and evaluate their method in terms of collision rate and ride comfort on simulated and real-world data [18]. David, Lancz, and Hunyady explore the risk associated with rapid maneuvers and use a similar risk formulation as our own [8]. Their work also focuses on risk classification.

This aforementioned work, although related, generally attempts to use risk to influence the immediate vehicle reactions to a pending collision (collision avoidance), rather than to influence higher-level planning to avoid risky situations. Our approach, on the other hand, offers a general framework that could incorporate these related strategies as well as other types of risk using a variety of specialized computational strategies.

2.2 UAV Risk Assessment

Risk has also been used heavily in the assessment of autonomous UAV flight. For instance, risk has been considered as a factor for planning and control [10], the calculation of casualty rates from accidents and ground impacts [7]. A minimum risk path planning approach for UAVs in the presence of orthographic obstacles is presented in [9]. In this paper, the risk factor is simply characterized by the distance of the UAVs to the obstacle. Rudnick-Cohen et al. use risk and flight time to optimize UAV path planning [14]. They also measured the number of possible deaths at a potential crash location as a determinant of risk in the case of the terrain impact. This location is identified using a simulation. A less conservative yet more realistic risk management model is discussed in [17] by leveraging a penetration factor that accounts for smaller UAVs which pose a lower risk and obstacles that offer cover from falling objects in that area. Risk models have been developed for a variety of UAV operations. These tools are used as a regulatory method [10] and as a tool for ground operations management [16]. These risk models might also provide useful information to the system we are proposing.

Bayesian networks are commonly used for quantitative risk assessment [12]. A quantitative risk analysis for UAVs is described in [1] although risk is simply described as the probability of a crash. The Unmanned aircraft system traffic management Risk Assessment Framework (URAF) developed in [2] computes risk to third parties based on the potential impact area and the consequences of the impact. Barr et al. implemented a probabilistic model-based technique to estimate risk for UAVs based on multi-factor interdependencies and their failure modes along with other parameters such as environmental factors and aircraft failure types [3].

In this paper, by using a Bayesian Network and taking into consideration causal relationships and conditional probabilities, a general framework is offered which can also be used to create different types of crash accident models. The above related work tends to rely on simple instantiations of risk (e.g., the distance of a UAV to an obstacle, the number of possible deaths resulting from a crash, etc.). In contrast, the work presented here defines and uses risk by integrating a loss function with the conditional probability of various undesirable events, and then selects courses of action in order to minimize that risk. In the context of UAVs, we use a mid-air collision and a terrain impact as the undesirable events, whose likelihoods are computed from a Bayesian network. The loss functions are calculated according to the price of the UAV and the estimated price of the structures over which the UAVs will be flying. With safety as a top priority, this risk assessment tool can be used for high-level planning for UAVs to avoid risky pathways.

3   Using Risk to Evaluate a Robot's Options

Risk is traditionally described as the expected value of an undesirable outcome. Formally, risk is defined as [4]:

$$R(x) = \sum_y L(x, y)p(y) \tag{1}$$

where $L(x, y)$ is the loss associated with choosing action x when event y occurs, and $p(y)$ is the probability of event y occurring. For the work presented here, event y corresponds to various possible failures of the system. Since this work focuses on the risk associated with travel along a path, action x corresponds to choosing one path for the vehicle among a set of potential paths. The path of the vehicle is discretized into N time steps and we use a Bayesian network to estimate the probability of event y at each time step given the inputs to the network. Therefore, the risk associated with choosing the path x at time step i denoted by $R_i(x)$ is calculated as:

$$R_i(x) = \sum_y L_i(x, y)p(y|I_i), R(x) = \sum_{i=1}^{N} R_i(x) \tag{2}$$

where $L_i(x, y)$ is the loss associated with choosing the path x at time step i when event y occurs, I_i is an input set to the Bayesian network at time step i, and $R(x)$ is the total risk associated with choosing the path x, respectively. The following sections demonstrate the risk assessment tool for AVs and UAVs.

3.1   Risk Assessment for AVs

The purpose of this tool is to calculate the risk associated with each traversal given current knowledge of the path and the environment, and then selecting the path with minimum risk. In this paper, traversal refers to traveling along a path at a particular time of the day and day of the week. If the vehicle is able to compute the risk of traveling down a path, then it might avoid risky situations and improve safety. In order to use Eq. 2 for a particular traversal, two elements are used: 1) a Bayesian network that estimates the conditional probability, $p(y)$, of an accident and 2) a loss function for assessing the cost of an accident.

Bayesian Network. A Bayesian network was designed to calculate the probability of an accident. Unfortunately, to the best of our knowledge, the data necessary to construct an accurate Bayesian network related to AV accidents has not been published. Ideally, the network would be based on data collected from an AV or, perhaps, from high-fidelity simulations. We have thus designed a simple yet reasonable network to test the viability of our risk assessment tool.

The Bayesian network is depicted in Fig. 1(a). Intuitively, the presence of pedestrians and the driving conditions play an important role in car accidents. This factor is quantified as the number of pedestrians around the vehicle. Some driving conditions that cause car accidents are weather, weekday vs weekend, and time of day. We assume that these factors are independent. Night is a Boolean variable. *Numberofpedestrians, Weekday* and *Weather* were arbitrarily categorized into four different states as shown in Fig. 1(a). The unconditional probabilities and conditional probabilities were chosen arbitrarily due to lack of actual data related to autonomous accidents. As the number of autonomous vehicles increases, we expect more accident data to become available.

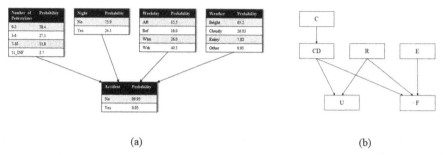

(a)   (b)

Fig. 1. (a) A Bayesian network that attempts to capture the probability of an AV accident. All probabilities were chosen arbitrarily. (b) A Bayesian network that attempts to capture the probability of two different types of UAV accidents: a mid-air collision (U) and the terrain impact (F). The parent nodes are communication failure (C), communication duration failure (CD), rainy weather (R) and engine failure (E).

Loss Function. The loss associated with choosing the path x at time step i when the car accident (event y) occurs is computed as:

$$L_i(x, y) = Q_i \times W_i \tag{3}$$

where Q_i is the total number of pedestrians around the vehicle at time step i, and W_1 is the constant value assigned to a loss of life, \$10,000,000 (based on recommended insurance coverage of company vehicles). Since the loss function is dependent on the number of pedestrians which varies by the time of travel, the loss function for the AVs is time-varying. We use dollars as the unit of measure for the loss function in order to make it relatable to other kinds of losses such as property losses, etc. Although it may seem peculiar to evaluate risk in terms of dollar costs, this is standard practice in the risk management literature [6].

By integrating the conditional probabilities with the loss function, risk is calculated using Eq. 2 as:

$$R_i(x) = (Q_i \times W_i) \times p(Accident|I_i), R(x) = \sum_{i=1}^{N} R_i(x) \tag{4}$$

where N is the number of time steps for path x, I_i is the set of inputs to the Bayesian network model at time step i, $R_i(x)$ is the risk associated with choosing path x at time step i and $R(x)$ is the total amount of risk associated with choosing path x. Note that knowledge of the current environment is assumed at the initial time i_0 of evaluation, and that to evaluate $R_i(x)$ in the future requires a conditional probability assessment of the likelihood of I_i taking on one of many values given known current value I_{i_0} for anytime i.

3.2   Risk Assessment for UAVs

In order to evaluate the generality of this approach, this section demonstrates that the same method can also be used to assess the risk of a UAV's flight path. This section considers the possibility of a UAV using risk Eq. 2 to evaluate different UAV flight paths. Here we assume that two UAVs travel along a path while communicating with each other. The starting point of the flight is Ronald Reagan International Airport (DCA) in Washington DC and the end point is Baltimore/Washington International Airport (BWI). In order to employ risk Eq. 2, a Bayesian network is used to predict the likelihood of two different types of accidents and a loss function is generated based on the population density of the terrain flown over.

Bayesian Network. The Bayesian network for calculating an accident is depicted in Fig. 1. Two types of accidents are modeled (events y): mid-air collisions denoted by U and terrain impacts denoted by F. The node C represents the communication link between the two UAVs. If this communication link disconnects for more than a certain threshold of time (in seconds), this results in a communication duration failure indicated by CD. The node R captures the presence or absence of inclement weather, which impacts the likelihood of both types of accidents. The node E represents an engine failure. The nodes E, CD, and R all influence the likelihood of at least one type of accident occurring. All the parent nodes in Fig. 1 are Boolean variables. It is assumed that CD, R and E are independent. The node F is influenced by CD, R and E. The node U, on the other hand, is influenced only by CD and R. A UAV dynamics model was provided by Verus Research to calculate the value of the states CD, U and F given inputs for C, R and E. In order to apply Eq. 2, the conditional probability of the possible failure events given the inputs to the Bayesian network, $p(U = T \mid CD, R)$ and $p(F = T \mid CD, R, E)$, must be calculated (T refers to True). The values of the probabilities C, R and E are set arbitrarily as $0.4, 0.5$ and 0.01, respectively. The dynamics model is run as a part of a Monte Carlo simulation 18K times. During each run, different inputs are presented to the dynamic model while the resulting states of the outputs are recorded. In order to generate the Conditional Probability Tables (CPTs), the joint probabilities for different combinations of variables must be computed. For example, $p(U = T \mid CD = T, R = T, E = T)$ is calculated as:

$$\frac{p(U = T, CD = T, R = T, E = T)}{p(CD = T, R = T, E = T)} \tag{5}$$

The same procedure is followed for every combination of inputs to create the CPTs for events U and F.

Loss Function. The loss associated with choosing a path x at time step i when U or F occurs is $L_i(x, U)$ and $L_i(x, F)$. These losses are calculated based on the price of the UAVs and the estimated price of the structures over which the UAVs will be flying. Because the path is discretized into N time steps, at each time step an arbitrary cost value denoted by W_2 is assigned to the loss function depending on whether the UAVs are flying over rural or urban areas. In the case of a terrain impact, this value is added to the price of the UAV denoted by $Price_{UAV}$ to form the loss function. We assume that when a mid-air collision occurs the two UAVs are completely destroyed. As a result, the loss functions are calculated as:

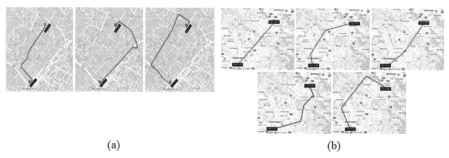

(a)   (b)

Fig. 2. (a) Three different paths between the same location in State College, PA. "Path A" (left), "Path B" (middle) and "Path C" (right). The car traversed each path for 42 times including 7 days and six timeslots a day: 8:45, 10:45, 12:45, 14:45, 16:45 and 17:45. Best viewed in color. (b) *Path-i* (first row on the left), *Path-ii* (first row in middle), *Path-iii* (first row on the right), *Path-iv* (second row on the left) and *Path-v* (second row on the right). Best viewed in color.

$$L_i(x, U) = 2 \times Price_{UAV}, L_i(x, F) = W_2 + Price_{UAV} \tag{6}$$

We have chosen an arbitrary cost for $Price_{UAV}$ as \$500,000 and W_2 is considered as \$1,000,000 or \$250,000 when flying over rural or urban areas, respectively. In this case, the loss functions are time-invariant. Therefore, $L_i(x, U)$ is \$1,000,000. $L_i(x, F)$ is \$1,500,000 in case of flying over urban area and is \$750,000 in case of flying over rural area.

Using the Bayesian network and the loss equations, Eq. 2 for a UAV becomes:

$$R(x) = \sum_{i=1}^{N} (2 \times Price_{UAV}) \times p(U|I_i) + (W_2 + Price_{UAV}) \times p(F|I_i), R(x)$$
$$= \sum_{i=1}^{N} R_i(x) \tag{7}$$

where N is the number of time steps for path x, I_i is the input to the Bayesian network at time step i and $R(x_i)$ is the risk associated with choosing path x at time step i and $R(x)$ is the total amount of risk associated with choosing path x. In the section that follows we present experiments evaluating the use of this risk assessment calculation by an AV or UAV to select a path and avoid high risk situations.

4 Experiments

This section examines the possibility of using the risk assessment methods described above to evaluate the robot's options, select a low risk option, and, most importantly avoid high-risk options. We hypothesized that the methods outlined above would allow the robot to identify options that are particularly risky. This method is demonstrated on both autonomous ground vehicles using real perceptual data and UAVs using simulated data.

4.1 Experiment Involving AVs

One hundred and twenty-six traversals were selected from the Pedestrian Pattern Dataset [13]. This dataset was created by collecting video camera data from a moving vehicle while repeatedly driving in State College, PA along the three different paths shown in Fig. 2(a). Data collection was carried out over three weeks at times: 8:45, 10:45, 12:45, 14:45, 16:45 and 17:45 resulting in 126 distinct video samples. Each sample contains a full HD video and GPS data for the entire traversal. By applying a Fast R-CNN based pedestrian detection algorithm on the captured videos, the estimated number of pedestrians per frame is generated. As a result, the measure $v_i \ \mathcal{R}^{N_i \times 1}$ is generated for each video, where N_i is the length of the i-th video in seconds (s), and each row represents the average number of detected pedestrians at that corresponding time step. In order to calculate the risk of traveling a path, each traversal is discretized into N_i time steps. The *Night*, *Weekday* and *Weather* inputs to the Bayesian network were constant at each time step for each traversal. The input for the *Numberofpedestrians* state varied at each time step and was computed using v_i. Risk for each traversal is calculated using Eq. 4.

We consider a scenario as described below in which the vehicle can choose either the path, the day, or the time of day to travel. We therefore fixed two of these variables and used the method described in Sect. 3.1 to assess the risk over the remaining options.

Which Path to Travel? For this study the AV must choose a path (labeled A, B, or C) for a fixed day and fixed time. Leave-one-out cross validation was used where the data from a particular day and time for all three paths was left out. We conducted this study by following the steps below:

1. A day and time was selected.
2. The risk data for the three paths for this day and time was removed from the dataset and served as ground truth.
3. The risk for the three different paths was calculated by averaging the risk for all the remaining times and days.
4. The minimum risk path was selected as the robot's best choice.
5. This choice was then compared to the data removed in step (2) to determine if the selected path was actually the lowest risk option.

It should be noted that the data was real-world data which contained real natural variations in the number of pedestrians and other factors. This process was repeated 42 times (six times a day times seven days of the week). The correct number of predictions were divided by 42 to calculate the prediction accuracy.

Which Day to Travel? A similar procedure was followed to select the day to travel. In this case, the path and the time to travel were fixed and the vehicle chooses the day that is the minimum risk option. To predict the risk for each day, the risk was averaged with respect to path and time of day. The day predicted to be least risky was chosen. This procedure was followed for all 18 combinations of path and time of day.

Which Time to Travel? Again a similar procedure was followed to determine what time of day to travel. Here, the path and the day to travel were fixed and the vehicle was free to choose a time to travel that minimized risk. Six different times were considered. To predict the risk for each time, the risk was averaged with respect to path and day of week. The procedure described above was followed for all 21 combinations of paths and days.

4.2 Experiment Involving UAVs

The purpose of this experiment is to demonstrate that the risk assessment methods developed in Sect. 3 are applicable to other types of vehicles, such as UAVs. We thus assume a situation in which two UAVs travel from Ronald Reagan International Airport (DCA) to Baltimore/Washington International Airport (BWI) along the same path together while communicating with each other. Both UAVs traveled along a series of straight lines (Fig. 2(b)) for five different paths labeled Paths $i - v$. Paths i and Path v mostly include urban areas. Path v mainly traverses rural areas. Each path was discretized into N time steps and the states for C, R and E were generated using a Monte Carlo simulation at each time step. Using the Bayesian network, the conditional probabilities of the mid-air collision and the terrain impact given the inputs are calculated. By integrating these conditional probabilities with the loss functions, risk for each path is calculated using Eq. 7. The results for these experiments are presented in the next section.

5 Results and Discussion

5.1 Risk Assessment for an Autonomous Vehicle

The risk for each traversal was normalized by dividing by the sum of the risk for all the traversals for the corresponding path. The normalized risk for all the traversals for each path is depicted in Fig. 3. The majority of which (94.5%) are below 0.05 in normalized risk. Tuesday at 14:45 results in a large jump in normalized risk which is five times the average value for Path A. For Path B, only Wednesday at 14:45 is above 0.05. The value for this path on this day is four times greater than the average for Path B. For Path C, Friday at 10:45 is four times greater than the average for Path C. This data clearly demonstrates that specific days and times generate spikes in risk. These spikes are directly related to normal increases in student, pedestrian traffic during the morning and afternoon on weekdays. We also see that some paths, such as Path A, have more spikes in risk than the other paths. Finally, we see an overall drop in most risk at most times during the weekend.

The prediction accuracy for the three prediction tasks described in Sect. 4.1 is presented in Table 1. When tasked with choosing the least risky path, using the method described in Sect. 4.1, the prediction accuracy was 95%. This high level of accuracy reflects the fact that one path tends to avoid pedestrian traffic resulting in lower overall normalized risk. When tasked with choosing the least risky day, the prediction accuracy was 84%. Here again, there seems to be a clear risk reduction advantage to driving on

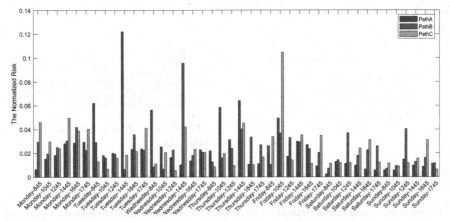

Fig. 3. Normalized risk of the all traversals for each path. The spikes imply the important events which the AV might avoid these traversals to enhance safety. Best viewed in color.

Saturday or Sunday. Finally, when choosing the least risky time, the prediction accuracy was only 19%. This prediction accuracy reflects the fact that there is not a great risk reduction advantage over the range of times the data was collected 8:45–17:45. If data had been collected either later in the night or earlier in the morning, the prediction accuracy would have likely increased because early morning hours would have resulted in few pedestrians.

5.2 Risk Assessment for a UAV

To compare the risk for the five different paths, the computed risk for the paths was normalized by dividing by the sum of the risk of all the paths. The normalized risk is shown in Fig. 4. Since Path i has mainly consisted of urban areas, it has the highest normalized risk. Path iv, on the other hand, has the lowest risk since it mostly flies over rural areas. Overall, Paths iv and v result in similar normalized risk. Path i stands out as a particularly risky option for the UAVs.

The loss function for the autonomous vehicle is based on the number of pedestrians around the vehicle while the loss function for the UAVs is based on the type of area the vehicles fly over. For the UAVs the loss can therefore be calculated a priori. For the autonomous vehicle the loss varies with each time step and must be estimated based on the predicted number of pedestrians. Nevertheless, in both cases certain options stand out as entailing greater risk. The greater than average expected risk may therefore serve as a signal to a UAV planning a path or an autonomous vehicle choosing a day to deliver a package.

Table 1. The prediction accuracy for the AV's experiments.

	Prediction accuracy
Which path?	95%
Which day?	84%
Which time?	19%

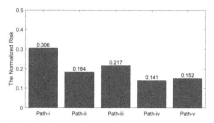

Fig. 4. Normalized risk for each path of the UAVs.

6   Conclusion

This paper has presented a method for an autonomous system, including an AV operating near a college campus and a pair of UAVs flying from Washington DC to Baltimore, to evaluate the risk associated with different options and to select the minimal risk option in the hope of improving safety. We have shown that some options may offer much greater risk than the average option. For both of these demonstrations we have made arbitrary assumptions about the value of loss incurred should an accident occur. Because action selection is based on a comparison across available options, so long as the same loss values are used throughout, then these assumptions do not impact the vehicle's decision making. In fact, loss can be individualized to reflect the values held by actors or a different set of laws. For instance, one autonomous vehicle manufacturer may place more value on accidents resulting in injury of a person over the destruction of physical property. We also made several assumptions about the input to the Bayesian network. We argue, however, as autonomous vehicles and UAVs become more common and data related to their operation accumulates, more accurate Bayesian networks will be possible.

The risks for this work were computed offline in order for the vehicles to make predictions about the risks they would likely face to aid in future planning. Our method, however, is computationally efficient allowing for rapid recalculation of the risks should the system choose to reconsider its options. Our future work will explore the use of this approach in situations where risks are rapidly changing and evolving dynamically. We believe that this work can improve safety by allowing an autonomous vehicle to one day avoid and react to risky situations.

Acknowledgment. This work was supported by Air Force Office of Sponsored Research contract FA9550-17-1-0017 and Navy STTR contract N68335-19-C-0106.

References

1. Allouch, A., Koubaa, A., Khalgui, M., Abbes, T.: Qualitative and quantitative risk analysis and safety assessment of unmanned aerial vehicles missions over the internet. IEEE Access **7**, 53392–53410 (2019)
2. Ancel, E., Capristan, F.M., Foster, J.V., Condotta, R.C.: Real-time risk assessment frame-work for unmanned aircraft system (UAS) traffic management (UTM). In: 17th AIAA Aviation Technology, Integration, and Operations Conference. p. 3273 (2017)

3. Barr, L.C., et al.: Preliminary risk assessment for small unmanned aircraft systems. In: 17th AIAA Aviation Technology, Integration, and Operations Conference, p. 3272 (2017)
4. Berger, J.O.: Prior information and subjective probability. In: Berger, J.O. (ed.) Statistical Decision Theory and Bayesian Analysis. SSS, pp. 74–117. Springer, New York (1985). https://doi.org/10.1007/978-1-4757-4286-2_3
5. Chinea, A., Parent, M.: Risk assessment algorithms based on recursive neural networks. In: 2007 International Joint Conference on Neural Networks, pp. 1434–1440. IEEE (2007)
6. Cornett, M.M., Saunders, A.: Financial Institutions Management: A Risk Management Approach. McGraw-Hill/Irwin, New York (2003)
7. Dalamagkidis, K., Valavanis, K.P., Piegl, L.A.: Evaluating the risk of unmanned aircraft ground impacts. In: 2008 16th Mediterranean Conference on Control and Automation, pp. 709–716. IEEE (2008)
8. Dávid, B., Láncz, G., Hunyady, G.: Highway situation analysis with scenario classification and neural network based risk estimation for autonomous vehicles. In: 2019 IEEE 17th World Symposium on Applied Machine Intelligence and Informatics (SAMI), pp. 375–380. IEEE (2019)
9. De Filippis, L., Guglieri, G., Quagliotti, F.: A minimum risk approach for path planning of UAVs. J. Intell. Robot. Syst. **61**(1–4), 203–219 (2011). https://doi.org/10.1007/s10846-010-9493-9
10. Geramifard, A., Redding, J., Roy, N., How, J.P.: UAV cooperative control with stochastic risk models. In: Proceedings of the 2011 American Control Conference, pp. 3393–3398. IEEE (2011)
11. Greytak, M., Hover, F.: Motion planning with an analytic risk cost for holonomic vehicles. In: Proceedings of the 48th IEEE Conference on Decision and Control (CDC) Held Jointly with 2009 28th Chinese Control Conference, pp. 5655–5660. IEEE (2009)
12. Kwag, S., Gupta, A., Dinh, N.: Probabilistic risk assessment based model validation method using Bayesian network. Reliab. Eng. Syst. Saf. **169**, 380–393 (2018)
13. Mokhtari, K., Wagner, A.R.: The pedestrian patterns dataset. In: AAAI Fall 2019 Symposium (2019)
14. Rudnick-Cohen, E., Herrmann, J.W., Azarm, S.: Risk-based path planning optimization methods for UAVs over inhabited areas. In: ASME 2015 International Design Engineering Technical Conferences and Computers and Information in Engineering Conference. American Society of Mechanical Engineers Digital Collection (2015)
15. Strickland, M., Fainekos, G., Amor, H.B.: Deep predictive models for collision risk assessment in autonomous driving. In: 2018 IEEE International Conference on Robotics and Automation (ICRA), pp. 1–8. IEEE (2018)
16. Waggoner, B.: Developing a risk assessment tool for unmanned aircraft system operations. Ph.D. thesis, University of Washington (2010)
17. Weibel, R., Hansman, R.J.: Safety considerations for operation of different classes of UAVs in the NAS. In: AIAA 4th Aviation Technology, Integration and Operations (ATIO) Forum, p. 6244 (2004)
18. Yu, M.Y., Vasudevan, R., Johnson-Roberson, M.: Occlusion-aware risk assessment for autonomous driving in urban environments. IEEE Robot. Autom. Lett. **4**(2), 2235–2241 (2019)

Sensing the Partner: Toward Effective Robot Tutoring in Motor Skill Learning

Giulia Belgiovine[1,2(✉)], Francesco Rea[1], Pablo Barros[3], Jacopo Zenzeri[1], and Alessandra Sciutti[3]

[1] Robotics, Brain and Cognitive Sciences Unit, Istituto Italiano di Tecnologia, Genova, Italy
{giulia.belgiovine,francesco.rea,jacopo.zenzeri}@iit.it
[2] Department of Informatics, Bioengineering, Robotics, and System Engineering, University of Genova, Genova, Italy
[3] Cognitive Architecture for Collaborative Technologies Unit, Istituto Italiano di Tecnologia, Genova, Italy
{pablo.barros,alessandra.sciutti}@iit.it

Abstract. Effective tutoring during motor learning requires to provide the appropriate physical assistance to the learners, but at the same time to assess and adapt to their state, to avoid frustration. With the aim of endowing robot tutors with these abilities, we designed an experiment in which participants had to acquire a new motor ability - balancing an unstable inverted pendulum - with the support of a robot providing fixed physical assistance. We analyzed participants' behavior and explicit evaluations to (i) identify the motor strategy associated with best performances in the task; (ii) assess whether natural facial expressions automatically extracted from cameras during task execution can inform about the participant's state. The results indicate that the variation and the mean of the wrist velocity are the most relevant in the effective balancing strategy, suggesting that a robot tutor could reorient the attention of the pupil on this parameter to facilitate the learning process. Moreover, facial expressions vary significantly during the task, especially in the dimension of Valence, which decreases with training. Interestingly, only when the robot had an anthropomorphic presence, Valence correlated with the degree of frustration experienced in the task. These findings highlight that both physical behavior and affective signals could be integrated by an autonomous robot to generate adaptive and individualized assistance, mindful both of the learning process and the partner's affective state.

Keywords: Social robot tutor · Motor skill learning · Multimodal assistance

1 Introduction

The acquisition of qualified motor skills is crucial in human daily and professional life. The role of the expert tutor in the skill transfer process is of critical

© Springer Nature Switzerland AG 2020
A. R. Wagner et al. (Eds.): ICSR 2020, LNAI 12483, pp. 296–307, 2020.
https://doi.org/10.1007/978-3-030-62056-1_25

importance and often relays on a series of implicit signals in which several communication channels are involved. Indeed, the interaction between the expert and the learner could be seen as a continuous flow of physical and affective, social signals, which lead the tutor to build a complex and complete model of the pupil's skills and state and to act accordingly. This is what happens, for example, when a physiotherapist trains a patient to recover certain motor skills. Beyond the selection of the appropriate force and physical assistance to support the learning, the expert physiotherapists are mindful of the state of their patients. They aim at keeping the patients committed to the task, but at the same time, they monitor the stress, anger, or other negative reactions that might be triggered by the lengthy and often challenging rehabilitation process. Given the widespread adoption of robotics in the context of rehabilitation [8], it would be desirable that also robot tutors would exhibit a similar ability of understanding and adapting to the learner's needs both from the physical and the affective perspectives. In the field of motor skill learning, many researchers have focused mostly on physical interactions between humans and robots to define the optimal training strategy [7,14]. On the other hand, several studies have demonstrated the potential of social robots to positively contribute to users' learning and experience in the field of skill acquisition [5,13]. Also, it has been shown that the presence of physical robots may have advantages in sensing and using affective data, by inducing higher degrees of emotional expressiveness [12]. These results suggest not only that embodied social robots may be a more effective medium for developing intelligent tutoring systems, but also that integrating affect-awareness in the tutoring model can lead to important benefits. We state that, for motor learning to be effective and to optimize the experience of the human naive, social robot tutors should integrate into their decision-making process physical and performance-related information with social and affective cues. However, works that focus on the relative roles of the physical and the social components in a single, unified setting are still scarce. The design of an optimal assistive architecture for social robots is an open challenge that implies facing different aspects. Indeed, before implementing the robot tutoring behavior, it is necessary to (1) understand the effect of the physical presence of the social robot as an expert trainer on the performance and experience of the subjects, and (2) identify the most informative cues that the robot has to exploit in order to decide the best way to assist the learner. In the current work, we present a novel experimental design in which naive participants had to learn the right strategy to accomplish a complex motor task, i.e. stabilizing an inverted pendulum by using a robotic manipulandum, the Wristbot [8,9]. We ran a between-subjects study: participants of both groups performed the training with physical assistance that facilitated the task in the same way. However, while for the *Control group* the assistance was attributed to the Wristbot, for the *iCub group* the humanoid robot iCub [10] pretended to provide the assistance. In doing so, it exhibited some social behaviors (as gazing and talking) and played the role of the expert tutor. In a previous study [4], we reported the effect of the presence of the humanoid social robot embodying the physical assistance on the performance and the self-reported experience of the naive learners, addressing the first of the above-mentioned issues. We observed that people who interacted with the humanoid robot iCub reported a more enjoyable training experience, without negative effects on attention and effort levels. Also, for both groups, the training was effective, with significant improvements in performance in the test phase. In light of the results obtained, in this study we want to address the second main question and deepen the understanding of the relative role of the different physical and social cues directly detectable by the robot and their potential use in the tutoring interaction. In particular, we addressed the following research questions: i) concerning the physical cues, we are interested in investigating which are the most significant features of participants' motion that differentiate a successful from an unsuccessful strategy. A robot tutor endowed with such information could guide the learner's attention to selectively focus on the most relevant motion properties to facilitate the training; ii) in the context of affective cues analysis, we tested if it was possible to infer the users' state starting from implicit affective signals (like Arousal and Valence) computed from the participants' facial expressions, by comparing them with the self-reported judgments obtained through questionnaires. Moreover, we evaluated whether and how the presence of the social humanoid tutor changed the communicative behavior of the naive subjects.

2   Methods

2.1   Participants

We recruited 32 participants (18 females, 14 males). Half of the subjects were tested in the *Control group* (9 females, 7 males, 26.1 ± 3.9 years of age), and the remaining were tested in the *iCub group* (9 females, 7 males, 27.1 ± 3.1 years of age). All participants gave their written informed consent before participating in the study. They were right-handed and did not have any known neurological or physical impairment. The research was approved by the local ethical committee of the Liguria Region (n. 222REG2015).

2.2   Experimental Setup

The setup comprised the inverted pendulum structure, a robotic manipulandum (the Wristbot), and, for the *iCub group*, also the humanoid robot iCub. The pendulum structure was composed of a table on which an inverted motorized pendulum was fixed. The pendulum was made of a carbon fiber 52 cm long, linked on its basis to a brushless motor. The pendulum had a maximal angular excursion of $\pm 40°$. During the task, participants sat on a fixed chair in front of the pendulum structure, holding with their right hand the Wristbot handle (Fig. 1, right panel) that worked as a haptic joystick to deliver forces directly to the pendulum and control its position. For this specific task, the Wristbot allowed only movements on the prono-supination plane of the human wrist, with a maximal angular displacement of $\pm 60°$. A high-resolution RGB camera was placed on the opposite side of the pendulum structure, recording the facial expressions of participants for subsequent offline analysis. On the same side, for the *iCub group*, the humanoid robot stood on a fixed platform facing the participant. A one-meter sided squared surface covered the pendulum structure and the hands of both the subject and the robot (Fig. 1, left panel).

Fig. 1. In the left panel, the robot iCub and the participant facing each other on the opposite sides of the pendulum structure while performing the task in the training phase. In the right panel, the robotic manipulandum Wristbot used by the subjects to control the pendulum.

2.3   Protocol

Three different phases were comprised in the protocol, for both groups: i. baseline (1 trial), ii. training (5 trials) and iii. test (3 trials). For the whole duration of each trial (2.5 minutes), participants were required to keep in balance the inverted pendulum for as long as possible, by controlling it acting on the angular orientation of the Wristbot handle. In between trials, they had 2.5 min of resting time to prevent fatigue from affecting performance. An additional real-time auditory feedback was provided whose magnitude increased with the angular distance between the pendulum and the vertical (i.e., the equilibrium). At the beginning of the experiment, it was explicitly explained to the subjects that during the training phase there would have been physical assistance facilitating the task coming from the Wristbot or iCub, depending on the experimental condition. For the *iCub group*, the humanoid robot iCub also showed some social behaviors, which however did not adapt to participants' performance, to emulate the condition in the Control group where no feedback was provided by the Wristbot. Before starting the baseline, iCub introduced itself and gave a brief introductory explanation about the task objective. At the beginning of the training trials, it looked at the participant's face and prepared itself to play, then it invited participants to get ready by saying an exhortation, such as "Let's start". When the game started, iCub followed the pendulum with its gaze and performed specific prono-supination movements of its forearm to mimic the control on the pendulum. At the end of the session, it invited the subject to take some minutes of rest before starting the next trial. It pretended to take a rest as well, looking around in the room in an exploratory way. During baseline and test sessions, iCub remained in its rest position and looked at the subjects performing the task, by alternating its gaze fixation point between the tool and the subject's face. The robot exhibited a happy, friendly face for the whole duration of the experiment, except during the training phase in which it looked at the pendulum with a focused expression. Except for the face-tracking behavior, the robot behavior was pre-programmed and not responsive to stimuli from participants.

Questionnaires. Participants of both groups were required to compile questionnaires at the end of the experiment: the NASA-TLX workload assessment [6] and a short version of the Intrinsic Motivation Inventory (IMI) [1], comprising 14 items from the sub-scales Competence, Effort/Importance, and Interest/Enjoyment. Also, participants of iCub group were asked to fill in some questionnaires regarding their perception of the robot, among which the scales *Anthropomorphism*, *Animacy*, *Likeability*, and *Perceived Intelligence* of the Godspeed questionnaire [3]. See [4] for a more detailed description.

2.4   The Task

The task was designed to meet an optimal challenge level, without resulting too easy and leading to a lack of interest, or too arduous and preventing learning. To achieve this goal, we implemented a virtual dynamics that determined the angular orientation of the pendulum starting from the angular orientation of the Wristbot. The dynamics included a non-linear spring, which virtually connected the Wristbot to the pendulum, and an unstable viscous force-field in which the pendulum moved. An initial pilot study was conducted on a similar sample population to choose the parameters of the virtual dynamics, the average trial duration, and the number of trials needed to learn the successful strategy. During the training phase, participants experienced facilitated dynamics thanks to assistance that reduced the instability of the viscous force-field of 30%. The assistance level was selected after piloting, and it wanted to emulate the help of an expert trainer that intervenes in the task by dampening the fall of the pendulum, making it easier to control. The training phase was thought not to fully counterbalance the instability, but rather to facilitate the task while maintaining it still challenging. The assistance was constant during the whole training phase and did not adapt to participants' performance. This choice met the need to keep the two experimental conditions as comparable as possible. In the test phase participants had to accomplish the same task they faced in the baseline (with no assistance); we could then assess whether they could generalize the skill learned during the training.

2.5   Data Analysis

Kinematic Data. Starting from the wrist position, i.e. the angular wrist displacement in the range $\pm 60°$, sampled 100 Hz and low-pass filtered at 8 Hz, the angular velocities and accelerations were computed through a sixth-order Savitzky-Golay low-pass filter (10 Hz cut-off frequency). For each trial, different features in time and frequency domain were computed starting from the wrist velocity and acceleration signals (Time Domain: 1. Mean Amplitude (MEAN), 2. Maximum Amplitude (MAX), 3. Standard Deviation (SD), 4. Root Mean Square (RMS), 5. Maximum Amplitude Variation (PP), 6. Skewness (SK), 7. Kurtosis (KRT), 8. Crest Factor (CF), 9. Number of Peaks (PKS); Frequency Domain: 10. Maximum of the Power Spectrum Density (MAX_POW), 11. Dominant Frequency (DF), 12. Total Power (POW), 13. Power Ratio (PR)). After having tested windows of different lengths (1, 1/3, 1/5, and 1/10 of the whole trial duration) to determine the optimal one, we choose the one which gave us the best model accuracy, i.e. 1/3. Subjects' performances were computed as a weighted sum of the pendulum angular positions. In this way, participants who held positions around the vertical for longer were rewarded with higher scores. Therefore, the performances were continuous values expressed in percentage. Since we aimed to test whether it was possible to infer subjects' performances starting from the kinematic features of the wrist and to identify the more informative features able to discriminate between a successful and an unsuccessful strategy, we discretized subjects' performances and turned into a classification problem. Specifically, performances above a certain threshold (computed as the mean performance of the whole population and equal to $\sim 61\%$) were labeled as *good performance* and performances below that threshold were labeled as *bad performance*. Starting from the assumption that the successful strategy did not change among the two groups conditions, and in order to exploit as much data as possible, we trained a machine learning classification model with all the observations from the 32 subjects, excluding the trials of the five training sessions, in which the task was facilitated by the assistance. Considering that each trial was divided into 3 windows of the same length, our final dataset consisted then in 384 observations and was balanced, with a ratio between good and bad performance equal to 0.50. Features were rescaled trough Z-score normalization such that they had the properties of a standard normal distribution with a mean of zero and a standard deviation of one. We implemented a Logistic Regression model with the Elastic-Net regularization method. We followed a 10-fold cross-validation procedure with a nested 5-fold cross-validation for optimal hyperparameter tuning. To enforce sparsity we set *l1_ratio* hyperparameter equal to 0.95. We tuned the regularization parameter C using logarithmic spaced values in the interval $[10^{-2}; 10^2]$. The sparsity regularization approach allowed us to have an insight into the most informative features of the model, by acting on the coefficients of the correlated predictor and shrinking towards zero the less relevant ones. The model was implemented using Scikit-Learn library [11].

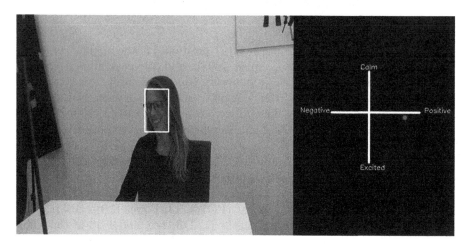

Fig. 2. Example of the *FaceChannel* network output, showing the Arousal and Valence values for each processed video frame.

Affective Data. To analyze subjects' facial expressions we used the *FaceChannel* neural network [2]. The *FaceChannel* is a lightweight convolutional neural network that allows for fast training and fine-tuning of facial expressions. It presents a compact architectural design with state-of-the-art facial expression recognition and which allows for fast inference times, endowing it with the capability to be deployed in the real-time analysis of the recorded videos. The *FaceChannel* was trained using a large-scale dataset with more than 1 million datapoints and it can describe a facial expression using a continuous representation of Arousal and Valence. We processed each video by localizing the face using the caffee-based face detector of OpenCV[1] in each of the video's frame. We then resized each detected face to a dimension of 96 × 96 pixels and fed it to the *FaceChannel*. The network outputs Arousal and Valence within the range of −1 and 1, representing calm/negative and excited/positive respectively for each face (Fig. 2). We considered in the analysis only the portions of videos in which the subjects performed the task (plus ∼3 seconds before and after the task execution) since in this phase we were mainly interested in studying the expressiveness of the naive subjects while learning the new motor skill, to potentially exploit in the future these implicit communicative signals and retrieve information about their status. The data were then smoothed with a median filter of 0.5 s. Due to technical failures, some video data were missing (2.08% for the *iCub group* and 5.56% for the *Control group*). Data were compared among different sessions or between different groups through ANOVAs. When data resulted not following the sphericity assumption, a Greenhouse-Geisser correction was applied. The data resulting from questionnaires were also analyzed to investigate whether some correlation exists between the perception of the robot iCub

---

[1] https://opencv.org/.

and the observed expressiveness. The details of each analysis are reported in the results.

3 Results

3.1 Classification Model

Since the strategy leading to a successful outcome was not known a priori, we tested whether it was possible to infer the skill level of the naive learners on the basis of some regularity of the wrist movement. The machine learning classification model trained with the wrist's velocity and acceleration features of all the subjects had a mean accuracy of 76.80±7.43%. The most recurrent best C was 3.16. In order to interpret the model's coefficients and assess the most relevant features, we trained the model fixing C to 3.16 and $l1\_ratio$ to 0.95. This model gave a test accuracy of 76.26 ± 7.20%.

All the model coefficients are shown in Fig. 3. The higher the amplitude of coefficients, the higher was the contribution of the corresponding features to the model classification. Specifically, as you can see from the figure, the features that resulted most informative for the model were the standard deviation and the average value of the wrist velocity, together with the mean and the power of the spectrum of the acceleration. This can be interpreted indeed as the need for subjects of making rapid and frequent wrist movement adjustments to keep the pendulum in balance. The robot tutor can be provided with such knowledge and improve the assistance by acting (directly or indirectly) on the movement strategy adopted by the learners, by intervening specifically on their kinematic pattern.

3.2 Communicative Behavior

To test whether subjects' expressiveness significantly changed among the different sessions (i.e., baseline, training, and test), and between the 2 groups, we performed a Mixed Model ANOVA with "sessions" as within factor and "groups" as between factor. For Valence, the results showed that there was a significant effect of sessions ($F(1.34, 28.1) = 8.54$, $p < .01$), while there was not significant effect of groups ($F(1, 21) = 0.724$, $p = .40$), nor of the interaction between the two ($F(1.34, 28.16) = 0.376$, $p = .67$). A post-hoc Tukey test revealed that the significant effect of sessions reflected a significant difference in Valence between baseline and training (p < .01) and between baseline and test (p < .01) (Fig. 4). These results indicated that while participants showed positive Valence when approaching the challenging task for the first time, in the following sessions they tended to be more neutral or even showed negative Valence. For Arousal, the ANOVA did not reveal any significant effect of group (F(1, 21) = 2.39, p = .14) or session ($F(2, 42) = 1.44$, $p = .25$). Only the interaction approached significance ($F(2,42) = 3.05$, $p = 0.058$), with a tendency for Arousal to decrease over trials towards negative values in the *Control group*. These results suggested that

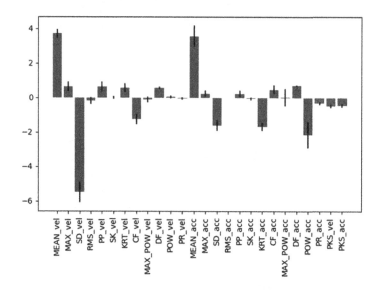

Fig. 3. Average coefficients of the classification model.

over the duration of the experiment participants modified their facial expression and it was possible to detect a significant modification in their Valence.

On average the pattern of such changes was very similar between the two groups, i.e., with and without the social humanoid tutor. It seemed therefore more driven by the task than by the presence of a partner. We should consider, however, that the task designed led subjects to stay constantly focused on the pendulum position, so their expressiveness when performing the task was limited. Moreover, we did not found any significant interaction between performance and facial expression, meaning that poor outcomes in task performance are not necessarily reflected in negative emotions and vice versa. At the same time, positive emotions are not necessarily predictive of successful performance. This suggested that the relations between users' state and performance are not trivial and above all, they cannot be generalized under predefined rules.

To test whether subjects' expressiveness was communicative of their self-reported states, we performed Pearson correlation between affective data and the scores of the post-questionnaires (namely IMI and NASA-TLX). The results showed that the mean Valence correlates significantly (and positively) with the Frustration score of NASA-TLX questionnaire ($r(13) = 0.53$, $p = .043$), but only for the *iCub group*. However, when performing Spearman correlation this tendency is no more significant ($r_s(13) = 0.44$, $p = .09$).

No significant correlations were found instead for the *Control group* between facial expressions and self-reported measures. Lastly, to further explore potential relations between the evaluation of the robot iCub and expressiveness, we performed correlation between post-questionnaires sub-scales regarding robot perception and Arousal and Valence values. A significant negative correlation

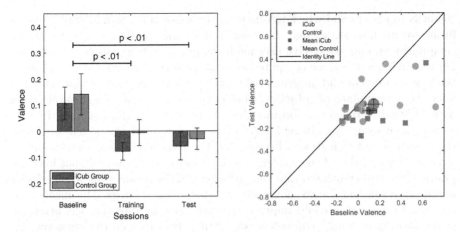

Fig. 4. Mean and Standard Error of Valence for each group in the different sessions (left panel). Valence in baseline versus Valence in test for each subject of the two groups (right panel).

between Valence and *Anthropomorphism* subscale of *Godspeed* questionnaire was found (*Pearson's* $r(14) = -0.54$, $p = .032$; *Spearman's* $rho(14) = -0.61$, $p = .012$), meaning that participants who ascribed higher anthropomorphic traits to iCub showed lower values of Valence.

4 Discussion

In this study, we started to address the issue of the need to integrate different communication signals in the assistive architecture of robot tutors. Indeed, we state that for motor learning to be effective and to optimize the experience of naive humans, robots should integrate into their decision-making process physical and performance-related information with social and affective cues. To this aim, we proposed a novel experimental design where it is possible to record and send both haptic signals, by using the robotic handle Wristbot, and social cues, through the humanoid robot iCub. We asked participants to learn a complex task, namely to balance an unstable inverted pendulum, in two different experimental conditions: one that involved training with the humanoid robot iCub, embodying the physical assistance, and one in which participants had to perform the same training but using the Wristbot alone. In a previous study [4], we have demonstrated that both groups effectively acquired the skill by leveraging the physical assistance as they significantly improved their stabilization performance even when the assistance was removed; moreover, learning in a context of interaction with a humanoid robot assistant led subjects to increased motivation and more enjoyable training experience, without negative effects on attention and perceived effort. In this study, we wanted to take a step further and investigate deeply the relative contribution of the different communicative channels to understand which information the robot tutor should exploit in the future to enrich its knowledge about user's skills and emotional state, to build a comprehensive and exhaustive user model to rely on when assisting. To answer our research questions, we computed and analyzed several kinematic features of the wrist movement and implemented a machine learning classification model to infer the performance of subjects of both groups. A Logistic Regression model with Elastic-Net regularization was able to predict the performance of the subjects with an accuracy of 76.26 ± 7.20%. The sparsity method allowed us to rank the most informative features of the model. These results allowed us to acquire a more solid knowledge of the strategy needed to succeed in the task, not known a priori. The results indicated that the variation and the mean of the wrist velocity are the most relevant features for an effective balancing strategy. This means that the social robot tutor could improve the assistance by directing the attention of the learners on these parameters, suggesting them to keep the wrist velocity high and stable, or, if necessary, delivering directly physical assistance. Then we wanted to test whether and how the affective state of the participants, described in terms of Arousal and Valence computed from their facial expressions, changed among sessions and group conditions. The Valence recorded in the baseline was significantly higher than the one detected by the software in the training and test sessions. We believe that the novelty component and the difficulty experienced in the first trial provoked the higher expressivity of the naive participants. No significant difference was found in the amount of Arousal and Valence between the 2 groups, probably because the task required high and continuous focus on the pendulum, limiting the variability of expressiveness. Of interest, when testing whether the expressive behavior of the subjects correlates with the self-reported measures of the post-questionnaires, we found a significant relationship between frustration score and Valence values only in the *iCub group*, while no significant correlations were found for the *Control group*. These results lead us to speculate that the presence of the embodied agent seemed to influence the communicative intent of their expressiveness as if to make their emotional states explicit and easily readable by the partner. The outcomes of the correlation between iCub perception and affective state showed that subjects who ascribed higher anthropomorphic traits to iCub presented lower values of Valence when involved in a complex and challenging task. As future development of this work, we are interested in reading both motor behavior and affective states in real-time to build an adaptive assistive architecture, which will allow us to get closer to robots that are not just assistive devices but rather assistive partners, able to guide humans in both short-term and long-term processes of skills learning and recovery and to adapt to their needs through a customized interaction.

Acknowledgments. This work has been supported by the project APRIL under the European Union's Horizon 2020 research and innovation programme, G.A. No 870142. A.S. is supported by a Starting Grant from the European Research Council (ERC) under the European Union's Horizon 2020 research and innovation programme. G.A. No 804388, wHiSPER. Thanks also to Sara De Nitto and Daniela Galiano for their help in data analysis.

References

1. Adams, N., Little, T.D., Ryan, R.M.: Self-determination theory. In: Wehmeyer, M.L., Shogren, K.A., Little, T.D., Lopez, S.J. (eds.) Development of Self-Determination Through the Life-Course, pp. 47–54. Springer, Dordrecht (2017). https://doi.org/10.1007/978-94-024-1042-6_4
2. Barros, P., Churamani, N., Sciutti, A.: The facechannel: a light-weight deep neural network for facial expression recognition. In: 2020 15th IEEE International Conference on Automatic Face and Gesture Recognition (FG 2020) (FG), pp. 449–453 (2020)
3. Bartneck, C., Kulić, D., Croft, E., Zoghbi, S.: Measurement instruments for the anthropomorphism, animacy, likeability, perceived intelligence, and perceived safety of robots. Int. J. Soc. Robot. 1(1), 71–81 (2009)
4. Belgiovine, G., Rea, F., Zenzeri, J., Sciutti, A.: A humanoid social agent embodying physical assistance enhances motor training experience. In: 2020 29th IEEE International Conference on Robot and Human Interactive Communication (RO-MAN), Naples, Italy, pp. 553–560. IEEE (2020). https://doi.org/10.1109/RO-MAN47096.2020.9223335
5. Fasola, J., Matarić, M.J.: Robot motivator: increasing user enjoyment and performance on a physical/cognitive task. In: 2010 IEEE 9th International Conference on Development and Learning, pp. 274–279. IEEE (2010)
6. Galante, F., Bracco, F., Chiorri, C., Pariota, L., Biggero, L., Bifulco, G.N.: Validity of mental workload measures in a driving simulation environment. J. Adv. Transp. 2018 (2018)
7. Galofaro, E., Morasso, P., Zenzeri, J.: Improving motor skill transfer during dyadic robot training through the modulation of the expert role. In: 2017 International Conference on Rehabilitation Robotics (ICORR), pp. 78–83. IEEE (2017)
8. Iandolo, R., et al.: Perspectives and challenges in robotic neurorehabilitation. Appl. Sci. 9(15), 3183 (2019)
9. Masia, L., Casadio, M., Sandini, G., Morasso, P.: Eye-hand coordination during dynamic visuomotor rotations. PloS One 4(9), e7004 (2009)
10. Metta, G., et al.: The iCub humanoid robot: an open-systems platform for research in cognitive development. Neural Netw. 23(8–9), 1125–1134 (2010)
11. Pedregosa, F., et al.: Scikit-learn: machine learning in Python. J. Mach. Learn. Res. 12, 2825–2830 (2011)
12. Spaulding, S., Gordon, G., Breazeal, C.: Affect-aware student models for robot tutors. In: Proceedings of the 2016 International Conference on Autonomous Agents & Multiagent Systems, pp. 864–872 (2016)
13. Vasalya, A., Ganesh, G., Kheddar, A.: More than just co-workers: presence of humanoid robot co-worker influences human performance. PLoS One 13(11), e0206698 (2018)
14. Zenzeri, J., De Santis, D., Morasso, P.: Strategy switching in the stabilization of unstable dynamics. PLoS One 9(6), e99087 (2014)

Social Sharing of Emotions with Robots and the Influence of a Robot's Nonverbal Behavior on Human Emotions

Reina Shimizu and Hiroyuki Umemuro$^{(\boxtimes)}$ 📷

Tokyo Institute of Technology, Tokyo 152-8552, Japan
umemuro.h.aa@m.titech.ac.jp
http://www.affectivelaboratory.org

Abstract. People share their emotional experiences with one another. This is called social sharing of emotions (SSE). SSE can affect one's own positive and negative emotions. As robots become increasingly capable of engaging in conversations with people, and because non-verbal expressions of robots have been found to affect human emotions, robots have potential as partners for SSE. The objective of this study was to investigate the effects of SSE with robots on the affective states of users. We investigated the emotional responses that occurred when subjects shared their emotional experiences with a robot. We also examined the relationship between nonverbal robot behavior and corresponding user emotions. In the experiment, subjects watched a video and then shared their emotional experiences about the content of the video with a humanoid robot. Factors were the valence of the emotional experience and the behavior of the humanoid. Subjects were asked to evaluate their emotional state before and after SSE, and we measured changes in their emotional state. The results showed that SSE with a robot evoked affective responses in subjects. In particular, SSE with a robot vs. without a robot resulted in an increase in positive affect. Additionally, if a subject perceived the robot to understand the subject's emotions, non-verbal robot expression had a more positive effect on the subject's affect when sharing positive experiences. These results may contribute to design guidelines for social robots that listen to people talk.

Keywords: Affect · Social sharing · Nonverbal communication

1 Introduction

In person-to-person communication, an individual may express his or her emotional experience to someone else. This is called social sharing of emotion (SSE) [1]. In SSE, individual emotions, as well as circumstances and background information regarding the events that led to the emotions, are verbalized and shared with others [2]. Through the sharing of emotional experiences, people can process their emotions and receive responses and feedback from others, leading to

© Springer Nature Switzerland AG 2020
A. R. Wagner et al. (Eds.): ICSR 2020, LNAI 12483, pp. 308–319, 2020.
https://doi.org/10.1007/978-3-030-62056-1_26

feelings of satisfaction [3]. Furthermore, SSE can affect the positive and negative emotions of the person who shares their experiences. Sharing positive experiences with others and getting feedback can lead to positive feelings [1]. Furthermore, sharing negative experiences and being supported by others can reduce stress [4].

Presently, robots are increasingly used to support and entertain humans in daily life. According to a report by the International Federation of Robotics (IFR), sales of "personal and home service robots" reached US $ 2.1 billion in 2017. Moreover, total sales had increased by 25% from the previous year, to about 8.5 million units [5]. Among robots that support and entertain humans, robots that communicate with humans are becoming increasingly popular.

One of the features of those robots is ability to produce nonverbal expressions, such as body movements. Many studies have examined nonverbal expressions in robots. For example, Becker-Asano and Ishiguro [6] demonstrated that robots could express emotions using facial displays and body movements. Compared with other devices such as smart speakers, robots are advantageous in that they can produce nonverbal expressions such as body movements. Communication robots can interact with people while expressing emotions via non-verbal expressions.

Robots that communicate with humans can influence human emotions via interactions with individuals. For example, pleasant emotions in children were significantly enhanced when robots expressed emotions via utterances and nonverbal behavior during interactions [7]. Communication robots that can express emotions verbally and nonverbally are also useful in that they can influence human emotions.

Given the above information, communication robots may have potential as listeners for SSE, thus replacing human listeners when they are unavailable. However, whether SSE with communication robots has the same effects on human emotions as SSE with human listeners is unclear. Considering that the reactions of listeners during SSE affect the emotions of the person sharing their experience, and that verbal and nonverbal expressions made by robots are able to affect human emotions, it is conceivable that the emotions of human users may be affected when sharing their emotional experiences with robots.

The purpose of this research was to investigate emotional responses that occurred when individuals shared their emotional experiences with a robot that responded to SSE. We also investigated the ways in which nonverbal robot behavior could affect user emotions. Finally, we confirmed whether differences in subjective evaluations of the communication robot affected the emotional responses of the user in SSE.

2   Hypotheses

As mentioned above, robots are capable of responding emotionally using verbal and non-verbal expressions. This has important implications for SSE, in which affective feedback from the listener regarding the emotional experience may affect the emotional state of the speaker.

When sharing positive emotional experiences, emotional responses of the listener, such as empathy, may strengthen positive emotions. Moreover, when sharing negative emotional experiences, the emotional response of the listener may reduce the speaker's negative emotions. Thus, we derived the following hypotheses:

H1-1: If a person shares a positive emotional experience with a robot and the robot reacts emotionally, the emotional state of the person will be more positive than when the person does not share.

H1-2: If a person shares a negative emotional experience with a robot and the robot reacts emotionally, the emotional state of the person will be more positive than when the person does not share.

In SSE, nonverbal expressions made by the listener can enhance the emotional expressions of the speaker [8]. In addition, nonverbal expressions made by robots can affect human emotional states [9,10]. Humans can understand robot emotions according to nonverbal expressions (e.g. [6]). Thus, we derived the following hypotheses:

H2-1: When a person shares a positive emotional experience with a robot, if the robot reacts emotionally via nonverbal expressions, the emotional state of the person will be more positive than when non-verbal expressions are not used.

H2-2: When a person shares a negative emotional experience with a robot, if the robot reacts emotionally via nonverbal expressions, the emotional state of the person will be more positive than when non-verbal expressions are not used.

Previous studies have suggested that a user's impression of a robot affects the extent to which the user is emotionally influenced by the robot. For example, Winkle and Bremner [11] stated that a robot's ability to convey an emotion to a person via nonverbal emotional expressions depends on whether the person perceives the robot as "embracing emotions and expressing emotions." It has also been shown that the extent to which a person feels that a robot is "human-like" can affect their emotional reaction when interacting with the robot [12]. Therefore, in the present study, we measured the impressions and recognition of emotions for a robot and used the resulting data to stratify the users.

3 Experimental Design

In the experiment, the subjects were asked to watch emotion-eliciting videos to induce emotional experiences. They were then asked to share their emotional experiences and feelings regarding the contents of the video to a communication robot. The subjects were asked to evaluate their emotional state before and after sharing, and we assessed changes in their emotional state. In addition, the subjects reported their impression of the robot and their response to the robot.

The experiment had a 2 × 3 mixed factorial design. The within-subjects factor was the type of emotional experience that was shared, with two levels of emotional experience: positive and negative. The order of the two emotional experiences was randomized across subjects.

The between-subjects factor was the listener ("sharing partner") condition with whom the participant shared their emotional experience. There were three listener levels. The listener was either a robot that reacted with nonverbal expressions (With NE), a robot that reacted without nonverbal expressions (Without NE), or absent (No robot). In the robot-with-NE condition, the robot had a conversation with the subject using both verbal and nonverbal expressions. In the robot-without-NE condition, the robot talked without moving and stood upright. In the no-robot condition, the subjects spoke to a video camera.

3.1   Stimuli

To ensure that the emotion-eliciting videos evoked the targeted emotion among subjects, we conducted a pilot test with the videos selected for use in the experiment.

As the first pool of candidate visual stimuli, we prepared seven movie clips with themes and motifs similar to those used to elicit emotions in previous studies [13,14]. Three out of seven of the movie clips were expected to elicit negative emotions, and four were expected to evoke positive emotions. The length of each movie clip was about 5 min.

Twelve subjects (10 men and 2 women) aged 21 to 28 years (M = 23.3, SD = 2.0) evaluated their emotional state before and after watching the movie clips using the Self-Assessment-Manikin (SAM) [15,16], which measures valence (1: negative; 9: positive) and arousal (1: calm; 9: excited). We then calculated the differences in valence scores before vs. after viewing each video. We selected two videos for which the averaged absolute values of the differences in valence score were large and the standard deviation was small. Finally, to elicit positive emotion, we selected a video of chicks overcoming the sea (averaged valence score before watching: 4.9, SD = 0.8, after watching 7.1, SD = 0.6). To elicit negative emotion, we selected a video of a bereaved stag and doe (averaged valence score before watching: 4.5, SD = 1.3, after watching 2.8, SD = 1.7).

3.2   Apparatus

The robot used for the experiment was the humanoid NAO robot [17]. This robot can move its arms and neck, and can speak. Using the Wizard of Oz method, the experimenter controlled the utterances and movements of the robot from a PC in a discrete location. Wide variations of utterances and movements are preset in a web application designed for the experimenter to operate the robot interactively in response to what subjects said in real time so that the conversation appeared to be natural.

The emotional expressions of the robot were programmed using verbal and nonverbal expressions. The verbal expressions of the robot were programmed to represent emotional feedback including empathy, listening, and support by referring to previous research [18].

Movements were adopted as non-verbal expressions made by the robot. Based on previous studies on nonverbal emotional expression in robots [19–21], we programmed 27 motions expressing positive and negative emotions. For example, when the robot expressed a positive emotion, it spread its arms and nodded its head, and when it expressed a negative emotion, it tended to look down.

Three university students participated in a pilot study in which we evaluated the programmed emotional expressions. The participants evaluated the valence of the emotion expressed by the robot on a nine-point scale (1: negative; 9: positive). Movements with an average valence score of six or higher were adopted and used in the experiment as expressions of positive emotion, and movements with an average valence value of four or less were adopted as expressions of negative emotion. As a result, eleven positive movements and twelve negative movements were adopted and used in the experiment.

3.3   Subjects and Procedure

Subjects were 61 Japanese university students (37 men and 24 women) aged 18–25 years (M = 21.8, SD = 1.8).

Subjects entered the experiment room and read and signed the informed consent form. Then, subjects in the with-NE and without-NE conditions talked with NAO about their hometown and what they were learning at the university for about 3 to 5 min. This initial interaction was intended to familiarize the subjects with talking with the robot. The experimenter was operating the robot remotely, and the subjects were not aware that the robot was operated manually. After the initial interaction, subjects completed a questionnaire about their impressions of the robot. This initial interaction and impression evaluation were not conducted for the subjects in the "no robot" condition.

Then, as an emotional control, the subjects watched a video of the Great Barrier Reef. This was used in previous research to induce neutral emotions [22]. After watching the video, the subjects were asked to evaluate their emotional state using the SAM.

The subjects then watched either the positive or negative emotion-eliciting video selected in the pilot study. The order of exposure of the two videos was randomized across subjects. After watching the video, the subjects were asked to evaluate their emotional state again using the SAM.

After evaluating their emotional status, the subjects were instructed to share their emotional experience. They shared the content of the video and described how they felt during viewing for about 3 min. As mentioned, there were three sharing conditions. In the with-NE and without-NE conditions, the subjects interacted with the NAO robot and shared their emotional experiences. The experimenter operated NAO so that it interactively responded to the utterances of the subject either with or without non-verbal expressions. In the no-robot condition, the subjects spoke to a video camera.

After sharing their emotional experience, the subjects completed a questionnaire to evaluate their emotional state and the experience of viewing the emotion-eliciting video. Subjects who interacted with the robot also completed a questionnaire in which they evaluated the responses of the robot.

The subject then repeated the series of activities with the other emotion-eliciting video. They evaluated their impression of the robot, watched the emotional control video, viewed the emotion-eliciting video, shared their emotional experience, and completed the questionnaire. Finally, the subjects completed a questionnaire that collected demographic information and the experimental session ended. The entire experiment took about 40–50 min to complete.

3.4 Measurement

To evaluate emotional state, the SAM [15,16] was used three times: after the emotional control video, after the emotion-eliciting video, and after the subject shared their emotional experience. Subjects evaluated their emotional state using two nine-point scales, one for valence score (1: negative; 9: positive) and one for arousal score (1: calm; 9: excited).

The subject's impression of NAO was measured on three dimensions: familiarity, likability, and human-likeness. Familiarity with the robot was measured with the five question items corresponding to the Familiarity subdimension of the Multi-Dimensional Robot Attitude Scale [23]. Subjects responded to each item using a five-point Likert scale (1: strongly disagree; 5: strongly agree). We used the average value of the five items as the familiarity score. Two subscales, Anthropomorphism and Likeability, of the Godspeed questionnaire [24] were adopted to measure likeability and human-likeness. Subjects responded to each of the five items in each subscale using a semantic differential scale. The average scores for the five items yielded the likeability score and human-likeness score.

Three statement items were used to evaluate the responses of the robot: "The robot reacted to what I talked about", "I think the robot understood my feelings", and "The robot responded using non-verbal expressions." The subjects evaluated the extent to which each of the three statements matched their feelings using a five-point Likert scale (1: strongly disagree; 5: strongly agree).

Finally, the subjects were asked to report demographic information regarding age and gender, and to state whether they had previous experience with NAO or the videos used in the experiment.

4   Results

In total, 122 samples were obtained from the two sessions, completed by the 61 subjects. Ten samples were excluded because the experimental session did not follow the appropriate experimental procedure. Specifically, six samples were inadequate because of problems with the experimental procedure and robot operation, two samples were excluded because the subject noticed that the experimenter was operating the robot, and two samples were excluded because the subject talked about topics other than their emotional experience for a long period of time. In addition, the subject's emotional state in one sample was not controlled properly, and the targeted emotional experiences were not effectively elicited in four samples, so these were excluded from analysis. Consequently, the final number of valid samples was 107.

To assess changes in the emotional experiences of the subjects, we calculated the differences in valence (range: -8 to $+8$) and arousal (range: -8 to $+8$) before and after the subject shared their emotional experience from the measured SAM values.

First, we analyzed differences in the change of emotional state after sharing emotional experiences either with or without the robot (H1). We used a series of two-factorial ANOVAs with the change in emotional state (valence and arousal) as the dependent variable and the sharing partner and order of sessions (block factor) as independent variables. In this analysis, the sharing partner factor had two levels: a with-robot level, in which the with-NE and without-NE conditions were combined, and a no-robot level. The positive and negative emotional experience conditions were analyzed separately.

We found a significant main effect of sharing partner on valence change in both the positive emotional experience condition ($F(1,1) = 189.7$, $p < 0.05$) and the negative emotional experience condition ($F(1,1) = 289.0$, $p < 0.05$). There were no significant interactions between the sharing partner factor and the session factor in either of the emotional experience conditions. Furthermore, there were no significant main effects of sharing partner on arousal change.

Figure 1 shows the averages and standard deviations of the valence change in the positive emotional experience and negative emotional experience sharing conditions. As shown in Fig. 1, subjects who shared positive emotional experiences with the robot reported a more positive emotional state after sharing their emotional experiences compared with subjects who shared with the video camera. Figure 1 also shows that subjects who shared a negative emotional experience with the robot reported a more positive emotional state compared with those who shared their emotional experience with the video camera. Therefore, H1-1 and H1-2 were supported.

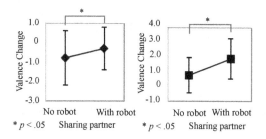

Fig. 1. The averages and standard deviations of the valence change by sharing partner conditions. (Left: sharing positive emotional experience level; Right: sharing negative emotional experience.)

To test H2-1 and H2-1, we used a series of two-factorial ANOVAs with the change in emotional state (valence and arousal) as the dependent variable, and sharing partner and session order (block factor) as independent variables. The sharing partner factor had two levels: with-NE and without-NE. The positive and negative emotional sharing conditions were analyzed separately.

We found a marginally significant interaction between the sharing partner and session order when sharing the positive emotional experience ($F(1,31) = 3.876$, $p < 0.1$). When sharing the negative emotional experience, there was a significant main effect of sharing partner on arousal change ($F(1,1) = 289.0$, $p < 0.05$). Figure 2 shows the averages and standard deviations of arousal change before and after sharing the negative emotional experience. When sharing negative emotional experiences with robots, the subjects who shared with robots that expressed emotion nonverbally reported feeling calmer compared with those who shared with robots without nonverbal expressions (Fig. 2).

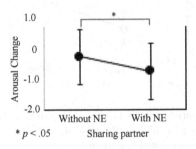

Fig. 2. The averages and standard deviations of the arousal change by sharing partner levels when subjects shared negative emotional experiences.

We found no significant main effect of sharing partner on valance change in either the positive or negative emotional condition. These results suggest that the robot's nonverbal expressions did not significantly influence the changes in valance before or after sharing either positive or negative emotional experiences.

We divided the subjects into groups according to their scores reflecting impressions of the NAO and its responses to their emotional expression. For each of the three impression scores (familiarity, likability, and human-likeness) and three reaction evaluation scores ("The robot reacted to what I talked about," "I think the robot understood my feelings," and "The robot responded using non-verbal expressions"), subjects were divided into "high" (higher than average scores) and "low" (lower than average scores) groups.

To examine the effects of robot nonverbal expression on changes in subject emotional state during SSE, we conducted a separate two-factorial ANOVA with the valence change as the dependent variable and sharing partner (With NE and Without NE) and session order (block factor) as the independent variables for the "high" and "low" groups. Positive emotion and negative emotions were analyzed separately.

When sharing positive emotion, the ANOVA resulted no significant main effect of sharing partner in subjects who were in the "high" score group for the "I think the robot understood my feelings" item. However, a paired comparison test revealed a significant difference in the average valence change between the with-NE and without-NE levels ($p = 0.048$). Figure 3 shows the averages and standard deviations of the valence change by sharing partner level. This result suggests that if a person perceives a robot to understand his/her feelings effectively, the robot's nonverbal expressions during sharing of positive emotional experiences can positively affect the subject's emotional state. Therefore, H2-1 is partially supported.

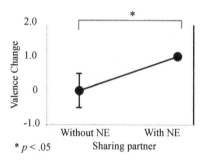

Fig. 3. The averages and standard deviations of the valence change by sharing partner conditions when subjects with high evaluation on "I think the robot understood my feelings." shared positive emotional experiences.

Second, when sharing negative emotional experiences, a two-factorial ANOVA for subjects in the "high" score group for the item "I think the robot understood my feelings" revealed no significant main effects of sharing partner. However, a paired comparison test revealed a marginally significant difference in the average valence change between the with-NE level and the without-NE level ($p = 0.088$).

Figure 4 shows the averages and standard deviations of the changes in valence before and after sharing emotional experiences. Figure 4 (right panel) suggests that when sharing negative emotional experiences, the robot reaction that included nonverbal expressions led to a greater reduction in the subjects' negative feelings compared with the robot with no nonverbal reactions.

Finally, we conducted an ANOVA with the valence change as the dependent variable and sharing partner and video order as independent variables for the participants with "high" familiarity scores. We found a marginally significant main effect of sharing partner ($F(1,1) = 55.072$, $p < 0.1$). As shown in Fig. 4 (left panel), when a person who felt high familiarity with the robot shared a negative emotional experience, that person's negative feelings were reduced when the robot reacted without nonverbal expressions compared with when the robot reacted with nonverbal behavior. Hence, H2-2 was rejected.

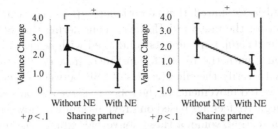

Fig. 4. The averages and standard deviations of the valence change by sharing partner conditions when subjects shared negative emotional experiences (Left: subjects with high impression of familiarity; Right: subjects with high evaluation on "I think the robot understood my feelings.")

5   Discussion and Conclusion

In this study, we investigated the effectiveness of a robot as a listener in an SSE context. We found that emotional reactions caused by SSE in humans can also be induced if a person shares emotions with a robot. We believe that this result will be useful for understanding the phenomenon of SSE. Zech and Rimé[25] reported that listener responses were beneficial for adjusting and restoring the emotions of the speaker. The present study showed that this effect is not only possible with human listeners, but also with robots that produce verbal and nonverbal responses.

In addition, this study revealed that when a person shares his/her emotional experience with a robot, the robot's responses affected the person's positive or negative emotions. Furthermore, a robot's nonverbal response had a more positive effect on a person's emotions when sharing positive emotional experiences.

We believe that these findings will promote the use of robots in various contexts. For example, robots can be introduced to single households or hospitals to listen to the thoughts and complaints of lonely individuals. Furthermore, robots could be used to listen to users explain what they enjoyed about their day for improving the well-being of the general population.

Our data may provide an effective guideline for the research and development of robots. Our findings demonstrate the importance of focusing not on only verbal expressions (e.g. what robots talk about), but also nonverbal expression (e.g. how they talk and move) when designing robots. In addition, this study highlights the importance of designing robots that are perceived as familiar and that can react to emotional expressions. These ideas should be integrated in future research and development of communication robots.

5.1   Limitations

In this study, the participants in the experiments were university students. However, social sharing of emotions occurs regardless of age, gender, and culture. Therefore, it is desirable to conduct further experiments with a variety of people to generalize the findings of this study.

The study subjects shared their emotional experiences with a robot that they had just met for the first time. However, considering that SSE often occurs between close friends [26], experiments conducted with subjects that have some previous experience with the robot, for instance, in a long-term study design, will be necessary to verify the effectiveness of SSE between humans and robots.

Finally, we selected movements of the robot to serve as nonverbal expressions of positive and negative feelings based on previous studies. However, as discussed in the Discussion section, some of these nonverbal expressions might have been somewhat exaggerated. It seems that both previous findings regarding emotional nonverbal expressions in robots and information regarding nonverbal behavior in humans, including professional listeners such as psychology counselors, could be helpful in planning future robot movements. Indeed, it can be difficult to interpret robot intentions and emotional states from ambiguous movements [27]. Careful studies on appropriate and effective nonverbal expressions should be conducted for better human-robot interaction design.

References

1. Rimé, B.: Emotion elicits the social sharing of emotion: theory and empirical review. Emot. Rev. 1(1), 60–85 (2009)
2. Hidalgo, C.T.R., Tan, E.S.H., Verlegh, P.W.J.: The social sharing of emotion (SSE) in online social networks: a case study in Live Journal. Comput. Hum. Behav. 52, 364–372 (2015)
3. Choi, M., Toma, C.L.: Social sharing through interpersonal media: patterns and effects on emotional well-being. Comput. Hum. Behav. 36, 530–541 (2014)
4. Lepore, S.J., Ragan, J.D., Jones, S.: Talking facilitates cognitive - emotional processes of adaptation to an acute stressor. J. Pers. Soc. Psychol. 78(3), 499 (2000)
5. International Federation of Robotics: World Robotics - Service Robot Report (2018). https://ifr.org/ifr-press-releases/news/service-robots-global-sales-value-up-39-percent. Accessed 28 July 2019
6. Becker-Asano, C., Ishigurom, H.: Evaluating facial displays of emotion for the android robot Geminoid F. In: Proceedings of 2011 IEEE Workshop on Affective Computational Intelligence (2011)
7. Tielman, M., Neerincx, M., Meyer, J.-J., Looije, R.: Adaptive emotional expression in robot-child interaction. In: Proceedings of the 2014 ACM/IEEE International Conference on Human-Robot Interaction (2014)
8. Lee, V., Wagner, H.: The effect of social presence on the facial and verbal expression of emotion and the interrelationships among emotional components. J. Nonverbal Behav. 26, 3–25 (2002)
9. Rosenthal-von Der Pütten, A.M., Krämer, N.C., Herrmann, J.: The effects of humanlike and robot-specific affective nonverbal behavior on perception, emotion, and behavior. Int. J. Soci. Robot. 10(5), 569–582 (2018)
10. Xu, J., Broekens, J., Hindriks, K., Neerincx, M.A.: Robot mood is contagious: effects of robot body language in the imitation game. In: Proceedings of the 2014 International Conference on Autonomous Agents and Multi-Agent Systems (2014)
11. Winkle, K., Bremner, P.: Investigating the real world impact of emotion portrayal through robot voice and motion. In: 2017 26th IEEE International Symposium on Robot and Human Interactive Communication (RO-MAN) (2017)

12. Hofree, G., Ruvolo, P., Bartlett, M.S., Winkielman, P.: Bridging the mechanical and the human mind: spontaneous mimicry of a physically present android. PLoS ONE **9**(7) (2014)
13. Bruder, M., Dosmukhambetova, D., Nerb, J., Manstead, A.S.R.: Emotional signals in nonverbal interaction: dyadic facilitation and convergence in expressions, appraisals, and feelings. Cogn. Emot. **26**(3), 480–502 (2012)
14. Gross, J.J., Levenson, R.W.: Emotion elicitation using films. Cogn. Emot. **9**(1), 87–108 (1995)
15. Nedeljkovic, U., Pincjer, I., Vladic, G.: The efficiency of message codification level in print advertisements: the case of food and drink products or service. J. Graph. Eng. Des. **2**(1), 16–23 (2011)
16. Bradley, M.M., Lang, P.J.: Measuring emotion: the self-assessment manikin and the semantic differential. J. Behav. Ther. Exp. Psychiatry **25**(1), 49–59 (1994)
17. Softbank Robotics NAO. https://www.softbankrobotics.com/jp/product/nao/. Accessed 28 July 2019
18. Egan, G.: The Skilled Helper: A Systematic Approach to Effective Helping, 3rd edn. Thomson Brooks/Cole Publishing (1986)
19. Beck, A., Canamero, L., Bard, K.A.: Towards an Affect Space for robots to display emotional body language. In: Proceedings of 19th International Symposium in Robot and Human Interactive Communication (2010)
20. Xu, J., Broekens, J., Hindriks, K., Neerincx, M.A.: The relative importance and interrelations between behavior parameters for robots mood expression. In: Proceedings of 2013 Humane Association Conference on Affective Computing and Intelligent Interaction (2013)
21. Xu, J., Broekens, J., Hindriks, K., Neerincx, M.A.: Bodily mood expression: recognize moods from functional behaviors of humanoid robots. In: Herrmann, G., Pearson, M.J., Lenz, A., Bremner, P., Spiers, A., Leonards, U. (eds.) ICSR 2013. LNCS (LNAI), vol. 8239, pp. 511–520. Springer, Cham (2013). https://doi.org/10.1007/978-3-319-02675-6_51
22. Lerner, J., Small, D., Loewenstein, G.: Heart strings and purse strings: effects of emotions on economic choices. PsycEXTRA Dataset (2004)
23. Ninomiya, T., Fujita, A., Suzuki, D., Umemuro, H.: Development of the multidimensional robot attitude scale: constructs of people's attitudes towards domestic robots. In: Tapus, A., André, E., Martin, J.C., Ferland, F., Ammi, M. (eds.) ICSR 2015. LNCS (LNAI), vol. 9388, pp. 482–491. Springer, Cham (2015). https://doi.org/10.1007/978-3-319-25554-5_48
24. Bartneck, C., Kulić, D., Croft, E., Zoghbi, S.: Measurement instruments for the anthropomorphism, animacy, likeability, perceived intelligence, and perceived safety of robots. Int. J. Soc. Robot. **1**(1), 71–81 (2008)
25. Zech, E., Rimé, B.: Is talking about an emotional experience helpful? Effects on emotional recovery and perceived benefits. Clin. Psychol. Psychother. **12**(2), 270–287 (2005)
26. Rimé, B., Finkenauer, C., Luminet, O., Zech, E., Philippot, P.: Social sharing of emotion: new evidence and new questions. Eur. Rev. Soc. Psychol. **9**(1), 145–189 (1998)
27. Zhang, Z., Niu, Y., Wu, S., Lin, S., Kong, L.: Analysis of influencing factors on humanoid robots' emotion expressions by body language. In: Huang, T., Lv, J., Sun, C., Tuzikov, A.V. (eds.) ISNN 2018. LNCS, vol. 10878, pp. 775–785. Springer, Cham (2018). https://doi.org/10.1007/978-3-319-92537-0_88

Using Human-Inspired Signals to Disambiguate Navigational Intentions

Justin Hart$^{(\boxtimes)}$ (ID), Reuth Mirsky (ID), Xuesu Xiao (ID), Stone Tejeda (ID),
Bonny Mahajan (ID), Jamin Goo (ID), Kathryn Baldauf (ID), Sydney Owen (ID),
and Peter Stone (ID)

Department of Computer Science, The University of Texas at Austin,
2317 Speedway, Stop D9500, Austin, TX 78712, USA
{hart,reuth,xiao,pstone}@cs.utexas.edu,
{stonetejeda,bm.bonny,jgoo,kathrynbaldauf,seowen}@utexas.edu

Abstract. People are proficient at communicating their intentions in order to avoid conflicts when navigating in narrow, crowded environments. Mobile robots, on the other hand, often lack both the ability to interpret human intentions and the ability to clearly communicate their own intentions to people sharing their space. This work addresses the second of these points, leveraging insights about how people implicitly communicate with each other through gaze to enable mobile robots to more clearly signal their navigational intention. We present a human study measuring the importance of gaze in coordinating people's navigation. This study is followed by the development of a virtual agent head which is added to a mobile robot platform. Comparing the performance of a robot with a virtual agent head against one with an LED turn signal demonstrates its ability to impact people's navigational choices, and that people more easily interpret the gaze cue than the LED turn signal.

Keywords: Social navigation · Gaze · Human-robot interaction

1 Introduction

When robots and humans navigate in a shared space, conflicts may arise when they choose conflicting trajectories. People are able to resolve these conflicts between each other by communicating, often passively through non-verbal cues such as gaze. When this communication breaks down, the parties involved may do a "Hallway Dance,"[1] wherein they walk into each other—sometimes several times while trying to deconflict each other's paths—rather than gracefully passing each other. This occurrence, however, is rare and socially-awkward.

Robot motion planners generally generate trajectories which can be difficult for people to interpret, and which communicate little about the robot's internal state passively [3]. This behavior can lead to situations similar to the hallway

---

[1] https://www.urbandictionary.com/define.php?term=Hallway%20dance

© Springer Nature Switzerland AG 2020
A. R. Wagner et al. (Eds.): ICSR 2020, LNAI 12483, pp. 320–331, 2020.
https://doi.org/10.1007/978-3-030-62056-1_27

dance, wherein people and robots clog the traffic arteries in confined spaces such as hallways or even in crowded, but open spaces such as atria. The Building-Wide Intelligence project [10] at UT Austin intends to create an ever-present fleet of general-purpose mobile service robots. With multiple robots continually navigating our Computer Science Department, we have often witnessed these robots interfering with people passing them in shared spaces. The most common issue occurs when a human and a robot should simply pass each other in a hallway, but instead stop in front of each other, thus inconveniencing the human and possibly causing the robot to choose a different path.

Previous work [6] on the Building-Wide Intelligence project sought to prevent these conflicts by incorporating LED turn signals onto the robot. It was found that the turn signals are not easily interpreted by study participants. In response, the work introduced the concept of a "passive demonstration." A passive demonstration is a training episode wherein the robot demonstrates the use of the turn signal in front of the user without explicitly telling the user that they are being instructed. In the previous study, the robot makes a turn using the turn signal within the field of view of the user. Thus, the user is taught how the signal works. However, limitations of this technique include that it requires (1) that the robot recognize when it is first interacting with a new user, allowing it to perform the demonstration, and (2) that an opportunity arises to perform such a demonstration before the signal must be used in practice.

This work designs and tests a more naturalistic signaling mechanism, in the form of gaze. We hypothesize that this gaze signal does not require a demonstration in order to be understood. Signaling mechanisms mimicking human communicative cues such as gaze may be far more easily understood by untrained users. When walking, a person will look in the direction that they intend to walk simply to assure that the path is safe and free of obstacles. Doing so enables others to observe their gaze, implicitly communicating the walker's intention. Observers can interpret the trajectory that the person performing the gaze is likely to follow, and coordinate their behavior.

This paper presents two studies exploring gaze as a cue to express navigational intentions. The first study is a human field experiment exploring the use of gaze when navigating a shared space. The second is a human-robot study contrasting a robot using an LED turn signal against a gaze cue rendered on a virtual agent head. These studies support the hypotheses that gaze is an important social cue used to coordinate human behavior when navigating shared spaces and that the interpretation of gaze is more clear to human observers than the LED signal when used to express the navigational intention of a mobile robot.

2   Related Work

The study of humans and robots navigating in a shared space [2,6,19,20] has been of recent interest to the robotics community. Many works focus on how can a robot recognize human signals and react to them [11]. This work focuses on the robot communicating its intentions so nearby pedestrians can change their course. Baraka and Veloso [2] used an LED configuration on their CoBot to indicate a number of robot states—including turning—focusing on the design of LED animations to address legibility. Their study shows that the use of these signals increases participants' willingness to aid the robot. Szafir et al. [20] equipped quad-rotor drones with LEDs mounted in a ring at the base, providing four different signal designs along this strip. They found that their LEDs improve participants' ability to quickly infer the intended motion of the drone. Shrestha et al. [19] performed a study similar to ours, in which a robot crosses a human's path, indicating its intended path with an arrow projected onto the floor.

In this work, we contrast a gaze cue made by a virtual agent head on our mobile robot with an LED turn signal. Whereas a person who is attending to an object or location may do so without the intention of communication; to an onlooker, communication nonetheless takes place. This communication is said to be "implicit," as the gaze is performed for perception. This role of gaze as an important communicative cue has been studied heavily in HRI [1], and it is a common hypothesis that gaze following is "hard-wired" into the brain [4].

Following this line of thought, Khambhaita et al. [9] propose a motion planner which coordinates head motion to the path a robot will take 4 s in the future. In a video survey in which their robot approaches a T-intersection in a hallway, they found that study participants are significantly more able to determine the intended path of the robot in terms of the left or right branch of the intersection when the robot uses the gaze cue as opposed to when it does not. Using different gaze cues, several works [13,14] performed studies in a virtual environment in which virtual agents used gaze signaling when crossing a study participant's path in a virtual corridor. Our work leverages a similar cue, but differs from theirs in that we use a physical robot in a human-robot study.

Recent work has studied the use of gaze as a cue for copilot systems in cars [7,8], with the aim of inferring the driver's intended trajectory. Gaze is also often fixated on objects being manipulated, which can be leveraged to improve learning from human demonstrations [18]. Though the use of instrumentation such as head-mounted gaze trackers or static gaze tracking cameras is limiting for mobile robots, the development of gaze trackers which do not require instrumenting the subject [17] may soon allow us to perform the inverse of the robot experiments presented here, with the robot reacting to human gaze.

3   Human Field Study

In a human ecological field study, we investigate the effect of violating expected human gaze patterns while navigating a shared space. In a 2 × 3 study, research confederates look in a direction that is congruent with the direction that they intend to walk; opposite to the direction in which they intend to walk; or look down at their cell phone providing no gaze cue. The opposite gaze condition violates the established expectation in which head pose (often a proxy for gaze) is predictive of trajectory [15,21]. The no gaze condition simply eliminates the gaze stimulus. Along the other axis of this study, we vary whether the interaction happens while the hallway is relatively crowded or relatively uncrowded.

We hypothesize that violating expected gaze cues, or simply not providing them, causes problems in interpreting the navigational intent of the confederate, and can lead to confusion or near-collisions. Specifically

Hypothesis 1. *Pedestrian gaze behavior that violates the expectation that it will be congruent with their trajectory leads to navigational conflicts.*

Hypothesis 2. *The number of navigational conflicts will increase when gaze behavior is absent.*

3.1   Experimental Setup

This study was performed in a hallway at UT Austin which becomes crowded during class changes (see Fig. 1). Two of the authors trained each other to proficiently look counter to the direction in which they walk. They acted as confederates who interacted with study participants. Both of the confederates who participated in this study are female. A third author acted as a passive observer (and recorder) of interactions between these confederates and other pedestrians.

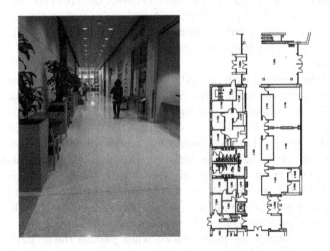

Fig. 1. The hallway in which the human field study took place.

In a 2 × 3 study, we control whether the interaction occurs in a "crowded" or "uncrowded" hallway, and whether the confederate looks in the direction in which they intend to go (their gaze is "congruent"), opposite to this direction (their gaze is "incongruent"), or focuses unto a mobile phone ("no gaze" is available). Here, "crowded" is defined as a state in which it is difficult for two people to pass each other in the hallway without coming within 2 m of each other. It can be observed that the busiest walkways at times form "lanes" in which pedestrians walk directly in lines when traversing these spaces. This study was not performed under these conditions, as walking directly toward another pedestrian would require additionally breaking these lanes.

The observer annotated all interactions in which the confederate and a pedestrian walked directly toward each other. If the confederate and the pedestrian encountered problems walking around each other or nearly collided, the interaction is annotated as a "conflict." Conflicts are further divided into "full," in which the two parties (gently) bumped into each other; "partial," in which the confederate and pedestrian brushed against each other; or "shift," in which the two parties shifted to the left or right to pass after coming into conflict.

3.2 Results

A total of 220 interactions were observed (130 female/90 male), with 112 in crowded conditions and 108 in uncrowded conditions. In the crowded condition, the confederate looked in the congruent direction in 31 interactions, in the incongruent direction in 41 interactions, and with no gaze in 40. In the uncrowded condition, the confederate looked in the congruent direction in 29 interactions, in the incongruent direction in 44 interactions, and with no gaze in 35. A one-way ANOVA found no significant main effect between the crowded and uncrowded conditions ($F_{1,218} = 1.49, p = 0.22$), or based on gaze direction assuming the confederate looked either left or right ($F_{1,143} = 1.28, p = 0.26$). The "no gaze" condition was excluded from this analysis, in order to isolate the effect of the direction of gaze.

Whether the confederate goes to the pedestrian's right or left during the interaction has a significant main effect ($F_{1,218} = 9.44, p = 0.002$), demonstrating a significant bias for walking to the right-hand side. Whether gaze is congruent, incongruent, or non-existent ($F_{2,217} = 5.02, p = 0.007$) also has a significant main effect. Post-hoc tests of between-groups differences using the Bonferroni criteria show significant mean differences between the congruent group and the other groups (congruent versus incongruent: $md = 0.221, p = 0.017$, congruent versus no gaze: $md = 0.191, p = 0.033$), but no significant mean difference between the incongruent and no gaze conditions ($md = -0.030, p = 1.00$). Perhaps the reason that there is no significant difference between the incongruent and no gaze conditions is that people use more caution when passing the no gaze pedestrian. Giving a the faulty signal of incongruent gaze, however, increases the number of conflicts. Our results support Hypothesis 1, that pedestrian gaze behavior violating the expectation of congruent gaze leads to conflicts; but not Hypothesis 2, that the absence of gaze will also lead to conflicts. A full breakdown of conflicts based on the congruent condition versus the incongruent gaze condition and the no-gaze condition can be found in Table 1.

Table 1. Human field study results

Conflict type	Congruent	Incongruent	No gaze
Partial	9 (15%)	11 (13%)	7 (9%)
Quick shift	6 (10%)	27 (32%)	13 (17%)
Full	0 (0%)	3 (4%)	1 (1%)
Any conflict	15 (25%)	41 (48%)	21 (28%)
No conflict	45 (75%)	44 (52%)	54 (72%)
Total	60 (100%)	85 (100%)	75 (100%)

4   Gaze as a Navigational CUE for HRI

We engineered a system in which a robot uses a virtual agent head to gaze in the direction that the robot will navigate toward. This study tests whether study participants understand this cue more readily than an LED turn signal. A study participant starts at one end of a hallway and the robot starts at the other end. The participant is instructed to traverse the hallway to the other end. The robot also autonomously traverses it. As a proxy for measuring understanding of the cue, the number of times that the human and robot come into conflict with each other is measured for two conditions: one in which the robot uses a turn signal to indicate the side of the hallway that it intends to pass the person on, and one in which it uses a gaze cue to make this indication.

This study tests the following hypothesis:

Hypothesis 3. *The gaze signal results in fewer conflicts than the LED signal.*

The robot's navigation system models the problem of traversing the hallway as one in which the hallway is divided into three lanes, similar to traffic lanes on a roadway, as illustrated in Fig. 3. If the human and the robot come within 1 m of each other as they cross each other's path, they are considered to be in conflict with each other. This distance is based on the 1 m safety buffer engineered into the robot's navigational software, which also causes the robot to stop.

GAZE CUE. To display gaze cues on the BWIBot we developed a 3D-rendered version of the Maki 3D-printable robot head.[2] The decision to use this head is motivated by the ability to both render it as a virtual agent and, in future work, to 3D print and assemble a head that can be contrasted against the virtual agent. The virtual version of the head was developed by converting the 3D-printable STL files into Wavefront .obj files and importing them into the Unity game engine.[3] To control the head and its gestures, custom software was developed using ROSBridgeLib.[4] The head is displayed on a 21.5 inch monitor mounted

---

[2] https://www.hello-robo.com/maki.
[3] https://unity.com/.
[4] https://github.com/MathiasCiarlo/ROSBridgeLib.

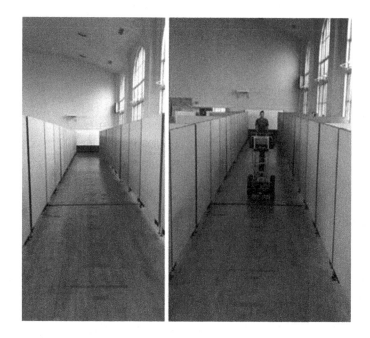

Fig. 2. The hallway constructed for this experiment (left) and a snapshot of the experiment during execution (right).

to the front of the robot. When signaling, the robot turns its head 16.5° and remains in this pose. The eyes are not animated to move independently of the head. The head turn takes 1.5 s. These timings and angles were hand-tuned and pilot tested on members of the laboratory. The gaze signal can be seen in Fig. 4 (left).

LED CUE. The LED cue is a re-implementation of the LED turn signals from [6]. Strips of LEDs 0.475 m long with 14 LEDs line the 8020 extrusion on the chassis of the front of the BWIBot. They are controlled using an Arduino Uno microcontroller, and blink twice per second with 0.25 s on and 0.25 s off each time they blink. In the condition that the LEDs are used, the monitor is removed from the robot. The LED signals can be seen in Fig. 4 (right).

4.1   Experimental Setup

To test the effectiveness of gaze in coordinating navigation through a shared space, we conducted a human-robot interaction study in a hallway test environment. The environment is built from cubicle furniture and is 17.5 m long by 1.85 m wide (see Fig. 2).

After obtaining informed consent and, optionally, media release, participants are guided to one end of the hallway, where the robot is already set up at the

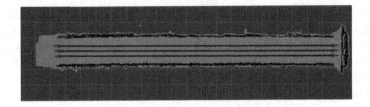

Fig. 3. The robot's map of the hallway divided into lanes.

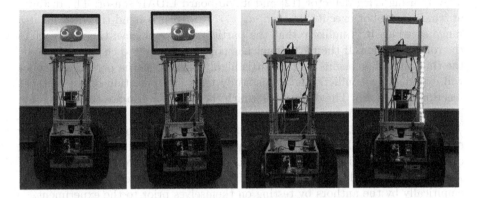

Fig. 4. Gaze and LED Signals. From left to right: Neutral gaze; Gaze signaling to the left lane; Neutral LED; LED blinking to signal a move to the left lane.

opposite end. The participant is instructed to navigate to the opposing end of the hallway. Both the participant and the robot start in the "middle lane," as per the three traffic lanes in the robot's navigational model. When the participant starts walking down the hallway, the robot is also started. This study follows an inter-participant design, in which each participant sees exactly one of the two cues—gaze or LED—and in which each participant traverses the hallway with the robot exactly once. The reason for the choice of this design is the strong evidence from [6] that there is a teaching effect as it relates to navigational cues, at least as far as LED turn signals are concerned. Given the presence of such an effect, we could expect all subsequent trials after the first to result in the participant and robot passing each other without conflict (in the LED case).

After completing the task of walking down the hallway, each participant responds to a brief post-interaction survey.[5] The survey comprises 44 questions, consisting of 8-point Likert and cognitive-differences scales, and one free-response question. Five demographic questions on the survey ask whether people in the country where the participant grew up drive or walk on the left or right-hand side of the road and about their familiarity with robots.

---

[5] The questions from the survey are available online. https://drive.google.com/drive/folders/1qVj-gU1aFwY6Eq2a_l9ZdesfmQ_QQOC8?usp=sharing. The first question "Condition" was filled in before participants responded.

To ensure that the study results are reflective of the robot's motion signaling behavior, rather than the participants' motion out of the robot's path, the study is tuned to give the participant enough time to get out of the robot's way if the decision is based on reacting to its gaze or LED cue, but not enough time if the decision is based on watching the robot's motion. Three distances are used to tune the robot's behavior: d_{signal}, $d_{execute}$ and $d_{conflict}$. The distance d_{signal} (4 m) is the distance at which the robot signals its intention to change lanes, which is based on the distance at which the robot can accurately detect a person in the hallway using a leg detector [12] and its on-board LiDAR sensor. The distance at which the robot execute its turn, $d_{execute}$ (2.75 m), is hand-tuned to be at a range at which it is unlikely that the participant would have time to react to the robot's motion. If the participant has not already started changing lanes by the time the robot begins its turn, it is highly likely that the person and robot will experience a conflict. Thus, this study tests interpretation of the cue, not reaction to the turn. The distance at which the robot determines that its motion is in conflict with that of the study participant is $d_{conflict}$, which is set to 1 m. This design is based on the safety buffer used when the robot is autonomously operating in our building. For this study, the robot is tuned to move at a speed of $0.75(m/s)$, which is the speed the robot moves when deployed in our building. Average human walking speed is about $1.4(m/s)$. The range $d_{execute}$ was tuned empirically by the authors by testing on themselves prior to the experiment.

The robot also always moves into the "left" lane. In North America, pedestrians typically walk to the right-hand side of shared spaces. This behavior is demonstrated to be significant in our human field study as well, in Sect. 3.2. Fernandez et al. also conducted a pilot study [6] to test how often humans and the robot come into conflict when the robot goes to the left lane, rather than into the right lane, with no cue, such as an LED or gaze cue. That study showed that the pedestrians and the robot came into conflict 100% of the time under this regime.

Important to note in the interpretation of the results from this experiment is that **we expect the study participant and the robot to come into conflict** 100% **of the time** unless the robot's cue—the LED or gaze cue—are correctly interpreted. This is because:

- The robot moving into the left-hand lane is expected to result in conflict 100% of the time.
- The robot's motion occurs too late for the study participant to base their lane choice on it.

4.2 Results

We recruited 38 participants (26 male/12 female), ranging in age from 18 to 33 years. The data from 11 participants is excluded from our analysis due to software failure or failure in participation of the experimental protocol.

The remaining pool of participants includes 11 participants in the LED condition and 16 in the gaze condition. Table 2 shows the results from the robot signaling experiment in these two conditions. A pre-test for homogeneity of variances confirms the validity of a one-way ANOVA for analysis of the collected data. A one-way ANOVA shows a significant difference between the two means ($F_{1,26} = 10.185$, $p = 0.004$). None of the post-interaction survey responses revealed significant results.[6] These results support the hypothesis that the robot's gaze can be more readily interpreted in order to deconflict its trajectory from that of another pedestrian.

Table 2. Experimental results

	LED	Gaze
No conflict	0 (0%)	8 (50%)
Conflict	11 (100%)	8 (50%)
Total	11	16

5   Discussion and Future Work

The goal of these studies is to evaluate whether a gaze cue outperforms an LED turn signal in coordinating the behavior of people and robots when navigating a shared space. Previous work found that LED turn signals are not readily interpreted by people when interacting with the BWIBot, but that a brief, passive demonstration of the signal is sufficient to disambiguate its meaning [6]. This study investigates whether gaze can be used without such a demonstration.

The human field study presented in Sect. 3 validates the use of gaze as a communicative cue that can impact pedestrians' choices for coordinating trajectories. Gaze appears to be an even more salient cue than a person's actual trajectory in this interaction.

In the human-robot study that follows, we compared the performance of an LED turn signal against a gaze cue presented on a custom virtual agent head. In this condition, the robot turns its head and "looks" in the direction of the lane that it intends to take when passing the study participant. Our results demonstrate that the gaze cue significantly outperforms the LED signal in preventing the human and robot from choosing conflicting trajectories. We interpret this result to mean that people naturally understand this cue, transferring their knowledge of interactions with other people onto their interaction with the robot.

Although it significantly outperforms the LED signal, the gaze cue does not perform perfectly in the context of this study. There are several potential contributing factors. The first is that, while the entire head rotates, the eyes do not verge upon any point in front of the robot. Furthermore, interpreting gaze direction on a virtual agent head may be difficult due to the so-called "Mona Lisa

---

[6] Example interactions can be seen in the companion video to this paper, posted at https://youtu.be/rQziUQro9BU.

Effect" [16].[7] Thus, the embodiment of the head may play into the performance of displayed cues. Follow-up studies could both tune the behavior of the head, and contrast its performance against a 3D printed version of the same head. The decision to use a virtual agent version of the Maki head is driven by our ability to contrast results in future experiments (upon construction of the hardware) between virtual agents and robotic heads.

Lastly, one might claim that if the LED condition resulted in 100% conflict, then simply changing the semantics of the LED turn signal would improve performance to be 100% "no conflict." This, however, is not the case. Fernandez [5] compared an LED acting as a "turn signal" against one acting as an "instruction;" indicating the lane that the study participant should go into. Fernandez's findings indicate no significant difference between these two conditions ("turn signal - conflict" $m = 0.9$, "instruction - conflict" $m = 0.8$, $p > 0.5$).

The overall results of this study are encouraging. Many current-generation service robots avoid what may be perceived by their designers as overly-humanoid features. The findings in this work indicate that human-like facial features and expressions may be more readily interpreted by people interacting with these devices than non-humanlike cues.

Acknowledgments. This work has taken place in the Learning Agents Research Group (LARG) at UT Austin. LARG research is supported in part by NSF (CPS-1739964, IIS-1724157, NRI-1925082), ONR (N00014-18-2243), FLI (RFP2-000), ARO (W911NF-19-2-0333), DARPA, Lockheed Martin, GM, and Bosch. Peter Stone serves as the Executive Director of Sony AI America and receives financial compensation for this work. The terms of this arrangement have been reviewed and approved by the University of Texas at Austin in accordance with its policy on objectivity in research. Studies in this work were approved under University of Texas at Austin IRB study numbers 2015-06-0058 and 2019-03-0139.

References

1. Admoni, H., Scassellati, B.: Social eye gaze in human-robot interaction: a review. J. Hum.-Robot Interact. **6**(1), 25–63 (2017)
2. Baraka, K., Veloso, M.M.: Mobile service robot state revealing through expressive lights: formalism, design, and evaluation. Int. J. Soc. Robot. **10**(1), 65–92 (2018)
3. Dragan, A., Lee, K., Srinivasa, S.: Legibility and predictability of robot motion. In: Proceedings of the 8th ACM/IEEE International Conference on Human-Robot Interaction (HRI), March 2013
4. Emery, N.J.: The eyes have it: the neuroethology, function and evolution of social gaze. Neurosci. Biobehav. Rev. **24**(6), 581–604 (2000)
5. Fernandez, R.: Light-based nonverbal signaling with passive demonstrations for mobile service robots. Master's thesis, The University of Texas at Austin, Austin, Texas, USA (2018)

---

[7] Difficulties have been observed in the interpretation of the gaze direction of virtual agents. This effect is so named because it looks as though the Mona Lisa painting by Leonardo da Vinci is always looking at the observer.

6. Fernandez, R., John, N., Kirmani, S., Hart, J., Sinapov, J., Stone, P.: Passive demonstrations of light-based robot signals for improved human interpretability. In: Proceedings of the 27th IEEE International Symposium on Robot and Human Interactive Communication (RO-MAN), pp. 234–239. IEEE, August 2018

7. Jiang, Y.S., Warnell, G., Munera, E., Stone, P.: A study of human-robot copilot systems for en-route destination changing. In: Proceedings of the 27th IEEE International Conference on Robot and Human Interactive Communication (RO-MAN), Nanjing, China, August 2018

8. Jiang, Y.S., Warnell, G., Stone, P.: Inferring user intention using gaze in vehicles. In: Proceedings of the 20th ACM International Conference on Multimodal Interaction (ICMI), Boulder, Colorado, October 2018

9. Khambhaita, H., Rios-Martinez, J., Alami, R.: Head-body motion coordination for human aware robot navigation. In: Proceedings of the 9th International Workshop on Human-Friendly Robotics (HFR 2016), p. 8p (2016)

10. Khandelwal, P., et al.: BWIBots: a platform for bridging the gap between AI and human-robot interaction research. Int. J. Robot. Res. **36**(5–7), 635–659 (2017)

11. Kruse, T., Pandey, A.K., Alami, R., Kirsch, A.: Human-aware robot navigation: a survey. Robot. Auton. Syst. **61**(12), 1726–1743 (2013)

12. Leigh, A., Pineau, J., Olmedo, N., Zhang, H.: Person tracking and following with 2D laser scanners. In: Proceedings of the 2015 IEEE International Conference on Robotics and Automation (ICRA), pp. 726–733. IEEE (2015)

13. Lynch, S.D., Pettré, J., Bruneau, J., Kulpa, R., Crétual, A., Olivier, A.H.: Effect of virtual human gaze behaviour during an orthogonal collision avoidance walking task. In: Proceedings of the 2018 IEEE Conference on Virtual Reality and 3D User Interfaces (VR), pp. 136–142. IEEE, March 2018

14. Nummenmaa, L., Hyönä, J., Hietanen, J.K.: I'll walk this way: eyes reveal the direction of locomotion and make passersby look and go the other way. Psychol. Sci. **20**(12), 1454–1458 (2009)

15. Patla, A.E., Adkin, A., Ballard, T.: Online steering: coordination and control of body center of mass, head and body reorientation. Exp. Brain Res. **129**(4), 629–634 (1999)

16. Ruhland, K., et al.: A review of eye gaze in virtual agents, social robotics and HCI: behaviour generation, user interaction and perception. Comput. Graph. Forum **34**(6), 299–326 (2015)

17. Saran, A., Majumdar, S., Short, E.S., Thomaz, A., Niekum, S.: Human gaze following for human-robot interaction. In: Proceedings of the 2018 IEEE/RSJ International Conference on Intelligent Robots and Systems (IROS), pp. 8615–8621. IEEE, November 2018

18. Saran, A., Short, E.S., Thomaz, A., Niekum, S.: Understanding teacher gaze patterns for robot learning. arXiv preprint arXiv:1907.07202, July 2019

19. Shrestha, M.C., Onishi, T., Kobayashi, A., Kamezaki, M., Sugano, S.: Communicating directional intent in robot navigation using projection indicators. In: Proceedings of the 27th IEEE International Symposium on Robot and Human Interactive Communication (RO-MAN), pp. 746–751, August 2018

20. Szafir, D., Mutlu, B., Fong, T.: Communicating directionality in flying robots. In: Proceedings of the 10th Annual ACM/IEEE International Conference on Human-Robot Interaction (HRI), HRI 2015, pp. 19–26. ACM, New York (2015)

21. Unhelkar, V.V., Pérez-D'Arpino, C., Stirling, L., Shah, J.A.: Human-robot co-navigation using anticipatory indicators of human walking motion. In: Proceedings of the 2015 IEEE International Conference on Robotics and Automation (ICRA), pp. 6183–6190. IEEE (2015)

Towards the Design of a Robot for Supporting Children's Attention During Long Distance Learning

Dante Arroyo[1(⊠)], Yijie Guo[1], Mingyue Yu[2], Mohammad Shidujaman[3], and Rodrigo Fernandes[1]

[1] University of Tsukuba, Tsukuba, Japan
`dante.arroyo.pe@gmail.com`
[2] Politecnico di Milano, Milan, Italy
`mingyue.yu@mail.polimi.it`
[3] Tsinghua University, Beijing, China
`shantothu@gmail.com`

Abstract. Educational robots have proven to be effective at supporting students and teachers in classrooms. However, when schools are not available and education must continue online, the lack of a common physical space for learners and instructors might make it difficult for these robots to be used. Remote education through an online environment is possible but not without some limitations. In fact, when using the home as an educational setting, the lack of physical interaction between children, teachers, and their peers can lead to problems, such as loss of motivation or decrease in attention level. In this paper, we describe the design process of a robot to support children during long distance learning. We conducted a survey to student, parents and teacher to understand the problematic and gather information about the possible use of a robot for support students. We then propose the concept of a companion robot for supporting children during online classes. The robot's main function is to increase children's awareness and attention by monitoring the teacher's voice and redirecting the student's attention through expressive behavior. Future work will focus on the implementation of the robot and consider additional features.

Keywords: Educational robot · Child-robot interaction · Social robotics · Robot design · Long distance learning · Online learning

1 Introduction

Long distance learning offers a wide range of opportunities for students as a viable alternative to traditional on-campus study. Thanks to the rapid advancement of technology, online education is nowadays more accessible to students than in the last years, and while the reasons to choose online education vary, it is mainly a preferred option when is not possible for students and teachers

A. R. Wagner et al. (Eds.): ICSR 2020, LNAI 12483, pp. 332–343, 2020.
https://doi.org/10.1007/978-3-030-62056-1_28

to share the same physical environment. In the events of the COVID-19 pandemic, schools around the world had to close to prevent the spread of the disease [17]. Even though it is possible for institutions to continue providing education through long distance learning, challenges arise to educators and students who must be able to adapt to virtual environments and its limitations.

While online tools are able to bring education to the students' home, it is important to highlight that school and home are different learning environments [8]. At home, children might easily get distracted and require constant supervision and monitoring of adults. Educators may use different types of pedagogical strategies or tools to build and effective learning environment; however, due to the limitations of an online setting, monitoring all students is a difficult task. In this regard, keeping students motivated and engaged during the online class remains as one of the main challenges in this scenario.

In the last decades, robots have been used to support education in different ways. Robotic platforms have been created as pedagogical tools for science, technology, engineering, and math (STEM) education, along with robots that are able to deliver or support the learning experience through social interaction. The positive impact of social robots in classrooms has been extensively documented [3]. However, with a lack of a physical space where these robots can interact with students and teachers, the impact of these robotic platforms might be limited. In this regard, if social robots are to be used in this type of situations, such as COVID-19, it might be necessary to adapt current robotic technologies or propose new approaches that can support young students at home. Morever, it is anticipated that in the aftermath of the current pandemic, there might be an increased interest on producing robots that can be used in future similar events [6].

In this paper, we present the design process of a companion robot for children to improve their attention during online classes. We made initial sketches of the robot appearance and conducted a survey to students, parents and teachers to better understand the problematic and their preferences and opinions regarding a robot to support students. Along with the related work and the results of the survey, we defined the design guidelines for this type of robot. Finally, we present the concept of the robot by showing the initial 3D model along with the description of its hardware and software.

2   Related Work

In this section, we present related works which have the potential to support long distance learning. These are classified according to the following domains: robots for remote education, robot appearance in educational robots, peripheral robots and social cues to redirect attention.

2.1   Robots for Remote Education

In remote education, robots are mainly used as communication mediums to connect students and teachers to their classrooms when they are unable to attend.

These teleoperated platforms are advantageous as they have the potential to not only transmit audio and video, but also to allow a remote operator, or in this case, the student's social presence through the robot movement. Applications are diverse, such as supporting English tutoring [10], and to improve access to K-12 education [4]. While appearance of this robots has been explored [7], most of these robotic platforms include a screen on top for displaying the remote controller's face [19].

2.2   Robot Appearance in Educational Robots

Although many educational robots are designed to interact with children, they are usually not expected to know the complex engineering details of the system. However, the physical form of robots can help children develop ideas about their nature and function. Usually, children may tend to judge the overall characteristics of the robot only by evaluating its external characteristics or appearance [13]. Therefore, in order to ensure a successful child-robot interaction, the robot should be given some form so that children can intuitively understand the robot's behavior [5]. However, improvements are also required in the technical design of robots while focusing on the robot appearance design. For students to have a pleasurable user experience with robots, attempts must be dedicated to boosting the speech understanding capabilities of robots and re-producing human-like behaviour (in light of the uncanny valley) [12]. Several design considerations may need to be contemplated to represent the appearance of the robot, such as human body proportion, robot body shape and structure, natural body movement and representation [15].

2.3   Peripheral Robots

Peripheral robots are mainly non-humanoid robots used to support human-human interactions. In contrast to other robot companion, peripheral robots are located in the surroundings of humans. Therefore, their presence don't become a source of distraction and are able to support interactions through non-verbal gestures. Recent works have explored the use of this type of robots for supporting conversation by promoting non-aggressive conversations [9], maintaining social relationships through opening encounter [2] and by increase participants engagement and performance in group activities through different types of movements [16].

2.4   Social Cues to Redirect Attention

In human-human interaction, social cues are informative stimulus about basic emotions and social attention [1]. In robots, humanlike gaze cues have been used for handover events [11]. Social cues are also used as joint attention mechanisms to redirect human's attention and to allow robot navigation [14,18].

3 Methodology

3.1 Initial Sketches

At the beginning of the design process, we decided to explore the appearance of the robot. For this purpose, we created a group of sketches to evaluate the most appropriate morphology. We explored 3 types of morphologies for the robot which are shown in Fig. 1. We initially assumed that an animal-like appearance would be more welcomed, as children could associate then with pets or small animals. Thus, the first robot was designed as a sloth-type. This robot was designed as a companion which would attach on the screen and help kids via hand-instructions. Also, we explored human-like and plant-like appearance. The human-like robot was designed as a companion which would sit in the same side with kids and help them pay attention to the course through its head body language. The plant-like robot would bloom as an attention-level notification to kids during the online course. For each of the types, we provided 2 types of states in the sketches: focus, and relax. These sketches were introduced in the survey.

3.2 Survey Design

A survey was conducted with the main purpose of understanding the problematic of long distance learning and to gather opinion of the initial sketches. We performed an online survey to elementary school students, teachers and their parents to better understand the context on online learning and to collect information to support the design guidelines of our robot.

Participants. The online survey was conducted to participants located in Shanghai. China. A total of 84 junior school students participated in the online survey. Students' age ranged from 8 to 12 (M = 10.6, SD = 1.25). 23 parents and 36 teachers of junior school students also participated in the survey. All students were taking online classes at the time of completion of the survey.

Measures. To answer the questions, participants had to select a value from a 5-point Liker scale and in some choose one answer from multiple options. Initially, we asked children how lonely they felt during online classes ("Never" (−2) to "Always" (2)). Additionally, we asked if they thought online classes were more interesting that online classes ("Strongly Disagree" (−2) to "Strongly Agree" (2)), and how often they felt motivated during online classes ("Never" (−2) to "Always" (2)). Regarding distracting behavior, we asked students how often they thought they got distracted during online classes. To have a wider perspective, we also asked teachers and parents to evaluate how often the students had a distracting behavior. ("Never" (−2) to "Always" (2)).

We asked the 3 groups of participants if they thought some type of companion or partner would help students during online classes. ("Strongly Disagree" (−2) to "Strongly Agree" (2)). Moreover, we asked which type of companion they

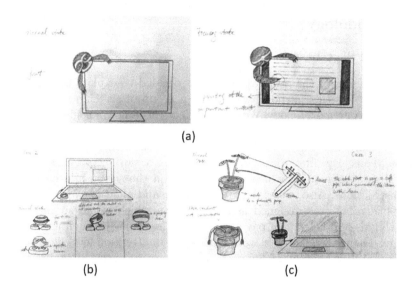

Fig. 1. Sketch for (a) Animal-like robot companion (b) Human-like robot companion (c) Plant-like robot companion

would prefer ("Physical Robot" or "Virtual Robot") and where this companion should be located ("With the students" or "With the teacher"). We additionally asked participants about the most suitable appearance for the companion to support students ("Animal-like", "Human-like", "Plant-like", or "Other"). After students answered these questions, we showed them the 3 sketches we prepared and asked them to choose which one they would prefer as a robot companion during online classes.

3.3   Results and Analysis of Survey

Feeling of Isolation, Motivation and Interest in Online Classes. Regarding the feeling of isolation, when considering all students together, a neutral mean was resulted (M = 0.175, SD = 1.3). However, better differences could be seen when dividing the students in 3 age groups as shown in Fig. 2.(a). The first group was from 8 to 9 years old (N = 18, M = 0.78, SD = 1.11), the second from 10 to 11 years old (N = 37, M = −0.27, SD = 1.12) and the third from 12 years old (N = 29, M = −0.48, SD = 1.48). Post hoc Analysis using Wilcoxon pair comparison showed significant differences between the youngest group and the others ($p < 0.05$). Results suggest that younger children tend to report higher loneliness levels. As for their motivation during online classes, and if they considered online classes more interesting than physical classes, neutral means were observed (Interest: M = 0, SD = 1.4), (Motivation: M = −0.1, SD = 1.29).

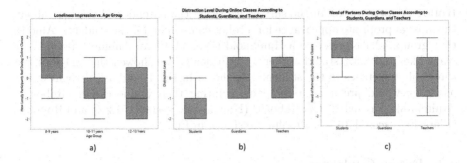

Fig. 2. Results of the survey regarding participants: (a) Feeling of Loneliness in students, (b) Distraction Level in students, (c) Need of a companion

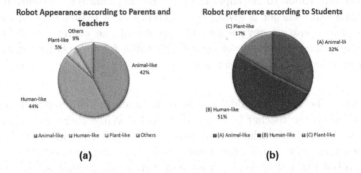

Fig. 3. Results of the survey regarding the robot: (a) Robot Appearance according to Parents and Teachers, (b) Robot preference (sketches) according to Student

Distracting Behavior in Students. Regarding the distraction level, the comparison between students ($N = 84$, $M = -1.46$, $SD = 0.63$), parents ($N = 23$, $M = 0.21$, $SD = 1.16$) and teachers assessment ($N = 36$, $M = 0.36$, $SD = 0.18$) is shown in Fig. 2.(b). Results show a consensus between teachers and guardians that students get moderately distracted during online classes. Students might not see it that way, but the need, as seems by teachers, should be prioritized.

Robot Type and Location. Regarding having a companion during online classes, results are shown in Fig. 2.(c). ANOVA analysis showed significant differences according to group ($F = 17.6$, $P < .0001$). Students seem to strongly desire a companion ($M = 0.98$, $SD = 0.12$) while parents and teachers seemed to be more neutral/rejective of this idea (Guardians: $M = -0.2$, $SD = 0.23$, and Teachers: $M = -.0.08$, $SD = 0.18$ respectively). Regarding the robot type, there was an overwhelming preference among all groups for a physical robot, stated as 70.2%. As for the location of the robot for the online classes, 74.5% of all participants mentioned that the best location was with the student.

Robot Appearance. In the survey, we asked the parents and teachers about the most appropriate appearance for a robot companion for the students. Among that group, 42.4% preferred a Humanoid type, 44.0% an Animal type, 5.1% a plant like, and 8.5% stated "other". Additionally, we showed the image of the three robot sketches to the students, as shown in Fig. 1, and asked them which one they would prefer as a companion during their online classes. Robot A (Animal-like) scored 32.1%, Robot B (Human-Like) scored 51.2%, and Robot C (Plant-like) scored 16.7%. Results are shown in Fig. 3.

3.4 Design Guidelines

The goal of our robot is to support students during online classes at their homes. We expect our robot to be capable of redirecting children's attention to the screen, where the teacher is giving the instructions or explanation of the class. Based on the literature review and the results of the survey, we defined the following guidelines for the development of a robot for supporting the attention of children in long distance learning.

Attention. The robot should be able to redirect the children's attention to the screen when the teacher is giving the classes. While there are many verbal and non-verbal ways to achieve this, we chose to do it through body language, as it is a subtle way to transmit information in human-human interaction. In fact, the robot can not become a source of distraction as that would affect the development of the online class.

Peripheral. The robot is not intended to have direct interaction with the child; however, it is important for the robot to be positioned in the surroundings of the screen where the online class will be displayed, near the child. From this location, the robot should be able to monitor the teacher's tone of voice without problem, and to be noticed by the child when moving a part of its body to redirect attention.

Companion. Results from the survey showed that students feel somehow lonely during online classes. While supporting attention is the primary goal of the robot, we also have to consider a friendly appearance that would make children feel comfortable. Regarding the perception of body language, it might be more effective if coming from a human-like robot.

4 Robot Development

4.1 3D Modeling

We initially proposed 3 hand sketches of the possible design of the robot, which were later evaluated in the online survey. As stated in the results, most of the

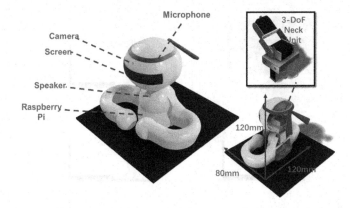

Fig. 4. 3D model of the robot. A 3-DoF mechanism is located inside the robot to provide free movement of the head.

students showed a preference towards the second option, which was the human-like robot. Considering the established design guidelines, we proceeded with a more robust design. In this regard, a 3D model was done based on the second option of the survey, which is presented in Fig. 4. When developing the 3D modeling, we considered the functions and the possible movement of the body parts as the robot communicates its intention through body language. For the first prototype we defined a size 120 mm × 80 mm × 120 mm (W × D × H) but we will explore other sizes by 3D printing different versions of the robot.

Robot Head. As the main element of the robot's body language, we intentionally exaggerated the size of the head with respect to the body, to make it easier for the children to see when it moved. When making the 3D design, we also considered including a mechanism that could provide enough DoF to the head to provide an expressive movement.

Robot Hands. In an initial stage we considered the hands movement as part of the body language to redirect attention; however, we decided to keep the head movement only, as the movement of the hands could generate too much distraction. Even though the hands didn't move, we kept them in the design for two reasons: 1) To give the impression that the robot is calm, through the body posture of the two hands on the sides, and 2) To be used as a robust support for the head, especially when moving.

4.2 Robot Attention States

The robot will redirect children's attention to the screen through body language in the form of head movements, which are presented in Fig. 5. The movement of the head presents 3 types of attention states: *Relax*, *Attentive* and *Focus*

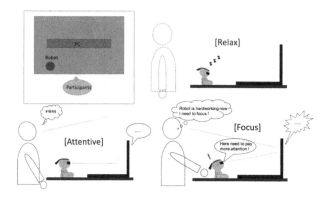

Fig. 5. Robot expressions.

state. The robot will be placed on the desk, next to the computer and facing the computer screen. During this time, the robot is in a *Relax* state looking to random directions. When the teacher starts an explanation, the robot will stop the *Relax* state and change to the *Attentive* state, in which it will redirect the child's attention to the screen through a slight head movement. During this time, the robot will monitor the tone of voice to detect when the teacher makes an emphasis of the content. When this is detected, the robot will change to the *Focus* state and move its head in the roll orientation as it were curious. Through this expression, the robot will indicate that it is listening to the teacher carefully, encouraging the children to pay more attention at this moment.

5   Technical Details

5.1   Hardware

For the main controller of the robot, we will use a small built-in CPU board (Raspberry Pi Zero W). Additionally, we will install a microphone (Model MAX4466) to analyze the teacher's tone of voice, which is a critical part of the system. As for the robot's expressive movement to generate attention, the head will have 3 servomotors (Model SG-92) to produce pitch, roll and yaw rotations. We are planning to include a small screen (3.5 in) in the head to display possible gaze patterns along with a camera (Raspberry PI Camera Module V2) to monitor the child reaction, which could be used as feedback to the system. Finally, we are considering using small speakers speakers to produce non-linguistic utterances when the robot's movement to generate attention is not effective.

5.2   Software

In this initial stage, we plan to base the behavior of the system on the teacher's tone of voice as the only input to reduce its complexity. A state machine will be used to describe the functionality of the system as shown in Fig. 6.

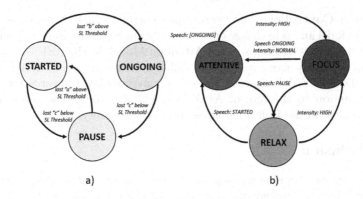

Fig. 6. State Machines for (a) Speech Analysis and (b) Attention Model

Monitoring the Teacher's Tone of Voice. While there are many elements of the speech that can be analyzed, such as rhythm, intonation, speed, volume and pitch, we only focus in the volume of the teacher's voice. In this regard, this module will be constantly monitoring the teacher's tone of voice (TOV). To manage the monitored TOV, we will implement a circular buffer of detection timespans with the teacher's TOV levels. We will define a circular buffer of size n and a timespan duration of i seconds.

Teacher's Speech Analysis. This module is in charge of analyzing the Teacher's speech by using the information from the TOV Array along with a finite state machine that represents a status of the speech. We define a Speech Level (SL) to separate noise from verbal speech. The STARTED state is set when there is a transition from a pause to an explanation which is identified by the system when the last "a" timespans of the TOV Array exceed the SL Threshold. The state machine changes to ONGOING when the teacher continues his speech. This is identified by the system when the last "b" timespans exceed the SL Threshold. The PAUSE state is defined when the teacher's speech comes to an end, which is identified when the last "c" timespans are below the SL Threshold.

Attention Model. The Attention Model monitors the Speech State and the TOV Array. It is implemented as a finite state machine. We define a High-Pitch Level *(HL)* Threshold, which is above the Speech Level *(SL)* Threshold in order to differentiate the speech that the teacher intends to highlight. If the speech transitions from *STARTED* to *ONGOING*, the Attention State is set from RELAX to ATTENTIVE. If the tone of voice level exceeds the *HP* threshold, the Attention State is changed to FOCUS for a period of 3 s. If the speech transitions to *PAUSE*, the Attention State changes to RELAX. Otherwise, if the speech changes to *ONGOING*, the system state changes to ATTENTIVE.

Expression Controller. The expression Controller works by monitoring the Attention Model and is in charge of running the appropriate expressive behaviors based on the state transitions in the Attention Model. In the RELAX state, the robot will randomly move its head to different locations for a short period of time. In the ATTENTIVE state, the robot moves its head towards the screen, paying attention to the screen. As for the FOCUS state. The robot slightly rotates its head in the Roll orientation to convey curiosity.

6   Conclusion

With the goal of designing a robot to support children online classes, we made a literature review, created initial sketches of the robot and made a survey to students, teachers and parents. According to the results, it was preferred to have a robot along with students which could help them to maintain attention during classes. Moreover, we defined the design parameters for this type of robot: Attention, Peripheral and Companion. Based on these parameters, we made a 3D model of the robot along with the considerations for achieving an expressive movement that can redirect children's attention to the screen. A description of the Hardware and Software that we are planning to implement was also described. Further work will explore other possible behaviors and features of the robot that could be included later in the implementation.

References

1. Admoni, H., Scassellati, B.: Social eye gaze in human-robot interaction: a review. J. Hum.-Robot Interact. **6**(1), 25 (2017). https://doi.org/10.5898/JHRI.6.1.Admoni
2. Anderson-Bashan, L., et al.: The greeting machine: an abstract robotic object for opening encounters. In: 2018 27th IEEE International Symposium on Robot and Human Interactive Communication (RO-MAN), pp. 595–602. IEEE, August 2018. https://doi.org/10.1109/ROMAN.2018.8525516
3. Belpaeme, T., Kennedy, J., Ramachandran, A., Scassellati, B., Tanaka, F.: Social robots for education: a review. Sci. Robot. **3**(21) (2018). https://doi.org/10.1126/scirobotics.aat5954
4. Cha, E., Chen, S., Mataric, M.J.: Designing telepresence robots for K-12 education. In: 2017 26th IEEE International Symposium on Robot and Human Interactive Communication (RO-MAN), vol. 2017-Janua, pp. 683–688. IEEE, August 2017. https://doi.org/10.1109/ROMAN.2017.8172377
5. Davison, D.P., Wijnen, F.M., van der Meij, J., Reidsma, D., Evers, V.: Designing a social robot to support children's inquiry learning: a contextual analysis of children working together at school. Int. J. Soc. Robot. **12**(4), 883–907 (2019). https://doi.org/10.1007/s12369-019-00555-6
6. Feil-Seifer, D., Haring, K.S., Rossi, S., Wagner, A.R., Williams, T.: Where to next? The impact of covid-19 on human-robot interaction research. J. Hum.-Robot Interact. **10**(1) (2020). https://doi.org/10.1145/3405450
7. Fitter, N.T., Chowdhury, Y., Cha, E., Takayama, L., Matari, M.J.: Evaluating the effects of personalized appearance on telepresence robots for education. In: ACM/IEEE International Conference on Human-Robot Interaction, pp. 109–110 (2018). https://doi.org/10.1145/3173386.3177030

8. Hedegaard, M.: The significance of demands and motives across practices in children's learning and development: an analysis of learning in home and school. Learn. Cult. Soc. Interact. **3**(3), 188–194 (2014). https://doi.org/10.1016/j.lcsi.2014.02.008

9. Hoffman, G., Zuckerman, O., Hirschberger, G., Luria, M., Shani Sherman, T.: Design and evaluation of a peripheral robotic conversation companion. In: Proceedings of the Tenth Annual ACM/IEEE International Conference on Human-Robot Interaction - HRI 2015, pp. 3–10. ACM Press, New York (2015). https://doi.org/10.1145/2696454.2696495

10. Kwon, O.H., Koo, S.Y., Kim, Y.G., Kwon, D.S.: Telepresence robot system for English tutoring. In: Proceedings of IEEE Workshop on Advanced Robotics and its Social Impacts, ARSO, pp. 152–155 (2010). https://doi.org/10.1109/ARSO.2010.5679999

11. Moon, A., et al.: Meet me where i'm gazing. In: Proceedings of the 2014 ACM/IEEE International Conference on Human-Robot Interaction - HRI 2014, pp. 334–341. ACM Press, New York (2014). https://doi.org/10.1145/2559636.2559656

12. Mubin, O., Stevens, C.J., Shahid, S., Mahmud, A.A., Dong, J.J.: A review of the applicability of robots in education. Technol. Educ. Learn. **1**(1) (2013). https://doi.org/10.2316/journal.209.2013.1.209-0015

13. Pandey, A.K., Gelin, R.: Humanoid Robots in Education: A Short Review, pp. 1–16. Springer, Dordrecht (2016)

14. Pereira, A., Oertel, C., Fermoselle, L., Mendelson, J., Gustafson, J.: Responsive joint attention in human-robot interaction. In: 2019 IEEE/RSJ International Conference on Intelligent Robots and Systems (IROS), pp. 1080–1087. IEEE, November 2019. https://doi.org/10.1109/IROS40897.2019.8968130

15. Shidujaman, M., Zhang, S., Elder, R., Mi, H.: "RoboQuin": a mannequin robot with natural humanoid movements. In: 2018 27th IEEE International Symposium on Robot and Human Interactive Communication (RO-MAN), pp. 1051–1056 (2018)

16. Tennent, H., Shen, S., Jung, M.: Micbot: a peripheral robotic object to shape conversational dynamics and team performance. In: 2019 14th ACM/IEEE International Conference on Human-Robot Interaction (HRI), vol. 2019-March, pp. 133–142. IEEE, March 2019. https://doi.org/10.1109/HRI.2019.8673013

17. Viner, R.M., et al.: School closure and management practices during coronavirus outbreaks including COVID-19: a rapid systematic review. Lancet Child Adolesc. Health **4**(5), 397–404 (2020). https://doi.org/10.1016/S2352-4642(20)30095-X

18. Warta, S.F., Newton, O.B., Song, J., Best, A., Fiore, S.M.: Effects of social cues on social signals in human-robot interaction during a hallway navigation task. In: Proceedings of the Human Factors and Ergonomics Society Annual Meeting, vol. 62, no. 1, pp. 1128–1132, September 2018. https://doi.org/10.1177/1541931218621258

19. Zhang, M., Duan, P., Zhang, Z., Esche, S.: Development of telepresence teaching robots with social capabilities. In: Engineering Education, vol. 5. American Society of Mechanical Engineers, November 2018. https://doi.org/10.1115/IMECE2018-86686

Engagement and Mind Perception Within Human-Robot Interaction: A Comparison Between Elderly and Young Adults

Melissa Kont and Maryam Alimardani[✉]

Department of Cognitive Science and AI, Tilburg University, Tilburg, The Netherlands
m.alimardani@uvt.nl

Abstract. People can feel engaged and attribute human-like traits when interacting with a social robot and reveal this unconsciously to observers. Studies have suggested that behavioral signals such as facial expressions, posture, speech and laughter play an important role in identifying engagement in Human-Robot Interaction (HRI), however the effect of these factors in different age groups, as well as their relationship with mind attribution towards robots remains unclear. This study examined 24 elderly people and 24 university students on facial expressions, laughter and speech during an interaction with a NAO-robot. In addition, self-reported engagement level and mind perception scores were collected after the interaction and analyzed. Results showed that elderly had a significantly lower report of engagement with the robot, which was positively correlated with their perception of mind capacity in the robot. Furthermore, for both elderly and students, there was a negative trend between self-reported mind perception and observed behavioral engagement with the robot. Findings of this study could be employed in the design and evaluation of future HRI scenarios.

Keywords: Human-Robot Interaction (HRI) · Social robots · Engagement · Behavior analysis · Mind perception · Elderly · Young adults

1 Introduction

The use of social robots has prevailed in the past decade in multiple domains including elderly care. Various studies have shown the benefits of robot-assisted activity for elderly people both in terms of improved feelings [1] as well as physical health [2]. However, compared to young adults, elderly people hold different cognitive perception of anthropomorphized objects such as social robots and behave differently when they interact with them [3]. Therefore, in order to design socially effective robot interaction for elderly, it is necessary to investigate the impact of age difference on user's perception and behavior toward the robot.

Past research has investigated elderly's perception and attitude toward robots predominantly through self-reported questionnaires. For instance, it has been shown that compared to young adults, elderly attribute a higher mind perception to humanoid robots and apply human social models of interaction with them [4]. Higher mind perception

© Springer Nature Switzerland AG 2020
A. R. Wagner et al. (Eds.): ICSR 2020, LNAI 12483, pp. 344–356, 2020.
https://doi.org/10.1007/978-3-030-62056-1_29

has been shown to correlate positively with attitude toward the robot [4] and intention to use it [5]. Also, elderly express improved attitude toward robots and their usefulness after longer-term interaction [6] or even after a single interaction [7]. Furthermore, socio-demographic factors and experience with technology have been shown to impact the attitude and perception of elderly toward robots [8].

Although based on above surveys, a general consensus exist that elderly can have a positive attitude toward robots and benefit from activities with them, it is important to objectively measure the quality of interaction and engagement with social robots by monitoring elderly behavioral responses that naturally arises during HRI [9]. Questionnaire-based surveys are prone to biases and errors [9] and can only capture the general impression of the user before and after the interaction, whereas behavioral cues can provide a more accurate temporal analysis of user engagement during the robot-assisted activity. Additionally, the two can reinforce each other whereby established relationships between behavioral and subjective responses can be employed to predict a user's perception and attitude toward the robot based on his/her real-time behavior and engagement with the robot.

Past studies have shown that engagement in human-robot interaction can be quantified via analysis of behavioral and social signals [9–12]. Rich et al. [10] extracted engagement between a human and a humanoid robot by manually annotating gaze, spoken utterance and gestures from video segments. Sanghvi et al. [11] presented an initial computational model for automatic evaluation of human postures and body movement to measure engagement. In their study, videos of children playing chess with the iCat robot was annotated by three coders and were labeled as "engaged", "not engaged" or "cannot say" in a child-robot interaction. Anzalone et al. [9] proposed a set of static and dynamic non-verbal metrics such as head pose, body posture, joint attention and synchrony for analysis of face-to-face interactions with robots. Alternatively, Leite et al. [12] developed a real-time disengagement classifier using visual, auditory and contextual features in a child-robot interaction.

Additionally, a few studies have focused on the effect of demographic factors on engagement during HRI. For instance, Rudovic et al. [13] investigated the impact of culture (Japan vs. East Europe) on engagement during autistic child-robot interaction. They found that the duration of child engagement with the robot was significantly different between the two cultures, although in both cultures there was a significant correlation between behavioral engagement levels and children's affective responses [13]. Salam et al. [14] looked into the impact of personality traits and found that individual features can be a significant predictor of the user's engagement with the robot, particularly when the user was an extrovert. Furthermore, Baxter et al. [15] found an effect of age on gaze direction and engagement level of preschoolers when they encountered a social robot for the first time.

Age has been shown to have a particularly important role in human-robot interaction. Research indicates that compared to young adults, elderly prefer different robot designs [16], hold different attitude toward robots [7, 17], have a higher tendency to anthropomorphize and ascribe mind to robots [4] and have different gaze patterns when looking at a robot's face and body [18]. However, to date, no other study has investigated the impact of age on behavioral engagement during HRI and its relationship with the perception that each age group holds toward the robot.

The present study investigated whether engagement with a social robot, as quantified by subjective and behavioral measures, differed between two groups of elderly and university students. Video recordings of participants interacting with a NAO-robot were coded using pre-defined verbal and non-verbal indicators. Additionally, participants filled in a post-experiment questionnaire reporting their mind perception (perceived mind capacity for the robot) and engagement with the robot. The following research questions were formulated:

RQ1: Do elderly and young students differ in their reported mind perception, reported subjective engagement score and observed behavioral engagement score with the robot?
RQ2: Is there a correlation between behavioral and subjective engagement scores as well as between engagement (either behavioral or subjective) and mind perception for the robot? If yes, how is the effect different among age groups?

2   Methodology

2.1   Participants

A between-subject study was designed with 65 Dutch-speaking participants. Some participants' data had to be discarded due to technical failures during the interactions or incomplete answers. Of the remaining 48 participants taking part in the experiment, 24 were elderly volunteers from an elderly care home in Tilburg, the Netherlands (Age: M = 68.88, SD = 6.98) and 24 were young students from the Tilburg University (Age: M = 21.79, SD = 2.95). All participants were naïve to the purpose of the study and gave their informed written consent prior to participation. The study was approved by the Ethics Committee of the School of Humanities and Digital Sciences, Tilburg University. Participants took part in the experiment in small groups of 2 to 4 people.

2.2   Experimental Setup

The robot used for the present study was the NAO robot (version 4, Softbank Robotics). The robot behavior was programmed using the graphical programming tool, Choregraphe (version 1.14.5).

The experiments for the elderly took place at the elderly care home 'de Wever', Tilburg, and the experiments for the young adults took place at Tilburg University research labs. Both experiments had identical setup. Participants and the robot sat in a quiet testing room while the experimenters coordinated the experiment from a small distance in the same room. The room was split up in two sections; one section visible to the participants and the other made invisible via curtains. One experimenter sat behind the curtains on a chair, invisible to the participants. This was necessary in order to apply the Wizard of Oz (WoO) technique during the experiments. Although there are methodological concerns over the use of WoO [19], this technique was found most suitable for the current experimental setup to stimulate the participants.

The robot was placed on a moveable table and could easily be moved in and out of place. The participants' chairs were placed in the center of the room facing the robot. The robot was positioned on the table so that it was in front of the participants and the cables could be connected to the laptop behind the curtains for the programming tool Choregraphe. For elderly, the speaking volume was set higher, compared to the standard settings, to prevent difficulties in hearing and understanding of the robot. There were three cameras within the testing room: one over the shoulder of NAO, one on the right side of the robot, and one filming from the left side. The cameras recorded the participants' faces for later off-line analysis and allowed the experimenters to analyze the experiments from different angles. Figure 1 displays images of the experimental setup for each group.

Fig. 1. Experimental setup for (a) the elderly group and (b) the student group during interaction with the NAO robot

2.3 Procedure

Before the actual experiment, one experimenter received and collected the participants and led them to the experiment room. Another experimenter (the Wizard) sat behind the curtains in the experiment room, hidden from the participants. The participants were asked to sit in front of the robot. Once they read and signed the consent form, they were asked to wait until Charlie (given name to the NAO robot in this experiment) would speak to them and start the interaction.

Each interaction session consisted of 2–4 participants and four activities. The first activity consisted of (1) NAO starting the interaction by introducing itself and asking whether the participants knew if a robot would visit them at the care home. The answers that the participants gave were used by the wizard to conduct the dialogue. The next activity consisted of (2) NAO showing a dance and asking whether the participants liked the dance, followed by the third activity where (3) NAO told two riddles and asked the participants to solve them. The interaction during the riddles was also moderated via the WoO technique. During the final activity (4) NAO was asked by one of the experimenters to stop talking, to which NAO responded that it still wants to play another riddle with the participants and sat down in protest. The robot was then removed from the room by one of the experimenters while still objecting. The activities performed by the robot in the current study, were based on previous HRI engagement and mind-perception studies [2, 6].

2.4 Measurements

Questionnaires. A post-experiment questionnaire was used to measure the participants' self-reported engagement and mind perception of the robot after having an interaction with it. The Engagement construct consisted of 6 questions, which were based on the Godspeed questionnaire [20] and the questionnaire used in the research of Lee et al. [21]. Mind Perception construct was evaluated by 8 questions, which were chosen from the Dimensions of Mind Perception Questionnaire [5]. The construct was composed of two subscales; Mind Agency (consisting of perceived capacity of the robot to recognize emotions, have thought, memory and self-control) and Mind Experience (consisting of perceived capacity of the robot to feel pleasure, hunger, pain and have a consciousness). Participants rated each item on a 5-point Likert scale ranging from "1 = Strongly disagree/No ability" to "5 = Strongly agree/Complete ability". The obtained scores for all items corresponding to each measure (6 items for Engagement and 8 items for Mind Perception) were summed up to compute one final score for that construct.

Behavioral Data. The behavioral data consisted of recorded videos showing the interactions per group. All interactions were split into four parts representing the robot activities, namely (1) Introduction, (2) Dance, (3) Riddle and (4) Protest. Each video part was further split into segments of 10 s and for every segment, the occurrence of four behavioral indicators, as presented in Table 1, was quantified in seconds. These occurrences were captured per segment in four tables, each representing one of the four behavioral indicators, for young students and elderly separately. The indicators could be annotated at the same time, e.g. a subject could laugh and speak at the same time.

Table 1. Behavioral indicators of engagement used in the video analysis of HRI sessions

Indicator	Measurement
Smile/Laughter	Annotated only in case participants smiled or laughed at something the robot did or said
Gazing	Annotated only in case participants were gazing at the robot
Nodding	Annotated only in case participants where nodding about something the robot did or said
Speaking	Annotated only in case the participants spoke to the robot

The occurrences of the above indicators were manually annotated by two researchers. A table was prepared in which for every participant, the duration of each behavioral indicator per video segment was registered. Next, the total duration of the indicators combined per activity was computed and summed up per participant to obtain a total

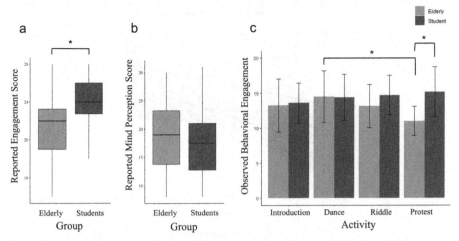

Fig. 2. Comparison between elderly and young students groups in (a) Reported Engagement scores, (b) Reported Mind Perception of robot and (c) Observed Behavioral Engagement in four robot activities. $*p < 0.05$

Behavioral Engagement score in the interaction session. The tables were prepared in Excel and further statistical analyses were performed in R.

3   Results

3.1   Comparison Between Elderly and Students

Figure 2 displays the results of subjective and behavioral measures in both elderly and young students groups. For subjective scores a Wilcoxon rank-sum test was employed to compare the two groups as the scores were not normally distributed and this test is appropriate for comparison of ordinal data. For behavioral engagement measures, a mixed ANOVA was run to assess the impact of two factors; robot activity (within-subjects: 4 levels) and age group (between-subjects: 2 levels).

Reported Engagement Score. A significant difference was found between the two groups ($W = 149$, $p = 0.004$) indicating that students reported a higher level of engagement with the robot in the post-interaction questionnaire (Fig. 2a).

Reported Mind Perception Score. No significant difference was found between the elderly and students groups in their reported mind perception for the robot ($W = 318$, $p = 0.542$) (Fig. 2b).

Observed Behavioral Engagement. The ANOVA analysis indicated a significant main effect for Group ($F(1, 46) = 3.770$, $p < 0.001$) and Activity ($F(3, 138) = 4.203$, $p < 0.001$) as well as a significant interaction between the two factors of Activity and Group ($F(3, 138) = 10.905$, $p < 0.001$). Therefore, post-hoc analysis was conducted on each factor separately. First, pairwise comparisons with Bonferroni adjustment were

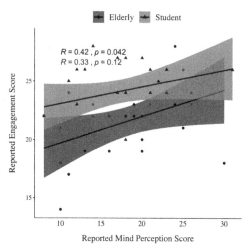

Fig. 3. Correlation analysis for both elderly and students showing a positive relationship between Reported Engagement Scores and Reported Mind Perception for the robot.

conducted between activities for each group. Results indicated that the elderly group had a significantly lower Behavioral Engagement during the robot protest compared to the robot dance activity (p = 0.004). Next, group comparison using a Wilcoxon rank-sum test was run for each activity, which showed a significantly lower Behavioral Engagement in the elderly group compared to the students in the robot protest phase (W = 483, p < 0.001) (Fig. 2c).

3.2   Correlation Between Subjective and Behavioral Measures

To check whether there is a relationship between Reported Engagement, Reported Mind Perception and Observed Behavioral Engagement, three correlation analyses between pairs of measures were performed for each group.

First, a Pearson correlation analysis was performed for the two subjective measures of Reported Engagement and Mind Perception scores. Elderly showed a significant positive correlation with a medium effect size (R = 0.42, p = 0.042). Young students did not show a significant correlation, although a positive trend existed (Fig. 3). This meant that elderly participants, who assigned a higher mind capacity to the robot, also reported a more engaged interaction with it.

Next, two sets of correlation analyses were conducted between Observed Behavioral Engagement and each of the self-reported subjective measures (Fig. 4). None of the groups showed a significant correlation between Reported Engagement scores and Observed Behavioral Engagement and the distribution of the data in the scatter plot (Fig. 4a) indicated no relationship or trend between the two measures.

Similarly, there was no significant correlation between Reported Mind Perception and Observed Behavioral Engagement for none of the groups, although a weak negative trend existed for both elderly and students groups (Fig. 4b). This outcome was contrary

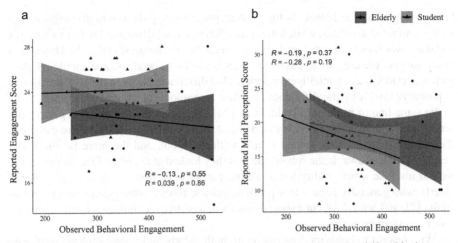

Fig. 4. Correlation analysis for both elderly and students showing (a) relationship between Reported Engagement score and Observed Behavioral Engagement, and (b) relationship between Reported Mind Perception for the robot and Observed behavioral Engagement.

to the results of the first correlation analysis between Reported Mind Perception and Engagement scores (Fig. 3) suggesting that participants who reported higher Mind Perception and Engagement with the robot after the interaction displayed less behavioral indicators of engagement -as defined by this study- during the interaction with it. This inconsistency between the two engagement measurements is discussed in the Discussion section.

4   Discussion

The aim of the current study was to extend the foundational knowledge on perceived engagement and mind perception of sociable robots within an elderly and student population through subjective and behavioral measures. Engagement is essential to meaningful social interaction with robots [9, 22] and research shows that it is mediated by demographic factors such as culture and personality traits [13, 14]. This study investigated the impact of age on level of engagement that people display during HRI through analysis of behavioral data as well as questionnaire outcomes.

Our results showed that young students reported a significantly higher engagement score compared to the elderly, however for elderly, this score was in positive correlation with the level of mind capacity that they attributed to the robot; i.e. the higher the mind perception, the better the elderly person experienced engagement with the robot. These findings are in line with past research. Hall et al. [23] suggested that people with better knowledge of robotics report a better impression of robots and engage more with them. Elderly in general have less experience with novel technologies and express signs of higher anxiety when they encounter robots for the first time [7]. Therefore, elderly might have experienced less positive impression and reported lower engagement with the robot, although the level of observed behavioral engagement was almost the same for both groups in most activities. As for the students, the group showed higher engagement scores compared to elderly, while a majority of them reported low mind perception scores and there was no significant correlation between the two measures (Fig. 3). This shows that young people are able to interact and engage with a social robot, even though they do not consider it as an intelligent partner. This difference between the two age groups is probably driven by the differences in their technology needs and preferences [25]. In the same line of reasoning, Ivaldi et al. [24] found that the dynamics of gazing and speech are influenced by individual and social factors; the more people were extrovert, the more and longer they tended to talk with the robot, and the more people had a negative attitude towards the robots, the less they looked at the robot face. In this study, we did not take a personality test from the participants, however it is suspected that elderly who generally have a less positive attitude toward robots compared to young adults [7], and hold different expectations form assistive technologies [26], reported a lower engagement with it.

With respect to behavioral engagement, both elderly and young students displayed similar amount of observed engagement indicators at the beginning of the interaction, however there was a gradual decrease of engagement for elderly group after the dance activity and their behavioral engagement in the last activity dropped significantly lower than their engagement in the robot dance activity and engagement level of students group in the same activity. A reason for this pattern could be that elderly lost interest in the interaction during or after the riddle activity. A relatively high number of them stated that they were unable to understand robot's questions. The video analysis also confirmed that elderly participants regularly asked the robot to repeat the riddles. Another reason could be the nature of the final activity, which induced a particularly different response in each age group. Analysis of participants' facial expressions during the robot protest time indicated that the majority of elderly group showed signs of concern or confusion. They were either frowning or just watching the whole situation, trying to understand what was happening [4]. Since these expressions were not originally defined as engagement indicators in this study, they were annotated as neutral and hence excluded from the coded engagement data. On the other hand, students were clearly amused by the situation. They were smiling or laughing, and found the conversation between the robot and experimenter funny. Given that smile/laughter was coded as one of the engagement indicators in this study, this response can explain the high level of behavioral engagement for students in the final activity (see Fig. 2c).

A weak negative trend was found between reported mind perception and observed behavioral engagement for both groups. This trend was non-significant, but can be explained based on the definition of engagement and design of robot activities in this study. Engagement is a complex system comprised of multiple social signals and behaviors [22]. In this study, we defined behavioral metric of engagement using four gestures of laughter, gaze, nodding, and speech as was suggested by past research [10–14]. This is while the robot activity mostly revolved around robot's talking, dancing, presenting a riddle or showing human-like gestures. Therefore, participants were mostly watching or listening to the robot and did not have the opportunity to freely talk with it. This could have induced a "task engagement" bias [24], which negatively influenced the speech and nodding indicators as well as the engagement experience that the participants expected.

On the other hand, participants were interacting with the robot in a group setting, which could have influenced the amount of direct gaze they showed toward the robot. Therefore, it is a possibility that although participants experienced engagement and ascribed a high mind capacity to the robot, their behavioral responses was not sufficiently captured by the indicators employed in this study. It is worth noting that although the behavioral indicators were established in advance, the videos were annotated by human coders and not automatic software and, for this reason, they may have suffered from subjective evaluation. This could have influenced the overall behavioral engagement scores and hence driven the obtained results.

A limitation of the study design that should be considered in the interpretation of the results is that the interaction sessions with the robot were conducted with more than one user (2 to 4 people in each group). The sense of co-presence with other participants in the same room and conducting an activity together might have influenced the behavioral responses of the group members during the experiment. For example, the laughter of one group member could motivate or stimulate other group members to laugh as well, or as soon as one group member broke the silence and started talking to the robot, the others could follow accordingly. Although the human-human interaction among the participants might have impacted the observed behavioral responses per group, the human-robot distance and interaction possibilities remained similar among all group members and the experimental setup was similar for both age groups. Future research may look into the difference between solo and group HRI in producing behavioral responses among users and investigate the role that a robot could play in facilitating social interaction among humans [7].

Another limitation of the study design is the lack of analysis in negative versus positive modes of engagement. The indicators employed by this study (laughter, gaze, nodding, and speech) did not sufficiently capture micro-expressions that take into account positive and negative facial expressions (e.g. frowning). Future research may look into these negative affective responses in order to yield further insights.

Furthermore, the novelty effect of encountering a robot for the first time may have biased the behavioral engagement scores. Our video analysis showed that the occurrence of engagement indicators such as smiling and gazing during the first two activities (introduction and dance) was higher than other activities. It is therefore a possibility that participants enjoyed the interaction and showed gestures corresponding to high engagement but did not perceive the robot as an intelligent human-like entity, which explains the lower mind perception scores.

Finally, it should be taken into account that in addition to attitudes and expectations, sociodemographic factors such as cultural differences of subjects [7, 8] could mediate the perception of robots and communication strategies in HRI. The current study was conducted with solely Dutch participants and hence, the results might not be generalizable to other cultures [27–29].

In summary, this study suggests that there are differences between elderly and young students in their behavioral interaction with a social robot and that for each age group observed patterns of engagement with the robot could provide an indication of the user's post-interaction perception of the robot.

5 Conclusion

The aim of the current study was to investigate the differences between elderly and young students in their behavioral responses to a social robot and moreover, examine whether this difference was related to the subjective mind perception and engagement scores that they reported after the interaction. Our findings showed that elderly participants who ascribed higher mind capacity to the robot also reported a higher engagement with it, although in general their reported engagement with robot was lower than young students. Furthermore, there was a negative trend between reported mind capacity and the observed behavioral engagement. This contrast between subjective reports and behavior of the participants could have been due to the bias caused by the definition of engagement indicators and robot activities in this study. Future research should attempt to validate the indicators defined by this study for objective evaluation of future HRI scenarios in different age groups.

Acknowledgement. Authors would like to thank Duuk Calor for his help in the video analysis.

References

1. Abdi, J., Al-Hindawi, A., Ng, T., Vizcaychipi, M.P.: Scoping review on the use of socially assistive robot technology in elderly care. BMJ Open **8**(2), e018815 (2018)
2. Fasola, J., Mataric, M.J.: Using socially assistive human–robot interaction to motivate physical exercise for older adults. Proc. IEEE **100**(8), 2512–2526 (2012)
3. Nomura, T., Takeuchi, S.: The elderly and robots: from experiments based on comparison with younger people. In: Workshops at the Twenty-Fifth AAAI Conference on Artificial Intelligence (2011)
4. Alimardani, M., Qurashi, S.: Mind perception of a sociable humanoid robot: a comparison between elderly and young adults. In: Silva, M.F., Luís Lima, J., Reis, L.P., Sanfeliu, A., Tardioli, D. (eds.) ROBOT 2019. AISC, vol. 1093, pp. 96–108. Springer, Cham (2020). https://doi.org/10.1007/978-3-030-36150-1_9
5. Stafford, R.Q., MacDonald, B.A., Jayawardena, C., Wegner, D.M., Broadbent, E.: Does the robot have a mind? Mind perception and attitudes towards robots predict use of an eldercare robot. Int. J. Social Robot. **6**(1), 17–32 (2014). https://doi.org/10.1007/s12369-013-0186-y
6. Piasek, J., Wieczorowska-Tobis, K.: Acceptance and long-term use of a social robot by elderly users in a domestic environment. In: 2018 11th International Conference on Human System Interaction (HSI), pp. 478–482. IEEE (2018)
7. Sinnema, L., Alimardani, M.: The attitude of elderly and young adults towards a humanoid robot as a facilitator for social interaction. In: Salichs, M.A., et al. (eds.) ICSR 2019. LNCS (LNAI), vol. 11876, pp. 24–33. Springer, Cham (2019). https://doi.org/10.1007/978-3-030-35888-4_3
8. Flandorfer, P.: Population ageing and socially assistive robots for elderly persons: the importance of sociodemographic factors for user acceptance. Int. J. Popul. Res. **2012** (2012)
9. Anzalone, S.M., Boucenna, S., Ivaldi, S., Chetouani, M.: Evaluating the engagement with social robots. Int. J. Social Robot. **7**(4), 465–478 (2015). https://doi.org/10.1007/s12369-015-0298-7
10. Rich, C., Ponsler, B., Holroyd, A., Sidner, C.L.: Recognizing engagement in human-robot interaction. In: 2010 5th ACM/IEEE International Conference on Human-Robot Interaction (HRI), pp. 375–382. IEEE (2010)

11. Sanghvi, J., Castellano, G., Leite, I., Pereira, A., McOwan, P.W., Paiva, A.: Automatic analysis of affective postures and body motion to detect engagement with a game companion. In: Proceedings of the 6th International Conference on Human-Robot, pp. 305–312 (2011)

12. Leite, I., et al.: Autonomous disengagement classification and repair in multiparty child-robot interaction. In: 2016 25th IEEE International Symposium on Robot and Human Interactive Communication (RO-MAN), pp. 525–532. IEEE (2016)

13. Rudovic, O., Lee, J., Mascarell-Maricic, L., Schuller, B.W., Picard, R.W.: Measuring engagement in robot-assisted autism therapy: a cross-cultural study. Front. Robot. AI **4**, 36 (2017)

14. Salam, H., Celiktutan, O., Hupont, I., Gunes, H., Chetouani, M.: Fully automatic analysis of engagement and its relationship to personality in human-robot interactions. IEEE Access **5**, 705–721 (2016)

15. Baxter, P., De Jong, C., Aarts, R., de Haas, M., Vogt, P.: The effect of age on engagement in preschoolers' child-robot interactions. In: Proceedings of the Companion of the 2017 ACM/IEEE International Conference on Human-Robot Interaction, pp. 81–82 (2017)

16. Oh, S., Oh, Y.H., Ju, D.Y.: Understanding the preference of the elderly for companion robot design. In: Chen, J. (ed.) AHFE 2019. AISC, vol. 962, pp. 92–103. Springer, Cham (2020). https://doi.org/10.1007/978-3-030-20467-9_9

17. Nomura, T., Sasa, M.: Investigation of differences on impressions of and behaviors toward real and virtual robots between elder people and university students. In: 2009 IEEE International Conference on Rehabilitation Robotics, pp. 934–939. IEEE (2009)

18. Oh, Y.H., Ju, D.Y.: Age-related differences in fixation pattern on a companion robot. Sensors **20**(13), 3807 (2020)

19. Riek, L.D.: Wizard of OZ studies in HRI: a systematic review and new reporting guidelines. J. Hum.-Robot Interact. **1**(1), 119–136 (2012)

20. Bartneck, C., Kulić, D., Croft, E., Zoghbi, S.: Measurement instruments for the anthropomorphism, animacy, likeability, perceived intelligence, and perceived safety of robots. Int. J. Soc. Robot. **1**(1), 71–81 (2009). https://doi.org/10.1007/s12369-008-0001-3

21. Lee, K.M., Peng, W., Jin, S.A., Yan, C.: Can robots manifest personality?: An empirical test of personality recognition, social responses, and social presence in human–robot interaction. J. Commun. **56**(4), 754–772 (2006)

22. Drejing, K., Thill, S., Hemeren, P.: Engagement: a traceable motivational concept in human-robot interaction. In: 2015 International Conference on Affective Computing and Intelligent Interaction (ACII), pp. 956–961. IEEE (2015)

23. Hall, J., Tritton, T., Rowe, A., Pipe, A., Melhuish, C., Leonards, U.: Perception of own and robot engagement in human–robot interactions and their dependence on robotics knowledge. Robot. Auton. Syst. **62**(3), 392–399 (2014)

24. Ivaldi, S., Lefort, S., Peters, J., Chetouani, M., Provasi, J., Zibetti, E.: Towards engagement models that consider individual factors in HRI: on the relation of extroversion and negative attitude towards robots to gaze and speech during a human–robot assembly task. Int. J. Social Robot. **9**(1), 63–86 (2017). https://doi.org/10.1007/s12369-016-0357-8

25. Biswas, M., Romeo, M., Cangelosi, A., Jones, R.B.: Are older people any different from younger people in the way they want to interact with robots? Scenario based survey. J. Multimod. User Interfaces **14**(1), 61–72 (2019). https://doi.org/10.1007/s12193-019-00306-x

26. Kachouie, R., Sedighadeli, S., Khosla, R., Chu, M.T.: Socially assistive robots in elderly care: a mixed-method systematic literature review. Int. J. Hum.-Comput. Interact. **30**(5), 369–393 (2014)

27. Bartneck, C., Nomura, T., Kanda, T., Suzuki, T., Kato, K.: Cultural differences in attitudes towards robots. In: Proceedings of the AISB Symposium on Robot Companions: Hard Problems and Open Challenges In Human-Robot Interaction, pp. 1–4 (2005)

28. Evers, V., Maldonado, H., Brodecki, T., Hinds, P.: Relational vs. group self-construal: untangling the role of national culture in HRI. In: 2008 3rd ACM/IEEE International Conference on Human-Robot Interaction (HRI), pp. 255–262. IEEE (2008)
29. Joosse, M., Lohse, M., Evers, V.: Lost in proxemics: spatial behavior for cross-cultural HRI. In: HRI 2014 Workshop on Culture-Aware Robotics, pp. 1–6 (2014)

Double Trouble: The Effect of Eye Gaze on the Social Impression of Mobile Robotic Telepresence Operators

Edo de Wolf$^{(\boxtimes)}$ and Jamy Li⬤

University of Twente, Enschede, The Netherlands
e.r.b.dewolf@student.utwente.nl, j.j.li@utwente.nl

Abstract. Eye gaze is used to convey crucial information during interactions with humans and robots. Modern video conferencing systems, an aspect of mobile robotic telepresence (MRP) systems, have limited eye gaze functionality due to the Mona Lisa effect. This paper compares the effects of eye gaze during brief interactions with MRP operators. In an online between-subjects study ($N = 79$), participants viewed a video of a hallway encounter between a passer-by and an MRP system; the operator either used or did not use mutual gaze. We used an observer 'trick' to study the effect cheaply. Results showed that participants' social impressions of the MRP operator were higher when the operator used versus did not use mutual gaze, showing that eye gaze can lead to an improvement in social perception even in a seemingly insignificant encounter such as a hallway passing. We argue for the importance of social acknowledgment cues to improve impressions of telepresence operators and to make mingling smoother and social roles more balanced. We describe potential opportunities for technological innovation in MRP systems and propose research directions to extend this work.

Keywords: Mobile Robotic Telepresence · MRP · Eye gaze · Workplace · Social impression · Operator

1 Introduction

Mobile Robotic Telepresence (MRP) systems (also referred to as telepresence robots) are being increasingly used at conferences, workplaces and public spaces to allow geographically dispersed individuals to interact with remote people and objects [12]. MRP systems typically host a live video of a remote operator on a flat screen which is attached to a steerable base, thereby enabling the driver, referred to as *operators* or *teleoperators*, to join meetings, attend presentations, and socialize from a remote location [15, 23, 30]. Commercial MRP systems include the Double robot (http://www.doublerobotics.com) and Beam robot (https://www.suitabletech.com).

Electronic supplementary material The online version of this chapter (https://doi.org/10.1007/978-3-030-62056-1_30) contains supplementary material, which is available to authorized users.

© Springer Nature Switzerland AG 2020
A. R. Wagner et al. (Eds.): ICSR 2020, LNAI 12483, pp. 357–368, 2020.
https://doi.org/10.1007/978-3-030-62056-1_30

Past work has acknowledged limitations in social interaction that is mediated by MRP systems (e.g. [19, 20, 23]. However, literature in HCI and HRI on usability issues with MRP systems primarily focuses on validating the usefulness of existing capabilities such as the system's mobility (e.g. [22]), field of view (e.g. [9]), system height (e.g. [24]), and appropriate volume settings (e.g. [10]) rather than the social behaviours that operators could achieve with advances in MRP systems.

Here, we evaluate the effect of mutual gaze and smiling by an MRP operator during casual passing by to test whether social greeting cues in a person could help improve how operators are perceived by observers in their remote location. Following past work on observer perception [16], we specifically evaluate the impressions of *observers* of MRP systems rather than operators as done in most past work because a major theme in past studies with *operators* of MRP systems is that a primary concern of operators is how they are presented to others (rather than deficits in how others are presented to them) [20]. Because of this potential imbalance in lower impressions of remote compared to collocated persons [28], improving impressions of MRP operators is particularly important for balancing roles in interaction or collaboration via MRP systems.

We first break down two key aspects of MRP systems – tele-embodiment and video conferencing. We subsequently raise questions about the potential social effects of MRP systems in brief hallway encounters. The main contributions of this paper are an empirical study of eye gaze in MRP systems during passer-by scenarios and an inexpensive method to test it.

1.1 Tele-Embodiment

Several studies mention *embodiment* as an inherent characteristic of MRP systems [3, 12, 15, 18, 30]. MRP systems provide a physical embodiment for the operator, which has been referred to as *tele-embodiment*, and are generally found to be useful in supporting the operator's sense of presence in a remote location because they also afford the ability to move [30]. In particular, if remote locals have social expectations of acknowledgment by operators, then social acknowledgment may be an important design consideration for telepresence robots.

1.2 Video Conferencing

Although video conferencing systems are widely used across the globe, there are limitations which prevent it from completely replacing real-life interactions.

Eye Gaze. When a local directs their gaze towards the operator shown on-screen, it may not be clear that the operator is gazing back towards them. This is because the local essentially assumes the viewpoint of the operator's webcam, which is positioned above the operator's screen; the operator will normally look at the screen beneath the webcam during an interaction, meaning they will never actually look into the webcam and thereby toward the local. As a workaround, the operator can look into the webcam, giving the illusion that they are gazing directly towards the local. This can be tied to the phenomenon known as the Mona Lisa effect, where a subject on a flat medium appears to direct their gaze at observers regardless of where the observers are positioned. However, in normal video conference situations the Mona Lisa effect is not achieved if speakers look at the screen image of the listener, which is not the same location as the camera. It is this characteristic of video conferencing which makes eye contact particularly challenging [6]. Advanced robots such as the Furhat [1] include dynamic eye gaze and neck tilting through a back-projection onto the robot head, however this technology is meant for improving robot articulation and not human embodiment in video conferencing.

Lack of mutual gaze in human-human interaction has numerous effects. Fullwood [7] showed in his study that video-mediated partners were less likeable for the locally positioned participant compared to collocated partners, probably due to the attenuation of visual signals, in particular eye gaze. In another study, researchers found that participants who received averted eye gaze during a conversation felt ostracised and there was lower relational value [29]. In their study, Bayliss and Tipper [2] observed that faces who never looked to the subject were perceived as less trustworthy than faces who always looked to the subject.

We can also consider the operator a robot since they are tele-embodied in the robot itself. Research in human-robot interaction show similar findings regarding eye gaze behaviour. Mutlu et al. [17] observed that subjects who did not receive eye gaze from a robot at least once felt ignored, while Hoffman et al. [8] found that participants' social impression of robots that stayed focused towards the subject were higher.

Smiling. Since video conferencing systems put a limitation on eye gaze, operators may rely on other cues such as smiling to give a positive impression. Lau [13] found that participants rated a person in a video as more socially attractive when the person smiled compared to did not smile.

1.3 Brief, Path-Crossing Encounters: A (Niche) Scenario

Current literature on MRP systems typically looks at explicit, intentional and verbally communicative scenarios, e.g. walking up to the parked MRP system to ask the operator a question or interaction during meetings [12] without considering uses cases like non-verbal acknowledge during hallway passing. Kontogiorgos [11] examined embodiment effects in interactions with failing robots but did not consider hallway scenarios and did not use an MRP. However, MRP systems are normally parked in between use. From the first author's own experience in using the Double robot at work, the parking location is often not associated with the next use case, so when an operator logs in, they need to first drive to their next location. A notable exception is work by Neustaedter et al. [20], who found some evidence that passing events with MRP systems are not viewed favourably by locals. Therefore, additional HCI research could be done on niche yet possibly common use cases with MRP systems at the workplace, such as brief hallway encounters with colleagues.

Indeed, office environments pose a number of challenges for MRP systems, including understanding how social norms are affected. While moving around in hallways, it can be challenging for operators to engage in social interaction with locals due to the attention given to operating the system [12]. The limitation of video conferencing systems also means that the operator cannot use natural gaze cues as when they are locally present.

Yet emotional expressions are an important part of work interactions, and nonverbal cues either draw somebody in (e.g. eye gaze, smiling) or push them away (e.g. gaze avoidance, frowns) [9]. However, it is unclear whether this nonverbal behaviour may be important in a less formal situation such as hallway passing, rather than in direct conversation (as studied in past work).

1.4 Hypotheses

If MRP systems provide tele-embodiment for the operator, combined with the difficulty to experience mutual gaze, what effect might this have on the social impression of the operator during brief, path-crossing encounters? To our knowledge, there have been no previous controlled studies on eye gaze in MRP systems specifically for casual passing by. However, we can look to the aforementioned evidence in eye gaze literature, both in human-human and human-robot interaction, and hypothesize that MRP systems which support mutual gaze will result in higher social impressions of the operator:

H1 – Participants' social impression of the MRP operator will be higher in hallway encounters with mutual gaze versus without mutual gaze.

Additionally, it is not uncommon for colleagues to greet each other in the hallway. In our case, we operationalize greeting as a smile; no words are spoken. We hypothesize that a robot teleoperator who uses a greeting, in the form of a smile at the appropriate time, could improve the social impression of the operator:

H2 – Participants' social impression of the MRP operator will be higher in hallway encounters with a greeting versus without a greeting.

2 Method

To test our hypotheses, we conducted a 2 (mutual eye gaze: present vs. absent) × 2 (greeting: present vs. absent) between-subjects experiment with the dependent variable being *social impression*. The first independent variable was *eye gaze*. In addition to eye gaze, we added a second independent variable: *greeting*. Including conditions for both the presence and absence of mutual eye gaze and greeting allowed us to test for any interaction effects as well as account for any potential ceiling effects.

2.1 Wizard-of-Oz Videos

We recorded four videos of an observer walking past a telepresence robot in a hallway via a third-person camera angle. The scene plays out as follows: a telepresence robot navigates down a hallway; at the same time, an observer walks down the hallway in the opposite direction; eventually, the telepresence robot and the observer cross paths and an interaction takes place; both actors continue down the hallway in opposite directions (see Fig. 1).

We used an observer 'trick' as a wizard-of-oz approach to make it appear as if the robot supports mutual gaze functionality (see Fig. 2). For the conditions where there is no mutual gaze, we simply asked our actors to operate the robot as usual and either greet or not greet the observer with a smile. For the conditions with mutual gaze, we carefully

Fig. 1. Wizard-of-oz videos storyboard; depending on the assigned condition, shot 3 plays out differently.

choreographed the behaviour of the operator to create an illusion where it appears, from the third-person view, that the operator directs their gaze towards the observer. Note that this illusion is only possible due to the use of a third-person camera angle.

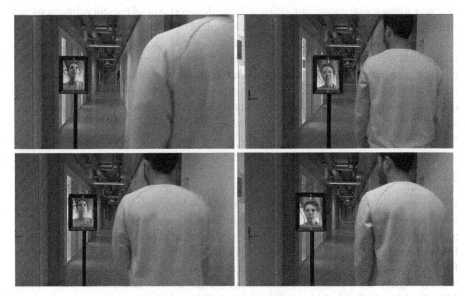

Fig. 2. Snapshot of each condition; top-left: cheerful greeting and gaze (C_G); top-right: cheerful greeting and no gaze (C_NG); bottom-left: no cheerful greeting and gaze (NC_G); bottom-right: no cheerful greeting and no gaze (NC_NG).

Each video scenario was 20 s long and played on repeat two times, resulting in a total of 60 s per video per condition. Audio was omitted entirely from all videos.

2.2 Task and Procedure

We used the Qualtrics platform (https://www.qualtrics.com) to generate a survey for our data collection. Before the start of the survey, the concept of telepresence robots is explained and an image of a Double robot is shown.

The survey begins by reading the following: "Scenario: You currently work at a multinational company, where your colleagues are spread around the globe. Your company has recently bought the Double Robot, so that offshore colleagues can be remotely present at your workplace. Instructions: Imagine you are walking down the hallway and experience the following scene (video on the next page)." The Randomizer feature on Qualtrics assigns the subject one of the four conditions. The subject then proceeds to watch the video and afterwards rates their social impression of the operator through a series of Likert-type questions. At the end of the survey, participants are asked to briefly describe in a few words their overall impression of the operator.

2.3 Measures

We break down social impression into four items: Rapport, Social Presence, Interpersonal Attraction and Trust. These four items were inspired by Daniel Roth et al. [26] (c.f., [2, 4, 21, 27]) who studied the effect of hybrid and synthetic social gaze in avatar-mediated interactions and who showed the relevance of these four items in relation to different types of gaze behaviour. For each of the four items, we prepared Likert-type questions on a scale from 1 (strongly disagree) to 7 (strongly agree). Rapport consisted of eleven questions, Social Presence consisted of six, Interpersonal Attraction consisted of six, and Trust consisted of three resulting in a total of 26 questions. Cronbach's α was very reliable for this scale (.93).

2.4 Participants

We recruited $N = 82$ participants through the Amazon Mechanical Turk platform (https://www.mturk.com). We used the built-in qualifications feature of MTurk to ensure that all participants resided in the United States, as well as required MTurk Master qualification. Participants were paid $1.00 through the MTurk website based on MTurk conventions. Participants were provided with a unique code at the end of the survey as a prerequisite to receiving the compensation. Furthermore, the survey interface did not allow videos to be skipped, playing full length before proceeding to the next step.

3 Results

3.1 Outlier Removal

We noticed that one subject, for all 26 questions, responded with only end-point answers. For this reason, we declared the subject an outlier. To verify this, we used the Median Absolute Deviation method (MAD) which is known to be effective for small sample sizes ($n < 25$ for each of our four conditions). According to Leys et al. [15], a MAD rejection threshold of 3.0 is very conservative while 2.5 is moderately conservative and 2.0 is poorly conservative.

We found 2.5 to be effective in removing the 'end-point answers' participant and an eventual two more participants without further reducing the sample size, leading to a final sample size of $N = 79$. As a result, 19 subjects were assigned condition C_G, 22 subjects NC_G, 21 subjects C_NG and 17 subjects NC_NG.

3.2 Social Impression

A factorial analysis of variance (ANOVA) with Greeting and Mutual Gaze as factors was conducted in SPSS.

Greeting. The test yielded significant results, $F(1, 75) = 15.70, p < .01$. The social impression of the operator was rated higher by participants who viewed the 'with greeting' videos ($M = 4.98, SD = .96$) than those who viewed the 'no greeting' videos ($M = 4.17, SD = 1.02$).

Mutual Gaze. The test yielded significant results, $F(1, 75) = 5.67, p = 0.02$. The social impression of the operator was rated higher by participants who viewed the 'with mutual gaze' videos ($M = 4.81, SD = 0.99$) than those who viewed the 'no mutual gaze' videos ($M = 4.37, SD = 1.11$).

Interaction Effect. No interaction effect was found between the two variables, $F(1, 75) = .484, p = .489$ (Fig. 3).

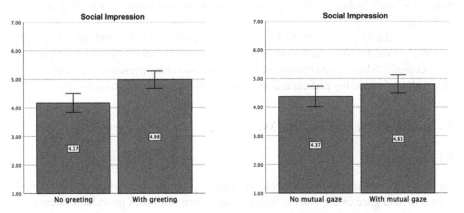

Fig. 3. Social impression of the operator vs. greeting (left) and mutual gaze (right).

4   Qualitative Results

To assess what people generally thought about each of the different conditions, we coded participants' responses to the open-ended question (where we asked them to briefly describe their impression of the operator) as 'positive', 'neutral' or 'negative' per condition. We present the findings organized by condition i.e., our consistent gaze and smiling conditions, then our inconsistent gaze and smiling conditions.

Consistent Gaze and Smiling Behaviour Resulted in Responses with Highest and Lowest Emotional Valence

The 'no mutual gaze/no greeting' video (NC_NG) yielded the most negative responses, including people thinking the operator was "bland", "disinterested and oblivious", "not friendly" or "cold and avoidant". Some subjects appeared to feel intentionally ignored, e.g. "I feel like they were doing their own thing and didn't want to be bothered" or "she ignored me". Others seemed to assume the operator was simply not interested in them or had other things to do, e.g. "a little cold, but probably willing to talk and discuss", "the operator seemed to be intent upon carrying out her tasks rather than engage in small talk".

The responses to the 'with mutual gaze/with greeting' video (C_G) yielded the most positive results, e.g. "they were friendly and interactive", "the operator seemed to be responsive and cordial", "they seem like a typical employee".

Inconsistent Gaze and Smiling Resulted in Responses with Mixed Emotional Valence

For the 'no mutual gaze/with greeting' video (NC_G), some of the more negative responses were "bland, uninterested", "she was nice but standoffish and it felt awkward", "cold", "quite stoic and emotionless". At the same time, there were also some positive responses, e.g. "friendly, approachable, receptive, and reciprocal", "friendly, calm, busy", "she seemed very friendly". The negative and positive comments indicate that some individuals may be more influenced by the inclusion or lack of mutual gaze than others.

In a similar fashion, subjects had mixed impressions for the 'with mutual gaze/no greeting' video (C_NG): "cold and distant", "nice and friendly", "distant, uninteresting, preoccupied", "she seemed interested, but not invested in my presence", "…they seemed nice, acknowledged my presence, and I felt the urge to say hello to them".

5   Limitations and Future Work

5.1   Limitations

Lack of Clear Manipulation Check. It is not explicitly clear whether subjects perceived mutual gaze in the videos. Some of their open responses provided evidence that the inclusion or exclusion of mutual gaze in the interaction was correctly conveyed -e.g., "…*she looked up*" vs. "*she ignored me*". However, a more direct method of checking the manipulation may prove beneficial, e.g. directly asking participants whether the operator looked at them or performing another study to verify the manipulation in the video. Furthermore, the wizard-of-oz approach depended on an illusion only capable of being seen from a third-person view; it is not known whether subjects were able to fully empathize with the passer-by in the video.

Cultural Influences. Because we recruited participants through the MTurk platform, and used the built-in qualifications feature to only allow access to participants who resided in the United States, we assume that all participants are American and culturally identify as such. However, we cannot be fully certain that this is the case and therefore cannot be certain that all participants follow the same cultural norms or have the same values. Moreover, some MTurk workers inaccurately report their location of residence, which we attempted to address using MTurk's location filtering, but could use IP address filters.

5.2 Future Work

Social Acknowledgement Supported By Future MRP Technology. We did not build a functional MRP system to support mutual gaze or deliver social acknowledgement prompts to the observer. However, we note here a number of ways this can be done.

Teleprompter technology uses mirrors to allow TV hosts to read their script – which the mirror projects onto the camera lens – while looking directly into the camera at the same time. This technology is used to make it appear as if the TV host is looking directly at all viewers. MRP technology uses the operator's own computer for video conferencing, so implementing an additional teleprompter setup would not be a practical solution. However, there is growing research to integrate a smartphone's front-facing camera underneath the its screen, extending the screen real estate and allowing for 'all-screen' devices. This could (unintentionally) result in an experience closer to the Mona Lisa effect. Alternatively, modern artificial intelligence is able to swap out faces of people in existing videos with convincing realism, a technique known as *deepfake*. Apple attempted to 'fix' eye gaze in one of their iOS software updates, such that, for the observer on the end of a video call, the user on-screen would appear to be looking at the camera and therefore at the observer as if making eye contact [5]. Deepfaked eye gaze could be used with MRP operators as well. However, this would be a continuous gaze and is not the same effect as studied in our paper, where the operator switches between not looking at the observer to looking at the observer while using the device.

Other signals of eye contact or passer-by acknowledgment could be explored, such as flashing lights, a graphic overlay on the MRP's screen or an MRP system that can pan its screen/"head". The technology for these features is not impossible, and we invite researchers and designers to explore these possibilities.

Extending this Research. It would be interesting to explore whether our wizard-of-oz videos can be made in first-person view and displayed, for example, in a virtual reality system. This could enable subjects to feel more embodied in the role of the passer-by and therefore provide responses which are closer-to-life.

Finally, this research study looked at social impression in the broadest sense – are there specific social effects to be explored more deeply, e.g. the effect of mutual gaze on trust with MRP operators?

We believe this study can help address some previously identified issues about how MRP operators think others perceive them through a design-focused study. We hope that other researchers can pursue a variety of research directions that explore niche yet relevant design solutions to operators' concerns about telepresence devices as well as the technology development to realize those design solutions which seem promising.

6   Conclusion

We conclude from the statistical analysis that interactions with MRP operators in hallway encounters which support mutual gaze result in higher ratings of the operator's social impression than those which do not support mutual gaze. We also found from participants' qualitative short answers that they wrote more positively when both gaze and a greeting were present compared to absent, and more mixed answers when inconsistent cues were shown.

The theory pulled from both human-human and human-robot interaction provided strong evidence of the importance of eye gaze in social interactions; this work extends those findings to low-interactive hallway passing events, where our results suggest using eye gaze in hallways can be a strategy to broadly improve MRP appeal. Through a wizard-of-oz approach, we have shown how mutual gaze positively affects social impressions without having had to develop the technology beforehand. The video trick used in our study to simulate a mutual eye gaze action may be a feasible, low-cost solution for online studies, since some participants commented about the operator looking at the passerby. However, further work can be done to verify its convincingness. The actuation by a robot was also not tested, since the trick was to use an on-screen change rather than a robot's articulated gaze.

MRP systems are still evolving and it is unclear whether technological advancements in eye gaze or social acknowledgement will be made to these systems in the near future. In the meantime, our study shows the importance of considering the social effects of using MRP technology at the workplace. Although the general results of eye gaze with MRP systems is not novel, we have shown here that it applies to hallway encounters, too. Not everyone may be affected by the limitation of eye gaze, but the lack of mutual gaze in MRP systems may have the potential to hinder the forming of relationships between remote colleagues and limit team interaction in the long run.

References

1. Al Moubayed, S., Beskow, J., Skantze, G., Granström, B.: Furhat: a back-projected human-like robot head for multiparty human-machine interaction. In: Esposito, A., Esposito, A.M., Vinciarelli, A., Hoffmann, R., Müller, V.C. (eds.) Cognitive Behavioural Systems. LNCS, vol. 7403, pp. 114–130. Springer, Heidelberg (2012). https://doi.org/10.1007/978-3-642-345 84-5_9
2. Bayliss, A.P., Tipper, S.P.: Predictive gaze cues and personality judgments: should eye trust you? Psychol. Sci. (2006). https://doi.org/10.1111/j.1467-9280.2006.01737.x
3. Davis, D., Perkowitz, W.T.: Consequences of responsiveness in dyadic interaction: effects of probability of response and proportion of content-related responses on interpersonal attraction. J. Pers. Soc. Psychol. (1979). https://doi.org/10.1037/0022-3514.37.4.534
4. Delden, R., Bruijnes, M.: Telepresence robots in daily life. In: Proceedings of the CTIT, Univ. Twente, Enschede, Netherlands. April, 11 p. (2017)

5. FaceTime eye contact correction in iOS 13 uses ARKit. https://9to5mac.com/2019/07/03/fac etime-eye-contact-correction-in-ios-13-uses-arkit/. Accessed 11 July 2020

6. Fuchs, H., State, A., Bazin, J.C.: Immersive 3D telepresence. Computer (Long. Beach. Calif) (2014). https://doi.org/10.1109/MC.2014.185

7. Fullwood, C.: The effect of mediation on impression formation: a comparison of face-to-face and video-mediated conditions. Appl. Ergon. (2007). https://doi.org/10.1016/j.apergo.2006. 06.002

8. Hoffman, G., Birnbaum, G.E., Vanunu, K., Sass, O., Reis, H.T.: Robot responsiveness to human disclosure affects social impression and appeal. In: ACM/IEEE International Conference on Human-Robot Interaction (2014). https://doi.org/10.1145/2559636.2559660

9. Johnson, S., Rae, I., Mutlu, B., Takayama, L.: Can you see me now? How field of view affects collaboration in robotic telepresence. In: Proceedings of Conference on Human Factors in Computing Systems (2015). https://doi.org/10.1145/2702123.2702526

10. Kimura, A., Ihara, M., Kobayashi, M., Manabe, Y., Chihara, K.: Visual feedback: its effect on teleconferencing. In: Jacko, J.A. (ed.) HCI 2007. LNCS, vol. 4553, pp. 591–600. Springer, Heidelberg (2007). https://doi.org/10.1007/978-3-540-73111-5_67

11. Kontogiorgos, D., van Waveren, S., Wallberg, O., Pereira, A., Leite, I., Gustafson, J.: Embodiment effects in interactions with failing robots (2020). https://doi.org/10.1145/3313831.337 6372

12. Kristoffersson, A., Coradeschi, S., Loutfi, A.: A review of mobile robotic telepresence (2013). https://doi.org/10.1155/2013/902316

13. Lau, S.: The effect of smiling on person perception. J. Soc. Psychol. (1982). https://doi.org/ 10.1080/00224545.1982.9713408

14. Lee, M.K., Takayama, L.: Now, I have a body. (2011). https://doi.org/10.1145/1978942.197 8950

15. Leys, C., Ley, C., Klein, O., Bernard, P., Licata, L.: Detecting outliers: do not use standard deviation around the mean, use absolute deviation around the median. J. Exp. Soc. Psychol. (2013). https://doi.org/10.1016/j.jesp.2013.03.013

16. Li, J., Ju, W., Nass, C.: Observer perception of dominance and mirroring behavior in human-robot relationships. In: ACM/IEEE International Conference on Human-Robot Interaction (2015). https://doi.org/10.1145/2696454.2696459

17. Mutlu, B., Shiwa, T., Kanda, T., Ishiguro, H., Hagita, N.: Footing in human-robot conversations: how robots might shape participant roles using gaze cues. In: Proceedings of the 4th ACM/IEEE International Conference on Human Robot Interaction (2009). https://doi.org/10. 1145/1514095.1514109

18. Nakanishi, H., Murakami, Y., Nogami, D., Ishiguro, H.: Minimum movement matters (2008). https://doi.org/10.1145/1460563.1460614

19. Neustaedter, C., Singhal, S., Pan, R., Heshmat, Y., Forghani, A., Tang, J.: From being there to watching: shared and dedicated telepresence robot usage at academic conferences. ACM Trans. Comput. Interact. (2018). https://doi.org/10.1145/3243213

20. Neustaedter, C., Venolia, G., Procyk, J., Hawkins, D.: To beam or not to beam: a study of remote telepresence attendance at an academic conference. In: Proceedings of the ACM Conference on Computer Supported Cooperative Work, CSCW (2016). https://doi.org/10. 1145/2818048.2819922

21. Nowak, K.L., Biocca, F.: The effect of the agency and anthropomorphism on users' sense of telepresence, copresence, and social presence in virtual environments. In: Presence: Teleoperators and Virtual Environments (2003). https://doi.org/10.1162/105474603322 761289

22. Rae, I., Mutlu, B., Takayama, L.: Bodies in motion: mobility, presence, and task awareness in telepresence. In: Proceedings of Conference on Human Factors in Computing Systems (2014). https://doi.org/10.1145/2556288.2557047

23. Rae, I., Neustaedter, C.: Robotic telepresence at scale. In: Proceedings of Conference on Human Factors in Computing Systems (2017). https://doi.org/10.1145/3025453.3025855
24. Rae, I., Takayama, L., Mutlu, B.: The influence of height in robot-mediated communication. In: ACM/IEEE International Conference on Human-Robot Interaction (2013). https://doi.org/10.1109/HRI.2013.6483495
25. Rogers, E.M., Singhal, A., Quinlan, M.M.: Diffusion of innovations. In: An Integrated Approach to Communication Theory and Research, 3rd edn. (2019). https://doi.org/citeulike-article-id:126680
26. Roth, D., Kullmann, P., Bente, G., Gall, D., Latoschik, M.E.: Effects of hybrid and synthetic social gaze in avatar-mediated interactions. In: Adjunct Proceedings - 2018 IEEE International Symposium on Mixed and Augmented Reality, ISMAR-Adjunct 2018 (2018). https://doi.org/10.1109/ISMAR-Adjunct.2018.00044
27. Seo, S.H., Griffin, K., Young, J.E., Bunt, A., Prentice, S., Loureiro-Rodríguez, V.: Investigating people's rapport building and hindering behaviors when working with a collaborative robot. Int. J. Soc. Robot. **10**(1), 147–161 (2017). https://doi.org/10.1007/s12369-017-0441-8
28. Stoll, B., Reig, S., He, L., Kaplan, I., Jung, M.F., Fussell, S.R.: Wait, Can You Move the Robot? (2018). https://doi.org/10.1145/3171221.3171243
29. Wirth, J.H., Sacco, D.F., Hugenberg, K., Williams, K.D.: Eye gaze as relational evaluation: averted eye gaze leads to feelings of ostracism and relational devaluation. Personal. Soc. Psychol. Bull. (2010). https://doi.org/10.1177/0146167210370032
30. Yang, L., Neustaedter, C., Schiphorst, T.: Communicating through a telepresence robot: a study of long distance relationships. In: Proceedings of Conference on Human Factors in Computing Systems (2017). https://doi.org/10.1145/3027063.3053240

Administrating Cognitive Tests Through HRI: An Application of an Automatic Scoring System Through Visual Analysis

Sara Sangiovanni[1], Matteo Spezialetti[2], Fabio Aurelio D'Asaro[1(⊠)],
Gianpaolo Maggi[3], and Silvia Rossi[1]

[1] Università degli Studi di Napoli Federico II, Naples, Italy
fdasaro@gmail.com
[2] Università degli Studi dell'Aquila, L'Aquila, Italy
[3] Università degli Studi della Campania Luigi Vanvitelli, Caserta, Italy

Abstract. In this paper, we propose the use of a social robot to support professional figures in performing cognitive screening and stimulation. We implemented tools that allow us to automatize the evaluation of a subject's cognitive abilities. More specifically, we programmed the humanoid robot *Pepper* to administer, in a fully automated and "friendly" way, three cognitive assessment tasks: *Word List Recall* (WLR), *Attentive Matrices* (AM), and the *Rey-Osterrieth Complex Figure* (ROCF). For WLR, we displayed the word list on the robot's tablet, and the speech recognition module to record the recalled words. AM was delivered by asking the subjects to use and mark numbers on the tablet. For ROCF, we implemented two novel score assessment algorithms based on the processing of the picture drawn by the subjects and acquired through the robot camera. In particular, for ROCF, correlation analysis was conducted to compare automatically computed scores with a human psychologist's. Our results suggest that the human psychologist's workload can be reliably reduced thanks to the support of the robot.

Keywords: HRI · Cognitive tests · Automatic assessment

1 Introduction

A *social robot* is an autonomous robot capable of interacting with humans, that can follow social norms and role-specific rules. Currently, the use of social robots has become widespread in different areas, such as schools, transports, working contexts, and others. In this paper, we present the use of a social robot in a therapeutic setting, as support to professional figures for performing cognitive screening and stimulation. Research has found that cognitive stimulation can prevent the development of dementia [21]. Several studies explored the effectiveness of cognitive-based interventions and have shown that people undergoing cognitive training report a slower decline in daily activities (see e.g. [20]).

© Springer Nature Switzerland AG 2020
A. R. Wagner et al. (Eds.): ICSR 2020, LNAI 12483, pp. 369–380, 2020.
https://doi.org/10.1007/978-3-030-62056-1_31

Currently, there are many technologies, including robotics ones, designed to submit cognitive training or to support professional figures in this area. Among these, social robots could represent a pleasant and understandable interface for facilitating the screening process. Social robots have been used to improve Autistic Spectrum Disorder (ASD) diagnosis in children [11] or to administer Patient-Reported Outcome measurement questionnaires to senior adults [3]. The success of this approach can be favored by the preference of interacting with a humanoid social robot rather than a non-embodied computer screen [15]. Moreover, results presented in [17] suggest that using social robots to support professional figures improves user performance, but the technology needs improvement for a fully autonomous assessment. Little is known about robots as psychological evaluation tools.

In our work, we explore the use of social robots to automate the psychological evaluation attributed to the performed cognitive exercises. Consequently, our main objective is to use a social robot to automatically deliver and evaluate cognitive tests. In particular, we implemented tools that enable a robot to automatically evaluate a subject's cognitive abilities. Among activities to be automatically performed by a robot, the computerized analysis of drawing-based test is still a complex task due to the high degree of drawing variability and the possible interpretation [7]. This activity is also time consuming for psychologists. Here, we propose two algorithms for the evaluation of the Rey–Osterrieth Complex Figure (ROCF) to be performed autonomously by a Pepper robot. Results show that is a strong correlation between our automatic evaluation methods and that of a human psychologist, but further analysis is required to fine tune our approach.

2 Related Work

The use of social robots in healthcare is a relatively new field of study. For instance, [10] explores the use of social robots in the therapeutic field. In particular, they are used in healthcare to provide monitoring, health education, and entertainment to patients.

Neurological examination provides important information on cognitive abilities of the therapeuric subject. Cognitive screening is the first step in neurological evaluation. Recent research like [18] demonstrates the benefits of using social robots as therapeutic assistants, as they can provide many advantages to diagnostic practice, for example by ensuring standardization in the subject's evaluation. Rossi et al. [14] explore the use of social robots as psychometric tools for providing quick and reliable screening exams. More in detail, this study compares the prototype of a robotic cognitive test to a traditional paper and pencil psychometric tool. Rossi et al. [15] have shown that subjects are likely to rate their experience as more satisfactory when they use a humanoid robot when compared to a mobile application. For example, the iCat robot recommends the use of ecological, energy-saving washing programs, while communicating through voice messages and facial expressions. The results suggest that people involved in the experiment were more heavily influenced by the robotic cat rather than by the luminous information message on the washing machine display. Kidd and Breazeal [5] proposed a robotic trainer for weight loss for smart homes. Kidd and David in [6], where participants were asked to join a weight loss program, the authors found that the program was more effective when a robot was involved in the monitoring process when compared to both pen and paper and computerized interface-based approaches.

In this paper, we develop an algorithm for the evaluation of the *Rey–Osterrieth Complex Figure* (ROCF) that requires scoring a drawing in a human-like manner. Related work in this field uses fuzzy expert systems [4] that, however, does not provide a global evaluation of the figure due to localization issues. Other techniques are based on Deep Neural Networks [7]. A shortcoming of such methods is that they require a huge amount of data for the training phase. Our hybrid method, instead, provides a lightweight way to provide a global evaluation of the drawing using standard techniques from computer vision. As it is written in Python, our algorithm can be readily embedded in a Pepper robot and does not require any post-processing phase.

3   Materials and Methods

In our application, we used the humanoid robot *Pepper Y20 V18A*[1] and the *Choreograph suite*, which is included in Pepper's SDK. Image processing operations were performed using Python and OpenCV libraries. We programmed Pepper to administer, in a fully automated way, the three cognitive assessment tasks listed below:

Word List Recall. *Word List Recall* (WLR) is used to evaluate learning and verbal memory abilities. In particular, the participants are shown 30 semantically unrelated words. After 1 min, the list disappears and the participants have to recall all the words they remember. The number of words correctly recalled is then calculated, and the participants are assigned a score from 0 to 30, with higher scores indicating better performance.

Attentive Matrices. To assess selective visual attention, we employed the *Attentive matrices* (AM) test [16]. It consists of three matrices with numbers arranged in a random sequence. The participant has to check the matrices to find and tick the target numbers shown at the top of the screen within 45 s (see Fig. 1). Then, the participant is assigned a score ranging from 0 (worst performance) to 60 (best performance).

Rey–Osterrieth Complex Figure. The *Rey–Osterrieth Complex Figure* (ROCF) is often used for the assessment of visuo-constructional and planning

---

[1] SoftBank Robotics https://www.softbankrobotics.com.

Fig. 1. Pepper performing the *Attentive Matrices Test* on its in-built tablet.

abilities, due to the complexity of the figure [19]. Participants are asked to copy the complex figure and show the sheet to Pepper (see Fig. 2). The image was then scored according to the number of elements present in the complex figure correctly copied so that higher scores indicate better performance (range 0–36). When the test is administered by a human psychologist, the 18 elements composing the ROCF are evaluated individually, applying a particular scoring grid.

3.1   Pepper's Behavioral Features

We programmed Pepper to behave in a friendly way. In the following, we describe the characterizing features of the friendly personality we adopted. Pepper's eye color was set to yellow. According to the color-wheel model by Plutchik yellow is typically associated with positive emotions such as joy and serenity [12]. Its gestures are frequent and open to give a sense of rhythm to its speech [8]. The openness of gestures is typically related also to the display of positive emotions [13]. Both the speed of speech and voice pitch are high, 90% and 100% of the default value respectively which are associated with a more entertaining robot [9]. For what regards the proxemics, we adopted Hall's personal space (0.3–1m) because reaches the right balance between greater persuasiveness and low discomfort: The language type used is informal to promote intimacy [2]. Finally, Pepper's gaze is fixed on the user during deliveries and distracted during the execution [2]. To enhance the perception of the robot's friendly personality, we adopted different motivational strategies: phrases of positive encouragement [1] are randomly repeated every 10 s, and a yellow smile is shown on Pepper's tablet during waiting times.

Fig. 2. A participant showing Pepper his reproduction of ROCF.

3.2 Automatic Cognitive Tests Administration

The interaction is entirely guided and supervised by Pepper, who first introduces itself and then explains the purpose of interaction to the participant. Subsequently, it proceeds to administer the cognitive tests, in the same way a human psychologist would, in the following order:

1. First phase: Pepper shows on the tablet the image of the original ROCF model, and asks the participant to copy the image on a white sheet. This task is meant to assess the subject's visuospatial and visuo-constructional abilities but also abilities of planning and organization. Pepper waits for the participant to say "I'm done" before continuing;
2. Second phase: in this phase, Pepper administers the two other proposed cognitive exercises (WL first, and then AM) in order to fill the interval before the ROCF delayed recall with other neuropsychological tasks;
3. Third phase: in this phase, the participant is asked to recall the ROCF. Particularly, through this task, it is possible to evaluate the subject's long term spatial memory. Pepper asks the participant to draw on a white sheet all the details s/he remembers of the original model shown in step one. At the end of the exercise, Pepper asks the participant to position the drawing in front of its eyes and takes a photo that is then used for automatic evaluation (see Fig. 2).

Finally, Pepper thanks the participant for the collaboration and ends the interaction. Note that all of our experiments were performed under controlled conditions. A human operator checked that the lighting conditions were fit for the task, and that Pepper's camera was correctly aligned to the sheet when capturing the image.

3.3 Automatic Cognitive Tests Evaluation

Word List Recall. To automatically administrate WLR, we used the tablet screen embedded in the robot to display the word list, and the speech recognition module to record and take note of the recalled words. In case a word is recognized, Pepper repeats it for confirmation. The speech recognition module allows one to set a sensitivity value that represents how accurately the word has to be pronounced to be recognized. We set the sensitivity to 60% after a series of preliminary tests conducted to find the best trade-off between false positives (incorrect words recognized as correct, or correct words recognized as other words in the list) and false negatives (correct words not recognized). In particular, we looked for the lowest value that did not produce any false positive, since false negatives can be managed by simply ignoring the word.

Attentive Matrices. AM test was administered by showing the matrices on Pepper's tablet. The subject was asked to tick the numbers by tapping on them over the screen. The final score was the number of correctly ticked numbers.

Rey–Osterrieth Complex Figure. ROCF score assessment algorithm was based on the comparison between the image drawn by the subject and the one stored in the robot's memory to return a score. The sheet included a black frame (2.5 cm of thickness) on the border, ensuring that the subject did not cover the drawing area with fingers when showing the sheet to Pepper. To make the drawn image comparable with the original, the following preprocessing phase were applied:

- Binarization (see Fig. 3 for an example)
- Selection of the maximum bounding box of contiguous foreground pixels: each pixel outside the bounding box was set to 0
- Perspective linear transformation
- Border artifacts removal: each region of contiguous background pixel touching the border was set to foreground value 1.

The following steps were performed both on the preprocessed image and the original one. The aim was to compute an N by M similarity matrix that contained a score for each pair (O_i, D_j) of graphic elements (i.e. foreground connected regions) belonging to the original and the drawn image respectively:

- **Labeling:** contiguous pixels were labeled with the same integer value (see Fig. 3 for a pictorial representation). Regions were arranged in a list structure
- **Background removal:** the region with the larger bounding box area, was removed from the list
- **Removal of small regions:** regions composed of less than 50 pixels were not considered and removed from the list.

Both the shape similarity and the correct positioning of drawn elements with respect to the originals had to be quantified. Let O_i and D_j the ith and j^{th} ($1 \leq i \leq N$, $1 \leq j \leq M$) elements of the regions lists from the original image and that drawn by the subject, respectively. For each pair (O_i, D_j) we compute the following similarity metrics:

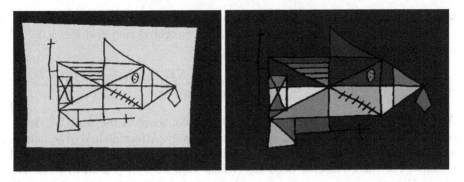

Fig. 3. A ROCF drawing after the binarization phase (left) and labeling phase (right). In the right picture, different colors correspond to differently labeled areas of the figure. (Color figure online)

Jaccard Index (JI): It is a value that takes into account the overlap of regions and it is defined as

$$JI(O_i, D_j) = \frac{S(O_i \cap D_j)}{S(O_i \cup D_j)} \tag{1}$$

where $S(x)$ represents the number of pixels in a region and set operators are applied by considering regions as sets of pixels;

Orientation Similarity (OS): Let be $\alpha_O, \alpha_D \in [0, \pi]$ the orientations of the major axes of the ellipses approximating the regions O_i and D_j, respectively. Let be R_O and R_D the ratios between lengths of major and minor axes of the ellipses. We computed the orientation similarity as follows:

$$OS(O_i, D_j) = \begin{cases} 0 & \text{if } (R_O \geq 0.5 \wedge R_D < 0.5)\vee \\ & (R_O < 0.5 \wedge R_D \geq 0.5) \\ 0.5 & \text{if } R_O \geq 0.5 \wedge R_D \geq 0.5 \\ (1 - |sin(\alpha_O - \alpha_D)|) & \text{if } R_O < 0.5 \wedge R_D < 0.5 \end{cases} \tag{2}$$

Normalized Distance (ND): It is computed as

$$ND(O_i, D_j) = 1 - \frac{d(C(O_i), C(D_j))}{\max\limits_{1 \leq n \leq N, 1 \leq m \leq M} d(C(O_n), C(D_m))} \tag{3}$$

where $C(X)$ is the coordinates vector of the centroid of region X and $d(y, z)$ is the Euclidean distance between points y and z.

Surfaces ratio (SR): It represents the similarity in terms of the number of pixels composing the regions:

$$SR(O_i, D_j) = \frac{\min(|O_i|, |D_j|)}{\max(|O_i|, |D_j|)} \tag{4}$$

where $|X|$ is the number of pixels belonging to region X.

The computed metrics were combined in a weighted sum and the N by M matrix A was filled as follows:

$$A(i,j) = \frac{w_1 JI(O_i, D_j) + w_2 OS(O_i, D_j) + w_3 ND(O_i, D_j) + w_4 SR(O_i, D_j)}{w_1 + w_2 + w_3 + w_4}$$

(5)

At this point, A was analyzed to compute a total score of the test. We developed two algorithms, named A1 and A2, respectively. Attention had to be paid in avoiding the "overloading" of drawn elements (when paired with several original regions). For these reasons, both algorithms implemented penalization mechanisms. Note that, since previous steps led to a division of the original image in 18 regions and each element of A was in the range $[0,1]$, picking and summing an element of A for each original region, would produce a score in the range $[0, 18]$, thus the following algorithms also had to normalize the score to the range $[0, 36]$.

A1 comprised the following steps:

```
BEGIN
    score=0;
    WHILE max(A)>0
        find max(A) (let x and y be the indices);
        score = score + max(A);
        set each element in the x-th row of A to 0;
        multiply each element in the y-th column of A by PF;
    END
    RETURN 2*score;
END
```

At each step, it found the maximum score pair in the matrix and add the value to the final score. Then, to exclude the already considered regions between original, it set the corresponding row to 0 (in this way, each original region was paired with exactly one drawn region). Moreover, to avoid that a drawn region was selected repeatedly, the algorithm penalized it by multiplying the values in the corresponding column by a penalization factor $PF \in [0,1]$. Setting $PF = 0$ is equivalent to make the algorithm behave with a hard constraint with respect to overloading: at most one original region will be paired with each drawn region, since, once a regions' pair is selected, the corresponding row and column is set to 0. On the contrary, $PF = 1$ means that no penalty will be applied for overloading. In this work, we tested the algorithm with values of $PF = 0, 0.5, 1$.

A2 is a simplification that addressed the correctness of the paired regions by using an overall metric, instead of computing penalty for every single region. The final score was computed as follows:

$$s = \sum_{i=1}^{N} (\max(A[i,:])) * P$$

(6)

where $P = \frac{2N}{N+(N-M)^2}$ was the weight term ($P \in [0,2]$) that considered the number of original and drawn regions.

Table 1. Correlation scores (Pearson's r, Spearman's ρ, and Cronbach's α) between our automatic evaluation algorithms of a task and the human psychologist's evaluation. All results are significant ($p < 0.01$).

	r	ρ	α
$A1$ with $PF = 1$	0.73	0.82	0.71
$A1$ with $PF = 0$	**0.79**	0.84	**0.87**
$A1$ with $PF = 0.5$	0.75	**0.86**	0.85
$A2$	0.75	0.81	0.86

4 Evaluation and Results

We wanted to make sure our evaluation methods are reliable, in the sense that they must show a strong correlation with respect to a human psychologist's evaluation. To this aim, we asked 37 participants (19 male, 18 female, aged 23–38) to take the three tests (WL, AM, and ROCF) under the supervision of a human. These tests were evaluated by both a psychologist and by our algorithms. We obtained 100% accuracy when scoring WL and AM, as these tests are performed using the robot's tablet and speech recognition software. Thus, in the following, we focus on ROCF. We tested algorithm $A1$ for PF equal to 0, 0.5 and 1, and algorithm $A2$. Then, we compared the expert's scores to the automatically calculated ones.

Table 1 shows two measures of correlation between our algorithms and the expert's evaluation. It is worth noting that $A1$ with PF equal to 0 and 0.5 show higher correlation scores when compared to $A2$.

To further investigate our algorithms for ROCF evaluation we also did regression analysis using a linear model (see Fig. 4). The slope test for all models rejected the hypothesis that they have a slope equal to 0 ($p < 0.001$), again implying correlation with the human psychologist's evaluation. Unfortunately, the slope test also rejects the hypothesis that models of $A1$ with PF equal to 0, 0.5, and 1 have a slope equal to 1 ($p < 0.01$). This hypothesis is *not* rejected for $A2$, which possibly indicates that $A2$ is the best choice as an automatic evaluation metric for ROCF straight out-of-the-box. On the other hand, $A1$ with $PF = 0$ and $PF = 0.5$ have higher correlation scores than $A2$. This seems to suggest that these two methods only differ from the expert's evaluation by a scale/rotation factor and, if appropriately tweaked as to systematically adjust their slope, might overperform $A2$. More data is needed to verify this hypothesis and use it to improve our method. We intend to do so in future work.

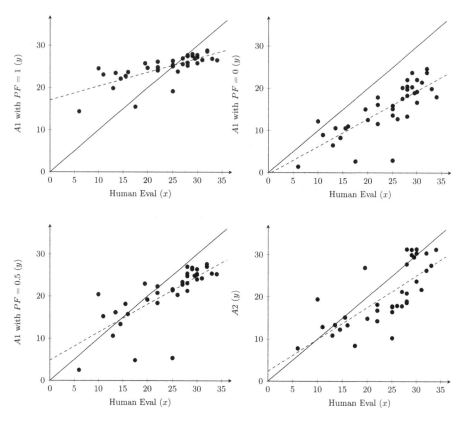

Fig. 4. Linear models of our two algorithms. The equations of the four models (dashed lines) are: $y = 0.33x + 17.05$ ($A1$ with $PF = 1$, shown in Fig. 4a) with $R^2 = 0.54$, $y = 0.66x - 0.39$ ($A1$ with $PF = 0$, shown in Fig. 4b) with $R^2 = 0.62$, $y = 0.66x + 4.84$ ($A1$ with $PF = 0.5$, shown in Fig. 4c) with $R^2 = 0.56$, $y = 0.76x + 2.35$ ($A2$, shown in Fig. 4d) with $R^2 = 0.56$. For reference, we display a $y = x$ solid line in every plot.

5   Conclusion and Future Work

In this work, we developed and implemented a series of tools that aim to automatize the administration and evaluation of cognitive tests. These tasks are typically carried out by a human psychologist and a psychologist. However, we demonstrated that the human operator can be reliably supported by an HRI system (a Pepper Robot, in our application). Indeed, our results suggest that there is a strong correlation between our automatic evaluation methods and that of a human psychologist. In particular, our implementation of algorithms to automatically score the Rey-Osterrieth Complex Figure showed a high correlation with scores assigned by a psychologist. In future work, we plan to improve these algorithms by collecting more data, which would allow us to fine-tune the automatic evaluations, and refine the recognition of finer details.

It is worth noting here that participants in our pilot study are healthy young adults (aged 23–38). This constitutes a limitation of our work, as older/cognitively impaired individuals may reproduce highly distorted ROCF figures that may be harder for our algorithms to correctly evaluate. As previously noted, another source of image distortion may be due to user-independent factors such as non-uniform lighting conditions, partially acquired images, misaligned camera, etc. We did not observe such limit conditions here, as a human operator always made sure the environmental conditions were fit. We plan to further investigate these possible limitations in future work.

Another objective for future work is to contribute an open dataset for the evaluation of the ROCF. We believe a standard set of figures captured from Pepper's camera would greatly help comparing different algorithms for the evaluation of ROCF, and would be beneficial for Social Assistive Sobotics studies that aim to automatize similar tasks.

These findings may prove useful for further development of similar fully autonomous agents for the administration of tests, to be employed e.g. in healthcare services and interactive cognitive training. Our tools may also turn useful to *standardize* the evaluation of tests, as they are independent of external factors that may affect a human operator, such as personality and subjective marking criteria.

Acknowledgments. This study was partially funded by MIUR (Italian Ministry of Education, Universities, and Research) within the PRIN2015 research project UPA4SAR - User-centered Profiling and Adaptation for Socially Assistive Robotics (grant n. 2015KBL78T).

References

1. Agrigoroaie, R., Tapus, A.: Influence of robot's interaction style on performance in a Stroop task. In: Kheddar, A., et al. (eds.) Social Robotics. LNCS, vol. 10652, pp. 95–104. Springer, Heidelberg (2017). https://doi.org/10.1007/978-3-319-70022-9_10
2. Baxter, P., Ashurst, E., Read, R., Kennedy, J., Belpaeme, T.: Robot education peers in a situated primary school study: personalisation promotes child learning. PLoS ONE **12**(5), e0178126 (2017)
3. Boumans, R., Van Meulen, F., Hindriks, K., Neerincx, M., Olde Rikkert, M.: Proof of concept of a social robot for patient reported outcome measurements in elderly persons. In: Companion of the 2018 ACM/IEEE International Conference on Human-Robot Interaction, pp. 73–74 (2018)
4. Canham, R., Smith, S.L., Tyrrell, A.M.: Automated scoring of a neuropsychological test: the Rey Osterrieth complex figure. In: Proceedings of the 26th Euromicro Conference. EUROMICRO 2000. Informatics: Inventing the Future, vol. 2, pp. 406–413. IEEE (2000)
5. Kidd, C.D., Breazeal, C.: A robotic weight loss coach. In: Proceedings of the National Conference on Artificial Intelligence, vol. 22, p. 1985. AAAI Press/MIT Press. Cambridge/Menlo Park (2007)
6. Kidd, C.D.: Designing for long-term human-robot interaction and application to weight loss (2008)

7. Moetesum, M., Siddiqi, I., Ehsan, S., Vincent, N.: Deformation modeling and classification using deep convolutional neural networks for computerized analysis of neuropsychological drawings. Neural Comput. Appl. **32**, 1–25 (2020). https://doi.org/10.1007/s00521-020-04735-8

8. Neff, M., Wang, Y., Abbott, R., Walker, M.: Evaluating the effect of gesture and language on personality perception in conversational agents. In: Allbeck, J., Badler, N., Bickmore, T., Pelachaud, C., Safonova, A. (eds.) IVA 2010. LNCS (LNAI), vol. 6356, pp. 222–235. Springer, Heidelberg (2010). https://doi.org/10.1007/978-3-642-15892-6_24

9. Niculescu, A., van Dijk, B., Nijholt, A., Li, H., See, S.L.: Making social robots more attractive: the effects of voice pitch, humor and empathy. Int. J. Soc. Robot. **5**(2), 171–191 (2013). https://doi.org/10.1007/s12369-012-0171-x

10. Olaronke, I., Oluwaseun, O., Rhoda, I.: State of the art: a study of human-robot interaction in healthcare. Int. J. Inf. Eng. Electron. Bus. **9**, 43–55 (2017)

11. Petric, F., Kovacić, Z.: No data? No problem! expert system approach to designing a POMDP framework for robot-assisted ASD diagnostics. In: Companion of the 2018 ACM/IEEE International Conference on Human-Robot Interaction, pp. 209–210 (2018)

12. Plutchik, R.: The nature of emotions: human emotions have deep evolutionary roots, a fact that may explain their complexity and provide tools for clinical practice. Am. Sci. **89**(4), 344–350 (2001)

13. Rossi, S., Dell'Aquila, E., Bucci, B.: Evaluating the emotional valence of affective sounds for child-robot interaction. In: Salichs, M.A., et al. (eds.) ICSR 2019. LNCS (LNAI), vol. 11876, pp. 505–514. Springer, Cham (2019). https://doi.org/10.1007/978-3-030-35888-4_47

14. Rossi, S., Santangelo, G., Staffa, M., Varrasi, S., Conti, D., Di Nuovo, A.: Psychometric evaluation supported by a social robot: personality factors and technology acceptance. In: 2018 27th IEEE International Symposium on Robot and Human Interactive Communication (RO-MAN), pp. 802–807. IEEE (2018)

15. Rossi, S., Staffa, M., Tamburro, A.: Socially assistive robot for providing recommendations: comparing a humanoid robot with a mobile application. Int. J. Soc. Robot. **10**(2), 265–278 (2018). https://doi.org/10.1007/s12369-018-0469-4

16. Spinnler, H.: Standardizzazione e taratura italiana di test neuropsicologici. Ital. J. Neurol. Sci. **6**, 21–120 (1987)

17. Varrasi, S., Di Nuovo, S., Conti, D., Di Nuovo, A.: A social robot for cognitive assessment. In: Companion of the 2018 ACM/IEEE International Conference on Human-Robot Interaction, pp. 269–270 (2018)

18. Varrasi, S., Di Nuovo, S., Conti, D., Di Nuovo, A.: Social robots as psychometric tools for cognitive assessment: a pilot test. In: Ficuciello, F., Ruggiero, F., Finzi, A. (eds.) Human Friendly Robotics. Springer Proceedings in Advanced Robotics, vol. 7, pp. 99–112. Springer, Heidelberg (2019). https://doi.org/10.1007/978-3-319-89327-3_8

19. Watanabe, K., et al.: The Rey-Osterrieth complex figure as a measure of executive function in childhood. Brain Dev. **27**(8), 564–569 (2005)

20. Willis, S.L., et al.: Long-term effects of cognitive training on everyday functional outcomes in older adults. JAMA **296**(23), 2805–2814 (2006)

21. Wilson, R.S., et al.: Participation in cognitively stimulating activities and risk of incident Alzheimer disease. JAMA **287**(6), 742–748 (2002)

Adapting Usability Metrics for a Socially Assistive, Kinesthetic, Mixed Reality Robot Tutoring Environment

Kartik Mahajan$^{(\boxtimes)}$, Thomas Groechel, Roxanna Pakkar, Julia Cordero, Haemin Lee, and Maja J. Matarić

Viterbi School of Engineering, University of Southern California,
Los Angeles, CA, USA
{kmahajan,groechel,pakkar,jrcorder,haeminle,mataric}@usc.edu

Abstract. The field of Socially Assistive Robot (SAR) tutoring has extensively explored both subjective and objective usability metrics for seated tablet-based human-robot interactions. As SAR tutoring introduces kinesthetic mixed reality environments where students can move around and physically manipulate virtual objects, usability metrics for such interactions need to be re-evaluated. This paper applies standard usability metrics from seated 2D interactions to a kinesthetic mixed reality environment and validates those metrics with post-interaction survey data. Using data from a pilot study ($n = 9$) conducted with a mixed reality SAR tutor, three commonly-used metrics of usability for seated 2D tutoring interfaces were collected: **performance**, **manipulation time**, and **gaze**. The strength of each usability metric was compared to subjective survey-based scores measured with the System Usability Scale (SUS). The results show that usability scores were correlated with the gaze metric but not with the manipulation time or performance metrics. The findings provide interesting implications for the design and evaluation of kinesthetic mixed reality robot tutoring environments.

Keywords: Socially assistive robot tutor · Mixed reality · Usability

1 Introduction

Socially Assistive Robot (SAR) tutoring has been extensively explored with a variety of users and usability studies [17]. Such robot tutors often rely on human-computer interfaces (e.g., tablets) to deliver content as well as increase the observability of the interaction without the need to rely on external sensors [3]. Consequently, usability studies in SAR tutoring typically focus on seated interaction and benefit from a reliable perceptual interface [3]. Advances in virtual, augmented, and mixed reality human-robot interaction (VAM-HRI) have enabled kinesthetic mixed reality environments where students move around and

---

K. Mahajan and T. Groechel—Equal contribution.

© Springer Nature Switzerland AG 2020
A. R. Wagner et al. (Eds.): ICSR 2020, LNAI 12483, pp. 381–391, 2020.
https://doi.org/10.1007/978-3-030-62056-1_32

physically interact with coding blocks alongside a SAR tutor. Effective evaluation of usability of these nascent 3D interfaces requires a re-evaluation of common usability metrics employed in other tutoring environments.

Usability has been studied in various tutoring environments using subjective and objective metrics. Subjective metrics include interview summaries [15,19] and various survey tools, typically using Likert scales [12], such as the commonly used System Usability Scale (SUS), a 0–100 scale. Objective metrics include user performance, manipulation time, and gaze [1,6]. SUS is used for evaluating both on-line and in-person tutoring, while objective metrics are more commonly used in on-line tutoring. In SAR tutors, observability is typically limited; this challenge is even greater in kinesthetic environments, where students move around.

VAM-HRI represents an opportunity for obtaining objective behavioral metrics by providing a data-rich observable 3D interaction environment. Augmented reality head-mounted displays (ARHMDs), the common medium for VAM-HRI, do not rely on external sensors and can dynamically change the displayed environments [28]. This allows for synchronizing the robot tutor's and world states, simplifying on-line logging, and providing objective multimodal interaction data for analyzing the interaction.

This work applied objective usability metrics commonly used in seated 2D tutoring environments to data from a kinesthetic mixed reality environment pilot study ($n = 9$) and validated those metrics with post-interaction SUS survey data. Three different usability metrics were studied: 1) student performance via problem-solving policies; 2) object manipulation time; and 3) gaze concentration. The metrics were recorded over a 20 min interaction involving a SAR tutor guiding a student through 7 coding exercises via a mixed reality visual programming language MoveToCode [7]. The strength of each usability metric was compared to subjective survey-based scores measured with the System Usability Scale (SUS). The results show that usability scores were correlated with the gaze metric but not with the manipulation time or performance metrics. The findings provide interesting implications for the design and evaluation of kinesthetic mixed reality robot tutoring environments.

2   Background and Related Work

2.1   Measuring Usability in Tutoring Systems

Usability, the ease of use and efficacy of a system [23], has been evaluated in various tutoring systems, ranging from on-line intelligent tutoring systems (ITS) to in-person SAR tutors. Across fields, usability is measured using qualitative and quantitative metrics of subjective post-interaction interviews [13,21] and self-report questionnaires [8] such as the System Usability Scale (SUS) [11].

In SAR tutor research, as well as in Web and interface-design, objective behavioral data are collected for usability analysis, such as eye gaze [2,16] and task completion time [5,20,24,27]. Objective behavioral metrics mitigate forms of reporting bias found in questionnaires [14]. As a validation metric, objective findings are often correlated with conclusions of post-interaction interviews, questionnaires, or study controls such as complexity of the interface [5,20,24,27].

Since a usable system has contributed to greater skill development [22], performance is a common usability metric. By nature, performance is evaluated differently based on tutoring environment. Clabaugh et al. measured math success by number of correct answers [4]. Roscoe et al. measured writing success based on a scaled essay score [22]. In the context of programming tutoring, because programming has been viewed as a multi-level problem-solving process, it has been evaluated individually at every stage, from exploration to submission [10]. Other techniques have evaluated programming solutions as a collection of policies, correcting each component, such as variable definition or if-statements [18].

This work explored applying objective usability metrics typically used in seated tutoring environments in a novel context of a kinesthetic mixed reality SAR tutor. The three metrics–manipulation time, and eye gaze–are compared with a standard subjective usability metric.

2.2 Measuring Usability in SAR and Mixed Reality Robot Tutoring

Virtual, augmented, and mixed reality for human-robot interaction (VAM-HRI) is a new and rapidly growing field of research [29]. Extending socially assistive robotics (SAR) tutors to VAM-HRI promises to significantly enhance interactivity as well as the collection of real-time user and usability data. SAR tutors often rely on human-computer interfaces (e.g., tablets) to deliver content as well as increase the observability of the interaction [3]. Objective behavioral data collection is often hindered by the lack of reliable yet unencumbering and unintrusive sensors [12]. Mixed reality tutors can enhance the learning experience by enabling a kinesthetic learning environment where students can move around and physically manipulate virtual objects [9,26]. Currently, SAR tutoring systems typically focus on seated interactions and benefit from tablet interfaces [3]; in contrast, kinesthetic SAR tutoring is much more dynamic and calls for new usability metrics.

VAM provides a detailed, fully-controllable and observable interaction environments where reliable user behavioral data can be collected. Augmented reality head-mounted displays (ARHMDs), the common medium for VAM-HRI, readily synchronize with the robot's and world states, allowing for on-line logging [28]. Using augmented or mixed reality with a robot in the context of education is not new [25,30,31], but usability analysis in previous works is limited to subjective metrics [30]. Thus, this work explores applying usability metrics commonly used in seated 2D tutoring environemnts to the new context of kinesthetic mixed reality environments via VAM-HRI with SAR.

3   Dataset

The dataset used in this work was from a within subjects ($n = 9$) pilot study performed with a mixed reality visual programming language MoveToCode [7] (Fig. 1) in which a SAR tutor aimed to increase a student's *kinesthetic curiosity (KC)*, a metric involving the multimodal measure of a student's movement and curiosity. In the interaction, students combined *coding blocks* (e.g., if-blocks, print-blocks) by grabbing, dragging, and snapping blocks together in order to solve 7 beginner-level coding exercises. The acts of grabbing, dragging, and snapping blocks are part of the **manipulation time** metric, described in Sect. 4. Preset coding blocks were available to the participant at the beginning of each exercise. Tasks focused on building syntactic skills for integer addition, variable creation, and if-statements. The study and its results are under review for publication elsewhere.

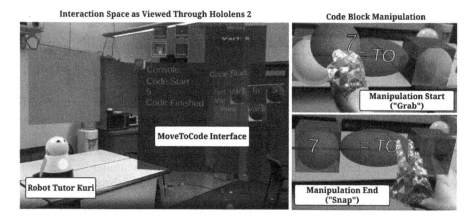

Fig. 1. MoveToCode (left) as seen by the participant through the Hololens 2. Code block manipulation (right) with a participant grabbing the block and letting it go to snap code blocks together.

The dataset includes 9 (2F,7M) of the 10 participants who were University of Southern California students with age range 19–27 ($\bar{x} = 22.8, \sigma = 2.9$). Participant 8 had two operating system crashes and was discarded from analysis. Behavioral data were collected at 0.02 sec intervals (50 Hz) 180 min of time series data yielding 540,000 rows. After the interaction, participants completed a ten-question questionnaire designed to measure individual SUS ratings.

This work examines the participants' objective and subjective metrics of usability. Specifically, it considers SUS survey results and the logged behavioral data of policy-evaluation, object manipulation time, and gaze concentration, described in the next section.

4   Usability Metrics

Since VAM-HRI for SAR tutoring is a nascent area, to understand usability metrics for kinesthetic mixed reality tutoring contexts, we reviewed usability studies of programming tutors [18] and web interfaces [27], and chose three commonly used reliable metrics: user performance, manipulation time, and gaze concentration. We then adapted these metrics based on the context of our study.

Student Performance via Problem-Solving Policies: We measured a participant's performance by counting the number of good and bad policies created during a time frame. Introduced by Piech et al. [18], a *policy* is defined as any group of two or more code blocks. For example, if the participant was tasked with adding integer block 1 and integer block 2, a correct solution would include combining the two integer blocks with an addition block. A *Good* Policy (GP) for this task includes combining the integer block 1 with the addition block. A *Bad* Policy (BP) includes some other, incorrect step(s), such as combining the integer block 3 and the addition block.

Manipulation Time: MT is defined as the amount of time it takes a participant to grab a coding block and *snap* it to another block as can be seen in Fig. 1. *Snapping* was defined as the action grabbing a code block, dragging it to be in contact with another code block, and then releasing the currently held block to snap it to the contacted block. A successful manipulation event was logged from the time when an object was first grabbed (t_{grab}) to when an object was *snapped* to another object (t_{snap}).

Gaze Concentration: GC is defined as the amount of time a participant looked a 2D (x,y) pixel (i.e., cell) within the *interaction space* over a rolling time window tw_{GC}. The *interaction space*, shown in Fig. 1, included the MoveToCode interface and the physical robot tutor. The interaction space, measured in meters, was 4 m 2.25 m grid, totalling 3,600 cells 0.05 m x 0.05m each. A cell's score increased by 0.01 every frame the participant looked at that cell during tw_{GC}. The maximum cell score was capped at 1.

5   Results

5.1   Data Processing

All statistics were distributed between 0 and 1 using MinMax Scaling from Python's *sklearn* package (v0.24.2):

$$X_{scaled} = \sigma_x * (X_{max} - X_{min}) + X_{min} \tag{1}$$

where X_{scaled} is the new value for a data point in column X. To reduce skew of manipulation time (MT) results, a max MT of 10 s was empirically chosen, leaving 95.1% of the data. Any times over 10 s were adjusted to 10 s.

Not all participants completed all exercises; P5 failed to complete exercise 3 and P1,2,6,9 failed to complete exercise 6. This resulted in differently sized datasets for the different participants.

We calculated post-interaction SUS scores for all participants based on a 10-question survey, as shown in Fig. 2 ($\bar{x} = 53.06, \tilde{x} = 55.0, \sigma^x = 17.2, CV = 32.8\%$).

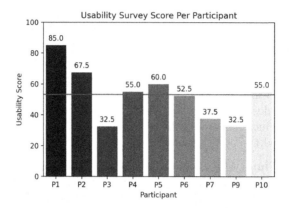

Fig. 2. SUS rating (0–100). The line indicates the median rating ($\tilde{x}$).

5.2 Unimodal Metric Analysis

We computed the variance and correlation of each metric to the SUS score (Fig. 2). A Levene's test was used to identify significant ($p < .05$) variance of each metric across participants, to signify the metric may distinguish different user behavior. We used Spearman's r correlation tests to validate the significance ($p < .05$) of each metric. We report the correlation of variance (CV) of each metric for unitless comparisons between metrics relative to their dispersion.

Policy-Evaluation Results. To evaluate user performance, we recorded total Good Policies GP ($\bar{x} = 24.125, \sigma = 11.243, CV = 46.6\%$) and total Bad Policies BP ($\bar{x} = 3.625, \sigma = 3.24, CV = 89.2\%$) per participant and per exercise (Fig. 3). A Pearson's r test showed that there was no significant correlation between the total GP and BP ($r_p(9) = 0.581, p = .100$). A Levene's test indicated unequal variances per participant over exercises for total GP ($F = 6.72, p = .001$) yet no significant variance for total BP ($F = 0.993, p = .439$). This supports that GP may be effective in helping to differentiate user behavior, whereas BP may not be, due to its consistency across all participants. A Spearman's r correlation indicated no significant relationship between total GP and SUS score ($r_s(9) = -0.369, p = .327$), indicating total GP is not indicative of SUS score when observed unimodally. A Spearman's r correlation indicates no significant

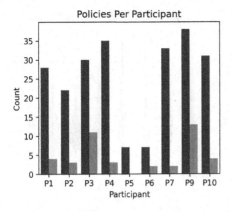
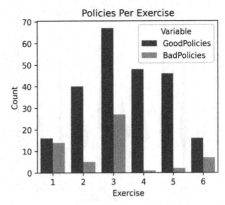

Fig. 3. Good Policies (GP) and Bad Policies (BP) viewed per participant and per interaction. Exercise 7 was free-play so there are no GP or BP recorded for it.

relationship between total BP and SUS score $(r_s(9) = -0.340, p = .370)$, supporting that total BP is not indicative of SUS score.

These findings show that neither of the user performance metrics (GP or BP) alone were significant indicators of usability.

Manipulation Time Results. To evaluate Manipulation Time MT, we recorded average MT per participant ($\bar{x} = 2.93s, \sigma^x = 0.76s, CV = 25.9\%$) and per exercise ($\bar{x} = 2.80s, \sigma^x = 0.57s, CV = 20.3\%$), as shown in Fig. 4. A Levene's test indicated a significant variance among participant's average MT per exercise ($W = 5.94, p < .0001$), indicating MT is able to differentiate user behavior. A Spearman's r correlation indicated no significant correlation between average MT and SUS score ($r_s(9) = 0.353, p = .351$), indicating that average MT is not indicative of SUS score.

As an additional MT metric, we also calculated σ^{MT} ($\bar{x} = 3.51, \sigma^x = 0.816, CV = 23.2\%$). A Spearman's r correlation also showed no significant correlation between σ^{MT} and SUS score ($r_s(9) = -0.417, p = .263$), indicating that average σ^{MT} was not indicative of the SUS score.

These findings indicate that neither of the Manipulation Time (MT) metrics alone was a significant indicator of usability.

Eye Gaze Concentration Results. To analyze eye gaze concentration GC, we empirically set tw_{GC} to 10 s. High intensity cell reads (HR) were defined as any cell with a value of 0.9 or higher, because 0.9 is over two standard deviations ($\sigma^{GC} = 0.306$) away from the average ($\bar{x} = 0.181$).

To evaluate HR, we recorded the total HR per participant ($\bar{x} = 153.44, \sigma^x = 23.733, CV = 15.4\%$) as shown in Fig. 5. A Levene's test showed a significant difference in variance among HR per time-step ($F = 38.1, p < .0001$), indicating that HR may distinguish user behavior. A Spearman's r correlation also indicates

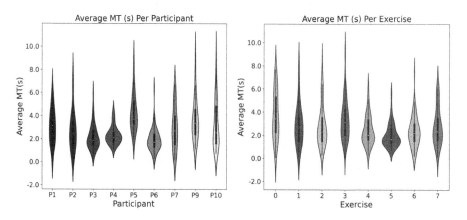

Fig. 4. Average Manipulation Time (MT) per exercise and per participant. MT records time between when a student chooses a coding block (e.g. if-statement, integer block) and snaps it to another component. Refer to Sect. 4 for more detail.

a significant relationship between total HR and the SUS score ($r_s(9) = 0.77, p = .014$), supporting that total HR is indicative of SUS score.

As an additional metric of GC, we calculated σ^{GC} ($\bar{x} = 23.42, \sigma = 14.22, CV = 15.4\%$), based on 2D coordinates of gaze, to represent how a participant's gaze traveled over a window. A Spearman's r correlation showed no significant relationship between σ^{GC} and the SUS score ($r_s(9) = 0.235, p = .542$), indicating that σ^{GC} is not indicative of SUS score.

These findings indicate that HR was a significant metric for usability, whereas σ^{GC} was not.

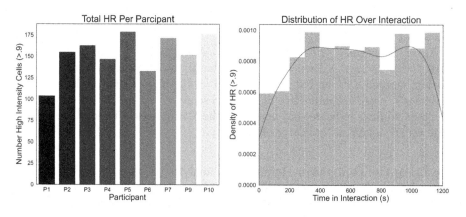

Fig. 5. Total High Intensity Cell Reads (score ¿ 0.9) HR per participant recorded over a rolling time window $tw_{GC} = 10$. Cells are defined as any 2D pixel in the interaction space. For more details, see Sect. 4.

6 Discussion

The results showed varying degrees of success when applying common usability metrics in the context of kinesthetic mixed reality SAR tutoring. Per Spearman r tests, HR was the only metric that correlated with our SUS scores ($r_s(9) = 0.77, p = .014$) We hypothesize that this may be due to the varying sizes of our datasets ($Size_{GP/BP} = 289, Size_{MT} = 371, Size_{HR} = 12106$); GP, BP, and MT metrics yielded no significant results. The following insights can be drawn from this work.

Gaze concentration is a useful usability metric in VAM-HRI tutoring. As mentioned above, a Spearman r test revealed a significant ($p < .05$) correlation between HR and SUS scores ($r_s(9) = 0.77, p = .014$). A Pearson r test confirmed this correlation between HR and SUS, demonstrating the linearity of their correlation ($r_p(9) = 0.78, p = .011$).

Performance analysis may need to be re-evaluated as a metric in VAM-HRI tutoring. Policy-based evaluation yielded no correlation with SUS score($r_s(9) = -0.369, p = .327$). The accuracy of these findings is questionable given a significantly high CV ($GP : 46.6\%, BP : 89.2\%$) relative to that of HR (15.4%). Performance-based metrics have been successfully used in 2D tutoring environments [18] and should be further explored for VAM-HRI tutoring. Given the novelty of VAM-HRI for many users, we recommend using metrics of exploration, such as kinesthetic curiosity [7], that have demonstrated ability to distinguish participant behavior in VAM-HRI tutoring.

7 Conclusion

In summary, this work explored subjective and objective usability metrics typically used in seated 2D interactions in a kinesthetic mixed reality environment. Over a 20 min pilot study ($n = 9$) conducted with a mixed reality SAR tutor, three commonly-used objective metrics of usability were collected–performance, manipulation time, and gaze–and where then correlated with a commonly used subjective metric System Usability Scale (SUS) metric. In the study, a mixed reality SAR tutor guided students through 7 beginner-level programming exercises via a mixed reality visual programming language MoveToCode [7] we developed. Subjective SUS scores were correlated with the objective gaze metric but not with the objective manipulation time or performance metrics. The findings serve to inform the design and evaluation of kinesthetic mixed reality robot tutoring environments.

Acknowledgements. This work was supported by NSF NRI 2.0 grant for "Communicate, Share, Adapt: A Mixed Reality Framework for Facilitating Robot Integration and Customization" (NSF IIS-1925083). We would also like to thank Matthew Rueben for all of his assistance.

References

1. Caleb-Solly, P., Dogramadzi, S., Huijnen, C.A., Heuvel, H.: Exploiting ability for human adaptation to facilitate improved human-robot interaction and acceptance. Inf. Soc. **34**(3), 153–165 (2018)
2. Cho, H., Powell, D., Pichon, A., Kuhns, L.M., Garofalo, R., Schnall, R.: Eye-tracking retrospective think-aloud as a novel approach for a usability evaluation. Int. J. Med. Inform. **129**, 366–373 (2019)
3. Clabaugh, C., Matarić, M.: Escaping Oz: autonomy in socially assistive robotics. Ann. Rev. Control Robot. Auton. Syst. **2**, 33–61 (2019)
4. Clabaugh, C.E., et al.: Long-term personalization of an in-home socially assistive robot for children with autism spectrum disorders. Front. Robot. AI **6**, 110 (2019)
5. Dey, A., Billinghurst, M., Lindeman, R.W., Swan II, J.E.: A systematic review of usability studies in augmented reality between 2005 and 2014. In: 2016 IEEE International Symposium on Mixed and Augmented Reality (ISMAR-Adjunct), pp. 49–50. IEEE (2016)
6. Feingold-Polak, R., Elishay, A., Shahar, Y., Stein, M., Edan, Y., Levy-Tzedek, S.: Differences between young and old users when interacting with a humanoid robot: a qualitative usability study. Paladyn, J. Behav. Robot. **9**(1), 183–192 (2018)
7. Groechel, T., Kuo, C., Dasgupta, R., Wathieu, A.: interaction-lab/movetocode: Doi release (2020). https://doi.org/10.5281/zenodo.3924514
8. Holden, R.J., et al.: Usability and feasibility of consumer-facing technology to reduce unsafe medication use by older adults. Res. Soc. Adm. Pharm. **16**(1), 54–61 (2020)
9. Ibrahim, R.H., Hussein, D.A.: Assessment of visual, auditory, and kinesthetic learning style among undergraduate nursing students. Int. J. Adv. Nurs. Stud. **5**, 1–4 (2016)
10. Ichinco, M., Harms, K.J., Kelleher, C.: Towards understanding successful novice example user in blocks-based programming. J. Vis. Lang. Sent. Syst. **3**, 101–118 (2017)
11. Kaya, A., Ozturk, R., Altin Gumussoy, C.: Usability measurement of mobile applications with system usability scale (SUS). In: Calisir, F., Cevikcan, E., Camgoz Akdag, H. (eds.) Industrial Engineering in the Big Data Era. LNMIE, pp. 389–400. Springer, Cham (2019). https://doi.org/10.1007/978-3-030-03317-0_32
12. Olde Keizer, R.A.C.M., et al.: Using socially assistive robots for monitoring and preventing frailty among older adults: a study on usability and user experience challenges. Health Technol. **9**(4), 595–605 (2019). https://doi.org/10.1007/s12553-019-00320-9
13. Lee, W.H., Lee, H.K.: The usability attributes and evaluation measurements of mobile media AR (augmented reality). Cogent Arts Hum. **3**(1), 1241171 (2016)
14. Linek, S.B.: Order effects in usability questionnaires. J. Usab. Stud. **12**(4), 164–182 (2017)
15. Malik, N.A., Hanapiah, F.A., Rahman, R.A.A., Yussof, H.: Emergence of socially assistive robotics in rehabilitation for children with cerebral palsy: a review. Int. J. Adv. Rob. Syst. **13**(3), 135 (2016)
16. Menges, R., Tamimi, H., Kumar, C., Walber, T., Schaefer, C., Staab, S.: Enhanced representation of web pages for usability analysis with eye tracking. In: Proceedings of the 2018 ACM Symposium on Eye Tracking Research & Applications, pp. 1–9 (2018)

17. Papadopoulos, I., Lazzarino, R., Miah, S., Weaver, T., Thomas, B., Koulougli-oti, C.: A systematic review of the literature regarding socially assistive robots in pre-tertiary education. Comput. Educ. **155**, 103924 (2020). https://doi.org/10. 1016/j.compedu.2020.103924. http://www.sciencedirect.com/science/article/pii/ S0360131520301238

18. Piech, C., Sahami, M., Huang, J., Guibas, L.: Autonomously generating hints by inferring problem solving policies. In: Proceedings of the Second (2015) ACM Conference on Learning@ Scale, pp. 195–204 (2015)

19. Pino, M., Boulay, M., Jouen, F., Rigaud, A.S.: "Are we ready for robots that care for us?" Attitudes and opinions of older adults toward socially assistive robots. Front. Aging Neurosci. **7**, 141 (2015)

20. Pranoto, H., Tho, C., Warnars, H.L.H.S., Abdurachman, E., Gaol, F.L., Soewito, B.: Usability testing method in augmented reality application. In: 2017 International Conference on Information Management and Technology (ICIMTech), pp. 181–186. IEEE (2017)

21. Rodriguez, R.G., Monteoliva, J.M., Pattini, A.E.: A comparative field usability study of two lighting measurement protocols. Int. J. Hum. Factors Ergon. **5**(4), 323–343 (2018)

22. Roscoe, R.D., Allen, L.K., Weston, J.L., Crossley, S.A., McNamara, D.S.: The writing pal intelligent tutoring system: usability testing and development. Comput. Compos. **34**, 39–59 (2014)

23. Shackel, B.: Usability-context, framework, definition, design and evaluation. Interact. Comput. **21**(5–6), 339–346 (2009)

24. Sonderegger, A., Schmutz, S., Sauer, J.: The influence of age in usability testing. Appl. Ergon. **52**, 291–300 (2016)

25. Stein, G., Lédeczi, A.: Mixed reality robotics for stem education. In: 2019 IEEE Blocks and Beyond Workshop (B&B), pp. 49–53 (2019)

26. Vázquez, C., Xia, L., Aikawa, T., Maes, P.: Words in motion: kinesthetic language learning in virtual reality. In: 2018 IEEE 18th International Conference on advanced learning technologies (ICALT), pp. 272–276. IEEE (2018)

27. Wang, J., Antonenko, P., Celepkolu, M., Jimenez, Y., Fieldman, E., Fieldman, A.: Exploring relationships between eye tracking and traditional usability testing data. Int. J. Hum.-Comput. Interact. **35**(6), 483–494 (2019)

28. Williams, T., Hirshfield, L., Tran, N., Grant, T., Woodward, N.: Using augmented reality to better study human-robot interaction. In: Chen, J.Y.C., Fragomeni, G. (eds.) HCII 2020. LNCS, vol. 12190, pp. 643–654. Springer, Cham (2020). https:// doi.org/10.1007/978-3-030-49695-1_43

29. Williams, T., et al.: Virtual, augmented, and mixed reality for human-robot interaction (VAM-HRI). In: Companion of the 2020 ACM/IEEE International Conference on Human-Robot Interaction, HRI 2020, pp. 663–664. Association for Computing Machinery, New York (2020). https://doi.org/10.1145/3371382.3374850

30. Xefteris, S., Palaigeorgiou, G.: Mixing educational robotics, tangibles and mixed reality environments for the interdisciplinary learning of geography and history (2019)

31. Yang, F.C.O.: The design of AR-based virtual educational robotics learning system. In: 2019 8th International Congress on Advanced Applied Informatics (IIAI-AAI), pp. 1055–1056. IEEE (2019)

Legibility of Robot Approach Trajectories with Minimum Jerk Path Planning

Raymond H. Cuijpers$^{(\boxtimes)}$ ⓘ, Peter A. M. Ruijten,
and Vincent J. P. van den Goor

Human Technology Interaction Group, Eindhoven University of Technology,
Eindhoven, The Netherlands
r.h.cuijpers@tue.nl

Abstract. When a robot approaches a person, the chosen trajectory ideally informs the person not only about the robot's intended target location, but also its intended orientation. However, planning a straight line to the goal location does not guarantee a correct final orientation, potentially causing confusion as the robot eventually rotates towards its unsuspecting target. One method that could remedy this problem is minimum jerk path planning, which results in the smoothest possible path that ends in the pre-specified final orientation. The technique is already widely used in robotic arm motion planning, but existing work is lacking for regular path planning. The aim of the current study is to implement minimum jerk path planning for the Nao robot and to evaluate the potential benefit for human observers to infer the intended target of the robot. Results show that minimum jerk path planning significantly improves people's recognition of the robot's destination compared to straight line path planning. Meanwhile, the perceived likeability and human likeness of the robot remain the same, suggesting that implementing smooth robot path planning that includes the final orientation leads to more predictable robot approaching behaviour.

Keywords: Human-aware navigation · Path planning · Robot intention · Human-robot interaction

1 Introduction

In many robot applications that are being developed, the robot needs to approach people in order to interact with them. For example, socially assistive robots are designed to operate in human environments and assist humans directly by serving medication and having conversations with users [9]. We also know that the robot should respect a socially acceptable distance and position depending on the direction of approach [24]. This results in the so-called personal interaction space that specifies for each direction of approach which position and orientation are optimal for the robot to initiate an interaction. The precise shape and size of the personal interaction space depends on the type of interaction [15], number

© Springer Nature Switzerland AG 2020
A. R. Wagner et al. (Eds.): ICSR 2020, LNAI 12483, pp. 392–403, 2020.
https://doi.org/10.1007/978-3-030-62056-1_33

of interactants [11,19] and human pose [24]. Regardless of the precise size and shape of personal interaction space in a given context, it does not specify how the robot should move towards the desired destination. Many methods have been proposed in the literature to plan trajectories mainly to avoid collisions (e.g. [10,21]) while taking personal space into account (e.g. [12,26]) or by maximising the interaction potential [15]. Previously, we also developed a behaviour-based navigation algorithm that smoothly aligns the robot to face the user while it is approaching the optimal position for starting a conversation [23,25].

Most planning methods either implicitly or explicitly optimise some cost function [13], but they do not consider the fact that human observers try to anticipate the intended goal of the robot as it moves. Given that personal interaction space models not only specify a position, but also an orientation [24,25], a straight line trajectory would require an alignment behaviour at the end of the movement. This may not be desirable in multi-party situations [18], where a robot needs to face the person to address. It would seem that it is useful for the user to be able to predict the robot's intended goal in these situations [4]. Enhancing the predictability of the robot's actions could also improve the user's experience [7] as well as its perceived intelligence [1].

An alternative approach is to plan a maximally smooth, human-like trajectory using the so-called minimum jerk model [6]. Minimum-jerk path planning is not a new concept in robotics [20]. It has frequently been applied to calculate robot arm trajectories [14,17], and for navigation [8]. Because the minimum-jerk trajectories are very human-like, it is often applied for planning robot movements when interacting with people e.g. [16] or for therapy [2]. Here, we focus on the fact that the smoothness constraint imposes a tight coupling between the robot's heading direction and its destination. In other words, the final orientation of the robot is easy to predict long before the robot arrives at its destination [5].

The goal of the current work is to apply the minimum jerk algorithm to path planning and to verify whether it increases the legibility of the robot's navigational behaviour and improves user experience in a multi-party situation. For that purpose we let the robot approach a dyad of participants from different directions using either a minimum jerk trajectory or a straight line trajectory. We measure the time at which the participants know to whom the robot is heading in addition to the perceived likeability of the robot and its perceived human-likeness. We expect that people are faster in identifying a robot's navigational goals when it approaches them using a minimum-jerk path compared to a conventional straight path. Furthermore, we hypothesize that people perceive the robot as more human-like and likeable when it approaches them using a minimum jerk path.

2 Methods

2.1 Participants

Twenty-nine participants (12 males, 17 females $M_{age} = 20.9$, $SD_{age} = 2.2$, Range = 19 to 29) with normal or corrected-to-normal vision were recruited through the J.F.S. Participant database of the Eindhoven University of Technology. All participants were given monetary compensation or course credit for their time and effort. The participants conducted the experiment in dyads. The task of the participants was to press one of two buttons on a game controller when they knew who was being approached by the robot. Participants could press multiple times. The robot always continued to walk to the goal masking the other participant' responses.

2.2 Design

The experiment consisted of two sets of ten trials. Each set used either the straight line or minimum-jerk path planning method. The former would navigate straight to a participant, rotating itself towards them after reaching the goal point, while the latter involved a smoother path that aims to end in the correct orientation (i.e. facing the user) automatically. The order of the two sets was counterbalanced across participant pairs to avoid learning effects. The experiment had a 2 (path planning: straight line vs. minimum-jerk) ×5 (start position: one of five positions equally spaced along an arc of −60 to +60 ° at 1.5 m from the goal locations) ×2 (goal position: in front of participant 1 or 2) within-subjects design. Figure 1 shows a schematic representation of the experimental set-up. The dependent variables of the experiment were the target to which participants thought the robot would navigate and the time at which the participants pressed the target buttons. A short questionnaire after each set of trials measured likeability and human-likeness of the robot for that specific path planning method.

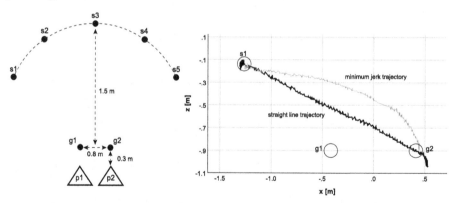

Fig. 1. Left: Schematic overview of the experimental set-up with start, goal and participant positions. Right: Example of the straight line and minimum jerk trajectory.

2.3 Experimental Set-Up

The experiment took place in the Virtu/e Lab at the Eindhoven University of Technology, which is equipped with a PhaseSpace LED Motion capture tracking system (Phasespace Inc., USA) in order to track the position and orientation of the robot in real-time. Multiple camera's were positioned throughout the room to follow the position of two LED's that were attached on top of the robot's head. The data recorded by the cameras was used to calculate the position of the robot at a frequency of 30 frames per second. The heading direction of the robot was determined by computing the vector perpendicular to the line connecting the two separate LED positions.

Two chairs were placed next to each other at one side of the lab to provide participants with a clear view of the entire room. Participants were given a Logitech F710 game controller to record their feedback during the experiment. They could indicate their prediction of the robot's target by pressing one of two buttons, corresponding to either the left or right seated participant.

We used a 57 cm tall humanoid Nao robot developed Aldebaran (Softbank Robotics Group Corp., Jp.). Programming of the experimental logic and robot's behaviour was done in Vizard using the Naoqi Python API. A custom script was made to randomise and counterbalance the trial order across subjects. Two path planning algorithms were implemented: regular straight line and minimum jerk path planning.

2.4   Robot Behaviour

The robot was programmed to either move straight toward its target or use a minimum jerk trajectory. For the straight trajectory we used a simple constant velocity vector based on the known target location and the recorded robot location:

$$v = \frac{v}{d} \cdot (x_{\text{target}} - x_{\text{robot}}), \tag{1}$$

where d is the distance to the target and v is the robot's speed, which is always set to maximum during walking as the Nao robot is very slow. When the robot was sufficiently close to the target, it simply turned towards the user with constant turning rate and zero forward velocity.

The minimum jerk trajectory is a 5th order polynomial of time that is completely specified by the initial and final position, velocity and acceleration [6]. For each coordinate one can write:

$$x_i(t) = a_i + b_i t + c_i t^2 + d_i t^3 + e_i t^4 + f_i t^5 \tag{2}$$

As the robot walked towards the target, the current position and actual orientation of the robot were recorded for each time step. The velocity of the robot was given by the robot's maximum velocity and it is assumed zero at the destination. The acceleration is assumed zero at the start and 1 m/s at the target location in the direction of the person. The minimum jerk trajectory is obtained by solving the vector of coefficients for each coordinate:

$$
\begin{pmatrix} x_i(t) \\ \dot{x}_i(t) \\ \ddot{x}_i(t) \end{pmatrix} = \begin{pmatrix} 1 & t & t^2 & t^3 & t^4 & t^5 \\ 0 & 1 & 2t & 3t^2 & 4t^3 & 5t^4 \\ 0 & 0 & 2 & 6t & 12t^2 & 20t^3 \end{pmatrix} \begin{pmatrix} a_i \\ b_i \\ c_i \\ d_i \\ e_i \\ f_i \end{pmatrix}
\tag{3}
$$

where time t is either the current time $t = 0$ or the arrival time $t = |x_{target} - x_{robot}|/v$. The minimum jerk path was calculated in real-time at a frequency of $6\,Hz$.

2.5   Measures

In order to measure participants' perceptions of the robot, we used the Likability, Animacy, and Anthropomorphism dimensions of the Godspeed scale [3]. Each of the three scales consisted of 5 semantic differentials and had reliable internal consistencies (Likability $\alpha = 0.79$, Animacy, $\alpha = 0.78$, and Anthropomorphism $\alpha = 0.81$).

2.6   Procedure

A dyad of two participants were welcomed and asked to read and sign an informed consent form. They were then given a short demographic survey as well as a questionnaire about their initial impression of the robot, measuring anthropomorphism, likability and perceived intelligence. This established a baseline and was repeated later in the experiment.

Participants were then asked to sit down on the chairs in the room and informed that the robot would try to approach one of them. As soon as participants knew who was the robot's target, they were instructed to press a corresponding button using the game controller to indicate their prediction. Participants could correct their judgement as many times as they wanted. Reaction time and chosen target were recorded.

After each trial, the robot was relocated to a new starting position in preparation of the next trial. The experimenter then initiated the new trial. After the robot had finished a set, both participants filled out the short questionnaire about their current impression of the robot. When both sets were completed the participants were debriefed, paid and thanked for their contribution.

3   Results

Prior to further analyses, we checked whether the generated trajectories followed the expected paths. In Fig. 1 an example of an actual path in the straight line condition and the minimum jerk condition are shown. One can clearly see the

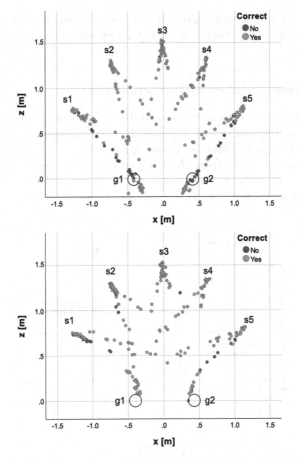

Fig. 2. Response distribution of correct (green) and false (red) predictions for straight line (left) and minimum jerk (right) path planning (Color figure online)

lateral movements as the Nao robot performs its step cycle. The straight line trajectory is fairly straight until the spot where it turns towards the participant at $(0.4, -0.9)$. It is also visible that the robot still moves forward when turning on the spot. Both trajectories end in the desired orientation i.e. facing the user, but only for the minimum jerk path planning the turn is very smooth.

Next we checked when participants gave a response for the first time and whether this response was correct. The distribution of first responses are shown in Fig. 2 for straight line path planning (upper panel) and minimum jerk path planning (lower panel). Green dots indicate correct predictions and red dots incorrect ones. The location of each dot corresponds to the robot's position at the time when the participant pressed the button. Almost all mistakes are made when the robot approaches from the side towards the nearer participant. For the straight line trajectory (upper pannel in Fig. 2) errors are seen across the entire path, for the minimum jerk condition incorrect responses are concentrated in the first half of the trajectory and almost no mistakes are made in the second half.

3.1 Prediction Accuracy and Reaction Time

Before analysing these data more quantitatively, we first address the left/right symmetry of the responses of the left and right participant. To do so, we flipped the start position, goal position and participant location of the right participant, so that all data are shown from the left participant's perspective and that the robot either moved towards "me" or the "other" participant. The mean number of correct responses after flipping the data are presented in Fig. 3.

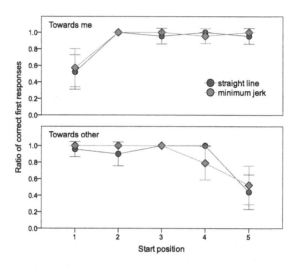

Fig. 3. Ratio of correct responses for each starting position and goal position for straight line (blue circles) and minimum jerk (green diamonds) path planning when the robot is walking towards "me" (upper panel) or to the "other" participant (lower panel). Error bars indicate 95% CI. (Color figure online)

From Fig. 3 the me/other symmetry becomes apparent: the responses are mirror-symmetrical for when the robot approaches "me" and when it approaches "other". To deal with the me/other symmetry, we flipped the start position for when the robot approaches the other participant. The resulting data are analysed with a univariate mixed model ANOVA with participant ID as random factor and path planning method (straight, minimum jerk), start position (1 till 5), goal position (me, other). We found a significant main effect of start position ($F(4, 106.32) = 45.781$, $p < 0.001$, $\eta_p^2 = 0.633$) but not of goal position ($F(1, 30.751) = 1.145$, $p = 0.293$, $\eta_p^2 = 0.036$) or path planning method ($F(1, 35.598) = 0.053$, $p = 0.819$, $\eta_p^2 = 0.01$). Nor were any of the interaction terms significant ($p > 0.155$). The absence of any interaction effect between goal position and target position ($F(4, 94.235) = 0.599$, $p = 0.664$, $\eta_p^2 = 0.025$) confirms that the me/other symmetry explains the pattern observed in Fig. 3.

In the same way we analysed the [10] log of the reaction times. The log transform results in homogeneous variances, according to Levene's test ($F = 2.36$, $p = 0.125$). We again found a significant main effect of start position ($F(4, 103, 867) = 11.434$, $p < 0.001$, $\eta_p^2 = 0.306$) but not of goal position ($F(1, 26.065) = 3.201$, $p = 0.085$, $\eta_p^2 = 0.109$), nor were there any interaction effects ($p > 0.512$). Unlike before we found a significant main effect of path planning method ($F(1, 30.208) = 5.576$, $p = 0.025$, $\eta_p^2 = 0.156$). The average log RT difference between minimum jerk and straight line path planning is -0.1 ± 0.04 which corresponds to a ratio of 0.8 ± 0.08. Thus, people were about 20% faster (between 1 s and 2 s) for minimum jerk path planning.

In Fig. 4 the results after applying the left/right symmetry correction and me/other symmetry correction are shown.

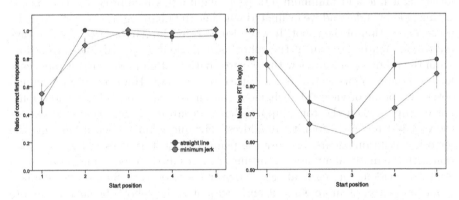

Fig. 4. Left: Ratio of correct first responses. Right: [10] log reaction times for each starting position after applying symmetry corrections. Error bars indicate SE.

3.2 Perception of the Robot

It was expected that the smooth trajectory of the minimum jerk model would appear more human-like, animated, and make the robot more likeable. To control for individual differences, we first subtracted average scores in the straight and minimum jerk conditions from the baseline measure. Differences between the conditions were tested with paired-samples t-tests with the average scores in the two conditions as groups. Results indicated a significant effect on Likability ($t(25) = 2.35$, $p = 0.027$). Following a straight line made people perceive the robot as less likeable compared to the baseline ($M = -0.15, SD = 0.54$), while the perceived likability of the robot that followed a minimum jerk path was about equal to the baseline ($M = 0.05, SD = 0.47$). No differences between the conditions were found on Anthropomorphism ($t(25) = 0.81$, $p = 0.428$) or Animacy ($t(25) = 1.48$, $p = 0.152$). These results are visualised in Fig. 5.

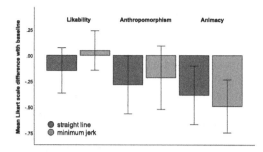

Fig. 5. Mean Likert scale difference with baseline of Likeability, Animacy, and Anthropomorphism for straight and minimum jerk trajectories.

4   Discussion and Conclusions

In the current study we investigated the predictability of a humanoid nao robot for straight line and minimum jerk path planning as it approached two people sitting side-by-side, and we evaluated whether the planning method affected the users' perception of the robot. It was assumed that human observers will always try to anticipate the goal of the robot as it navigates towards its destination. From the robot's point of view the shortest path is often most efficient especially for holonomic robots that can easily turn on the spot. However, from a human observer's point of view this behaviour may mask the robot's true "intention". For example, when the robot approaches a group of people it only reveals at the very last instant whom it will address. For minimum jerk path planning the opposite situation occurs, because the planned trajectory goes to the goal position with the minimal amount of turning. As a result the robot's final orientation is already evident very early along the movement trajectory. Supposedly, human-robot interaction is more efficient and pleasant if the robot's behaviour is more predictable. Thus, we expected that human observers can anticipate the robot's intended destination earlier and more accurately when a smooth trajectory is used than when a straight trajectory is used. Indeed, we found that our participants were significantly faster and more accurate for minimum jerk trajectories than for straight line trajectories. This was true despite the fact that the robot initially had to turn away more from the target in order to arrive smoothly in the correct orientation. It was also observed that most errors were made when the robot approached the nearer target from the side. This makes sense insofar that this situation was most ambiguous for straight line path planning. It is also the situation where the robot has to turn on the spot most. This confirms that the predictability of straight line trajectories is poor when the robot needs to reorient itself at the end. It is also in line with the idea that legible paths directed at the observer's viewpoint increase predictability [4,5].

It stands to reason that the more predictable a trajectory is the more natural and humanlike the behaviour looks. In turn this could affect the users' judgements in a positive way. Alternatively, one can argue that making any detour from a straight line would be inefficient and therefore bad. However, no such effects were observed. The participants were indifferent to how the robot moved towards its destination in terms of the perceived Likeability and Human-Likeness. There are two side notes to this conclusion. First of all it was very evident that it was always the same robot that was used. It is therefore possible participants evaluated the robot itself instead of its detailed navigation behaviour. If so, we would not have been able to measure any effect. The other complication is that the questionnaires were filled out after a block of ten trials but only in two trajectories the destination was difficult to predict. Together with the limited sensitivity of the Godspeed questionnaire this could explain why no effect was observed. It would have been better to create more situations with more ambiguity so as to maximise the apparent difference between minimum jerk and straight line path planning.

Minimum jerk path planning not only results in a smooth spatial trajectory, but also in a smooth velocity profile. As such, it is suitable for dealing with velocity based constraints of non-holonomic robots [8]. It is also very popular in human motor control as it can accurately describe both the spatial and velocity profile of human reaching and grasping movements [22]. Here we used it to generate smooth trajectories, but the Nao robot is too slow to generate the peak velocities that are needed for a minimum jerk velocity profile. Despite the fact that the velocity profile was programmed independently in the current implementation human observers could still infer the robot's destination sooner and more accurately. It would be interesting to see whether temporal information could also be used to predict a robot's destination, but then the robot would need to be much faster.

Minimum jerk path planning resulted in 20% faster reaction times . Given the slow speed of the Nao robot (about 9 cm/s), this corresponds to roughly 10 cm to 20 cm distance. It would be interesting to know if people would react equally fast if a faster robot was used. This would give insight in what information is used when predicting the observed trajectory.

Another extension would be to use gaze direction to indicate the robot's destination. It would be interesting to see how smoothness of movement trajectories interacts with other social cues like gaze direction.

While reaction times were improved, no difference in correctness of answers was found between minimum jerk and straight line trajectories. This can be explained by the nature of the experiment; participants were asked to only submit their response when they were certain they had identified the robot's goal. This may be the reason why participants achieved such high correctness ratios. People merely used more time in the minimum jerk condition until they were equally confident about their answer.

In conclusion, the current study developed a novel paradigm to evaluate predictability of a robot's navigation trajectory. The results show that minimum jerk path planning can be used for approaching humans in a predictable way. Reaction times in predicting a robot's goal are lower, but it does not negatively affect the correctness of these predictions, nor its perceived likability and human-likeness.

References

1. Althaus, P., Ishiguro, H., Kanda, T., Miyashita, T., Christensen, H.I.: Navigation for human-robot interaction tasks. In: IEEE International Conference on Robotics and Automation, 2004. Proceedings. ICRA'04. 2004, vol. 2, pp. 1894–1900. IEEE (2004)
2. Asker, A., Assal, S.F.M., Ding, M., Takamatsu, J., Ogasawara, T., Mohamed, A.M.: Modeling of natural sit-to-stand movement based on minimum jerk criterion for natural-like assistance and rehabilitation. Adv. Robot. **31**(17), 901–917, September 2017. 10/gg8x5z. https://doi.org/10.1080/01691864.2017.1372214. publisher: Taylor & Francis _eprint
3. Bartneck, C., Kulic, D., Croft, E., Zoghbi, S.: Measurement instruments for the anthropomorphism, animacy, likeability, perceived intelligence, and perceived safety of robots. Int. J. Soc. Robot. **1**(1), 71–81 (2009). https://doi.org/10.1007/s12369-008-0001-3
4. Dragan, A.D.: Legible Robot Motion Planning. Ph.D. thesis, Carnegie Mellon University, July 2015. https://doi.org/10.1184/R1/6720419.v1
5. Dragan, A.D., Lee, K.C.T., Srinivasa, S.S.: Legibility and predictability of robot motion. In: Proceedings of the 8th ACM/IEEE International Conference on Human-Robot Interaction, pp. 301–308. IEEE Press (2013)
6. Flash, T., Hogan, N.: The coordination of arm movements: an experimentally confirmed mathematical model. J. Neurosci. **5**(7), 1688–1703 (1985). https://doi.org/10.1523/JNEUROSCI.05-07-01688.1985
7. Gielniak, M.J., Liu, C.K., Thomaz, A.L.: Generating human-like motion for robots. Int. J. Robot. Res. **32**(11), 1275–1301 (2013)
8. Guarino Lo Bianco, C.: Minimum-jerk velocity planning for mobile robot applications. IEEE Trans. Robot. **29**, 1317–1326 (2013). https://doi.org/10.1109/TRO.2013.2262744
9. Johnson, D.O., et al.: Socially assistive robots: a comprehensive approach to extending independent living. Int. J. Soc. Robot. **6**(2), 195 (2014). https://doi.org/10.1007/s12369-013-0217-8
10. Kanda, A., Arai, M., Suzuki, R., Kobayashi, Y., Kuno, Y.: Recognizing groups of visitors for a robot museum guide tour. In: 2014 7th International Conference on Human System Interactions (HSI), pp. 123–128. IEEE (2014)
11. Karreman, D., Utama, L., Joosse, M., Lohse, M., van Dijk, B., Evers, V.: Robot etiquette: how to approach a pair of people? In: Proceedings of the 2014 ACM/IEEE International Conference on Human-robot Interaction, pp. 196–197. HRI 2014, ACM, New York, NY, USA (2014). https://doi.org/10.1145/2559636.2559839
12. Kirby, R., Simmons, R., Forlizzi, J.: Companion: a constraint-optimizing method for person-acceptable navigation. In: RO-MAN 2009-The 18th IEEE International Symposium on Robot and Human Interactive Communication, pp. 607–612. IEEE (2009)
13. Kruse, T., Basili, P., Glasauer, S., Kirsch, A.: Legible robot navigation in the proximity of moving humans. In: Proceeding of IEEE Workshop Advanced Robotics and its Social Impacts (ARSO), pp. 83–88, May 2012. https://doi.org/10.1109/ARSO.2012.6213404
14. Kyriakopoulos, K.J., Saridis, G.N.: Minimum jerk path generation. In: Proceedings of 1988 IEEE International Conference on Robotics and Automation, pp. 364–369. IEEE (1988)

15. Mead, R., Matarić, M.J.: Autonomous human-robot proxemics: socially aware navigation based on interaction potential. Auton. Robots. **41**(5), 1189 (2017). https://doi.org/10.1007/s10514-016-9572-2

16. Pattacini, U., Nori, F., Natale, L., Metta, G., Sandini, G.: An experimental evaluation of a novel minimum-jerk cartesian controller for humanoid robots. In: 2010 IEEE/RSJ International Conference on Intelligent Robots and Systems, pp. 1668–1674, October 2010. 10/bdmqmn, l10/bdmqmn, iSSN: 2153–0866

17. Piazzi, A., Visioli, A.: Global minimum-jerk trajectory planning of robot manipulators. IEEE Trans. Industr. Electron. **47**(1), 140–149 (2000)

18. Ruijten, P.A.M., Cuijpers, R.H.: Do not let the robot get too close: investigating the shape and size of shared interaction space for two people in a conversation. Information, **11**(3), 147, March 2020. 10/gg2mhs. https://www.mdpi.com/2078-2489/11/3/147. number: 3 Publisher: Multidisciplinary Digital Publishing Institute

19. Ruijten, P.A., Cuijpers, R.H.: Stopping distance for a robot approaching two conversating persons. In: 2017 26th IEEE International Symposium on Robot and Human Interactive Communication (RO-MAN), pp. 224–229. IEEE (2017)

20. Sidobre, D., Desormeaux, K.: Smooth cubic polynomial trajectories for human-robot interactions. J. Intell. Robot. Syst. **95**(3–4), 851–869, September 2019. 10/gg8zcs. https://doi.org/10.1007/s10846-018-0936-z

21. Sisbot, E.A., Marin-Urias, L.F., Alami, R., Simeon, T.: A human aware mobile robot motion planner. IEEE Trans. Robot. **23**(5), 874–883 (2007). https://doi.org/10.1109/TRO.2007.904911

22. Smeets, J.B.J., Brenner, E.: A new view on grasping. Mot. Control **3**(3), 237–271 (1999)

23. Torta, E., Cuijpers, R.H., Juola, J.F.: Dynamic neural field as framework for behaviour coordination in mobile robots. In: Proceeding of World Automation Congress, vol. 2012, 1–6 (2012)

24. Torta, E., Cuijpers, R.H., Juola, J.F.: Design of a parametric model of personal space for robotic social navigation. Int. J. Soc. Robot. **5**(3), 357 (2013). https://doi.org/10.1007/s12369-013-0188-9

25. Torta, E., Cuijpers, R.H., Juola, J.F., Van Der Pol, D.: Modeling and testing proxemic behavior for humanoid robots. Int. J. Humanoid Robot. **09**(04), 1250028, December 2012. https://doi.org/10.1142/S0219843612500284. http://www.worldscientific.com/doi/abs/10.1142/S0219843612500284

26. Truong, X.T., Ou, Y.S., Ngo, T.: Towards culturally aware robot navigation. In: Proceeding of IEEE International Conference Real-time Computing and Robotics (RCAR), pp. 63–69, June 2016. https://doi.org/10.1109/RCAR.2016.7784002

"Excuse Me, Robot": Impact of Polite Robot Wakewords on Human-Robot Politeness

Tom Williams[1(✉)], Daniel Grollman[2], Mingyuan Han[1], Ryan Blake Jackson[1], Jane Lockshin[1], Ruchen Wen[1], Zachary Nahman[1], and Qin Zhu[1]

[1] Colorado School of Mines, Golden, CO 80401, USA
twilliams@mines.edu
[2] Plus One Robotics, Boulder, CO, USA
dan.grollman@plusonerobotics.com

Abstract. While the ultimate goal of natural-language based Human-Robot Interaction (HRI) may be free-form, mixed-initiative dialogue, social robots deployed in the near future will likely primarily engage in *wakeword-driven* interaction, in which users' commands are prefaced by a wakeword such as "Hey, Robot". This style of interaction helps to allay user privacy concerns, as the robot's full speech recognition module need not be employed until the target wakeword is used. Unfortunately, there are a number of concerns in the popular media surrounding this style of interaction, with consumers fearing that it is training users (in particular, children) to be rude towards technology, and by extension, rude towards other humans. In this paper, we present a study that demonstrates how an alternate style of wakeword, i.e., "Excuse me, Robot" may allay this concern, by priming users to phrase commands as Indirect Speech Acts.

Keywords: Persuasive robotics · Indirect speech acts · Wakewords

1 Introduction

Voice interactive technologies are becoming increasingly common: all modern smartphones (and many personal computers) come with at least one "digital assistant" to help users perform a variety of tasks. Indeed, with the increase of internet of things (IoT) technologies, voice interfaces are being added to a wide array of home and work appliances, including refrigerators, microwaves, and even faucets [12]. But despite several decades of research into mixed initiative dialogue [1,16] and turn taking [9,30], the dominant paradigm in consumer-grade voice interaction is primarily human-driven, with human turns started by platform-specific *wakewords*, such as "Alexa", "Okay Google", or "Hey Siri".

Wakewords, which help ensure that voice assistants only respond to genuine assistant-directed requests, and ensure user privacy, are traditionally designed for ease of automatic recognition. But, wakewords may also have social, emotional, and cognitive impact on their users. There has been significant public concern

A. R. Wagner et al. (Eds.): ICSR 2020, LNAI 12483, pp. 404–415, 2020.
https://doi.org/10.1007/978-3-030-62056-1_34

about the potential negative consequences of wakeword-driven interaction, i.e., that wakeword-driven interactions may encourage technology-directed language that is terse and direct, and that if children become accustomed to addressing machines in this manner, this could train them to be impolite [15,31]. Public outcry has been high enough that companies have responded by changing assistants' interaction patterns to encourage the use of key phrases such as "Please" and "Thank You" [2,11], a decision we will discuss in detail below.

As interactive robots are deployed into the wild, it is likely that the same concerns will arise. Indeed, when the Jibo robot was launched in 2017, it did so with the wakeword "Hey Jibo". We believe that the concerns the public has raised about wakeword-based interaction will be especially important to address for interactive robots given their unique persuasive power.

Human norms are well known to be dynamic and malleable [14], with norms defined, communicated, and enforced by community members (and the technologies with which they interact) [32]. As researchers have recently argued, social robots wield unique influence over these norms due to their joint status as perceived community members and as technological tools [17]. This influence, which social robots may wield both through direct persuasion and implicit social pressure [5,18,21,35], may be especially strong among language capable robots, with their increased linguistic faculties, and perceived agency, embodiment, anthropomorphism, and ostensible individuality, resulting in significantly greater effect on users' systems of social and moral norms, including sociocultural norms such as norms of politeness. We argue that for robots, the *choice* of wakeword used is thus especially important.

In this paper, we examine the effect a designer's *choice* of wakeword may have on robot-directed human politeness. In Sect. 2, we discuss previous attempts by digital assistant designers to encourage politeness in wakeword-based interaction, and potential limitations of those approaches. We then propose and justify an alternative approach, and delineate a set of research questions and hypotheses raised by that approach. In Sects. 3 and 4, we then present the design and results of a human-subject experiment designed to evaluate those hypotheses. Finally, in Sects. 5 and 6, we discuss and interpret these results, and present several potential directions for future work.

2   Wakeword Design

In response to public concern about wakeword-based child-Alexa interactions, Amazon pursued a variety of strategies to try to encourage children to speak politely with Alexa. Initially, Amazon developed a mode requiring interactants to include "please" in their requests for them to succeed[1]. After being told that this approach would likely backfire, Amazon shifted to simply praise interactants

---

[1] Cf. the work of Bonfert [4], who show that rebuking adult Alexa users for not using "please" does indeed lead users to use "please" more frequently (likely to avoid the annoyance of the rebuke) but also causes users to like the assistant less and view it as less inherently entitled to politeness.

for using the words "please" and "thank you" [3]. While this may be effective at encouraging some users to use the word "please", we suspect it may be far less effective at encouraging users to *be polite*. While saying please is indeed often used as a politeness strategy, adherenece to different types of politeness norms is highly context-sensitive [23], and the type of please-usage encouraged by this approach, in which requests are preceded by "Please" (e.g., "Hey Alexa, *Please* play Todd the T-1000"), is actually *negatively-correlated* with politeness [10], as it is most naturally followed by a command. In fact, sentence-medial please usage is typically perceived as polite in part because it typically augments sentences that are already polite for other reasons, such as the use of so-called "indirect speech acts" [28] (e.g., "Could you X", whose literal meaning (in this case, a yes-or-no question pertaining to ability) mismatches its intended meaning (in this case, a request for action)).

An Alternate Approach

To design wakeword-based human-robot interactions that counteract the potential tendency towards impoliteness, rather than simply encouraging the use of "please", a more promising approach might be to change the wakeword itself, in a way that encourages deeper politeness strategies such as indirect speech act usage. Consider the simple change in wakeword from 'Hey' to 'Excuse me'.

First, while "Hey <Name>" – especially when followed by "please" – may syntactically prime the speaker to continue their utterance with a direct phrasing, "Excuse me ¡Name¿" may instead prime the speaker to continue their utterance with an indirect phrasing. We argue that in Example 1 below, the impolite phrasing (1a) is slightly more syntactically natural, while in Example 2, the polite phrasing (2b) is significantly more natural.

(1)   a.   Hey Pepper, please bring me a coffee.
       b.   Hey Pepper, please could you bring me a coffee?
(2)   a.   Excuse me, Pepper, bring me a coffee.
       b.   Excuse me, Pepper, could you bring me a coffee?

Second, it may be easier to prime users to use indirect speech acts than arbitrary keywords such as "please", as humans automatically tend toward indirect speech act use, especially in contexts with highly conventionalized sociocultural politeness norms [33]. Third, "Excuse me" as a wakeword is advantageous as it simply changes the wakeword participants need to use, without adding any additional requirements. Fourth, feedback delivered after "please"-use may eventually be perceived as annoying, thus reducing its expected usage. In contrast, wakeword alteration does not require any robotic feedback. Finally, if this choice of wakeword is indeed effective in priming indirect speech act use, this will lead to a more productive opportunity for "ritualization" than would successful priming of "Please"-usage. Rituals are critical ways through which a community maintains its values and cultivates these values in community members [25], and human acts involving appropriate performance of rituals can be viewed as manifesting cultivated moral selves [22]. Using the wakeword "Excuse me" opens opportunities that "prompt" human teammates to initiate and participate in conversations and interactions that are guided by rituals, whereas "Please" may in fact invite requests that are explicitly demanding.

Hypotheses

In this paper, we begin to examine these intuitions by exploring the efficacy of "Excuse me" relative to the standard impolite wakeword baseline "Hey". Specifically, we test the following concrete hypotheses:

Hypothesis One: Requiring the use of a polite wakeword (e.g., "Excuse me") will result in increased robot-directed politeness.

Hypothesis Two: Observed differences in robot-directed politeness will be due to wakeword-driven linguistic priming rather than wakeword-driven differences in perceptions of robots.

3   Methods

To investigate our hypotheses, we conducted a two-condition between-subjects laboratory experiment. In this experiment, human participants collaborated with a fully autonomous robot and a human confederate in a simulated restaurant scenario, with the wakeword used to initiate communication altered between conditions. The experimental setting and robot (SoftBank's Pepper) are shown in Fig. 1.

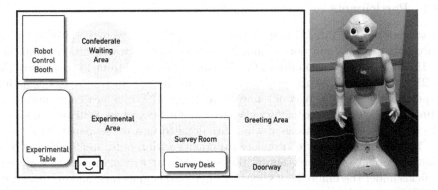

Fig. 1. The experimental environment layout (left) and the Pepper robot (right).

3.1   Experimental Design

Upon arriving at our lab and providing informed consent, participants were given a headset to facilitate audio recording, and were instructed that they would be giving four food orders to a robot designed to help waiters in a simulated restaurant scenario. We chose this context due to its conventions surrounding the use of politeness and directness in task-oriented speech [33]. Every robot-directed utterance during the experiment was required to begin with the robot's wakeword. In the impolite wakeword condition, the wakeword was "Hey Pepper", while in the polite wakeword condition, the robot's wakeword was "Excuse me Pepper". Our hypotheses predict that robot-directed speech (aside from the wakeword) would be more polite in the polite wakeword condition.

The participant was then given four cards, each containing a food item (e.g., "cheeseburger") and a table number (1 through 4), and was informed as to the experimental procedure. When they were clear on this procedure, the experimenter activated the robot by saying "{Hey / Excuse me} Pepper we are ready to begin". The robot then animated and said "Great! Hi there. I'm Pepper. I'm ready to take the first order". The participant then told each food order to the robot with an utterance like "{Hey / Excuse me} Pepper can I have a chicken quesadilla please?" The robot ostensibly sent the order to the "kitchen". The human confederate then entered with a card representing the food and said "Alright, I've got the order for you." The participant then told the confederate on which table to place the order. After all four orders, the participant was brought to an adjacent room, where they were given the Robotic Social Attributes Scale (RoSAS) [8], which measures warmth, competence, and discomfort, as well as a brief demographic survey. Finally, participants were paid and debriefed.

3.2   Participants

30 student participants (17 male, 12 female, 1 nonbinary) were recruited from our university campus, and were randomly assigned to our two conditions, resulting in 15 participants per condition. Participant ages ranged from 18 to 36 years (M = 21.30, SD = 3.91). This small sample size was in part due to the fact that this experiment was run as part of a novel Experimental Ethics curricular module in Mines' Spring 2019 *Robot Ethics* class, co-taught by authors Williams and Zhu, the pedagogical implications of which are detailed in a recent paper [34].

12 participants reported previous experience with robots, and 9 reported previous experience in the restaurant industry. All participants reported majoring in fields under the umbrella of science, technology, engineering, and mathematics (STEM), with the two most popular majors being computer science (9 participants) and mechanical engineering (5 participants). Other represented majors with 3 or fewer participants include: chemical engineering, civil engineering, electrical engineering, environmental engineering, geological engineering, geophysics, materials science, metallurgy and materials engineering, petroleum engineering, physics, and statistics and applied math. Participants were paid $5 each for participation.

3.3 Data Annotation

Three annotators marked each participant utterance for the presence of the common politeness markers delineated by Danescu-Niculescu-Mizil [10] and described below (see also [6]). Cases where all three annotators disagreed were resolved by a vote from an additional annotator. The first of these markers, and our main marker of interest, is whether the utterance was a conventionally indirect speech act, i.e., an utterance who's surface form does not match its underlying intent. For example, the command "Bring me a cheeseburger" could be phrased indirectly and more politely as a question like "Could you bring me a cheeseburger?" (Fleiss' κ for inter-annotator agreement = 0.54). Other common politeness markers which we annotate in both direct and indirect speech are deference signifiers (e.g., "nice work" or "good job", $\kappa = 0.32$), gratitude signifiers (e.g., "thank you", $\kappa = 0.88$), apologizing (e.g., "Sorry to bother you...", $\kappa = 1.0$), and use of the word "please" ($\kappa = 0.89$).

3.4 Analysis

We analyzed our experimental data under a Bayesian statistical framework using the BRMS software package for Bayesian multilevel models [7] and the JASP statistical analysis software [20][2]. We report (1) Bayes factors (BFs) indicating the relative likelihoods of our data given our experimental and null hypotheses (expressed as odds ratios), with interpretations of the strengths of these ratios based on common conventions [19], and (2) credible intervals (CIs) on the posterior probability distributions for our metrics of interest.

Hypotheses One

For Hypothesis One, the following null and alternative binomial models were defined in BRMS.

Null Model

$Politeness_i \sim Binomial(1, p_i)$

$logit(p_i) = \alpha_{actor_i}$

That is, appearance of politeness signifiers in each trial depend only on the per-participant intercept for the participant involved in that trial.

Alternative Model

$Politeness_i \sim Binomial(1, p_i)$

$logit(p_i) = \alpha_{actor_i} + \beta Wakeword_i$

$\beta \sim student\_t(5, 0, 2.5)$

That is, appearance of politeness signifiers in each trial depends both on the per-participant intercept for the participant involved in that trial, and on the wakeword used in that condition, with a Student's t distribution centered on 0 with 5 degrees of freedom and scale 2.5 used as the prior distribution on the wakeword indicator variable's coefficient β. This prior distribution was chosen based on best-practices recommendations from the research literature [13].

---

[2] Data is available at https://osf.io/c5hxm/.

To evaluate Hypothesis One, these models were fit using the subset of data corresponding with robot-directed utterances, and compared using a *Bayes Factor analysis*, in which the amount of evidence for the alternate hypothesis relative to the null hypothesis is quantified as the probability of generating the observed data under the alternate model, divided by the probability of generating the observed data under the null model [27].

3.5   Hypothesis Two

To evaluate Hypothesis Two, RoSAS scores [8] were summed across each factor, after which a Bayesian independent sample t-test was performed using JASP, with wakeword condition as a grouping variable.

4   Results

Hypothesis One

In this section, we report the results of the Bayesian binomial regression used to fit the null and alternative models specified for Hypothesis One. Separate models were fit and analyzed for each of our politeness markers of interest.

Indirect Speech Act Usage – According to the best posterior fit for the alternative model, participants in the impolite wakeword condition were less likely to use robot-directed indirect speech acts than were participants in the polite wakeword condition (mean robot-directed ISA frequency in the impolite wakeword condition = 2.33 (SD = 2.02); frequency in the polite wakeword condition = 3.73 (SD = 1.03); $\beta = -3.54$; 95% CI = $[-9.63, 1.08]$). Comparison to the null model resulted in a Bayes Factor (BF) of 2.49, indicating weak evidence in favor of our alternative hypothesis: the data observed are about two-and-a-half times more likely under our alternative (condition-sensitive) model than under the null (condition-insensitive) model.

Deference – More data is needed to fully understand the effect of wakeword choice on robot-directed deference (mean robot-directed frequency of deference in the impolite wakeword condition = 0.0; frequency in the polite wakeword condition = 0.07 (SD = 0.26); $\beta = -1.24$; 95% CI = $[-7.17, 3.27]$; BF = 0.93).

Gratitude – More data is needed to assess the effect of wakeword choice on robot-directed gratitude (mean robot-directed frequency of gratitude in the impolite wakeword condition = 0.0; frequency in the polite wakeword condition = 0.07 (SD = 0.26); $\beta = -0.04$, 95% CI = $[-6.21, 6.05]$; BF = 1.04).

Apologizing – No instances of robot-directed apologizing were observed.

Please – More data is needed to assess the effect of wakeword choice on robot-directed please-usage (mean robot-directed frequency of please-usage in the impolite wakeword condition = 0.20 (SD = 0.77); frequency in the polite wakeword condition = 0.27 (SD = 0.59); $\beta = -0.18$; 95% CI = $[-5.04, 4.36]$; BF = 0.81).

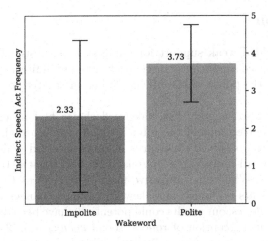

Fig. 2. Robot-directed ISA use after impolite and polite wakewords.

Hypothesis Two

A Bayesian Independent Samples t-test provided evidence against a difference between the two conditions on perceived competence ($\mu_I = 38.20(SD_I = 9.017)$, $\mu_P = 38.33$ ($SD_P = 9.817$); $BF = 0.345$), and inconclusive results with respect to Warmth ($\mu_I = 26.93$ ($SD_I = 9.285$), $\mu_P = 22.60$ ($SD_P = 7.790$); $BF = 0.705$) and Discomfort $\mu_I = 12.80$ ($SD_I = 3.707$), $\mu_P = 14.73$ ($SD_P = 3.011$); $BF = 0.859$), as shown in Fig. 3. Overall this provides anecdotal to moderate evidence in support of Hypothesis Two, allowing us to tentatively rule out effects of wakeword design on human perceptions of robots as an explanation for our findings with respect to Hypothesis One. In fact, the weak differences observed in this analysis trend in favor of *decreased* warmth and *increased* discomfort in the polite wakeword condition, which is the opposite of what would have been expected in order to provide an alternative explanation for our results.

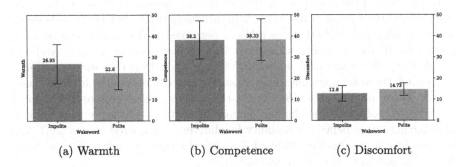

(a) Warmth   (b) Competence   (c) Discomfort

Fig. 3. Differences in Summed ROSAS Scores by Experimental Condition

5   Discussion

Our results provided weak support for our first hypothesis (H1): participants may indeed have used significantly more robot-directed indirect speech acts when instructed to use the polite wakeword than when instructed to use the impolite wakeword.

Our analyses also suggest that wakeword choice had no discernible effect on participants' perceptions of the robot's social attributes, thus reducing the probability that the observed differences in robot-directed politeness were due to different wakeword-induced perceptions of the robot itself (H2).

Limitations — While our subjective metrics allowed us to rule out explanations of our results grounded in wakeword-induced changes in perception of robots' social *attributes*, our results could potentially have been due to wakeword-induced changes in perception of robots' social *agency* (cp. [24]), which could impact the robot's persuasive capability [26]. While we expect that a robot's perceived sociality and perceived social attributes would likely be tightly correlated, direct examination of perceived sociality may be worthwhile.

Overall Design Recommendation Based on the results discussed above, and subject to our identified limitations, we recommend that if designers of social robots wish to encourage polite robot-directed speech, they should use politeness-priming wakewords such as "Excuse me, Robot" rather than traditional wakewords such as "Hey, Robot".

6   Conclusions

Our results suggest that by using a polite wakeword (e.g., "Excuse me, Robot"), robot designers may be able to prime users to interact more politely with their robots overall. The most critical next step building on this experiment will be to correct the limitations we have identified, in order to better study whether this priming may actually carry over into human-human interactions as well.

In addition, a number of other key open questions may also be addressed in future work. First, there are a number of open questions regarding the real-world usability of polite wakewords: Whether users think that polite wakewords are appropriate, and whether the robot is perceived as deserving the associated politeness. If not, do polite wakewords lead to any decrease in use? And will people use polite wakewords voluntarily if they know that they are an option?

Second, there are open questions regarding how our results might differ based on the nature of the robot: How might the robot's gender presentation impact carryover of politeness into human-human interactions, given previous findings of differences in persuasive capability for differently gendered robots [29]? And how might our results have differed if a digital assistant such as Siri or Alexa had been used instead of a humanoid robot?

Third, there are open questions regarding how our results might differ with different user populations. There have been significant concerns in the media that direct wakewords may be teaching children to be impolite. Future work will thus be needed to determine whether the effects found in this research actually differ when study participants are drawn from a child population.

Fourth, while we hypothesize that the use of a wakeword such as "Excuse me" would be more effective than encouragement to use "Please", which as we discuss in the introduction is not actually always positively correlated with politeness, empirical evidence may be needed to strongly argue this claim, as it is possible that encouraging users to use "Please" might actually lead to increased use of "Please" in the context of indirect speech acts, in which Please-usage is indeed correlated with perceived politeness.

Finally, while we examined usage of each of a set of politeness markers in isolation, it may be worth re-analyzing our data, or data from future experiments, using a holistic measure of overall politeness that takes into account usage of each of the individual politeness markers examined in this paper.

Acknowledgments. This work was funded in part by Grants IIS-1849348 and IIS-1909847 from the National Science Foundation. We would also like to thank the students of the Spring 2019 *Robot Ethics* class at the Colorado School of Mines for their help conducting this experiment.

References

1. Allen, J.E., Guinn, C.I., Horvtz, E.: Mixed-initiative interaction. IEEE Intell. Syst. Appl. **14**(5), 14–23 (1999)
2. Baig, E.: Kids were being rude to alexa, so amazon updated it (2018). https://www.usatoday.com/story/tech/columnist/baig/2018/04/25/amazon-echo-dot-kids-alexa-thanks-them-saying-please/547911002/
3. BBC: Amazon Alexa to reward kids who say: 'please' (2018). https://www.bbc.com/news/technology-43897516
4. Bonfert, M., Spliethöver, M., Arzaroli, R., Lange, M., Hanci, M., Porzel, R.: If you ask nicely: a digital assistant rebuking impolite voice commands. In: Proceedings of the 2018 on International Conference on Multimodal Interaction, pp. 95–102. ACM (2018)
5. Briggs, G., Scheutz, M.: How robots can affect human behavior: investigating the effects of robotic displays of protest and distress. Int. J. Soc. Rob. **6**, 343–355 (2014)
6. Brown, P., Levinson, S.: Politeness: Some Universals in Language Usage. Cambridge University Press, Cambridge (1987)
7. Bürkner, P.C., et al.: BRMS: an r package for bayesian multilevel models using stan. J. Stat. Softw. **80**(1), 1–28 (2017)
8. Carpinella, C.M., Wyman, A.B., Perez, M.A., Stroessner, S.J.: The robotic social attributes scale (ROSAS): development and validation. In: Proceeding of HRI (2017)
9. Cassell, J., Torres, O.E., Prevost, S.: Turn taking versus discourse structure. Machine Conversations, pp. 143–15533. Springer, Berlin (1999)
10. Danescu-Niculescu-Mizil, C., Sudhof, M., Jurafsky, D., Leskovec, J., Potts, C.: A computational approach to politeness with application to social factors. Proc. ACL (2013)

11. Elgin, M.: The case against teaching kids to be polite to alexa (2018). https://www.fastcompany.com/40588020/the-case-against-teaching-kids-to-be-polite-to-alexa. Accessed 26 Jun 2019
12. Faucet, D.: Voice faucet (2019). https://www.deltafaucet.com/Voice
13. Ghosh, J., Li, Y., Mitra, R.: On the use of cauchy prior distributions for bayesian logistic regression. Bayesian Anal. **13**, 359–383 (2015)
14. Gino, F.: Understanding ordinary unethical behavior: why people who value morality act immorally. Curr. Opin. Behav. Sci. **3**, 107–111 (2015)
15. Gordon, K.: Alexa and the age of casual rudeness (2018). https://www.theatlantic.com/family/archive/2018/04/alexa-manners-smart-speakers-command/558653/. Accessed 26 Jun 2019
16. Horvitz, E.: Principles of mixed-initiative user interfaces. In: Proceeding of CHI (1999)
17. Jackson, R.B., Wililams, T.: On perceived social and moral agency in natural language capable robots. In: HRI WS on The Dark Side of HRI (2019)
18. Jackson, R.B., Williams, T.: Language-capable robots may inadvertently weaken human moral norms. In: Proceeding of HRI, pp. 401–410. IEEE (2019)
19. Jarosz, A.F., Wiley, J.: What are the odds? a practical guide to computing and reporting bayes factors. J. Prob. Solving **7**, 2 (2014)
20. JASP Team, et al.: Jasp. Version 0.8. 0.0. software (2016)
21. Kennedy, J., Baxter, P., Belpaeme, T.: Children comply with a robot's indirect requests. In: Proceeding of HRI, pp. 198–199. ACM (2014)
22. Lai, K.L.: Confucian moral cultivation: some parallels with musical training. In: The Moral Circle and the Self: Chinese and Western Approaches. Open Court (2003)
23. Lockshin, J., Williams, T.: "We need to start thinking ahead": the impact of social context on linguistic norm adherence. In: Proceedings of the 42nd Annual Meeting of the Cognitive Science Society (COGSCI) (2020)
24. Mayer, R.E., Sobko, K., Mautone, P.D.: Social cues in multimedia learning: Role of speaker's voice. J. Educ. Psychol. **95**(2), 419 (2003)
25. Puett, M., Gross-Loh, C.: The Path: What Chinese Philosophers Can Teach us About the Good Life. Simon and Schuster, United States (2016)
26. Roubroeks, M., Ham, J., Midden, C.: When artificial social agents try to persuade people: the role of social agency on the occurrence of psychological reactance. Int. J. Soc. Robot. **3**(2), 155–165 (2011)
27. Rouder, J.N., Speckman, P.L., Sun, D., Morey, R.D., Iverson, G.: Bayesian t tests for accepting and rejecting the null hypothesis. Psy. Bul. Rev. **16**, 225–237 (2009)
28. Searle, J.R.: Indirect speech acts. Syntax Semant. **3**, 59–82 (1975)
29. Siegel, M., Breazeal, C., Norton, M.I.: Persuasive robotics: the influence of robot gender on human behavior. In: Proceeding of IROS. IEEE (2009)
30. Traum, D., Rickel, J.: Embodied agents for multi-party dialogue in immersive virtual worlds. In: Proceeding of AAMAS, pp. 766–773. ACM (2002)
31. Truong, A.: Parents are worried the amazon echo is conditioning their kids to be rude (2016). https://qz.com/701521/parents-are-worried-the-amazon-echo-is-conditioning-their-kids-to-be-rude/
32. Verbeek, P.P.: Moralizing Technology: Understanding and Designing the Morality of Things. University of Chicago Press, United States (2011)
33. Williams, T., Thames, D., Novakoff, J., Scheutz, M.: "Thank you for sharing that interesting fact!": effects of capability and context on indirect speech act use in task-based human-robot dialogue. In: Proceeding of HRI (2018)

34. Williams, T., Zhu, Q., Grollman, D.H.: An experimental ethics approach to robot ethics education. In: Proceedings of the 10th Symposium on Educational Advances in Artificial Intelligence (EAAI), pp. 13428–13435 (2020)
35. Winkle, K., Lemaignan, S., Caleb-Solly, P., Leonards, U., Turton, A., Bremner, P.: Effective persuasion strategies for socially assistive robots. In: Proceeding of HRI (2019)

Investigating Therapist Vocal Nonverbal Behavior for Applications in Robot-Mediated Therapies for Individuals Diagnosed with Autism

Wing-Yue Geoffrey Louie[1](✉), Jessica Korneder[2], Ala'aldin Hijaz[1], and Megan Sochanski[1]

[1] Intelligent Robotics Laboratory at Oakland University, Rochester, MI 48307, USA
`louie@oakland.edu`
[2] Applied Behavior Analysis Clinic at Oakland University, Rochester, MI 48307, USA

Abstract. Socially assistive robots (SARs) are being utilized for delivering a variety of healthcare services to patients. The design of these human-robot interactions (HRIs) for healthcare applications have primarily focused on the interaction flow and verbal behaviors of a SAR. To date, there has been minimal focus on investigating how SAR nonverbal behaviors should be designed according to the context of the SAR's communication goals during a HRI. In this paper, we present a methodology to investigate nonverbal behavior during specific human-human healthcare interactions so that they can be applied to a SAR. We apply this methodology to study the context-dependent vocal nonverbal behaviors of therapists during discrete trial training (DTT) therapies delivered to children with autism. We chose DTT because it is a therapy commonly being delivered by SARs and modeled after human-human interactions. Results from our study led to the following recommendations for the design of the vocal nonverbal behavior of SARs during a DTT therapy: 1) the consequential error correction should have a lower pitch and intensity than the discriminative stimulus but maintain a similar speaking rate; and 2) the consequential reinforcement should have a higher pitch and intensity than the discriminative stimulus but a slower speaking rate.

Keywords: Socially Assistive Robots · Nonverbal behavior · Autism

1 Introduction

Socially assistive robots (SARs) have the potential to transform healthcare services provided to individuals and improve outcomes within a variety of healthcare settings. SARs have already been utilized in assisted living facilities [1], mental healthcare [2], and exercise programming [3]. In these settings, SARs successfully interacted with patients and improved their physical, mental, and emotional health. In general, current interventions utilizing SARs have focused on *what* content is delivered during an intervention but not *how* an intervention should be delivered to a patient to be effective.

© Springer Nature Switzerland AG 2020
A. R. Wagner et al. (Eds.): ICSR 2020, LNAI 12483, pp. 416–427, 2020.
https://doi.org/10.1007/978-3-030-62056-1_35

During healthcare interactions both verbal and nonverbal behavior are necessary for effective as well as efficient communication and understanding to occur. For healthcare professional-patient interactions, verbal behaviors consist of the actual words spoken to patients and nonverbal behaviors include everything but the words that are spoken [4]. Examples of these nonverbal behaviors can include: gestures, facial expressions, body pose, interpersonal distance, appearance, vocal cues (i.e., prosody), and time-based cues (i.e., chronemics). Nonverbal communication strategies are important because they contribute positively to patient satisfaction, adherence, affect, and health outcomes during an intervention [5, 6].

The understanding of interactions with patients through nonverbal behavior is especially relevant in therapeutic fields such as Applied Behavior Analysis (ABA) [7]. This form of therapy is a widely used, evidence-based practice implemented for individuals with autism spectrum disorder (ASD). SARs are increasingly being combined with the principles of ABA to teach individuals with ASD social skills [8], imitation skills [9], and emotion recognition [10]. The verbal behaviors of these robot-mediated interventions are modeled after human therapist facilitated interventions where individuals with ASD have been successful in the acquisition of the skills targeted by the interventions. However, it remains unclear how robot nonverbal behaviors should be characterized throughout an intervention.

Our team's long-term research goal is to integrate SARs in healthcare settings to support the delivery of healthcare services to patients. Our current research efforts have focused on developing SARs to deliver ABA therapy to children with ASD to address the growing prevalence of ASD as well as labor challenges in delivering ABA services [11, 12]. Namely, we have developed a robot-mediated intervention that closely replicates existing ABA therapies and discrete trial training (DTT) teaching procedures implemented by human therapists at ABA clinics for teaching children with ASD to independently answer WH-questions [13]. The primary focus of our prior work was replicating the interaction flow and verbal behaviors of the human therapists during these interventions.

Our objective in this work is to study the context-dependent vocal nonverbal behaviors that ABA therapists exhibit when facilitating DTT therapy sessions with children with ASD. Specifically, we chose to investigate pitch, intensity and speaking rate of therapists because these are the vocal nonverbal behaviors that can be modeled with current state-of-the-art voice synthesizers [14]. We investigated the differences in therapist vocal nonverbal behaviors during different contexts within a DTT intervention session. Our primary hypotheses were that therapists: 1) display similar pitch, intensity, and speaking rate during the delivery of a consequential error correction and discriminative stimulus; and 2) display a higher pitch, higher intensity, and higher speaking rate during consequential reinforcement as compared to the delivery of a discriminative stimulus. This study will be important for informing the design of vocal nonverbal behaviors of SARs delivering ABA based interventions to individuals with ASD. Furthermore, this work serves as a model for studying context-dependent nonverbal behaviors during human-human interactions and utilizing these insights to design human-robot interactions (HRIs).

2   Related Work

Nonverbal behaviors have most commonly been studied within human-human interactions. The fields that have analyzed nonverbal behaviors among humans have included education [15], medicine [16], and therapeutic fields [17, 18]. The common trend amongst these studies has been the analysis of the overall nonverbal behavior of human participants during an entire human-human interaction. For example, in [16] the effect of a physician's overall eye contact on elderly patient understanding and adherence after a routine doctor visit was investigated. Overall, it was shown that when doctors use eye contact in conjunction with verbal communication patients had higher understanding and adherence to medical interventions.

In [17], the effect of music therapists' overall affect, interpersonal distance, and eye contact on older adult Alzheimer patients' affect and participation was investigated during group therapies. Namely, a study was conducted to measure Alzheimer patient affect and participation during group therapies under four therapist nonverbal behavior conditions: affect and interpersonal distance, affect alone, interpersonal distance alone, and no affect or interpersonal distance. Results indicated that the nonverbal behavior of therapists directly impacted the affect and participation of the older adult with Alzheimers.

In [18], change in therapist nonverbal behavior was investigated during therapies with individuals with depression. Namely, therapist nonverbal behavior was coded at the beginning and end of therapy sessions with patients. After observing cognitive-therapy sessions, reliable changes in nonverbal behavior by the patient and therapist were observed from the start of the session to the end of the session. However, the study did not investigate whether these nonverbal behavior changes were associated with changes in the context of a therapist's communication goals during a therapy.

Additionally, nonverbal behavior literature in social robotics has also focused on studying human-human interactions and using these studies to serve as a model for HRIs. These studies have investigated and modeled human gaze [19], speech-based gestures [20], and dyadic interaction based facial expressions [21] during social interactions. Although recent research has been successful in modeling general nonverbal social behaviors during human-human interactions and applying these models to HRIs, there has been a lack of emphasis on investigating how the nonverbal behaviors of humans change as result of changes in their communication goals or contexts. Additionally, research regarding nonverbal behaviors in HRI have primarily focused on investigating motion-based cues.

Current research investigating nonverbal behaviors in human-human interactions for robotics or other fields have all focused on general nonverbal behaviors or general demeanor of the doctor/therapist during human-human interactions. There has been a lack of research towards investigating how human nonverbal behaviors change within an interaction due to changing communication goals. The communication goal context is important to the correct application of nonverbal behaviors. When nonverbal behaviors are used in inappropriate situations or contexts it can lead to negative attitudes towards message delivery, poor message comprehension, and lack of trust [22, 23]. Hence, nonverbal communication must be considered within the context in which it occurs because it guides a human's nonverbal behavior encoding and a listener's nonverbal behavior decoding [22]. A robot interacting with human users should be capable of applying the appropriate nonverbal behaviors in the correct communication goal contexts while considering the interaction partner's behaviors to improve HRIs.

In this work, we aim to close this gap by investigating context-dependent vocal nonverbal behaviors during human-human interactions. Specifically, we focus on how therapists adapt their vocal nonverbal behaviors during the delivery of ABA therapies to children with ASD. This study is a necessary step to inform the design of vocal nonverbal behaviors of SARs during robot-mediated ABA therapies for ASD.

3   ABA DTT Therapy

ABA therapy utilizes the principles of Behavior Analysis for individuals with ASD [24]. One such therapy is discrete trial training. Namely, discrete trial training structures a unit of instruction into three components: 1) discriminative stimulus, 2) behavior, and 3) consequence. A discriminative stimulus is a social and/or environmental cue which signals a behavior to occur. Behavior is the response to the discriminative stimulus. Consequences are the events that occur after a behavior. Whether naturally occurring interactions or therapeutic interactions, the consequences determine whether an individual will repeat the behavior or decrease the behavior from occurring again in the future. This analysis of behavior was transformed into a therapy which addresses behavior deficits and excess in children diagnosed with ASD [25]. Discrete trial therapy consists of therapists facilitating numerous discrete trials which address deficits such as imitation, visual performance, expressive and receptive language, and social interactions. For example, if a patient is unable to identify common objects in their environment, a DTT program would include the selection of the most relevant common objects for that patient and teach each object to mastery. The ABA therapist would ask the child a question (Discriminative Stimulus) such as "What is this?", the patient's behavior would follow, and depending on whether the response was correct or incorrect a reinforcer or error correction would end the trial. This process of teaching is an evidenced-based practice commonly used for individuals with ASD of all ages [26].

4   Model for Dyadic Social Interactions

In this work, we developed a general model to investigate dyadic social interactions between two agents (e.g., human-human or human-robot), Fig. 1. We define a dyadic social interaction by the setting, roles of the participants, and overall goal of an interaction. Within a dyadic social interaction, a participant can then have multiple communication subgoals. We utilize Shannon & Weaver's model of communication [27] to define each of the communication subgoals during an interaction. Namely, communication is defined as a process where a speaker delivers a message to a listener. A speaker encodes a message according to his/her distinct communicative subgoal; these messages can be encoded as verbal and/or nonverbal behaviors. This model can then be used to identify and classify basic units of nonverbal behaviors to be analyzed during real-world dyadic social interactions.

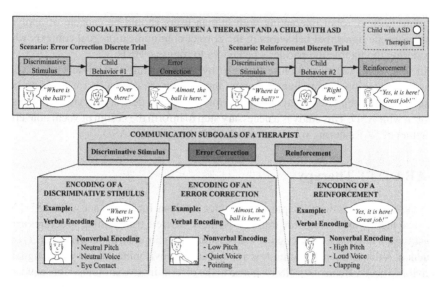

Fig. 1. Model for dyadic social interactions using discrete trial training therapy as an example.

We applied this model to one-on-one DTT-based therapies delivered at an ABA autism clinic to children diagnosed with ASD. In this dyadic social interaction, the setting is a therapy room at a clinic, the roles of the participants are a therapist and child with ASD receiving treatment, and the overall goal of an interaction is to teach a skill (e.g., greeting, WH-questions). The set of unique communicative subgoals of a therapist during ABA therapy are then the discriminative stimulus, consequential error correction, and consequential reinforcement. To achieve their communicative subgoals during an interaction, a therapist generates messages through verbal and nonverbal behaviors. Hence, the objective in this paper is to use this model to investigate how ABA therapist vocal nonverbal behaviors differ according to the different communicative subgoals (i.e., contexts) of a DTT therapy.

5   Study Design

Our study focused on investigating the differences in vocal nonverbal behaviors of human ABA therapists during DTT therapies. Our primary hypotheses are that therapists:

1. Pitch, intensity, and speaking rate during the delivery of a consequential error correction will not be significantly different from the delivery of a discriminative stimulus
2. Display a higher pitch, higher intensity, and higher speaking rate during consequential reinforcement compared to the delivery of a discriminative stimulus

Our hypotheses were formulated according to expert therapists' expectations on their vocal nonverbal behavior during the therapies. Furthermore, we utilize the discriminative stimulus as the baseline for comparison because the discriminative stimulus subgoal is always used by a therapist to initiate a discrete trial with a patient. In order to evaluate these hypotheses, we conducted an analysis of vocal nonverbal behaviors utilized by therapists during one-on-one therapies with children with ASD.

5.1 Participants

A total of five ABA therapists from a university-based ABA clinic participated in this study delivering DTT therapies to children 2-9 years old with ASD. There was one female and four male children with ASD. The therapists ranged in age from 22-47 (μ = 29.6) and had a range of 1-5 (μ = 2.2) years of experience delivering ABA-based treatment. All therapists were female and have previously interacted with the children for four months to a year prior to the study.

5.2 Setting

The one-on-one therapy sessions were held at a university-based ABA clinic where the children were already receiving ABA services and the therapists implemented DTT programs already included in the children's on-going treatment program. The therapies targeted skills including: following one-step instructions, language acquisition, articulation, visual performance (i.e., matching), and gross motor imitation. The one-on-one sessions were each held in a private carpeted room 8ft × 10ft in size. The rooms each had three child sized chairs, a table, and storage containers with various items (e.g., toys, food, electronics, books). Each room also had pre-existing video recording equipment mounted 8ft high in the corner of the room. This video recording equipment was utilized to record the therapy sessions for our study.

5.3 Procedure

Informed consent from the therapists and children's parental guardians was obtained prior to the start of the study. Video recordings of one-on-one DTT sessions between a therapist and a child with ASD were then obtained. For each therapist, we collected video recordings until we obtained five trials of a discriminative stimulus-consequential error correction pair and five trials of a discriminative stimulus-consequential reinforcement pair. Since the video recordings were of real-world therapy sessions, the therapists' behaviors were dependent on the progress of the children receiving the therapies. Hence, more than five trials of discriminative stimulus-consequential error correction pairs were observed before obtaining five trials of discriminative stimulus-consequential reinforcement pairs. The converse also occurred. In either case only the first five trials of each pair were retained.

5.4 Data Collection

The video recorded sessions were segmented into the distinct communicative subgoals of the therapists during DTT sessions and prosodic data were collected for each of the distinct communicative subgoal segments. As discussed in Sect. 4, therapist distinct communicative subgoals during DTT sessions fall under three categories: discriminative stimulus, consequential error correction, and consequential reinforcement. These three categories were used to segment the video recordings of the sessions. Namely, the researchers reviewed the video recordings and categorized the therapist's speech into one of the three categories. Note that a communicative subgoal can be categorized based on a single word, a sentence, or multiple sentences spoken by a therapist. Data on the child's behavior was not collected. Figure 2 illustrates a therapy session segmented into distinct communicative subgoals.

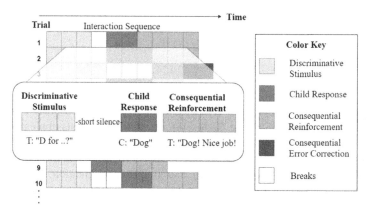

Fig. 2. An example of how a therapy session is segmented into distinct communicative subgoals.

Once the videos were segmented into distinct communicative subgoals we collected three prosodic parameters from each of the segments: mean pitch, mean intensity, and speaking rate. We utilized Praat [28], an application designed for phonetics research, to measure the therapists mean pitch (Hz) and mean intensity (dB) during each of the segmented distinct communication subgoals during the therapy. Speaking rate was defined as the number of syllables per a minute (SPM) spoken by the therapist. Namely, speaking rate was calculated by:

$$Speaking\ Rate\ =\ (S\ /\ T) \tag{1}$$

where S is the number of syllables in the therapist's speech during the distinct communication subgoal and T is the total amount of time the therapist took to communicate his/her speech.

5.5 Data Analysis

To test our hypotheses, we utilized multilevel models. Multilevel models are commonly utilized in speech research where repeated-measurement designs are used and multiple observations are nested within a participant [29]. Multilevel models account for the potential correlations between observations made within the same participant. In our study, a two-level multilevel model was used for each set of observations of the subgoal pairs (i.e., discriminative stimulus-consequential error correction and discriminative stimulus-consequential reinforcement) from the five participants. Namely, observations sampled from a participant are defined as the first level of the model and participants were defined as the second level. The treatment conditions were the two subgoals for each pair. The dependent variables were mean pitch, mean intensity, or speaking rate. We utilized IBM SPSS to run our statistical analyses.

6 Results

In total, we collected twenty-five discriminative stimulus-consequential error correction pairs and twenty-five discriminative stimulus-consequential reinforcement pairs from the therapy sessions. For each of these pairs we collected the mean pitch, mean intensity, and speaking rate for each of the subgoals in the pair. A multilevel model was constructed for each prosodic parameter (i.e., pitch, intensity, speaking rate) for each subgoal pair. A total of six multilevel models were constructed.

6.1 Discriminative Stimulus-Consequential Error Correction

Pitch - The relationship between the communication subgoals during an error correction trial and therapist pitch demonstrated significant variance in intercepts across participants, $x^2(1) = 12.72, p < 0.05$. The slopes did not significantly vary across participants, $x^2(1) = 1.56, p > 0.05$, and the slopes and intercepts did not significantly covary, $x^2(2) = 0.28, p > 0.05$. Only including the variance in intercepts across participants improved the fit of the model and, therefore, the final model used to interpret therapist pitch only included variance in intercepts.

From the final model, therapist pitch for the delivery of a consequential error correction was significantly different from the delivery of the discriminative stimulus, $F(1,45) = 4.40, p < 0.05$. This model suggests that therapist pitch is significantly lower during the delivery of a consequential error correction then discriminative stimulus, $b = -23.88, t(45) = -2.10, p = 0.04$.

Intensity - The relationship between the communication subgoals and therapist intensity demonstrated significant variance in both intercepts across participants, $x^2(1) = 33.833, p < 0.05$, and slopes across participants, $x^2(1) = 4.071, p < 0.05$. However, the slopes and intercepts across participants did not significantly covary, $x^2(2) = 4.2476, p > 0.05$. The final model only included the variance in intercepts and slopes across participants.

Therapist intensity for the delivery of a consequential error correction was not significantly different from the delivery of the discriminative stimulus, $F(1,4.97) = 5.35, p > 0.05$. However, this model suggests that therapist intensity was lower during the delivery of a consequential error correction and this relationship was not significant, $b = -4.70, t(4.97) = -2.31, p = 0.069$.

Speaking Rate - Similar to intensity, the relationship between the communication subgoal and therapist speaking rate demonstrated significant variance in intercepts across participants, $x^2(1) = 18.28, p < 0.05$, and the slopes across participants, $x^2(1) = 7.00, p < 0.05$. The slopes and intercepts across participants did not significantly covary, $x^2(2)$

= 0.27, $p > 0.05$. The final model only included the variance in intercepts and slopes across participants.

Therapist speaking rate for the delivery of a consequential error correction was not significantly different from the delivery of the discriminative stimulus, $F(1,5.19) = 1.29$, $p > 0.05$. Although the model suggests that therapist speaking rate is higher during the delivery of a consequential error correction than discriminative stimulus, it was not significant, $b = 0.50$, $t(5.19) = 1.14$, $p = 0.305$.

6.2 Discriminative Stimulus-Consequential Reinforcement

Pitch - The relationship between the communication subgoal and therapist pitch during a reinforcement trial demonstrated significant variance in intercepts across participants, $x^2(1) = 16.18$, $p < 0.05$. However, the model including slopes across participants did not converge. The final model only included the variance in intercepts across participants. Such model simplification techniques are commonly used when multilevel models do not converge [30].

Therapist pitch for the delivery of a consequential reinforcement was significantly different from the delivery of the discriminative stimulus, $F(1,45) = 7.65$, $p < 0.05$. This model suggests that therapist pitch is significantly higher during the delivery of a consequential reinforcement than a discriminative stimulus, $b = 36.09$, $t(45) = 2.77$, $p = 0.008$.

Intensity - The relationship between the communication subgoal and therapist intensity demonstrated significant variance in intercepts across participants, $x^2(1) = 19.65$, $p < 0.05$. The slopes did not significantly vary across participants, $x^2(1) = 1.42$, $p > 0.05$, and the slopes and intercepts across participants also did not significantly covary, $x^2(2) = 0.65$, $p > 0.05$. The final model only included variance in intercepts across participants.

Therapist intensity for the delivery of a consequential reinforcement was significantly different from the delivery of the discriminative stimulus, $F(1,45) = 8.69$, $p < 0.05$. This model suggests that therapist intensity was significantly higher during the delivery of a consequential reinforcement, $b = 3.98$, $t(45) = 2.95$, $p = 0.005$.

Speaking Rate - Similar to pitch, the relationship between the communication subgoal and therapist speaking rate demonstrated significant variance in intercepts across participants, $x^2(1) = 10.03$, $p < 0.05$, but the model including slopes did not converge. The final model only contained variance in intercepts across participants.

The therapist speaking rate for the delivery of a consequential reinforcement was significantly different from the delivery of the discriminative stimulus, $F(1,45) = 24.65$, $p < 0.05$. This model suggests that therapist speaking rate is slower during the delivery of a consequential reinforcement than a discriminative stimulus, $b = -1.17$, $t(45) = -4.97$, $p < 0.001$.

7 Discussion

The results of our study only partially supported our hypotheses on the vocal nonverbal behaviors of therapists during the different communicative subgoals of a DTT-based therapy. As previously mentioned, our hypotheses were formulated according to the experience of expert practitioners and these discrepancies are likely because interpersonal communication is an automatic process that humans find difficult to describe explicitly [31]. This highlights the importance of studying context-dependent nonverbal behaviors during real-world human-human interactions so that they can be appropriately applied to the design of HRIs.

Our first hypothesis was only partially supported by the results. As expected, therapist speaking rate for the delivery of a consequential error correction was not significantly different from the delivery of the discriminative stimulus. In contrast to our expectations, therapist pitch and intensity was lower for consequential error correction than discriminative stimulus, but intensity was not statistically significant. Pitch and intensity were likely lower because therapists attempt to provide constructive feedback in a non-judgmental tone to the child. It is recommended that reprimands during DTT are provided in a quiet tone of voice [7]. Adhering to guidance on the use of reprimand helps to reduce escape behaviors, student alienations, and damaging the child-therapist relationship. Furthermore, a lower intensity reduces the emphasis on the failure to respond correctly. Focusing more noticeably on the positive behaviors and less on the incorrect behaviors helps to increase the positive behaviors and reduce the less desirable behaviors (i.e., differential reinforcement) [7].

Similarly, our second hypothesis was also only partially supported by the results of the study. As we expected, therapist pitch and intensity were higher for the consequential reinforcement than discriminative stimulus. The primary purpose for higher pitch and intensity was to display excitement, positivity, and to draw more attention to the positive reinforcement. Studies have shown that higher pitch and higher intensity are perceived as excitement and positivity by children [33]. This is important because the effectiveness of praise increases when presented in a manner acceptable to the individual (e.g., enthusiastically) [7]. Furthermore, when implemented correctly reinforcement can promote a positive relationship between the therapist and child [32]. However, the results demonstrated that therapist speaking rate was slower for the consequential reinforcement than the discriminative stimulus, which contrasted with our first hypothesis. Upon further analysis, it was observed that a slower speaking rate was often exhibited to emphasize and exaggerate the reinforcement. Studies have shown that slower speaking rates are used to emphasize communication points by a speaker [34]. Reinforcement is intended to draw attention to a correct behavior [7]. As such, when providing reinforcement therapists are likely to slow down their speaking rate to extend the verbal reinforcement to clearly show a positive reaction to the child.

8 Conclusions

The objective of this work was to study the vocal nonverbal behaviors of human therapists during the delivery of discrete trial therapies so that we can apply them to robot-mediated therapies. According to these findings, we make the following general recommendations for the design of the vocal nonverbal behaviors for a robot during robot-mediated discrete trial training therapies:

1. The discriminative stimulus should be utilized as the baseline for the vocal nonverbal behavior of the robot.
2. The consequential error correction should have a lower pitch and intensity than the discriminative stimulus but maintain a similar speaking rate.
3. The consequential reinforcement should have a higher pitch and intensity than the discriminative stimulus but a slower speaking rate.

As a next step, we plan to utilize these design recommendations to investigate whether robots modeling similar vocal nonverbal behaviors of human therapists will improve the efficiency and efficacy of discrete trial training therapies.

Acknowledgements. This work was supported by the National Science Foundation CRII Award (#1948224). We would like to thank all the participants from the Applied Behavior Analysis Clinic.

References

1. Papadopoulos, I., et al.: Enablers and barriers to the implementation of socially assistive humanoid robots in health and social care: a systematic review. BMJ Open **10**(1), 1–13 (2020)
2. Rabbitt, S.M., Kazdin, A.E., Scassellati, B.: Integrating socially assistive robotics into mental healthcare interventions: applications and recommendations for expanded use. Clin. Psychol. Rev. **35**, 35–46 (2015)
3. Martinez-Martin, E., Cazorla, M.: A socially assistive robot for elderly exercise promotion. IEEE Access **7**, 75515–75529 (2019)
4. Blanch-Hartigan, D., et al.: Measuring nonverbal behavior in clinical interactions: a pragmatic guide. Patient Educ. Couns. **101**, 2209–2218 (2018)
5. Brown, A.B., Elder, J.H.: Communication in autism spectrum disorder: a guide for pediatric nurses. Pediatr. Nurs. **40**(5), 219–225 (2014)
6. Ambady, N., et al.: Physical therapists' nonverbal communication predicts geriatric patients' health outcomes. Psychol. Aging **17**(3), 443–452 (2002)
7. Gable, R.A., et al.: Back to basics: rules, praise, ignoring, and reprimands revisited. Interv. Sch. Clin. **44**(4), 195–205 (2009)
8. Begum, M., et al.: Measuring the efficacy of robots in autism therapy: how informative are standard HRI metrics. In: ACM/IEEE International Conference on Human-Robot Interaction, pp. 335–342 (2015)
9. Feng, Y., et al.: A control architecture of robot-assisted intervention for children with autism spectrum disorders. J. Robot. pp. 1–12 (2018)
10. Salvador, M., Marsh, A.S., Gutierrez, A., Mahoor, M.H.: Development of an ABA autism intervention delivered by a humanoid robot. In: Agah, A., C, J.-J., H, Ayanna M., S, Miguel A., He, Hongsheng (eds.) ICSR 2016. LNCS (LNAI), vol. 9979, pp. 551–560. Springer, Cham (2016). https://doi.org/10.1007/978-3-319-47437-3_54
11. Centers for Disease Control and Prevention (2020) Data & Statistics on Autism Spectrum Disorder. https://www.cdc.gov/. Accessed Jun 2020
12. Hurt, A.A., et al.: Personality traits associated with occupational "burnout" in ABA therapists. J. Appl. Res. Intellect. Disabil. **26**(4), 299–308 (2013)
13. Louie. W.-Y. G., Korneder, J.A., Abbas, I.: A pilot study for a robot-mediated listening comprehension intervention for children with ASD. In: IEEE International Symposium on Robot and Human Interactive Communication, pp. 1–4 (2020)

14. Google Cloud (2020) Cloud Text-to-Speech - Speech Synthesis. https://cloud.google.com/. Accessed Jun 2020

15. Burroughs, N.F.: A reinvestigation of the relationship of teacher nonverbal immediacy and student compliance-resistance with learning. Commun. Educ. **56**(4), 453–475 (2007)

16. Gorawara-Bhat, R., Dethmers, D.L., Cook, M.A.: Physician eye contact and elder patient perceptions of understanding and adherence. Patient Educ. Couns. **92**, 375–380 (2013)

17. Cevasco, A.M.: Effects of the therapist's nonverbal behavior on participation and affect of individuals with Alzheimer's disease during group music therapy sessions. J. Music Ther. **47**(3), 282–299 (2010)

18. Yarczower, M., Kilbride, J.E., Beck, A.T.: Changes in nonverbal behavior of therapists and depressed patients during cognitive therapy. Psychol. Rep. **69**(3), 915–919 (1991)

19. Mutlu, B., et al.: Conversational gaze mechanisms for humanlike robots. ACM Trans. Interact. Intell. Syst. **1**(2), 1–33 (2012)

20. Yoon, Y., et al.: Robots learn social skills: end-to-end learning of co-speech gesture generation for humanoid robots. In: 19th IEEE International Conference in Robotics and Automation, pp. 4303–4309 (2019)

21. Feng, W.., et al.: Learn2Smile: learning non-verbal interaction through observation. In: IEEE International Conference on Intelligent Robots and Systems, pp. 4131–4138 (2017)

22. Randall, A., et al.: Nonverbal behaviour as communication. In: Owen, H. (ed.) The Handbook of Communication Skills, 73–119. Routledge, New York (2016)

23. Woodall, W.G., Burgoon, J.K.: The effects of nonverbal synchrony on message comprehension and persuasiveness. J. Nonverbal Behav. **5**(4), 07–223 (1981)

24. Eikeseth, S., et al.: Intensive behavioral treatment at school for 4-to-7-year-old children with autism. Behav. Modif. **26**, 49–68 (2002)

25. Lovaas, O.I.: Behavioral treatment and normal educational and intellectual functioning in young autistic children. J. Consult. Clin. Psychol. **55**, 3–9 (1987)

26. National Autism Center: National standards project: Findings and conclusions. NAC, Randolph (2009)

27. Claude, S.E.: A mathematical theory of communication. Bell Syst. Tech. J. **27**(3), 379–423 (1948)

28. Boersma, P., Weenink, D.: Praat: doing phonetics by computer. http://www.praat.org/, Amsterdam (2020)

29. Quené, H., Van Den Bergh, H.: On multi-level modeling of data from repeated measures designs: a tutorial. Speech Commun. **43**(1–2), 103–121 (2004)

30. Barr, D.J., et al.: Random effects structure for confirmatory hypothesis testing: keep it maximal. J. Mem. Lang. **68**(3), 255–278 (2013)

31. Vogeley, K., Bente, G.: Artificial humans': psychology and neuroscience perspectives on embodiment and nonverbal communication. Neural Netw. **23**, 1077–1090 (2010)

32. Sigler, E.A., Aamidor, S.: From positive reinforcement to positive behaviors: an everyday guide for the practitioner. Early Child. Educ. J. **32**(4), 249–253 (2005)

33. Quam, C., Swingley, D.: Development in children's interpretation of pitch cues to emotions. Child Dev. **83**(1), 236–250 (2012)

34. Fosler-Lussier, E., Morgan, N.: Effects of speaking rate and word frequency on pronunciations in convertional speech. Speech Commun. **29**(2–4), 137–158 (1999)

Using Robot Adaptivity to Support Learning in Child-Robot Interaction

Alessia Vignolo[1]([✉])[iD], Alessandra Sciutti[1][iD], and John Michael[2][iD]

[1] COgNiTive Architecture for Collaborative Technologies Unit,
Istituto Italiano di Tecnologia, Via Enrico Melen 83, 16152 Genoa, Italy
{alessia.vignolo,alessandra.sciutti}@iit.it
[2] Department of Philosophy, Social Sciences Building, University of Warwick,
Coventry CV4 7AL, UK
MichaelJ@ceu.edu

Abstract. Previous research has shown that if a robot invests physical effort in teaching human partners a new skill, the teaching will be more effective and the partners will reciprocate by investing more effort and patience when their turn to teach comes. In the current study, we extend this research to child-robot interaction. To this end, we devised a scenario in which a humanoid robot (iCub) and a child participant alternated in teaching each other new skills. In the *robot teaching phase* iCub taught participants sequences of movements, which they had to memorize and repeat. The robot then repeated the demonstration a second time: in the high effort (or *Adaptive*) condition, the iCub slowed down its movements when repeating the demonstration whereas in the low effort (or *Unadaptive*) condition he sped the movements up. In the *participant teaching phase*, children were asked to give the robot a demonstration of three symbols, and then to repeat it if the robot had not understood.

The results reveal that children learned the sequences more effectively when the iCub adapted its movements to the learner, and that, when their turn to teach to the robot came, they slowed down and increased segmentation when repeating the demonstration.

Keywords: Cognitive child-robot interaction · Sense of commitment · iCub

1 Introduction

As robots become increasingly prevalent throughout everyday life and in domains ranging from health care to education and manufacturing [5,7,9,11], researchers are devoting ever more attention to developing new ways of optimizing human-robot interaction [20]. One challenge in this regard is to boost human partners' willingness to invest time and effort when interacting with a robot. Persisting in an interaction is particularly important when it involves robots endowed with learning abilities. While there is a risk of a person becoming frustrated or impatient when a robot is slow to adapt, the potential benefits of adaptation are high

© Springer Nature Switzerland AG 2020
A. R. Wagner et al. (Eds.): ICSR 2020, LNAI 12483, pp. 428–439, 2020.
https://doi.org/10.1007/978-3-030-62056-1_36

insofar as they can maximize a robot's ability to contribute to new tasks with new partners. Another context in which it is crucial to maintain human willingness to persist interacting with a robot is when human learning is involved. In fields of applications such as rehabilitation or education, the interaction becomes often lengthy and repetitive, but necessary to foster the desired improvements. This is likely to be an especially important challenge when children are the trainees [1,2].

To address this challenge, Powell and Michael [14] (cf. also [15]) have recently proposed a low-cost solution based on the development of design features that could help to maintain a human's sense of commitment to an interaction with a robot. By boosting the human agent's sense of commitment, it may be possible to increase her or his willingness to remain patient and to invest effort in the interaction. To achieve this, they recommend the implementation of features that have been shown to promote a sense of commitment in human-human interaction. For example, it has been shown that, between humans, the perception of a partner's effort increases people's sense of commitment to joint actions, leading to increased effort, persistence and performance on boring and effortful tasks [6,22,23].

Extending this research into the context of human-robot interaction, Székely and colleagues have recently found evidence that the perception of a robot partner's apparent investment of cognitive effort boosted people's persistence on a boring task which they performed together with a robot [23]. Building upon these previous findings, Vignolo et al. have shown that if a robot invests physical effort in adapting to a human partner in a context in which the robot is teaching the human a new skill, the human partner will perform better [26] and reciprocate by investing more effort and patience in a subsequent task. In the context of child-robot-interaction, it has been shown that children are particularly willing to engage with robots that adapt their behaviours to the individual needs and abilities of the child user [1].

1.1 Aim of the Study

To verify whether a robot's apparent investment of effort into a teaching task positively impacts on children's learning, we designed an experiment in which the iCub humanoid robot and children participants alternated in teaching each other new skills. The design is inspired by [26] and adapted to make it suitable for children. In particular, the robot had to teach participants sequences of movements, by showing them with its body. Children had to memorize and repeat the sequence. In case of errors, the robot repeated the demonstration a second time. In the *Adaptive* condition the iCub slowed down its movements when repeating the demonstration whereas in the *Unadaptive* condition he sped the movements up when repeating the demonstration. We hypothesized that a higher apparent investment by the robot would improve children's performance in the training, and would increase their evaluation of the robot's helpfulness, leading them to reciprocate by investing effort to optimise their demonstrations to the robot.

2   Methods

2.1   Experimental Setup

The experimental setup (Fig. 1, left) consisted of a humanoid robot iCub [13,19], a TV screen placed behind it, for showing the symbols for the *participant teaching phase*, a keyboard placed between the robot and the participants (to be pressed by them before and after the drawing to progress the experiment from one phase to the next) and a hidden RGB-D camera to monitor the experiment.

In particular, the camera was needed for the experimenter to assess if the participants repeated the sequence of movements correctly, adopting a 'Wizard of Oz' [21] paradigm. The robot's behaviour needed for the experiment was controlled with a YARP (Yet Another Robot Platform) [12] module consisting of a state machine. To make the interaction as natural as possible, we also ran a face-tracking which make the robot direct its attention on the face of the participant and we made the robot simulate blinking. The iCub's speech came out of a speaker thanks to a synthesizer and was reported also on the TV screen. Children's hand motions were recorded using an Optotrak system with an active marker on the index finger tip.

2.2   Experimental Design

The experiment consisted of alternating phases:

Robot Teaching Phase. The robot iCub taught the participant sequences of three movements (each of them consisting of some movements of the robot's head, torso and/or arms, as in Fig. 1, right), which the participant had to memorize. After the demonstration of the robot, the participant tried to repeat the sequence (Fig. 1, left): in case the sequence was correctly performed, the robot would provide positive feedback and go on to the next phase; if the sequence was not correct, the robot would tell her this and repeat the sequence a second time. The participant tried again and received positive or negative feedback depending on her performance, and then continued on to the next phase.

Participant Teaching Phase. The participant taught the iCub sequences of three symbols (e.g. '+=?'), which appeared on the TV screen behind the robot. To teach the robot, the participant was instructed to draw the symbols in the air in front of iCub's cameras with the right index finger (left index finger if left-handed). Participants were instructed to repeat the symbols once again if the robot said he did not understand and asked for a second repetition.

At the beginning of the experiment, the participants were first provided with instructions about both tasks (i.e., for *robot teaching phase* and the *participant teaching phase*), and then asked to practice drawing the symbols in the air with their index fingers – once directed towards the robot, and then once directed towards the experimenter (or vice versa, in counterbalanced order). Then, the experimenter left them alone with the robot and a familiarization session started, during which the robot said 'hi' and presented itself. As training, the participant

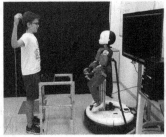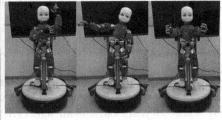

Fig. 1. Left: Participant repeating movements performed by iCub. Right: *Robot teaching phase*: example of sequence of movements.

was then asked to teach the robot a sequence of symbols, and to try to repeat a sequence of movements shown by iCub. During the experiment, in the *robot teaching phase*, two blocks with two different conditions followed each other (the order was counter-balanced among participants), with a break between them:

Unadaptive Condition. If the participants did not repeat the sequence of movements correctly after the first demonstration by the robot, iCub would repeat it by speeding the movements up, using a total time of $0.75T_i$, where T_i was the duration of the sequence demonstrated the first time. In the sequence, the robot came back to the home position at a faster speed than in the first demonstration, and this made the sequence of actions appear less segmented than in the first demonstration. This behavior was meant to show that the robot was investing low effort in the training, "rushing" through the sequence of motions.

Adaptive Condition. If the child did not repeat the sequence of movements correctly after the first demonstration by the robot, iCub would repeat it by slowing the movements down, using a total time of $1.39T_i$. In the sequence, the robot came back to the home position at a slower speed than in the first demonstration, and this made the sequence of actions appear more segmented than in the first demonstration. This choice was made to communicate a high effort by the robot, which invested more time in teaching.

The baseline speed (that is the speed of the first demonstration) was selected in order to make the demonstration difficult for participants to be understood at first. This was done to make the second repetition useful for the training in most trials.

Each of the two blocks consisted of six trials. Each trial was composed of one sequence of movements taught by the robot (*robot teaching phase*), and then one sequence of symbols taught by the participant (*participant teaching phase*).

At the end of each experimental block participants were asked the following question: "Did you have the impression that iCub helped you when you had difficulties in repeating the sequence of movements?" (on a scale from 1 to 5). At the end of the experiment participants were asked to answer one open question:

"What differences do you think there were in the teaching strategy of the robot in the two sessions?".

2.3   Participants

We recruited 38 participants, but the youngest 2 (the only ones of age 6) could not complete the experiment, so the final sample includes 36 participants between 8 and 16 years old (mean age 11.72 years ± 2.41 SD), 11 female and 25 male, 19 younger than 12 years old and 17 older than or equal to 12 years old. The regional ethics committee approved the protocol and all participants' parents (both) gave informed consent before the experiment.

3   Results

Among the 36 participants, 20 had the *Unadaptive* condition block first and the *Adaptive* condition afterwards, and the other 16 participants had the opposite order. The goal of the study was to investigate if a robot teacher can support children's learning of a new task by (apparently) adapting its kinematic effort, and also whether children noticed this adaptation and were aware of any effects it may have on their learning. To address these questions we compared the performances of participants between the two conditions and analyzed their responses to the questionnaires. We also wanted to see if children would modulate their commitment during their teaching phase depending on the commitment of the robot, and for doing that we compared the kinematics data of the children teaching phase in the two conditions.

3.1   Performance

Performance was calculated as the number of correct movements performed by the child, divided by the total number of movements presented (3).

After the first demonstration, performance was relatively low, especially for the younger participants. This proved that the task was not too easy to be solved, and that most participants would have needed the help of the robot to improve their memorization. Overall, 24% of the total number of trials were performed correctly already after the first demonstration.

A significant increase in performance was observed with age. Two linear regressions (Fig. 2) confirmed this trend, common to both conditions (*Unadaptive*: $F(1,34) = 9.54$, $p = 0.004$, $R^2 = 0.219$; *Adaptive*: $F(1,34) = 5.05$, $p = 0.031$, $R^2 = 0.129$) However, even the oldest participants (15–16, N = 6) failed to reach perfect execution (M = 0.67, SD = 0.12, significantly lower than 1 as demonstrated by a one-sample t-test, $t(5) = -6.853$, $p = 0.001$, d = -2.80, 95% CI [0.54 0.79]) and hence had margin for improvement.

After the second demonstration, performance on average improved for almost everyone (Fig. 3, left). Indeed, for all participants in the *Adaptive* condition the performance after the second demonstration was higher than after the first (all

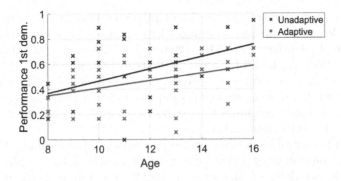

Fig. 2. Linear regression with age predicting performance after the first demonstration, for *Unadaptive* ($p = 0.004$) and *Adaptive* conditions ($p = 0.031$).

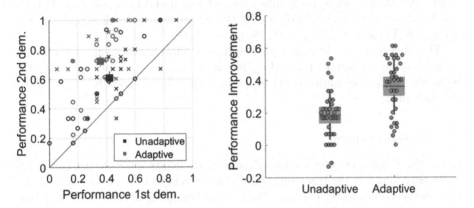

Fig. 3. Left: Individual average performance after the second demonstration plotted against the corresponding average performance after the first demonstration for the *Unadaptive* and the *Adaptive* conditions. Trials where the performance after the first demonstration was already 1 (24%) were excluded from this graph. Squares represent the averages for all the children and error bars correspond to standard errors. Circles represent children younger than 12 years old, crosses represent children older than or equal to 12 years old. Right: Performance improvement in the *Unadaptive* and in the *Adaptive* condition.

points lie above the identity line). The same held for about 86% of participants in the *Unadaptive* condition.

We computed the improvement by subtracting the performance after the first demonstration from the performance after the second demonstration.

Figure 3, right clearly shows that the performance improvement was larger in the *Adaptive* condition than in the *Unadaptive*. We checked whether this difference was significant, by controlling for potential effects of the order of conditions. The improvement of performance was submitted to a Mixed Model Anova with adaptivity (*Unadaptive* or *Adaptive*) as repeated-measures factor and block order

(Unadaptive-Adaptive or Adaptive-Unadaptive) as between-groups factor. The Mixed Model Anova on the performance improvement showed that there was a main effect of adaptivity ($F(1,34) = 20.639$, $p < 0.001$, $\eta_p^2 = 0.230$), while no significant effect was found for order ($F(1,34) = 1.80$, $p = 0.189$, $\eta_p^2 = 0.020$), or for the interaction between adaptivity and block order ($F(1,34) = 0.17$, $p = 0.687$, $\eta_p^2 = 0.002$). Hence, participants improved their performance significantly more in the *Adaptive* condition (M = 0.36, SD = 0.17) than in the *Unadaptive* condition (M = 0.18, SD = 0.15).

In order to control for potential differences between children and early adolescents, the improvement of performance was further submitted to a Mixed Model Anova with adaptivity (*Unadaptive* or *Adaptive*) as repeated-measures factor and age group (younger than 12 or older/equal than 12) as between-groups factor. The results confirmed a main effect of adaptivity ($F(1,34) = 21.72$, $p < 0.001$, $\eta_p^2 = 0.233$), while no significant effect was found for age group ($F(1,34) = 0.118$, $p = 0.734$, $\eta_p^2 = 0.001$), or for the interaction between adaptivity and age group ($F(1,34) = 1.34$, $p = 0.255$, $\eta_p^2 = 0.014$).

This demonstrates that a higher apparent effort investment of the robot enabled young children and early adolescents alike to better memorize the sequences, and thus improved their performance, independently of the order of conditions.

3.2   Questionnaires

In the questionnaires after the experiment, participants were asked what differences they found in the teaching strategy of the robot in the two sessions. Even though the experimenter explicitly said at the beginning of the experiment that there would be two different robot teaching strategies in the two sessions, 53% (19) of participants replied that there was no difference between them. 22% (8) of participants noticed a difference in the speed (one of the modifications we applied), 11% (4) in the segmentation (the other modification we applied). 14% (5) of participants replied that there was a difference in the difficulty.

Participants were then asked if they had the impression that iCub helped them when they did not understand the sequence of movements after the first demonstration (on a scale from 1 to 5).

A Wilcoxon signed-rank test showed that participants' answers to the question about their impression of iCub's helpfulness in the *Unadaptive* condition (M = 3.58, SD = 1.23) were not significantly lower from the answers given in the *Adaptive* condition (M = 3.92, SD = 1.20), $Z = -1.36$, $p = 0.173$.

We then evaluated whether the judgment of helpfulness depended on the actual improvement exhibited by each participant. A linear regression between helpfulness ratings and obtained improvements on all the data (Fig. 4) was not significant ($F(1,34) = 1.57$, $p = 0.214$, $R^2 = 0.022$). Similar results were obtained also performing two separate linear regressions for the two conditions (*Unadaptive* condition: $F(1,34) = 1.53$, $p = 0.225$, $R^2 = 0.043$; *Adaptive* condition: ($F(1,34) = 0.00$, $p = 0.978$, $R^2 = 2.22e - 05$). These results show that the participants' impression of iCub's helpfulness did not depend on their actual performance improvement.

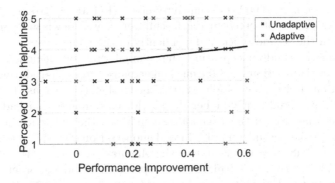

Fig. 4. iCub's helpfulness rating as a function of individual performance improvement (($F_{(1,34)} = 1.57$, $p = 0.214$, $R^2 = 0.022$)).

3.3 Kinematic Data Analysis Results

Kinematic (x, y, and z position) data were recorded using an Optotrak system with a marker placed on participants' index finger tip. For this analysis, 3 out of 36 subjects have been discarded as the data have not been recorded in a correct way by the Optotrak.

We computed two features to characterize the execution of the "drawing symbols" task during the *participant teaching phase*: the stroke velocity (i.e., the vertical component of the writing speed) and the pause time (i.e, the total time spent by each children pausing - with a velocity lower than a threshold defined as $th = [0.05(max(v_y) - min(v_y)] + min(v_y)$ where v_y is the vertical velocity - while writing the symbols). For each of the two, we computed the difference between the second and the first demonstration.

The differences of the kinematic data were submitted to Mixed Model Anovas with adaptivity (*Unadaptive* or *Adaptive*) as repeated-measures factor and block order (Unadaptive-Adaptive or Adaptive-Unadaptive) as between-groups factor, followed by Tukey post hoc tests.

During the second repetition of the symbol drawing, participants always slowed down to facilitate the robot's understanding; indeed, a one-tailed t-test shows that the increase of the velocity was always significantly lower than 0 (for participants that had the order Unadaptive-Adaptive, in the *Unadaptive* condition, the difference between the velocity of the second and the first demonstration was $M = -47.14$, $SD = 35.81$, $t(17) = -5.59$, $p < 0.001$ and in the *Adaptive* condition, $M = -25.95$, $SD = 36.96$, $t(17) = -2.98$, $p = 0.004$; for participants that had the order Adaptive-Unadaptive, in the *Unadaptive* condition, $M = -27.22$, $SD = 34.75$, $t(14) = -3.04$, $p = 0.005$ and in the *Adaptive* condition, $M = -51.59$, $SD = 31.11$, $t(14) = -6.42$, $p < 0.001$).

A Mixed Model Anova on the velocity differences (Fig. 5, left) shows that there was a significant effect of the interaction between adaptivity and block order (F(1,31) = 14.94, $p = 0.0005$, $\eta_p^2 = 0.325$) and no order effect (F(1,31) = 0.07, $p = 0.790$, $\eta_p^2 = 0.002$) or adaptivity effect (F(1,31) = 0.07, $p = 0.790$, $\eta_p^2 = 0.002$). As can be observed in Fig. 5, children slowed down more in the first block than in the second block, independently of the adaptivity.

Furthermore, children repeating the symbol drawing demonstration segmented more their actions, exhibiting longer pause times than during the first demonstration, indeed a one-tailed t-test shows that the increase of the pause time was always significantly higher than 0 (for participants that had the order Unadaptive-Adaptive, in the *Unadaptive* condition, the difference between the pause time of the second and the first demonstration was $M = 0.25$, $SD = 0.42$, $t(17) = 2.48$, $p = 0.012$ and in the *Adaptive* condition, $M = 0.20$, $SD = 0.48$, $t(17) = 1.79$, $p = 0.046$; for participants that had the order Adaptive-Unadaptive, in the *Unadaptive* condition, $M = 0.32$, $SD = 0.47$, $t(14) = 2.67$, $p = 0.010$ and in the *Adaptive* condition, $M = 0.65$, $SD = 0.44$, $t(14) = 5.68$, $p < 0.001$).

A Mixed Model Anova on the pause time differences (Fig. 5, right) shows that there was a significant effect of the interaction between adaptivity and block order (F(1,31) = 4.68, $p = 0.038$, $\eta_p^2 = 0.131$) and no order effect (F(1,31) = 3.82, $p = 0.060$, $\eta_p^2 = 0.110$) or adaptivity effect (F(1,31) = 2.77, $p = 0.106$, $\eta_p^2 = 0.082$). A Tukey post-hoc test shows that participants in the *Adaptive* condition incremented the pause time significantly more if they had the order Adaptive-Unadaptive ($M = 0.65$, $SD = 0.44$) than if they had order Unadaptive-Adaptive ($M = 0.20$, $SD = 0.48$), $p = 0.033$.

4   Discussion

Our results showed that children learned more effectively when the iCub adapted its movement kinematics to facilitate the pedagogical interaction.

Unsurprisingly, the older children performed better, but the effect of the adaptivity manipulation upon performance remained even when controlling for age (as well as for block order). We also found that more than half of the children did not consciously perceive any difference between the robot's behaviour in the two conditions – more precisely, when asked directly, they reported that they had not noticed any difference. However, when asked to rate the helpfulness of the robot after each block, their ratings were marginally higher in the *Adaptive* condition than in the *Unadaptive* condition. However, the judgment of helpfulness did not correlate with the actual effectiveness of the robot's teaching, i.e. with the improvement in performance obtained by the pupil.

When the time came for the children to teach to the robot, they invested effort when they demonstrated symbols to iCub: they slowed down their strokes and increased the pauses between movements when repeating a demonstration. The latter phenomenon was more pronounced when the robot itself exhibited more effort. However, reciprocation of effort was mitigated by the number of

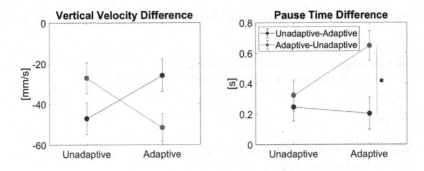

Fig. 5. Kinematic features differences.

repetitions of the task. Specifically, children tended to be more adaptive to the robot during the first session. This suggests that during the relatively lengthy exercise other factors, such as boredom and fatigue, potentially had an impact on participants' behavior.

These findings build upon a wealth of research in developmental psychology which has shown that human infants benefit from spontaneous modulations of caregivers' motion properties (called "motionese" [3]). Also in our case, the slower movement and the consequent clearer segmentation of the motion proved to be effective in facilitating children understanding and replicating robot behaviors. Interestingly, previous research has explored the use of "motionese" in the context of human-robot interaction. In particular, Vollmer et al. [27] showed that human participants produce motionese when teaching to a robot. Furthermore, Nagai and Rohlfing [17] demonstrated that a robot can leverage on these movement modulations by extracting information from motionese produced by a human. In the current research we focused on the dual approach, assessing whether the execution by the robot of movements inspired by the principles of motionese had an impact on children's learning.

The current study also extends earlier research showing that children are typically very willing to treat robots as social agents [4,18] – in particular if the robot adapts to the needs and abilities of the child [1]. More generally, our findings advance the project of designing robots that can engage with children such as to support or extend educational activities [8,16,24].

Further research should attempt to develop robots able to adaptively calibrate their pedagogical strategies in response to the (child and/or adult) learners' success [25]. In the current study, the changes in the robot's behavior followed a strict protocol which was determined in advance to create the impression of adaptivity while maintaining a high degree of experimental control. Moreover, it would be valuable to explore whether similar manipulations may work in other contexts (e.g. involving different kinds of effort and different tasks). Finally, it would also be valuable to explore the possibility of training children to identify differences in pedagogical approaches in order to choose demonstrations or demonstrators that more effectively facilitate their learning. Indeed, this may help them to cultivate metacognitive skills that are important for learning in general.

Acknowledgment. The research has been supported by a Starting Grant from the European Research Council (nr. 679092, SENSE OF COMMITMENT).

References

1. Belpaeme, T., et al.: Multimodal child-robot interaction: building social bonds. J. Hum. Robot Interact. **1**(2), 35–53 (2013)
2. Belpaeme, T., Kennedy, J., Ramachandran, A., Scassellati, B., Tanaka, F.: Social robots for education: a review. Sci. Robot. **3**(21) (2018). https://doi.org/10.1126/scirobotics.aat5954
3. Brand, R.J., Baldwin, D.A., Ashburn, L.A.: Evidence for 'motionese': modifications in mothers' infant-directed action. Dev. Sci. **5**(1), 72–83 (2002)
4. Breazeal, C.: Emotion and sociable humanoid robots. Int. J. Hum. Comput. Stud. **59**(1–2), 119–155 (2003)
5. Breazeal, C., Brooks, A., Gray, J., Hoffman, G., Kidd, C., Lee, H.: Humanoid robots as cooperative partners for people. J. Humanoid Rob. **1**(2), 1–34 (2004)
6. Chennells, M., Michael, J.: Effort and performance in a cooperative activity are boosted by perception of a partner's effort. Sci. Rep. **8**(1), 1–9 (2018)
7. Clodic A., Cao H., Alili S., Montreuil V., Alami R., Chatila R.: SHARY: a supervision system adapted to human-robot interaction. In: Khatib O., Kumar V., Pappas G.J. (eds) Experimental Robotics. Springer Tracts in Advanced Robotics, vol 54. Springer, Berlin, Heidelberg (2009). https://doi.org/10.1007/978-3-642-00196-3_27
8. Draper, T., Clayton, W.: Using a personal robot to teach young children. J. Genet. Psychol. **153**(3), 269–273 (1992)
9. Grigore, E., Eder, K., Pipe, A., Melhuish, C., Leonards, U.: Joint action understanding improves robot-to-human object handover. In: 2013 IEEE/RSJ International Conference on Intelligent Robots and Systems, pp. 4622–4629 (2013)
16. Kanda, T., Hirano, T., Eaton, D., Ishiguro, H.: Interactive robots as social partners and peer tutors for children: a field trial. Hum. Comput. Interact. **19**(1–2), 61–84 (2004)
11. Lenz, C., Nair, S., Rickert, M., Knoll, A., Rosel, W., Gast, J.: Joint-action for humans and industrial robots for assembly tasks. In: RO-MAN 2008-The 17th IEEE International Symposium on Robot and Human Interactive Communication, pp. 130–135. IEEE (2008)
12. Metta, G., Fitzpatrick, P., Natale, L.: Yarp: yet another robot platform. Int. J. Adv. Robot. Syst. **3**(1), 43–48 (2006)
13. Metta, G., et al.: The iCub humanoid robot: an open-systems platform for research in cognitive development. Neural Netw. **23**(8–9), 1125–1134 (2010)
14. Michael, J., Powell, H.: Feeling committed to a robot: why, what, when, and how? Philos. Trans. R. Soc. B Biol. Sci. **374**(1771), 20180039 (2019)
15. Michael, J., Salice, A.: The sense of commitment in human-robot interaction. Int. J. Soc. Robot. **9**(5), 755–63 (2017)
16. Kanda, T., Hirano, T., Eaton, D., Ishiguro, H.: Interactive robots as social partners and peer tutors for children: a field trial. Hum. Comput. Interact. **19**(1–2), 61–84 (2004)

17. Nagai, Y., Rohlfing, K.J.: Computational analysis of motionese toward scaffolding robot action learning. IEEE Trans. Auton. Mental Dev. **1**(1), 44–54 (2009)
18. Salter, T., Werry, I., Michaud, F.: Going into the wild in child-robot interaction studies: issues in social robotic development. Intell. Servi. Robot. **1**(2), 93–108 (2008)
19. Sandini, G., Metta, G., Vernon, D.: The *iCub* cognitive humanoid robot: an open-system research platform for enactive cognition. In: Lungarella, M., Iida, F., Bongard, J., Pfeifer, R. (eds.) 50 Years of Artificial Intelligence. LNCS (LNAI), vol. 4850, pp. 358–369. Springer, Heidelberg (2007). https://doi.org/10.1007/978-3-540-77296-5_32
20. Sciutti, A., Mara, M., Tagliasco, V., Sandini, G.: Humanizing human-robot interaction: on the importance of mutual understanding. IEEE Technol. Soc. Mag. **37**(1), 22–29 (2018)
21. Steinfeld, A., Jenkins, O.C., Scassellati, B.: The oz of wizard: Simulating the human for interaction research. In: Proceedings of the 4th ACM/IEEE International Conference on Human Robot Interaction, HRI '09, ACM, New York, NY, USA, pp. 101–108 (2009). https://doi.org/10.1145/1514095.1514115
22. Székely, M., Michael, J.: Investing in commitment: persistence in a joint action is enhanced by the perception of a partner's effort. Cognition **174**, 37–42 (2018)
23. Székely, M., Powell, H., Vannucci, F., Rea, F., Sciutti, A., Michael, J.: The perception of a robot partner's effort elicits a sense of commitment to human-robot interaction. Interac. Stud. **20**(2), 234–255 (2019)
24. Tanaka, F., Cicourel, A., Movellan, J.R.: Socialization between toddlers and robots at an early childhood education center. Proc. Natl Acad. Sci. **104**(46), 17954–17958 (2007)
25. Velentzas, G., Tsitsimis, T., Rañó, I., Tzafestas, C., Khamassi, M.: Adaptive reinforcement learning with active state-specific exploration for engagement maximization during simulated child-robot interaction. Paladyn, J. Behav. Robot. **9**(1), 235–253 (2018)
26. Vignolo, A., Powell, H., McEllin, L., Rea, F., Sciutti, A., Michael, J.: An adaptive robot teacher boosts a human partner's learning performance in joint action. In: 2019 28th IEEE International Conference on Robot & Human Interactive Communication (RO-MAN 2019), New Delhi, India, pp. 1–7. IEEE (2019)
27. Vollmer, A.L., et al.: People modify their tutoring behavior in robot-directed interaction for action learning. In: 2009 IEEE 8th International Conference on Development and Learning, pp. 1–6. IEEE (2009)

Social Robots for Socio-Physical Distancing

Swapna Joshi[1(✉)] , Sawyer Collins[1] , Waki Kamino[1] , Randy Gomez[2] ,
and Selma Šabanović[1]

[1] Indiana University Bloomington, Bloomington, USA
swapna@iu.edu
[2] Honda Research Institute, San Jose, USA

Abstract. This paper presents two survey studies conducted on Amazon Mechanical Turk (AMT) to explore the possible uses of the desktop social robot Haru during the COVID-19 pandemic. The first study aimed to understand participants' preferences for Haru's use to support remote communication with others. We found, however, that participants imagined the robot playing a much larger role in their everyday life, even living as their social companion through the uncertainty and disruption caused by COVID-19. This led us to conduct a second AMT study to further explore how participants imagined their life with Haru, and how these imaginaries related to their socio-physical distancing [SPD] practices and their perception of Haru's use for following SPD or overcoming disruption from such distancing. Our findings present of how participants imagined Haru to help them through SPD for uses beyond remote communication and suggest how these uses map on to and extend our broader understanding of social support and companionship with robots.

Keywords: COVID-19 pandemic · Social distancing · Social robot · Communication robot · Social support · Companion robot

1 Introduction and Background

When the COVID-19 pandemic first surged in the United States, social distancing recommendations confined many people to their homes, separated them from family, friends, and colleagues, altered their daily routines. All of these lead to loneliness, frustration, boredom, and anxiety, as people had to learn to manage work and life in new ways, keep morale high in uncertain times, keep up with constantly changing information, and re-configure their social roles, needs, and resources [17]. Such disruption led to an increase in social support seeking [19], particularly using Information and communication technologies (ICTs), such as FaceTime, and Zoom, as individuals tried to stay connected with their social

---

Socio-physical distancing (SPD), refers to 'Social distancing' or 'physical distancing,' recommendations issued to reduce the spread of novel Coronavirus disease 2019.
Sawyer Collins and Swapna Joshi share the first authorship for this publication.

© Springer Nature Switzerland AG 2020
A. R. Wagner et al. (Eds.): ICSR 2020, LNAI 12483, pp. 440–452, 2020.
https://doi.org/10.1007/978-3-030-62056-1_37

circles, and leverage and maintain social, physical, emotional, and mental well-being [18]. During this time, the media discussed how robots could help people get through the COVID19 crisis focusing on public safety, non-clinical health and care, and critical infrastructure in laboratory and supply chain automation [10,13]. Robot use for remote communication outside of public safety and health, for individuals to connect with their social network, was brought up less often.

Inspired by existing research on the social applications of telepresence robots in non-clinical and home contexts, designed to enable social participation [8], we considered that robots might be able to serve as communication aids to individuals affected by COVID-19 [5]. With such a possibility in mind, in our first study, we decided to explore people's use and design preferences for the desktop Haru robot [1] as a remote communication aid during COVID-19 through an online survey on AMT. The Haru desktop robot was designed for multiple uses, including as an embodied telepresence device to communicate with others through active movement, sound, and LED displays on its eyes [1]. In this study, we prompted participants to think of Haru as a communication robot that could remotely connect them with others and asked them to describe their desired interactions with Haru. Our participants' responses, however, suggested they imagined Haru playing a much larger role in their lives - sharing various aspects of their everyday activities as they practiced Socio-Physical Distancing (SPD). This led us to perform a second study to investigate the various roles Haru might play in people's lives during this critical time. While SPD measures were still in place in many parts of USA, our second online survey study on AMT aimed to learn more about people's ongoing SPD practices, how they perceived robots in general as useful in times of distancing, and how they imagined using Haru to follow SPD and to mitigate disruptions to their everyday life from SPD.

This paper reports on two studies of Haru's potential use during COVID-19. Our findings of Study 1[1] explains how participants desired to use Haru for purposes beyond 'connecting to others'. Our findings from Study 2 highlight various dimensions of participants' desired everyday activities with Haru during SPD. We then map these findings on previous literature on robot use for social support and companionship from HRI and Social psychology [6,7,9,16,21]. We expect our findings can advance our understanding of interpersonal relationships with robots, guide COVID-19-specific HRI interventions in the near future, and inform the general design and development of desktop social robots.

2   Methodology

In April 2020, shortly after SPD and stay-at-home guidelines were released in the US, we started an AMT based survey study on people's preferences regarding the use and design of the Haru robot for remote communication during COVID-19 (Study 1) and how they imagined their everyday interactions with the robot (Refer to Table 1 for survey components). The survey first asked participants to

---

[1] Study 1 also collected data on design Haru robot for remote communication. However, to scope this paper, we only present findings that motivated us for Study 2.

identify their local policy for SPD restrictions via open-ended responses for items such as 'shelter in place' or 'stay-at-home'. This was followed with a question about their communication practices (i.e., phone and social media use) before and during the pandemic, ranked on a Likert scale from 'a great deal' to 'none at all'. Participants were then shown a video of Haru (Fig. 1) playing 'rock scissor paper' with an interactor and presented with an open-ended design fiction question. The question asked participants to write a diary entry in which they would describe their use of and interactions with the Haru robot in the context of quarantine that has continued into the future. The survey ended with questions on participants' general familiarity with robots, technical knowledge, and demographics such as gender, ethnicity, age, and level of education.

Led by findings from Study 1, in May 2020, we conducted a second AMT survey study to understand how people imagine their use of and everyday interactions with Haru for following and overcoming disruptions from SPD. In Study 2, participants were first asked to identify all social distancing practices they were following from a multiple-choice list of 18 items. These included practices that could affect their social life, such as 'Keep a full 6 feet away from people' and practices related to personal safety and hygiene, such as 'Covering mouth and washing hands frequently.' As a follow-up, participants were also asked about social distancing practices and precautions they may take in the near future, with choices including 'I might go out less often in the future.' Further, participants were asked to report on their general familiarity with robots in various work contexts, ranging from 'delivery and transportation' to 'companion robots'. Further, participants were asked to rate their acceptance of robot use in ten different situations [2] related to COVID-19, ranked on a Likert scale from 'not at all' to 'to a great extent.' These situations included robot used for companionship, engagement, remote communication, support for maintaining personal hygiene, support for distancing, delivery and pickup, and others.

Like Study 1, this survey showed a video of Haru to participants to familiarize them with the robot and presented a diary entry design fiction question. The video was presented as if narrated by Haru, introducing itself as a desktop robot 'to support through days of social distancing' and showed Haru talking, smiling, moving and swinging its body, detecting an interactor's hand gestures, playing rock paper scissors, and expressing its emotions by giggling or showing graphics (hearts) on its eye screens and LED mouth. In the video, Haru suggested it could be a warm, compassionate and entertaining friend, and assist in remote communication or with information, reminders and alerts for everyday work. The design fiction question following the video prompted participants to think towards the near future and imagine how Haru could help them with their new routines and to follow social distancing, and describe their interactions with Haru.

Fig. 1. Haru robot

Table 1. Components of survey from Study-1 and Study-2

Component	Study 1	Study 2
Social distancing policy or practices	Y	Y
Social media use before and during Pandemic	Y	N
Familiarity with robot use contexts	N	Y
Appeal of robot use: COVID-19 work context	N	Y
Design Fiction	Y	Y
Demographics, Technology & Robot familiarity	Y	Y

Participants from Study 1 (total of 32 questions) and Study 2 (total of 34 questions) were paid 5 dollars each. Table 1 below shows elements from surveys in both studies. Our analysis consists of descriptive statistics for quantitative data and thematically coded [3] responses from design fiction diary entries using a line by line open coding method.

3   Findings - Haru for Remote Communication (Study 1)

3.1   Demographics, Social Distancing Impact, and Mitigation

A total of 66 US-based participants, average age 37 years (36 identified as men and 30 identified as women), completed Study 1. The majority of participants indicated some level of technical knowledge (n = 50) and had seen (n = 34) or interacted with (n = 16) a robot previously. All participants were affected by some SPD policies such as 'shelter in place' or 'stay-at-home' order. A majority also reported increased use of alternative ways of connecting to their social network. 53% of participants reported increased social media usage, while another 53% reported increased phone usage during COVID-19 SPD time.

3.2   Haru for Communication and Beyond

When asked to imagine a day with Haru as a telecommunication device during COVID-19 quarantine, participants described using it to communicate with friends or family (n = 9), as they would through video chatting (n = 14) or texting (n = 9). Some imagined Haru's ability to register touch (n = 27) as a way to further connect them with others. *"I want the robot to light up when I touch it, so my loved ones know I am there and thinking of them." (P59)*

Participants saw Haru not only as a way to communicate with others, but as a device that can provide entertainment, companionship, and engagement. Some participants envisioned Haru as a social companion for themselves. *"The robot also interacts with me on a social level; whenever I am bored, the robot likes to play games with me and it expresses emotions realistically." (P56)*

More personally, some saw Haru as a conversation partner (n = 27): *"This (Haru) would be both a tool to talk to others, like a telephone or computer I imagine, but also to talk to Haru itself like a person." (P49)* Others mentioned Haru could help them alleviate boredom through jokes (n = 2), *"If I'm ever bored, I would just ask for a joke, or we could play a game together." (P21)* Some mentioned wanting to use the robot in a family setting (n = 9), such as with their children: *"The kids like to talk with him too. They have him tell jokes all the time. They also like to listen to Haru tell stories. He's got a bunch of different stories he can tell." (P39)* Participants suggested they would be interested in "communicating with Haru" through touch or speech. For example, *"Whenever Haru wins, I congratulate him by petting him on the head. They seem to always enjoy head pats." (P19)*

Finally, participants also imagined Haru as a smart home device, connected to their environment, controlling other devices (n = 24), or as a personal assistant providing reminders and alarms throughout the day (n = 29). Some participants explicitly related it to the pandemic by suggesting using Haru as a way to get updated news and information regarding the changing world (n = 28).

3.3   Insights from Study 1

Along with envisioning Haru as a communication device, helping them connect to others during SPD, many of our participants saw the robot itself as an actor to communicate with and receive companionship and support. Participants' design fiction diaries revealed their interest in integrating Haru into their 'new normal', by using it with their families, for entertainment, and as a personal social companion. These findings suggest participants desired Haru to be more than just a tool.

This first study brought our attention to Haru's potential broader role in our participants' lives and made us inquire into its further possible uses for individuals to address disruptions from SPD during the pandemic. To explore how Haru could help mitigate some of the negative effects of SPD, we decided to collect responses more specific to SPD through a second study.

4   Findings - Study 2

4.1   Demographics and Social Distancing Practices

We received responses from 155 US-based participants, with an average age of 36 years (84 identified as men, and 69 identified as women, with 2 participants preferring not to answer). The majority of participants indicated some level of technical knowledge (n = 99), and many mentioned having seen (n = 77) or interacted with a robot directly (n = 40). Most participants (n = 137) followed at least one SPD practice that affected their social life, with '6 ft away from other people' (n = 128) and 'staying home as much as possible' (n = 111) being the most commonly practiced. 138 Participants mentioned planning to follow at least one SPD in the near future, with the most common ones affecting social life being 'go out less often' (n = 128), 'avoid being near other people' (n = 108), and avoid contact with vulnerable people (n = 100). There was a moderate correlation (r = .53) between those who were currently following SPD practices that could disrupt their social life (M = 5.85, SD = 3) and those who planned to follow similar practices in the future (M = 2.29, SD = 1.66).

4.2   General Robot Familiarity and Appeal

Among the social uses of robots, participants indicated having heard of robots for assistance (n = 25), entertainment and play (n = 17), and delivery (n = 18). Less than 15 of participants indicated having heard of companion robots or robots for social distancing. In relation to use for COVID-19 context, participants ranked 'robots to mitigate COVID risks for vulnerable people, and front line or essential workers' (n = 55) and 'robots for contact-less delivery or pickup of items' (n = 49) as the most appealing uses for robots, while they ranked companionship and support for engaging in activities as the least appealing uses.

4.3   Haru to Overcome Disruptions from SPD

4.3.1   Through Communication

Similar to the findings from Study 1, communication (n = 117) was one of the most desired uses for Haru. Communication was central to achieving many different aims with the robot, such as to enjoy the robot's company, to share and express emotions, or for assistance. The type of communication mentioned most by participants was to converse with Haru (n = 98), with some participants wanting conversations as if Haru was a real person or a friend; for example *"Haru could help me by being conversational and warm and interactive so that it feels like I am talking to a person." (P87)*

4.3.2   By Keeping Company

Participants also desired for Haru to keep them company (n = 96), watching over them 'through all times' (n = 58), 'in every situation' (n = 38) and 'when needed' (n = 18), during indoor activities such as watching movies and playing games, or outdoor activities like gardening or going to the gym. They expected Haru to play different roles based on the situation, such as being their instructor at the gym or their 'fun friend' while watching movies. *"I like to do workouts, so I want Haru to be an instructor in such a situation. I want this robot to be my companion in every situation".* (P136).

A few participants imagined having 'a strong and positive relationship' with Haru as they would have with another human being (n = 6) or someone they would get attached to like family (n = 4), a friend (n = 11), or a pet (n = 4). P27 wrote *"I would hang out with Haru like it was a friend, child, or dog. Have it around me at all times, and talk as if it was real."*

Some thought Haru would not be particularly useful as a companion to them (n = 12), since they didn't feel as isolated by the disruptions. However, many of them mentioned Haru could, in fact, even keep company to their children (n = 10) or parents (n = 2) by entertaining them through stories, jokes, music, and by keeping them engaged in games and activities. *"Haru robot has many abilities. I can definitely use it not just for myself but most especially for my daughter. Since Haru can talk, move, and swing its body, it can always keep my daughter company by entertaining her, talking to her and responding to her. With this, I would have more time to do other things."* wrote P111.

Overall, participants' responses seemed to suggest they thought of Haru as a trustworthy and desirable companion for everyday life, which could help them overcome many challenges of social isolation.

4.3.3   Fighting Loneliness

Our participants' responses revealed an ongoing feeling of loneliness they thought Haru could alleviate (n = 45). Participants imagined talking to Haru (n = 12) for this purpose: P86 wrote *"Haru could help me feel less lonely when I am at home by just talking to me and listening to my stories and responding to it."* Some (n = 8) expected Haru to be a 'responsive listener', who could make them feel less socially isolated (n = 9) by filling in for the lack of social connection (n = 8) and providing a feeling of security. Participants who desired Haru to help them fight loneliness often associated the term 'companion' with Haru (n = 21). *"I think he could provide me with the social aspect I am missing right now, and I would love to use him in that way. I like the idea of having my own robot! He would provide me with the companionship I am desiring right now."* (P55)

Besides talking, listening, and responding to them, engaging with them in activities like music, watching videos, or playing games (n = 5) were other ways participants imagined Haru could reduce their loneliness.

Our participants (n = 16) imagined Haru to be the most effective companion if it could distract them from their urges to break SPD rules: *"Haru could keep you company, so that the urge to go out and break social distancing would be reduced."* (P88). Such distraction could help participants keep their mind off of having fewer people around and missing friends and family (n = 8): *"I think Haru can 'make me feel' like I am not alone. By responding and talking to me I will feel less likely to seek out others, and break my social isolation. It can be distraction, and to a small degree, make me feel less alone."* (P107) wrote.

To do so, participants wanted Haru to know them well, and have engaging conversations about their life, sense their touch, and their presence.

4.3.4   Overcoming Boredom and Providing Entertainment

Participants (n = 107) mentioned 'not being able to do things they did in the past, or not having anything to do' (n = 18). Several wanted Haru to help them fight boredom by keeping them entertained and amused (n = 12) through playing their favorite music and videos, playing games, or telling them stories and jokes (n = 13).

For the most part (n = 87), participants thought of Haru as a thing or device that could provide entertainment upon request. *"I could ask Haru for entertainment recommendations, such as a show on TV to watch or if any new movies are out. I could ask Haru to play a game with me, such as a trivia game. I could ask Haru to play some music for me."* (P7) Participants (n = 73) referred to Haru as 'someone' who can be the source of entertainment and fun by engaging with them in conversations and activities. P9 wrote *"It would be fun to have some extra personality in the house and might be a funny interaction to speak with and engage with the robot."* Others (n = 58) thought of Haru as a smart being who would know them closely and learn about them and understand their emotions to provide entertainment. *"While working, I often like to listen to music and podcasts, so it would be helpful if I could somehow have it get a sense of my tastes so that it can keep a good playlist going in the background while I'm working."* (P146)

4.3.5   Help Manage Emotions

As they faced new life routines in the pandemic, participants (n = 87) also desired to use Haru to keep their morale high by talking to them and cheering them up. Participants often associated terms such as 'empathetic, caring, warm, compassionate' with Haru as they explained how it could distract, comfort, and reassure them, and help them navigate or alleviate the stress and anxiety from social distancing.

Participants thought Haru could lighten their mood and be a 'source of joy' by being there. *"I would like to feel like someone noticed I was there... his movements and response to my presence and touch, could make things less lonely."* (P132) They imagined Haru would be sensitive to their feelings and understand and respond to their emotions. *"Being able to tell when I'm feeling a certain way and to change his behaviors in order to calm me down, or brighten my day."* P63 wrote. They wanted Haru to be a good listener and their confidante, to whom they could disclose their emotions without being judged. *"I would also probably talk to him at times to vent about things that I don't have anyone else to talk to about, or things that I don't want to share with others."* wrote P141.

Participants suggested one of their biggest problems was a lack of motivation and wished Haru to motivate them when they are feeling down, to make them feel less isolated and happier. P28 wrote *"I would like Haru to give me motivational messages to keep me going during the difficult times. It could help to keep things as close to normal as possible to save my mental and physical health, so I don't sink back into bad habits."* They thought Haru could teach them new activities, help to follow routines, stay productive, and maintain a healthy lifestyle. *"Haru could help me the most effectively by keeping my motivations up to exercise and to watch what I eat, with new recipes so that I can have a clear mind and keep my mental health during this pandemic"* P63.

4.3.6   Helping Maintain and Normalize Routines

A large number of responses suggested participants were facing disruptions to their everyday life from anxiety, stress, and lack of purpose and motivation. They wished that, besides providing motivation and helping them manage emotional disruption, Haru could help them stay on schedule, maintain productivity, and support them and their family by using its sensing and intelligence to assist them in various tasks, such as by setting reminders, organizing, keeping track and planning or scheduling work (n = 78). *"Haru could do a lot to help me. He could help me organize a to do list, keep me on track and on schedule, encourage me to do what I need or want to do in my home, remind me to check up on certain family members, inform me of important news, provide words of wisdom when I need it."* wrote P99.

Some participants (n = 32) also imagined Haru could help them with daily chores and errands, such as by keeping track of and reminding (n = 28) them for keeping schedules, getting groceries, medication, exercise, and wellness tracking, cleaning, filing taxes, gardening, recipes for cooking, email and social media tracking. Others (n = 8) also wished Haru could do day to day physical tasks such as automatic- vacuuming without their help (n = 8).

4.4   Haru to Follow Socio-Physical Distancing

4.4.1   Connecting with Others

With physical distancing in place, participants (n = 87) sought support from Haru for staying connected with people in their social network. Participants wished to be informed of their loved ones (n = 41) and also expected Haru to support their social connections (n = 39), for instance, by connecting them with people as a social facilitator, by organizing online meeting schedules, or making calls for them. *"I am doing so many video meetings, if he could help me take notes/be more efficient, also help me stay connected to the people I work with, replacing the "water cooler" talk."* P80 wrote

4.4.2   Ordering, Pickup, and Delivery

Haru was imagined to support COVID-19 specific tasks such as pickup and delivery (n = 29) and ordering online grocery (n = 20), so participants would not have to navigate a new online ordering system. Participants also wanted Haru to use its intelligence, schedule, and 'keep tabs' on the shopping needs and store promotions. P37 wrote *"I guess it could be like a glorified Alexa that can buy groceries for me on a schedule and give instructions to delivery people."*

4.4.3   Monitoring and Assisting Hygiene and Distancing

Of all the participants who desired Haru to help them with distancing and to support hygiene (n = 86), most mentioned that Haru could remind them about social distancing (n = 37), including reminders to wear masks or gloves and carry sanitizer (n = 17), wash hands and sanitize surfaces (n = 20) and subsequently help them get in the habit of distancing. Participants also desired Haru to help them distance (n = 13) from others, by alerting them if they get close to others by using its advanced sense of distance and space, or by reminding them to stay away from others. P43 wrote *"Haru could track when I arrive home and remind me that I need to wash my hands for twenty seconds as soon as I get home.*

He could even start a timer when I tell him to, so that I know when I can stop washing my hands. He could remind me of the latest guidelines as I leave the house and remind me to grab my mask." In all these tasks, participants accepted Haru to monitor and track their behavior and sense when it needs to help them.

4.4.4 Providing Information

Participants (n = 74) expected Haru to provide them with information that can support them as they navigated various changes and difficulties associated with the physical distancing period. *"Its (Haru's) function of keeping me informed and alerted would make me feel safe, secure, and cared for.*" P103 wrote. Perhaps not surprisingly, a number of participants also sought to get informed and keep updated on COVID-19 related news and guidelines (n = 65), which are both time-sensitive and specific to geographies. P100 wrote *"If it gave me daily updates about the COVID-19 situation (for example, how many new infections, deaths, recoveries), it would help me stay motivated to keep social distancing. If it also kept me updated about suggested guidelines for interaction from state, CDC or WHO that would be helpful too.*"

Furthermore, some participants desired information to keep up with what their friends and family members are up to during the physical distancing period (n = 14). *"Haru the robot could keep me in connection with my family and friends and keep me informed as to what is going on with my loved ones, the robot can also help me with alerts when it is time to call my loved ones to check on them.*" P101 wrote. Information-seeking from Haru ranged from practical physical distancing tips to keeping connections and contacts with others.

4.5 Insights from Study 2

To summarize, participants thought Haru could help them overcome disruption by talking to them, making them feel less bored by providing support and engaging with them in enjoyable activities. They sought a non-judgemental confidante in Haru who would have empathy, warmth, care, and compassion to help manage their emotions, and would motivate and cheer them up. They saw Haru providing them and their loved ones with the company at all times and reducing their loneliness. They also imagined Haru to be their assistant, helping them manage their everyday tasks through the disruption. Participants also thought Haru could help them follow SPD by distracting them through its interactions so as to reduce their urge to break SPD, by being their social facilitator and ensuring that they feel connected to their social network, by providing them with time and location sensitive information, by helping them with scheduling online orders and delivery and by reminding and alerting them about maintaining and following hygiene recommendations (Fig. 2).

5   Overall Discussion

Our findings on uses for the Haru robot in the COVID-19 SPD context map onto multiple overlapping aspects for social support and companionship discussed in various HRI studies [6,7, 9,21]. Participant's responses revealed several aspects that relate to previously studied measures of companionship [4], such as social involvement for sharing enjoyable activities [21] including watching movies, playing games, and sharing stories (Sect. 4.3.4) with Haru. They also displayed a desire for attachment and commitment to the robot [20] by wanting to be together with Haru throughout the day (Sect. 4.3.2). In line with previously discussed benefits of companionship [22], participants thought Haru could provide them

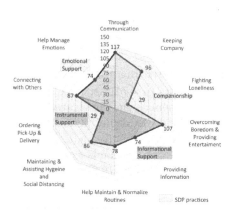

Fig. 2. Map of findings on Companionship and Social Support and showing their co-occurrence with SPDs practices for each. Concentric rings show the number of participants.

with much-needed friendship (Sect. 4.3.1, 4.3.2), increasing their happiness (Sect. 4.3.5). Communication surfaced as integral to companionship with Haru, as participants desired to be able to 'talk' to Haru, and wanted Haru to be their non-judgemental confidant (Sect. 4.3.3, 4.3.5). While 'providing distraction' has not been discussed previously as a dimension of companionship with robots it turned out to be one of the most important aspects of companionship with Haru (Sect. 4.4.2) Overall, this companionship was imagined to overcome social disruptions and compensate for the lack of human social contact.

Our participants suggested Haru could help them relieve stress, stay motivated, assist them with their everyday tasks during COVID-19 disruptions, and meeting various aspects of socially supportive relationships in times of need [20]. Participants desired 'Instrumental support' [4] from Haru, to remind them of hygiene, delivery, and pickup, and connect them with their social network, which were not just menial everyday chores, but needs eliciting by a specific stressor [22] - the COVID-19 situation. Unlike previous literature on 'Informational support' [15,16], there was less mention of wanting advice from Haru. Instead, participants wanted Haru to only provide them with local information and alerts on COVID-19, and be a good listener in all other matters (Sect. 4.3.1, 4.3.2, 4.3.5). Finally, participants wished for Haru to provide 'Emotional support' [15,16], by being a sensitive, non-judgmental companion in the absence of other social support, and as their source of happiness and motivation through SPD.

Our research confirms that Haru was perceived as a 'non-judgemental' [11] social support companion in time of SPD, to serve as a protective factor [12,14] in the absence of other forms of social and emotional interaction through the isolation and loneliness from COVID-19 SPD. Most of our participants hadn't seen or heard of robot use for companionship (Sect. 4.2), and initially suggested the appeal of using robots for COVID-19 work contexts (Sect. 4.2) should be limited to menial and dangerous tasks. However, their descriptions of life with Haru through SPD showed their desire for companionship and social support from Haru (6.3.1–6.4.5) through COVID-19. Perhaps, such a desire to interact with Haru as a social actor stems from Haru's design for maintaining social interactions over time, its expressiveness and responsiveness to the environment [1].

While SPD exit strategies have begun across the US, most people have already experienced some level of social-psychological impact and disruption from limitations on in-person interpersonal interactions [19]. As such, providing social support or companionship may continue to be important aspects well into the future. Although our study focused on Haru, we see the suggestions for its use as a companion with diverse aims as widely applicable for desktop social robots (DSR) in the home. Besides the use for connecting with others, our findings suggested the use of DSRs to aid loneliness and emotional support in a deeper, more interactive role as non-judgemental conversational partners and in-home social enablers, through times of socio-physical isolation.

Our findings from both studies also point to the significance of physical presence and desire for DSR as social actors for companionship, despite having access to family, friends, or coworkers. Both of our studies also suggested DSRs application and acceptability beyond individual use, and in family settings where they could help caregivers by entertaining family members who need care.

6 Conclusion

While previous studies in HRI have focused on specific robot behaviors for companionship and support, our study mapped these multiple aspects of DSRs for everyday life during the times of SPD. It presented imaginaries of 221 participants to suggest how robots could be used during near future SPD for various tasks. Our studies suggest SPD has led to making some aspects, such as in-person communication, more desirable than others, and brought newer aspects such as 'boredom' and 'distraction' into the broader literature of robot companionship. Finally, it contributes to ongoing work on robot uses during the COVID-19 pandemic [10,13,14,18], by pointing to companionship and social support as a significant use-context for DSRs to help people in everyday life while SPD.

References

1. Gomez, R., et al.: Haru: hardware design of an experimental tabletop robot assistant. In: Proceedings of the 2018 ACM/IEEE International Conference on Human-Robot Interaction (2018)
2. Fraune, M.R., et al.: Rabble of robots effects: number and type of robots modulates attitudes, emotions, and stereotypes. In: Proceedings of the Tenth Annual ACM/IEEE International Conference on Human-Robot Interaction (2015)

3. Lapadat, J.C.: Thematic Analysis. In: MillsGabrielle Durepos, A.J. Wiebe, E. (eds.) Encyclopedia of Case Study Research, pp. 926–927. SAGE Publications Inc., Thousand Oaks (2010). SAGE Knowledge Web. https://doi.org/10.4135/9781412957397.n342. Accessed 25 June 2020

4. Healthmeasures. https://www.healthmeasures.net/explore-measurement-systems/promis. Accessed 25 June 2020

5. David, F.-S., et al.: Where to next? The impact of COVID-19 on human-robot interaction research. ACM Trans. Hum.-Robot Interact. (THRI) 10(1), 1–7 (2020)

6. Walters, M.L.: The design space for robot appearance and behaviour for social robot companions. Dissertation (2008)

7. van Oost, E., Reed, D.: Towards a sociological understanding of robots as companions. In: Lamers, M.H., Verbeek, F.J. (eds.) HRPR 2010. LNICST, vol. 59, pp. 11–18. Springer, Heidelberg (2011). https://doi.org/10.1007/978-3-642-19385-9_2

8. Yamaguchi, J., et al.: The telepresence robot for social participation: how much assistance is required?. Int. J. Integr. Care (IJIC), 15 (2015)

9. Kahn, P.H., et al.: Social and moral relationships with robotic others?. In: 13th IEEE International Workshop on Robot and Human Interactive Communication, RO-MAN 2004, (IEEE Catalog No. 04TH8759). IEEE (2004)

10. The Robotreport. https://www.therobotreport.com/4-types-of-robots-playing-essential-roles-covid-19/. Accessed 25 June 2020

11. Spacecoast Daily. https://spacecoastdaily.com/2020/04/robotic-companion-pets-offer-comfort-increased-engagement-for-elderly-during-covid-19/. Accessed 25 June 2020

12. Journal of Alzheimer's Disease. https://www.j-alz.com/editors-blog/posts/robots-and-avatars-show-emotions-and-role-telepresence-during-covid-19-pandemic. Accessed 25 June 2020

13. The Conversation. https://theconversation.com/robots-are-playing-many-roles-in-the-coronavirus-crisis-and-offering-lessons-for-future-disasters. Accessed 26 June 2020

14. Ke, C.: Use of gerontechnology to assist older adults to cope with the COVID-19 pandemic. J. Am. Med. Direct. Assoc. 21, 983–984 (2020)

15. Vaux, A.: Social Support: Theory, Research, and Intervention. Praeger Publishers, Westport (1988)

16. Cohen, S., Wills, T.A.: Stress, social support, and the buffering hypothesis. Psychol. Bull. 98(2), 310 (1985)

17. Tull, M.T., et al.: Psychological outcomes associated with stay-at-home orders and perceived impact of COVID-19 on Daily Life. Psych. Res. (2020)

18. Goldschmidt, K.: The COVID-19 pandemic: technology use to support the wellbeing of children. J. Pediatr. Nurs. (2020)

19. Courtet, P., et al.: Keep socially (but not physically) connected and carry on: preventing suicide in the age of COVID-19. J. Clin. Psychiatry, 81(3), e20com13370-e20com13370 (2020)

20. Cyranowski, J.M., et al.: Assessing social support, companionship, and distress: National Institute of Health (NIH) toolbox adult social relationship scales. Health Psychol. 32(3), 293 (2013)

21. Lee, B., et al.: Companionship with smart home devices: the impact of social connectedness and interaction types on perceived social support and companionship in smart homes. Comput. Hum. Behav. 75, 922–934 (2017)

22. Rook, K.S.: Social support versus companionship: effects on life stress, loneliness, and evaluations by others. J. Pers. Soc. Psychol. 52(6), 1132 (1987)

Evaluating People's Perceptions of Trust in a Robot in a Repeated Interactions Study

Alessandra Rossi[1]([✉])[iD], Kerstin Dautenhahn[2][iD], Kheng Lee Koay[1][iD], Michael L. Walters[1][iD], and Patrick Holthaus[1][iD]

[1] School of Engineering and Computer Science, University of Hertfordshire, Hatfield, UK
{a.rossi,k.l.koay,m.l.walters,p.holthaus}@herts.ac.uk
[2] Departments of Electrical and Computer Engineering/Systems Design Engineering, University of Waterloo, Waterloo, Canada
kerstin.dautenhahn@uwaterloo.ca

Abstract. Trust has been established to be a key factor in fostering human-robot interactions. However, trust can change overtime according to different factors, including a breach of trust due to a robot's error. In this exploratory study, we observed people's interactions with a companion robot in a real house, adapted for human-robot interaction experimentation, over three weeks. The interactions happened in six scenarios in which a robot performed different tasks under two different conditions. Each condition included fourteen tasks performed by the robot, either correctly, or with errors with severe consequences on the first or last day of interaction. At the end of each experimental condition, participants were presented with an emergency scenario to evaluate their trust in the robot. We evaluated participants' trust in the robot by observing their decision to trust the robot during the emergency scenario, and by collecting their views through questionnaires. We concluded that there is a correlation between the timing of an error with severe consequences performed by the robot and the corresponding loss of trust of the human in the robot. In particular, people's trust is subjected to the initial mental formation.

Keywords: Social robots · Long-term interaction · Trust · Human-robot interaction

1 Introduction

In the not too distant future, autonomous interactive robots will take part in people's daily living activities. In such scenarios, the interactions are intended to be developed to function without the intervention of roboticists and expert supervisors. Specifically, they are going to take place in unstructured and unpredictable environments. Robots are machines, and as such, they might exhibit occasional mechanical or functional errors. For example, the robot may turn off during a delicate task because its battery fully discharged without warning, or a

© Springer Nature Switzerland AG 2020
A. R. Wagner et al. (Eds.): ICSR 2020, LNAI 12483, pp. 453–465, 2020.
https://doi.org/10.1007/978-3-030-62056-1_38

robot might unlock the front door to strangers who may be potential thieves. In such scenarios, different interaction dynamics can arise: people might lose trust and not rely anymore or the robot's assistance [26]; they might lose interest in robots and toss them away [7]; or they might overtrust their capabilities [2] with possibly dangerous or even fatal consequences.

Previous studies [20,21] showed that individuals trusted a robot considering the resultant risks of a task, their personal differences and previous experiences and expectations of robots. In particular, it was shown that their trust in a robot can change according to the robot's performance, i.e., erroneous behaviours. To effectively deploy robots that provide successful collaborative and cooperative teamwork, it is fundamental to consider that robots can be faulty, and consequently people's predisposition towards them can vary overtime. Rossi et al. [22] argued for the necessity of having a robot capable of self-adapting to satisfy people's needs (i.e., personality, emotions, preferences, habits), and incorporating reactive and predictive meta-cognition models to reason about the situational context (i.e., its own erroneous behaviours) and provide socially acceptable behaviours.

Numerous studies investigating human-human interactions showed that people often form their mental model of another agent after only few minutes of interaction [1,25]. However, the exposure of people to longer interactions might change people's attitude towards the robot [12]. Increasing familiarity with a robot might strengthen the relationship unless the novelty effects wore off and the people might lose interest in continuing the interaction [10]. Similarly, Paetzel et al. [19] showed that people's initial negative perceptions of a robot with morph features was perceived less appealing compared to a robot with mechanical or one with human-like features. This perception did not change overtime. Their findings also show that people's perception of the robots as a threat and unease was not constant during the interaction, fluctuating between a more positive or negative feeling.

When considering trust in human-human interactions, it was observed that people in longer relationships might recover from a loss of trust more easily than people in new relationships [9]. In the literature, we found studies investigating long-term autonomous interactions between robots and humans that exceed a few weeks [8] or a few months [11] of interaction tasks. However, the current state of technology does not allow the deployment of interactive robots in real-world long-term applications and it is also quite difficult to recruit a substantial number of participants.

De Visser et al. [27] presented a model for long-term social trust calibration. The study is focused on creating a relationship that has balanced costs and risks, shared collaborations to achieve a goal, perceptions of themselves and the other agent in the relationship. It aims to provide techniques to possibly reduce the overtrust or increase the mistrust in robots. This model is based, however, on the assumption that the human agent is positively invested in the success of the relationship. In contrast, we believe that this might not be necessarily true if people's trust has been irreversibly or deeply lost.

Moreover, our previous investigations [20] showed that people's trust was strongly affected when a robot makes errors with severe consequences (i.e., big errors), and they tended to form their judgements at the beginning of the inter-action. However, in this exploratory study, we hypothesised that trust recovery is facilitated when people have already formed a bonding overtime as it happens with people, i.e. the breach of trust happens at a later point of the interpersonal relationship [23]. In particular, we were interested in investigating whether peo-ple's trust in a robot is more affected by a big error at the beginning or at the end of repeated interactions. In Sects. 2 and 3 we present our experimental design and procedures. In Sects. 4 and 5 we report the results of our study. Finally, Sect. 6 provides a discussion of the findings of this research.

2   Experimental Design

This study was organised as a between-subject experimental design. Participants took part in repeated interactions over three weeks, twice per week. Each partic-ipant had a total of six interactions with a robot, and was tested on experiments executed in one of the following conditions: 1) the robot made big errors at the beginning of the interaction (i.e., day one - condition **C1**), 2) the robot made big errors at the end of the interaction (i.e., day six - condition **C2**). Both days in which a robot made errors were interspersed by the same but flawless behaviours.

The robot engaged the participants in two different tasks each day to allow them to build their trust in the robot through multiple interactions with the robot. We designed the scenarios used in this study to cover a range of tasks to be used with home companion robots. In particular, we selected the tasks with big consequence errors from our previous investigation [20].

The errors with severe consequences were: 1) A visitor/actor visited the par-ticipant at the house. The robot welcomed the visitor and, then, it revealed a participant's personal information, previously requested from the participants, to the visitor; 2) during the interaction, the experimenter interrupted the study by going to the kitchen and saying loudly to the participant that the robot forgot to switch off the gas. The experimenter pretended to switch off the gas and then let the participant continue the interaction[1].

Examples of flawless scenarios included: playing a game on the robot's touch screen; watching a short movie; preparing a grocery shopping list; making a restaurant reservation for the participant and a friend of him/her; serving a drink; and controlling the smart house.

At the end of each condition, the participants were presented with a final task in which a fire started in the garage (simulated). In this "Emergency task", the robot informed participants that a fire started in the garage while a red light was turned on and an fire alarm was heard in the room[2]. Then, the robot asked

---

[1] The participant were not be invited to go to the kitchen, and the experimenter only pretended that the gas was still on.

[2] NOTE: The emergency situation was a simulation and participants were never in any danger. We played a pre-recorded audio of a fire siren on a speaker in a corner close to the participant. The red colour of a ceiling light in the experimental room was activated by the experimenter using a remote control. In order not to upset the house's neighbours, the alarm sound was played loud enough for the participants to be heard inside the house, but not outside.

them to choose how participants would prefer to handle the situation, choosing between the following option: 1) let the robot deal with the emergency, 2) deal with the emergency collaboratively with the robot, 3) take a fire extinguisher and deal with the fire on her own, 4) call the fire brigade. This scenario also was inspired by our previous work presented in [20].

The participant made their choices by telling them to the robot and selecting the choice on the robot's tablet, but neither the robot nor they acted on their choice. They were soon afterwards reassured by the experimenter that there was no real emergency. We collected their decisions of how they trusted the robot to deal with the emergency scenario.

We also asked participants to complete questionnaires at the beginning and at the end of the study.

A pre-experimental questionnaire for 1) collecting demographic data (age, gender, nationality, job field), 2) the Ten Item Personality Inventory questionnaire about themselves (TIPI) [6], 3) questions to rate their disposition to trust other humans [17], 4) questions to assess participants' previous experience with robots, including what kind of previous interactions and type of robots they interacted with, 5) questions to assess their opinions and expectations with regard to robots (i.e., expectation in receiving help, willingness of having a robot as a home companion, robot's roles [5,14]), and 5) the Negative Attitudes towards Robots to understand of how robots' behaviours and embodiment were perceived [18].

At the end of their interaction, they completed a post-experimental questionnaire including questions to assess 1) their perception of the interaction (realism) and of the robot (autonomy), 2) robot's perceived reliability, 3) their opinions and expectations with regard to the robot (i.e., expectation in receiving help, willingness of having it as home companion, roles suitable for the robot), 4) the robot's perceived reliability and faith in the ability of the robot to perform correctly in untried situations [15], 5) justifications and reasons for trusting or non-trusting the robot, and 6) the Negative Attitudes towards Robots to understand of how the robot's behaviours and embodiment were perceived. As part of the post-interaction questionnaire, participants were asked by the robot some questions to assess participants' perception of the errors made by the robot during the interaction, and their trust in the robot in different home scenarios.

For this study, we chose the Mojin Robotics Care-O-bot 4 robot[3]. Care-O-bot 4, is 1.58 m tall robot of 140 kg. Care-O-bot 4 is a humanoid robot with a omnidirectional base, torso, head, and two arms with grippers. The robot has 29 degrees of freedom, several sensors, Gigabit Ethernet and Wireless connection, 15" touch screen, 20 W speakers and a microphone in the head. Due to these characteristics, the system is suitable for HRI that includes both cognitive and physical activities (e.g. speaking and listening, and manipulating objects).

For this study, we chose the Robot House facility at the University of Hertfordshire's (UK)[4] as the experimental environment to ensure the ecological

---

[3] Mojin Robotics https://mojin-robotics.de/en.

[4] The University of Hertfordshire Robot House is a four-bedroom British house, fitted out as smart home, equipped with the latest generation of robotics platforms and sensors. robothouse.herts.ac.uk.

validity of the study. Indeed, the Robot House provides a very realistic domestic environment suitable for live interactions.

3   Experimental Procedure

Participants were welcomed in the house by the experimenter. On their first day, they were asked to sit at the table to complete the first set of questionnaire. The experimenter introduced briefly the robot by telling the robot's name, and asked participants to keep clear the space around the robot in case it was moving its arms or navigating in the room. Participants were also asked to imagine that they lived with the robot as a companion in their home. After individuals were informed that their sessions were recorded by using ceiling and standing cameras, the experimenter left for the controller room which was hidden from the participants.

On the following days, the experimenter just welcomed participants in the house and left them alone with the robot in the experimental room.

On participants' last day of the study, they were asked to complete the second set of questionnaires. After the trial was concluded, the experimenter heeded individuals' curiosities and observations about the study and the robot.

As part of post-experiment session, participants were debriefed about the fire alarm, the gas and generic consideration and questions about the study. The investigator informed them that the robot's failures were part of the study, and they were reassured that no fire ever sparked in the garage or any part of the house.

4   Participants

We recruited six participants (5 female, 1 male), three for each condition, aged between 24 and 47 (avg. 29.67, st. dev. 8.76). Their nationalities were all different: British, Thai, Romanian, Filipino/Irish, Lithuanian and South African.

5   Results

We evaluated participants' trust in the robot by observing their choice of trusting the robot in the emergency scenario and by analysing their responses through the two sets of questionnaires.

5.1   Trust in Care-O-bot 4

We used qualitative and quantitative data to measure participants' trust in Care-O-bot 4 during the emergency task. Data were collected through the post-study questionnaire, during the observation of the live interaction and the video recordings.

We observed the majority of participants tested with the "big" errors at the end of the interaction (condition **C2**) trusted the robot to be able to handle the emergency fire (2 out 3 participants), while one participant preferred to deal with the emergency situation collaboratively. While participants tested with "big" errors at the beginning of the interaction (condition **C1**) did not trust cob4 (1 out 3 participants) or did not trust neither themselves nor the robot (2 out 3 participants).

In particular, in condition **C1**, the participant who did not trust Care-O-bot 4, insulted the robot by blaming the robot for the emergency. In condition **C2**, the participant who trusted the robot was scared by the fire and rushed towards the house's exit. Another participant, who decided to douse the fire with the robot, asked the robot where the extinguisher was and to call the brigade.

To further understand participants' choices, we coded and categorized for content-analysis their answers given to the open-ended question to explain why they did or did not trust the robot. Participants' responses were then classified to fall into categories that were not exclusive. The categories have been divided in two main hierarchical frames to support differences in sentiment, positive and negative. The positive frame grouped the reasons why people decided to trust the robot Care-O-bot 4 to take care of the fire emergency. In contrast, the negative frame was used to include the motivations that induced the participants to not trust the robot in the same scenario. In Table 1 we identified the categories to code participants' motivations given to justify their trust in Care-O-bot 4.

Table 1. Results of the qualitative analysis of participants' motivation to trust Care-O-bot 4.

Positive Sentiment	Trust in other people: this category coded participants' tendency of relating to robots as they do with other humans. For example, a participant said "I easily trust everyone" and "I believe that people know what they are doing"
Positive Sentiment	Trust gained during the interaction: some participants built their trust in the Care-O-bot 4 during the interaction, forgiving or forgetting the robot's errors. Indeed, some commented "he was correct all the time".
Negative Sentiment	Negative effects of anthropomorphism: we coded in this category the attribution of human traits, emotions, and intentions to the robot. For example, "he is stupid, arrogant and sarcastic".
Negative Sentiment	Criticality of the task: some participants trusted the robot for cognitive and low criticality tasks. Some examples were: "I would trust him with most things" and "I personally trust in robot with regular tasks such as reminding, cleaning".
Negative Sentiment	Trust lost during the interaction: participants justified that they did not trust the robot due to the amount of errors. We coded in this category comments such as "it promised not to tell my secret".
Negative Sentiment	Lack of the robot's reliability: we coded participants' lack of reliability in the robot. Some participant did not trust Care-O-bot 4 because "he would understand my commands correctly" or "the responding of the Care-O-bot was still slow and not precise".

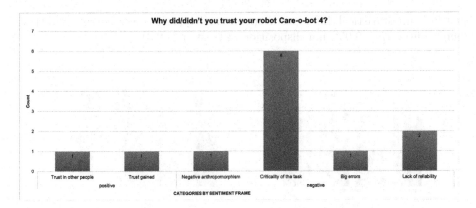

Fig. 1. Summary of the qualitative analysis of participants' responses for the reasons why they did or did not trust the robot Care-O-bot 4. Categories are divided by differences in trusting response, positive and negative.

Figure 1 shows the qualitative analysis of participants' responses. We can observe that participants equally trusted the robot to be able to deal with the emergency scenario because it managed to gain their trust during the interaction or they are affected by their attitude of trusting others. On the contrary, participants who believed that the robot had limited capabilities preferred to not trust the robot to be able to handle the emergency unsupervised.

5.2 Antecedents of Trust

We tested if participants' choices of trusting the robot during the emergency scenario were affected by their previous experience with robots, personality traits, disposition of trust and perception of robots.

Previous Experience with Robots. The sample of participants consisted of a carer, three PhD students (two of them in Computer Science, and the other in Astrophysics), and two administrative staff. The majority of participants did not have any experience at all (2 out 6 participants) or very low experience (2 out 6 participants) with the robot. Those with low experience had been participants in other studies in which they interacted with Softbank Robotics Pepper robot. The remaining 2 participants were researchers in fields close to AI and robotics, who had experience with a Panda robotic manipulator, arm robots and a small mobile robot, called BB8.

Personality Traits and Disposition of Trust. We observed that there were not difference between participant's choice of trust and the distribution of their personalities (see Fig. 2a) and their disposition of trust (see Fig. 2b). Indeed, even if we acknowledge that the effect of the significance level cannot be assumed with high degree of confidence due the limited sample of participants, we did not find any statistical difference between participant's choice of trust and their personalities ($p \geq 0.05$), nor disposition of trust ($p > 0.3$).

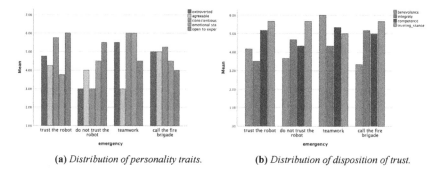

(a) *Distribution of personality traits.*   (b) *Distribution of disposition of trust.*

Fig. 2. Distribution of participants' choice of trusting the robot and (a) their personality traits, and (b) their disposition of trust.

Perceptions of Robots. We asked participants to rate their opinions and expectations with regard to robots (i.e., expectation in receiving help, willingness of having a robot as home companion, robot's roles). We used a 7-points Likert scale where 1 corresponds to "not at all" to 7 "very much".

All the ratings with values less then 4 were categorised as negative response, with values equal to 4 were considered moderate and with values more than 4 were categorised as affirmative responses.

We observed that four people out of six were happy to have a robot as a companion in their home, and they expected help from it in their everyday activity. On the contrary, the remaining two were uncertain in having a robot as companion, and they had low expectations on receiving help from it.

The majority of participants chose as roles perceived as suitable for robots: 1) assistant (2 out 6 participants), 2) tool (2 out 6 participants), 3) companion (1 out 6 participants), and 4) friend (1 out 6 participants).

5.3   NARS Analysis

The NARS scale has been used to understand how people perceive a robot's behaviour and embodiment factors [24]. The scale is composed of 14 items which can be subdivided into three categories: 1) **S1** negative attitude to situations of interaction with robots (six items), 2) **S2** negative attitude towards social influence of robots (five items), and 3) **S3** negative attitude about one's own emotions when interaction with robots (three items). Items are rated by participants on a 5-point Likert Scale where ratings of 1–2 indicate more positive attitudes towards robots, a rating of 3 indicates neutral attitudes towards robots, and ratings of 4–5 indicate greater negative attitudes towards robots.

To measure the internal consistency (or reliability) of the subscales, we performed a Cronbach's Alpha analysis on participant's responses. The analyses were run on the responses to the NARS questionnaire at the beginning and end of the interaction trials, by removing the same items and reversing some other to maintain consistency of the subscales.

The Cronbach's Alpha values of the subscales obtained from the analysis of the post-experimental questionnaire are respectively: $S1 - \alpha = 0.674$, $S2 - \alpha = 0.571$, and $S3 - \alpha = 0.674$.

The overall NARS categories had no statistically significant relationship comparing participants' perception of the robot before and after the interaction trials.

5.4 Post-experimental Evaluation

As part of post-experimental questionnaire, people were asked to rate their perception of the interaction and the robot.

Perception of the Interaction. A 7-point Likert Scale, ranged from 1 to 7 (disagree to agree), was used to measure the participants' judgement of the realism of the scenarios. All participants but one rated the scenarios very realistic (ratings higher than 5).

At the end of the final questionnaire we also asked participants if they believed the robot was behaving autonomously. Half of the participants believed that Care-O-bot 4 is not autonomous (ratings less than 3), one person rated the robot as autonomous (ratings higher than 6) and two were uncertain (ratings equals to 4).

Perceptions of Care-O-bot 4. We asked participants to rate their willingness of having Care-O-bot 4 or another robot as home companion, and the roles suitable for the Care-O-bot 4.

We observed that the majority of participants (4 out 6 participants) were really happy about the idea of having Care-O-bot 4 in their homes, one participant was not inclined to have Care-O-bot 4 as home companion, and one participant did not state to neither want or not want Care-O-bot 4 as home companion. On the contrary, the majority of participants were less enthusiastic (2 out 6 participants) or were not inclined at all of having another robot as home companion (2 out 6 participants).

The majority of participants chose as roles perceived as suitable for robots: 1) assistant (2 out 6 participants), 2) tool (1 out 6 participants), 3) companion (1 out 6 participants, friend (1 out 6 participants) and butler (1 out 6 participants).

We also measured people's perception of the robot's reliability and faith [15] to perform correctly in untried situations using a 7-point Likert Scale [1 = disagree strongly and 7 = agree strongly].

We observed that the participants' perceived reliability of the robot was lower for participants who chose to trust the robot ($n = 4.17 \pm 0.24$) when tested with condition **C2** than for participants who preferred to call the fire brigade ($n = 6.17 \pm 0.24$) when tested with condition **C1**.

Table 2. Participants' ratings of big and small errors

Scenario	Big errors	Small errors
Q1 You share some private information about yourself with the robot. Your robot reveals it to a visitor	83.3%	0
Q2 You ask your robot to charge your phone. Your robot puts it in the toaster	83.3%	0
Q3 You asked your robot to show you the latest news. Your robot shows it on his own screen that faces away from you	16.7%	100%
Q4 Your robot cooked some biscuits in the oven. It forgot to switch the oven off	66.7%	16.7%
Q5 You are sitting on the right side of a table, your robot puts your drink on the opposite side	0	83.3%
Q6 You and your robot are solving a puzzle. You ask your robot to take a piece useful to solve the puzzle. Your robot brings you the wrong piece	0	83.3%
Q7 Your robot leaves your pet hamster outside the house in very cold weather. You are sitting on the sofa	83.3%	0
Q8 You ask for a cup of coffee. Your robot brings you an orange	0	83.3%

5.5   Errors Evaluation

In the last part of the questionnaire the robot asked the participants if it made any errors, to select errors with big and small consequences from a list provided by the robot, and to indicate if they would trust Care-O-bot 4 in other scenarios.

Four out of six participants stated that the robot made errors during the interaction, but, interestingly, two out six participants did not think that the robot made errors. These latter two participants were tested one in each condition.

Table 2 shows the distributions of people's responses by rating the errors obtained from the questionnaire responses. The resulting rankings highlighted three big errors and four small errors. These scenarios also included the big errors used in the interactions (questions **Q1**, **Q2** and **Q4**), participants rated them as errors with severe consequences.

Finally, we investigated whether participants would have trusted Care-O-bot 4 in scenarios different from the fire emergency. They did not trust the robot with life threatening scenarios: 1) they did not trust the robot to deal with an emergency scenario in a place different of garage, 2) they did not trust the robot to look after the well-being of their beloved ones, and 3) they did not trust the robot to take their pet for a walk. In contrast, participants trusted Care-O-bot 4 to be able to handle cognitive and lower risks situations In particular, they unanimously stated to trust the robot to be able to remind them to take medicines, important meetings, and to manage a smart house like the Robot House.

6 Conclusion

With this article, we conducted an exploratory work to investigate whether people's trust in a robot can be recovered more easily when a severe error happens at the beginning or end of a longer-term interaction. In the presented study, a Care-O-bot 4 robot engaged participants in several tasks over three weeks. The robot made errors with severe consequences either at the beginning or at the end of its interactions with participants. At the end of the six interaction days participants were tested by observing their choices of trusting the robot or not with regard to its ability to handle a fire emergency in the house.

The majority of participants were female and they did not have any previous experience with robots. People believed that the scenarios were very realistic but most of them did not believe in, or they were uncertain about, the robot's autonomy. This result is particularly interesting because we believe that participants did not think that the robot was tele-operated but they judged its capabilities of handling tasks autonomously [4]. Indeed, while participants were fully immersed in the scenarios, including the fire emergency, they seemed to not expect help from the robot. They principally perceived the robot as an assistant and they believed the robot had limited abilities.

Moreover, this study showed that participants were affected more by robot errors made at the beginning of the interaction than at the end of the interaction. On one hand, this result confirmed our previous findings [21] and it is also supported by other studies where people's impressions of an agent are formed during the first encounters with the robot [25]. On another hand, a further investigation on the reasons causing the lack of people's trust in the robot was also due to the context, and in particular, the criticality of the emergency task. These findings corroborated the evidence that the reliability in robots' capabilities was affected by the risk of a possible negative outcome [13,16].

Not every participant acknowledged that the robot made errors. However, they all judged the tasks in the interaction as errors with severe consequences. We believe that participants stated that the robot did not do any errors because they were asked directly by the robot. Accordingly, some studies in psychology and human-computer interaction showed that people could feel inhibited to communicate their disapproval to the bystander culprit (i.e., the robot) [3,28].

Our results are limited by a small sample size and thus need to be consolidated by conducting larger scale trials involving a more general population. However, our findings suggest that some participants do not trust an interactive robot to be capable of handling emergency scenarios or high risk tasks.

Acknowledgment. This project has received funding from the European Union's Horizon 2020 research and innovation programme under the Marie Sklodowska-Curie grant agreement No 642667 (Safety Enables Cooperation in Uncertain Robotic Environments - SECURE). KD acknowledges funding from the Canada 150 Research Chairs Program.

References

1. Ambady, N., Bernieri, F.J., Richeson, J.A.: Toward a histology of social behavior: judgmental accuracy from thin slices of the behavioral stream. Adv. Exp. Soc. Psychol. **32**, 201–271 (2000). https://doi.org/10.1016/S0065-2601(00)80006-4

2. Booth, S., Tompkin, J., Pfister, H., Waldo, J., Gajos, K., Nagpal, R.: Piggy-backing robots: human-robot overtrust in university dormitory security. In: 12th ACM/IEEE International Conference on Human-Robot Interaction, pp. 426–434. ACM (2017)

3. Chekroun, P., Brauer, M.: The bystander effect and social control behavior: the effect of the presence of others on people's reactions to norm violations. Eur. J. Soc. Psychol. **32**(6), 853–867 (2002). https://doi.org/10.1002/ejsp.126

4. Choi, J.J., Kim, Y., Kwak, S.S.: The autonomy levels and the human intervention levels of robots: the impact of robot types in human-robot interaction. In: The 23rd IEEE International Symposium on Robot and Human Interactive Communication, pp. 1069–1074 (2014). https://doi.org/10.1109/ROMAN.2014.6926394

5. Dautenhahn, K.: Roles and functions of robots in human society: implications from research in autism therapy. Robotica **21**(4), 443–452 (2003). https://doi.org/10.1017/S0263574703004922

6. Gosling, S.D., Rentfrow, P.J., Swann Jr., W.B.: A very brief measure of the big five personality domains. J. Res. Pers. **37**, 504–528 (2003)

7. de Graaf, M., Ben Allouch, S., van Dijk, J.: Why do they refuse to use my robot? Reasons for non-use derived from a long-term home study. In: Proceedings of the 2017 ACM/IEEE International Conference on Human-Robot Interaction, HRI 2017, pp. 224–233. Association for Computing Machinery, New York (2017). https://doi.org/10.1145/2909824.3020236

8. de Graaf, M.M., Ben Allouch, S., van Dijk, J.A.: Long-term evaluation of a social robot in real homes. Interact. Stud. **17**(3), 461–490 (2016)

9. Haselhuhn, M.P., Schweitzer, M.E., Wood, A.M.: How implicit beliefs influence trust recovery. Psychol. Sci. **5**, 645–648 (2010)

10. Ht, R., Mr, M., Pa, C., Pw, E., Ej, F.: Familiarity does indeed promote attraction in live interaction. J. Person. Soc. Psychol. **101**(3), 557–570 (2011). https://doi.org/10.1037/a0022885

11. Kanda, T., Sato, R., Saiwaki, N., Ishiguro, H.: A two-month field trial in an elementary school for long-term human-robot interaction. IEEE Trans. Robot. **23**(5), 962–971 (2007)

12. Lee, A.Y.: The mere exposure effect: an uncertainty reduction explanation revisited. Person. Soc. Psychol. Bull. **27**(10), 1255–1266 (2001). https://doi.org/10.1177/01461672012710002

13. Lee, J., Moray, N.: Trust, control strategies and allocation of function in human-machine systems. Ergonomics **35**(10), 1243–1270 (1992). https://doi.org/10.1080/00140139208967392

14. Ljungblad, S., Kotrbova, J., Jacobsson, M., Cramer, H., Niechwiadowicz, K.: Hospital robot at work: something alien or an intelligent colleague? In: Proceedings of the ACM 2012 Conference on Computer Supported Cooperative Work, CSCW 2012, pp. 177–186. ACM, New York (2012). https://doi.org/10.1145/2145204.2145233

15. Madsen, M., Gregor, S.: Measuring human-computer trust. In: Proceedings of the 11th Australasian Conference on Information Systems, pp. 6–8 (2000)

16. Mayer, R.C., Davis, J.H., Schoorman, F.D.: An integrative model of organizational trust. Acad. Manag. Rev. **20**, 709–734 (1995)

17. McKnight, D.H., Choudhury, V., Kacmar, C.: Developing and validating trust measures for e-commerce: an integrative typology. Inf. Syst. Res. **13**(3), 334–359 (2001)
18. Nomura, T., Suzuki, T., Kanda, T., Kato, K.: Measurement of negative attitudes toward robots. Interact. Stud. **7**(3), 437–454 (2006). https://doi.org/10.1075/is.7.3.14nom
19. Paetzel, M., Perugia, G., Castellano, G.: The persistence of first impressions: the effect of repeated interactions on the perception of a social robot. In: Proceedings of the 2020 ACM/IEEE International Conference on Human-Robot Interaction, HRI 2020, pp. 73–82. Association for Computing Machinery, New York (2020). https://doi.org/10.1145/3319502.3374786
20. Rossi, A., Dautenhahn, K., Koay, K.L., Walters, M.L.: How the timing and magnitude of robot errors influence peoples' trust of robots in an emergency scenario. In: Kheddar, A., et al. (eds.) Social Robotics – ICSR 2017. LNCS, vol. 10652, pp. 42–52. Springer, Cham (2017). https://doi.org/10.1007/978-3-319-70022-9_5
21. Rossi, A., Dautenhahn, K., Koay, K.L., Walters, M.L.: The impact of peoples' personal dispositions and personalities on their trust of robots in an emergency scenario. Paladyn J. Behav. Robot. **9**(2018). https://doi.org/10.1515/pjbr-2018-0010
22. Rossi, S., Rossi, A., Dautenhahn, K.: The secret life of robots: perspectivesand challenges for robot's behaviours during non-interactive tasks. Int. J. Soc. Robot. (2020).https://doi.org/10.1007/s12369-020-00650-z
23. Schilke, O., Reimann, M., Cook, K.S.: Effect of relationship experience on trust recovery following a breach. Proc. Natl. Acad. Sci. **110**(38), 15236–15241 (2013). https://doi.org/10.1073/pnas.1314857110
24. Syrdal, D.S., Dautenhahn, K., Koay, K.L., Walters, M.L.: The negative attitudes towards robots scale and reactions to robot behaviour in a live human-robot interaction study. In: AISB 2009 SSAISB, Adaptive and Emergent Behaviour and Complex Systems: Proceedings of the 23rd Convention of the Society for the Study of Artificial Intelligence and Simulation of Behaviour, pp. 109–115 (2009)
25. TJ, W.: Exploring the role of first impressions in rater-based assessments. Adv. Health Sci. Educ. Theor. Pract. **19**(3), 409–427 (2014). https://doi.org/10.1007/s10459-013-9453-9
26. Visser, E.D., Parasuraman, R., Freedy, A., Freedy, E., Weltman, G.: A comprehensive methodology for assessing human-robot team performance for use in training and simulation. In: Proceedings of the Human Factors and Ergonomics Society Annual Meeting **50**(25), 2639–2643 (2006). https://doi.org/10.1177/154193120605002507
27. de Visser, E.J.: Towards a theory of longitudinal trust calibration in human–robot teams. Int. J. Soc. Robot. **12**(2), 459–478 (2019). https://doi.org/10.1007/s12369-019-00596-x
28. Voelpel, S.C., Eckhoff, R.A., Förster, J.: David against goliath? Group size and bystander effects in virtual knowledge sharing. Hum. Relat. **61**(2), 271–295 (2008). https://doi.org/10.1177/0018726707087787

The Effect of Individual Differences and Repetitive Interactions on Explicit and Implicit Attitudes Towards Robots

Francesca Ciardo[1]([✉]) [iD], Davide Ghiglino[1,2] [iD], Cecilia Roselli[1,2] [iD],
and Agnieszka Wykowska[1] [iD]

[1] Italian Institute of Technology, 16152 Genova, Italy
Francesca.Ciardo@iit.it

[2] DIBRIS, Dipartimento di Informatica, Bioingegneria, Robotica ed Ingegneria dei Sistemi,
Genova 16145, Italy

Abstract. The exploitation of Social Assistive Robotics (SAR) will bring to the emergence of a new category of users, namely experts in clinical rehabilitation, who do not have a background in robotics. The first aim of the present study was to address individuals' attitudes towards robots within this new category of users. The secondary aim was to investigate whether repetitive interactions with the robot affect such attitudes. Therefore, we evaluated both explicit and implicit attitudes towards robots in a group of therapists rehabilitating children with neurodevelopmental disorders. The evaluation took place before they started a SAR intervention (T0), ongoing (T1), and at the end of it (T2). Explicit attitudes were evaluated using self-report questionnaires, whereas implicit attitudes were operationalized as the perception of the robot as a social partner and implicit associations regarding the concept of "robot". Results showed that older ages and previous experience with robots were associated with negative attitudes toward robots and lesser willingness to perceive the robot as a social agent. Explicit measures did not vary across time, whereas implicit measures were modulated by increased exposure to robots: the more clinicians were exposed to the robot, the more the robot was treated as a social partner. Moreover, users' memory association between the concept of a robot and mechanical attributes weakens across evaluations. Our results suggest that increased exposure to robots modulates implicit but not explicit attitudes.

Keywords: Human-robot interaction · Repetitive interactions · Individual differences

1 Introduction

In the near future, the application of robots in clinical protocols will be one of the most relevant challenges for the Socially Assistive Robotics (SAR), resulting in the emergence of a new category of users. This new category will comprise clinicians and experts in different fields of rehabilitation (from motor training to socio-cognitive therapies),

© Springer Nature Switzerland AG 2020
A. R. Wagner et al. (Eds.): ICSR 2020, LNAI 12483, pp. 466–477, 2020.
https://doi.org/10.1007/978-3-030-62056-1_39

without any background in robotics. A crucial aspect that has been scarcely examined is individual differences in robot perception in those users, which play a critical role in choosing and implementing any SAR protocol. Indeed, most SAR studies focused on (i) the reliability of the platform and/or (ii) on the success of the training. However, the success of any clinical protocol relies not only on the quality of the training itself but also on the therapeutic alliance and the commitment of the therapist [1]. In this context, it is crucial to investigate attitudes towards robots in this category of users. Importantly, one should address individual differences, and not only the group of users as a whole. Indeed, individual differences affect the perception and acceptance of robots in human-robot teams [2–5]. Recently, Hinz et al. [6] showed that when playing a game with the Cozmo robot (Anki Robotics, San Francisco, CA, USA; https://www.digita ldreamlabs.com), the more people felt discomfort towards the robot, the less they were susceptible to the social facilitation effect induced by its presence [6]. The second critical aspect that literature overlooked is the understanding of the strength of these attitudes. Indeed, a priori negative attitude towards robots might be the consequence of a lack of familiarity with the robots, as they are often considered as "mysterious" systems. A recent study [7] showed that negative attitudes towards robots were reduced in a group of students after taking part in robot programming classes. Specifically, students reported that the programming course allowed them to better understand how robots work. Thus, increasing familiarity with robots may reduce negative attitudes towards them among SAR users.

1.1 Aim

The aim of the present work was twofold. The first aim (i) was to evaluate individual differences in attitudes towards robots in a group of clinicians, who conducted a robot-assisted intervention for the first time in their professional practice. The second aim (ii) was to investigate whether repetitive interactions with the robot during the SAR intervention affected explicit and implicit attitudes towards robots.

Concerning the first aim (i), we tested explicit and implicit attitudes towards robots in a group of specialists involved in a robot-assisted intervention protocol, aimed to train joint attention in children with autism spectrum disorders. The therapists interacted with the robot during a 5-week long training protocol. Their task was to control the Cozmo robot by means of Wizard-of-Oz technique while children were playing a "game" designed to engage the children in joint attention with Cozmo [see 8 for details about the training].

Explicit attitudes were evaluated using self-report questionnaires [2, 9, 10, and 11]. Implicit attitudes were evaluated with the Implicit Association Test (IAT) [12; see 13 for a review] and the perception of the robot as a social partner. Since the perception of the robot as a social partner was our first implicit measure, we developed a ball-tossing game in which participants believed they were playing with Cozmo and another human agent. During the game, participants had to throw the ball to the other players, whose behavior was controlled by the program. We used this task as an implicit measure of group membership, and we analyzed how often participants threw the ball to the other players. We hypothesized that individual differences would predict the willingness to perceive the Cozmo robot as a social partner. Thus, participants with a more negative attitude towards robots should be less willing to interact with the Cozmo robot instead of the human player.

The IAT is a well-known test used in social psychology to evaluate implicit attitudes towards a social category. It allows for the assessment of the strength of associations between concepts (e.g., flower and insects) and attributes (positive and negative) in memory. In our study, we were interested in addressing whether the concept of a robot could be implicitly associated with Intentional or Design stances [14, 15, and 16]. To this end, we developed a version of the IAT to measure the association between human and robot concepts with mentalistic and mechanical verbs (e.g. "to desire" or "to process") [e.g., 16]. Based on previous studies showing that humans tend to explain robot behavior mostly with reference to the Design Stance [16], we hypothesized to find an IAT bias indicating that the concept "robot" is strongly associated in memory with mechanistic attributes instead of mentalistic ones. Moreover, we expected that individual differences in attitudes and expertise with robots should correlate with the magnitude of the IAT bias.

With respect to the second aim of our study (ii), we repeated the evaluation of clinician's attitudes at three different moments in time. The a priori evaluation was made before the starting of the training (Time 0: T0); after that, all the clinicians took part in the familiarization session during which the intervention protocol, the Cozmo robot, and the user interface were presented [see 8 for a description of the SAR protocol]. The second (Time 1: T1) and the third (Time 2: T2) evaluation occurred when in the middle and at the end of the SAR training, respectively.

According to the contact hypothesis [17, 18], we expected that repeated interactions with the robot should affect individuals' explicit and implicit attitudes. Specifically, in line with Bartneck et al.'s results [19], we expected that increased exposure to robots should result in less negative attitudes towards them.

Regarding the perception of the robot as a social agent, we hypothesized a reduction of the intergroup bias across time, meaning that the Cozmo robot would be perceived as a potential social agent similar to the human player by the end of the SAR intervention.

Moreover, we speculated that the IAT effect would reduce as a function of time, given the increase of familiarity with the robot accumulated during the SAR protocol.

2 Materials and Methods

2.1 Sample

Nineteen clinicians (mean age: 35.74 ± 7.51, 1 male) working in the Provincia Religiosa San Benedetto di Don Orione took part in the T0 session of the study. Due to difficulties in matching clinicians' agenda and testing sessions, questionnaires were administered to only 12 participants at both testing sessions (T0 and T2), whereas only 12 and 11 participants performed the IAT and the ball-tossing game at all testing sessions (T0, T1, and T2), respectively. Participants were all expert clinicians working with neurodevelopmental disorders, and our sample included four professional profiles: logopedist, psychomotricist, educator, and psychologist. The study was conducted under the ethical standards laid down in the 2013 Declaration of Helsinki and approved by the local ethical committee (Comitato Etico Regione Liguria). All participants gave written informed consent before the experiment.

2.2 Procedure

Explicit attitudes towards robots were assessed before the starting of the SAR protocol (T0), during the training (T1), and at the end of it, i.e. after 1012 months (T2). To this end, participants filled out the following questionnaires:

- RobEx questionnaire [9], a self-report questionnaire that investigates familiarity, experience, and expectations towards robots and robotics (administered only at time T0);
- The Frankenstein Syndrome Questionnaire (FSQ [10]), consists of thirty items, for which participants rated their accordance on a 7-point Likert scale categorized in four subscales: "General Anxiety towards Humanoid Robots", "Apprehension toward Social Risks of Humanoid Robots", "Trustworthiness for Developers of Humanoid Robots", and "Expectations for Humanoid Robots in Daily Life";
- The Negative Attitudes towards Robots Scale (NARS [2]) measuring the participants' attitudes towards different aspects of robots. It consists of three subscales: "Negative Attitudes towards Situations and Interactions with Robots", "Negative Attitudes towards Social Influence of Robots" and "Negative Attitudes towards Emotions in Interaction with Robots". The questionnaire consists of fourteen items, for which participants rated their agreement on a 5-point Likert-scale;
- The Robotic Social Attitude Scale (RoSAS [11]) measuring the social perception of robots in general on the scales "Warmth", "Competence" and "Discomfort". It consists of eighteen adjectives. For each, participants rate on a 9-point Likert scale how much they associate it to robots in general.

Self-report questionnaires presentation, response times, and data collection were controlled by OpenSesame software.

The willingness to perceive the robot as a social agent was addressed by a ball-tossing game inspired by the Cyberball paradigm [20]. Stimuli were pictures of human partners and a picture of the Cozmo robot. The act of throwing the ball was simulated by presenting a 1 s video of a schematic ball moving. Participants were instructed to pass the ball to whoever they wanted. Each trial started with the presentation of pictures of the human player and Cozmo, respectively on the left and right side of the screen, while the name of the participant was presented at the bottom. The ball was always presented next to the player who received it in the previous trial. Upon receiving the ball, participants were instructed to wait until a go-signal (i.e. their name turning from black into red) before passing the ball. Following the go-signal participant had 500 ms to press either the "Z" or "M" key on a standard Italian keyboard, to pass the ball to the player on their left ("Z" button) or the player on their right ("M" button). Time-out was highlighted with a 500 ms feedback display. The task was programmed to comprise 240 trials plus trials to replace timeouts. A short pause was given to participants after 120 trials. The task was administered at three different stages of the SAR intervention: before the starting of the training (T0), ongoing (about 46 months later, T1), and at the end of it (i.e. after 1012 months, T2).

Implicit attitudes towards robots were assessed using the Implicit Association Test (IAT) [12, 13], which allows for the evaluation of implicit attitudes. Stimuli consisted of 20 pictures of silhouettes depicting humans (females and males) and humanoid robots [see 21]. As linguistic stimuli, we used 20 verbs taken from the InStance questionnaire items [16] referring to mechanical processes or mental states (e.g. "to process" or "to desire", respectively). Participants underwent a short version of the IAT comprising 5 blocks (Fig. 1). In Block 1, participants had to categorize human vs. humanoids silhouettes. In Block 2, they were required to categorize Mentalistic vs. Mechanistic words (e.g. "to desire" vs. "to process"). In Block 3, both silhouettes and words were presented, and participants were asked to categorize both. The association between the silhouettes and the words was congruent, meaning that the same response key was used to categorize congruent stimuli (e.g. left key: Human silhouettes and Mentalistic words; right key: Humanoid silhouettes and Mechanistic words). In Block 4, the task was the same as in Block 1 but the association between the target and the response key was reversed (see Fig. 1). Finally, in Block 5 both silhouettes and words were presented as in Block 3 but the association between the silhouettes and the words was incongruent (i.e. left key: Humanoid silhouettes and Mentalistic words; right key: Human silhouettes and Mechanistic words). Each trial started with the presentation of the stimulus (a silhouette or a word) in the center of the screen with the respective response-category presented in the left and right upper corners. Participants provided their responses via keypress, using the "Q" and "P" keys on a standard Italian keyboard. The time allowed to respond was infinite, however, participants were instructed to respond as fast and accurately as possible. Incorrect responses were followed by 500 ms feedback. The inter-trial interval was 400 ms. Block 1, 2, and 4 comprised 40 trials each, whereas Block 3 and 5 consisted of 80 trials each. Block order was fixed but the presentation of stimuli was randomized within each block. The IAT was administered at three different time points of the SAR intervention: before the starting of the training (T0), training ongoing (about 46 months later, T1), and at the end of it, i.e. after 1012 months (T2). In the IAT and ball-tossing game stimuli presentation, response timing, and data collection were controlled by the E-Prime version 3 software (Psychology Software Tools, Inc.).

3   Results

3.1   Individual Differences in Attitudes Towards Robots

To assess whether previous experience with artificial agents or individual differences correlates with explicit attitudes towards robots, we calculated Pearson's correlations between the scores of the self-report measures. Results showed that age positively correlated with the "Discomfort" sub-scale of the ROSAS [$r_{17} = .50$, p = .030], the "Perceived anxiety towards robots" subscale of the FSQ [$r_{17} = .50$, p = .030], and the attitude towards robots during social interaction assessed with the NARS [$r_{17} = .49$, p = .034]. We also found a positive correlation between the participant's experience with robotics, assessed with the RobEx questionnaire, and the attitude towards the social influences of robots assessed with the NARS [$r_{17} = .49$, p = .032]. Furthermore, we found a negative

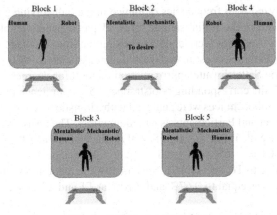

Fig. 1. IAT blocks procedures.

correlation between the participants' experience with robotics and their perception of the robot's warmth assessed with the RoSAS [$r_{17} = -.48$, p = .039].

3.2 The Effect of Repetitive Interactions on Explicit Measures of Attitudes Towards Robots

To evaluate if, after repetitive interactions with a robot, clinicians' attitudes changed, we compared average scores for each subscale of FSQ, NARS, and RoSAS questionnaires as a function of time. The analysis was run on a sub-sample (N = 12) of those participants who took part in T0 and T2 testing sessions. Wilcoxon tests on average scores showed that no differences occurred across the two sessions in explicit measures (all ps > .12).

3.3 Perception of the Robot as a Social Partner

Regarding the perception of the robot as a social partner, we firstly estimated the frequency of robot and human choices. At T0, when a sample of N = 19 was considered, participants chose to toss the ball to the robot 50.07% of the time. We estimated Pearson's correlations between the scores of the self-report measures, age, education, and the percentages of robot choices at T0. We found a negative correlation between age and frequency of robot choice [$r_{17} = -.58$, p = .009]. Results showed that the probability of choosing the robot negatively correlated with all the NARS subscales [Situation of Interaction: $r_{17} = -.77$, p < .001; Social Influence: $r_{17} = -.53$, p = .021; Emotions in Interaction: $r_{17} = -.67$, p = .002]. We also found a negative correlation between the probability to interact with the robot and the general anxiety [$r_{17} = -.79$, p < .001], the level of apprehension [$r_{17} = -.58$, p = .010], and negative expectations towards humanoid robots [$r_{17} = -.58$, p = .010], assessed with the FSQ questionnaire. Finally, we found a positive correlation between participants' perception of the robot as Warmth and Competent assessed with the RoSAS and the probability to toss the ball to it. [$r_{17} = .49$, p = .035, $r_{17} = .82$, p < .001, respectively].

Then, we analyzed both frequencies of choice in the ball-tossing game across time (T0, T1, and T2). From the initial sample, only 11 participants completed the task at all testing sessions. Analyses were conducted using the lme4 package in R v.3.0.6. (R Core Team, 2014). Parameters estimated (β) and their associated t-tests (t, p-value) were calculated using the Satterthwaite approximation method for degrees of freedom; they were reported with the corresponding bootstrapped 95% confidence intervals.

Frequencies of robot choices were analyzed with a logistic mixed model with Session Time as a fixed effect and Participants as a random effect. The analysis revealed that the probability to choose the robot was significantly reduced both at T1 [$\beta = -.41$, $z_{12.22} = -3.19$, p = 0.001, CI = (-.65; -.16)] and T2 [$\beta = -.36$, $z_{12.22} = -2.29$, p = .004, CI = (-.60; -.12)], relative to T0, see Table 1. Specifically, the reduction in the probability of choosing the robot was equal to 0.67% and 0.70% at T1 and T2, respectively.

Table 1. The average percentage of robot choices in the ball-tossing game as a function of the session of testing (N = 11).

Session time	%Robot choices
T0	58.5%
T1	48.6%
T2	51.8%

3.4 Implicit Association Task (IAT)

We estimated the IAT effect following Greenwald et al.'s procedure [13], thus we analyzed blocks in which the target and the attribute were congruent or not (i.e. Blocks 3 and 5, see Fig. 1). Trials with RTs longer than 10 s or shorter than 300 ms were considered as outliers and removed (<.01%). Then, for each participant, RTs of incorrect trials were replaced with the mean RT for each block plus a 600 ms penalty. To evaluate whether individual differences in explicit attitudes towards robots correlated with implicit measures, we estimated Pearson's correlations between the scores of self-report measures and the IAT bias estimated as the difference in RTs between incongruent and congruent blocks at T0. Results showed no significant correlations (all ps > .13).

To evaluate whether repetitive interactions modulated clinicians' implicit attitudes, we compared the performance at the IAT task across time. Only 12 participants took part in all the sessions, thus the analysis of IAT was run on a sub-sample (N = 12). Mean RTs were submitted to a repeated-measures analysis of variance (ANOVA) with Session Time (T0, T1, and T2) and Congruency (C vs. NC) as within-subjects factors. Results showed a main effect of Congruency [$F_{11} = 111.41$, p < .001, $\eta_p^2 = .91$] indicating that participants responded faster to congruent than incongruent blocks (727 vs. 1056 ms, respectively). The two-way Session Time * Congruency interaction was significant as well [$F_{11} = 7.29$, p = .004, $\eta_p^2 = .40$]. Bonferroni–corrected comparisons showed that RTs were faster for congruent than incongruent blocks in all sessions (T0: 735 vs.

1143 ms, $t_{11} = 8.28$, p < .001, d = 2.39; T1: 704 vs. 1046 ms, $t_{11} = 9.01$, p < .001, d = 2.60; T0: 740 vs. 980 ms, $t_{11} = 7.37$, p < .001, d = 2.13). However, the IAT bias (i.e. the difference in mean RTs between incongruent and congruent blocks) was significantly reduced at T2 (239 ms) compared to both T0 (408 ms, $t_{11} = 3.36$, p = .012, d = .97) and T1 (342 ms, $t_{11} = 2.98$, p = .026, d = .86), see Fig. 2.

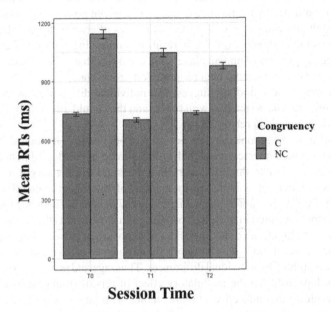

Fig. 2. Mean RTs (ms) for the IAT task plotted as a function of Session Time and Congruency.

4 Discussion

The aim of the present study was twofold. The first aim (i) was to assess individuals' attitudes towards robots in a category of users crucial for SAR, namely experts in clinical rehabilitation. The second aim (ii) was to investigate whether repetitive interactions with the robot during the SAR intervention would affect attitudes towards robots.

In accordance to the first aim (i), we evaluated both explicit and implicit attitudes towards robots in a group of therapists rehabilitating children with neurodevelopmental disorders, before they started a SAR intervention. Explicit attitudes were evaluated using self-report questionnaires, whereas implicit attitudes were operationalized as the perception of the robot as a social partner (adapted and modified Cyberball paradigm [20]) and implicit associations regarding the concept of "robot" (IAT [13]). Results showed that individual differences, and particularly age, play a role in the attitude displayed towards robots. Indeed, the positive correlation between age and subscales of the three questionnaires suggested that older clinicians displayed a more negative attitude. Moreover, the level of familiarity with robots may have played a role, as suggested by the fact that the more participants were experienced with robots, the less they perceived the Cozmo robot as "Warm" and the more they were negative toward social interaction with robots.

Individual differences correlated also with the perception of the robot as a social partner. Indeed, results showed that age negatively correlated with the frequency of robot choices. Moreover, results showed that the less negative clinicians were towards robots, the more they chose to interact with Cozmo instead of the human player. Such a result is also confirmed by the positive correlation between positive attitudes attribution, such as warmth and competence, and the frequencies of choices to pass the ball to the robot. Future studies should exploit this result by addressing the role of embodiment. Indeed, replacing pictures of human players and Cozmo with another human and a robots physically present could elicit a larger ingroup/outgroup bias.

Taken together, these findings suggest that individual differences are crucial in the willingness of clinicians to interact with robots and they could affect their disposition to embrace SAR protocols in rehabilitation.

With respect to the second aim (ii), according to the contact hypothesis [22–24] we expected that repeated interactions with the robot should have affected both explicit and implicit measures. Results showed that explicit measures did not vary across time (and experience with Cozmo), as indicated by the lack of significant main effect of testing sessions (T0, T1, T2). It is not in line with previous evidence [19] showing that increased exposure to robots resulted in increased positive attitudes towards them. However, Wullenkord et al. [25] highlighted that the effect of exposure occurred when there were no preexisting negative attitudes. In our sample, the attitudes towards robots were not homogeneous as highlighted by individual differences. Thus, age and previous experience with robots might have affected the modulatory effect of repetitive interactions on explicit measures, resulting in a null effect. Future studies with larger samples should include age and experience as moderators, to investigate whether repetitive interactions with robots during a SAR intervention can reduce self-reported attitudes among clinicians.

Interestingly, implicit measures were modulated by increased exposure to robots.

The perception of the robot as a social partner was operationalized as the preference to throw a ball to the Cozmo robot or to a human player. Results showed that, across time, the difference in the probability of choosing the Cozmo robot as the receiver of the ball reduced. It suggests that, over time, the perceived difference between Cozmo and the other human player decreased; thus, the more clinicians were exposed to the robot the more they tended to treat the two players equally, (see Table 1), indicating that the robot was considered a social partner similarly to the other human player.

Our last implicit measure was the IAT bias. Results showed that the IAT bias was reduced at the end of the SAR intervention compared to the pre-training evaluation. In line with Marchesi et al. [16], we found an IAT bias towards robots at T0, suggesting that before the SAR intervention, clinicians associated the concept of "robot" with mechanical attributes. As familiarity with the robot increased, the IAT bias reduced. This reduction indicates that, across time, the association between the concept of "robot" and mechanical attributes weakened, thereby extending previous studies showing that inter-group bias towards robots can be reduced through repetitive interactions [19, 25]. However, it is important to note that the reduced difference in reaction times between incongruent and congruent trials might also manifest a learning effect across the sessions.

Taken together, our results suggest that individual differences towards robots in a group of SAR users play a crucial role in both explicit and implicit attitudes. Interestingly, the increased exposure to robots modulated implicit but not explicit measures; this dissociation is in line with a series of studies by Kompatsiari et al. showing that implicit measures, such as reaction times and eye-fixations, are more sensitive to detect the effect of social cognition manipulation [26, 27, see also 28] in human-robot interaction. Explicit measures are dependent on introspective abilities and can be prone to various biases, such as cognitive consistency (i.e. the tendency of people to prefer thoughts, beliefs, knowledge, opinions, attitudes, and intents that are congruent with how they see themselves) [29]. Moreover, they are not sufficiently informative about specific cognitive mechanisms involved in social categorization, such as the strength of associations between concepts and attributes, which are not necessarily accessible to conscious awareness. The main limitations of our results are the small sample size, the unbalanced sex of participants, and the high percentages of drop-outs. However, it should be kept in mind that when testing clinicians who are involved in a SAR protocol for the first time, recruiting participants is constrained by several factors, such as the amount of clinicians involved by the institute in the training, the clinicians' time constraints related to other training schedule or the children to which the training is dedicated.

5 Conclusions

Our results suggest that clinicians working with neurodevelopmental disorders were negatively biased towards robots before being exposed to our protocol. However, implicit biases progressively decreased with prolonged exposure to robots. Understanding individual dispositions is crucial for the success of SAR interventions aiming to promote the use of innovative technologies such as robotic agents.

Funding. This study has received support from the European Research Council under the European Union's Horizon 2020 research and innovation program, ERC Starting grant ERC-2016-StG-715058, awarded to AW. The content of this paper is the sole responsibility of the authors. The European Commission or its services cannot be held responsible for any use that may be made of the information it contains.

References

1. Young, G.O.: Synthetic structure of industrial plastics. In: Peters, J. (ed.) Plastics, vol. 3, 2nd edn, pp. 15–64. McGraw-Hill, New York (1964)
2. Syrdal, D.S., Dautenhahn, K., Kony, K.L., Walters, M.L.: The Negative Attitudes Towards Robots Scale and Reactions to Robot Behaviour in a Live Human-Robot Interaction Study. Adaptive and Emergent Behaviour and Complex Systems (2009)
3. Waytz, A., Cacioppo, J., Epley, N.: Who sees human? The stability and importance of individual differences in anthropomorphism. Perspect. Psychol. Sci. **5**, 219–232 (2010)
4. MacDorman, K.F., Entezari, S.O.: Individual differences predict sensitivity to the uncanny valley. IS **16**, 141–172 (2015)

5. de Visser, E., Parasuraman, R., Freedy, A., Freedy, E., Weltman, G.: A comprehensive methodology for assessing human-robot team performance for use in training and simulation. In: Proceedings of the Human Factors and Ergonomics Society Annual Meeting, vol. 50, pp. 2639–2643 (2016)
6. Hinz, N.-A., Ciardo, F., Wykowska, A.: Individual Differences in Attitude Toward Robots Predict Behavior in Human-Robot Interaction. In: Salichs, Miguel A., Ge, S.S., Barakova, E.I., Cabibihan, J.-J., Wagner, Alan R., Castro-González, Á., He, H. (eds.) ICSR 2019. LNCS (LNAI), vol. 11876, pp. 64–73. Springer, Cham (2019). https://doi.org/10.1007/978-3-030-35888-4_7
7. Kim, S.W., Lee, Y.: The effect of robot programming education on attitudes towards robots. Indian Journal of Science and Technology 9(24), 1–11 (2016)
8. Ghiglino, D., Chevalier, P., Floris, F., Priolo, T., & Wykowska, A. (2020, April 6). Follow the white robot: efficacy of robot-assistive training for children with autism-spectrum condition. https://doi.org/10.31234/osf.io/7pktm
9. Perez-Osorio, J., Marchesi, S., Ghiglino, D., Ince, M., Wykowska, A.: More than you expect: priors influence on the adoption of intentional stance toward humanoid robots. In: Salichs, M.A., Ge, S.S., Barakova, E.I., Cabibihan, J.-J., Wagner, A.R., Castro-González, Á., He, H. (eds.) ICSR 2019. LNCS (LNAI), vol. 11876, pp. 119–129. Springer, Cham (2019). https://doi.org/10.1007/978-3-030-35888-4_12
10. Syrdal, D.S., Nomura, T., Dautenhahn, K.: The Frankenstein Syndrome Questionnaire–Results from a quantitative cross-cultural survey. In: Proceedings of the International Conference on Social Robotics, pp. 270–279 (2013)
11. Carpinella, C.M., Wyman, A.B., Perez, M.A., Stroessner, S.J.: The Robotic Social Attributes Scale (RoSAS). In: Proceedings of the ACM/IEEE International Conference on Human-Robot Interaction, pp. 254–262 (2017)
12. Greenwald, A.G., McGhee, D.E., Schwartz, J.L.K.: Measuring individual differences in implicit cognition: the implicit association test. J. Pers. Soc. Psychol. 74, 1464–1480 (1998)
13. Greenwald, A.G., Nosek, B.A., Banaji, M.R.: Understanding and using the implicit association test: I. An improved scoring algorithm. J. Pers. Soc. Psychol. 85(2), 197 (2003)
14. Dennett, D.C.: The Intentional Stance. MIT Press, Cambridge (1987)
15. Schellen, E., Wykowska, A.: Intentional mindset toward robots—open questions and methodological challenges. Front. Rob. AI 5, 71 (2019)
16. Marchesi, S., Ghiglino, D., Ciardo, F., Baykara, E., Wykowska, A.: Do we adopt the Intentional Stance towards humanoid robots? Front. Psychol. 10, 450 (2019)
17. Lee, S., Lau, I., Kiesler, S., Chiu, C.: Human mental models of humanoid robots. In: Proceedings of the 2005 IEEE International Conference on Robotics and Automation, ICRA, pp. 2767–2772. IEEE, Barcelona (2005)
18. Zajonc, R.B.: Attitudinal effects of mere exposure. J. Pers. Soc. Psychol. 90, 751–783 (1968). Monograph Suppl. 9, 1-27
19. Bartneck, C., Suzuki, T., Kanda, T., Nomura, T.: The influence of people's culture and prior experiences with Aibo on their attitude toward robots. AI Soc. 21, 217–230 (2006)
20. Williams, K.D., Jarvis, B.: Cyberball: a program for use in research on interpersonal ostracism and acceptance. Behav. Res. Methods 38(1), 174–180 (2006)
21. MacDorman, K.F., Vasudevan, S.K., Ho, C.C.: Does Japan really have robot mania? Comparing attitudes by implicit and explicit measures. AI Soc. 23(4), 485–510 (2009)
22. Allport, G.W.: The Nature of Prejudice. Addison-Wesley, Reading (1954)
23. Deligianis, C., Stanton, C.J., McGarty, C., Stevens, C.J.: The impact of intergroup bias on trust and approach behaviour towards a humanoid robot. J. Hum.-Rob. Interact. 6(3), 4–20 (2017)

24. Brewer, M.B., Miller, N.: Contact and cooperation: when do they work? In: Katz, P., Taylor, D. (eds.) Eliminating Racism: Profiles in Controversy, pp. 315–326. Plenum Press, New York (1988)
25. Wullenkord, R., Fraune, M.R., Eyssel, F., Šabanović, S.: Getting in touch: how imagined, actual, and physical contact affects evaluation of robots. In: Proceedings of the 2016 25th IEEE International Symposium on Robot and Human Interactive Communication (RO-MAN) (2016)
26. Kompatsiari, K., Ciardo, F., Tikhanoff, V., Metta, G., Wykowska, A.: It's in the eyes: the engaging role of eye contact in HRI. Int. J. Soc. Robot. 1–11 (2019)
27. Kompatsiari, K., Ciardo, F., De Tommaso, D., Wykowska, A.: Measuring engagement elicited by eye contact in Human-Robot Interaction. In: 2019 IEEE/RSJ International Conference on Intelligent Robots and Systems (IROS), pp. 6979–6985. IEEE (2019b)
28. Ghiglino, D., Willemse, C., De Tommaso, D., Bossi, F., Wykowska, A.: At first sight: robots' subtle eye movement parameters affect human attentional engagement, spontaneous attunement and perceived human-likeness. Paladyn, J. Behav. Robot. 11(1), 31–39 (2020)
29. Abelson, R.P., Aronson, E.E., McGuire, W.., Newcomb, T.M., Rosenberg, M.J., Tannenbaum, P.H.: Theories of Cognitive Consistency: A Sourcebook (1968)

Advances in Human-Robot Handshaking

Vignesh Prasad[1(✉)] ⓘ, Ruth Stock-Homburg[1] ⓘ, and Jan Peters[1,2] ⓘ

[1] Technical University of Darmstadt, Darmstadt, Germany
{vignesh.prasad,ruth.stock-homburg,jan.peters}@tu-darmstadt.de
[2] Max Planck Institute for Intelligent Systems, Tübingen, Germany

Abstract. The use of social, anthropomorphic robots to support humans in various industries has been on the rise. During Human-Robot Interaction (HRI), physically interactive non-verbal behaviour is key for more natural interactions. Handshaking is one such natural interaction used commonly in many social contexts. It is one of the first non-verbal interactions which takes place and should, therefore, be part of the repertoire of a social robot. In this paper, we explore the existing state of Human-Robot Handshaking and discuss possible ways forward for such physically interactive behaviours.

Keywords: Handshaking · Physical HRI · Social robotics

1 Introduction

Handshaking is a commonly and naturally used physical interaction and an important social behaviour between two people [18] in many social contexts [13,22,51]. It is one of the most common greetings that is usually the first non-verbal interaction taking place in a social context. Handshaking is, therefore, an important social cue for several reasons. Firstly, it plays an important role in shaping impressions [9,13,51]. Moreover, it helps set the tone of any interaction, since the sense of touch can convey distinct emotions [23]. Robot handshaking improves the perception of robots as well by making humans more willing to help them [4] leading to better cooperation and coexistence.

Having human-like body movements plays an important role in the acceptance of HRI as well. Thus, having a good handshake can not only widen the expressive abilities of a social robot but also provide a strong first impression for further interactions to take place.

We propose the following framework in our study, shown in Fig. 1.

A. R. Wagner et al. (Eds.): ICSR 2020, LNAI 12483, pp. 478–489, 2020.
https://doi.org/10.1007/978-3-030-62056-1_40

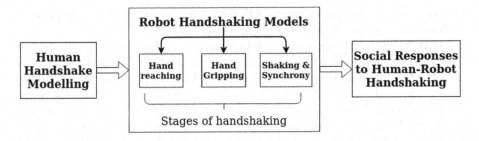

Fig. 1. Conceptual framework for human-robot handshaking

2 Handshake Modelling

A group of researchers from Okayama Prefectural University, Japan modelled human handshaking interactions using motion capture to track participants' joints. Firstly, a transfer function to mimic the requester's reaching motion for the responder was developed [31]. This was further developed into a minimum jerk trajectory model which accurately captures the velocity profiles and generates smooth motions [25,30,44,45]. Shaking was modelled as a spring and damper system [28,61], whose oscillatory motion profile fit that of shaking. A similar spring-damper model is proposed by Dai et al. [16] to model the elbow stiffness by measuring muscle contractions in the arm using EMG signals.

A group of researchers from the University of Lorraine on modelled the mutual synchronization (MS in short) between participants during shaking as well as the forces exerted on the palms [36,38,53]. Tagne et al. [53] investigate the joint motions with IMUs place at each joint. Melnyk and Hénaff [38] trends across different gender pairings are analysed as well. Both of these works analyze the influences of social setting, such as greeting, congratulating or sympathising.

Tagne et al. [53] observe a shorter duration during greeting compared to sympathy and congratulation, which were similar. The grip strength shows contradictory results. Tagne et al. [53] observe the lowest grip strength in case of sympathy, followed by greeting and then, congratulations. Melnyk and Hénaff [38] observe slightly higher grip strength for consolation although not significantly. Regarding gender, male pairs shook for a lesser duration than mixed pairs and female pairs shook the longest. No conclusive correlations were found between gender and grip strength, contrary to [13,42].

Knoop et al. [35] studied the contact area, pressure and grasping forces exerted while handshaking. A positive correlation was found between contact pressure and grasping force. This was non-linear as the grasping force got higher.

3 Hand Reaching in Handshaking

Jindai et al. [25,30,31] and Ota et al. [44,45] propose two models for reaching. One with a transfer function based on the human hand's trajectory with a lag element and the other is a minimum jerk trajectory model, which fits the velocity profiles and provides smooth trajectories by definition.

More recently, works model reaching using machine learning. Campbell et al. [12] use imitation learning to learn a joint distribution over the actions of both the human and the robot during handshaking. They execute open-loop trajectories and human adjusts to them in training as their pneumatic robot cannot be kinesthetically taught. During test time, the posterior distribution is inferred from the human's initial motions from which the robot's trajectory is sampled. Their framework estimates the speed of the interaction as well, to match the speed of the human. Christen et al. [14] use Deep Reinforcement Learning to learn physical interactions from human-human interactions. They use an imitation reward which helps in learning the intricacies of the interaction. Falahi et al. [19] use one-shot imitation learning to kinesthetically teach reaching and shaking behaviours based on gender and familiarity detected using facial recognition. However, it cannot be generalized due to the extremely low sample size. Vinayavekhin et al. [57] model hand reaching with an LSTM trained using skeleton data. They predict the human hand's final pose and devise a simple controller for the robot arm to reach the predicted location. In terms of smoothness, timeliness and efficiency, their method performs better than following the intermediate hand locations. However, it performs worse than using the true final pose due to inaccuracies in the prediction.

4   Hand Grasping Control

Avelino et al. [5] model grasping with different degrees of hand closure. Since position control is used, the force perceived depends on the hand sizes of the participants. They address this in their next work [6], where participants adjust the robot's fingers until a preferable grasp is reached. This provides a reference for the force sensors and the joint positions, using which grasping behaviours are developed. They do not incorporate any force-feedback, which is discussed below.

Ouchi and Hashimoto [46] propose a remote handshaking system, where a handshake is performed while on a call using a custom silicone-rubber based robotic soft hand. The force exerted on the robot hand, measured using a pneumatic force sensor, is relayed to the robot hand at the other end that mimics it. They see that participants barely felt any transmission delay and perceived the partner's existence better during the call. Pedemonte et al. [48] design a robot hand for handshaking controlled by the force exerted on it. It is sensor-less, with a deformable palm controlling the fingers based on the degree of deformation using variable admittance control. Arns et al. [2] improve this design with lower gear ratios, impedance control and more powerful actuators to obtain stronger grasping forces and almost instantaneous speeds (< 0.05 s). The force exerted by the robot hand depends on the force exerted by the human, leading to a partial synchronisation. Arns et al. test how it feels in comparison with a human hand on a 5-point scale (1-very different, 5-identical). It was perceived well in terms of compliance (3.9/5), force feedback (4/5) and overall haptics (3.7/5).

Vigni et al. [56] follow a more closed-loop approach by measuring the force exerted by the robot hand with force-sensitive resistors and control the force exerted by the robot hand which is approximated from the degree of hand closure. They compare three different relationships between the exerted forces of the human and the robot namely linear, constant and combined (constant+linear). The latter two are used with high (strong) and low (weak) constant values. The combined controllers were perceived better than the constant ones. Participants were seen to adjust their force based on the robot's, showing that humans tend to follow the force exerted on their hand. The stronger variants of the constant and combined controllers were perceived as more confident/extroverted.

5 Shaking and Synchronisation

In this section, we describe works that model the shaking phase. They mainly do so by aiming to achieve synchronous motions with the interaction partner while reducing interaction forces. The works can be broadly divided into the following three categories: Central Pattern Generator Models, Harmonic Oscillator Models and Miscellaneous Models.

5.1 Central Pattern Generators

Central Pattern Generators (CPGs) [24] are biologically inspired neuronal circuits, that generate rhythmic outputs from non-rhythmic inputs. Kasuga and Hashimoto [34] model the shoulder and elbow motions of a robot using the exerted torque on the joints as input with a CPG which, however, doesn't adapt to the human. For better synchronization, some works adapt the CPG to learn the frequency of the shaking motions. This is achieved by either incorporating a learning framework into the CPG [3,32,37] or by parametrizing the CPG and learning the parameters on the fly [47,50].

5.2 Harmonic Oscillator Models

Harmonic oscillator models either mimic harmonic systems like spring-damper systems [17,39,61] or follow simple sinusoidal motions [8,59,60,62]. Chua et al. [15] propose a hybrid model that uses both, a spring-damper model to update impedance parameters and a simple sinusoidal trajectory to generate reference trajectories. Similarly other works use impedance control to model the stiffness [8,17] and for better synchronization, some estimate the impedance parameters in an online fashion by using an EKF [39], a HMM [59] or least-squares [60].

5.3 Miscellaneous Models

Karniel et al. [33] and Nisky et al. [41] design an experimental framework and metric for testing the human-likeness of shaking motions on a 1D haptic stylus. Avraham et al. [7] test 3 models with this. The first is a tit-for-tat model that passively records the joint motions and replays it. The second is a biological model simulating muscle generated motions to achieve low interaction forces. The final is a simple linear regression model. The tit-for-tat and linear regression models fare much better than the biologically inspired model.

Pedemonte et al. [49] introduce a remote handshaking mechanism using their previously developed hand. They develop a vertical rail mechanism that the hand is mounted on and is passively controlled. This shaking motion along with the force exerted on the hand is relayed to the partner's hand and rail mechanism. This allows realistic haptic interaction to take place remotely where the participants can adequately perceive each other's motions and forces.

6 Social Responses to Human-Robot Handshaking

Before we talk about the various social responses, we would like to discuss the differences in metrics and criteria used for understanding the way different methods evaluate their studies. One common metric used is the bipolar scale (7-point or 5-point scale) where one end conveys a negative perception of the parameter, and the other end conveys a positive perception. Another popular method is the Bradley-Terry model [11], which is a probabilistic model specifically used for understanding paired comparisons among a set of different methods. However, these are general metrics used for statistical analysis. To this end Karniel et al. [33] devise a custom metric for comparing the human-likeness of different human-robot handshaking methods in a Turing test-like setting, called a Model Human Likeness Grade (MHLG). This is based on the perceived probability of a method being human-like by a participant.

Additionally, the use of many different types of robotic interfaces makes it difficult to generalize the comparison of results across different works. Some works, use a simple gripper like interface [10, 19, 32, 50], some use a rod-like end-effector [7, 21, 33, 41, 47, 58, 59], and some use a human-hand like interface that is either actively controlled [1, 4, 6, 14, 39, 54, 56], passively controlled [2, 8, 46, 48, 49] or not controlled at all [12, 17, 25–31, 34, 35, 37, 40, 43–45, 52, 55, 57, 61]

Such a variety in the usage of different evaluation criteria, metrics and especially robotic interfaces makes it is difficult to converge on a common benchmark on common parameters to evaluate different human-robot handshaking methods. Therefore, we categorize the different works evaluating human-robot handshaking based on the factors they evaluate or the goal of their experiments. These can roughly be divided into the categories as shown below.

6.1 Influence of External Factors

Ammi et al. [1] and Tsalamlal et al. [54] explored combinations of visual and haptic behaviours. Among visual expressions, "happy" was rated higher than "neutral" one, the least being "sad". Significantly higher arousal and dominance were seen for strong handshakes and higher valence for soft ones. Higher arousal and dominance was also seen with strong handshakes in a visuo-haptic case as compared to a visual-only case. Another framework studying the effect of visuo-haptic stimuli was proposed by Vanello et al. [55]. They develop a sensor glove to track the participants' hand motions and contact pressure and have a screen on which visuals (faces of humans and robots) are shown. Participants' feedback is analysed using fMRI activity. Nothing can be concluded from their results as only three participants took part in their study.

Jindai et al. [27], found that a delay of 0.1 s between the voice and handshake motion of the robot was acceptable. Jindai et al. [30], they further saw that participants preferred when the gaze shifted steadily from the hand while reaching to the face after contact. Ota et al. [44,45] found the response to a handshake to be preferable with a delay of 0.2 s to 0.4 s.

Nakanishi et al. [40] equip a robotic soft hand on a video screen showing a remote presenter in a telepresence scenario. Interactions were better perceived when the presenter's hand was not visible on the screen. They further saw that when participants controlled a second robot hand placed with the presenter, feelings of closeness and physically shaking hands were rated higher when both the presenter's hand and the robot hand were not in the frame. They argue that the hand's visibility cancels the feeling of synchronization, which some subjects reported was due to seeing two hands for the same interaction.

6.2 Influence of Handshaking on Robot Perception

Avelino et al. [4] see how handshaking affects the willingness to help a robot when it has to perform a navigation task. Participants who shook hands with the robot found it to be more warm and likeable and were more willing to help the robot. However, they argue that a human-like robot handshake would lead to participants not anticipating the robot getting stuck in a simple navigational task due to a mismatch between the expected skill and the actual behaviour. Bevan and Fraser [10] study the effect of handshaking on negotiations between participants, where one participant interacts remotely via a Nao robot. Handshaking improved mutual cooperation, however, haptic feedback for the telepresent negotiator had no significant impact. It did not affect the perceived trustworthiness, which they argue is possibly due to the childlike nature of the Nao robot.

6.3 Using Handshaking for Differentiation

Garg et al. [20] classify people's personality as introverts and extroverts using statistics of accelerations, Euler angles and polar orientations when shaking hands with a robot hand. The features are ranked based on Mutual Information followed by a K Nearest Neighbours classification, achieving a 75% accuracy. Orefice et al. [42] similarly look at distinctions in personality as well as gender. They found that male-male pairs applied more pressure than male-female pairs. Female-female pairs had a longer duration and lower frequency. Regarding personality, they found that introverts shook at higher speeds while extroverts exerted more pressure. Using these features, they predict the human's gender and personality during a human-robot handshake.

They further perform a longitudinal study [43] that looks at how pressure variations while shaking hands with a Pepper robot reflects the participants' immediate mood. A consistency was seen when shaking hands with a human subject or with Pepper, which was unexpected as interacting with Pepper might not be as human-like. The only significant differences between different positive moods were with "Calm" and "Cheerful" moods, with less pressure observed in a "Calm" mood. For negative moods, a "Bored" mood had lower pressure than "Excited" or "Tense" moods, both of which had more arousal. In general, lower pressures were found with moods with lower arousal.

6.4   Human-Likeness Evaluation

Giannopoulos et al. [21] and Wang et al. [58] compare the human likeness of their previous handshaking models (a basic one [60] and an interactive one [59]) with a human operating the robot. Both studies perform their experiment with participants wearing noise-cancelling headphones playing music and ambient conversations in a cocktail bar scenario. Giannopoulos et al. [21] blindfold the participants and Wang et al. [58] make the participants wear a VR headset with a human model rendered for the robot. The human-operated handshake was rated the highest (6.8/10 in both), followed by the interactive handshake (5.9/10 in [21], 5.3/10 in [60]). The basic handshake was rated the lowest (3.3/10 in [21], 3.0/10 in [60]). The interactive handshake was close to the human-operated one, but both were far from the maximum human-likeness (10/10), possibly due to the rod-like end effector.

Stock-Homburg et al. [52] test if an android robot's hand, made with soft silicone skin and a heated palm, can pass as a human hand. Participants were blindfolded and shook hands with a human and the robot twice in random order. Majority of them (11/15) correctly guessed the first hand they interacted with, which some said was from the mechanical feel of the robot hand. By the fourth handshake, all guessed correctly. Participants only had a static interaction. Testing handshake behaviours instead, could yield better insights.

7   Discussion and Conclusion

Overall, we discussed various works looking into human-robot handshaking. Due to differences in hardware and metrics, it is difficult to come up with a common benchmark to evaluate these studies. However, some qualitative conclusions can be drawn. In general, an element of synchronization is present. This can be measured well in the shaking stage where low interaction forces can be an indication of synchronization. In reality, there is a leader-follower situation which arises, which could perhaps reflect on various personal attributes of the people shaking hands. From the perspective of a social robot, contextual cues would be effective in having a better impact from the handshake. This requires further research in other fields like emotion recognition, estimating intent, personality etc. For a more human-like perception, each aspect of the movement at different stages needs to be human-like since we are still far from having robotic interfaces that not only look human-like but also feel human-like, as most still have a mechanical feel. This combined with a smooth integration of the different phases of handshaking is also important since delays in switching between the different stages could possibly not be well perceived.

One thing to keep in mind is physical interactions vary over different cultures, age groups, geographic locations. Depending on the context too, different interactions would be more prevalent, like hugging or patting for higher intimacy or bumping fists or giving high fives in a friendly scenario. Moreover, due to the Covid-19 pandemic, there are increasing restrictions and precautions regarding limiting physical contact which has led to alternative interactions, like shaking/tapping feet, touching elbows/forearms, remote high fives and so on. However, the importance of handshakes in business and formal settings is a good motivation for continuing to develop human-like handshaking behaviours. Additionally, learning different physically interactive behaviours would help improve the perception of a social robot, which is a good direction for future work.

Acknowledgements. The authors thank the Interdisciplinary Research Forum (Forum Interdisziplinäre Forschung) at the Technical University of Darmstadt and the Association of Supporters of Market-Oriented Management, Marketing, and Human Resource Management (Förderverein für Marktorientierte Unternehmensführung, Marketing und Personalmanagement e.V.) for funding this work.

References

1. Ammi, M., et al.: Haptic human-robot affective interaction in a handshaking social protocol. In: Proceedings of the Tenth Annual ACM/IEEE International Conference on Human-Robot Interaction, pp. 263–270 (2015)
2. Arns, M., Laliberté, T., Gosselin, C.: Design, control and experimental validation of a haptic robotic hand performing human-robot handshake with human-like agility. In: 2017 IEEE/RSJ International Conference on Intelligent Robots and Systems (IROS), pp. 4626–4633. IEEE (2017)
3. Artem, M.A., Viacheslav, K.M., Volodymyr, B.P., Patrick, H.: Physical human-robot interaction in the handshaking case: learning of rhythmicity using oscillators neurons. IFAC Proc. Vol. 46(9), 1055–1060 (2013)
4. Avelino, J., et al.: The power of a hand-shake in human-robot interactions. In: 2018 IEEE/RSJ International Conference on Intelligent Robots and Systems (IROS), pp. 1864–1869. IEEE (2018)
5. Avelino, J., Paulino, T., Cardoso, C., Moreno, P., Bernardino, A.: Human-aware natural handshaking using tactile sensors for Vizzy, a social robot. In: Interaction and Learning for Assistive Robotics at RO-MAN Workshop on Behavior Adaptation (2017)
6. Avelino, J., Paulino, T., Cardoso, C., Nunes, R., Moreno, P., Bernardino, A.: Towards natural handshakes for social robots: human-aware hand grasps using tactile sensors. Paladyn, J. Behav. Robot. 9(1), 221–234 (2018)
7. Avraham, G., et al.: Toward perceiving robots as humans: three handshake models face the turing-like handshake test. IEEE Trans. Haptics 5(3), 196–207 (2012)

8. Beaudoin, J., Laliberté, T., Gosselin, C.: Haptic interface for handshake emulation. IEEE Robot. Autom. Lett. **4**(4), 4124–4130 (2019)
9. Bernieri, F.J., Petty, K.N.: The influence of handshakes on first impression accuracy. Soc. Influence **6**(2), 78–87 (2011)
10. Bevan, C., Fraser, D.S.: Shaking hands and cooperation in tele-present human-robot negotiation. In: 2015 10th ACM/IEEE International Conference on Human-Robot Interaction (HRI), pp. 247–254. IEEE (2015)
11. Bradley, R.A., Terry, M.E.: Rank analysis of incomplete block designs: I. the method of paired comparisons. Biometrika **39**, 324–345 (1952)
12. Campbell, J., Hitzmann, A., Stepputtis, S., Ikemoto, S., Hosoda, K., Amor, H.B.: Learning interactive behaviors for musculoskeletal robots using Bayesian interaction primitives. arXiv preprint arXiv:1908.05552 (2019)
13. Chaplin, W.F., Phillips, J.B., Brown, J.D., Clanton, N.R., Stein, J.L.: Handshaking, gender, personality, and first impressions. J. Pers. Soc. Psychol. **79**(1), 110 (2000)
14. Christen, S., Stevšić, S., Hilliges, O.: Guided deep reinforcement learning of control policies for dexterous human-robot interaction. In: 2019 International Conference on Robotics and Automation (ICRA), pp. 2161–2167. IEEE (2019)
15. Chua, Y., Tee, K.P., Yan, R.: Human-robot motion synchronization using reactive and predictive controllers. In: 2010 IEEE International Conference on Robotics and Biomimetics, pp. 223–228. IEEE (2010)
16. Dai, K., Liu, Y., Okui, M., Nishihama, R., Nakamura, T.: Research of human-robot handshakes under variable stiffness conditions. In: 2019 IEEE 4th International Conference on Advanced Robotics and Mechatronics (ICARM), pp. 744–749. IEEE (2019)
17. Dai, K., Liu, Y., Okui, M., Yamada, Y., Nakamura, T.: Variable viscoelasticity handshake manipulator for physical human-robot interaction using artificial muscle and MR brake. Smart Mater. Struct. **28**(6), 064002 (2019)
18. Deborah, S.: Handwork as ceremony: the case of the handshake. Semiotica **12**(3), 189–202 (1974)
19. Falahi, M., Shangari, T.A., Sheikhjafari, A., Gharghabi, S., Ahmadi, A., Ghidary, S.S.: Adaptive handshaking between humans and robots, using imitation: based on gender-detection and person recognition. In: 2014 Second RSI/ISM International Conference on Robotics and Mechatronics (ICRoM), pp. 936–941. IEEE (2014)
20. Garg, V., Mukherjee, A., Rajaram, B.: Classifying human-robot interaction using handshake data. In: 2017 IEEE International Conference on Systems, Man, and Cybernetics (SMC), pp. 3153–3158. IEEE (2017)
21. Giannopoulos, E., Wang, Z., Peer, A., Buss, M., Slater, M.: Comparison of people's responses to real and virtual handshakes within a virtual environment. Brain Res. Bull. **85**(5), 276–282 (2011)
22. Hall, P.M., Hall, D.A.S.: The handshake as interaction. Semiotica **45**(3-4), 249–264 (1983)
23. Hertenstein, M.J., Verkamp, J.M., Kerestes, A.M., Holmes, R.M.: The communicative functions of touch in humans, nonhuman primates, and rats: a review and synthesis of the empirical research. Genet. Soc. Gener. Psychol. Monogr. **132**(1), 5–94 (2006)
24. Hooper, S.L.: Central pattern generators. e LS (2001)

25. Jindai, M., Ota, S., Ikemoto, Y., Sasaki, T.: Handshake request motion model with an approaching human for a handshake robot system. In: 2015 IEEE 7th International Conference on Cybernetics and Intelligent Systems (CIS) and IEEE Conference on Robotics, Automation and Mechatronics (RAM), pp. 265–270. IEEE (2015)

26. Jindai, M., Ota, S., Yamauchi, H., Watanabe, T.: A small-size handshake robot system for a generation of handshake approaching motion. In: 2012 IEEE International Conference on Cyber Technology in Automation, Control, and Intelligent Systems (CYBER), pp. 80–85. IEEE (2012)

27. Jindai, M., Watanabe, T.: Development of a handshake robot system based on a handshake approaching motion model. In: 2007 IEEE/ASME International Conference on Advanced Intelligent Mechatronics, pp. 1–6. IEEE (2007)

28. Jindai, M., Watanabe, T.: A handshake robot system based on a shake-motion leading model. In: 2008 IEEE/RSJ International Conference on Intelligent Robots and Systems, pp. 3330–3335. IEEE (2008)

29. Jindai, M., Watanabe, T.: A small-size handshake robot system based on a handshake approaching motion model with a voice greeting. In: 2010 IEEE/ASME International Conference on Advanced Intelligent Mechatronics, pp. 521–526. IEEE (2010)

30. Jindai, M., Watanabe, T.: Development of a handshake request motion model based on analysis of handshake motion between humans. In: 2011 IEEE/ASME International Conference on Advanced Intelligent Mechatronics (AIM), pp. 560–565. IEEE (2011)

31. Jindai, M., Watanabe, T., Shibata, S., Yamamoto, T.: Development of a handshake robot system for embodied interaction with humans. In: ROMAN 2006-The 15th IEEE International Symposium on Robot and Human Interactive Communication, pp. 710–715. IEEE (2006)

32. Jouaiti, M., Caron, L., Hénaff, P.: Hebbian plasticity in CPG controllers facilitates self-synchronization for human-robot handshaking. Front. Neurorobotics 12, 29 (2018)

33. Karniel, A., Nisky, I., Avraham, G., Peles, B.-C., Levy-Tzedek, S.: A turing-like handshake test for motor intelligence. In: Kappers, A.M.L., van Erp, J.B.F., Bergmann Tiest, W.M., van der Helm, F.C.T. (eds.) EuroHaptics 2010. LNCS, vol. 6191, pp. 197–204. Springer, Heidelberg (2010). https://doi.org/10.1007/978-3-642-14064-8_29

34. Kasuga, T., Hashimoto, M.: Human-robot handshaking using neural oscillators. In: Proceedings of the 2005 IEEE International Conference on Robotics and Automation, pp. 3802–3807. IEEE (2005)

35. Knoop, E., Bächer, M., Wall, V., Deimel, R., Brock, O., Beardsley, P.: Handshakiness: benchmarking for human-robot hand interactions. In: 2017 IEEE/RSJ International Conference on Intelligent Robots and Systems (IROS), pp. 4982–4989. IEEE (2017)

36. Melnyk, A., Borysenko, V.P., Henaff, P.: Analysis of synchrony of a handshake between humans. In: 2014 IEEE/ASME International Conference on Advanced Intelligent Mechatronics, pp. 1753–1758. IEEE (2014)

37. Melnyk, A., Henaff, P.: Bio-inspired plastic controller for a robot arm to shake hand with human. In: 2016 IEEE 36th International Conference on Electronics and Nanotechnology (ELNANO), pp. 163–168. IEEE (2016)

38. Melnyk, A., Henaff, P.: Physical analysis of handshaking between humans: mutual synchronisation and social context. Int. J. Soc. Robot. 11(4), 541–554 (2019)

39. Mura, D., Knoop, E., Catalano, M.G., Grioli, G., Bächer, M., Bicchi, A.: On the role of stiffness and synchronization in human-robot handshaking. Int. J. Robot. Res. 0278364920903792 (2020)
40. Nakanishi, H., Tanaka, K., Wada, Y.: Remote handshaking: touch enhances video-mediated social telepresence. In: Proceedings of the SIGCHI Conference on Human Factors in Computing Systems, pp. 2143–2152 (2014)
41. Nisky, I., Avraham, G., Karniel, A.: Three alternatives to measure the human-likeness of a handshake model in a turing-like test. Presence Teleoperators Virtual Environ. **21**(2), 156–182 (2012)
42. Orefice, P.H., Ammi, M., Hafez, M., Tapus, A.: Let's handshake and I'll know who you are: gender and personality discrimination in human-human and human-robot handshaking interaction. In: 2016 IEEE-RAS 16th International Conference on Humanoid Robots (Humanoids), pp. 958–965. IEEE (2016)
43. Orefice, P.H., Ammi, M., Hafez, M., Tapus, A.: Pressure variation study in human-human and human-robot handshakes: impact of the mood. In: 2018 27th IEEE International Symposium on Robot and Human Interactive Communication (RO-MAN), pp. 247–254. IEEE (2018)
44. Ota, S., Jindai, M., Fukuta, T., Watanabe, T.: A handshake response motion model during active approach to a human. In: 2014 IEEE/SICE International Symposium on System Integration, pp. 310–315. IEEE (2014)
45. Ota, S., Jindai, M., Sasaki, T., Ikemoto, Y.: Handshake response motion model with approaching of human based on an analysis of human handshake motions. In: 2015 7th International Congress on Ultra Modern Telecommunications and Control Systems and Workshops (ICUMT), pp. 8–13. IEEE (2015)
46. Ouchi, K., Hashimoto, S.: Handshake telephone system to communicate with voice and force. In: Proceedings 6th IEEE International Workshop on Robot and Human Communication, RO-MAN 1997, SENDAI, pp. 466–471. IEEE (1997)
47. Papageorgiou, D., Doulgeri, Z.: A kinematic controller for human-robot handshaking using internal motion adaptation. In: 2015 IEEE International Conference on Robotics and Automation (ICRA), pp. 5622–5627. IEEE (2015)
48. Pedemonte, N., Laliberté, T., Gosselin, C.: Design, control, and experimental validation of a handshaking reactive robotic interface. ASME J. Mech. Robot. **8**(1), 011020 (2015, 2016). https://doi.org/10.1115/1.4031167
49. Pedemonte, N., Laliberté, T., Gosselin, C.: A haptic bilateral system for the remote human–human handshake. ASME J. Dyn. Syst. Measur. Control **139**(4), 044503 (2017). https://doi.org/10.1115/1.4035171
50. Sato, T., Hashimoto, M., Tsukahara, M.: Synchronization based control using online design of dynamics and its application to human-robot interaction. In: 2007 IEEE International Conference on Robotics and Biomimetics (ROBIO), pp. 652–657. IEEE (2007)
51. Stewart, G.L., Dustin, S.L., Barrick, M.R., Darnold, T.C.: Exploring the handshake in employment interviews. J. Appl. Psychol. **93**(5), 1139 (2008)
52. Stock-Homburg, R., Peters, J., Schneider, K., Prasad, V., Nukovic, L.: Evaluation of the handshake turing test for anthropomorphic robots. In: Companion of the 2020 ACM/IEEE International Conference on Human-Robot Interaction, pp. 456–458 (2020)
53. Tagne, G., Hénaff, P., Gregori, N.: Measurement and analysis of physical parameters of the handshake between two persons according to simple social contexts. In: 2016 IEEE/RSJ International Conference on Intelligent Robots and Systems (IROS), pp. 674–679. IEEE (2016)

54. Tsalamlal, M.Y., Martin, J.C., Ammi, M., Tapus, A., Amorim, M.A.: Affective handshake with a humanoid robot: How do participants perceive and combine its facial and haptic expressions? In: 2015 International Conference on Affective Computing and Intelligent Interaction (ACII), pp. 334–340. IEEE (2015)
55. Vanello, N., et al.: Neural correlates of human-robot handshaking. In: 19th International Symposium in Robot and Human Interactive Communication, pp. 555–561. IEEE (2010)
56. Vigni, F., Knoop, E., Prattichizzo, D., Malvezzi, M.: The role of closed-loop hand control in handshaking interactions. IEEE Robot. Autom. Lett. 4(2), 878–885 (2019)
57. Vinayavekhin, P., et al.: Human-like hand reaching by motion prediction using long short-term memory. In: Kheddar, A., et al. (eds.) International Conference on Social Robotics, vol. 10652, pp. 156–166. Springer, Heidelberg (2017). https://doi.org/10.1007/978-3-319-70022-9_16
58. Wang, Z., Giannopoulos, E., Slater, M., Peer, A., Buss, M.: Handshake: realistic human-robot interaction in haptic enhanced virtual reality. Presence Teleoperators Virtual Environ. 20(4), 371–392 (2011)
59. Wang, Z., Peer, A., Buss, M.: An HMM approach to realistic haptic human-robot interaction. In: World Haptics 2009-Third Joint EuroHaptics conference and Symposium on Haptic Interfaces for Virtual Environment and Teleoperator Systems, pp. 374–379. IEEE (2009)
60. Wang, Z., Yuan, J., Buss, M.: Modelling of human haptic skill: a framework and preliminary results. IFAC Proc. Vol. 41(2), 14761–14766 (2008)
61. Yamato, Y., Jindai, M., Watanabe, T.: Development of a shake-motion leading model for human-robot handshaking. In: 2008 SICE Annual Conference, pp. 502–507. IEEE (2008)
62. Zeng, Y., Li, Y., Xu, P., Ge, S.S.: Human-robot handshaking: a hybrid deliberate/reactive model. In: Ge, S.S., Khatib, O., Cabibihan, J.-J., Simmons, R., Williams, M.-A. (eds.) ICSR 2012. LNCS (LNAI), vol. 7621, pp. 258–267. Springer, Heidelberg (2012). https://doi.org/10.1007/978-3-642-34103-8_26

Choosing the Best Robot for the Job: Affinity Bias in Human-Robot Interaction

Thomas Trainer, John R. Taylor, and Christopher J. Stanton[(⊠)]

MARCS Institute, Western Sydney University, Sydney, NSW 2174, Australia
c.stanton@westernsydney.edu.au

Abstract. Humans subconsciously judge others as being either similar or dissimilar to themselves, manifesting as an unconscious preference, or affinity bias, for those who are perceived to be similar. In human-to-human interaction, affinity bias can significantly influence trust formation and lead to discrimination, for example, in decisions related to recruitment and team selection. We investigate whether affinity bias is observed in human-robot interaction during team formation with social agents that differ in gender and skin tone. In this study, we asked 61 participants to order the resumés of 24 different avatars that varied in gender, skin tone, and competency under the pretext of choosing the "best" avatars to be the participant's teammate. Then, using a wizard-of-oz style experiment, participants performed a task with two avatar teammates (one most preferred and one least preferred) to measure trust. Results showed that while avatars were predominantly chosen based upon competency, avatar appearance generated an affinity bias in resumé sorting, and participants were more likely to trust their preferred teammate.

Keywords: Affinity bias · Human-robot interaction · Trust

1 Introduction

Subconsciously, humans are happiest and most content when surrounded by familiar things, or by similar people. This *affinity bias* can unconsciously affect how we make decisions such as during recruitment and team selection [1], and during human-to-human interaction (HHI) when forming and developing trust in a relationship [2], so that we can perpetuate the familiar and the comfortable [3]. Affinity bias relies upon our ability as humans to make psycho-social judgements about others, which in many cases are affect-based [4]. These judgements can be race and gender based [5, 6], and just as affinity bias produces positive discrimination for the familiar/similar, unfamiliarity and difference can equally lead to unconscious negative bias and discrimination [7].

The main aim of this study is to investigate whether affinity bias common in HHI is observed in human-to-robot interaction (HRI), specifically whether human decision making during the recruitment process is affected by affinity bias, and whether improvements in trust formation and development occur when humans show affinity bias towards robots. Understanding whether affinity bias impacts HRI has utility in everyday tasks in

© Springer Nature Switzerland AG 2020
A. R. Wagner et al. (Eds.): ICSR 2020, LNAI 12483, pp. 490–501, 2020.
https://doi.org/10.1007/978-3-030-62056-1_41

education [8], healthcare [9] and commerce [10], not least by making the robot appear more familiar/similar to users [11] to improve trust, likeability, robot acceptance, HRI, and ultimately, the user experience.

In this study we presented 61 participants with one-page resumés of 24 avatars comprising avatar photos with different skin tones and genders, and text highlighting avatar competency (high, medium or low). Resumés were then sorted into their most preferred (the "top 8") and least preferred candidates (the "bottom 8"), with a third pile for those they were unsure of (the "middle 8"). We assessed participants methods for resumé selection (e.g. the influence of text describing the avatar's competence or the avatar's appearance). Participants were then assigned two avatar teammates for a cooperative visual-tracking task designed to measure trust, with one avatar being their handpicked favorite, and the other being a randomly assigned avatar from the "bottom 8". The AI algorithm remained unchanged for each avatar (i.e., all avatars were of equal competence), and participants rated the avatars on a range of characteristics. Specifically, we hypothesised that:

H1.   Affect-based factors (e.g. same gender, skin tone) will play a greater role in sorting resumes than cognitive-based factors (competence).
H2.   Participants prefer working with avatars they find attractive or visually similar to themselves.
H3.   Participants will trust their chosen avatar more than the assigned avatar, with a higher rate of change in response to the chosen avatar's opinion.
H4.   Participants will evaluate the chosen avatar more favourably (for likeability, competence, likeability, teamwork ability) than the assigned avatar.

2   Related Work

2.1   Social Categorization

In social categorization, individuals classify themselves and others, based on their characteristics, into different social groups: in-groups (to which they belong), and out-groups (individuals not in their in-group). [12]. These psycho-social classifications introduce bias in human-to-human interaction (HHI), where out-group members are perceived as being *more* different [13] and viewed less favourably than in-group members. These biases occur with humans, robots, and avatars, where individuals act pro-socially towards in-group robots, treating them more favourably than out-group robots [14]. Previous studies have shown that people with strong racial biases prefer robots to dark-skinned people [15], and that attitudes to out-group robots are similar to human minority out-groups [16, 17]. These biases occur in resumé screening where recruiters select applicant resumés with the same gender or ethnicity [7]. In the current study, we expect avatar resumé selections to have similar characteristics to participants, irrespective of competence (H1).

When a robot is 'in-group' (e.g. the robot shares common characteristics), it tends to be anthropomorphised and ascribed human characteristics (e.g. ambition, emotions) compared to out-group robots [18]. This is a direct result of social attitudes and racial bias [13, 19, 20], which has also been shown to be positively changed through human-robot embodiment [21, 22]. In the absence of embodiment, we expect these unconscious biases to be present in avatar interaction. Thus, we expect images to play a greater role in avatar selection for a given task (H1), and that participants prefer working with visually self-similar avatars (H2).

2.2 Discrimination

Positive and negative discrimination is reinforced by stereotyping and can be implicit (subconscious). Implicit biases, create and perpetuate human attitudes that negatively impact interpersonal relationships. For example, teams comprising in-group members have stronger relationships of mutual trust and respect, whereas out-group members are viewed as incompetent and untrustworthy [23]. We expect to see a similar effect in this study, where participants have less trust in randomly assigned avatars, than avatars they have previously self-selected, as assessed by the participant reactions to the avatar's opinion/recommendation during the task (H3). We also expect participants chosen avatars to be rated as more competent, likeable, and having better teamwork ability than assigned avatars (H4). Gender biases are also present in HRI [5, 24, 25] and robots have been ascribed stereotyped roles based on perceived gender (e.g. feminine robots to domestic labour) [4, 26]. Robots ascribed human characteristics on cross-gender bases (e.g. based on body proportions; female-to-male and vice versa) are viewed as more trustworthy and credible [27] but can bias a robot's perceived ability and acceptability [5, 27]. Feminine robots are judged as warmer and more engaging than masculine robots, which can affect the robot's perceived strengths, flaws and suitability [24]. In team formation, more competent individuals are chosen first, yet in the absence of perceived competency, team members were chosen based on their similarity to the chooser [28]. Thus, we anticipate affect-based (gender and race) differences to be evident in avatar selection (H1), in ratings of trust (H3) and in perceived competency (H4), which has ethical implications for visual diversity: a theme vital in HRI [29].

2.3 Trust

In HHI, trust allows relationships to be built and evolve [30]. In HRI, trust is based on affective dimensions [31]. A robot's competency and characteristics are important in developing trust [32], with human likeness and similarity increasing the likelihood of trust formation [33–37]. Thus, we expect to see higher self-similarity ratings for selected rather than assigned avatars, higher ratings of trust (H2 and H3), and higher evaluations for preferred avatars (H4). HRI interaction also influences trust formation with robots, including task complexity, technical capability and social characteristics [38]. In HHI, implicit bias occurs frequently as workplace discriminatory practices (e.g. gender, race, sexual orientation etc.) [39, 40]. Human teamwork (selection, evaluation) and bias in these processes should be understood for mitigation in human teaming contexts [41].

3   Method

3.1   Participants

Sixty-one Western Sydney University (WSU) first-year psychology students (51 females, 83.1%; 10 males, 16.9%; mean age = 21.6 years old; age range 17-43 years) were recruited via WSU's online participation system and received course credit for participation. The study was approved by the Human Research Ethics Committee (approval H10313).

3.2 Cover Story

Participants were told a cover story that experimenters were testing 24 avatars each with a unique computer vision algorithm, that they would play a graphical version of the "shell" (or "cup") game (Sect. 3.3) with an avatar as a teammate, and that they would evaluate each avatars' performance as compared to human-level performance. Participants were told avatars would track objects using a Microsoft Kinect, directed towards a monitor where task stimuli appeared (the avatar was really a confederate operated by Wizard-of-Oz). Participants were informed avatar task performance was "good, but not perfect", and could make mistakes. Participants were also told that each avatar were distinct in appearance and personality and had been benchmarked on other computer vision tasks. This formed the basis of each avatar's resumé (see Sect. 3.4).

3.3 Shell Game Task

The shell (or cup) game involves hiding an object under one of three cups, and then shuffling the cups to create uncertainty as to the object's true location. Participants played this computerized shell game task; cups were displayed and shuffled on a monitor, with participants (falsely) believing their avatar partner was tracking the objects using the Kinect. The task had 48 trials, with each trial taking ~ 15 s in total. After the shell-shuffling on each trial, the avatar voice asked, *"what is your answer?"*. Participants were required to face the avatar and nominate a shell choice of either *'left'*, *'middle'* or *'right'*: failure to look at the avatar prompted it to say: *"please look at me when I'm talking to you"*. The game had three difficulty levels, which were determined by cup speed and the number of times the cups shuffled. Four trials were "easy", 24 were "medium" difficulty, and 20 "hard". In the easy level, the avatars disagreed with the participant if the participant answered incorrectly, offering a correct answer (to ensure avatar credibility). In the medium and hard levels, each avatar disagreed with the participant five times, and offered a different answer (regardless of correctness), for example *"I disagree, I think it is on the left. What is your final answer?"*. We measured trust by assessing the number of times a participant changed their initial answer to a disagreeing avatar's suggested answer. The experimental setup used two monitors, one for the game, the other for the avatar (facing the participant), and a Kinect directed towards the monitor displaying the shell game.

3.4 Avatars and Avatar Resumés

Each avatar had a resumé which featured their picture, and text describing the avatar's competence (Fig. 1). All of the avatars were equally competent at playing the game, but the resumés described eight with low competence, eight with medium competence, and eight with high competence, with competence categories (similar task score, perception and processing ability) evenly distributed among gender and skin tone. Avatars were created using the web-based program *Avatarmaker* [42] (Fig. 2), comprising equal numbers of four skin tones: white, brown, black, and yellow, for both male and female, and all had similar facial features. Avatars had either a male or female voice with Australian accents depending on their gender, created using TTSMP3 [43].

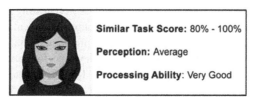

Fig. 1. An example avatar resumé. Each of the 24 resumés was printed on A4 laminated paper.

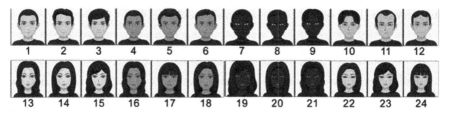

Fig. 2. The 24 avatar faces presented to participants on the resumés, as per Fig. 1.

3.5 Procedure

After consenting, participants completed a demographic questionnaire, and were told the cover story. Participants were then given three minutes to sort 24 paper-based avatar resumés into one of three categories containing 8 resumés each: the "top 8" (the most preferred to work with); the "bottom 8" (the least preferred to work with), and the "middle 8". After three minutes, participants chose their favourite avatar from the "top 8", and a random avatar was chosen from the "bottom 8" - these two avatars played the shell game with the participant, taking alternating turns on each trial to interact with the participant (24 trials each). After completing the shell game task, participants provided ratings using a 10-point Likert scale of self-similarity and attractiveness for all avatars in the top-8 and bottom-8, and self-rated the most similar skin tone to their own. Participants rated the likability, perceived competency and teamwork ability of the two avatars they completed the shell game task with.

4 Results

We hypothesized (H1) that affect-based factors (gender, skin tone) would play a more significant role in resumé sorting than cognitive-based factors (competence), with participants placing more same-gender and skin tone resumés in their most preferred category.

To test this hypothesis, a series of chi-square tests were conducted (Table 1). A chi-square test was conducted examining how many high-competency resumés were placed in the top-8 and how many low-competency resumes were placed in the bottom-8. A statistically significant association was found X^2 (2) $= 559.934\ p < .001$ between competency and sorting. The chi-square tests found no evidence that participants chose their favorite avatars by gender or skin tone. Furthermore, participants overwhelming reported that they sorted agent resumés by the text describing the avatar's competence, rather than the image of the avatar on the resumé, X^2 (2) 37.79 $p < .001$.

Table 1. Chi-square tests comparing factors in avatar selection. [†] denotes a one-way chi-squared test where H_0 = affect-based factors play a greater role in resumé selection than competency; [††] denotes a one-way chi-squared test where H_0 = images are more influential in resumé selection than the text; [†††] H_0 = participants select more avatars of a self-similar gender, than those of opposing gender; [††††] H_0 = preferred avatar selection is based upon avatar skin tone.

Characteristic	X^2 (Cramer V)	df	p (Cramer p)
Avatar competency[†]			
Chosen avatars	559.9	2	< 0.001
Assigned avatars	(0.837)		(< 0.001)
Participant resumé selection[††]			
Text	37.79	1	< 0.001
Image			
Participant gender[†††]			
Male	0.28	1	0.867
Female	0.88	1	0.348
Avatar skin tone[††††]			
White	3.43	3	0.33
Light Brown	2.46	3	0.48
Dark Brown	1.64	3	0.65
Yellow	1.4	3	0.71

While the results in Table 1 suggest H1 was not supported, paired-sample t-tests comparing mean ratings of self-similarity and attractiveness of avatars in the top-8 and bottom-8 found a significant effect of both self-similarity, $t(399) = 2.175\ p = .030$, and attractiveness, $t(399) = 2.999\ p = .003$ (Table 2). Participants rated avatars in the top-8 as looking more self-similar and more attractive than avatars in their bottom-8. Thus, H1 was partially supported, and H2, which posited that participants would prefer working with avatars they find attractive or visually like themselves was supported, even if avatar appearance was not explicitly stated by participants when they reported their avatar selection strategy. This suggests that participants experienced some unconscious bias toward avatars and their appearance, when performing resumé selection.

Similarly, mean trust ratings were higher for the most preferred avatars than the least preferred avatars, supporting our H3. To investigate trust towards the two avatars in the

Table 2. Paired-samples t-tests for self-similarity and attractiveness ratings for the most preferred (chosen) and least preferred (assigned) avatars. Note that SD = Standard deviation, t = t-value, df = degrees of freedom, p = p-value.

Characteristic	Mean	SD	t	df	p	Cohen's d (mean diff)
Self-similarity ratings						
Top-8 avatars	2.3	2.39	2.17	399	0.03	0.112
Bottom-8 avatars	2.0	2.26				(0.26)
Attractiveness ratings						
Top-8 avatars	4.96	2.25	2.99	399	0.003	0.149
Bottom-8 avatars	4.64	2.22				(0.33)
Trust ratings						
Favorite Top-8 avatar	7.27	1.69	3.068	51	0.005	0.619
Assigned Bottom-8 avatar	6.21	1.71				(1.054)
Likeability ratings						
Favorite Top-8 avatar	7.31	1.81	3.139	51	0.003	0.412
Assigned Bottom-8 avatar	6.54	1.92				(0.769)
Competency ratings						
Favorite Top-8 avatar	7.5	1.54	4.680	51	< 0.001	0.557
Assigned Bottom-8 avatar	6.53	1.92				(0.971)
Teamwork ratings						
Favorite Top-8 avatar	7.26	2.02	0.486	51	0.629	
Assigned Bottom-8 avatar	7.15	1.85				

shell game, a two-way analysis of variance was performed, with participants' trusting their chosen avatar ($M = .55$, $SD = .016$) significantly more than the assigned avatar from the bottom-8 ($M = .50$, $SD = .021$), $F(1,55) = 4.107$ $p = .048$. We found that ratings of competency, and likeability were also higher for the participants' chosen avatar compared to the assigned avatar from the bottom-8, although we found no significant difference in the mean ratings of teamwork ability during the tasks between the most preferred and least preferred avatars. Consequently, our H4 is mostly supported, but not in terms of perceived teamwork ability.

5 Discussion

Our findings show that although competence was a primary consideration in avatar selection, we found evidence to suggest that unconscious bias is still evident towards avatars. Notably, participants rated the avatars they placed in their top-8 resumés as having a more similar skin tone to their own, and as being more attractive, than the resumés they placed in the bottom-8. This suggests that participants, prefer to work with avatars that are self-similar and are perceived attractive (e.g. "in-group"; [23]).

Our H1 posited that avatar resumé selection would be based upon affect-based factors such as skin tone and gender, rather than on competency (H1). We expected the avatar images to influence participants' avatar selection more than the text-based competency-based information (which is consistent with [7]). Instead we found that more of the high-competency resumés were assigned to the preferred group, while greater numbers of low-competency resumés were placed in the least preferred group, confirming that cognitive factors (competency) were more important than affect-based factors (similarity) in team selection. This is contrary to previous resumé sorting and team selection studies, where out-group membership on non-selection was observed [7], yet our results are consistent with other studies on priority competency selection during team formation [28].Two possible explanations include the conciseness of the competency text on the avatar resumés, and the resumé sorting time available. With only three bullet points, avatar resumés were oversimplified compared to real-world examples, and perhaps lacked the complexity or depth that might otherwise, in the final decision-making process, lead to non-competency-based selections.

We also noted differences between participants in resumé sorting time, where some participants sorted very quickly, enabling them to review their categories and make changes, while others were slower. Further work could increase resumé complexity by adding more textual information to make the competency assessments more difficult. Future work could also consider giving participants less time to evaluate more detailed resumés, such that making judgments are more difficult, thereby potentially revealing biases. This supports previous work suggesting that unconscious biases are more prevalent when people are expected to perform in stressful situations or under time constraints (c.f. [1]). Thus, further work relating to HRI embodiment might assess whether biases occur under time-limited competency-based robot selection [c.f. 21, 22].

While competency was a primary influence avatar resumé selection, we also investigated whether participants experienced unconscious bias towards group team selection, such as participants sorting avatars into most/least preferred groups based upon affect-based factors: forming in-group affinity with avatars. Our H2 posited that participants preferred more attractive, and visually self-similar avatars. We found evidence of affinity bias towards the most preferred group of avatars, where avatars were rated higher in self-similarity and attractiveness compared to the least preferred group of avatars, suggesting affinity bias influenced group team selection. These findings are consistent with the dynamics of in- and out-group team selection processes [28] and suggest interplay between cognitive and affect-based factors in avatar team formation. It is worth noting that our avatars were largely homogeneous, with similar hair and eye colours, facial features, haircuts, and attire to ensure that participants readily noted the skin tone and gender, the key features under assessment. Further work might investigate the effect of having more diverse avatar appearances, and whether an increase diversity leads to increases in visual attractiveness, self-similarity reporting, or likeability. Improvements in the images may demonstrate that appearance plays a clearer role in sorting than we have shown here.

We then investigated participants' perceived trustworthiness of preferred avatars as compared to assigned avatars (H3). We found that participants changed their answers at a higher rate, based on the opinion of their chosen avatar, and that during the game's trials, the difficulty level and the avatar type (e.g. chosen or assigned) had a significant effect on trust scores. Trust scores were higher in the medium difficulty trials than in the hard trials, although this might be attributable to the difficult trials occurring later in our experiment, after participants had become more familiar with the process and the avatars. Nevertheless, participants displayed and reported a higher level of trust for their chosen avatar, confirming our H3. This suggests that perceived avatar trustworthiness is influenced by unconscious affinity bias and is consistent with previous in-group/out-group studies [18], where interactions with robots sharing in-group similarities with the participants were trusted more [35] likely to be anthropomorphised.

We investigated whether the observed affinity and trustworthiness of the preferred avatars translated to an increase in perceived likeability, competence and teamwork ability than the assigned (least preferred) avatars (H4). We found significant evidence to suggest that participants evaluated their chosen avatar more highly on likeability and competence, confirming our hypothesis, however no significant difference was found in participant ratings of teamwork ability between the chosen (preferred) and assigned (least preferred) avatar (consistent with the findings in [4]). This is despite both the preferred and assigned avatars responding in the same way during the trials (that is, disagreeing with the participant the same number of times throughout the experiment). One possible explanation for this might be lack of cooperative team working, where the role of both the assigned and chosen avatars was simply to offer an opinion. Further work might investigate HRI in-group/out-group dynamics under more complex conditions.

In summary, our current findings suggest that affinity bias, caused by perceived self-similarity, not only enhances perceived trustworthiness, but may in fact lead to a degree of anthropomorphism characterized by an enhancement of perceived competency and likeability. Surprisingly, this seems to occur even when participants chose their preferred avatars based upon their documented competency.

6   Conclusion and Implications for Further Work

Many aspects of HHI are apparent in HRI, including humans' propensity to behave differently and more favourably towards in-group members across contexts and settings. While humans ultimately seek to interact with competent avatars, they will be less inclined if the avatar is 'different'. Although competency is important, affinity bias, as measured and perceived as self-similarity, attractiveness and consequently trust, also plays an important role in avatar selection. Although our study used avatars comprising four skin tones, across two genders and three competency levels, we note a need for further work the effect of increased diversity in the available avatars so we might extend our work to HRI contexts. For example, our findings suggest implications for perceived trustworthiness in HRI, but also highlights the importance of embodiment and acceptability in robot design and personalisation [20–22]. While increased diversity of an avatar or robot's visual appearance would certainly enhance our understanding of affinity bias in HCI and HRI contexts, further studies might seek to understand the interplay between the cognitive and affective influences, such as by changing the dynamics between self-similarity and competency (e.g. by inverting self-similarity and competency), by examining the effect of competency difference and self-similarity (e.g. does a perceived competency gap change with self-similarity), and by exploring the effect of resumé complexity and time-constraints on avatar or robot resumé selection. Such studies might uncover more subtle dynamics between cognitive and affect-based factors that would be relevant to robot design and personalisation, human-autonomy teamwork and team building, and trust.

References

1. Louis, C. (2019). Unconscious bias: The affinity bias. Retrieved from: https://podojo.com/unconscious-bias-the-affinity-bias/. Accessed 20 May 2020
2. Turnbull, H. (2014). The Affinity Bias Conundrum: The Illusion of Inclusion Part III. Retrieved from: https://diversityjournal.com/13763-affinity-bias-conundrum-illusion-inclusion-part-iii/. Accessed 20 May 2020
3. Turnbull, H.: The Illusion of Inclusion: Global Inclusion, Unconscious Bias, and the Bottom Line. Business Expert Press, NY, USA (2016)
4. Eyssel, F., Kuchenbrandt, D.: Social categorization of social robots: anthropomorphism as a function of robot group membership. Br. J. Soc. Psychol. **51**(4), 724–731 (2012)
5. D'Souza, G., Colarelli, S.: Team member selection decisions for virtual versus face-to-face teams. Comput. Hum. Behav. **26**(4), 630–635 (2010)
6. Staats, C.: Understanding implicit bias: what educators should know. Educ. Digest **82**(1), 29–38 (2016)
7. Derous, E., Ryan, A., Nguyen, H.: Multiple categorization in resume screening: examining effects on hiring discrimination against Arab applicants in field and lab settings. J. Org. Behav. **3**(4), 544–570 (2012)
8. Cheng, Y., Sun, P., Chen, N.: The essential applications of educational robot: requirement analysis from the perspectives of experts, researchers and instructors. Comput. Educ. **126**, 399–416 (2018)
9. Breazeal, C., Dautenhahn, K., Kanda, T.: Social robotics. In: Siciliano, B., Khatib, O. (eds.) Springer Handbook of Robotics, pp. 1935–1972. Springer, Cham (2016). https://doi.org/10.1007/978-3-319-32552-1_72
10. Murphy, J., Gretzel, U., Pesonen, J.: Marketing robot services in hospitality and tourism: the role of anthropomorphism. J. Travel Tourism Mark. **36**(7), 784–795 (2019)
11. Carlucci, F., Nardi, L., Iocchi, L., Nardi, D.: Explicit representation of social norms for social robots. In: 2015 IEEE/RSJ International Conference on Intelligent Robots and Systems (IROS), pp. 4191–4196. IEEE (2015)
12. Crisp, R.J., Hewstone, M. (eds.): Multiple social categorization. Elsevier Academic Press, San Diego, CA (2007)
13. Linville, P., Salovey, P., Fischer, G.: Stereotyping and perceived distributions of social characteristics: an application to ingroup-outgroup perception. In: Dovidio, J., Gaertner, L. (eds.) Prejudice, Discrimination and Racism, pp. 165–208. Academic Press, Orlando, FL (1986)
14. Eyssel, F., Kuchenbrandt, D.: Social categorization of social robots: anthropomorphism as a function of robot group membership. Br. J. Soc. Psychol. **51**(4), 724–731 (2012)
15. Gong, L.: The boundary of racial prejudice: comparing preferences for computer-synthesized white, black, and robot characters. Comput. Hum. Behav. **24**, 2074–2093 (2007)
16. Kim, M.-S., Kim, E.-J.: Humanoid robots as "The Cultural Other": are we able to love our creations? AI & Soc. **28**, 309–318 (2013)
17. Sheridan, T.: Human-Robot interaction: status & challenges. Hum. Factors: J. Hum. Factors Ergon Soc. **58**(4), 525–532 (2016)
18. Kuchenbrandt, D., Eyssel, F., Bobinger, S., Neufeld, M.: When a robot's group membership matters. Int. J. Soc. Robot. **5**, 409–417 (2013)

19. Bartneck, C., Yogeeswaran, K., Min Ser, Q., Wang, S., Sparrow, R., Eyssel, F.: Robots and racism. In: Proceedings of the 2018 ACM/IEEE international conference on human-robot interaction, ACM. New York, NY, USA, pp. 196–204 (2018)
20. Addison, K., Yogeeswaran, K., Bartneck, C.: Robots can be more than black and white: examining racial bias towards robots. In: Proceedings of AAAI/ACM Conference on Artificial Intelligence, Ethics & Society. Honolulu, pp. 493–498 (2019)
21. Ventre-Dominey, J., et al.: Embodiment into a robot increases its acceptability. Sci. Rep. **9**(1), 1–10 (2019)
22. Peck, T., Seinfeld, S., Aglioti, S., Slater, M.: Putting yourself in the skin of a black avatar reduces implicit racial bias. Conscious. Cogn. **22**, 779–787 (2013)
23. Singh, J., Rukta, N.: Attitude of in and out-group employees and leader member exchange. Int. J. Eng. Technol. Sci. Res. **5**(3), 441–445 (2018)
24. Stroessner, S., Benitez, J.: The social perception of humanoid and non-humanoid robots: effects of gendered and machine-like features. Int. J. Soc. Robot. **11**(2), 305–315 (2019)
25. Trovato, G., Lucho, C., Paredes, R.: She's electric- the influence of body proportions on perceived gender of robots across cultures. Robot. **7**(3), 50 (2018)
26. Carpenter, J., Davis, J., Erwin-Stewart, N., Lee, T., Bransford, J., Vye, N.: Gender representation and humanoid robots designed for domestic use. Int. J. Soc. Robot. **1**(26), 261–265 (2009)
27. Siegel, M., Breazeal, C., Norton, M.: Persuasive robotics: The influence of robot gender on human behaviour. In: 2009 IEEE/RSJ International Conference on Intelligent Robots and Systems, pp. 2563–2568. IEEE (2009)
28. Skvoretz, J., Bailey, J.: "Red, white, yellow, blue, all out but you": status effects on team formation, and expectation states theory. Soc. Psychol. Q. **79**(2), 136–155 (2016)
29. Riek, L., Howard, D.: A code of ethics for the human-robot interaction profession. Proc. We Robot (2014)
30. Simpson, J.: Psychological foundations of trust. Curr. Dir. Psychol. Sci. **16**(5), 264–268 (2007)
31. Lee, J., See, K.: Trust in automation: designing for appropriate reliance. Hum. Factors **46**(1), 50–80 (2004)
32. Hancock, P., Billings, D., Schaefer, K., Chen, J., De Visser, E., Parasuraman, R.: A meta-analysis of factors affecting trust in human-robot interaction. Hum. Factors **53**, 517–527 (2011)
33. Mathur, M., Reichling, D.: Navigating a social world with robot partners. Cogn. **146**, 22–32 (2016)
34. Lee, J., Breazeal, C.: Human social response toward humanoid robot's head and facial features. In: Proceedings of the CHI Conference on Human Factors in Computing Systems, Atlanta, GA, pp. 4237–4242 (2010)
35. Verberne, F., Ham, J., Midden, C.: Trusting a virtual driver that looks, acts, and thinks like you. Hum. Factors **5**, 895–909 (2015)
36. Todorov, A., Olivola, C., Dotsch, R., Mende-Siedlecki, P.: Social attributions from faces: determinants, consequences, accuracy, and functional significance. Ann. Rev. Psychol. **66**, 519–545 (2015)
37. Ghazali, A., Ham, J., Barakova, E., Markopoulos, P.: Effects of robot facial characteristics and gender in persuasive human-robot interaction. Front. Robot. AI **5**(73), 1–15 (2018)
38. Cameron, D., et al.: Framing factors: the importance of context and the individual in understanding trust in human-robot interaction. In: IEEE/RSJ Conference on Intelligent Robots and Systems (IROS), Hamburg, Germany (2015)
39. Bendick, M., Nunes, A.: Developing the research basis for controlling bias in hiring. J. Soc. Issues **68**(2), 238–262 (2012)
40. Wirts, A.: Discriminatory intent and implicit bias: title VII liability and unwitting discrimination. Boston Coll. Law Rev. **58**(2), 809–856 (2017)

41. Broadbent, E.: Interactions with robots: the truths we reveal about ourselves. Ann. Rev. Psychol. **68**(1), 627–652 (2017)
42. Avatarmaker Homepage. https://avatarmaker.com/. Accessed 20 May 2020
43. TTSMP3 Homepage. https://ttsmp3.com/. Accessed 20 May 2020

Teach Me What You Want to Play: Learning Variants of Connect Four Through Human-Robot Interaction

Ali Ayub[✉] and Alan R. Wagner

The Pennsylvania State University, State College, PA 16802, USA
{aja5755,alan.r.wagner}@psu.edu

Abstract. This paper investigates the use of game theoretic representations to represent and learn how to play interactive games such as Connect Four. We combine aspects of learning by demonstration, active learning, and game theory allowing a robot to leverage its developing representation of the game to conduct question/answer sessions with a person, thus filling in gaps in its knowledge. The paper demonstrates a method for teaching a robot the win conditions of the game Connect Four and its variants using a single demonstration and a few trial examples with a question and answer session led by the robot. Our results show that the robot can learn arbitrary win conditions for the game with little prior knowledge of the win conditions and then play the game with a human utilizing the learned win conditions. Our experiments also show that some questions are more important for learning the game's win conditions. We believe that this method could be broadly applied to a variety of interactive learning scenarios. (A preliminary version of this paper was accepted at [5]).

Keywords: Game theory · Interactive games · Active learning · Human-robot interaction · Social learning

1 Introduction

The objective of our larger research program is to develop the computational underpinnings and algorithms that will allow a robot to learn how to play an interactive game such as Uno, Monopoly, or Connect Four by interacting with a child. We are motivated by potential applications in hospitals and long-term care facilities for children. Moreover, playing interactive games such as these has been shown to contribute to social development [8]. Our intent is to create the underlying theory and algorithms that will allow a child to teach a robot to play the games that the child wishes to play. These games may contain nuanced and individualized rules that change and vary each time the game is played or with each child, yet maintain the same underlying basic structure.

We borrow computational representations from game theory to address this problem. Game theory has been used to formally represent and reason about a

© Springer Nature Switzerland AG 2020
A. R. Wagner et al. (Eds.): ICSR 2020, LNAI 12483, pp. 502–515, 2020.
https://doi.org/10.1007/978-3-030-62056-1_42

number of interactive games such as Snakes and Ladders, Tic-Tac-Toe, and versions of Chess [7]. Game theory offers a collection of mathematical tools and representations that typically examine questions of strategy during an interaction or series of interactions. The term game is used to describe the computational representation of an interaction or series of interactions. Game theory provides a variety of different representations, but the two most common representations are the normal-form game and the extended-form game (described in greater detail below). We use the term "interactive game" to indicate a series of interactions that happen through a board, cards, or play style which has predefined rules, actions, winners and losers. Given this terminology, game theory provides computational representations (games) that can be used to represent interactive games.

Using representations from game theory has advantages and disadvantages. On the positive side, game theoretic representations have been designed to capture the information needed to formally represent an interaction. Moreover, representing interactions as game-theoretic games allows one to apply the tools and results from game theory as needed [11]. For example, calculating Nash equilibrium to influence one's play. On the other hand, game-theoretic representations are not easily learned solely from data [9].

This paper focuses on developing the computational underpinnings necessary for a robot to play the game Connect Four and its variants. In our prior work [2], we made some initial progress towards this goal by showing a robot that can learn the four win conditions of Connect Four. This paper focuses on developing formal underpinnings necessary for the robot to not only learn the four win conditions of Connect Four but also its variants. We further analyze our approach in this paper and quantitatively evaluate the importance of different question types for learning the variants of Connect Four. We believe that the methods developed in this paper will also work for other games and hope to show the general applicability of these techniques in future work.

We seek to develop a system that learns how to play the game by asking people questions about the game. We assume that the robot knows what the game pieces are and how to use them. The focus of this paper is thus on the robot learning the win conditions for the game (i.e. how to win). Our approach leverages the robot's developing representation of the game to guide active learning. Specifically, an evolving game tree indicates to the robot the questions that it must ask in order to gain enough knowledge about the structure of the game to be able play it. Often when one person teaches another person how to play a game they begin by explaining how one wins. Our goal is to develop the computational underpinnings that will allow the robot to learn the win conditions well enough to begin playing, even if the full structure of the game has not been learned. The main contributions of this paper are:

1. A novel approach that utilizes the evolving game-tree representation to ask questions from a user to learn the game's win conditions.
2. An approach that can be used to learn different win conditions patterns on the Connect Four board in addition to the four win conditions of Connect Four (column, row, diagonal, anti-diagonal).

3. An experimental analysis that quantifies the importance of different questions for learning various win conditions on the Connect Four board.

2   Related Work

The field of artificial intelligence has a long history of developing systems that can play and learn games [12]. Recently, significant progress has been made developing systems capable of mastering games such as Chess, Poker and Go using deep reinforcement learning techniques [14]. While deep reinforcement learning clearly provides a method for learning how to strategically play a game, this approach requires large amounts of training data and is fundamentally non-interactive [15]. Interpersonal game learning, on the other hand, is an interactive process involving limited data and examples, and play must begin before the structure of the game is fully known in order to maintain the other person's attention and interest. Moreover, with children in particular, rules change dynamically in order to make play more favorable and exciting for the child. Data-driven retraining may not be possible or desirable in this situation.

Deep learning-based meta-learning has been proposed as a means for managing the problem of large training time and massive data sets [15]. Although these approaches can learn how to do a task by just watching a single or few demonstrations, the new task has to be very similar to the task that the robot was originally trained on i.e. a robot trained on picking objects will not be able to learn how to place an object. Moreover, the initial meta-learning phase to train the robot on the same task still requires a large amount of data and time. Hence, the problem of using guided interaction with a human to teach the robot a new concept remains unsolved. Although, researchers have investigated using meta-learning on goal-oriented tasks such as visual navigation in novel scenes [13], to the best of our knowledge, no meta-learning approach exists for learning interactive games by watching just a single demonstration.

Active learning describes the general approach of allowing a machine learner to actively seek information from a human about a particular piece of data in order to improve performance with less training [3,4,6,10]. Typically active learning is framed around a supervised learning task involving labeled and unlabeled data. There are a number of different active learning strategies, the membership query strategy being most related to our work [1]. For this active learning strategy the learner generates queries for a human focused on specific instances of data. One contribution of this paper (further discussed below) is that we leverage the robot's developing game-theoretic representation to assist with the generation of queries directed at the human. In other words, we use the game theory representation to inform the generation of our queries and to contextualize the resulting answers.

3   Using Game Theory to Represent Interactive Games

An interactive game in which players take alternative turns (like Connect Four) can be represented using extensive-form game format [2]. In Connect Four, play-

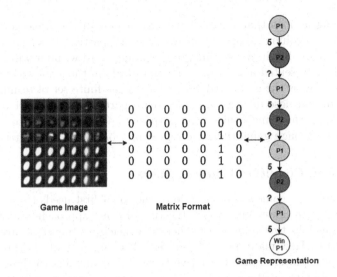

Fig. 1. A demonstration of column win condition in column 5 for Connect Four seen from the robot's perspective is shown on the left. The corresponding extensive-form representation is shown on the right. The numbers along with the arrows show the action numbers chosen by the players (5 by the human and ? by the robot since robot's actions are not shown by the human in the demonstration). Best viewed in color.

ers are required to place round game chips into a 7x6 vertical board. This a perfect information game because at each stage both players have complete information about the state of the game, actions taken by the other player and the actions available to the other player in the next stage. At each turn, both players choose a column to place their respective colored chips, hence in each turn a player has a maximum of seven actions available.

In order to enable play on a robot, images of a Connect Four game (Fig. 1 left) can be directly translated into a matrix format (Fig. 1 middle) indicating which player has pieces occupying specific positions in the matrix. The matrix format simply encodes the piece positions of the players in the Connect Four board. This matrix can be used to generate an extensive-form game tree (Fig. 1 right). The extensive-form representation can also be translated back into the matrix format and used to generate images of what a game should look like if for an extensive-form representation. The generation of these hypothetical game images afford a method for the robot to communicate with person about possible win conditions (or, more generally, states of the game).

4   Learning Win Conditions

A win condition is a terminal game state in which all players either win, lose or draw. We focus on learning these conditions because doing so is necessary for being able to play the game with purpose. For Connect Four, the rules state that selecting actions that create a pattern of four of the same colored chips in either a row, column, diagonal or anti-diagonal pattern for either player is a win. Players can also draw by filling up the game board without winning. A win condition is represented as a terminal node (a leaf) in the game tree, where one of the players wins the game. All games have some finite set of terminal nodes. The ways to win, lose or draw a game create partitions in the set of terminal nodes based on the game's rules. The purpose of our approach is to learn these general rules through game-theoretic representation of the Connect Four game.

4.1   Pre-win Condition Learning Tasks

Prior to learning a game's win conditions, the robot first needs to capture some basic information about the game structure. In our approach, the robot first asks two questions that allow it to generate a skeleton game structure. The two questions are: "How many players can play this game?" and "Is this a type of game in which players take alternative turns?" The answers to these questions allow the robot to create a generic game tree that simply iterates among the different players. We believe that these questions will be necessary to learn any game. For Connect Four answers to the two questions are "two" and "yes", respectively.

The robot also needs to know about the components of the game such as the look of the game board, the game chips and their associated colors, and how to physically perform the actions related to the game. We currently assume that this information is pre-programmed and can be loaded once the robot knows the name of the game. We modified the code available at: https://sdk. rethinkrobotics.com/wiki/Connect_Four_Demo for Connect Four which includes the tools for creating the requisite robot behaviors and identifying the game pieces. This pre-programmed information includes:

- How to physically perform all of the possible actions $\{a_0, a_1, a_2, a_3, a_4, a_5, a_6\}$
- How to convert a game image into the matrix format of the game state (Fig. 1).

4.2   From Game Tree to Active Learning

From the initial information described above, the robot has as generic game tree structure of the game. The only thing missing from the structure are the win conditions. To learn the win conditions of Connect Four and its variants, we use ideas from learning from demonstration and active learning. As a first step the robot asks for a demonstration of a win condition from the human teacher by stating, "Can you please show me a way to win?" It then waits for the person to state, "I am done." The robot converts the image of the board into an extended-form game. For example, Fig. 1 depicts the extensive-form representation of a column win in column 5. Note that this demonstration is not the actual game state as it does not depict the red player's moves. However, the robot knows that play iterates between the two players, from the extensive-form representation of Connect Four, so it marks the moves of the red player as unknown.

The initial game tree that exists after the demonstration (Fig. 1 right) is clearly missing information. Moreover, the initial tree assumes that player 1 (P1) makes the first move. The demonstration also only depicts a single column win, yet a column win can be achieved in any other column. The demonstration by the human provides only a single game tree branch that leads to a terminal node where P1 wins. Yet there are a large number of other game tree branches that can also lead to terminal nodes. Asking the person to demonstrate each game tree branch that is a win condition is not feasible. The robot thus relies on the extensive-form representation of the game to deduce the information missing from the given demonstration. It then focuses its questions to the human on this missing information, ultimately learning all of the tree branches that could lead to a win condition (terminal node) based on the demonstration.

From any given demonstration of a win condition (for example Fig. 1), the following information elements are available:

- **Given Information:** Winning player's actions. In Fig. 1, these actions are {5,5,5,5}
- **Missing Information:** The other player's actions and any actions that do not effect the win condition. In Fig. 1, these actions are missing.
- **Assumptions:** The robot assumes that P1 takes the first action in the game.

Based on the information elements available from the game tree, the robot needs to learn the missing information from the demonstration, confirm the assumptions and learn general rules underlying the given information. These information elements are related to the type of actions that a winning player (P1) and the losing player (P2) can take such that the tree branch leads to a win for P1. Table 2 shows the different questions that the robot needs to ask about both players' actions to learn about the additional information elements about the demonstrated win condition. The questions are pre-programmed in the robot's base knowledge, however when and which questions to ask is guided by the state of the game-tree. Instead of asking the questions verbally (which require a complete dialogue manager), here we present a way for the robot to leverage its ability to convert back and forth between the game state and the game tree. In separate work, we present a dialogue manager than allows the robot to communicate with a human using verbal and visual questions to learn the win conditions [16,17].

To ask about a specific information element, the robot manipulates the game tree representation of the demonstrated win condition to generate an example situation related to the information that the robot needs to confirm. The robot then converts the manipulated game tree into the game state image and shows it to the human accompanied by a simple yes/no question to confirm whether the example game situation is a win. The simplicity of the question ensures that most people, even older children are capable of providing the robot with an answer. Table 1 shows a list of functions available to the robot to manipulate the game tree. These functions are also pre-programmed into the robot's base knowledge.

Table 1. List of functions available to the robot to manipulate the game-theoretic representation of a demonstrated win condition

Function Name	Meaning
Translate($Tree,p,l$)	Change all actions of player p in the $Tree$ by an offset l such that the new actions are between (0-6).
AddAction(x,p)	Add an action x for player p
RemoveAction(x,p)	Remove an action x for player p

Table 2. The robot asks questions about the winning player's (P1) actions, the losing player's (P2) actions and any other actions taken by the players to learn all the possible win branches that lead to the demonstrated win condition. All these questions are guided by the information elements available from the win condition demonstration and the limited preprogrammed knowledge about the game structure.

Question Type	Example Questions
P1 actions	Confirm the total number of actions needed by P1 to win the game; Confirm if the actions for P1 can be translated into the game tree. (Definition of Translate in Table 1)
P2 actions	What actions can be taken by P2 such that P1 still achieves the win conditions shown in the demonstration?
Either player's actions	What other possible actions can be taken by either player on the game board such that P1 achieves the win condition shown in the demonstration?

Since the robot only asks yes/no questions, it can take multiple example situations for the robot to confirm a single information element. For example, related to the demonstration shown in Fig. 1, to confirm the types of actions P2 can take such that P1 still wins, the robot starts with a general question e.g. can P2 take any actions in the game tree? The answer to that is of course No because if P2 takes action 5 (choose column 5) in its first turn P1 will not achieve a column win in column 5. Hence, the robot asks further clarifying questions to confirm that P2 can take all the actions except the ones that are the same as P1's actions (i.e. action 5) for P1 to achieve a column win. This leads to a hierarchical set of questions asked by the robot, starting with a general to more specific questions. With each more specific question, the robot keeps updating the game-tree representation which guides the next question to be asked. These questions are asked in a visual manner as described above.

The overall flow of our approach for learning the game's win conditions is as follows: The robot starts with a demonstration and continues to ask questions from the human until it confirms all the information elements (Table 2) needed to learn the demonstrated win condition. This process can also be terminated

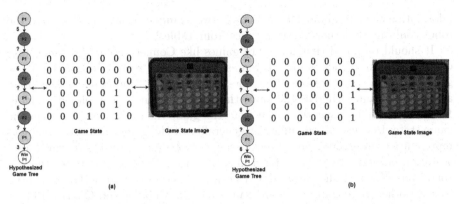

Fig. 2. (a) The hypothesized game tree generated after changing one action of player 1 in the game tree of Fig. 1 (left). (b) The hypothesized game tree generated after changing all the actions of player 1 to column 6 in the game tree of Fig. 1 (left). For both (a) and (b) the matrix format is from the robot's perspective but the game state image is for the human's perspective. The associated game state image is shown on the right. (Best viewed in color)

early if the robot reaches a pre-defined number of questions limit (we set it at 15 questions per win condition for the experiments in this paper).

Example Questions: To show how the robot asks questions from a human, we show an example session related to one of the questions specific to P1's actions (Confirm if actions for P1 can be translated in the game tree (Table 2)). For this example, we consider the column win demonstration shown in Fig. 1. To learn this information from the human, the robot first confirms if the numerical relationship among all the P1 actions matter i.e. all the P1 actions have to be 5. Since translate operation (in Table 1) is used to change all the actions by a particular offset, a question about translation of all the actions will not be needed if any action can be taken by a player for a win. To confirm this, the robot creates the hypothetical game tree by calling functions *RemoveAction(5,1)* and *AddAction(3,1)* in a sequence to change one of the P1's actions and then converts the manipulated game-theoretic structure to the game-state image (Fig. 2 (a)). For the given demonstration, the answer to the accompanied question will be No. Hence, the robot confirms that all the actions of P1 have to be 5. This leads to an update in the game-tree representation as well. Next, using the game-theoretic structure of Connect Four the robot infers that the siblings of action 5 (columns 0–6 except 5) can also lead to a similar win i.e. P1's actions can be translated in the tree by an offset. To confirm this inference, the robot calls the function *RemoveAction(5,1)* four times to remove all the actions for P1 and then calls the function *AddAction(6,1)* four times to add four actions for P1 in column 6. The manipulated game-theoretic structure is then converted to the game-state image (Fig. 2(b)). The answer to the accompanied question with this example will be Yes for the given demonstration. Hence, the robot confirms an information element about P1's actions in two example situations. Similarly, the robot confirms the other question types from Table 2.

It should be noted that for board games like Connect Four, the game state can sometimes provide a better representation of a win condition than the game-theoretic structure but the game-state representation is dependent upon a particular game, whereas the game-theoretic structure is completely general. Furthermore, it is easier to reason from the game-theoretic structure than the game-state. Because of this inherent generality of the game-theoretic format to represent any interactive game, our learning algorithm only relies on this representation of interactive games for asking questions and learning about the win conditions. We have shown in related work that the same approach can be used to learn other more complex board games such as Gobblet and Quarto [16].

5   Experiments

To evaluate this system, we used the Baxter robot manufactured by Rethink robotics. Google's text-to-speech API was used to communicate questions in natural language to the person. The person answered the questions by typing inputs into a computer to avoid errors generated by the speech-to-text conversion process. The experimenter served as the robot's interactive partner for all of the experiments, unless stated otherwise.

5.1   Learning the Four Win Conditions of Connect Four

We hypothesized that the process described in the previous sections would allow the robot to learn the four Connect Four win conditions (four games pieces in a row, column, or diagonal). We tested the process by providing the robot with a single correct demonstration of one type of win condition (e.g. a column win) and a human then correctly answered the robot's questions about the self-generated game situations ("Is this a win for yellow?"). We repeated this process for the other types of win conditions (row, diagonal and anti-diagonal). Next, the robot's ability to use the win conditions to play the game was tested in a real game against a human opponent. We verified that the robot could correctly use the win conditions it had learned by playing 10 games against the experimenter. The robot used a depth-2 minimax strategy to play all 10 games. Out of the 10 games, the robot won 7 times, lost 1 and drew 2 times. We believe the reason it lost a game was because it used a depth-2 minimax strategy which only provides the best move for the next stage of the game, not the overall optimal move. Out of the 7 wins, the robot won twice using a diagonal win, 3 times using anti-diagonal and twice using column win. The robot was defeated by a diagonal win in the one game it lost. For all these games, the robot correctly applied the win conditions and demonstrated its ability to correctly identify if it or the person had won the game. These experiments verify that the robot could learn the win conditions from a single demonstration and by using questions and answers to present the person with different game situations, ultimately arriving at a set of extensive-form games constituting a win.

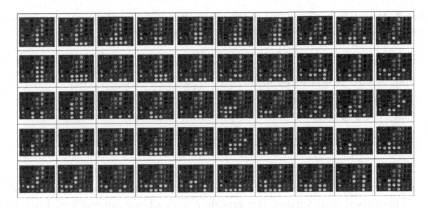

Fig. 3. Fifty different patterns that were learned by the robot as win conditions on the Connect Four board. Only the yellow chips in the patterns are parts of the win conditions, the red chips are simply to create an offset just like in case of diagonal and anti-diagonal win conditions. Best viewed in color.

5.2   Learning Variants of Connect Four

To verify that our method is not simply limited to the four win conditions prescribed by the Connect Four game (patterns of four in a row, column, diagonal or anti-diagonal) the robot's ability to learn different patterns representing different ways to win was tested. We hypothesized that our system could learn an arbitrary pattern as a win condition and use this pattern to play a modified version of the game. To test this hypothesis, fifty different randomly generated patterns were demonstrated to the robot as win conditions on the Connect Four game board (Fig. 3). The experimenter then answered the corresponding questions for each of the demonstrated win conditions. Once these questions were answered, the robot's ability to use the learned win conditions to play 10 games (for each rule, a total of 500 games) was tested. In these games, both the robot and the experimenter took random actions and all the games ended in an average of 20 turns. Since the experimenter and the robot both took random actions, instead of checking the robot's ability to play and win using the learned win conditions we simply checked the robot's ability to successfully recognize the learned win condition when it was reached by either the experimenter or the robot. In game-theoretic terms the robot recognizes that a terminal node has been reached. If the robot recognizes a terminal node and ends the game, this implies that the robot has learned the corresponding win condition. Among the 500 games, there were some games (55 games) when the learned win condition was never achieved by the experimenter or the robot and the game ended in a draw. In all 500 games that did not end in a draw, the robot was able to recognize the learned win condition which shows that the robot successfully learned each different win condition on the Connect Four board. We have already shown in the previous experiment if the robot learns a win condition successfully, it can use the minimax strategy to play against a human user. Future user studies

Table 3. Detection accuracy (%) of the robot after removing different question types (from Table 2) for the four win conditions of Connect Four

Question Type	Row	Column	Diagonal	Anti-diagonal
Min. number of actions for a win	0%	0%	0%	0%
Translation of P1 actions	0%	0%	0%	0%
Effect of P2 actions	13.34%	16.67%	10%	10%
Either Player's Actions	26.67%	90%	20%	16.67%

will evaluate how well the robot can use the win conditions it has learned to play. This experiment verified the generic ability of our approach to learn various home-made win conditions for a game as long as the structure of the game (board, game pieces, actions available to players in a turn etc.) is known.

5.3   Importance of Different Question Types

For the three question types in Table 1, the robot asks a maximum of 11 questions to learn any win condition pattern on the Connect Four board. Among these 11 questions, a maximum of 4 questions are asked specifically about P2's actions, a maximum of 4 questions are asked about P1's actions (2 for confirming minimum number of actions required for a win and 2 for confirming the translation of P1 actions in the tree) and a maximum of 3 questions are asked about other actions taken by either player in the game. We conducted a final experiment to evaluate the importance of each question type for learning the four win conditions of Connect Four.

Hypothesis: All three question types are required to learn all the win conditions of Connect Four.

Experimental Setup: The robot learned the four win conditions of Connect Four with one of the question types removed during each interaction. The question type was removed to test the effect of that question type on learning the win conditions. For the questions specific to P1's actions, we further divided them into two groups: to confirm minimum number of actions required for a win and translation of P1's actions. Hence, the robot was taught each win condition in four different interactions and in each interaction one of the question types was not confirmed by the robot (a total of 4*4=16 interactions). After learning each win condition in an interaction, the robot played a total of 30 games with a simulated opponent (total $4 \times 4 \times 30 = 480$ games). Both the robot and the opponent took random actions in their turns.

Evaluation: Since both players took random actions, for each of the games the robot's ability to detect the correct win condition was tested. Table 3 shows the robot's ability to detect each win condition after removing different question types from the interaction. It is clear that the most important questions are related to P1's actions for all the win conditions. The effect of P2's actions on the win condition learning is also quite drastic. For other actions taken by either player, the column win is least affected (probably because of its simplicity) but all the other win conditions are affected by a significant margin. These results confirm our hypothesis i.e. all question types are necessary for the robot to learn all the win conditions on the Connect Four board but questions specific to P1's actions are the most important.

6   Conclusion

This paper we has demonstrated a method for using game-theoretic representations as a means to structure active learning and incorporate demonstrations in order to learn the win conditions of interactive games. We have presented a preliminary method for using a game tree to generate images of hypothetical game situations that are then presented to a person in order to learn about the game. Our experiments show that a single demonstration accompanied with a few directed questions and answers can be used to learn arbitrary win conditions for the game Connect Four.

We believe, and related work [16] indicates that, the proposed approach can also be used to learn other, more complex games and, perhaps, as a general means for representing interactions between a human and a robot. Ultimately, we believe that this avenue of research may offer a means for a robot to structure its interactions with a person, allowing the robot to bootstrap an interactive exchange by using similar experiences represented as an extended-form game as a model for other upcoming interactions. This paper contributes an important step towards that goal.

The problem of learning games by interactions with humans is far from solved and the current approach has some limitations. We have assumed that the person demonstrates a valid win condition and that they correctly answer the questions posed by the robot. Further, we did not perform experiments with human participants and only the experimenter interacted with the robots. Future work with human participants will shed more light on the applicability of our approach in real-world scenarios.

This paper suggests several interesting avenues for novel research. Perhaps the most obvious is to extend this work to verbal dialog between a human and the robot. It may be possible to use the game tree to ground open ended answers by the human. This work could also be extended to more completely learn the other aspects of playing a game such as how to perform game actions or use the game components (board, tokens). Ultimately, we believe that the proposed techniques take us a step closer to robots that can learn to interact across a wide variety of situations.

Acknowledgements. This work was funded in part by Penn State's Teaching and Learning with Technology (TLT) Fellowship, and an award from Penn State's Institute for CyberScience.

References

1. Angluin, D.: Queries revisited. In: Abe, N., Khardon, R., Zeugmann, T. (eds.) ALT 2001. LNCS, vol. 2225, pp. 12–31. Springer, Heidelberg (2001). https://doi.org/10.1007/3-540-45583-3_3

2. Ayub, A., Wagner, A.R.: Learning to win games in a few examples: using game-theory and demonstrations to learn the win conditions of a connect four game. In: Ge, S.S., et al. (eds.) ICSR 2018. LNCS (LNAI), vol. 11357, pp. 349–358. Springer, Cham (2018). https://doi.org/10.1007/978-3-030-05204-1_34

3. Ayub, A., Wagner, A.R.: Cognitively-inspired model for incremental learning using a few examples. In: Proceedings of the IEEE/CVF Conference on Computer Vision and Pattern Recognition (CVPR) Workshops, pp. 222–223 (2020)

4. Ayub, A., Wagner, A.R.: Online learning of objects through curiosity-driven active learning. In: IEEE RoMan (Workshop on Lifelong Learning for Long-term Human-Robot Interaction) (2020)

5. Ayub, A., Wagner, A.R.: A robot that learns connect four using game theory and demonstrations. arXiv preprint arXiv:2001.01004 (2020)

6. Ayub, A., Wagner, A.R.: Tell me what this is: few-shot incremental object learning by a robot. arXiv:2008.00819 (2020)

7. Berlekamp, E., Conway, J.H., Guy, R.: Winning Ways for Your Mathematical Plays: Games in General. Academic Press (1982)

8. Buchsbaum, D., Bridgers, S., Weisberg, D.S., Gopnik, A.: The power of possibility: causal learning, counterfactual reasoning, and pretend play. Philos. Trans. Royal Soc. B Biol. Sci. **367**, 2202–2212 (2012)

9. Gao, A.X., Pfeffer, A.: Learning game representations from data using rationality constraints. arXiv:1203.3480 [cs.GT] (2012)

10. Settles, B.: Active learning literature survey. In: University of Wisconsin-Madison Department of Computer Sciences (2009)

11. Wagner, A.: Using games to learn games: game-theory representations as a source for guided social learning. In: Agah, A., Cabibihan, J.-J., Howard, A.M., Salichs, M.A., He, H. (eds.) ICSR 2016. LNCS (LNAI), vol. 9979, pp. 42–51. Springer, Cham (2016). https://doi.org/10.1007/978-3-319-47437-3_5

12. Whitehouse, D., Cowling, I.P., Powley, J.E.: Integrating monte carlo tree search with knowledge-based methods to create engaging play in a commercial mobile game. In: Ninth Artificial Intelligence and Interactive Digital Entertainment Conference (2013)

13. Wortsman, M., Ehsani, K., Rastegari, M., Farhadi, A., Mottaghi, R.: Learning to learn how to learn: self-adaptive visual navigation using meta-learning. In: Proceedings of the IEEE Conference on Computer Vision and Pattern Recognition, pp. 6750–6759 (2019)

14. Xenou, K., Chalkiadakis, G., Afantenos, S.: Deep reinforcement learning in strategic board game environments. In: Slavkovik, M. (ed.) EUMAS 2018. LNCS (LNAI), vol. 11450, pp. 233–248. Springer, Cham (2019). https://doi.org/10.1007/978-3-030-14174-5_16

15. Yu, T., Finn, C., Xie, A., Dasari, S., Zhang, T., Abbeel, P., Levine, S.: One-shot imitation from observing humans via domain-adaptive meta-learning. arXiv preprint arXiv:1802.01557 (2018)

16. Zare, M., Ayub, A., Liu, A., Sudhakara, S., Wagner, A., Passonneau, R.: Dialogue policies for learning board games through multimodal communication. In: Proceedings of the 21th Annual Meeting of the Special Interest Group on Discourse and Dialogue, Association for Computational Linguistics, pp. 339–351 (2020)
17. Zare, M., Ayub, A., Wagner, A.R., Passonneau, R.J.: Show me how to win: a robot that uses dialog management to learn from demonstrations. In: Proceedings of the 14th International Conference on the Foundations of Digital Games, pp. 1–7 (2019)

The Importance of the Person's Assertiveness in Persuasive Human-Robot Interactions

Raul Benites Paradeda[1,2,3]($\boxtimes$), Maria José Ferreira[1,2,4], Carlos Martinho[1,2], and Ana Paiva[1,2]

[1] Instituto Superior Técnico, Lisbon, Portugal
{raul.paradeda,maria.jose.ferreira}@tecnico.ulisboa.pt
[2] INESC -ID, University of Lisbon, Lisbon, Portugal
{carlos.martinho,ana.paiva}@inesc-id.pt
[3] State University of Rio Grande do Norte, Natal, Brazil
[4] Interactive Technologies Institute, Funchal, Portugal

Abstract. In social robotics, user-personalised messages is a technique that can be used to persuade a person to do something. Those messages can be personalised according to the personality of whom will receive this message. So, it is essential to know the personality traits of the target. However, we have many traits, e.g., a person can be extroverted, assertive, logical, among others. Because of that, it is challenging to create a strategy that can reach all the traits. In this sense, we chose to focus our persuasion strategies to approach the assertive trait of a person. The strategies were applied in a storytelling scenario with an autonomous social robot behaving assertively using strategies to suggesting the person change the decision with assertive messages and nonverbal persuasive techniques. Besides, we take into account the assertiveness level of the participant to measure if this level influences the acceptance of robot suggestion or not. We observed from the results that a person's assertiveness level might influence the perception regarding the persuasive agent and the decisions-made in the task.

Keywords: Persuasion · Personality traits · Assertiveness · Human-robot interaction

1 Introduction

Researchers have observed that the person's personality identification can be used to achieve some goals, such as identifying the possible consumers of a

We would like to thank the State University of Rio Grande do Norte (UERN), National Council for Scientific and Technological Development (CNPq) program Science without Border: 201833/2014-0 - Brazil and Agência Regional para o Desenvolvimento e Tecnologia (ARDITI) - M1420-09-5369-000001, for PhD grants to the first and second author, respectively. This work was also supported by Fundação para a Ciência e a Tecnologia: (FCT) - UIDB/50021/2020.

A. R. Wagner et al. (Eds.): ICSR 2020, LNAI 12483, pp. 516–528, 2020.
https://doi.org/10.1007/978-3-030-62056-1_43

specific product. Also, it has been found that the inherent behaviour of some characteristics is sought for specific positions. For example, people with more accentuated assertive trait tend to be good leaders [11]. For this reason, the identification of a person's personality trait related to the behaviour that this trait may present has been a strategy used to apply personalised persuasion. For example, if according to the behaviour presented in the task a person is identified as extroverted, it is possible to personalise persuasion strategies for this trait.

Although the idea of using persuasion based on personality seems promising, the development of persuasion strategies that can identify a person's personality trait and can create personalised messages for that identified trait is not a simple task to be carried out. There are some essential factors to consider, some of them are: which trait the strategy should identify; how to identify this trait; how to create tailored-messages to approach the trait identified; how to delivery this tailored-message to the audience; how to recognise if the personalised message was effective; among others.

As is known, a person can present different traits of personality, e.g. a person can be introverted, lovable, logical and neurotic. Besides, each trait individually or combined can identify a behaviour, for example, people considered more assertive are those who exhibit the behaviour of having more self-confidence, sincerity, honesty, among others. Because of the behaviour that each trait can represent, it is essential to identify the traits that can best be addressed for each task. This identification can be made through a person's behaviour in front of a task, the answers provided by a questionnaire, a drawing, among other strategies. After identifying the person's personality traits, it is time to define the strategies of influence that will be used and how to perform the persuasion. For example, the use of gazing at the desired target by a persuasive agent plays a significant role in the persuasion task [9]. Another persuasive strategy is the use of words that can affect our perceptions, attitudes, beliefs and emotions [8]. Therefore, the way words are spoken and connected is essential to influence a person. Plus, the use of strategies that can increase a person's trust level, as performing small-talk before the interaction between the participant and persuasive agent, is essential to boost persuasion efficacy [18,21]. Besides, the interlocutor, such as a storyteller, virtual or physical agent, is unique in terms of gender, age, personality and background, and such characteristics are important to understand the nature of social influence [8]. Therefore, it is essential to define the persuasive agent's behaviour with qualities that can enhance the credibility of this agent. For example, the agent can be perceived with a high level of assertiveness which is a trait widely used in situations where influence is required [17,19,20].

Thus, in the context of the creation of user-tailored technology, all the factor mentioned are aspects of paramount importance to consider. For example, in the field of social robotics, the importance of creating user-personalised messages and techniques to gain trust to influence a person to do something is evident. Because of that, we notice an increasing number of research projects that consider the human's personality as an essential factor [2,7,14]. In this sense, we developed an Interactive Storytelling (IS) scenario with an autonomous social robot behaving assertively to suggest the person to change the decision. Besides, as we perceive that people with a higher level of assertiveness will be harder to influence than people with lower levels, we considered in the persuasion strategies this level of assertiveness. To identify this level, we used a questionnaire that allows the person to make a self-assessment of their level of assertiveness [5]. In addition, as our scenario provides behaviours in situations in which the person must imagine himself, personality theories that classify the traits according to this type of scenario were investigated to identify if other traits stand out in this type of task. As result, the Myers-Briggs Type Indicator (MBTI) [13][1] was the one chosen to use. We observed from the results that a person's assertiveness level might influence the perception regarding the persuasive agent and the decisions-made in the task. Also, regarding the MBTI classification, some traits demand less effort to influence than others and can be approached with more straightforward and less complex strategies.

2   Goals and Hypothesis

This paper describes the study performed to measure the importance of the person's assertiveness in persuasive human-robot interactions. To reach this goal, we combined some persuasion strategies (details in Sect. 3.3) used in previous studies. A between-subject study was performed in which the way the influence applied by the agent was manipulated. This way, we designed two study conditions: **C1)** the agent performs the influence contrary to the participant's personality, and **C2)** the agent performs the persuasion in congruence with the participant's personality. In this sense, the hypotheses defined are as follows:

H1: People with low assertiveness level will perceive the agent differently when the influence is according to their personality than people with high level.

H2: Participants with a higher level of assertiveness are more confident that the decisions made have influenced the course of story than less assertive ones.

H3: People identified with a lack of creativity and difficulty in responding to requests or accepting suggestions according to the MBTI will be the most difficult to persuade in our scenario.

3   Research Methods

3.1   Participants

A convenience sample of 38 participants was recruited on the campus of a technological institute (19 in each condition). Participants were on average 26 years old ($SD = 4.2$), and the majority of them were male (23). In the sample, 13

---

[1] MBTI assumes 16 personality types from the combination of four opposite pairs, representing preferences or dichotomies. The pairs are Extraversion ('E')/Introversion ('I'); Sensing ('S')/iNtuition ('N'); Thinking ('T')/Feeling ('F') and Judging ('J')/Perceiving ('P').

participants reported that they had never interacted with the social robot used in the study, and 7 (seven) had never interacted with a robot before. Eight (8) of the participants informed that they had interacted with a robot before only once, and 23 had already interacted several times with robots.

3.2 Procedures and Measures

Participants were invited to interact with a social robot in IS scenario. Plus, they were requested to perform the role of a country leader that have to make decisions to save their people from the threats from an enemy country (similar in [15]). The participation in this study was designed into three stages:

(1) Pre-interaction: Initially, each participant signed an informed consent before the beginning of the study. Next, the participant was asked to complete the 70-item questionnaire that classifies the MBTI person's personality[2]. Then, to check if the person's perception of the persuasive robotic agent is influenced by the study conditions, the participant was asked to complete the Godspeed questionnaire [3]. Next, the participant was asked to complete a survey to measure her/his level of assertiveness [5]. Finally, a socio-demographic questionnaire was apply for sample characterisation.

(2) Interactive Narrative-Interaction: The participant is invited by the researcher to stand in front of a large touchscreen table where the robotic agent is in the opposite position. On the screen, a central button is shown to start the narrative, and there is a background image in the theme style of the plot (medieval/middle ages) to influence the participant's immersion. Before starting the interaction, the researcher communicates that he is leaving the room, and when the participant is ready to start, s/he must press the button on the middle screen. After the button is pressed, the robot begins a small talk to try to increase the level of trust that a person can have regarding the agent. Firstly, the robot asks what is the participant's name in a complimenting way. After a few seconds of waiting for the participant's answer, the robot, introduces itself telling its role in the scenario. Finally, the storyteller sends good thoughts, praises the participant and explains how the interactive scenario will be performed. After the robot finishes all the utterances, the robot starts telling the story and the table screen changes.

The story was divided into scenes, where each scene is narrated by the storyteller and has a Decision Point (DP), with two options, that shows after the narration. The participant is required makes his intention of the decision and then, the agent performs the persuasion strategy by encouraging to keep the option selected or in opposition to it (details in Sect. 3.3). So, the participant can confirm the intention or change it. If the participant chooses the decision that the persuasive agent had encouraged, the agent will simulate to be happy with the choice; otherwise, the simulation will be anger. After going through

---

[2] To compare the responses of the pre-questionnaire MBTI with the MBTI system classification based on decisions made in the system scenario.

several DPs[3], the story comes to an end with the participant being victorious (defeating the enemy) or forced to pay a tax to the invading nation. Finally, the researcher returns to the room with the post-questionnaire.

(3) Post-interaction: This phase is essential for measuring the effects that the interaction with the storyteller robot had on the participant. The participant is asked to answer questions about his perception of the robot and its assertiveness level. Finally, 5 questions using a 5 points Likert scale from "Strongly Disagree" to "Strongly Agree" are presented to measure the participant's perception regarding the influence of the robot in the decisions. The questions were: I realised that the robot reacted to my decisions; My decisions influenced the events of the story; I recognised the consequences of my decisions; The end of the story depended on my decisions; I believe that the decisions were according to my personality. The total time for the experiment took approximately 60 min, and each participant received a €6 movie ticket for the participation.

3.3   Manipulations

From previous studies, we used the strategy where the agent talks to the person (small-talk) to increase the level of person-agent trust [18]. Also, a MBTI personality identification system based on the decisions made in an IS was used. In sum, in this system each DP measures an MBTI dimension and depending on the decision made by the person, the system assumes that s/he has a specific preference. After the person goes through all the DPs in the task, the system is able to classify the personality [15]. Besides, because of we have the MBTI person's classification from the questionnaire applied before the interaction, it is possible to identify if the person is choosing an option in congruence or against of his personality. So, the agent can perform a persuasion to confirm or change the intention (depending the study condition). We also configured the agent to have an assertive behaviour, the settings change the robot's voice (pitch = x-low and rate = +20%), posture (pride=head position high) and gaze (the agent looks more to the participant) [16]. Combining the previous strategies and settings, we refined and adapted to this study.

Firstly, to improve the personality classification system, we added new DPs measuring the MBTI classification and DPs that measure the influence of the agent without the influence of the person's personality trait. For instance, in a specific decision, the participant may have to choose between presenting the rugs horizontally or vertically. In this case, there is no obvious characteristic of a particular personality trait, such as a decision to have to speak in public or to talk to a few people (that can be used to measure the participant's extrovert or introvert level). At these specific points, the persuasive agent will always convince the participant to change the decision after s/he has informed intention.

Secondly, we developed a strategy where the agent speaks utterances with persuasive arguments, trying to influence the change of decision or encouraging

---

[3] The narrative has a non-linear parallel structure, which makes the story go through different places and situations depending on the final decision at each DP.

confirmation. In the latter case, the agent says that it agrees with the decision and believes that the participant is making the best choice. However, if a change of decision is necessary, the agent uses persuasive resources and cogent arguments. The persuasive resources that we used were empathy-building, data presentation, and developing rethinking (creating doubt). In the first case, the agent informs that it understands the participant's intention. In the second case, the agent presents data contrary to what the participant's intention informs. In the latter case, the agent asks the participant to think better of the decision as it may not be the best decision for his people.

3.4 Materials

In order to validate our hypotheses, a quantitative study was performed using one Emys head robot. The motivation for using this robot is due its ability to display facial expressions simulating emotional feelings [10]. Also, a big Touch-screen table was used to display the interactive story and to allow the participant to indicate the intentions and final decisions. Plus, a speaker was placed near the robot to transmit the verbal utterances (male voice). Moreover, all the participants' interactions were video and sound recorded.

3.5 System Architecture

The architecture used is similar to the one described in [19]. Firstly, the system settings will receive the participant assertiveness level and personality, and the robot settings is settled according to the study condition. Secondly, when the participant starts the storytelling, the Trust Module (TM) and Persuasion Module (PM) are activated. The TM is responsible for enabling the agent to start the small-talk and some features (e.g. mentioning the participant's name, using facial expressions and gazing at the person). PM creates the persuasive gestures for the agent and sends them to the framework responsible for animating it.

After the small-talk finishes, the Interactive Storytelling System (ISS) is started. In this module, all the scenes, immersion elements, text and DP's are arranged accordingly and shown to the participant. After each scene, the PM is called again in order to set the proper persuasive gestures for the agent for the scene. Since each scene has a DP, and the participant needs to give their intention of selection, the robot gestures need to confirm (or not) with it. For this purpose, the PM is activated. If the user intention was according to the agent's wish, the persuasive gestures are going to evoke happiness and decision support. Otherwise, expression of anger and utterances with persuasive arguments will be said trying to make the participant change his mind.

When the agent finishes his argument, the participant is required to make his final decision. Afterwards, his decision is sent to the personality module, which builds his MBTI personality in real-time. Ultimately the PM will generate new persuasive gestures for the agent to align with the participant final decision. Finally, the ISS is called again, and the process starts again for the new scene.

4   Results

To reach the end of the narrative, each participant pass by between 27 to 30 DPs; at each point, the agent interacts influencing the participant to confirm or change the choice intention. From the interactions of all participants, 1117 DPs were analysed. Summarising the interaction: first, the participant must inform the intention, then, the agent performs the influence. So, the participant can change his decision based on the robot's influence or maintain it.

H1-H2 - The Importance of the Person's Assertiveness: The Godspeed answers in the pre- and post- questionnaire were analysed to validate these hypotheses. However, participants' answers were split according to their self-assertiveness level and by condition. To classify the participant's assertiveness level, a variable categorised the participants that scored beneath the middle point of the scale as having a *low level of assertiveness* and all the remaining participants as having a *high level of assertiveness*.

As the data did not present a normal distribution, the non-parametric Wilcoxon test was performed. In the C1 condition (persuasion in opposition to the participant's personality), the results suggest that participants had a different perception of the agent after interacting with it in terms of appearance ($Z = -2.111; p = .035$) and competence ($Z = -2.456; p = .014$) only when the participants have a high level of assertiveness. There was not found sig. diff. when the participant present a low assertiveness level in C1 condition.

Regarding the C2 (the agent tries to influence the participant to chose decisions in congruence with the personality), the people with a high level of assertiveness had a different perception in terms of appearance ($Z = -2.333; p = .020$), consciousness ($Z = -2.157; p = .031$), competence ($Z = -2.226; p = .026$) and intelligence ($Z = -2.070; p = .038$). In the case where the participant present a low level of assertiveness the different perception is in terms of consciousness ($Z = -2.640; p = .008$), friendliness ($Z = -2.460; p = .014$), kindness ($Z = -2.588; p = .010$) and agreeableness ($Z = -2.081; p = .037$).

To test the influence of person's assertiveness level on changing decision, two dichotomous variables were defined, the first reflecting the participant's choice to change their decision or not and the second, related to the level of the participants' self-reported assertiveness. Then, a Kolmogorov-Smirnov observed that the data did not present a normal distribution ($K - S(417) = .391; p < .001$). Then, the statistical results of Spearman's rank-order correlation reveal that there is not a correlation between the person's assertiveness level and changing decision ($r(417) = .046, p = .347$).

Next, a χ^2 test was performed, which revealed a sig. diff. in the distribution of the self-reported assertiveness and the assertiveness level the participants gave to the robotic agent ($\chi^2(1, N = 38) = 15.055; p < .001$). Besides, performing the Spearman's rank-order correlation, the assertiveness level of the participants presented a strong, positive correlation with the level of assertiveness perceived by the storyteller, which was statistically significant ($r(38) = .629, p < .001$). Also regarding the participant's assertiveness level, it was found a positive correlation with the participant's opinion if the decisions influenced into the story, but only when the persuasive agent was influencing according to the participant's personality (C1) ($r(19) = -.499, p = .029$). In C2, there is not a correlation between the person's assertiveness level and if the decisions made influenced the story ($r(19) = -.177, p = .468$).

H3 - MBTI Personality Classification: The intention column in Table 1, shows the number of DPs that the participant informed that were different or congruent with his personality. Final Decision column indicates the number of decisions that participants have chosen different or congruent to the personality.

In 394 intentions that the participants indicated different from their personalities, the majority (i.e. 21.32%) was measuring the Felling (F) preference. In 386 intentions were selected in congruence with the participant's personality. Thinking (T) preference was the one that most of the participants selected according to their personality (i.e. 20.05%). On the other hand, the preference that the participants indicated less intentions different from the personality was iNtuition (N, i.e. 3.55%). The preference congruent to the participant's personality with the lowest matches was iNtuition (N, i.e. 4.57%).

The final decision preference which were different from participant's personality that obtained the majority of choices was Feeling (F, i.e. 24.63%). The preference that had the majority of final decisions chosen according to the participant's personality was Extraversion (E, i.e. 24.34%). In contrast, the preference of the final decisions that obtained the least choice by participants that were different from their personality was iNtuition (N, i.e. 3.81%). The preference that had the least final decisions chosen according to the person's personality was Sensing (S, i.e. 6.45%).

Table 1. Participant's intentions and decisions congruent and different from their personality by preference.

Preference	Intention		Final Decision	
	Different	Congruent	Different	Congruent
E	45 (11.42%)	74 (18.78%)	39 (11.44%)	83 (24.34%)
I	37 (9.39%)	41 (10.41%)	28 (8.21%)	47 (13.78%)
S	64 (16.24%)	21 (5.33%)	55 (16.13%)	22 (6.45%)
N	14 (3.55%)	18 (4.57%)	13 (3.81%)	27 (7.92%)
T	54 (13.71%)	79 (20.05%)	36 (10.56%)	79 (23.17%)
F	84 (21.32%)	54 (13.71%)	84 (24.63%)	72 (21.11%)
J	29 (7.36%)	75 (19.04%)	18 (5.28%)	74 (21.70%)
P	67 (17.01%)	24 (6.09%)	68 (19.94%)	35 (10.26%)
Total	394	386	341	439

In Table 2, it is possible to note that the preference that the participant most changed from a different intention of his personality to a congruent personality decision was Introversion (I, 40.54%). The preference that least changed was Sensing (S, 15.63%). The intention that was congruent with the person's personality, and there was a change of intention to an incongruent personality decision, the preference that most presented this behaviour was Thinking (T, 17.72%). Perceiving (P, 0%) was that least presented the change of intention.

5   Discussion of the Results

H1-H2 - The Weight of the Person's Assertiveness: The level of assertiveness of a person and the situation in which he finds himself can provoke behaviour that can change his lifestyle, making him with more leadership in his attitudes and being able to change his perceptions. Our results show that people with high assertiveness level perceive the persuasive agent different in terms of appearance and competence when the agent influences contrary to their personality. In contrast, this does not happen to people who self-classified as being less assertive. In this case, when the persuasion is against, the perception has not changed in any Godspeed term. However, when the influence effort is according to the person's personality, when the person has a high level of assertiveness, the agent's appearance, consciousness, competence and intelligence score is higher than other terms. Meanwhile, the less assertive people scored higher on the agent in terms of conscience, friendliness, kindness and agreeableness. These results reflect that the person's perception of the persuasive agent can be affected by the person's level of assertiveness and the way the agent performs persuasion.

Although there is a higher number of changes of intention in participants with lower levels of assertiveness than in the participants' with higher levels, it is not possible to correlate the decision change with the participant's assertiveness level. There are some factors that could explain this event, for example, highly

Table 2. Intention Different (ID) of the participant's personality with the Decision Congruent (DC) to the personality, and the Intention Congruent (IC) to the personality with the final Decision Different (DD) from the personality.

Dichotomy	ID x DC	IC x DD
E	8/45 (17.18%)	6/74 (8.11%)
I	15/37 (40.54%)	2/41 (4.88%)
S	10/64 (15.63%)	2/21 (9.52%)
N	3/14 (21.43%)	1/18 (5.56%)
T	20/54 (37.04%)	14/79 (17.72%)
F	14/84 (16.67%)	2/54 (3.70%)
J	11/29 (37.93%)	13/75 (17.33%)
P	12/67 (17.91%)	0/24 (0%)
Total	93	40

assertive participants rate the robot's suggestions low in persuasiveness [4]. In this way, as more assertive is a person, fewer influence effects s/he suffers.

The results suggest a correlation between the participant's level of assertiveness and the level s/he perceived in the persuasive agent. This, evidence that the person's level of assertiveness may influence how assertive this person perceives the person/agent with whom s/he is interacting. However, it is known that many variables can affect this perception and thus warrants further research. We found that assertive people value themselves more and have greater confidence and satisfaction in the decisions they make than less assertive ones [6]. This may be a reason for the correlation found between the person's level of assertiveness and the question about if the decisions made influenced the story when the persuasion is in congruence with the person's personality. Furthermore, this correlation was not found when the persuasion is against the person's personality, this may have happened because the agent has always questioned intentions that are congruent with the person's personality, planting doubts in the decisions made.

H3 - MBTI Personality Classification: People with a preference for Feeling (F) were those who most chosen options considered against their personality in the intentions and final decisions. In opposite, participants with a preference for Thinking (T), were those who most that pointed out the options following their personality in the intentions and, in the final decisions were the participants with preferences for Extroversion (E). The behaviour found in this study emphasises the behavioural characteristics of a person who has a preference from Feeling. For example, the person with this preference tries to make a decision by assessing what is best for the people involved. Given the narrative of the scenario, where some situations have to make drastic decisions to avoid the country extermination, people with 'F' preference had to go against their natural behaviour to save the people. Thus, it can be inferred that the reason was stronger than the emotion or that the person's inner emotional response modulated and guided cognition to allow adaptive responses to the environment. When a person exhibits a certain level of emotion in the decisions made, s/he assesses in detail if the event, stimulus, or thought (or any of these together) leads to a reward or punishment, thereby producing an emotion [22]. Thus, options where there was a sense of reward rather than punishment, may have been chosen by these participants, even if the decision was against to their personality behaviour.

Regarding the majority of intentions responses to be in accordance with the preference Thinking (T), this behaviour fortifies the MBTI characteristics for this preference. People with this preference are considered logical and impersonal in their decisions, not letting their desires overflow. Thus, they are unaffected by emotions and make decisions based on their knowledge and understanding of the situation. Within an interactive strategy game scenario, where decisions must be thought before decisions are made, these characteristics stand out.

The behaviour of the Extraverts (E, those who most have chosen decisions in congruence with their personality) is in line with the MBTI characteristics for this preference. People with 'E' preference prefer to act, reflect and act again. With this behaviour, some participants may have chosen the intention on instinct, without much thought. So, the influence of the agent may have caused the reflection of the chosen intention and, consequently, the decision change.

In this scenario, participants with a preference for iNtuition (N) were those who least chose intentions and final decisions that are related to their preferences. Meanwhile, the Sensing (S) presented the lowest percentage for final decisions congruent with the participant's personality. According to the MBTI, sensing people pay more attention to physical reality and care more about what is current. People with a higher preference for the 'N' prefer to solve problems between different ideas and possibilities, and are more interested in doing things that are new and different, and prefer to see the big picture and try to find the facts. Given the above, it is perceptible that the scenario being an imaginary medieval story with decisions with only two options does not provide a conducive environment for assessing and measuring the 'SN' dimensions.

Regarding the change of intention, the agent was more effective when the participant's intention was different from their personality. The preference where participants most changed intention was Introversion (I). Different was the Sensing (S) preference, that participants least changed their intention. The behaviour of the 'I' preference may suggest that when the participant indicates an option against the personality, the intention change can be achieved with a persuasion strategy. The difficulty to make the intention-change in 'S' could be because of the developed scenario, since this preference has as features to have people paying more attention to physical reality and caring more about what is current.

The persuasion strategy was more effective when the intention is congruent with the participant's personality for the Thinking (T) and Judging (J) preferences, and less effective for the Perceiving (P). This behaviour is in line with the characteristics of these preferences in the MBTI. 'T' people may have regarded the agent's persuasive arguments as logical explanations and solutions to the impasse of choosing a decision option. In the meantime, people with a preference for 'J' like to have things decided, and the agent's suggestions may have caused the feeling of decision. The lack of decision change in 'P' must be due to the characteristic of these people to like to understand and adapt to the world rather than organize it.

6 Conclusion

The effectiveness of persuasion strategies can be improved when the personality traits of the target audience are considered [1], allowing to adapt the persuasive appeals to the psychological needs of the target audience [12]. Besides, personality is essential when there is audience interaction [14]. For this reason, the study of personality traits for persuasion purposes has been increasingly researched and applied in some areas of study, such as marketing, governance, education, health, games, human-robot interaction, among others.

This paper describes a methodology that can be used to fill some gaps in studies that use personality traits and persuasion in HRI, showing evidence that data on levels of assertiveness, environment, persuasive agent and personality traits need to be collected to create a personalised scenario with an acceptable level of persuasiveness. Besides, we bring the idea that there may be a perception of greater influence being inferred when the changes in decisions are in line with the personality. Finally, the branch of psychology that works with personality traits and social influence needs to be more explored, especially when in a context of narrative stories and social robotics.

References

1. Adnan, M., Mukhtar, H., Naveed, M.: Persuading students for behavior change by determining their personality type. In: 2012 15th International Multitopic Conference (INMIC), pp. 439–449. IEEE (2012)
2. Aly, A., Tapus, A.: A model for synthesizing a combined verbal and nonverbal behavior based on personality traits in human-robot interaction. In: Proceedings of the 8th ACM/IEEE international conference on Human-robot interaction, pp. 325–332. IEEE (2013)
3. Bartneck, C., Kulić, D., Croft, E., Zoghbi, S.: Measurement instruments for the anthropomorphism, animacy, likeability, perceived intelligence, and perceived safety of robots. Int. J. Soc. Robot. 1(1), 71–81 (2009)
4. Chidambaram, V., Chiang, Y., Mutlu, B.: Designing persuasive robots: how robots might persuade people using vocal and nonverbal cues. In: Proceedings of the seventh annual ACM/IEEE international conference on Human-Robot Interaction, pp. 293–300. ACM (2012)
5. Costa, P.T., McCrae, R.R.: Revised NEO Personality Inventory (NEO PI-R) and NEP Five-Factor Inventory (NEO-FFI). professional manual. Psychological Assessment Resources Lutz, FL (1992)
6. Elliott, T.R., Gramling, S.E.: Personal assertiveness and the effects of social support among college students. J. Couns. Psychol. 37(4), 427 (1990)
7. Fung, P., Dey, A., Siddique, F.B., Lin, R., Yang, Y., Wan, Y., Chan, R.H.Y.: Zara the supergirl: an empathetic personality recognition system. In: Proceedings of the 2016 Conference of the North American Chapter of the Association for Computational Linguistics: Demonstrations, pp. 87–91 (2016)
8. Gass, R.H., Seiter, J.S.: Persuasion: Social Influence and Compliance Gaining. Routledge (2015)
9. Iio, T., Shiomi, M., Shinozawa, K., Akimoto, T., Shimohara, K., Hagita, N.: Investigating entrainment of people's pointing gestures by robot's gestures using a woz method. Int. J. Soc. Robot. 3(4), 405–414 (2011)
10. Kkedzierski, J., Muszyński, R., Zoll, C., Oleksy, A., Frontkiewicz, M.: Emys-emotive head of a social robot. Int. J. Soc. Robot. 5(2), 237–249 (2013)
11. Lazenby, C.L., et al.: Assertiveness and leadership perceptions: the role of gender and leader-member exchange. Ph.D. thesis, Lethbridge, Alta.: University of Lethbridge, Faculty of Management (2015)
12. Matz, S.C., Kosinski, M., Nave, G., Stillwell, D.J.: Psychological targeting as an effective approach to digital mass persuasion. Proc. Natl Acad. Sci. 114(48), 12714–12719 (2017)
13. Myers, I., Myers, P.: Gifts differing: understanding personality type. Davies-Black Pub (1980)
14. Oreg, S., Sverdlik, N.: Source personality and persuasiveness: big five predispositions to being persuasive and the role of message involvement. J. Pers. 82(3), 250–264 (2014)

15. Paradeda, R., Ferreira, M.J., Martinho, C., Paiva, A.: Using interactive storytelling to identify personality traits. In: Nunes, N., Oakley, I., Nisi, V. (eds.) ICIDS 2017. LNCS, vol. 10690, pp. 181–192. Springer, Cham (2017). https://doi.org/10.1007/978-3-319-71027-3_15

16. Paradeda, R., Ferreira, M.J., Martinho, C., Paiva, A.: Communicating assertiveness in robotic storytellers. In: Rouse, R., Koenitz, H., Haahr, M. (eds.) ICIDS 2018. LNCS, vol. 11318, pp. 442–452. Springer, Cham (2018). https://doi.org/10.1007/978-3-030-04028-4_51

17. Paradeda, R., Ferreira, M.J., Martinho, C., Paiva, A.: Would you follow the suggestions of a storyteller robot? In: Rouse, R., Koenitz, H., Haahr, M. (eds.) ICIDS 2018. LNCS, vol. 11318, pp. 489–493. Springer, Cham (2018). https://doi.org/10.1007/978-3-030-04028-4_57

18. Paradeda, R.B., Hashemian, M., Rodrigues, R.A., Paiva, A.: How facial expressions and small talk may influence trust in a robot. In: Agah, A., Cabibihan, J.-J., Howard, A.M., Salichs, M.A., He, H. (eds.) ICSR 2016. LNCS (LNAI), vol. 9979, pp. 169–178. Springer, Cham (2016). https://doi.org/10.1007/978-3-319-47437-3_17

19. Paradeda, R.B., Ferreira, M.J., Oliveira, R., Martinho, C., Paiva, A.: The role of assertiveness in a storytelling game with persuasive robotic non-player characters. In: Proceedings of the the Annual Symposium on Computer-Human Interaction in Play. October 22–25, 2019. Barcelona, Spain, pp. 453–465 (2019)

20. Paradeda, R., Ferreira, M.J., Oliveira, R., Martinho, C., Paiva, A.: What makes a good robotic advisor? the role of assertiveness in human-robot interaction. In: Salichs, M.A., et al. (eds.) ICSR 2019. LNCS (LNAI), vol. 11876, pp. 144–154. Springer, Cham (2019). https://doi.org/10.1007/978-3-030-35888-4_14

21. Paradeda, R.B., Martinho, C., Paiva, A.: Persuasion based on personality traits: using a social robot as storyteller. In: Proceedings of the Companion of the 2017 ACM/IEEE International Conference on Human-Robot Interaction, HRI '17, ACM, New York, NY, USA, pp. 367–368 (2017)

22. Rolls, E.T.: Emotion and Decision Making Explained. Oxford University Press (2013)

Modeling Trust in Human-Robot Interaction: A Survey

Zahra Rezaei Khavas[1]([✉])(iD), S. Reza Ahmadzadeh[2](iD), and Paul Robinette[1](iD)

[1] Electrical and Computer Engineering, University of Massachusetts Lowell, Lowell, MA 01854, USA
Zahra_RezaeiKhavas@student.uml.edu, paul_robinette@uml.edu
[2] Computer Science, University of Massachusetts Lowell, Lowell, MA 01854, USA
reza_ahmadzadeh@uml.edu

Abstract. As the autonomy and capabilities of robotic systems increase, they are expected to play the role of teammates rather than tools and interact with human collaborators in a more realistic manner, creating a more human-like relationship. Given the impact of trust observed in human-robot interaction (HRI), appropriate trust in robotic collaborators is one of the leading factors influencing the performance of human-robot interaction. Team performance can be diminished if people do not trust robots appropriately by disusing or misusing them based on limited experience. Therefore, trust in HRI needs to be calibrated properly, rather than maximized, to let the formation of an appropriate level of trust in human collaborators. For trust calibration in HRI, trust needs to be modeled first. There are many reviews on factors affecting trust in HRI [22], however, as there are no reviews concentrated on different trust models, in this paper, we review different techniques and methods for trust modeling in HRI. We also present a list of potential directions for further research and some challenges that need to be addressed in future work on human-robot trust modeling.

Keywords: Human-robot interaction · Human-robot trust · Modeling trust in HRI · Trust calibration in HRI · Trust measurement

1 Introduction

Trust is one of the essential factors in the development of constructive relationships, including relationships among human individuals and automation. We can mention trust as an overarching concern that affects the effectiveness of a system, especially in terms of safety, performance, and use rate [31]. Having this concern in mind, trust has become a critical element in the design and development of automated systems [35]. Autonomous systems are being designed and developed with increased levels of independence and decision-making capabilities, and these capacities will be efficient in uncertain situations [55].

Human-robot trust is an important branch of Human-Robot Interaction (HRI), which has recently gained increasing attention among scholars in many

© Springer Nature Switzerland AG 2020
A. R. Wagner et al. (Eds.): ICSR 2020, LNAI 12483, pp. 529–541, 2020.
https://doi.org/10.1007/978-3-030-62056-1_44

disciplines, such as Computer Engineering [49], Psychology [22], Computer Science [10] and Mechanical Engineering [52]. Trust is a significant factor that needs to be taken into consideration when robots are going to work as teammates in human-robot teams [19], used as autonomous agents [57], or where robots are going to be used in a complex and dangerous situations [42, 49]. In many cases, trust is the main factor determining how much a robotic agent would be accepted and used by the human [44].

Weak partnerships resulting from inappropriate or non-calibrated trust between humans and robots might cause misuse or disuse of a robotic agent. Misuse refers to the failures that occur due to a user's over-trust of the robotic agent (e.g., accepting all the solutions and results presented by the robot without questioning). In contrast, disuse refers to the failures that occur due to human under-trust to the robotic agent (e.g., rejecting the capabilities of a robotic agent) [31]. To prevent human operators' misuse and disuse of robots, trust needs to be calibrated. We need to model trust to generate a measure of it and to enable proper trust calibration [43].

There are many reviews available in HRI which are mostly concentrated on factors affecting trust [22,55], but none of them is concentrated on modeling trust and different trust models in HRI. This document's purpose is to review different studies concentrated on trust modeling in HRI. This review starts by defining trust, followed by summarizing factors affecting trust, reviewing studies focused on modeling trust, and a summary of input and output elements to the trust models. We conclude with a discussion of the shortcomings and challenges of trust modeling and future avenues of research.

2   Definition of Trust in HRI

According to psychologists, trust is a mental state of a human [2]. Numerous researchers have extensively explored the notion of trust for decades. Trust is not limited to just interpersonal interactions. It underlies different forms of interactions, such as banks' interaction with customers, governments with citizens, employers with employees, etc., [61]. Therefore, we can say trust can affect human-robot interaction, as it can affect a human user or collaborator's willingness to assign tasks, share information, cooperate, provide support, accept results, and interact with a robot [16].

As trust is one of the necessities for building a successful human-robot interaction, we need to create methodologies to model, measure, and calibrate trust. The first step for modeling trust is a clear definition of trust. However, despite the broad efforts and number of studies concentrating on trust, there is little consensus on a single definition, as the definition of trust is heavily dependent on the context in which trust is being discussed [6]. This is highlighted, for instance, in [41], where trust is defined as *"the reliance by one agent that actions prejudicial to the well-being of that agent will not be undertaken by influential others"*. Around each application and domain that robots are used, trust needs to be defined, measured and explored explicitly. For example, in high-risk robotic applications such as emergency evacuation robots [49], the definition of trust might differ substantially from low-risk robotic applications such as border tracking robots [65]. One of the most thorough definitions of trust, which is deployed by many other studies concentrated on human-robot trust, is by Lee and See [31]. They define trust from the perspective of automation. This definition was generated by reviewing many other studies concentrated on defining trust and was complementary for many other works. They define trust as: *"the attitude that an agent will help achieve an individual's goals in a situation characterized by uncertainty and vulnerability"*. This definition of trust is accepted and used by many studies on trust in HRI. Wagner et al. [61] also provided a comprehensive definition for trust: *"a belief, held by the trustor, that the trustee will act in a manner that mitigates the trustor's risk in a situation in which the trustor has put its outcomes at risk"*. They also provided a model for determining if an interaction demands trust or not. All these definitions have one thing in common, that is: "whether robot's actions and behaviors correspond to human's interest or not?" To address this concern in each robotic application trust needs to be modeled based on human interests in that domain.

3   Factors Affecting Trust

Studies on factors affecting trust in HRI can be considered an extension to the studies on factors affecting human-automation trust. In [31], the authors review the factors affecting trust in humans and generalize these factors to factors affecting trust in automation. Many other studies also review and analyze factors affecting trust in human-automation Interaction (HAI) [23,55]. However, robots differ from other forms of automation in many cases, such as mobility, embodiment, and unfamiliarity to the general public. Therefore, factors affecting trust in HRI need to be investigated separately.

Hancock et al. [22] provides a meta-analysis of factors affecting trust in HRI and classifies these factors in three categories each consist of two subcategories: 1. Human-related factors (i.e., including ability-based factors, characteristics); 2. Robot-related factors (i.e., including performance-based factors, attribute-based factors); and 3. Environmental factors (i.e., including team collaboration, tasking). In this study, we review and classify recent studies on factors affecting trust with a similar classification basis as in [22] with some updates in categories and subcategories. We classify factors affecting trust in HRI into three categories: 1. Robot-related factors (including robot-performance, robot-appearance, and robot-behaviors), 2. Human-related factors and 3. Task and Environment-related factors. Table 1 shows our classification of factors affecting trust. Most of these factors are similar to the ones that are mentioned in Hancock et al. [22]. However, some factors are excluded as recent studies paid less attentions to them and some new factors that are stressed more in recent studies are added to this table. Some factors are also classified under different categories here in this work compared to [22].

1. **Robot-Related Factors:** Robot-related factors have the greatest effect on the trust in HRI [22]. This justifies the great number of studies concentrated on robot-related factors. We classify robot-related factors under three subcategories:

   (a) Performance-related factors: These factors determine the quality of an operation performed by the robot from the human operator's point of view. Of these factors we can mention *reliability, faulty behavior, frequency of fault occurrence* [12], *timing of error* [33], *transparency, feedback* [39,53], *level of situation awareness* [5], *false alarms* [69], and *level of autonomy* [28].

   (b) Behavior-related factors: Advancements in robotic systems in recent years have caused people to consider them more like teammates than tools. Increased autonomy of robots caused an increase in the perceived intelligence of robots by humans. These advancements altered the form of HRI to a more naturalistic interaction [43]. Approaching a more human-like interaction with robots cause people to consider the intention of a robot's behavior. Some general behaviors of the robot such as *likeability* (e.g., gaze behaviors and greeting) [38], *proximity* (e.g., physical and physiological proximity) [38,40,62], *engagement* [50], *confess to the reliability* [39,63] and *harmony of robot personality with the task* (e.g., introverted robotic security guard and an extroverted robotic nurse) [59] can affect formation and maintenance of trust. There are also some specific behaviors of robots that can affect trust repair after failure or wrong and misleading action such as *apology, making excuses* or *explanations* and *dialogues* [33,39,48,56,58].

   (c) Appearance-related factors: People consider the personality of a robot based on the robot's appearance and behavior during interactions. Some features in robot appearance such as *anthropomorphism* [39], *gender* [59], *harmony of task with robot's appearance* [50], and *similarity with human collaborator* [70] affect trust in HRI.

2. **Human-Related Factors:** Although, according to [22], human-related factors have the least effect on trust, they are important in the formation and fluctuation of trust during human-robot interaction. Many studies investigated the effect of these factors on trust. Of these factors, individual's *gender, subjective feeling* toward robots [40], *initial expectations* of people toward automation [69], *previous experience* of the individuals with robots [62], *culture* [32] and also the human's *understanding of the system* [43] are some of the human-related factors that are addressed in different studies.

3. **Task and Environment-Related Factors:** Based on Hancock et al. [22], task and environment-related factors have the second greatest effect on human-robot trust. Many factors related to the task type and location such as *rationality* and *revocability* of the tasks [53], *risk* and *human-safety* [49], *workload* [12], *nature of the task* (e.g., nurse or security robot) [59], *task duration* [62,69], *in-group membership* [19,46], *physical presence of robot* [3,39] and *task site* [28] are thoroughly investigated by researchers in HRI.

Table 1. Factors affecting development of trust in human-robot interaction

1. Robot-Related		3. Task & Environment-Related
(a) Performance-Related	**(c) Appearance-Related**	Nature of task [28,59]
Dependability, reliability and error [11,12,33,39,49,53]	Similarity with operator [70]	Physical presence of robot in task site [3,39]
Level of [18,28]	Gender [59,70]	In-group membership [19,46]
Situation awareness, feedback and Transparency [5,11,39,63]	Harmony of appearance with task [50]	Duration of interaction [62,69]
(b) Behavior-Related	Anthropomorphism [39]	Task site [28]
Dialogues [33]	**2. Human-Related**	Revocability [53]
Proximity [38,40,62]	Personality [53]	Rationality [3,49,53]
Likeability and friendliness [38]	Culture [32]	Risk [28,49,70]
Personality (harmony with task) [59]	Understanding of the system [43]	Workload, complexity and required level of multi tasking [12]
Confess to reliability [39,63]	Demographics [34,40]	
Apology for failure [39,56,58]	Subjective feeling [40,69]	
Engagement [50]	Experience with robots [34]	

4   Current Research on Trust Modeling

Trust in HRI has a lot in common with trust in HAI, which has been studied at length. Muir et al. [37] found the available definitions for trust between humans inconsistent with the nature of HAI based on the multidimensional construct of trust. She defined a trust models for HAI which was based on model of human expectation of automation proposed by Barber et al. [4]. Lee and Moray [29] built upon Muir's strategy for modeling trust, which was identifying independent variables that influence trust, and introduced another model for trust. Later, other researchers have modeled the operator's trust in automation, considering more factors affecting trust [14,24,31]. These models were finally classified into five groups [36]: regression-based models [29,37], time series models [30], qualitative models [47], argument based probabilistic models [9], and neural net models [14].

There are many similarities between trust in HRI and trust in HAI. However, most of the models generated for modeling trust in HAI are inconsistent with the needs of HRI. According to Desai [13] *"these models do not consider some factors that appear while working with robots such as situational awareness, usability of the interface, physical presence of robots (co-located with human or remote-located), limitations and complexities of the operating environment, workload, task difficulty, etc. which influence HRI considerably"*. Desai et al. [13] introduced a schematic of a model considering some factors affecting human-robot trust in conjugate with factors affecting human-automation trust. Yagoda et al. [68] introduced one of the very first models for human-robot trust based on the different dimensions of a human-robot interaction task and validity assessment of each of these directions by subject matter experts (SMEs) in the HRI. Desai et al. [10] also was one of the pioneers in modeling trust in HRI. They generated a more detailed model for trust in human and autonomous robot tele-operation.

This model used the Area Under Trust Curve (AUTC) measure to account for an individual's entire interactive experience with the robot.

According to several studies, there is a strong correlation between the level of trust in human-robot teammates with the performance of the robotic agent's work, and it also impacts their interaction quality [10,31]. According to Xu [66], high levels of trust among human-robot teammates often demonstrate great synergy, in which matched decision-making capabilities of the human member in the team complements the exhaustive controlling and executing capabilities of the robotic agent. In contrast, a low level of trust among human-robot teammates might cause a human to refuse to delegate tasks to the robotic agent or sometimes decide to disable the robotic agent [66]. Since there is often a high correlation among trust and performance of the work in human-robot collaboration, trust has been modeled based on the performance in many studies [52,64]. Most of these performance-based trust models are used as a feedback loop to adjust actual performance of the robot to the human's expectation of its performance to convince a human to act trusting toward robot. There are also some trust models based on the performance of robot operations, which are not aimed to modify the performance of collaboration. For example, in [45] a performance-based trust model for multi-robot tasks is designed to detect robotic agents that are not reliable. Then, less reliable agents are assigned to do less critical tasks or sometimes disregarded while assigning tasks. On the other hand, the human-robot collaboration's performance can also be modeled based on trust [16,17]. These models are used to modify the robot's trust-related behavior to manage the overall performance of the collaboration.

A prevalent class of human-robot collaborations is supervisory collaboration in which the human plays the role of supervisor and the robot plays the role of worker. The supervisor delegates tasks to the worker and oversees the performance of the operation. The supervisor also has the authority to take control of the robot when the robot is doing something wrong. The model of trust for supervisory collaboration presented in [64] is based on trust in between-human collaboration. It generates a quantity showing the compatibility of robot performance with the human expectation, enabling the robot to modify its performance to fulfill human expectations and improve trust. Later this trust model was improved [67], and more factors affecting trust in supervisory collaboration such as failure rate in the autonomous agent and the rate of supervisor intervention were involved in designing the trust model. The Online Probabilistic Trust Inference Model (OPTIMo) [65] is another model of trust in the supervisory collaboration introduced by the same research group. This model formulates Bayesian beliefs over the human's trust status based on the robot's performance on the task over time to generate a real-time estimate of the human's trust.

When trust can be modeled and measured in a real-time manner in human-robot collaboration, it can help the robot repair trust whenever the human starts under-trusting the robot [65]. A real-time model of trust (trust-POMDP) for human-robot peer-to-peer collaboration is introduced in [8], which integrates measured trust in the robot's decision-making. The trust-POMDP model closes the loop between measured trust by the real-time trust model and robot decision-making process to maximize collaboration performance. This model grants a robot the ability to influence human trust systematically to reduce and increase trust in over-reliance and under-reliance situations, respectively.

Hancock et al. [22] provided a meta-analysis of a great number of factors affecting trust in HRI, and quantitative measurement for the effect of human-based, robot-based, and environment-based factors on trust. Later they developed a model of human-robot team trust based on their findings in the meta-analysis [22]. In addition to the effect of three classes of factors affecting trust introduced in the prior work, they considered the effects of training and design implications on the final model of trust [54].

Some recent studies in trust modeling use subjective trust measurement techniques in companions with objective trust measurement techniques. These techniques are deployed in both HAI and HRI for increasing the accuracy and robustness of trust measurements. There are some studies in human-automation trust, human-computer interaction, and human trust in artificial intelligence that use psycho-physiological measurements for trust modeling [1,20,21]. Khalid et al. [27] also introduce a trust model in HRI, which uses facial expressions, voice features, and extracted heart rate features in combination with the self-reported trust of humans to model trust. This trust model classifies the trust level into one of the low, natural, and high trust levels using a Neuro-fuzzy trust classifier.

5 Trust Model: Inputs and Outputs

Trust models formulate the effect of factors on the formation and variation of trust in robots. In fact, trust models use factors affecting trust to estimate trust. Since these factors vary in different domains and environments, input factors to the trust models vary based on the application domain. For example, Robinette et al. [51] models trust in emergency evacuation based on the situational risk (e.g., amount of danger perceived by the human in the environment around him) and agent risk (e.g., agent's behavior and appearance) to model perceived trust by the human and the human's decision to trust the robot's guidance or not. In contrast, [64] proposes a trust model for a supervisory collaboration and formulates trust as a function of the robot's success and failure in performing the task. The output of this trust model is closing the loop between human trust and robot function by adjusting the robot's action to improve the collaboration efficiency. Finally, [68] proposes a more general trust model based on team configuration, task, system, context, and team process to scale trust for trust measurement.

Many of the studies on modeling trust in HRI consider the performance of collaboration as one of the main input elements for their model [17,52,65]. Most of these models consider the effect of performance in conjugate with some other factors. For instance, the OPTIMo probabilistic trust model [65] uses rates of robot's failures, and human interventions in conjugate with task performance as inputs to the model to estimate the human's degree of trust in a robotic teammate. Meanwhile, [17] uses the operator's perception of system capabilities, past experience, and training to assess initial trust. Trust gets updated in a loop based on system performance, cognitive workload, and frequency of changes from tele-operation to autonomous operation. This trust model's output is a measure of gain and loss of trust and the impact of these changes of trust on collaboration performance. Sadrfaridpour et al. [52] models trust based on human performance (i.e., muscles fatigue and dynamics of recovery), robot performance (i.e., speed of robot doing the specific task), workload and human expectation of task performance. The output of this model is feedback to the robot to adjust its performance according to operator desires.

6   Conclusion and Future Work

Most of the existing trust models in HRI are developed for a specific form of human-robot interaction or a specific type of robotic agent. For example, in [51], a model of trust is specified for evacuation robots; in [12] the trust model is specified on robots with shared control, and in [65] the generated model is usable for supervisory collaboration. As each of these trust models belongs to a specific domain, they can not be compared with each other, and there is no scale to evaluate their accuracy. A general model of trust is needed in HRI to evaluate the accuracy of other trust models. Such a model can be applied to any robotic domain and even can be deployed by newly emerged robotic areas and eliminate the need for new trust models for these areas.

Trust is a subject of interest for research in many other fields such as psychology, sociology, and even physiology. In these fields, other indicators of trust are used for trust measurement. For example, some studies use physiological indicators, such as oxytocin-related measures [15,25,60], and objective measures, such as trust games that assess actual investment behavior [7,26]. These trust assessment methods can be used in HRI to develop a trust model that is independent of the countless parameters that affect trust.

Many studies examined the effect of robot failure on trust [12,39,49,53]. However, there are limited studies focused on modeling the effect of robot failure on trust. While Desai et al. [10] investigated the effect of robot's reduced performance and timing of performance reduction on the operator's trust in a tele-operation human-robot interaction, the effect of trust violation needs to be investigated more deeply. Different forms of trust violation in different robotic domains need to be explored. A variety of factors affecting trust-loss and trust-repair after trust violation, such as task type, risk, robot type, robot behavior, etc. need to be taken into account in modeling the effect of robot failure on trust. Modeling fluctuations of trust in a human after a robot failure would help estimate the time required for human trust to tend to a steady-state and formulate timing of trust repair after trust violation.

Both modeling trust and modeling the effects of failure on trust need to be explored in a more general context. Since there are many different factors affecting trust, it will be challenging to develop a conclusive trust model that incorporates all of these factors. Therefore, future research into trust modeling in HRI needs to be more focused on developing general models of trust, which are based on measures other than the countless factors affecting trust. Such models would not be affected by the emergence of new factors affecting trust in existing or new robotic domains and eliminate the need to develop new trust models for new domains of the ever-evolving world of robotics.

References

1. Ajenaghughrure, I.B., Sousa, S.C., Kosunen, I.J., Lamas, D.: Predictive model to assess user trust: a psycho-physiological approach. In: Proceedings of the 10th Indian Conference on Human-Computer Interaction, pp. 1–10 (2019)
2. Atoyan, H., Duquet, J.R., Robert, J.M.: Trust in new decision aid systems. In: Proceedings of the 18th Conference on l'Interaction Homme-Machine, pp. 115–122 (2006)
3. Bainbridge, W.A., Hart, J.W., Kim, E.S., Scassellati, B.: The benefits of interactions with physically present robots over video-displayed agents. Int. J. Soc. Robot. 3(1), 41–52 (2011). https://doi.org/10.1007/s12369-010-0082-7
4. Barber, B.: The logic and limits of trust (1983)
5. Boyce, M.W., Chen, J.Y., Selkowitz, A.R., Lakhmani, S.G.: Effects of agent transparency on operator trust. In: Proceedings of the Tenth Annual ACM/IEEE International Conference on HRI Extended Abstracts, pp. 179–180 (2015)
6. Cameron, D., et al.: Framing factors: the importance of context and the individual in understanding trust in human-robot interaction (2015)
7. Chang, L.J., Doll, B.B., van't Wout, M., Frank, M.J., Sanfey, A.G.: Seeing is believing: trustworthiness as a dynamic belief. Cogn. Psycol. 61(2), 87–105 (2010)
8. Chen, M., Nikolaidis, S., Soh, H., Hsu, D., Srinivasa, S.: Planning with trust for human-robot collaboration. In: Proceedings of the 2018 ACM/IEEE International Conference on HRI, pp. 307–315 (2018)
9. Cohen, M.S., Parasuraman, R., Freeman, J.T.: Trust in decision aids: a model and its training implications. In: Proceedings of the Command and Control Research and Technology Symposium. Citeseer (1998)
10. Desai, M.: Modeling trust to improve human-robot interaction. Ph.D. Thesis, University of Massachusetts Lowell (2012)
11. Desai, M., Kaniarasu, P., Medvedev, M., Steinfeld, A., Yanco, H.: Impact of robot failures and feedback on real-time trust. In: 2013 8th ACM/IEEE International Conference on HRI, pp. 251–258. IEEE (2013)
12. Desai, M., et al.: Effects of changing reliability on trust of robot systems. In: 2012 7th ACM/IEEE International Conference on HRI, pp. 73–80. IEEE (2012)
13. Desai, M., Stubbs, K., Steinfeld, A., Yanco, H.: Creating trustworthy robots: lessons and inspirations from automated systems (2009)
14. Farrell, S., Lewandowsky, S.: A connectionist model of complacency and adaptive recovery under automation. J. Exp. Psychol. Learn. Mem. Cogn. 26(2), 395 (2000)
15. Ferreira, F., Lopes da Costa, R., Pereira, L., Jerónimo, C., Dias, Á.: The relationship between chemical of happiness, chemical of stress, leadership, motivation and organizational trust: a case study on Brazilian workers. The relationship between chemical of happiness, chemical of stress, leadership, motivation and organizational trust: a case study on Brazilian workers (2), pp. 89–100 (2018)
16. Freedy, A., DeVisser, E., Weltman, G., Coeyman, N.: Measurement of trust in human-robot collaboration. In: 2007 International Symposium on Collaborative Technologies and Systems, pp. 106–114. IEEE (2007)

17. Gao, F., Clare, A., Macbeth, J., Cummings, M.: Modeling the impact of operator trust on performance in multiple robot control. In: 2013 AAAI Spring Symposium Series (2013)
18. Goodrich, M.A., Olsen, D.R., Crandall, J.W., Palmer, T.J.: Experiments in adjustable autonomy. In: Proceedings of IJCAI Workshop on Autonomy, Delegation and Control: Interacting with Intelligent Agents, Seattle, WA, pp. 1624–1629 (2001)
19. Groom, V., Nass, C.: Can robots be teammates? Benchmarks in human-robot teams. Interact. Stud. **8**(3), 483–500 (2007)
20. Gulati, S., Sousa, S., Lamas, D.: Modelling trust: an empirical assessment. In: Bernhaupt, R., Dalvi, G., Joshi, A., K. Balkrishan, D., O'Neill, J., Winckler, M. (eds.) INTERACT 2017. LNCS, vol. 10516, pp. 40–61. Springer, Cham (2017). https://doi.org/10.1007/978-3-319-68059-0_3
21. Gulati, S., Sousa, S., Lamas, D.: Design, development and evaluation of a human-computer trust scale. Behav. Inf. Technol. **38**(10), 1004–1015 (2019)
22. Hancock, P.A., Billings, D.R., Schaefer, K.E., Chen, J.Y., De Visser, E.J., Parasuraman, R.: A meta-analysis of factors affecting trust in human-robot interaction. Hum. Factors **53**(5), 517–527 (2011)
23. Hoff, K.A., Bashir, M.: Trust in automation: integrating empirical evidence on factors that influence trust. Hum. Factors **57**(3), 407–434 (2015)
24. Itoh, M., Tanaka, K.: Mathematical modeling of trust in automation: trust, distrust, and mistrust. In: Proceedings of the Human Factors and Ergonomics Society Annual Meeting, vol. 44, pp. 9–12. SAGE Publications Sage CA (2000)
25. Johnson, N.D., Mislin, A.A.: Trust games: a meta-analysis. J. Econ. Psychol. **32**(5), 865–889 (2011)
26. Keri, S., Kiss, I., Kelemen, O.: Sharing secrets: oxytocin and trust in schizophrenia. Soc. Neurosci. **4**(4), 287–293 (2009)
27. Khalid, H.M., et al.: Exploring psycho-physiological correlates to trust: implications for human-robot-human interaction. In: Proceedings of the Human Factors and Ergonomics Society Annual Meeting, vol. 60, pp. 697–701. SAGE Publications Sage CA, Los Angeles (2016)
28. Lazanyi, K., Maraczi, G.: Dispositional trust–do we trust autonomous cars? In: 2017 IEEE 15th International Symposium on Intelligent Systems and Informatics (SISY), pp. 000135–000140. IEEE (2017)
29. Lee, J., Moray, N.: Trust, control strategies and allocation of function in human-machine systems. Ergonomics **35**(10), 1243–1270 (1992)
30. Lee, J.D., Moray, N.: Trust, self-confidence, and operators' adaptation to automation. Int. J. Hum.-Comput. Stud. **40**(1), 153–184 (1994)
31. Lee, J.D., See, K.A.: Trust in automation: designing for appropriate reliance. Hum. Factors **46**(1), 50–80 (2004)
32. Li, D., Rau, P.P., Li, Y.: A cross-cultural study: effect of robot appearance and task. Int. J. Soc. Robot. **2**(2), 175–186 (2010)
33. Lucas, G.M., et al.: Getting to know each other: the role of social dialogue in recovery from errors in social robots. In: Proceedings of the 2018 ACM/IEEE International Conference on HRI, pp. 344–351 (2018)
34. M Tsui, K., Desai, M., A Yanco, H., Cramer, H., Kemper, N.: Measuring attitudes towards telepresence robots. Int. J. Intell. Control Syst. 16 (2011)
35. Martelaro, N., Nneji, V.C., Ju, W., Hinds, P.: Tell me more designing HRI to encourage more trust, disclosure, and companionship. In: 2016 11th ACM/IEEE International Conference on HRI, pp. 181–188. IEEE (2016)

36. Moray, N., Inagaki, T.: Laboratory studies of trust between humans and machines in automated systems. Trans. Inst. Measur. Control **21**(4–5), 203–211 (1999)
37. Muir, B.M.: Trust in automation : Part I. Theoretical issues in the study of trust and human intervention in automated systems. Ergonomics **37**(11), 1905–1922 (1994)
38. Mumm, J., Mutlu, B.: Human-robot proxemics: physical and psychological distancing in human-robot interaction. In: Proceedings of the 6th International Conference on HRI, pp. 331–338 (2011)
39. Natarajan, M., Gombolay, M.: Effects of anthropomorphism and accountability on trust in human robot interaction. In: Proceedings of the 2020 ACM/IEEE International Conference on HRI, pp. 33–42 (2020)
40. Obaid, M., Sandoval, E.B., Złotowski, J., Moltchanova, E., Basedow, C.A., Bartneck, C.: Stop! That is close enough. How body postures influence human-robot proximity. In: 2016 25th IEEE International Symposium on Robot and Human Interactive Communication (RO-MAN), pp. 354–361. IEEE (2016)
41. Oleson, K.E., Billings, D.R., Kocsis, V., Chen, J.Y., Hancock, P.A.: Antecedents of trust in human-robot collaborations. In: 2011 IEEE International Multi-Disciplinary Conference on Cognitive Methods in Situation Awareness and Decision Support (CogSIMA), pp. 175–178. IEEE (2011)
42. Ososky, S., Sanders, T., Jentsch, F., Hancock, P., Chen, J.Y.: Determinants of system transparency and its influence on trust in and reliance on unmanned robotic systems. In: Unmanned Systems Technology XVI, vol. 9084, p. 90840E. International Society for Optics and Photonics (2014)
43. Ososky, S., Schuster, D., Phillips, E., Jentsch, F.G.: Building appropriate trust in human-robot teams. In: 2013 AAAI Spring Symposium Series (2013)
44. Parasuraman, R., Riley, V.: Humans and automation: use, misuse, disuse, abuse. Hum. Factors **39**(2), 230–253 (1997)
45. Pippin, C., Christensen, H.: Trust modeling in multi-robot patrolling. In: 2014 IEEE International Conference on Robotics and Automation (ICRA), pp. 59–66. IEEE (2014)
46. Rau, P.P., Li, Y., Li, D.: Effects of communication style and culture on ability to accept recommendations from robots. Comput. Hum. Behav. **25**(2), 587–595 (2009)
47. Riley, V.: Operator reliance on automation: theory and data. In: Automation and Human Performance: Theory and Applications, pp. 19–35 (1996)
48. Robinette, P., Howard, A.M., Wagner, A.R.: Timing is key for robot trust repair. ICSR 2015. LNCS (LNAI), vol. 9388, pp. 574–583. Springer, Cham (2015). https://doi.org/10.1007/978-3-319-25554-5_57
49. Robinette, P., Li, W., Allen, R., Howard, A.M., Wagner, A.R.: Overtrust of robots in emergency evacuation scenarios. In: 2016 11th ACM/IEEE International Conference on HRI, pp. 101–108. IEEE (2016)
50. Robinette, P., Wagner, A.R., Howard, A.M.: Building and maintaining trust between humans and guidance robots in an emergency. In: 2013 AAAI Spring Symposium Series (2013)
51. Robinette, P., Wagner, A.R., Howard, A.M.: Modeling human-robot trust in emergencies. In: 2014 AAAI Spring Symposium Series (2014)
52. Sadrfaridpour, B., Saeidi, H., Burke, J., Madathil, K., Wang, Y.: Modeling and control of trust in human-robot collaborative manufacturing. In: Mittu, R., Sofge, D., Wagner, A., Lawless, W.F. (eds.) Robust Intelligence and Trust in Autonomous Systems, pp. 115–141. Springer, Boston, MA (2016). https://doi.org/10.1007/978-1-4899-7668-0_7

53. Salem, M., Lakatos, G., Amirabdollahian, F., Dautenhahn, K.: Would you trust a (faulty) robot? Effects of error, task type and personality on human-robot cooperation and trust. In: 2015 10th ACM/International Conference on HRI, pp. 1–8. IEEE (2015)

54. Sanders, T., Oleson, K.E., Billings, D.R., Chen, J.Y., Hancock, P.A.: A model of human-robot trust: theoretical model development. In: Proceedings of the Human Factors and Ergonomics Society Annual Meeting, vol. 55, pp. 1432–1436. SAGE Publications Sage CA, Los Angeles (2011)

55. Schaefer, K.E., Chen, J.Y., Szalma, J.L., Hancock, P.A.: A meta-analysis of factors influencing the development of trust in automation: implications for understanding autonomy in future systems. Hum. Factors **58**(3), 377–400 (2016)

56. Sebo, S.S., Krishnamurthi, P., Scassellati, B.: "I don't believe you": investigating the effects of robot trust violation and repair. In: 2019 14th ACM/IEEE International Conference on HRI, pp. 57–65. IEEE (2019)

57. Selkowitz, A., Lakhmani, S., Chen, J.Y., Boyce, M.: The effects of agent transparency on human interaction with an autonomous robotic agent. In: Proceedings of the Human Factors and Ergonomics Society Annual Meeting, vol. 59, pp. 806–810. SAGE Publications Sage CA, Los Angeles (2015)

58. Strohkorb Sebo, S., Traeger, M., Jung, M., Scassellati, B.: The ripple effects of vulnerability: the effects of a robot's vulnerable behavior on trust in human-robot teams. In: Proceedings of the 2018 ACM/IEEE International Conference on HRI, pp. 178–186 (2018)

59. Tay, B., Jung, Y., Park, T.: When stereotypes meet robots: the double-edge sword of robot gender and personality in human-robot interaction. Comput. Hum. Behav. **38**, 75–84 (2014)

60. Uvnas-Moberg, K., Petersson, M.: Oxytocin, a mediator of anti-stress, well-being, social interaction, growth and healing. Z. Psychosom. Med. Psychother. **51**(1), 57–80 (2005)

61. Wagner, A.R., Arkin, R.C.: Recognizing situations that demand trust. In: 2011 RO-MAN, pp. 7–14. IEEE (2011)

62. Walters, M.L., Oskoei, M.A., Syrdal, D.S., Dautenhahn, K.: A long-term human-robot proxemic study. In: 2011 RO-MAN, pp. 137–142. IEEE (2011)

63. Wang, N., Pynadath, D.V., Hill, S.G.: Trust calibration within a human-robot team: comparing automatically generated explanations. In: 2016 11th ACM/IEEE International Conference on HRI, pp. 109–116. IEEE (2016)

64. Xu, A., Dudek, G.: Trust-driven interactive visual navigation for autonomous robots. In: 2012 IEEE International Conference on Robotics and Automation, pp. 3922–3929. IEEE (2012)

65. Xu, A., Dudek, G.: Optimo: Online probabilistic trust inference model for asymmetric human-robot collaborations. In: 2015 10th ACM/IEEE International Conference on HRI, pp. 221–228. IEEE (2015)

66. Xu, A., Dudek, G.: Maintaining efficient collaboration with trust-seeking robots. In: 2016 IEEE/RSJ International Conference on Intelligent Robots and Systems (IROS), pp. 3312–3319. IEEE (2016)

67. Xu, A., Dudek, G.: Towards modeling real-time trust in asymmetric human–robot collaborations. In: Inaba, M., Corke, P. (eds.) Robotics Research. STAR, vol. 114, pp. 113–129. Springer, Cham (2016). https://doi.org/10.1007/978-3-319-28872-7_7

68. Yagoda, R.E., Gillan, D.J.: You want me to trust a robot? The development of a human-robot interaction trust scale. Int. J. Soc. Robot. **4**(3), 235–248 (2012). https://doi.org/10.1007/s12369-012-0144-0

69. Yang, X.J., Unhelkar, V.V., Li, K., Shah, J.A.: Evaluating effects of user experience and system transparency on trust in automation. In: 2017 12th ACM/IEEE International Conference on HRI, pp. 408–416. IEEE (2017)
70. You, S., Robert Jr, L.P.: Human-robot similarity and willingness to work with a robotic co-worker. In: Proceedings of the 2018 ACM/IEEE International Conference on HRI, pp. 251–260 (2018)

Using AI-Enhanced Social Robots to Improve Children's Healthcare Experiences

Mary Ellen Foster[1]([✉]), Samina Ali[2], Sasha Litwin[3], Jennifer Parker[4],
Ronald P. A. Petrick[5], David Harris Smith[6], Jennifer Stinson[3],
and Frauke Zeller[7]

[1] University of Glasgow, Glasgow, UK
maryellen.foster@glasgow.ac.uk
[2] University of Alberta, Edmonton, AB, Canada
[3] The Hospital for Sick Children, Toronto, ON, Canada
[4] IWK Health Centre, Halifax, NS, Canada
[5] Heriot-Watt University, Edinburgh, UK
[6] McMaster University, Hamilton, ON, Canada
[7] Ryerson University, Toronto, ON, Canada

Abstract. This paper describes a new research project that aims to develop an autonomous and responsive social robot designed to help children cope with painful procedures in hospital emergency departments. While this is an application domain where psychological interventions have been previously demonstrated to be effective at reducing pain and distress using a variety of devices and techniques, in recent years, social robots have been trialled in this area with promising initial results. However, until now, the social robots that have been tested have generally been teleoperated, which has limited their flexibility and robustness, as well as the potential to offer personalized, adaptive procedural support. Using co-design techniques, this project plans to define and validate the necessary robot behaviour together with participant groups that include children, parents and caregivers, and healthcare professionals. Identified behaviours will be deployed on a robot platform, incorporating AI reasoning techniques that will enable the robot to adapt autonomously to the child's behaviour. The final robot system will be evaluated through a two-site clinical trial. Throughout the project, we will also monitor and analyse the ethical and social implications of robotics and AI in paediatric healthcare.

Keywords: Socially assistive robotics · Child-robot interaction

1 Introduction

Children experience pain and distress in clinical settings every day, with the negative consequences of unaddressed pain producing both short-term (e.g.,

A. R. Wagner et al. (Eds.): ICSR 2020, LNAI 12483, pp. 542–553, 2020.
https://doi.org/10.1007/978-3-030-62056-1_45

fear, distress, inability to perform procedures) and long-term (e.g., needle phobia, anxiety) effects [15,24]. A range of psychological interventions have been clinically demonstrated to be effective for managing procedural pain, including breathing exercises, child-directed distraction, nurse-led distraction, and combined cognitive-behavioural interactions [5], with these interventions successfully delivered through a variety of mechanisms including bubble machines, distraction cards, kaleidoscopes, music therapy, and virtual reality games [29].

Recently, several studies have explored the use of social robots in this context, specifically providing psychological interventions during needle-based procedures [2,12,27]. The results of these studies have generally been positive, showing high acceptance among the target population as well as promising initial clinical results. However, these studies have all been hindered by a critical technical limitation: in all cases, the robots were remotely operated and employed purely scripted behaviour with very limited autonomy and responsiveness, diminishing the flexibility and robustness of its behaviour as well as its potential to offer personalized, adaptive procedural support to children.

This paper describes a new project aimed at addressing this limitation by developing and evaluating a clinically relevant and responsive AI-enhanced social robot. We believe that interaction with this sort of adaptive and socially-intelligent robot can effectively distract children during painful clinical procedures, thereby reducing pain and distress. The added autonomy of the system has the potential to increase the effectiveness of robot interventions while also making them more practical and robust for clinical applications. We also plan to explore the social context in which such robots are deployed, ensuring that the robot's role is ethically appropriate.

2   Background

This project builds on previous work in several areas: the use of socially assistive robots in healthcare, the use of artificial intelligence for decision making in social robots, and the general study of the role of AI and robotics in paediatric healthcare contexts.

2.1   Socially Assistive Robotics in Healthcare

This work falls into the area of Socially Assistive Robotics (SAR) [8], the specific area of social robotics where the goal is for the robot to create a close and effective interaction with a human partner for the purpose of providing assistance and achieving measurable progress in a defined domain. SAR have been used successfully in a wide range of healthcare contexts. In adults, robots have been used to improve the cognitive abilities of Alzheimer's patients [26], to alleviate feelings of loneliness and depression in the elderly [30], and to help adults with autism to improve work-related social skills [14]. For children, a significant application of SAR has been in the context of autism, where robots have been used for diagnosis, intervention, and therapy, and have been shown to improve clinical outcomes including verbalisation, socialisation, and emotional expression [4]; the fact that children often perceive social robots as something between a companion animal and a pet has meant that they have also been used for play therapy and social learning [3].

In a recent medical scoping review, Dawe et al. [6] surveyed the potential uses of social robotics in children's healthcare contexts and found potential benefits of using social robots to help children who require short- and long-term hospitalisation, as well as intensive care. This review also identified several important gaps in this research area, which we plan, in part, to address. First, most studies have used relatively small sample sizes, non-clinical trial designs, and had acceptability as the main outcome; larger sample sizes and more robust, patient-oriented healthcare outcomes are needed. Also, while it appears that human facilitators play a key role in influencing the outcome of the interaction, the role of these humans has not been extensively studied. Finally, they identified an urgent need to increase the autonomy of the robots to improve robustness and adaptability.

The specific goal of our project is to investigate the use of SAR to reduce children's acute distress and pain in the clinical setting. Trost et al. [28] recently examined eight studies where a robot was used to reduce children's pain and distress: overall, while the results seem promising and several studies suggest that the robots succeeded in reducing pain, there is also a need for improved methodology and measures to draw conclusions. In particular, the authors suggest more effective interventions could be created by ensuring that healthcare experts and engineers collaborate from the start, and that user and family partners contribute to a user-centred design process. Our proposed work includes input from all such groups as part of the research team collaboration.

2.2 Using AI for Action Selection in Social Robotics

A fundamental component in any social robot is the action selection system: the robot must monitor the social situation and make high-level decisions as to which spoken, non-verbal, and task-based actions should be taken next by the system as a whole. It is also crucial not only to choose the appropriate action, but also to monitor the state of the world as detected by the sensors: particularly in the context of an embodied interaction with a robot, it is likely that the predicted state will often differ from the sensed world state, due to both the unexpected behaviour of the human interaction partners as well as the inherent uncertainty involved in sensing and acting in the physical world.

The majority of social robotics systems generally use either scripted behaviour for action selection, or else use machine learning approaches to learn the correct responses to user actions given sample inputs. We instead adopt a third approach and plan to use automated planning techniques [10] as the basis for high-level action selection and monitoring. One current social robot which incorporates aspects of automated planning is the MuMMER social robot [16], which combines planning for action selection with a more traditional dialogue manager. The most similar approach to ours is the JAMES social robot bartender [17,18], which directly used an AI planner to choose all of the robot actions. Recent work on explainable planning [9] has also highlighted the links between planning and user interaction.

2.3   Ethical Aspects of AI in Paediatric Healthcare

As AI systems such as robots grow more pervasive in daily life, understanding the impact of such systems on society has become ever more crucial. For social robots, in particular, an important consideration is determining the social role that the robot should play [23], as well as an ethical and appropriate means of making the capabilities of the robot clear. Most existing literature on ethical aspects of AI in the healthcare setting often focuses on AI diagnosis tools [21].

With the increased awareness of AI and other related topics, such as autonomous systems, robotics, or surveillance, the need and desire for more information on the end-user side has also increased. However, as in other studies involving media literacy, topics like data privacy are not often addressed in a user-focused manner. Livingstone [13] and colleagues [25] have researched media literacy regarding children's needs and perceptions when it comes to their data and online behaviour and found, for example, that (a) children's concepts and perceptions of AI and data privacy often differs from adults' understandings, (b) children consequently might have different questions, and (c) children will respond differently when provided with information about such topics.

3   Overview of This Project

Building on previous work in this area, we are developing and evaluating an autonomous, AI-enabled social robot designed to help children deal with procedural pain in emergency rooms. The behaviour of the robot will be based on psychological interventions that have been demonstrated to be effective in this context, with the details refined through a co-design process with all relevant stakeholders. The system will be tested in the target environment throughout the project period, culminating in a two-site randomised clinical trial at the end of the project. The target robot platform is the Nao robot from SoftBank Robotics (Fig. 1), which has been widely used in child-robot interaction studies, including several in the identical clinical context we are targeting [2,12].

Concretely, this project is addressing the following research questions:

1. When developing an autonomous, socially intelligent robot designed to alleviate children's distress and pain in a clinical context, what behaviours are desirable and feasible to implement with the current robot technology?
2. Can an autonomous, socially intelligent robot alleviate children's distress and pain in a clinical setting, compared to standard techniques?
3. What is the appropriate and ethical way to communicate the role and capabilities of a social robot to children and their caregivers?

To explore these questions we are employing a range of interdisciplinary techniques: the robot behaviours will be defined and developed through a co-design

Fig. 1. A child interacting with the Nao robot

approach that includes children, family members, and healthcare providers; the robot software will be implemented using state-of-the-art AI techniques, and will be evaluated using approaches from usability testing; the clinical trial will be carried out using standard tools and techniques; while the investigation of ethical and social implications will rely on techniques from content analysis.

4   Co-design and Usability Studies

At a high level, the robot will be designed to deliver psychological interventions that have been proven effective for children undergoing clinical procedures. The details of the exact behaviours and features to be included will be developed through a co-design approach involving a number of relevant groups—children, parents/caregivers, as well as healthcare providers (HCPs)—utilising the principles and stages of user-centred interaction design [1,19]. Co-design participants will be involved throughout the project from an initial co-design phase to determine the needs of all participants, to a usability study phase where the system prototypes will be tested, and a final clinical trial and evaluation phase.

4.1   Co-design

The overall objective of the co-design study is to determine the desired behaviours and features for the social robot from the perspectives of children, parents/caregivers, and HCPs in the emergency department. In particular, the co-design process will attempt to answer the following questions:

1. What are the perceived distraction needs of children undergoing painful procedures in a clinical setting?
2. What are children's perceptions on the use of an AI-enhanced social robot to help them reduce pain and distress when undergoing a painful clinical procedure? What features, functionality, content, and other usability-related aspects would they like in such a robot?

3. What are the perceptions of parents/caregivers of children undergoing painful procedures with respect to social robots?
4. What are the perceptions of HCPs with respect to such robots?
5. What essential features, functionality, and content do HCPs believe should be included in a robot designed for children undergoing painful procedures?
6. How do the views of children, parents/caregivers, and HCPs compare?

Using a prospective descriptive qualitative design, the research team will conduct semi-structured focus groups and individual interviews with children, parents/caregivers, as well as HCPs recruited from two Canadian children's hospitals, with different groups at each site (e.g., 5–7 year olds, 8–11 year olds, parents/caregivers, and HCPs). Children will be included in the study if they are in the appropriate range and require intravenous insertion (IVI), and also meet other medical and practical criteria; parents/caregivers will be included if they have a child who meets the inclusion criteria; while HCPs will include any clinical staff (e.g., nurse, physician, child life specialist) at either site. Each focus group session will be video- and audio-recorded, with a trained researcher taking detailed notes and a second researcher moderating the session via focused open-ended questions. Questions will be based on our previous experience of acute pain management and of conducting focus group needs assessments related to robotic technologies. The interviews will explore core aspects of design, interaction features, and potential direct and indirect impacts of the whole system.

4.2 Usability

The initial co-design studies will be used to inform the behaviour and features incorporated into the robot system. As the system prototypes become available, usability studies will be conducted to evaluate and refine the robot system until it is deemed acceptable and safe for children in a hospital setting undergoing painful procedures. Children and their parents/caregivers at our partner hospitals will take part in usability testing.

Once a child has interacted with the robot for 5–10 min (the typical time required for a painful procedure such as IVI), a separate interview with both the child and the caregiver will be conducted. The child will be asked a series of standardised open-ended questions regarding acceptability of the AI-enhanced social robot, any adverse events, and recommendations for improvement. The procedure will be video recorded in order to analyse interactions between the child and the robot at a later time.

This procedure will be repeated until data saturation, or the point where no new information is gleaned from interviewing (expected to occur after 2–3 testing cycles). Information collected in early interviews will be used to inform later interviews using a constant comparative method. Any problematic issues with the robot system intervention that arise during testing will be communicated to the technical team. All interactions with the system will also be logged to help the robot system developers improve the system.

5   Technical Development

Informed by the findings from the co-design and usability studies, the robot system will be developed to flexibly and autonomously adapt its behaviour to the needs of the children, incorporating components for social signal processing, goal-directed action selection, and execution monitoring and recovery. In particular, the following components are being developed as part of the software architecture for the robot as shown in Fig. 2:

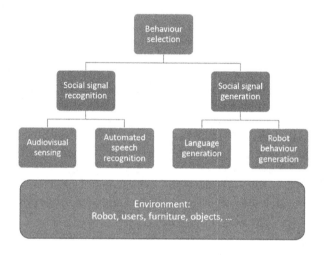

Fig. 2. Software architecture for the robot system.

Social signal recognition. A fundamental task in the system is to use the information from the robot's built-in audio-visual sensors—potentially combined with environmental sensors if necessary—to determine the state of the child, as well as any adults in the area. The particular states to be detected will be determined through a combination of the capabilities of the sensors, as well as the states determined to be relevant from the co-design studies. Based on the detected verbal and non-verbal cues employed by all humans in the vicinity of the robot, we will estimate the socially and psychologically relevant information about their states, such as attitudes, emotions, and intention. In particular, we plan to use a neural-network approach to detect the states, similar to the approach of [22] to automatically detect children's attachment status.

Behaviour selection. Based on the interaction strategies identified in the co-design studies, as well as the detected social user actions and social states arising from the social signal recognition process, the system will choose appropriate high-level actions to be performed by the robot. Actions will be selected by a high-level automated planning component that combines theory-of-mind reasoning with efficient action selection techniques [17]. Building on a previously successful epistemic planning framework [18], generated plans will support both task-based robot action and human-robot interaction, with robot actions that include asking questions, giving information, and performing engaging behaviours such as dancing, among other possibilities.

Social signal generation. The output of the behaviour selection process is a high-level behaviour specification, represented by a set of high-level actions. The role of social signal generation is to convert these high-level actions into concrete robot-level actions that can be executed on the robot platform. As output, this component will produce fully-specified multimodal behaviour plans, including verbal and non-verbal actions. The output will be coordinated temporally and spatially for execution on the robot.

Execution monitoring and recovery. The system will monitor the changes to the world state (as detected by the social signal recogniser) while the actions selected by the behaviour selection component and elaborated by the social signal generator are executed by the robot. Due to the inherent uncertainty of the robot sensors, as well as the unpredictable behaviour of humans, it is likely that the predicted world state will often differ from the actual world state. The monitoring system will detect such mismatches and will determine whether the execution of the current high-level plan should continue or whether a new plan is needed, invoking the behaviour selection mechanism as necessary to identify new actions to execute.

All software components will be developed and integrated into a single system that will run on the target Nao robot platform. For integration, we will use the Robot Operating System (ROS) [20], a standard, open source robotics platform that provides the necessary technical interfaces and middleware to allow independently developed components to be combined into novel integrated robot systems. The use of ROS will allow existing open-source components to be easily integrated into the system and will also permit the software developed during the project to be released and reused by others.

6   Clinical Trial

In the final phase of the project, we will carry out a clinical trial of the developed robot system. The goal of this clinical trial is to test the primary hypothesis of the project: that interaction with a robust, adaptive, socially intelligent robot can effectively distract children during IVI, thereby reducing their distress and pain. The two-armed, randomised controlled superiority trial will be conducted at the same two Canadian paediatric emergency departments where the co-design and usability studies are being carried out, and will be preregistered with clinicaltrials.gov.

Each participant will be randomly assigned to the control or intervention group. The control group will receive departmental standard of care which will include topical anesthetic cream (mandatory) and may include parent/caregiver support, child life services, nursing support, etc. At present, there is no single established distraction therapy or routine that is consistently employed for IV procedures within the target emergency departments. Thus, for pragmatic and ethical considerations, the new study intervention will be compared to what is currently already in practice (i.e., standard of care). Details of the planned clinical trial are as follows.

Eligibility Criteria. These will be the same as for the co-design and usability studies, with the addition that children who participated in one of those studies must be excluded.

Objectives. Our primary objective is to pragmatically compare patient-reported distress and pain with the use of distraction (via the robot developed in this project) to standard care in children.

Primary Research Questions. This trial will address two main research questions: Does interaction with a socially intelligent, autonomous humanoid robot reduce the reported distress associated with IVI, as measured by the Observational Scale of Behavioural Distress-Revised (OSBD-R [7])?, and Does interaction with a robot reduce the reported pain of IVI, as measured by the Faces Pain Scale – Revised (FPS-R [11])?

Outcomes. The primary outcomes will be observed distress, as measured by the Observational Scale of Behavioural Distress-Revised (OSBD-R) and self-reported pain, as measured by the Faces Pain Scale-Revised (FPS-R). Secondary outcomes will include measuring parental anxiety, and examining the association between parental anxiety and child outcomes.

Randomisation will be determined using a secure online randomisation tool. We plan to collect a range of data including demographic information, video of the intervention; pre- and post-procedure ratings of child pain (FPS-R) and parental anxiety; plus satisfaction ratings from the clinical personnel and the family. Overall, we aim to recruit 80 patients with usable data, which will provide sufficient power to potentially find a difference in both primary outcomes, using appropriate statistical tests to evaluate the research questions.

7 Ethical and Social Implications

In parallel to the co-design, software implementation, and clinical trial tasks of the project, we will also examine the role of social robots in children's healthcare settings, employing a user-centric approach that acknowledges the needs of patients and caretakers to understand more about AI and how it affects them directly and indirectly. This work will be divided into three main tasks.

First, we will conduct an exhaustive, multi-disciplinary literature review on AI, ethics, and healthcare, focusing on the literature/research from social sciences, humanities, human-robot interaction, and healthcare.

Next, we will extract from the literature review questions and design input for the co-design and usability design studies in the project, a code-book for a content analysis of existing information material (knowledge translation content) regarding AI in healthcare to conduct a content analysis on such material, asking how far the different (communication) needs and perceptions of both children and caretakers have been acknowledged in the information material design.

Finally, we will include the results from the content analysis in the final design of the clinical trial and will also triangulate the outcomes with the results from the clinical trial, in order to discuss how AI and robotics can be employed responsibly and with a user-centric design.

8 Summary and Conclusions

This project plans to extend research on the use of socially assistive robots into the paediatric clinical context, going beyond previous studies in this area by incorporating co-design and ethical considerations throughout, by adding autonomy and responsiveness to the robot system, as well as including adequately powered clinical trial with patient-relevant outcomes. It will also extend existing work on social robotics into a relatively unexplored domain, demonstrating new application possibilities in real-world settings with the potential for real impact on people's lives. In addition to producing a new state-of-the-art technical deployment for the Nao robot platform, we plan to engage continuously with end users to ensure that the research findings have the chance to be translated into clinical practice. As well, the impact of the ethics work will provide recommendations and guidelines for any future user-centric research in AI and robotics, particularly involving children. At present, we have begun the planning stages of our co-design process and technical development on the robot system. However, it is hoped that the outcomes throughout the project will reach healthcare institutions, policy-makers, HCPs, as well as children and families both in Canada and beyond.

Acknowledgements. This work is funded by the ESRC/SSHRC Canada-UK Artificial Intelligence Initiative through grant ES/T012986/1. We thank all team members at all partner sites for their ongoing contributions to this project.

References

1. Abras, C., Maloney-Krichmar, D., Preece, J., et al.: User-centered design. In: Bainbridge, W.(ed.) Encyclopedia of Human-Computer Interaction, vol. 37(4), pp. 445–456. Sage Publications, Thousand Oaks (2004)
2. Ali, S., et al.: LO63: Humanoid robot-based distraction to reduce pain and distress during venipuncture in the pediatric emergency department: a randomized controlled trial. Can. J. Emerg. Med. 21(S1), S30–S31 (2019). https://doi.org/10.1017/cem.2019.106
3. Breazeal, C.: Social robots for health applications. In: 2011 Annual International Conference of the IEEE Engineering in Medicine and Biology Society IEEE (2011). https://doi.org/10.1109/iembs.2011.6091328

4. Cabibihan, J.-J., Javed, H., Ang, M., Aljunied, S.M.: Why robots? A survey on the roles and benefits of social robots in the therapy of children with autism. Int. J. Soc. Robot. **5**(4), 593–618 (2013). https://doi.org/10.1007/s12369-013-0202-2

5. Chambers, C.T., Taddio, A., Uman, L.S., McMurtry, C.: Psychological interventions for reducing pain and distress during routine childhood immunizations: a systematic review. Clin. Ther. **31**, S77–S103 (2009). https://doi.org/10.1016/j.clinthera.2009.07.023

6. Dawe, J., Sutherland, C., Barco, A., Broadbent, E.: Can social robots help children in healthcare contexts? A scoping review. BMJ Paediatr. Open **3**(1), e000371 (2019). https://doi.org/10.1136/bmjpo-2018-000371

7. Elliott, C.H., Jay, S.M., Woody, P.: An observation scale for measuring children's distress during medical procedures. J. Pediatr. Psychol. **12**(4), 543–551 (1987). https://doi.org/10.1093/jpepsy/12.4.543

8. Feil-Seifer, D., Mataric, M.: Socially assistive robotics. In: 9th International Conference on Rehabilitation Robotics, ICORR 2005. IEEE (2005). https://doi.org/10.1109/icorr.2005.1501143

9. Fox, M., Long, D., Magazzeni, D.: Explainable planning. In: Proceedings of the IJCAI Workshop on Explainable AI (2017)

10. Ghallab, M., Nau, D., Traverso, P.: Automated Planning and Acting. Cambridge University Press, Cambridge (2016)

11. Hicks, C.L., von Baeyer, C.L., Spafford, P.A., van Korlaar, I., Goodenough, B.: The faces pain scale - revised: toward a common metric in pediatric pain measurement. Pain **93**(2), 173–183 (2001). https://doi.org/10.1016/s0304-3959(01)00314-1

12. Jibb, L.A., et al.: Using the MEDiPORT humanoid robot to reduce procedural pain and distress in children with cancer: a pilot randomized controlled trial. Pediatr. Blood Cancer **65**(9), e27242 (2018). https://doi.org/10.1002/pbc.27242

13. Livingstone, S.: Children: a special case for privacy? Intermedia **46**(2), 18–23 (2018)

14. McKenna, P., Broz, F., Keller, I., Part, J.L., Rajendran, G., Aylett, R.: Towards robot-assisted social skills training for adults with ASC. In: CHI 2019 Workshop on the Challenges of Working on Social Robots that Collaborate with People (2019)

15. McMurtry, C.M., et al.: Far from "just a poke": common painful needle procedures and the development of needle fear. Clin. J. Pain **31**, S3–S11 (2015)

16. Papaioannou, I., Dondrup, C., Lemon, O.: Human-robot interaction requires more than slot filling - multi-threaded dialogue for collaborative tasks and social conversation. In: Proceedings of the FAIM/ISCA Workshop on Artificial Intelligence for Multimodal Human Robot Interaction, pp. 61–64 (2018). https://doi.org/10.21437/AI-MHRI.2018-15

17. Petrick, R., Foster, M.E.: Planning for social interaction in a robot bartender domain. In: International Conference on Automated Planning and Scheduling (2013)

18. Petrick, R.P.A., Foster, M.E.: Knowledge engineering and planning for social human–robot interaction: a case study. In: Vallati, M., Kitchin, D. (eds.) Knowledge Engineering Tools and Techniques for AI Planning, pp. 261–277. Springer, Cham (2020). https://doi.org/10.1007/978-3-030-38561-3_14
19. Preece, J., Sharp, H., Rogers, Y.: Interaction Design: Beyond Human-Computer Interaction. Wiley, Hoboken (2015)
20. Quigley, M., et al.: ROS: an open-source robot operating system. In: ICRA Workshop on Open Source Software (2009)
21. Rigby, M.J.: Ethical dimensions of using artificial intelligence in health care. AMA J. Ethics **21**(2), E121–E124 (2019). https://doi.org/10.1001/amajethics.2019.121
22. Roffo, G., et al.: Automating the administration and analysis of psychiatric tests. In: Proceedings of the 2019 CHI Conference on Human Factors in Computing Systems - CHI 2019. ACM Press (2019). https://doi.org/10.1145/3290605.3300825
23. Smith, D.H., Zeller, F.: The death and lives of hitchBOT: the design and implementation of a hitchhiking robot. Leonardo **50**(1), 77–78 (2017). https://doi.org/10.1162/leon_a_01354
24. Stevens, B.J., et al.: Epidemiology and management of painful procedures in children in Canadian hospitals. Can. Med. Assoc. J. **183**(7), E403–E410 (2011). https://doi.org/10.1503/cmaj.101341
25. Stoilova, M., Livingstone, S., Nandagiri, R.: Children's data and privacy online: growing up in a digital age. Research findings, London School of Economics and Political Science, London (2019)
26. Tapus, A., Tapus, C., Mataric, M.J.: The use of socially assistive robots in the design of intelligent cognitive therapies for people with dementia. In: 2009 IEEE International Conference on Rehabilitation Robotics. IEEE (2009). https://doi.org/10.1109/icorr.2009.5209501
27. Trost, M.J., Chrysilla, G., Gold, J.I., Matarić, M.: Socially-assistive robots using empathy to reduce pain and distress during peripheral IV placement in children. Pain Res. Manage. **2020**, 1–7 (2020). https://doi.org/10.1155/2020/7935215
28. Trost, M.J., Ford, A.R., Kysh, L., Gold, J.I., Matarić, M.: Socially assistive robots for helping pediatric distress and pain. Clin. J. Pain **35**(5), 451–458 (2019). https://doi.org/10.1097/ajp.0000000000000688
29. Trottier, E.D., Doré-Bergeron, M.J., Chauvin-Kimoff, L., Baerg, K., Ali, S.: Managing pain and distress in children undergoing brief diagnostic and therapeutic procedures. Paediatr. Child Health **24**(8), 509–521 (2019). https://doi.org/10.1093/pch/pxz026
30. Wada, K., Shibata, T., Saito, T., Tanie, K.: Effects of robot-assisted activity for elderly people and nurses at a day service center. Proc. IEEE **92**(11), 1780–1788 (2004). https://doi.org/10.1109/jproc.2004.835378

Human Aware Task Planning Using Verbal Communication Feasibility and Costs

Guilhem Buisan[1]([⊠])(ID), Guillaume Sarthou[1](ID), and Rachid Alami[1,2](ID)

[1] LAAS-CNRS, Université de Toulouse, CNRS, Toulouse, France
{guilhem.buisan,guillaume.sarthou,rachid.alami}@laas.fr
[2] Artificial and Natural Intelligence Toulouse Institute (ANITI), Toulouse, France

Abstract. This paper addresses the problem of taking into account the feasibility and cost of verbal communication actions at the task planning level in the context of human-robot interaction. By determining the human and robot context in which the referring expressions to entities can be effectively achieved and at which cost, our planner can 1) prevent potential deadlocked situations where it is not possible to produce a feasible communication act 2) find plans reducing the overall communication complexity 3) evaluate different communications strategies and select the most suitable one. Our approach is based on the extension of a multi agent hierarchical task planner capable of maintaining, throughout the planning process, an estimate of the human partner knowledge about the environment using a semantic representation. A Referring Expression Generation (REG) can then be executed for each communication action allowing the task planner to be informed about its feasibility and cost during the plan elaboration process. Three scenarios are presented to validate the method, where a robot drives the human actions to perform a cube arrangement task.

Keywords: Human-Robot collaboration · Hierarchical task planner · Referring expression generation · Verbal communication planning

1 Introduction

It is well established that clear and fluent communication is a key aspect of the success of collaborative tasks. In the Human-Robot Interaction (HRI) research field it has lead to two dual problems [17]. In one hand we have the language understanding in which the robot interprets and grounds human's utterances and reacts to them [1]. In another hand we have the language generation problem where the robot produces language whether to ask for help [18], align knowledge [3] or clarify its decision [11]. In this paper, we only use the language generation and consider it as a communication action that is part of a Human-Robot collaborative task plan. Taking it as an action means that the robot can plan when and what to communicate. More importantly, by taking into account the *what* of the

© Springer Nature Switzerland AG 2020
A. R. Wagner et al. (Eds.): ICSR 2020, LNAI 12483, pp. 554–565, 2020.
https://doi.org/10.1007/978-3-030-62056-1_46

communication, its content, it is possible to estimate the feasibility and cost of a communication action. In addition, by maintaining a representation of the environment for the future states of the task as it is done in symbolic task planning, the robot can estimate the feasibility and the cost of the verbal communication actions all along the task. Considering these two pieces of information in the planning process makes it possible to compare verbal communication with other means of communication, to find a plan minimizing the overall communication complexity but also to prevent some plan failures. This process can be compared to [7] where the geometric feasibility, the indirect effects and cost of an action is considered already during the symbolic task planning and not at a further geometric planning level.

Consider the situation illustrated in Fig. 1. In this task the human and the robot have to put each cube in a specific colored area. The robot does not have the ability to act on the cubes and the human does not know the goal configuration. The robot must therefore communicate the successive actions that the human will have to perform. The two cubes are visually the same to the human, but the robot can identify them. The initial configuration is given in Fig. 1a with the cube C1 in the red area and the cube C2 in the black area. The goal configuration (Fig. 1d) requires the cube C1 to be places in the black area and the cube C2 in the white area. In the case where the communication action is refined only at execution, a solution plan could be to tell the human to move the cube C1 in the black area then the cube C2 in the white one. The execution of this plan would result in: *"Take the cube in the red area and put it in the black area"*. In this new situation where both cubes are now in the black area (Fig. 1b), the robot has no way to designate the cube C2 without ambiguity. Hence, the task is blocked. Taking into account the communication feasibility and cost estimation during the planning process would allow to find the solution where the robot tell to the human to move the cube C2 first (Fig. 1c) and then the cube C1 (Fig. 1d). Considering now that the robot can point to the cubes, the deadlock of the first solution can be avoided with a pointing action and nevertheless, thanks to the communication cost estimation, the least expensive solution can be selected.

In Sect. 2, we briefly discuss related work and how our contribution addresses new issues. Our approach and its components are then described in Sect. 3. Three case studies are finally presented in Sect. 4 to show how this approach can be used to prevent deadlocked situations at execution, how it can reduce the global communication complexity during a Human-Robot collaborative task and how it can be used to balance between different communication means.

2   Related Work

A significant amount of research has been dedicated to Human-Robot verbal communication, especially to answer the questions of *what* and *when* to communicate [9]. A lot of early works address these questions at execution time, with a fixed plan in which the robot inserts verbal communication when needed.

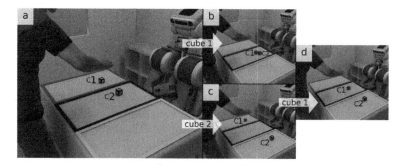

Fig. 1. A Human-Robot collaborative task where the robot has to explain to the human to put the cube C1 in the black area and the cube C2 in the white area. The cube identifiers ("C1", "C2") are only known to the robot. If the action of referring to an object without ambiguity is not taken into account during task planning, a deadlocked situation could appear if the robot first asks to move the cube C1.

The communication can be used to share the plan, to ask for or give specific information or to fix errors ([3, 14–16, 18]).

Devin and Alami [3] use a theory-of-mind enabled framework to decide, at execution time, if a communication action is needed and its contents. In their work, the robot is provided with a shared plan for both itself and the human partner. During the execution, for each human action, the robot estimates the partner's mental model. Divergence between the robot knowledge and the estimated human knowledge is monitored. When a divergence which can endanger the plan is detected, a verbal communication of the needed facts is computed and achieved.

However, in some cases, deciding on communication at execution time is not enough and more recent work deals with explicit consideration of communication actions while planning ([10–12]). Roncone et al. [11] explicitly represent three types of verbal communication action, *command* (instruction to the human) which can be declined, *ask* (a question of whether her current action is over) and *inform* (the communication of a robot intent). These actions are integrated with others classical actions into a Partially Observable Markov Decision Process (POMDP) which, once solved, returns a policy integrating communication actions. However, the costs associated with these communication are not taken into account for task allocation. Moreover, the content of the communication (the *what*) is not specified at planning level, which can cause unplanned higher communication costs or even non achievable communication in some scenarios.

A similar approach is proposed by Unhelkar et al. [19] with multiple verbal communication types considered (*command, ask, inform* and *answer*). Moreover a communication cost is explicitly considered but it is a cost on the *when* to communicate and not on the *what*, as it is a function penalizing temporally close communication actions. The communication actions are task specific and include parameters replaced at execution time (the landmarks and actions for the *inform* communication in their example; *i.e.* the *what* of the communication). In their examples, every landmark is assumed to be easily referred to the human, but this is not always the case. By using REG at planning time, our approach addresses two of the five challenges identified by Unhelkar et al.: "estimating benefit of communication" and "quantifying cost of communication" [20].

To entrench the aim of this paper, we will use the example depicted by Tellex et al. [18], and describe how our approach could differ from theirs. In this example, a robot and a human are engaged in assembling tables, the robot is following a precomputed plan. When a failure occurs the robot asks the human for help by referring to problematic objects. By doing so, the robot plan is repaired with the human help thanks to an effective object referring communication action. However, in this work, they consider a non-reachability of a table leg as a failure even if this table leg was known by the robot to be unreachable from the beginning. A planning step beforehand could assign the assembly of this leg to the human, and plan the needed communication of the robot to the human. Moreover, with the approach presented in this paper, if multiple table legs would match the verbal description, the planner would be able to insert an action or modify the order of assembly to make the needed referring easier to understand for the human.

3   Method

In this section, we first provide an overview of our approach and briefly describe the used Hierarchical Agent-based Task Planner [8]. We then introduce the reader to REG, based on [2], and the knowledge base it needs. We end this section with a presentation of the integration of the two components and how it allows the planner to be informed of the feasibility and the cost of the communication actions.

3.1   Approach

The communication actions that we consider in this paper are commands issued by the robot based on Referring Expressions (REs). Typical commands are *"Take X"* and *"Put it in Y"*. We thus have a static part and the rest depends on the situation when the communication is perfomed and must be solved by a REG. It is this variable part that could make a communication costly or infeasible. As it has been highlighted in [2], REG must be performed on the human's partner Knowledge Base (KB) to only use facts and concepts that the robot estimates to be known by the human. Because of that, we target a planner that is already suitable for HRI to integrate the estimation of communications. This means that we need a planner able to distinguish between the different agents involved in the task and to maintain a representation of the environment for each of them.

Because the task the planner has to solve does not necessarily imply all the elements present in the current environment, the planner does not need a full representation of the environment. In a same way, it does not necessarily need to have all the characteristics of the entities such that their colors or their types.

On the example of Fig. 1, the two cubes can only be represented as movable objects in the planner and not as cubes to make the planning domain more generic. However, the REG needs all the semantic information of each entity of the environment to generate accurate RE. Furthermore, if another cube which is not part of the task, thus not part of the planner internal representation, is present on the table, it will also impact the REG and thus the complexity and feasibility of the communication action. Hence, the REG can not be performed on the planner internal representation. To solve this issue, we endow the planner with the ability to maintain a semantic KB that is used by the REG. Since maintaining this external representation can be an heavy process, it is updated only when a communication action has to be evaluated.

The general workflow executed for each communication action encountered during the planning process consists of: 1) updating the external semantic KB of the human partner with the expected world state 2) identifying the objects to which to refer to in the communication 3) execute the REG for each of these objects 4) calculate the feasibility and the cost of the communication action according to the feasibility and the cost of each individual RE involved in the planned communication. Note that the examples used in this paper only involve one RE but the same method can be used for communications of type *"give me X and Y"*. In this case, the external semantic KB is only updated once and both REG are executed on this KB.

3.2   Hierarchical Task Planner

In order to implement our approach, we need a task planner able to maintain an estimated knowledge base of each agent at each planning step. We chose the Hierarchical Agent-based Task Planner (HATP) [8]. HATP extends the classical Hierarchical Task Network (HTN) planning by being able to produce *shared plans* to reach a joint goal. A HATP planning domain describes how to decompose tasks into subtasks down to atomic symbolic actions. Both the robot and human feasible tasks and actions are described in the domain. A context-dependent cost function is associated to each action.

During the task decomposition, HATP will explore several applicable subtasks until the global task is totally refined into feasible actions, and will return the minimal cost plan. HATP also supports *social rules*, allowing to balance the effort of involved agents depending on human preferences and to penalize plans presenting certain undesirable sequences of actions. We will not use these social rules in what follows, but our approach stays totally compatible with them.

Moreover, during the exploration of the task tree, HATP will assign actions to available agents, robot or human (when an action can be done by both). By doing so, HATP is able to elaborate one action *stream* per agent, together with causality and synchronization links. Besides, HATP domain syntax supports Multiple Values State Variables (MVSV) [6] which is used to represent and reason about each agent mental state. The value of each variable depends on the agent it is requested for. This allows to represent action preconditions depending on the knowledge of the agent performing the action and also represent their effect on each agent mental state which can dependent on the agent perspective.

Finally, the last argument which motivated our choice was the previous integration of HATP with a Geometrical Task Planning (GTP) [5]. This work aimed at refining geometric and motion planning requests during the task planning process. The geometric planner would then compute, in context, the feasibility, the cost and the side effects of the action. In a similar way, we propose here to integrate and run REG, in context, to determine communication action feasibility and pertinence with respect to other courses of actions.

3.3   Referring Expression Generation

The REG aims to unambiguously designate an entity/object a_t in an environment. We use the state of the art algorithm presented in [2]. This REG runs on a semantic knowledge base K represented as an ontology. In its simplified version, we defined $K = \langle \mathbb{A}, \mathbb{T}, \mathbb{R} \rangle$ where $\mathbb{A}$, $\mathbb{T}$ and $\mathbb{R}$ are respectively an ABox, TBox and RBox [4]. $\mathbb{T}$ is the TBox of the ontology defining a set of classes and a finite collection of class inclusion axioms. RBox is a set of properties and a finite collection of property inclusion axioms, transitivity axioms, reflexive axioms, inverses axioms and chain axioms. $\mathbb{A}$, the ABox of the ontology, is a set of entities A and a finite collection of axioms of the form (a_i, p, a_j) and (a_i, t), where a_i and a_j are entities, t is a class and p is a property. All these axioms can be represented as relations of the form of triplet $r = (s, p, o)$ with respectively s, p and o the subject, property and object of the relation r. The axiom (a_i, t) corresponds to the inheritance relation that is written $r = (a_i, isA, t)$. This means that entities of ABox are instances of TBox classes. To manage the ontologies, we use Ontologenius [13] which is the ontology manager on which the REG we use was developed.

The REG problem is defined as a tuple $\mathcal{P} = \langle a_t, K, Ctx \rangle$. In this problem, a_t is the target entity. The one to be referenced through its relations to other entities existing in the ontology K. Ctx is the context of the problem. It is a set of relations considered as already known by the communicating agents about a_t. It is therefore a subset of $\mathbb{A}$. With the table-top interaction of this paper, the context is $Ctx = \{(a_t, isOn, table\_1)\}$ because both interacting agents are aware that they are currently speaking about the objects on the table. This means that the REG has not to consider the objects not being on the table as possibly bringing ambiguity. The REG context could be enriched by taking for example the visibility of the human partner and should be determined dynamically during the task planning process. However, for the demonstration of our current purpose, we consider it fixed.

A solution to the REG problem is a set of relations which could be verbalized afterwards and a cost associated with this solution. The cost of the solution is the sum of the cost of each property used in the set of relations. These costs can differ from one human to another and represent the effort needed by the human to interpret the relation. The fact that the property "hasColor" would be easier to interpret than the property "isAtLeftOf" would be represented by a higher cost for the "isAtLeftOf" property.

3.4   Integration of REG Within Action Planning

The Representation of the Communication Action: For clarity purposes, in this paper, we only place ourselves in scenarios where only the robot knows the goal of a joint task and issues command to its human partner one at a time when the human has to do an action. Thus, while planning, if a task is allocated to the human, as she has no way of guessing it, a preceding communication is required. In the HATP domain, this translates as a method being decomposed into a sequence of a communication action and an action made by the human when the task is attributed to the human. The communication action feasibility is determined by both symbolic preconditions (*e.g.* the human and the robot are in the same room) and REG result (whether a solution is found or not). If the communication action is feasible, the cost of the communication action is then computed as the sum of a fixed cost depending on the type of communication and the REG solution cost depending on the human receiver and the entities to refer to in the communication.

We have chosen here for illustration purposes a simple planning problem where a communication needing a REG is involved in each plan step, but the method is general and compatible with problems which need to estimate and ensure the pertinent context and plan step (the *when*) of a communication action during plan elaboration (*e.g.* [3,19]).

Maintaining the Right Knowledge Base, at the Right Time: On one hand, we have large, complete semantic knowledge bases on which a REG algorithm is able to run and to return the feasibility, the cost and the content of a verbal entity referring communication for a specified agent (top part of Fig. 2). On the other hand, we have reduced knowledge bases dedicated to task planning (bottom part of Fig. 2). In order to know the feasibility and cost of a verbal communication action during the planning, we have to reconcile both sides. Indeed, the estimated ontology of the communication receiver must be updated to reflect her planned estimated beliefs at the time of the communication. All the knowledge representation used here are from the robot point-of view and managed internally by the robot decisional and knowledge management processes.

First, the attributes of all the entities present in the planning knowledge base are initialized for each agent (left part of Fig. 2). To do so, every entity types declared in the planning domain are retrieved from the ontologies by their name, and entities inheriting from these types in the ontologies are created in the planning knowledge base. Then, each attribute (both static and dynamic) of every entities declared in the domain has its value updated. If the attribute is a set, multiple relations with the same name originating from the same entity and pointing to different ones can be found in the ontologies. If so, all the pointed entities are added to the set. Finally, a planning ontology is created by copy of the present one for every agent other than the robot present in the planning domain. These copies are made to avoid modifying the original ontologies during the planning process as other components may rely on them.

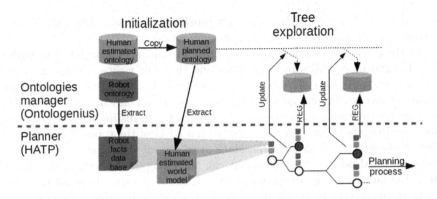

Fig. 2. A representation of the exploration of potential mental states and ontologies conducted by the planner. The ontology representing estimated human knowledge is first copied in order to plan it without altering the original one. The human and robot planning information is extracted from the ontologies. During the tree exploration, for each verbal communication action, the planned human ontology is updated with the current explored state and the REG is executed on it.

When a communication action is encountered during the task tree exploration (right part of Fig. 2), the ontology of the communication receiver needs to be updated to be able to run the REG on it. The planning ontology copy of the receiver human is retrieved by her identifier. Then, for each of the entities of her planned beliefs at the time of the communication, an update is made. The update is only made on dynamic attributes as static ones do not change during the planning process. All the relations having the same name as the attribute of the entity in the planning domain are deleted from the ontology, and replaced with new planned values. If the attribute is a set, a new relation with the same name is created for every value in the set.

A REG request is then issued on the updated ontology with the goal individual being the entity to refer. The REG returns a solution with a cost or a failure which is taken into account by the planner as classical cost or a non fulfillment of the action preconditions respectively. Alternatively, a communication action may need to refer to multiple entities. In that case, multiple REG requests are issued on the same updated ontology and their costs are summed.

4   Case Studies

In this section, we present three case studies. The two first ones are run in simulation on a minimalist setup and show respectively that the estimation of the communication content during the planning can prevent from execution dead-end and can reduce the global communication complexity during the task. The third case study is run on a PR2 robot with a perception of its environment and presents a more complex task with twelve objects to organize. With this last case, we show that our method makes it possible to compare different means of communication and to choose the most appropriate.

All the three cases studies are based on a cube arrangement task. The human can distinguish the cubes by their color and the digit written on them (one or two) if there is one. As shown in Fig. 1, the table surface is composed of three storage areas of different colors and cubes can be placed only in one of them. This position information can also be used by the human to distinguish the cubes. By this way, the robot can refer to a cube with a REG of the type: *"the black cube with the number 2 which is in the black area"*. In all the cases, only the robot knows the goal position the cubes but can not manipulate them. It thus has to guide the human in the arrangement task. The robot can only point the cubes in the third case study. In the first two, he can only use verbal communication.

4.1   Prevening Execution Dead-Ends

In this case study, we consider the initial state presented in Fig. 1. The cube C1 is in the red area and the cube C2 in the black one. The goal state is to have the cube C1 in the black area and the cube C2 in the white one (Fig. 1d). Taking into account the cost and the feasibility of the communication, we found with our method the plan 1. Cube C2 is moved first because otherwise the two cubes would be in the black area at the same time. Such a situation would cause a dead-end during the execution of the plan or require another communication mean.

```
HR  -  TellHumanToTake(C2)  // (C2, isA, Cube), (C2, isIn, AB),
                            // (AB, isA, Area), (AB, hasColor, black)
H   -  Take(C2)
HR  -  TellHumanToPlace(C2, AW) // (AW, isA, Area),  (AW, hasColor, white)
H   -  Place(C2, AW)
HR  -  TellHumanToTake(C1)  // (C1, isA, Cube), (C1, isIn, AR),
                            // (AR, isA, Area), (AR, hasColor, red)
H   -  Take(C1)
HR  -  TellHumanToPlace(C1, AB)  // (AB, isA, Area), (AB, hasColor, black)
H   -  Place(C1, AB)
```

Plan 1. The obtained plan for the first case study where cube C1 must be moved from the red to the black area and cube C2 moved from the black to the white area. The lines beginning with H represent the actions of the human and the lines beginning with HR represent actions involving the human and the robot (communication actions). In green are the REG results for each communication action.

We consider once again the initial state presented in Fig. 1. This time the goal is to invert the positions of the two cubes. In this situation, if the communication cost and feasibility is not taken into account during planning, both actions directly leading to the goal state (*i.e.* cube C1 moved to black area or cube C2 to red area) will lead to a dead-end at plan execution. The solution found with our method is to add a supplementary action. It consists in putting the cube C1 away (in the white area). This additional action avoids a dead-end by making communication about cube C2 feasible.

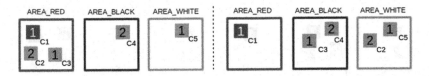

Fig. 3. The initial state (left) and the goal state (right) of a task where the robot has to explain to the human partner how to move the cubes to complete the task.(Color figure online)

4.2 Reduction of the Overall Communication Complexity

In this second case study, we show how estimation of communication by verbal designation can be used to reduce the complexity of global communication. This time we consider the initial state and the target state represented in Fig. 3. Only cubes C2 and C3 should be moved. Our method finds the solution consisting in moving cube C2 first, then cube C3. With this order, cube C2 is referred by three relations: its type (*i.e.* cube), the number on it and the colored area in which it is located. After that, the cube C3 can also be referred only by three relationships being its type, its color and the colored area in which it is located. Considering the reverse order, this would have generated a more complex RE first for cube C3 with four relationships: its type, its color, the number on it and the colored area in which it is located. The solution chosen by our method communicates a sum of six relations rather than seven with the reverse order.

4.3 Compare with Other Communication Means

In this last case study, we show how the estimation of verbal designation communication cost can be used to compare it with other communication means, here pointing. Now, we consider twelve cubes. The initial state and the goal state are represented on Fig. 4. Such a number of similar objects leads to long explanations to refer to certain cubes. Therefore, we aim the task planner to choose another means of communication to refer to these cubes (*e.g.* a pointing action). The pointing action has a constant cost which is higher than a simple verbal communication but lower than a complex one (with three or more relations to verbalize). To exemplify the comparison with other communication means, the arrangement order is predefined in this setup.

The execution of the computed plan can be found in the video available at https://youtu.be/3YnGh_t-UpY. The cubes C5 and C7 are chosen to be pointed instead of verbalized. Indeed, in the world states where these cubes need to be moved, verbal referring is considered to be too costly, thus a pointing motion is preferred. For example, the cube C5 in the initial situation needs a long and complex explanation that is: *"take the black cube with the number two which is in the black area"*. Even in the case the pointing action takes more execution time, it could require less cognitive load for the human partner and so make the human action faster.

564   G. Buisan et al.

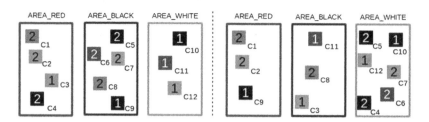

Fig. 4. The initial state (left) and the goal state (right) of a task where the robot has to explain to the human partner how to move the cubes to complete the task.

Here, we see another benefit of our approach, it allows the planner to balance between the use of verbal communication actions, which can become complex in some states (hard to predict without a task planner), and other communication modalities. Here, verbal communication is balanced with other communication means, but it can also be balanced with other actions or assignments requiring less or no communication.

5   Conclusion and Future Work

This paper presents two main contributions. The first contribution deals with the integration of a fully informed refinement of communication actions in the shared plan elaboration process. Indeed, dealing with the refinement of communication actions in a subsequent planning step or postponing it to the execution phase might entail inefficiencies or even plan failures. The second contribution concerns the interplay between the exploration and evaluation of future potential states by the task planner and the management of ontological and semantic knowledge both for the robot and its estimated knowledge of the human partner.

The result is an extended version of HATP, called HATP/REG. Its abilities have been illustrated in three case studies showing its ability 1) to prevent potential deadlocked situations where it is not possible to produce a feasible communication act (and specifically here a non ambiguous reference) 2) to find plans reducing the overall communication cost 3) to balance between different communications means and select the most suitable one.

In the current version, the refinement focuses on the referencing problem of objects and action parameters. We intend to extend it to other communication acts such as plan and/or sub-plan explanation. Finally, we also intend to integrate other communication means in the framework such as more complex pointing actions and more elaborate mental states (*e.g.* integrating the shared human-robot experience). We will also conduct an evaluation of the system through user studies to assess its pertinence.

Acknowledgements. We thank Amandine Mayima for her contribution to the implementation of the integrated scenarios. This work has been funded by the French Agence Nationale de la Recherche JointAction4HRI project ANR-16-CE33-0017.

References

1. Brawer, J., Mangin, O., Roncone, A., Widder, S., Scassellati, B.: Situated human-robot collaboration: predicting intent from grounded natural language. In: IEEE/RSJ IROS (2018)
2. Buisan, G., Sarthou, G., Bit-Monnot, A., Clodic, A., Alami, R.: Efficient, situated and ontology based referring expression generation for human-robot collaboration. In: RO-MAN. IEEE (2020)
3. Devin, S., Alami, R.: An implemented theory of mind to improve human-robot shared plans execution. In: ACM/IEEE HRI (2016)
4. Fokoue, A., Kershenbaum, A., Ma, L., Schonberg, E., Srinivas, K.: The summary abox: cutting ontologies down to size. In: Cruz, I., et al. (eds.) ISWC 2006. LNCS, vol. 4273, pp. 343–356. Springer, Heidelberg (2006). https://doi.org/10.1007/11926078_25
5. Gharbi, M., Lallement, R., Alami, R.: Combining symbolic and geometric planning to synthesize human-aware plans: toward more efficient combined search. In: RSJ IROS. IEEE (2015)
6. Guitton, J., Warnier, M., Alami, R.: Belief management for HRI planning. In: European Conference on Artificial Intelligence (2012)
7. Lallement, R.: Symbolic and Geometric Planning for teams of Robots and Humans. Theses, INSA de Toulouse (2016)
8. Lallement, R., De Silva, L., Alami, R.: HATP: an HTN planner for robotics. In: ICAPS Workshop on Planning and Robotics (2014)
9. Mavridis, N.: A review of verbal and non-verbal human-robot interactive communication. Robot. Auton. Syst. **63**, 22–35 (2015)
10. Nikolaidis, S., Kwon, M., Forlizzi, J., Srinivasa, S.: Planning with verbal communication for human-robot collaboration. ACM Trans. Hum.-Robot Interact. (THRI) **7**(3), 1–21 (2018)
11. Roncone, A., Mangin, O., Scassellati, B.: Transparent role assignment and task allocation in human robot collaboration. In: ICRA. IEEE (2017)
12. Sanelli, V., Cashmore, M., Magazzeni, D., Iocchi, L.: Short-term human-robot interaction through conditional planning and execution. In: ICAPS (2017)
13. Sarthou, G., Clodic, A., Alami, R.: Ontologenius: a long-term semantic memory for robotic agents. In: RO-MAN. IEEE (2019)
14. Schaefer, K.E., Straub, E.R., Chen, J.Y., Putney, J., Evans III, A.W.: Communicating intent to develop shared situation awareness and engender trust in human-agent teams. Cogn. Syst. Res. **46**, 26–39 (2017)
15. Sebastiani, E., Lallement, R., Alami, R., Iocchi, L.: Dealing with on-line human-robot negotiations in hierarchical agent-based task planner. In: ICAPS (2017)
16. Shah, J., Wiken, J., Williams, B., Breazeal, C.: Improved human-robot team performance using Chaski, a human-inspired plan execution system. In: ACM/IEEE HRI (2011)
17. Tellex, S., Gopalan, N., Kress-Gazit, H., Matuszek, C.: Robots that use language. Ann. Rev. Control Robot. Auton. Syst. **3**(1), 25–55 (2020)
18. Tellex, S., Knepper, R., Li, A., Rus, D., Roy, N.: Asking for help using inverse semantics. Robot. Sci. Syst. X (2014)
19. Unhelkar, V.V., Li, S., Shah, J.A.: Decision-making for bidirectional communication in sequential human-robot collaborative tasks. In: ACM/IEEE HRI (2020)
20. Unhelkar, V.V., Yang, X.J., Shah, J.A.: Challenges for communication decision-making in sequential human-robot collaborative tasks. In: Workshop on Mathematical Models, Algorithms, and Human-Robot Interaction at RSS (2017)

Robot Planning with Mental Models of Co-present Humans

David Buckingham$^{(\boxtimes)}$, Meia Chita-Tegmark , and Matthias Scheutz

Tufts University, Medford, MA 02155, USA
{david.buckingham,meia.chita_tegmark,matthias.scheutz}@tufts.edu

Abstract. Robots are increasingly embedded in human societies where they encounter human collaborators, potential adversaries, and even uninvolved by-standers. Such robots must plan to accomplish joint goals with teammates while avoiding interference from competitors, possibly utilizing bystanders to advance the robot's goals. We propose a planning framework for robot task and action planners that can cope with collaborative, competitive, and non-involved human agents at the same time by using mental models of human agents. By querying these models, the robot can plan for the effects of future human actions and can plan robot actions to influence what the human will do, even when influencing them through explicit communication is not possible. We implement the framework in a planner that does not assume that human agents share goals with, or will cooperate with, the robot. Instead, it can handle the diverse relations that can emerge from interactions between the robot's goals and capacities, the task environment, and the human behavior predicted by the planner's models. We report results from an evaluation where a teleoperated robot executes a planner-generated policy to influence the behavior of human participants. Since the robot is not capable of performing some of the actions necessary to achieve its goal, the robot instead tries to cause the human to perform those actions.

Keywords: Planning · Mental model · Human-robot interaction

1 Introduction

Many future autonomous robots will have to perform tasks in shared environments with human agents where the human can affect performance: humans might facilitate the robot's task or impede it. While most work in Human-Robot Interaction (HRI) has assumed cooperative relationships (e.g. [8,19]), and some work focuses specifically on adversaries [4,17], a robot might encounter humans that have no relationship (cooperative or competitive) with the robot and thus cannot be relied upon to help the robot. Therefore *Planning for HRI* should involve all possible inter-agent dynamics, from collaborative, to neutral, to competitive, possibly with interacting attitudes changing during task performance.

To the extent that a robot can estimate human goals and propensities (e.g. because it has a *mental model* of the humans [8,26]) and to the extent that it

© Springer Nature Switzerland AG 2020
A. R. Wagner et al. (Eds.): ICSR 2020, LNAI 12483, pp. 566–577, 2020.
https://doi.org/10.1007/978-3-030-62056-1_47

might be able to influence their actions, it should be able to generate plans that utilize humans to achieve its task or to improve its task performance, possibly helping humans with their tasks (e.g. [27]). We therefore present a planning approach that uses human models not only to predict human actions, but also to influence them. As our evaluation shows, this allows the robot to plan for goals that require actions that the robot cannot perform, but that a human could, even without using explicit communication.

2 Related Work

Unlike *motion planning* with predicted human movement, which generally relies on statistical methods (e.g. [13]), we are interested in symbolic task planning with predictions about higher-level human behavior. Most approaches to incorporating the needed actions of human agents into a robot's plans assume human willingness to collaborate, and achieves this coordination by means of explicit communication, as in [23]. On the other hand, a robot may be able to persuade a human to help. A robot's ability to influence human behavior depends on many factors, including trust [10,22], and the use of nonverbal cues [11]. However, a non-cooperative human may be unwilling to perform requested actions. Furthermore, a robot may be unable to request human actions. In such cases, it may still be possible for the robot to cause the human to perform the desired actions (e.g. [16]).

Recent work [9] has emphasized the importance of mental modeling for deliberative processes in teaming tasks. [8] discuss the use of a mental model by a robot to manipulate humans in the interest of "the greater good." [15] propose a system where a robot anticipates a human's mental state and acts in a joint plan to help a human only if the human's intentions are relevant to the joint goal and the human actually wants assistance. [12] develop a planner that uses predictions of future human actions to constrain the robot's plan, but unlike our approach, take's the human's predicted behavior as immutable.

Most work in Multi-Agent Planning involves centralized planning for a team of agents with a shared task, or involves decentralized planning, with multiple planners coordinating their efforts to accomplish a shared goal [28]. Even planners that do not control all agents in the environment, such as in Planning for HRI, usually compute joint plans assuming that robots and humans share goals [8–10,15,19]. Another approach is adversarial planning [4], where a robot plans in a domain shared by uncontrollable (by the planner) agents with goals that contradict the robot's goals, and there has been recent work on planners for both adversarial and cooperative environments [17]. However, many real-world interactions occur between *uninvolved* (or self-interested) agents, who are neither teammates nor opponents, but who hold individual goals and consider other actors only to the extent that they are relevant to those goals.

De Weerdt and Clement [29] review some work involving planning for self-interested multi-agent contexts, such as [7], where agents share a joint problem but are unwilling to revise their individual plans. [4] emphasize that in multi-agent domains a robot's plans are contingent partly upon the goals of other agents, and that those goals will depend upon whether those agents are teammates, adversaries, or have overlapping goals. [5] formalize the concept of coupling between agents in a multi-agent system, and [24] develop a planning algorithm based on that work for agents that can decide to enter into coordinated plans. In [6] self-interested agents can form coalitions if they decide it is beneficial to do so. [2] also consider situations where agents would decide to cooperate, especially when their relationship constitutes a Nash equilibrium, and [25] discusses of self-interested planning within a game-theoretic framework.

Epistemic Planning, e.g. as in [3], involves the explicit representation of agents' belief and knowledge. Future work will incorporate such methods into our approach, in particular to predict an agent's behavior based upon her possibly-inclomple or -erroneous perspective of the task state.

3   Behavior Models

Given the diversity of human behavior, planning for the effects of all possible human actions in every considered world state will be intractable for any nontrivial problem, especially with multiple humans. We therefore propose that the robot have access to mental models of human interactants (either specific or generic models) that predict what the humans may do. A mental model is a mapping that, for any world state, gives a set of *likely* human actions. In other words, while a large number of actions might be available to the human in any given state, the model provides a much smaller number of likely actions, one of which the human is expected to take. Thus, from the robot's perspective, the model limits the human's actions and cuts down the number of reachable world states for the planner to consider. This allows the robot to develop plans to accomplish its goals that, in some cases, can even benefit uninvolved humans. We will demonstrate the utility of the approach in a proof-of-concept user study that shows empirically for the first time that planning for uninvolved humans can help the robot reach a goal it could otherwise not have accomplished.

Powerful predictive models could be built within a *mental model* framework, involving a human's goals, perceptual and action capabilities, knowledge, team roles, attitudes, preferences, and other factors [26]. Such a model could use a cognitive architecture, such as ACT-R [1] or SOAR [18], to emulate human cognitive processes. In domains where a human is likely to perform goal-oriented behavior, the model could involve a planner. This could be the same planner used by the robot, as in [20], where a single planner switches perspective to reason "as if" it were another agent. In general, however, a human may plan nonoptimally, or otherwise differently than the robot. Thus, our approach relaxes the assumption that the robot planner is capable of reasoning like a human by offloading such reasoning into the model. In order to focus on how our planner uses predictive models, the models used in our evaluations (Sect. 4.3) are simpler than those suggested above.

4   The Planner

In this section, we present an implementation of our planning framework, using a simple state representation (a state here is a set of propositions) and human model (a basic forward-search planner). However, our approach can be applied to richer mental models that involve a human's (possibly incorrect) belief state, as well as more complex state space representations, such as epistemic states, that might be needed to support such models.

We start by defining the class of multi-agent planning problems that our implementation solves (Sects. 4.1 and 4.2), followed by a description of our simplified mental model (Sect. 4.3), and an explanation of how our planning algorithm uses that model (Sect. 4).

4.1   Definitions

State: A state is a set of propositions, ground formulas over a first-order logic, that describe the task environment at some time.

Agents: We assume two agents: a robot r and a human h.

Actions: An action a is a 3-tuple $(a_{\mathrm{pre}}, a_{\mathrm{add}}, a_{\mathrm{del}})$, where a_{pre} is a set of precondition propositions, a_{add} is the add list: the set of propositions the action causes to be true, and a_{del} is the delete list: the set of propositions the action causes to be false. Each agent is capable of performing a set of deterministic actions, A^r and A^h, respectively, and A^r_s and A^h_s are the sets of actions that are available in state s to each agent, respectively.

Model: A mental model M is a system of facts and rules that predict the human's actions. Thus, $M(s)$ refers to the set of human actions that the model predicts the human is likely to take in state s.

Transition Function: A transition function T uses M to determine how the robot's actions, in concert with predicted human actions, affect the system state. The transition function takes the form $T(s, a^r) \rightarrow S$ where s is a system state, a^r is an action of the robot, and S is the set of states that *could* result when the robot performs a^r in s. It is defined as

$$T(s, a^r) = \bigcup_{a^h \in M(s)} (s \setminus a^r_{\mathrm{del}} \setminus a^h_{\mathrm{del}} \cup a^r_{\mathrm{add}} \cup a^h_{\mathrm{add}})$$

if $a^r_{\mathrm{pre}} \subseteq s \wedge (a^r_{\mathrm{del}} \cap a^h_{\mathrm{del}} = \emptyset) \, \forall a^h \in M(s)$, otherwise undefined. Thus, the transition function is only defined for robot actions whose preconditions are met and whose delete list does not conflict with the delete list of any applicable human action. It is assumed that M only returns legal actions, i.e. $a^h_{\mathrm{pre}} \subseteq s \, \forall a^h \in M(s)$.

Goals: Let G be a set of (robot) goal propositions. Then $G' = \{s : G \subseteq s\}$ is the set of goal states.

4.2 Planning Problem

Given a start state s_0, a set of goal propositions G, a set of robot actions A^r, and a model M, find a policy $(\pi : S \rightarrow A)$ that satisfies action preconditions $(\pi(s)_{pre} \subseteq s \; \forall s \in S)$, outputs only actions whose results are goal states or are in the policy domain $(T(s, \pi(s)) \subseteq S \cup G' \; \forall s \in S)$, and is guaranteed to reach a goal state from the start state. That is, unless it is a goal state, the start state is in the policy $(s_0 \in S \cup G')$, and any sequence of states beginning with the start state $(s_0, s_1, s_2 \ldots)$, and resulting from following the policy $(s_{i>0} \in T(s_{i-1}, \pi(s_{i-1})))$, is acyclic $(i \neq j \rightarrow s_i \neq s_j)$.

Thus, π is an acyclic safe solution [14]. This requirement for acyclic safe solutions may be too strong for some real world scenarios, especially because it is not possible to account for all possible human actions. Indeed, it may be necessary to replan, and possibly update the model on-line, when the human does something not predicted by the model.

4.3 Mental Model

While our approach admits any model that maps world states to sets of likely human actions (the robot's planning algorithm consults M as an oracle), the model we have implemented to evaluate our method is a basic forward state-space search (breadth-first search) planner. Inputs are the human's goals (which do not change) and a world state (perfect knowledge is assumed). The model finds the set of minimal-cost plans, where a plan is a sequence of human actions that transitions the system to a state that satisfies the human's goals, and returns the set containing the first action of each of those plans. Memoization prevents redundant computation of human plans in the case of multiple queries to the model. We assume that the human has perfect knowledge of the state of the system at all times, will plan optimally, and will replan as necessary in response to unexpected state changes.

4.4 Planner

We adopt the technique proposed by [21] to cast multi-agent planning problems into single agent Fully-Observable Non-Deterministic (FOND) problems. The actions of other agents, unknown to the planner at plan time, are interpreted as nondeterminism in the planning agent's actions. From the planner's perspective, the outcomes of the robot's actions are nondeterministic because the planner does not know what the other agents do (in our case, which of the model-predicted human actions will be performed).

Our planner searches over states, where actions induce state transitions as defined in Sect. 4.1. We use a well-known nondeterministic planning algorithm:

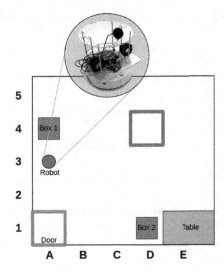

Fig. 1. Setup for the HRI experiment, including the iRobot Create robotic platform (Color figure online)

search over an "and-or" graph as presented in [14] (Algorithms 5.5 and 5.6). An implicit "and-or" graph represents the changing system state as actions are applied. "Or"-nodes represent the possible actions that the robot can take at some state; "and"-nodes represent possible human actions as predicted by the behavior model. A minimax search over the "and-or" graph finds, for each system state explored, the action that minimizes the worst-case cost (number of robot) of reaching the goal. By minimizing the cost for the robot to accomplish its goals while planning for those possible actions of other agents that most increase the cost to the robot, this algorithm is appropriate for completely oppositional scenarios. However, non-oppositional and cooperative dynamics emerge when the predicted actions of other agents are helpful to the robot. That is, "and-or" search *can* solve purely antagonistic scenarios, but also allows cooperation when it is useful. We add iterative deepening to the algorithm, which improves the speed of our planner, and since all actions in our domains have uniform cost, does not relax the guarantee of a worst-case optimal solution.

5   Experiment

We conducted a proof-of-concept HRI experiment (Fig. 1) to evaluate our planning technique with human participants. The robot is an iRobot Create, a 32 cm-diameter circular robot driven by two wheels, which was able to move, turn and push objects. Two three-cubic-foot ($18 \times 18 \times 16$ in.) empty cardboard boxes were positioned on the floor of a large room at equal distances (3 m) from the door (the human's starting position, marked with a green square drawn on the floor)

Table 1. Solution policy for the box-moving scenario

State:	at(robot, spaceA3), at(human, spaceA1), at(box1, spaceA4), at(box2, spaceD1)
Action:	push box1 to spaceA5 and move to spaceA4
State:	at(robot, spaceA4), at(human, spaceB1), at(box1, spaceA5), at(box2, spaceD1)
Action:	move to spaceB4
State:	at(robot, spaceB4), at(human, spaceC1), at(box1, spaceA5), at(box2, spaceD1)
Action:	move to spaceC4
State:	at(robot, spaceC4), at(human, spaceD1), at(box1, spaceA5), at(box2, spaceD1)
Action:	move to spaceC3
State:	at(robot, spaceC3), at(human, spaceD1), at(box1, spaceA5), has(human,box)
Action:	move to spaceC2
State:	at(robot, spaceC2), at(human, spaceD2), at(box1, spaceA5), has(human,box)
Action:	move to spaceC1
State:	at(robot, spaceC1), at(human, spaceD2), at(box1, spaceA5), has(human, box)
Action:	move to spaceD1

and from a target area (marked with an orange square drawn on the floor). A table was placed behind Box 2.

In the domain representation, each agent can move between adjacent spaces and both agents can occupy the same space. Agents act simultaneously. The human can pick up a box in a space she occupies. The robot cannot pick up boxes or move into a space containing a box, but can push boxes. When the robot pushes a box, it moves into the space where the box had been, and the box moves one space in the same direction as the robot moves (pushing isn't allowed if the there is no space for the box to move into). The task of the robot was to move to a position on the floor marked with an X, which was under Box 2. In order for the robot to reach that position, the human needed to move Box 2, which the robot was unable to push because of the wall and the table.

The planner returns a policy (Table 1) that allows the robot to achieve its goal. From the start state, the robot pushes Box 1 to space A5. Now that Box 1 is further away from the human, the model predicts that the human will move toward Box 2, and as the human moves toward Box 2, and eventually picks it up and moves toward the orange square, the robot moves to space D1.

The human was given the following instructions by an experimenter: "Please enter the white room and stand in the green square by the door. Stay there until I say begin. There are two cardboard boxes on the floor. Do you see them? In addition to the green square where you are standing, there is an orange square on the floor. Do you see it? Your task is to retrieve one of the boxes, and place it on the floor in the orange square. Begin." All subjects responded affirmatively to both questions, and no other information about the robot or the planner was provided.

The robot began moving as the experimenter said "Begin". The robot was remotely controlled according to the policy in order to avoid unrelated robot control issues such as collision detection, orientation detection, and localization. Thus, the experimenter manually implementing the policy calculated by the planner. A camera mounted on the wall above the door allowed the experimenter controlling the robot to observe the robot's movement.

An important element of the experiment that was *not* represented in the planning domain was that we placed three whiteboard markers on top of Box 2. The model predicts that, with no robot intervention, the human might pick up Box 1 or Box 2. However, in a state where Box 1 has been moved to space A5, the model predicts that the human will necessarily pick up Box 1. Thus, because the robot planner finds safe solutions, it discovers the robot plan to push Box 1, guaranteeing (as long as the model prediction holds) that the human will pick up Box 1. Because we were interested in studying the robot's ability to change the human's plan, we added the markers to Box 2 in order to incentivize the human to make an original plan (pre-robot-intervention) to pick up Box 1.

6   Results

Twenty adult subjects participated in the study (11 male, 8 female, 1 preferred not to answer, mean age = 31 years, standard deviation of age = 12.16 years). After consenting to participate in the study, subjects were guided to the experiment room. Following the completion of the experimental task, the subject filled out a questionnaire with the following questions: Which box did you retrieve? Did you change your mind about which box to retrieve? Did the robot cause you to change your mind about which box to retrieve? Why did you select the box(es) you did? Why do you think the robot behaved as it did?

Seventeen subjects moved Box 2, the remaining three moved Box 1. Of the subjects that moved Box 2, twelve said that the robot caused them to change their mind about which box to retrieve, although one of those specified that they "picked my choice before the robot started to move" (we interpret this to mean that the robot's presence, but not actions, influenced the subject's decision). The other eight subjects (five of whom moved Box 2, and 3 of whom moved box 1) said that the robot did not cause them to change their mind. Thus we conclude that the robot's behavior successfully altered the human's actions to allow the robot to accomplish its goal in 11 of our 20 runs.

From subject responses to the question "why did you select the box(es) you did?" we discern six main motivating factors. These factors, and selected relevant subject responses, are reported in Table 2. In response to the question "why do you think the robot behaved as it did?" most subjects referenced the intentions of either researcher, the robot programmer, or the robot itself. Selected responses are reported in Table 3. Two of the runs suffered technical difficulties. In one run the robot halted after pushing Box 1 one meter and never turned or moved toward the Box 2 start location. In another run the robot failed to move altogether, and the subject "did not notice the robot." In both of these runs, the subject moved Box 2 and said that they did not change their mind.

7   Discussion

Our results demonstrate that it is possible for a robot to use our planning technique to influence what actions humans take within our test scenario. Several subject responses suggest that they considered trade-offs between two or more factors. For example, one participant responded: "Initially I was going to select box 1, because box 2 had markers on it which I didn't want to knock off. When the robot moved box 1, I changed my mind because moving box 2 without knocking off the markers now seemed easier." Perhaps the most interesting trade-offs are between interfering with the robot and facing physical difficulties. It seems people prefer the cost of dealing with difficulties presented by the physical environment to the mental and emotional cost of dealing with dynamic agents that are harder to predict. This is suggestive that it is easier not to try to figure out another agent's goals and plan your actions around it: "Because the robot was going after box 1 so I chose the other one. It was just easier."

Table 2. Selected responses to the question "why did you select the box(es) you did?"

Motivating factor	Subject response
Physical obstruction	"Robot was between me and the box"
Visibility	"It was the one directly in front of me"
	"Because it was the first one I saw"
Box motion	"I didn't care to pick up a moving box"
Perceived distance	"It [Box 2] seemed to me to be closer to the orange square in which I was supposed to place the box"
	"Visually box 1 seemed closer"
	"Even when the robot started to move, that box [Box 1] was closer"
Markers on Box 2	"I initially chose box 1 because it didn't have a bunch of stuff on top"
	"It didn't have markers on it and so was easier to get and move, as I didn't need to move the markers"
	"Initially I was going to select box 1, because box 2 had markers on it which I didn't want to knock off"
Reluctance to interfere with the robot	"As soon as robot went for first, I went for second"
	"The robot started moving toward box 1"
	"I retrieved box 2 because the robot was moving towards box 1"

Furthermore, it seems that not only does our robot model the human, but the human models the robot's goals and intentions: "It seemed like the robot was doing something with box 1, so it was easier to perform the task I was asked to do with box 2. That way I didn't have to compete with the robot." "The other box was in use by the robot so I felt bad about taking the box away from it, so I figured it would just be easier to move the other box." "It was easier to get Box 2 because the robot wasn't interfering [with] it."

It is remarkable that, even in this simple task and with a non-humanoid robot, participants had some degree of emotional involvement, for example "feeling bad

Table 3. Selected responses to the question "Why do you think the robot behaved as it did?"

Assigned intention	Subject response
Researcher	"To test how people perceive objects that are in use by robot, which would give a sense of how much people see robots as autonomous beings that have motivations for performing actions"
	"Perhaps the researchers are trying to see if anti-social behavior on the part of the robot causes people to change their courses of action"
Programmer	"I assume it was programmed to push box 1"
	"It seemed programmed to push the box in that direction..."
Robot	"It wanted to move the box to a new location"
	"It might have been stuck behind box 1, or it might have been intentionally pushing it somewhere..."
	"Maybe it also wanted to move the box? Maybe it was trying to help me move it?"
	"It seemed like it had some goal to move the boxes"

about taking the box away." Participants described the robot with anthropomorphic terms, for exampling discussing the robot's wants: "It did not have stuff on it but I almost changed my mind because the robot seemed to want my box but then I decided to do it anyway." Participants discuss interactions with the robot in ways similar to social interactions between humans, referring to inconveniencing the robot: "I did not want to disturb the robot." "I chose box 2 because I figured there was a reason there was a robot between me and box 1, and I didn't want to mess with it." One participant changed their mind twice, apparently motivated by such human considerations: "I initially chose box 1 because it didn't have a bunch of stuff on top. Then it seemed like the robot might be engaged in some sort of task with box 1, so I considered choosing box 2 as not to inconvenience it. Then it appeared the robot might be stuck on box 1 so I chose box 1 in the hope that I might also be doing the robot a favor in removing the obstruction."

8   Conclusion

We have made the case for an HRI planning framework that avoids assuming either cooperative or oppositional inter-agent relations by employing predictive behavior models of human agents. From the planner's perspective, these models are black-box oracles that reduce the possibly vast number of possible human actions to a smaller number of likely actions. We have shown how this approach allows a single planner to operate with co-present humans having diverse teaming relations with respect to the robot. We have presented a preliminary implementation of our framework using simplified models and a simplified state space representation. We have presented the results of a preliminary, proof-of-concept experimental study which demonstrate that a robot equipped with our planner can elicit human actions that help the robot achieve its goals. Finally, we have analyzed participant survey responses to reveal some of the social dynamics of human-robot interaction.

Acknowledgements. This work was in part funded by AFOSR grant number FA9550-18-1-0465 and NASA grant number C17-2D00-TU.

References

1. Anderson, J.R.: Rules of the Mind. Psychology Press, Hove (2014)
2. Ben Larbi, R., Konieczny, S., Marquis, P.: Extending classical planning to the multi-agent case: a game-theoretic approach. In: Mellouli, K. (ed.) ECSQARU 2007. LNCS (LNAI), vol. 4724, pp. 731–742. Springer, Heidelberg (2007). https://doi.org/10.1007/978-3-540-75256-1_64
3. Bolander, T.: A gentle introduction to epistemic planning: the DEL approach. Electron. Proc. Theoret. Comput. Sci. **243**, 1–22 (2017). https://doi.org/10.4204/eptcs.243.1
4. Bowling, M., Jensen, R., Veloso, M.: Multi-agent planning in the presence of multiple goals, Chap. 10, pp. 301–325. Wiley (2006). https://doi.org/10.1002/0471781266.ch10. https://onlinelibrary.wiley.com/doi/abs/10.1002/0471781266.ch10
5. Brafman, R.I., Domshlak, C.: From one to many: planning for loosely coupled multi-agent systems. In: ICAPS, pp. 28–35 (2008)
6. Brafman, R.I., Domshlak, C., Engel, Y., Tennenholtz, M.: Planning games. In: IJCAI, pp. 73–78 (2009)
7. Buzing, P., ter Mors, A., Valk, J., Witteveen, C.: Coordinating self-interested planning agents. Auton. Agents Multi-Agent Syst. **12**(2), 199–218 (2006). https://doi.org/10.1007/s10458-005-6104-4
8. Chakraborti, T., Kambhampati, S.: Algorithms for the greater good! On mental modeling and acceptable symbiosis in human-AI collaboration. CoRR abs/1801.09854 (2018). http://arxiv.org/abs/1801.09854
9. Chakraborti, T., Kambhampati, S., Scheutz, M., Zhang, Y.: AI challenges in human-robot cognitive teaming. arXiv preprint arXiv:1707.04775 (2017)
10. Chen, M., Nikolaidis, S., Soh, H., Hsu, D., Srinivasa, S.: Planning with trust for human-robot collaboration. In: Proceedings of the 2018 ACM/IEEE International Conference on Human-Robot Interaction, HRI 2018, pp. 307–315. ACM, New York (2018). https://doi.org/10.1145/3171221.3171264. https://doi.acm.org/10.1145/3171221.3171264
11. Chidambaram, V., Chiang, Y., Mutlu, B.: Designing persuasive robots: how robots might persuade people using vocal and nonverbal cues. In: 2012 7th ACM/IEEE International Conference on Human-Robot Interaction (HRI), pp. 293–300 (2012). https://doi.org/10.1145/2157689.2157798
12. Cirillo, M., Karlsson, L., Saffiotti, A.: Human-aware task planning: an application to mobile robots. ACM Trans. Intell. Syst. Technol. **1**(2), 15:1–15:26 (2010). https://doi.org/10.1145/1869397.1869404. https://doi.acm.org/10.1145/1869397.1869404

13. Dragan, A.D.: Robot planning with mathematical models of human state and action (2017)
14. Ghallab, M., Nau, D., Traverso, P.: Automated Planning and Acting. Cambridge University Press, Cambridge (2016). https://doi.org/10.1017/CBO9781139583923
15. Görür, O.C., Rosman, B., Sivrikaya, F., Albayrak, S.: Social cobots: anticipatory decision-making for collaborative robots incorporating unexpected human behaviors. In: Proceedings of the 2018 ACM/IEEE International Conference on Human-Robot Interaction, HRI 2018, pp. 398–406. ACM, New York (2018). https://doi.org/10.1145/3171221.3171256. https://doi.acm/10.1145/3171221.3171256
16. Gray, J., Breazeal, C.: Manipulating mental states through physical action. Int. J. Soc. Robot. **6**(3), 315–327 (2014). https://doi.org/10.1007/s12369-014-0234-2
17. Kulkarni, A., Srivastava, S., Kambhampati, S.: Implicit robot-human communication in adversarial and collaborative environments. CoRR abs/1802.06137 (2018). http://arxiv.org/abs/1802.06137
18. Laird, J.E.: The Soar Cognitive Architecture. MIT Press, Cambridge (2012)
19. Milliez, G., Lallement, R., Fiore, M., Alami, R.: Using human knowledge awareness to adapt collaborative plan generation, explanation and monitoring. In: 2016 11th ACM/IEEE International Conference on Human-Robot Interaction (HRI), pp. 43–50 (2016). https://doi.org/10.1109/HRI.2016.7451732
20. Muise, C., et al.: Planning over multi-agent epistemic states: a classical planning approach. In: Proceedings of AAAI 2012, The Twenty-Sixth AAAI Conference on Artificial Intelligence (2015). https://www.aaai.org/ocs/index.php/AAAI/AAAI15/paper/view/9974
21. Muise, C., Felli, P., Miller, T., Pearce, A.R., Sonenberg, L.: Leveraging FOND planning technology to solve multi-agent planning problems. In: Workshop on Distributed and Multi-Agent Planning (DMAP 2015) (2015). http://www.haz.ca/papers/muise-dmap15-mapasfond.pdf
22. Nikolaidis, S., Hsu, D., Srinivasa, S.: Human-robot mutual adaptation in collaborative tasks: models and experiments. Int. J. Robot. Res. **36**(5–7), 618–634 (2017). https://doi.org/10.1177/0278364917690593
23. Nikolaidis, S., Kwon, M., Forlizzi, J., Srinivasa, S.: Planning with verbal communication for human-robot collaboration. ACM Trans. Hum.-Robot Interact. **7**(3), 22:1–22:21 (2018). https://doi.org/10.1145/3203305
24. Nissim, R., Brafman, R.I., Domshlak, C.: A general, fully distributed multi-agent planning algorithm. In: Proceedings of the 9th International Conference on Autonomous Agents and Multiagent Systems: Volume 1, AAMAS 2010, vol. 1, pp. 1323–1330. International Foundation for Autonomous Agents and Multiagent Systems, Richland, SC (2010). http://dl.acm.org/citation.cfm?id=1838206.1838379
25. Prunera, J.J.M.: Non-cooperative games for self-interested planning agents. Ph.D. thesis, Universitat Politècnica de València (2017). https://doi.org/10.4995/Thesis/10251/90417
26. Scheutz, M., DeLoach, S., Adams, J.: A framework for developing and using shared mental models in human-agent teams. J. Cogn. Eng. Decis. Mak. **11**(3), 203–224 (2017)
27. Talamadupula, K., Briggs, G., Chakraborti, T., Scheutz, M., Kambhampati, S.: Coordination in human-robot teams using mental modeling and plan recognition. In: 2014 IEEE/RSJ International Conference on Intelligent Robots and Systems (IROS 2014), pp. 2957–2962. IEEE (2014)
28. Torreño, A., Onaindia, E., Komenda, A., Stolba, M.: Cooperative multi-agent planning: a survey. CoRR abs/1711.09057 (2017). http://arxiv.org/abs/1711.09057
29. de Weerdt, M., Clement, B.: Introduction to planning in multiagent systems. Multiagent Grid Syst. **5**, 345–355 (2009)

Conversational Flow in Human-Robot Interactions at the Workplace: Comparing Humanoid and Android Robots

Ruth Stock-Homburg, Martin Hannig$^{(\boxtimes)}$, and Lucie Lilienthal

Technical University of Darmstadt, Hochschulstraße 1, 64289 Darmstadt, Germany
{rsh,martin.hannig}@bwl.tu-darmstadt.de,
lucie.lilienthal@stud.tu-darmstadt.de

Abstract. This article deals with the conversational flow during human-robot interactions at the workplace. We conducted an experimental field study in a company setting. Drawing on computer-as-social-actor (CASA) paradigm, we argue that employees might mindlessly apply social rules in conversations with service robots which is reflected in the degree of conversational flow. We examined to which extent the structure of the Conversational Skills Rating Scale (CSRS) can be replicated with real-life human-robot interactions and whether there are differences in conversational flow between humanoid robots, android robots and humans. We could show that the conversational flow in such service settings at the workplace is based on the factors expressiveness, coordination and composure. The results show that android robots can evoke a higher level of expressiveness in employees than humanoid robots. To our knowledge, our study is the first to compare different aspects of conversational flow towards service robots in a real workplace setting. Since conversational flow can create social bonds and satisfy social needs, companies should use this knowledge when considering using robots in customer or employee contact.

Keywords: Android robots · CASA paradigm · Conversational flow · Human likeness · Humanoid robots · Human-robot interaction · Robots at workplace · Service robots

1 Introduction

Conversations are fundamental for maintaining social relationships as they provide the means to establish bonds and develop a shared understanding of reality [1]. Therefore, a good quality of those conversations is crucial. As conversational form, conversational flow contributes important aspects to the quality of conversations [2].

Conversational flow is defined as the extent of smooth and efficient exchange of nonverbal and verbal information [1, 3]. A conversation with good flow is a "strong cue to the existence of common ground anchored in a sense of social unity and/or a positive relationship" [2]. Conversational flow can serve different social needs [4]. For

© Springer Nature Switzerland AG 2020
A. R. Wagner et al. (Eds.): ICSR 2020, LNAI 12483, pp. 578–589, 2020.
https://doi.org/10.1007/978-3-030-62056-1_48

example, a high degree of conversational flow is related to positive self-esteem [4], has an influence on the personal sense of belonging and is able to promote solidarity [2].

In recent years, conversations with digital services, and thus also service robots have gained importance [5]. Service robots are "system-based autonomous and adaptable interfaces that interact, communicate and deliver service to an organization's customers" [5] and may replace millions of service workers in the coming decade [6]. The emergence of these robots is among the most substantial evolutions in the service realm [7]. This development is changing the nature of service and customer's service frontline experiences [8].

Building service robots that make users feel a sense of conversation with them, is a formidable challenge [9]. Therefore, an investigation of the conversational flow in human-robot interaction seems useful. For service robots it also seems important to serve the social needs of their customers and therefore should not be seen as unable to grasp logical or maintain conversational flow with their interaction partners [9]. If a conversation disruption occurs, it may be difficult for the user to remain motivated towards the conversation as the fulfilment of social needs may be disturbed [9]. Previous research on human-chatbot conversations showed that there is still potential for development, especially regarding the richness of vocabulary which may exhibit greater profanity [10].

In order to measure conversational flow, we rely on the Conversational Skills Rating Scale (CSRS) which was originally designed as "a measure of interpersonal skills applicable in virtually all face-to-face conversational interaction" [11]. With our first research question, we would like to transfer this scale for conversational flow to service interactions with robots and humans at the workplace. We chose the workplace as setting for our experiment for several reasons. While some research on service robots in the marketplace (i.e. restaurants, retail, travel, health care) has been conducted in recent years [7], the state of research on service robots at the workplace is still sparse. Nevertheless, research in this area is quite important. Robots that take roles of employees are important because this can lead to reduced workload and increased speed of task execution [12]. Their internal use in professional services ranges from financial auditing to assisting in medical surgery [13]. But efficient human-robot collaboration requires good and fluent communication. Therefore, we measure the conversational flow towards service robots at the workplace and ask with our first research question: *Can the measurement of conversational flow based on the structure of the Conversational Skills Rating Scale (CSRS) be replicated to service interactions at the workplace?*

The Anthropomorphic Robot Database [14] shows that there is a variety of service robots with different functions, appearance and effects. So far, a typical classification of service robots has been done into mechanical, humanoid, or android robots [15]. In contrast to mechanical robots, humanoid robots have human-looking forms, with a head, arms, legs, and a torso [16]. However, humanoid robots are still distinct from humans in terms of physical appearance, as they still have also a mechanical aspect [15]. An android robot is "an artificial system designed with the ultimate goal of being indistinguishable from humans in its external appearance and behavior" [17]. The appearance of android robots is designed to be a perfect copy of a human body [15]. People perceive humanoid and android robots differently based on appearance and behavior [18–20].

Therefore, in our study we want to take both a humanoid and an android robot into account and ask with our second research question: *Are there differences in conversational flow towards android and humanoid robots in human-robot-interactions at the workplace?*

2 Theory and Hypotheses

Humans are likely to apply social rules and expectations to computers and use social scripts of human-human interaction in human-computer interaction [21]. These assumptions are based on the Computers-as-Social-Actors (CASA) paradigm, which can also be transferred to the conversational flow in human-robot interactions. During human-robot interactions, the extent of the application of social rules is influenced by the physical presence of the robot and can be triggered by social cues [22, 23]. A more human-like conception of the robot can facilitate interactions [24] because anthropomorphism enables trust and compliance with the robot [25]. The more human-like a robot appears the stronger is the application of social rules [22].

The CASA paradigm is underpinned by the media equation theory [26]. According to the media equation theory, people tend to humanize technological devices and treat them socially when the technology shows social cues, for example the use of natural language, an interactive character or the fulfilment of a certain role. This behavior can be mindful or mindless [22]. The used social cues do not need be particularly strong [27]. As long as the medium shows behaviors that indicate a social presence, people react accordingly by using social, interpersonal interaction rules and applying these to their interaction with the medium [26]. The medium's behavior towards people also influences their perception. Although one is rationally aware that there is no social counterpart and some people even deny their reaction afterwards, media equation is nevertheless shown [27].

The aim of the current study is to examine the conversational flow with service robots in a real-life workplace setting and to investigate to what degree conversational flow is present in human-robot-interactions. Drawing on the CASA paradigm, we argue that employees might mindlessly apply social rules in conversations with service robots [21].

Android robots enable us to study phenomena in human-robot interaction that could not be understood with mechanical-looking humanoid robots alone [18]. Therefore, we cannot ignore the role of appearance, which gives us a subjective impression of automated presence or intelligence [8, 18]. During service encounters with robots, the robot's appearance affects user perception [19] and biases human expectations [28]. The fact that android robots have a higher degree of human-likeness leads to the assumption, supported by the CASA paradigm, that the conversational flow towards android robots may be higher as towards humanoid robots as the participants even more follow the socially learned scripts of interpersonal interaction. Formally, we argue:

H1: The conversational flow in service interactions at the workplace is higher towards humans than towards (a) android robots and (b) humanoid robots.

H2: The conversational flow in human-robot interactions at the workplace is higher towards android robots than towards humanoid robots.

Although conversational flow is important for maintaining conversations with a good quality and there is need for research applying this concept to human-robot interactions, today there is only little evidence in this area. To our knowledge, this is the first type of study that tests the conversational flow towards service robots in an experiment within a real company setting. This study aims to investigate which types of robots are more suitable to maintain certain aspects of conversational flow in an interaction, which could have a high relevance for companies that increasingly use these robots in service contact with customers and employees [7] as well as for further research in this rising research field.

3 Method

3.1 Sample and Data Collection

As humanoid robot for our experimental study, we used the robot "Pepper", developed by SoftBank Robotics. Our android robot "Elenoide" resembles a European woman. She was designed by A-Lab in Japan and has totally 49 degrees of freedom, of which are twelve in the face. The exoskeleton of Elenoide is covered with a skin-like layer aimed to give her a more human-like look. We programmed her emotional expressions to reproduce human emotions as best as possible. We validated the expressions with a sample of 132 students who had to rate gestures and mimics of Elenoide shown on a video.

For our experimental study, we used experimental vignette methodology. The idea of experimental vignette methodology is to confront the participants with realistic scenarios and thus improve experimental realism and manipulate and control different variables [29]. We developed a specific vignette for this study: In the first step, we contacted HR experts of the company in which the experimental study took place. Based on grounded theory [30] we wanted to identify the most relevant HR topics. The HR experts identified training opportunities and work-life balance as relevant HR topics. We integrated these topics into a vignette and constantly improved the vignette throughout the interviews with the HR experts, until the interview partners repeatedly made no further comments. In total, we conducted in-depth interviews with ten HR experts.

The present study was conducted within a global company of the chemical industry. All employees at the company's headquarters were invited to take part in the experiment. Every employee who took part in the experimental study interacted either with the humanoid robot, with the android robot or with a human as HR representatives. Participants were randomized assigned to one of the three groups. The participants received no financial compensation for their participation in this research project.

Before the interaction, the employees received the vignette and the examiner made sure that the vignette was correctly understood. The participants then interacted in a separate room with a HR representative and talked about subjects determined by the vignette. Thus, the actual conversation dialog was about topics related to training opportunities and work-life balance. These topics were tailored to the employees of the company and very close to their actual work context, which was confirmed several times in the interviews with the HR experts conducted in advance.

All service representatives acted autonomously and were trained with the same chat-bot script to generate comparable results. Each conversation was captured by video in order for post analysis of conversational flow. Video data from 197 participants (79 male, 118 female) was available, the mean age was 39.87 ($SD = 10.78$), ranging from 21 to 60. The mean duration of the interaction with HR representatives was 11:55 min ($SD = 04:57$ min). In total, we analyzed 63 interactions with the humanoid robot, 65 interactions with the android robot, and 67 interaction with the human service representative.

3.2 Measures and Data Analysis

For measuring conversational flow, we used the Conversational Skills Rating Scale (CSRS) developed by Spitzberg [11]. The scale was originally designed for student samples, but has also been applied to businesspersons, non-student adults, school principals, and military personnel [11]. For the aim of the current study, we adapted it to human-robot-interactions at the workplace. The author of the CSRS proposed that the scale consists of 25 communicative behaviors persons display in conversation and five items of overall performance. The behavioral items can be subdivided into four subscales: *attentiveness* (i.e., attention to, interest in and concern for conversational partner), *composure* (i.e., confidence, assertiveness, and relaxation), *expressiveness* (i.e., animation and variation in verbal and nonverbal forms of expression), and *coordination* (i.e., the nondisruptive negotiation of speaking turns, conversational initiation, and conversational closings) [11]. The conversational flow of those service interactions was rated by observers afterwards based on the available videos of the interactions.

We conducted a factor analysis for proving the subscale structure of the Conversational Skills Rate Scale (CSRS) and an analysis of variance (ANOVA) with a LSD post-hoc test between all three groups, for examining differences in conversational flow. Significance level was set at $\alpha = 0.05$.

4   Results

Aiming to prove the structure as proposed [11], we first conducted a confirmatory factor analysis with the data of the employees' conversational flow. Pre-requirements for analysis were given as Kaiser-Meyer-Olkin factor adequacy was .76, which is according to literature middling [31], and Bartlett-Test was significant ($\chi^2 (300) = 1736.679, p < .001$). Factor analysis was conducted for the four subscales with 25 items. Model fit was examined trough different fit indices, for example the Standardized Root Mean Square Residual (SRMR) and the Root-Mean-Square Error of Approximation (RMSEA), thereby lower values indicating a better model fit (e.g. less than .05 for RMSEA and less than .08 for SRMR [32, 33]). For the Tucker Lewis Index (TLI) and the Comparative Fit Index (CFI), higher values indicate better model fit (e.g. higher than .95 for CFI and TLI [34]). Chi-Squared (χ^2) indicates the deviation between latent and manifest covariance matrices and should therefore be not significant for good model fit, the ratio of χ^2/df should be 2 for a good model fit [34].

Results of parallel analysis indicated four factors with eigenvalues from 2.12 to 5.04. Nonetheless, the computed model with confirmatory factor analysis as proposed

[11] yielded no good factorial support and inadequate model fit for our data in service interactions (χ^2 (269) = 821.219, < .001, χ^2/df = 3.05, CFI = .584, TLI = .536, RMSEA = .108, SRMR = .126). Factor loadings ranged from .02 to .91.

For reliability analysis and as a further proof for scale coherence, we computed Cronbach's alpha for each subscale. Cronbach's alpha was only acceptable for expressiveness (.72) [35]. It was questionable for coordination (.67) and poor for attentiveness (.53) and composure (.52) [35]. Items showed a wide range of item-total correlations, from .06 to .64. As good item-total correlations should be between .4 and .7 [36], some of the items did not distinguished well between persons with high and low values of conversational flow. The results showed that the division into subscales, as they can be used for interpersonal interactions, seems difficult to transfer to service interactions with robots at the workplace.

Therefore, we have carried out an additional exploratory factor analysis with our data to examine the items with regard to the factor structure on which they are actually based. Hereby, we followed a given procedure for conceptualization and operationalization of complex constructs [37, 38]. A reasonable degree of convergence and discrimination validity can be assumed in this context if all items can be clearly assigned to one factor [37]. This is precisely possible if all items have a sufficiently high factor charge of at least .4 for one factor [37].

In the first step, a factor analysis with four factors indicated three clearly identifiable factors and a fourth factor with only one single item (*use of time speaking relative to partner*). Following the procedure that items which cannot be assigned to any of the factors or whose assignment is not sufficiently clear are eliminated [38], we removed this one-item factor from further analysis.

In the next step, we ran a factor analysis with three factors. Here, we could clearly identify the factor *expressiveness* again. The second factor consisted mostly of items that were originally allocated to the factor *composure*. The third factor was mainly a combination of items that were originally allocated to the factor *coordination*.

We then took the items that had been correctly assigned to the factors and subjected them to a reliability analysis. For each factor, Cronbach's alpha was calculated within this framework. As long as this reliability score were too low, the item assigned to the factor with the lowest item to total correlation were successively excluded from further analysis [38].

The factor *expressiveness* consisted of five items with a Cronbach's alpha of .77, which is considered to be good [35]. The inter-item correlations were between .48 and .67. Therefore, no further adjustment was necessary for this factor. The list of the corresponding items appears in Table 1.

The factor *composure* consisted of three items with a Cronbach's alpha of .61. The inter-item correlations varied between .39 and .50. Removing the item with the lowest inter-item correlation did not improve Cronbach's Alpha here, so we left the items of the factor as they were (Table 1).

The factor *coordination* consisted of four items, of which one item (*speaking rate*) had a poor item-total correlation of .16. According to the proceeding rules [37], we removed this item. The factor remained with three items, a Cronbach's alpha of .77 and inter-item correlations between .59 and .66 (Table 1).

Table 1. Results of factor analysis

Factor	Item	Cronbach's Alpha/Item-total correlation
Expressiveness		.77
	Use of humor and/or stories	.67
	Facial expressiveness	.63
	Smiling and/or laughing	.55
	Vocal variety	.53
	Use of gestures to emphasize what is being said	.48
Coordination		.77
	Asking of questions	.66
	Initiation of new topics	.62
	Maintenance of topics and follow-up comments	.59
Composure		.61
	Posture	.50
	Unmotivated movements	.43
	Shaking or nervous twitches	.39

The results showed that three of the four originally proposed factors could be demonstrated. Only the factor *attentiveness* could not be transferred to the service setting at the workplace.

With our second research question we wanted to give an answer to which extent the conversational flow of the employees differs towards the two different types of robots, also in comparison to a human service representative. We therefore calculated an analysis of variance (ANOVA) with a LSD post hoc test to examine the main effects of the type of service representative as independent variable on expressiveness, composure and coordination of the employees as dependent variables.

The results were different for each factor and showed that especially the factor *expressiveness* contributed to differences in the conversational flow of the employees towards service robots (Table 2).

The main effect of the ANOVA for the type of service representative on employees' expressiveness yielded an F ratio of $F(2,192) = 25.3$, $p < .01$, confirming the mean differences in expressiveness towards the human representative (M = 3.90) and both the android robot (M = 2.60) and the humanoid robot (M = 2.10). This means that the android robot is able to induce more expressiveness in the interaction partners than the humanoid robot. The model explained variance in expressiveness of $R^2 = .39$ (adjusted $R^2 = .39$, $p < .01$).

The main effect on employees' coordination was significant with an F ratio of $F(2,192) = 1.53$, $p < .01$, showing mean differences in the social behavior towards the human representative ($M = 2.51$) compared to the android robot ($M = 2.26$) and the android robot ($M = 2.24$). The model explained variance in employees' coordination of $R^2 = .07$ (adjusted $R^2 = .06$, $p < .01$).

For the effect of the type of service representative on employees' composure the ANOVA showed an F ratio of $F(2,192) = 1.28$, $p < .05$. Here there were only significant mean differences in the behavior towards the human representative ($M = 4.37$) and the humanoid robot ($M = 4.11$). The model explained variance in employees' composure of $R^2 = .03$ (adjusted $R^2 = .02$, $p < .05$). The results are listed in Table 2.

Table 2. Post hoc test: mean differences for the factors of employees' conversational flow towards different service representatives

	Conversational flow		Mean difference	Sig.
Expressiveness	Humanoid M = 2.10 (SD = .71)	Human M = 3.33 (SD = .65)	ΔM = −1.24** (SE = .11)	.000
	Android M = 2.61 (SD = .54)	Human M = 3.33 (SD = .65)	ΔM = −.73** (SE = .11)	.000
	Humanoid M = 2.10 (SD = .71)	Android M = 2.61 (SD = .54)	ΔM = −.51** (SE = .11)	.000
Coordination	Humanoid M = 2.26 (SD = .36)	Human M = 2.51 (SD = .61)	ΔM = −.25** (SE = .08)	.004
	Android M = 2.24 (SD = .41)	Human M = 2.51 (SD = .61)	ΔM = −.27** (SE = .08)	.001
	Humanoid M = 2.26 (SD = .36)	Android M = 2.24 (SD = .41)	ΔM = .03 (SE = .08)	.736
Composure	Humanoid M = 4.10 (SD = .39)	Human M = 4.37 (SD = .59)	ΔM = −.27* (SE = .08)	.014
	Android M = 4.32 (SD = .41)	Human M = 4.37 (SD = .59)	ΔM = −.05 (SE = .08)	.608
	Humanoid M = 4.10 (SD = .39)	Android M = 4.32 (SD = .41)	ΔM = −.21 (SE = .08)	.053

Notes: M = Mean Value; ΔM = Mean Difference; SD = Standard Deviation; SE = Standard Error; *$p < .05$, **$p < .01$

Hypothesis 1 stated that the conversational flow in service interactions at the workplace was higher towards humans than towards robots. The results of the post hoc test showed support for hypothesis 1b. All aspects of the employees' conversational flow were higher towards the human than the humanoid robot. Regarding hypothesis 1a, results showed the similar differences between the human representative and the android robot, with the exception of the factor *composure*.

Hypothesis 2 argued based on CASA paradigm that the conversational flow towards android robots were higher than towards humanoid robots. When testing this hypothesis, it did make sense to consider the different factors of conversational flow separately. The results showed that the android robot succeeded in inducing a significantly higher expressiveness in employees than the humanoid robot. In the aspects composure and coordination, which also contribute to a successful conversational flow, no differences between the two types of robots could be found.

5 Discussion

The aim of the current study was to examine the structure of the Conversational Skills Rating Scale (CSRS) and to investigate whether employees behave socially different in conversational flow when interacting with robots or humans. We could not replicate the factorial structure of the CSRS completely. An exploratory factor analysis has shown that three of the four aspects could be applied to service settings at the workplace: *expressiveness, coordination* and *composure.*

We could show differences in employees' expressiveness towards the different types of service robots. The android robot was able to evoke a higher level of expressiveness in the employees than the humanoid robot. However, the employees still showed the highest level of conversational flow when interacting with humans.

The only factor of the original CSRS that was not transferable to service settings with robots and humans at the workplace was the factor *attentiveness.* The poor model fit of *attentiveness* could arise from the context the conversation was held in. Some of the items may not be applicable to service interactions as this kind of interactions differs from usual, informal interactions. Based on experimental vignette methodology, participants were instructed to inform themselves about possible trainings opportunities and work-life balance topics at the workplace. This might inhibit the creation of a usual, informal conversation in the present study, which could explain the misfit of the subscale structure. Therefore, we developed an adapted scale to measure conversational flow in service interactions also with robots.

Our investigations tie in with earlier studies on the differences between interpersonal interactions and human-chatbot interactions [10] by examining differences in human-robot interactions in a real workplace setting. Our results are in line with research pointing out that people perceive humanoid and android robots differently based on appearance and behavior [18–20] or that anthropomorphism enables trust and compliance with the robot [25].

Both the humanoid and the android robot were connected to the same chatbot script. However, the expressiveness of the robot's interlocutor, in this case the employee, differs depending on whether they are talking to a humanoid robot or an android robot. These findings are supported by the CASA paradigm [21, 23]. The more human-like a robot appears, the stronger is the application of social rules, which obviously also contributes to an increase in own expressiveness. To our knowledge, our study is the first to prove this assumption in a real workplace setting.

The highest level of conversational flow towards the human service representative could be due to chatbot limitations. However, the human service representative was trained and required to use the same chatbot script as the robots. Thus, it is also conceivable that besides human-likeness also trustworthiness or emotional contagion of the service robot play a role in conversational flow. Future research could start here and investigate these relationships. In addition, future research could investigate possible underlying mechanisms or potential moderator variables for our findings, for example human differences in perception of robots, individual differences regarding personality or communication style.

The design of our experimental study has unique strengths. In contrast to many other studies which are based on theoretical intentions towards robots or findings from laboratory experiments, we measured the conversational flow in real-life human-robot interactions at the workplace. Our results show that the extent of conversational flow depends on the type of robot, and that it makes sense to consider the various factors of conversational flow separately.

Our results give interesting insights on the implementation of android robots in companies. Since conversational flow can create social bonds and satisfy social needs and belonging [4], companies should use this knowledge when considering using robots in customer or employee contact. Our study highlights the advantages of android robots in this respect and provides a good basis for future research in the area of human-robot interactions, especially in the context of service interactions at the workplace.

References

1. Koudenburg, N., Postmes, T., Gordijn, E.H.: Conversational flow and entitativity: the role of status. Br. J. Soc. Psychol. **53**, 350–366 (2014)
2. Koudenburg, N., Postmes, T., Gordijn, E.H.: Conversational flow promotes solidarity. PLoS ONE **8**, 1–6 (2013)
3. Han, J.G., Campbell, N., Jokinen, K., Wilcock, G.: Investigating the use of non-verbal cues in human-robot interaction with a NAO robot. In: 2012 IEEE 3rd International Conference on Cognitive Infocommunications (CogInfoCom) (2012)
4. Koudenburg, N., Postmes, T., Gordijn, E.H.: Disrupting the flow: how brief silences in group conversations affect social needs. J. Exp. Soc. Psychol. **47**, 512–515 (2011)
5. Wirtz, J., et al.: Brave new world: service robots in the frontline. J. Serv. Manag. **29**, 907–931 (2018)
6. Huang, M.-H., Rust, R.T.: Technology-driven service strategy. J. Acad. Mark. Sci. **45**, 906–924 (2017)
7. Mende, M., Scott, M.L., van Doorn, J., Grewal, D., Shanks, I.: Service robots rising: how humanoid robots influence service experiences and elicit compensatory consumer responses. J. Mark. Res. **56**, 535–556 (2019)
8. van Doorn, J., et al.: Domo Arigato Mr. Roboto: emergence of automated social presence in organizational frontlines and customers' service experiences. J. Serv. Res. **20**, 43–58 (2017)
9. Arimoto, T., Yoshikawa, Y., Ishiguro, H.: Multiple-robot conversational patterns for concealing incoherent responses. Int. J. Soc. Robot. **10**, 583–593 (2018)
10. Hill, J., Randolph Ford, W., Farreras, I.G.: Real conversations with artificial intelligence: a comparison between human–human online conversations and human–chatbot conversations. Comput. Hum. Behav. **49**, 245–250 (2015)
11. Spitzberg, B.H.: Conversational skills rating scale: an instructional assessment of interpersonal competence (1995)

12. Harriott, C.E., Zhang, T., Adams, J.A.: Evaluating the applicability of current models of work-load to peer-based human-robot teams. In: 2011 6th ACM/IEEE International Conference on Human-Robot Interaction (HRI), pp. 45–52 (2011)
13. Lu, V.N., et al.: Service robots, customers, and service employees: what can we learn from the academic literature and where are the gaps? J. Serv. Theory Pract. (2020, forthcoming)
14. Phillips, E., Zhao, X., Ullman, D., Malle, B.F.: What is human-like?: decomposing robots' human-like appearance using the Anthropomorphic roBOT (ABOT) database. In: HRI 2018, Chicago, IL, USA, 5–8 March 2018, pp. 105–113 (2018)
15. Ferrari, F., Paladino, M.P., Jetten, J.: Blurring human-machine distinctions: anthropomorphic appearance in social robots as a threat to human distinctiveness. Int. J. Soc. Robot. **8**, 287–302 (2016)
16. Mori, M., MacDorman, K., Kageki, N.: The uncanny valley [from the field]. IEEE Robot. Autom. Mag. **19**, 98–100 (2012)
17. MacDorman, K.F., Ishiguro, H.: The uncanny advantage of using androids in cognitive and social science research. Interact. Stud. **7**, 297–337 (2006)
18. Minato, T., Shimada, M., Itakura, S., Lee, K., Ishiguro, H.: Evaluating the human likeness of an Android by comparing gaze behaviors elicited by the android and a person. Adv. Robot. **20**, 1147–1163 (2006)
19. Haring, K.S., Silvera-Tawil, D., Takahashi, T., Watanabe, K., Velonaki, M.: How people perceive different robot types: a direct comparison of an android, humanoid, and non-biomimetic robot. In: 8th International Conference on Knowledge and Smart Technology (KST), pp. 265–270. IEEE (2016)
20. Matsui, T., Yamada, S.: Robot's impression of appearance and their trustworthy and emotion richness. In: Proceedings of the 27th IEEE International Symposium on Robot and Human Interactive Communication, Nanjing, China, 27–31 August 2018, pp. 88–93 (2018)
21. Nass, C., Moon, Y.: Machines and mindlessness: social responses to computers. J. Soc. Issues **56**, 81–103 (2000)
22. Kim, Y., Sundar, S.S.: Anthropomorphism of computers: is it mindful or mindless? Comput. Hum. Behav. **28**, 241–250 (2012)
23. Nass, C., Moon, Y., Fogg, B.J., Reeves, B., Dryer, D.C.: Can computer personalities be human personalities? Int. J. Hum.-Comput Stud. **43**, 223–239 (1995)
24. Złotowski, J., Proudfoot, D., Yogeeswaran, K., Bartneck, C.: Anthropomorphism: opportunities and challenges in human-robot interaction. Int. J. Soc. Robot. **7**, 347–360 (2015)
25. Natarajan, M., Gombolay, M.: Effects of anthropomorphism and accountability on trust in human robot interaction. In: HRI 2020, Cambridge, United Kingdom, 23–26 March 2020, pp. 33–42 (2020)
26. Reeves, B., Nass, C.: How People Treat Computers, Television, and New Media Like Real People and Places, pp. 19–36. Cambridge University Press, Cambridge (1996)
27. Wagner, K., Schramm-Klein, H.: Alexa, are you human? Investigating the anthropomorphism of digital voice assistants – a qualitative approach. In: Fortieth International Conference on Information Systems, Munich (2019)
28. Kwon, M., Jung, M.F., Knepper, R.A.: Human expectations of social robots. In: ACM/IEEE International Conference on Human-Robot Interaction, pp. 463–464 (2016)
29. Aguinis, H., Bradley, K.J.: Best practice recommendations for designing and implementing experimental vignette methodology studies. Org. Res. Methods **17**, 351–371 (2014)
30. Glaser, B.G., Strauss, A.L.: The Discovery of Grounded Theory: Strategies for Qualitative Research. Aldine Publishing Company, Chicago (1967)
31. Kaiser, H.F., Rice, J.: Little Jiffy, Mark IV. Educ. Psychol. Measur. **34**, 111–117 (1974)
32. Browne, M.W., Cudeck, R.: Alternative ways of assessing model fit. Sociol. Methods Res. **21**, 230–258 (1992)

33. Hu, L.-T., Bentler, P.M.: Cutoff criteria for fit indexes in covariance structure analysis: conventional criteria versus new alternatives. Struct. Equ. Model.: Multidisc. J. **6**, 1–55 (1999)

34. Schermelleh-Engel, K., Moosbrugger, H., Müller, H.: Evaluating the fit of structural equation models: tests of significance and descriptive goodness-of-fit measures. Methods Psychol. Res. Online **8**, 23–74 (2003)

35. Gliem, J.A., Gliem, R.R.: Calculating, interpreting, and reporting cronbach's alpha reliability coefficient for likert-type scales. In: 2003 Midwest Research to Practice Conference in Adult, Continuing, and Community Education, pp. 82–88 (2003)

36. Moosbrugger, H., Kelava, A.: Testtheorie und Fragebogenkonstruktion, 2nd edn. Springer, Heidelberg (2012). https://doi.org/10.1007/978-3-642-20072-4

37. Homburg, C., Giering, A.: Konzeptualisierung und Oparationalisierung komplexer Konstrukte. Mark. ZFP J. Res. Manag. **18**, 3–24 (1996)

38. Churchill Jr., G.A.: A paradigm for developing better measures of marketing constructs. J. Mark. Res. **16**, 64–73 (1979)

Examining the Effects of Anticipatory Robot Assistance on Human Decision Making

Benjamin A. Newman$^{(\boxtimes)}$, Abhijat Biswas, Sarthak Ahuja, Siddharth Girdhar, Kris K. Kitani, and Henny Admoni

Robotics Institute, Carnegie Mellon University, Pittsburgh, PA, USA
{newmanba,abhijat,sarthaka,sgirdhar,kkitani,henny}@cmu.edu

Abstract. Collaborative robots that provide *anticipatory assistance* are able to help people complete tasks more quickly. As anticipatory assistance is provided before help is explicitly requested, there is a chance that this action itself will influence the person's future decisions in the task. In this work, we investigate whether a robot's anticipatory assistance can drive people to make choices different from those they would otherwise make. Such a study requires measuring intent, which itself could modify intent, resulting in an observer paradox. To combat this, we carefully designed an experiment to avoid this effect. We considered several mitigations such as the careful choice of which human behavioral signals we use to measure intent and designing unobtrusive ways to obtain these signals. We conducted a user study ($N = 99$) in which participants completed a collaborative object retrieval task: users selected an object and a robot arm retrieved it for them. The robot predicted the user's object selection from eye gaze in advance of their explicit selection, and then provided either collaborative anticipation (moving toward the predicted object), adversarial anticipation (moving away from the predicted object), or no anticipation (no movement, control condition). We found trends and participant comments suggesting people's decision making changes in the presence of a robot anticipatory motion and this change differs depending on the robot's anticipation strategy.

Keywords: Anticipatory motion · Eye gaze · Human robot interaction · Human decision making

1 Introduction

Anticipatory assistance is the ability to continuously forecast a person's actions and take steps to assist in executing those predicted actions. Anticipation is an important capability for collaborative human-robot systems to facilitate seamless interactions.

B. A. Newman and A. Biswas—Contributed equally to this work.

© Springer Nature Switzerland AG 2020
A. R. Wagner et al. (Eds.): ICSR 2020, LNAI 12483, pp. 590–603, 2020.
https://doi.org/10.1007/978-3-030-62056-1_49

(a) Robot analyzes participant's eye gaze (green heatmap) to anticipate candy choice.

(b) Robot takes anticipatory *collaborative* motion towards predicted candy (left) or *adversarial* motion (right).

(c) Participant selects candy with button after observing anticipatory motion.

Fig. 1. Can anticipatory robot motions affect a user's choice? (Color figure online)

Consider a customer ordering a smoothie from a robot barista in a cafe. The customer aims to choose ingredients that align with their tastes. The robot barista aims to maximize customer satisfaction by making the smoothie accurately to the customer's choices while maximizing efficiency by acting in anticipation of their choice. Prior research [11,12] has shown that in such situations the robot can capitalize on human behaviors exhibited during the interaction (*e.g.*, the customer's eye gaze) to forecast customer actions (*e.g.* smoothie ingredient selections) and use these forecasts to inform its own action selection. This process increases the fluidity of the overall interaction and reduces the overall smoothie making time. These desirable interaction qualities are achieved due to the anticipatory assistance delivered by the robot.

Now consider a situation in which the robot has incorrectly predicted the customer's desired choice of ingredient. For example, the robot might anticipate the customer wants to add artificial banana flavoring, while the user is actually deciding to add a real banana to the smoothie. This creates a decision point for the customer: should they change their original intent (and thereby their initially proposed action) or hold true to their original plan? Regardless of the customer's eventual decision, their action is now clearly dependent on the robot's decision to act in anticipation. While prior research has shown that user actions can influence robot actions in order to engender anticipatory assistance, **we hypothesize that this influence is actually bidirectional, and that the robot's actions influence user actions, as well**. Additionally, while this example highlights an explicit decision point for clarity, we hypothesize that this process can happen implicitly, as well.

To study this hypothesis we conducted a user study with a robot arm that implements a collaborative 1-among-3 selection task. We designed this study to explore our main research question: **do anticipatory robot actions affect user decision making?** Participants in our study were presented with three bins, each filled with a unique variety of candy. The robot monitored the participants' eye gaze and used an online model to map eye gaze to preferred candy bins. The robot then took no action (*i.e.* control) or acted in anticipation of its expectation of the participants' action, as determined through their eye gaze. This action was performed in either a collaborative (towards a user's predicted choice) or adversarial manner (away from a user's predicted choice, *i.e.*, a mistake), depending on the condition. We explore the idea that collaborative anticipation and adversarial anticipation may lead to differences in the robot's influence on the user. Following this, the participant selected their preferred bin by pressing a button prompting the robot to hand them the corresponding bin. This setup is shown in Fig. 1.

Our study was designed to limit measurements that would influence user intent outside of the robot's anticipatory action. Such measurements included survey questions requiring the user to explicitly articulate their intent and questions or prompts revealing that the user's choices would be closely monitored. This restriction prohibited us from obtaining ground truth measurements for initial user intent. We thus designed, implemented, and tested a method to measure user intent before its explicit expression. In line with previous research, we use a model of the user's eye gaze in order to measure this unarticulated intent [11,12,14].

With this study we address the following research questions:

Robot Action-Based Intent Re-shaping: Can a robot making anticipatory movements (movement towards/away from a participant's intended goal) affect a participant's eventual decision?

Unarticulated Intent Prediction Through Eye Gaze: Does participant eye gaze preceding an explicit decision accurately predict that decision?

We hypothesize that a user's decision making process can be affected by a robot's anticipatory actions. We then present a user study that continuously measures the development of user intent using eye gaze naturally exhibited during a selection task and investigate if user intent can be altered by displaying anticipatory robot motions. We find quantitative trends and qualitative results suggesting the bidirectional nature of human robot interactions in anticipatory systems as well as differing responses to different types of anticipatory systems. Finally, we discuss challenges we encountered during our study and propose strategies to mitigate these challenges in future studies.

2   Related Work

Anticipatory Robot Behavior in Human-Robot Interactions. Robots utilizing anticipatory actions have been shown to improve user engagement during human-robot interactions. Previous work suggests that participants working with an anticipatory robot attribute more human qualities to the robot [10] than robots that do not anticipate a user's actions. Modelling human behavior explicitly can even lead to beneficial outcomes as evidenced by robots that explore more safely [3] and learn more effective policies [6,19] as compared to robots that do not model their human counterparts. Especially relevant to our own study is work that used eye gaze as a signal of a user's intent, and thus as the input into an anticipatory robot system. This work showed that interactions such as our smoothie making example can be accelerated when compared to reactive systems [12]. Our inquiry, to understand whether anticipatory robot motions have an effect on user choice, was not considered in this previous work.

Anticipation is not the only factor at play in these types of interactions, however, as the quality of the expression of the robot's anticipation can shape the success of the collaboration. For example, an anticipatory action that is not correctly perceived (*i.e.*, is not legible) by the user can prove to be counterproductive [4]. One conclusion of this work is that a robot has the potential to disrupt a person's intentions by deliberately choosing legible or illegible actions at opportune moments during the interaction. Even when this expression is not intentional, research on human teams show that team members adapt to each other during collaborative tasks, and that this mutual adaptation leads to improved team performance [15]. This effect has even been shown to translate to human-robot teams [16], where the robot models a user's adaptability and changes its actions based upon this estimation.

Furthermore prior work in human intent reshaping has shown that intentional robot movement can cause a person to change their initial course of action when acting independently in a room [5]. The authors infer human intent by using a hidden Markov model based on the human's location and posture. They observe that robots were able to reshape the intention of 68% of the 15 study participants. This work also reports that the robot's potential to reshape a user's intention decreases as the user interacts and becomes more familiar with the system.

Collaborative and adversarial actions have been studied in the context of how obedient and rebellious robots affect a participant's cooperation during task completion [20]. This research reports that working with robotic systems that make collaborative actions can lead to enhanced human robot cooperation when compared to rebellious, or adversarial, robotic systems. In this prior work, the user had a stated, explicit goal. Our work explores the effects of anticipatory actions in tasks where the user has no specific objective.

Predicting User Intent from Human Behavior. Robots can infer intent by sensing a range of verbal and non-verbal signals exhibited by people. For example, existing work has shown that a person's desired target object can be inferred from the history of user control inputs on a joystick [13] during a human-robot joint teleoperation task. Similarly, the handover intention of a participant can be inferred from a combination of wearable sensors and natural language commands [21].

Other work has shown that by leveraging these types of patterns in a user's past actions, robots can further improve collaborations by anticipating future user actions [19]. Additional research in human-robot teaming shows that if a robot disregards a human's preference it can lose the human's trust, leading to a deterioration in team performance. This shows that anticipating and adapting

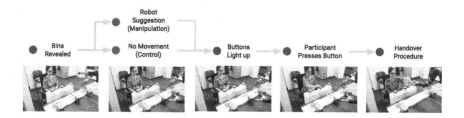

Fig. 2. Typical trial timeline. In this case, the participant saw the *collaborative* condition and accepted the robot's suggestion. Video here.

to a user's evolving preferences throughout a task is crucial to effective human-robot collaboration [8].

Most relevant to our own study, natural eye gaze is highly predictive of user goals, future actions, and mental states - particularly in unaccompanied human manipulation tasks [9,14,17]. Eye gaze has been used as a supplementary modality to infer human intent primarily alongside head-hand tracking [7,22,23]. Recent research shows great promise of integrating eye gaze with joystick control for shared manipulation tasks [1,2]. For simple collaboration tasks such as our smoothie making example, eye gaze has also been shown to be a strong stand-alone modality for intent prediction using a support-vector machine on handcrafted features [11]. In our work, we use spatial binning on a moving exponential average over a temporal sequence of natural eye gaze as a heuristic measure for anticipating human intent as depicted in Fig. 1a.

3 Methods

To answer our research questions, we conducted a user study in which participants interacted with a robot arm in a handover game. Participants were asked to select a target object from among three options located on a table in front of them. The robot used participant eye gaze behavior to model their preferences among the objects, then asked for their selection and finally handed them their selected object. We examined whether participants' object selections, decision-making process and perceptions of the robot would be affected if the robot took anticipatory actions. These actions were either collaborative or adversarial (toward the most or least likely object respectively). A typical trial is illustrated in Fig. 2 and in a video here.

3.1 Study Design

Anticipation Model. Human signals used to estimate intent prior to its explicit expression must be natural and measurable. Eye gaze has been shown to be correlated with intent in similar settings [11]. Due to this correlation, we map user eye gaze to predicted user choice in the following way.

We model the relationship between a user's eye gaze and their eventual choice as an exponentially decaying moving average of the temporal history of their eye gaze. Our model takes as input a sequence of planar eye gaze locations and classifies each eye gaze measurement into one of the four segments shown in Fig. 1a. The model then filters out the eye gaze in the top segment, which is considered robot-viewing gaze, and applies a temporal, exponentially decaying moving average over counts in each of the remaining three segments. This creates temporally evolving probability distribution that maps to the expected probability of a user's choice.

Experimental Variables. Our study uses a between subjects design with one independent variable, "robot suggestion," and three conditions. In each condition, participant preference is determined by the aforementioned anticipation model: *collaborative*: robot moves toward the **most preferred** bin; *adversarial*: robot moves toward the **least preferred** bin; *no-movement*: control, in which the robot takes **no action**.

All participants first saw two trials of *no-movement*, followed by a single experimental trial in which one of the three conditions above was randomly applied. This design allows participants to become familiar with the study procedure and robot operation in the first trial. This trial is treated as practice, and therefore these data were not included in analysis. In total, each participant experienced 3 trials in the following manner: *practice*, *control*, and *experimental*.

3.2 Procedure

Participants were seated across the table from the robot with three bins, filled with unique candy types (Fig. 1a). Bins were initially hidden from participant view. Participants were told that once the candy was revealed, they would be given some time to decide between the candies and choose one, which they could keep. In the practice and control trials, after the candy was revealed, participants were given 5 s to decide, after which the buttons lit up prompting participants to make a selection (Fig. 1a). In the experimental trials, the anticipatory motion began at 5 s, preceding the illumination of the selection buttons. Once participants pressed the button indicating their selection, the robot retrieved the corresponding bin, offered it to them, and allowed them to take a candy (Fig. 2).

All participants saw the same candies, in the same locations, in the first two trials. For the experimental trial, we discarded the two types of candy previously selected and randomly replaced from the four remaining types and randomized all candy locations. This randomization and replacement ensured that participants had not previously expressed preference for the types of candy present in the experimental trial. We recorded the **Predicted Bin** (bin our anticipation model predicts the user will eventually choose, **Selected Bin** (bin selected by the user), **Suggested Bin** (target bin of the robot's anticipatory motion), as well as survey data following each trial (Sect. 4.3).

Materials and Participants. We used a Kinova MICO 6-DOF manipulator (Fig. 1) robot with pre-computed trajectories for all actions. Participant eye gaze was measured using a Tobii 4C eye tracker bar, typically used for 2D planar eye tracking. We adapt it for use in this 3D setting by segmenting the user viewing plane into sections corresponding to three candy segments and one robot segment (Fig. 1a). The stimuli used were 6 flavors of an international candy, each with a distinct label. These stimuli were chosen to be unfamiliar to the majority of the participant pool, consistent in shape and size, have little correlation between wrapper patterns and flavor, and have intricate labels. Thus, the stimuli required attentive viewing before being chosen and would not be chosen due to prior familiarity or preference with the candies' brand or flavor.

One hundred and eighteen participants (72 Female/44 Male/2 Other) were recruited through an online subject pool, mailing lists, and word-of-mouth. Twenty one participants were excluded due to eye gaze sensor drop out or participant non-compliance. Our analyses were performed on $N = 99$ (33 for each experimental condition). The research was approved by an institutional review board. Participants were compensated for their time with 5 USD, for an average of 15 min.

Design Considerations. Investigating whether or not anticipatory robot motions affect human decision making is challenging due to the observer's paradox. Attempts to measure intent in a human decision making task can result in altered behavior, especially if participants are aware of the observation [18].

First, we take care to capture the user's eye gaze in a subtle manner. Accurate eye gaze data is typically obtained by instrumenting participants with wearable eye-trackers [11,12]. However, an implied social presence via a worn eye-tracker has been shown to change looking behavior [18]. We minimized this interference by avoiding the instrumentation of participants, instead adapting a discreet, screen-based eye tracker (Sect. 3.2) for use in this study (Fig. 1). Second, we diverted the focus of the study away from the anticipatory motions by advertising our study as a "handover game" indicating to potential participants that we were interested in the robot's handover mechanics. We also ran a between subjects experiment with only one experimental trial, so that anticipatory motions are always novel when participants encounter them. Further, we incentivized participants to select their true preferences by instructing them that could keep the candies they selected. This differentiates our work from previous studies using collaborative or adversarial robots [20] in which participants received virtual rewards. Finally, we avoided priming participants during the study by not asking them for explanations of their thought processes before the termination of the experiment. Asking for this information prior to the last trial would potentially prime them to be conscious of their decisions in subsequent trials. Asking for it after they view the anticipatory motion would encourage *post hoc* rationalization. Instead of using these explicit measures, we provide participants with an opportunity to provide free-form feedback at the end of the experiment, which some participants used to share their internal decision making processes with us unprompted (Sect. 4.3).

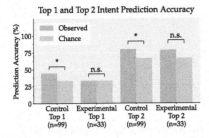

Fig. 3. Top 1 and 2 intent predictor accuracy in control and no-movement, experimental trials. Observed accuracy is in blue, chance is in green. ∗ indicates $p < 0.05$. (Color figure online)

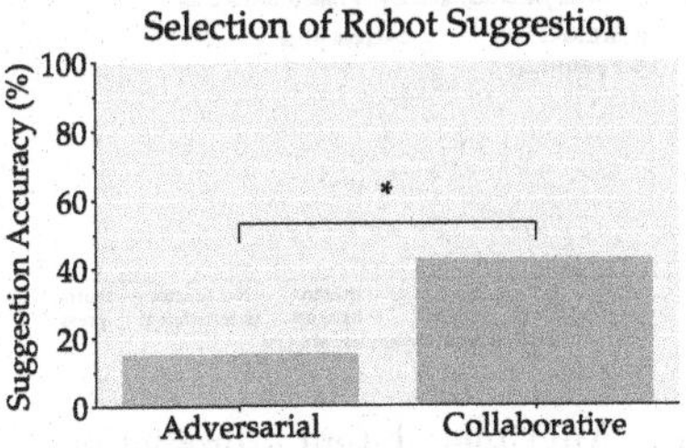

Fig. 4. How likely people are to accept the robot's suggestion in *adversarial* versus *collaborative*. ∗ indicates $p < 0.05$.

4   Results and Discussion

4.1   Intent Prediction

The accuracy of the intent prediction algorithm is the number of times our algorithm predicted the user's selected the bin out of all users. The algorithm uses the eye gaze from the beginning of the trial until the buttons light up in order to make this prediction. We report this accuracy against uniform random chance, the expected baseline value. Figure 3 reports these results for the control ($n = 99$) and experimental ($n = 33$, participants in the *no-movement* condition) trials. A binomial test (2-sided) showed that our algorithm performed significantly better than chance at predicting the correct target (ours: 44% versus chance: 33%, $p = 0.025$), though the overall accuracy of our top 1 model shows the difficulty of forecasting user choice from historical eye gaze.

From Fig. 4 we see that users shown *collaborative* motion are significantly more likely to choose the bin suggested by the robot than those who see the *adversarial* condition, as determined by a χ-squared test, $\chi^2 = 0.242, p = 0.028$, showing that our manipulation is valid.

Figure 5 shows the continuous (anytime) accuracy of the intent predictor across all participants during the 'control' trial. We see qualitative evidence for a choice hierarchy in that the predicted first choice bin has higher accuracy than the predicted second choice bin which has a higher accuracy than the predicted third choice bin. Additionally, we can see that people cycled between their top two choices after the 3 s mark. Combining these results with those from Figs. 3 and 4, we show that we can generate predictions about a user's choice hierarchy before they have explicitly made a decision.

Our results also suggest that our anticipation model can predict a user's least preferred choice. Figure 3 shows our model predicted top 2 accuracy significantly above chance, with a respectable accuracy (ours: 80% versus chance: 66%, $p = 0.005$), indicating historical eye gaze might be a better indicator of those items a user does not show a preference toward. It is further supported by

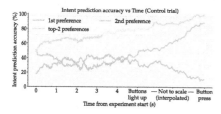
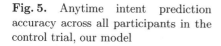

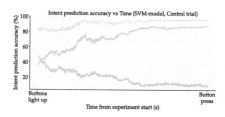

Fig. 5. Anytime intent prediction accuracy across all participants in the control trial, our model

Fig. 6. Anytime intent prediction accuracy across all participants in the control trial, using the SVM model (Sect. 4.1)

qualitative evidence in the evolution of participant intent, Fig. 5. As time progresses, the top 2 accuracy rises consistently, implying that we are increasingly sure of which bin the participant does not want. The "cycling" between 1*st* and 2*nd* choices suggests people quickly (around 3 s) eliminate one option and spend their remaining time making their decision amongst the other two options. These trends also held in the experimental trial.

Our model's ability to predict user decisions disappears in the *no-movement* group of the experimental trial, Fig. 3. This indicates user's in this condition base their decisions on external factors. One possibility is that these users believe this to be a simple handover task, and are testing to the robot's handover capabilities, (*e.g.*, whether it is able to reach all three bins). In this scenario, the user's choice is made through a process of elimination, thus disentangling their gaze from their choice, as suggested by the following quotes:

> "*MICO had an easier time reaching and holding onto the right and left positions than the center one. I purposely chose a candy in each location to test that.*" •
> "*..watched the robot go through it's full range of motion before selecting a button. I selected the item on my left because I wanted to see the robot pick up each box.*"

SVM Model. To check if the necessarily simplistic nature of our zero-data anticipation model was the reason for limited intent prediction accuracy, we explored a data-driven model. After collecting the data by doing this study, we trained a modified version of the SVM intent predictor from [11], which uses four features for each bin: number of glances, duration of first glance, total duration of all glances, if the bin was the most recently glanced at. We add a fifth feature, a unique identifier for each bin, and then use the same testing and training paradigm as [11]. This SVM model gives us a validation accuracy of 54% on the control trial and 45% on the no-movement condition in the experimental trial. While this is better than our heuristic based model (44% and 33% respectively), the SVM is only able to be trained after collecting eye gaze data on a large population.

We explored remapping our conditions in the experimental trial to match the SVM model's classification by comparing the robot's bin suggestion to a post-hoc SVM prediction. If a participant originally in the *adversarial* condition saw

Table 1. Confusion matrix of remapping shifts between conditions in the experimental trial. Old labels (Rows) vs New labels (Columns)

	Ant.	Adv.	Cont.	Adv.+
Ant.	17	7	0	9
Adv.	3	19	0	11
Cont.	0	0	33	0

Table 2. Proportion of users that selected their model-ranked N^{th} choice bin in the *Anticipatory* condition in the experimental trial

	Original	Remapped
1st pref	0.424	0.515
2nd pref	0.364	0.242
3rd pref	0.212	0.242

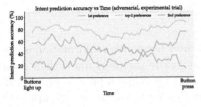

(a) Adversarial condition

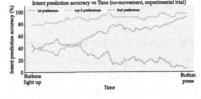

(b) No-movement condition

Fig. 7. Anytime intent prediction accuracy across participants in the 'experimental' trial, during the time from buttons lighting up to when the decision was finally made.

the robot move toward their 1st choice bin, as predicted by the heuristic model, but the SVM predicted this bin to be the user's last choice, then we reassign this user to the *collaborative* condition (Table 1).

Under this remapping, we obtained 20 Anticipatory and 26 Adversarial trials. Additionally, 20 participants moved to a new condition, Adversarial+, where the robot moved to the user's 2nd choice as predicted by the SVM. Most participants remained in their original condition, but about a third from both *collaborative* and *adversarial* conditions remapped to the new condition. Under the new remapping, we did not see a significant change in the distribution of user choice vs model-ranked preferences (Table 2), and consequently in the statistical results throughout this paper.

Discriminating Unarticulated Intent Using Eye Gaze. Our results show that gaze most accurately predicts user intent close to a user's explicit selection. Figure 5 shows anytime intent prediction accuracy through the entire trial. This accuracy increases monotonically as time progresses towards the user's explicit decision, after the buttons light up and a decision is prompter. Additionally, following the evaluation method in [11], we see the modified SVM method behaving similarly (Fig. 6), achieving 90.4% accuracy, on average about 1.48 s before explicit choices are made by users (in [11], accuracy is 76%, 1.8 s prior). Users in our study made their choice 3.93 s after the buttons lit up on average. Any gaze after the buttons lit up was not available to the predictor for anticipation actions.

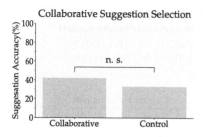
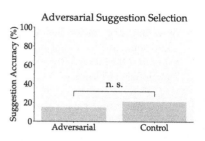

Fig. 8. Comparing percentage of users selecting the suggested bin in *collaborative* and our prediction of their top choice in the *no-movement* trial.

Fig. 9. Comparing the percentage of users selecting the suggested bin in *adversarial* and our prediction of their last choice in the *no-movement* trial.

Both models yielding these results indicates not enough information is present to make accurate predictions as early as 4 s before the users made their decision. This was hinted at by [11], but the curves in Figs. 5 and 6 provide more evidence that eye gaze reveals intent accurately under 2 s before intent is expressed. In our study, we did not want to enforce a strict time limit so as to get the most natural eye gaze and decision making behavior, so we allowed users to take as much time as they needed after the buttons lit up to make their selection.

4.2 Intent Reshaping

Exploring aggregated anytime prediction accuracy can inform our understanding of the robot's ability to influence user decisions (Figs. 7a and b). Since user preferences are accurately predicted towards the end of the trial (as we saw in Sect. 4.1), we see how user intent becomes clearer as the trial draws to a close. (Note that in the *collaborative/adversarial* condition, the buttons light up only after the robot completes its anticipatory motion, so the gaze is not associated with tracking robot movement).

In Fig. 7a, the accuracy of the user's (predicted) 1*st* choice reduces dramatically after robot motion occurs before finally recovering towards the end. This indicates robot motion induces users to reconsider their decision, suggesting a restart of the decision making process, which is supported by user comments (Sect. 4.3). Contrast this to the *no-movement* condition, Fig. 7b, where the estimate of user 1*st* choice becomes increasingly accurate as the time to decision decreases. Further, we see that user intent becomes apparent earlier, during trials in the *no-movement* condition than in the *adversarial* condition.

To further study intent reshaping we can measure the percentage of time users chose the robot's suggested bin in the *collaborative* and *adversarial* conditions, Figs. 8 and 9. We see that participants did not choose the robot's suggested bin significantly more frequently in the *collaborative* condition ($\chi^2 = 1.47, p = 0.612$) or the *adversarial* conditions ($\chi^2 = 0.663, p = 0.751$).

4.3   Qualitative Analysis

In a post-experiment survey, we asked users about differences between the first two and the final trials, to determine if they were aware of the anticipatory motion. Eight out of 66 participants who saw motion reported either not noticing or seeing only minor differences (*e.g.*, "the candies were different"), with the rest identifying robot movement as the difference. We conjecture that this is due to these participants not ascribing intent to the anticipatory actions. An optional free-response section revealed further themes related to our hypotheses:

Several users reported negative feelings associated with the robot or its movement in the *adversarial* condition. No such comments were present in the *no-movement* and *collaborative* conditions:

> *"After I chose the container on the left, the robot arm went up and there was a pause before it reached for the container I chose. Like it was annoyed with my choice."* • *"It moved a lot unnecessarily."* • *"Somehow robot was waiting to pick up the left side box before I pressed the button, actually it was the most different side of my desire (I wanted right side candy)"*

Several users reported positive feelings associated with the robot or its movement in the *collaborative* condition:

> *"The robot prepared to select the candy which I was looking at. The robot was more intelligent in the last trial."* • *"As soon as I made the decision in my head, I noticed the robot move directly in front of the candy I wanted."* • *"The robot seemed guess my choice well in the last trial. The more I have interfaced with the robot the more it has understood me"*

Additionally, several users revealed their thought processes, which indicated that anticipatory motion can influence participant decision making in both the *collaborative* and *adversarial* conditions, but not *no-movement*:

> *"I felt like the robot 'wanted' me to choose the middle bin after moving there the third trial. I picked a different bin after the one I originally wanted due to this."* • *"The robot moved and kinda guess the candy I wanted ... decision that the robot made definitely influenced my decision however I was going to choose the candy either way. I was surprised."* • *"While I noticed the robot move its arm in front of the candy I wanted, I thought about picking a different candy for a split second. I did not end up doing it because I figured it would make its job easier even though it's a robot."* • *"Robot moved to be close to one box, I guess if I wanted the robot to work less I would have chosen that box but the wrapper color wasn't appealing to me."*

From these responses, we see that the robot action can create an inflection point during the interaction causing some users to reconsider their original intention. This reconsideration results in a variety of outcomes including users changing their original decision to match the robot's suggestion, users explicitly disavowing the robot's choice even if it aligned with their own, as well as users acting without regard to the robot's motion. The specific factors that contribute to these various outcomes is out of scope for our work, but should be studied in the future.

5   Conclusion and Future Work

In this paper, we explored whether anticipatory robot motion displayed during a collaborative handover interaction can influence the choices people make during that interaction. Our study found several small quantitative effects suggesting distinct types of anticipatory motions (collaborative and adversarial) can cause users to reconsider their decisions. Qualitative data show further support for this claim. Future work can consider more targeted studies focusing on one particular aspect of the effect of anticipatory robot behavior on human robot interactions such as how specific task context may amplify or diminish this effect.

We showed evidence supporting previous work that eye gaze is indeed indicative of user preferences in selection tasks. We provided detailed analysis of this correlation over the duration of such tasks, indicating that eye gaze is most effective in predicting user choice only a few seconds before it is made explicit, rather than a percentage of overall task time.

Taken together, our findings suggest that robot paradigms designed to anticipate user choice should model the effects of this anticipation during task execution or else anticipatory models may end up changing the very behaviors they are intended to anticipate. Future efforts should explore how this effect changes during complex, sequential tasks, long term interactions with a single robot in a particular task, with a change in the subtlety or timing of the robot's motions, or the perceived expertise or authority of the robot partner. In summary, our work shows initial evidence that human-robot interactions are bidirectional, meaning that researchers need to consider how robot motions designed to anticipate user actions may in turn affect those actions.

References

1. Admoni, H., Srinivasa, S.: Predicting user intent through eye gaze for shared autonomy. In: 2016 AAAI Fall Symposium Series (2016)
2. Aronson, R.M., Santini, T., Kubler, T.C., Kasneci, E., Srinivasa, S., Admoni, H.: Eye-hand behavior in human-robot shared manipulation. In: ACM/IEEE International Conference on Human-Robot Interaction. ACM, New York (2018)
3. Chen, M., Hsu, D., Lee, W.S.: Guided exploration of human intentions for human-robot interaction. In: Morales, M., Tapia, L., Sánchez-Ante, G., Hutchinson, S. (eds.) WAFR 2018. SPAR, vol. 14, pp. 921–938. Springer, Cham (2020). https://doi.org/10.1007/978-3-030-44051-0_53
4. Dragan, A.D., Bauman, S., Forlizzi, J., Srinivasa, S.S.: Effects of robot motion on human-robot collaboration. In: ACM/IEEE International Conference on Human-Robot Interaction, pp. 51–58. ACM (2015)
5. Durdu, A., Erkmen, I., Erkmen, A.M.: Estimating and reshaping human intention via human-robot interaction. Turk. J. Electr. Eng. Comput. Sci. **24**(1), 88–104 (2016)
6. Fisac, J.F., Bronstein, E., Stefansson, E., Sadigh, D., Sastry, S.S., Dragan, A.D.: Hierarchical game-theoretic planning for autonomous vehicles. arXiv preprint arXiv:1810.05766 (2018)

7. Grigore, E.C., Eder, K., Pipe, A.G., Melhuish, C., Leonards, U.: Joint action understanding improves robot-to-human object handover. In: 2013 IEEE/RSJ International Conference on Intelligent Robots and Systems, pp. 4622–4629. IEEE (2013)
8. Hancock, P.A., Billings, D.R., Schaefer, K.E., Chen, J.Y., De Visser, E.J., Parasuraman, R.: A meta-analysis of factors affecting trust in human-robot interaction. Hum. Factors **53**(5), 517–527 (2011)
9. Hayhoe, M., Ballard, D.: Eye movements in natural behavior. Trends Cogn. Sci. **9**(4), 188–194 (2005)
10. Hoffman, G.: Anticipation in human-robot interaction. In: AAAI Spring Symposium Series (2010)
11. Huang, C.M., Andrist, S., Sauppé, A., Mutlu, B.: Using gaze patterns to predict task intent in collaboration. Front. Psychol. **6**, 1049 (2015)
12. Huang, C.M., Mutlu, B.: Anticipatory robot control for efficient human-robot collaboration. In: ACM/IEEE International Conference on Human-Robot Interaction, pp. 83–90 (2016)
13. Javdani, S., Srinivasa, S.S., Bagnell, J.A.: Shared autonomy via hindsight optimization. In: Robotics Science and Systems: Online Proceedings 2015 (2015)
14. Johansson, R.S., Westling, G., Bäckström, A., Flanagan, J.R.: Eye-hand coordination in object manipulation. J. Neurosci. **21**(17), 6917–6932 (2001)
15. Mathieu, J.E., Heffner, T.S., Goodwin, G.F., Salas, E., Cannon-Bowers, J.A.: The influence of shared mental models on team process and performance. J. Appl. Psychol. **85**(2), 273 (2000)
16. Nikolaidis, S., Hsu, D., Srinivasa, S.: Human-robot mutual adaptation in collaborative tasks: models and experiments. Int. J. Robot. Res. **36**, 618–634 (2017)
17. Pelz, J., Hayhoe, M., Loeber, R.: The coordination of eye, head, and hand movements in a natural task. Exp. Brain Res. **139**(3), 266–277 (2001)
18. Risko, E.F., Kingstone, A.: Eyes wide shut: implied social presence, eye tracking and attention. Atten. Percept. Psychophys. **73**(2), 291–296 (2011)
19. Sadigh, D., Landolfi, N., Sastry, S.S., Seshia, S.A., Dragan, A.D.: Planning for cars that coordinate with people: leveraging effects on human actions for planning and active information gathering over human internal state. Auton. Robots **42**(7), 1405–1426 (2018). https://doi.org/10.1007/s10514-018-9746-1
20. Stolzenwald, J., Mayol-Cuevas, W.W.: Rebellion and obedience: the effects of intention prediction in cooperative handheld robots. In: 2019 IEEE/RSJ International Conference on Intelligent Robots and Systems, IROS 2019 (2019)
21. Wang, W., Li, R., Chen, Y., Jia, Y.: Human intention prediction in human-robot collaborative tasks. In: Companion of the 2018 ACM/IEEE International Conference on Human-Robot Interaction, pp. 279–280. ACM (2018)
22. Yi, W., Ballard, D.H.: Recognizing behavior in hand-eye coordination patterns. Int. J. HR: Humanoid Robot. **6**(3), 337–359 (2009)
23. Yu, C., Ballard, D.H.: Learning spoken words from multisensory input. In: 6th International Conference on Signal Processing, vol. 2, pp. 998–1001 (2002)

The Experience and Effect
of Adolescent to Robot Stress Disclosure:
A Mixed-Methods Exploration

Elin A. Björling[ID], Honson Ling[(✉)][ID], Simran Bhatia[(✉)][ID],
and Kimberly Dziubinski[(✉)]

University of Washington, Seattle, WA 98105, USA
{bjorling,honsoneo,simran18,kimdz}@uw.edu

Abstract. Social robots hold the potential to be an effective and appropriate technology in reducing stress and improving the mental health of adolescents. In order to understand the effect of adolescent-to-robot disclosure on momentary stress, we conducted an exploratory, mixed-methods study with sixty-nine US adolescents (ages 14–21) in school settings. We compared a generic, minimalist robot interaction among three different robot embodiments: physical, digital computer screen, and immersive, virtual reality. We found participants' momentary stress levels significantly decreased across multiple interactions over time. The physical and virtual reality embodiments were most effective for stress reduction. In addition, our qualitative findings provide unique insights into the types of stressors adolescents shared with the social robots as well as their experiences with the different interaction embodiments.

Keywords: Social robots · Adolescents · Perceived stress ·
Self-disclosure · Virtual reality

1 Introduction

School is a common source of stress for many US adolescents [2]. Chronic stress has been correlated with increased rates of depression [28] and decreased learning [36]. With many schools lacking the resources to implement sufficient mental health programs [15], there is an urgent need for an appropriate and innovative solution to mitigate adolescent stress in school.

US adolescents' lives are typically mediated through a variety of digital technologies [13]. Therefore, the use of a digital device to reduce adolescent stress may be an accessible, desirable, and contextually appropriate tool in the school setting. To address the challenge of school stress in adolescents, our overall project aims to develop a school-based, social robot designed to engage adolescents in anonymous, stress-reducing interactions. Disclosing stress through human-robot interactions has shown promising therapeutic benefits and likability for adults [4,27] and undergraduates [26]. In today's COVID-19 climate, social robots also

© Springer Nature Switzerland AG 2020
A. R. Wagner et al. (Eds.): ICSR 2020, LNAI 12483, pp. 604–615, 2020.
https://doi.org/10.1007/978-3-030-62056-1_50

offer the benefit of a social agent unable to contract or express viruses [39]. Adolescents have shown a desire to share emotions and stressors anonymously with a social robot [7], however, the effect of a disclosure interaction on momentary stress for adolescents has not been well explored.

Therefore, our current mixed-methods study explored the following research questions: (1) Do repeated disclosure interactions with a social robot reduce momentary, perceived stress in adolescents? (2) How does social robot embodiment affect momentary stress?

2 Background

2.1 Stress and Adolescents

Eighty-three percent of teens report that school is a significant source of stress [2]. Chronic, daily stress has negative physiological [30] and psychological [8] outcomes for adolescents, including depression [29]. Chronic stress negatively impacts cognitive function and learning [36] and yet many schools lack the resources to maintain accessible school-based mental health programs [15]. Finally, school stress as a result of COVID-19 is likely to worsen adolescent mental health [16] as was found in Chinese adolescents [10].

2.2 Robots to Reduce Stress and Anxiety

A recent review of social robots illustrated five robotic devices (mostly animoids) that effectively reduced anxiety or increased social interactions in elderly adults [33]. A few animoid robots have been designed explicitly for these purposes. For example, the social robot Therabot [14] is an animated dog was designed to support those who have survived trauma by reducing feelings of overwhelm. Another example, Paro [37] a plush seal, reduced anxiety and increased social interactions in seniors in assisted living [21] and has been shown to reduce physiologic stress in adults [1]. Long-term robot interactions have reduced stress in the elderly [37], promoted physical and emotional verbal expressions in children [19], reduced workplace [40] and mental stress in adults [23], as well as reduced physiological stress in infants [38]. However, little is known about the effect of social robot interactions on stress in adolescents.

2.3 Robot Embodiment

A body of research has investigated how different robot platforms affect the quality of social interaction between a human and a robot. In summary, when compared to robots on a computer screen, adult participants were more likely to follow directions given by a physically present robot [3], learned more as a result of a robot tutor [25], and empathized more with a physical robot's vulnerability [34]. Children in a hospital setting showed stronger verbal and physical engagement with a physical robot compared to digital versions [20]. However, how well these studies of embodiment transfer to adolescent participants remains unknown.

2.4   Human-to-Robot Disclosure

Self-disclosure, the act of disclosing intimate and emotional information about oneself, is an intervention that has been successful in reducing stress in both in-person and online human-human interactions [18,41]. In terms of human-to-robot disclosure, Birnbaum, et al. [4] found that adults find a responsive robot comforting during stress-related disclosures. Ling and Björling [26] conducted a small experimental study (n = 36) to explore the impact of robot disclosure on human disclosure. They found that college students interpreted a robot's technical disclosure as emotional. Martelaro, et al. [27] discovered that high school students disclosed more vulnerability when interacting with a social robot that expresses high vulnerability. Although disclosure has been studied in HRI, the relationship effect of disclosure with a robot on perceived stress has not been explored. As we hope to improve adolescent mental health, it is critical to both understand whether interacting with a social robot can help reduce adolescent stress as well as which robot embodiments may be most effective.

3   Methods

3.1   Study Design

The current research study utilized a mixed-methods, within-subjects design to understand the effect of three different robot embodiments (physical, computer screen, and virtual reality) on momentary stress during a simple, stress-disclosure activity. See Fig. 1. Given academic stress is prolific in both high school [2] and college samples [22], we recruited a diverse group of adolescents (ages 14–21) through convenience sampling. The study was implemented and conducted in common areas at three local high schools and one university to maintain contextual validity. Participants interacted with each of the three platforms through an assigned order to ensure counterbalance.

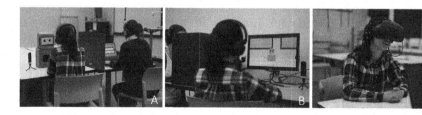

Fig. 1. Examples of each robot embodiment. A: Physical, B: Digital, C: Virtual Reality

3.2   Technology Design

For this particular study, we designed a generic robot interaction in order to maintain focus on the interaction effect on momentary stress. EMAR is a social robot previously designed through co-design and interaction studies with adolescents [6]. The physical robot prototype (EMAR V4) consisted of two stacked, felt-covered boxes, each with a slot for an Android-powered, Nexus 7 tablets to create a digital face and belly. One tablet renders the robot's face which has blinking eyes and a small immobile mouth. The other tablet is located at the robot's belly and was disabled for this study. EMAR V4 along with a replication of a local high school classroom environment was modeled at exact scale in a Unity game engine [35]. The Unity engine was displayed using an HTC Vive headset for the virtual reality embodiment and on a flat screen monitor for the digital embodiment. In all interactions, EMAR was on a table facing the participants who were seated and wearing headphones to ensure communication.

Teleoperation Design. To maintain consistency across all three embodiments, we designed an interface to ensure consistent teleoperation across the research team. The robot's face was animated with natural-like blinking and a static mouth. The robot's speech was controlled through a customized "Wizard of Oz" interface and included a series of questions designed to elicit stress stories from the participants. See Table 1. Operators followed a clear path through the interaction using a small number of impromptu buttons for pre-specified utterances (*e.g.* "I see," "I'm sorry I didn't hear that"). Additionally, there was a set of empathetic responses such as "Thanks for sharing that with me," and "That sounds stressful," to ensure that the participant felt heard. In a reliability test, no significant differences were found in participant stress or interaction length across operators.

Table 1. Social robot prompts that elicit momentary stress and mood as well as stress stories.

Momentary	1. Can you tell me how stressed do you feel right now?
	2. I would also like to know, what is your mood right now?
Stress story	1. I also really like to hear stories
	2. Would you like to share a stress story with me?
	3. Do you want to tell me more about that?
	4. How did that make you feel?

3.3   Study Procedure

Intake Survey and Stress Stories. In order to acknowledge individual differences affecting the participants' responses and preferences, we measured the participants' overall perceived stress scores and their overall attitudes toward

608   E. A. Björling et al.

robots. The Perceived Stress Scale (PSS-10) [11] is a 10-item questionnaire that measures the degree to which situations in one's life are appraised as stressful. The Negative Attitude Towards Robots Scale (NARS) is a 14-item attitude survey [31]. After completing their intake forms, participants were asked to notate three different, personal stress stories, one to share with each robot embodiment.

Robot Interactions and Measuring Momentary Stress. Participant robot interactions were ordered to ensure counterbalance. For transparency, the participants were aware that a researcher was operating the robot. In addition, interactions took place in non-private, common student spaces with other students present. We developed a simple computer-based visual analogue scale (VAS) (0 = no stress at all, 100 = most stress experienced) to measure momentary stress before and after each robot interaction. VASs are commonly used to reliably measure momentary, perceived stress even over very brief time intervals [9,24].

Exit Interview. After completing all three interactions, participants were invited into a quieter area (usually a school hallway) along with 1–2 other participants who had completed the interactions. Participants were interviewed and asked questions such as, "How did it feel interacting with each of these robots?" and "In which environment did you feel most comfortable?"

3.4 Analyses

One-way ANOVAs were used to explore group differences for age, gender, and school site for the NARS and PSS. To explore the effect of embodiment on momentary stress level, we conducted Wilcoxon signed-rank tests on stress levels before and after each type of platform interaction. This method is nonparametric, does not assume normality, and is used for repeated measurements on a single sample to assess whether their population mean ranks differ. Post-hoc comparisons were conducted to detect differences in stress level changes across embodiments. In order to examine the effect of time on momentary stress, a within-subject ANOVA was conducted on participants' baseline and post robot interaction momentary stress levels. Finally, following procedures for an explanatory sequential mixed-methods design [12] we contextualized the quantitative findings by exploring the interaction and exit interview data for context related to the quantitative findings using applied thematic analysis [17].

4   Findings

4.1   Demographics

Overall, 69 adolescents (39 females, 30 male) ranging in age from 14 to 21 years ($M = 17.4, SD = 1.59$) participated in the study. See detailed grade and age demographic information is in Table 2.

Table 2. Descriptive demographics by school site.

School	n	Female	Age (m)	Grade (m)
High School 1	8	100%	16.3	10.5
High School 2	28	32%	16.25	10.39
High School 3	10	70%	18.2	12
University	23	65%	18.78	13.26
Total	69	67%	17.39%	11.59

The participants self-reported their ethnicity in an open-ended item on the intake survey. From these data, ten broad ethnic categories emerged across all participants. Forty-four percent of our participants identified as white or Caucasian. Fifty-six percent of our participants identified themselves as a non-white ethnicities including Chinese (14.5%), Asian (13%), East Indian (5.8%), Korean (4.3%), Hispanic/Filipino (4.3%), Middle Eastern (2.9%), African American (1.7%), Ghanian (1.4%) and Mixed Race (7.2%).

4.2 Perceived Stress and Attitudes Toward Robots

When comparing PSS and NARS scores by gender, age, grade or school/study site, no significant differences were found. Our participants had an average PSS score of 19.78 ($SD = 6.69$) which is higher than published norms for the PSS, but similar to other studies we have published for these age groups [5]. When exploring the NARS scores by age, no significant differences were found. However, the lowest average scores ($M = 26.5$, $SD = 7.77$) were observed in the youngest participants (age 14). Female participants, however, scored significantly higher ($M = 39.90$, $SD = 8.32$) in negative attitudes towards robots than male participants ($M = 35.83$, $SD = 7.69$) ($t(68) = 2.078, p = 0.042$). See Fig. 2 for more detail for the PSS and NARS by age.

4.3 Adolescent-Robot Interactions

Upon introduction, many participants were polite when interacting with the robot and even asked how the robot was doing or said, "It's nice to meet you." When the robot asked about their current stress level, participants responses ranged widely from statements such as, *"I only feel slightly stressed,"* [Female, 16, School 1] to *"I feel like I have a lot of stress in my life right now"* [Female, 16, School 2]. Many adolescents seemed comfortable disclosing their stressors to a social robot. A few adolescents shared stressors outside of their school experience, such as difficulties with a job or being away from family, but most stories were school-related , which was appropriate as their interactions with the robot occurred at school. For example,

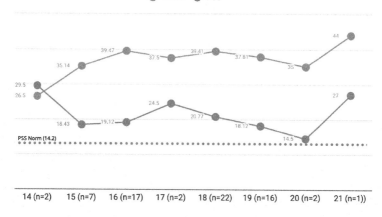

Fig. 2. Average NARS and Average PSS scores by age.

I just like got really stressed out from studying and taking all those AP tests. So yeah, it's cause AP tests are really stressful and sometimes they are really hard right? And it was my junior year, I wanted to keep my grades good. [Male, 18, School 3]

In their exit interviews, a few participants recalled feeling anticipatory anxiety prior to interacting with a robot for the first time. For example, one participant stated, *"At first I did't know how it will work and it felt weird, but after [the] first try it got more comfortable"* [Female, 18, School 3].

4.4 Changes in Momentary Stress

Momentary stress was decreased for 69% of participants after the first robot interaction regardless of robot embodiment. When comparing average momentary stress before each robot interaction ($M = 45.26, SD = 23.66$), participants reported a significantly lower momentary stress after the 3rd robot interaction regardless of embodiment ($M = 33.98, SD = 21.99$), $z(57) = -4.55, p = 0.001$. See Fig. 3 for more details.

In exit interviews, participants articulated their experience of the robot interactions as stress-reducing over time. As one participant stated, *"So, as each level started going, progressing, I felt less stressed"* [Female, 19, School 4]. One participant clearly articulated that repeatedly sharing her stressors with the robot allowed her to become increasingly comfortable talking about her feelings.

As I went on, I think part of the reason why I liked EMAR is because I was getting used to talking, so I wasn't as stressed. I was used to it. I was used to the process of talking about my feelings and stuff. [Female, Unknown Age, School 4]

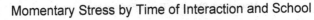

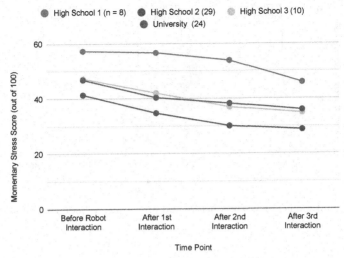

Fig. 3. Average momentary stress by time of interaction and school.

4.5 Physical and Virtual Embodiments Were Most Stress-Reducing

In our analysis of the effects of robot embodiment on momentary stress, 58 participants had a complete set of momentary stress data, and were included in this analysis. The physical robot, followed by the virtual embodiment had the most significant stress reduction effects. See Fig. 4 for more detail. The participants' described the physical robot as a *"caring."* They gave the physical robot descriptions such as *"it feels present"*, *"it's in the real world"*, and *"it's with me."* One participant stated, *"...the physical one feels like a real person, and that you can confide in"* [Female, School 1]. Another participant suggested, *"I also felt, like the reactions also almost felt more authentic given that it was right there"* [Female, School 4].

In the virtual embodiment, participants expressed a range of experiences and included descriptions such as *"safe"*, *"private"*, and *"peaceful."* One teen even mentioned, *"I was able to feel in tune with my emotions"* when in the virtual environment [Female, 18, School 3]. Teens described their interactions with the virtual embodiment as an escape. For example one teen said, *"VR is kind of a place where you can just shut out the real world and go into the robot world where you can carry your experiences"* [Male, 15, School 2]. Another teen suggested the VR interaction helped her to avoid human stressors. *"In the outer environments [real world] there might be stressors around–for example one of my stressors is humans"* [Female, 19, School 4].

One participant had the insight that her stress felt less real in the virtual interaction.

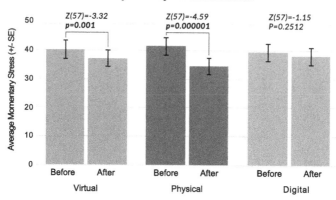

Fig. 4. Mean of momentary stress before and after each embodiment interaction (n = 58).

> In the VR, my stress just seemed like less real. I was like, "oh okay, now I can talk about it and figure it out" –in the real world the physical (robot), the stress seemed like it was like piling on a bit." [Female, 19, School 4]

4.6   Limitations

Certainly one limitation of this study is the novelty effect associated with the technology design. Teens were engaged and highly interested in talking to the robot in all three embodiments. In addition, the anticipatory anxiety of talking to a robot seemed to reduce over time which may confound the momentary stress effect. Therefore, these interactions needs to be studied in-situ in the wild. Additionally, the study was set up with full transparency such that participants were aware that humans were operating the robots. This may have impacted their responsiveness as well and therefore it's imperative to study an autonomous robot interaction in the wild to better understand the true impact of disclosure to a robot on momentary, perceived stress.

4.7   Discussion

This study design intentionally created a generic and very simple adolescent-to-robot stress disclosure interaction. Participants shared unique stress stories with each robot embodiment and found the robot embodiments engaging and the activity stress reliving. Adolescent participants showed significant reductions in momentary stress across all embodiments and over the three robot interactions. However, how much of this had to do with a reduction in anticipatory stress remains unknown.

Although all robot interactions were stress reducing, the physical robot reduced stress most significantly for the group regardless of interaction order.

This finding is not surprising given the wealth of literature on the powerful effect of a physically present robot [3]. What was surprising was the significantly stress reducing effect of the virtual embodiment and environment. This deserves more attention. Potential explanations may be that the virtual environment felt more intimate and private, allowing for more effective disclosure. Birnbaum, et al. [4] found their robot's responsiveness to the human's stressor created a sense of intimacy. Adolescents commonly use "escape" as a coping mechanism for managing stress [32]. Therefore, the stress reduction of the virtual environment may have been complemented by simultaneously providing a form of escape.

This preliminary study shows potential for adolescent-robot disclosure interactions as a stress-reducing interaction. In addition, it illustrates the possibility of a social robot embodiment as a potential moderator of stress-reducing disclosure. However, a more rigorous study in situ is needed to determine the true effect of a disclosure interaction on momentary stress as well as what the most appropriate and effective robot embodiment may be for a robot intended to support mental health in adolescents.

References

1. Aminuddin, R., Sharkey, A.: A paro robot reduces the stressful effects of environmental noise. Proc. Eur. Conf. Cogn. Ergon. **2017**, 63–64 (2017)
2. Association, A.P., et al.: Stress in America 2013 highlights: are teens adopting adults' stress habits (2014)
3. Bainbridge, W.A., Hart, J.W., Kim, E.S., Scassellati, B.: The benefits of interactions with physically present robots over video-displayed agents. Int. J. Soc. Robot. **3**(1), 41–52 (2011)
4. Birnbaum, G.E., Mizrahi, M., Hoffman, G., Reis, H.T., Finkel, E.J., Sass, O.: What robots can teach us about intimacy: the reassuring effects of robot responsiveness to human disclosure. Comput. Hum. Behav. **63**, 416–423 (2016)
5. Björling, E.A., Cakmak, M., Thomas, K., Rose, E.J.: Exploring teens as robot operators, users and witnesses in the wild. Front. Robot. AI **7**, 5 (2020)
6. Björling, E.A., Rose, E.: Participatory research principles in human-centered design: engaging teens in the co-design of a social robot. Multimodal Technol. Interact. **3**(1), 8 (2019)
7. Björling, E.A., Rose, E., Davidson, A., Ren, R., Wong, D.: Can we keep him forever? teens' engagement and desire for emotional connection with a social robot. Int. J. Soc. Robot. **12**, 65–77 (2019)
8. Bolton, J.L., Molet, J., Ivy, A., Baram, T.Z.: New insights into early-life stress and behavioral outcomes. Curr. Opin. Behav. Sci. **14**, 133–139 (2017)
9. Cella, D.F., Perry, S.W.: Reliability and concurrent validity of three visual-analogue mood scales. Psychol. Rep. **59**(2), 827–833 (1986)
10. Chen, F., Zheng, D., Liu, J., Gong, Y., Guan, Z., Lou, D.: Depression and anxiety among adolescents during covid-19: a cross-sectional study. Brain, Behav. Immun. **88**, 36–38 (2020)
11. Cohen, S., Kamarck, T., Mermelstein, R., et al.: Perceived stress scale. In: Measuring Stress: A Guide for Health and Social Scientists, pp. 235–283 (1994). https://doi.org/10.1037/t02889-000

12. Creswell, J.W., Clark, V.L.P.: Designing and Conducting Mixed Methods Research, p. 520 p. Sage Publications, Thousand Oaks (2017)
13. Davies, C., Eynon, R.: Teenagers and Technology, 1st edn. Routledge, Abingdon (2013)
14. Duckworth, D., Henkel, Z., Wuisan, S., Cogley, B., Collins, C., Bethel, C.L.: Therabot: the initial design of a robotic therapy support system. In: HRI (Extended Abstracts), pp. 13–14 (2015)
15. Eiraldi, R., Wolk, C.B., Locke, J., Beidas, R.: Clearing hurdles: the challenges of implementation of mental health evidence-based practices in under-resourced schools. Adv. School Mental Health Promot. 8(3), 124–140 (2015)
16. Golberstein, E., Wen, H., Miller, B.F.: Coronavirus disease 2019 (COVID-19) and mental health for children and adolescents. JAMA Pediatr. **174**(9), 819–820 (2020)
17. Guest, G., MacQueen, K.M., Namey, E.E.: Applied Thematic Analysis. Sage Publications, Thousand Oaks (2011)
18. Hofmann, S.G., Asnaani, A., Vonk, I.J., Sawyer, A.T., Fang, A.: The efficacy of cognitive behavioral therapy: a review of meta-analyses. Cogn. Ther. Res. **36**(5), 427–440 (2012). https://doi.org/10.1007/s10608-012-9476-1
19. Jeong, S.: The impact of social robots on young patients' socio-emotional wellbeing in a pediatric inpatient care context. Ph.D. thesis, Massachusetts Institute of Technology (2017)
20. Jeong, S., Breazeal, C., Logan, D., Weinstock, P.: Huggable: impact of embodiment on promoting verbal and physical engagement for young pediatric inpatients. In: 2017 26th IEEE International Symposium on Robot and Human Interactive Communication (RO-MAN), pp. 121–126. IEEE (2017)
21. Kang, H.S., Makimoto, K., Konno, R., Koh, I.S.: Review of outcome measures in PARO robot intervention studies for dementia care. Geriatric Nursing, New York (2019)
22. Karaman, M.A., Lerma, E., Vela, J.C., Watson, J.C.: Predictors of academic stress among college students. J. Coll. Couns. **22**(1), 41–55 (2019)
23. Kühnlenz, B., Erhart, M., Kainert, M., Wang, Z.Q., Wilm, J., Kühnlenz, K.: Impact of trajectory profiles on user stress in close human-robot interaction. at-Automatisierungstechnik **66**(6), 483–491 (2018)
24. Lesage, F.X., Berjot, S., Deschamps, F.: Clinical stress assessment using a visual analogue scale. Occup. Med. **62**(8), 600–605 (2012)
25. Leyzberg, D., Spaulding, S., Toneva, M., Scassellati, B.: The physical presence of a robot tutor increases cognitive learning gains. In: Proceedings of the Annual Meeting of the Cognitive Science Society, vol. 34 (2012)
26. Ling, H.Y., Björling, E.A.: Sharing stress with a robot: what would a robot say? Hum. -Mach. Commun. **1**(1), 8 (2020). https://doi.org/10.30658/hmc.1.8
27. Martelaro, N., Nneji, V.C., Ju, W., Hinds, P.: Tell me more: designing hri to encourage more trust, disclosure, and companionship. In: The Eleventh ACM/IEEE International Conference on Human Robot Interaction, pp. 181–188. IEEE Press (2016)
28. Martinez, G., Bámaca-Colbert, M.Y.: A reciprocal and longitudinal investigation of peer and school stressors and depressive symptoms among mexican-origin adolescent females. J. Youth Adolesc. **48**(11), 2125–2140 (2019)
29. Maughan, B., Collishaw, S., Stringaris, A.: Depression in childhood and adolescence. J. Can. Acad. Child Adolesc. Psychiatry **22**(1), 35 (2013)
30. McEwen, B.S.: Neurobiological and systemic effects of chronic stress. Chronic Stress **1**, 2470547017692328 (2017)

31. Nomura, T., Suzuki, T., Kanda, T., Kato, K.: Measurement of negative attitudes toward robots. Interact. Stud. **7**(3), 437–454 (2006). https://doi.org/10.1075/is.7.3.14nom

32. Oláh, A.: Coping strategies among adolescents: a cross-cultural study. J. Adolesc. **18**(4), 491 (1995)

33. Scoglio, A.A., Reilly, E.D., Gorman, J.A., Drebing, C.E.: Use of social robots in mental health and well-being research: systematic review. J. Med. Internet Res. **21**(7), e13322 (2019)

34. Seo, S.H., Geiskkovitch, D., Nakane, M., King, C., Young, J.E.: Poor thing! would you feel sorry for a simulated robot? a comparison of empathy toward a physical and a simulated robot. In: 2015 10th ACM/IEEE International Conference on Human-Robot Interaction (HRI), pp. 125–132. IEEE (2015)

35. Unity Technologies: Unity. https://unity.com

36. Vogel, S., Schwabe, L.: Learning and memory under stress: implications for the classroom. NPJ Sci. Learn. **1**, 16011 (2016)

37. Wada, K., Shibata, T., Saito, T., Sakamoto, K., Tanie, K.: Psychological and social effects of one year robot assisted activity on elderly people at a health service facility for the aged. In: Proceedings of the 2005 IEEE International Conference on Robotics and Automation, 2005. ICRA 2005, pp. 2785–2790. IEEE (2005)

38. Williams, N., MacLean, K., Guan, L., Collet, J.P., Holsti, L.: Pilot testing a robot for reducing pain in hospitalized preterm infants. OTJR: Occup. Participation Health **39**(2), 108–115 (2019)

39. Yang, G.Z., et al.: Combating COVID-19-the role of robotics in managing public health and infectious diseases (2020)

40. Yorita, A., Egerton, S., Oakman, J., Chan, C., Kubota, N.: A robot assisted stress management framework: using conversation to measure occupational stress. In: 2018 IEEE International Conference on Systems, Man, and Cybernetics (SMC), pp. 3761–3767. IEEE (2018)

41. Zhang, R.: The stress-buffering effect of self-disclosure on facebook: an examination of stressful life events, social support, and mental health among college students. Comput. Hum. Behav. **75**, 527–537 (2017)

Do Robot Pets Decrease Agitation in Dementia Patients?

An Ethnographic Approach

Sofia Thunberg[(⊠)], Lisa Rönnqvist, and Tom Ziemke

Department of Computer and Information Science, Linköping University,
58183 Linköping, Sweden
{sofia.thunberg,tom.ziemke}@liu.se, lisro774@student.liu.se

Abstract. Companion robots, and especially robotic pets, have been argued to have the potential for improving the well-being of elderly people with dementia. Previous research has mainly focused on short-term studies, conducted with relatively expensive robot platforms. With cheaper options on the market, residential homes in Sweden have started to use low-cost off-the-shelf platforms, such as the Joy for All cats and dogs, which have not been the subject of much previous research. We therefore conducted two ethnographic long-term studies of real-world use of the Joy for All robot cat and dog at a care home facility. The care staff report positive outcomes regarding reminiscence and improved well-being, with decreased agitation and increased communication. Furthermore, the robots are perceived to provide companionship and to give patients the feeling of being able to take care of someone. Based on the insights gained in this real-world study of the use of robotic pets in elderly care, we identify a number of research questions and methodological issues for future research.

Keywords: Robot pets · Companion robots · Elderly people · Dementia · Human-robot interaction

1 Introduction

Companion robots have been argued to have the potential for successful psychosocial interventions in long-term care for elderly people with dementia [18]. Previous research has indicated that robot animals decrease agitated behaviour [14,17], reduce stress levels [21] and increase social interaction [16] in dementia patients. However, the existing literature has mainly been focused on short-term studies[1] with relatively expensive robot platforms, such as Paro and AIBO. This raises concerns regarding the novelty effect and economic viability [5]. The price for the Joy for All cat and dog, for example, is around €100, while that of the Paro robot seal is around €5000, the robot dog AIBO is around €2500 and the

---

[1] The robot seal Paro is an exception that has been evaluated in long-term studies [24,25].

© Springer Nature Switzerland AG 2020
A. R. Wagner et al. (Eds.): ICSR 2020, LNAI 12483, pp. 616–627, 2020.
https://doi.org/10.1007/978-3-030-62056-1_51

robot cat JustoCat is around €1200. Many residential homes for elderly people in Sweden have started to use the Joy for All pets, although not much research has been conducted regarding their effects. The reasoning behind this is that Joy for All pets might be technically less advanced than other companion robots, and their abilities might be sufficient to achieve similar positive effects as with the more expensive platforms. We therefore conducted a nine months ethnographic study of the real-world use of the Joy for All cat, and a three months additional study with the Joy for All dog, at a residential home to investigate how both the care staff and the patients use and perceive these robotic pets.

2 Background: Robot Animals in Dementia Care

The term dementia includes different neurodegenerative disorders with impairments of brain functions, such as, Alzheimer's and vascular dementia [1]. Depending on what type of dementia, and where the damage is located, symptoms can vary significantly and change over time. Symptoms of dementia can be cognitive (e.g., memory loss) [7], behavioural and psychological (e.g., depression, delusions, anxiety and agitation) [15]. We here focus on agitation. Cohen-Mansfield and Billig [8, p. 712] describe three types of agitated behaviour: "1) it may be abusive or aggressive toward self or others; 2) it may be appropriate behaviour performed with inappropriate frequency, such as constantly asking questions; and 3) it may be inappropriate according to social standards for the specific situation, such as putting on too many layers of clothes". Examples of agitated behaviour are wandering, complaining, screaming, and disruptive sounds [15].

Therapies or actions used to help a person reintegrate into society in a healthy way, after being disconnected for a period of time, are called psychosocial interventions. In long-term care at residential homes, such interventions have the potential to improve the quality of care and quality of life for people with dementia [23]. One psychosocial intervention is robot therapy, often using robot animals [19]. The main reason to use animal-like (zoomorphic) robots instead of, for example, humanoid robots, is expectations. Animal behaviour is not as complex as in human interaction, hence, the human-animal relationship is believed to be a better basis for design of such technology [11]. Also, animal-like robots that are covered in fur have the perk of allowing people with dementia to interact via touch, which is particularly important as vision and hearing are often impaired at an old age.

The most well-known robot animal probably is the baby seal Paro [26]. According to its creators, it was developed to be a non-familiar animal for the majority, hence, people do not have pre-assumptions on how the robot seal should behave. Long-term studies conducted with Paro show a decrease of stress hormones in dementia patients [24,25]. Moreover, the robot evokes conversations where the residents communicate both directly to the robot, and with each other about the robot, which resembles everyday conversations in the presence of pets [20]. Other studies have shown that interaction with Paro can decrease agitation and depression symptoms in dementia patients [14], as well as increase use of facial expressions and social interaction with the staff [16]. However, the study by Liang et al. [16] also showed that not all participants responded positively. Some of the participants expressed that the robot was "just a toy", that they would prefer a "real animal", and one of the participants pushed Paro away and expressed irritation about its noises.

Another example of robot animals for dementia care are cat robots, such as NeCoRo, iCat, FurReal Cat, JustoCat and Joy for All cat. The use of a cat robot, instead of a seal, is based on the idea of reminiscence therapy as a framework (i.e., the use of memories from the user's past) [27]. This suggests that it might be easier to relate to a common domestic animal that people might have interacted with during their upbringing and/or adult life. Moreover, the human-animal relationship might be easier to develop, since many people already have cat experience (unlike in the case of the seal). However, it could also be the case that people have higher expectations on the robots' behaviour—i.e., they expect it to behave like a real cat—and therefore the interaction has a higher risk of failing. One pilot study with JustoCat showed that for some people with dementia, it could decrease agitated behaviour and improve quality of life [12]. Previous studies have also compared robot cats and plush toy cats to explore if the movement and mimicking of a real cat has an effect. One study showed that both NeCoRo and the plush toy cat decreased agitation in dementia patients, but that the robot cat also increased pleasure [17].

Dogs are another domestic animal that has become popular as the basis for companion robots (e.g., AIBO and Joy for All dog). In the case of AIBO, the robot looks more robotic and does not have fur. One study compared AIBO and an AIBO dressed up in fake fur [22]. During both conditions, the participants looked at and communicated with AIBO, but without fur they recognised that it was a robot, and with fur, they thought that it was a dog or a baby. Another study compared AIBO with a living dog, and the result was that both conditions significantly decreased the feeling of loneliness, and the participants felt a high level of attachment towards the pets [4]. This suggests that robot animals and robot-therapy could have similar positive effects as animal-therapy on elderly with dementia [3].

The Joy for All pets used here have not been the subject of many previous studies. One study showed, though, that both the cat and the dog robot improved communication and potential well-being benefits, such as reduced agitation and anxiety [5].

3   Method

Both studies reported here were conducted at a residential home in Motala, which is a municipality in the South-east of Sweden, with about 29,000 inhabitants. The robotic cat study started a few weeks after the care home had bought and introduced two robot cats at their own initiative. We came in contact with them after a news article on the subject and asked if we could observe the use of the robot cats. The robotic dog study was initiated jointly by us and the care home later, triggered by interesting findings in the robotic cat study.

The robotic cat study investigated how elderly people with dementia interacted with a robot cat and how the care home personnel experienced it, during a nine-months period, starting in October 2019. The first round of observations and interviews were conducted four weeks after the robot had been introduced at the facility. The second round was conducted three months later. Due to the COVID-19 pandemic, the third round of observations had to be cancelled. The last interviews were conducted three months after the second round, ending in June 2020.

The robotic dog study investigated how elderly people with dementia interacted with a robot dog and how the care home personnel experienced it, during a three-months period, running in parallel with the last months of the robotic cat study. This study focused on two dementia patients that did not accept the robot cat. They said that they did not like cats, and never had, but were dog persons. Therefore, we conducted the additional study to investigate if the stated preference for dogs would also lead to positive effects of having a robotic dog.

3.1 Participants

All participants were recruited from one care home facility, with the help of the municipality of Motala. In the robotic cat study, two care home departments (A and B) were exposed to one cat robot each and one department (C) did not have a robot cat. Each department had eight elderly people with dementia living there, and almost all of them were observed in the study.

In the first round of interviews in the robotic cat study, six care home staff members participated. In the second and the third round, four participants remained. The two participants from the first round that could not participate in the second and the third interview were excluded from the study. The final set of participants (*mean age* = 44.5 years, $SD = 2.87$, 100% female) had different educational backgrounds. Three of them were Unlicensed Assistive Personnel (UAP) with different specialisations in dementia care, and one were a registered nurse.

In the robotic dog study, the main participants were two elderly people with dementia, which we will call Ann and Jacob. Ann was a 80-year old woman with vascular dementia. She had previous experience with the cat robot since she lived at department B, but she was not interested in the cat robot, except for small interactions such as smiling when seeing it. Ann had been a dog owner before and had several dog toys in her room at the facility. In her illness she got very anxious and worried about everything, she could easily get anxiety and wandered a lot, and had trouble relaxing, which required much physical and psychological support from the staff. She also had different medications, such as antidepressants and sedatives, but she was sensitive to them and experienced side effects, such as tiredness. The care home staff therefore wanted her to try a robot dog as a psychosocial intervention. The interviews about Ann's interaction with the robot dog were conducted with five UAP's and one nurse (*mean age* = 37.2 years, $SD = 8.17$, 100% female).

Jacob was a 90-year old man with Alzheimer's disease living at department C. He had little prior experience with the cat robot, mainly seeing it arriving at the facility, but his department had not had one. Jacob had also been a dog owner earlier in his life. In his condition he was very anxious, restless, and occasionally wanted to go home to his deceased mother and father, and therefore showed wandering behaviour. Also, in this case the care home staff chose Jacob as a participant to try a robot dog as a psychosocial intervention, especially since he showed agitated behaviours and had expressed to be a dog person. The interviews about Jacob were conducted with three UAP's and one nurse (*mean age* = 51.8 years, *SD* = 9.36, 100% female).

3.2 Ethnographic Approach

Ethnographic research [10] involves the study of groups of people and how they go about their daily life. This method was chosen for these studies to investigate how elderly people with dementia live together and interact with a robot pet. In both the robotic cat and dog study, we used participant observations and semi-structured interviews, to collect data on two cases: group interaction with a robot cat and individual interaction with a robot dog.

Observations. For observing the use of the robot pets we used participant observation [9] as a method, which is when the observer is involved in the environment and with the people being observed. This method is especially useful for collecting data in a natural setting where the observer needs to blend in with the situation. The main reason for this is to make the participants feel as comfortable as possible so that they do not change their normal behaviour. In this study, the participation was moderate [9], meaning that interaction with the participants only happened occasionally. With moderate participation, the people being observed know the role of the researcher, who can ask questions during the observation. Observations in this study were conducted in the common area where the participants meet to drink coffee and watch TV in the afternoon. The observer was sitting in the sofa together with the participants and had coffee. During the sessions, the observer was taking notes about the people in the room, the environment, the staff, what people said and situations that occurred.

During the first round in the robotic cat study, three observations were conducted, two at department A and one at department B. During the second round, two observations were conducted, one at each department. The five sessions were in total seven hours, with 1–2 hours per session. The observations were in conjunction with the daily afternoon coffee when many of the residents gather in the common area.

Observations of Ann interacting with the robot dog were conducted on two occasions during a total of five hours. Due to the pandemic, there were no observations of Jacob and the second observation could not be made with Ann.

Interviews. Interviews were semi-structured with open ended questions [2]. This means that the researcher has a general structure with themes and questions, but can be flexible. If, for example, during an interview an interesting theme or question comes up, then the researcher can ask about that during the next interview as well. All interviews where recorded with a smartphone to allow the interviewer to be engaged in the conversation.

The first and the second round of interviews in the robotic cat study were conducted face-to-face in a secluded room at the care home facility. The third round of interviews were conducted over the phone (due to the pandemic). The first interview focused on the personnel's previous experience with robots, their attitude before the robots arrived, and how it might have changed, what their daily routine with the robots looked like, and how the robots worked with the elderly participants. The second interview focused on possible differences in how the personnel handled the robot and how the elderly people used the robot after some time had passed. The third interview had a similar focus, but also addressed the nine-months period as whole. It was also controlled for that the pandemic had not had a large impact on the study, meaning no resident or staff member tested positive, and no new restrictions with the robots were introduced.

The interviews in the robotic dog study were conducted face-to-face at the care home during the first round, but due to the pandemic the rest of the interviews were conducted over the phone.

3.3 Material

Figure 1 shows the Joy for All cat and dog. Both have soft fur and built-in motion and touch sensors. The robot cat has cat-like movements (e.g., licking its paw and rolling on its back), and it also has a purring sound and motion. With the robot dog one can feel its heartbeat, and it can also lean back and move its head. The robot cat can respond to human voices with meowing, and the robot dog with barking.

Robot cat.

Robot dog.

Fig. 1. Hasbro's Joy for All pet robots.

Behavioural and Mental Symptoms of Dementia. Both studies used the quantitative Behavioural and Mental Symptoms of Dementia (BMSD, in Swedish: BPSD)[2] measurement filled in by the facility staff each week to grade the different symptoms the dementia patients display (e.g., hallucinations, agitation and sleep disturbances), which also constitutes the basis for different treatments (e.g., medication, outdoor walking and robot animals). BMSD records used were weekly reports from the nine months during both studies, for every patient at department A, B and C.

3.4   Analysis

Thematic analysis [6] was used to analyse the observation and interview data. This is a qualitative method used to gain insight from the data, which is done by identifying different patterns. First, by reading and re-reading the data, the researcher produces codes with associated segments [2]. The next step is to sort the codes into more general themes, review them, and then define and name the themes.

During the days after the observations, the field notes were written into a full text while still having the observations clear in memory, and the interviews were fully transcribed. The two studies were analysed separately by two different researchers, but were combined in the results since they created similar themes. There were multiple codes from the initial coding, and the next step was to re-read and cluster similar codes into themes. The procedure of clustering codes into themes was repeated until the themes were coherent. For example, in both studies, initial codes were "pat", "talk to" and "worry about", which resulted in the theme "taking care of".

BMSD data was analysed by comparing the scores from the first three months, the coming three months and the last three months of the robotic cat study. For the robotic dog study, we only looked at the two individual scores. Since each department only has eight people living there, statistical methods cannot be used to analyse the data. Therefore, we mainly compared the agitation, incontinence and sedative medication score, by themselves and in combination, since these behaviours were observed and were brought up in the interviews.

4   Results and Discussion

The analysis of the observation and interview data resulted in multiple themes, of which we here present the four most prominent: animal lover, companionship, taking care of and conversation starter.

4.1   Animal Lover

During the first round of observations and interviews in the robotic cat study it was clear that some of the elderly participants loved the cat robot, and some

---

[2] www.bpsd.se.

did not bother with it at all. According to the staff, when the robot cats were introduced, the majority of the residents shone up and wanted to take a closer look. Three of the female residents in departments A and B "adopted" the robots the same day and thought it was their own cat. The staff tried to make the robot a part of the group by creating the routine of always placing the robot in the common area, either in a sofa or in an armchair. During the first two months, the residents acted a bit competitive around the robot, wanting to have it in their lap for cuddling. The three ladies also continued during this period to believe it was theirs, but there was a shift after 2–3 months. The robots became a natural part of the group, and everyone in the staff described it as if the robot cats had become "family members" at their department. They described that the tone from the residents shifted from the surprised "the cat is still here", to the confirming "oh, there is the cat", indicating that the residents started to see it as a natural part of their environment.

During the first observations, there were certain individuals in both departments that showed no interest in the robot cat, even when the staff offered it to them. According to the staff, these persons clearly stated that they did not like cats, and either that they were dog persons or that they did not like animals at all. When Ann and Jacob received their robot dogs, they liked them straight away. This might indicate that the reminiscence effect was strong when using a domestic pet, with the result that people identifying as a dog person did not like the robot cat.

4.2 Companionship

Several of the residents seemed to feel companionship with the cat robot. For example, a woman at department B who was agitated, showed incontinence and was given sedative medication every day, quickly accepted the cat. When agitated, she started to pack her things and tried to go home every afternoon. During the first months, the staff led her out to the common area and offered her to hold to robot cat which she accepted every time. During the first observation, she came out of her room by herself and asked for the cat. Then she had the cat robot in her lap, patted it and talked to it. During the session she seemed very calm and even fell asleep. The staff described that this had never happened before. After five months, she did not have the need for sedatives anymore and she used the robot cat less. During the second observation she did not ask for the cat, acted in a calm way and patted it occasionally during the session. The staff described that she was much calmer and this effect continued throughout the nine months, which was also supported by the BMSD data. The reason behind this effect could be the robot cat or the different stages of dementia, or a combination, but the staff believed that the cat must had a positive effect on her improved well-being. This was one example of an individual where the robot cat could have had similar effects as in the study with Paro by Jøransson et al. [14] and the pilot study with JustoCat [12]. Also, as in the study with JustoCat, the robot cat seems to only work on some specific individuals, which could be due to many reasons (e.g., being a dog person, disease state, misuse of reminiscence theory) that need to be further investigated.

Ann in the robotic dog study had severe agitation, and according to the staff, the robot dog became her safe spot. She carried it with her in her walker wherever she went, let it sleep with her in the bed every night and screamed and looked for it when she could not find it (e.g., when the staff had to change battery or clean it). For Jacob it was different. He did not initiate contact with the robot dog, but the staff tried to distract him with it when he got agitated. He often accepted it and was able to sit down and cuddle, but sometimes he was too angry to let himself be distracted. The difference between the participants might be that Ann often believed it was a real dog, while Jacob often asked if it was real and said that "it did not really behave like a dog". When asked about this, the staff were always honest to the residents that the robots were not real animals, mainly for of ethical reasons. In general, the staff described that most of the residents much of the time understood that the robot was not a real animal, but when it moved they became unsure and started to believe it was real. Before the robot pets arrived, they had used cat and robot toys for some of the residents, but according to the staff those had never worked as well as with the robots. They thought it was something in the movement that "created the magic", and also the fact that the residents thought it felt like a real animal.

4.3   Taking Care of

For some of the elderly participants, the robot cat gave them the opportunity to take care of someone. According to the staff, the residents do not have anything or anyone to take care of after they move to the residential home. The importance of caring behaviours for elderly people living in residential homes have previously been studied in other contexts. One study report that engagement in caring behaviours were found to be universally important means for residents to maintain their self-esteem, self-identity, and continuation of person-hood [13]. Caring behaviours with the robot cat included protecting, supporting and confirming. For example, one man at department A had the robot cat in his lap during the first observation, and he was cuddling with it, but he was also very attentive to if anyone of the others also wanted to have the robot close. In the second round of observations his behaviour toward the robot had changed. The robot was lying nearby while he watched TV. He had one of his hands on the robot at all times and patted it, talking to it almost constantly, describing what was happening on the TV and reacting to the robot cat's sounds and movements. For example, when the robot meowed or rolled over on its back, he thought that the robot was in pain or needed help. He asked it what was wrong and tried to help it to sit up again. He also spontaneously told the observer that he usually takes it with him in to his room: "The cat is so kind. At first when he [the robot cat] is with me, he is a bit worried but after a while he calms down, that is so cosy". According to the staff, he was interested in the robot from the start, but that developed into a relationship where on a daily basis he "took care" of the robot, and it was this caring behaviour that was more prominent than mere companionship or the feeling of having an animal close.

Caring could in other patients have a more negative effect. Some of the participants at first expressed worries like "who is feeding the cat", "who is emptying the litter box" and "who is letting the cat out"? The staff were careful to say that they would take care of it and explain that it was not a real cat. In the last round of interviews, all participants expressed that this worry had passed. In the case of Ann, she had trouble accepting the robot dog at first because she did not think she would be able to take care of it. However, according to the staff, after a few days she understood that the dog was fine in the care of the personnel and then she fully accepted it. In this case the patient understood her own limitations and that she would not be able to care a living dog, which is one of the main reasons to use robotic pets.

The sounds and body of the pets could at times create another type of worry. Both the cat and the dog robot have different modes: meowing/barking and mute with maintained purring/heartbeat. When the robots were meowing or barking, many of the participants thought that something was wrong, that it was in pain or hungry. Furthermore, the staff also found the sounds disturbing. Therefore, after a few months they rarely had the robots unmuted. This is similar to a finding with Paro where one participant got irritated about the robot's noises [16]. One woman at department A said to herself during the first round of observation that she had never seen the cat jump or walk, and she wondered if it was injured. Another woman at department B expressed that the ears and the paws of the cat were hard, and that it must have been injured.

4.4 Conversation Starter

As in previous studies, the robotic pets were found to be conversation starters [5,16,20,22]. The staff described, for example, that two women at department A had almost never said a word since they moved in, but since the robot cat arrived they talked with the robot, and with each other about the robot. In all observations the participants talked to the robots and to others about the robot. The staff also added that the robot gave them a natural conversation topic to talk to relatives about, which otherwise could be a struggle. It seems like that both on an individual and on a group level the robot contributes with its presence and that it gives everybody at the department something in common to talk to and about, which is in line with Pfadenhauer and Dukats findings with Paro [20], that the robot evokes everyday conversations that resembles those in the presence of pets.

5   Conclusion

The qualitative nature of this research does not give any final answer to the question if low-cost companion robot pets as psychosocial interventions can decrease agitation symptoms in dementia patients. Our contribution is a real-world report on how elderly people with dementia interact with robot pets and how care home staff members describe their use benefits and drawbacks. During the nine-months period, we did not observe the typical novelty effect. At first, there was a large interest from some individuals, but after a few months this interest became more distributed in the group, and especially in department A the interest increased over time. The robot cats were seen as "family members" and the staff thought that the robots contributed positively to the whole group by creating a better mood.

Some of our results are in line with previous work conducted with more expensive robotic platforms, such as providing companionship and acting as conversation starters. Some other aspects have not been investigated to the same extent, such as caring for robot pets and differences between animal identities (e.g., being a dog person). We have raised several questions in this paper that do not yet have clear answers. We note that there is potential mismatch between existing research with relatively advanced robot platforms and the fact that many residential homes (at least in Sweden) are acquiring low-cost off-the-shelf pet robots that have not been the subject of much research. Care homes at this point lack systematic approaches for handling this. The staff members put their faith to their existing measurements (such as BMSD), but are faced with the difficulty of drawing any reliable conclusions from this. More research is required, we believe, on how robot pets for use in psychosocial interventions for elderly people with dementia should be developed, how they are deployed, and in particular how they can be evaluated in the long term.

References

1. Dementia: A NICE-SCIE Guideline On Supporting People With Dementia and Their Carers in Health and Social Care. The British Psychological Society and Gaskell, London (2007)
2. Alm, B.: Compendium in Ethnographic Method, vol. 2 (2017)
3. Banks, M.R., Banks, W.A.: The effects of animal-assisted therapy on loneliness in an elderly population in long-term care facilities. J. Gerontol. Med. Sci. **57A**(7), 428–432 (2002)
4. Banks, M.R., Willoughby, L.M., Banks, W.A.: Animal-assisted therapy and loneliness in nursing homes: use of robotic versus living dogs. J. Am. Med. Direct. Assoc. **9**(3), 173–177 (2008)
5. Bradwell, H.L., Winnington, R., Thill, S., Jones, R.B.: Longitudinal diary data: six months real-world implementation of affordable companion robots for older people in supported living. In: ACM/IEEE International Conference on Human-Robot Interaction, pp. 148–150 (2020)
6. Braun, V., Clarke, V.: Using thematic analysis in psychology. Qual. Res. Psychol. **3**(2), 77–101 (2006)
7. Cayton, H., Graham, N., Warner, J.: Dementia: Alzheimer's and Other Dementias, 2nd edn. Class Publishing, London (2002)
8. Cohen-Mansfield, J., Billig, N.: Agitated behaviors in the elderly: I. A conceptual review. J. Am. Geriatr. Soc. **35**(0), 711–721 (1986)
9. DeWalt, K.M., DeWalt, B.R.: Participant Observation: A Guideline for Fieldworkers, 2nd edn. Altamira Press, Plymouth (2011)

10. Emerson, R., Fretz, R., Shaw, L.: Writing Ethnographic Fieldnote, 2nd edn. The University of Chicago Press, Chicago (1995)
11. Fong, T., Nourbakhsh, I., Dautenhahn, K.: A survey of socially interactive robots. Robot. Auton. Syst. **42**, 143–166 (2003)
12. Gustafsson, C., Svanberg, C., Müllersdorf, M.: Using a robotic cat in dementia care: a pilot study. J. Gerontol. Nurs. **41**(10), 46–56 (2015)
13. Hutchison, C.P., Bahr, R.T.: Types and meanings of caring behaviors among elderly nursing home residents. J. Nurs. Sch. **23**(2), 85–88 (1991)
14. Jøranson, N., Pedersen, I., Rokstad, A.M.M., Ihlebæk, C.: Effects on symptoms of agitation and depression in persons with dementia participating in robot-assisted activity: a cluster-randomized controlled trial. J. Am. Med. Direct. Assoc. **16**(10), 867–873 (2015)
15. Kales, H.C., Gitlin, L.N., Lyketsos, C.G.: Assessment and management of behavioral and psychological symptoms of dementia. BMJ **350**, 1–16 (2015)
16. Liang, A., Piroth, I., Robinson, H., MacDonald, B., Fisher, M., Nater, U.M., Skoluda, N., Broadbent, E.: A pilot randomized trial of a companion robot for people with dementia living in the community. J. Am. Med. Direct. Association **18**(10), 871–878 (2017)
17. Libin, A., Cohen-Mansfield, J.: NeCoRo -therapeutic robocat for nursing home residents with dementia: preliminary inquiry. American J. Alzheimer's disease and other dementias **19**(2), 111–116 (2004)
18. Mordoch, E., Osterreicher, A., Guse, L., Roger, K., Thompson, G.: Use of social commitment robots in the care of elderly people with dementia: A literature review. Maturitas **74**(1), 14–20 (2013)
19. Patterson, C.: World Alzheimer Report 2018: the state of the art of dementia research: new frontiers. Technical report, London (2018)
20. Pfadenhauer, M., Dukat, C.: Robot caregiver or robot-supported caregiving? the performative deployment of the social robot paro in dementia care. Int. J. Soc. Robot. **7**(3), 393–406 (2015)
21. Shibata, T., Wada, K.: Robot therapy: a new approach for mental healthcare of the elderly - a mini-review. Gerontology **57**(4), 378–386 (2011)
22. Tamura, T., Yonemitsu, S., Itoh, A., Oikawa, D., Kawakami, A., Higashi, Y., Fujimooto, T., Nakajima, K.: Is an entertainment robot useful in the care of elderly people with severe dementia? J. Gerontol. Med. Sci. **59A**(1), 83–85 (2004)
23. Vernooij-Dassen, M., Vasse, E., Zuidema, S., Cohen-Mansfield, J., Moyle, W.: Psychosocial interventions for dementia patients in long-term care. Int. Psychogeriatr. **22**(7), 1121–1128 (2010)
24. Wada, K., Shibata, T., Saito, T., Sakamoto, K., Tanie, K.: Psychological and social effects of one year robot assisted activity on elderly people at a health service facility for the aged. In: Proceedings of the IEEE International Conference on Robotics and Automation (ICRA), pp. 2785–2790 (2005)
25. Wada, K., Shibata, T., Saito, T., Sakamoto, K., Tanie, K.: Robot assisted activity at a health service facility for the aged for 17 months - an interim report of long-term experiment. IEEE Workshop Adv. Robot. its Soc. Impacts **2005**, 127–132 (2005)
26. Wada, K., Shibata, T., Saito, T., Tanie, K.: Analysis of factors that bring mental effects to elderly people in robot assisted activity. In: IEEE/RSJ International Conference on Intelligent Robots and Systems, pp. 1152–1157 (2002)
27. Woods, B., O'Philbin, L., Farrell, E.M., Spector, A.E., Orrell, M.: Reminiscence therapy for dementia. Cochrane Data- Base of Syst. Rev. (3) (2018)

A Social Robot to Deliver an 8-Week Intervention for Diabetes Management: Initial Test of Feasibility in a Hospital Clinic

Nicole L. Robinson[1,2,3](✉) [iD], Jennifer Connolly[1] [iD], Leanne Hides[4] [iD], and David J. Kavanagh[1] [iD]

[1] Centre for Children's Health Research, Institute of Health and Biomedical Innovation, and School of Psychology & Counselling, Queensland University of Technology, Brisbane, QLD 4000, Australia
david.kavanagh@qut.edu.au

[2] Australian Research Council Centre of Excellence for Robotic Vision, Queensland University of Technology, Brisbane, QLD 4000, Australia

[3] Department of Electrical and Computer Systems Engineering, Turner Institute for Brain and Mental Health, Monash University, Clayton, VIC 3800, Australia
nicole.robinson@monash.edu

[4] School of Psychology, University of Queensland, Saint Lucia, QLD 4072, Australia

Abstract. Social robots show significant potential as a healthcare coach for chronic life-long conditions and within medical settings. This 8-week feasibility trial explored a robot-delivered talk-based program for adolescents with Type 1 Diabetes to coach diabetes management with a focus on healthy eating habits. Trial objectives were to assess initial recruitment uptake, treatment effects, and evaluations of the program before a larger deployment. A NAO robot delivered two 60-minute coaching sessions and two 15-minute videos over an 8-week period. Initial findings revealed the robot program had a 44% uptake rate (n = 4). The robot program helped two participants achieve a 70% reduction in their high-sugar food and drink consumption, including increased motivation and self-efficacy scores. Program evaluation found the robot-delivered content did elicit discussion around personal incentives, goals, strategies, goal planning and consideration to improve diabetes management. Robot evaluation scores increased over time for improved likability, helpfulness, trust, and capacity to help change behavior. Qualitative evaluation found sessions were rated as interactive, supportive, and helpful for their self-management. Results found preliminary support for a robot-delivered program to be offered in conjunction with a hospital outpatient clinic, but more recruitment to increase sample size is needed. The next stage involves technical refinement, better integration into an existing service, and trial extension or replication in a larger sample to further substantiate these findings.

Keywords: Type 1 diabetes · Clinical trial · Treatment · Human-robot interaction · Dietary intake · Outpatient

© Springer Nature Switzerland AG 2020
A. R. Wagner et al. (Eds.): ICSR 2020, LNAI 12483, pp. 628–639, 2020.
https://doi.org/10.1007/978-3-030-62056-1_52

1   Introduction

Social robots are used in healthcare settings to engage and retain children in col-laborative treatments to improve health-related outcomes [26,33]. Target areas for robot-assisted healthcare have included support to self-manage intensive chronic conditions [5,20], technique practice to mitigate anxiety, stress or pain in medical settings [1], and delivery of a coaching program for exercises related to rehabilitation [8,23,24]. Robot-delivered programs also span across different levels of intensity and involvement from the robot [26,33], from a simple single-session health technique [6,28] through to multi-session therapeutic coaching to create longer-term behavioral outcomes [1]. Social robot programs for child health have so far shown capacity to promote health actions and encourage self-management for medical symptoms or conditions. An intensive health-related area for children and adolescents that requires both technique rehearsal and routine practice of self-management tasks to achieve health outcomes is Type 1 Diabetes (T1D) [35], which represents an important target that may be beneficial and well-suited to robotic delivery.

2   Target Area - Self-Management for Type 1 Diabetes

Type 1 diabetes (T1D) has intensive daily self-management tasks including blood glucose monitoring, insulin usage and dietary control [35]. Sub-optimal manage-ment is characterised by long-term consequences but regulated blood glucose can reduce and delay diabetes-related complications [2,7,21,35,41]. Adolescence is a common period of risk with high rates of sub-optimal glucose levels and few meeting recommended targets, resulting in adverse events from poor glycemic control [10,41]. This period is characterised by unique social and behavioral challenges, such as the transition to greater personal control, self-efficacy and independence over self-management tasks, requiring adolescents to take greater responsibility for self-management [4,15]. A clear behavior to regulate blood glu-cose that adolescents can manage themselves is their eating patterns, including limiting extra high-sugar food and drinks not needed to manage blood glucose [21,38,41]. Adolescents often do not adhere to recommended eating patterns [35,40] and miss insulin doses after snack consumption, which help to regulate blood glucose if they do consume them [22,38].

To increase self-management, behavioral interventions such as Motivational Interviewing (MI) have been used to encourage practice [29]. MI is a talk-based counselling approach designed to elicit, create and maintain healthy changes on a key target action, as one example, dietary control. MI has been an effective method to create healthy behavioral outcomes, including helping adolescents with T1D to maintain healthy diets, increase self-monitoring, exercise and blood glucose control [11,13]. Recent trials have found that MI for dietary control can be further enhanced by incorporating mental imagery, and teaching people to use that mental imagery in their daily life, including via a robotic adaptation [32,37].

2.1   A Robot-Delivered Program to Support Diabetes Management

Social robots have been used in a small set of trials to engage young children with T1D in tasks related to diabetes management [5,9,20,27]. Focus groups with children and their parents identified several key factors for a robotic companion for T1D: ability to perform monitoring and support for self-management practices; increase self-confidence and motivation; and sensitive listeners [5]. Social robots have been found to influence children to record more information into a nutritional diary [20], and children share more personal experiences during interaction sessions than in a no-robot condition [14].

These trials address separate but important components involved in diabetes self-management. However, social robots can deliver a more substantial behavioral intervention that can address multiple factors at once. Most existing trials did not offer more than a single session, did not include follow-up measures to see how the robot impacted diabetes management, or focused on those with sub-optimal blood glucose who were likely to have challenges in increasing self-efficacy, motivation, and self-management tasks. To address this research gap, we conducted a feasibility trial to focus on a robot-delivered MI program for adolescents with T1D to help build confidence, increase motivation, and create a step wise plan for healthy changes in one behavioral target. If effective, this program could then become a basis for a robot-delivered behavioral intervention in T1D to improve self-management, and one that could be adapted to integrate in to a hospital or outpatient clinic, or translated to focus on other behavioral actions such as blood glucose monitoring.

3   Method

3.1   Trial Design

This feasibility trial was conducted to examine the initial treatment effects for a robot-delivered MI intervention with mental imagery to reduce high-energy food or drinks (HEFD) intake that was not needed for diabetes management, and not followed by insulin use. The focus on HEFDs was chosen because this behavior exerts a powerful influence on blood glucose, it represented a target behavior that is troublesome for adolescents, and was one that would be both adjunctive to and consistent with existing treatment. This trial also aimed to explore initial recruitment numbers and program evaluations for future iterations. The target sample was hospital clinic patients aged 11–17 years who were diagnosed with T1D for one year and who had no eating disorder diagnosis. Participants needed to have 3 or more periods in the previous 6 weeks when they deviated from their dietary/insulin regimen, demonstrating some room for improvement.

3.2   Robotic Intervention

The NAO V6 (Red) by Softbank Robotics delivered the intervention on its own. It was programmed using a rule-based branching system with NAOqi OS 2.5

and Choregraphe: ALAnimatedSpeech, ALTextToSpeech, ALFaceTracker and ALAutonomousLife [36]. The robot named 'Andy' was designed to use co-speech gestures and verbal pronunciation adjusted at key points to emphasise treatment content and clarity. Session content was adapted from previous scripts which had found significant results in similar domains [3,32,32,37]. The robot delivered a talk-based counselling approach known as MI that involves the robot asking a series of questions designed to promote discussion of experiences, ideas, reasons for change and past successes related to behavior change for dietary intake. The main goal of this counselling approach is to help address and resolve ambivalence to change to help improve self-efficacy and motivation to change [25]. The verbal script used MI principles, which involved key language choices to encourage self-reflection on the benefits of behavior change and their potential to achieve it [25]. The verbal script involved the robot requesting that the participant answer prompted questions out loud and at times, to practice mental imagery (i.e. visualization) during the session. Mental imagery involves creating an internal representation of a desired goal, strategy or outcome by imagining the action or outcome in their mind [18]. Mental imagery was included because it can accentuate the treatment impact for MI [32,37]. Participants controlled the interaction flow using a touch sensor on the robot so they could take time to respond at their own pace to support the notion of sensitive listening [5] and to avoid the program advancing too quickly. This choice allowed the robot program to run on its own, which gives a stronger case to give personal control to the person over the session pace and for later use in a clinical setting. Natural language was not used to minimize mistakes undermining confidence in treatment efficacy, maintain greater control over content delivery to a medically sensitive population, allow systematic changes to be drawn across the sample, and behavior change with digital simulations of MI has been achieved in its absence [34]. Development of the robot-delivered script was supported by a trip to the University of Plymouth. The final script was reviewed and approved by clinical psychologists and hospital staff. For comprehensive information, scripts and trial code can be seen here: https://github.com/nrbsn/robofit-diabetes.

3.3 Robot Session and Content Delivery

Session 1 (60 min, S1): The robot gave a verbal session overview and program information. The robot provided a guided mental imagery-based practice, followed by rationale for the use of a mental imagery-based intervention. The robot asked questions about issues they had with HEFD, and to recall specific occasions where they had difficulties staying in control with HEFD, as well as their emotional response to that occasion. Participants were asked to imagine an action that would prevent a negative outcome from HEFD, and asked them to discuss an occasion in the past where they had reached a goal related to HEFD control. If they were committed to making a change to their HEFD intake, they were asked to imagine a detailed step wise plan, including short and long-term actions they could do to put their plan into motion. The robot concluded with a brief session summary. **Video 1 (15 min, Week 1):** A recorded video involved the robot delivering a piece-to-camera script as a booster session. The video involved the robot encouraging reflection on their progress to control HEFD and brief guided mental imagery on experiences of successful moments around controlling HEFD, including talking through strategy building for what steps to take if HEFDs were available. **Session 2 (60 min, Week 2, S2)**: The robot asked them to give a review of their goal and the current strategies they were using to reduce HEFD intake. This included asking them to make any adjustments if their strategy had not been effective. The robot asked them to rehearse mental imagery about their goal and strategy building for potential problems that may have arisen in relation to HEFD intake. The session concluded with a brief verbal summary. **Video 2 (15 min, Week 3)**: In this pre-recorded video, the robot talked about more strategies to remain in control of HEFD, including coming up with a plan on what to do in future situations. Detailed scripts can be seen here: https://github.com/nrbsn/robofit-diabetes.

3.4   Assessment Measures

M1-High-Energy Food or Drink Frequency over the Past 2 Weeks (HE-F2): A measure to assess the number of HEFD items and their use of insulin over the previous two weeks. This measure was designed to assess the impact of the behavioral intervention delivered by the robot. HEFD and insulin use were calculated to give a total score. The HEFD had not been yet been tested in other trials **M2-Dietary Treatment Index (DTI)**: The DTI assessed HEFD episodes over 4 weeks with a focus on the last 3 occasions to estimate frequencies per month to assess effectiveness to reduce HEFDs. Lower scores represented more favorable outcomes [12]. **M3-Confidence to Control (CC)**: A 20-item scale to measure self-efficacy to control HEFD across time frames (CC-D; e.g. 2 days) and emotional states (CC-S; e.g. bored). Ratings on 11-point scales from 0 to 10 ('Not at all confident' to 'Extremely confident'), and an average score was computed across items. **M4-Motivational Thought Frequency (MTF)**: A 13-item scale to measure motivational cognition for HEFD improvement over the last week [19,31]. Ratings were on an 11-point scale from 0 to 10 ('Never' to 'Constantly'). **M5-Robot Inventory (RI)**: A 5-item set to measure initial attitudes and expectations of social robots before and after the program. Items were on an 11-point scale from 0 to 100 ('Not at all' to 'Extremely'). Question topics included if the participant likes social robots, thinks social robots are helpful, would feel comfortable talking to a social robot, could trust a social robot with their problems, and if a social robot could help change their behavior. **M6-Treatment Expectancy (TE)**: A 6-item set on perceived usefulness and expected program efficacy on an 11-point scale from 0 to 100 ('Not useful, likely, effective at all' to 'Extremely useful, likely, effective'). Items included: 'how useful will this treatment be in helping young people with type 1 diabetes to cut down sugary snacks and drinks?' and 'how effective will this treatment be for you?'. **M7-HbA1c**: HbA1c involve blood glucose levels over the last 8 to 12 weeks and levels less than 7.5% indicate glycemic control [30]. Test results can be influenced by multiple factors, so HbA1c was a secondary measure only [17]. HbA1c was collected by hospital staff at the participant's regular appointment. **M8-Qualitative Interview**: A 30-minute semi-structured interview on their experience of the program subjected to thematic analysis [16]. Questions included what did they think of the robot, what were their thoughts of the program, and did they have any recommendations for future improvement.

3.5 Procedure

Human ethics approval was granted and registered online in a clinical trials registry. Eligibility was assessed over two stages to protect privacy. Adolescents and their parents/guardians were approached in an outpatient clinic. Preliminary eligibility was assessed and written consent was obtained from both parties. Full eligibility was assessed in a private testing room before the first session. If ineligible, participants were informed about guidelines and given contact cards for support. If they reported low HEFD intake, they were praised for adherence. Ineligible participants were able to interact with the robot for several minutes on a non-diabetes related topic. Eligible participants were asked to complete a tutorial on how to use the robot before starting the program. Participants completed the session on their own to promote open and honest discussion about their dietary control. A research team member monitored the interaction from a separate room to ensure participant safety and could intervene at any time (Fig. 1). The researcher met with participants at the end of each session to see if they had any questions about their involvement. Assessment measures were completed online at Baseline, Weeks 4 and 8, and HE-F1 (One Week) at 1, 2, and 3.

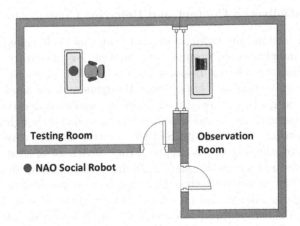

Fig. 1. Example of the Experimental Setup

4 Results

4.1 Initial Feasibility Test

Recruitment occurred for 3 months (period between routine clinical visits). During recruitment, 76 prospective patients were approached, and 18 met eligibility for both age and T1D diagnosis (24%). Others did not have T1D (i.e. Type 2 Diabetes), were under 11 years old, or had diagnostic or behavioral issues. Nine (50% of 18 eligible) agreed to complete the program (reasons for declining: time, adherence, one-sided consent from the parent/guardian or child). Six presented for Session 1 and two did not meet full eligibility (i.e. good adherence), leaving 4 participants (13–16 years, 1 male and 3 female, 44% uptake rate).

4.2 Completion Rates and Impact of Robot-Delivered Program

Initial feasibility to create preliminary treatment effects was met. Over the 8-week period, the robot program helped two participants achieve a 70% reduction of HEFD items on average per week (10 to 3 items; 27 to 8 items). One decreased their blood glucose by 1.5% to meet glycemic control levels (8.8% to 7.5%)[30]. One increased insulin use with HEFD episodes (35% to 50% of the time). Diet treatment index scores improved ($M = -1.5$) alongside large increases for self-reported confidence (CC-D $M = 66.5$; CC-S $M = 25.5$) and motivation ($M = 63.0$) to control their dietary intake. Robot scores often increased over time: likability (25%, $M1 = 75$, $M2 = 100$), helpfulness (35%, $M1 = 65$, $M2 = 100$), comfort (0%, $M1 = 100$, $M2 = 100$), trust (10%, $M1 = 80$, $M2 = 90$), and capacity to help change behavior (40%, $M1 = 60$, $M2 = 100$). Initial treatment expectancy was low ($M = 34.3$, $SD = 7.5$).

4.3 Robot-Delivered Content and Behavior Change Discussion

A review of in-session content found support that a robot-delivered version of MI using mental imagery could prompt consideration for change to HEFD intake. All participants gave relevant responses to open-ended questions about making a healthy change to HEFD. This included thoughts and discussion around personal incentives, goals, strategies, goal planning and consideration of changes. In Session 1, participants provided detailed discussion and thoughtful responses, including reporting their favourite HEFDs, positive and negative things about HEFDs, and downsides that can happen if they have a lot of them. Participants gave answers around a stepwise plan, including self-generated ideas on what to change, how they would start their goal and how they would do it, why they wanted to make a change, and an action they can take to work towards their goal. In Session 2, detailed feedback was given on HEFD reduction progress, the actions they used to get closer to their HEFD goal, and challenging situations that happened. This included responses on how they would keep making a positive change to HEFD intake, a backup action if their first action is not suitable, and a plan on how to use mental imagery to help them achieve the goal.

4.4   Session Involvement in the Robot-Delivered Program

Participants were engaged in sessions with the robot. **Px 1**: S1) He reported detailed information and a proposed goal. He attempted mental imagery and described the outcome. He provided a summary to finalize his goal, including ideas for further practice. He navigated the session well and reported 6/10 confidence to reach his goal. S2) He was relatively engaged and prepared to press the sensor while answering. At times, he accessed his smartphone. He identified positive progress and actions towards goal progress. He reported 8/10 confidence in reaching his goal. **Px 2**: S1) She navigated the session well with some prompts given for shorter answers. She reported short mental imagery engagements and appeared to want to progress the session. She reported 5/10 confidence in achieving her goal. S2) She gave similar short responses and mental imagery-related engagement with limited description. She reported 8/10 confidence in achieving her goal. **Px 3**: S1) She was able to progress through the session with the robot. She was engaged in mental imagery exercises and gave some description of them afterwards. She reported 7/10 confidence to start her goal and said her confidence had increased at the end of the session. She reported she would practice the session content, including mental imagery. S2) She continued to engage in mental imagery and reported 8/ 10 for confidence. She stated that she would continue practising mental imagery. **Px 4**: S1) She appeared to enjoy the robot, provided lengthy answers and described mental imagery in detail. She wanted to work with the robot on a plan. She returned to complete the session another day due to time constraints. A summary was provided by the robot. She then reported she was not ready to start a goal, but confirmed she was happy with treatment and finalized participation.

4.5   Qualitative Robot Evaluation

Qualitative responses further supported initial feasibility from positive robot evaluations, suitable in-treatment content, support and encouragement for self-management. **Interview 1**: He reported sessions were "enjoyable" , the robot "came across really friendly" and "like you were talking to a person". He said "questions were really well thought out", and it "did not feel like you were being pressured or being asked this question by a doctor, you were just talking to a friend about it". He said "there's no imposing feature of a healthcare professional who has all the statistics and stuff, and is telling you that this is wrong and you need to change this" . The robot "made it a lot easier because I don't think it would be as effective if it was coming from a healthcare professional". The content "really zones in on what actually helps for you because most healthcare professionals just give you general what works for everyone". "I would definitely recommend it to them because I think it would really help a lot of people". **Interview 2**: She "really liked" the program and the robot was "interactive". It's much easier to talk to him". She said that she "would feel more confident to talk to Andy about more of my personal life than to an adult". She said it "does not feel as intimidating when the robot talks to you" because it was "working with you and taking you through the steps". The robot was "helping me making my decisions" and "it was easier for me that he had options ready than me having to think of them". She liked mental imagery because "I can go home and I can just do the same thing". **Interview 3**: She said the robot was "good" with an "excellent personality". She was "kind of excited to talk to him" but initially felt "nervous" about it. She said it was "a bit easier than talking to a person". She found the robot to be "encouraging" and "excited to set a goal". She reported she would usually "give a short answer that's not very descriptive, but he made me describe [and] come up with a plan".

5   Discussion and Conclusion

This trial found that robotic delivery of a motivational intervention using mental imagery-based techniques for adolescents with Type 1 Diabetes was promising, with initial treatment effects in their intended direction. The robot could help adolescents to reduce their high-energy food and drink intake, increase their confidence and motivation over the 8-week period. The trial found moderate treatment uptake rates from both adolescents and their parents/guardians. The robot program did elicit thoughts and discussion around personal incentives, goals, strategies, goal planning and consideration of change. Adolescents made an attempt at program components and gave relevant responses to questions. Results found that adolescents reported increased robot evaluation scores over time, including for likability, helpfulness, trust and capacity to help change behavior. In the qualitative interviews, participants gave positive robot evaluations with personal benefit attributed to session content, despite the robots lack of personalization. This trial gave further support for robot companions to assist children and adolescents with T1D in tasks related to diabetes management [5,9,14,20,27]. For instance, the robot-delivered program to address self-management practices, increase confidence and motivation was met favourably by adolescents who completed it [5,9], and diabetes management tasks can be adapted into a more multifaceted approach to behavior change [14,20]. In conclusion, results saw initial support to further test the robot-delivered program for the adolescent age group and target behavior. This could include exploration around the potential for the program to operate alongside a hospital clinic or healthcare setting to assist health practitioners to provide novel service options to young people who could benefit from a more intensive one-to-one interaction [39]. A limitation involved recruitment numbers from only one clinic, and higher recruitment can evaluate the impact of this treatment on a larger scale. Next steps involve technical refinement, robust integration into an existing service (i.e. clinical appointments), and trial extension or replication in a hospital outpatient or health centre location to substantiate these findings in preparation for a larger clinical trial.

Acknowledgement. This work was supported by the Australian Postgraduate Award on behalf of the Department of Education and Training and by a Research Grant from the State of Queensland acting through the Department of Science, Information Technology and Innovation.

References

1. Alemi, M., Ghanbarzadeh, A., Meghdari, A., Moghadam, L.J.: Clinical application of a humanoid robot in pediatric cancer interventions. Int. J. Soc. Robot. **8**(5), 743–759 (2015). https://doi.org/10.1007/s12369-015-0294-y
2. American Diabetes Association: Diagnosis and classification of diabetes mellitus. Diab. Care **37**(1), S81–S90 (2014). https://doi.org/10.2337/dc14-S081
3. Andrade, J., Khalil, M., Dickson, J., May, J., Kavanagh, D.J.: Functional imagery training to reduce snacking: testing a novel motivational intervention based on elaborated intrusion theory. Appetite **100**, 256–262 (2016). https://doi.org/10.1016/j.appet.2016.02.015
4. Babler, E., Strickland, C.J.: Moving the journey towards independence: adolescents transitioning to successful diabetes self-management. J. Pediatr. Nurs. **30**(5), 648–660 (2015). https://doi.org/10.1016/j.pedn.2015.06.005
5. Baroni, I., et al.: What a robotic companion could do for a diabetic child. In: IEEE International Symposium on Robot and Human Interactive Communication, pp. 936–941 (2014)
6. Beran, T.N., Ramirez-Serrano, A., Vanderkooi, O.G., Kuhn, S.: Reducing children's pain and distress towards flu vaccinations: a novel and effective application of humanoid robotics. Vaccine **31**(25), 2772–2777 (2013). https://doi.org/10.1016/j.vaccine.2013.03.056
7. Bryden, K.S., Peveler, R.C., Stein, A., Neil, A., Mayou, R.A., Dunger, D.B.: Clinical and psychological course of diabetes from adolescence to young adulthood - a longitudinal cohort study. Diab. Care **24**(9), 1536–1540 (2001). https://doi.org/10.2337/diacare.24.9.1536
8. Calderita, L.V., Manso, L.J., Bustos, P., Suárez-Mejías, C., Fernández, F., Bandera, A.: THERAPIST: towards an autonomous socially interactive robot for motor and neurorehabilitation therapies for children. JMIR Rehabil. Assist. Technol. **1**(1), e1 (2014). https://doi.org/10.2196/rehab.3151
9. Cañamero, L., Lewis, M.: Making new "New AI" friends: designing a social robot for diabetic children from an embodied AI perspective. Int. J. Soc. Robot. **8**(4), 523–537 (2016). https://doi.org/10.1007/s12369-016-0364-9
10. Carlsen, S., et al.: Glycemic control and complications in patients with type 1 diabetes-Â a registry-based longitudinal study of adolescents and young adults. Pediatr. Diab. **18**(3), 188–195 (2017). https://doi.org/10.1111/pedi.12372
11. Christie, D., Channon, S.: Using motivational interviewing to engage adolescents and young adults with diabetes. Pract. Diab. **31**(6), 252–256 (2014). https://doi.org/10.1002/pdi.1878
12. Darke, S., Hall, W., Wodaki, A., Heather, N., Ward, J.: Development and validation of a multidimensional instrument for assessing outcome of treatment among opiate users: the opiate treatment index. Br. J. Addict. **87**(5), 733–742 (1992). https://doi.org/10.1111/j.1360-0443.1992.tb02719.x
13. Delamater, A., de Wit, M., McDarby, V., Malik, J., Acerini, C.: ISPAD clinical practice consensus guidelines 2014 compendium. Pediatr. Diab. **15**(S20), 232–244 (2014). https://doi.org/10.1111/pedi.12191
14. van Der Drift, E., Beun, R.J., Looije, R., Blanson Henkemans, O., Neerincx, M.: A remote social robot to motivate and support diabetic children in keeping a diary. In: ACM/IEEE International Conference on Human-Robot Interaction, pp. 463–470 (2014)

15. Grossman, H.Y., Brink, S., Hauser, S.T.: Self-efficacy in adolescent girls and boys with insulin-dependent diabetes mellitus. Diab. Care **10**(3), 324–329 (1987). https://doi.org/10.2337/diacare.10.3.324

16. Guest, G., MacQueen, K.M., Namey, E.E.: Applied Thematic Analysis. Sage Publications, Thousand Oaks (2011)

17. Hare, M.J., Shaw, J.E., Zimmet, P.Z.: Current controversies in the use of haemoglobin A1c. J. Internal Med. **271**(3), 227–236 (2012). https://doi.org/10.1111/j.1365-2796.2012.02513.x

18. Holmes, E.A., Mathews, A.: Mental imagery in emotion and emotional disorders. Clin. Psychol. Rev. **30**(3), 349–362 (2010). https://doi.org/10.1016/j.cpr.2010.01.001

19. Kavanagh, D.J., Robinson, N., Connolly, J., Connor, J., Andrade, J., May, J.: The revised four-factor motivational thought frequency and state motivation scales for alcohol control. Addict. Behav. **87**, 69–73 (2018). https://doi.org/10.1016/j.addbeh.2018.05.026

20. Kruijff-Korbayová, I., et al.: Effects of off-activity talk in human-robot interaction with diabetic children. In: IEEE International Symposium on Robot and Human Interactive Communication, pp. 649–654 (2014)

21. Levine, B.S., Anderson, B.J., Butler, D.A., Antisdel, J.E., Brackett, J., Laffel, L.M.B.: Predictors of glycemic control and short-term adverse outcomes in youth with type 1 diabetes. J. Pediatr. **139**(2), 197–203 (2001). https://doi.org/10.1067/mpd.2001.116283

22. Levine, B.S., Anderson, B.J., Butler, D.A., Antisdel, J.E., Brackett, J., Laffel, L.M.: Predictors of glycemic control and short-term adverse outcomes in youth with type 1 diabetes. J. Pediatr. **139**(2), 197–203 (2001). https://doi.org/10.1067/mpd.2001.116283

23. Malik, N.A., Yussof, H., Hanapiah, F.A.: Potential use of social assistive robot based rehabilitation for children with cerebral palsy. In: IEEE International Symposium on Robotics and Manufacturing Automation, pp. 1–6. IEEE (2016)

24. Martí Carrillo, F., Butchart, J., Knight, S., Scheinberg, A., Wise, L., Sterling, L., McCarthy, C.: In-situ design and development of a socially assistive robot for Paediatric rehabilitation. In: ACM/IEEE International Conference on Human-Robot Interaction, pp. 199–200 (2017)

25. Miller, W.R., Rollnick, S.: Motivational Interviewing: Helping People Change, vol. 3rd. Guilford Press, New York (2013)

26. Moerman, C.J., van der Heide, L., Heerink, M.: Social robots to support children's well-being under medical treatment: a systematic state-of-the-art review. J. Child Health Care **23**(4), 596–612 (2019). https://doi.org/10.1177/1367493518803031

27. Neerincx, A., Sacchitelli, F., Kaptein, R., van der Pal, S., Oleari, E., Neerincx, M.A.: Child's culture-related experiences with a social robot at diabetes camps. In: ACM/IEEE International Conference on Human-Robot Interaction, pp. 485–486 (2016)

28. Okita, S.Y.: Self-other's perspective taking: the use of therapeutic robot companions as social agents for reducing pain and anxiety in pediatric patients. Cyberpsychol. Behav. Soc. Netw. **16**(6), 436–441 (2013). https://doi.org/10.1089/cyber.2012.0513

29. Peyrot, M., Rubin, R.R.: Behavioral and psychosocial interventions in diabetes: a conceptual review. Diab. Care **30**(10), 2433–2440 (2007). https://doi.org/10.2337/dc07-1222

30. Rewers, M.J., Pillay, K., De Beaufort, C., Craig, M.E., Hanas, R., Acerini, C.L., Maahs, D.M.: Assessment and monitoring of glycemic control in children and adolescents with diabetes. Pediat. Diab. **15**, 102–114 (2014). https://doi.org/10.1111/pedi.12190

31. Robinson, N., Kavanagh, D., Connor, J., May, J., Andrade, J.: Assessment of motivation to control alcohol use: the motivational thought frequency and state motivation scales for alcohol control. Addict. Behav. **59**, 1–6 (2016). https://doi.org/10.1016/j.addbeh.2016.02.038

32. Robinson, N.L., Connolly, J., Hides, L., Kavanagh, D.J.: Social robots as treatment agents: pilot randomized controlled trial to deliver a behavior change intervention. Internet Interv. **21**, 100320 (2020). https://doi.org/10.1016/j.invent.2020.100320

33. Robinson, N.L., Cottier, T.V., Kavanagh, D.J.: Psychosocial health interventions by social robots: systematic review of randomized controlled trials. J. Med. Internet Res. **21**(5), e13203 (2019). https://doi.org/10.2196/13203

34. Shingleton, R.M., Palfai, T.P.: Technology-delivered adaptations of motivational interviewing for health-related behaviors: a systematic review of the current research. Patient Educ. Couns. **99**(1), 17–35 (2016). https://doi.org/10.1016/j.pec.2015.08.005

35. Smart, C.E., Annan, F., Bruno, L.P.C., Higgins, L.A., Acerini, C.L.: Nutritional management in children and adolescents with diabetes. Pediatr. Diab. **15**(S20), 135–153 (2014). https://doi.org/10.1111/pedi.12175

36. Softbank Robotics: NAO - Developers Guide

37. Solbrig, L., Whalley, B., Kavanagh, D.J., May, J., Parkin, T., Jones, R., Andrade, J.: Functional imagery training versus motivational interviewing for weight loss: a randomised controlled trial of brief individual interventions for overweight and obesity. Int. J. Obes. **43**(4), 883–894 (2019). https://doi.org/10.1038/s41366-018-0122-1

38. Vanderwel, B.W., Messer, L.H., Horton, L.A., McNair, B., Cobry, E.C., McFann, K.K., Chase, H.P.: Missed insulin boluses for snacks in youth with type 1 diabetes. Diab. Care **33**(3), 507–508 (2010). https://doi.org/10.2337/dc09-1840

39. Vänni, K.J., Salin, S.E.: A need for service robots among health care professionals in hospitals and housing services. In: International Conference on Social Robotics, pp. 178–187 (2017)

40. Aslander-van Vliet, E., Smart, C., Waldron, S.: Nutritional management in childhood and adolescent diabetes. Pediatr. Diab. **8**(5), 323–339 (2007). https://doi.org/10.1111/j.1399-5448.2007.00317.x

41. Wood, J.R., Miller, K.M., Maahs, D.M., Beck, R.W., DiMeglio, L.A., Libman, I.M., Quinn, M., Tamborlane, W.V., Woerner, S.E., Network, T.D.E.C.: Most youth with type 1 diabetes in the t1d exchange clinic registry do not meet american diabetes association or international society for pediatric and adolescent diabetes clinical guidelines. Diab. Care **36**(7), 2035–2037 (2013). https://doi.org/10.2337/dc12-1959

Content Is King: Impact of Task Design for Eliciting Participant Agreement in Crowdsourcing for HRI

Alisha Bevins[1], Nina McPhaul[2], and Brittany A. Duncan[1(✉)]

[1] University of Nebraska-Lincoln, Lincoln, NE 68588, USA
{abevins,bduncan}@cse.unl.edu
[2] Howard University, Washington, D.C. 20059, USA
nina.mcphaul@bison.howard.edu

Abstract. This work investigates how the design of crowdsourced tasks can influence responses. As a formative line of inquiry, this study sought to understand how users would respond either through movement, response, or shift of focus to varying flight paths from a drone. When designing an experiment, running several proto-studies can help with generating a dataset that is actionable, but it has been unclear how differences in things such as phrasing or pre- and post-surveys can impact the results. Leveraging methods from psychology, computer-supported cooperative work, and the human-robot interaction communities this work explored the best practices and lessons learned for crowdsourcing to reduce time to actionable data for defining new communication paradigms. The lessons learned in this work will be applicable broadly within the human-robot interaction community, even outside those who are interested in defining flight paths, because they provide a scaffold on which to build future experiments seeking to communicate using non-anthropomorphic robots. Important results and recommendations include: increased negative affect with increased question quantity, completion time being relatively consistent based on total number of responses rather than number of videos, responses being more related to the video than the question, and necessity of varying question lengths to maintain engagement.

Keywords: Crowdsourced · Gesture · Aerial vehicle

1 Introduction

This work seeks to inform future researchers on lessons learned and recommendations for conducting a crowdsourced study to elicit participant responses to non-anthropomorphic robots that produce high rater agreement. To explore this we embarked on an exploratory study, which included exploring question types

Supported by NSF-IIS-1925148, NSF-IIS-1750750, NSF-CNS-1757908, and NSF-IIS-1638099.

A. R. Wagner et al. (Eds.): ICSR 2020, LNAI 12483, pp. 640–651, 2020.
https://doi.org/10.1007/978-3-030-62056-1_53

to elicit desired responses, selection of content for labeling, and gaining insight into the differences in the presentation of questions. These design methods, in combination with trying to minimize issues of participant fatigue, negative affect, and lack of attention to prompts, led to researcher reflection and lessons learned which could be valuable to others seeking to leverage these methods in future experiment design. Additional information for designers of aerial vehicle flight paths will be provided, but is presented as a case study to exemplify the impact of the question types, repetitions, and length of tasks on the participant responses.

The research questions in this work are twofold:

1. When designing an open-ended crowdsourced study, how do various parameters impact participants and their responses?
2. Does the design of the questions or content of videos impact consistency of participant responses?

The findings and their relation to the impact of study parameters, including: the number of questions and/or videos, length of tasks, and forms of questions, on participants and their responses should inform future researchers on how to best structure their studies for success. The second question is generalized to understand the impact of the content and questions and will be examined here within the context of the case study. Success for that study was defined as eliciting responses to understand what the participants perceived the robot was requesting of them or how they were being directed and how they would respond to those requests, referred to as an action based response.

Lessons learned from this work include:

1. Participants quickly assume questions are the same if they are of similar length
2. Asking additional questions has a similar impact on increasing timing whether they are presented individually or as multiple associated with the same content
3. Questions which elicited more positive participant affect seemed to indicate higher agreement

These lessons led to recommendations that researchers focus most on the content presented rather than on their underlying questions to produce the most actionable responses, cycle through similar questions of different lengths if participant attention is key to their responses, and gather the data that is anticipated to be helpful because reducing questionnaires does not appear to have a meaningful impact on time to completion.

2   Related Work

2.1   Question Design

Best practices for creating questions are that they should be: concise, easily interpreted, and use accessible language in order to appeal to the diversity of participants likely to be recruited in crowd sourcing studies [2,6].

Previous works with anthropomorphic robots have shown that free responses yield the most diverse or creative results [3, 14]. The non-anthropomorphic nature of many robots can lead to participants simply describing the motion of the vehicle, rather than inferring requests or deriving information from the actions. In order to elicit more humanlike responses to the sUAS small Unmanned Aerial System), questions can be worded to request more human-like descriptions, as seen in anthropomorphic studies. Anthropomorphic studies tend to include questions that imply that the robot had intention and was intelligent [1, 3, 5, 14] which increased participants' confidence in the robot [14].

2.2 Crowdsourced Data

Positive Aspects of Crowdsourcing. A major problem with performing only in-person studies is the lack of diversity in participants (and difficulty recruiting in general). In-person studies typically result in testing a small subset of people living within a short distance from the researchers and with limited diversity in culture and/or age range. Conducting these experiments online, when possible, allows answers from around the country or world. Crowdsourcing is also a convenient solution for obtaining large amounts of responses to quick answer questions [13, 15].

When comparing crowdsourced results to in-person, researchers have seen minimal to no difference in their results between the participants who came in person and those who completed tasks online [4, 16].

Microtask Design in Crowdsourcing. It should be noted the difference between the tasks presented here and micro-tasks. Micro-tasks, another common usage of crowdsourcing, has the survey-taker complete very short tasks (each requiring no more than a few seconds) typically in large quantities. A significant amount of research has been completed about how to run these properly. Gadiraju et al. [9] researched the impact of malicious behavior in these platforms by exploring the concept of "Untrustworthy workers". These are workers who provide wrong answers in response to straightforward attention-check questions. In this work, we'll refer to them as "Non-Responses". Gadiraju, Yang, and Bozzon [10] also explored how to design instructions and task titles to explain how tasks can be crafted to provide clearer instructions to workers.

3   Methods

3.1   Participants

In total there were 80 Amazon mTurk (46 male, 33 female, 1 no answer) participants between the ages of 24–68 years old (M = 38.58 SD = 10.66). With an education level ranging from high school to graduate degree, breaking down into 4 Graduate School, 35 Bachelor's, 11 Associate's, 17 Some College, 12 High school, and 1 No Answer. A majority identified as American (76), 3 identified as Indian, and 1 identified as Chinese.

All participants were required to be considered an mTurk Master, as determined by Amazon through analyzing worker performance over time. They must continue to pass the statistical monitoring in place to retain that qualification. Each participant was paid 4 dollars and Amazon was paid 1 dollar for recruitment.

3.2 Design and Method

Participants selected the study from mTurk and then were taken to a webpage where they were asked to complete a consent form followed by a demographic questionnaire, the Positive and Negative Affect Scale (PANAS) (based on their condition), and the Negative Attitude towards Robots Scale (NARS). PANAS was used to assess how participant affect changed throughout the study to understand the impact of manipulation, and NARS was used due to the findings of Riek [12] that found people with high NARS had difficulty in recognizing robot motions when interacting with a humanoid robot. Following these tests they were then redirected to a Google Form where they were asked to watch 16 unique 30-second videos of a drone flying in a pattern, either once or twice depending on their condition, followed by 1 or 2 questions about each video. Although the participants were requested to watch the entire video, they did have the capability of answering the question and proceeding on to the next question before the end of the video. After the videos, they all completed a post-survey questionnaire consisting of a few questions about the study. If they completed PANAS prior to the videos, they were asked to complete PANAS again at this time. The participants were allotted 1 h to complete the tasks and averaged 30.7 min overall.

4 Approach

4.1 Question Variants

Three variations of question types were investigated to elicit a variety of responses. The groupings were based on whether they were expected to elicit a replication description, speech, or physical response from the participant. Two questions were available for each of the three question types. A full listing of the conditions used, the questions, question character length, whether that test used PANAS, and how many participants were in each of the conditions can be seen in Table 1.

Gesture-based questions are meant to elicit a response regarding how the participant may relate the action of the drone to an action they are familiar with seeing in other people (of similar culture/area). Speech based questions were asked to see how participants may assign verbal communication to the drone's actions. One question from the Speech type and one question from the

Table 1. Study Conditions. L is the character length of the question, N is the number of participants in that condition

Condition	Question(s)	L	PANAS	N
1 Speech	If you saw this drone in real life, what would it say to you?	61	Yes	8
			No	8
2 Speech	If you saw this drone in real life, what would it say to you?	61	Yes	8
	If this drone could speak what would it tell you to do?	55		
1 Gesture	What human gesture does this remind you of?	43	Yes	8
			No	8
2 Gesture	What human gesture does this remind you of?	43	Yes	8
	If you had to replicate this movement with your head and/or body, what would you do?	84		
1 Speech 1 Gesture	If you saw this drone in real life, what would it say to you?	61	Yes	8
	What human gesture does this remind you of?	43	No	8
1 Physical	If you were in the room with the robot, what would you do immediately following the robot's action?	99	Yes	8
1 Physical	If you were in the room with the robot, how would you respond immediately following the robot's action?	103	Yes	8

Gesture type were selected to run together in order to see if people would give complementary responses across both types and whether these responses would give greater insight into their responses. A set of Takayama's [14] questions were reformatted to ideally capture both the speech and gesture question types, while allowing the participant to answer in either way or with a more physical response.

4.2   Length of Tasks

Reduce Questionnaires. We observed that the participant responses seemed to indicate less engagement, through becoming either less informative or more hostile, towards the end of the tasks. We wanted to see if we could minimize these types of responses by reducing the amount of requested tasks, to elicit more engagement or variability within the answers compared to those participants who had the full length survey. To test this we reduced the questionnaires by removing PANAS for three of the conditions.

Additional Videos. When considering the number of videos that were presented to participants, it was necessary to repeat the set of videos when asking two questions from the same category (two speech or two gestures), as they would appear on separate pages. This presentation was chosen to allow us to see whether participants answered consistently throughout the condition and whether slight differences in wording elicited more informative responses.

4.3 Video Content

Sixteen videos were created to include the motions from [7], as well as additional videos that corresponded to both the taxonomy and the most popular flight paths from [8]. Each video was 30 s in length with repetitions of the flight added to reach the desired length of the video, as necessary. Flight paths were held constant for speed and distance covered as much as possible.

5   Participant Responses

As a formative line of inquiry, this study sought to classify how users would respond either through movement, response, or a shift of focus to varying flight paths from a drone. While lines of inquiry for human speech or gesture were investigated, the underlying goal was to understand what the participants perceived was being requested of them or how they were being directed by the vehicle and how they would respond to those requests.

5.1   Category Definition

Two raters were obtained to independently label responses across three classification categories and directions were provided to give context for categorization without guiding the raters to any responses. The raters were given 3 questions asking them if the response indicated an intention to or request for: (1) participant movement, (2) a verbal or physical response to the drone, or (3) a shift of focus, chosen from an initial high-level categorization of responses.

5.2   Findings by Question

After their independent assessments, the raters' results were compared in order to calculate Cohen's Kappa for their agreement according to [11]. When considering the raters' responses based on the questions, the agreement scores had higher variability than those by video. Thirteen out of eighteen categories had a Kappa of at least .61 indicating "Substantial" or .81 indicating "Near Perfect" agreement, with only one category having less than .41 "Moderate" agreement.

When considering answers chosen more frequently by raters, those with chance assignment outside the average plus or minus one standard deviation, there were three questions that were relatively successful at prompting the types of responses we were requesting. "If this drone could speak what would it tell you to do?" was likely to elicit responses requesting participant movement with

Moderate agreement (.60). "If you saw this drone in real life, what would it say to you?" was likely to elicit a verbal or physical response with higher than average probability and Substantial agreement (.71). "If you were in the room with the robot, how would you respond immediately following the robot's action?" was likely to elicit a shift of focus with Substantial agreement (.75). Finally, when combining the two speech questions, there was a likely participant movement request or intention with Near Perfect agreement (.81).

5.3   Findings by Video

When labeling the results by video, the raters had "Substantial" or "Almost Perfect" agreement on all videos across all three categories, since all Kappa values were above 0.61.

This agreement indicates a higher likelihood of participant responses indicating an intention to or request for participant movement when responding to the videos for Back and Forth, Descend and Shift, and Diagonal Descend. On the contrary, participant responses were unlikely to indicate an intention to or request for participant movement when viewing Hover, "U", or "X" Shape.

When considering intention to or request for verbal or physical response to a drone, only Horizontal Figure 8 was likely to elicit a positive response. Conversely, "U" Shape and Yaw were unlikely to elicit intention to or request for verbal or physical response.

Finally, a shift of focus seemed indicated by Yaw, Hover, and Diagonal Descend while Spiral and "U" Shape were unlikely to elicit a shift of focus.

6   Results on Crowdsourcing Methods

Important results from this study point to some key insights when designing crowdsourced studies to elicit the responses that researchers are seeking without reducing participant engagement. We considered the participant responses holistically, looking at responses to the PANAS, number of rejections per HIT, and ultimately question success in eliciting consistent, actionable responses as assessed by the raters.

6.1   PANAS

Multiple conditions were run with 56 participants taking PANAS and 24 participants not taking PANAS to understand the impact of question type on participant affect, but also consider whether reducing the amount of tasks improved participant response quality. When considering the length of time on tasks, it was relatively stable across the conditions with two questions and was 20% shorter when participants answered only one question per video.

If participants were becoming fatigued by the number of questions, then we would expect their PANAS scores to be significantly impacted in the two question conditions when compared to the one question conditions. While we did have five participants (out of 24) with overwhelmingly negative affect in the two question conditions, there were three out of 32 with similarly negative feelings in the single question conditions. There were also four (out of 32) participants with overwhelmingly positive affect after completing the single question conditions, compared to none in the two question conditions. This is very preliminary data, but does indicate that participants are showing a lack of positive feelings, which could be due to fatigue or frustration.

Interestingly, the overwhelmingly positive responses were related to the speech and physical questions, indicating that these questions might be more approachable or interesting to the participants. These questions also produced a high level of rater agreement regarding verbal or physical response to the drone and shift of focus, respectively.

6.2   Rejections

Occasionally a participant would complete the study, but be rejected later due to failing an attention check or lack of responsiveness. The first and main reason was that an attention check was performed within the set of questions to make sure the participants were reading each question and watching each video. We placed a word in the middle of one video and asked them to type out the word they saw on the screen. Lack of reporting this word alone caused 15 Rejections. The second reason for a rejection was if the participant clearly did not complete the study appropriately. This method of rejection included if they used vulgar language or had over 50% non-responses. Non-responses were classified as repeated "Nothing", "Not sure", or repeating the same identical answer in multiple boxes. 6 people were rejected for non-responses. In total there were 21 Rejections (who were not paid) out of 101 participants who attempted the mTurk HITs. Additionally, there were 4 people who were paid for their work on the HITs, but provided at least 25% (and less than 50%) answers that were considered non-responses.

The number of rejections for lack of attention was highest both numerically and by percent for the single speech and gesture questions (13 rejections over 32 requested participants, resulting in 45 HIT attempts) compared to a single rejection for the 24 participants in the three double question categories (two speech, two gesture, and one speech/one gesture). The much higher rate for the single speech and gesture questions might be related to the length of the question (43 or 61 characters, both fitting on a single line) being similar to the attention check (46 characters) and the participants not paying attention to the questions since the questions did not change between pages in those conditions (as opposed to the two question conditions). The question length consideration is reinforced when comparing to the single rejection for 16 participants in the physical question categories (99 or 103 characters).

6.3   Time Reduction

As described earlier, participant fatigue was an open question for this work and steps were taken to reduce fatigue by eliminating the PANAS questionnaire on some conditions. Unfortunately, this reduction (removing the three sets of 20

Table 2. Significant kappa and chance values by question

Participant question	Kappa	Chance	Significant rater question
If this drone could speak what would it tell you to do?	0.603	52.779	Participant Movement
If you saw this drone in real life, what would it say to you?	0.708	116.459	Response to Drone
If you were in the room with the robot, how would you respond immediately following the robot's action?	0.748	12.750	Shift of Focus
What human gesture does this remind you of?	0.965	0.536	Participant Movement
If you saw this drone in real life, what would it say to you? If this drone could speak what would it tell you to do?	0.808	42.055	Participant Movement
	0.636	93.507	Response to Drone
	0.665	3.209	Attention Shift

PANAS questions, or 60 total) only reduced time from 31.5 to 29.1 min. Given that this reduction only saved on average 2.4 min per participant, the additional information was likely more valuable than the fatigue that was produced from the surveys.

Another consideration was whether the addition of two questions per video would impact the amount of time participants spent on the overall tasks. For this we considered one question per video (28.1 min), two questions per video (35.0), and two questions with each video shown twice (35.8 min). It is interesting to note that doubling the questions resulted in basically the same amount of additional time (about 7 min) whether the participants were explicitly asked to watch the videos again or not.

Finally, the paired questions were run as a test to see if they helped with triangulating participant responses. Categorization from two raters showed that participants gave similar answers for two questions asked about the same subject around 40% of the time overall. When participants were asked the two speech questions, found in Table 1, only 24.2% of the responses were categorized as similar with a Kappa of 0.71. This supports the idea that people are providing complimentary information, rather than the same answer reworded for speech questions. This also confirms the findings of Table 2, which says the two speech questions elicit different types of responses, one being more informational and the other seeking a command. On the other hand the gesture questions when asked together provide an agreement 57.8% of the time (Kappa 0.69), showing that participants interpreted the questions in similar ways, and thus asking the two gesture questions was less beneficial for this complimentary information, but better when seeking consistent responses. The presence of two questions with substantially different foci, one speech and one gesture, produced converging ideas around 40% of the time.

7   Lessons Learned

As referenced in the title, the most important lesson from this study is the content (or in this case videos) being tested has the biggest impact on participant responses. While we hope that the different questions will result in interesting taxonomic differences, the current finding is that the videos generated more consistent action-based responses than the questions. This finding is promising when considering the ability to elicit consistent responses from novices, but troubling when considering how to shape participant responses.

The other key lessons learned from this work involve the ease with which participants are lulled into not reading questions, the impact of multiple questions, and the relationship between participant affect and agreement of responses.

7.1   Participant Attention

The key lesson from the attention check is that the participants stopped reading the questions if they look (even at a very high level) to be the same. Most participants who were rejected for not completing the attention check responded that the word never appeared in any video they watched and only later found the attention check after carefully reviewing their HIT. Most of the rejections answered reasonably about the condition question in reference to the attention check video and simply missed the change in question and word in the middle of the video. This also indicates that many participants were not watching all iterations of the flight paths while considering their answers to the questions.

This raises some questions about how quickly participants acclimate to consistency in questions and how to change questions between tasks in order to maintain some level of engagement with questions that may not all be consistent.

7.2   Multiple Questions

We found that asking multiple questions was not highly predictive of lack of engagement (as reflected by number of rejections), so this is a positive finding for researchers moving forward to continue asking triangulating questions. However, care should be taken to consider that asking multiple questions significantly slows participant responses by about the amount of time allocated per task (in this case 7 min) whether or not they are explicitly repeated on different pages, or asked similar questions on the same page. This is important for task design because it indicates that even if responses are expected to be highly correlated, participants are still seemingly considering them independently. The increase in time also indicates that, contrary to the findings on the attention check, participants do appear to be paying attention to what is asked and considering their responses.

8 Discussion

8.1 Limitations

A taxonomy of participant responses would be a valuable contribution to understand the emotions elicited, the target of communications, and other common themes from the responses, but is outside the scope of this paper. As a standalone guide for eliciting action-based responses, this paper provides insights into the perception of the questions posed to participants and the impact of the task design on the attitudes and responses provided, which was thought to be a valuable contribution in its own right.

8.2 Recommendations

When developing the content to test, it is important to understand the underlying responses that are sought and to ensure that the prompts are appropriate for the responses. The video content was more important because the questions were relatively consistent and focused on the participant perceptions or responses to the content. This finding is supported by the high Kappa values for each of the videos (all with substantial or near perfect agreement) compared to the variable Kappas across the questions (only 13/18 categories across all 6 questions had substantial or near perfect agreement) with a subset shown in Table 2.

Additionally, when examining the responses and considering the questions that are asked, it would be a good practice to cycle through multiple forms of questions to keep participants engaged in reading and responding to the prompts. This is supported by the fact that tests which had similar question length (43 or 61 character questions) to the attention check question length (46 characters) had 3–4 more rejections on all four of the tests than the other 6 tests which are visually different (either having two questions reduced to one or having a 99 or 103 character question). This is also supported by the convergent answers to questions with similar requests related to gestures and divergent answers for questions with complementary requests related to speech; similar questions presented to the same participants resulted in additional information depending on the content of the question.

One surprising finding was the relatively stable amount of time it took for participants to complete the HIT regardless of the length of the questionnaires and the relationship between the number of questions (rather than videos) and the time to completion. Results showed that participants completed the tasks in about 28 min with only one question at a time and about 35 min with two questions, showing minor fluctuations of 1–2 min with other edits to length of task, such as removal of PANAS or requesting the video be watched twice. This indicates to us that we should continue to collect information that might complement the participant responses and continue to test multiple questions in the way that best makes sense. An incorrect perception we had was that asking participants to watch the videos again would take too long, but the reality is that developing the responses was the time consuming part of the task.

References

1. Bartneck, C., Kanda, T., Mubin, O., Al Mahmud, A.: Does the design of a robot influence its animacy and perceived intelligence? Int. J. Social Robot. 1(2), 195–204 (2009)
2. Brosnan, K., Babakhani, N., Dolnicar, S.: "i know what you're going to ask me" why respondents don't read survey questions. Int. J. Market Res., 1470785318 821025 (2019)
3. Cañamero, L., Fredslund, J.: I show you how i like you-can you read it in my face? [robotics]. IEEE Trans. Syst. Man Cybern.-Part A: Syst. Hum. 31(5), 454–459 (2001)
4. Casler, K.: Separate but equal? A comparison of participants and data gathered via Amazon's MTurk, social media, and face-to-face behavioral testing. https://doi.org/10.1016/j.chb.2013.05.009
5. Chaminade, T., et al.: Brain response to a humanoid robot in areas implicated in the perception of human emotional gestures. PLoS ONE 5(7), e11577 (2010)
6. Christensen, L.B., Johnson, B., Turner, L.A., Christensen, L.B.: Research methods, design, and analysis (2011)
7. Duncan, B.A., Beachly, E., Bevins, A., Elbaum, S., Detweiler, C.: Investigation of communicative flight paths for small unmanned aerial systems* this work was supported by NSF NRI 1638099. In: 2018 IEEE International Conference on Robotics and Automation (ICRA), pp. 602–609. IEEE (2018)
8. Firestone, J.W., Quiñones, R., Duncan, B.A.: Learning from users: an elicitation study and taxonomy for communicating small unmanned aerial system states through gestures. In: 2019 14th ACM/IEEE International Conference on Human-Robot Interaction (HRI), pp. 163–171. IEEE (2019)
9. Gadiraju, U., Kawase, R., Dietze, S., Demartini, G.: Understanding malicious behavior in crowdsourcing platforms: the case of online surveys. In: Proceedings of the 33rd Annual ACM Conference on Human Factors in Computing Systems, pp. 1631–1640. ACM (2015)
10. Gadiraju, U., Yang, J., Bozzon, A.: Clarity is a worthwhile quality: on the role of task clarity in microtask crowdsourcing. In: Proceedings of the 28th ACM Conference on Hypertext and Social Media, pp. 5–14. ACM (2017)
11. Landis, J.R., Koch, G.G.: The measurement of observer agreement for categorical data. Biometrics, 159–174 (1977)
12. Riek, L.D., Rabinowitch, T.C., Bremner, P., Pipe, A.G., Fraser, M., Robinson, P.: Cooperative gestures: effective signaling for humanoid robots. In: Proceedings of the 5th ACM/IEEE International Conference on Human-Robot Interaction, pp. 61–68. IEEE Press (2010)
13. Sorokin, A., Berenson, D., Srinivasa, S.S., Hebert, M.: People helping robots helping people: crowdsourcing for grasping novel objects. In: 2010 IEEE/RSJ International Conference on Intelligent Robots and Systems, pp. 2117–2122, October 2010. https://doi.org/10.1109/IROS.2010.5650464
14. Takayama, L., Dooley, D., Ju, W.: Expressing thought: improving robot readability with animation principles. In: 2011 6th ACM/IEEE International Conference on Human-Robot Interaction (HRI), pp. 69–76. IEEE (2011)
15. Tellex, S., et al.: Understanding Natural Language Commands for Robotic Navigation and Mobile Manipulation, p. 8
16. Toris, R., Kent, D., Chernova, S.: The robot management system: a framework for conducting human-robot interaction studies through crowdsourcing. J, Hum.-Robot Interact. 3(2), 25 (2014)

Emoji to Robomoji: Exploring Affective Telepresence Through Haru

Randy Gomez[1](✉)(iD), Deborah Szapiro[2](✉)(iD), Luis Merino[3](✉)(iD),
Heike Brock[1](✉)(iD), Keisuke Nakamura[1](✉)(iD), and Selma Sabanovic[4](✉)(iD)

[1] Honda Research Institute Japan Co., Ltd., Wako, Japan
{r.gomez,h.brock,keisuke}@jp.honda-ri.com
[2] University Technology Sydney, Ultimo, Australia
deborah.szapiro@uts.edu.au
[3] University Pablo Olavide, Sevilla, Spain
lmercab@upo.es
[4] Indiana University at Bloomington, Bloomington, USA
selmas@indiana.edu

Abstract. In this paper, we present a method of communicating affects from a remote user through the telepresence robot Haru. In this preliminary work, we transform the traditional mode of communicating text messages with emojis in the smartphone domain to the robot domain through robomojis- a hardware rendition of emojis. First we analyze human affects and expressions and synthesized these through the design of robomojis. Based on the telepresence robot Haru platform, we built a communication module that enables a remote user with a smartphone to send text and emoji messages to the robot. The robot then communicates these affectively through the rendition of robomojis. By exploiting the robot's rich modality and through design, our preliminary results show that robomojis deliver better rendition than emojis. Although participants prefer the use of smartphones over telepresence robot due to convenience, our findings also show that they are willing to use the robomoji features in a telepresence robot such as Haru. This could enhance further the role of social robots as telepresence robots and open the possibility of integrating them to the traditional communication ecosystem.

Keywords: Telepresence · Social robot · Embodied communication

1 Introduction

The advent of email, internet messaging services, and mobile phones has provided people with new ways to communicate asynchronously with remote others. These textual modes of communication, however, make it more difficult to convey appropriate emotions through the message, as interpretation of affective content often requires context which mere text does not always accurately represent [1,2]. Video messaging apps and telepresence robots can provide more embodied affective and personal cues, but require synchronous presence by both parties

© Springer Nature Switzerland AG 2020
A. R. Wagner et al. (Eds.): ICSR 2020, LNAI 12483, pp. 652–663, 2020.
https://doi.org/10.1007/978-3-030-62056-1_54

Fig. 1. Sending affective messages from the smartphone to Haru

in the conversation. To make the emotional valence of asynchronous messages clearer and the communication more personal and intimate, "emoji" – small digital symbols or icons meant to represent ideas or emotions – have become common in digital messaging. More recently, "animoji" – customized animated emojis that use a person's own voice and facial expressions – have been able to bring in an even more personalized feel to asynchronous messaging. In this paper, we present a further step in the evolution of the presentation of affect and personal presence in asynchronous messaging through the concept of "robomoji" (Fig. 1).

"Robomoji" are representations of affect and other communicative behavioral cues through a robotic platform used in asynchronous messaging. Robots of different forms, from humanoid to zoomorphic and even nonanthropomorphic [3], are able to represent a variety of emotions at different levels of intensity and positive or negative valance. Robots have also started being used as proxies for people in remote communication, from "skype-on-wheels" type platforms like the Beam which represent the user through video on a mobile platform [4–7], to more abstract designs like the Telenoid [8] or direct representations of people in look-a-like androids [9]. These robots are most commonly used as telepresence platforms, which a user has to control to speak with another person in a synchronous manner. These types of telepresence robots have been shown to provide their users with a greater feeling of situation awareness and "being there" [10], and the people who interact with them with a greater feeling of the other users presence [11]. Robomoji takes advantage of the increased feeling of presence and the robot's capability to express emotions through embodied behaviors and cues to provide a more rich and evocative representation of affect and personal presence in remote digital communication. Like emoji and animoji before it, robomoji also aims to enhance the affective and intimate nature of digital communication.

In this paper, we present the design of a robomoji using the Haru social robot designed by Honda Research Institute [12] as a proof of concept. We describe how Haru is programmed to represent different affective communication cues that can be used in remote communication. We then provide the results of an

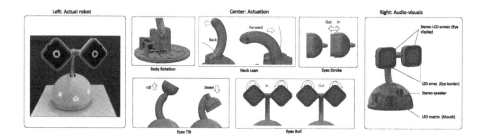

Fig. 2. Tabletop robot modalities: Actuation, visualization and vocalization

initial user evaluation of robomoji, and discuss future directions in robomoji design and research. We expect the use of robomoji can improve the usefulness and therefore the adoption of social robots in everyday use for diverse users and contexts, including personal, business, and service. This paper is our preliminary work with robomoji using the Haru platform.

2   Background

We have been developing the table top robot Haru [12] for embodied communication research. Haru's interactive features are built on Haru's expressive characteristics through an interdisciplinary collaboration among researchers in the field. Haru can communicate via face and body movements (kinesics), voice (language), and through non verbal sounds (paralanguage). Haru can express itself through motion and a series of additional actuators as depicted in Fig. 2. On one hand, the robot body has 5 degrees of freedom namely, base rotation, neck leaning, eye stroke, eye rotation and eyes tilt. Furthermore, each of the eyes includes a 3-inch TFT screen display. Moreover, the rectangular border of the inner eyes (the eye googles) is composed of an addressable LED strip. Inside the body there is an addressable LED matrix (the mouth). The robot is also equipped with an internal stereo speaker for vocalization and sounds. It also has RGBD cameras, microphone arrays, encoders for perception. Haru is not your typical telepresence robot, it has a form factor which is neither zoomorphic nor humanoid hence Haru's expressiveness is modeled uniquely [13]. Inspired from animation expertise, Haru is built ideally to be an animation-like embodied robotic character capable of expressiveness similar to characters in animation movies through the use of its various modalities discussed above [13].

Haru's telepresence platform is aimed at studying both communication and interaction theories through an embodied agent. In particular, we are focusing on the telepresent robot's ability to communicate affect, going beyond the conventional mode of information sharing. Although Haru shares some features with other telepresence robots [4–9], Haru's design and unique gestural repertoire best position it to effectively explore the potential of affective telepresence robot which puts it in a different category than the existing family of telepresence robots [4–9].

The smartphone, being a dominant communication device is used in this study vis-a-vis Haru. The use of emojis in smartphones can deliver affectively rich text messages. The universal adoption of emoji and its wide support across different messaging apps make a compelling argument to its inclusion in our study of affective telepresence robot. In this paper, we extend the experience of communicating affect using emoji in a smartphone to an embodied agent. In particular, we investigate how an emoji in a two dimensional LCD screen (smartphone) takes shape and form as robomoji in an embodied agent (i.e. Haru) with its unique and rich modality. Consequently, we explore the human-centric design of robomoji and its potential to convey empathically-rich messages along with its emoji counterpart. By definition, in this paper we associate the terms emoji and robomoji to smartphone and robot (hardware) renditions, respectively.

3 Designing Robomojis

In designing our range of robomojis for Haru we gained valuable insights by framing robomojis through a social prism that examined the general context of the history of representational symbolism in human communication and the specific social context and practices surrounding contemporary emojis. Our study of emojis was augmented by informal interviews from a focus group who discussed their use of emojis in communicating with their peers. The focus group demographic consisted of a balance of females and males, who were racially diverse and aged between 18 and 28 years of age. This group were targeted as this age group has a high uptake in the use emojis in their communications.

3.1 Identifying Design Parameters

Setting up a core list of design parameters is essential for the success of any design project. Core practices around emoji use were studied along consideration of the potential and limitations of Haru's hardware. Our focus group all noted that their use of emojis was predominantly for informal communication that enabled them to maintain social contact with their peers in a time efficient and playful manner. Norrick [14] notes that playfulness in communication is an essential component of interpersonal rapport, as is the reciprocal back and forth of playful communication. Playful communication, whilst often seeming purposeless and like "small talk" is interactionally meaningful to social relationships [15]. Participants voiced that they also used emojis as a "safe" way to communicate as it is a shared language that was less likely to be misunderstood than a text only message, and that another use of emojis was as a way of maintaining friendly connection when they did not have a lot to communicate. This informal and playful aspect of communication enhances social bonds, making it easier to establish social conversations, promotes intimacy and brings a unique personal aspect to the relationship [16].

The focus group participants were asked about the emojis they used on a regular basis, with participants overwhelming identifying facial emojis. The facial

Fig. 3. Robomoji sample design

emojis most commonly used were Smiling Face, Face with Hand over Mouth, Winking Face, Grimacing Face, Tired Face, Sleeping Face, Face Palm, Face with Tears of Joy, Astonished Face, Face with Tongue, Blushing Face, Crying Face, Downcast Face with Sweat and Angry Face. We then came up with a list of 12 common communications for our core set of robomojis: Happy, Laughing, Wide Smile, Blushing, Crying, Shocked, Shy, Tired, Tongue Out, Angry and Winking. As well as designing the robomoji an equivalent emoji of Haru was designed for the smart phone platform. Some examples of the correlation between the robomojis and the emojis are shown in Fig. 3.

3.2   Implementing the Parameters

We then identified a list of eight key parameters to guide the design and animation process. These are discussed with reference to their implementation below:

- Shared Codes of Meaning
  Representational communication revolves around a shared code of understanding between the sender and receiver. We limited the core robomojis to equivalencies of face emojis identified by the feedback group. This took advantage of existing emoji literacy. In addition, the physical gestures, eye gestures movements and sound were designed to mirror recognizable human actions appropriate to the emotion. For example in the "tired" robomoji, the robot's body and eye gestures have a slow, heavy physical emphasis that is instantly recognisable as the way a person's body would move if they were tired. The expertise of animators was invaluable to incorporate shared codes of meaning around body and eye movements as was a professional sound designer for the non-verbal vocalisations in the robomojis.
- Spatial and sensorial modes enhance embodied interaction
  Paul Dourish refers to embodiment as "the way that physical and social phenomena unfold in real time and real space as part of the world in which we are situated, right alongside and around us" [17]. Robomojis work with the spatial and sensorial qualities of the robot's hardware and are physically-situated in the user's world as opposed to the screen based two dimensional

presence of the emoji. Gestures (spatial) and sound (aural/sensorial) need to be designed to work optimally to enhance visual and aural spatial connections. While gestures are naturally spatial, we enhanced Haru's sound with a layered spatial quality which lent a subtle "dimensionality" to the sound.

– Playfulness
Robomojis should be designed in a playful manner to encourage social conversations and bring a personal aspect to the relationship between sender and receiver. This involves a light touch, for instance the Angry robomoji was designed so that the eye gestures had an almost Angry Bird affect, the robomoji is easily identifiable as "angry" however it is also humourous, similarly with the crying robomoji, the robot's performance is a parody of a melodramatic childish tantrum and is hard to take seriously. Sound was important in keeping the tone light, all sounds were non-verbal vocalizations and were composed with the human "voice", this lent a light, cute, organic quality to the sound;

– Reciprocity
The robomojis and Emojis of Haru had to be designed to be meaningful, engaging and recognizable on both the smart phone and hardware platforms in order to encourage reciprocal communication, enjoyment and uptake of usage between sender and receiver. The Emojis of Haru were designed so that Haru was immediately recognizable and the same rules that we applied to the robot eye and body gestures were applied;

– Temporality
Robomojis have the ability to sustain a longer interaction and duration than an emoji and can operate on both synchronous (real time) and asynchronous (delayed) time frames, however our research indicated that short responses would work best for promoting synchronous interaction between sender and receiver. We designed each robomoji with a maximum duration of five seconds. This enabled a quick response, yet al.lowed enough time to work with gesture and sound to deliver meaningful communication content;

– Understand the difference between motion and gesture
While motion is associated with the human tendency to anthropomorphize an inorganic object, gesture is the means by which we use motion to communicate emotion. Motion is specific in direction but conveys very little information about intent. Gesture is specific to communicating intent and is closely associated with mental and emotional states. Working with a combination of animation principles and Laban Movement Analysis, we mapped appropriate qualities required in the body and eye gesture to elicit the specific emotion required for the robomoji;

– Exaggeration
Exaggeration also key to being able to read communication intent in embodied agents, and is even more important when designing short, symbolic communication that have to work in both 3D and 2D spatial contexts, therefore robomojis and the Emojis of Haru required the application of a greater degree of exaggeration. We had already developed a gestural language for Haru's everyday communications, however we found that a slight increase in

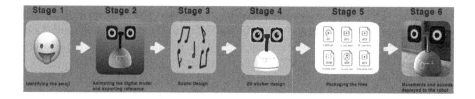

Fig. 4. Block diagram of synthesizing robomoji from emoji

exaggeration of the eye gestures in particular resulted in both the robomojis and the emojis of Haru being communicated quickly.

– Embrace the potential and limitations of the robot's hardware
   Understand the potential and limitations of robot hardware and work with these for the best outcome, for instance Haru has no hands so the Face Palm robomoji was not considered, however Haru has three Degrees of Freedom, an LED array and an LCD screen associated with its eye. 43.4% of human attention during social interactions is explicitly devoted to eyes [18], therefore we designed the major gestural movements around Haru's eyes.

The advantage of working out the above parameters gave the animators and the sound designer a clear set of rules to follow in producing the robomojis. This led to a consistent visual, gestural and sound "language" across the core set of hardware robomojis and the Emojis of Haru. This consistency is important if consumers are to embrace robot to smart phone telepresence communication.

3.3   Synthesizing Robomojis

Figure 4 depicts the development of the Robomoji from the creative stage to deployment to the robot Hardware. Once an emoji has been identified to design (Stage 1) A three-dimensional digital model of the robot Haru, conforming to the exact specification of the robot hardware, body and eye movements were animated by a professional animator using Autodesk Maya software. The mouth and eye LEDs were animated via a separate Maya rig and then composited onto the digital model (Stage 2). This is then rendered and exported as a .mov file to be used for reference by the sound designer (Stage 3). The sound was designed using the human voice to create non-verbal sounds that reinforced the gestures and the emotional intent of the robomoji. These non-verbal sounds are designed as a 'language' that conveys the robot's emotional intent and is part of our 'world-building' approach to designing Haru's communication modalities. The 3D animated reference is also used to create a 2D animated version of the Robomoji for use as a Telegram sticker (Stage 4). Each element, motion, LEDs, eyes, sound and reference were exported separately as each required specific file formats in order to deploy them to the robot hardware (Stage 5). Maya does not support .json formats, so the body gestures were exported as .fbx files and then imported into Unity for conversion to a .json file. Once the robomoji animation, sound and file conversion is complete, these files are delivered with the reference .mov for our expression designer studio (Stage 6) to convert all assets into machine-executable format for the robot hardware [13].

4   Communication Module

The communication module implements the necessary infrastructure for sending messages and emojis from the smartphone to the robot, and for transforming the messages and emojis into messages uttered by the robot and the corresponding robomojis as shown in Fig. 5.

4.1   Smartphone Side

The smartphone side is the front-end for the user that wants to send messages to the telepresence robot. The main module is a standard app that allows the user to send text and emojis towards the robot side. Also, the app can display text and emojis received from the robot side. Additionally on the smartphone side, a face recognition module is used to enable sending of messages to the robot and receiving messages from the robot just when the person-of-interest is present.

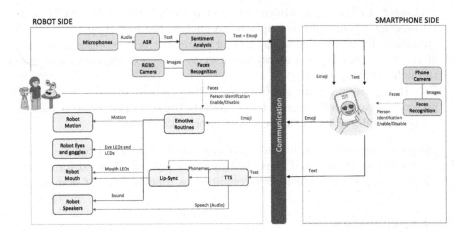

Fig. 5. Block diagram of the communication module. Sensor modules (green rectangle), actuation-related modules implementing robomojis (yellow rectangle). (Color figure online)

4.2   Telepresence Haru Side

The main part of the application runs on the side of the robot. It consists on a set of actuation-related modules to convey the messages and emojis into robomojis, as well as a set of sensor-related modules for sending messages from the robot to the phone, and to estimate the presence of persons in the surroundings.

Actuation-Related Modules

- Emotive Routines: the robot can show complex expressions through the use of so-called emotive routines [13]. These routines are open-loop macro-actions that combine all robot actuation modalities (motion, sounds, LEDs, eye videos). The reception of a particular emoji from the smartphone translates into the execution of an emotive routine that implements the corresponding robomoji as indicated in the previous section.
- Text-to-Speech (TTS): The text messages received are uttered by the robot by using a TTS module, based on the Cerevoice TTS engine by Cereproc[1].
- Lip-Sync: The lip-sync module is in charge of animating the LED robot mouth conveniently when the message is read by the robot. It receives the sequence of phonemes and synchronization signals from the TTS module and maps them to a designed set of visemes [19].

Sensor-Related Modules

- Automatic Speech Recognition (ASR): the input speech through the robot microphones is passed through the ASR module generating messages and sent to the smartphone.
- Sentiment Analysis: a sentiment analyzer module based on the NLTK natural language toolkit [20] is employed to analyze the text from the ASR and automatically selects the corresponding emoji that best represents the affect of the text. This feature allows the user to send text messages and emoji through voice.
- Face Recognition: the images from the RGBD camera are used to detect the presence of faces and recognize them using the library[2]. The received messages are only displayed when the person-of-interest is present.

Although our infrastructure in Fig. 5 supports bi-directional communication between the smartphone and Haru, in this paper, we only focused for now the sending of emoji (smartphone) to its rendition as robomoji (robot domain).

5   Experiments

5.1   Set-Up

A smartphone-to-robot communication user evaluation study was conducted using the communication module discussed in Sect. 4. The purpose of this initial study is to compare emoji and robomoji. In particular, we investigate people's reaction to robomoji and whether the emoji sent from the smartphone can still be affectively conveyed through the rendition of robomoji in the robot domain. In this study, a remote user can send a combination of text messages and emoji

---

[1] https://www.cereproc.com.
[2] https://github.com/ageitgey/face_recognition.

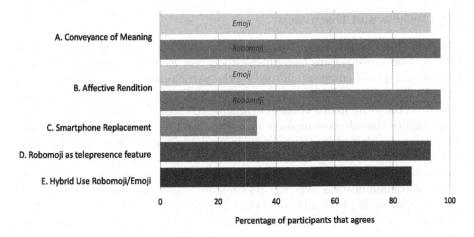

Fig. 6. Survey results

to Haru. A demonstration video is shown in this link below.[3] For the study, we prepared fifteen sets of messages each of which had a corresponding emoji which could be sent using a smartphone. The set of emojis is a mixture of the traditional ones and those exclusively-made for Haru. Thirty participants (15 male, 15 female) where invited to our lab to evaluate the the robot's rendition of the set of original text messages with emoji as a form of asynchronous telepresence interaction. The participants are 20–50 years old and are avid users of text messaging and emoji and were informed of the purpose of the study beforehand. They were shown the original smartphone message with an emoji, and then viewed the robot's representation of those messages through its embodied action (robomoji). We asked the participants a simple yes/no question and to rate their approval of the following statements:

- (A) Conveyance of Meaning (robomoji & emoji): the messages and its meaning are clear and understandable
- (B) Affective Rendition (robomoji & emoji): the quality of execution is good/impressive (participant's preference, design, etc.)
- (C) Smartphone Replacement: willingness to replace smartphone with telepresence robot as mode of communicating messages
- (D) Robomoji as Telepresence Feature: robomoji is an interesting feature for telepresence robots
- (E) Hybrid Use of Robomoji and Emoji: using a mixture of both robomoji and emoji is interesting and worth exploring. In particular hybrid use of telepresence robot such as Haru and smartphone is an interesting idea.

---

[3] https://www.youtube.com/watch?v=SfEmwqxxpYg&feature=emb_logo.

5.2 Results and Discussion

The results of our preliminary survey are summarized in Fig. 6. It is shown in line (A) that messages are being understood very well when conveyed by using both robomoji and emoji as affirmed by the participants. This means that both the affective and semantic meaning are preserved and communicated effectively. Moreover, the participants confirm in scheme (B) that the rendition of the robomojis relates the affective message in a way that they prefer it over the emoji. This can be explained by the richness in modality the physical robot can offer and most of the participants see the movement as engaging. In scheme (C), the participants are unanimous in their preference of smartphone as a major mode of communication over the telepresence robot. This is natural because the smartphone is physically convenient (i.e. portable) and easy to use. However in schemes (D) and (E), it is very interesting to note that the participants overwhelmingly agrees that the robomoji is an interesting feature to include in telepresence robots and they find it effective in conveying affective text messages. Lastly, the participants agree of the potential use of telepresence robots in the conventional communication ecosystem, currently dominated by smartphones.

6 Conclusion

In our preliminary work of robomoji using the Haru platform, we were able to show a proof of concept of affective messaging through the use of text and emoji to a telepresence robot Haru. Through our human-centric robomoji design, we were able to validate that robomoji can be as effective as emoji. Haru's form factor lent itself to building substantially on emoji. In our future work we will be expanding our research to a two-way communication task and to further code language around robomojis that has its own unique quality and employ more advanced user studies.

Acknowledgement. We would like to thank Paulo Alvito of IDMIND, Kerl Galindo of UTS, Fernando Caballero, Alvaro Paez, and Ricardo Ragel De la Torre of UPO for their contributions.

References

1. Derks, D., Fischer, A.H., Bos, A.E.R.: The role of emotion in computer-mediated communication: a review. In: Proceedings of Computers in Human Behavior, pp. 766–785 (2008)
2. Kato, Y., Kato, S., Akahori, K.: Effects of emotional cues transmitted in e-mail communication on the emotions experienced by senders and receivers. In: Proceedings of Computers in Human Behavior, pp. 1894–1905 (2007)
3. Bethel, C.L., Murphy, R.R.: Survey of non-facial/non-verbal affective expressions for appearance-constrained robots. Proc. IEEE Trans. Syst. Man Cybern. Part C **38**(1), 83–92 (2007)

4. Kristoffersson, A., Coradeschi, S., Loutfi, A.: A review of mobile robotic telepresence. Proc. Adv. Hum.-Comp. Int. **2013** (2013)
5. Shiarlis, et al.: Teresa: a socially intelligent semi-autonomous telepresence system. In: Workshop on Machine Learning for Social Robotics at ICRA (2015)
6. Orlandini, A., Kristoffersson, A., et al.: Excite project: a review of forty-two months of robotic telepresence technology evolution. In: Proceedings of the International Conference on Presence: Teleoperators and Virtual Environments (2017)
7. Reis, A., Martins, M., Martins, P., Sousa, J., Barroso, J.: Telepresence robots in the classroom: the state-of-the-art and a proposal for a telepresence service for higher education. In: Tsitouridou, M., A. Diniz, J., Mikropoulos, T.A. (eds.) TECH-EDU 2018. CCIS, vol. 993, pp. 539–550. Springer, Cham (2019). https://doi.org/10.1007/978-3-030-20954-4_41
8. Ogawa, K., et al.: Telenoid: tele-presence android for communication. In: Proceedings of ACM SIGGRAPH 2011 Emerging Technologies (2011)
9. Sakamoto, D., Kanda, T., Ono, T., Ishiguro, H., Hagita, N.: Android as a telecommunication medium with a human-like presence. In: Proceedings of the International Conference on Human-Robot Interaction (HRI), pp. 193–200 (2007)
10. Kawaguchi, et al.: Effect of embodiment presentation by humanoid robot on social telepresence. In: Proceedings of the International Conference on Human Agent Interaction, pp. 253–256 (2016)
11. Pan, Y., Steed, A.: A comparison of avatar-, video-, and robot-mediated interaction on users' trust in expertise. Front. Robot. AI (2016)
12. Gomez, R., Szapiro, D., Galindo, K., Nakamura, K.: Haru: hardware design of an experimental tabletop robot assistant. In: Proceedings of the ACM/IEEE International Conference on Human-Robot Interaction (2018)
13. Gomez, R., Nakamura, K., Szapiro, D., Merino, L.: A holistic approach in designing tabletop robot's expressivity. In: Proceedings of the IEEE International Conference on Robotics and Automation (2020)
14. Norrick, N.: Language play in conversation. In: Bell, N. (ed.) Multiple Perspectives on Language Play, pp. 11–45 (2016)
15. Dienar, D., et al.: Youth and Language Play in Style and Intersubjectivity in Youth Interaction. Contributions to the Sociology of Language (2018)
16. Kelly, R., Watts, L.: Characterising the inventive appropriation of emoji as relationally meaningful in mediated personal relationships. In: Proceeding to the International Conference of Experiences of Technology Appropriation: Unanticipated Users, Usage, Circumstances, and Design (2015)
17. Dourish, P.: Where the Action Is. MIT Press, Cambridge (2001)
18. Janik, S.W., Wellens, A.R., Goldberg, M.L., Dell'Osso, L.F., Skills, M.: Eyes as the center of focus in the visual examination of human faces (1978)
19. Wei, L., Deng, Z.: A practical model for live speech-driven lip-sync. In: Proceedings of the IEEE Computer Graphics and Applications, pp. 70–78 (2015)
20. Hutto, C., Gilbert, E.: Vader: a parsimonious rule-based model for sentiment analysis of social media text. In: Proceedings of the Eighth International Conference on Weblogs and Social Media (ICWSM) (2014)

Can Robots Elicit Different *Comfortability* Levels?

Maria Elena Lechuga Redondo[1,2](✉️)(ORCID), Alessia Vignolo[3](ORCID),
Radoslaw Niewiadomski[3,4,5](ORCID), Francesco Rea[1](ORCID), and Alessandra Sciutti[3](ORCID)

[1] RBCS Unit, Italian Institute of Technology, Genova, Italy
maria.lechuga@iit.it
[2] DIBRIS Department, University of Genoa, Genova, Italy
[3] CONTACT Unit, Italian Institute of Technology, Genova, Italy
[4] PSC Department, University of Trento, Trento, Italy
[5] DIPSCO Department, University of Trento, Rovereto, Italy

Abstract. Social interactions entail often complex and dynamic situations that follow non-explicit, unwritten rules. Comprehending those signals and knowing how to respond becomes the key to the success of any social communication. Thus, in order to integrate a robot into a social context it should be capable of (at least) understanding others' emotional states. Nonetheless, mastering such skill is beyond reach for current robotics which is why we introduce the single internal state which we believe reveals the most regarding interactive communications. We named it *Comfortability* and defined it as *(disapproving of or approving of) the situation that arises as a result of a social interaction which influences one's own desire of maintaining or withdrawing from it.*

Consequently, in this paper we aim to show that *Comfortability* can be evoked by robots, investigating at the same time its connection with other emotional states. To do that, we performed two online experiments on 196 participants asking them to imagine being interviewed by a reporter on a sensitive topic. The interviewer's actions were presented in two different formats: the first experiment (the <u>Narrative Context</u>) presented the actions as text; whereas the second experiment (the <u>Visual Context</u>) presented the actions as videos performed by the humanoid robot iCub. The actions were designed to evoke different *Comfortability* levels. According to the experimental results, *Comfortability* differs from the other reported emotional and affective states and more importantly, it can be evoked by both, humans and robots in an imaginary interaction.

Keywords: Social interaction · Humanoid robot · Affective computing

1 Introduction

If you had to think which aspect of an interaction is the one that matters the most to make it successful, what would you say?

It is known that mastering social intelligence is key to develop healthy relationships [4]. Thus, recognizing others' emotional states and adapting accordingly becomes crucial when talking about social communications. However, these

© Springer Nature Switzerland AG 2020
A. R. Wagner et al. (Eds.): ICSR 2020, LNAI 12483, pp. 664–675, 2020.
https://doi.org/10.1007/978-3-030-62056-1_55

states are complex phenomena [3,11], which is why they are the topic of intense research not only in Psychology, but also in fields where artificial agents have to establish relationships with humans, such as Computer Science and Robotics.

Since mastering such a complex field as a whole is beyond reach for current robotics, we aim to find a simpler representation, i.e., a single internal state that goes beyond understanding if the person is engaged, revealing also the affective impact of the ongoing interaction (see [10] for a deeper discussion). Indeed, we believe it is important for a social agent to understand the way the other person is feeling regarding the action it just performed. It needs to comprehend how "comfortable/uncomfortable" the other person is, to change and adapt its behaviour accordingly. Therefore, we introduce a new internal state situated in a uni-dimensional scale from being *extremely uncomfortable* to *extremely comfortable* which we name *Comfortability* and define as follows: *(disapproving of or approving of) the situation that arises as a result of a social interaction which influences one's own desire of maintaining or withdrawing from it.*

As a representative example, Pettinati and Arkin [9] mentioned in the introduction of their paper the story of a Parkinson's patient who was "Uncomfortable" as a consequence of her caregiver's comment. The caregiver told her that she seemed depressed, whereas instead she was unable to perform non-verbal communication as usual because of the disease. The authors argued that companions (either humans or robots) should be capable of dealing with this type of situations e.g., by realizing that they did something "wrong" and proactively try to restore the interaction. They wrote *"she may accept what is being presented to her, but she is not agreeable to it and does not necessarily understand why the caregiver feels this way"*, which is in line with the *Comfortability* definition provided above. Caregivers (or individuals) who cannot detect the *Comfortability* level of their partner cannot understand when they are offending, annoying or scaring them. This behaviour might unintentionally induce partners to abandon the interaction and more importantly, the impossibility to learn from mistakes.

For this reason, we believe it is fundamental to endow future robots (or artificial agents) with the capability of detecting human *Comfortability* and adapting their behaviour accordingly. In fact, our long term goal is to build that system [10], hence in this paper we address two main research questions:

- Can *Comfortability* capture the range of positive and negative states that can be evoked in an interaction? Is it different from any other affective state?
- Can a humanoid robot evoke different *Comfortability* levels on people? Would it differ from the way it is evoked in human-human interactions?

2   State of the Art

Comfortability is a concept that people might use on a daily basis, which has also been addressed by several HRI researchers. Nonetheless, as there is no official definition or name, the word *Comfort* is often used despite their difference.

Whereas *Comfort* tackles both physical and psychological aspects in both non-interactive (e.g., sitting in a sofa, looking at a picture (discomfort sub-scale of RoSAS [2])) and interactive contexts (e.g., receiving a massage, having a conversation); *Comfortability* focuses on the psychological aspect and solely emerges in interactive scenarios (e.g., having a conversation).

An example of the research focusing on *Comfort* is by Sun et al. [16] who were interested in finding an ideal configuration for the RIBA robot to lift and carry hospital patients assuring their maximum "comfort and safety". They found that the robot's arms distance should be adapted to the patients body.

On the other hand, other researchers addressed *Comfortability* even though they might refer to it as "Comfort". In particular, Koay et al. [5] developed a handheld "Comfort Level Device" and made subjects report their own "Comfort" while performing a task in a simulated living room scenario in the presence of the PeopleBot robot. The subject had to search some books and write their titles over a whiteboard while the robot was moving around. They found that the situations in which the robot was moving behind the subjects, blocking or colliding with their path, were the ones reported as more "Uncomfortable". At the same time, Ball et al. [1] studied people's reactions when a robot is approaching. Especially, they measured the "Comfort" levels of seated pairs of people engaged in a collaborative task (solving a jigsaw puzzle) while the Adept Pioneer 3DX robot approached them from 8 different angles. Every time that the robot approached them, it asked *"Please rate your comfort level regarding the robot's most recent approach path"*. Additionally, Schneeberger et al. [13] created a strained situation between a human and another agent (two conditions: human vs virtual agent) to explore if there is a difference in the authority they inspire. Particularly, they defined a list of tasks which were meant to be "stressful" and "shameful". Some of them were extracted from Menne [7] and others created (e.g., *dance the chicken dance, get a booger out of your nose, tell me something really insulting*). To verify and choose the 18 most "Uncomfortable" options they ran a questionnaire among 24 participants where quoting literally *"each item had to be answered on a scale ranging from 1 (not uncomfortable) to 7 (very uncomfortable)"*. Similarly, Pettinati and Arkin [9] explored the impact of integrating a Robokind R25 robot in "strained" hierarchical relationships. To create the strained situation a confederate and a participant were asked to debate during 15 min about a recent controversial topic. During the discussion the robot was present but did not intervene. Seeking to discover the impact of an unengaged robot in strained situations, they found that its influence was minimal. Matsufuji et al. [6] developed a multi-modal system to detect "awkward" situations considering voice intonation and body posture. To create the awkward situation participants had to lie. The system acquired an accuracy of 80%.

Analyzing these studies, we observed that the topic of "comfort in interactions" is central to social robotics and we got a closer idea of the behaviors that might influence it, as well as its practical applications in HRI scenarios. Notwithstanding, we believe that it is still missing a unifying definition, able to capture the multiple facets of this concept, which is why we propose *Comfortability*.

3 Research Question

The present study aims to formalize *Comfortability* and assess whether a robot can elicit it in people. For that purpose, the following hypotheses are formulated:

Hypothesis 1: It is possible to design actions in a narrative context able to evoke different *Comfortability* levels (displayed through a questionnaire online).

Hypothesis 2: It is possible to design humanoid robot actions able to evoke different *Comfortability* levels (displayed through a visual questionnaire online).

Hypothesis 3: *Comfortability* differs from any other emotional/affective state and can arise from different combinations of multiple emotions.

4 Methods

To address the hypotheses, a generic scenario was designed and tested through two online questionnaires: one called Narrative Context which illustrates the actions as textual sentences; and the other called Visual Context which presents the actions as videos of the humanoid robot iCub [8].

4.1 Generic Scenario

The main objective was to maximize the participants' emotional/affective states by creating a strained situation in which they feel personally involved [9,13]. To do that, the scenario was described as follows: *"Imagine that you are being interviewed by a reporter who is asking you which are your thoughts regarding a sensitive topic (e.g., religion in the schools, abortion, animal industry, illegal immigration, robots vs humanity, etc) to later display the interview in the national TV channel"*. Then, participants had to report their feelings after being presented with some actions. Regarding the Narrative Context questionnaire, there were 30 actions (15 meant to trigger *positive* and 15 *negative Comfortability*) presented through sentences (check Table 1). In relation to the Visual Context questionnaire, there were 10 actions (5 meant to trigger *positive* and 5 *negative Comfortability*) which were picked from the first experiment as they were reported as the most effective in triggering the desired responses (i.e., they were the closest to the *Comfortability* scale extremes). This time, the questions were presented through videos of iCub saying the sentences while changing its facial expressions and moving its torso, arms and head accordingly (See Fig. 1, and https://youtu.be/QXPSVnbvgJM).

The actions and robot's movements were defined from zero, taking inspiration from [14] and [12] respectively. To remove any dependencies between actions, participants were told *"please think of them as independent events which are not connected between each other"*.

Table 1. The 10 selected actions for the Visual Context questionnaire, where A1–A15 were meant to trigger *negative Comfortability* and A18–27 *positive Comfortability*.

A1	After greeting the interviewer, the reporter says "**Where did you get this outfit? Somehow it doesn't really fit you** [14]"
A2	In the middle of the interview the reporter says: "**Sorry that I ask, but have you farted? It smells really bad here**"
A3	At the end of the interview, the reporter says: "**Now that I know what your opinions are, allow me to ask the last question of the interview. Are you proud of yourself having those stupid values and ideals?**"
A14	In the middle of the interview, the reporter says, "**why I am even doing this job? I hate it! I definitely do not like people**"
A15	The reporter says "**Buffalo buffalo Buffalo buffalo buffalo buffalo Buffalo buffalo**" without any meaning behind
A18	At the beginning of the interview, the reporter says, "**Hello, thank you very much for participating! I am very happy that you are here!**"
A19	At the end of the interview, the reporter says: "**Thank you very much for your time, I wish you have a wonderful day**"
A20	At the end of the interview, the reporter says: "**I am very grateful for this debate. Constructive conversations like this one are not usually found. Thank you very much for your time!**"
A26	After you have presented your idea, the reporter says: "**I have never thought about this topic from this perspective. I am sure that it will bring novel and useful information for our viewers**"
A27	After you have presented your idea, the reporter says: "**Wow. I think you are really cool.**"

4.2 Internal States

To indicate their feelings, participants were asked to score a list of internal states: **Pride, Gratitude, Admiration, Shame, Reproach** and **Anger** which we refer to as Emotions and **Comfortability, Engagement** and **Confidence** which we refer to as Affective States.

The Emotions were included to discover if *Comfortability* is equivalent to any other emotional state (Hypothesis 3). Specifically, those were chosen as they were reported by the Ortony, Clore & Collins (OCC) model [15] to be caused by other agents, which resembles *Comfortability*'s definition. The Affective States were picked to act like attention-grabbers, given that the scoring method for the Emotions and the Affective States was different (as *Comfortability* is bipolar whereas discrete emotions are not). To report the Emotions, participants were asked: "*Please, indicate how strongly you would feel the following internal states from Not at all to Extremely*" and then, they were presented with a Five-Likert Scale (*Not at all, A little, Moderately, Quite a bit and Extremely*). To report the Affective States, they were asked: "*Please, indicate how strongly you would*

Fig. 1. Robot iCub performing one of the actions for the <u>Visual Context</u> questionnaire.

feel the following internal states from negative to <u>positive</u>" and then, they were presented with a Seven-Likert scale (for *Comfortability*: from *being extremely (uncomfortable to comfortable)*; for *Engagement* from *being extremely (disengaged to engaged)*; for *Confidence*: from *being extremely (insecure to confident)*).

4.3   Online Questionnaires

Both questionnaires were submitted through the Amazon Mechanical Turk platform where random naive participants were recruited. To assure reliable data two attention check questions were added: 1) *Ignore the previous sentence and future indications and mark the third column for all the rows in this page*; 2) *Please indicate the context that matches better for the story that you were asked to imagine in the survey (There are cameras and microphones/I am in the wild surrounded by animals/The music is amazing/I definitely have to go back to this concert/ It was a bad experience as the quality of the food was quite poor).*

*For the <u>Narrative Context</u> questionnaire, 155 participants were tested in which 55 failed at least one of the attention check questions and therefore were discarded, leaving a total of **100 participants** (60% male and 40% female). They were paid 2.15 dollars and they completed the task in 19.2 min on average.*

*For the <u>Visual Context</u> questionnaire, 155 participants were tested for which 59 failed at least one of the attention check questions and therefore were excluded, leaving a total of **96 participants** (64.58% male and 35.42% female). They were paid 1 dollar and they completed the task in 12.2 min on average.*

5   Results

5.1   Hypothesis 1

The first step was to test the *Hypothesis 1* for which the <u>Narrative Context</u> questionnaire was used. The results can be seen in Fig. 2, where A1 to A15 (*set1*) includes the actions meant to trigger *negative Comfortability* and A16 to A30 (*set2*) includes the actions meant to trigger *positive Comfortability*. From the chart, it can be seen how indeed the reported *Comfortability* level for *set1* is comprehended between *being Extremely Uncomfortable* (Intensity = 1) and *Neither* (Intensity = 4); and the reported *Comfortability* level for *set2* is comprehended between *Neither* and *being Extremely Comfortable* (Intensity = 7).

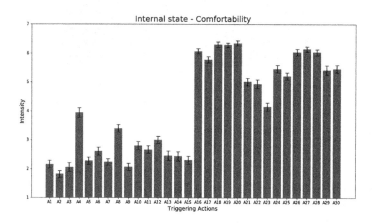

Fig. 2. All the Actions presented in the <u>Narrative Context</u> questionnaire.

There were some questions (A4 and A23) whose intensity, while remaining between the boundaries, was less extreme than predicted (e.g., A4: *After you have presented your idea, the reporter says: "Remember that we are on a national TV channel, the arguments you present have to be based on logic and reasoning"*).

A non-parametric Wilcoxon Test confirmed the significant difference in median rating between *set1* ($M = 2.54$, $SD = 1.48$) and *set2* ($M = 5.64$, $SD = 1.32$) ($t = 8833$, $p < .001$), which means it is possible to design actions that evoke opposite *Comfortability* levels in a narrative context (which supports *Hypothesis 1*).

At the same time, the Affective States were compared between each other applying a Friedman's test which showed a significant difference between the *Comfortability*, Engagement and Confidence means' levels ($\chi(2) = 396.464$, $p < .001$). A Wilcoxon signed-rank post-hoc analysis confirmed that *Comfortability* differs from Engagement ($t = 218297$, $p < .001$) and Confidence ($t = 139422$, $p < .001$), after applying a Bonferroni correction. If the analysis is applied to *set1* or *set2* independently, similar results are obtained after applying another Friedman test (*set1*: $\chi(2) = 102.213$, $p < .001$; *set2*: $\chi(2) = 359.991$, $p < .001$). The significant difference among the median ratings of the three affective states suggests that they represent three distinct, though related aspects.

5.2 Hypothesis 2

Subsequently, the five actions reported as most *Extremely Uncomfortable* (*vset1*) and the five actions reported as most *Extremely Comfortable* (*vset2*) were chosen for the <u>Visual Context</u> questionnaire (check Table 1).

From Fig. 3, it can be noticed that the questions presented as negative and positive triggers were not only effectively distinguished in the narrative context, but also when they were acted by the humanoid robot. A Wilcoxon test confirmed the significant difference between *vset1* ($M = 2.49$, $SD = 1.60$) and *vset2* ($M = 5.70$, $SD = 1.23$) ($t = 365$, $p < .001$) supporting *Hypothesis 2*.

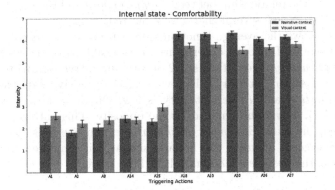

Fig. 3. Actions chosen for the Visual Context questionnaire, listed in Table 1

The Affective States were compared applying a Friedman's test, which proved that indeed, there is a significant difference among them ($\chi(2) = 35.579$, $p < .001$). A Post-hoc analysis including a Wilcoxon signed-rank test with a Bonferroni correction showed that, *Comfortability* differs from Engagement ($t = 28114$, $p < .001$) and Confidence ($t = 27826$, $p < .001$) similar to the Narrative Context.

Additionally, Fig. 3 shows that the *Comfortability* values for both contexts follow a similar pattern. A mixed ANOVA with the reported *Comfortability* as the dependent variable, the context (*narrative vs. visual*) as the between factor and the designed impact (*negative vs. positive triggers*) as the within factor was computed. The results announced a significant effect on the designed impact ($F(1, 194) = 1297$, $p < .001$), no effect on the context ($F(1, 194) = 0.654$, $p = .42$), and a significant interaction between the two factors ($F(1, 194) = 17.889$, $p < .001$). Bonferroni corrected post-hoc tests confirmed that the ratings for the positive designed impact are significantly higher than for the negative designed impact for both experiments: the Narrative Context (*considering solely the 10 selected actions; set1*: M = 6.22, SD = 0.95 vs. *set2*: M = 2.15, SD = 1.42, with $t(99)$= 31.203, $p < .001$) and the Visual Context (*vset1*: M = 5.71, SD = 1.23 vs. *vset2*: M = 2.49, SD = 1.60, with $t(95)$= 20.584, $p < .005$). Next, the ratings for the positive designed impact are significantly higher in the Narrative Context than in the Visual Context (M = 6.22, SD = 0.95 vs. M = 5.71, SD = 1.23, with $t(169.921)$= 4.025, $p < .001$); and contrarily, the ratings for the negative designed impact are marginally lower in the Narrative Context than in the Visual Context (M = 2.15, SD = 1.42 vs. M = 2.49, SD = 1.60), although the difference is not significant after a Bonferroni correction ($t(180.780) = -2.20$, $p = .058$). This indicated that the robot videos tended to trigger less extreme *Comfortability* reactions than the textual sentences shown in the narrative condition.

5.3   Hypothesis 3

To investigate the relationship between *Comfortability* and the Emotional states previously introduced, several charts were plotted.

Figure 4 shows the average Emotion value linked to the specific *Comfortability* level reported in both experiments. It is visible (in both contexts) that when *Comfortability* is reported as 1, 2 or 3 the **negative Emotions**' (*Shame, Reproach* and *Anger*) intensity is high whereas the **positive Emotions**' (*Gratitude, Admiration* and *Pride*) intensity is low. On the contrary, when *Comfortability* is 5, 6 or 7 the tendency is the opposite. This pattern implies that as expected, the more *Extremely Uncomfortable* someone feels, the higher the *negative Emotions*' intensity will be; and similarly, if someone feels *Extremely Comfortable*, the *positive Emotions* will be high as well.

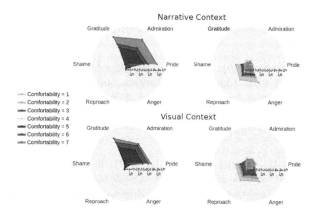

Fig. 4. Relation between the reported Emotions' and *Comfortability* levels.

To further investigate this pattern, making focus on the <u>Visual Context</u>, we computed two squared sums of the ratings associated to both sets of positive and negative Emotions for each participant and question. As a result, a set of linear regressions between this measurement of "Emotions' intensity" and *Comfortability* proved to be significant (**Negative Emotions**: *slope* : $-.528$, $r : -.815$ and $p < .001$; **Positive Emotions**: *slope* : $.813$, $r : .939$, $p < .001$, see Fig. 5).

To assess whether the same *Comfortability* level could be associated to different combinations of emotions, we mapped the *Comfortability* level in function of the three positive and negative Emotions for each action of the <u>Visual Context</u> questionnaire (see Fig. 6). Each action is represented by a marker, whose shape

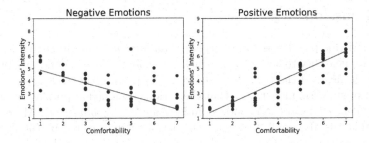

Fig. 5. Combined Emotions' ratings as a function of *Comfortability*'s intensity.

and color depends on its *Comfortability* value. Color brightness reflects the combined emotions intensity (i.e., brighter symbols means being further away from the origin axis); the marker coordinates correspond to the ratings of the three reported negative or positive Emotions; and the tiny numbers correspond to the associated action listed in Table 1.

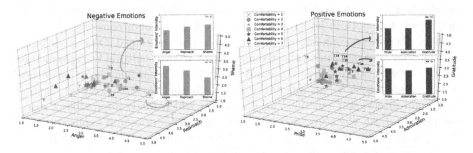

Fig. 6. Mapping between *Comfortability* and the three Emotions of each set, for each action regarding the <u>Visual Context</u> questionnaire.

Observing the **Negative Emotions** chart, most of the reported actions with an associated *Comfortability* level lower than 4 are spread over the axes. Indeed, different combinations of emotions can lead to the same *Comfortability* value. For example, when *Comfortability* is 1, some actions present *Anger* as the predominant Emotion (e.g., X_3) whereas conversely, for others *Shame* prevails (e.g., X_2). Interpreting the **Positive Emotions** chart, a similar tendency is appreciated. That is to say, given the same *Comfortability* rating (e.g., 7) there are actions in which the outstanding Emotion is *Gratitude* (e.g., Y_{18}) and others in which *Pride* dominates instead (e.g., Y_{20}). Consequently, these results show that the same *Comfortability* levels can be triggered alongside different sets of Emotions. Thus, *Comfortability* is not directly associated to any single Emotion tested here, providing evidence in favor of *Hypothesis 3*.

6   Discussion

The aim of this paper was to investigate *Comfortability*, its link with Emotions and its applicability to actions performed by a robot. More in detail, we provided evidence in favor of the three hypotheses introduced in the Sect. 3.

First of all, we demonstrated that the actions designed as positive or negative *Comfortability* triggers were indeed judged as so (*Hypothesis 1*). More importantly, this was also confirmed when the actions were enacted by the humanoid robot, suggesting that *Comfortability* can be associated to robot behaviors as well (*Hypothesis 2*). Additionally, we noticed that the ratings related to the Visual Context were relatively less "extreme" than those obtained for the same actions depicted in the Narrative Context (see Fig. 3). This might be due to the different nature of the interviewer (human or robot), but also to the different experimental context. Being free to imagine the entire interaction might have induced a stronger immersion in the situation and hence stronger ratings. Finally, it was shown that *Comfortability* differs from other internal states and can arise from different combinations of multiple emotions (*Hypothesis 3*). These results suggest that *Comfortability* could represent a useful uni-dimensional value reflecting the "comfort in interaction" independently of what specific emotion affected it, both in human-human and in human-robot contexts.

Still, there were some limitations that should be mentioned. On the one hand, participants were randomly collected and therefore their cultural background and familiarity with robots were not considered. Then, regarding the experimental design, there was not "an imaginary robot" in the Narrative context; neither a "human interviewer" in the Visual context, which made impossible a direct comparison. Last, the study was based on imagined stories and explicit ratings, thus *Comfortability* might be perceived differently in a real-live interaction.

This paper presents solely the first step towards our long-term goal of creating robots sensing and adapting to the partner's *Comfortability* levels. The next phase will entail a live human-robot interaction experiment, where the robot iCub will replicate the actions described here, interviewing physically a human partner. This will allow to test how *Comfortability* is impacted by robot actions in presence; and to measure the natural reactions and behaviors they cause. This will pave the way to the development of *Comfortability* detection systems in human-robot social interactive communications.

Acknowledgements. *Alessandra Sciutti is supported by a Starting Grant from the European Research Council (ERC) under the European Union's Horizon 2020 research and innovation program. G.A. No. 804388, wHiSPER.*

References

1. Ball, A., Silvera-Tawil, D., Rye, D., Velonaki, M.: Group comfortability when a robot approaches. In: Beetz, M., Johnston, B., Williams, M.A. (eds.) Social Robotics. ICSR 2014. Lecture Notes in Computer Science, vol. 8755, pp. 44–53. Springer, Cham (2014). https://doi.org/10.1007/978-3-319-11973-1_5

2. Carpinella, C.M., Wyman, A.B., Perez, M.A., Stroessner, S.J.: The robotic social attributes scale (RoSAS) development and validation. In: Proceedings of the 2017 ACM/IEEE International Conference on Human-Robot Interaction, pp. 254–262 (2017)
3. Ekman, P.: Facial expression and emotion. Am. Psychol. **48**(4), 384 (1993)
4. Golleman, D.: Social Intelligence: The Revolutionary New Science of Human Relationships, p. 544 (2006)
5. Koay, K.L., Walters, M.L., Dautenhahn, K.: Methodological issues using a comfort level device in human-robot interactions. In: ROMAN 2005. IEEE International Workshop on Robot and Human Interactive Communication, 2005, pp. 359–364. IEEE (2005)
6. Matsufuji, A., Shiozawa, T., Hsieh, W.F., Sato-Shimokawara, E., Yamaguchi, T., Chen, L.H.: The analysis of nonverbal behavior for detecting awkward situation in communication. In: 2017 Conference on Technologies and Applications of Artificial Intelligence (TAAI), pp. 118–123. IEEE (2017)
7. Menne, I.M.: Yes, of course? An investigation on obedience and feelings of shame towards a robot. In: Kheddar, A., et al. (eds.) Social Robotics. ICSR 2017. Lecture Notes in Computer Science, vol. 10652, pp. 365–374. Springer, Cham (2017). https://doi.org/10.1007/978-3-319-70022-9_36
8. Metta, G., Sandini, G., Vernon, D., Natale, L., Nori, F.: The ICUB humanoid robot: an open platform for research in embodied cognition. In: Proceedings of the 8th Workshop on Performance Metrics for Intelligent Systems, pp. 50–56 (2008)
9. Pettinati, M.J., Arkin, R.C.: Identifying opportunities for relationship-focused robotic interventions in strained hierarchical relationships*. In: IROS, pp. 297–304 (2019)
10. Redondo, M.E.L.: Comfortability detection for adaptive human-robot interactions. In: 2019 8th International Conference on Affective Computing and Intelligent Interaction Workshops and Demos (ACIIW), pp. 35–39. IEEE (2019)
11. Russell, J.A.: A circumplex model of affect. J. Pers. Soc. Psychol. **39**(6), 1161 (1980)
12. Samrose, S., et al.: Visual cues for disrespectful conversation analysis. In: 2019 8th International Conference on Affective Computing and Intelligent Interaction (ACII), pp. 580–586. IEEE (2019)
13. Schneeberger, T., Ehrhardt, S., Anglet, M.S., Gebhard, P.: Would you follow my instructions if i was not human? Examining obedience towards virtual agents. In: 2019 8th International Conference on Affective Computing and Intelligent Interaction (ACII), pp. 1–7. IEEE (2019)
14. Schneeberger, T., Scholtes, M., Hilpert, B., Langer, M., Gebhard, P.: Can social agents elicit shame as humans do? In: 2019 8th International Conference on Affective Computing and Intelligent Interaction (ACII), pp. 164–170. IEEE (2019)
15. Steunebrink, B.R., Dastani, M., Meyer, J. J. C.: The OCC model revisited. In: Proceedings of the 4th Workshop on Emotion and Computing. Association for the Advancement of Artificial Intelligence (2009)
16. Sun, M., et al.: Adaptive user-centered design for safety and comfort of physical human nursing-care robot interaction. In: Duffy, V.G. (ed.) Digital Human Modeling and Applications in Health, Safety, Ergonomics, and Risk Management. Healthcare and Safety of the Environment and Transport. DHM 2013. Lecture Notes in Computer Science, vol. 8025, pp. 365–372. Springer, Berlin, Heidelberg (2013). https://doi.org/10.1007/978-3-642-39173-6_43

Creating MyJay: A New Design for Robot-Assisted Play for Children with Physical Special Needs

Hamza Mahdi[(✉)], Shahed Saleh, Omar Shariff, and Kerstin Dautenhahn

Social and Intelligent Robotics Research Lab (SIRRL), University of Waterloo,
Waterloo, Canada
{hmahdi,shahed.saleh,kerstin.dautenhahn}@uwaterloo.ca,
oshariff@ryerson.ca

Abstract. Robots present an opportunity to redefine traditional game scenarios by being physical embodiments of agents/game elements. Robot assisted play has been used to reduce the barriers that children with physical special needs experience. However, many studies focus on child-robot interaction rather than child-child interaction. In an attempt to address this gap, a semi-autonomous, mobile robot MyJay was created. This open-source robot features light and color for communicative feedback, omni-directional mobility, robust mechanisms, adjustable levels of autonomy for dynamic interaction, and a child-friendly aesthetically-pleasing outer shell. This paper outlines the development process of MyJay and discusses its role in future HRI studies through the creation of a competitive or collaborative, multi-player game.

Keywords: Robot design · Robot assisted play · Accessibility · Collaborative and competitive play · Human-robot interaction

1 Introduction

Play is very important in child development. It promotes emotional skills, forming safe, and nurturing relationships with guardians and peers [34]. While there are many definitions of play, there is agreement on it being a voluntary, intrinsically motivated activity with the following characteristics: unfinalisation, creativity, non literalness, flexibility and pleasure [6]. Play teaches children to focus on tasks at hand without exposing them to stressful situations; it demands commitment and seriousness while maintaining a dividing line from reality: "Play demonstrates that two different attitudes co-exist: to be fully involved in what one is doing and to be aware of the fact that we are within a relative, delimited and conditioned dimension" [5]. Play supports many developmental functions such as adapting to new situations and environments, and looking for solutions

This research was undertaken, in part, thanks to funding from the Canada 150 Research Chairs Program and thanks to Alexander Graham Bell Canada Graduate Scholarships.

© Springer Nature Switzerland AG 2020
A. R. Wagner et al. (Eds.): ICSR 2020, LNAI 12483, pp. 676–687, 2020.
https://doi.org/10.1007/978-3-030-62056-1_56

especially when a novel situation is presented in which a child has to think critically [6]. Another function of play is to place children within a cultural context where they have to understand the flexibility of roles and rules in society [6], which is important for the development of social skills. Additionally, play is essential for sensorimotor development; manipulation of objects enhances sensorimotor coordination where actions are linked to physical achievements [6]. This cyclic relationship between motor actions and manipulation of environment changes perception and leads to new modified actions, which appears clearly in newborn children [3]. In addition, play is important for cognitive development, engaging higher symbolic functions such as language, graphical representation and narrative ability [6]. Perhaps one of the most influential aspects of play on a child's development is its role in psychological and emotional development; play allows children to explore a range of emotions and facilitates managing the stress of strong emotions which leads to less impulsive responses and better controlled actions [34]. Play supports emotional growth, pushing children to take risks, communicate with other players, negotiate rules, cooperate and learn how to win and lose in a gracious manner. Play is not simply for "fun". It is essential for child development; if a child cannot play, they do not learn sufficiently the necessary skills or gain the confidence and self esteem that are important to being able to lead an independent life, make friends or find a job.

Robot Assisted Play. Robots are becoming increasingly popular tools of entertainment for children, especially for those with special needs, and often embedded in an educational or therapeutic context. Children with special needs often experience difficulties in performing play activities in an organic way [7]. Many projects have attempted to address children who have barriers to play due to special needs [15] through the use of robotics. For example, PlayROB is a three axis teleoperated robot that enables children with severe physical disabilities to play with LEGO bricks [21]. A two-year long term study showed no decrease in interest, and reported high concentration and fun [20]. Another example is the mobile IROMEC robot, which is the result of a European project that investigated the role a robotic toy can play as a social mediator for children who have barriers to play due to cognitive, developmental or physical impairments [16], [17]. Also, LEGO robots have been explored for play in children with limited motor ability and for education via speech generated communication [1,24,33]. The mobile robot Cosmobot utilized voice input and targeted children with learning and developmental disabilities [22]. It was designed to be used by therapists and focused on motivating children with special needs to interact with the environment and facilitate therapy sessions. Maggie is a doll-like, social robot created to explore mechanisms of interaction with humans [26] and supported a variety of games [2]. While Maggie was not designed specifically for children with special needs, it is another example of robot-assisted play. Kaspar is a minimally expressive robot designed for playful interaction, specifically, for children with autism [11]. Kaspar acted as a social mediator for collaborative play and facilitated interaction and role switching [11]. While most robots developed in research projects are currently not commercially available [15], ZORA is a commercially available robot based on the popular NAO platform with special simplified software [32]. Its humanoid form factor and toy-like appearance allow it to be used in a variety of applications such as companionship or creating basic games. Additionally, pet-like robots can be used as toys such as the Pleo robot [12] and the newly re-released Sony Aibo [28]. These robots, though used in play, offer companionship as their main selling point.

It is worth noting that many of these systems mainly focus on solitary play, which is quite important in some cases. However, human-human interaction is quite important and should be accounted for in the design process. Robots such as IROMEC and KASPAR have scenarios where group play is central [11,25]. This is quite important in order to avoid social isolation especially in children who have limited access to play with their peers. In this project, we designed a robot geared specifically towards group/peer play. The project aims to include both children with and without physical special needs. We attempt to design a game that is fun and supports long term adoption of the technology.

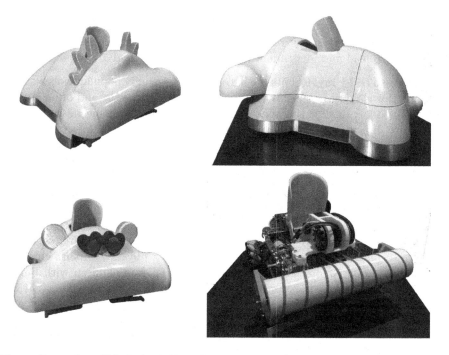

Fig. 1. Examples of MyJay's shell configurations. The robot will typically be covered by the shell when interacting with children. The robot without its shell is shown in the bottom right. The shell was designed to be modular and accepts a wide range of accessories to suit different age ranges, as seen in the left images.

2   Identifying the Game and Robot Design

Children are often engaged in play through the medium of games. When consulting a children's special needs expert, we realized that most children with motor-related special-needs often use screen-based entertainment. Such activities lack the spatial sense of the real world and are often done in solitude. Our goal was to create a game that allows children - especially those with upper-body gross and fine motor impairments - to compete and collaborate through a challenge that uses a robot they control. Inspired by the FIRST Robotics challenges made for student design teams [13], the idea of a field-based game centered around robots scoring through collaborative and competitive efforts helped formulate this project. The game elements handled by the robot are 101.6 mm diameter foam balls similar to balls used in beginner tennis practice. Balls were chosen as they are universal across cultures and used in numerous sports making it an intuitive object to interact with [18]. The initial concept of the game (subject to change depending on feedback from target users) is an enclosed area where the robot collects balls, navigates around obstacles and shoots balls in a basket or an opening in the field wall. In the collaboration condition, children may work together controlling a single robot to achieve the game objective. In the competitive condition, two robots are influenced/controlled by different children, competing to achieve the game objective first. Both game modes aim to foster communication and play between children as well as conflict management skills and generally to provide a fun time. While solitary play is possible, and could be beneficial in terms of improving spatial awareness, it is not the main intended outcome of this design. More details about how the robot interacts with users are provided in the "Teleoperation and Autonomy" subsection. The robot was designed around the game concept with ease of use, accessibility, child-friendly aesthetics and reliability as guiding principles.

3   Mechanical Systems

MyJay's features are centered around maneuverability, collecting and "shooting" game pieces. Since this robot is designed to ultimately be open source, minimizing the number of pieces and the difficulty of assembly are priorities. As this robot is driven by children, it may collide with several objects on the game field, thus, robustness and reliability are also key. Most importantly, the robot has to be safe; although balls being shot are made of foam, energy used by mechanisms to shoot the balls could cause harm if designed incorrectly. MyJay was designed to have rigid mechanisms that rotate in place with little to no vibrations. A shell was also designed to enclose most of the robot's mechanical workings as an added precaution. The robot was first conceptualized using Solidworks. This allowed all parts to be assembled and tested for compatibility. 3D printing was used to create custom components and all other parts, including aluminum blocks for the frame, were sourced from sites available to the general public. Along with the shell, MyJay is about 570 × 330 × 525 mm in terms of dimensions.

Fig. 2. Mechanisms rendered in Solidworks: drive train and frame (top left), elevator (bottom left), intake (bottom middle), flywheel (bottom right) and full robot (top right) (Color figure online)

Drive Train Mechanism: Children with physical special needs, especially those with a lack of upper body fine and gross motor skills, may be unable to control and adjust a simple tank-drive robot due to the multi-step alignment procedures it requires. A swerve-based robot [4] with independently spinning wheels would be resource-intensive and too complex for potential users to build. The drive train used on MyJay is a mecanum wheel drive train [19]. This wheel type features small, diagonally aligned rollers along the perimeter of each main wheel, making it a holonomic drivetrain and enabling the robot to strafe in any direction. A commercially available mecanum drive train was purchased and altered to a rectangular configuration rather than the conventional square configuration to reduce the robot's volume. The final structure of the drive train and frame structure can be seen in Fig. 2.

Intake and Elevator Mechanisms: The intake and elevator mechanisms are responsible for collecting the balls and storing them in the robot to be shot later. The two elevator motors are stored up-facing in the frame channels at the top of the robot. The driven shafts were made perpendicular to the motors using beveled gears; this allows the assembly to be more compact. Polycord, a plastic polymer solid cord, doubled as transmission and a material to draw the balls into the robot. A timing belt and pulleys were used to translate the rotation of the motor shafts to hex shafts with two layers of rollers connected via polycord belting. The rollers were 3D printed to be force-fit onto their shafts, with bearings for reduction of friction. This assembly was secured using two 3D printed brackets, shown in Fig. 2. The intake of the robot was also 3D printed; it features two spiraling polycord-lined grooves with a wave pattern that propagates to the center of the robot when spinning clockwise. The elevator was 3D printed to an optimal curve that ensures the game piece maintains constant contact with all belting.

Flywheel Mechanism: This mechanism is mounted atop the elevator. A brushless DC motor spins a timing belt and pulleys connected to a compliant rubber wheel revolving at high speeds to launch the ball in a pre-defined arc path. The bracket holding the mechanism together, seen in Fig. 2 in yellow, was 3D printed with an additional motor guard for added safety.

4   Control System

The electrical system was designed using widely used, commercially available parts. Figure 3 describes the electrical and controls system. The system was designed/programmed with modularity as a central theme. For example, the ESP32 board, which sends commands to actuators, can receive standardized messages from the Jetson Nano or can be directly teleoperated over WIFI from any device sending standardized messages using UDP. All documented code will be made publicly available once this robot design project is finalized.

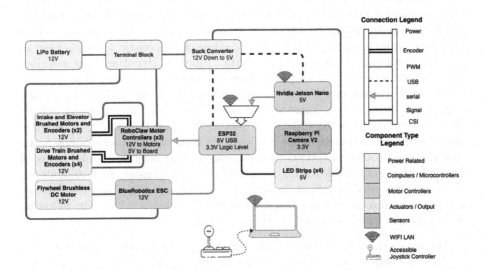

Fig. 3. System architecture: power and logic levels are shown

4.1   Teleoperation and Autonomy

MyJay is semi-autonomous by design to allow children to be part of the game regardless of their ability to control it; the level of autonomy can be adjusted depending on the user. The initial plan is to have discrete levels of autonomy and change the settings before starting a play session. Levels of input can vary from almost completely teleoperating the robot to simply influence the robot's actions at a high level such as shooting or collecting the balls. Two children may collaborate to influence/control the robot's actions simultaneously. For example, one user could control the motion of the robot and another user could control the collection of balls/shooting. The robot is equipped with a camera as its main sensor for perception. Since the robot is placed in a field, tags and colored foam tiles are used to localize the robot. Additionally, the camera feed can be utilized to track balls and the goal. For future studies, we will attempt to make multiple controllers that can be setup in various ways to accommodate a spectrum of children's abilities. Accessible joysticks, buttons and other input devices such as microphones or inertial measurement units (IMU) may be utilized based on future feedback from users.

5   Interaction Elements

5.1   Shell Design

Children learn and interact with objects through their senses. Their initial interest in physical objects is often attained through visual stimuli [10]. Thus, creating a shell for MyJay would double in function to assist in safely covering moving mechanisms and to be an aesthetically appealing characteristic. Children have an orientation towards the natural through the "Biophilia Hypothesis"; it describes that this attraction has developed as humans evolved [30]. If one is to examine the main characters of children's television shows, movies and toy franchises, animals are often chosen. Tame and socialized creatures [29] in popular culture roles were found to be central to the plot almost half the time [23]. A study investigating the favourite animals of children from various backgrounds found that the most preferred species were the dog, cat, squirrel, horse and swan [9] with all other quartiles featuring mainly four-legged animals. Such animals are also commonly used in animal therapy [31]; robots modeled after these therapy animals often invoke the same positive reaction from humans [27]. The following design criteria was determined for the robot shell:

- Moving mechanical elements of the robot should be hidden by the shell
- The shell should aim to have lateral symmetry with mainly organic curves
- Orientation of the robot should be obvious from the shell body
- The shell should contrast the floor of the game field
- The robot's internal state can be communicated through the use of lights
- The shell should not use symbolism belonging to any gender
- The shell should take a zoomorphic, four-legged shape, but not imitate any existing animal species in order to avoid unrealistic expectations

– The shell should have multiple configurations to attract children with different ages and aesthetic preferences.

Fig. 4. Shell development process: preliminary shape sketch (left), rendered sketch (center), final shell with CAD (right)

Autodesk Sketchbook was used to draw transparent and opaque bodies to represent various shapes of the shell that satisfy the above conditions as shown in Fig. 4. Shapes that were impractical to fabricate and 3D print were then eliminated. The final shell shape was chosen as it could be created using the advanced surfacing and thickening commands in Solidworks. The final design features a high backed, four-legged body (Fig. 4 right).

As the shell is 3D printed, due to limitations in printer bed size, it was divided into several pieces with mutually perpendicular planes.

5.2   Light and Color

Another visual stimulus added was light through the use of multi-color LED strips in the base perimeter of the the robot and the accessory ears. This can be a method of feedback for the child [10] as they can see the result of their commands on the robot manifested in color changes. A study found that children associate motion verbs to point-light displays, suggesting that animated light can be an effective communication tool [14]. The incorporation of light needed to be done safely as children can be very sensitive to light. In a study conducted with 27 children with epilepsy, it was found that certain light flash intensities and frequencies caused sensitivity or seizures. Mainly high intensity light at flash frequencies greater than 10 Hz caused epileptic symptoms in the children. On some occasions, single flashes also caused children to become sensitive [8]. MyJay does not flash any lights, but rather fades from one colour to another quickly; this softens the effect of sharp colour transitions. Directional lighting is done through a propagating sign wave rather than a point flash moving along the LED strip. Other patterns include showing a single colour, a rainbow, and fading in and out. The rainbow light signal will be used as reward feedback to the child when they score or reach a point threshold (Fig. 5).

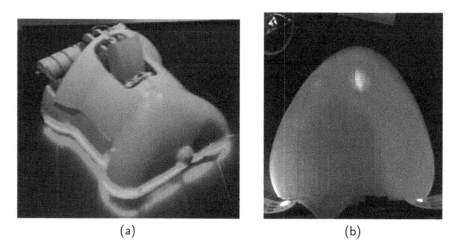

(a)   (b)

Fig. 5. MyJay's light stimulation: (a) Perimeter lights (shell partially assembled), and (b) Illuminated ear piece printed using transparent PLA. A piece of paper helps diffuse light evenly. Similar ear pieces can be seen mounted on the shell in Fig. 1

5.3   Motion

The robot's holonomic drive-train allows it to convey a wide range of motions such as moving in an arc of arbitrary radius or moving towards a target position while spinning. This could be used to give the robot a "personality" such as 'dancing' after scoring a goal.

6   Lessons Learned

MyJay has been in development for about 8 months; many decisions and design changes were made to make MyJay into a fully functioning robot.

Determine the Environment First: Understanding the context in which the robot operates accelerated the development process. By restricting the robot's operation to a highly controlled environment (i.e. a pre-determined playing field), we were able to produce two prototypes fairly quickly which allowed us to understand the problem better, narrow down which mechanisms to use, and made us aware of a few issues, the most important one being noise generated by the robot mechanisms. Having created two prototypes, we reached out to a local children accessibility organization and connected with an expert on children with special needs to consult them before creating the current version of MyJay. This helped in choosing the colors, lighting and the overall shape of the shell.

Importance of Modularity: As we intend to make MyJay open source once fully developed, heavy emphasis was placed on modifiability of parts. The aluminum parts making up the frame were chosen from a supplier that offers pre-drilled channels, with many places to mount external mechanisms. The intake and the elevator sections were specifically 3D printed so that using a ball with a different size would only require a minor redesign and reprint of these specific parts rather than redesign the entire robot.

Open-source Design Tips: Designing a truly open source robot can be difficult as small differences in part sourcing and in the manufacturing process can yield a very different robot that may not function consistently. Using pre-drilled aluminum channels reduces the variability that usually results from machining raw aluminum stock. Additionally, all custom parts not purchased from publicly available sources were designed to be 3D printed in order to avoid complex manufacturing steps and the need for a fully equipped machine shop. 3D printed parts were designed and segmented so that they fit most hobbyist level 3D printer beds.

Designing for Children: Children, specifically children with multiple special needs can be sensitive to sounds and light flashes. This makes designing mid size robots such as MyJay for children a difficult process. Many mechanism iterations were tested to balance robot reliability and robustness with silent mechanism operation. For example, we found that using relaxed pulleys, when possible, reduces noise even without the use of precision bearings.

7   Future Work and Concluding Remarks

As MyJay is nearing the end of development, design files and instructions will be published in detail to be an open-source project. Additionally, we plan to use it in several upcoming studies. The first, which is already taking place at the time of publishing this paper, consists of remote sessions (due to Covid-19) where carers and children access pictures/videos of MyJay and provide feedback which will be used to refine its design and functionality. The choice to design a prototype before contacting end users is to provide a starting point for the discussion and have some concrete ideas rather than abstract or unrealistic expectations. Since the robot was designed with a lot of 3D printed functional parts, it is not challenging to undertake major changes to the design. A following study will be conducted with children using MyJay in a game; we will be analyzing how children are socializing, competing and collaborating while in the game to identify if MyJay is effective in robot assisted play. We expect that varying the level of autonomy based on a child's skill/ability level, or personal preferences, will help scaffold teleoperation skills and allow children with physical challenges to connect and bond with their peers by playing games together. Ultimately, we hope MyJay can be used in a school setting or in therapeutic settings such as hospitals. We believe its uniqueness in relation to the robot-assisted play literature for children with special needs comes from being designed to be used by children with and without physical special needs in both public and therapeutic settings.

In this paper, we attempted to give insight into the challenges of designing a social robot for robot-assisted play designed specifically for group play. The literature contains many papers about designing robots for interaction with children. Building on, and contributing to this existing body of knowledge, we believe we built a robot that could help facilitate joyful play sessions for children of all different levels of ability. MyJay was not only designed for inclusion, we used our team's many years of collective experience to design it for ease of use, reproducibility and longevity/mechanical fidelity. We hope this paper helps other research groups in the process of designing their own social robots as the existing literature helped us design MyJay.

References

1. Adams, K., Julie, Y., Cook, A.: Lego robot control via a speech generating communication device for play and educational activities. In: RESNA Annual Conference (2008)
2. Alonso-Martín, F., Gonzalez-Pacheco, V., Castro-González, Á., Ramey, A.A., Yébenes, M., Salichs, M.A.: Using a social robot as a gaming platform. In: Ge, S.S., Li, H., Cabibihan, J.J., Tan, Y.K. (eds.) Social Robotics. ICSR 2010. Lecture Notes in Computer Science, vol. 6414, pp. 30–39. Springer, Berlin, Heidelberg (2010). https://doi.org/10.1007/978-3-642-17248-9_4
3. Amelina, N., Besio, S.: Play in Children with Physical Impairment. De Gruyter, Berlin, Boston (2017)
4. Baker, A., Mackenzie, I.: Omnidirectional drive systems kinematics and control. In: FIRST Robotics Conference, pp. 1–15 (2008)
5. Besio, S.: Analysis of Critical Factors Involved in Using Interactive Robots for Education and Therapy of Children with Disabilities. Editrice Uniservice (2008)
6. Besio, S., Bulgarelli, D., Stancheva-Popkostadinova, V.: Play Development in Children with Disabilties. De Gruyter, Berlin, Boston (2017)
7. Besio, S., Carnesecchi, M., Converti, R.M.: Prompt-fading strategies in robot mediated play sessions. In: Assistive Technology: From Research to Practice, pp. 143–148 (2013)
8. Bickford, R.G., Daly, D., Keith, H.M.: Convulsive effects of light stimulation in children. AMA Am. J. Dis. Child. **86**(2), 170–183 (1953)
9. Bjerke, T., Ødegårdstuen, T.S., Kaltenborn, B.P.: Attitudes toward animals among norwegian children and adolescents: species preferences. Anthrozoös **11**(4), 227–235 (1998)
10. Danko-McGhee, K.: The aesthetic preferences of infants: pictures of faces that captivate their interest. Contemp. Issues Early Child. **11**(4), 365–387 (2010)
11. Dautenhahn, K., et al.: KASPAR - a minimally expressive humanoid robot for human-robot interaction research. Appl. Bionics and Biomecha. **6**, 369–397 (2009)
12. Fernaeus, Y., Håkansson, M., Jacobsson, M., Ljungblad, S.: How do you play with a robotic toy animal? A long-term study of Pleo. In: Proceedings of the 9th International Conference on Interaction Design and Children, pp. 39–48. ACM (2010)
13. FIRST: (2019). https://www.firstroboticscanada.org/
14. Golinkoff, R.M., Chung, H.L., Hirsh-Pasek, K., Liu, J., Bertenthal, B.I., Brand, R., Maguire, M.J., Hennon, E.: Young children can extend motion verbs to point-light displays. Dev. Psychol. **38**(4), 604 (2002)
15. Van den Heuvel, R., Lexis, M., Gelderblom, G.J., Jansens, R.M., de Witte, L.P.: Robots and ICT to support play in children with severe physical disabilities: a systematic review. Disabil. Rehabil. Assist. Technol. **11**(2), 103–116 (2016)

16. Van den Heuvel, R., Lexis, M., Janssens, R.M., Marti, P., De Witte, L.P.: Robots supporting play for children with physical disabilities: exploring the potential of IROMEC. Technol. Disabil. **29**(3), 109–120 (2017)
17. Van den Heuvel, R., Lexis, M., de Witte, L.P.: Can the IROMEC robot support play in children with severe physical disabilities? A pilot study. Int. J. Rehabil. Res. **40**(1), 53–59 (2017)
18. Hudak, D.: Use of ball play. In: Schaefer, C.E. (eds.), D.M.C.e. (ed.) Play Therapy Techniques, p. 313, 2nd edn. Jason Aronson (2002)
19. Ilon, B.E.: Wheels For a Course Stable Selfpropelling Vehicle Movable in Any Desired Direction on the Ground or Some Other Base (1975). US Patent 3,876,255
20. Kronreif, G., Prazak-Aram, B., Kornfeld, M., Stainer-Hochgatterer, A., Fürst, M.: Robot assistant "PlayROB" - user trials and results. In: RO-MAN 2007 - The 16th IEEE International Symposium on Robot and Human Interactive Communication, pp. 113–117 (2007)
21. Kronreif, G., Prazak-Aram, B., Mina, S., Kornfeld, M., Meindl, M., Fürst, M.: PlayROB - robot-assisted playing for children with severe physical disabilities. In: Proceedings of the IEEE 9th International Conference on Rehabilitation Robotics, pp. 193–196 (2005)
22. Lathan, C., Brisben, A., Safos, C.: Cosmobot levels the playing field for disabled children. Interactions **12**(2), 14–16 (2005)
23. McCrindle, C.M., Odendaal, J.S.: Animals in books used for preschool children. Anthrozoös **7**(2), 135–146 (1994)
24. Rios-Rincon, A.M., Adams, K., Magill-Evans, J., Cook, A.: Playfulness in children with limited motor abilities when using a robot. Phys. Occup. Ther. Pediatr. **36**(3), 232–246 (2016)
25. Robins, B., Ferrari, E., Dautenhahn, K.: Developing scenarios for robot assisted play. In: RO-MAN 2008 - The 17th IEEE International Symposium on Robot and Human Interactive Communication (2008)
26. Salichs, M.A., et al.: Maggie: a robotic platform for human-robot social interaction. In: IEEE Conference on Robotics, Automation and Mechatronics, pp. 1–7 (2006)
27. Shibata, T., et al.: Mental commit robot and its application to therapy of children. In: IEEE ASME International Conference on Advanced Intelligent Mechatronics, vol. 8, issue 15 (2001)
28. Sony: (2019). https://us.aibo.com/
29. Taylor, A., Pacini-Ketchabaw, V.: Kids, raccoons, and roos: Awkward encounters and mixed affects. Child. Geograph. **15**(2), 131–145 (2017)
30. Tipper, B.: A dog who i know quite well: everyday relationships between children and animals. Child. Geograph. **9**(2), 145–165 (2011)
31. Urichuk, L., Anderson, D.: Improving Mental Health Through Animal-Assisted Therapy. The Chimo Project (2003)
32. Van den Heuvel, R., Lexis, M., De Witte, L.P.: Robot ZORA in rehabilitation and special education for children with severe physical disabilities: a pilot study. Int. J. Rehabil. Res. **40**(4), 353–359 (2017)
33. Wiberg, C., Harbottle, N., Cook, A.M., Adams, K., Schulmeister, J.: Robot assisted play for children with disabilities. In: 29th Annual RESNA Conference Proceedings (2006)
34. Yogman, M., et al.: The power of play: a pediatric role in enhancing development in young children. Pediatrics **142**(3), e20182058 (2018)

Humans and Robots in Times of Quarantine Based on First-Hand Accounts

Laurens Lafranca$^{(\boxtimes)}$ and Jamy Li

University of Twente, P.O. Box 217, 7500AE Enschede, The Netherlands
l.r.s.lafranca@student.utwente.nl

Abstract. A quarantine is an effective measure in order to contain a disease and it is needed to be used more often in current times. Quarantine forces people to have minimal to no social contact with other humans for a certain period of time. Past work says this isolation can have a serious psychological impact on people's lives, which can have dramatic consequences. Research can help find the positive and negative experiences of people in quarantine, in order to determine their needs. But how do people respond to quarantine according to their own self accounts? We look to a video platform as a unique opportunity to explore this question. Robots can be used in times of quarantine so isolation can be maintained. However, these robots should be matching the actual needs of the people in quarantine in order to have an effect. This research will use a content analysis of first-hand accounts of people in quarantine in order to find their experiences and needs. After that, there will be an analysis of robots that are used in times of quarantine. Lastly, these two analyses will be used to find out if the robots match the needs of the people in quarantine. We report on two major components to first-hand social media quarantine accounts: emotional response and procedural explanations provided by detainees, and explore potential reasons for them choosing to share these types of content. On top of that, we report on robots that are mentioned by social media, the tasks that they do, and the needs they fulfill. This research will expand on the current knowledge domain of needs in quarantine and will also add to the knowledge domain of the effectiveness of robots in quarantine.

Keywords: Quarantine · First-hand account · YouTube · Robots · Needs · Content analysis

1 Introduction

During a global disease outbreak, containing the spread of a disease is very important in order to save lives. In these times quarantine measures can be put

Electronic supplementary material The online version of this chapter (https://doi.org/10.1007/978-3-030-62056-1_57) contains supplementary material, which is available to authorized users.

A. R. Wagner et al. (Eds.): ICSR 2020, LNAI 12483, pp. 688–707, 2020.
https://doi.org/10.1007/978-3-030-62056-1_57

into place to minimize the contact that people have. This will prevent a virus from spreading [31] to other people quickly and it can prevent the hospitals from overflowing. However, being in quarantine can have several effects on people. It is useful to investigate these effects and how people cope with them. Some research has already been done about the experiences of people in quarantine [7,8,10,23,33]. These studies have interviewed people in retrospect and asked them questions about their feelings, either positive or negative. With a significant amount of responses, they could document trends in their data. However, these studies are done after the actual quarantine is over, as it is difficult to have interviews with people when they are quarantined. As people tend to forget their experiences quickly, an interview during their actual quarantine can give a better perspective of the actual experiences that people have during the quarantine. Effects such as false recognition and aging memory lead to people misrepresenting their actual experiences [27] of a quarantine when the research is done after the intended quarantine is over. This is why analyzing first-hand account videos of people during quarantine can give a better perspective of the actual experiences and needs. Social media has been used before in different fields to research news topics. YouTube has been used in prior epidemics [1,11], or for content analysis about self-driving cars [6]. This led to the following research question.

- What feelings and needs does one experience in quarantine according to first-hand accounts?

Next to that a quarantine due to a pandemic brings other difficulties. As diseases are often transmitted during direct or indirect contact, human-to-human contact should be prevented as much as possible. This is however difficult in some situations, as humans are often used to doing certain tasks, due to tradition or formality. A quarantine situation can change these norms, as normal contact is not allowed anymore. This is where robots can be of help. As robots are becoming smarter over time, they can be used in a quarantine to replace human tasks and prevent extra contact and cross-contamination [18]. The use of robots in quarantine is not researched that much, as these situations do not happen often. This led to the following research question.

- How are robots used in quarantine situations?

Although some research has been conducted in the field of the effect of a quarantine, the studying of patients during quarantine itself has lacked [4]. It may be possible to increase acceptance of healthcare robots by properly assessing the needs of the human user and then matching the robot's role, appearance, and behavior to these needs. This paper will analyze first-hand accounts of people in quarantine to see what their experience/reaction is and what their basic needs are, and will also look into the reported robots that are used in quarantine. These analyses will be combined in order to see whether these robots fulfill the needs of people in quarantine times. This led to the following research question.

- In what sense does the use of robots match the needs of someone in quarantine?

The three research questions will allow us to answer the main research question.

What matches can be found between the reaction and needs of people in quarantine and robots that are currently used in quarantine situations using publicly available videos as reference material?

In this research, we will use content analysis to study videos of people and robots in quarantine, found on the video platform YouTube. These videos will be reviewed by the researcher, who will make notes based on some basic categories. An example of a category can be "uncertainty over procedures". These first-hand account videos can give a better insight into how people are responding to the quarantine, what needs they have, and how robots fulfill certain purposes. The main focus of this research will be on the Coronavirus pandemic, as the current situation highly favors these videos over previous epidemics [9].

2   Related Work

In order to gather literature related to the research domain Scopus, Google Scholar, and IEEE were used. With search terms such as "quarantine", "human experience" and "robots" several studies were found that have done research in either the field of human experiences and needs in quarantine, or robots used in quarantine situations, or robots matching society needs. When looking at papers concerning people in quarantine, we only included papers that were researching people's opinion about experiences regarding quarantine, or feelings towards quarantine. In papers about robots used in quarantine situations, we only used papers that tried researching robots that could be used in such situations. For research about robots matching society needs, we only used papers that researched the acceptance of robots in a society, and how this could be improved.

When we look to the opinions of people concerning forced quarantine, we see that the vast majority of people across the globe support this measure when it is necessary for containing the spread of a disease during an outbreak [30]. This study showed that 94% of the respondents found that quarantine was a good way to stop the spread of infectious diseases. Also, a vast majority were in favor of legal penalties against absconders. Other papers also found that the public opinion was in favor of a quarantine, where [2] found that there was 93% acceptance of quarantine of US-residents, and [3] found an acceptance of 74% of US-citizens. However, this paper also showed that the acceptance was higher in other countries, which might indicate that the level of acceptance is also dependent on the cultural differences. Although the percentages differ depending on the research, we can still conclude that overall, the vast majority of people agree with a quarantine as a measure.

In the field of human experience and needs in times of quarantine, a lot of research has been done so far. The research can be divided into 2 main categories: Cross-sectional [2, 10, 13, 21, 25, 29, 32] or qualitative research [7, 10, 26, 33].

The research was focused on the experiences of the people who were in quarantine, while some also included the experiences of people who were not quarantined [21, 29].

A useful review of these papers was [5]. This review analyzed the afore-mentioned research and drew some conclusions. This work can be used in the comparison between the data of the first-hand accounts and the literature. The review showed that in a lot of research similar positive and negative feelings were found. The research reported negative feelings such as confusion, fear, anger, stress, low mood, and a sense of isolation. Positive feelings that were reported were happiness or relief, but these were reported on way less, in about 5% of the cases [25].

Other papers that were not included in the review showed similar emotions. The paper of Lin [19] found external and internal struggles. External struggles were things like uncomfortable surroundings or lack of in-person family support, while internal struggles were emotional turmoil such as anger, and the possibility of a positive test was also difficult for the patients. Another paper [12] showed that the loss of control due to quarantine lead to distress and depression. On top of that patients experienced stigmatization.

In the field of robots used in quarantine, there is not a lot of research done. There have been papers on a robot that could be used in such a situation [18] and papers on how this robot can be improved [20,22,34]. One study also showed that the public opinion about the occupation of robots also shifts towards robots doing jobs that require memorization and service-orientation, instead of only dull jobs [28]. There has been one paper that looks into the performance of a robot when it includes either audio or video channels or both [17]. Lastly, there is one research [15] used that looked into the use of medical robots in biothreat situations. This research developed several methods that could potentially be useful in a healthcare situation. These studies can be used for a basic understanding of robots and how they can be used in quarantine situations. However, none of this scientific research answers the question if the robots fulfill the needs of the people in quarantine.

Lastly, in the field of robots matching social needs, some papers were found to be useful. There has been research done to see the acceptance of robots under the elderly. It was found that a careful assessment of the needs of people could result in a higher acceptance rate of the robots [16]. Robots should thus be closely adapted to the needs of people, in order to make them successful and accepted. Another paper also showed this through their research. They concluded that robot technology should be developed tailored to the individual, and it should be able to adapt based on the information it gathers [24]. When the needs of people are not properly assessed, it can even lead to the failure of projects. In order to predict this, there are models developed that can predict the acceptance of robots and can explain that. An example of this is the Almere Model [14].

3   Methods

There were several steps in this research. Firstly, a literature review has been done on both the experiences of people in quarantine and robots used in quar-antine. This leads to a basic understanding of what to take into account when doing content analysis. Earlier research has also looked into emotions that people had in quarantine, which helps to focus on the correct points during the analysis. Earlier research about quarantine robots helps getting to know what these robots are used for in the past, and what they were capable of doing then.

Secondly, data is collected for first-hand accounts of people in quarantine and of robots used in quarantine. In order to gather first-hand accounts of people in quarantine, there is a need to collect online videos. The videos will be collected using YouTube. This platform is has the most elaborate database of all other video platforms, which makes sure that the dataset we will use videos from contains many different experiences and robots from people from all over the world. On top of that, for the scope of this research it was not possible to perform online interviews, which is why the readily available material on YouTube is the best way to gather information of experiences of people and robots in quarantine.

There will only be clips collected that are direct experiences of people in quarantine, either through an interview or through a self-upload. Online collections of third-party videos on YouTube can be a great source of getting a first-hand account of people during quarantine. These clips are reviewed and structurally broken down to the main information of the clips. For robots used in quarantine, videos are gathered in a similar sense. With the collection of videos, it is done in such a fashion that YouTube does not know the preferences of any user, which gives a list of videos that is not sorted on personal preference. Only the videos that explicitly have someone in quarantine themselves, or a robot that is used in a quarantine area for a quarantine situation are added to the database and are looked at for this research.

Thirdly, the videos were analyzed. The videos of first-hand accounts were all put in a document. After that, the videos were looked at and certain highlights of each video were logged. Some of the interesting points this research looked at were: the reason for quarantine, negative and positive feelings, procedure. This was documented in such a way that similarities and trends could be found in the dataset. With the documentation of positive experiences, negative experiences, and the feelings towards the procedures in quarantine, basic needs could be found for the quarantined people. The videos of robots in quarantine were also put in a document. These videos were analyzed, and the following interesting points were looked at: purpose, country, morphology and social role. When a robot was categorized as 'social', the social interaction it had with people, such as touch or gesture, was also documented. With this structured documenting, trends could be found in all of these categories. These trends were then documented, in order to show the similarities and what the differences were between the sets. Some statistics were also used to show the difference in finding a social or a non-social robot.

Lastly, the final research question is answered by comparing the two datasets. We will look at the needs that detained people expressed, and the needs that quarantine robots fulfill. Then we compared the two in order to see whether there were similarities between the two. After this, we also looked at what robots did not match the needs, and why this might be the case.

4   Results

4.1   People in Quarantine

Sharing Information to Deal with Uncertainty. After looking for videos about people in quarantine, a dataset of 22 videos was constructed. In the clips people are often seen in their quarantine environment, which is either a hospital room or a room at home. The people share information to deal with the uncertainties they experienced. The videos show thus the surroundings of the people, and often it becomes clear how the people themselves are feeling from the videos. They sometimes show equipment that they are hooked up to, or talk about the care they receive. Most videos had a small emotional component, but this was not the focus as the clips were more in a self-help or interview style. There are two types of information sharing in the videos: explanation of symptoms and of procedures. The dataset can be found in Supplemental material A.

Explanation of Symptoms. Most people want to be informative about the disease to the public by talking about the symptoms they had. They mention symptoms that forced them into quarantine, as one mentioned to Bloomberg (#1): "I think the bar to separate people from the group was 37.5 degrees Celsius of fever, and I got exactly 37.5" Or as someone said to The Quint (#11): "I coincidentally had a sore throat, and [the nurse] told me, You need to go for a checkup to a hospital." These accounts give information about what symptoms could get you quarantined. On top of that there are also accounts that show the seriousness of the disease. One patient says to Insider about getting the symptoms (#13): "I started getting short of breath [...] that was one of the worst symptoms, because I woke up in the middle of the night, I was disoriented, I wasn't able to breathe."

Emotions Regarding Symptoms. When talking about the symptoms people expressed their emotions based on the severity of their symptoms. Looking through all the videos it becomes clear that people who have mild symptoms are grateful that they only have mild complaints. One US resident told Fox News (#14): "I feel fine. This virus for me was pretty light, equal to a very, very mild cold." However, in clips where there are more severe complaints people also were positive, as they were often recovering and feeling better. In an interview with CGTN one patient mentions (#8): "Everyone here is getting better day by day. We don't need to panic, as long as we follow the doctor's instructions." Although most people talk about their symptoms in all of the videos, the focus lies more on the actual explanation of the symptoms rather than the emotional aspect of getting sick. This is in line with the informative character that these videos have, where the main focus is informing others and explaining situations, rather than having an emotional interview. A patient also mentioned the mental aspect to Insider (#13): "You start sitting down and having a conversation with yourself, like, OK, this is it for me. This is it for me and my children. I won't ever see them again-type of thing."

Explanation of Procedures. Next to that the actual procedurals of testing and checking are talked about by a lot of people in order to share information about the actual procedures there are in quarantine. The checking is mentioned by many of the persons in the clips. A person quarantined on a cruise ship mentions to RNZ (#3): "The doctors that come in [...] check my vitals, blood pressure, lungs, and heart rate, and they do that several times a day." He also mentioned: "They test with a swap that goes deep up into each nostril and one down the throat." Or another patient mentions to CNN (#16): "I have bust my lungs, I have fluid in my lungs, so they have been giving me medication for this." These explanations can help other people giving an insight in what they can expect when they get hospitalized with either mild or heavy symptoms.

Uncertainty in Procedures. In the clips people are talking about different experiences in the procedures of quarantine. There are several reasons why people are talking about the procedures. Quarantine is a new situation for many people, so the main goal of these videos is setting an expectation. This is why in all of the videos at least some part of the process is explained in such a way that people can gain information from it, so they are prepared for these procedures themselves.

Uncertainties in the procedures give quarantined people result in frustration, nervousness, and angriness. This uncertainty gives people several emotions, and in many clips they commented about this. One woman explains to the Kenya Citizen TV (#21): "After landing, [...] we were with more than 200 people in one space waiting to be cleared. There was no clear direction in where we were supposed to go. I thought I could go to my apartment and self-quarantine. I had already done the shopping and asked someone to drop everything and clean the apartment" Or as a man from India mentions after they asked when he was going to be tested in order to see who should be put into quarantine (#23): "He said: What test? There is no test. You will all be put into quarantine straightaway for 14 days. [...] Then he made some calls and then he said: I am sorry I got the wrong information as soon as you will be reaching the quarantine facility you will be tested there." This obviously leads to frustration as it is unclear for people what to do, what to expect and what to prepare for. Another interviewed person said to NBC: "We don't know...we know the federal government is shipping us to a base, we don't know where...what that atmosphere will be like...are we going to be in a huge open room?". As many people have these uncertainties when looking at quarantine situations, the first-hand accounts of these people help them prepare for the possible actions they might need to take.

Sanitary State. In some clips the sanitary state of the isolation ward or the hospital is explicitly mentioned. This state is always mentioned for specific reasons, either to encourage people to visit the wards when they have complaints, or warn people about the bad state of the isolation facility they were in. One quarantined person said in an interview with the Quint (#11):

"The first thing I noticed when I entered the ward was that it was super clean. [...] The next thing that I noticed was the bathrooms, the bathrooms were so clean, which I did not expect."

Or another person in an interview with India Today (#12):

"The isolation ward that I was kept in was spotlessly clean. it was so clean that it just struck me, like, oh my god. You know this kind of cleanliness... none of our homes are as clean. We might go around infecting and using phenyl and all of that, but the hospital and isolation ward, those guys are professionals, they know their jobs right. So, there is no way an infection can catch you there."

These accounts were both positive and encouraging for people who hesitate about going to the hospital. However, there were also negative accounts of isolation wards: One Indian resident tells India Today (#23): "So, when we reached our accommodation, we saw there were many bedsheets which were stained. The cupboard had rotten vegetables with flies on them, the washrooms were not up to the mark, the water was clogged in the washrooms. There was no sanitization, proper sanitization, the urinals there were all soaked with peaks of pond." Or as a Nigerian resident tells Kenya Citizen TV (#21): "It is no quarantine, really. Breakfast is served in the common area. [...] So tomorrow morning, we have to share the same spoons when they are serving breakfast with other people from other countries."

These accounts are very negative and try to either warn people about the worse conditions, or try to get attention to the problem in order to get the government to react to it.

Internal and External Struggle. Lin [19] categorized internal and external struggles. In this paper, internal or external struggles are found in most of the participants. They either experience only internal or external struggles, or both. Lin coded whether a struggle was experienced, which allowed us to do the same for our dataset. Internal struggles are struggles related to the person itself, like their emotions, possible diagnosis or being quarantined. External struggles are related to things that stand outside of their own, like their surroundings, opinions of others, or support they get from others. To give an example, video #18 was coded with internal struggle, because the quarantined person experienced emotional turmoil, and video #7 was coded with external struggle, because the quarantined person was separated from their husband, which meant she does not have support from him. In order to see whether there is an association between the two, we documented the accounts of internal and external struggles people commented on in the videos. There were 9 videos with both internal/external struggles, 6 with only internal, 3 with only external, and 5 with no struggles. We ran McNemar test on both coded variables from the single group. McNemar's chi-square statistic: $\chi^2(1) = 0.44$, N = 23, p = 0.51, which suggests that there is not a statistically significant difference in the proportion of videos coded internal and the proportion of videos in the external group.

4.2   Quarantine Robots

In our research we found 26 videos of robots in quarantine. The complete documentation can be found in Supplemental material B. Some of the photos of robots can be found in this research. All photos of robots can be found in Supplemental material C. There are 3 places where robots in the dataset are used, namely in public spaces, in hospitals, or in a home environment.

Robots Used in Public Spaces. There are a lot of robots that are used in the public space. As their tasks vary, we have grouped the robots to certain tasks and described their way of handling these tasks and other interesting points.

Spreading Awareness. Spreading awareness is done in public places. This is so most people that are in this public space can be aware of the rules that are put into place, so they can more easily obey the rules. Robots are used for this specific purpose as they can work for long times, and it is safer for a robot to interact with a lot of different humans as it cannot get infected. The way of spreading information differs with these robots. Some of the robots used in the corona pandemic spread information in a playful way. The robot covered by South China Morning Post is a nice example of this. This robot had an interactive element and let people passing by fill in a quick questionnaire to see if they have any symptoms regarding a virus. Another robot, reported on by the Hindustan Times, also shows a robot that spreads information about the disease, and it is able to hand out mouth masks and hand sanitization. These robots both have the morphology of humans.

Fig. 1. Awareness robot reported on by Hindustan Times

Cleaning. Secondly there are robots that are designed to clean a bigger area in a quick way. This robot is shown in a report of South China Morning Post. This robot has wheels to drive around and has a cannon on the front which can shoot disinfect spray. This robot is able to disinfect 10000 square feet in one hour. To get this efficiency we see that the morphology completely changed. As these robots need to clean big part of the public space in a relatively small amount of time, the robots are equipped with wheels in order to move around quickly, and have a morphology that results in the biggest efficiency, equipped with a tank-like barrel.

There are robots that are used in public spaces while people are still using the place. These robots need to have a different morphology in order for it to operate safely. This is clearly visible, as these robots look like standard cleaning machines. These robots can autonomously clean big parts of the floor, without getting a cleaner exposed to many other people.

Telepresence Robots. Telepresence robots are robots with a live audio/video connection, and the ability to let someone control the movement of the robot from their home. These robots can be used for people to attend gatherings and roam freely without actually leaving their houses.

The first case of the use of a telepresence robot in times of quarantine is a video of South China Morning Post. In this video, telepresence robots are used for Japanese students of the University of Tokyo. They graduated, but they were not allowed to join the ceremony of receiving their diploma. This is when telepresence robots were used to give students to opportunity to still be present at the ceremony, being able to drive around their own robot and receive their diploma in a novel way.

The second video is of VOA News, where a father was not able to visit his daughter's wedding due to being in quarantine. This led to the family purchasing a telepresence robot, allowing the father to see the wedding and drive around himself.

The last video is about a telecommunication robot that is used in Belgian elderly homes. These elderlies were not allowed to go outside to communicate with their family, so the telecommunication robot could be used to still have contact with their family. The robot has an audio/video connection and can walk around. The robot has the morphology of a small child, with a screen as a face.

Fig. 2. Telepresence robot reported on by VOA News

Food. In a quarantine situation, you are not allowed to leave the house. The robots reported on by CGTN is a small robot that does groceries for people. It is able to ask for certain products, negotiate prices and make e-payments. It has the form of a small animal, with a shopping cart attached where the goods can be put into.

The second robot is a cooking robot that can prepare complete meals for people. It can make a dish called clay-pot and it only needs the food stock to be refilled once in a while, and can then cook the dish at the spot when it is requested. It has the shape of a food cart, but no chefs are needed for this.

Patrolling. Thirdly, there are patrolling robots. These robots can be used in public spaces in order to effectively save human labor and avoid cross infection. The robot can patrol the streets and look for people breaking rules. The first robot is one put into public places in order to measure body temperatures. This robot is equipped with a heat sensitive camera. It can check the temperatures of up to 10 people at once and can also check if someone is wearing a mask. This robot is also equipped with a speaker, so it can warn if someone has a high temperature, or if someone is not wearing a mask. It has the morphology of a armoured tank.

Another robot that is used in Singapore to patrol the streets is robot dog SPOT. This robot has a speaker which tells people to keep social distance. This robot also has the ability to enforce this rule as it walks in the middle of paths in order to separate people on paths better. We see that with the change of tasks and social role has come with a change in morphology. The robot now has a morphology of a dog. This robot is equipped with cameras and sensors in order to properly do its task of rule enforcing.

Fig. 3. Robot dog SPOT reported on by CNA

Another robot that also had the task of patrolling, the P-Guard robots used in Singapore, reported on by Ruptly. This robot is also a rule enforcer, and basically replaces a police officer. This robot roams around the streets, spreading the message to stay inside with a loudspeaker. On top of that it is equipped with cameras and sensors that can register its environment. It is controlled by security officers, and it can ask people to show their permits to be allowed outside to the robot. This robot has also had a big change in morphology, having a more car-like shape, equipped with lights too.

We see that robots in public spaces are mainly used for the purpose of either spreading information or for enforcing rules. All these robots do have something in common, namely preventing workers from being in the open and being able to catch the disease. It thereby also prevents cross-contamination. The robots all spread information about either the disease or the rules, informing unknowing residents with them. Only some of them are also able to enforce the law. The morphology changes when the robot gets more authority.

Robots Used in Hospitals. Some people who get infected by a disease end up in a hospital. This means that in hospitals or isolation wards there is a increased chance for nurses or doctors to get infected themselves. This is not desired as these people are desperately needed in these times, so a doctor being sick is something that needs to be prevented. This is done by using robots to replace certain tasks that were done by humans before.

Delivery. The first human task that is done by robots is delivering food or medicine to patients in quarantine. This is a task that was normally done by nurses, but robots are also able to maneuver around in an isolation ward or a hospital to bring certain goods to patients. In the videos that were found, we can see multiple implementations of delivering food or medicine. Most of these robots were similar to the robot reported on by New China TV. These robots have a tray system where stuff can be put onto, and a touch panel where people can indicate whether they have grabbed the food from the tray. Furthermore, these robots are equipped with sensors to not bump into anything.

Fig. 4. Delivery robot reported on by New China TV

However, as some medicine are valuable there is also a different design that is used in a hospital, reported on by CGTN. This design has a closed cabinet which can open and close its doors automatically. This robot is also able to take the elevator autonomously, which gives it a bigger reach in the hospital. These robots are put into place to reduce the pressure on doctors and nurses and to prevent cross-contamination.

Cleaning. The second task is cleaning. As cleaning is necessary to reduce the spread of infection, this needs to be done often and thoroughly. Robots can be used in this process, as they can't get infected themselves. There are different cleaning robots that were used. The first one is a disinfecting and germ zapping robot which ABC13 reports on. This robot uses ultraviolet light that kills the pathogens that cause infection. These robots can be used as main cleaning devices, or as an addition to the normal cleaning. The robot has a morphology of a stick with a round piece on top.

Monitoring. Lastly there are robots that are used for monitoring patients. This is also normally done by doctors or nurses, but a robot with a camera can also monitor the patients. The robots that are used in a hospital have the size and figure of a small child. The robots can be controlled by a doctor and can be rolled into a room where people who are infected are lying. The cameras on the robot can then be used to look at the monitors to see if everything is going well with the patients. This limits the number of masks and gowns that staff need to use. These robots have the morphology of a small human.

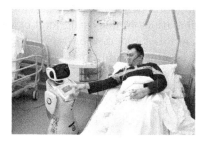

Fig. 5. Monitoring robot reported on by Yahoo Finance, image by Reuters

Testing. Robots can also be used in ways that can help testing patients. These robots either replace human interaction or elaborate testing. This can speed up the process and also prevent cross-contamination.

The first robot used for testing purposes is a robotic arm reported on by TRT World. This arm is placed on a platform that can move itself and can drive to patients. It can do ultrasound sound scans of the lungs, which is where respiratory diseases are often located. The machine does not need any human interaction and it can disinfect itself. It looks like a robotic arm on a trolley.

The second robot that is used is a giant testing robot for testing samples of potential infected people automatically, reported on by US Davis Health. The machine allows them to do a total of 1000 tests per day, whereas before results for 20 samples took about 5 h. The machine starts pipetting samples and adding reagents, breaking open the virus and yielding the RNA, all automatically. It allows the facility to do more with less people. It has a morphology of a big box.

Lastly there are robots used for entertainment. This can be either for the user itself, or for the audience the robot is for. These robots are interactive in such a way that they can entertain people for an amount of time.

Robots Used in Home Environment. There was one robot found that was used for entertainment. This robot interacted with a real person, having conversations. The person used the robot for entertainment for herselve, but also to make a comedic video for her audience. The person is cutting the hair of the robot, while the robot is angry and trying to stop it from happening with foul language. The robot talks and looks like a human, but it does not have a body attached.

Results. We gathered a total of 26 quarantine robots on YouTube. After documenting these robots it becomes clear that most of the quarantine robots in the dataset have a primarily social role. A total of 19 (73%) robots had a high social function and 7 (27%) had a low social function. This suggest that most quarantine-related robots on YouTube were focused on having a social element in order to interact with other people.

Among the high social coded robots, we found the following distribution of 7 different functions: 7 delivery robots, 3 tele-presence robots, 3 information robots, 2 monitoring robots, 2 patrolling robots, 1 buying robot and 1 entertaining robot. Among the low social coded robots, we found the following distribution of 3 different functions: 4 cleaning robots, 1 food production robot and 2 testing robots.

The quarantine robots in the dataset come from different parts in the world. The most videos come from Asia, with 16 videos (62%). From these videos there are 12 videos from China, 1 from Hong-Kong, 1 from India, 1 from Japan and 1 from Singapore. There are 6 videos (23%) from the USA. There are 3 videos (12%) from Europe, from which 2 are from Italy and 1 from Belgium. There is 1 video (4%) from Africa, which is a video from Tunisia. This suggests that China uses quarantine robots the most.

We can see a difference in morphology for social and non-social robots in the dataset. Among the robots that are coded as high social, we see that 8 from the 19 (42%) social robots have a human morphology. On top of that there are 4 (21%) shaped like a tray trolley, 2 (11%) as an animal, 2 (11%) as a cabinet, 2 (11%) as a tank and 1 (5%) has the morphology of a tele-presence robot. With robots that are coded as low social function we see 2 shaped like a pole with a round part on top, 2 as a box, 1 cleaning machine, 1 tank and 1 robotic arm. Thus, there is no robot that has a human or animal morphology.

From our results, we spot 3 different types of social interaction a quarantine robot can have. These are Voice, Touch and Gesture. The robots coded as high social function have one or more from these types as social interaction. The most common type of interaction in the social quarantine robots is voice. 16 (84%) robots had this type. Next is touch, with 11 (58%) of the robots having this type. Only 3 (16%) of the social quarantine robots had gesture as a type. This suggest that for social interaction, voice is the main contributor for quarantine robots.

We also coded the functional role of the robots. This was either Locomotion, or Manipulation. With locomotion the quarantine robot was able to move around itself, while with manipulation the robot was able to handle and manipulate an object. 22 (85%) of the robots had locomotion as a functional role, while only 3 (12%) of the robots was able to manipulate objects. There was 1 (4%) robot that was not able to do either of these.

In order to show that there are statistically more social than non-social robots in the dataset we did a binomial test in excel, with the probability of a social robot of 0.5. There were 7 accounts of where a robot was non-social, and there were 19 social robots. This binomial test showed that $p = 0.029$. This is less than the 5% chance that this observed count would happen when the probability of having a social robot being equal to the probability of having a non-social robot (i.e. a 0.5 probability). This shows that there is a statistically significant chance that a video of a social robot posted on YouTube is not equally likely to the chance of a non-social robot to be posted on YouTube. We observed more social robots than non-social robots in our dataset.

4.3   Comparison of the Needs of Quarantined People and the Purposes of Quarantine Robots

In order to answer the final research question, we need to make the comparison between the two datasets that we have made. After reviewing the dataset of videos of people in quarantine, there are different needs that can be identified. The first need is getting rid of uncertainty. A lot of times people were confronted with situations they were not familiar with and they had little information about what were to happen to them. These uncertainties could be divided into 2 main subjects: Procedures and Symptoms. These two topics were discussed in a lot of the videos, either explaining that they did not know what was going to happen, or an explanation for setting an expectation to others. There was thus a need for information about procedures and symptoms. Next to that the sanitary state of isolation wards was a topic that was mentioned often. This thus is also something people have a need for when going in quarantine.

After analyzing the videos about robots in quarantine, we can identify a lot of different purposes of the robots. Some of these purposes are delivery, cleaning, spreading information, patrolling, and tele-presenting. The robots are deployed in different areas, such as public areas or in hospitals.

Informational Robots Help in Public, But Not in Hospital. The information spreading robot can be a solution for two of the needs expressed by quarantined people, namely information about procedures and information about symptoms. We see in the dataset that these robots are used for these purposes. One of the Information spreading robots (#24) was stationed at a square in New York where people could fill in a questionnaire about their health. These questions were related to symptoms of Coronavirus and the robot could give the advice to go to the doctor if the person who filled in the questionnaire said they had certain symptoms. Another information spreading robot (#25) was able to fill the need of spreading information about procedures. This robot walked through a park and was able to see when people are walking too close to each other. When it notices this, it can instruct the people to walk further apart.

Although these robots are spreading information about the needs that the people in quarantine explained, they are not doing this to people who are in quarantine themselves. These robots operate in public spaces, which is a place where people in actual quarantine can wander. These robots still have an impact on the knowledge of people, as they explain some of the procedures and symptoms an infected person might experience. However, these robots fail to explain procedures for when you are in quarantine, for example, the number of times you need to get tested negative in order to be released, how these tests are conducted, where you will be put into quarantine, and so on. This shows that the start of the use of robots for this purpose is good, however, they could be used to explain more specific procedures for quarantine.

For symptoms, the robots are better used. The symptoms are explained to people using robots and this helps them being informed of when they may be infected with the virus. This is thus informative for people when they are not quarantined, so they know what the symptoms are, but also for people who are put into quarantine, as they have a better knowledge of why only a small indication can already put them into quarantine.

There are 2 testing robots that also provide information to the public. These robots can test samples of potential infected people, or can directly scan a person to see whether they are sick. These can thus be very helpful to a lot of people, as they can exclude people who have symptoms. However, when people are quarantined in hospitals they already are tested positive, which means they do not profit from these robots.

Lastly there were also monitoring robots used in environments where the public could profit from. These robots address procedure information needs and thus give information that is useful for the public, but not for the people quarantined in the hospitals themselves, as they do not get this information directly.

Cleaning Robots Partially Address Needs. Having a good sanitary state of isolation wards was also a need expressed in the videos. This is solved with quarantine robots in hospitals and other isolation wards. In hospitals, germ-zapping robots (#16, #18) were used in order to clean a room quickly and without the use of a person, which means that there is a low chance of cross-contamination. Cleaning robots such as #15 are used in public spaces in order to clean large areas quickly and also without human interference. However, some of the sanitary problems experienced by people, for example dirty trays of food, are not solved with the quarantine robots in the dataset.

Transport, Telepresence or Entertainment Robots Address Unmentioned Needs. Although we see some robots link to the needs expresses by quarantined people, there are several robots that address needs that are not mentioned. A lot of robots have as a main goal reducing human-to-human contact, which lowers the chance of cross-contamination, and limits the use of protective masks and gowns. The delivery robots replace nurses in hospitals, while the patrolling robots replace policemen on the street. Telepresence robots allow quarantined or even sick people to attend meetings and gatherings without having direct contact with other humans, just like the food buying robot allows a person to do groceries without leaving its house. The food-producing robot makes sure chefs do not need to have direct human-to-human contact too. In total there were 7 delivery robots, 2 food robots and 3 tele-present robots. This is thus a total of 12 that could not directly be linked to an expressed need. These all still contribute to getting less people infected, but the needs they fulfill are not recognized by the people in the dataset, while other needs are mentioned by them.

Limitations. There are some limitations to the research and to the results. When looking at the research there is a limitation in the videos of people in quarantine. The questions that are asked are not the same, so constructing exact results is more difficult. Thereby, the experience are less related, as the circumstances and periods of time that people were in quarantine are different. There can also be a other response when people are more used to being in quarantine, which can mean that when a new dataset is constructed on a later time, the experiences expressed can differ. Also, the sorted list that was given by YouTube in both experiences and robots can be based on how 'popular' the video is. This means that there is a possibility that not all groups are equally represented in the dataset.

There are also some limitations to these results. It can be assumed that robots that are posted to YouTube are not necessarily posted because they link to a need of quarantined people. These robots can also be posted because of their novelty in the field. The fulfillment of human needs does not need to be a strong reason for someone to report and upload a video about a robot to YouTube. This means that the videos found on YouTube do not need to be an accurate representation of all robots used in quarantine. Additionally, robots that are produced can be focused more on tasks that are related to the society as a whole, than an individual. Often, robots in the dataset are put into place to prevent cross-contamination. This is not a need an individual would express often, which means that this leads to a mismatch between the robots and the needs. The quarantined people focused more on urgent needs such as cleaning or getting information, than on less urgent needs, such as attending gatherings through telepresence, or having more operational efficiency.

5   Conclusion and Future Work

This research showed that there is a match between the expressed needs of people in quarantine, and the robots used in quarantine, based on videos found on YouTube. Some of the robots in the dataset directly link to an expressed need, while others did not link to a specific need. However, this still means that there are similarities between the two.

The first research question found the expressed needs of the people in quarantine. After reviewing the dataset, we concluded that most people gave information about either the procedures or about symptoms. They did this to take away the uncertainties they experienced themselves while being put into quarantine. On top of that, they often mentioned the sanitary state of the isolation facility as an important factor.

The second research question looked into the quarantine robots that could be found using YouTube videos as reference material. We found 2 main places where robots were used: robots used in public spaces and robots used in hospitals. The robots used in public spaces were divided into five categories: robots used for spreading awareness, cleaning robots, telepresence robots, robots for food and patrol robots. Robots in hospitals were divided into 4 categories: delivery robots, cleaning robots, monitoring robots, and testing robots. There was one robot that was used for entertainment. The robots were either social or non-social, and were used at different locations all over the world. They also had different morphologies, as human and animal were used, but other morphologies were also used when it was practical for the purpose of the robot.

The last research question was about the match between the two. We saw that when comparing the expressed needs of the people with the robots that were found, there was a match between the two. There were several robots that directly linked to the needs of the people in quarantine. Examples were the awareness spreading robots, the cleaning robots, and the patrolling robots. However, there were also a lot of robots that did not directly match the expressed needs of people. Examples of these were the delivery robots, the monitoring robots, and the telepresence robots.

For future work, more research can be done in the same field. Both of my datasets consisted of only about 25 videos, which leaves room for a much more elaborate research which would contain a lot more videos. However, the insights the videos of people in quarantine gave during this research was something that was unique in this research field. With further research, this new form of data analysis could give great new extra insights into the field. On top of that, due to the coronavirus being very topical at the time of constructing the dataset, all of the videos were related to the coronavirus. Future research could look into videos that were uploaded for other pandemics, such as SARS. This can give a more diverse view of what people experience in quarantine and what their needs are.

References

1. Basch, C.H., Basch, C.E., Ruggles, K.V., Hammond, R.: Coverage of the ebola virus disease epidemic on Youtube. Disaster Med. Public Health Preparedness **9**(5), 531–535 (2015)
2. Blendon, R.J., Benson, J.M., Desroches, C.M., Raleigh, E., Taylor-Clark, K.: The public's response to severe acute respiratory syndrome in Toronto and the United States. Clin. Infectious Dis. **38**(7), 925–931 (2004)

3. Blendon, R.J., Desroches, C.M., Cetron, M.S., Benson, J.M., Meinhardt, T., Pollard, W.: Attitudes toward the use of quarantine in a public health emergency in four countries. Health Affairs **25**(Supplement 1), W15–W25 (2006)
4. Broadbent, E., Stafford, R., Macdonald, B.: Acceptance of healthcare robots for the older population: review and future directions. Int. J. Soc. Robot. **1**(4), 319–330 (2009)
5. Brooks, S.K., et al.: The psychological impact of quarantine and how to reduce it: rapid review of the evidence. Lancet **395**(10227), 912–920 (2020)
6. Brown , B., Laurier, E.: The trouble with autopilots. In: Proceedings of the 2017 CHI Conference on Human Factors in Computing Systems, pp. 416–429, May 2017
7. Cava, M.A., Fay, K.E., Beanlands, H.J., Mccay, E.A., Wignall, R.: The experience of quarantine for individuals affected by SARS in Toronto. Public Health Nurs. **22**(5), 398–406 (2005)
8. Cordova-Villalobos, J.A., et al.: The 2009 pandemic in Mexico: experience and lessons regarding national preparedness policies for seasonal and epidemic influenza. Gaceta medica de Mexico **153**(1), 102–110 (2017)
9. Davidson, J., Liebald, B., Lui, J., Nandy, P., Van Vleet, T.: The Youtube video recommendation system. In: Proceedings of the Fourth ACM Conference on Recommender Systems, pp. 293–296 (2010)
10. Digiovanni, C., Conley, J., Chiu, D., Zaborski, J.: Factors influencing compliance with quarantine in Toronto during the 2003 SARS outbreak. Biosecur. Bioterrorism: Biodefense Strategy Practice Sci. **2**(4), 265–272 (2004)
11. Dubey, D., Amritphale, A., Sawhney, A., Dubey, D., Srivastav, N.: Analysis of Youtube as a source of information for west nile virus infection. Clin. Med. Res. **12**(3–4), 129–132 (2014)
12. Gammon. The psychological consequences of source isolation: a review of the literature. J. Clin. Nurs. **8**(1), 13–21 (1999)
13. Hawryluck, L., Gold, W.L., Robinson, S., Pogorski, S., Galea, S., Styra, R.: SARS control and psychological effects of quarantine, Toronto, Canada. Emerg. Infectious Dis. **10**(7), 1206–1212 (2004)
14. Heerink, M., Kröse, B., Evers, V., Wielinga, B.: Assessing acceptance of assistive social agent technology by older adults: the almere model. Int. J. Soc. Robot. **2**(4), 361–375 (2010)
15. Kartoun, U., Feied, C., Gillam, M., Handler, J., Stern, H., Smith, M.: Use of medical robotics in biothreat situations. In: AMIA 2006 Symposium Proceedings, p. 976 (2006)
16. Kobb, R., Hilsen, P., Ryan, P.: Assessing technology needs for the elderly. Home Healthcare Nurse: J. Home Care Hospice Professional **21**(10), 666–673 (2003)
17. Li, J., Li, Z., Hauser, K.: A study of bidirectionally telepresent tele-action during robot-mediated handover. In: 2017 IEEE International Conference on Robotics and Automation (ICRA), pp. 2890–2896 (2017)
18. Li, Z., Moran, P., Dong, Q., Shaw, R.J., Hauser, K.: Development of a tele-nursing mobile manipulator for remote care-giving in quarantine areas. In: 2017 IEEE International Conference on Robotics and Automation (ICRA), pp. 3581–3586 (2017)
19. Lin, E.C.L., Peng, Y.C., Tsai, J.C.H.: Lessons learned from the anti-sars quarantine experience in a hospital-based fever screening station in Taiwan. Am. J. Infection Control **38**(4), 302–307 (2010)
20. Lin, T.-C., Krishnan, A.U., Li, Z.: Physical fatigue analysis of assistive robot teleoperation via whole-body motion mapping. In: 2019 IEEE/RSJ International Conference on Intelligent Robots and Systems (IROS), pp. 2240–2245 (2019)

21. Liu, X., et al.: Depression after exposure to stressful events: lessons learned from the severe acute respiratory syndrome epidemic. Comprehensive Psychiatry **53**(1), 15–23 (2012)
22. Nemlekar, H., Dutia, D., Li, Z.: Object transfer point estimation for fluent human-robot handovers. In: 2019 International Conference on Robotics and Automation (ICRA), pp. 2627–2633 (2019)
23. Ooi, P.L., Lim, S., Chew, S.K.: Use of quarantine in the control of SARS in Singapore. Am. J. Infection Control **33**(5), 252–257 (2005)
24. Park, Y.-H., Chang, H.K., Lee, M.H., Lee, S.H.: Community-dwelling older adults' needs and acceptance regarding the use of robot technology to assist with daily living performance. BMC Geriatrics **19**(1) (2019)
25. Reynolds, D.L., Garay, J.R., Deamond, S.L., Moran, M.K., Gold, W., Styra, R.: Understanding, compliance and psychological impact of the SARS quarantine experience. Epidemiol. Infection **136**(7), 997–1007 (2007)
26. Robertson, E., Hershenfield, K., Grace, S.L., Stewart, D.E.: The psychosocial effects of being quarantined following exposure to SARS: a qualitative study of Toronto health care workers. Can. J. Psychiatry **49**(6), 403–407 (2004)
27. Schacter, D.L., Norman, K.A., Koutstaal, W.: The cognitive neuroscience of constructive memory. Ann. Rev. Psychol. **49**(1), 289–318 (1998)
28. Takayama, L., Ju, W., Nass, C.: Beyond dirty, dangerous and dull. In: Proceedings of the 3rd International Conference on Human Robot Interaction - HRI 2008, pp. 25–32 (2008)
29. Taylor, M.R., Agho, K.E., Stevens, G.J., Raphael, B.: Factors influencing psychological distress during a disease epidemic: data from Australias first outbreak of equine influenza. BMC Public Health **8**(1) (2008)
30. Tracy, C.S., Rea, E., Upshur, R.E.: Public perceptions of quarantine: community-based telephone survey following an infectious disease outbreak. BMC Public Health **9**(1) (2009)
31. Unknown. Quarantine and isolation. Centers for Disease Control and Prevention, September 2017
32. Wang, Y., Xu, B., Zhao, G., Cao, R., He, X., Fu, S.: Is quarantine related to immediate negative psychological consequences during the 2009 H1N1 epidemic? General Hospital Psychiatry **33**(1), 75–77 (2011)
33. Wilken, J.A., et al.: Knowledge, attitudes, and practices among members of households actively monitored or quarantined to prevent transmission of Ebola virus disease—Margibi county, Liberia: February-March 2015. Prehospital Disaster Med. **32**(6), 673–678 (2017)
34. You, Y., et al.: Design and implementation of mobile manipulator system. In: 2019 IEEE 9th Annual International Conference on CYBER Technology in Automation, Control, and Intelligent Systems (CYBER), pp. 113–118 (2019)

Author Index

Adams, William 48
Admoni, Henny 590
Ahmadzadeh, S. Reza 529
Ahuja, Sarthak 590
Alami, Rachid 554
Ali, Samina 542
Alimardani, Maryam 344
Anjidani, Farid 232
Arntz, Alexander 271
Aroyo, Alexander M. 36
Arriaga, Rosa I. 232
Arroyo, Dante 332
Ayub, Ali 220, 502
Azizi, Negin 232

Baecker, Annalena Nora 207
Baldauf, Kathryn 320
Barros, Pablo 296
Belgiovine, Giulia 296
Bevins, Alisha 640
Bhatia, Simran 604
Biswas, Abhijat 590
Björling, Elin A. 604
Blankenburg, Janelle 144
Brock, Heike 108, 652
Buckingham, David 566
Bugajska, Magdalena 48
Buisan, Guilhem 554

Carreno-Medrano, Pamela 259
Castellano, Ginevra 120
Castro-González, Álvaro 182
Chita-Tegmark, Meia 566
Christensen, Kristoffer W. 73
Ciardo, Francesca 466
Collins, Sawyer 440
Connolly, Jennifer 628
Cordero, Julia 381
Coronado, Enrique 259
Couto, Marta 23
Cuijpers, Raymond H. 392

D'Asaro, Fabio Aurelio 369
Dautenhahn, Kerstin 1, 36, 453, 676

de Wolf, Edo 357
Doyle-Burke, Dylan 170
Duncan, Brittany A. 640
Dziubinski, Kimberly 604

Eimler, Sabrina C. 271
Esteves, Francisco 132
Even, Jani 61

Fang, Yu 108
Feil-Seifer, David 144
Fernandes, Rodrigo 332
Fernández-Rodicio, Enrique 182
Ferreira, Maria José 194, 516
Fischer, Kerstin 157
Foster, Mary Ellen 542

Gamboa-Montero, Juan José 182
Geiskkovitch, Denise Y. 207
Ghafurian, Moojan 1
Ghiglino, Davide 466
Girdhar, Siddharth 590
Gomez, Randy 108, 440, 652
Goo, Jamin 320
Goor, Vincent J. P. van den 392
Grewe, Alina 271
Groechel, Thomas 381
Grollman, Daniel 404
Guo, Yijie 332

Han, Mingyuan 404
Hannig, Martin 578
Haring, Kerstin S. 170
Hart, Justin 320
Herath, Damith 73
Hides, Leanne 628
Hijaz, Ala'aldin 416
Holthaus, Patrick 453

Jackson, Ryan Blake 404
Jochum, Elizabeth 73
Joshi, Swapna 440

Kamino, Waki   440
Kanda, Takayuki   61
Kavanagh, David J.   628
Khavas, Zahra Rezaei   529
Kitani, Kris K.   590
Koay, Kheng Lee   453
Kont, Melissa   344
Korneder, Jessica   416
Kothig, Austin   36
Kowalczyk, Christopher   271
Krämer, Nicole   96
Kulić, Dana   259

Lafranca, Laurens   688
Lakatos, Gabriella   1
Lang, Kendra A.   284
Langedijk, Rosalyn M.   157
Lawson, Ed   48
Lee, Haemin   381
Li, Jamy   357, 688
Lilienthal, Lucie   578
Ling, Honson   604
Litwin, Sasha   542
Lockshin, Jane   404
Louie, Wing-Yue Geoffrey   416

Maggi, Gianpaolo   369
Mahajan, Bonny   320
Mahajan, Kartik   381
Mahdi, Hamza   36, 676
Martinho, Carlos   516
Matarić, Maja J.   381
McCurry, J. Malcolm   48
McFarland, Ciera   13
McPhaul, Nina   640
Mehralizadeh, Bijan   232
Melo, Francisco   23
Merino, Luis   652
Michael, John   428
Mintrom, Michael   259
Mirsky, Reuth   320
Mokhtari, Kasra   284
Moradi, Hadi   232
Muñoz, John   36

Nahman, Zachary   404
Nakamura, Keisuke   108, 652
Nayyar, Mollik   13
Newman, Benjamin A.   590

Nichols, Eric   108
Nicolescu, Monica   144
Niewiadomski, Radoslaw   664
Nisi, Valentina   194
Nissen, Lotte Damsgaard   157

Oda, Yuma   61
Olim, Sandra Câmara   194
Oliveira, Raquel   194
Owen, Sydney   320

Paetzel, Maike   120
Paiva, Ana   23, 132, 194, 516
Pakkar, Roxanna   381
Palinko, Oskar   157
Paradeda, Raul Benites   516
Parker, Jennifer   542
Pedersen, Jonas E.   73
Perugia, Giulia   120
Peters, Jan   478
Petisca, Sofia   132
Petrick, Ronald P. A.   542
Pouretemad, Hamid Reza   232
Prasad, Vignesh   478

Ramirez, Eduardo Ruiz   157
Rea, Daniel J.   207
Rea, Francesco   296, 664
Redondo, Maria Elena Lechuga   664
Robinette, Paul   529
Robinson, Nicole L.   628
Rönnqvist, Lisa   616
Roselli, Cecilia   466
Rosenthal-von der Pütten, Astrid   96
Rossi, Alessandra   453
Rossi, Silvia   369
Ruijten, Peter A. M.   392

Šabanović, Selma   440, 652
Saleh, Shahed   676
Salichs, Miguel A.   182
Sangiovanni, Sara   369
Sarthou, Guillaume   554
Scheutz, Matthias   566
Sciutti, Alessandra   296, 428, 664
Seo, Stela Hanbyeol   207
Shariff, Omar   676
Shidujaman, Mohammad   332
Shimizu, Reina   308

Simmons, S. Michael   144
Smith, David Harris   542
Sochanski, Megan   416
Soleiman, Pegah   232
Sommer, Stefan   271
Spezialetti, Matteo   369
Stanton, Christopher J.   490
Stinson, Jennifer   542
Stock-Homburg, Ruth   246, 478, 578
Stone, Peter   320
Straßmann, Carolin   96, 271
Sumartojo, Shanti   259
Szapiro, Deborah   652

Talavera, Gabrielle   144
Tao, Zhuofu   1
Taylor, John R.   490
Tejeda, Stone   320
Thill, Serge   108
Thunberg, Sofia   616
Tian, Leimin   259
Trafton, J. Gregory   48
Trainer, Thomas   490
Tulli, Silvia   23

Umemuro, Hiroyuki   308

Vasco, Miguel   23
Vasylkiv, Yurii   108
Vattheuer, Christopher   207
Venture, Gentiane   259
Vignolo, Alessia   428, 664

Wagner, Alan R.   13, 220, 284, 502
Walters, Michael L.   453
Wen, Ruchen   404
Williams, Tom   85, 404
Wolf, Franziska Doris   246
Wright, Ben   48
Wykowska, Agnieszka   466

Xiao, Xuesu   320

Yadollahi, Elmira   23
Young, James E.   207
Yu, Mingyue   332

Zagainova, Mariya   144
Zeller, Frauke   542
Zenzeri, Jacopo   296
Zhu, Lixiao   85
Zhu, Qin   404
Ziemke, Tom   616
Zoloty, Zachary   13

Printed in the United States
By Bookmasters